Early Modern Japanese Literature

TRANSLATIONS FROM THE ASIAN CLASSICS

Early Modern Japanese Literature

An Anthology, 1600–1900

Edited with Introductions and Commentary by Haruo Shirane

TRANSLATORS

James Brandon, Michael Brownstein, Patrick Caddeau, Caryl Ann Callahan,
Steven Carter, Anthony Chambers, Cheryl Crowley, Chris Drake, Peter Flueckiger,
Charles Fox, C. Andrew Gerstle, Thomas Harper, Robert Huey, Donald Keene,
Richard Lane, Lawrence Marceau, Andrew Markus, Herschel Miller,
Maryellen Toman Mori, Jamie Newhard, Mark Oshima, Edward Putzar,
Peipei Qiu, Satoru Saito, Tomoko Sakomura, G. W. Sargent, Thomas Satchell,
Paul Schalow, Haruo Shirane, Jack Stoneman, Makoto Ueda, Burton Watson

COLUMBIA UNIVERSITY PRESS

NEW YORK

Columbia University Press wishes to express its appreciation
for assistance given by the Japan Foundation toward the cost
of publishing this book.

Columbia University Press wishes to express its appreciation
for assistance given by the Pushkin Fund toward the cost
of publishing this book.

Columbia University Press
Publishers Since 1893
New York   Chichester, West Sussex
Copyright © 2002 Columbia University Press
All rights reserved
Library of Congress Cataloging-in-Publication Data
Early modern Japanese literature : an anthology, 1600–1900 / [edited with introduction
by Haruo Shirane].
p. cm. — (Translations from the Asian classics)
Includes bibliographical references and index.
ISBN 0-231-10990-3 (cloth : alk. paper)
I. Shirane, Haruo, 1951–   II. Series.
PL782.E1   E23   2002
895.6′08003—dc21
2001053725

♾

Columbia University Press books are printed on permanent
and durable acid-free paper.
Printed in the United States of America
c 10 9 8 7 6 5 4 3 2 1

CONTENTS

PREFACE

This anthology, one of two planned volumes of Japanese literature from the ancient period through the nineteenth century, brings to the reader carefully chosen examples of literature from the Edo period (1600–1867). Except for such late-seventeenth-century writers as Saikaku, Bashō, and Chikamatsu, the three centuries of early modern Japanese literature have often been neglected by Western readers, and most of the texts here have been translated for the first time. It is my hope that this volume will stimulate interest in one of the most exciting periods in world literature.

This book pays particular attention to *gesaku* (playful writing), the popular literature of the late eighteenth and early nineteenth centuries, which includes *dangibon, kyōka, senryū, kibyōshi, sharebon, yomihon, kokkeibon, gōkan,* and *ninjōbon*. Also integral to early modern culture were the poetry and prose written in Chinese or classical Japanese by those in the literati (*bunjin*), Chinese studies (*kangaku*), and nativist studies (*kokugaku*) movements that came to the fore in the eighteenth century and are well represented here. The anthology's focus on these "high" genres, especially poetics and literary treatises, reveals their close connection to the popular literature and culture.

Nine selections from *jōruri* (puppet theater) and kabuki by major playwrights are an important part of this book as well. Today in Japan, jōruri and kabuki plays are rarely viewed in their entirety. Instead, favorite scenes or acts are performed, often as a medley. This book takes the same approach, thereby allowing the reader to sample a wide variety of plays. The jōruri and kabuki selections also were chosen to demonstrate their close connection to the fiction of this period.

Early modern Japanese fiction was accompanied by pictures that existed in a dialogic relationship to the printed text. In this anthology, I have tried to create the same relationship and provide commentary on the images. The drama selections likewise include both photographs from modern performances and Edo-period *ukiyo-e* and print illustrations.

Much of Japanese literature, particularly the poetry, is highly allusive and elliptical. Consequently, considerable effort has been made not just to translate important and interesting texts but also to offer critical introductions to the various genres, sociocultural phenomena, and authors. Almost all the poetry is accompanied by commentary in the footnotes. Except where indicated, I have written all the introductions and commentaries, and I bear full responsibility for the accuracy and quality of the translations.

This anthology owes its existence to Jennifer Crewe, editorial director at Columbia University Press, who many years ago urged me to take on this project. Because of various other commitments, however, I did not begin working on it seriously until 1997. Since then, I have accumulated many debts.

My greatest debt is to Chris Drake, with whom I had long discussions about the texts, who took on a lion's share of the translations, and, indeed, without whom this anthology would not exist. A number of scholars in Japan gave generously of their time, particularly Horikiri Minoru, Hori Nobuo, Ibi Takashi, Kawamoto Kōji, Kurozumi Makoto, Momokawa Takahiro, Nagashima Hiroaki, Ogata Tsutomu, Ōoka Makoto, Shirakura Kazuyoshi, Suzuki Jun, and Torii Akio. My gratitude goes as well to Lewis Cook, Andrew Gerstle, Howard Hibbett, Donald Keene, Lawrence Kominz, Lawrence Marceau, Mark Oshima, Thomas Rimer, Edward Seidensticker, Tomi Suzuki, and the anonymous readers who provided invaluable feedback.

Many thanks go to my graduate students—particularly Anne Commons, Cheryl Crowley, Torquil Duthie, Peter Flueckiger, Christina Laffin, Herschel Miller, Jamie Newhard, Satoru Saitō, Tomoko Sakomura, Michael Scanlon, and Akiko Takeuchi, all of whom assisted with the manuscript at various stages. I-Hsien Wu checked the pinyin, and Wei Shang helped with the Chinese references. Special thanks go to Tomoko Sakomura, who did extensive research on and wrote the legends for the ukiyo-e prints and for the *kana-zōshi, jōruri,* late *ukiyo-zōshi,* literati, *kibyōshi, gōkan,* late *yomihon,* and late kabuki illustrations. Melissa McCormick and Barbara Ford assisted with the illustrations. I am grateful to Sakaguchi Akiko, who helped obtain for me the illustrations from the National Theatre in Tokyo. Barbara Adachi, who recently donated her jōruri collection to C. V. Starr East Asian Library at Columbia University, allowed me to use her superb photographs, and Amy Heinrich, the director of the library, provided much assistance with the photographs and other matters. Mihoko Miki, the Japanese studies librarian at the C. V. Starr Library, obtained important materials for this book. Yuiko Yampolsky helped me in many ways. Winifred Olsen was an invaluable editor and consultant for the first draft. Margaret B. Yamashita was a superb copy editor. Irene Pavitt at Columbia University Press provided invaluable advice.

My thanks to all the translators for their contributions and patience with what turned out to be an enormously complex and time-consuming project and for the seemingly endless revisions.

Most of all, my thanks to Shinchōsha for providing generous support to make these two volumes possible. Funding was also provided by Itoh Foundation (Tokyo) and the Daidō Life Foundation (Osaka).

HISTORICAL PERIODS, MEASUREMENTS,
AND OTHER MATTERS

MAJOR HISTORICAL PERIODS

Nara	710–784
Heian	794–1185
Kamakura	1185–1333
North and South Courts	1336–1392
Muromachi	1392–1573
Warring States	1477–1573
Early Modern / Tokugawa	1600–1867
Meiji	1868–1912

MAJOR ERA NAMES IN THE
EARLY MODERN PERIOD

Kanbun	1661–1673
Genroku	1688–1704
Kyōhō	1716–1736

Hōreki	1751–1764
An'ei-Tenmei	1772–1789
Tenmei	1781–1789
Kansei	1789–1801
Bunka-Bunsei (Ka-Sei)	1804–1829
Tenpō	1830–1844
Bakumatsu	1853–1867

DISTANCE

ri	36 *chō*: approximately 2.5 miles or 4 kilometers
chō	36 *jō*: approximately 120 yards or 110 meters
jō	10 *shaku*: approximately 3.28 yards or 3 meters
shaku	10 *sun*: approximately 1 foot or 30 centimeters
sun	0.1 *shaku*: approximately 1.2 inches or 3 centimeters

WEIGHTS

kan or kanme	1,000 *monme* or 6.25 *kinme*: approximately 8.3 pounds or 3.76 kilograms
kin or kinme	160 *monme* or 16 *ryō*: approximately 1.3 pounds or 600 grams
ryō	10 *monme*: approximately 1.3 ounces or 37.6 grams
monme	0.1 *ryō* or 0.001 *kanme*: approximately 0.13 ounce or 3.76 grams

CAPACITY

koku	10 *to*: approximately 47.5 gallons or 180 liters
to	10 *shō*: approximately 4.75 gallons or 18 liters
shō	10 *gō*: approximately 3.8 pints or 1.8 liters
gō	0.1 *shō*: approximately 0.38 pint or 180 milliliters

AREA

chō	10 *tan*: approximately 2.5 acres or 1 hectare
tan	10 *se*: approximately 0.25 acre or 0.1 hectare
se	30 *tsubo*: approximately 119 square yards or 99.3 square meters
tsubo	100 *shaku*: approximately 3.95 square yards or 3.31 square meters

COINS

ōban, bankin	largest "gold" coin (not pure gold), used only on special occasions, weighed 44 *monme* (5.8 ounces, 165.4 grams)
koban	second largest "gold" coin, largest in everyday use, weighed 4.8 *monme* (63 ounces, 18 grams), equivalent to 1 *ryō*
ichibukin	smallest gold coin, equivalent to one-quarter *ryō*
chōgin	largest silver coin, weighed about 43 *monme* (5.7 ounces, 161.64 grams)
zeni	small copper coin, weighed 1 *monme* (0.13 ounce, 3.76 grams), smallest monetary unit

DATES AND SEASONS

The First through the Third Month of the lunar calendar (roughly the equivalent of February through April): spring

The Fourth through the Sixth Month (roughly May through July): summer

The Seventh through the Ninth Month (roughly August through October): autumn

The Tenth through the Twelfth Month (roughly November through January): winter

Conversion from the lunar to the solar calendar is complex. For example, the eighteenth day, Twelfth Month, in the third year of the Jōkyō era, was January 31, 1687.

TERMS AND TITLES

Whenever possible, a Japanese term or title is translated in its first appearance. Japanese literary terms are listed and defined in the index.

ROMANIZATION

The romanization of Japanese words is based on the Hepburn system, and the romanization of Chinese words follows the pinyin system.

NAMES

Names are given in the Japanese order, surname first, followed by personal or artistic name. After the first occurrence, artists and poets are referred to solely by their artistic name or pen name. Thus, Matsuo Bashō is referred to by his haikai name (*haigō*), Bashō, and not Matsuo, his family name.

ABBREVIATIONS OF MODERN SERIAL EDITIONS

KHT   *Koten haibungaku taikei* (Tokyo: Shūeisha, 1970–)

MNZ   *Motoori Norinaga zenshū*, 21 volumes (Tokyo: Chikuma shobō, 1968–1977)

NKBT   *Nihon koten bungaku taikei*, 102 volumes (Tokyo: Iwanami shoten, 1957–1968)

NKBZ   *Nihon koten bungaku zenshū*, 60 volumes (Tokyo: Shōgakukan, 1970–1976)

NKT   *Nihon kagaku taikei*, 10 volumes (Tokyo: Kazam shobō, 1956–1963)

NST   *Nihon shisō taikei*, 81 volumes (Tokyo: Iwanami shoten, 1970–1995)

RZ   *Ryōkan zenshū*, 2 volumes, edited by Toyoharu Tōgō (Tokyo: Tōkyō Sōgensha, 1959)

SNKBT *Shin Nihon koten bungaku taikei* (Tokyo: Iwanami shoten, 1989–)

SNKBZ *Shinpen Nihon koten bungaku zenshū* (Tokyo: Shōgakukan, 1994–)

SNKS   *Shinchō Nihon koten shūsei*, 79 volumes (Tokyo: Shinchōsha, 1976–1989)

Citations are followed by an abbreviation of the series title, the volume number, and the page. For example, NKBZ 51: 525 refers to page 525 of volume 51 of the *Nihon koten bungaku zenshū*.

Early Modern Japanese Literature

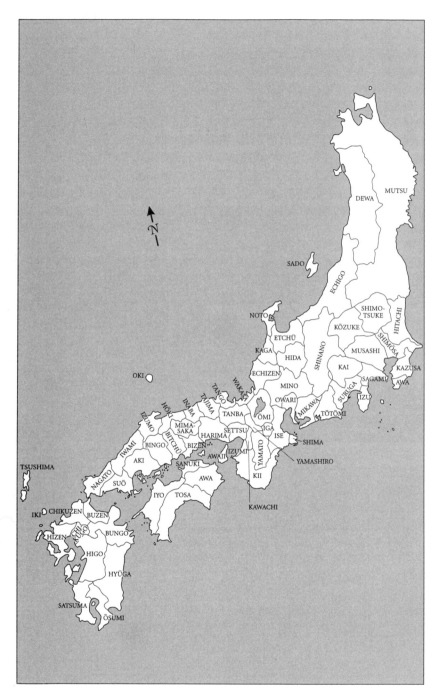

Provinces in the Early Modern Period

Chapter 1

EARLY MODERN JAPAN

One of the most dramatic transformations in Japanese history was the transition from the medieval period (thirteenth to sixteenth century) to the early modern era (1600–1867), when literary and cultural paradigms gave birth to a whole new body of vernacular literature. During the seventeenth century, urban commoners (*chōnin*) emerged as an economically and culturally powerful class; mass education spread, especially through the domain (*han*) schools for samurai and the private schools (*terakoya*) for commoners; and printing was introduced—all of which led to the widespread production and consumption of popular literature, which became a commodity for huge markets. As a result, traditional Japanese and Chinese literary texts were widely read for the first time.[1]

Until the seventeenth century, literary texts had been shared through limited quantities of handwritten manuscripts, almost all of which belonged to a small group of aristocrats, priests, and high-ranking samurai. In the medieval period, traveling minstrels (*biwa hōshi*) had recited military epics such as *The Tale of the Heike* to a populace that could neither read nor write. Even most samurai

---

1. Before 1590, almost no printing existed except in Buddhist monasteries. But within a century, more than ten thousand books were in print and sold or rented by more than seven hundred bookstores.

were illiterate, as were farmers and craftsmen. But in the seventeenth century, with the creation of a new socioeconomic structure, the government promotion of education, and the spread of print capitalism, this situation changed drastically. By midcentury, almost all samurai—now the bureaucratic elite—were able to read, as were the middle to upper levels of the farmer, artisan, and merchant classes.

The seventeenth century brought not only a dramatic rise in the standard of living for almost all levels of society but also a dramatic change in the nature of cultural production and consumption. In the medieval period, although provincial military lords were able to learn about the Heian classics from such traveling *renga* (classical linked verse) masters as Sōgi (1421–1502), the acquisition of these classical texts was limited to a relatively small circle of poet-priests and aristocrats, who were deeply rooted in the traditional culture of Kyoto. A monopoly—epitomized by the Kokin denju, the secret transmission of the *Kokinshū* (*Anthology of Old and New Japanese Poems*, ca. 905)—was established over a significant part of so-called refined culture, which was often passed on through carefully controlled lineages in one-to-one transmissions to the elected few. In the seventeenth century, by contrast, anyone who could afford to pay for lessons could hire a "town teacher" (*machi shishō*) in any one of the many arts or fields of learning. The transmission of learning was no longer dependent, as it had been in the medieval period, on the authority or patronage of large institutions such as Buddhist temples or powerful military lords. Such cultural activities as writing *haikai* poetry, singing nō (*utai*), and performing the tea ceremony (*chanoyu*) became not only available to commoners but highly commercialized.

THE SHŌGUNATE AND THE DOMAINS

The Tokugawa shōgunate (1603–1867), the third and last of three warrior governments (the first two being the Kamakura and Muromachi shōgunates), was founded by Tokugawa Ieyasu three years after he vanquished his rivals at the battle of Sekigahara in 1600. The first of fifteen successive Tokugawa shōguns, Ieyasu took the title of *seii-tai shōgun* (barbarian-subduing generalissimo), and his military government was referred to as the *bakufu*, generally translated as "shōgunate." To control foreign trade and diplomacy, the shōgunate restricted many of the foreign contacts, under the seclusion (*sakoku*) edicts of 1633 to 1639, and to preserve social order at home, it attempted to establish a four-class system (*shi-nō-kō-shō*) in which samurai, farmer, artisan, and merchant were viewed as existing in a strict hierarchy.

By the beginning of the eighteenth century, Japan's population had reached nearly 30 million. Of this number, roughly 10 percent were samurai, who were organized along feudal hierarchical lines, with ties of vassalage linking every man to his lord and ultimately to the shōgun, who ostensibly stood at the top.

Immediately under the shōgun were two groups of vassals: the daimyō, or domain (*han*) lords, and the shōgun's direct vassals. The total number of daimyō, to whom the shōgun entrusted most of the work of provincial administration, was around 260. At the top were the collateral houses (*shinpan*), or cadet houses of the Tokugawa, which eventually numbered 23, followed by the "house" (*fudai*) daimyō, who had been Tokugawa vassals before the battle of Sekigahara and who numbered 145 by the end of the eighteenth century. The remainder were "outside" (*tozama*) daimyō, who had gained eminence before the rise of the Tokugawa. Many of these daimyō ruled their domains like private princes. To help maintain control over them, in the 1630s and 1640s the shōgunate institutionalized the alternate attendance (*sankin kōtai*) system, which required daimyō to reside in Edo in alternate years in attendance on the shōgun. To perform this obligation, a daimyō had to maintain in Edo a residential estate (*yashiki*)—which consumed about 70 to 80 percent of his income—where his wife and children were permanently detained by the shōgunate as political hostages. The typical daimyō traveled to the capital every other year with a large retinue, using the main highways, which were under shōgunal control, and expending a considerable amount of money. For example, Kaga Domain (now Ishikawa Prefecture), on the Japan Sea side, belonging to the Maeda family, with an income of 1,030,000 *koku*, required a retinue of 2,500 when the daimyō traveled to Edo.

The Tokugawa house itself formed the largest power bloc. The direct Tokugawa vassals were the *hatamoto*, the enfeoffed bannermen and the higher-ranking direct vassals; and the *gokenin*, the stipended housemen and the lower-ranking direct vassals. The hatamoto, about five thousand in number, occupying a position analogous to an officer corps in a standing army, drew annual stipends of at least one hundred *koku* and usually were descendants of warriors who had helped the Tokugawa before the battle of Sekigahara. Their civil positions ranged from grand chamberlain (*sobayōnin*), directly under the senior councillor (*rōjū*), to financial clerks. The gokenin, who numbered about twenty thousand in 1800, received annual stipends that were usually less than one hundred *koku*. Under the gokenin and the provincial daimyō came the bulk of the samurai class.

With a few exceptions, such as Tokugawa Tsunayoshi (r. 1680–1709), Tokugawa Yoshimune (r. 1716–1745), and Tokugawa Ienari (r. 1787–1837), who wielded nearly absolute power, the shōgun was usually overshadowed by others in the shōgunal administrative system, particularly the senior councillors, most often house daimyō who met in formal council and conducted national affairs, foreign relations, and control of the daimyō. From time to time, powerful senior councillors such as Tanuma Okitsugu (1719–1788), Matsudaira Sadanobu (1758–1829), and Mizuno Tadakuni (1794–1851) were able to dominate the council and control shōgunal policy.

Politically and financially, the Tokugawa shōgunate was at its peak in the seventeenth century. Thereafter, many of its daimyō controls lost their efficacy, and its revenues began to decline. Periodic attempts were made to restore both authority and solvency, first with the Kyōhō Reforms (1716–1736), carried out by the eighth shōgun, Tokugawa Yoshimune; then with the Kansei Reforms (1787–1793), executed by the senior councillor Matsudaira Sadanobu; and finally with the Tenpō Reforms (1830–1844), administered by the senior councillor Mizuno Tadakuni. Although the Kyōhō Reforms temporarily restabilized the finances of the Tokugawa shōgunate, none of these measures had lasting success. They generally did, however, have a greater impact, in terms of censorship and other limitations, on cultural and literary production. Accordingly, the high points of early modern literature—the Genroku era (1688–1704), the Hōreki-Tenmei era (1751–1789), and the Bunka-Bunsei era (1804–1829)—tended to come precisely between these major reforms.

THE SOCIAL HIERARCHY

In order to strengthen their power and authority, the bakufu and the provincial domains created a rigid, hierarchical class society made up of samurai, farmers, artisans, and merchants, in descending order. (Nobility were treated separately, and Buddhist and Shintō priests were given a position equal to that of the samurai.) Below the four classes were outcasts called *eta* and *hinin* (nonpersons). By the end of the early modern period, about 75 percent of the population were farmers; 10 percent, samurai; about 7 to 8 percent, urban commoners; 2 percent, priests; and 4 percent, a miscellaneous mix. To reinforce this social hierarchy, extremely harsh rules were instituted. Only samurai were given surnames; they also had the right to cut down a farmer or chōnin for an insult. Every aspect of clothing and living was regulated to bring each individual within the class system.

Among the samurai, a strict hierarchy was established as well, beginning at the top with the shōgun, daimyō, hatamoto, and gokenin and working down to the servants of middle-rank samurai families, each pledging absolute fidelity to his immediate superior. Similar hierarchies based on fidelity also existed in commoner society: between the main family (*honke*) and the branch family (*bunke*) in regard to kinship structure, between the master and the apprentice in artisan society, and between the employee and the employer in the merchant world. Strict laws governing residence and clothing were applied also to the eta, who were confined to farming and jobs related to dead animals (such as leather making) or criminals, and the hinin, who cleaned up waste and performed other demeaning tasks.

The fundamental social unit in the early modern period was the *ie* (house), which was centered on the family and governed by the house head (*kachō*), with preferential treatment given to the eldest son, who usually inherited the property and became the next head of the house. The ie included nonblood relations such as employees and servants, and it was possible, and not uncommon, for an adopted heir with no blood tie to become the kachō. The younger sons, who did not inherit any property, frequently left the house to be adopted by a family that lacked sons. The house was the principal unit within each class category (samurai, farmer, artisan, and merchant), with each house pursuing a hereditary "house occupation" (kagyō). The members of the house considered themselves as both individuals and part of the larger social unit of the house, with a sense of obligation toward other members of the house similar to that between child and parent or retainer and lord.

The income for a samurai house—which came from a stipend—was fixed according to hereditary criteria, leaving rōnin (masterless samurai) and second or third sons in a precarious financial situation. One result was that they often took up scholarship, literature, religion, or the arts, in which they could establish a house of their own. Many of the leading writers and scholars of the early modern period—such as Gion Nankai, Hiraga Gennai, and Koikawa Harumachi—were samurai who had either lost or become disillusioned with their inherited positions or were of extremely low status, with insufficient means for survival, and consequently sought alternative professions in scholarship and the arts.

The social position of women was low. In a samurai family, a woman had no right to inherit the family name, property, or position. In the medieval period, when the samurai lived on the land as property owners and producers, samurai wives had an important position sustaining the household and family. But under the Tokugawa bakufu system, the samurai were no longer tied to the land, and so they gathered in the castle towns and became bureaucrats. The shōgun and the domain lords took over direct control of the farmers, who became the producers. In the seventeenth century, the samurai became similar to aristocrats in that they had male and female servants who took care of them. One consequence was that the role of the wife was reduced to that of a protected lady, with any power she might have had going entirely to her husband, who was master of the house. As the position of women declined and that of men rose, it became normal for the samurai, as head of the house, to have a mistress or to spend considerable time in the pleasure quarters.

The literature of the early modern period is often thought to be the literature of and by urban commoners (chōnin). Although some writers—such as Ihara Saikaku, Santō Kyoden, and Shikitei Sanba—were from artisan or merchant families, an overwhelming number came from samurai families. Asai Ryōi, Chikamatsu Monzaemon, Gion Nankai, Hattori Nankaku, Hiraga Gennai, Koikawa Harumachi, Jippensha Ikku, and Takizawa Bakin—to mention only the most prominent names—were from warrior families, usually ones in severe decline. Even those not normally associated with samurai, such as Matsuo Bashō, were descendants of warriors. The literature of the early modern period is thus as much by the samurai as by the chōnin. A few writers had a peasant background, perhaps the best known being Issa, a haikai poet. Buson was the son of a well-to-do farmer.

THE ECONOMY AND THE THREE CITIES

At the end of the sixteenth century, foundries for minting gold and silver coins were built, leading to a unified gold- and silver-based currency. In 1636, the bakufu opened a foundry for minting *zeni*, or bronze coins, which provided the basis of a common currency. The bakufu and the daimyō, who were in need of cash, established large warehouses (*kurayashiki*) in cities such as Osaka, Edo, Tsuruga, and Ōtsu, to which merchants transported and in which they sold the rice and goods stored in the warehouses. The domain lords distributed the rice grown by their farmers to their vassals and sent the remainder to the warehouses in these large cities, where they exchanged it for hard currency which was used to pay the domain's expenses. These merchants, referred to as "warehouse people" (*kuramoto*), also extended loans to the domain lords, thus becoming a key part of the domain's financial structure. In the Genroku era, this system prospered, particularly in Osaka, which became known as the "kitchen of the country" because it contained as many as ninety-seven domain warehouses. Ideally positioned, Osaka became the national trading center for goods from the provinces, mainly rice, the country's most important staple. As a result, gigantic sums of currency circulated through Osaka and provided enormous profits for the city's merchants.

Before the mid-seventeenth century, when the supply routes and the financial (currency exchange) institutions still were inadequate, a special class of urban commoners—like those involved in minting gold and silver, managing the domain warehouses, and trading in Nagasaki—were the exclusive beneficiaries of the new currency and market economy, in which fortunes were made through the accumulation of capital. In 1671/1672, however, Kawamura Zuiken (1618–1699), receiving orders from the bakufu to create shipping routes for its annual rice tributes, successfully created an eastern shipping lane, from the Ōshū (the northeastern region of Honshū) to Edo and, more important, a western shipping lane from Sakata, at the northern end of the Japan Sea coast, down to Osaka. These new shipping lanes formed a national trade network that revolutionized the economy and made the Kamigata (Kyoto-Osaka) region the center of the new economy. In 1660, Yagobei of Tennōji was the only currency dealer in Osaka to exchange the currency from one part of the country for that from another, but ten years later, both a system of exchange dealers and a *zeni* exchange had been established. The 1670s through the 1680s gave rise to new, more financially powerful urban commoners and to such family businesses as the Kōnoike, Mitsui, and Sumitomo, which later became the huge Kamigata financial cartels.

The capital that accumulated at this time in the hands of Kyoto-Osaka chōnin also indirectly affected the farm villages in the provinces. The urban commoners hired the second and third sons of farming families as assistants who would work to become assistant managers and then, after many years of service, would set up their own business, thereby becoming members of the middle- or upper-class chōnin. These middle- to upper-class chōnin enjoyed such arts as *waka* (thirty-one-syllable verse), *haikai, nō, kyōgen* (comic drama), *chanoyu,* and *kadō* (incense). The vitality of the economy at this time was a major reason for the flourishing of literature and arts.

A salient feature of the late seventeenth century was the growth of an urban culture. The deliberate policy of the Tokugawa bakufu to place the samurai class in the regional castle towns and to force the daimyō to maintain residences in the new capital of Edo, combined with the new transportation networks and commercial infrastructure, resulted in the rapid development of the cities. Particularly significant was the enormous growth of Edo, Osaka, and Kyoto, where the local domain products and the rice that the daimyō collected as taxes were sent and stored, particularly in Edo and Osaka, where they were exchanged for currency. To facilitate the circulation of goods, special markets sprang up in the cities: a rice market at Dōjima in Osaka, fish markets at Zakoba in Osaka and Nihonbashi in Edo, and vegetable markets at Tenma in Osaka and Kanda in Edo. This commerce led, in turn, to the development of chains of wholesalers, middlemen, and retailers.

Edo was the home of the daimyō, hatamoto, and gokenin and their retainers and servants. Merchants and artisans gathered in Edo to supply this substantial population, which was a large source of their income. After the Great Meireki Fire of 1657, which destroyed most of Edo, including Edo Castle, the city was redesigned and reconstructed, leading to further expansion and growth. By the mid-eighteenth century, Edo had become a center for not only consumption but also commerce and production. In 1634 the population of Edo was about 150,000; by 1721 it had more than tripled to exceed 500,000; and by 1873 the inhabitants of Edo numbered nearly 600,000. (By contrast, the population of Paris in 1801 was 548,000.) Unlike Edo, which was populated by samurai and its supporters, Osaka was largely a merchant city, with a population of more than 380,000 in 1721. Its streets lined with domain warehouses, Osaka became in the seventeenth century the trade and distribution center for not only western Japan but also the entire nation and, by the early eighteenth century, had a population of more than 350,000. Kyoto, which had been the cultural capital of Japan for more than six hundred years and was the site of the imperial palace, had a thriving craft industry that produced dyed cloth and other wares. In addition, Shintō shrines and Buddhist temples were concentrated in Kyoto, giving it a religious character and making it a common destination for pilgrims from around the country. Nonetheless, the population of Kyoto, reflecting its shrinking economic and political importance, gradually decreased, from 410,000 in 1634 to 340,000 in 1721 to less than 240,000 in 1873.

THE LICENSED QUARTERS

The licensed quarters, particularly those in the three largest cities, played a major role in Japan's early modern culture and literature. In a deliberate effort to bring prostitution under control and to separate it from society at large, the bakufu consolidated the existing brothels and placed them in designated licensed quarters (*yūkaku*), which were usually located on the periphery of the large cities, surrounded by a wall or moat, as in the case of Shimabara and Yoshiwara. Because of their construction, they were popularly referred to as the *kuruwa* (literally, castle wall). The licensed quarter had only one large gate, which controlled the clientele entering and prevented the courtesans from leaving at will. The bakufu eventually designated roughly twenty such areas throughout the country, of which the largest and most noteworthy were Shimabara in Kyoto, Yoshiwara in Edo, and Shinmachi in Osaka, followed by Maruyama in Nagasaki.

In 1589 the shōgun, Toyotomi Hideyoshi, gathered together the dispersed brothels in Kyoto, the capital, in a single area called Yanagi-machi. In 1640, under the Tokugawa shōgunate, the houses were moved to the western part of the city, dubbed the Shimabara. A similar licensed quarter called Shinmachi, whose facilities were unrivaled throughout Japan, was built in Osaka. In contrast to Kyoto's Shimabara, which served mainly upper-class and well-educated gentlemen, Shinmachi, which was situated near the provincial daimyō storehouses and the commercial port, served local wealthy merchants as well as those who came for business from all over Japan. Then, around 1618 the bakufu established the Yoshiwara licensed quarter in the Nihonbashi area of Edo. After the Great Meireki Fire of 1657, Yoshiwara was moved to the Asakusa area where, like Shimabara and Shinmachi, it became a major center of urban culture. The daimyō and the hatamoto stationed in Edo spent lavishly at Yoshiwara, as did wealthy townsmen.

Throughout most of the early modern period, the licensed quarter and the theater district were the two major entertainment centers, and they were closely connected. The kabuki, for example, drew its subject matter from the licensed quarters, and *ukiyo-e* (literally, pictures of the floating world) depicted courtesans and kabuki actors. Equally important, the licensed quarters became gathering places for intellectuals, artists, and performers, whose work had a profound impact on contemporary literature, drama, music, and art as well as on the fashion and customs of the times. During the 1770s and 1780s, as the center of popular culture increasingly shifted from Kyoto-Osaka to Edo, there was an explosion of popular literature in Edo, including the *sharebon* (books of wit and fashion) such as *The Playboy Dialect* (*Yūshi hōgen*, 1770), which described the ideal of *tsū*, or connoisseurship of the licensed quarters, specifically that of Yoshiwara. In contrast to the wealthy merchant and daimyō customers who had supported the golden age of high courtesan culture in the seventeenth century, the customers in Edo included petty merchants and middle- or lower-level samurai like the one found in *The Playboy Dialect.*

THE COURTESANS AND FEMALE ENTERTAINERS

The most general terms for women who worked in the licensed quarters were *yūjo* (literally, women who play or entertain) and *jorō* (women). Another general term was *keisei* (literally, castle toppler, a Chinese term alluding to the power of a woman to bring down a kingdom), which came to refer to high-ranking courtesans. In the licensed quarter, these women were arranged in a strictly hierarchical order that reflected their status and price.

Until the 1750s, *tayū*, a term generally used for a superior artist, was the highest rank of courtesan. Tayū were highly trained and educated performers skilled in such arts as music, dance, poetry, calligraphy, tea ceremony, and flower arrangement. Because there were very few, access to them was very difficult. Tayū could also reject men, who could see them only by special appointment. It is said that out of a thousand *kamuro* (preteenage attendants) in training, only three or five ever were elevated to the rank of tayū.[2]

Immediately below the tayū were the *tenjin*, called *kōshi* in Yoshiwara. Although kōshi also were considered to be of high rank and highly skilled, their price was 30 to 50 percent less than that of a tayū. They sat in the latticed parlors, where prospective customers could view them from outside, hence the name *kōshi* (lattice). In 1668 a new system, which incorporated hitherto illegal prostitutes, was established in Yoshiwara, adding the ranks of *sancha* (powdered tea) and *umecha* (plum tea) beneath those of tayū and kōshi. The sancha were originally teahouse waitresses who worked as prostitutes and did not reject clients, but under the new system their status rose. Their services cost half or less than what a kōshi charged.

By the 1760s, the situation had changed significantly. The tayū and kōshi had disappeared in Yoshiwara and been supplanted by the *oiran*, the highest-ranking courtesans. The highest oiran were the *yobidashi* (literally, persons on call), who could be seen only by making an appointment through a teahouse. The next level of oiran was the *chūsan*, who were displayed for selection in the latticed parlor. The third level, originally beneath that of an oiran, was the *zashikimochi* (parlor holder), who had her own parlor and anteroom, and the *heyamochi* (room holder), who had only one room, where she lived and met her clients.[3]

---

2. According to one Genroku source, Shimabara could claim 13 taiyū out of a total of 329 courtesans, and Shinmachi, 17 taiyū out of a total of 983 courtesans.

3. In the new system, the former sancha became yobidashi and chūsan, and the former umecha became zashikimochi and heyamochi.

In the late eighteenth century, the oiran, like the tayū before them, were typically accompanied by kamuro and *shinzō* (literally, newly launched boat), who were apprentices from fourteen to twenty years of age. In Yoshiwara, a kamuro became a shinzō at the age of fourteen. The kamuro and shinzō took lessons in the arts, trained to become courtesans, and performed various tasks for their "elder sisters" (*anejorō*), who looked after them. The shinzō who attended the highest-ranking oiran sometimes entertained a client with talk and music until the oiran arrived.

In the seventeenth century, when customers wanted to visit a high-ranking yūjo, they did not go to her residence but instead went to a teahouse and made an appointment to visit a place called an *ageya* (performance house). In Yoshiwara, the ageya lined Nakanochō, the main street of the licensed quarter. At the ageya, the customers were entertained by geisha and professional jesters and were served food and drink while they waited for the tayū, who arrived with her retinue in an elaborate procession called the *ageya-iri*, or "entering the performance house." By 1760 the ageya system, along with the tayū and kōshi, had disappeared in Yoshiwara (although it continued in Osaka until the end of the nineteenth century) and been replaced by a cheaper system: customers went to a guiding teahouse (*hikitejaya*) where they were entertained until they were taken to see the high-ranking courtesan at a courtesan residence (*yūjoya*).

The *geisha* (skilled person) was a professional entertainer in one or more of the traditional Japanese arts such as music, dance, and storytelling. The town (*machi*) geisha worked freelance at parties outside pleasure quarters, and the quarter (*kuruwa*) geisha entertained at parties in the pleasure quarters. The role of the quarter geisha (both men and women), who first appeared in Osaka in the 1710s and in Edo in the 1750s, became more important as the artistic talents of the high-ranking courtesans declined. Initially there were more male geisha (sometimes referred to as *hōkan*, who were often jesters and storytellers) than female geisha in Yoshiwara, but by 1800 female geisha outnumbered the men by three to one, and the term eventually applied only to women, as it does today. Geisha were performers, not prostitutes, although in the late Edo period, the line between these callings was often crossed.

Further down the social scale were the illegal courtesans who worked outside the licensed quarters. Those in unlicensed quarters, such as Fukagawa and Shinagawa in Edo, also were arranged in ranks. At the bottom of the scale were the various unlicensed prostitutes not connected to any quarter. They ranged from "bath women" (*yuna*), who washed and entertained bathers, to street-walkers (*tsujikimi*) and night hawks (*yotaka*), who solicited on the streets.

LITERACY, SCHOLARSHIP, AND PRINTING

Through the sixteenth century, the average samurai was illiterate, as were farmers and urban commoners. But with the transformation of the samurai from warriors to bureaucrats, politicians, and the social elite, education became a primary concern. A school was established in Edo for the hatamoto; the various domains created domain schools for their own samurai; and by the mid-seventeenth century, almost all samurai were literate. In contrast to their medieval counterparts, the new Tokugawa rulers adopted a policy of rule by law and morality—by letter rather than force—a policy that required mass education. With the introduction of a currency-based economy, a knowledge of reading, writing, and arithmetic became essential to farmers, artisans, and merchants, and as a result, private schools (*terakoya*) sprang up in both the cities and the farming villages. By the middle of the seventeenth century, middle- to upper-class chōnin and farmers were literate, and by the late seventeenth century, when Matsuo Bashō and Ihara Saikaku were writing, the audience of readers was large.

Earlier popular literature—such as *The Tale of the Heike* and the *Taiheiki*—often were texts orally presented (*katarimono*) by raconteurs and blind minstrels. But with the spread of literacy, both samurai and commoners had access to a literate culture, including various forms of refined or elite literature (such as *waka, renga, monogatari, kanshi,* and *kanbun,* which earlier had been the exclusive possession of the nobility, priests, and elite samurai) and a variety of new popular literature. Perhaps the most important form of popular literature in the seventeenth century was *haikai* (popular linked verse), which in the Muromachi period had been an adjunct to *renga* (classical linked verse). *The Puppy Collection (Enoko shū)*, a collection of haikai edited in 1633 by two Kyoto urbanites, Matsue Shigeyori and Nonoguchi Ryūhō (disciples of Matsunaga Teitoku), was the first anthology of poetry by commoners.

Haikai masters such as Matsunaga Teitoku (1571–1653), who were teachers and specialists in waka and renga, wrote commentaries on the classics to make them accessible to their students, who needed a fundamental knowledge of the classics to be able to compose haikai. Teitoku, for example, wrote influential commentaries on *Essays in Idleness (Tsuzuregusa)* and *One Hundred Poets, One Hundred Poems (Hyakunin isshu)*, while his noted disciple Kitamura Kigin compiled commentaries on *The Tale of Genji,* the *First Eight Imperial Waka Anthologies (Hachidaishū), Japanese and Chinese Poems to Sing (Wakan rōeishū),* and Sei Shōnagon's *Pillow Book*. Knowledge of the Japanese classics, which had been socially restricted through the sixteenth century, now became the foundation for writing haikai and created a mass audience that could appreciate such complex and allusive writers as Saikaku and Bashō.

With the exception of some Buddhist sutras, Japanese literature before the seventeenth century existed only in the form of hand-copied manuscripts. Then, using the printing technology imported by Christian missionaries from Europe, a romanized version of *Isoho monogatari,* a Japanese translation of *Aesop's Fables,* was printed in 1594. Inspired by this development, the first shōgun, Tokugawa Ieyasu, began printing important Confucian, military, and administrative texts in the early seventeenth century, using movable type. In Kyoto, Hon'ami Kōetsu (1558–1637), a court artist, with the help of a calligraphy disciple, Suminokura Sōan (1571–1632), who lived in Saga, printed luxury editions of thirteen different texts, including *The Tales of Ise*, an abridged version of *The Tale of Genji*, the *Shinkokinshū*, and *Essays in Idleness*. Although they represented a major step in the canonization process, these private editions (commonly referred to as the Saga, Kōetsu, or Suminokura texts) were not available to general readers.

In the 1630s, movable type, which could be used for *kanji* (Chinese characters) but not for the cursive *kana* (Japanese syllabic writing), was replaced with multiple-use woodblocks, which were more suitable for reproducing Japanese texts. At about the same time, commercial publishing houses opened, mainly in Kyoto. The result was that by the 1660s, major premodern Japanese texts, key Chinese texts, medical books, calendars, and dictionaries, along with the new vernacular fiction and haikai handbooks, were being published and sold in bookstores and publishing houses in the three largest cities. With the rise of the publishing industry—which had become fully developed by the time Ihara Saikaku published *Life of a Sensuous Man* in 1682—prose fiction acquired a fixed size and length. The commercialization of literature also meant that publication was based on an expected profit, for which the author was promised a certain amount of money. This development gave birth to the professional writer, who had to produce a certain number of pages within a set period of time and to write for a mass audience. As a result, this tended to lead—with the exception of works by a handful of writers and in special genres—to literature of low quality. In addition, the mass circulation of literature caused literary works to become the object of government censorship, which had a further negative effect on the range and quality. During each of the three major bakufu reforms—Kyōhō (1716–1736), Kansei (1787–1793), and Tenpō (1830–1844)—the bakufu issued orders to stop certain types of publications. Works that touched on the Tokugawa family and other sensitive matters or that contained erotic material were banned, and writers who violated these rules could be imprisoned.

WOMEN, READERSHIP, AND LITERATURE

Compared with the Heian period, in which there were many prominent women writers, the early modern period produced almost no women writers in the field of vernacular fiction. The only exception was Arakida Reijo (1732–1806), who wrote historical tales (*monogatari*) and Heian court romances between 1772 and 1781 and was a contemporary of Motoori Norinaga, Takebe Ayatari, and Ueda Akinari. The same is true in the field of drama. Legend has it that Ono no Otsū was the author of the Muromachi-period *Tale of Prince Jōruri* (*Jōruri hime monogatari*), considered to be the origin of jōruri narration, but there are no known women playwrights of *jōruri* (puppet plays) or kabuki. The only field in which women had some presence as writers was in poetry, particularly waka and hai-kai, and in literary diaries and travel literature, often by the same authors. Women did, however, play a major role as characters in drama and fiction and became an important audience for both drama and fiction, which had more readers than did waka and haikai.

The audience for *ukiyo-zōshi* (books of the floating world), of which Ihara Saikaku's writings are the most famous and that dominated vernacular fiction from the late seventeenth century until the middle of the eighteenth century, appears to have been overwhelmingly male. With the exception of works such as *Women's Water Margin* (*Onna suikoden*, 1783) which was aimed at female readers, the late-eighteenth-century *yomihon* (reading books) in the Kyoto-Osaka region were targeted at male readers as well. However, in the nineteenth century, when the audience for fiction expanded, two major genres of fiction, *gōkan* (bound picture books) and *ninjōbon* (books of sentiment and romance), catered to a largely female audience, and Tamenaga Shunsui, the principal writer of ninjōbon, had an assistant writer who was a woman.

In the eighteenth century, literacy rates for women appear not to have been high, even for those who were economically well off, and even literate women lagged significantly behind men in their level of education. Japanese classics such as *Hyakunin isshu*, *Kokinshū*, *The Tales of Ise*, *The Tale of Genji*, and *A Tale of Flowering Fortunes* (*Eiga monogatari*) are said to have been the basic reading for women in the Edo period, but these works, particularly the longer ones, were generally read in digest form with pictures, such as *Child Genji* (*Osana Genji*, 1665), a popular *kana-zōshi* (kana booklet) by Nonoguchi Ryūho, and *Women's Genji, Lessons for Life* (*Onna Genji kyōkun kagami*, 1713), which combined plot summaries of each chapter of *The Tale of Genji* with lessons from *Record of Treasures for Women* (*Onna chōhōki*), a woman's guide to ev-eryday life. Ethical textbooks such as *Women's Great Learning* (*Onna daigaku*), which reinforced conservative Confucian values, were used in schools, while illustrated digests such as *Lessons and Good Manners for Women* (*Onna kyōkun shitsukekata*), which combined didactic tales with commentary on classical stories, were the most popular among women.

Of particular interest here is the fact that theater, kabuki, and jōruri, in which the difference in educational background was not so serious a handicap, were extremely popular among women in the Edo period. In contrast to kabuki, whose scripts were for internal consumption only, the texts for jōruri were pub-lished at the time of the first performance and were sometimes followed by illustrated, easy-to-read digests, thereby making jōruri an important form of popular *literature*. Jōruri chanting also became a popular practice among am-ateurs. Indeed, when the numbers of texts and performances, including kabuki performances of jōruri plays, are combined, jōruri may have had the widest audience of any artistic genre in the Edo period, and women accounted for a large percentage.

In his jōruri, Chikamatsu generally casts the female protagonist as a person who loves her husband and makes every sacrifice for him. A similar type appears in prose fiction. For example, in Ueda Akinari's "Reed-Choked House," from his *Tales of Moonlight and Rain (Ugetsu monogatari)*, Miyagi waits faithfully for her husband and endures difficulties to the point of sacrificing her own life. Many eighteenth-century jōruri depict women who must suffer as a result of their husband's infidelity or lack of concern, although the actions of these men are rarely punished. In eighteenth-century society, the position of a woman was inferior to that of her husband, who had the right to take her life for any transgression, thus making it difficult for her to protest. Women in jōruri rarely commit adultery, and when they do, as in Chikamatsu's *Drums of the Waves of Horikawa*, the adultery is the result of accident and circumstance. But these female characters are not simply exemplaries of Confucian self-sacrifice and devotion; instead, they reveal the extremely difficult position of women. Significantly, Ueda Akinari portrays another type of woman in *Tales of Moonlight and Rain*, a type introduced largely from Chinese vernacular fiction—the strong woman who, feeling betrayed by the man whom she has loved, takes revenge, as Isora does in "Caldron of Kibitsu." This kind of angry, vengeful woman does not appear in eighteenth-century jōruri but marks a new development in Japanese fiction and emerges in such nineteenth-century kabuki and fiction as Oiwa in Tsuruya Nanboku's *Ghost Stories at Yotsuya*.

WARRIOR AND URBAN COMMONER ATTITUDES

Much of the thought and writing of the early modern period tends to be "this-worldly" in outlook, affirming life in this world and looking forward to future improvement, compared with the "other-worldly" attitudes of the medieval period. The "this-worldly" perspective was reflected in the literature of the period: in the focus on contemporary society and in the pursuit of hedonistic pleasures. Warrior attitudes were reinforced by Confucian ethics, with its emphasis on humaneness (*jin*) and rightness (*gi*), and so tended to be highly moralistic, self-sacrificing, and concerned with honor and obligation. Chōnin attitudes, formed from the new commercial and urban economy, were oriented toward the present and physical needs.

The ethical system that emerged and was supported by the bakufu was fundamentally Confucian, and at the base of the Confucian virtues were filial piety (toward parents) and loyalty (toward the master or ruler), which gave the bakufu an ethical basis for reinforcing both the status hierarchy and the hereditary system. From the bakufu's perspective, the greatest threat to this morality and social structure was the notion of individual love or desire. The bakufu thus passed a law stating that "a person who falls in love with the daughter of the master of the house can, at the request of the master, be executed, exiled, or, at the very least, bodily removed." Those youths who did not obey their parents and fell in love could be legally disowned. If the husband discovered his wife in an act of adultery, he had the right to kill her on the spot. If she ran away with a lover, the master could capture her, have her tied to a stake, and stabbed.

The attitudes of the warrior and of the urban commoner overlapped and influenced each other. Although samurai society was built on a lord–retainer relationship, with the disappearance of war and the need for income beyond the monthly stipend, particularly for lower-ranking samurai, traditional values and structures began to collapse. The pleasure seeking that marked wealthy chōnin life infiltrated samurai life, and the samurai became interested in the customs and culture of the urban commoners, such as pipe smoking, jōruri, kabuki, and *kouta* (popular songs), and in the licensed quarters, in ransoming prostitutes and committing double suicide. And with their finances falling apart, the samurai turned to wealthy chōnin for support as adopted sons.

Likewise, samurai values—for example, the notion of lord and vassal and the ideas of duty and loyalty—deeply infiltrated chōnin life: the relationship between the employer and the employee in a merchant business, or between master and apprentice in an artisan house, became infused with the notion of duty/obligation (*giri*) and service (*hōkō*). As commoners became wealthy and had more leisure time, they indulged in cultural activities that earlier had been the province of elite samurai—nō, tea, and *ikebana* (flower arranging)—and took Buddhist names (*ingo*), as samurai did. More important, the ideals of the samurai as they were transformed by Confucianism were reflected in the popular literature and drama of the period. Jōruri, or puppet theater, also was centered on the notions of duty as they became entangled and conflicted with love and human passion (*ninjō*). Much of kabuki as well as popular fiction took the form of samurai narratives, succession disputes in great samurai houses (*oiesōdō*), or vendettas (*kataki-uchi*), such as that found in *Chūshingura: The Storehouse of Loyal Retainers*, with the samurai spirit and values usually winning in the end. It was only toward the end of the early modern period, in the nineteenth century, that a more degenerate image of the samurai, no doubt reflecting their deteriorating financial condition, appeared on stage in kabuki plays such as Tsuruya Nanboku's *Ghost Stories at Yotsuya* and Kawatake Mokuami's *Benten the Thief.*

In the end, these two tendencies—the samurai emphasis on ethics, self-sacrifice, and concerns with political stability and social order, and that of urban commoners, with their focus on contemporary society, finances, and the play of human passions—mixed together in interesting and often creative ways. For example, genres such as jōruri, kabuki, and yomihon are always divided into two basic formats, that of the contemporary-life drama (*sewamono*) and that of the historical or period drama (*jidaimono*), with the former reflecting urban commoner interests and the latter more samurai values, at least on the surface. The playwright Chikamatsu is today known for his contemporary-life dramas, such as *The Love Suicides at Amijima*, but in his day, his historical plays like

The Battles of Coxinga were of far greater importance and occupied the bulk of his repertoire. Even when jōruri and kabuki shifted to historical plays after the prohibition of love-suicide plays in the early eighteenth century, contemporary-life scenes were inserted into the larger historical drama so that "samurai" plays such as *Chūshingura* and *Chronicle of the Battle of Ichinotani* revolved around chōnin themes of money and love. In both these formats, the desires and passions (*ninjō*) of the individual conflicted with duty and responsibility (*giri*) and the pressures and restraints of society, a clash that reflected the larger social and political hierarchy of ruler and ruled, as well as the commingling of the chōnin and samurai cultures.

POPULAR AND ELITE LITERATURES

In the early modern period, there were two distinct genealogies of literature: popular (*zoku*) literature and elegant or refined (*ga*) literature. Popular literature consisted of the new genres, generally used kana-based vernacular language, tended to focus on the urban chōnin society, and reflected the ebullient, erotic, comic, and violent side of contemporary culture. In poetry, the popular genres were haikai, *senryū* (satiric haiku), *kyōka* (wild poetry), and *kyōshi* (wild Chinese poetry); in drama, they were jōruri and kabuki—in contrast to nō, which became the refined or classical form of drama in the Edo period—and in prose fiction, they included *kana-zōshi* (kana booklets), *ukiyo-zōshi* (books of the floating world), *kibyōshi* (satiric and didactic picture books), *sharebon* (books of wit and fashion), *gōkan* (bound illustrated books), *yomihon* (reading books), and *kokkeibon* (comic fiction). The refined literature, by contrast, consisted of the long-standing, authoritative genres such as Chinese poetry (*kanshi*), Chinese prose (*kanbun*), classical poetry (thirty-one-syllable waka), and *gikobun* (neo-classical prose). These more elegant genres, which had a long tradition going back to the ancient period and tended to stress more aristocratic topics (such as nature, the four seasons, and love), relied heavily on classical Chinese or classical Japanese.

The distinction between elite and popular literature was underscored by the close association of popular literature with humor, vulgar topics, and the two "bad places" (*akusho*), the theater and the licensed pleasure quarters, both of which became major sources of popular culture and literature. Kabuki, reflecting urban commoner interests, began as a drama of prostitute buying (*keiseikai*), and its music and dialogue were heavily erotic. The ukiyo-zōshi, the first major vernacular fictional genre, likewise were based largely on the courtesan critiques (*yūjo hyōbanki*) and guides to the licensed quarters. The ukiyo-e, an art form also reflecting urban commoner interests, similarly focused on actors and courtesans.

Popular genres such as kyōka, senryū, and kyōshi had a strong tendency to parody their classical counterparts—waka and kanshi—even as they focused on and satirized the immediate, contemporary world. Indeed, one of the principal characteristics of seventeenth-century literature was the tendency of popular literature to transform the past into the present, the high into the low, and the sacred into the profane, or to move in the opposite direction, as Matsuo Bashō did, by seeking the high or spiritual in the low and everyday.

Chinese studies (*kangaku*) and Japanese nativist studies (*kokugaku*) were an integral part of "refined" literary studies and were closely associated with kanshi and waka, respectively. The early modern period was a great age of Chinese learning that was without precedent and never matched again. Chinese studies in the seventeenth century concentrated on the study of Confucianism, particularly that branch influenced by the Song-period Confucian philosopher Zhu Xi (1130–1200) and his followers. Two major Confucian scholars who opposed this school of Song Confucianism were Itō Jinsai (1627–1705) and Ogyū Sorai (1666–1728), who tried to return directly to the Confucian classics through a systematic philological and historical study of ancient Chinese texts and who are today referred to as members of the Ancient Studies (*kogaku*) school. Kokugaku, which came to the fore in the late seventeenth century, was similar to Ancient Studies in its attempt at a systematic philological and historical study of ancient texts. In contrast to Jinsai and Sorai, however, the kokugaku scholars examined ancient and classical Japanese texts and were crucial to the excavation of such ancient texts as the *Man'yōshū* (*Anthology of Ten Thousand Leaves*) and the *Kojiki* (*Record of Ancient Matters*). During the eighteenth century, nativist learning—led by scholars such as Kada no Arimaro (1706–1751), Kamo no Mabuchi (1697–1769), and Motoori Norinaga (1730–1801)—gradually began to take philosophical and ideological positions opposed to those found in Chinese studies, stressing a "Japanese," or nativist, cultural identity and closely associating Japanese texts with Shintō (the way of the Japanese gods).

Ogyū Sorai's school of Chinese studies, which dominated the first half of the eighteenth century, centered on the literary composition of Chinese poetry and prose, thereby feeding into the *bunjin* (literatus) movement that began in the early eighteenth century, and was led by kanshi poet-artists like Hattori Nankaku (1683–1759). Kokugaku likewise was the field of scholars like Kamo no Mabuchi (1697–1769), who was one of the best-known waka poets of the eighteenth century. Scholarship and commentary, in fact, were inseparable from these elegant genres, kanshi and waka, which had been associated in the medieval period with nobility and priesthood but were now the province of educated samurai and urban commoners. Significantly, the waka composed by Mabuchi and others in his school consciously attempted to address contemporary needs and to establish new ground for poetry.

The eighteenth century was thus marked by the interaction and fusion of refined and popular cultures and literatures. A new kind of commoner culture gradually developed that sought refinement and elegance. Well-to-do urban commoners, rich farmers, and samurai attempted through the elegant classical genres to adopt aspects of elite culture for themselves. This striving for elegance and refinement (*ga*) was closely tied to two salient movements: a deepening interest in Chinese poetry, fiction, and art and a renewed interest in ancient and classical Japanese culture and literature. The newly literate classes, which included the samurai, sought expression for their everyday lives in vernacular popular forms such as haikai, but they found cultural legitimacy in the acquisition of classical Japanese or Chinese culture that had hitherto been the property of either the nobility or the Buddhist clergy. Thus a popular genre like the late-eighteenth-century sharebon, the vernacular fiction of the licensed quarters, had a highly sinicized cast, including Chinese prefaces, that reflected a desire for the high culture associated with China. Accordingly, the trend, embodied most obviously in the bunjin movement, was toward cultural elegance and refinement, toward the development of "Chinese" or "classical Japanese" tastes, even as the deep interest in the vulgar and everyday dimensions of contemporary life continued.

PERIODIZATION

The early modern period can be said to begin either in 1600, when Tokugawa Ieyasu unified Japan by achieving an overwhelming military victory at the battle of Sekigahara, or in 1603, when Ieyasu founded a new military government, or shōgunate, in Edo. The period came to an official end in 1867 when the Tokugawa shōgunate turned over its power to the new Meiji emperor, who became the symbolic head of a nation-state. These 260 years are variously referred to as the Tokugawa period (after the ruling military family), the Edo period (after the new city of the shōgunate), the *kinsei* period (literally, recent period), and the early modern period, implying the first stage of modernization. Each of these terms is incomplete: Tokugawa is a political label, stressing the ruling house; Edo is primarily a geographic designation; early modern emphasizes the notion of the modern; and kinsei does not make sense in English. As a consequence, this book uses three terms—Tokugawa, Edo, and early modern—depending on circumstance.

The early modern period, from 1600 through the late nineteenth century, can be roughly divided into four subperiods. The first, which stretched from the late sixteenth century to the late seventeenth century, was a cultural extension of the medieval period. Politically, the country moved from war to peace and started on the path to economic and urban development that would be the mark of early modern society. The popular literature of this time, however, represented most prominently by haikai and kana-zōshi, closely resembles the popular literature of the sixteenth century. It was not until the second subperiod, from the late seventeenth century through the first two decades of the eighteenth century, that the early modern culture began to flourish, especially in the Kyoto-Osaka area. The third subperiod, roughly covering the remainder of the eighteenth century, came to a climax in the latter half of the century and had bases in both Kyoto-Osaka and Edo. The fourth subperiod, encompassing the first half of the nineteenth century and centered primarily in Edo, had peaked by 1830 but lasted until the end of the Tokugawa regime in 1867.

Most literary histories consider the two high points of early modern culture to be the Genroku era (1688–1704) in the first half of the period and the Bunka-Bunsei era (1804–1829) in the second half. The major figures in the first peak are generally agreed to be Ihara Saikaku (1642–1693), Matsuo Bashō (1644–1694), and Chikamatsu Monzaemon (1653–1724), while the major figures in the second peak are considered to be Takizawa Bakin (1767–1848), Shikitei Sanba (1776–1822), and Jippensha Ikku (1765–1831). This view of literary history, however, heavily reflects the perspective of modern Japanese writers and scholars who are interested in the origins and development of the modern novel or are looking for a modern dramatic prototype.

As this anthology demonstrates, the third subperiod, the century between the Genroku and the Bunka-Bunsei eras, peaking in the latter half of the eighteenth century, should be considered one of the high points of early modern literature and culture. Significantly, this literature is not marked by the kind of realism found in the other periods but by a deep interest in other worlds, by a complex fusion of Chinese and Japanese cultures, and by a mixture of elite and popular cultures. The unusual combination of humor, moral didacticism, and the fantastic signals an exceptional achievement in fiction, poetry, and drama, producing such diverse and remarkable writers as Namiki Sōsuke (1695–1751), Hiraga Gennai (1728–1779), Yosa Buson (1716–1783), and Ueda Akinari (1734–1809). As Nakano Mitsutoshi argued, if the Genroku and the Bunka-Bunsei are eras of popular literature characterized by an interest in contemporary society and immediate reality, then the literature of the eighteenth century, which Nakano considers to be the high period, marks a remarkable fusion of high and popular styles and cultures.

The tremendous growth of kangaku (Chinese studies) in the eighteenth century, particularly the study of vernacular Chinese, created a profound interest in China and led, among other things, to the bunjin (literatus) movement, which sought freedom in elegant and imaginary worlds. The eighteenth century also produced nativist studies (kokugaku), which sought an ideal world or community in ancient Japan, and witnessed the emergence of rangaku (Dutch studies), which stirred interest in science, medicine, and yet another distant country. Hino Tatsuo pointed out that even the licensed quarters, which played a major role in cultural production throughout the early modern period, became fertile ground for the imagination. In the Genroku era, fiction and drama such as Chikamatsu Monzaemon's Love Suicides at Amijima explored the domestic consequences of a man's involvement in the licensed quarters and its impact on his wife and family. In late-eighteenth-century sharebon like The

Playboy Dialect, such unpleasant realities disappear, and the licensed quarters become a self-enclosed world separate from realities of everyday life.[4]

The literature and culture of the Bunka-Bunsei era, by contrast, marks the gradual loss of these imaginary worlds and a return to everyday reality and language. The fusion of elite and popular that characterized much of eighteenth-century literature was gradually replaced by a broad-based popular culture and literature aimed at a wide audience of both men and women. In kanshi (Chinese poetry), for example, poets moved away from the difficult neoclassical style of Ogyū Sorai's Ancient Rhetoric school, which had governed most of eighteenth-century kanshi poetics, into a relaxed, everyday style of the Fresh Spirit (*seishin*) movement, making possible the emergence of such down-to-earth kanshi poets as Ryōkan (1757–1831). The vernacular romance likewise shifted from the cerebral sharebon, based on the tightly defined notion of the connoisseur of the licensed quarters, to the more popular love romances of the ninjōbon widely read by women. If Buson's haikai represent a "departure from the common" (*rizoku*), Issa's haikai mark a return to the common and everyday. There are, of course, notable exceptions. Eighteenth-century genres such as senryū and dangibon cast a satiric and realistic eye on the contemporary world, and Takizawa Bakin's monumental *The Eight Dog Chronicles* (1814–1842) was heavily influenced by the Chinese vernacular novel of the Ming period and so might be called the ultimate exploration of other worlds. But as a general trend, the early nineteenth century marked a movement away from the richly imaginative tendencies of the eighteenth century toward a solid refocusing on this not-always-so-pleasant, everyday world.

---

4. Hino Tatsuo, "Kinsei bungakushiron," *Iwanami kōza Nihon bungakushi,* vol. 8 (Tokyo: Iwanami shoten, 1996), pp. 3–46.

Chapter 2

KANA BOOKLETS AND

THE EMERGENCE OF A PRINT CULTURE

The culture and literature of the early Tokugawa period, from 1600 to 1680, belongs as much in the medieval as in the early modern period. Politically during this time, the country moved from the military hegemony of Oda Nobunaga and Toyotomi Hideyoshi to the founding of the Tokugawa bakufu in Edo, from war to peace. Commercially, this period brought the rapid development of communication, transportation, and economic exchange on a national scale; the growth of three major cities (Kyoto, Osaka, and Edo); and the emergence in these cities of the "bad places" (*akusho*), the pleasure quarters (*yūkaku*), and the theater area (*shibaimachi*), which were cordoned off and controlled by the Tokugawa military government. Nonetheless, the popular literature of this time, represented most prominently by *haikai* (comic linked verse) and *kana-zōshi* (kana booklets in vernacular prose), still closely resembled the popular literature of the sixteenth century, with one distinct difference: the emergence of printing. Many of the noted medieval literary forms such as the *otogi-zōshi*, the Muromachi tales, were in fact printed for the first time in the early seventeenth century. In short, a distinctive early modern literature and culture did not fully emerge until the end of the seventeenth century.

In the sixteenth century, Japan increased its trade with other East Asian countries, importing technologies for ceramics, weaponry, metallurgy, and printing. The first form of printing was movable type, which resulted in a flood of publications, spurred the new consumption of printed goods, and established a publishing industry. Movable type was then abandoned in favor of woodblock printing, with nonmovable type, which allowed for mass printing and further expanded the market. At first, the publications were primarily Buddhist and Confucian texts, then medical books and literary classics, and eventually contemporary vernacular literature. The decline of movable type, the rise of the publishing industry, and the mass production of printed goods all occurred at the same time, in the mid-seventeenth century.

A direct descendant of the folk narratives (*setsuwa*) and otogi-zōshi of the late medieval period, the seventeenth-century kana-zōshi were noted for their diversity, ranging from literary parodies like *The Dog Pillow Book* (*Inu makura*) and *Fake Tales* (*Nise monogatari*) to humorous tales such as *Today's Tales of Yesterday* (*Kinō wa kyō no monogatari*) to didactic tales like Asai Ryōi's *Tales of the Floating World* (*Ukiyo monogatari*) to supernatural tales such as Asai Ryōi's *Hand Puppets* (*Otogi bōko*). Some kana-zōshi were pedagogical, intended, for example, to teach the principles of Buddhism or Confucianism to a popular audience. Others served as travel guides (*meishoki*), such as Asai Ryōi's *Famous Sights Along the Eastern Seaboard* (*Tōkaidō meishoki*).

PARODIES

Parodies were one of the earliest kana-zōshi genres and transformed texts of Heian or medieval court culture into humorous comic versions of contemporary popular culture. The first parodies appeared in the early sixteenth century, along with haikai, or comic linked verse, which parodied classical waka poetry. With the rise of print culture in the seventeenth century, which made classical texts available to a wider audience, literary parody gained new life, with *Fake Tales* (1640s), a word-for-word parody of *The Tales of Ise*; *Dog Hundred Poems* (*Inu hyakunin isshu*), a parody of *Hyakunin isshu* (*One Hundred Poets, One Hundred Poems*), edited by the noted poet Fujiwara Teika; *The Dog Pillow Book*, a takeoff on Sei Shōnagon's famous *Pillow Book*; and *Dog Essays in Idleness* (*Inu tsurezuregusa*, 1653), an extended comic twist on Yoshida Kenkō's *Tsurezuregusa*. Another new literary form at this time was the easy-to-read digests or modern renditions of the classics for popular audiences. The most salient examples are *Ten-Chapter Genji* (*Jūjō Genji*, 1661), *Child Genji* (*Osana Genji*, 1665), and *Tales of Ise in Easy Words* (*Ise monogatari hirakotoba*, 1678), which turned *The Tales of Ise* into a continuous narrative instead of the episodic sections found in the original.

In strong contrast to Ihara Saikaku, the pioneer of the late-seventeenth-century vernacular prose and a professional writer of merchant background who profited financially from writing, most of the authors of kana-zōshi were intellectuals, usually Confucian scholars, Buddhist priests, doctors, and samurai (mainly former samurai), who, with the exception of a few writers like Asai

Ryōi, did not leave their names on their works, suggesting that for most of them, writing kana-zōshi was a hobby.

THE DOG PILLOW BOOK (*INU MAKURA*, 1607?)

The Dog Pillow Book, whose author is unknown, was printed during the Keichō era (1696–1715) and so is one of the earliest kana-zōshi and a good example of literary parody. Consisting of some seventy sections, it parodies Sei Shōnagon's *Pillow Book*, specifically her "detailing of things" (*mono wa tsukushi*) sections, in which she introduces a topic (*mono*) and then details (*tsukushi*) its possibilities, as in the following example:

Elegant Things

A white coat worn over a violet waistcoat.
Duck eggs.
Shaved ice mixed with liana syrup and put in a new silver bowl.
A rosary of rock crystal.
Wisteria blossoms. Plum blossoms covered with snow.
A pretty child eating strawberries.

This kind of "detailing of things" became a popular literary practice in the seventeenth century. In *The Dog Pillow Book* each entry within a section is linked to the next in an unexpected fashion, with the sections themselves often juxtaposed in contrastive or parallel fashion, as in haikai. The result is a text that derives its pleasure from its terseness, surprising juxtapositions, and unexpected humor.

Disagreeable Things

Being invited to a clumsy tea ceremony.
A woman who falls asleep after making love.
Accompanying the master on a sightseeing trip to the hills.
A grievance that goes unheard.
A long-staying guest on a night when one has other matters in mind.
A bad friend.

Things That Stand One's Hair on End

Talking about ghosts.
In winter, putting on armor without underclothes.
A river of unknown deeps and shallows.
Malaria.
The prospect of an evening's conversation with one's boy favorite.[1]
The house where a faith healer is praying.

---

1. One's boy favorite (*wakashu*) was a young boy who was a sexual partner for an adult male.

Dangerous Things

Leaving one's boy favorite in a priest's charge.
A one-log bridge.
A skipping race on stone steps.
Gossip about one's master.

Things One Would Like to Send Away

An old wife.
Someone who appears in the middle of a conversation.
A beggar standing at the gate.
The officious parent of one's boy favorite.
A woman who falls asleep after making love.

Things the Bigger the Better

Roof beams.
The heart of the master's son.
The penny cakes of a teahouse where one stops on a tiring journey.
Blossoms on trees—the fruit, too.
The sword of a strong man.

Things the Smaller the Better

The youth who is one's personal servant.
The sword worn in a reception hall.
The wine cup of a weak drinker.
Acolytes and serving boys.

> [*Kana-zōshi shū*, NKBT 90: 35–48, adapted from a translation by Edward Putzar]

FAKE TALES (*NISE MONOGATARI*, 1640s)

Fake Tales is a word-for-word parody of the 125 sections of *The Tales of Ise*, the Heian poem-tale about the noted lover Ariwara no Narihira. The parody derives its interest from not only the witty twists on the original text, which in those times most readers knew by heart, but also its reflections on contemporary life in the mid-seventeenth century. The following passage, which turns on the notion of "burning alive," the preferred method of executing Christians, is about the ban on Christianity that went into effect in 1612 and continued to the end of the Edo period. The repression of Christians was most severe between 1615 and 1644, when this parody was written. The episode translated here is probably based on the actual execution of more than forty Christians in 1638. Section 12 of *The Tales of Ise* also has been reproduced here in full.

This woodblock illustration from *Fake Tales* is a comic variation on the deluxe *Sagabon* edition of *The Tales of Ise*, first published in Kyoto in 1608. This scene from *Fake Tales* shows a commoner couple tied up in the fields of Musashino—replacing the elegant courtier couple in the *Sagabon* edition—while two officials prepare to set fire to the fields. Musashino was associated in classical poetry with autumn grass (reflected in the pampas grass and bush clover). Clouds frame the scene at the top and bottom, a convention used in the *Sagabon* and earlier illustrated books.

In the past there was a man who ran off with someone's daughter and led her to the fields of Musashi.[2] Since this made him a thief, he was arrested by the governor of the province. He left the woman in a grassy place and ran away. Some people who came along the road said, "We hear there is a thief in this field" and started to set fire to it. The woman was distraught and composed the following:

Musashino wa	Don't burn
kyō wa na yaki so	the fields of Musashi!
wakakusa no	My spouse, as tender as
tsuma mo komoreri	young grass, is hidden here
ware mo komoreri	and so am I.[3]

When they heard this, they took the woman and led the pair off together.

Edict Against Christianity (section 12)

It was amusing: since there was an edict against Christianity, a man fled with a woman into the fields of Musashi. Because his actions made him a criminal, he was apprehended by the magistrate. They put both the woman and the man

---

2. In a region now occupied by Tokyo, Saitama Prefecture, and part of Kanagawa Prefecture.

3. This poem differs from *Kokinshū*, no. 17, an anonymous poem in the first book of Spring, only in that the word "Musashino" replaces "Kasugano" (fields of Kasuga), in Yamato Province (Nara). In the *Kokinshū* poem, men are setting fire to the fields not out of malice but in order to clear away dead growth before the spring planting. *Wakakusa no* (tender grass) is a pillow word, or epithet, for *tsuma* (spouse).

in the field to be executed and were about to set fire to it when the woman pleaded:

Musashino wa	Don't burn
kyō wa na yaki so	the fields of Musashi!
Asakusa ya	At Asakusa
tsuma mo koroberi	my spouse has renounced his faith
ware mo koroberi	and so have I.[4]

[*Kana-zōshi shū*, NKBT 90: 172–173, translated by Jamie Newhard]

HUMOROUS STORIES

The long tradition of humorous stories (*waraibanashi*) took on special importance in the late medieval period when powerful generals and domain lords employed professional storytellers (*otogi-shū*) as jester-critics to entertain, inform, and provide them with interesting company. This tradition of storytelling, which emphasized humor, gradually spread from the elite samurai to the populace, and with the advent of printing in the seventeenth century, humorous stories became extremely popular, reaching an even wider audience than did other comic genres such as *senryū*, *kyōka*, and *kibyōshi*. Professional storytellers such as Anrakuan Sakuden (1554–1642) began to publish collections of stories that they had heard of or had used. Since these storytellers did not consider their stories to be literature, they were not bound by the conventions or language of the classical genres and so presented these stories in a style that closely reflected colloquial Japanese as well as contemporary, commoner interests.

TODAY'S TALES OF YESTERDAY
(*KINŌ WA KYŌ NO MONOGATARI*, CA. 1615)

Today's Tales of Yesterday is a kana-zōshi collection of humorous stories that was widely popular between 1615 and 1630. While similar to earlier *setsuwa* (folk narrative) collections, which often contained humorous stories, *Today's Tales of Yesterday*, like *Wake Up Laughing* (*Seisuishō*, 1623, published between 1624 and 1644) — another collection of humorous stories — represented a departure from the past in its specialized focus on humor and in its more "modern" repertoire of humorous types. The break with the past is symbolized by the title *Kinō wa kyō* (literally, yesterday is today), which reverses the temporal formula *ima wa mukashi* (now is the past) from the early-twelfth-century

---

4. "Asakusa" (literally, Shallow Grass), replacing *wakakusa* (tender young grasses) in *The Tales of Ise* poem, was used as an execution ground in Edo until the early 1650s. *Koroberi*, replacing *komoreri* (hidden), literally means "tumble down" or "fall to the ground," an action used at the time to indicate a renunciation of Christianity.

setsuwa collection *Tales of Times Past* (*Konjaku monogatari shū*). Although the identity of the editor is unknown, some scholars have suggested that it was Anrakuan Sakuden, the author of *Wake Up Laughing*. Indeed, the style and subject matter suggest a compiler like Sakuden, either an itinerant storytelling monk (*dangi-sō*) or perhaps a merchant-class professional storyteller. The work has been called Japan's first best-seller, with numerous editions (including some printed from woodblocks) and variations in the number and order of the stories. Many of the stories rely on puns and wordplays for their humor, making them difficult to translate. In the first of the two following selections, the humor of the passage hinges on a punch line, a device employed frequently in *Today's Tales of Yesterday*. The second selection is unlike most passages in the collection in that the humor relies on the Solomon-like wisdom of the legal resolution to the story it describes.

Dangerous Things in the World (episode 20)

"There are many dangerous things in the world: A crippled pottery seller. A heavily laden packhorse making its way down a narrow path on a riverbank. A blind man walking downhill. A young mother-in-law who gets along too well with her son-in-law. A widower on close terms with his daughter-in-law. A young widow who worships frequently at a temple. That's about it."

A monk heard this and carelessly said, "Yes, each of the things you mentioned is certainly dangerous. Why, there is a young widow who worships at our temple, and she is definitely dangerous." He covered his mouth as soon as he had spoken.

The Woman Who Cut Off Her Nose (episode 35)

A certain man suffered from a certain illness. As death approached, he called his wife to his side.

"I feel that I will not survive more than a day or two. It is hard to say good-bye, but most unbearable is the thought that you might one day remarry and make love to another man."

"Put your mind at rest. If you should die, I will shave my head and become a nun, and devote myself to thoughts of the afterlife and prayer for your soul's repose."

"Your words give me great joy, but hair grows back after it's been shaved off. If you agree, please show your devotion to me while I breathe, by cutting off your nose. If you do so, I swear that my birthright, my storehouse, and my entire earthly fortune will be yours."

"I will gladly do so," she said, and, to prove her devotion to him, she cut off her nose.

He wrote a detailed last will and testament in which he bequeathed everything to his wife and handed it to her. "Now I can die in peace," he said.

He waited for death, but to everyone's surprise, within one or two days his appetite had improved and his spirits had lifted. Before long, he had completely recovered.

Everyone rejoiced over his recovery, but there was one thing the man could not escape: the sight, day and night, of his wife's noseless face. One day he called her to his side: "I am ashamed to tell you this, but seeing your face makes me wish I were dead. There is no kind way to say it: I want you to leave."

His wife could not believe her ears. "I was born with that nose, and what about our happy years together? After all, you are the one who made me cut it off. If you find me so repulsive, you should be the one to leave."

"What you say is true," he said, "but I still must ask you to leave. Do it for the sake of our past love."

The woman refused and decided to petition the local authorities. Shortly an inquiry was begun, and she was summoned for questioning.

The man then stepped forward and said, "What the woman told you is true, but I am still young. It is not fair that I should be made to look at her, day and night, in her present condition. Please order her to leave me as I requested."

The magistrates heard him and discussed the case among themselves for some time. They then handed down their judgment: "Off with the man's nose."

The man was terrified and tried to escape, but guards captured him, sliced off his nose, and turned him over to the woman. "There should be no cause for animosity between you now," the head magistrate said, and he dismissed the couple.

The man was in low spirits and thought to himself." Now I have no hope of ever being married to a beautiful woman again. But as the saying goes, 'No go-between is needed to reconcile with your wife.'"

Hand in hand, the noseless man and the noseless woman returned home and lived happily ever after without incident.

[*Edo shōwa shū*, NKBT 100: 61–63, introduction and translation by
Paul Gordon Schalow]

ASAI RYŌI

Asai Ryōi, the most prominent of the kana-zōshi writers, was a samurai in Edo before becoming a *rōnin*, or masterless samurai. In the 1650s, he entered the Buddhist priesthood and made his home in Kyoto. It was during this later period that he wrote most of the pieces that have survived. Although many kana-zōshi at this time were written by amateurs who did not leave their names on their works, Asai Ryōi, who wrote a large number, including *Tales of the Floating World* (*Ukiyo monogatari*) and *Hand Puppets* (*Otogi bōko*), was an important exception.

TALES OF THE FLOATING WORLD (*UKIYO MONOGATARI*, 1666)

Tales of the Floating World, a loose collection of stories, centers on a wealthy young man of Kyoto named Hyōtarō, who engages in various dissolute activities from gambling to sex and squanders his fortune in the process. He manages to become a minor samurai but loses his position as a result of a dispute, and after wandering about, he becomes a lay-priest with the name Ukiyobō (Floating-World Priest). Finally, he is employed by a daimyō as a kind of jester-critic in residence. Although *Tales of the Floating World* are didactic narratives that have Confucian and Buddhist underpinnings and satirize contemporary society, particularly the rōnin and the pleasure-loving townsmen, they also reveal the new "commoner" focus on the present moment. A good example is the episode "Regarding Advice Against Wenching." This story is typical of the kana-zōshi genre in its mixture of entertainment, humor, and moral purpose and in the way laughter generated by failure is used as an opportunity for didactic or educational persuasion.

In contrast to the otherworldly, Buddhist attitude of medieval society, which stressed "seeking the Pure Land" (*gongu jōdo*) and "turning away from the dirty world" (*enri edo*), the military leader Oda Nobunaga (1534–1582) pursued an active, anti-Buddhist policy, which was inherited and continued by Toyotomi Hideyoshi (1536–1598) and Ieyasu, the first Tokugawa shōgun. Then, in the seventeenth century, urban commoners began to formulate their own view of this world, one that came to be embodied in the word *ukiyo* (floating world), as opposed to its homonym the "sorrowful world" (also *ukiyo*). The famous preface to *Tales of the Floating World* articulates this difference in the form of a debate between a person who holds a darker, more medieval view and the author/narrator who takes a lighter, more optimistic, contemporary perspective embodied in the metaphor of the floating gourd (*hyōtan*), with final approval going to the latter. Significantly, the nickname of the protagonist is Hyōtaro (Gourd Boy), who "bobs along with the current."

Preface

"In days now past," someone said, "There was a folk song:

> Such a strange thing—
> My heart is my own,
> But it won't do as I want it.

"This popular love song was sung by all, high and low, men and women, old and young. There was also a poem:

> When nothing goes
> As you want it to go—
> It's a sorrowful world.

"It seems that they call this a sorrowful world [*ukiyo*] because in all things, nothing can be fulfilled; nothing goes as you want it to go. It's like that saying, 'Scratch the soles of your feet with your shoes still on.' You feel an itch, but you can't scratch it. It seems within reach, but you can't reach it. It's such an irritating thing. You are yourself, but you have no control over your body and soul. What a strange thing! Needless to say, in this world there is not one thing that goes as one desires it to. That's precisely why it's called a sorrowful world," the person concluded.

I responded: "No, that's not the meaning of it at all. When we live in this world, we see and hear the good and the bad in all things; everything is interesting, and we can't see more than one inch in front of us. It's not worth the skin of a gourd to worry about it; fretting just causes indigestion. So cross each bridge as you come to it; gaze at the moon, the snow, the cherry blossoms, and the bright autumn leaves; recite poems; drink saké; and make merry. Not even poverty will be a bother. Floating along with an unsinkable disposition, like a gourd bobbing along with the current—this is what we call the floating world [*ukiyo*]."

An expert on the subject was impressed at this and exclaimed, "Truly, that's it, that's it!"

Regarding Advice Against Wenching (book 1, episode 6)

Once upon a time a hitherto unknown itch attacked Hyōtaro, the Gourd Boy, and he began frequenting the pleasure houses of the Shimabara quarter.[5] He would leave home looking for all the world as though he were setting out on some respectable business. But en route he would hail a crossroads sedan-chair and, in this, ride south along Ōmiya Street and follow the Tanba Highway up to the entrance of the Shimabara. Then he would send back the palanquin and, putting on a large woven-reed hat, walk quickly over Slicking-up Grounds and Rumor Lane, soon arriving at Assignation-House Street. Climbing to the second floor of one of the houses, he would meet with a courtesan he had known well for a long time.

Not infrequently they would engage in lovers' quarrels, but he knew better than to take the girl's reproaches seriously and laughed away all thoughts of ever being able to please her entirely. At other times, being promised her true love until the end of time, he became so intoxicated with joy as to think less of his own life than of dirt. And all the while he was being fawned on and flattered by the hired jesters, to the very end of his nose on his boastful face. In this way he visited the pleasure quarter every day and used up his gold and silver as one would use water, spending everything his father had so carefully saved. He

---

5. The licensed quarter in Kyoto.

Three samurai approach the main gate of the Shimabara licensed quarter in Kyoto. Three bearded footmen (*yakko*)—their kimonos bunched up at the hips, exposing their thighs—follow, carrying their master's sedge hat and extra clothes. The samurai are visiting incognito, wearing large sedge hats and covering their mouths with cloths. Each wears a long *haori* jacket over his kimono and two swords, one short and one long, a sign that he is a samurai.

carried the treasure blithely from his house and, when he was really under the spell, cared not at all who saw him.

His coat was in the latest style, with the hem pulled high and his wide sash tied in back. In a fine scabbard he carried a short sword with a glittering gold sword guard. The stockings he wore were elegant, with foreign-style buttons attached, as he clacked along on his high wooden clogs. Taking a better look, we see the *sakayaki* style of coiffure, shaved all the way down to his ears, the sideburns thinned, and his moustache trimmed in his own special way. On his head he wore a great woven-reed hat, pulled low over his eyes. Can we call his appearance good or bad? Certainly it was little more than the epitome of the crude style of the menservants of lesser samurai.

His brothers and relatives, pained by his behavior, cautioned him in private in the following manner:

"Of late we hear that you've been frequenting some such totally unbelievable place as the Shimabara! This is really not the proper thing to do. By her nature a courtesan is a woman who attends herself well, dresses up and adorns herself, and so is quite alluring. For this reason it is readily understandable that a man's heart should be conquered and that he should fall head over heels in love. Her charming willowy tresses, her face lovely as a cherry blossom, her eyebrows with mascara recalling the deep green treetops of the distant mountains. Her laughing crimson lips like the first opening of the hibiscus petals, her polished teeth shining white just like the driven snow. Her arms and legs slim, not at all differing in beauty from the Chinese dianthus just beginning to bloom in the hedge. Her lips languorous like a loose-wound spool, the fragrance of her perfume reaching to the skies. And how lovely when she moves, swaying back and forth; truly she could easily be mistaken for the living incarnation of the Amida Buddha! When compared with this creature, a man's wife can hardly seem more than a salted fish long past its prime!

"And so, tired of one's spouse and unable to put the courtesan from one's mind, one goes again to meet with her. Her voice of greeting is lovely, like the first sound of the nightingale as it darts forth from a narrow valley:

"'You've come at last! Come to me quickly!'

"And the thankfulness you feel just to hear the sound of her voice! What great priest could bestow on you words of enlightenment equal to this? You two coming close together, your conversation is intimate though still somewhat restrained, and her manner is intoxicating. As she plays the shamisen close to you, strumming the strings 'tsuru-ten,' one thinks the sound of the plectrum must make the lover almost paralyzed with joy. Truly awesome! When she finally begins her song, your heart's as if afloat; fired by the song and her voice, it's as if you're in a dream, thinking, 'Ah, were I to die tomorrow, what would I regret! When one's bones are drying in the sun, there's no more glory anyway. Ah, this is the life! Pass the saké cup over here.' And so she stretches forth her arm, lovely and white as a bamboo shoot, holding the wine cup for you. 'Please drink a bit,' she murmurs, and you feel that life will never be so fine again, your heart so much afloat.

"And thus do many men go to their ruin.

"A certain Kameya something-or-other, a famous millionaire here in the capital, was in love with a courtesan, but his wife became exceedingly jealous, saying, 'Well, I'm going to buy a courtesan too!' Husband and wife each night summoned two of the finest courtesans of the city as companions, hiring also the lesser courtesans, such as half-night courtesans, kept courtesans, lordship courtesans, as well as masseurs, thus spending all their time in gay merriment. Before long, his estate was completely used up, and now, so the story goes, the fellow's no longer able even to live in the capital and has gone down to Nagasaki, to live on whatever he can manage to make as a day laborer!

"But from olden times, there've been many others thus ruined. One, perhaps knifing the courtesan to death and then killing himself; another (one Yoshinoya something-or-other) eloping with his courtesan, only later to be captured and lose his life—not to mention having his property confiscated by the government. Besides these are the many who, pursued by debts from the courtesan quarter, must hide in barrels, commit theft, and finally are beheaded. Or we might mention yet others who, having neither gold nor silver, sold all their household goods and ruined their families and then were reduced to begging, clad in a cheap hemp gown or torn paper robe, so that no one will even talk to them. And these are only the recent cases.

"So please, we beseech you, cease this folly!" Thus they admonished him at length.

Having listened to their long harangue, Hyōtaro answered as follows:

"Truly, I am most grateful for your kind advice. Henceforth, I will not go there anymore." Having thus made his solemn pledge, he sent the elders home and, without a pause, hurried out on his way to the Shimabara and, before long, using up all he had, ended up as yet another of those thread-bare bums, to the tune of the samisen's *"te-tsuru-ten"*!

[*Kana-zōshi shū*, NKBT 90: 244, 253–255, translated by Jack Stoneman
and Richard Lane, respectively]

HAND PUPPETS (*OTOGI BŌKO*, 1666)

Asai Ryōi wrote *Hand Puppets*, a collection of sixty-eight supernatural tales, in 1666, after his writing career had been well established. The title refers to the dolls traditionally placed by children's pillows to ward off harmful spirits. Eighteen of the stories in Asai's collection, including "The Peony Lantern," were drawn from the noted Ming collection of ghost tales, *Jiandeng Xinhua* (J. *Sentō shinwa*; *New Stories After Putting out the Lamp*, 1378) by Qu You. Ryōi was the first Japanese writer to use this Chinese collection extensively, and it became a source for narrative fiction into the late Tokugawa and Meiji periods. The three main types of ghost stories—the Buddhist tales of karmic causality beginning with *An Account of Rewards and Retribution for Good and Evil in Japan* (*Nihon ryōiki*, 810–824), ghost stories from various provinces, and adaptations from Chinese ghost stories—were represented in the seventeenth century by *Tales of Karmic Causality* (*Inga monogatari*, 1661–1673), *Hundred Tales* (*Hyaku monogatari*, 1659), and Ryōi's *Hand Puppets*, the last being the most sophisticated and innovative in literary terms. Whereas the earlier medieval ghost stories had been heavily influenced by the Buddhist doctrine of karmic causality—which rewards religious piety and punishes evil—Asai's ghost stories focused on human psychology, using the supernatural to reflect intense emotional states, particularly resentment and jealousy, and thus established a new style of ghost story, which had a profound impact on later writers such as Ueda Akinari.

Asai Ryōi did not directly translate his Chinese sources. Instead, he gave them Japanese characters and settings and employed an elegant Japanese style (*gabun*) that distanced his narratives from their Chinese origins. "The Peony Lantern," one of Ryōi's best-known stories, was an adaptation of the Chinese tale "Botan tōki" (Account of a Peony Lantern), with the setting shifted to Kyoto during the turmoil of the Ōnin War (1467–1477), which devastated the capital. Employing waka poetry and a classical style, Ryōi created the atmosphere of a courtly Heian romance. The noted *rakugo* (comic oral storyteller) performer Sanyūtei Enchō rewrote the story in the late nineteenth century, altering and expanding it considerably.

The Peony Lantern

Every year from the fifteenth through the twenty-fourth of Seventh Month, the people of Kyoto set up altars in their homes and perform memorial services for the spirits of their deceased ancestors. Paper lanterns are made as festival dec-orations. People place the lighted lanterns on their altars or hang them from the eaves of their homes, and when they visit the graves of their departed, they set one in front of the tombstone. These lanterns are elegantly painted with designs of flowers and birds or trees and plants. Throughout the festival season they are left burning all night long. Sightseers drift through the city streets incessantly, and now and then a troupe of festival dancers comes dancing grace-fully along, their charming voices raised in hymns of praise to the buddhas and saints. The entire capital from one end to another is thus transformed during the Festival of the Dead.[6]

It was the Seventh Month of the seventeenth year of Tenbun [1548].[7] At this time there lived on Fifth Avenue in the Kyōgoku district a man named Ogihara Shinnosuke. He had recently lost his wife; his breast smoldered with longing for her; and his sleeves were always soaked with tears. He lingered forlornly by his window, pining for the days they had passed so happily together. This year the seasonal festivities moved him more deeply than ever before. To think that his own wife was now among the souls of the departed! He spent his time offering sutras for her repose and had no desire to set foot outside his home. His friends tried to entice him out, but he did not have the heart. He just lingered at his gate, lost in thought. Once he composed a verse: "The apparition of my precious wife remains ever before me; Why, then, am I heartbroken, though she still clings to me so?" Murmuring these lines, he wiped away his tears.

It was very late at night on the fifteenth of the Seventh Month. The number of passersby had dwindled and the streets were nearly silent. Just then Ogihara noticed a lovely woman around twenty years old gracefully strolling along. She was accompanied by a girl of fourteen or fifteen who was carrying an exquisite paper lantern inscribed with a peony design. The woman's eyes were bright as lotus blossoms, her figure lithe as a willow, her eyebrows lovely as a laurel tree, her jet black tresses indescribably alluring. As he gazed at her beneath the moonlight, Ogihara wondered whether she was a goddess who had descended from heaven to amuse herself among humans, or the Princess of the Dragon Palace who had risen from the ocean depths to divert herself on earth. Truly, she seemed a creature not of this world! Ogihara lost his senses; he was so entranced by the woman that he could not resist following her.

He began subtly flirting with her, now overtaking her, now falling behind. After they had walked westward a short distance the woman turned around, and with a faint smile, she spoke to him: "It's not that I am waiting anxiously for a

---

6. During the Obon Festival, or the Feast of Spirits, the living pay respects to the spirits of the dead, who were thought to return for the occasion.

7. The Tenbun era (1532–1555).

man who promised to meet me. I was lured out by the moon tonight and lost track of time. I dread walking home so late at night. Won't you keep me company?" Ogihara slowly approached her. "Your home must be far from here, and it's dangerous to return at this late hour. I live in a dusty, ramshackle place, but if you don't mind, please spend the night there," he offered. The woman smiled and replied, "One who leads a dreary life, gazing alone at the moonlight seeping through her window, is delighted to receive such an invitation. The human heart is moved by kindness." She drew a little closer to him.

Ogihara was elated. He took the woman's hand and led her to his home. He brought out some liquor, asked the young maid to serve them, and he and the woman drank a bit together. The moon hung low in the sky, and as Ogihara listened to the woman's charming conversation, he thought, "Would that this day together were the last day of my life!"[8] Little did he realize that his wish would prove prophetic. Then Ogihara tried composing a verse: "Must we wait until the hour of our next meeting to share a pillow? No, this very night may be our one opportunity." The woman responded: "If only you pledge you will wait night after night, I'll come without fail; Why should parting make you fret and cast such rueful glances?"

Ogihara was more and more enchanted. He and the woman bared their innermost feelings to each other, then they disrobed and shared a pillow for the first time. Before they could exchange all the words of love in their hearts, dawn had come.

"Where do you live?" asked Ogihara. "My house is no 'rough-hewn wooden palace,' but do tell me your name!"[9] The woman replied, "I am a descendant of Nikaidō Masayuki, whose ancestors were Fujiwaras. In Masayuki's day our family was influential and prosperous. Times changed, and now I dwell very humbly, barely managing to stay alive. My father, Masanobu, was slain in battle during the uprisings in Kyoto.[10] After all my brothers died, our house was ruined. Now only I am left. I live with my maid near the Manju Temple.[11] Even introducing myself makes me feel sad and ashamed."

Her speech was refined and her manner frank and endearing. Already the moon, veiled in trailing clouds, was about to slip behind the mountain crest,

---

8. Ogihara is alluding to a love poem in the early-thirteenth-century imperial anthology, the *Shinkokinshū*. The poem was written by a woman to a man who had just begun courting her: "Though you firmly swear your love will last forever, I cannot be sure; would that this day together were the last day of my life" (no. 1149).

9. Alludes to a poem written by Emperor Tenji (r. 668–671) while he was staying at a temporary palace in a rustic area far from the capital: "While way out here in this rough-hewn wooden palace in Asakura, I wonder who that lad is who gives his name as he passes by" (*Shinkokinshū*, no. 1687).

10. She is referring to the Ōnin War (1467–1477).

11. A Buddhist temple of the Zen (Rinzai) sect in eastern Kyoto.

and the lamplight in the room had grown faint. The woman arose, reluctantly bid farewell, and left. After that, the woman came to Ogihara at dusk and departed at dawn; every night she kept her vow to visit. Ogihara's heart was in turmoil, his reason had flown. He was thrilled that the woman cared for him so deeply and never failed to come. He lost interest in seeing anyone else, even during the day. For more than twenty days he remained in this state.

Next door to Ogihara lived a wise old man. He thought it strange that lately, night after night, he could hear the voice of a young woman, laughing and singing, coming from Ogihara's house. He became so suspicious that finally he went and peeked through a crack in his fence. Lo and behold, there in the lamplight sat Ogihara, face to face with a skeleton! When Ogihara spoke, the skeleton would move its arms and legs, nod its skull, and reply in a voice that seemed to come from its mouth. The old man was aghast. As soon as it was daybreak he sent for Ogihara.

"These days you seem to have a guest every evening. Who on earth is it?" he asked. But Ogihara stayed silent, wishing to keep his affair a secret. So the old man spoke his mind: "You are headed for disaster. It's no use trying to hide anything. Last night I peeked through the fence and saw everything. You know, human beings are energetic and pure while they're alive, but after they die and become ghosts they turn gloomy and vicious. That's why corpses are taboo. Now you're dallying with a gloomy ghost and you don't realize it. You're sleeping with a filthy evil enchantress, but you're blind to it. Soon your energy will be gone, your vigor depleted, and misfortunes will beset you. You'll fall ill, and

Ogihara, wearing a black lozenge-pattern robe, sits relaxed with one knee folded and his sword placed by his side (non-samurai were allowed to carry only one sword), engrossed in conversation with the skeleton by the light of a lamp. Ogihara's neighbor is standing in the next room, peeking through a crack in the wall, rather than through a fence, as noted in the text. From the 1666 edition.

A votive paper lantern, with peony flowers on the top, hangs from the eaves of a small shrine. The lattice doors are open, revealing flowers and other offerings in front of the mortuary tablet, which Ogihara is reading.

no amount of medicine or moxa or acupuncture will do you any good. Consumption will set in, and in the bloom of your youth, robbed of a long life, you'll find yourself in the netherworld, your bones buried beneath the moss. Oh, what a pity!"

Ogihara was stunned, then fear gripped his heart, and he revealed his recent experiences. After hearing the story the old man said, "If she said she lives near the Manju Temple, you ought to go there and look for her." So Ogihara headed westward on Fifth Avenue and scoured the entire area around Madé Avenue. He trudged over riverbanks and through willow groves and made many inquiries, but no one could tell him a thing. When dusk fell he entered the Manju Temple precincts to rest for a while. As he wandered northward, beyond the bathhouse, he came upon an old burial shrine. He went up to it and read the inscription on the coffin: "Here lies Iyako, daughter of Imperial Palace Guard Nikaidō Masanobu; Buddhist name, Ginshōin Reigetsu."[12] Beside the coffin was an old doll, a child's amulet; on its back was written the name "Asaji." An old paper lantern, inscribed with a pattern of peonies, hung on the front of the shrine. Here were the woman and her little maid; there was no doubt about it. Ogihara was so horrified that his hair stood on end. Without looking back, he fled from the temple grounds and raced home.

The passion that had consumed him for weeks was utterly quenched. Ogihara was now petrified to be at home. Gone was the lover who had longed for

12. According to Buddhist custom, the deceased receive a religious name.

dusk and lamented the dawn; Ogihara could only tremble at the thought of the woman appearing that evening. He went next door to the old man's house and asked to spend the night there. "What on earth shall I do?" he moaned. The old man gave him this advice: "Kyō no kimi, a monk at the Tō Temple,[13] is both a holy man and a scholar. What's more, he's known for his healing powers. Hurry and ask for his help."

Ogihara lost no time in going to meet the man. Kyō no kimi declared, "A fiendish spirit is sucking your blood and confusing your mind. You have only ten days to live." Then Ogihara related the whole story to him. Kyō no kimi wrote a talisman to ward off evil and told Ogihara to attach it to his gate. After that the woman did not visit him again.

Around fifty days later Ogihara called on Kyō no kimi at the Tō Temple to express his gratitude. The monk treated him to some liquor, and Ogihara left rather intoxicated. Naturally enough, he found himself yearning for a glimpse of the woman's face. He staggered to the Manju Temple and peered through the gate. At once the woman appeared before him and reproached him severely:

"Your recent vows of love have soon become empty words, and you've shown your heartlessness. At first, since your feelings were deep, I yielded myself to you. I came to you faithfully at twilight and departed at dawn. Although you promised you would cling to me forever, someone called Kyō no kimi cruelly drove us apart and turned your heart against me. But how happy I am that you have come to see me tonight! Please come in." The woman took Ogihara by the hand and led him through the gate and into the darkness.

Ogihara's manservant took to his heels in fright. He raced home and told everyone what he had witnessed. They all were appalled and rushed to the scene. But by the time they arrived, Ogihara had already been lured into the woman's grave and had died embracing her bones. The monks at the temple were highly perplexed by the incident, and they had the grave moved to Toribeyama.

After that, on dark, rainy nights Ogihara and the woman were seen walking hand in hand, accompanied by a girl carrying a lantern with a peony design. People who encountered them fell gravely ill, and their neighbors were terror stricken. Ogihara's family was greatly dismayed by these occurrences. They recited the Lotus Sutra a thousand times, and they visited Ogihara's grave to offer sutras copied for the repose of his soul.[14] From that time on, it is said, the spirits ceased to appear.

[*Kana-zōshi shūsei* 7: 196–203, translated by Maryellen Toman Mori]

---

13. A Buddhist temple of the Shingon sect in southern Kyoto.

14. The sutra copies offered at his grave are the product of *ichi nichi tonsha* (one-day hasty copying), the practice in which a group of people gather for a day to transcribe a sutra.

MILITARY STORIES

At the beginning of the Edo period, various types of military stories were written and widely read. Particularly prominent were regional and individual records of those who had directly participated in the battles leading to the unification of the country in 1600. In contrast to the medieval military tales, which celebrated the bravery and accomplishments of war heroes, these accounts — such as *Mikawa Narrative* (*Mikawa monogatari*), *Daté Diary* (*Date nikki*), and *O-An's Stories* (*Oan monogatari*) — were attempts at faithful reportage and provide a rare glimpse of everyday life during battle.

O-AN'S STORIES (OAN MONOGATARI, 1737)

O-An's Stories, which was frequently printed and widely read in the Edo period, includes an account of the battle of Sekigahara written from the perspective of an elderly woman looking back on her experience as a teenage girl. In the autumn of 1600, Tokugawa Ieyasu, the leader of the forces in the East, defeated Ishida Mitsunari (1560– 1600), the leader of the forces in the West, in a decisive battle at Sekigahara in Mino Province (Gifu). Following his overwhelming victory, Ieyasu united the country and became shōgun three years later. O-An, the daughter of a samurai in the service of Ishida Mitsunari, survived the siege and fall of Ōgaki Castle in Mino, which was being defended by Ishida Mitsunari's forces. In the following passage, which recounts the events on the eve of the battle of Sekigahara, O-An describes the firing of cannons (recently imported from the West), the making of bullets for rifles, and the dressing of the severed heads of enemy warriors. Tanaka Yoshimasa, whom O-An identifies, was one of the commanders of Ieyasu's Eastern army, which was attacking Ōgaki Castle.

After escaping from the castle with her parents, O-An went to Tosa (Kōchi), where she was married. (O-An is the title of respect accorded her after she was widowed and became a nun.) She died during the Kanbun era (1661–1673) when she was in her eighties. The name of the scribe, who recorded the memoir as a colloquial narration, is not known. The text presented here is based on a 1737 woodblock edition.

The children would gather round her and plead, "Miss O-An, tell us a story of the olden days." And so she would begin.

"My father, Yamada Kyoreki, was in the service of Lord Ishida. At first we were in the castle at Hikone, in Ōmi, on the shores of Lake Biwa; but later, when Lord Ishida rose in rebellion, he gathered his forces in Ōgaki Castle, in the province of Mino.

"We all were there in the castle together when a strange thing happened. Night after night, in the midnight hour, the voices of perhaps thirty people — both men and women, although who they were we could not tell — would wail, 'Lord Tanaka, ka-a-a-a! Lord Tanaka, ka-a-a-a!' And then, 'Waaaa!' they would shriek. It happened night after night. It was eerie, oh it was eerie, and so frightening. After that, a vast force sent by Lord Ieyasu approached and beset the castle, and the fighting continued night and day. The commander of that force, it turned out, was called Lord Tanaka.

"Whenever our men were going to fire the cannon, they would make the rounds and warn us. Do you know why? Because when they fired those cannon, it was horrendous; the turrets would shiver and sway, and the very earth seemed as if it would split open. For the frailer-spirited sorts of ladies, that was enough to make them faint on the spot. So they would warn us in advance. Once we'd been warned, we felt as if we were waiting for lightning to flash and thunder to crash. At first I was utterly terrified, so frightened I hardly felt I was alive. But after a while, it didn't bother me at all.

"All of us, my mother and the wives and daughters of the other vassals, were in the Great Keep, molding bullets for the musketeers. The severed heads taken by our side also were collected in the Keep. We attached name tags to all of them, to keep track of whose they were. Then we would carefully blacken the teeth of each head. Do you know why? In the old days, a head with black teeth was prized as the head of a man of rank, so they asked us to blacken the teeth of any head that had white teeth. We weren't frightened of the heads. We would lie down and sleep with blood-stinking heads all around us.

"One day the attackers opened fire on us with their muskets. This will be the day, people were saying; now the castle will fall. There was incredible panic throughout the castle. Then Father's young retainer came to us.

"'The enemy has withdrawn without a trace,' he said. 'Don't panic; calm down.' And at that instant a musket ball flew in and struck my little brother, who was fourteen; he crumpled in pain and died on the spot. Oh, I've seen some ghastly things.

"That same day an arrow with a letter tied to it landed in the sector of the castle that my father was defending. It said:

> Inasmuch as you, Kyoreki, once served as teacher of writing to Lord Ieyasu, you will be permitted, should you so desire, to escape from the castle. Make your escape in whichever direction you please; you will meet with no hindrance en route. Orders to this effect have been issued to all units.

Sometime tomorrow they'll attack, we thought, and then they'll take the castle by storm. Everyone was weak with despair. I, too, was desolate, quite certain that I'd be killed the next day.

"My father came in secret to fetch us from the Keep. He told my mother and me where we were to go and put up a ladder at the far end of the northern ramparts; from there he lowered us with a rope into a tub, and we crossed to the other side of the moat.

"There were only the four of us, my two parents, me, and our young retainer. The other vassals remained behind. When we had gone about five or six *chō* from the castle, Mother felt a pain in her belly and gave birth to a daughter. Our young man, not wasting a moment, washed the baby in some water that lay in a rice field, then hoisted her up and wrapped her in a scrap of cloth. Father picked up Mother on his back, and we made our escape across Aono-gahara. What a terrifying experience that was. Oh, those old days. . . . Praise be to Amida Buddha, Praise be to Amida Buddha."

"Tell us another story of Hikone," the children would say.

"My father's stipend was 300 *koku*, but there were so many wars in those days that everything was in short supply. Of course, we all were careful to put by whatever we could, but most of the time we ate some sort of gruel, morning and night. Sometimes my elder brother would go hunting in the mountains with his musket. In those days we would cook up a batch of rice and greens in the morning, and that would last us through our midday meal. I got nothing to eat but rice and greens, so I was always pestering my brother to go shooting, and when he did I'd be beside myself with joy.

"We had nothing to wear, either. When I was thirteen I had one hand-stitched, unlined pink kimono and nothing else. I wore that one kimono until I was seventeen, by which time my legs were sticking out the bottom; it was dreadful. How I longed to have just one kimono that would at least cover my legs. That's how hard up we were in the old days. And eating lunch was something we never even dreamed of, nor did we have anything to eat after nightfall.

"Young people nowadays—they waste all their time and spend all their money on whims of fashion, and they're terribly fussy about what they'll eat. It's just outrageous."

Over and over again she would tell them tales of Hikone and then scold them. Which is why, after a while, the children nicknamed her "Granny Hikone." Even now, when people contrast times past with the way things are now, people call that a "Hikone." The expression originated with this woman. That's why people from other provinces don't understand it. It's a local expression.

[*Zōhyō monogatari, Oan monogatari*, translated by Thomas Harper]

Chapter 3

IHARA SAIKAKU AND THE
BOOKS OF THE FLOATING WORLD

The term *ukiyo-zōshi* (books of the floating world) refers to a vernacular fictional genre that originated in the Kyoto-Osaka area and spanned a hundred-year period from the publication in 1682 of Ihara Saikaku's *Life of a Sensuous Man* (*Kōshoku ichidai otoko*) to the late eighteenth century. Although originally synonymous with *kōshokubon* (books on love or sexual pleasures), ukiyo-zōshi covered a much wider range of subjects, and in accordance with the restrictions imposed by the Kyōhō Reforms (1716–1736), this term replaced kōshokubon. The genre now includes both long and short works as well as essays. Likewise, in modern literary histories, the word *ukiyo* (floating world), which originally referred to the world of sexual pleasures (*kōshoku*), has been expanded to include the contemporary world.

In the 1640s and 1650s, courtesan critiques (*yūjo hyōbanki*) became popular (more than sixty-nine survive), beginning with *Tale of the East* (*Azuma monogatari*), a critique of Edo's Yoshiwara district, published in 1641, and leading up to the publication of *Life of a Sensuous Man* in 1682. Yūjo hyōbanki were guides to the pleasure quarters (Shimabara in Kyoto, Yoshiwara in Edo, Shinmachi in Osaka), which had become, as noted earlier, a cultural place for aesthetic pursuits. The guides to the pleasure quarters also provided entertaining reading, with their emphasis on both hedonism and reality that the other forms of vernacular writing could not provide. As titles such as *Tales of Osaka* (*Naniwa monogatari*, 1656) and *Tales of Kyoto* (*Miyako monogatari*, 1656) suggest, these guides took the form of fictional tales (*monogatari*). The eventual result was the birth of a new urban commoner literature. Saikaku's ukiyo-zōshi, particularly his tales of love (*kōshoku mono*), beginning with *Life of a Sensuous Man*, represent both an extension of and a departure from the pleasure quarter guides. Here Saikaku borrowed the subject matter of the courtesan guides, drew on a long tradition of love literature (stretching from *The Tale of Genji* and *The Tales of Ise* to seventeenth-century kana-zōshi), and employed an experimental, dramatic form of *haibun*, or haikai prose, for which there was no precedent in the prose literature of his time.

IHARA SAIKAKU

Ihara Saikaku (1642–1693), born into a well-to-do merchant family in Osaka, also became a merchant, running a mid-size business with four or five full-time assistant managers. But he eventually abandoned his family business to become a haikai master and then a writer of vernacular fiction. Saikaku started composing *haikai* (linked verse) when he was fifteen and became a haikai master in 1662, at the age of twenty. Using the pen name Ihara Kakuei, Saikaku became a member of the Teimon circle of haikai, which was in fashion at the time and was known for its wordplay and links by phonic and lexical associations. Around 1670, Saikaku became one of the leading disciples of Nishiyama Sōin, a *renga* (classical linked verse) master in Osaka who established the Danrin style, which used more colloquial language, looser rules, and earthy humor, deliberately parodying the classical poetic tradition and actively depicting contemporary commoner life. In 1673, Saikaku established himself as a publicly recognized haikai master with his own distinctive style (derisively labeled by his former Teimon companions the "Dutch style," or heretical style) and led a large group of poets in composing ten thousand haikai in twelve days at the Ikudama Shrine in Osaka. In the same year, Saikaku changed his haikai name from Kakuei to Saikaku (the *sai*, or "west," being the Sino-Japanese reading for *nishi* in Nishiyama), thereby signifying his affiliation with Nishiyama Sōin and the Danrin school.

In 1675, Saikaku's wife, whom he loved dearly, died of a fever at only twenty-five, leaving behind three very young children (one of whom was blind). Five days later, Saikaku composed an impromptu but passionate thousand-verse haikai requiem in about twelve hours (averaging about forty seconds per verse), which he published as *Haikai Single-Day Thousand Verses* (*Haikai dokugin ichinichi senku*). It was Saikaku's first long work, and in it he merged his narrative and lyric interests. Soon afterward, he shaved his head in mourning and became a lay monk, apparently turning over his domestic affairs to his assistants. From this time on, Saikaku dedicated himself to writing and remained a haikai master until his death.

The success of *Haikai Single-Day Thousand Verses* led Saikaku in 1677 to compose another single-day solo speed sequence (in hundred-link units) of sixteen hundred linked haikai, which was published as *Many Verses* (*Ōku kazu*), and on a single day in 1680 he wrote a four-thousand-verse sequence entitled *Saikaku Many Verses* (*Saikaku ōyakazu*). He was able to write these sequences so quickly because a particular topic could be developed over a number of links, thus creating a kind of panoramic prose poem, in 5–7–5 and 7–7 alternating verse. It was a short step from this kind of speed haikai to vernacular haikai fiction, to which Saikaku turned next, in his *Life of a Sensuous Man*. Saikaku here employed a form of haibun characterized by its elliptical quality, use of colloquial language, rapid descriptive movement, and interest in everyday, commoner life.

Two years later Saikaku wrote *Great Mirror of Female Beauty* (*Shoen ōkagami*, 1684), a book on the licensed quarters and its performing women and customers, which functioned as a sequel to *Life of a Sensuous Man*. This was followed by books such as *Five Sensuous Women* (*Kōshoku gonin onna*, 1686) and *Life of a Sensuous Woman* (*Kōshoku ichidai onna*, 1686). Until this time, Saikaku had been a local author whose works were published exclusively in Osaka, but after the appearance of *Life of a Sensuous Woman*, he became a national author whose books were published and read in the three major cities. Interestingly, *Great Mirror of Male Love* (*Nanshoku ōkagami*), published in 1687 in Osaka and Kyoto, purports to have been written in Edo. Tsunayoshi, who became the fifth shōgun in 1680, had a fondness for beautiful boys who were talented in nō drama and gathered them in Edo Castle. A number of domain lords followed suit, keeping young boys as lovers and making Edo the place for male–male love among samurai. Hoping, therefore, to extend his audience from the Kyoto-Osaka region to Edo, Saikaku pretended that he had written the book in Edo. *Twenty Unfilial Children in Japan* (*Honchō nijū fukō*, 1687), written in the same year, was published in both Osaka and Edo, as were all his subsequent works.

As he gained a national audience, Saikaku was pressured to write on demand and in great volume. At first he produced only one or two works a year, but in the two years from 1687 to 1688 he published twelve books, for a total of sixty-two volumes. Saikaku's style and approach also changed at this point. Until 1686, he had written mainly extended, fictional narratives—*Life of a Sensuous Man*, *Five Sensuous Women*, and *Life of a Sensuous Woman*—which were unified by the life of a single protagonist or a group of protagonists and in which the use of classical literature, haikai-esque allusion, parody, and rhetorical devices was conspicuous. After 1686, however, Saikaku turned for his material to a medieval genre, collections of *setsuwa* (recorded folktales), which enabled him to make use of his talents as a short-story writer and rework existing stories that he had heard or read about.

These later works, which had shifted stylistically away from the emphasis on classical parody and rhetoric, are collections of autonomous short stories unified by a particular theme or format. They include *Great Mirror of Male Love, Japan's*

Eternal Storehouse (*Nippon eitaigura*, 1688), *Tales of Samurai Duty* (*Bukegiri monogatari*, 1688), and *Worldly Mental Calculations* (*Seken munezan'yo*, 1692). In these collections, different tales are linked by a single theme, a single time, a single social class, or a single form of sexual or economic desire.

This tendency toward collecting parallel short tales existed also in Saikaku's earlier longer fiction. Even *Life of a Sensuous Woman*, his longest and most unified work, is not a novel in the modern sense so much as it is a collection of interconnected short stories about different women. The short-story format may, in fact, have been more suitable or natural for Saikaku, who spent twenty years of his life as a haikai poet, linking together in sequences fragmentary, momentary slices of life. At the same time, by using only a single theme in each collection, Saikaku was able to approach the same subject from a variety of perspectives, a technique resembling the poetic practice of composing on established topics.

Saikaku's prose works were not regarded as high literature by the literary establishment of the time, although they enjoyed a wide readership. Then in the late eighteenth century, there was a Saikaku revival in Edo, inspiring Santō Kyōden and other fiction writers. Saikaku is now generally considered the greatest fiction writer of the Edo period, and his works have influenced many modern Japanese writers, from social realists to humorists to romantic sensualists.

LIFE OF A SENSUOUS MAN (*KŌSHOKU ICHIDAI OTOKO*, 1682)

Life of a Sensuous Man, which Saikaku published in Osaka in 1682, initiated what came to be called books of the floating world (*ukiyo-zōshi*). It was Saikaku's first work of prose fiction and included his own pictures in a light, haikai-sketch style.[1] The protagonist, Yonosuke, is a second-generation, well-to-do Osaka-Kyoto chōnin whose father, Yumesuke, is an expert in the ways of love and whose mother is a famous, high-ranking performing woman (tayū) in the licensed quarter in Kyoto. Tayū were not strictly courtesans, since they could refuse to serve men they did not like. Although they could not leave the semipublic confines of the licensed quarters, they were outstanding artists who had mastered everything from discerning rare incenses to writing waka and haikai poetry. Outside the quarters, tayū were widely revered, and their charisma resembled those of modern media stars. Thus it is no surprise that Yonosuke also embarks on a wild life of love at the early age of seven. Because of his reckless ways, he shows himself unfit to become a merchant and is disowned at the age of nineteen. He then wanders, impoverished, from one end of Japan to the other, meeting women of many classes and professions. When Yonosuke is thirty-four, his father dies

---

1. The 1684 Edo printed edition includes a different set of illustrations, done in a heavier, more literal style with thicker lines, by Hishikawa Moronobu (d. 1694), the first great ukiyo-e print artist.

and Yonosuke unexpectedly comes into an enormous inheritance. Drawing on his extensive experience of love and his newly found wealth, Yonosuke visits famous tayū in licensed quarters, such as Yoshino in Misujimachi (Kyoto), Yūgiri in Shinmachi (Osaka), Takahashi in Shimabara (Kyoto), and Takao in Yoshiwara (Edo). Finally, in 1682, at the same time the book was published, he boards a ship and heads for the Island of Women.

Life of a Sensuous Man has five volumes and fifty-four sections, one for each year of Yonosuke's life and reminiscent of the fifty-four chapters of The Tale of Genji, one of its many allusions to Genji. The Heian classic The Tales of Ise is referred to even more often, probably because Narihira, its hero, was considered an even greater lover than Genji. Told in a unique mixture of colloquial styles and haibun, with an overlay of classical rhetoric and allusion, Life of a Sensuous Man can be divided into two parts. The first describes Yonosuke's youthful affairs and life of wandering. The second follows his life as a big spender in various licensed quarters and focuses on the famous women performers in a complex, realistic, and often humorous way that goes well beyond the stereotypes found in contemporary courtesan critiques. If the life of Yonosuke (literally, man of the world) is an unapologetic affirmation of the constantly changing "floating" world of the senses, then the licensed quarters, the site of most of the second part, similarly represent a place of partial liberation, a "bad" area, that allowed wealthy males to temporarily leave the rigid class system of Tokugawa society and to fulfill dreams not achievable in the everyday world. Yonosuke embodies these ideals and fantasies in, sometimes, their most imaginative and extreme form, although more often he ironically or parodically shows their limitations. He is an endlessly energetic prodigy who can act as a man of refinement (sui), raising erotic life to an aesthetic and cultural ideal, but also willfully, breaking the quarters' rules or showing his true feelings when he should not. Included here are the first chapter of the first half, which describes Yonosuke's early awakening to love as a young boy; the first chapter of the second half, which focuses on Yoshino (d. 1643), one of the most famous tayū of the seventeenth century; and the last chapter of the second half, in which Yonosuke sails off to the Island of Women. In Yonosuke's meetings with tayū (and occasionally with kabuki actors) in the second half, he cedes the stage to famous women in the quarters from the 1630s to the 1670s (most already were dead by the time the book was published), who display their intelligence, creativity, humor, and capacity for emotion in colorful ways. Saikaku often describes these women as violating the quarters' etiquette. In Yoshino's case, it was a strict rule that a tayū could not meet a man of low status: in her day, a tayū in Kyoto could meet only an aristocrat or a very wealthy, cultured merchant. According to Fujimoto Kizan's Great Mirror of the Way of Love (Shikidō ōkagami, 1678), an encyclopedia of life in various licensed quarters, Yoshino broke this rule and was consequently forced to leave the Misujimachi quarter in Kyoto. In Saikaku's imaginative reworking of the story, it is the breadth and depth of Yoshino's true feelings and her fearless willingness to violate this rule through her acceptance of a man of extremely low status who has yearned for her intensely that endear her to Yonosuke, who decides immediately to buy out her contract and marry her. Above all, Yonosuke sees in Yoshino's act a fidelity to her true feelings that suggests that her feelings for him also go beyond the usual coquetry and monetary calculations. Yoshino's flouting of the quarters' rules ironically implies that money—the primary means by which urban commoners gained power—cannot, in the end, buy love. At the same time, like other commoners, Yoshino achieves her refinement and her high position through her individual talent as a performer, intense training, and emotional integrity rather than, as in medieval aristocratic society, through family connections and inheritance.

Putting Out the Light, Love Begins

AGE SEVEN (VOL. 1: SEC. 1)

Blossoms scatter soon after they bloom, and people grieve. The moon, too, always sinks down behind the mountains. Near Mount Irusa in the province of Tajima,[2] in a silver-mining settlement, lived a man who came to be known as Yumesuke, Man of Dreams. Weary of making money, he put aside his worldly duties as a mine manager and moved to Kyoto, where he dreamed, asleep and awake without reserve, along the double path of female and male love.

Yumesuke drank hard with Nagoya Sanza[3] and Kaga no Hachi,[4] two of the most wild, free-roving warriors around, and the three and their followers showed their closeness by wearing robes with seven lozenge crests on them. Long past midnight, they would head back north across the Modoribashi Bridge[5] on First Avenue on their way home from the Misujimachi licensed quarter dressed in outrageous fashions that reversed the styles men usually wore when they visited the district. Sometimes the friends made themselves up as beautiful young men waiting for older male lovers; sometimes they dressed as Buddhist monks in black, long-sleeved robes; and sometimes they wore wigs of long, unkempt hair. The bridge was famous for spectral sightings, but these three were true ghosts if there ever were ones. But the friends listened to this and similar attributions as calmly as the medieval warrior Hikoshichi, who never even flinched when the woman he carried on his back revealed herself to be a demon. The friends assured the great tayū that they wanted nothing so much as to feel the women's teeth on their bodies unto death.[6]

The men's passion grew stronger with every visit to the quarter until finally

---

2. Northwest of Kyoto, facing the Japan Sea.

3. Famed for his good looks and for being the reputed lover of Okuni (the woman founder of kabuki) and the tayū Kazuraki. A masterless samurai most of his life, he died in a sword fight in 1603.

4. The licensed quarters' nickname for Kagae Yahachirō, famed for his fearlessness. According to legend, he died in a sword fight in 1584 while on a mission to assassinate Tokugawa Ieyasu, later the first Tokugawa shōgun.

5. Northeast Kyoto, the area through which demons were believed to enter and leave the city.

6. Both the men and the tayū are thus ghostly, demonic lovers.

they bought out the contracts of three of the most famous women there, Kazuraki, Kaoru, and Sanseki.[7] They gave the women retirement villas in wooded areas outside Kyoto at Saga, Higashiyama, and Fujinomori, where they could live quietly and privately. But the lovemaking continued, and one of the women gave birth to a baby boy. His parents named him Yonosuke, Man of the World. There's no need to go into the details. They're familiar enough to those who know about these things.

The child's parents loved him deeply. They amused him by clapping his tiny hands for him or gently rocking his small head, which rapidly took shape. In the frost of the Eleventh Month of the boy's fourth year, they performed his first hair-binding ceremony, and at the following New Year's, he put on his first formal divided skirt. Later, when he caught smallpox, his parents prayed fervently to the smallpox god, who left the boy scarless.

Yonosuke passed through his sixth year and entered his seventh. One night that summer he woke on his pillow and pushed it away. Soon the silence was broken by the sound of the metal latch on the sliding door of his bedroom. Then the latch opened, and there were yawning sounds. The night attendants in the next room knew immediately what was happening and followed the boy. One of them lit a candle in a holder with a long handle and walked in front of Yonosuke as he stamped down the wooden floor of the long corridor.

In the deep-shadowed northeast corner of the large house, the Demon Gate— through which ghosts were believed to come and go—spread the leafy branches of some low barberry trees planted there to ward off harmful spirits. Then, from nearby came the sound of piss trickling down onto freshly strewn pine needles in a pot. Later, as Yonosuke washed his hands in the wood basin, the attendant, worried that the head of an iron nail might be sticking up from the rough, split bamboo floor, moved her candle so that she could light it more brightly.

"Put out the light," Yonosuke said. "Come closer."

"Please allow me to protect your feet," she protested. "How could I possibly let you walk in darkness?"

Yonosuke seemed to understand and nodded. But then he added, "Don't you know? They say 'Love is darkness.'"

The other attendant, a bodyguard with a short sword, was standing nearby. She heard what Yonosuke had said and blew out the candle. When she did, Yonosuke tugged on her long left sleeve and anxiously asked, "Isn't that strict old nurse around here somewhere?"

It was almost too funny for the women to bear. He still had a boy's body, but he was beginning to feel the real thing, as in the ancient myth of the first two primal parent gods as they stood at the bottom of the Heavenly Floating Bridge,

---

7. Actual Kyoto tayū in the late sixteenth and early seventeenth centuries.

Yonosuke—preceded by his personal attendant and followed by his bodyguard and nursemaid, carrying a candle—goes to the privy with the lattice window (*lower left*). The corridor takes the form of a bridge, suggesting the mythological Heavenly Floating Bridge that connects the world of the gods to that of humans. The illustration is attributed to Saikaku. From the 1682 edition.

knowing they had to give birth to the cosmos but unsure of how to do it.[8] Later the maids recounted everything to the boy's mother. It must have been the beginning of a great joy for her.

Yonosuke daily grew more aware of the "thing" inside him. He had no actual lovers yet, so for the moment he collected alluring portraits of beautiful women. Soon he'd put so many into his book cart that it was a complete mess. He refused to show them to anyone, however, and he protected the door to his room—to which he now gave the elegant name Chrysanthemum Chamber—as closely as a guard at a road barrier in a romantic old tale. No one, he ordered, was to enter it unasked.

Once, while Yonosuke was folding paper into *origami*, he presented one of his creations to a maid, saying it was the fabled double bird, half male and half female, that flew in the form of two lovers in one body. He also folded paper into blossoms and fastened them to a limb. This he also gave it to the maid, declaring it to be the legendary linking limb that grew between two lover trees, connecting them so closely that they shared the same grain and became one.

In all that Yonosuke did, this was the one thing he never forgot. He tied his loincloth privately, refusing to let any of the maids help him, and he carefully knotted his waistband by himself in front and then slid it around to the back, the way grown men did. Remembering the artful scents used by the amorous prince Niou in *The Tale of Genji*, he wore pouches of fine incense on his body and also scented his sleeves. His stylish appearance put adult men to shame, and he moved the hearts of the women who saw him.

---

8. According to the *Kojiki* and later works retelling the myth, the two gods learned how to procreate by watching a pair of wagtails (birds with a thin body and a very long tail that they habitually flick up and down) mate.

When he played with friends his own age, Yonosuke hardly noticed the kites they sent up into the sky. Instead, he asked questions like "When people talk about 'building bridges to the clouds,'[9] do they mean that in the old days up in heaven there were men who actually traveled at night like shooting stars to their lovers' houses?" Or "The oxherd star can meet the weaver woman star on only one night a year.[10] How does he feel if rain clouds cover the sky that night and they're kept apart?" The farthest points of heaven made Yonosuke grieve.

Willingly racked by love, by the time Yonosuke was fifty-four, his notebooks show he had slept with 3,742 women[11] and 725 men. After resting against the edge of a well wall with the girl next door, Yonosuke went on to drain every drop of vital fluid from his kidneys.[12] It is amazing to think that he ever lived that long.

Yonosuke shows a precocious desire for life, companionship, and lovemaking. At nineteen, he becomes a monk but quickly forgets his meditations and travels, poor and without connections, from one end of Japan to the other, meeting women of many classes and professions. After a near-death experience and an unexpected inheritance, he is transformed into a big spender whose job it is to give his fortune to the leading tayū in the major licensed quarters. The first chapter of the fifth book, translated next, opens with a requiem waka poem written by the noted Kyoto ash merchant and aesthete Sano Jōeki (son of the famous sword polisher Kōeki), who fell in love with Yoshino, one of the most famous tayū of the seventeenth century, and bought out the remainder of her contract in 1631, when she was twenty-six. They married and lived happily until 1643, when Yoshino died. Readers were expected to discern the overlap of the two times and two men, Jōeki and the younger Yonosuke. "Honored" indicates that Yonosuke has changed from a vagabond into an "honored visitor" to the quarter, and Yoshino comes to be called "honored wife."

Afterward "Honored" Is Added to Their Names

AGE THIRTY-FIVE (5:1)

After the great tayū Yoshino died, a bereaved man wrote this poem: "She turned the capital into a village without blossoms—now Yoshino blooms in the other world."

---

9. Yonosuke does not yet understand the meaning of this metaphorical expression indicating an impossible love.

10. Celebrated as the Tanabata Festival on the seventh day of the Seventh Month.

11. A number similar to that commonly used for the number of gods in Japan as well as for the number of women loved by Narihira, who became the god of love during the medieval period.

12. In East Asian medical thought, the seat of desire and passion.

Near and far, people remembered Yoshino as a truly outstanding woman. She was talented in every way and fully lived up to her name, which she took from Mount Yoshino with its endless clouds of cherry blossoms.[13] There had never been a tayū like her before. Above all else, the depth of her feeling was beyond compare.

On Seventh Avenue in Kyoto stood the workshop of a lowly smith of daggers and knives who used the grand-sounding title Kinzuna, lord of Suruga. One of his apprentice smiths had seen Yoshino at a distance in the Misujimachi licensed quarter and had fallen in love with her. Unable to express his love, the apprentice turned over and over in his mind an old poem: "A guard blocks my secret path to my love—may he fall right asleep night after night!"[14] Night after night, the apprentice himself worked furiously, beating out fifty-three short sword blades in fifty-three days and saving fifty-three *monme* in silver coins, enough to buy an audience with Yoshino, who was a performer of the highest rank. He waited and waited for a chance to meet Yoshino, but finally he was forced to give up his fantasy that he could, like an ancient Chinese king, simply order a carpenter to build him a magical ladder to the clouds. Down on the ground, cold rain fell on his sleeves—bitter tears of true love that he swore to the gods were not false.

The apprentice had the day off for the Bellows Festival on the eighth of the Eleventh Month, when all forges were extinguished and purified with prayers before being relit. In the afternoon he discreetly made his way once more to the licensed district. There, someone heard the apprentice lamenting the fact he had enough money yet couldn't arrange an audience with the great Yoshino because of his low social position as a manual worker. This person told Yoshino about the apprentice, and Yoshino, moved by the strength of the man's feeling, pitied him and secretly called him to her.

As their conversation became more intimate, the nervous apprentice began to shake. He was so awed by Yoshino that he no longer knew what he was doing, and tears ran down his smudged face. "You can't imagine how grateful I am," he told Yoshino. "I'll never forget this, no matter how many times I'm reborn. Meeting you is the only thing I've been thinking about for years, and now it's finally happened."

The overwhelmed apprentice got up to leave the room, but Yoshino took hold of his sleeve and stopped him. Then she blew out the lamp. Without even undoing her sash, she put her arms around him. "Please," she said, "do as you wish."

At Yoshino's touch, the lower part of the man's body moved uncontrollably.

---

13. Probably the most famous mountain in Japan, located south of Nara.

14. From *The Tales of Ise*, sec. 5, and *Kokinshū*, no. 632, by Narihira. Yoshino is implicitly compared with the empress whom Narihira wants to visit.

But his anxiety continued. Even as he began to undo his cotton loincloth, he whispered, "Someone's coming" and tried to stand up again. Yoshino pulled him back to her.

"Unless we make love," she said, "I'm not going to let you go, even if I have to wait here all night and the sun comes up. You really are a man, aren't you? You're not going to climb up on Yoshino's belly[15] and then go back empty-handed, are you?" She pinched the man's sides, stroked his thighs, massaged the back of his neck, and caressed the small of his back.

At dusk Yoshino arranged two pillows, and they lay down together. Then at last, around the time the ten o'clock bell was booming outside, somehow or other, after many twists and turns, she managed a successful conclusion. And later, before she sent the apprentice back, she formally exchanged parting cups of saké with him.[16]

The performance house[17] protested strongly. "What you did," they said, "was outrageous."

"But tonight I'm meeting Yonosuke," Yoshino said. "He knows about things, and he'll understand me. I won't hide anything from him. And none of you needs to worry, either. He won't blame anyone." As they went on talking like this, the night deepened. Then a voice came up from the entrance: "We're honored by Suke's[18] arrival."

Yoshino talked with Yonosuke and explained everything, including how she'd made love earlier. "You acted like a perfect tayū," Yonosuke said. "Now I'll never let you go."

Hurriedly, Yonosuke went through the proper negotiations that very night and bought out the remainder of Yoshino's contract. He had decided to make Yoshino his wife.

Yoshino was sensitive and refined, but she'd also learned much about the world outside the quarters, and her intelligence never ceased to amaze people. She had always been fervent in her prayers to be born in the Buddhist paradise in the next world, and later she joined the same Flower of the Law[19] temple to which Yonosuke belonged. She thought of his feelings in everything she did and even gave up smoking her pipe for him.

---

15. The overlapping of Yoshino with Mount Yoshino continues throughout the chapter.

16. A symbolic ritual indicating that the two had become husband and wife in the fictional space of the quarter during the time they were together.

17. The *ageya*, where a tayū entertained customers, as opposed to the house where she lived, which was owned by her manager. Yoshino has broken several rules: (1) she has slept with and even exchanged vows of symbolic marriage with a low-class man, one, moreover, in a "dirty" profession; (2) she has done it in a room rented by another man (Yonosuke); and (3) she has not hidden her act, thereby forcing the performance house to take joint responsibility.

18. Yonosuke's nickname in the quarter. A house attendant announces him.

19. The Nichiren sect, popular with Kyoto craftspeople, artists, and merchants, including Jōeki.

Yoshino and Yonosuke talk while Yoshino's
assistants attend them.

The relationship greatly displeased Yonosuke's relatives. Shocked that Yono-suke planned to marry a former woman of the quarter, they refused to meet him or recognize her as being in any way related to them. Yoshino grieved, and finally she proposed to Yonosuke that they separate, ". . . or, at the very least, that you put me in a villa somewhere and just come to see me from time to time. They'll relent as long as you don't formally make me your legal wife." But no matter how hard Yoshino pleaded, Yonosuke refused to consent.

"Well, then," she said, "I'll just have to deal with your relatives myself."

"And just how do you plan to persuade them?" Yonosuke asked. "They refuse to listen even to the Buddhist monks and Shintō priests I've been sending to see them."

"Well," Yoshino said, "first you write to each of them very politely. Something like, 'Tomorrow I will proceed to separate myself from Yoshino and send her back to her home. Therefore I earnestly pray that you think of me once more as you always have.' And then you send around a circular invitation saying, 'The cherry blossoms in the garden are at their peak. I beg the kind attendance of all the gentlewomen.' Your women relatives aren't really opposed at all."[20]

And they weren't. That day all of them, without exception, came to Yono-suke's mansion, riding in fine enclosed palanquins. Soon they were sitting for-mally in rows in the great guest room built on a framework of pillars that projected out from the slope of a hill which, in the space of the large garden, seemed as high as a mountain. How long it had been, they all exclaimed, since

---

20. Yonosuke's male relatives oppose the marriage, presumably because they want him to marry into a wealthy family with access to the aristocracy.

they'd been able to look out over it! When Yoshino saw that the saké had been going around for a while and the women were feeling relaxed, she appeared in the great room wearing a serving woman's blue green wadded cotton robe with a red apron and a folded kerchief on top of her head. She carried a plain-wood tray heaped with thinly cut slices of dried abalone arranged in portions for each guest to eat with her saké. Going first to the oldest woman there, she got down on her knees and bowed low, pressing her hands to the floor.

"Please allow me to speak about myself," she said very politely. "I am a performing woman who once lived in the Misujimachi quarter. My name is Yoshino. I realize I am unworthy to appear in such esteemed company as this, but today I have been allowed to go back to my mother's home, and I would like to leave you with a parting memory." Then she sang a song from long ago:[21]

> Common, oh, common
> common, oh, common
> reel of mulberry thread
> winding on and winding
> turning the past into the present—
> ah, would that it could!

All who heard her felt as if their souls were about to leave their bodies.

Later Yoshino played her *koto*, a kind of zither, recited waka poems, and performed the tea ceremony with utter grace. She arranged fresh flowers in artistic designs, showed the women how to adjust the weights in a mechanical clock, fixed the hair of the young girls, played *go*, a kind of checkers game, with them, and performed on her bamboo mouth organ. She also told stories about mortality and faith in the Lotus Sutra and even gave advice on balancing household accounts. In everything, she took great care to see that the women enjoyed their time with her. Yoshino directed the whole entertainment by herself, and she would no sooner go into the kitchen than the women would call her out again.

Yoshino's guests completely forgot the time until the dawn sky began to brighten. Then at last, they began to declare they'd better be getting back home. As the women left, they offered their deeply felt advice to their host.

"Yonosuke," one said, "how could you even think of separating from Yoshino? You must never, never let her go."

---

21. Sung at Mount Yoshino by the medieval dancer Shizuka Gozen in the nō play *Two Shizukas*. By singing the song, the humble, "common" Yoshino pays homage to the shirabyōshi (a type of song-and-dance performance) performing women of long ago and testifies to her love for Yonosuke, whom she loves as truly as Shizuka once loved Yoshitsune.

"Even to other women," another said, "she's incredibly interesting to be with."

"She's so warm and gentle and intelligent, she'd make an excellent wife for any man in any position."

"There isn't a single woman among all thirty-five or -six of us who compares with her. Please pardon us all. You really ought to marry her."

The women did their best to smooth things over, and soon Yonosuke and Yoshino were rushing to complete preparations for a wedding in front of all their relatives. Casks of saké and cypresswood boxes of cakes and delicacies sent as gifts piled up like mountains. As decoration, they placed a stand in the center of the room with a model of the Mountain of Eternal Youth that rises in the Eastern Sea. At the end, everyone chanted together from a nō play: "Delighting in the rustling of the wind in twin pines growing old together." Finally Yoshino sang, "Until you are a hundred and I am ninety-nine."

Aids to Lovemaking: Sailing to the Island of Women

AGE SIXTY (8:5)

Twenty-five thousand *kanme* of good silver. More than twenty tons of it. Yono-suke's mother had urged Yonosuke to use as much of his dead father's money as he wanted. For twenty-seven years, day and night, he'd abandoned himself with women. He'd traveled great distances to every licensed quarter in the land, seen every one. His body was worn down by love, and since he had no wife or children, nothing held his mind any longer to the impermanent floating world. Yonosuke had thought deeply about this and realized the way of physical love that his soul had been following was actually a path winding through the forty-nine days after death between this world and the next. Still, it was hard for him to leave behind forever the burning house of material forms and human desires that people call the physical world.

The next year would be his sixty-first. Already. His feet faltered; his ears barely heard even the creaking of wobbling cart wheels; and he leaned on a mulberry cane. He definitely wasn't what he'd once been. And he wasn't alone. White frost now covered the hair of the women he'd loved, and wrinkles crossed their foreheads. Surely there wasn't a day the women didn't feel upset by how they'd changed. Even the little girls I used to carry on my shoulder under great parasols at festivals, he realized; they're already attracting men and making families. The world itself is change. How many times have I heard that? Still, could things really have changed this much?

Yonosuke had never done anything that would justify reciting last-minute prayers for rebirth in the Pure Land paradise. After he died, he knew perfectly well, he'd be food for hungry demons. A change of heart, sudden piety—well, entering the Buddhist path wasn't that easy. No, he wouldn't worry about whatever miserable end was coming. He'd spent practically his whole fortune, and he took the remaining six thousand silver coins and buried them in the hills east of Kyoto. On the site he placed a rock quarried in Uji[22] and planted morning glory vines that would climb up it. Into the rock he carved a poem he'd written: "Lit at dawn and sunset, these morning glories bloom above the shining of six thousand silver coins." At least that's what people in the greedy human world said for some time. But none of them knew exactly where it was.

Then Yonosuke gathered around him seven friends of like mind, and he had a ship built on Enokojima, a small island in Osaka Harbor that local people referred to as Penis Island. He christened it *Yoshiiro maru*, the Ship of Good Desire. Its scarlet silk crepe pennant was made from an underskirt that the great tayū Yoshino had left behind for Yonosuke long ago. For bunting and curtains, Yonosuke sewed together and hung up robes given to him as remembrances by other performing women who now were dead. The baseboards of the cabin were papered with pages from evaluation books comparing the virtues of famous quarters women, and the hawser was made by braiding together lengths of hair that women had offered to Yonosuke.

The galley was filled with stamina-stretching foods. Loach, a kind of carp, swam in boat-shaped tubs of fresh water, surrounded by stores of burdocks, yams, and eggs carefully preserved in earth and sand. Into the hold were placed fifty large jars of Kidney Combustion Pellets and twenty crates of Women Delighter Pills, both powerful herbal aphrodisiacs for men. They also took aboard 250 pairs of metal masturbation balls for women, 7,000 dried taro stalks to be soaked in warm water and used by pairs of women, 600 latticed penis attachments, 2,550 water-buffalo-horn dildos, 3,500 tin dildos, 800 leather dildos, 200 erotic prints, 200 copies of *The Tales of Ise*, 100 loincloths, and 900 bales of tissue paper.[23]

Checking, they found they'd forgotten many things. So then they brought aboard 200 casks of clove-oil lubricant; 400 packets of hot-sliding pepper ointment; 1,000 roots of cows-knee grass for inducing abortions; 133 pounds each of mercury, crushed cotton seeds, red pepper, and imported amaranthus roots for the same purpose; as well as various other lovemaking aids and implements. Then they loaded great numbers of stylish men's robes and diapers.[24]

"You know," Yonosuke said, "we'll probably never get back to the capital again. So let's drink some parting cups of saké." Six of the men, astounded, asked exactly where it was he intended to take them and why it was they weren't ever going to return.

"Well," Yonosuke replied, "we've seen every kind of quarters woman, dancing woman, or streetwalker there is in the floating world. Look around you.

---

22. Southeast of Kyoto. "Lit" in the poem refers to rays of the sun at dawn and sunset.
23. For use after lovemaking.
24. Presumably expressing the hope for rebirth after their deaths on the island.

Yonosuke and his friends sail to the legendary Island of Women, with Yoshino's petticoat at the prow. Yonosuke sits on the upper
deck beneath a flag bearing his crest, a wild
pink.

There are no more mountains anywhere to block any of our hearts' horizons.
Not yours, not mine. Our destination's the Island of Women. The one with
only women living on it.[25] There'll be so many women there, well, all you'll
have to do is just reach out your arms." At that the men were delighted.

"You may exhaust your kidneys and vital fluids," Yonosuke continued, "and
get yourself buried there, but, well, what of it? All of us here happened to be
born to live our whole lives without ties or families. Really, what more could
we ask for?"

The men finally found fair weather at Izu, at the southern tip of eastern
Japan. From there, following the winds of love, they sailed out into the ocean
at the end of the Tenth Month, the Godless Month, in 1682, and disappeared,
whereabouts completely unknown.

[*Saikaku shū jō*, NKBT 47: 39–41, 129–132, 212–214, translated by Chris Drake]

SAIKAKU'S TALES FROM VARIOUS PROVINCES
(SAIKAKU SHOKOKUBANASHI, 1685)

Saikaku's Tales from Various Provinces, published in 1685, is a collection of five books,
the last major prose fiction Saikaku himself illustrated. It contains thirty-five short
stories about strange and unusual events in various provinces. In the preface, Saikaku
writes, "The world is wider than we can imagine, and I went to many provinces looking
for story material." After briefly describing some amazing people he has encountered,

---

25. A legendary island believed to lie far to the east of Japan in the Pacific. The women there
were said to be impregnated by the east wind and to bear only female babies.

Saikaku concludes, "In my opinion, humans are spooks. There's nothing you won't find somewhere in the world." The half-humorous term "spooks" suggests a transformation, as if humans were capable of being or turning into an infinite number of shapes. The majority of these stories deal with small happenings that have large consequences, as if nothing could be so strange as ordinary human life. Saikaku consciously draws on contemporary oral comic storytelling, but unlike the written story collections of his time, he does not simply pretend to transcribe oral legends or narrative performances but makes it obvious, as suggested in the title, that he is writing his own creative revisions of motifs and figures already known to readers. The story translated here is typical in that an artifact from one context bursts into another, distant one, in which it is interpreted in new ways that turn out to look foolish but that contain their own local reversal.

The Umbrella Oracle (vol. 1: sec. 4)

Believing that mercy is the most important thing in the world, the monks at the Kakezukuri Kannon Temple in Kii Province[26] hang out twenty umbrellas beside the road to help those in need. Someone donated the umbrellas long ago, and to this day the temple replaces the oiled paper on them every year and puts them out for passersby. If it begins to rain or snow, anyone at all is free to take one and use it on the way home. All the borrowers are honest people, and they return them when the weather clears.

Not a single umbrella had ever disappeared until the spring of 1649, when a villager from Fujishiro[27] borrowed an umbrella and was walking home on the shore road along Waka Bay and Fukiage Beach. A very strong divine wind began blowing from the direction of the nearby Tamatsushima Shrine,[28] and one hard gust took the umbrella with it up into the sky and out of sight. The borrower was horrified, but there was nothing he could do to retrieve the umbrella. Carried by the wind, it crossed the entire Inland Sea and finally landed far to the west in the village of Ana[29] in the mountains of Higo Province.[30]

The villagers here had long lived in isolation with virtually no knowledge of other areas. The world is a big place, and even Buddhism had never spread this far. The villagers were astounded by the umbrella. It was the first one they had ever seen. The wise elders conferred, but none of them had ever heard of anything like it in all their years.

Then one man with a smattering of learning spoke up. "I counted the bamboo ribs," he said. "There are exactly forty. The paper isn't ordinary, either. I

---

26. Today in the city of Wakayama in modern Wakayama Prefecture.
27. Not far from the temple.
28. Dedicated to the goddess Sotoorihime, one of the three gods of waka poetry.
29. Homophonous with "hole."
30. In the western part of Kyūshū.

Oiled-paper umbrellas hang outside a tem-
ple wall for local people to use. Two pas-
sersby cover their heads as it begins to rain.
The illustration is attributed to Saikaku.
From the 1685 edition. (From SNKBZ 67,
Ihara Saikaku shū 2, by permission of
Shōgakukan)

now tremble to speak a holy name, one known everywhere in the outside world.
This object is the manifest body of the great sun god[31] from the inner precincts
of the Ise Grand Shrine, which is surrounded by forty outer shrines. It has flown
all the way here to us."

When the villagers heard that, they were filled with awe and immediately
purified the umbrella with saltwater and placed it on a clean new straw mat.
Everyone in the village went up into the surrounding mountains and felled
trees for timber and cut long grass for thatching. Soon the shrine to the Ise god
was completed. As the villagers began to worship before it day after day, the
umbrella's divinity became increasingly apparent. By the time the summer rains
came, the shrine was repeatedly giving off portentous sounds.

Finally an oracle was delivered: "The area in front of the divination cauldrons is filthy. This summer you have neglected to keep it clean, and it is
teeming with roaches. Even the inner sanctum has been defiled. Henceforth
you must rid the entire province of roaches. Not a single one must remain. And
I have a further request. You must send a beautiful young woman to serve as
the shrine shaman. Otherwise, before seven days have passed, rain as thick as
cart axles will fall with such force not a single human among you will remain
alive."

The frightened villagers met to discuss the oracle. They gathered the prettiest
young women in the village and tried to choose who would serve. None of the
women was married, and they wept loudly. "How could we possibly survive

---

31. Amaterasu, the female sun god and head of all the Yamato gods. Humorous in view of
the different gender attributed to the deity later in the story.

that?" they protested. They'd noticed something peculiar about the umbrella's divine shape when it was folded up.

A widow known for her passionate nature came forward. "It is, after all, a divine command," she said. "It's not something we can refuse. Let me go instead of these young women."

And so the widow went to the shrine. There she waited the whole night for the god, but it did not show the slightest sign of affection. Her anger grew, and finally she stormed into the inner sanctum and took hold of the umbrella. "So," she said, "you're nothing but a nice-looking body!" Then she ripped it apart and threw it away.

[*Ihara Saikaku shū* 2, NKBZ 39: 78–80, translated by Chris Drake]

FIVE SENSUOUS WOMEN (*KŌSHOKU GONIN ONNA*, 1686)

Ihara Saikaku published *Five Sensuous Women* in the second month of 1686, at the age of forty-four, shortly before the appearance of *Life of a Sensuous Woman* and four years after *Life of a Sensuous Man*, his first ukiyo-zōshi. (Saikaku's name is not given on the cover of *Five Sensuous Women*, perhaps because of the controversial nature of the actual scandals it deals with.) *Five Sensuous Women* belongs to Saikaku's books on "love" or "sexual desire" (*kōshoku*), but here he moves away from the licensed quarters, which had been at the heart of *Life of a Sensuous Man* and his previous works, to explore the world of illicit love among ordinary women in urban commoner society.

Late-seventeenth-century Tokugawa society regarded marriage primarily as a means of bonding two houses and ensuring the welfare of its descendants. Love affairs between individuals outside the institution of marriage were strictly forbidden, and adultery by a woman was often punished by death. In *Five Sensuous Women*, Saikaku evokes the lives of five merchant-class women who broke these strict rules. One married woman runs away with a clerk from her father's store; two commit adultery; one starts a fire in order to meet the man she loves; and another abandons her family and goes off to seduce a monk. The consequences are severe. Two of the women are executed for their offenses; one commits suicide; and the fourth goes crazy. Only one of the women, in the last story (which, by convention, was usually celebratory), is able to live happily with her man.

In *Five Sensuous Women*, Saikaku creates a tight structure based on five volumes (five women in five places: Himeji, Osaka, Kyoto, Edo, and Kagoshima), each with five sections. Saikaku's recent involvement, in 1685, in writing five-act jōruri puppet plays for the noted chanter Kaganojō is evident in the emphasis here on tragedy, the employment of stage conventions such as the *michiyuki* (travel scene), the focus on dramatic scene and dialogue, and the use of *sekai* (established world) and *shukō* (innovation), in which an established story is given a new twist or interpretation. Indeed, like many of Chikamatsu's contemporary-life plays (*sewamono*), *Five Sensuous Women* draws directly on recent scandals (one as recent as the year before its publication), with which his readers were familiar through contemporary ballads (*utazaemon*), popular songs (*hayariuta*), and hearsay. Saikaku entertained his audience by presenting a new version of a well-known incident while retaining the basic facts.

"The Calendar Maker's Wife," the third volume of *Five Sensuous Women*, which is translated here, is loosely based on a famous incident that had occurred three years earlier, in 1682. It involved a prestigious Kyoto printer who maintained a virtual monopoly on the printing and marketing of almanac calendars, widely coveted because of the yin-yang divinations and warnings given for each day. According to a contemporary ballad, Osan committed adultery with the clerk Mohei (Moemon in Saikaku's narrative) with the aid of the maid Tama (Rin in Saikaku's version) while her husband was away on business in Edo. Osan and Mohei escaped to Tanba (east of Kyoto) with Tama when Osan's pregnancy became apparent, but they were finally discovered, brought back to Kyoto, and quickly tried and executed. The crime of adultery was compounded by Mohei's violation of the strict boundary between employer and employee and by Osan's absconding with her husband's money. In 1683, both were crucified and then speared; the maid Tama was beheaded. Saikaku uses only the bare outlines of this incident, however, fabricating almost all the interesting details, such as Osan's first appearance before a group of men, her substitute letter writing, the faked suicide, the story of Zetarō, and Moemon's trip back to the capital. Only the ending, reinforced by historical fact, is never in doubt.

Before World War II, Japanese scholars stressed the tragic dimension of *Five Sensuous Women*, pointing out that the protagonists struggled valiantly but ultimately futilely against a brutal feudal system that condemned the pursuit of love. Saikaku is clearly sympathetic to these women's rebellious spirit and energy in the face of seemingly inhumane laws and customs. Late-seventeenth-century readers appeared to have an interest in lovers who could devote themselves to love despite the inevitability of death—a situation similar to the double suicides in Chikamatsu's contemporary-life plays. Postwar scholars, by contrast, have tended to emphasize the comic elements, pointing out, for example, that Saikaku generally avoids condemning the lovers for their actions and instead focuses on the humorous nature of their amorous pursuits. Indeed, *Five Sensuous Women* reveals the heavy influence of *haikai* (comic linked verse), which generated humor and wit through parody and comic inversion. The opening scene can be read as a parody of the popular critiques of courtesans (*yūjō hyōbanki*) or of the famous discussion of women in the "Broom Tree" chapter of *The Tale of Genji*. The third section, in which Moemon and Osan visit Ishiyama Temple, opens with a *michiyuki*, with highly stylized language, but instead of ending with a tragic double suicide, as in the love-suicide plays, the passage finishes on a comic note, as the couple cleverly deceive their pursuers. The highlight of the fourth section is the comic figure of Zetarō, a savage country bumpkin who takes Osan as his prospective bride. At the end of the same section, the Monjushiri deity appears to Osan in a dream, warns her of her sins, and urges her to take holy vows, but in a comic inversion of the traditional revelation tale, Osan dismisses the god's warning, claiming that Monju, whose full name (Monjushiri) is associated with buttocks (*shiri*), may understand the love of men for men but not that of men for women. Saikaku seems to observe the characters from a distance, with irony and detachment, often giving romantic or tragic situations a sardonic touch. His occasional moral comments were probably intended to put the reader's conscience at ease. As in haikai linked verse, the narrative deliberately undercuts itself, establishing a serious tone only to follow it quickly with a lighthearted scene. The result is entertaining tragicomedy in haikai prose.

The Calendar Maker's Wife
(Written in the Calendar's Middle Column)

JUDGES OF BEAUTY STRICT AS BARRIER GUARDS (1)

"New Year's Day: Write for the first time this year," begins the lower column of the Kyoto Daikyōji almanac calendar for 1682.[32] "On this day everything will go well. The second: Make love for the first time this year."[33] In ancient times a pair of amorous wagtails taught the first gods how to make love for the first time, and the gods later gave birth to humans. Ever since, men and women have never stopped pursuing this pleasure.

In the year 1682 the woman married to the owner of the Daikyōji shop that printed these famous Kyoto calendars, was widely known as "the calendar maker's beautiful wife." Her reputation had begun to spread while she was still young, and she aroused a mountain of desire among the men of Kyoto. To them, her eyebrows curved as gracefully as the crescent new moon high atop a float in the Gion Summer Festival; her face had the freshness of cherry buds at Kiyomizu Temple just as they burst into bloom; and her scarlet lips rivaled the autumn leaves on Mount Takao at the height of their color. She grew up on Muromachi Avenue, a street of prosperous clothiers, and her robes were always so novel and imaginative that she set fashions in the capital. No other woman in all Kyoto could compare with her.

One year, when spring was at its height, people were feeling lighthearted and restless, and many went to the eastern hills of Kyoto to see the wisteria in bloom. At Yasui Temple, the blossoms on their trellises trailed through the air

---

32. The top column of printed calendars contained the date and zodiacal signs; the middle column displayed for each day one of twelve fortune-telling signs; and the bottom column suggested actions proper for the total configuration. Saikaku compares his book with a calendar, and "The Calendar Maker's Wife," the third and middle episode of five, with the "middle column" of the calendar-like book.

33. Actual quotations from the 1682 calendar. The middle column on the first had *naru*, a sign suggesting that the day was good for beginning projects; the go-between Naru takes her name from this sign. On the second, the middle column had *osan*, a day on which all activities were predicted to go well; it is also the name of the heroine, Osan. Both names are thus ironic.

like purple mist and made even the brilliant green of the pines almost invisible. After the sun went down, the blossoms became still more beautiful, floating endlessly in the gathering dimness. So many wisteria viewers were gathered together then that they turned the eastern hills into living hills of attractive women.

In Kyoto in those days there were four famous playboy friends nicknamed the Four Heavenly Kings.[34] They all were noted for their stylish appearance, and they'd inherited so much money from their parents that they caroused throughout the year. One day they would go to the Shimabara licensed quarter and spend the night with leading tayū like Morokoshi, Hanasaki, Kaoru, or Takahashi, and the next day they would tryst with star kabuki actors such as Takenaka Kichizaburō, Karamatsu Kasen, Fujita Kichizaburō, or Mitsuse Sakon, who played young women's and young men's roles. They loved both women and men night and day in almost every imaginable way. Today they'd spent the day at a kabuki performance,[35] and now they all sat together at the Matsuya teahouse[36] nearby, along the Kamo River by the Fourth Avenue.

"I've never seen so many good-looking ordinary women[37] out before," one of the men said. "If we looked, who knows, we might even see one who'd really impress us." The men decided to try this new diversion and asked a discriminating kabuki actor to be head judge. Then they sat back and waited for women to pass by on their way back to the city after blossom viewing.[38]

Most of the women rode in enclosed palanquins, and the disappointed men tried to guess what kind of woman sat inside each. Then some women walked by in a loose group. They all had pleasant looks, the men felt, but none, they judged, was truly beautiful.

"However this turns out," one man said, "we ought to keep a list of the striking ones." So the men got ink and paper from the teahouse and began writing brief descriptions of their choices. The first woman they recorded looked thirty-four or thirty-five. The nape of her neck was long and slender, and she had large, bright eyes and a beautiful natural hairline, although the bridge of her nose, they felt, could have been a bit less prominent. She wore three satin robes with the material turned under at the cuffs and hems. Next to her skin was a white robe, then one of blue green, and over this a deep orange outer robe with traditional ink paintings on it. The painting on her left sleeve of the

---

34. Originally four guardian deva-kings who protect Buddhism, also the "outstanding four" in any field. The playboy guardians come to resemble road barrier guards, inspecting women in the street, and ironically, in the last chapter, one of them literally becomes a guard.

35. Performances began soon after sunrise and finished shortly before sunset.

36. The teahouse, run by the theater, arranged tickets and meals during the performance.

37. That is, not working in the licensed quarter.

38. The women walk westward along the Fourth Avenue back toward the downtown area of the city.

On the right, two men carry a women's palanquin, preceded by a merchant's wife wearing an elegant shawl. A male servant carries a luggage box with a folded rug for them to sit on while flower viewing. Fastened to his carrying pole is a container for lunch boxes. A young woman (*left*) wears a rush hat and a sash tied stylishly in front. To her right is a nun in black robes watching over the young women, who are followed by a maid. In the teahouse, a young woman boils water on a stove. In the entrance, one of the playboys watches the women, as does his footman. The illustrations are attributed to Yoshida Hanbei (act. 1684–1688). From the 1686 edition.

writer-monk Kenkō showed him just as he described himself,[39] sitting alone at night poring over old books below a wick lamp. And it was done with remarkable invention! Around her waist was a velvet sash woven in a multicolored checkered pattern. Over her head she elegantly wore a thin silk shawl dyed with a colorful courtly pattern. Her socks were pale purple silk, and she seemed to glide without a sound in her leather sandals with thongs braided from cord of three colors. And how natural the motion of her hips was as she walked! Just as the men were exclaiming at how lucky her husband was, the woman opened her mouth to say something to one of her maids—and showed she was missing a lower front tooth. The men's desire cooled rapidly.

Soon afterward, the men recorded a young woman of fifteen or sixteen. Surely, they thought, she couldn't have been seventeen yet. The older woman on her left looked like her mother, and on her right walked a black-robed nun who would take responsibility in case she did something wrong in public. The woman trailed several maids, and male servants walked vigilantly, as if they

---

39. In sec. 13 of Yoshida Kenkō's *Essays in Idleness* (*Tsurezuregusa*, fourteenth century).

were guarding an unmarried woman. But her teeth were blackened, so she had to be married. She must have a child, too, since she'd shaved off her eyebrows. She had a round, pretty face; intelligent, bright eyes; cute, clearly formed earlobes; and smooth, white, fleshy fingers and toes. She also had a stunning way of wearing her clothes. Above her inner robe, yellow on both sides, was a completely dapple-dyed purple robe. Over that she wore a gray satin outer robe covered with swallow-shape patches. Her wide silk sash was stripe-dyed horizontally in many colors. Her loose robes were suggestively open at the neck, and she moved in them very gracefully. Her wide-brimmed, lacquered paper hat was lined inside, and from it hung a finely braided paper cord.

The men were drawn to this glamorous woman, but when they looked again they saw a scar almost an inch long on the side of her face, where she'd struck something. They were sure she hadn't been born with it. "She must have quite a grudge against the nurse who was taking care of her when that happened," one of the men remarked. They all laughed and let the woman pass by without further comment.

Next they recorded a woman of twenty-one or twenty-two wearing a single homemade striped cotton robe. As she walked by, the wind lifted it, exposing all the ragged, improvised patchwork on the inside. Her pitifully narrow sash seemed to be made from cloth left over from a cloak, and she wore what were obviously her only pair of shabby, out-of-date purple leather socks in nonmatching straw sandals. On top of her head was an old cloth headpiece, and her messy, uncombed hair had obviously been gathered up in a hurry. She walked alone without putting on the slightest airs, enjoying herself regardless of what others might think. When the men looked more closely they saw she had a perfect face. They all wondered if a more beautiful woman had ever been born and were quite taken with her.

"If you gave her some nice clothes to wear," one of the men said, "she'd be an absolute killer. It's not her fault she's poor, after all." They felt very concerned, and after the woman had passed by, they sent someone to follow her. She lived, it turned out, at the end of Seiganji Street, where she worked in a small shop chopping tobacco leaves. The men felt very sad to hear that, but their concern was mixed with desire.

The next woman the men recorded was twenty-seven or twenty-eight and dressed with impeccable elegance. All three of her robes were of the finest black silk, edged at the hems with scarlet from the inner sides. On her outer robe, sewn in gold thread, was a discreetly embellished version of a very private crest. Her wide, striped sash was of Chinese silk, tied conspicuously in front. Her stylish chignon with a low topknot was tied far back with a wide, folded paper cord. In her hair were two matching decorated combs, and over her head was a kerchief dyed with a brush-stroke design. Above this she wore a wide rush hat in the style of the female-role kabuki actor Kichiya, tied with a four-color cord. She wore the hat tilted up to show her face, and she imitated the deliberate, wide-stepping walk of tayū in the licensed quarters, complete with a swaying hip motion.

"She's the one, she's the one."

"She's got to be the best one."

"Calm down, will you?"

As the men waited for the woman to come closer, they noticed that each of the three maids behind her carried a baby. Suddenly they found the woman amusing and joked that she was having one a year. The woman walked past without turning her head, pretending not to hear the shouts of "Mommy! Mommy!" behind her.

"All dressed up like that," one of the men said, "she must really hate to hear them—even though they're hers."

"A woman can look very nice," said another man, "until she has children." The men laughed so hard the woman must have been deeply shocked.

Later a young woman of thirteen or fourteen came walking along at a leisurely pace in front of her palanquin, which the carriers brought along after her. Her hair was combed straight down in back, gathered up at the end, and tied with a folded strip of crimson silk. In front her high-combed hair was parted in the middle like a young man's, and the chignon at the top of her head was secured with gold paper cord and accented in front with a large decorated comb. She gave off an immediate, overwhelming impression of beauty, and her features left the men speechless. Next to her skin she wore a white satin robe ink-painted with various scenes. Above that was a satin robe shimmering with various shades of purple and green and sewn with peacock shapes. Over it all was a transparent netting of gold Chinese silk. The novel design showed striking imagination. She had on a soft, twelve-color sash and walked along barefoot in paper-thonged sandals, while behind her a maid carried her wide-brimmed sedge hat. In her hand she held a wisteria branch with many blooming tassels hanging from it, obviously to show to people at home.

None of the other women the men had seen that day compared with this one. The men asked her name.

"She's the daughter of a prominent merchant on Muromachi Avenue," said a man in her group as he went by. "Don't you know? Everyone's calling her the 'modern Komachi.'"[40]

Soon the men reached their decision. This last young woman was truly the flower of all the women they'd seen that whole day. The passionate Komachi lamented long ago in one of her poems that without her lover she was spending her days in vain,[41] and those who saw the modern Komachi that day later came to realize how far she, too, was willing to follow her own desire.

---

40. In the Edo period, Ono no Komachi, the noted Heian woman poet who, as a young woman, was thought to have had many suitors. She became a symbol of female beauty.

41. Alludes to a poem by Komachi: "The blossom's colors all have faded in vain as I gaze,

SLEEPERS DONE IN BY THEIR DREAMS (2)

A bachelor living with other men leads a carefree life, but without a wife at home he can get awfully lonely in the evenings. The owner of the shop that printed prestigious Daikyōji almanac calendars[42] had remained a bachelor for many years. Living in the capital, he saw many women dressed with great imagination and sensitivity, but his tastes were so exacting that he had yet to meet a woman he considered stylish and beautiful enough to marry.

The calendar maker had begun to feel, as he put it, as melancholy as the free-floating river grass to which Komachi had compared herself in a poem centuries before,[43] and he wanted to know more about the young woman who was getting quite a reputation as the modern Komachi. The calendar maker asked someone who knew her family to help him get a look at her, and when he went and saw her, she was indeed the same young woman he and the other playboys had judged most attractive of all on Fourth Avenue that spring, when her beauty had been as delicate as the wisteria she carried. Her name was Osan. The calendar maker immediately fell completely in love with her and couldn't find the slightest thing to criticize. People were amused to see how quickly this sophisticated bachelor tried to arrange a marriage.

In those days there was a famous go-between who was known as Smooth-Talking Naru because of her high success rate. The calendar maker went to see her at her office just north of the intersection of Shimo-Tachiuri and Kara-sumaru Streets in uptown Kyoto and begged her to do her best for him. Naru succeeded in arranging an engagement,[44] and to seal it, the calendar maker sent Osan's family the traditional pair of double-handled kegs of saké and other gifts. A wedding was agreed on, a felicitous day was chosen, and finally the calendar maker and Osan were married.

From then on, the calendar maker gazed only at his wife, ignoring every other beautiful sight, even cherry blossoms at night and the moon at dawn. The two became intimate and got along well as husband and wife for three years. From morning to night, Osan applied herself to directing the housework, and she herself carefully bought and prepared imported pongee thread and oversaw the maids as they wove it into striped silk cloth. She always made sure her husband looked his very best. She also was frugal, never letting too much fire-

---

longing for endless summer rains" (*Kokinshū*, no. 113). In Saikaku's day, "act in vain" was also a euphemism for an adulterous affair.

42. The printer produced calendars for the court in Kyoto and the shōgun in Edo and had an extensive printing and distribution network for commoners as well.

43. He recalls a poem by Komachi: "Comfortless, alone a floating plant cut at the root—if a river should ask, I think I would go" (*Kokinshū*, no. 938).

44. The calendar maker is an attractive candidate, since he has both money and, with his connections at court, an enviously high social status for a commoner, a status higher than that of Osan's parents.

wood burn in the ovens and keeping detailed daily records in her expenditures book. She was the kind of wife a city merchant loves to have.

The calendar business prospered, and the couple was extremely happy. But then the calendar maker had to make an extended trip to Edo and other eastern areas.[45] The thought of leaving Kyoto grieved him, but the calendar business made hard demands. Finally he resigned himself to going, and before he left, he went to see Osan's parents on Muromachi Avenue and explained the situation to them.

When they heard about the calendar maker's long business trip, Osan's parents worried about how their daughter would get along during his absence. They felt that she needed someone who knew a lot about everything and who could oversee the printers and the shop out front and help Osan with practical advice about running the big house in back. Out of the same deep concern that parents everywhere have for their daughters, Osan's parents decided to send over Moemon, a trustworthy clerk who'd worked in their store for many years, to their son-in-law's house.

Moemon was so honest and straightforward that the gods came, as they say, and lived in his head. Unconcerned with styles, he let hairdressers do what they wanted with his hair, and he didn't pluck out the hairs on his temples trying to look desirable to women. He was a conscientious worker who wasn't interested in robes with flashy, wide-hanging sleeves. He carefully kept his sleeve openings narrow at the cuffs. And never, in all the time since he'd begun to grow his hair long as a young boy, had he ever borrowed a wide sedge hat from a teahouse and gone, face hidden, to the licensed quarter. Neither did it occur to him to gaudily decorate his short sword the way many men did. During the day he thought only of business, and at night his abacus was his pillow. Even his dreams were about new ways to make money.

Autumn deepened, and at night bitter winds began to blow. Moemon, wanting to stay healthy through the winter, decided to have some moxibustion treatment to strengthen his body's resistance. Osan's personal maid Rin was supposed to be very skillful at burning the tiny cones of grass on special points, so he asked her to do it. Before they began, she rolled a supply of the little cones between her fingers and draped a striped quilt over both sides of the mirror on her low dressing table so Moemon could hold on to it during the treatment.

The first couple of burning cones on his back were too hot for Moemon to bear. The nurse, the middle maid, and even Také, the kitchen helper, all pressed on Moemon's skin around the spot to help dull the pain, but they couldn't help laughing at his grimaces. Smoke rose thickly from one cone after another, and at last the treatment was almost over. Moemon could hardly wait for Rin to

---

45. His job required him to negotiate with distributors in Edo and the surrounding region. In Edo he would meet his most prestigious customer, the shōgun.

Rin gives moxibustion treatment to Moemon, who sits on the mat floor with his robe pulled down to his waist. On an acupoint she has lighted a small cone of moxa grass, which gives off smoke, and she will soon remove the hot ashes with special wooden chopsticks. She looks back at Osan, who wears a fine robe decorated with a pattern of stylized wheels. Beside Osan is a nursemaid in a cotton cap. On the board floor is a female servant standing and a parlor maid sitting.

light the final cone, which she put on top of a smear of salt to prevent swelling. But when Rin lit the little cone, it fell off the salt and tumbled down Moemon's spine. His skin twitched wherever the burning grass touched, but he closed his eyes, grit his teeth, and did his best to endure it silently because Rin was being very kind. Rin saw Moemon being considerate, and she pitied him. She kept rubbing his lower back until finally she'd managed to put out all the shreds of burning grass.

It was the first time Rin had ever touched a man, and in the days that followed she found herself falling in love with Moemon. She suffered alone with her feeling, but someone noticed, and soon everyone in the house, including Osan, knew about it. But even that didn't deter Rin.

Rin's parents were poor, and she'd never learned how to write. It pained her deeply not to be able to send Moemon a letter telling him how she felt, and she envied Kyūshichi, the odd-jobs man, his ability to brush out a few basic phrases. Secretly she went to him and asked him to write a love letter to Moemon in her name. Kyūshichi, however, tricked her and tried to make her love him instead. For Rin, the days that followed were long and hard.

Onc cold, rainy day at the beginning of winter, Osan was writing a letter to her husband in Edo. It was the Tenth Month, when all the gods were believed to leave and gather in Izumo and when ancient poets wondered whether their lovers were as true to them as the cold rains that always fell at that time. For Osan, it was the beginning of a season of untruth. After she finished her letter to her husband, she wrote one for Rin as well, with rapid, flowing strokes of her brush. She folded the letter several times and on the outside fold wrote simply "To Mo," using the first character of Moemon's name, followed by an equally intimate "From Me." Rin was overjoyed when Osan gave her the letter, and she waited for a chance to ask someone to give the letter to Moemon.

Later, when Moemon called from the shop in front for someone to bring him a fire to light his pipe, Rin found she was the only one in the kitchen. It was too good a chance to miss, and when she took the flame to Moemon, she gave him the letter herself. Moemon read the long, involved letter, completely unaware it was written by Osan. He thought Rin was a cute young woman, but she was only a maid, and he didn't take her seriously. His reply was brief and quickly written.

Unable to read the letter, Rin waited until Osan was in a good mood and asked her to read it for her. "I perused your letter," Osan began, "and was surprised to learn of your special feelings for a person in my position. Being a clerk and still unmarried, I am not averse to responding to your wishes. If we make love often, however, we will soon be bothered by a visit from the midwife. Still, if you are prepared to pay for my robes, cloaks, visits to public baths, and personal items, then most grudgingly I will accede to your request." It was a very blunt letter.

"Really," Osan said, "what a disgusting thing to write! There's no shortage of men around, Rin. And you have decent looks. There isn't a reason in the world you can't get a man at least as good as this Moemon to marry you." So Osan wrote another love letter for Rin to Moemon and then a series of letters filled with the most passionate thoughts repeated in ever new ways, all designed to deceive and seduce Moemon. Even the brush strokes in the letters were beautiful, and Moemon soon fell deeply in love with Rin and regretted his earlier insulting letter. Now his replies were filled with keenly felt emotion.

At last Rin got a letter from Moemon suggesting a secret meeting on the night of the fourteenth of the Fifth Month. It was a night of ceremonies when people stayed up and prayed to the dawn sun, and Moemon promised to slip away at a suitable moment and meet Rin. As Osan read, she and the other women all laughed at the top of their voices.

"Listen," Osan said, "here's what we ought to do. It'll be fun and help us pass the night."

When the evening of the fourteenth arrived, Osan changed places with Rin, disguising herself in a simple cotton robe. She lay awake almost the whole night in the place where Rin usually slept, but no one came. At last she fell soundly asleep. All the women of the house waited according to plan in various places nearby, holding sticks, clubs, and even candleholders. At a word from Osan they would descend on Moemon and give him a well-deserved beating. But they were tired from helping with the night's rituals, and they all began to snore where they waited.

Sometime after the three-thirty bell, Moemon slipped away in the dark and went to Rin's sleeping place, loosening his loincloth as he went. All he could think about was getting under the covers, and by the time he got inside he was completely naked. Burning with excitement, he made love without saying a single word to the woman he thought was Rin. As he pulled the covers back over the sleeping woman, he was momentarily surprised by a delicate scent of perfume coming from her sleeves. Then he walked back the way he'd come as softly as he could.

There certainly are a lot of cunning people in the world, Moemon thought to himself. Rin's so young I would never have imagined she'd be man-crazy already. I wonder what kind of men she's done it with before me? Afraid of what he might be getting into, Moemon vowed to himself never to make love with Rin again.

What Osan saw when she woke shocked her. Her pillow had been knocked away in a very rough way. Her sash had been untied and was nowhere in sight. Used tissue paper littered the floor. Suddenly Osan realized what had happened and was overcome with shame. There was no way, she was sure, that the others didn't know. And there was nothing she could do about it now. So Osan decided to give up everything. She would spend the rest of her life loving Moemon, even if people called them adulterers. She made up her mind to set out on a final journey with Moemon that would end only when they both reached the other world together.[46]

Resolved not to turn back, Osan told Moemon about her plan to commit love suicide together. Moemon was as amazed as she at how things had turned out. He'd started a relationship with Rin, but he realized things had gone too far with Osan already, and he changed his affections to her from that moment on. Night after night he ignored the cold looks and words he got from people in the house and went to her room. Losing their heads and leaving right and wrong behind, Osan and Moemon would soon be forced to stake their lives against all odds on a single gamble. Nothing could have been more dangerous.

LAKE OF DECEPTION (3)

Love drives women and men to do things beyond their comprehension or control. This can be found written even in *The Tale of Genji*. At Ishiyama Temple, where Murasaki Shikibu began her tale, the statue of the merciful bodhisattva Kannon was being shown to the public,[47] and people from nearby Kyoto crowded into the temple. The famous cherries in the eastern hills of Kyoto were in full bloom, but on their way to the temple, people walked right

---

46. Adultery, as Osan knows, is a capital crime, so she chooses love suicide and possible rebirth with Moemon in Amida Buddha's Pure Land paradise.

47. The statue was shown every thirty-three years and was very popular with Kyoto people, since Kannon was believed to have inspired Murasaki Shikibu to begin writing while she was staying at Ishiyama Temple, near the shores of Lake Biwa, a short distance east of Kyoto.

by them with hardly a second look. At Kyoto's eastern border, where a check-point had stood centuries before, streams of pilgrims passed out of the city and back into it, but if you looked closely, you could see that most of the pilgrims were women wearing the very latest styles. Not one looked as if she were visiting the temple to pray for rebirth in Amida Buddha's Pure Land after she died. The women were trying so hard to look beautiful in their fine robes that Kannon, knowing what was in their minds, must have been beside herself with laughter.

Osan, too, made a pilgrimage to Ishiyama Temple and took Moemon with her. They gazed at the cherry blossoms and felt they understood why human life was so often compared with the fragile, delicate blossoms that fell to the ground so quickly. Osan and Moemon, sure they would never again see the inlets and mountains around Lake Biwa, decided to make their last day on earth their best.

Not far from the temple, in Seta, they left Osan's attendants behind and rented a small fishing boat. As they rowed out onto the lake, they passed the Seta Long Bridge.[48] It made them wish they could be together alone forever, although they knew that could never happen. With little time left in this world, they lay down in the boat and made love on the water, rocked by the waves. By the time the boat passed Toko Mountain, Osan's hair was so wild that people could have seen it from shore. Later, trying to make herself neat again, Osan could barely see her worried face in the tear-streaked surface of her mirror, while on the shore, clouds closed around Kagami[49] Mountain. When they passed Shark Point,[50] its name reminded Osan of the extreme danger they were in. Even the sounds of boatmen calling to one another at Katada[51] Inlet fright-ened her—were they people from Kyoto in pursuit? As she gazed at Nagara[52] Mountain, she found herself wishing she could somehow, after all this, live a long life. But how could that possibly happen? Beyond Nagara rose Mount Hiei, imposing yet only a twentieth the height of Mount Fuji. She wasn't even twenty yet herself, but she was about to disappear as quickly as the last trace of snow on Hiei's peak. Again and again she cried into her sleeves.

They passed the shore along which the Shiga capital[53] had once stood. But the court had disappeared forever, leaving only legends. Soon, Osan thought,

---

48. Crosses the southern part of the lake, part of the Tōkaidō route. The first in a series of place-names along the west side of the lake that are woven into the text for their poetic associations in *michiyuki* style.

49. Literally, mirror.

50. There were no sharks in Lake Biwa. Rather, the name comes from the Wani (Shark) clan, one branch of which moved to the area from Izumo, where Japan sea sharks were worshiped as gods.

51. Literally, hard fields, suggesting the difficulty of escape.

52. Literally, long shape.

53. The court presided over by Emperor Tenchi (r. 668–671).

Osan, Moemon, and Osan's attendants sightsee on Lake Biwa. Osan (*left*), with a cap and outer cloak, sits on a small rug near Moemon, who wears his finest short sword. Behind her sits Rin and other household women, with two male servants in the stern. The boat nears Seta Long Bridge. On shore is the Ishiyama Temple compound.

they'll talk about us as though we were nothing but people in legends, and she grew even more melancholy.

Evening was approaching by the time they arrived at the Shirahige Shrine along the shore, and lanterns were being hung up in front of the main shrine and in the trees around it. They made their prayers to the shrine god, a white-bearded deity believed to grant long life. Long life? The thought made them feel even closer to death.

"Whatever happens to us," Osan told Moemon, "I'm very sure of one thing. The longer we live, the more we're going to suffer. Let's jump into the lake together and live forever as wife and husband in the Pure Land along with all the buddhas."

"Please don't think I'm attached to living," Moemon said, "but considering all we've done, I don't think it's the Pure Land we'll be heading for after we die. I have an idea, though. We'll leave a joint message addressed to the people back in Kyoto, and then we'll start a rumor that we've committed double suicide by jumping into the lake. Meanwhile we'll go somewhere far away. Anywhere, who cares where. That way we'll be able to live the rest of our lives together."

Osan was overjoyed. "Actually," she said, "I've been thinking something similar, myself, ever since we left the house. Inside the luggage box there are five hundred gold coins. I put them there."

"Then we have something to live on!" Moemon said. "We'd better get ready to leave this place."

Together the two left a final message. "Evil thoughts," they wrote, "came into our minds, and we have committed adultery. We fully realize we cannot escape the punishment of heaven, and there is no place in this world left for us to go. Today we take our leave of it."

Each left behind things people would recognize. Osan took off the two-inch buddha statue she always wore around her neck for protection and placed it together with some strands of her hair. Moemon left behind his best short sword, made by the famous swordsmith Seki Izumi no Kami.[54] It was ornamented with bronze and had a fine iron hand guard engraved with a coiled dragon. And under a willow beside the lake, they placed two outer cloaks, a pair of women's brightly colored sandals, and a pair of men's leather sandals. Then, very secretly, they met with two local fishermen who were skilled at diving off high rocks. After they paid them a sizable sum and explained the job, the fishermen accepted willingly. The men then hid and waited for the agreed-on time to arrive.

Osan and Moemon made their preparations, taking care to leave open the woven-branch door of the simple house where they and the servants were staying the night. When they were ready, they shook everyone inside awake and told them they were in a hopeless situation and were going to end their own lives. Before anyone could stop them, they ran outside through the open door. Faint voices chanting Amida Buddha's name were soon heard from the top of a steep crag, and then the sounds of two bodies hitting the surface of the lake. While everyone was shouting and wailing, Moemon, with Osan on his back, made his way through the underbrush at the foot of the mountain and disappeared into a thick grove of cedars. The two divers, meanwhile, swam a great distance underwater and came ashore in a place no one could have connected with the splashes.

Osan's attendants struck their hands together in grief. They asked the local fishermen to look for the bodies in various places, but none of the searches turned up anything. It was already dawn by then, so they gathered up what the two had left behind and carried it in a bundle back to Kyoto. There they related what had happened, and the people in both houses were sworn to strict secrecy about the shameful incident. The world, however, has sharp ears. Rumors about Osan and Moemon spread in no time, and the two became a standard topic of New Year's small talk year after year. Still, it couldn't have been otherwise. The two truly were adulterers.

A TEAHOUSE WHERE THEY'D NEVER SEEN GOLD COINS (4)

Osan and Moemon headed northwest into Tanba Province, staying away from roads and walking through field after field of high grass. When they reached a

---

54. Active until 1520. As a commoner, Moemon cannot wear a long sword.

high mountain, Moemon held Osan's hand, and finally they reached the top. They never stopped looking back anxiously as they went. They'd chosen to do this, but only now did they begin to realize how hard it would to be to live on in the world after they'd already died.

Soon there were not even woodcutters' tracks to follow. Osan and Moemon wandered on completely lost, despairing of ever finding their way again. Finally Osan's strength gave out, and her woman's body in great pain, she collapsed. Her breathing grew fainter and didn't seem as if it could last much longer. Moemon grieved to see her completely pale face, and with a leaf, he cupped water trickling from some rocks and poured it into her mouth. He tried to revive Osan in many other ways as well, but her pulse grew steadily weaker.

Moemon had nothing with him he could use as medicine, and he resigned himself to waiting for Osan's life to end. But then he leaned close to her ear and whispered, "We only need to go a little farther. Up ahead there's a village where I know someone. If we can just get that far, we'll be able to sleep together and forget all this."

Osan seemed to have heard what Moemon had said. Then she spoke. "You make me very happy," she said. "You love me more than your own life." Soon she felt much better, and her whole soul filled with desire. Moemon could see how much she wanted him then, and that made him want to care for her all the more. He carried her on his back as he had earlier, and they continued on through the forest.

Soon they reached the hedge around a house in a small mountain village along a road. Moemon asked and learned that this was the main pack road leading from Tanba to Kyoto. It was only just wide enough for two horses to squeeze past each other, and in places it wound around the edges of steep cliffs. Finally they saw a small, thatched house with bundles of cedar needles hanging from the eaves and a sign saying "Best-Quality Saké." The once-white rice cakes for sale at the entrance were covered with many days' worth of dust. The other side of the small house was a tea shop that also sold tea whisks, painted clay dolls, and toy drums from Kyoto. These reminded Osan and Moemon of home, and as they rested and drank their tea, their spirits rose. In their exuberance, they gave the old man who ran the teahouse a gold coin, but the surprised man scowled and said gruffly, "Please, pay for your tea!" The place couldn't have been forty miles from Kyoto, yet the people here had never seen gold coins. Osan and Moemon thought it quite amusing.

They continued on to a place called Kayabara, where they went to the house of Moemon's aunt, whom he hadn't seen for many years. He wasn't even sure she was still alive. She was, and soon they were talking about the old days. The woman treated Moemon warmly, since he was her nephew. She went on and on about Moemon's father Mosuke, and they spent the whole night talking, stopping only to clear tears from their eyes. Around dawn, Moemon's aunt became curious about the attractive woman he was with and asked who she

Moemon carries Osan on his back in the mountains of Tanba. At the top of the slope stands a small teahouse with an iron pot of water over a stove. Teacups are on a rack to the right. Two horsemen, one with a whip in hand, lead packhorses loaded with crates.

was. Moemon hadn't thought through an answer to this question yet and was caught off guard.

"Oh, she's my younger sister," he answered, saying the first thing that came into his mind. "She served for several years in an aristocrat's mansion, but she felt very depressed by the solemn, formal life in the capital. She's left Kyoto because she'd rather marry a man living in a quiet mountain village like this. She says she'd like to work in the kitchen of a farmhouse from now on and doesn't care about her husband's social class, no matter how low it is. That's why I brought her here. She has a dowry of two hundred gold coins with her."

People everywhere are moved by greed, and Moemon's aunt was no exception. The dowry was simply too good for her to ignore. "Well," she said, "this really is a stroke of good luck. My only son still isn't married yet, you know. Moemon, you're kin, so please bless their marriage and do your part to help out."

Things were going from bad to worse. Osan cried, but she hid her tears. Late that night, while she was still trying to think of a way to avoid the marriage, the woman's son came back. He looked ferocious. He was very tall, and the wavy hair standing out from his head made him look like a lion. His beard was thick as a bear's, and his bloodshot eyes gleamed brightly. His arms and legs were as gnarled and sinewed as pine trees; his clothes were made from rags; and his belt was braided from strips of wisteria bark. With one hand he held a rifle and cotton fuses; with the other, a straw bag full of dead rabbits and raccoons. He obviously made his living as a hunter.

The man introduced himself. His name, he said, was Cliff-Leaping Zetarō, and he was the toughest and meanest man in the village. But when his mother told him he had a chance to marry a woman from Kyoto, even this fearsome, grimy brute was delighted.

"If it's good," he exclaimed, "grab it while you can. That's what I always say. Let's have the wedding tonight!" The man looked almost gentle as he took out his pocket mirror and examined his face.

His mother immediately began preparing for the ritual exchange of saké that would seal the marriage. After getting out salted tuna and an old bottle with a chipped mouth for pouring saké, she made a small wedding bedroom by partitioning off a corner of the room big enough for two people. Inside the straw standing screens, she put down two wooden pillows, two straw sleeping mats, and a striped quilt. Then she came back and lit a brazier with split pinewood kindling. That night she was in very high spirits.

Osan was distressed, and Moemon completely gave up hope. "This all happened because I spoke without thinking," he said. "I must have done something in a former life that made me say what I did. But still, if only I hadn't! If I'd known something this bad was going to happen, I would have died in Lake Biwa. There's no sense living any longer now. Heaven's not going to let me get away!" He unsheathed his short sword and started to stand up.

Osan pulled him back down again before he could cut himself open. "Don't be so emotional," she said. "Use your head. Right now I have several ideas. As soon as it starts to get light, we'll be far away from this place. Just leave everything up to me." This calmed Moemon's mind.

That night, as the ritual cups of saké were being exchanged, Osan acted as if she were very happy. Then very casually, she remarked, "Zetarō, I must tell you I was born in the year of the fiery horse.[55] Most men don't want to marry me because of that. You know what they say about women like me."

"I don't care if you were born in the year of the fiery cat," Zetarō said, "or even the year of the fiery wolf.[56] I love poisonous green lizards myself. In fact, I eat them all the time. And they haven't killed me yet. I'm twenty-eight, and I've never even had a bellyache. Hey, Moemon, you really ought to become tough like me. Just look at this woman. She was raised in Kyoto, and actually she's much too soft and gentle for me. But I have to marry her because of you. Talk about bad luck! I'm only doing this as a favor because you're family."[57] He put his head on Osan's lap, closed his eyes, and dozed off contentedly.

Osan was as amused as she was sad. She could hardly wait for Zetarō to fall

---

55. A double-fire year in the zodiacal cycle. Women born in this year were said to be so passionate that they sometimes killed their husbands with too much lovemaking.

56. Zetarō shows his ignorance, since such years did not exist.

57. Zetarō attempts to make Moemon feel indebted and thus gain leverage over him.

soundly asleep, and when he did she and Moemon slipped out of the house. They headed north and disappeared into the depths of Tanba Province.

Several days later they returned to the main road and followed it north into Tango Province. Not much later they reached the shores of the Japan Sea. That night they went to the Monju Hall in Kireto, located near the break in the long, sandy arm of land known as the Amanohashitate,[58] and there they spent the night in prayer with other pilgrims. Sometime around what must have been the middle of the night, when Osan was beginning to feel drowsy, she saw a vision of the revered Monju, the bodhisattva of wisdom. "You both have committed flagrant adultery," the bodhisattva told her. "No matter where you go, you will never be able to escape pain and suffering. You cannot go back into the past now and change what you have done, but from this time on, you must give up your worldly ties. Cut off the long black hair you love so much and take Buddhist vows. If you and he live separately, abandon your bad thoughts, and meditate on the path to enlightenment, people will surely be willing to spare your lives."

Osan listened to the revelation, unsure whether she was dreaming or awake. Then she thought she heard her voice saying, "Don't worry about what's going to happen to me in the future, Monju. I'm doing this because I want to. I like it. I chose to love that man outside my marriage and my social rank, and I'm willing to die for it. Monju, it's common knowledge that you know all about love between men.[59] But you don't understand a thing about love between women and men!" Just then Osan was aware that an unpleasant dream had ended. All she could hear was the sea wind blowing through the pines on the long spit of land nearby.

"Buddhists say the world's all dust and dirt," Osan said to Moemon. "Well then, so what if we're dirt? The wind blows everyone away, anyway."

Osan's love continued and grew even stronger.

EAVESDROPPING ON HIMSELF (5)

When things go badly, people act as if nothing has happened. Gamblers never talk about the times they've lost, and men who've been taken for everything by a woman in the licensed quarter strut around as though they were too smart ever to visit a place like that. Professional toughs don't mention fights they've lost, and speculating merchants hide their bad investments. People commonly call this "pretending you haven't stepped on dog shit in the dark."

---

58. Now called Amanohashidate (literally, Bridge to Heaven), one of the three most famous vistas in Japan.

59. Osan refers to Monju's full name, Monjushiri (from the Sanskrit Manjusri); in Japanese, *shiri* means "rear end," and Monju had an unofficial reputation as a proponent of male homosexual love.

Nothing humiliates a married man as much as finding that his wife has been having an affair, and the calendar maker was no exception. But he couldn't pretend Osan was still alive. She was dead, and that wouldn't change, so he dutifully notified the authorities and everyone else involved of the facts of her love suicide just as they had been reported to him. After that he acted as if nothing had happened and tried to keep any new rumors from starting. When he remembered how he and Osan had once lived, his heart filled with hatred for her, but he did the proper thing and invited monks to come to his house to say prayers for the repose of her soul. How sad people were when they saw all Osan's inventive silk robes given to the family temple and, following custom, cut up into Buddhist streamers and canopies. As people saw them turning and fluttering emptily in the wind, they realized Osan really was dead, and their grief grew even deeper.

Humans can be very reckless creatures. Moemon was an honest, responsible man, and so cautious he refused to go outdoors after dark for fear something might happen, but as time passed he began to forget he was a dead man hiding from the world. Gradually he found himself longing to see the capital again. So one day he disguised himself in some shabby clothes, pulled his wide sedge hat down over his face, left Osan with some neighbors in the village, and set off for Kyoto, where he had no business at all going.

Moemon walked along more fearfully than someone being chased by avenging enemies. By the time dark had fallen, he was at the edge of Kyoto. The double reflection of the moon on the surface of Hirosawa Pond[60] made him think of Osan, and he began crying uncontrollably into his sleeve. As he passed Narutaki Falls roaring nearby, he was weeping so hard his tears mixed with the water frothing at the foot of the falls.[61] He pressed on and made good time through Mimuro and Kitano along a route he knew well, and soon he was walking down city blocks. They made him feel strangely uneasy. Several times his whole body froze in terror at the sight of a figure following right behind him—and each time it turned out to be his own shadow in the bright light of the moon, which was only two nights past full.

Moemon kept walking until he reached the block on which Osan's parents' store was located, a block on which he'd spent so much of his own life. There he found a dim spot and stood trying to overhear what people there were saying. First he heard some men wondering why a payment from Edo was late arriving, and then he heard clerks talking, comparing their hairstyles and the cut and fit of their cotton robes. They all were interested in women and wanted to look as

---

60. In Saga in west Kyoto. Double or even triple reflections of the moon were sometimes seen on its surface.

61. "Tears" and "froth" are homophones in Japanese, as is the word for "soul" (*tama*). Through an allusion to *Shinkokinshū*, no. 1141, and *Goshūishū*, no. 1163, Saikaku suggests that Moemon's soul is leaving his body.

sexy as they possibly could. After discussing various things, they finally began to talk about what he was waiting to hear.

"Hey, now, wasn't that Moemon something?" One said. "First he runs off with the most beautiful woman anybody's ever seen, and then he doesn't even hesitate to give up his life. He's dead, but still, he was a lucky, lucky man."

"You can say that again. He must have had the time of his life."

Then Moemon heard a pompous-sounding voice: "Really," the man said, "you shouldn't even mention that man's foul name upwind of normal people. He betrayed his own employers and seduced their daughter, even though she was married. I've never heard of such a disgusting thing in my whole life." The voice went on and on, criticizing Moemon and saying that he was thoroughly immoral.

Moemon was sure it was Kisuke, who worked at the Daimonjiya dry goods store nearby. What an insensitive bastard he is, Moemon thought, saying things like that without any regard for the person he's talking about. He borrowed ten and a half ounces of silver from me and gave me a receipt for it, but he still hasn't paid it back. Moemon ground his teeth together in anger. Kisuke, he swore to himself, you're not going to get away with this. I'll get that money back from you if I have to wring your neck to get it. But Moemon had no choice. He just stood there hiding, barely managing to endure his rage. Then he heard another voice.

"From what I hear," the clerk said, "Moemon's still alive. They say he escaped together with Osan. They probably went somewhere near Ise, and he's living there with Osan right now. That's a very sweet thing he's getting away with, isn't it."

When Moemon heard that, his body began shaking uncontrollably, and he broke out in a cold sweat. He left as quickly as he could and went to Third Avenue, where he found a cheap inn for the night. He was so afraid of being discovered that he went directly to his room, without going to the bath. Later, when a beggar passed by in the street crying out for donations during the seventeenth-night moon-viewing ceremonies,[62] Moemon went out and gave him a folded paper with twelve copper coins inside and asked him to deliver a written prayer for him to the fire god at the Atago Shrine. As the beggar moved his brush, Moemon dictated a prayer asking the god to "keep my matter very secret forever." But how could he possibly expect the god who protects against fires to help someone who had done such grievous wrong?

Early the next morning Moemon set out to take a last look at Kyoto. Hiding his face, he walked through the eastern hills and then down through the kabuki theaters along the river near the Fourth Avenue. "Come right in," cried one

---

62. The full moon on the fifteenth day of the Eighth Month was considered the most beautiful of the year, and ceremonies were also held on the seventeenth day.

ticket seller. "See a true-life three-act play starring Fujita Koheiji.[63] Show's start-ing, show's starting!" Curious, Moemon went in, thinking he could tell Osan about it when he got back. He rented a round straw mat and went to the back of the open seating area, where he sat down nervously and watched the play from a distance, half-trembling with fear that someone in the theater would recognize him.

The play was about a man who was running off with another man's daughter. As he watched, Moemon grew more and more uneasy, and then he noticed that the man sitting near the stage several rows directly in front of him was Osan's husband. Moemon was so shocked his soul almost left his body, and he struggled to stay conscious. He felt as if he were leaping from the top of one cliff to the top of another with all hell down below. Large beads of sweat were running down his body. Managing to stand up, he rushed out of the theater, and he didn't stop until he was back in the village in Tango Province where he and Osan lived. After that he was so afraid of Kyoto that he never went there again.

A few days before the Chrysanthemum Festival on the ninth of the Ninth Month, a chestnut seller from Tanba Province on a trip to Kyoto stopped at the calendar maker's house, as he did every year at that time. After rambling on about all sorts of things, he asked about the calendar maker's wife. No one in the house was willing to say anything, and they all stood awkwardly in silence. "Her?" the calendar maker finally said, a bitter look on his face. "Oh, she dropped dead."

"Well now, I guess some people are just born into this world to be doubles," the salesman exclaimed as he was leaving. "In Tango, near where the ocean flows through at the end of the Amanohashitate land spit, there was a woman who was the perfect look-alike for your wife. And the young man with her, he was the living image of Moemon."

The calendar maker was very interested in what he'd heard, and he sent some men to Tango to see if it was true. When the men came back and reported that the two really were Osan and Moemon, the calendar maker gathered to-gether all the men he had working for him and had them go capture the fugitives.

Osan and Moemon were unable to escape punishment for their serious crimes, and after an investigation they were condemned to death, along with Tama, the woman who had acted as their go-between. Like a dream at dawn on the twenty-second of the Ninth Month, all three were bound and paraded on horseback around the capital as a lesson to others and then taken to the Awataguchi execution grounds, where they disappeared like the dew on the morning grass. But they lived their last moments with such dignity that they

---

63. Famous for male lead roles in the 1760s through the early 1690s in Kyoto.

became a legend. Even now people talk about Osan and describe her as if she were again before their eyes riding along in her plain blue green prisoner's robe.

[*Saikaku shū jō*, NKBT 47: 260–280, translated by Chris Drake]

LIFE OF A SENSUOUS WOMAN (*KŌSHOKU ICHIDAI ONNA*, 1686)

Ihara Saikaku wrote *Life of a Sensuous Woman* at the peak of his career. Published in Osaka, the work, in six volumes and twenty-four chapters, marks one of the last in a series of "books on love" (*kōshoku-mono*), a subgenre of books of the floating world (*ukiyo-zōshi*), which began with *Life of a Sensuous Man*. *Life of a Sensuous Woman* is an aging woman's extended confession to two young men. She describes her various experiences, beginning with her childhood (as the daughter of a former aristocrat in Kyoto) and her life as an attendant in the imperial palace through a series of increasingly low positions, until in the end she falls to the position of a streetwalker. If *Life of a Sensuous Man* is seen as a parody of the noted Heian male lovers Genji and Narihira, *Life of a Sensuous Woman* can be regarded as a seventeenth-century version of the legendary Ono no Komachi, known for her transformation from a stunning beauty with many lovers to an unattractive old woman. In contrast to *Life of a Sensuous Man*, about a man who seems to remain forever young and optimistic, *Life of a Sensuous Woman* looks at the world of love and sexuality from the perspective of a woman who is growing older and whose outlook is becoming increasingly bleak.

Life of a Sensuous Woman, the only major narrative that Saikaku wrote in the first person, structurally echoes the Buddhist *zange*, or confession narrative, as found, for example, in the late medieval tale *The Three Priests* (*Sannin hōshi*) or the early-seventeenth-century *Two Nuns* (*Nininbikuni*, ca. 1632), in which someone who has become a priest or nun recounts a past life of sin, particularly the crisis that led to spiritual awakening. Instead of a religious confession, the aged woman narrator is implicitly initiating the two young men visitors into the secrets of the way of love, describing a life of vitality and sexual desire. Some of the earlier chapters, in fact, reveal the influence of courtesan critiques. It is not until the end, when the sight of the statues of the five hundred disciples causes the woman to have a vision of many of the men with whom she has had relations, that the narrative takes the form of a Buddhist confession.

Significantly, the two young male listeners ask the aged woman to tell them about her past experience in "the style of the present" (*imayō*). Instead of describing her life in the past as it happened, she transforms it into the present, telling it as if she were repeatedly living "today." In this fashion, Saikaku explores many of the positions that a woman could have at the time—as a palace attendant, a dancer, a mistress of a domain lord, a high-ranking woman of the licensed quarter (*tayū*), a priest's wife, a teacher of calligraphy and manners, a nun who performs Buddhist chants (*utabikuni*), a hairdresser, a seasonal house cleaner, a go-between for marital engagements, a seamstress, a waitress at a teahouse, a streetwalker, and many other professions—providing a remarkable portrayal of a cross section of contemporary commoner society. *Life of a Sensuous Woman* has in fact been described by many modern scholars as a novel of manners. Sometimes with the names of actual people barely disguised, Saikaku satirically reveals the underside of the lives of domain lords, powerful samurai, wealthy priests, and upper-level merchants. Throughout the work, Saikaku's main interest remains the woman's resourcefulness and imagination in these concrete social circumstances and how these contexts evoke or frustrate her irrepressible desire.

An Old Woman's Hermitage (1:1)

A beautiful woman, many ages have agreed, is an ax that cuts down a man's life. No one, of course, escapes death. The invisible blossoms of the mind[64] finally fall and scatter; the soul leaves; and the body is fed like kindling into a crematorium fire in the night. But for the blossoms to fall all too soon in a morning storm—ah, how foolish are the men who die young of overindulgence in the way of sensuous love. Yet there is no end of them.

On the seventh of the First Month, the day people go out to have their fortunes told, I had to visit Saga[65] in northwest Kyoto. As if to show that spring had truly come, the plums at Umezu Crossing[66] were just breaking into blossom. On the eastbound ferry to Saga I saw an attractive young man dressed in the latest style but unmistakably disheveled. His face was pale, and he was thin and worn, obviously from too much lovemaking. He looked as if he didn't have much time left and was getting ready to leave his inheritance to his own parents.

"I've never lacked anything at all," he said to the man with him. "But there's one thing I really would like. I wish my pledging liquid could keep flowing on and on like this river and never stop."

His friend was startled. "What I'd like," he said, "is a country without women. I'd go there and find a quiet place to live, far from any town. There I'd take good care of myself, so I could live to a decent old age. The world keeps changing, and I'd really like to see a lot of different things."

The two men had opposite attitudes toward life and death. One sought as much sensual pleasure as he could get, even though he knew that it was shortening his life, and the other wanted to give up love altogether and live many more years. Both longed for the impossible, and they talked in a dazed way, halfway between dreaming and waking.

After we reached the other side, the men joked and horsed around, staggering along the path on the bank and stamping without a thought on the parsley and thistles that were coming into leaf. Finally they turned away from the river,

---

64. Alludes to a poem by Ono no Komachi: "They fade invisibly and change, these blossoms of the mind in our human world" (*Kokinshū*, Love 5, no. 797).

65. A wooded area of temples and the huts of recluses.

66. On the Katsura River, a major collecting point for lumber from the northwest.

left the last houses behind, and entered the shadows of the mountains to the north. I felt curious about them and followed at a distance. Eventually we came to a grove of red pines and, within it, an old fence made of bundled bush-clover stalks that were beginning to come apart. Beside the braided bamboo gate a gap had been opened so a dog could pass through. Inside the fence, in deep silence, stood a meditation hut, its front roof sloping down from a boulder above the mouth of a natural cave. Ferns grew in its thatched eaves, and vines clung to the roof, their leaves still tinted with last fall's colors.

To the east stood a willow tree, and from below it came a soft sound. Clear, pure water was flowing naturally through a raised pipe of split bamboo from a source nearby. I looked around for the venerable monk that I assumed must live there and was surprised to see an old woman, one whose face the years had given a refined beauty. Her back was bent, but her frost-touched hair was well combed. Her eyes were as soft and hazy as the moon low on the western horizon. Over an old-style sky blue wadded-silk robe embroidered with gold thread, she wore another splashed with a dappled pattern of thickly petaled chrysanthemums. Her medium-width sash, with flowers in a lozenge design, was tied in front—stylish even at her age. To the crossbeam above the front of what seemed to be her bedroom was attached a weathered plaque that read "Hut of a Sensuous Hermit." A scent of incense lingered in the air. I think it must have been First Warbler's Cry, a very fine aloeswood.[67]

I found a place outside a window and stood there, so overcome with curiosity that my mind strained to leap out of myself and into the hermitage. As I watched, the two men, looking thoroughly at home, went right inside without even announcing themselves.

"So, you've come again today," the woman said smiling. "There are so many pleasures in the world to captivate you men. Why have you come all the way here to see me, like wind visiting a rotting old tree? My ears are bad, and words no longer come easily. It's just too difficult for me now to keep up relationships properly, the way I'd need to do if I wanted to stay in the world. I've been living in this place for seven years already, and the plum trees are my calendar. When they bloom, I know spring's come. When the mountains are white with snow, I know it's winter. I almost never see anyone any more. Why do you keep coming here?"

"He's being tortured by love," said one of the men. "And I get very depressed. Neither of us understands the way of sensuous love deeply enough yet. We've heard many things about you, and we've followed the same path you've traveled. Right here to your door. You're so very experienced, won't you please tell us the story of your life in the words people use now? Please do it in a way that will help us understand more about life and the world today."

---

67. Temple incense chosen to match the early spring season, when the warblers return.

The old woman plays her koto while a censer burns on a small table. One of the two young men accompanies her on a short shakuhachi, a type of flute. Both men seem to be well-off commoners and wear short swords. The narrator, standing outside, peers furtively though a latticed window. The illustrations are attributed to Yoshida Hanbei (act. 1684–1688). From the 1686 edition.

One of the men poured some fine saké into a beautiful gold wine cup and strongly urged the old woman to drink. She relented and gradually lost her reserve and began to play on her koto. She was so skillful it was obvious she played it often. For a while she sang a short song about deep love. Then overcome with emotion, she began to relate, as if in a dream, all the loves in her own life and the various things that had happened to her.

I didn't come from a low-class family, she began. My mother was a commoner, but my father was descended from middle-ranking aristocrats who mixed with high officials at the court of Emperor GoHanazono.[68] Families, like everything else in the world, go up and down. Mine came down very hard, and we were so miserable we didn't want to go on living. But I happened to be born with a beautiful face, so I went to Kyoto to serve a court lady of the highest rank, and I learned most of those elegant, refined ways of aristocrats. If I'd continued to serve there for a few more years, I'm sure I would have had a very happy future.

From the beginning of the summer when I was eleven, I became very loose and forgot I was supposed to concentrate on serving my employer. When people did my hair, I wouldn't be satisfied and I'd redo it myself. I was the one, you

---

68. Presumably she is referring to Emperor GoHanazono both while he reigned (1428–1464) and while he was a cloistered emperor until his death in 1470.

know, who invented the version of the Shimada hairstyle that has the hair swept up behind and the chignon tied and folded flat in back. It became quite stylish. I also created that way of tying the topknot without showing the cord that became so popular. I'm sure you know the white silk robes with colorful Gosho-dyed patterns. Well, in the beginning only court ladies wore them. But I spent all my time and energy making new patterns and colors for them, and soon they became quite popular with ordinary women.

Aristocrats, you know, are always thinking about love, whether they're composing poems or playing kickball. Those women's pillows, why, they're always in use. Whenever I saw women and men lying together, I'd feel excited, and when I'd hear them in the dark, my heart pounded. Naturally I began to want to make love myself. Just when I was beginning to feel love was the most important thing in my life, I also began to get love letters from a lot of men. They all were full of deep feelings and tender thoughts, but I got so many I had no way to get rid of them all. I had to ask a guard to burn them for me. Of course I made him promise to keep it secret. Later, you know, he told me something strange. The places in the letters where the men swore by their patron gods that their love for me was true and would never change, those places, he said, didn't burn. They rose up with the smoke and came down in the Yoshida Shrine, where all the gods of Japan gather together.[69] There's nothing as strange as love. Every one of the men who longed for me was handsome and knew how to look attractive, but I didn't have special feelings for any of them. I was interested in a young samurai who was working for one of the aristocrats. He was of low rank and wasn't good-looking, but his writing, even in his very first letter, sent me into another world. He kept on writing more and more letters, and before I knew it I was beginning to suffer and yearn for him, too.

It was hard for us to meet, but I managed to arrange things sometimes, and we were able to make love. Rumors started, but I couldn't stop myself. In the faint light early one morning, someone saw both of us together out in the shifting mist,[70] as they say, and while the mist swirled ever more thickly, my employer secretly fired me and had me discreetly left beside the road at the end of Uji Bridge.[71] I was merely punished, but the man—how cruel they were! He lost his life for what we'd done.

For four or five days I couldn't tell whether I was sleeping or awake. I couldn't sleep, but I couldn't get up either. Several times I was terrified when I saw the man's resentful-looking shape in front of me. It refused to even speak. I was in complete shock, and I thought about killing myself. But the days went by, and

---

69. The Yoshida Shrine, in Kyoto, claimed to include all 3,132 gods in Japan.

70. Ironically alludes to a poem by Sadayori: "In faint early light, mist on the Uji River begins to break, and through its gaps: weir poles in the shallows" (*Senzaishū*, no. 420).

71. The woman was born in Uji, just south of Kyoto.

you know, I completely forgot about that man. It's amazing how quickly a woman's mind can change. But I was thirteen at the time, and people looked on me leniently. Ridiculous, they'd think, surely she hasn't done *that* already. And what could have been more ridiculous than their own thoughts!

In the old days, when it came time for a bride to leave for the groom's house, she would grieve at leaving her parents' house and cry at the gate until her sleeves were all wet. But these days young women know a lot more about lovemaking. They grow impatient with the slow bargaining of the go-between woman, rush to get their trousseaus ready, and can't wait for the fancy palanquin to come and take them away. When it arrives, they practically leap in, excitement glowing everywhere, to the tips of their noses. Until forty years ago, young women used to play horse outside their front doors until they were eighteen or nineteen. And young men didn't have their coming-of-age ceremonies until they were twenty-five. My goodness, the world certainly does change quickly!

I was very young when I learned about love. I was still a flower in bud, you could say. And after that I had so many experiences that the pure water of my mind turned completely the color of sensuous love, like the water in the Uji River where it turns yellow from all the mountain roses on the banks. I just followed my desires wherever they went—and I ruined myself. The water will never be clear again. There's no use regretting it now, though. I certainly have managed to live a long time, but my life, well, it wasn't what you'd call exemplary.

Mistress of a Domain Lord (1:3)

The land was at peace, and calm breezes drifted through the pines of Edo. One year the daimyō lord of a certain rural domain was in Edo spending his obligatory year living near the castle of the shōgun. There he was able to be with his wife, who was required to live permanently in Edo, but during the year she died. Since she'd left no male heir, the lord's worried retainers gathered more than forty beautiful young women from leading warrior families in Edo, hoping one of them would bear a boy baby for the lord and ensure the continued rule of the lord's clan over the domain—and the retainers' own employment. The head chambermaid was resourceful, and whenever she saw the lord feeling good, she brought a young woman near his sleeping chamber and did her best to put him in the mood. All the women were fresh as budding cherry blossoms, ready to burst into full bloom if wet by the slightest rain. Most men would have gazed at any of these women and never grown tired, yet not a single one suited the lord, and his retainers began to grow anxious.[72]

The retainers didn't bother to look for other women among the commoners

---

72. If a daimyō lord died without a male heir, the domain administration was transferred to a new clan, forcing the retainers to become unemployed rōnin.

in Edo. Ordinary women raised in the eastern provinces,[73] you know, they're rough and insensitive. They have flat feet and thick necks, and their skin is hard. They're honest and straightforward, but they don't feel deep passion and don't know how to express their desire to men or attract them by acting afraid. Their minds are sincere, but they're ignorant of the way of sensuous love and can't share it with a man who knows it.

I've never heard of any women more attractive than those in Kyoto. For one thing, Kyoto women have a beautiful way of speaking. It's not something they study. They pick it up naturally living in the capital, where women have talked that way for centuries. Just look at how different Kyoto is from Izumo Province. In Izumo they have an ancient tradition of love and courtship going back to the days of the gods, but the men and women there slur their words so badly it's hard to understand them. But then just go offshore from Izumo to Oki Island. The islanders there look like country people, but they speak the way people do in the capital. And Oki women are gentle and know how to play the koto, play *go*, distinguish fine incense, and compose and appreciate waka poems. That's because long ago Emperor GoDaigo was exiled to Oki with his entourage,[74] and the islanders maintain the customs from that time even now.

So the daimyō's councillors thought that in Kyoto, at least, there must be a woman their lord would like. To look for one, they sent the lord's old and trusted retainer, the overseer of the inner chambers. The overseer was more than seventy. He couldn't see a thing without glasses and had only few front teeth. He'd forgotten what octopus tasted like, and the only pickled vegetables he could still eat were finely grated radishes. Day after day he lived without any pleasure, and as for sensuous love, well, he did wear a loincloth, but he might as well have been a woman. The best he could do was excitedly tell a few sexy stories. As a samurai, he wore formal divided skirts and robes with starched, high shoulders, but since he served in his lord's wife's private chambers and in the women's quarters, he wasn't allowed to wear either a long or a short sword. Too old to be a warrior, he was put in charge of watching the silver lock on the doors to the inner chambers. That's why the councillors chose him to go to Kyoto to find a mistress—and to chaperon her all the way back to Edo. It would be like putting a precious buddha statue in front of a puzzled cat. You just can't let a young man alone with a woman, you know, even if he's Shakyamuni Buddha.

The old retainer finally arrived in the capital, which looked to him like the Pure Land paradise on earth. He went directly to one of the exclusive Sasaya clothiers on Muromachi Avenue that caters to aristocrats and warrior lords. There he announced himself and was led to a private room.

---

73. Edo was located in the eastern provinces, an area considered by Kyoto people to be rustic and unrefined.

74. GoDaigo was exiled to Oki in 1332.

"I cannot discuss my business with any of the young clerks," he told the person who received him. "I need to talk very confidentially with the owner's retired parents."

The old retainer, who knew nothing of how things worked, felt uneasy as he waited. Finally the retired shop owner and his wife appeared. With a grave expression on his face, the old retainer said, "I've come to choose a mistress for my lord." "But of course," the retired owner said. "All the daimyō lords have them. Exactly what kind of woman are you looking for?"

The retainer opened a paulownia-wood scroll box and took out a painting of a woman. "We want to find someone," he said, "who looks like this."

The retired couple saw a woman between fifteen and eighteen with a full, oval face of the kind so popular then, skin the light color of cherry blossoms, and perfect facial features. The lord's councillors wanted round eyes; thick eyebrows with plenty of space between them; a gradually rising nose; a small mouth with large, even white teeth; ears a bit long but not fleshy and with clearly formed earlobes; a natural forehead and unaltered hairline; as well as a long, slender nape with no loose hairs. Her fingers were to be long and delicate with thin nails, and her feet, about seven inches long, with the large toes naturally curved the way a truly sensuous woman's are and with arched soles. Her torso was to be longer than most women's, her waist firm and slim, and her hips full. She should move and wear her clothes gracefully, and her figure should show dignity and refinement. She was to have a gentle personality, be skilled at all the arts that women learn, and know something about everything. The old retainer added that she was not to have a single mole on her body.

"The capital is a big place," the retired owner said, "and a lot of women live here. Even so, it won't be easy to find a woman who meets all these requirements. But it's for a domain lord, and expense is no concern. If the woman exists, we'll find her for you." The retired couple then went to see an experienced employment agent named Hanaya Kakuemon on Takeyamachi Street. They discreetly explained all the conditions and asked him to search for suitable candidates.

Employment agencies live off commissions. If an employer pays one hundred large gold coins as a down payment, the agency takes ten. This is broken down into silver coins, and even the errand woman gets 2 percent. An applicant for a mistress job has to have an interview, and if she has no proper clothes, she has to rent what she wants. For two and a half ounces of silver a day, she can rent a white silk robe or one of figured black satin, a dapple-dyed robe to wear over that, a wide brocade sash, a scarlet crepe underskirt, a colorful dye-pattern shawl to cover her head like an elegant lady, and even a mat to sit on in her hired palanquin. If the young woman makes a good impression and is hired, she has to pay the agency a large silver coin as its fee.

A woman from a poor family needs to have a new set of foster parents who own property and will vouch for her. The agency negotiates with the owners of a small house, and the young woman formally becomes their daughter. In return, the foster parents receive money and gifts from the lord or rich merchant who employs their new daughter. If the woman works for a lord and bears a baby boy, she becomes an official domain retainer, and the lord gives a regular rice stipend to her foster parents.

Competition is intense, and candidates try very hard to make a good impression at the interview. In addition to renting clothes, they have to spend half an ounce of silver for a palanquin and two carriers—no matter how short the ride is, the rate is the same to anywhere in Kyoto. And the woman needs a girl helper at two grams of silver a day and an older maid at three. She also has to pay for their two meals. After all this, if the woman is not hired, not only does she still have no job, but she's lost well over three ounces of silver. It's a very hard way to make a living.

And that's not the only thing the woman has to worry about. Well-off merchants from Osaka and Sakai constantly come to Kyoto to visit the Shimabara licensed quarter or party with boy kabuki actors near the theaters along the river by the Fourth Avenue Bridge. Sometimes these men have some free time and prey on women applicants to amuse themselves. The merchant pays a jester with a shaved head to pretend to be a wealthy visitor from the western provinces and has him ask women from all over Kyoto to come interview to be his mistress. The merchant attends the interview, and if a woman catches his eye, he asks her to stay and secretly negotiates with the owner of the house for a secluded room. Then he asks the woman to sleep with him for just that one time. The surprised woman is terribly angry and disappointed, but when she tries to leave, he says all sorts of things to persuade her. Finally he mentions money, and since the woman has paid so much for the interview, she gives in. For selling herself, she gets two small gold pieces. There's nothing else she can do. But women who aren't from poor families don't do that.

The employment agency carefully chose more than 170 attractive young women and sent them to the old retainer for interviews, but he wasn't satisfied with a single one. Desperately, the agency kept on searching, and when they heard about me, they contacted someone in the village of Kohata on the Uji River. Together they came to see me at my parents' house in an out-of-the-way part of Uji, where we were trying to live inconspicuously away from the world until people had forgotten what I'd done. But I agreed to an interview, and I went right back to Kyoto with the anxious agents just as I was, without putting on good clothes or makeup. When I got there, the old retainer thought I was even better than the woman in the painting, so the search was called off. Everything was decided on the spot, and I got to set the conditions myself. I became an official domain mistress.[75]

---

75. She becomes the daimyō lord's semiofficial second wife. Normally the mistress would

A woman is interviewed by a daimyō's retainer in a spacious Kyoto inn. The retainer sits in front of an alcove with flowers and a hanging scroll, and the clothier sits at bottom left. The woman stands in robes bearing the crest of the Itakura clan, suggesting the daimyō's clan. A maid kneels (*right*), and two palanquin bearers sit at the gate.

And so I went with the retainer all the way to Edo, far off in Musashi Province in the east. There I lived very happily day and night in the lord's third mansion[76] in Asakusa, on the outskirts of the city. Everything was so luxurious, well, in the day I couldn't believe my eyes. I felt I must be seeing the most beautiful cherry blossoms in the world on the Mount Yoshino in China[77] that people talk about. And at night they had top kabuki actors from Sakai-chō come, and we'd watch their plays and variety shows and laugh hour after hour. Everything was so luxurious you couldn't imagine anything else you'd want.

But women, you know, are very basic creatures. They just can't forget about physical love, even though warriors have very strict rules keeping women and men apart. The serving women who live in the inner rooms of those mansions almost never even see a man and don't have the slightest idea what the scent of a man's loincloth is like. Whenever they look at one of Moronobu's suggestive prints, they'll feel a rush and go dizzy with desire. Without even imagining they're really making love, they'll twist and push their own heels or middle fingers way around and move their implements. And when they're finished,

---

live with the daimyō while he was in his home domain on alternate years, but in this case the lord's wife has died, so she goes to Edo.

76. A daimyō lord usually had three mansions in Edo: the first was for his family and formal audiences; the second was for emergencies; and the third was for relaxation and a mistress.

77. Mount Yoshino, south of Nara, was believed to have the most beautiful cherry blossoms in Japan—prompting the belief in an even more beautiful, ideal Mount Yoshino in China.

they still feel unsatisfied. They want to make love with a flesh-and-blood man all the more.

Daimyō lords usually spend most of their time in the front rooms of their mansions overseeing domain business, and without knowing it, they become attracted to the young pages with long hair who are constantly waiting on them. The love a lord feels for a page is deeper than anything he feels for a woman. His wife is definitely in second place. In my opinion, this is because a lord's wife isn't allowed to show her jealousy the way commoner women do. Men, high or low, fear a jealous woman more anything else in the world, and those warriors take strict precautions.

I've always been an unlucky woman, but with the lord I was fortunate. He was tender to me, and we enjoyed our lovemaking. But things didn't work out. Before I could get pregnant, he started taking herbal pills. They didn't do much good, though. He was still young, but in bed he just couldn't do anything anymore. It was just extremely bad luck. I couldn't talk about it with anyone, so I spent all my time regretting what had happened. The lord kept losing weight, and finally he became so weak and haggard he was just awful to look at.

I was amazed to discover that the councillors thought it was my fault. They said I was a woman from the capital who liked fancy sex and had worn out their lord. Those old men didn't know the first thing about love, but they made the decisions. I was suddenly dismissed and sent all the way back to my parents—again. If you look closely at the world, you'll see that a man who's born sexually weak is a very sad thing for a woman.

A Monk's Wife in a Worldly Temple (2:3)

I have a small build, so I unstitched the sewn-up openings under the arms of the robes I'd worn as a girl[78] and put them on again. I looked so young people called me a female version of the Daoist wizard Tie-guai.[79]

In those days Buddhism was at its proverbial high noon, and truly, even in broad daylight, women dressed as temple pages[80] would walk right into temple precincts and visit the monks there. I, too, finally overcame my shame and had my hair done up like a boy, with thick, long hair in front and the top of my

---

78. Girls wore long, loose sleeves with an opening under the arms that was sewn up when they became adults, usually in their late teens. In this chapter, the woman is about twenty-five or twenty-six years of age.

79. A Daoist wizard from the Sui dynasty who, according to legend, was able to breathe out earlier versions of himself from his own mouth.

80. Boy assistants to high-ranking monks. They often were sexual partners of the older men, but in the seventeenth century, women were able to enter temples more easily, and a new type of page flourished.

The woman (*right*) stands inside the precincts of the temple dressed as a young samurai with a long and a short sword. She wears a sedge hat trimmed with leather. Behind her is the sandal bearer, holding her sandals. Beyond a cherry tree, the jester (*left*) negotiates with the head priest, who wears a black robe over a wadded white silk robe.

head shaved. I learned to speak like a boy and move my body almost like one, too. When I put on a loincloth, I was surprised to see how much like a boy I looked! I also changed to a boy's narrow sash, but the first time I stuck long and short swords through it, they were so heavy I couldn't keep my waist and legs steady. And when I put on a boy's cloak and wide-rimmed sedge hat, I began to wonder whether I was really myself.

I hired a young man with a long ink moustache painted on his face to carry my spare sandals and other things, and I set out together with a professional jester from the licensed quarter who knew a lot about how things worked in Kyoto. We asked around and found a temple known to have wealth and a sex-loving head monk. We walked right through the gate in the earth walls surrounding the temple, pretending we were going inside to see the small cherry tree in the temple garden. Then the jester went to the head monk's quarters and began whispering with the monk, who seemed to have a lot of free time on his hands. Soon I was called into the reception room, where the jester introduced me to the monk.

"This young warrior," the jester said, "has lost his lord, and he has no one to depend on. He's been able to make some contacts, but while he's waiting for an offer from another lord, he'll drop in here from time to time for a little recreation. I most sincerely ask you to take care of him to the best of your ability." He went on and on about a lot of similar things.

The head monk was flushed with excitement. "Just last night," he blurted out, "I got someone to teach me how to make an herbal mixture to induce abortions. It's something you women really need to. . . ." Then he clapped his hand on his mouth. It was all quite amusing.

Later we drank some saké and spoke more freely. As we savored the smells of meat and fish coming from the temple kitchen, my fee was set at two small gold coins[81] per night. Later, the jester and I went around to temples of every persuasion suggesting they switch to the Woman-Loving sect, and we didn't find a single monk who didn't convert.

Eventually the head priest of one temple fell in love with me, and I agreed to become his temporary wife for three years in exchange for twenty-five pounds of silver. I became what people call an "oven god."[82] As the days went by, I was more and more amazed by what I saw and heard at this floating-world temple. In the past, a group of monk friends who lived in various halls around the temple compound had gotten together on the six days a month when special purifications and austerities are required. They all solemnly pledged that on days except for these six, they would strictly obey their abstentions. And they vowed to rigorously limit their fish and poultry and their sex with women to the nights of these six days, except, of course, when the days fell on the memorial days for various buddhas and the sect founder. To pursue their pleasures, they went all the way to Third Avenue in downtown Kyoto and visited places like the Koiya Inn.[83] On other days, the men acted like model monks. The buddhas, who know all, looked on them leniently, and everything went smoothly.

But in the last few years, this large temple had been growing very prosperous, and the monks were losing all restraint. At night they replaced their black robes with long cloaks and went to the licensed quarter pretending to be shaven-headed herbal doctors. And the head priest would bring his secret wife of the moment right into the monks' living quarters. He'd had his monks dig far down below one corner of the main living room and built a secret underground room for the wife. Between the ground and the raised floor of the quarters, they'd constructed a narrow window in a place that no one could see from the outside. That way the woman could have a little light. They'd also filled the space between the ceiling of the underground room and the quarters floor with earth and constructed soundproof walls more than a foot thick all the way around to the back of the room. During the day the head priest forced me down into this

---

81. Two *bu*.

82. Daikoku, one of the seven gods of fortune, was often worshiped as a kitchen or an oven god. It was also a euphemism for a woman living and cooking in a temple, a custom that was widespread but officially forbidden. The priest pays the woman a substantial sum.

83. Koiya Inn, a popular seafood restaurant, had many private rooms where the monks could meet women.

underground cell. When the sun went down, I was allowed up and could go as far as his bedroom.

Living like this was depressing enough, but sleeping with the priest made me even sadder. It was just a job, and there was no love in it. I had to give myself to that disgusting priest day and night, whenever he wanted to have sex, and I began to lose interest in living. Nothing gave me pleasure any more, and I gradually lost weight and grew weaker. But the priest didn't let up in the least. His expression showed that as far as he was concerned, if I died he'd just have me secretly buried somewhere on the temple grounds without even a proper cremation. And that would be that. It was frightening.

Later I got used to the situation, and I even came to enjoy it. When the priest went out to chant sutras at a parishioner's house on the night after a death or on a memorial day, I found myself waiting up late, wishing he would come back. And when he went out at dawn to pray over the ashes of a cremated person, I felt as if we were saying good-bye to each other, and I hated for him to be away, no matter how short a time it was. Even the smell of incense on his white robe clung to my body and seemed dear to me. After a while I forgot my loneliness, and I started to like the sounds of gongs and cymbals at the ceremonies. At first, you know, I would hold my hands over my ears whenever I heard them. And my nose got used to the smell from the crematory. The more deaths there were, well, the happier I was, since they meant more offerings for the temple. Early each evening, I called in fish peddlers and made suppers of duck meat with and without bones, blowfish soup, cedar-broiled fish, and other fine seafood.[84] I did take one small precaution, though. I always put a cover on the brazier so the nice smells wouldn't escape.

The young monks in training saw our loose way of living and imitated us. They hid salted red herrings in their sleeve pockets and wrapped them in pieces of old calligraphy practice paper covered with half-written buddha names. After soaking the papers, they would place them in warm ashes to bake and would eat herrings from morning until night. It gave them wonderful complexions and lustrous skin and kept them vigorous and healthy. Some monks go off for long periods to a mountain or forest where they eat only berries and plants. Other monks are so poor they have no choice but to eat only vegetables. You can spot these kinds of monks right away from their lifeless expressions. They look like rotting trees.

I'd worked at the temple from spring until early fall. At first the priest was terribly afraid I would run away, and while I was up out of my underground room, he would lock the living quarters each time he went out. But later he came to trust me and just glanced in at me from the kitchen from time to time.

---

84. All prohibited foods.

Gradually I became bolder, and when parishioners came to visit the priest I no longer rushed underground but simply slipped out of sight into another room.

One evening I went out onto the bamboo verandah to get some fresh air, and a strong wind was moaning in the trees and ripping the thin leaves of the plantains in the garden. It was an eerie sight. Everything in the world really does change, I felt, just as they preach. I lay down on the porch with my head on my arm and was soon very drowsy. Then I saw what looked like a phantom shape. Her hair was completely gray, and her face was covered with wrinkles. Her pathetic arms and legs were thin as tongs, and she was bent over with a crooked back. She came toward me crawling on all fours.

"I've lived in this temple for many, many years," she said in a voice so full of sorrow I could hardly bear to listen. "The priest told people I was his mother. I'm not from a low-class family, but I decided to do a disgraceful thing, and I came here. I was twenty years older than he was, and I'm ashamed to say I was so poor I couldn't get by any more, and I began to sleep with him. Later we became close and exchanged many pledges, but they. . . . For him, all those pledges were nothing, nothing at all. When I got old like this, he pushed me into a dark corner of the temple. He gives me nothing but old rice offerings he's taken down from the altars. And now he sees I'm not about to die eating only that, so he glares resentfully at me. He's treated me terribly, but still, you know, it isn't really so bad. There's something else that gnaws at me until I can't stand it. Every single day. It's you! You don't know anything about me, but whenever I hear you and the priest saying little things to each other in bed, well, you see, even at my age I just can't forget sex. So I've decided to get rid of this terrible longing I have and feel good again. I'm going to bite right into you. Tonight!"

I was completely shaken. I knew I had no business being in that temple a minute longer. Finally I devised a method of escape that impressed even me. I stuffed a lot of cotton wadding between the outer and inner layers in the front part of my robe. That made me look quite heavy. Then I went to see the head priest.

"I haven't told you until now," I said, "but I'm several months pregnant. I'm not sure exactly when, but the baby could come any time now."

The priest lost his usual composure. "Please go back to your parents' house," he said. "Have a safe delivery and then come back here." He gathered up a lot of offertory coins from different places and gave them to me, swearing he was very worried about all the needs I'd have at home. Then he gave me some tiny silk robes that grief-stricken parents had left as offerings after their babies died. The priest said he couldn't stand to look at them any more, and he gave me all he had, telling me to sew them into things for his baby instead. Then he began celebrating and named the child Ishijiyo—Everlasting Rock—a boy's name, even though it hadn't been born yet.

I'd had enough of that temple. There was a lot of time left on my contract, but I never went back. The priest must have been very upset, but in a situation like that, well, there was no legal action he could take.

A Teacher of Calligraphy and Manners (2:4)

"The irises you sent are exquisite.[85] Watching them gives me endless pleasure in ways too many to begin to count." This is the kind of thing a woman has to write to begin a respectable thank-you letter in early summer.

In Kyoto, ordinary women can learn to write in a flowing woman's hand from women calligraphy teachers, who also sell their skills transcribing letters. These commoner teachers start their careers when they're young, serving for several years in the mansion of an aristocrat and learning from experience all the proper ways of elegant comportment, writing, and speech as well as the various traditional ceremonies that mark off the year. When they finish their service, most of these women are models of respectability and make a decent living teaching what they've learned. Parents tell their daughters to emulate these teachers and send their girls to study under them.

I, too, had once worked for a high-ranking aristocratic family. Although I'd been through a lot since then, some very kind people thought it would be a shame for me to waste my experience and knowledge, and they helped me establish my own calligraphy school for girls. It consisted of a single room, which served as my bedroom at night, but it was a pleasant place, and I was extremely happy to finally have a house of my own. I pasted a notice on the doorpost announcing that I taught calligraphy to women, and to help me, I hired a young woman from the country who'd just arrived in Kyoto.

Taking care of other people's daughters isn't an easy job. Day after day you continually have to exert yourself correcting brush strokes on the girls' practice papers and generally act as an example, demonstrating and explaining to them the cultured manners and decorum they're expected to learn. To avoid rumors, I completely gave up relationships with men and managed to overcome every temptation to meet them.

Then one day an obviously vigorous young man in a state of extreme passion came to me and asked me to write a letter to a certain woman with whom he fervently wished to become intimate. Since I'd worked in the licensed quarter, I knew how to compose love letters that would reach their readers' hearts. I could make a woman reader want to fly together with a man, sharing the same wings and eyes, or make her desire to become one with him, like two trees linked by a shared limb. Choosing precisely the right expressions, I could make the woman who read one of my letters fall deeply in love with the man who'd asked me to write it. I could see directly into the feelings of young women still living with their parents and persuade even the most experienced woman who knew everything about men. I used different ways of affecting each woman, but there was none my letters didn't move.

---

85. Sending in-season flowers was one sign of the good taste and manners required of upper-class women, who were imitated by commoners in the seventeenth century.

Nothing shows a person's feelings better than a letter. No matter how far away the person you're thinking of is, you can communicate your thoughts with your brush. You may write at length, using phrase after polished phrase, but if your letter is filled with falsehoods, it will show and soon be forgotten. Truthful brush strokes go straight to the heart. As you read, you will feel as if you're meeting the writer, who's right there with you.

When I was working in the licensed quarter, there was one man among my many customers whom I loved very much. Whenever I met him I forgot I was performing and opened my heart completely to him. I trusted him and told him everything. The man also opened himself to me, but when his parents discovered our relationship, they forced him to stop his visits. I was so sad I wrote him every day and had the letter secretly delivered to him at home.

Later he told me that while he was confined in his parents' house he felt as if we were still together—as if I were right there with him. After reading each of my letters several times, he would go to sleep at night with it pressed against his skin. Sooner or later the same dream would come. In it, the letter would take on my shape, and we would talk and hold each other all night. The people guarding the man slept near him, and they would hear two voices coming from the place where he was sleeping. They certainly had a hard time believing what they heard!

Eventually the man's parents relented, and when we met again he told me about everything he'd experienced. I discovered that the thoughts I'd been thinking each day had also reached his mind—exactly as I'd thought them. Actually, though, there's nothing strange about that. When you spend a long time writing a letter, you forget about everything else. If you put your whole mind into thinking something, it will always reach the other person.

I turned to the young man who'd visited my school. "Since I'm taking on the full responsibility for writing your letters," I said, "I can assure you that sooner or later the woman will respond to your love, no matter how uninterested she seems now." I put all of myself into composing the best letters I possibly could. But as I wrote more and more letters, I found I'd lost control. The man who'd asked me to write the letters had become very, very dear to me.

During one of the man's visits, I was unable to continue writing. I sat there holding my brush and thinking only about him. Then I abandoned all shame. "What an incredibly coldhearted woman she is," I said. "She's torturing you and not showing the slightest sensitivity to your feelings. You're just not getting anywhere with her. Why don't you love me instead? We'd have to talk about it, of course, and we'd have to set looks aside. But I'm kindhearted, and with me you can realize your love without even waiting. You've got a lot to gain with me right now."

The man looked surprised, and he remained silent for some time. He didn't know whether the woman he was writing to so often to would ever agree to meet him, and he realized it would be a lot quicker with me. He didn't seem

The sign on the door announces: "calligraphy Taught to Women." Outside, two girls leave after a lesson, with a maid carrying calligraphy practice books and a brush case. Inside is a low writing table with a black lacquer box (for brushes and an inkstone). Sitting in front of her kimono rack and her koto, the woman writes a love letter for a male customer, who, like many well-off merchants, wears a short sword. While the woman's helper brings tea to the customer, the woman writes on a thick sheaf of paper, with her inkstone box in front of her. Another rolled sheaf of paper lies on the floor.

to think I was a bad substitute, either. Judging from my wavy hair, curving large toes, and small mouth,[86] he thought I must be a very passionate woman.

"Please let me be frank," he finally said. "Even in relationships I begin myself, money's out of the question. I won't be able to give you even one new sash. And after we've known each other a short time, if you start inquiring whether I know any dry goods dealers and ask me for two rolls of ordinary silk or a roll of crimson silk, I just won't be able to promise you that. I've got to make that absolutely clear right from the beginning."

How insensitive and mean, I thought to myself, to say an arrogant thing like that to someone he wants to make love with! There was no shortage of nice men in the capital, and I decided I'd have to look somewhere else.

It was the rainy season, and just then a soft rain began to come down. Suddenly it became very quiet outside. A sparrow flew in through the window, and the flame in the lamp went out. Taking advantage of the darkness, the man threw himself on me and grabbed me tightly. He was breathing heavily as he forced himself on me, and as he began, he took some expensive tissue paper out of his robe and placed it near the pillow. After he finished, he slapped me gently on the small of the back, apparently thinking I'd enjoyed it. He even

---

86. All believed to be signs of a sensuous temperament.

sang an old wedding song, saying he'd love me till I was a hundred and he was ninety-nine.

What an idiot, I thought. You have no idea how fragile life is. Do you really think life is an old song and you're going to live to be ninety-nine? You said some pretty disrespectful things just now. You won't last even one year. Pretty soon you'll have a sunken jaw and be walking with a stick. And then you'll leave the floating world altogether.

I made love with the man day and night. When he lost his desire, I strengthened him with loach broth, eggs, and yams, and we continued. Gradually, as I expected, he ran dry. It was pitiful to see him shivering in the Fourth Month of the next year, still wearing thick winter robes when everyone else had changed into early summer things. Every doctor he'd seen had given up on him. His beard was long and unkempt; his nails lengthened unclipped; and he had to cup his hand to his ear in order to hear. At the slightest mention of an attractive woman, he turned his head away with a look of endless regret.

A Stylish Woman Who Brought Disaster (3:2)

Kickball has long been a sport for aristocratic men and warriors, but I discovered that women play it, too. At the time, I was working as the outside messenger for the wife of a daimyō domain lord in the lord's main mansion in Edo.[87] My job was running errands and dealing with people outside the women's quarters, and once I went with the lord's wife to their third mansion in Asakusa,[88] where she sometimes went to relax. In the large garden inside the mansion, azaleas were beginning to bloom, turning all the small fields and hills a bright crimson. Nearby I saw some waiting women wearing long divided skirts of a matching crimson. Their long sleeves were fluttering and swaying as they played kickball inside a high, rectangular fence. They lifted the deerskin ball almost noiselessly with special shoes, and using only their feet, they strained to keep it moving in the air for as long as they could. They were extremely good and used the Multiple Cherry, the Mountain Crossing, and other difficult kicks. I was amazed that women were doing this. It was the first time I'd seen anything like it.

Earlier, in Kyoto, I'd been quite surprised to see court ladies practicing indoor archery, but people at court said it was quite natural. The women were following a venerable tradition begun in China by the imperial consort Yang Guifei.[89] Still, I'd never heard of women in Japan playing football in all the

---

87. The lord's wife and children were required to live in Edo as virtual hostages of the shōgunate, and the lord himself had to live here every other year.

88. An oblique reference to Lord Mizuno Mototomo and his wife.

89. The musically gifted, beloved consort of the eighth-century Tang emperor Xuanzong. Many legends became attached to her name.

At the domain lord's mansion in Edo, four serving women (*right*), wearing special pants and leather shoes for football, play inside a high, cage-like structure. The lord's wife (*left*), sitting with her hands on her knees, watches the game. Since only women are present, the hanging bamboo blind is raised. Three of the wife's attendants sit outside on a low porch. The painting on the sliding door to the right shows a white heron in a river under a willow, and the painting to the left depicts bush clover.

centuries since it was first played here by Prince Shōtoku.[90] But the wife of a domain lord is free to do any thing she wants. How magnificent she was!

Later, as evening approached, a strong wind began to blow, bending the trees in the garden. The kickers had a hard time controlling the ball, which wouldn't spin and constantly swerved off course, and soon everyone lost interest in the game. The lord's wife had just taken off her kickball robes and put them away when her face suddenly took on a fierce expression as if she'd remembered something. Nothing her attendants said cheered her up, so finally they stopped speaking and tried not to move or make any noise. Then a lady in waiting named Kasai, who'd served for many years, spoke up in an obsequious tone of voice. Her head moved back and forth and her knees trembled with excitement.

"Tonight," she said, "please honor us by holding another jealousy meeting.[91] Until the tall candle burns itself out!"

The lord's wife's face suddenly took on a pleasant expression. "Yes," she said. "Yes indeed!"

---

90. Shōtoku (574–622), the second son of Emperor Yōmei (r. 585–587), was active in spreading Buddhism as well as Chinese and Korean culture. According to legend, he watched or played kickball.

91. Such meetings, at which women spoke of their bitterness and shared their resentment, were commonly held in the seventeenth century by women of the upper merchant and warrior classes, who were particularly restricted.

An older woman named Yoshioka, the head waiting woman, pulled on a brocade-tufted cord that ran along the wall of a corridor. At the far end a bell rang, and soon even the cooks and bath maids appeared and sat without the slightest hesitation in a circle around the lord's wife. There must have been thirty-four or thirty-five women in all. I also joined them.

"You may speak about anything at all," Yoshioka told us. "Don't hold anything back. Confess something you yourself did. How you blocked another woman's love for a man and hated her. How you were jealous of a man going to see another woman and spoke badly of him. Or the pleasure you felt when a man and woman broke up. Stories like these will bring great joy to our mistress." This certainly was an extraordinary kind of meeting, I thought, but I couldn't laugh, since it was being held at the command of the lord's wife.

Soon they opened a wooden door with a painting of a weeping willow on it and brought out a life-size doll that looked exactly like a real woman. The artisan who made it must have been a master. It had a graceful figure and a face more beautiful than any blossom in full bloom. I myself am a woman, but I was entranced and couldn't stop gazing at it.

One by one, each woman spoke what she felt. Among them was a lady in waiting named Iwahashi[92] who had a face so classically unattractive it invited disaster.[93] No man would want to make love with her in the daytime, and she hadn't slept with a man at night for a very long time. In fact, during all that time she hadn't even seen a man. Now she ostentatiously pushed her way through the other women and volunteered.

"I was born and raised in Tōchi in Yamato," she said, "where I also married and lived with my husband. But that damn man started making trips to Nara. Then people began to tell me he was seeing the daughter of one of the lower priests at the Kasuga Shrine[94] there. She was exceptionally beautiful, they said. So one night I secretly followed my husband. My heart pounded loudly as I went, and when he arrived, I stood nearby and listened while the woman opened the small back gate and pulled him inside.

"'Tonight,' the woman says, 'my eyebrows kept on itching and itching. No matter how hard I rubbed them. I just knew something good was going to happen.' And then, with no shame at all, she calmly rests her slender little waist against his.

---

92. "Rock Bridge" is probably a nickname alluding to a classical poem by Sakon: "The rock bridge promised at night also ended unfinished—like the god of Mount Kazuraki I am downcast at dawn" (*Shūishū*, no. 1201). According to legend, the god of Mount Kazuraki promised to build a long bridge, but to hide their ugly faces, the god and his demon helpers worked only at night, and the bridge, like the love affair in the poem, was never finished.

93. An ironic reference to the title of the chapter. It is not Iwahashi who brings disaster to the lord's wife.

94. One of the largest Shintō shrines in Japan.

"I couldn't bear any more of that and ran right over to them. 'Hey,' I shouted, 'that's my husband!' I opened my mouth wide to show her my blackened teeth and prove I was married, and before I knew it, I'd bitten into her as hard as I could!" Then Iwahashi fastened her teeth around the beautiful doll and refused to let go. The way she did it made me feel that right there in front of me, with my own eyes, I was seeing exactly what had happened that night long ago. I was terrified.

The jealousy meeting had begun. The next woman walked very slowly out in front of us as if she hardly knew where she was. She was a typical woman who lets her emotions run away with her. I don't know how she was able to say the things she did.

"When I was young," she confessed, "I lived in Akashi in Harima Province.[95] My niece got married and took in her husband as part of her own family.[96] What a tramp he turned out to be. And a complete lecher! He slept with every single maid and with the helping women, too. It was perfectly obvious—they were dozing off all the time. My niece tried to keep up appearances, you know, so she let things go and didn't criticize him. Inside, though, she was very upset at not being able to do anything. So every night I would go and try to help her. I got someone to nail iron fasteners to her bedroom door, and after asking my niece and her husband to go inside, I'd shout, 'Please sleep together tonight!' Before I'd go back to my own room, I'd lock their door from the outside.

"Soon my niece was looking thin and exhausted. She didn't even want to see her husband's face any more. 'If he keeps on like this,' she told me, 'I'm not going to live much longer.' Her body was shaking when she said that. She was born in the year of the fiery horse,[97] so she should have caused her husband to die young, but he was the one who was wearing her down. She got very sick because of that despicable man and his endless urges. I'd like to make him do it again and again right now with this doll here. Until he falls over dead!" She hit the doll and knocked it over, and then she screamed at it for some time.

Then another lady in waiting named Sodegaki got up. She was from Kuwana[98] in Ise Province. She told us she'd been a jealous person even before she got married. She was so jealous of her parents' maids she wouldn't let them put on makeup or use mirrors when they did their hair or put white powder on their skin. If a maid had a pretty face, she forced the woman to make herself look as unattractive as she could. Stories about how she acted got around,

95. On the Inland Sea, just west of present-day Kobe.

96. Among commoners, a groom often took his wife's name and legally became a family member.

97. A "double fire" year in the sixty-year zodiacal cycle. It was believed that a woman born in such a year would be so passionate she would wear out her husband. Such years occurred in 1606 and 1666.

98. On the Tōkaidō route between Kyoto and Edo.

though, and people began avoiding her. No men in her hometown or for miles around would think of marrying her. So she came all the way to Edo to look for work.

"Hey, beautiful doll," the woman yelled. "Yes, you're so very, very smart, aren't you. You even know how to make another woman's husband stay overnight at your house!" Then she began to disfigure the innocent doll.

Each woman tried to speak more jealously than the rest, but none of their stories satisfied the lord's wife. When my turn came, I went directly to the doll and pulled it down onto the floor. Then I got on top of it.

"You!" I said. "You're just a mistress. But the lord likes you, so you act as if you're more important than his wife, sleeping with him on the same long pillow just as you like without thinking anything about it. Listen, you, I'm not going to let you get away with it!" I glared at the doll, ground my teeth, and acted as if I truly hated the doll from the bottom of my heart.

What I'd said turned out to be what the lord's wife herself had been thinking. "Exactly," she said, "exactly!99 Let me tell you about this doll. You see, the lord treats me now as if I hardly existed. He's had his beautiful mistress from the domain brought all the way here to Edo, and he doesn't think about anyone but her day and night. It's very sad being a woman—complaining does no good at all. But I did have this doll made to look like her. At least I can cause pain to it."

Before the lord's wife had finished, something strange happened. First the doll opened her eyes and extended her arms. She looked around the room for a while, and then she seemed to stand up, although by that time no one was watching closely anymore. All the frightened women were scrambling away as fast as they could. Then the doll grabbed the front of the lord's wife's outer robe and wouldn't let go. I only barely managed to separate them. After that, nothing more happened.

Perhaps because of this incident, a few days later the lord's wife fell ill and began to speak deliriously of terrible things. The waiting women thought she must be possessed by the doll's soul. If they didn't stop the resentful doll, it might cause even more serious harm, so they secretly decided to get rid of it. In a far corner of the mansion they burned the doll so completely that nothing at all remained, but they showed their respect and buried the ashes in a formal grave. After that, people began to fear the burial mound, and they claimed that every evening they could clearly hear a woman's wailing voice coming from inside it. The rumor spread beyond the mansion walls, and the lord's wife became the object of widespread ridicule.

---

99. The woman narrator is able to guess what the lord's wife was worrying about because she herself once served as a lord's mistress. The woman's subsequent actions suggest sympathy, perhaps unconscious, for the mistress.

Word of the affair eventually reached the lord, who was at his second Edo mansion with his mistress from his home domain. Astounded, he started an investigation and ordered the outside messenger to report to him. Since that was my job, I had to appear. I couldn't hide what I knew, and I related everything about the doll, just as it had happened.[100] The people who heard me clapped their hands together in amazement.

"There's nothing as nasty as a woman's vengeance," the lord told his aides. "I have no doubt at all that very soon my mistress won't be safe from my wife's avenging soul. Her life is in danger here. Explain the situation to her and have her return to the domain."

When the woman appeared and sat nervously on her knees before the lord, I saw she was far more graceful and beautiful than the doll had been. I was a bit proud of my own looks, you know, and we both were women, but I was so overwhelmed I could hardly bear to look at her. Such great beauty, I thought to myself, and yet the lord's wife, out of jealousy, is trying to kill her with curses. The lord declared that women were fearsome creatures, and he never again entered the women's quarters of his main mansion in Edo. His wife became a virtual widow while her husband was still alive.

I had to watch all this and try to take messages between them. Soon I grew very weary of my job, prestigious as it was, and I submitted my resignation. It was accepted, and I returned to Kyoto feeling so disappointed with the world I thought I might become a nun. Jealously is something you must never, never give in to. Women should be very careful to resist it.

Ink Painting in a Sensual Robe (4:2)

The first standards for sewing court women's elegant robes were laid down in the eighth century during the reign of Empress Kōken,[101] the forty-sixth ruler in the imperial line. After that, clothes in Japan became quite attractive. Even today, when women sew a silk robe for an aristocrat or a warrior, they're extremely careful. The first thing they do is count the exact number of needles in the pin cushions. Then when they're finished, they count them all over again to make sure not a single one has been left in the robe to do any harm. They're meticulous about every detail and purify themselves before they begin. A woman who's having her period isn't even allowed to enter the sewing room.

I was good at sewing, and without really intending to, I became a seamstress in one of the big daimyō mansions in Edo. I made an effort to live with a calm

---

100. It is thus the woman narrator who invites disaster by causing the doll to seem to come alive and by reporting about it to the lord.

101. Empress Kōken (718–770, r. 749–758). The first standards for women's robes were set in 719 and revised in 730.

mind, just the way I was supposed to, and I forced myself to abstain from the pleasures of love. I enjoyed the bright sunlight coming through the southern window of the sewing room in the women's quarters of the mansion, and from time to time I rested my eyes from the needlework and gazed at the green leaves of irises that had been placed there in a pot of water.

All the seamstresses contributed a little money, and when we took our rest, we would drink delicious Abe tea and eat jam-filled buns we'd ordered from the Tsuruya store in Iidamachi. None of the seamstresses working for the mansion got more than a pittance, but we didn't think bad thoughts, and we had no real worries to weigh on us. Living together, with no men, our hearts were as clear and unbounded as the cloudless moon above us shining down on the warrior mansions in the Yamanote heights.[102] I felt we were like buddhas living freely and joyfully in perfect enlightenment beyond worldly desire and attachment.

Then one day I was asked to finish an inner robe for the lord's son. It was pure white silk, and on the inner lining was a painting so finely done that, well, it must have been brushed by an extremely skilled painter. In it, a man and woman, completely naked, were making love. The woman was showing all the beautiful skin she had, and her heels were raised high in the air. She was so totally involved she was bending the ends of her toes. I stared at the couple, entranced. They no longer looked like painted figures, and I was sure I could hear soft, sweet words coming from their unmoving lips. I began to feel dizzy, and my mind rose and swirled like mist. For some time I just sat there, leaning on my needle box.

I'd remembered once more what it was like to want a man. I didn't touch my leather thimble or my spool that day, and I forgot about sewing the robe. My mind began to wander, and soon I was overcome by longing and imagining. That night I could hardly bear to sleep alone. All those wonderful nights I'd hoped would never end, well, they still continued on, unending, inside me. I relived experience after experience from the past, and even though they all were from my own mind, their sadness moved me to cry as I remembered real loves, and I laughed all over again at those that weren't so real. But true loves or false, all those men were precious to me. It grieved me deeply to think that as soon as I loved a man, he grew so dear to me that I caused him to make love too hard or to drink and eat too much. I completely ruined some men's careers and made others die much too young.

I couldn't count the number of men I'd known, even the ones with whom

---

102. Literally, Edge of the Mountains, a hilly area west of Edo Castle with many warrior mansions, in one of which the woman works. She alludes to a poem by the Zen priest Musō Kokushi: "I think of neither the rising nor the setting moon—no mountain edges hide my mind" (*Fūgashū*, no. 2076). The moon, a traditional Buddhist trope for mind, here implies a calm, detached speaker.

Seamstresses (*left*) sew robes in the spacious sewing room of a daimyō's Edo mansion. A needle box, a bobbin, a measure, and pin cushions are visible. A well-dressed young woman (*right*), who seems to be the daimyō's daughter, stands with her parlor maid. Behind them, robes hang on a rack, waiting to be sewn.

I'd had special relationships. Many women know only one man their whole lives. Even if they divorce, they don't look for a new husband, and if their husband dies, they leave the world behind and become nuns. They're able to control their desire and live decently, enduring the change and their separation from their beloved husbands. I, on the other hand, how pathetic I'd been, endlessly pulled along by one strong desire after another. I made up my mind that this time I absolutely would not to give in.

As I lay swearing this to myself, dawn came, and the other women sleeping beside me woke. I folded up my bedding, stacked it in a pile, and waited impatiently for my third of a pint of breakfast rice. I looked around for still-live logs from the previous night's fire, lit my pipe, and puffed hard on it without bothering to smoke in the elegant way. I wasn't planning to show my messy hair to anyone anyway, so I gathered it up roughly and tied it with an old paper cord. The chignon on top was leaning sideways, but I didn't even care.

Later I went out to throw away what was left of the oily water we'd used for smoothing down our sidelocks. As I was standing there in the shade of the grove of bamboos growing just outside the window, I caught sight of a man on the far side of the trees. He looked like a hired man who did odd jobs for the warrior retainers living in the mansion barracks.[103] Unaware he was being watched, he'd

---

103. Unmarried samurai retainers of daimyō lords staying in Edo lived in long barracks inside the mansion walls.

put down the basket of fresh fish he'd bought early that morning by the shore in Shibaura and stood with the bottom of his plain, dark blue robe hitched up beside the barracks drainage ditch. In one hand he held a flask of vinegar and sulfur-tipped staves for kindling, and in the palm of the other he held his thing, pissing. The pure stream fell like a strand of sacred Otowa Falls,[104] knocking lose a rock at the edge of the ditch and hollowing out the dirt beneath it.

As I watched, longings came up from deep within me. Ah, I thought, that poor man. He never got any glory putting down the Shimabara Rebellion, and he's certainly never made enough money to be able to raise his fine spear in the Shimabara licensed quarter.[105] He's getting old without ever making a name for himself with the women there. He and I, how pathetic we are. We're both just wasting our lives!

In the next few days my desire grew so strong I found it impossible to do my job. I claimed I was seriously ill, and with that excuse I managed to get discharged before my seasonal contract was up. I found a room for myself in a back-street tenement in an out-of-the-way part of Hongō, in the sixth block.[106] On a post at the entrance to the alleyway leading to the tenement I put up a sign saying, "Seamstress for Every Need—Inquire Within." I'd gotten out of my contract for the sole purpose of meeting men, and now I planned to enjoy whatever man came into my little shop. But things didn't turn out that way. All my customers were women wanting me to sew the latest fashions! I had to take their orders, but I whipped their seams very sloppily, only here and there. My work was outrageous.

My soul constantly ached to make love, but I couldn't mention it to anyone. Then one day I remembered something. I told my helper to come along and carry my purse for me, so I would look proper, and I went downtown to Nihonbashi. There I dropped in at the Echigoya, a big dry goods store I knew about because it delivered cloth to the mansion where I used to work.

"I stopped working at the mansion," I told the clerks, "and now I live alone. There's no one else in my room, not even a cat. The people in the next room to the east are almost always out, and on the west side there's a woman who's over seventy. Her ears are bad, you know. On the other side of the alley in front there's only a prickly hedge. No one's ever over there. I might as well be living by myself. Whenever you go up to the mansions on the main avenue in Hongō on business, be sure to drop by my place and relax for a while." Before I left, I chose a roll of Kaga twisted silk, enough scarlet silk for one sleeve, and a sash

---

104. A waterfall in Kiyomizu Temple in Kyoto that was regarded as the body of the patron god of the temple and was famous for its purity and spiritual power.

105. The Shimabara Rebellion was an uprising of Christians and farmers in 1637/1638 in Shimabara (in Kyūshū), after which was named the Shimabara licensed quarter in Kyoto. "Spear" is a sexual pun.

106. At the time, a poor residential area in Edo.

of thick Ryūmon silk. Retail stores are very strict about not selling on credit, but the young clerks there, they were pretty infatuated with me. They handed over the merchandise without even thinking of asking for cash.

Time passed, and there weren't many days left before the fall collection day on the eighth of the Ninth Month. Fourteen or fifteen clerks stood arguing about who was going to get the chance to go collect from the seamstress.[107] One was an older man who didn't know the slightest thing about love or passion. He counted with his abacus even in his dreams, and he spent his waking hours brushing figures into the shop books. He was so loyal to the owner of the head store in Kyoto that people called him White Mouse.[108] He was the main support of the store, and as head clerk he would watch and judge all the customers, something he could do better than anyone else. The way the other clerks were wasting time talking irritated him.

"Leave the woman's payment up to me," he told the young clerks. "If she doesn't pay up, I'll pull off her head and bring that back instead." So the head clerk went to the woman's place himself. He yelled at her and ordered her roughly to produce the money, but she remained calm and relaxed.

"I deeply apologize for causing you to come so far for so little," she said and began to take off her plum red silk robe. "I dyed it this color myself, but I've only had it next to my skin for two days—yesterday and today. And here's the sash!" She threw them at the man. "Right now I have no money at all to give you. I know you won't be satisfied. Actually, I sympathize with you. But please take these instead." She was crying and practically naked, with only her crimson petticoat on.

Her body was quite attractive. She was neither fat nor thin, and her smooth, light skin glowed, with no scars from moxibustion anywhere on it. The head clerk was a serious and self-controlled man, but when he saw the woman like that, he began to shake uncontrollably.

"How could I possibly take these with me?" he said. "I'm afraid you'll catch cold." When he picked up the clothes and tried to get the woman to put them on again, he already belonged to her.

"By the gods, what a compassionate man you are!" she said, leaning against him.

The man was visibly excited. He called his assistant Kyūroku, who was waiting outside, and had him open the carrying case. He reached in and pulled out a small silver coin.

"Here," he said to the young man, "this is yours. Just keep walking down Shitaya Street until you get to the Yoshiwara quarter. And once you get there,

---

107. From here to the end of the chapter, the woman narrator talks about herself in the third person, presumably because she is a bit ashamed of what she does.

108. Daikoku, the god of fortune, was believed to use a white mouse as his messenger.

why don't you take a good look around? There's no need to come back right away."

Kyūroku's heart was pounding. He couldn't believe what the head clerk was telling him. He blushed and didn't know what to say. Finally he realized the man was serious and wanted him out of the way while he was making it with this woman. The skinflint had never given him anything before, but here was his chance at last.

"The licensed quarter?" he said. "How could I possibly go there in this cheap cotton loincloth?"

"You have a point there," the clerk said. He estimated roughly and cut a length of wide Hino silk. Without even hemming the edges, the young man tied it right on and ran off to do as he wished.

After the young man was gone, the woman closed the latch on her door and hung a broad-rimmed sedge hat in the window. She and the man then pledged a very plain love. No one had even formally brought them together. Later the man forgot all about material gain and lost his head over the woman. There was no way he could blame it on youthful ardor, and when so much cloth was found missing that the store was on the verge of collapse, he was relieved of his post and sent back to the main store in Kyoto.

The woman still advertised herself as a seamstress, but now she went here and there to nice houses, doing whatever made her customers happy. She set her price at one small gold coin per day, but she never once opened the needle box she always had her helper carry along. She made a fairly decent living for a while. As they say, though, if you don't knot your threads at the end, they will come unraveled.

Luxurious Dream of a Man (4:4)

Even for women, there's nothing as interesting as being a wandering seasonal house worker. For a long time I worked in houses in Edo, Kyoto, and Osaka, but one year at the beginning of the fall contract period on the fifth of the Ninth Month, I went south from Osaka to the port of Sakai.[109] I imagined that if I lived there for a while, I might see some things I'd never come across before. The first thing I did was go to a placement agency run by a man named Zenkurō in Nakabama, in the west part of Nishikinochō,[110] and asked them to help me find something, although I had to pay by the day for my room and board while I waited.

After a few days someone came looking for an odd-jobs maid for the retired

---

109. In Saikaku's time, a flourishing commercial city just south of Osaka.
110. Just west of the city's commercial center.

former owner of a big shop on the main avenue. My job would consist only of staying near my employer's room in the retirement house,[111] getting out the bedding in the evening, and putting it away again in the morning. I met the employer's representative, and the woman looked me over.

"She's the right age," the woman said finally. "Her appearance is good, and she knows how to act and speak. Everything about her is in order. I'm sure my employer will like her."

The woman agreed to pay part of my salary in advance and didn't even try to bargain me down. She seemed to be a nursemaid who'd worked for the family for many years, and she looked happy with me as we walked back together to the house. On the way she gave me some advice she thought I'd find useful. She had a forbidding face, but she spoke gently. Well, I thought to myself, they say the world isn't all demons. I guess there really are kind people here and there wherever you go. So I listened carefully.

"Above all," the woman said, "remember that the retiree is very jealous and can't stand to see women servants talking with clerks from the shop in the main house. So never repeat rumors about people's love affairs. Don't even stare at the hens and roosters when they're going at it in the yard. Also, your employer believes in the Lotus sect. Never, never chant Amida Buddha's name.[112] The white cat wearing a collar is the retiree's darling, so let it do what it wants. Don't chase it even if it runs off with a fish from your tray while you're eating. The eldest son's wife in the main house likes to act big, but no matter how arrogant she gets, don't take her seriously. Her name is Shun. She used to be the parlor maid for the son's first wife, but after his wife died from a bad case of influenza, he got infatuated with that Shun and married her. Maybe if she were at least pretty—but you know, she isn't at all, and yet she's quite uppity. She says nothing but self-centered things, and when she rides in a palanquin, she sits up on extra cushions. It's a wonder she doesn't break her hip!" The woman went on and on, but I had to listen. The more I heard, the more ridiculous it got.

Finally the nurse changed the subject. "At other houses," she said, "all you'll get is cheap red rice morning and night, but here we eat special reserve rice from Harima Province. And bean paste, why, we get as much as we need from the saké store run by the daughter's husband. The bath here, well, it's heated every single day. If you're too lazy to use it, then you're the loser. And the last day of the year is really something. You should see all the rice cakes and special dishes that arrive from the relatives and former employees.

"Sakai's a big place, you know, but every house south of Ōshōji Avenue[113]

---

111. Located behind the larger main house, which contains the shop fronting on Sakai's main avenue.

112. The Nichiren (Lotus) sect and the Pure Land (Amidist) sects were vigorous rivals.

113. Ran east to west and crossed the main avenue, which ran north to south.

owes us money. And if you go two blocks from here, you'll see a big house on the northeast corner. The owner used to be our head clerk. And oh yes, there's the big Sumiyoshi Festival[114] along the shore. I'm sure you've never seen that before. It's at the end of the Sixth Month, so there's still quite a while before it comes around. The whole household goes to the initial god-descent ceremonies on the night before the festival, and we all stay overnight. Before that, though, in the Third Month, everyone in the house goes to see the wisteria blooming down near the harbor. The cooks cover the bottoms of big lacquered picnic boxes with nandin leaves and heap them full of steamed rice with red beans in it, and the men carry the boxes with us. Then we have a very nice lunch under the wisteria.

"If you have to work, then you're very lucky to be at a house like ours. Don't you dare leave here without here asking your employer to set you up with a house and a husband. Just be sure to make your employer like you. Never ignore an order, no matter what it is. And never even dream of talking about private family things to people outside the house. Your employer is old and rather short-tempered, but remember, it's just something that flares up for a moment. It never lasts very long. No one else knows this, but there's a good deal of silver. If your employer happened to die tomorrow, think of what good fortune you might have. The retiree is already seventy and covered with wrinkles—definitely not long for this world. So whatever your employer says, remember, it's just wishful thinking. You know, I still don't know you very well, but I'm telling you this because I think I like you already." The nurse opened her heart to me and told me everything she could think of to mention.

After hearing all this, I felt confident I'd be able to handle the old man, who was obviously looking for a younger woman. I told myself that if I got along well with him and he renewed my contract, I'd have plenty of chances to find a young man for myself on the side. When I got pregnant, I'd tell the old man it was his and get him to write his will so his money went to me. I'd be set for the rest of my life. As I walked along, I had everything already decided.

"Well, we're here," the nursemaid said, interrupting my thoughts. "Please come in." We passed down a corridor through the shop at the front of the main house and went as far as the door to the living quarters in back. After taking off our sandals, we went around to a wooden-floored room next to the kitchen and sat down. Soon an old retired woman[115] of about seventy who looked very healthy and energetic came into the room. She stared at me so intently she seemed to be boring a hole into me.

"Everything about her is excellent," she said to the nurse. "I'm very pleased."

---

114. The chief god's palanquin was carried from the Sumiyoshi Shrine in south Osaka down the coast to nearby Sakai.

115. A widow and grand dame of the house.

The woman goes to work as a servant for a retiree. The woman (*right*) is shown to the house of her new employer by the family nursemaid, wearing a cotton cap. The two women are about to enter the lattice-windowed main house, in which the eldest son and his wife live and manage the family business. A hired man (*left*) hulls rice in a mortar by stepping on a beam that moves the pestle up and down.

This was something I was completely unprepared for. I would never have agreed to take the job if I'd known my employer was a woman, and I regretted coming. Yet the old woman's words were full of feeling, and my six-month contract would be up in no time. Having to endure it might even be a worthwhile experience. Walking on salt, as they say, is hard, but it's supposed to be good for you, and there was plenty of salt in this harbor town. So I decided to stay there and work.

On the outside, Sakai people look as easygoing as the people in Kyoto, but actually they're stingy and small-minded. The hired men in that house stepped incessantly on their foot pestles, hulling rice in mortars without ever getting any rest; and the hired women were always sewing cotton socks whenever they had any free time at all. The employers in Sakai train their workers very strictly and make them work as hard as they can.

There were six or seven other women working at the house, each with her specific duties. I was the only one who simply watched and waited, looking as if I didn't have anything to do. That night I was told to get out the retiree's mattresses and bedding and spread them so she could sleep. That much made sense to me. But when I was told, "Please go sleep with her on the same pillow," I didn't really understand any more. It was my employer's orders, though, so I couldn't very well refuse.

I expected the old woman would ask me to massage her lower back or something like that. But I certainly was wrong. She had me be the woman while she took the part of the man. Then she made love to me all through that night.[116] Well now, I'd certainly gotten myself into a real fix!

The world's a big place, and I'd worked inside a lot of houses, but this woman had a wish I'd never heard before. "After I die," she told me, "I want to be reborn at least once as a man.[117] Then I can openly do what I really want."

Streetwalker with a False Voice (6:3)

By this time I'd worked at just about every kind of job there was, and wrinkles covered my face like waves on the ocean. Somehow I found my way back to Osaka again and to the Shinmachi licensed quarter, a sea of endlessly young love that never seems to change. I knew a lot about the place and how things worked there, and I looked up some people I once knew and asked them to help me out. I managed to get work as a lowly matron at a performance house, but unlike before, when I worked there catching customers and hated the matrons, I now felt ashamed to be in the quarter.

All matrons wear the same thing and are easy to spot. Like the others, I also put on a light red apron and tied my medium-width sash far to the left. From my sash dangled a whole collection of different keys. I didn't need to be elegant any more, and I would reach right around underneath my robe and pull up the back hem of my robe. I couldn't afford a hood, so I usually wore a small folded cotton cloth on top of my head and walked as silently as I could, hoping no one would notice me. I made it a habit to go around with a sour look on my face. That way, the high-ranking tayū feared me even when I wasn't angry. I taught the young ones many things, though, and took care of them. I trained even the timid ones to be self-aware and sophisticated, and I showed them how to make their customers like them. My job was to get them to work hard so they would have a customer every single day and make their manager happy.

As a former tayū myself, I knew all too well what the tayū were doing and thinking, and after a while I began to stare and criticize them when they were having secret meetings with their real lovers. The women feared me, and the men were embarrassed and annoyed, so they all gave me special tips of two gold pieces even before the seasonal festival days came around. But when they handed me the coins, they looked at me as if I were the old demon woman who guards the river between this world and the next and grabs coins from the

---

116. Using a dildo.

117. The ironic chapter title thus refers to both the narrator, who wants to believe that she is working for a rich old man, and to the old woman, who, though rich, dreams of true luxury in the next life.

souls of those who'd recently died.[118] If you treat people badly, you can't expect to continue doing what you're doing very long. Everyone around me began to hate me, and I felt uncomfortable in the quarter, so I left and went to live in Tamazukuri, at the edge of Osaka, where no one would know me. It was a dismal place, with no shops and nothing but small, poor houses and bats flying around even in the daytime. I found a room there in a tenement on a back alley, but I hadn't been able to save anything, so I had to sell my one and only nice robe to pay for it. To light my cooking fire in the morning, I gradually broke up the shelves in my room, and for supper I had nothing to drink but hot water as I chewed on my parched soybeans.

One rainy night, a tremendous thunder and lightning storm descended on us, and while other people were shuddering with fear, I prayed to the lightning and asked it, if it had any compassion at all, to fall directly on me and kill me. At that moment I felt utterly tired of the world and no longer wanted to live. I was already sixty-five, although people took me for just over forty because of my smooth, fine skin and small build. That was small comfort to me then.

As I sat there, I began to remember all the lovers I'd had in my life, and I fell into deep thought. Then I happened to look out my window and saw the shapes of children wearing what looked like wide lotus-leaf hats. They had their placentas on their heads. From the waist down, the children were stained with blood. I looked at each one of them. All together, there were ninety-five or ninety-six children standing there.

They were calling out something through their tears. I was sure they were saying, "Carry me on your back! Carry me on your back!" They must be the souls of women who died in childbirth, I thought. I'd heard about them. They're supposed to fly around holding their dead children and weeping in the night. I watched and listened closely.

"You terrible Mommy!" one suddenly said to me. Then each of them spoke to me in a voice filled with resentment.

Then I realized these must be all the children I'd aborted over many years, and I began to feel very remorseful. If I'd had them and brought them up, I'd have more children now than the famous warrior Wada Yoshimori,[119] who fathered ninety-three, and everyone would be congratulating me. While I sat there wishing I could return to the past, the shapes disappeared completely without a trace. I thought about this and decided it must have been a sign I didn't have much time left in this world, and I made up my mind to accept my death. But when the sun came up the next morning, well, how pathetic I was. Once again I felt myself wanting to live.

---

118. Coins were put in coffins so that dead souls could pay the woman and thus be allowed to cross the river to the other world instead of staying attached to their former habitations.

119. A twelfth-century warrior.

The woman (*left*) looks out the window of her room in a poor tenement and has a vision of small children wearing lotus-leaf hats, the spirits of the babies she has aborted who are crying out to her. Their lotus-leaf hats resemble placentas, and the dark strips tied around their waists represent blood. Three streetwalkers (*right*) living in the opposite room boil water while windblown rain pelts the board roof held in place by stones.

The woman notices that her neighbors live surprisingly well and discovers they are streetwalkers. Finally she tries the job herself and has her young male bodyguard sing in a female voice in the dark to make men think she's young. Failing to get a single customer the whole night, however, she decides to leave the profession forever.

Five Hundred Disciples of the Buddha—I'd Known Them All (6:4)

In winter the mountains sleep beneath leafless trees, and the bare limbs of the cherries turn white only with snow at dusk. Then spring dawns come once more, filled with blossoms. Only humans get old as the years pass and lose all pleasure in living. I especially. When I recalled my own life, I felt thoroughly ashamed.

I thought I at least ought to pray for the one thing I could still wish for—to be reborn in Amida Buddha's Pure Land paradise. So I went back to Kyoto one more time and made a pilgrimage to the Daiunji temple[120] in the northern hills. It was supposed to be a visible Pure Land right here in this world. My mind was filled with pious feelings, and I'd chosen a good time to visit. It was

---

120. A Tendai temple in the northern hills of Kyoto, believed to be a place where the bodhi-sattva Kannon manifested herself, making it a Pure Land on earth. The temple was famed for cures of mental problems and was a refuge for those considered mentally ill.

the end of the Twelfth Month, when people gathered to chant the names of all the buddhas and to confess the bad deeds they'd done during the year and ask for forgiveness.[121] I joined in their chanting.

Afterward, as I walked down the steps of the main hall, I noticed a smaller hall devoted to the Five Hundred Disciples of Shakyamuni Buddha.[122] All were wise and worthy men who had achieved enlightenment, and I went over and looked inside. Each virtuous disciple was distinctly individual and differed from all the others. I wondered what marvelous sculptor could have carved all these many unique statues.

People say there are so many disciples that if you search hard enough, you're bound to find someone you know. Wondering if it might be true, I looked over the wooden statues and saw disciples who obviously were men with whom I'd shared my pillow when I was younger. I began to examine them more closely and found a statue that looked like Yoshi from Chōjamachi in Kyoto.[123] When I was working in the Shimabara quarter, we exchanged very deep vows, and he tattooed my name on his wrist where no one would notice. I was beginning to remember all the things that had happened between us when I saw another disciple sitting under a large rock. He looked exactly like the owner of the house in uptown Kyoto where I worked as a parlor maid. He loved me in so many ways that even after all those years I couldn't forget him.

On the other side of the hall I saw Gohei. Even the disciple's high-ridged nose was exactly his. I once lived together with him. We loved each other from the bottoms of our hearts for several years, and he was especially dear to me. Then, closer to me, I saw a wide-bodied disciple in a blue green robe with one shoulder bared. He was working very hard—and he looked familiar. Yes, yes, it was definitely Danpei, the man who did odd jobs for a warrior mansion in Kōjimachi.[124] While I was working in Edo, I used to meet him secretly six nights a month.

Up on some rocks in back was a handsome man with light skin and the soft, gentle face of a buddha. Finally I remembered. He was a kabuki actor from the theaters down along the riverbank near the Fourth Avenue in Kyoto who'd started out as a boy actor selling himself to men on the side. We met while I was working at a teahouse, and I was the first woman with whom he'd ever made love. I taught him all the different styles women and men use, and he learned well, but pretty soon he just folded up. He grew weaker and weaker,

---

121. A ceremony held annually between the nineteenth day and the end of the Twelfth Month.

122. The original disciples of Shakyamuni Buddha who propagated his doctrines after his death.

123. A wealthy area of uptown Kyoto, west of the imperial palace, famous for its many money brokers.

124. The narrator lived there herself as a seamstress. See "Ink Painting in a Sensual Robe" (4:2).

The woman (*left*), with a cotton winter hat of the type worn by older women, stands in front of the Five Hundred Disciples of the Buddha, gazing intently at the statues inside the hall. Before the largest statue, representing Shakyamuni, stand two vases of lotus flowers and incense holders. A commoner (*right*) chants a prayer on the porch of the main temple hall, fingering his prayer beads, while a monk in black outer robe and surplice walks through the temple yard.

like a flame in a lantern, and then he was gone. He was only twenty-four when they took his body to the crematory at Toribe Mountain.[125] The disciple I saw had just his hollow jaw and sunken eyes. There was no doubt about it.

Farther on was a ruddy-faced disciple with a mustache and bald head. Except for the mustache, he looked just like the old chief priest who'd kept me in his temple as his mistress and treated me so badly.[126] By the time I met him I was used to every kind of sex, but he came at me day and night until I was so worn down I lost weight and had fevers and coughs and my period stopped. But even he had died. Endless storehouse of desire that he was, he, too, finally went up in crematory smoke.

And there, under a withered tree, a disciple with a fairly intelligent face and prominent forehead was shaving the top of his head. He seemed to be on the verge of saying something, and his legs and arms looked as though they were beginning to move. As I gazed at him, I gradually realized he, too, resembled someone I'd loved. While I was going around dressed up like a singing nun, I would meet a new man every day, but there was one who became very attached to me. He'd been sent from a western domain to help oversee the domain's rice

125. A large cemetery in eastern Kyoto.
126. See "A Monk's Wife in a Worldly Temple" (2:3).

warehouse sales in Osaka, and he loved me so much he risked his life for me. I could still remember everything about him. The sad things as well as the happy ones. He was very generous with what people begrudge the most,[127] and I was able to pay back everything I owed my manager.

Calmly I examined all five hundred disciples and found I recognized every single one! They all were men I'd known intimately. I began to remember event after event from the painful years when I was forced to work getting money from men. Women who sold themselves, I was sure, were the most fearful of all women, and I began to grow frightened of myself. With this single body of mine I'd slept with more than ten thousand men. It made me feel low and ashamed to go on living so long. My heart roared in my chest like a burning wagon in hell,[128] and hot tears poured from my eyes and scattered in every direction like water from one of hell's cauldrons. Suddenly I went into a sort of trance and no longer knew where I was. I collapsed on the ground, got up, and fell down again and again.

Many monks had apparently come to where I was, and they were telling me that the sun was going down. Then the booming of the big temple bell finally returned my soul to my body and startled me back to my senses.

"Old woman, what grieves you so?"

"Does one of these five hundred disciples resemble your dead child?"

"Is one your husband?"

"Why were you crying so hard?"

Their gentle voices made me feel even more ashamed. Without replying, I walked quickly out the temple gate. As I did, I suddenly realized the most important thing there is to know in life. It was all actually true![129] The Pure Land, I was sure then, really does exist. And our bodies really do disappear completely. Only our names stay behind in the world. Our bones turn to ash and end up buried in wild grass near some swamp.[130]

Some time later I found myself standing in the grass at the edge of Hirosawa Pond.[131] And there, beyond it, stood Narutaki Mountain. There was no longer anything at all keeping me from entering the mountain of enlightenment on the far side. I would leave all my worldly attachments behind and ride the Boat of the Buddhist Dharma[132] across the waters of worldly passions all the way to

---

127. That is, money.

128. The woman fears that she will soon go to Buddhist hell, not the Pure Land. Fiery carts were believed to carry condemned souls to the assigned part of hell.

129. The woman cites the nō play *Tomonaga*, in which a monk prays for the soul of the dead warrior Tomonaga. Tomonaga's soul returns and exclaims that the Pure land, Kannon's mercy, and other Buddhist beliefs are "actually true!"

130. The woman alludes to "Nine Stages of the Corpse," a meditative Buddhist poem on the reality of death attributed to Su Dongpo, and then literally arrives at some swamp grass.

131. A large pond in Saga in western Kyoto.

132. Buddhist teachings, commonly compared to a boat. The Other Shore is both the realm

the Other Shore. I made up my mind to pray, enter the water, and be reborn in the Pure Land.[133]

I ran toward the pond as fast as I could. But just then someone grabbed me and held me back. It was a person who'd known me well many years before.[134] He persuaded me not to end my own life and fixed up this hermitage for me.

"Let your death come when it comes," he said. "Free yourself from all your false words and actions and return to your original mind. Meditate and enter the way of the Buddha."

I was very grateful for this advice, and I've devoted myself to meditation ever since. From morning to night I concentrate my mind and do nothing but chant Amida Buddha's name. Then you two men came to my old door, and I felt drawn to you. I have so few visitors here. Then I let you pour me some saké, and it confused my mind. I actually do realize how short life is, you know, though I've gone on and on, boring you with the long story of my own.

Well, no matter. Think of it as my sincere confession of all the bad things I've ever done. It's cleared the clouds of attachment from me, and I feel my mind now shining bright as the moon. I hope I've also managed to make this spring night pass more pleasantly for you. I didn't hide anything, you know. With no husband or children, I had no reason to. The lotus flower in my heart[135] opened for you, and before it closed it told everything, from beginning to end. I've certainly worked in some dirty professions, but is my heart not pure?

[*Saikaku shū jō*, NKBT 47: 326–454, translated by Chris Drake]

GREAT MIRROR OF MALE LOVE (*NANSHOKU ŌKAGAMI*, 1687)

After the publication of *Life of a Sensuous Woman* in 1686, Saikaku suddenly stopped writing vernacular fiction concerned with male–female love in urban commoner society and began to explore new topics. One of these was male–male love (*nanshoku*) in both chōnin and samurai societies, which he wrote about in 1687 in *Great Mirror of Male Love*, his longest work. Because marriage in Tokugawa society was usually a

---

of enlightenment and the other world. To the woman, the pond looks like the sea of existence itself.

133. In the medieval period, many people believed that they could reach the Pure Land by sailing out to sea in a small boat or by jumping into rivers or ponds while meditating on Amida and Kannon. It was a form of religious suicide chosen most commonly by outcasts, sick people, or monks.

134. Gender unspecified; "he" is used because the person has enough money to buy the woman a hut.

135. A Buddhist metaphor. Just as the lotus rises from the mud, the pure mind experiences enlightenment amid the delusions of the world. Exemplified by Kannon, the lotus-holding female bodhisattva.

formal arrangement to ensure heirs for the continuation of the ancestral household, an urban man's "romantic" urges tended to be satisfied outside marriage with female or male prostitutes. Men pursued romantic relations with women in the licensed quarters and, in the manner of a connoisseur cultivating Confucian virtues, called it the "way of loving women" (nyodō). Or they pursued romance with male youths in the theater districts, calling it the "way of loving youths" (wakashudō or shudō). Male–male love in samurai society usually meant a sexual and emotional relationship between an adult man (nenja) and an adolescent youth (wakashu), who was recognized by his long, glossy forelocks. Then, when he reached manhood, around the age of nineteen, he shaved the crown of his head in the manner of an adult, signaling the end of his status as a wakashu. Because of the scandalous mingling of social classes in these places and the spending of money in exchange for sexual access, both the licensed quarters and the theater districts were regarded by the authorities as "bad places" (akusho). The fact that a hard-earned fortune could also be dissipated there rather quickly by a profligate son made it a genuinely "bad place" for the merchant class as well.

Reflecting the social division between samurai and merchant in their practice of male–male love, Saikaku divided *Great Mirror of Male Love* into two parts. The first consists of twenty stories focusing on the world of the samurai, and the second contains another twenty stories dwelling on young kabuki actors, boy prostitutes in the theater district. In all probability, Saikaku began *Great Mirror of Male Love* with the intention of depicting kabuki wakashu and the world of the theater and chōnin that he knew so well, but in the process he was drawn into the world of the samurai, which had a long tradition of nanshoku beginning in the medieval period when young pages served samurai warriors in battle. The result was a new exploration of the world of the samurai, which Saikaku continued to write about in subsequent years. *Great Mirror of Male Love*, which no doubt appealed to the samurai in Edo as well as the wealthy merchants in Osaka and Kyoto, thus stands between Saikaku's earlier chōnin fiction on male–female love and his later works on the samurai.

In the samurai world, male–male love relationships were bound by the samurai code of loyalty, devotion, and honor in action, in which the relationship between lord and retainer, or samurai and page, was often transferred to that between a man and a youth. In this context, the mature man offered protection, support, or employment, and the youth in turn was expected to be loyal and dedicated to him. A close reading of *Great Mirror of Male Love* shows that Saikaku distinguished between two types of nenja. Those called "connoisseurs of boys" (shōjin-zuki) were usually married and had sexual relations with women in addition to youths, whereas those called "woman haters" (onna-girai) rejected women as sexual partners and loved only young boys. Interestingly, Saikaku chose to structure *Great Mirror of Male Love* around the exclusive viewpoint of the woman haters, who represented the single-minded devotion to "the way of loving youths" that he sought to romanticize for his readers. In a fashion reminiscent of Chikamatsu's puppet plays, the result of Saikaku's efforts often depicts a dramatic conflict, as in the following short story, between duty/obligation (giri), which was determined by a strict social code, and human emotion/desire (*ninjō*), which violated that social code.

Though Bearing an Umbrella (1:2)

How Nagasaka Korin, a filial son, made a living.
He killed a creature in the cherry-viewing teahouse.
He traded his life for a secret lover.

The sea at Urano Hatsushima grew rough and the winds blew strong on Mount Muko.[136] Thunderheads billowed up in layers, as if the ghost of Tomomori might appear at any moment.[137] Soon rain began to fall. Travelers on the road found themselves in unforeseen distress.

An envoy named Horikoshi Sakon, who was on his way back to Amagasaki from Akashi, took shelter from the rain under some hackberry trees in a field by Ikuta Shrine. Just then, a handsome boy of twelve or thirteen came running up with an unopened umbrella of the type called "fall foliage" (even though it was summer).

The boy noticed Sakon. "Allow me to lend you this umbrella," he said, and handed it to an attendant.

"I am most grateful," Sakon responded. "But it strikes me as odd that you let yourself get rained on, even though you have an umbrella."

At this, the boy began to cry.

"Now, now. There must be some reason for this. Tell me what it is," Sakon coaxed.

"I am the son of Nagasaka Shuzen," the boy said. "My name is Korin. My father became a masterless samurai and had to leave Kai for Buzen to take up a new position, but he became sick and died on board ship. My mother and I had no choice but to bury him in this coastal town. The local people were kind enough to help us build a crude hut on the beach. The black bamboo outside our window became our only means of making a living. We watched the artisans making umbrellas and learned to do it ourselves. When I think of my mother doing a man's work with her own hands, I cannot bring myself to use an umbrella for fear of inviting the wrath of heaven, even if it means getting wet."

So that was it. Not unlike an old lady selling fans who would rather shade

---

136. Mount Rokkō, in Kobe.

137. Taira no Tomomori, fourth son of Kiyomori, died in the Heike defeat at Dannoura in 1185. In the nō play *Funa Benkei* his spirit tries to sink the ship of Minamoto Yoshitsune, the enemy leader, during a powerful storm but is foiled by Benkei's (Yoshitsune's retainer) fervent prayers.

the sun with her hand or the winnow seller who prefers to do his winnowing with a hat! Sakon was much impressed with the boy's filial sense and sent one of his attendants to accompany the boy back to the village where he lived with his mother.

When Sakon returned to Akashi, he immediately presented himself at the lord's castle and delivered the other daimyō's reply. Since the lord seemed to be in a good mood, Sakon mentioned Korin and told him the boy's story. The lord was very impressed and ordered the boy to be brought to him. It was Sakon's joyful task to fetch Korin. Obediently, the boy came to the lord's castle with his mother.

When he appeared before the lord, his lordship was smitten immediately with the boy's unadorned beauty, like a first glimpse of the moon rising above a distant mountain. The boy's hair gleamed like the feathers of a raven perched silently on a tree, and his eyes were as lovely as lotus flowers. One by one, his other qualities became apparent, from his nightingale voice to his gentle disposition, as obedient and true as a plum blossom. The lord increasingly had the boy attend to him, and soon Korin was sharing his bed at night.

The night guard stationed next to the lord's bed chamber listened carefully for signs of trouble, but all he heard were the unrestrained sounds of the lord amusing himself with the boy. When it was over, the lord could be heard to say, "I would gladly give my life for you."

Korin's response showed none of the gratitude that one would expect from a boy receiving the lord's favor. "Forcing me to yield to your authority is not true love. My heart remains my own, and if one day someone should tell me he truly loves me, I will give my life for him. As a memento of this floating world, I want a lover on whom I can lavish real affection."

The lord was slightly irritated with the boy but dismissed what he said as a joke. Korin insisted, however, that he was serious.

"I swear by the gods of Japan that I meant every word of it."

The lord was astonished, but he could not help but admire even this stubborn streak in the boy.

One evening, the lord assembled a large group of his pages to enjoy the breeze at a teahouse in the garden. There they sampled several varieties of saké from throughout the domain. After several rounds, the party was becoming quite lively. Suddenly, the stars disappeared from the sky and the pines at Hitomaru's shrine[138] began to shake noisily. The air stank of death. Clouds spread swiftly overhead, and out from them leaped a one-eyed goblin. It landed on the eaves nearby and tweaked the noses of everyone there, stretching its

---

138. A shrine in Akashi dedicated to the early-seventh-century poet Kakinomoto no Hitomaro, called Hitomaru in the Edo period.

hand out more than twenty feet. The boys stopped their amusement and immediately surrounded their lord to protect him. They then rushed him to his chambers. Later, the ground shook violently with the sound of a mountain being rent asunder.

Shortly after midnight, word was sent to the lord that an old badger had broken down a cedar door in the teahouse used for cherry blossom viewing west of the man-made hill in the garden. Even though it had been decapitated, the head was still gnashing its tusks and screeching in an unearthly manner.

"Well then, the quake earlier must have been the badger's doing. Who killed the beast?" the lord asked. Everyone in the household was questioned, but no one came forward to claim merit for the feat.

One night seven days later, at the hour of the ox, around 2 A.M., the voice of a young girl was heard coming from the boxlike ridge of the great assembly hall. "Korin's life is in danger; it is he who murdered my blameless father." The voice screamed the words three times, then disappeared.

So, it was Korin who performed the deed, everyone thought in awe.

Sometime afterward, the magistrate in charge of buildings and grounds spoke to the lord about fixing the door damaged by the badger. The lord had other plans, however.

"Long ago," he said, "Marquis Wen of Wei got boastful and bragged, 'No one dares oppose a single word I say.' But the blind musician Shi Jing struck a wall with his harp and made him realize his arrogance. Marquis Wen left the damaged south wall as a reminder of his faithful subject.[139] I command that the broken door be left as it is so that all may see the evidence of Korin's brave warrior spirit."

The lord rewarded Korin generously, and his love for the boy grew even stronger.

A man named Sōhachirō, second son of Captain of the Standard Bearers Kan'o Gyōbu, had for some time recognized Korin's true feelings. He told Korin of his love by letter, and they were soon in constant communication. They waited for an opportunity to consummate their love, and the year drew to a close.

On the night of the thirteenth of the Twelfth Month, a day set aside for house cleaning, the lord's presentation of silk for New Year's garments was to take place. One of Korin's attendants had the idea of concealing Sōhachirō inside the basket for worn-out clothing to be sent to Korin's mother for washing and repair. In this way, Sōhachirō was able to make his way to the room next to the lord's bedchamber.

---

139. The story is based on one in *Han Feizi* in which Duke Ping of Jin (Jin Pingpong) was admonished for his pride by the blind musician Shi Kuang. The wrong Chinese names have been given.

Toward evening, Korin complained of stomach pains and secluded himself in his room. When the lord retired, he could not sleep at first because of the constant opening and closing of the door and creaking of the wheels,[140] but soon he was snoring. Able to make love at last, Korin embraced Sōhachirō. In their passion, Korin gave himself to the man without even undoing his square-knotted sash. They pledged to love each other in this life and the next.

The sound of their voices woke the lord from his sleep. He removed the sheath from a spear he kept near his pillow and shouted, "I hear voices. Whoever it is, do not let him escape!" As he rushed out in pursuit, Korin clung to the lord's sleeve.

"There is no need to be alarmed. No one is here. It was merely a demon that came in the agony of my illness and threatened to kill me. Please forgive me."

The boy spoke calmly, giving Sōhachirō time to climb an oak tree and jump across the spiked fence surrounding the mansion. The lord spotted him, however, and demanded an explanation, but Korin insisted that he knew nothing.

"Well then," the lord said, "perhaps it was just another of that badger's tricks."

The lord was willing to let the matter rest there, but a secret agent[141] named Kanai Shinpei came up just then with some information.

"The sound of footsteps just now was made by a man with loose hair tied by a headband. That much I could tell for sure. Without a doubt, he was someone's lover."

The lord's interrogation of Korin suddenly changed. Deadly earnest now, he commanded the boy to confess.

The boy said, "He is someone who swore his life to me. I would not identify him even if you tore me limb from limb. I told you from the beginning that you were not the one I loved." Korin's expression showed no trace of regret as he spoke.

Three days later, on the morning of the fifteenth, the lord summoned Korin to the hall where martial arts were practiced. He assembled his attendants to watch as a lesson to the entire household. Lifting a halberd, he said to the boy, "Korin, you have reached your end."

Korin smiled brightly. "I have enjoyed your favor for so long, to die at your hands would be one more honor. I have no regrets."

As the boy attempted to stand, the lord cut off Korin's left arm. "Still no regrets?" he taunted.

---

140. Korin's feigned gastrointestinal distress required frequent trips to the toilet, apparently located beyond wheeled doors that ran on a track.

141. Secret agents (*kakushi yokome*) were employed by daimyō lords to spy on members of the household in order to catch violators of house laws and protect against intrigue.

The lord (*left*) cuts off Korin's arm. Like the other young men (*bottom left*), Korin wears a long-sleeved robe (*furisode*) and has a "boy's hairstyle" (*wakashu mage*), with a partially shaved head, thick topknot, and two protruding folds of hair at the forehead and the nape of the neck. The illustrations are attributed to Yoshida Hanbei (act. 1684–1688). From the 1687 edition. (From NKBZ 39, *Ihara Saikaku shū 2*, by permission of Shōgakukan)

Korin stretched out his right arm. "I stroked my lover's body with this hand. Surely, that must anger you terribly."

Enraged, the lord slashed it off.

Korin spun around and cried out to the people assembled there. "Take one last look at the figure of this handsome youth. The world will never see his likes again."[142] His voice grew weaker and weaker.

The lord then cut off the child's head.

The lord's sleeve became a sea of tears, like the Sea of Akashi visible before him, and the weeping of the assembled retainers echoed like waves upon the shore.

Korin's corpse was sent to Myōfuku-ji for burial. His brief life had evaporated like the dew. At this temple in Akashi is Morning Glory Pond, named for the flower whose life, if it survives the morning frost, lasts but a single day. In ancient times there was a man banished to Suma for his seductive mischief in the capital.[143] He did not learn his lesson but fell in love with the daughter of a lay

---

142. The implication is that these words were spoken by a possessing spirit, probably related to the murdered badger. Saikaku is drawing on a tradition in setsuwa literature of supernatural fantasy as a metaphor for psychological or social conflict.

143. A reference to Genji, hero of *The Tale of Genji*, who was banished to Suma and then to Akashi. The poem does not appear in *The Tale of Genji*.

priest there. On one of his visits to her, he wrote a poem: "Braving autumn wind and waves, I came each night by the light of the moon on Akashi's hill: morning glories." If this poem had been composed for the sake of boy love, it would surely be remembered today. Unfortunately, it was written for a woman and naturally has been forgotten.

Korin's unknown lover became the subject of severe criticism. "Korin died for his sake, yet he does not come forward and announce himself like a man. He could not possibly be a samurai, just a stray dog who happened to be reincarnated into human form."

In the New Year, on the night of the fifteenth, Sōhachirō attacked Shinpei and cut off both his arms. He then administered the coup de grâce and made a clean escape. After hiding Korin's mother where no one would find her, he fled to Morning Glory Temple. In front of Korin's tomb, he set up a signboard and wrote on it a detailed account of his love for the boy. There, at the age of twenty-one, he ended his life, a dream within a dream; like one gone to sleep, he cut open his belly and died.

At dawn the next day, the morning of the sixteenth, people found the body. The wound was distinctly cut in the shape of a diamond with three crosscuts inside. This was Korin's family crest. "If one is going to fall that deeply in love," people said approvingly, "then this is exactly the way to show it."

Within seven days, the anise branches[144] that people gathered from hills throughout the province filled the entire pond.

[*Ihara Saikaku shū 2*, NKBZ 39: 369–372, translated by Paul Schalow]

TALES OF SAMURAI DUTY (*BUKEGIRI MONOGATARI*, 1688)

After publishing *Great Mirror of Male Love*, Saikaku published two samurai narratives, *Transmission of Martial Arts* (*Budō denraiki*) in 1687 and *Tales of Samurai Duty*, in the next year. Saikaku's shift from stories of love to samurai narratives has been variously attributed to the government ban in 1686 on books dealing with erotic matters, to Saikaku's personal exhaustion with the topic of love and need for fresh material, and to the crisis that faced the samurai at the time. This was the period in which the "Way of the samurai" (*bushidō*), combining the earlier medieval samurai code with Confucian ethics and values, was being established and promoted, particularly by the Tokugawa bakufu, as a means of preserving the rapidly corroding authority of the samurai. This new samurai ethics influenced even the urban commoner or chōnin class, leading to the birth of the "samurai plays" (*budō-mono*) in the world of kabuki.

Transmission of Martial Arts, with the subtitle *Vendettas in Various Provinces*, is a

---

144. Branches of the Japanese star anise (*shikimi*) were used as decorative greenery to mourn the dead.

collection of thirty-two stories about samurai vendettas, vastly expanding a theme that appeared in the first half of *Great Mirror of Male Love*. In the bakufu-domain system, each domain had relative administrative autonomy and its own standing military force. If someone committed an offense and escaped into the neighboring domain, that person was unlikely to be arrested or punished. Consequently, the system permitted a vendetta if the purpose was to compensate the victimized family and if the avenging group received permission in advance from the lord and followed the rules. Although Saikaku tended to idealize the vendetta, in *Transmission of Martial Arts*, he examines both sides, the pursuers and the pursued, and is particularly interested in the suffering caused to both by the vendettas, which were sometimes unjust, often drawn out over months and years, and not always successful. One theme of the book is the strength and brutality of the samurai, who kill or are killed for extremely trivial reasons and who think nothing of taking a life—an ethos and attitude carried over from the Warring States period (1477–1573).

In *Tales of Samurai Duty*, however, which contains twenty-six stories in six volumes, Saikaku focuses on the issue of *giri* (duty, responsibility, obligation), which had become an important value for everybody in Edo society. It was one of the five Confucian principles (humaneness, ritual decorum, rightness, wisdom, and sincerity), but it had a special value for the samurai at this time. In contrast to the older way of the samurai depicted in *Transmission of Martial Arts*, in which the samurai took up the sword for themselves out of their need for revenge, *Tales of Samurai Duty* depicts the new way of the samurai based on the higher principle of giri and self-sacrifice, in which giri meant sacrificing oneself in the service of the lord or one's house. A second level of giri existed in one's responsibility toward one's fellow samurai. In both instances, giri implied never breaking a promise and being ready to give up one's life in order to carry out one's obligations and duties. *Tales of Samurai Duty* draws on material from as early as the Kamakura period and an incident as recent as eight months before its publication. Saikaku portrays idealized samurai who have, in both distant and recent times, honestly upheld this new ideal of giri and managed to overcome the pull of human emotions. In one story (1:2), an older sister who has been promised in marriage to Hidemitsu falls ill and becomes blind in both eyes. Her younger sister is then sent as a substitute, but Hidemitsu, who notices the difference and feels that taking the younger sister would go against giri, sends her back and marries the older sister.

Saikaku's samurai narratives were not handbooks for samurai; rather, they were intended for urban commoners who were interested in and influenced by the customs and psychology of the samurai, who were the ruling elite and their commercial customers. Some of the stories are overconceptualized, perhaps because they look from the outside at idealized samurai, a perspective that may have been a result of Saikaku's position as an urban commoner. In the following story, it may appear that Saikaku is lamenting the unreasonable, inhumane demands of duty on the samurai, but the focus instead is on the conflict between Shikibu's determination to carry out his duty toward Tango and his grief over his child, as well as on the sympathy that Tango subsequently shows his fellow samurai.

In Death They Share the Same Wave Pillow (1:5)

> The Ōi River where life is in passage.
> Six people enter the religious life suddenly.

Although all human beings are allotted a fixed span of life, the code of the samurai requires them to die, if necessary, before their time, to preserve their honor. No one wants to die, but a samurai is prepared for the moment when it comes and dies with dignity.

There was once a samurai by the name of Kanzaki Shikibu who was in the service of Araki Murashige, lord of Itami Castle in Settsu.[145] Shikibu worked as an inspector, an office that required him to watch over the conduct and affairs of all the retainers. That he possessed the ability and intelligence to manage the affairs of such a distinguished household so long and so well was all due to his impeccable lineage.

One day the lord's second son, a boy named Muramaru, expressed a desire to visit the Chishima Islands far to the northeast,[146] and Shikibu was ordered to accompany him. Shikibu's only son, Katsutarō, was also granted his wish to go along on the journey. After completing all their preparations for departure, father and son traveled with the party along the road to the east.

It was during the rainy season, at the end of the Fourth Month, and they had been traveling for many days. The party was trying to reach the post station at Shimada in Suruga, where arrangements had been made for their lodging. The heavy downpour gave them no respite even as they traversed the high Sayo Pass. White waves broke ceaselessly against the small bridge spanning the Kiku River, and the wind buffeted the pines like breaking waves and blew the servants' sleeved capes inside out. It was only with the greatest difficulty that the travelers managed to cross the mountain.

Reassembling the group at the Kanaya post station directly across the Ōi River from Shimada, young Lord Muramaru prepared to hurry the party across the river. Shikibu had been following in the rear to make sure that all was well, and he arrived just at that moment. Looking at the roaring torrent and realizing that the river was rising by the minute, Shikibu tried to stop the boy, saying, "My lord, please let us lodge here tonight." But Muramaru was young and high-spirited and refused to listen to reason. He insisted on having his own way and ordered the crossing to commence. As they waded through the raging current, many in the party were swept away and were never seen again. The young man refused to turn back despite all the difficulties, and at long last his bearers brought him to the far bank.

---

145. Araki Murashige captured Itami Castle in 1574 and made it his own. Four years later, he unsuccessfully rebelled against Nobunaga and fled to Aki.

146. It is commonly believed that these islands were located near Hokkaidō.

As was his custom Shikibu followed in the rear. Now before Shikibu departed from Itami, a fellow inspector, Morioka Tango, had entrusted him with the safety of his son, sixteen-year-old Tanzaburō, who had never left home before. Concerned for the boy's safety, Shikibu made his own son, Katsutarō, cross the river first and had Tanzaburō follow behind him. He carefully chose a horse and men to take Tanzaburō across, and he himself brought up the rear.

Darkness began to fall as they crossed, and in the dim light, the men leading Tanzaburō's horse stumbled into the deep part of the river. As Tanzaburō's saddle slipped down, a wave hit the boy from the side, and he was swept away by the current to disappear into the water. Shikibu was overcome with confusion and grief, but the boy had been lost and nothing could be done to aid him. The tragedy was all the greater because Tanzaburō had nearly reached the far bank. Shikibu was devastated when he realized that his own son had safely reached shore while his own charge had drowned.

He thought for a while and then summoned his son. "Tanzaburō's father entrusted his son's safety to me," he said, "but I let him die. If you remain alive, I will not be able to fulfill my duty to Lord Tango and preserve my honor as a samurai. And so you yourself must die at once."

Katsutarō, with true samurai spirit, showed not the slightest hesitation. He turned back, dove into the seething waves, and was never seen again. For some time, Shikibu stood by the river and contemplated the way of the world.

"Truly, nothing is so heartbreaking as fulfilling the claims of duty. There were any number of men Tango could have chosen to look after his son. Just because he asked me, just because of my few words of agreement, I was bound to live up to his trust and see my only son, who had already safely crossed the mighty river, drown in front of my eyes. What a bitter place this world is! Tango has other sons, and they will help him forget his grief. But I have been parted from my only son, and now I have no pleasure or hopes to look forward to in my old age. His mother's grief will be boundless. It breaks my heart to think of this cruel and untimely parting. I too would like to die here, but it would be a terrible thing if I disobeyed my lord's orders to accompany his son."

And so Shikibu devoted himself to his responsibilities, showing nothing of his emotions, but in his heart he was painfully aware of the transience of human existence. After safely bringing the young master back to the castle in good health, Shikibu pleaded illness and confined himself to his quarters. A short time afterward, his request for termination of his services was granted, and he left Itami. Near Kiyomizu, deep in the mountains of Harima, he and his wife turned their backs on the world and devoted themselves to the Way of the Buddha.

Until that time, no one really knew what had happened at the river, but when Tango learned the details of Katsutarō's death, he was deeply moved by Shikibu's resolve. Tango also asked that his service be terminated and entered the religious life. His wife and children put on the black robes as well, and they

Katsutarō (*left*) and Tanzaburō (*right*), each on horseback and each assisted by five male carriers and a footman in the back carrying a covered spear, cross the rough waves of the Ōi River. From the 1688 edition. (From SNKBZ 69, *Ihara Saikaku shū 4*, by permission of Shōgakukan)

followed Shikibu to the mountains. There they were awakened from their dreamlike existence in this world of suffering by the sound of the wind soughing in the pines. The tears that they shed together for their sons took the place of the ritual offering of water. Joined by destiny in a most mysterious fashion, Tango and Shikibu worked together toward enlightenment. Like the moon disappearing behind the edge of the mountain,[147] their pure and bright hearts joined in a unique friendship, and they aspired to be born together in paradise. Thus the months and the years passed as they performed their religious austerities.

These people are now gone and nothing of them remains in this world. And those who lingered in this world to tell their tale have also vanished into the great beyond.

[*Ihara Saikaku shū 4*, SNKBZ 69: 340–344, adapted from the translation by Ann Callahan in *Tales of Samurai Honor*, pp. 45–48]

JAPAN'S ETERNAL STOREHOUSE (*NIPPON EITAIGURA,* 1688)

In the 1660s, a national network of transportation and communication was formed, and the economy in the Kyoto-Osaka area grew quickly. At the same time, a new type

---

147. Alludes to a poem by Izumi Shikibu (ca. 970–1030) in the *Shūishū*: "I enter the dark road from darkness. Far off shines the moon on the edge of the mountain."

of merchant, who made his fortune in the new currency-based capitalist economy in which capital was invested and circulated, came to the fore, replacing those who had made their fortunes earlier in the century through monopolistic privileges and special connections to domain lords. These enterprising merchants were active not only in Edo, Kyoto, and Osaka but also in the smaller cities and in farm villages in the provinces, where they accumulated wealth that far exceeded that held by the samurai. The first of Saikaku's so-called chōnin narratives, *Japan's Eternal Storehouse*, published in 1688, suggests the techniques for achieving wealth in this new economy. The subtitle of *Japan's Eternal Storehouse* is *Fortune, Gospel of the New Millionaire* (*Daifuku shin chōja kyō*), indicating that it is a sequel to *Gospel of the Millionaire* (*Chōjakyō*), a short book published in 1627 describing how three merchants had become millionaires. The word "millionaire" (*chōja*) meant a self-made man, but the term "eternal generations" (*eitai*) also suggests that the objective was to establish a prosperous family line. The book is a "storehouse" (*kura*) of such models.

The virtues that Saikaku advocates here are ingenuity (*saikaku*), thrift, diligence, and honesty. The word *saikaku* (written differently from Saikaku's name, although he may have chosen his pen name for this association) implies cleverness and quickness of mind, as exemplified in the first selection, "In the Past, on Credit, Now Cash Down" (1:4), in which the draper Mitsui Kurōemon sells goods for cash, eliminating the cost of the usual credit sales. He has each of his clerks specialize in a different cloth and divides the store into departments, thereby inventing the notion of the department store. Mitsui Kurōemon's real name was Mitsui Hachirōemon, who opened the Echigoya store in 1683, beginning what became the Mitsukoshi Department Store chain.

Japan's Eternal Storehouse is, however, ultimately a contradictory text. The book begins by purporting to reveal the means of amassing a fortune in the new economy, but in the end, Saikaku shows how difficult it is to achieve that objective and even questions its validity as a goal for urban commoners. Many of the stories, in fact, criticize the worship of money and advocate an honest, frugal, and steady lifestyle. Even though only a few people could make a fortune, all merchants could benefit from the virtue of thrift, which Saikaku ends up making one of his central themes. The most famous example is Fuji-ichi in "The Foremost Lodger in the Land" (2:1). Even if one can make a large profit, if it is by dishonest means, it is better to be poor, as demonstrated by "All Goodness Gone from Tea" (4:4). Saikaku also emphasizes diligence and steady work, which can help anyone, rich or poor. There is a strong tendency to think of the Genroku chōnin as the pleasure-seeking, spendthrift consumers found in the drama and ukiyo-zōshi of the period, particularly Saikaku's love tales, but the portrait that Saikaku draws here of the honest, steady, and frugal urban commoner is probably more appropriate. Saikaku even provides a number of stories about financial failures, anticipating his more pessimistic view of commoner economic life in *Worldly Mental Calculations*.

Japan's Eternal Storehouse was written as much to entertain as to teach. If Saikaku had simply shown examples of those who had succeeded in accumulating a fortune, he would not have been able to attract the interest of his urban commoner readers.

Instead, he placed at the center of *Eternal Storehouse* those who, having broken with normal standards of behavior, enjoyed great success or suffered disastrous failure. As with much of Saikaku's fiction, the appeal of these stories frequently derives from the humorous twists that he gives to them. (For guidance on currency, see the front matter.)

In the Past, on Credit, Now Cash Down (1:4)

Ancient simplicity is gone. With the growth of pretense, the people of today are satisfied with nothing but finery, with nothing but what is beyond their station or purse. You have only to look at the way our citizens' wives and daughters dress. They can hardly go further. To forget one's proper place is to invite the wrath of heaven. Even the august nobility are satisfied with clothes made of nothing more splendid than Kyoto *habutae* silk,[148] and in the military class the formal black dress of five crests[149] is considered ill suited to none, from minor retainers to the greatest daimyō. But in recent years, ever since some ingenious Kyoto creatures started the fashion, every variety of splendid material has been used for men's and women's clothes, and the drapers' sample books have blossomed in a riot of color. What with delicate stylish stencil-patterns, multicolored imperial designs, and dapple-dyed motifs, one must seek an exotic effect in other worlds, for every device on earth has been exhausted. Paying for his wife's wardrobe or his daughter's wedding trousseau has lightened the pocket of many a merchant and dampened his hopes in business. A courtesan's daily parade of splendor is made in the cause of earning a living. Amateur beauties — when they are not blossom viewing in spring, maple viewing in autumn, or getting married — can manage well enough without dressing in layers of conspicuous silks.

Not long ago, in a tailor's shop set back a little from Muromachi Street and displaying on its curtains the crest of a fragrant citron, there was a craftsman who tailored stylish clothes with even more than the usual Kyoto dexterity. Such piles of silk materials and cotton wadding were deposited with him that he enjoyed a constant prospect of Silk Clothes Mountain[150] without stirring from his shop. Although it was always a rush to remove the tacking stitches and apply the smoothing iron in time, each year on the first day of the Fourth Month —

---

148. A smooth, strong silk woven in Kyoto, the center of the weaving industry at the time.

149. At an audience with the shōgun, it was the custom for every samurai, regardless of rank, to wear the same formal black kimono. The five crests were arranged one on each sleeve, one on each lapel, and one on the back.

150. Kinukake-yama, more commonly known as Kinugasa-yama (Clothes and Hat Mountain), a hill on the northwestern outskirts of Kyoto. According to legend, the retired emperor Uda wanted to see the sight of snow on this mountain in the summer and so had white robes hung up on the mountain.

even as the impatient cuckoo sounded its first notes in the skies above Mount Machikane—he had in his shop a fresh array of splendidly colored summer kimono ready for the season's Change of Clothes.[151] Among them one might have seen garments of three distinct layers—scarlet crepe inside translucent layers of delicate white silk—and garments with sleeves and collars stiffened with padding. Such things were unheard of in earlier days. One step further and we might have been wearing imported Chinese silks as work clothes. The recent clothing edicts[152] were truly for the good of every one of us, in every province in the land, and on second thought, we are grateful. A merchant wearing fine silks is an ugly sight. Not only is homespun better suited to his station, but he also looks smarter in it.

With samurai, of course, for whom an imposing appearance is essential in the course of duty, even those without any servants should not dress like ordinary persons. In Edo, where peace reigns changeless as the pine, on foundations as firm as the ageless rocks of Tokiwa Bridge, drapers' establishments were recently opened in Hon-chō to cater to the great lords. As branches of Kyoto firms, they proudly advertised their crests in all the trade guides. Managers and clerks, in single-minded devotion to duty, were united in their efforts to secure orders from the various great mansions that favored them with patronage. Never relaxing for a moment from matters of business, they displayed eloquence and finesse, judgment and ingenuity. Expert in accountancy and never deceived by a dubious coin, they would gouge the eyes from a living bull for profit. To pass beneath the Tiger Gate in the darkness of the night, to prowl a thousand miles in search of custom—such things they accepted as no more than necessary duties. Early next day, while the stars were still shining overhead, they would be hard at work in the shops, checking the weights on the rods of their scales. From dawn until dusk they courted the favor of customers—but things were no longer as they used to be. The broad and fertile plain of Musashi was still there, but every inch of the ground had been exploited, and there were no easy pickings left. Earlier, on the occasion of a lord's wedding or a distribution of presents, it had been possible for the contractor—with the friendly cooperation of the lord's chamberlain—to do a little trade on satisfactory terms, but nowadays, with offers invited from all sides, the expected profits were meager and more than outweighed by incidental expenses. The true condition of these businesses told a sad story, and orders were supplied to the great households for prestige only. Not only that, but the greater part of the sales were on credit, and accounts remained unsettled year after year. Such money would have been more prof-

---

151. The first day of the Fourth Month marked the beginning of summer, when it was customary to change from padded to unpadded garments.

152. Clothing edicts, setting out lists of clothing materials deemed suitable for respective classes and prescribing penalties for extravagant display, were issued regularly by the shōgun's government.

itably invested even with a Kyoto banker. Because the shops were in constant difficulty because of the shortage of ready cash to negotiate new bills of exchange and because it was unthinkable suddenly to close down businesses that had only just been opened, they were obliged to limit themselves to small-scale transactions. But do what they might, the accounts balanced no better, and before long, the main shops in Kyoto were closed and only the Edo branches remained, with their losses running into hundreds and thousands of *kanme*. Each firm began devising methods of cutting expenses while they were still in business. Had they only known that other ways of trade existed.

In Suruga-chō—a name that brings back memories of the gleam of old *koban*[153]—a man called Mitsui Kuröemon risked what capital he had in hand to erect a deep and lofty building of eighteen yards frontage and eighty yards depth and to open a new shop. His policy was to sell everything for cash, without the inflated charges customary in credit sales. More than forty skilled clerks were in his service, constantly under the master's watchful eye, and to each he assigned full charge of one type of cloth: one clerk for gold brocades, one for Hino and Gunnai silks, one for *habutae*, one for damask, one for scarlets, one for hempen overskirts, one for woolen goods, and so on. Having divided the shop into departments in this manner, he willingly supplied anything his customers asked for, however trifling—a scrap of velvet an inch square, a piece of imported damask suitable for the cover of an eyebrow tweezers, enough scarlet satin to make a spear-head flag, or a single detachable cuff of *ryūmon* silk.[154] Whenever a samurai required a formal waistcoat for an immediate audience with his lord or someone was in urgent need of a gown for a dress occasion, Kuröemon asked the messenger to wait, marshaled a score or so of the tailors on his staff, manufactured the garment on the spot, and delivered it immediately to the customer. By such means the business flourished, and the average daily sales were said to amount to 150 *ryō*. The shop was a marvel of convenience to all. To look at, the master was no different from other men—he had the usual eyes, nose, hands, and feet—but a difference lay in his aptitude for his trade. He was the model of a great merchant.

Neatly folded in the alphabetically arranged drawers of his shop were all the materials of Japan and countries overseas, a varied selection of antique silks, Lady Chūjō's homespun mosquito net, Hitomaro's Akashi crepe, Amida's bib, a strip of Asahina's flying-crane kimono, the mattress which Daruma Taishi used for meditation, Rin Wasei's bonnet, and Sanjō Kokaji's sword sheath.[155] Absolutely nothing was missing. A firm with such well-filled stock books is indeed fortunate!

---

153. A gold coin circulating primarily in Edo.
154. A thick, strong silk, rather like *habutae*, often used for summer kimono and sashes.
155. The articles in the list are nonsensical.

In Mitsui Kurōemon's drapery (kimono) store, two salesclerks, one using an abacus and the other displaying various rolls of uncut fabric, attend a samurai customer in a hemmed cap. His servant, wearing a lozenge-pattern robe and holding a sedge hat and a walking stick, crouches beside the pillar. Two other samurai customers, sitting on a bench (*lower left*), talk to the salesclerks, who are busy weighing coins and entering sales into a ledger. On the earthen floor, a footman with a pole-bound lacquered box (*hasamibako*), for carrying accoutrements, waits for his master. From the 1688 edition.

The Foremost Lodger in the Land (2:1)

"This is to certify that the person named Fuji-ichi,[156] tenant in a house belonging to Hishiya Chōzaemon of Muromachi is, to my certain knowledge, the possessor of one thousand *kanme* in silver. . . ."

Such would be the style of his testimonial when Fuji-ichi sought new lodgings. He was unique, he claimed, among the wealthy of this world, for although he was worth one thousand *kanme*, he lived in a rented house no more than four yards wide. In this way he had become the talk of Kyoto. One day he accepted a house in Karasuma Street[157] as surety for a fixed-time loan of thirty-eight *kanme*. As the interest mounted, the surety became forfeit, and for the first time Fuji-ichi became a property owner. He was much vexed at this. Until now he had achieved distinction as "the rich man in lodgings," but now that he had a house of his own, he was nobody—his money in itself was mere dust by comparison with what lay in the strong rooms of Kyoto's foremost merchants.

Fuji-ichi was a clever man and made his substantial fortune in his own lifetime. But first and foremost he was a man who knew his own mind, and this was the basis of his success. In addition to carrying on his regular business, he kept a separate ledger, bound from odd scraps of paper, in which, pen in

---

156. Fuji-ichi is an abbreviated form of the name Fujiya Ichibei, a celebrated merchant of Goike-machi, Muromachi Street, Kyoto, who died about twenty years before the publication of *Nippon eitaigura*.

157. Karasumaru—or in the Kyoto pronunciation "Karasuma"—is a long street running north to south through the center of Kyoto.

hand, he entered a variety of chance information as he sat all day in his shop. As the clerks from the money exchanges passed by, he noted down the market ratio of copper and gold; he inquired about the current quotations of the rice brokers; he sought information from druggists' and haberdashers' assistants on the state of the market at Nagasaki; and he noted the various days on which the Kyoto dealers received dispatches from the Edo branch shops for the latest news on the prices of ginned cotton, salt, and saké. Every day a thousand things were entered in his book, and people came to Fuji-ichi if they ever had questions. He became an invaluable asset to the citizens of Kyoto.

His dress consisted invariably of a thin undervest beneath a cotton kimono, the latter stuffed if necessary with three times the usual amount of padding. He never put on more than one layer of outer garments. It was he who first started wearing detachable cuffs on the sleeves—a device that was both fashionable and economical. His socks were of deerskin, and his clogs were fitted with thick leather soles, but even so, he was careful not to walk too quickly along the hard main roads. Throughout life his only silk garments were of pongee, dyed plain dark blue—there was one, it is true, that he had dyed an undisguisable seaweed brown, but this was a youthful error of judgment, and he was to regret it for the next twenty years. For his ceremonial dress he had no settled crests, being content with a three-barred circle or a small conventional whirl, and even during the summer airing time, he was careful to keep these from direct contact with the floor mats. His overskirts were of hemp, and his starched jacket of an even tougher variety of the same cloth, so that they remained correctly creased no matter how many times he wore them.

When there was a funeral procession that his whole ward was obliged to join, he followed it to the cemetery on Toribe Hill, but coming back he hung behind the others, and on the path across the moor at Rokuhara, he and his apprentices pulled up sour gentian herbs by the roots.[158]

"Dried in the shade," he explained, "they make excellent stomach medicine."

He never passed by anything that might be of use. Even if he stumbled, he used the opportunity to pick up stones for fire lighters, and tucked them in his sleeve. If the head of a household is to keep the smoke rising steadily from his kitchen, he must pay attention to a thousand things like this.

Fuji-ichi was not a miser by nature. It was merely his ambition to serve as a model for others in the management of everyday affairs. Even in the days before he made his money, he never had the New Year rice cakes prepared in his own lodgings. He considered hiring a man to pound the rice, and to bother over the various utensils was too much trouble at such a busy time of the year; so he

---

158. Toribeyama, an old cremation ground in the vicinity of Kiyomizu Temple, in eastern Kyoto. Rokuhara was a vaguely defined area of open land near Toribeyama.

placed an order with the rice-cake dealer in front of the Great Buddha.[159] How-ever, with his intuitive grasp of good business, he insisted on paying by weight—so much per *kanme*. Early one morning, two days before New Year's Day, a woman from the cake maker arrived at Fuji-ichi's shop. Hurrying about her rounds and setting down her load, she shouted for someone to receive the order. The newly pounded cakes, invitingly arrayed, were as fresh and warm as spring itself. The master, pretending not to hear, continued his calculations on the abacus, and the woman, who begrudged every moment at this busy time of the year, shouted again and again. At length a young clerk, anxious to demonstrate his businesslike approach, checked the weight of the cakes on the large scales with a show of great precision and sent the woman away.

About two hours later Fuji-ichi asked, "Has anyone taken in the cakes which arrived just now?"

"The woman gave them to me and left long ago," said the clerk.

"Useless fellow!" cried Fuji-ichi. "I expect people in my service to have more sense! Don't you realize that you took them in before they had cooled off?"

He weighed them again, and to everyone's astonishment, their weight had decreased. Not one of the cakes had been eaten, and the clerk stood gazing at them in open-mouthed amazement.

It was the early summer of the following year. The local people from the neighborhood of Tōji temple, in southern Kyoto, had gathered the first crop of eggplants in wicker baskets and brought them to town for sale. "Eat young eggplants and live seventy-five days longer" goes the saying; they are very pop-ular. The price was fixed at two *zeni* for one eggplant or three *zeni* for two, which meant that everybody bought two. But Fuji-ichi bought only one, at two *zeni*, because—as he said—"With the one *zeni* now in pocket I can buy any number of larger ones when the crop is fully grown." That was the way he kept his wits about him, and he seldom made a mistake.

In an empty space in his grounds he planted an assortment of useful trees and flowers such as willow, holly, laurel, peach, iris, and bead beans. This he did as an education for his only daughter. Morning glories started to grow of their own accord along the reed fence, but Fuji-ichi said that if it was a question of beauty, such short-lived things were a loss, and in their place he planted runner beans, whose flowers he thought an equally fine sight. Nothing delighted him more than watching over his daughter. When the young girl grew into womanhood, he had a marriage screen constructed for her, and (since he con-sidered that one decorated with views of Kyoto would make her restless to visit the places she had not yet seen and that illustrations of *The Tale of Genji* or *The Tales of Ise* might engender frivolous thoughts) he had the screen painted

---

159. A famous rice-cake shop in front of the Daibutsu (Great Buddha) of Hōkō-ji temple, in Higashiyama, on the east side of Kyoto.

Women (*right*) deliver rice cakes to Fuji-ichi's shop. A young clerk (*upper right*) measures cakes on a scale. Various vendors—a fishmonger, a kitchenware merchant, and an herb seller—approach Fuji-ichi's shop, followed by a man carrying a bag of coins (*far right*). Inside the shop, Fuji-ichi (*upper left*) is looking through his account book, placed next to a box labeled Daikoku-chō (God of Wealth Account Book). His assistants are weighing silver pieces and making calculations on an abacus. Masked beggars (*sekizoro*), who wear paper hoods and visit households at the end of year, are dancing on the earthen floor and chanting New Year's blessings (*lower left*).

with busy scenes of the silver and copper mines at Tada, in Settsu Province. He composed instructional verses[160] on the subject of economy and made his daughter recite them aloud. Instead of sending her to a girls' temple school, he taught her how to write himself, and by the time he had reached the end of his syllabus, he had made her the most finished and accomplished girl in Kyoto. Imitating her father in his thrifty ways, after the age of eight she no longer spilled ink on her sleeves, no longer played with dolls at the Doll Festival, or joined in the dancing at the Bon Festival.[161] Every day she combed her own hair and bound it in a simple bun. She never sought others' help in her private affairs. She mastered the art of stretching silk padding and learned to fit it perfectly to the length and breadth of each garment. Since young girls can do all this if properly disciplined, it is a mistake to let them do as they please.

---

160. *Iroha-uta* were instructional poems, each of which began with a different syllable in the order of the famed *Iro ha nihohedo . . .* poem.

161. The Doll Festival (Hinamatsuri) was on the third day of the Third Month. The Bon Festival, the festival for the spirits of the dead, was usually on the twentieth day of the Seventh Month.

Once, on the evening of the seventh day of the New Year, some neighbors asked permission to send their sons to Fuji-ichi's house to seek advice on how to become millionaires. Lighting the lamp in the sitting room, Fuji-ichi sat down his daughter to wait, asking her to let him know when she heard a noise at the private door from the street. The young girl, doing as she was told with charming grace, first carefully lowered the wick in the lamp. Then, when she heard the voices of the visitors, she raised the wick again and retired to the scullery. By the time the three guests had seated themselves, the grinding of an earthenware mortar could be heard from the kitchen, and the sound fell with pleasant promise on their ears. They speculated on what was in store for them.

"Pickled whaleskin soup?" hazarded the first.

"No. As this is our first visit of the year, it ought to be rice-dumpling gruel," said the second.

The third listened carefully for some time and at last confidently announced that it was noodle soup. Visitors always go through this amusing performance. Fuji-ichi then entered and talked to the three of them about the requisites for success.

"Why is today called the Day of the Seven Herbs?"[162] one asked him.

"That was the beginning of economy in the age of the gods: it was to teach us the ingredients of a cheap stew."

"Why do we leave a salted bream hanging before the god of the kitchen range until the Sixth Month?"[163] asked another.

"That is so that when you look at it at mealtimes you may get the feeling of having eaten fish without actually doing so."

Finally he was asked the reason for using thick chopsticks at New Year.

"It is so that when they become soiled they can be scraped white again, and in this way one pair will last the whole year. They also signify the two divine pillars of the state, Izanagi and Izanami."

"As a general rule," concluded Fuji-ichi, "give the closest attention to even the smallest details. Well now, you have kindly talked with me from early evening, and it is high time that refreshments were served. But not providing refreshments is one way of becoming a millionaire. The noise of the mortar that you heard when you first arrived was the pounding of starch for the covers of the account book."

---

162. On the festival day of the seventh day of the First Month, rice gruel is served flavored with the "seven herbs of spring" (*nanakusa*).

163. *Kake-dai*, a pair of salted bream on a wooden spit, decorated with ferns, was hung over the kitchen range from New Year's Day until the first day of the Sixth Month as an offering to the god Kōjin, who was popularly worshiped as a deity who warded off starvation and fire.

A Feather in Daikoku's Cap (2:3)

One for his bales of rice,
Two for his two-floor mansion,
Three for his store-sheds, three floors high. . . .[164]

So ran the Daikoku dancers' song, and if you looked for someone to fit it, in
Kyoto there was the wealthy merchant called Daikokuya. When Gojō Bridge
was being changed from wood to stone,[165] he purchased the third plank from
the western end and had it carved into a likeness of the god Daikoku, praying
that by spending his life, as this plank had done, in useful service beneath the
feet of customers, he might attain to great wealth. In faith there is profit,[166] and
his household steadily grew more prosperous. He called himself Daikokuya
Shinbei, and the name was known to all.

He had three sons, all safely reared to manhood and all gifted with intelligence. The old man, delighted at such good fortune, was passing his declining
years in great satisfaction and getting ready for retirement when the eldest son,
Shinroku, suddenly started to spend recklessly, visiting the brothel quarters
again and again with no account of the expense. After half a year, the clerks
discovered that 170 *kanme* of the money recorded in their cashbooks had disappeared. When it became clear, however, that Shinroku could never repay
the money, they worked secretly together in his behalf and, by falsifying the
prices of goods being held in stock, managed to get him safely through the next
reckoning day in the Seventh Month. But for all their earnest pleas that he
should live less extravagantly in the future, he took no notice, and at the last
reckoning for the year the cash was short again—by 230 *kanme*. A fox with his
tail exposed, Shinroku could play his tricks no more, and he sought refuge with
a friend who lived by the Inari Fox Shrine at Fushimi, south of Kyoto. His
father, a straitlaced old man, was furious, and no amount of pleading softened
his temper. Summoning the neighborhood group to come to his house in formal dress, he publicly disowned his son and abandoned him to his own devices.
When a father dissociates himself in this way from his own son, it is for no
trifling misdemeanor. Shinroku was now in sorry straits: it was impossible for
him to remain in the vicinity, even in his present refuge, but if he was to leave

---

164. A variation on the traditional verses of the Daikoku dance. Daikoku, a god of good
fortune, is customarily depicted smiling while sitting on two bales of rice, a mallet in one hand
and a sack over his shoulders. At New Year's, companies of begging street performers wearing
Daikoku masks and carrying mallets moved from house to house serenading and dancing for the
residents.

165. Gojō Bridge, across the Kamo River in Kyoto, was rebuilt in 1645.

166. "In faith there is profit" (*shinjin ni toku ari*), a well-known proverb, reflecting the current
utilitarian attitude toward religion.

and make for Edo he must have money, and at the moment he had not even the price of a pair of sandals for the journey.

"Was there ever a more unhappy case than mine?" he moaned. But self-pity did nothing to mend his fortune.

It was on the evening of the twenty-eighth of the Twelfth Month, soon after Shinroku had entered the bathtub in his lodgings, that someone shouted the dread alarm of his father's approach. Terrified, Shinroku leaped from the tub, hastily draped a padded kimono about his dripping body, and fled into the street. He held his sash in one hand but had somehow forgotten to retrieve his underwear—and now that Shinroku was eager at last to get ready for the walk to Edo, the absence of his loincloth was truly unfortunate.

It was not until the twenty-ninth that he finally set out. The skies were overcast, and as he passed Fuji-no-mori, south of Kyoto, the snow that had long threatened began to fall and settle on the pines. Shinroku was hatless, and icy drops oozed past his collar. By sundown, his spirits still further depressed by the booming of temple bells, he was gazing with longing at the steaming tea urns in the cozy rest houses of Ōkamedani and Kanshuji. A sip of tea, he felt, was the very thing to ward off this bitter cold. Having no money, however, he bided his time until he noticed a house before which the palanquins from Fushimi or Ōtsu were drawing up with particular frequency. It was jammed tight with customers, and in the general confusion he quenched his thirst free of charge, and as he left he took the opportunity to appropriate a straw cape that someone had momentarily laid aside. After this initiation into the art of thieving he proceeded along the road toward the village of Ono. There, beneath the branches of a desolate, leafless persimmon tree, he came across a group of children bewailing some misfortune.

"What a shame!" he heard one say. "Poor old Benkei's dead!"

Stretched on the ground before them was a huge black dog, the size of a carter's ox. Shinroku went up to the children and persuaded them to let him have the carcass. Wrapping it in the straw cape he had stolen, he carried it with him as far as the foot of Otowa hill and there addressed some laborers who were digging in the fields.

"This dog," said Shinroku, "should make a wonderful cure for nervous indigestion. For more than three years I've fed him on every variety of drug, and now I intend to burn him into black medicinal ash."[167]

"Well, that's something we should all profit from!" exclaimed the laborers, and fetching brushwood and withered bamboo grass from around them, they produced their tinder wallets and started a fire.

Shinroku gave a little of the ash to each of them, flung the remainder across

---

167. *Kuroyaki*. Concoctions made from the ash of plants, birds, beasts, fishes, and the like were popular at this time as medicines or ointments, for internal or external use.

Shinroku is chased out of the bathtub by his enraged father, who is waving a long stick. The surprised landlady (*upper right*), wearing a cotton cap (*unagi-wata*, or eel cap), and her two attendants are attempting to bring the old man back to his senses. A clerk (*left*) follows Shinroku with his clothes.

his shoulders, and set off again. Crying "Burned wolf powder!" mimicking the curious local dialect, he proceeded to hawk his wares along the road. Passing the Osaka barrier gate, where "people come and people go, both those you know and those you know not,"[168] he persuaded all and sundry to stop and buy. Even peddlers of needles and hawkers of writing brushes, who had long experience themselves in swindling travelers, were taken in by him, and between Oiwake and Hatchō he sold 580 *zeni'* worth of ash.

What a pity, he told himself, never to have realized until now what a born genius he was! If he had used his wits like this in Kyoto, no wearisome walk to Edo would ever have been necessary. Laughing at the thought and at the same time on the verge of tears, he pressed on across the long bridge at Seta and steeled himself to think only of what lay eastward. He passed New Year's Day at a lodging house in Kusatsu, where even as he refreshed himself on the local Uba cakes, he caught a glimpse of Mirror Mountain and wept again for Kyoto and the old familiar mirror cakes of home. But soon, like those first blossoms on Cherry Hill, buds of hope were stirring in his breast, and then, as he sensed the fragrance and the color of his full-flowering youth, he knew that he was ready and able to work, and he laughed at the weak-kneed, ancient god of poverty behind him struggling to keep pace. At Oiso, even the age-old shrine was young with the spirit of spring, its trees white with sacred festoons, and the moon above, so sad in autumn, shone bright with promise for the future. Doubts

168. Saikaku weaves into his text a quotation from a celebrated poem on the Osaka Barrier by Semimaru in the *Ogura hyakunin isshu* (ca. 1200).

lay demolished like the old barrier gates he passed at Fuwa, and day in, day out, he trudged onward. Taking the Mino Road to Owari, and hawking his powder around every town and village on the Tōkaidō, the Eastern Seaboard Highway, at last, on the sixty-second day after leaving Kyoto, he arrived at Shinagawa.

Now that he not only had supported himself all this way but also had made an overall profit of 2,300 *zeni*, he threw the unsold remains of the black powder into the waves by the shore and hurried on toward Edo. But it grew dark and as he had nowhere in Edo to stay, he passed the night before the gate of the Tōkai-ji temple at Shinagawa. Beneath its shelter a number of outcasts were lying, stretched out under their straw capes. It was spring, but the wind from the sea was strong, and the roar of the waves kept him from closing his eyes until midnight. The others were recounting their life stories, and lying awake, he listened to them. Although all of them were beggars now, it seemed that none was so by inheritance. One was from the village of Tatsuta in Yamato and had formerly been a small brewer of saké, supporting a family of six or seven in tolerable comfort. However, when the money he had been steadily putting by amounted to one hundred *koban*, he decided that getting rich by running a local business was a slow process, and—disregarding all that his relations and friends said to dissuade him—he abandoned his shop and came down to Edo. Following his own foolhardy impulses, he rented a shop from a fishmonger in Gofuku-chō and started a business alongside all the high-class saké stores. He could not, however, compete with the products of Kōnoike, Itami, and Ikeda, or with the cedar-barreled saké of the long-established, powerful Nara breweries,[169] and when the capital with which he had started his shop had dwindled to nothing, he took the straw matting from a sixteen-gallon tub of saké to serve as a coat and took to the road as a beggar.

"I thought I should go back to Tatsuta in embroidered scarlet silks, but now I'd go back if I had even so much as a new cotton kimono," he wailed. "It just shows that you should never abandon a business you're used to."

But words were useless. Although the time of wisdom had come, it was too late.

Another of the outcasts was from Sakai, to the south of Osaka, in Izumi Province. A master of a thousand arts, he had come to Edo in high hopes, swollen with conceit. In calligraphy he had been granted lessons by Hirano Chūan.[170] In tea he had drunk at the stream of Kanamori Sōwa. Chinese verse and prose composition he had learned under Gensei of Fukakusa, and for

---

169. Kōnoike, Itami, and Ikeda are localities near Osaka, and each brewed a much-esteemed saké, which was exported by sea to all parts of Japan.

170. The names in the following passage are those of contemporary scholars, aesthetes, actors, and so forth, mostly from Kyoto and Osaka.

linked verse and haikai he had been a pupil of Nishiyama Sōin. In nō drama he had mastered the dramatic style of Kobatake and the drum technique of Shōda Yoemon. Mornings he had listened to Itō Genkichi expounding on the classics, evenings he had practiced kickball under Lord Asukai; during the afternoon he had joined in Gensai's chess classes; and at night he had learned koto fingering from Yatsuhashi Kengyō and blowing the flute as a pupil of Sōsan. In jōruri recital he learned the style of Uji Kadayū, and in dancing he was the equal of Yamatoya no Jinbei. In the art of love he had been trained by the great Shimabara courtesan Takahashi, and in revels with boy actors he had copied to perfection the mannerisms of Suzuki Heihachi. Under the guidance of the professional entertainers in both the Shimabara and the unlicensed quarter he had developed into a pleasure seeker of exquisite refinement. If there was anything that man could do he had sought out a specialist in it and had copied his technique, and he now proudly regarded himself as one qualified to succeed in any task to which he might turn his hand. But these years of rigorous training proved of little use in the immediate business of earning a living, and he soon regretted that he had never used an abacus and had no knowledge of the scales. At a loss in samurai households, useless as a merchant's apprentice, his services were scorned by all. Reduced to his present plight, he had cause to reconsider his opinion of himself, and he cursed the parents who had taught him the arts but omitted any instruction in the elements of earning a living.

A third beggar was Edo born and bred, like his father before him. Although he had once owned a large mansion and grounds in Tōri-chō, drawing a regular income of six hundred *koban* per annum from house rents, he had no conception of the meaning of the simple word "economy," and before long he had sold everything except the walls and roof of his house. Left without a means of support, he abandoned society and his home and took to the life of a beggar — an outcast in practice, even if not registered as one with Kuruma Zenshichi's guild.[171]

Listening to each of these life stories, different though they were from one another, Shinroku felt that all were very like his own, and his sympathy was aroused. He moved nearer to where the others were lying.

"I too am from Kyoto," he said and added, concealing nothing of his disgrace, 'I have been disowned by my father and was going to Edo to try my luck — but listening to your stories has disheartened me.'

"Was there no way of excusing yourself?" the beggars exclaimed. "Had you no aunt to intercede for you? You would have been far better advised never to have come to Edo."

"That is past, and I cannot retrace my steps. It is advice for the future that I

---

171. Kuruma Zenshichi of Asakusa was the hereditary chief of the *hinin*, or outcaste, community north of Nihonbashi Bridge in Edo.

require. It surprises me that men so shrewd as each of you should be reduced to such distress. Surely you could have made a living of some sort, no matter what trade you chose."

"Far from it. This may be the great castle town of the shōgun, but it is also the meeting place for all the sharpest men in Japan, and they won't give you three *zeni* for nothing. In Edo you cannot get anywhere without capital."

"But during all the time you've been looking about, have no fresh ideas for trade occurred to you?"

"Well, you could pick up the empty shells that people scatter all over the town, burn them at Reigan-jima, and sell the ashes as lime. Or since people are hard pressed for time in this place, you could shred edible seaweed or shave dried bonito into 'flower strips' and sell them by the plateful. Or you could buy a roll of cotton and sell it piecemeal as hand towels. Apart from things like this, there seems to be no way of starting trade on an almost empty pocket."

Their words had given him the idea he wanted. At dawn he took his leave, and when he gave the three of them a parting gift of one hundred *zeni* each, their delight knew no bounds.

"Your luck has come!" they cried. "You'll make a pile of money as high as Mount Fuji!"

After this he went to visit an acquaintance who had a cotton-goods shop in Tenma-chō, and there he related the details of his present predicament and his plans. The shopkeeper was sympathetic.

"In a case like this, honest work is the only answer," he said. "Try your luck at trade for a bit."

Taking heart, Shinroku purchased a roll of cotton on which he had set his mind and cut it up for sale as hand towels. On the twenty-fifth of the Third Month, the festival day of the Tenjin Shrine at Shitaya, he started his new business. Seated at the base of the holy-water font by the entrance, he offered his towels for sale. The pilgrims, believing that this was another way of improving their luck, bought them gladly, and at the end of the first day he had already made a profit. Every day thereafter he made more money, and within ten years he was rumored to be worth five thousand *koban*. For shrewdness he was considered in a class of his own. People took Shinroku's advice on many matters, and he became a treasured asset in the area. On his shop awnings he printed a picture of the god Daikoku wearing a reed hat, and his firm was known as the Hatted Daikokuya. . . .

> Eight for the daimyō's agent,
> Nine for the nuggets of gold in his stock,
> Ten for a tale's happy ending.

And happy too was his lot in living in this tranquil age!

All the Goodness Gone from Tea (4:4)

One gold *bankin* a day—that, they say, is the average toll levied on cargoes arriving at the port of Tsuruga in Echizen. The daily toll on freighters up and down the Yodo River is no higher. Tsuruga is a place where wholesalers of every kind flourish, but its period of greatest activity is in the autumn, when rows of temporary shops are erected for the annual market. The streets take on a truly metropolitan air, and to look at the women, strolling at ease amid crowds of men and bearing themselves with feminine grace and restraint, you might think that a new Kyoto had sprung up in the north. This also is the season for traveling players to converge on the town and for pickpockets to gather in strength. But people have learned to keep their wits about them: they have abandoned altogether the practice of hanging valuable *inrō* ornaments from their belts and hide their money wallets far out of reach in the folds of their kimono. These are hard times indeed, if even the brotherhood of thieves can no longer make a dishonest penny in a crowd this size. But honesty still reaps its reward, and a skillful tradesman, humbly inviting buyers to inspect his wares, treating each customer with courtesy and respect, need not despair of making a living.

On the outskirts of the town lived a man called Kobashi no Risuke. With no wife or children to support, his only care each day was to provide a living for himself. In his approach to this he displayed considerable ingenuity. He had built a smart portable tea server, and early every morning, before the town was astir, he set the contraption across his shoulders and set out for the market streets. His sleeves were strapped back with bright ribbon; he wore formal divided skirts, tightly bound at each ankle—the picture of efficiency—and on his head he set a quaint *eboshi* cap.[172] He might have passed for the god Ebisu himself. When he cried "Ebisu tea! A morning cup of Ebisu tea!" the superstitious merchants felt obliged to buy a drink for luck, even if they were not at all thirsty, and from force of habit they tossed him twelve *zeni* for each cup. His luck never changed, day after day, and before long he had enough capital to open a retail tea shop and do business on a larger scale. Later he hired several assistants, and he rose to be a leading merchant in the wholesale trade.

So far, as a man who had made a fortune by his own efforts, he had earned nothing but admiration and respect. He even received, and rejected, requests from influential citizens to marry their daughters.

"I shall take no wife before I have ten thousand *ryō*," he used to say, calculating that matrimony might involve inconvenient expenses at the moment. "There is plenty of time left before I pass forty."

For the time being, he found sufficient pleasure in watching his money grow,

---

172. Ebisu, the merchant's favorite god of luck, invariably wore an *eboshi*, a tall black cap of lacquered paper or stiffened cloth. Worshiping Ebisu, the god of luck, early in the morning was a common practice among merchants.

and he lived in solitary bachelorhood. As time passed he became less scrupulous in his business methods: sending his assistants to all parts of Etchū and Echigo Provinces, he bought used tea leaves on the pretext they were needed for Kyoto dyes, and he mixed these with the fresh leaves in his stock. People could see no difference, and his sales brought tremendous profits. For a period, at least, his household enjoyed great prosperity, but heaven, so it would seem, did not approve. Risuke became stark-raving mad, gratuitously revealing his private affairs to the whole province and babbling about tea dregs wherever he went. People cut him dead: they would have no dealings with a man whose fortune was so disreputably made. Even when he summoned a doctor, no one would come. Left to himself he grew steadily weaker, until he did not have even the strength to drink hot or cold water. Once, toward the end, he begged tearfully for a mouthful of tea to cleanse him of worldly thoughts, but although they held the cup before him, a barrier of retribution was firmly settled in his throat. Then, scarcely able to breathe, he ordered his servants to bring the money from his strong room and lay it about his body, from head to foot.

"To think that all this gold and silver will be someone else's when I die!" he sobbed. "What a sad and dreadful thought that is!"

He clasped the money to his breast; he clenched it between his teeth; his tears trailed crimson streaks across his ashen face; and he needed only horns to be the image of a white devil. In his madness he leaped wildly about the room, a shadow of his former self, and even though he sank down again and again in exhaustion, no one could hold him still for long. He revived and started searching for his money once more. Thirty-four or thirty-five times he repeated this performance. By then even his own servants could find no more pity for him. They were terrified, and one by one they gathered in the kitchen, grasping sticks and clubs to defend themselves. They waited for two or three days, and when they could no longer hear any sounds, they rose together and peeped into the room. Risuke lay there with staring eyes, still clutching his money. Nearly dead with fright they bundled his body, just as it was, into a palanquin and set off for the cremation ground.

It was a mild spring day, but suddenly black clouds swirled into view; sheets of rain sent torrents racing across the flat fields; gusts of wind snapped withered branches from the trees; and lightning lit the skies. Perhaps it was the lightning that stole away the body even before they had a chance to burn it. In any event, nothing remained now except the empty palanquin. With their own eyes they had witnessed the terrible truth that this world of the senses is a world of fire.[173] They turned and fled, and every one of them became a devout follower of the Buddha.

---

173. The present existence, being insecure and subject to change, was likened in the Lotus Sutra, a Buddhist scripture, to a "house afire."

The frenzied Risuke has leaped out of his sickbed, clasping a packet of silver in his right hand and a piece of gold coin in his left. Other bundles of money and coins are scattered around his bedding. Three servants, each holding a stick, attempt to restrain Risuke while a bald doctor in a black robe and three female servants flee. In the shop front are a large tea bushel, a gigantic tea jar, a basket filled with tea leaves, and a tea-leaf scale.

Later, all of Risuke's distant relatives were summoned and asked to divide the deceased's property, but when they heard what had happened they shook with fright, and none of them would take so much as an odd chopstick. They told the servants to split the property among themselves. But the servants showed no enthusiasm at all; on the contrary, they left the house and even the articles of clothing that Risuke had given them during their service. Since the laity, trained in the world of greed, had shown themselves to be so stupid, there was nothing to do but sell the whole property at a loss and donate the proceeds to the local temple. The priests were delighted with their windfall. Because the money could not be used for sacred purposes, they went to Kyoto, where they had the time of their lives with boy actors and brought smiles of happiness to the faces of the Higashiyama brothel keepers.

Strangely enough, even after his death Risuke made regular rounds of the various wholesale stores to collect his dues on previous credit sales. The proprietors knew well enough that he was dead, but from sheer terror at seeing him in his old form they settled their accounts at once, without attempting to give him short weight. The news of his reappearance caused wide alarm. They called Risuke's old house a "ghost mansion," and when nobody would take it even as a gift, it was left to crumble and become a wilderness.

It is easy enough, as may be observed, to make money by shady practices. Pawning other people's property, dealing in counterfeit goods, plotting with confidence tricksters to catch a wife with a large dowry, borrowing piecemeal from the funds of innumerable temples, and defaulting wholesale on a plea of bankruptcy, joining gangs of gambling sharks, hawking quack medicines to country bumpkins, terrorizing people into buying inferior ginseng roots, conniving with your wife to extort money from her lovers, trapping pet dogs for skins, charging to adopt unweaned babies and starving them to death, collecting the hair from drowned corpses[174]—all these are ways of supporting life. But if we live by subhuman means, we might as well never have had the good fortune to be born human. Evil leaves its mark deep in a man's heart, so that no kind of villainy seems evil to him any longer. And when he has reached that stage, he is indeed in a pitiful state of degradation. The only way to be a man is to earn one's livelihood by means appropriate to a man. Life, after all, is a dream of little more than fifty years, and whatever one does for a living, it is not difficult to stay so brief a course.

[*Saikaku shū ge*, NKBT 48: 46–49, 59–63, 125–129, adapted from the translation by G. W. Sargent in *The Japanese Family Storehouse*]

WORLDLY MENTAL CALCULATIONS (*SEKEN MUNEZAN'YŌ*, 1692)

Worldly Mental Calculations, the last major prose work published in Saikaku's lifetime, appeared in the first month of 1692, a year before Saikaku's death. With only a few exceptions, the twenty short stories in *Worldly Mental Calculations* focus on the twenty-four hours of the last day of the year. By the end of the seventeenth century, buying and selling on credit was standard practice, with certain days set as the deadline for returning loans.[175] The last day of the year was by far the most important day, when expenses and debts for the entire year had to be settled. There was a widespread belief that if one survived the last day of the year, one could survive the next year. One consequence was that many people with little money pawned their clothing and other possessions on the last day of the year.

Worldly Mental Calculations focuses on this tumultuous day in the Kyoto-Osaka region, the two major merchant cities at the time, looking specifically at the middle- and lower-class urban commoners who had been left behind by the new economy and for many of whom urban life had become a kind of hell on earth. Unlike *Japan's Eternal Storehouse*, which describes upper-class merchants who had made fortunes in the old and new economies, *Worldly Mental Calculations*, probably Saikaku's darkest and most pessimistic text, deals mostly with city dwellers who cannot make ends meet. Here, the interest of the narrative has shifted from imaginative ways of making money to the elaborate ruses and schemes to avoid debt collectors and to the psychological

---

174. To be sold to wig makers.

175. The third day of the Third Month, the fifth day of Fifth Month, the sixteenth day of Seventh Month, the ninth day of Ninth Month, and the last day of the Twelfth Month.

and social effects of extreme poverty. As revealed in "In Our Impermanent World, Even Doorposts Are Borrowed" (2:4), even when the characters engage in devious behavior, the narrator reacts with amazement or occasional pity rather than with words of condemnation. At the same time, Saikaku shows, as in "His Dream Form Is Gold Coins" (3:3), that not all impoverished commoners are ready to sell themselves for money. Significantly, relatively few of the characters in *Worldly Mental Calculations* have names, and many appear only briefly. Instead, as in "Holy Man Heitarō" (5:3), anonymous individuals are often linked by a common sense of desperation and loss. In this story, a priest is about to give a special New Year's Eve sermon about Heitarō, a disciple of Shinran, the founder of the True Pure Land sect (Jōdo shinshū), which, along with the Nichiren sect, was the most popular Buddhist institution. He attracts only three listeners, however, each of whom "confesses" his or her nonreligious motives for coming to the temple. Here, as in the other stories, Saikaku mixes humor, surprising twists, and irony even in his darkest stories, ultimately creating the effect of tragicomedy.

In Our Impermanent World, Even Doorposts Are Borrowed[176] (2:4)

Familiarity takes away our fear of things. In Kyoto there is a rice-field path called the Narrow Path of Shujaka that has become very famous and is often sung about in popular short songs because it leads to the Shimabara licensed quarter. One fall at harvest time, a farmer whose field was near the path put up a scarecrow with an old wide rush hat and bamboo walking stick. But the crows and kites were so used to seeing big spenders with their friends and attendants walking to and from the quarters discreetly wearing rush hats down over their faces that the birds thought the scarecrow was just another visitor who'd decided to come alone. They weren't the slightest bit afraid, and later they began to perch on its hat, flattering and cajoling it as if it were a rich patron.

For most people, there's nothing more frightening than a visit from a bill collector, but one Kyoto man who'd been in debt for many years stayed home even on the last day of the year and didn't try to dodge the collectors. "Not a single person in history," he told the assembled collectors, "has ever had his head cut off for owing money. I'll definitely pay back what I have. Honestly speaking, I'd like to pay it all back. But I can't pay what I don't have. What I'd really like right now," he said, walking over to a tree in a sunny corner of the garden, "is a money tree. But I haven't planted any seeds, so I'm not counting on finding one." Then he unrolled an old straw mat and got out a pair of iron fish skewers and a kitchen knife, which he began to sharpen.

"Now, there, so much for the rust," he said. "But I can't even afford dried

---

176. The title juxtaposes the Buddhist sense of transience (*kari*) of all things with the capitalist notion of borrowing (*kari*) to make a living.

sardines this New Year's, so I'm not going to chop a single one with this. You just never know about emotions. Right now I might suddenly be feeling extremely angry about something, and this knife might very well help me kill myself. I'm getting pretty old. I'm fifty-six already, and I'm certainly not afraid of dying. You all know that fat, greedy merchant in the business district who's going to die young for something he's done. Well, if he'll pay back all my debts for me, completely, just like that, then I swear, in all truthfulness before the great fox god Inari, I swear I'll take all the responsibility for whatever it was the man did. I'll cut myself wide open and die instead of him."

The man waved the knife around, and his eyes gleamed wildly as if he were possessed by the fox god. Just then a large cock came by, clicking its beak.

"Hey," he shouted at the bird. "Today you're my sacrifice. Bring me good luck on my journey to the other world, will you!" Then he cut off its head.

The debt collectors were shaken. It would be dangerous to try to negotiate with the man in the state he was in, and one by one they began to leave. On their way out each collector stopped in front of the teapot boiling on the kitchen hearth and told the man's wife how much he sympathized with her for being married to such a short-tempered man. The aggressive strategy the man had used for getting rid of the bill collectors was a common one, yet it was a shabby way to settle his accounts for the year. He hadn't said a single word of apology, and he'd finished everything all too simply.

Among the bill collectors was an apprentice to a lumber dealer in Horikawa.[177] He was still eighteen or nineteen and hadn't yet begun to shave the top of his head. He kept his hairlines at ninety-degree angles at the temples to show he was already a young man, but he still wore his hair long, and his body looked as delicate and frail as a woman's. In actuality, he was strong willed and fearless. While the owner of the house was threatening the other collectors with his act, the young man sat on the low bamboo verandah, not paying the slightest attention. Nonchalantly he took a string of prayer beads out of his long, hanging sleeve and began to count the number of times he'd chanted Amida Buddha's holy name. Later, after the other collectors had left and the house had returned to normal, he went over and addressed the owner.

"Well," he said, "the play seems to have ended. Now it's time to pay me the money you owe so I can leave."

" 'Pay'?" the owner replied. "What right have you got to stay here with that smirking, know-it-all look on your face when all the grown men have had the good sense to leave?"

"I'm very busy right now," the young man said, "and yet I was forced to sit through a useless farce about a man pretending to threaten suicide."

"You're wasting your time prying around."

---

177. An area in western Kyoto near the Horikawa River, down which timber from the mountains was floated.

The owner goes to the front gate to stop the debt collector, holding a large mallet for knocking out the gateposts. Having pretended to disembowel himself, the owner stands with his robe half off. Two felicitous pines, a New Year's decoration, stand in front of the gate. A peddler of decorative pine branches (*left*), a woman carrying a New Year's decorative paddle and arrow (*right*), a fish seller, a man delivering saké, and a crockery peddler, resting his load on a pole, all look on. From the 1692 edition.

"Whatever. I won't leave until you give it to me."

"Give what?"

"The money."

"And who's going to make me give it?"

"I am. Listen, my job is getting what others can't get. I was hired especially to collect from twenty-seven hard-core cases. Look at my book here. I've already collected from twenty-six, and I'm not going back without collecting from all twenty-seven. By the way, the lumber you used to remodel your house—until you pay, it belongs to the lumberyard. If you're not going to pay for it, I'll have to take it back with me." The young man picked up a large mallet and went to the front gate, where he began knocking out one of the gateposts.

The owner ran out to the gate shouting, "You won't get away with this!"

"You know," the young man said, "your approach to extortion is really out of date. You don't know the slightest thing about advanced methods. Taking back gatepost lumber is the latest thing in bill collecting."

At that, the owner realized there was nothing more he could do to threaten the young man. He promptly apologized to him and paid back the full amount.

"You've paid what you owed," the young man told him, "so I don't have any right to say this, but your method of evading payment is awfully old. You're quite an extortionist, and it just doesn't seem right. Allow me to make a few suggestions. First you talk over everything with your wife, and then you and she begin fighting at around noon on the last day of the year, before the collectors arrive. Your wife changes into street clothes and says, 'There's no reason I have to stay in this house forever. But if I go, two, maybe three, people are going to end up dead. Is that all right with you? Do you understand how serious this is? Listen, you. Are you absolutely sure you want me to get out? You don't even need to tell me, you know. I'll be out of here before you can tell me anything— and happy to be gone!' Then you say, 'Please, please understand. I need all the money we have to pay back my debts. I want people to speak kindly of me when I'm dead, after all. We live only once, but our reputations live forever. I have exactly one choice. I'll clear my debts and then kill myself. Today's my last day on earth. It has to be done. Still, just thinking about it makes me very angry!' Then you take some papers, any old papers, and rip them up one by one as if they were extremely important documents. When the collectors see that, even the most hardened veteran isn't going to stay long."

"In all these years," the owner exclaimed, "that plan never even occurred to me. Thanks to you," and then he turned to his wife, "we're going to use it to get us through the last day of the year next year just fine, aren't we?" Then he turned back to the young man. "You haven't lived many years, but you're wiser than we are. And your wisdom's gotten us through the end of the year. Won't you please celebrate the coming new year with us for a moment? It's not much, just a token of our gratitude."

The couple plucked the headless cock and served a delicious broth to the young man, and then they exchanged cups of saké. The young bill collector had already left by the time the man exclaimed to his wife, "Why should we wait until next year? It's still early, and every year the toughest collectors come late."

The two promptly invented an argument, and they managed to fend off every collector who came that night. Eventually they became famous as the Brawlers of Ōmiya Street.[178]

His Dream Form Is Gold Coins (3:3)

"Never forget about business," advised one very rich man, "even in your dreams." The things people think about always appear in their dreams, whether they're happy or sad. So there's something sleazy about dreaming of picking up money someone else has dropped. And even if you actually went out and looked, you wouldn't find anything. Nobody drops coins any more. People regard money as life itself and take the greatest care with it. Not a single copper coin reaches the ground when crowds gather at Buddhist temples and toss

---

178. An area west of Horikawa Street and south of Fifth Avenue with many tatami (floor mat) makers.

offerings into collection boxes on those special days when prayers are supposed to have a thousand times their normal effect. And the ground is bare even on the day after the big Tenma Festival[179] in Osaka. Money, it seems, only appears after you've worked for it.

Just south of Kyoto in Fushimi, there was a poor man who slighted his trade and spent his time thinking of ways to get rich all at once. He couldn't forget a sight he'd seen once in Suruga-chō[180] when he was living in Edo. There, in one moneychanger's shop, he'd seen stacks of unwrapped coins rising up like a small mountain. Now he lay on his cheap paper bedding obsessed with the desire to have that heap of coins to get him through the end of the year. In his mind he once more saw stack after stack of freshly reminted coins rising up from the buckskin mat in the shop—so many coins he was sure they must have been the size of his own body when he was lying down.

At dawn on the thirty-first of the Twelfth Month, the last day of the year, the man's wife woke first, worrying about how her family would manage to get through the day. As she tried to think of ways they might come up with some money, she happened to look over at the sunlight falling onto the floor through the eastern window. There, in its rays, rose a heap of gold coins.

It had actually happened! She decided it must be a gift from heaven. Elated, she called to her sleeping husband again and again. "What is it?" he finally answered. As he spoke, the coins disappeared. The woman was filled with remorse for what she'd done, and she explained to her husband what had happened.

"It must have been the gold coins I saw when I was living in Edo," her husband said. "Even now, all I can think about is having that money. My desire must have taken the shape of those coins for a while. Actually, just now I was beginning to think bad thoughts, and my bad soul overcame my good soul. I was thinking, well, if it were the only way out of this poverty, I'd be willing to make money by ringing the Bell of Eternal Torment at Sayo-no-Nakayama. I'd do it, even though I knew I'd have to go to hell for it later and could never get reborn in the Pure Land. For rich people this world is paradise, but for poor people it's already hell. Unlike hell, though, in this world we poor people don't even have enough firewood under our cauldrons! I was lying there half asleep thinking what an awful year this was when I saw two demons, one black and one white, coming to meet me in a roaring, fiery chariot. They took me all the way to the edge of the other world and were showing me along the border of hell."

When the woman heard this, she grew even sadder. "No one lives to be one hundred," she said firmly, admonishing her husband. "It's just plain foolish to

---

179. The largest annual festival in Osaka is on the twenty-fifth day of the Sixth Month, climaxing with a nocturnal procession of lantern-decked riverboats carrying the gods.

180. An area where many money-changing houses were located.

waste your time with that ridiculous wish. As long as we don't change our feelings for each other, I'm sure we'll have happy new years in the future. I understand your deep disappointment as a man at not being able to support me and our daughter, but if we don't do something, all three of us are going to starve. We're in luck, though. Luckily, there's a job opening for a live-in servant I can take. We have only one child, and this will also be good for her future. While I'm away, if you'll take care of her and raise her, I'm sure we'll all have better times in the future. It would be cruel to give her away to someone else. Please, I beg you." Tears were running down her face.

The man, his pride hurt, was unable to reply or even look into his wife's face. While he was sitting there with his eyes closed, a woman from Sumizome-chō in Fushimi, an employment agent, arrived together with a wealthy retired woman in her sixties and began talking with his wife.

"As I said yesterday," the agent began, "you have good breasts, so you'll receive your whole year's salary of eleven and a quarter ounces of silver in advance. And you'll get new clothes quarterly. Most wet nurses get to change their robes only twice a year, you know. You should feel grateful. Those big women who work in the kitchen get only four and a quarter ounces for six months, plus they have to weave cloth at night. It's all because of your breasts. You should realize that. If you don't want the job, I've found another woman in northern Kyō-machi who can do it. It has to be settled today. I'm not coming back here again."

"I'm only doing this to help my family get by," the woman said cheerfully. "Do you really think I'll be able to take care of their baby boy properly? If it's a job I can really do, then I accept the offer."

"Then we'd better go over to the house right away," the agent answered, without bothering to speak to the woman's husband. The agent borrowed a brush and inkstone from a neighbor and wrote out a formal one-year contract for the woman. Then she paid the full amount in silver.

"Oh, I might as well do this now as later. It's the standard rate," the agent said, taking back the package, which was marked "Thirty-seven Silver Coins: Eleven and a Quarter Ounces." Carefully she measured out her commission, exactly 10 percent. "Well now, wet nurse, we must be going. Come along just as you are."

Tears came to the man's eyes, and his wife's face was red and swollen from crying. "Goodbye, Oman," she said to her daughter. "Mommy's going to her new employer's nice mansion. She'll come back soon, on the sixteenth of the First Month.[181] We'll be together then." She asked the neighbors on both sides to look after a few things, and then she started crying again.

---

181. Servants had two three-day vacations a year, beginning on the sixteenth day of the First and Seventh Months.

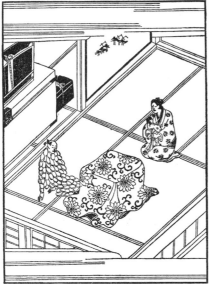

An employment agent leads a prospective employer and her parlor maid into the earthen space at the entrance to the couple's home. Behind them are three earthen ovens and cooking utensils. In the living room, the wife sits and holds her daughter while her husband, covered with gold coins representing his desire and his wife's dream, sits with his feet under a foot warmer.

"Children can grow up without parents," the agent said brusquely. "Even if you try to beat them to death, the ones that aren't going to die won't. And good day to you, sir." Then the agent turned and began to leave.

The retired woman, the wife's new employer, looked back once more at the baby. She understood well how many sorrows there were in the world. "My motherless grandson certainly deserves pity," she said, "but that little girl, how pitiful she's going to be without her own mother's milk."

"If the girl dies," the agent said, without caring in the least that the child's mother was listening, "then she's just fated to die, that's all. If you want to blame something, blame money." She hurried the other two women out of the house.

As evening deepened on the last day of the year, the man began to feel he had no reason to go on living. First I get a big inheritance, he told himself, and then I lose it all because of my bad attitude and my stupid mental calculations. I even had to run away from Edo.[182] Fushimi's a run-down place, but thanks to my wife, I've been able to settle down here. Everything that's happened has been because of her love. Even if all we had was some nice tea to celebrate with, we could still have a wonderful New Year's just being together and making

---

182. Presumably to escape his creditors.

love. And over there. What's that on the end of the shelf? How sweet of her! She's bought two pairs of special chopsticks for us to eat New Year's food with. I certainly won't need both. The man broke one pair in two and fed it into the fire under the pan he was heating.

It grew late, but the baby refused to stop crying, and women from next door dropped by to help. They taught the man how to boil rice flour into gruel, mix it with sweet barley syrup, and then boil the whole mixture. Then they showed him how to feed it to the baby through a bamboo tube with silk tied around the end that was the same size as her mother's nipple.

"Am I imagining things," one woman asked, "or has her little chin grown thinner just today?"

The man was tending the fire with a pair of tongs. "This just isn't going to work," he said, angry at himself. Suddenly he hurled the tongs onto the dirt floor of the kitchen.

"I sympathize with you," another woman said. "Your wife is lucky, though. The son of the old woman who hired her likes pretty women, so he'll treat her well."

"Treat her very, very well," the first woman said. "She looks a lot like his own wife who just died."

"Actually," the second woman said, "when you look at your wife from behind, with that attractive way she has, yes, she looks exactly like the dead woman."

"The money's still all there," the man declared abruptly. "I haven't touched it. After hearing what you've said, I'd rather starve to death than take it!" He ran out of the house and came back later with his wife. They were still crying when the year changed.

Holy Man Heitarō (5:3)

Buddhism has long been considered by monks and believers alike to be a means of making a living. This continues to be true today. Every year, for example, on the last night of winter, sermons are given at True Pure Land sect temples to recount the life of the pious disciple Heitarō[183] and retell the story of his vision of Saint Shinran, the sect's founder. Men and women of all ages go to the temples in great numbers to hear these sermons, which are never new but are always felt to be worth listening to.

In 1673 the last night of winter happened to fall on the last night of the year, as happens every so often.[184] The calls of year-end bill collectors competed with

---

183. On the last night of winter in 1240, Heitarō prayed at the Kumano Shrine and saw a dream vision of Saint Shinran (1173–1262) and the Kumano god sitting together, indicating Shinran's divinity.

184. In the lunar calendar, the two were independent of each other, and the date of each changed slightly every year.

the voices of beggars singing purifying charms in doorways on the last night of winter, and the sharp sounds of merchants tapping on their scales with mallets, weighing out the silver they owed, clashed with the clattering of dried beans thrown in every direction to ward off bad fortune as spring approached. There was something uncanny about it all, as if a demon had been tied up and was struggling to get loose somewhere out in the dark. People felt vaguely but distinctly nervous about what might happen.

The sound of the large drum in one True Pure Land temple reverberated far and wide. The monks lit lanterns in front of the buddha image in the main hall and waited for believers to arrive, but when the great bell boomed out at seven-thirty, only three believers could be seen. The head monk led the early evening services, and after he had finished he sat silently for a while, pondering what was happening out in the world.

"Well," he finally said, "tonight people have to finish off the year's business. Everybody seems to be too busy to come worship. But all the old women out there who've already left their household duties to their children and grandchildren, they have enough time. Nothing should be keeping them home tonight. When they die and Amida Buddha comes for them in that boat of his, none of them are going to say they're too busy then to get on board and ride to the Pure Land paradise! How foolish humans are. How pitiful and shortsighted.

"There's no use giving a sermon to only three of you. Temples are devoted to the buddhas, but we also have to make mental calculations, you know. Your offerings won't even cover the cost of the lamp oil. No matter how hard I flapped my mouth, it would be a complete loss. Please take back your offerings and carry them home with you. Each of you came here even though you were very worried about trying to make ends meet. And you don't even belong to the temple. I'm impressed beyond words at the sincerity of your belief. You've come all the way here when you must be so very, very busy! Amida Buddha won't forget your devotion. He'll make sure it gets written down in the golden ledger of good deeds consulted by Enma, the judge of souls.[185] It will be calculated in your favor once you get to the other world, no doubt about it. Never, never think your offerings were in vain. Amida is merciful above all else. That's the absolute truth. Trust me."

One of the visitors, an old woman, was crying. "After hearing your precious words," she told the monk, "I feel ashamed from the bottom of my heart. I didn't come here tonight out of any deep belief. I came because my only son is lazy and careless about his work. He's always being hounded by bill collectors, you know. Until now he's managed to escape the collectors on all the settlement days by making up stories, but at the end the year they get very serious. He just couldn't think up a good enough story.

"So he asked me to make a short pilgrimage to a True Pure Land temple.

---

185. King of the nether world and judge of where recently dead souls go after death.

'I'll shout and wail that I can't find my aged mother,' he said. 'Then I'll ask the neighbors to help me look for you. We'll walk around all night banging on drums and gongs, and by the time the sun comes up the collectors will be gone. Pretending someone's lost is an old technique,' he bragged, 'but I'll be the first one ever to escape my creditors by going around shouting for someone to bring back my elderly mother.'

"And that's just what that son of mine's done. He claims it's all right because neighbors have to help out one another in emergencies, no matter how much of an imposition it is. But my son's deceiving them and causing them a frightful amount of trouble. It's a great sin."

Moved by the old woman's confession, another visitor spoke. "I'm from Ise Province," he said. "You know, the way husbands and wives meet is the strangest thing in the whole world. I have no relatives at all in Osaka, but an Ise traveling priest who has a lot of customers here for his amulets hired me to be his porter. I was amazed to see all the business going on in this city, and I judged it would pretty easy for me to make enough to feed myself and have a wife and a child, too. Luckily for me, a salesman I knew who used to sell Osaka goods in the countryside around Nara died. He left behind a two-year-old son, and his wife had a fair complexion and was strong and energetic. Well, we decided to live and work together. I was counting on the boy to take care of me when I got older, so I took the woman's last name and entered her family as her husband.[186] I didn't know very much about the area around Nara, though. Or about being a traveling salesman! In less than six months I'd used up all the little money we had. Around the beginning of the Twelfth Month, I realized I really ought to find a new line of business.

"Once while I was sitting there thinking about what type of business I ought to try, my wife began talking to the child. 'You've got ears, too,' she said, 'so listen well to what I say. Your real daddy was small, but he was very intelligent. And he even did the woman's work of cooking. He let his wife go to bed early while he stayed up until dawn making straw sandals to sell. He himself never wore anything fancy, but he made sure his wife and child had nice cotton clothes at New Year's. This brown robe is something he gave me. Everything used to be better in the old days, didn't it? Cry, child. Cry that you want your daddy.'

"How I regretted then that I'd given up my family for hers! It was very hard to endure each day, but I had no choice. Finally I confessed to my wife that I had a little money that I had lent out back in Ise. I promised her I'd use that to pay off our debts and get us through to the New Year. So I went all the way back to Ise. But the people there to whom I'd lent the money had left, and I

---

186. In the seventeenth century, this was still a widespread form of marriage among commoners, reflecting earlier, more matrilocal customs and bilateral descent.

The son of the elderly woman visiting the temple bangs on a gong (*left*) and leads a group of neighbors through the streets, pretending to look for his lost mother. In front of him, two neighbors carry lanterns. The man holding the long staff is the block elder.

had to come back to Osaka with nothing at all to show for my trip. I finally got home just before supper tonight. Somehow my wife had managed to pound some fresh rice cakes and buy firewood. And the small tray of offerings to the gods was spread with green ferns. Well, I thought, the world has more than worries in it. When you're down, some people look the other way, but others will pick you back up. It made me very happy to see that my wife had managed to pay off our debts and was preparing nicely for New Year's.

'I'm back,' I said, 'and all in one piece.' My wife was in an unusually good mood, and she came with warm water so I could wash my feet. A moment later she brought a tray with sliced raw anchovies on one plate and grilled dried ones on another to celebrate the last night of winter. As I picked up my chopsticks and began to eat, she asked me, 'Did you bring back the money from Ise?' She interrupted me before I could even begin to explain why I hadn't. 'You have a lot of nerve coming back here,' she said. 'A lot. We have to pay for this rice, half a bushel of it, by the end of the Second Month—a month earlier than usual. And because of your bungling, I had to buy it on credit at the year-end rate. That's two and a half times normal. And I'm the collateral! It's illegal, but I had to sign my name. It was the only way I could get the rice. So now I'm going to be that man's servant for life! But don't worry. The only thing you brought with you when you came to this house was your loincloth, so you won't be losing anything. At night it gets very dark, you know. Get out while you can see where you're walking.'

"She took away the tray I was eating from and threw me right out of the house. The neighbors quickly gathered round. 'This is very hard for you as a husband,' one said, 'but unluckily you married into her family.' 'Show you're a real man,' said another. 'Give up and go.' Still another assured me I'd 'find another nice place to go to.' They, too, drove me out—with their words. I was so sad I couldn't even cry. I made up my mind to go back to my hometown tomorrow, but tonight I have no place to stay. So I came here to your temple. Actually, though, I'm registered with your biggest rival, the Lotus sect." The man's frank confession was as touching as it was amusing.

The third visitor laughed loudly. "There's just no way," he said, "I could tell you all about myself. I owe so much, well, if I were at home tonight, my creditors wouldn't let me see the dawn. No one will lend me even ten coppers. I need some saké badly, but I don't have a coin to my name. I thought up a lot of dumb plans this year, but I just couldn't manage to pay back my debts. Then I came up with an idea. A very, very shameful one. I thought a lot of people would come to your temple tonight to hear the story of Holy Man Heitarō, and I planned to take the straw and leather sandals the believers left at the entrance and sell them for the price of some saké. But there's no one here at all. Or at any of your other temples, either. Tonight I couldn't steal the eyes off a buddha statue." The man wept as he revealed himself.

The head monk clapped his hands together in amazement. "Well, well," he said, "poverty leads people to think so many unvirtuous thoughts! Each of you is a buddha in your own body, but you've all had to do bad things in order to get along in the floating world." He was overcome with thoughts about how difficult life was for sentient beings passing through the human realm. Being reborn as humans was a wonderful chance for people to meditate and do good deeds and improve their karma, yet how easy it was for them to go astray.

Just then a woman rushed excitedly into the room. "I would like to inform you," she told the monk, "that your niece has just given birth to a healthy baby. It was a very easy delivery." A moment later someone came in saying, "Just now the cabinetmaker Kuzō got into a terrible argument with a bill collector. He strangled the collector and then committed suicide himself. Tomorrow's New Year's, so his funeral's going to be held later tonight. We're very sorry to trouble you, but we need you to chant some sutras at the crematory."

Into the midst of this commotion came someone from the tailor's. "Unfortunately," he said, "the wadded white silk you gave us to sew into a formal underrobe[187] was, well, stolen. We're investigating, but if it doesn't reappear, we'll compensate you in silver. Rest assured, sir, you won't lose a thing."

"Please pardon the imposition," came the voice of a neighbor from the house to the east, "but tonight our well suddenly caved in. We can't get diggers to come until the fourth, so we'd like to use your well over New Year's."

---

187. To be worn beneath an outer black robe.

Later, the only son of the temple's largest benefactor came in. He'd squandered an outrageous amount of money, and his father had disowned him and told him he never wanted to see him again. His mother had intervened, and a message from her asked the revered head monk to kindly keep the young man with him until the fourth. The monk couldn't refuse this request, either. People like to say that in the Twelfth Month, everyone is too busy finishing the year's business to think about making donations to temples, leaving monks with lots of time on their hands. But monks live in the floating world and are actually just as busy as everyone else at this time of year.

[*Saikaku shū ge*, NKBT 48: 235–239, 254–259, 300–306, translated by Chris Drake]

EJIMA KISEKI AND THE HACHIMONJIYA

Hachimonjiya Jishō (d. 1745), an ukiyo-zōshi writer and a publisher, was born in Kyoto, the son of the Kyoto publisher Hachimonjiya Hachisaemon (1648–1652). After inheriting the business around 1688, Jishō expanded it to include the publication of jōruri texts (*jōruribon*) and illustrated kabuki summary books (*eiri kyōgenbon*), and he eventually surpassed the other publishers in terms of number of titles and copies. The commercially savvy Jishō discovered Ejima Kiseki and formed an alliance with him that had a profound influence on vernacular fiction in the first half of the eighteenth century.

Ejima Kiseki, also born in Kyoto, was the son of a wealthy family of rice-cake merchants (*mochiya*), and in 1694 he became the fourth-generation owner of his family business. As a youth, Kiseki loved drama, and he began to write jōruri in the late 1690s, about the time he became involved with the Hachimonjiya House. At the request of Jishō, who saw the talent in the as-yet unrecognized author, Kiseki wrote *Actor's Vocal Shamisen* (*Yakusha kuchijamisen*), a new kind of actor's critique (*yakusha hyōbanki*), which was published in 1699 and became an enormous hit. From this time until the end of the Tokugawa period, the Hachimonjiya became the main publisher of actor critiques. Following the success of *Actor's Vocal Shamisen*, Jishō asked Kiseki to write ukiyo-zōshi, which resulted in the publication of *Courtesan's Amorous Shamisen* (*Keisei irojamisen*) in 1701. This book was followed by a series of similar "love stories" (*kōshoku mono*) about the pleasure quarters. The Hachimonjiya, which made these books both portable and affordable and added attractive touches such as illustrations by the contemporary artist Nishikawa Sukenobu, flourished as a result of these publications, becoming by the beginning of the eighteenth century the leading publisher of ukiyo-zōshi.

At first, Kiseki's works appeared anonymously, but then they began to appear under the name of Jishō, an unsatisfactory situation for Kiseki. When his family rice-cake business began to decline around 1710, Kiseki sold it and used the money to establish his own publishing house under the name of his son, thus creating a rivalry with the Hachimonjiya. He began to sign his works in 1714, and the rivalry with the Hachimonjiya spurred him to even greater productivity. Kiseki wrote urban commoner (*chōnin mono*) collections such as *Tradesman's War Fan* (*Akindo gunbai uchiwa*, 1712) and "character" pieces (*katagi mono*) such as *Characters of Worldly Young Men* (*Seken musuko katagi*, 1715) and *Characters of Worldly Young Women* (*Seken musume katagi*, 1717). At the end of 1718, Kiseki reconciled with Hachimonjiya Jishō, and the two publishers brought out publications jointly, under both their names. Kiseki's own publishing house closed in 1723, and from then on, the Hachimonjiya house published a number of his books under both his and Jishō's names.

Kiseki's best pieces, such as *Characters of Old Men in the Floating World* (*Ukiyo oyaji katagi*, 1720), part of which is included here, are katagi mono in which he examines a particular social type that was representative of a larger group or category in contemporary chōnin society. In the beginning, Kiseki concentrated on family roles, on daughters in *Characters of Worldly Young Women*, on sons in *Characters of Worldly Young Men*, and on fathers in *Characters of Old Men in the Floating World*. Later ukiyo-zōshi writers wrote about mothers, mistresses, doctors, tea masters, and other occupational categories. Using the names of real places and people, Kiseki describes in concrete and vivid details certain habits and characteristics that he exaggerates to heighten the humor. The katagi mono focus on a specific vice or folly—in this case, miserliness—in preparation for the surprise ending, in the manner of oral storytelling (*rakugo*). *Characters of Old Men in the Floating World*, which contains fifteen stories and is signed by both Kiseki and Jishō, is believed to be the work of Kiseki alone.

In the modern period, Kiseki's works have tended to be overshadowed by those of Saikaku, although Kiseki's influence on late Tokugawa writers was greater than that of Saikaku. After Kiseki's death in 1735, the Hachimonjiya turned, in 1739, to Tada Nanrei (1696–1750) as its ghost writer and continued to publish ukiyo-zōshi.

CHARACTERS OF OLD MEN IN THE FLOATING WORLD
(UKIYO OYAJI KATAGI, 1720)

A Money-Loving, Loan-Sharking Old Man (2:1)

The splendor of the capital—viewed from Kiyomizu Temple's West Gate, this splendor glitters forth in row upon row of tiled roofs that stretch off into the distance. It is also seen in the white walls of the treasure-filled storehouses as they reflect the morning sun, a sight that evokes, even in summer, thoughts of a snowy dawn. No wind pines among the evergreens of this realm,[188] and

---

188. There is a pun here on *matsu* (pine), the first character of Matsudaira and the original

thousand-year birds sport among its clouds,[189] marking the munificence of the present regime.

The city fans out below as far as the eye can see, and the number of dwellings, once said to total 98,000,[190] has so risen that this figure is but ancient history. Now even the bamboo grove beyond Hideyoshi's earthwork stands within its boundaries.[191]

The people of the capital labor, each at his own family trade, and enjoy in moments of leisure refined diversions and entertainments that chase from their minds the pain of the year's toil. Thanks to their work, they are able to earn fair sums of money with which they can provide their families comfort and put their own minds to rest, all because they dwell here in the capital with its myriad freedoms.

Here in the city of opportunity, here among the numerous masters for whichever of the arts one might wish to learn, there was an old man who lacked all artistic accomplishment and whose sole pleasure in life was the accumulation of wealth. He was naturally robust, like a pine that cleaves with its roots to a craggy boulder. And in Matsunaga Teitoku's own Hanasaki Ward,[192] next door to the very house in which the poet had long dwelled, this old man had opened a moneylender's shop under the name of Koishiya Mataemon.[193] There he made his living, convinced that there was nothing more important than his work, and although he cared not at all for the cherry blossom viewing in spring, he still chose to wear blossom-hued padded clothes because they were durable. An abacus of twenty-five rows served as his constant plaything by day; his pillow, at night. He and Teitoku had lived in the same ward for forty years, but the fact that Teitoku composed haikai merely indicated, this old fogy believed, that the poet was a man of discernment who was consulted about provincial legal suits.

"Teitoku may live just next door," he thought, "but never in my life will I

---

name of the ruling Tokugawa family. Hence the line praises the shōgunate and no doubt pleased the censors.

189. A reference to cranes, popularly believed to have a life span of a thousand years and therefore to be auspicious symbols of longevity.

190. This number, which appears in the *Nihon ryakki* (1596), refers to the number of dwellings in Kyoto in the second half of the fifteenth century.

191. This earthwork, built by Toyotomi Hideyoshi in 1591, once marked the outer boundary of the capital. These first two paragraphs have been lifted almost verbatim from Saikaku's *Twenty Unfilial Children of Japan* (Honchō nijū fukō).

192. Matsunaga Teitoku (1571–1653) was a noted scholar and haikai poet, the founder of the Teimon haikai school. Hanasaki Ward (also known as Inari-chō) is located in present-day Shimogyō-ku, in Kyoto. The "matsu" of Matsunaga is a pivot word, serving as the "pine," a symbol of longevity, of the previous clause as well as the first character of the poet's name. Kiseki took this section about Teitoku from *Saikaku nagori no tomo*.

193. Koishiya, or House of the Pebbles, suggests a comic contrast with the craggy boulder of the previous phrase.

start a legal suit, so there's not a chance I'll ever beg him to write me any of those haikai." If even in our flowering capital there can live such a codger as this, how can we laugh at a country bumpkin who mistakes a miniature flint box for a *hina* doll's cotton-scrap spool?[194]

Although advancing years had left him as shrunken and shriveled as a dried salmon, this oldster had lost nothing on top. Rather than look to some future world, he set his sights squarely on this one, and since his youth he had never known an idle moment. He would pound flat a damaged pipe bowl to insert in place of one *sen* in a string of a hundred and would take old pieces of string even from the scrap heap to refashion as money cords.[195] Having thus strung out his moneymaking ways over many years, he had become the second richest man in the capital, well known for the loans he negotiated with the military lords. The rumor that the old man's fortune had reached thirty thousand *kanme* certainly could not have been far wrong. Despite his great wealth, he had never bought a new house or made a single improvement on his crude shingle-roofed dwelling, a small place, barely twelve feet across, that he had inherited from his parents. Here he resided with a single diminutive (not to mention light-eating) man-servant and also a sixtyish maid about whom he would never have to worry about the possibility of loose behavior. To the pickles he ate the year around, he added nothing out of the ordinary, not even one Third Month sea bream[196] or a single bunch of mushrooms, even when they could be had for a pittance. "Look, don't touch" was his rule. When thirsty, he drank hot water flavored with rice powder. As for lighting, he set a single oil lamp in the center of the house and snuffed it out at bedtime, for the wild scampering of mice in the dark did not bother him in the least.

Even for his loincloth, silk was out of the question, and he usually wore old padded garments of cotton. For ceremonial functions in the district or for dinners with other moneyed souls to discuss loans to straitened lords, he did, however, take into account what others thought. Despite his miserliness, he would adjourn to a used-clothing store in his debt and force the proprietor to lend him some ill-fitting garments. There he would put together an outfit, even down to the tissue paper he carried. His return from these social functions took him immediately back to the shop to exchange these borrowed clothes for his old cotton ones.

---

194. Hina dolls, made of paper or porcelain and dressed in aristocratic dress, were set out on display during the Doll Festival. The bumpkin mistakenly believes that an incense burner is a cotton-scrap spool being used by the nearest doll.

195. The copper *sen* coin had a hole in the middle so that a hundred of them (actually ninety-six were normally accepted for the value of one hundred) could be strung together on a cord. By inserting the flattened pipe bowl, the old man cheated by making up cords of only ninety-five *sen*.

196. The Third Month was when bream were caught in great quantities in the Inland Sea and so were cheap.

His sole interest was in accumulating interest, and he pursued it as avidly as a connoisseur of the pleasure quarters follows his crazed quest for beauty. He lent money to east-bank teahouses[197] and actors at 50 percent interest and, as if that was not enough, set the repayment period at three months. "Who needs festivals?" the old man might have asked, for when it came time, those who could not pay up did their dancing to the tune of doubled interest. It was with such schemes that this old boy made seventeen months' profit within twelve months.

Hoarding money alone brought him pleasure. With hair white as snow, he ran about the capital doing his lending and collecting with more vigor than a young man not yet twenty.[198] He squeezed a 10 percent handling fee even from Buddhist mourners ordering a funeral bier for a departed parishioner. The jeweled eyes of a statue of a devil? Gouge them out! The gold leaf of a statue of the Buddha? Strip it off! Nothing escaped untouched by this greedy old man.

For most people, the desire for money is the desire to enjoy security in life and to have a few modest diversions and amusements that will provide pleasure for the body and comfort for the soul. But the uppermost thought in the old man's mind was that a family would only be a drain on the household finances, so he had no wife and thus no children, either.

"This fortune of yours—who were you thinking of leaving it to?" queried the head priest of his family temple in a sermonizing tone. "You can't take it with you when you die. Give a thought to choosing an heir and making arrangements to have the proper services performed on your behalf after your death. If you don't, your riches will go to a total stranger. Now is that what you want?"

Perhaps the old man took these words to heart, for afterward he made a nephew his adopted son, but even so, he did not take the youth into his home. Rather, he turned right around and apprenticed the boy to another shop. "Upon my death," the old man told the boy, "all my wealth will pass to you. And as a sign of your appreciation of this great favor, you will bring me a gift of one hundred *mon* at both the Bon Festival and New Year's."

No, while he lived, the old man was in no way generously inclined toward the boy. In fact, he even went so far as to lay claim to the possessions of this apprentice, whose clothes had been provided by his new master.

One day the leading actor of an itinerant troupe invited the old man to his inn to ask for a loan of five *ryō* in gold, but he said nothing beforehand of his purpose. He treated the old man to a bowl of noodles and proceeded to use on him all the flattery at his command. In the end, when the actor made his

---

197. Many small theaters and teahouses were located on the east bank of the Kamo River around the Shijō area in downtown Kyoto.

198. Alludes to a line in *The Tales of Ise*, sec. 9, that gives the height of snow-covered Fuji as equal to twenty mountains the size of Mount Hiei stacked one on top of another.

request, the old man's answer as he sat there with wine cup in hand was noncommittal.

"If I don't raise this money," thought the actor, "how can I hope to get my costumes out of hock? And without costumes there's no way I can do the tour I've been hired for."

He therefore asked a fellow actor to approach the old man again with his request. "I'll come by this evening, and we can discuss it then," the old man replied.

"Surely he wouldn't say he'd come again if he was going to refuse," said the actor to himself. "But just in case, tonight I'll go all out on a meal that will shame him into agreeing. Once in my net, he won't be able to say no."

As bait for this fish, he had various delicacies prepared—soup made from carp, a light rice dish with grilled eel, and bamboo shoots with skewered abalone that had been stewed. When the old man arrived, the actor gave him the royal treatment, and having from the outset replaced the small wine cups with large ones, he plied his guest with saké.

"If I may be so bold," the actor said when the drinking had reached a peak, "there is the matter of the five *ryō* that we discussed the other day. It is my most earnest desire that you bestow upon me your kind favor in the form of a loan of this amount." And he bowed low, humbly touching the floor with his hands.

"Although I have never before lent to itinerant actors," the old man answered, "I am willing to grant you the loan you feel so compelled to seek. But as for the seven-months' interest that will accrue between the present Fifth Month and the Eleventh Month repayment date you have proposed, I shall withdraw this sum from the principal at the outset and then turn over to you the remainder. Are we in agreement on this matter?"

Although this would put him in a bind, the actor thought that were he to object, the old goat might withdraw from the transaction altogether. "Please, if you will allow me to be so presumptuous, might I ask that you accept the interest together with the principal in the Eleventh Month?" he requested.

"Impossible, I fear," replied the old man, to whom compassion was an unknown quality. "Here, bring me your abacus, and I'll work it out for you. I'll show you how the money can come in handy that much sooner."

"This is welcome news indeed," said the actor. "We actors lack any talent for arithmetic. Therefore I ask only that a beneficial arrangement be made for me, whatever it may be." And he handed over his abacus to the old man, who took charge of the instrument and started to calculate, explaining the details of his scheme to the actor, the would-be borrower.

"First, bear in mind that for every *ryō* gold piece, the interest comes to six *monme* in silver. Figuring at the exchange rate of sixty *monme* to the *ryō*, we have a total in silver of three hundred *monme*, and the interest on this principal comes to thirty *monme* per month. Now, when we subtract a 10 percent handling charge of thirty *monme* from the principal, we are left with 270 *monme*.

The moneylender (*upper right*) is busy counting his interest on an abacus while the actor entertains him with refreshments. Moneylender: "The abacus has spoken." Actor: "Every piece of silver disappears when calculated on that abacus!" Woman: "The noodles have arrived." Deliveryman: "I came as quickly as I could." From the 1720 edition. (From NKBZ 37, *Kana-zōshi shū, ukiyo-zōshi shū,* by permission of Shōgakukan)

And from that principal must be subtracted and turned over to me immediately, as agreed, interest at the rate of thirty *monme* per month, with a month's interest being added at the end of each of the two-month intervals in which the principal is still outstanding. That means, therefore, a total of ten months' interest, hence a total interest in silver of three hundred *monme*.

"However, it's impossible to subtract that from a principal of 270 *monme*. As the principal is short by thirty *monme*," he concluded, flicking the abacus's beads into place and showing his calculation to the actor, "I ask that you turn over this amount to me immediately to cover the deficit."

The actor was astounded. "If there's a thirty-*mon* lack that I am to make up before I've borrowed even a single *mon*," he said furiously, "what, may I ask, are you lending me now?"

The old man eyed him doubtfully. "The abacus has spoken. This is what happens when you deal with people unschooled in numbers," he muttered as he took his leave. "Such slow wits. . . ."

In the end, alas, not only did the actor fail to obtain his loan; he lost as well the two carefully prepared feasts that the old man had gobbled down.

[*Kana-zōshi shū,Ukiyo-zōshi shū,* NKBZ 37: 483–489, translated by Charles Fox]

Chapter 4

EARLY HAIKAI POETRY AND POETICS

Haikai is both a specific poetic genre and a particular mode of discourse, an attitude toward language, literature, and tradition. It is an approach that is most prominently displayed in linked verse, the seventeen-syllable *hokku* (later called *haiku*), *haibun* (haikai prose), and *haiga* (haikai painting) but that also pervaded much of early modern Japanese culture and literature. Haikai, which originated in the medieval period and peaked in the early modern period, grew out of the interaction between the vernacular and the classical language, between the new popular, largely urban, commoner- and samurai-based culture and the residual classical tradition, with its refined aristocratic associations, which haikai parodied, transformed, and translated into contemporary language and form. Haikai imagination, which took pleasure in the juxtaposition and collision of these two seemingly incongruous worlds and languages, humorously inverted and recast established cultural associations and conventions, particularly the "poetic essence" (*hon'i*) of classical poetic topics.

The seventeen-syllable (5–7–5) hokku, or opening verse, could be composed as an independent poem or as the beginning of a haikai linked-verse sequence. In addition to the 5–7–5 structure, the hokku required a *kigo* (seasonal word), an encoded sign that indicated a specific season and had specific poetic associations (the autumn wind, for example, suggesting loneliness or desolation), and a *kireji* (cutting word), which divided the hokku into two parts, usually after the first or second line. The cutting word, which causes a syntactic break and is marked by a dash in the English translations, creates a space between the two parts of the hokku, often causing the two parts to resonate and forcing the reader to find some internal connection. The hokku could be either a "single-object" poem, focusing on a single image, or a "combination" poem, juxtaposing two different elements. But even "single-object" poems usually have two parts, and the different parts of the "combination" poem are, at least on one level, elements of a larger single scene. Frequently, one part of the hokku, most often the part with the seasonal word, has a classical seasonal topic, and the other part features an image from contemporary, popular culture, thus creating a tension between the two, with the popular image or vernacular phrase giving new life or perspective to the classical topic or the classical topic giving poetic shape or overtones to the contemporary image.

Waka, the thirty-one-syllable classical poem, generally excluded all forms of language not found in the refined, aristocratic diction of the Heian classics, particularly the *Kokinshū*, *The Tales of Ise*, and *The Tale of Genji*. The subject matter was likewise confined to a cluster of highly elegant topics, usually pertaining to love and the four seasons. The same restrictions applied to *renga*, or classical linked verse, which continued the classical tradition into the late medieval period. By contrast, haikai freely used "haikai words" (*haigon*)—vernacular, Chinese, Buddhist terms, slang, common sayings—which challenged, inverted, or otherwise subverted classical poetry and often were scatological, bawdy, or corporeal. The *Mongrel Tsukuba Collection* (*Inu tsukuba shū*, 1532), one of the earliest anthologies of haikai, begins with

| kasumi no koromo | A robe of mist |
| suso wa nurekeri | soaked at the hem |

The added verse (*tsukeku*) composed by Yamazaki Sōkan (d. 1538), one of the pioneers of haikai and thought to be the editor of the *Mongrel Tsukuba Collection*, is

Sahohime no	Princess Saho
haru tachinagara	with the coming of spring
shito o shite	stands pissing

It was a convention of classical poetry that Sahohime, the beautiful goddess of spring, should stand in the midst of a spring mist, which became her robe. The added verse, which uses the vernacular phrase *shito o su* (to piss), parodies that classical convention by having the princess urinate while standing, as commoner women did in those days. The same homonym *tatsu*, which means both "to stand" and "to begin" (as in the coming of spring), applies to both socio-cultural worlds.

MATSUNAGA TEITOKU AND THE
TEIMON SCHOOL

In the first half of the seventeenth century, haikai radically changed with the founding of the Teimon school by Matsunaga Teitoku (1571–1653), a noted scholar, waka poet, and teacher of classical literature. Teitoku and his disciples wanted to maintain and encourage haikai as a popular art, one that would be accessible to a wide but not necessarily highly educated audience, and also to make it a respectable form and part of the larger poetic tradition. Their answer was to concentrate on using "haikai words," which gave haikai its popular character, while rejecting or tempering the kind of ribald, irreverent humor and language found in earlier haikai, which they regarded as immoral and vulgar. The Teimon school continued the lexical play and parody that characterized earlier haikai but restricted the haikai words to Chinese words (*kango*) and acceptable vernacular Japanese, excluding vulgar and highly colloquial phrases. The *New Mongrel Tsukuba Collection* (*Shinzō inu tsukuba shū*, 1643), a haikai anthology edited by Teitoku, presented Teitoku's response to the "robe of mist" poem cited earlier:

> kasumi no koromo   A robe of mist
> suso wa nurekeri   soaked at the hem

> tennin ya   Heavenly creatures
> amakudaru rashi   descending it seems—
> haru no umi   the sea of spring

Except for the haikai word *tennin* (heavenly creatures), a Chinese compound with no vulgar implications, the content is the same as that of an elegant verse in classical renga. *The Puppy Collection* (*Enoko shū*, 1633), edited by Teitoku's disciples, contains the following hokku by Teitoku under the topic of New Year's Day (*ganjitsu*):

> kasumi sae   Even the spring mist
> madara ni tatsu ya rises in spots and patches—
> tora no toshi   Year of the Tiger

In this poem, Teitoku links "spring mist" (*kasumi*), a classical word, to "tiger" (*tora*), a haikai word, through two "pivot words" (which are used twice): *madara ni* (in spots and patches), associated with both mist and tiger, and *tatsu* (to stand, rise, begin), a verb for the tiger "getting up," the mist "rising," and the New Year (the seasonal topic) "beginning." In Teimon fashion, the gap between the classical image (spring mist) and the contemporary vernacular is humorously bridged through puns and lexical associations.

KITAMURA KIGIN

Kitamura Kigin (1624–1705), a disciple of Matsunaga Teitoku and a prominent member of the Teimon school of haikai, was a noted poet, scholar, and commentator on such Heian classics as *The Tale of Genji* and Sei Shōnagon's *Pillow Book*. One of the important objectives of the Teimon school and of Kigin in particular was educating commoners in the poetic and literary tradition, specifically the poetic and literary associations of seasonal words, which were required in each hokku for linking by means of word association. In *Essential Style for Haikai* (*Haikai yōi fūtei*, 1673), Kigin wrote:

> In haikai, words are used to describe the ways of the present world, but that style must also be one with the poetry of the *Kokinshū*. Since haikai is a poetic art, the heart of the poet should enter into the way of classical poetry, admire the cherry blossoms, yearn for the moon, and establish the way of father and son, ruler and subject. It should not forget love between men and women. . . . If one does not read books of poetry like *The Tale of Genji* or *The Pillow Book*, if one does not soak one's spirit in the ancient style, if one does not use that language in various ways, how can one know true haikai?

THE MOUNTAIN WELL (*YAMA NO I*, 1648)

The Mountain Well, a haikai manual written by Kigin in 1648, categorizes poetic words and topics by season, explains their poetic associations and use, and gives illustrative examples of haiku. Its elegant prose passages have also been considered an early form of haibun, or haikai prose. *The Mountain Well*, which was extensively used by later haikai poets, is the forerunner of *kiyose* or *saijiki*, poetic seasonal almanacs, which modern haiku poets still use to learn seasonal words and poetic associations. The following passage alludes to the various classical sources and legends related to the summer topic of the firefly, associated in the literary tradition with burning passion. It also demonstrates the method of haikai linking in which the participant uses a word from the previous verse as a link to a new verse. Here the writer moves from "firefly" to "Hyōbukyō" to "Itaru" to "buttocks of monkeys" to "fox fires," as one would in haikai linked verse.

Fireflies

In composing haikai about fireflies, those that mingle among the wild pinks are said to share the feelings of Prince Hyōbukyō[1] and the ones that jump at the

---

1. This passage alludes to the "Fireflies" chapter in *The Tale of Genji*, in which Prince Hyōbukyō, the brother of the Shining Genji, catches a glimpse of the young Tamakazura in the light of the fireflies that Genji released behind her screen, causing Prince Hyōbukyō to immediately fall in love with her. The wild pinks (*tokonatsu*) refer to Tamakazura.

lilies are said to be like the amorous Minamoto Itaru.[2] The ones that fly on Mount Hiyoshi are compared to the red buttocks of monkeys,[3] and the ones that glitter on Mount Inari are thought to be fox fires.[4] Fireflies are also said to be the soul of China's Baosi[5] or the fire that shone in our country's Tamamo no mae.[6] Furthermore, poetry reveals the way in which the fireflies remain still on a moonlit night while wagging their rear ends in the darkness, or the way they light up the water's edge as if camphor or moxa were in the river, or the way they look like stars—like the Pleiades or shooting stars.

> Kōyasan   At Mount Kōya
> tani no hotaru mo   Even the fireflies in the valley
> hijiri kana   are holy men[7]

[*Kinsei haiku haikai bunshū*, NKBZ 42: 455–464, translated by Haruo Shirane]

NISHIYAMA SŌIN AND DANRIN HAIKAI

Danrin haikai became popular in the 1670s, especially in the Enpō era (1673–1681), and dominated the haikai world after the decline of the Teimon school in the late 1660s. It used many of the techniques found in Teimon haikai: word association (*engo*), homophonic wordplay (*kakekotoba*), parody, and visual comparisons (*mitate*). However, for Nishiyama Sōin (1605–1682), the founder of

---

2. This passage refers to episode 39 in the Heian-period *Tales of Ise* in which Minamoto Itaru peers into a woman's carriage with the aid of light from fireflies.

3. Mount Hiyoshi, also known as Mount Hiei, is a mountain in Ōmi (Shiga) Province, behind Hiyoshi Shrine. The messenger to the god of Hiyoshi Shrine is the monkey.

4. Inari Shrine is at the western foot of Mount Inari, north of Fushimi in Kyoto. The word "foxfire" (*kitsunebi*), which originally referred to the fire that was thought to come from the mouth of a fox, refers to strange fires or lights that appear in the hills and fields at night. Inari Shrine was associated with both foxes and foxfire.

5. Baosi (J. Hōji) was the beloved daughter of Emperor You (J. Yūō) of Zhou. According to the *Kagakushū*, a Muromachi-period dictionary, after Baosi died, he became Japan's Tamamo no mae.

6. Tamamo no mae was a nine-tailed golden fox that bewitched the cloistered emperor Toba by disguising itself as a beautiful woman. The emperor loved Tamamo no mae, but the light that shone from her pained him, and he had to call on Miura no suke Yoshiaki to exorcise her. Tamamo no mae, according to legend, was turned into the rock Sesshōseki ("The rock that kills") in Nasuno in Shimotsuke Province.

7. Kōyasan, in Wakayama Prefecture, is the headquarters of the Buddhist Shingon sect. The hokku plays on the word *hijiri*, which means both "holy men" and "fire buttock" (lower part of a hearth), implying homosexuality, which was not uncommon among priests in the medieval period. *Hijiri*, *hotaru*, and *Kōya* are *tsukeai*, or associated words used for verse linking.

Danrin haikai, haikai was not an intermediary stage for entering the world of classical poetry. Unlike the haikai of the Teimon school, which was based in Kyoto, the center of aristocratic culture, and evoked the classical tradition, Danrin haikai developed in Osaka, the new center of commerce, where a new society of increasingly wealthy and powerful urban commoners was creating its own culture. If Teitoku tried to impose order on linked verse, Sōin, who came from Osaka, stressed spontaneity and freedom of form and movement, linking verses without excessive concern for rules or precedent. Indicative of the Danrin's iconoclastic character was the practice of using an excessive number of syllables (*jiamari*)—surpassing the formal limit of seventeen—usually adding to the last five syllables of the hokku. Instead of placing constraints on haikai's language or avoiding the vulgarity of the *Mongrel Tsukuba Collection*, Danrin poets explored the myriad aspects of contemporary culture, including that of the pleasure quarters and the popular kabuki theater.

Like the Teimon poets before them, the Danrin poets also parodied classical poetry and narratives like *The Tales of Ise* and well-known historical events, but they did this in a bolder and more dynamic fashion, not hesitating to concentrate on the popular or vulgar. Far less educated than their Teimon predecessors, the Danrin poets' knowledge of the classics was extremely circumscribed, limited almost entirely to the famous classical poems in the *Kokinshū* and *Shinkokinshū* (*New Collection of Old and New Poems*, 1205); to well-known passages from nō plays, *The Tales of Ise*, and *The Tale of Genji*; or to some of the Chinese poetry by Bo Juyi (772–846) and others. Danrin poets used these classical fragments, along with *yoriai* (established lexical associations), to link verses, and it was these kinds of associations that helped Ihara Saikaku to engage in rapid solo sequences of immense length—the *yakazu haikai*, or "countless arrow," haikai.

Danrin poets deliberately heightened the tension between haikai words and classical diction, believing that the greater the collision was between the two languages, the greater the haikai effect would be. *Teachings Collection* (*Indōshū*, 1684), a Danrin haikai handbook edited by Saikoku (1647–1695), a merchant from Bungo (Kyūshū) and a disciple of Saikaku, uses the following verse as an example of the Danrin method:

mine no hana	Making sea lions and whales
no nami ni ashika	swim in the cherry blossom waves
kujira o oyogase	at the hilltop

This hokku links cherry blossoms—which were closely associated with waves and hilltops in classical poetry—with sea lions (*ashika*) and whales (*kujira*), two haikai words. The poem comically deconstructs a familiar classical convention, "the waves of cherry blossoms," by using this figurative cliché in its original, literal meaning as the "waves of water" in which sea lions and whales swim. The resulting disjunction, in which two different socially inscribed languages inhabit the same word, produced not only haikai humor but what Itchū (1639–1711), a Danrin spokesman, referred to as *gūgen* (allegory), making possible what is not possible. Saikoku observed that it is easy to combine deer with mountain but that it takes ingenuity to make the sea lions and whales swim in the waves of flowers at the mountain peak.

nagamu tote	Gazing at
hana ni mo itashi	the cherry blossoms
kubi no hone	I hurt my neck bone

Sōin here alludes to a noted Saigyō poem in the *Shinkokinshū* (1205; Spring 2, no. 126): "Thinking to gaze at them, I grew extremely close to the cherry blossoms, making the parting ever so painful" (*nagamu to te hana ni mo itaku narenureba chiru wakare koso kanashikarikere*). He then explodes the serious tone and content of the foundation poem: the classical word *itashi* (extremely) becomes the haikai vernacular word *itashi* (it hurts), and the sorrow of parting with the short-lived cherry blossoms is replaced by the neck pain resulting from gazing up at the cherry blossoms for too long.

OKANISHI ICHŪ

When Nishiyama Sōin published a hundred-verse sequence entitled *Swarming Mosquitoes: One Hundred Verses* (*Kabashira hyakku*, 1674), the Teimon school immediately criticized it in a work called *Astringent Fan* (*Shibu-uchiwa*), whose title suggests a fan to beat off the Danrin mosquitoes. *Astringent Fan* also takes to task Sōin's verses for "having lost the essence of poetry" and notes: "Isn't haikai after all a form of *waka*? Poetry is a way to assist government and to edify people." It fell to Okanishi Ichū (1637–1711), a disciple of Sōin and the leading Danrin theoretician, to defend the Danrin's position.

HAIKAI PRIMER (HAIKAI MŌGYŪ, 1675)

In the passage from *Haikai Primer* translated here, Ichū argues that the wild humor, the unrestrained expression of imagination and spirit, and the relativity of perspective found in the *Zhuangzi* represent the essence of haikai.

The essence of the *Zhuangzi* is completely embodied in haikai. Lin Xiyi writes in his notes on the "Carefree Wandering" chapter of the *Zhuangzi*: "Most readers don't understand the place where the author intends to be humorous;

it is a technique that people today call disconnected speech."[8] Lin also writes in his notes: "When reading the *Zhuangzi*, one finds that the essence of the text lies in allegory [*gūgen*]."

The spirit of the *Zhuangzi* can, for example, be seen in the passage "In the Northern Depth there is a fish called Kun. The fish is so huge that no one knows how many thousand *li* it measures. The fish changes and becomes a bird called Peng. No one knows how many thousand *li* the back of the bird measures. When the sea begins to move, Peng sets off for the Southern Depth from the north. Its wings beat the water for three thousand *li*, and riding on the wind, the bird rises up ninety thousand *li*."[9] Here is the heavenly wandering of mind, the ultimate freedom of change and spontaneity. In the same way, today's haikai should free itself from the narrow mind and leap into the vastness of heaven and earth. It should mix things that exist with those that do not and be unrestricted in its methods and styles. That is the truth of haikai. We should maintain this spirit when composing verses on mountain travel, outings in the fields, cherry blossom viewing, and appreciating the autumn leaves. Isn't this the *carefree wandering* of haikai? Let us take the great length of the five mountains of Mount Tai that extend over Qi and Lu and make it tiny, and let us make the tip of an autumn hair huge. Let us take the short life of a child who died at three months and make it long, and let us make the seven hundred years of Pengzu's life a passing moment.[10] Such mixing of big and small, of the eternal and the ephemeral, the making of fabrication truth and of truth fabrication, the taking of right as wrong and of wrong as right—these not only are the allegories found in *Zhuangzi* but also the very nature of haikai.

[*Koten haibungaku taikei* 4: 83, 98, translated by Peipei Qiu]

---

8. Lin Xiyi was a scholar and official of Song China. His dates of birth and death are unknown. His commentary on the *Zhuangzi, Zhuangzi Juanzhai kouyi* (1253), was reprinted in Japan during the seventeenth century and was widely read by the haikai poets.

9. Ichū's quotation seems to be an altered version of the original. For an English translation of the original, see Burton Watson, trans., *The Complete Works of Chuang tzu* (New York: Columbia University Press, 1968), p. 29.

10. These two sentences allude to specific passages in *Zhuangzi*: "There is nothing in the world bigger than the tip of an autumn hair, and Mount Tai is tiny. No one has lived longer than a dead child, and Pengzu died young." (Watson, *Complete Works of Chuang tzu*, p. 43). As Watson notes, the strands of animal fur were believed to grow particularly fine in autumn; hence "the tip of an autumn hair" is a metaphor for something extremely tiny.

Chapter 5

THE POETRY AND PROSE OF MATSUO BASHŌ

Matsuo Bashō (1644–1694) was born in the castle town of Ueno, in Iga Province (Mie), approximately thirty miles southeast of Kyoto. Although Bashō's grand-father and great-grandfather had belonged to the samurai class, for reasons that are unclear, they were disenfranchised. By Bashō's generation, the family had fallen so low that they had become farmers with only tenuous ties to the samurai class. Bashō at first served as a domestic employee of the Tōdō house, presum-ably as a companion to Toshitada (better known by his haikai name, Sengin), the son of the Tōdō lord. During this time, Bashō adopted the haikai name Munefusa, or Sōbō, and became a devotee of the Teimon style of haikai, the school led by Matsunaga Teitoku. In 1666, Sengin died prematurely, at the age of twenty-five, apparently forcing Bashō to leave the Tōdō house and severing his last connection with the samurai class.

In the spring of 1672, at the age of twenty-eight, Bashō moved to Edo to establish himself as a haikai master who could charge fees for his services. There he came under the influence of Nishiyama Sōin, with whom he composed poetry in 1675. By the mid-1670s, Bashō had attracted the nucleus of his disciples and patrons—notably Kikaku, Ransetsu, Sanpū, and Ranran—who played a major role in the formation of what later came to be known as the Bashō circle (Shōmon). In the winter of 1680, at the age of thirty-six, Bashō left Edo and retreated to Fukagawa, on the banks of the Sumida River. By moving to the outskirts of Edo, Bashō also left behind the urban haikai, which by then had become highly commercialized. During the next four years, he wrote in the so-called Chinese style, creating the persona of the recluse poet who was opposed to the materialism and social ambitions of the new urban culture. One of Bashō's literary achievements was fusing the earlier recluse poet tradition established by waka and kanshi poets like Saigyō, Sōgi, and Ishikawa Jōzan with the new commoner genre of haikai and haibun (haikai prose). He took his poetic name from the *bashō* plant, or Japanese plantain, whose large leaves sometimes tear in the wind, thus representing the fragility of the hermit-traveler's life.

In the fall of 1684, Bashō began the first of a series of journeys that occupied much of the remaining ten years of his life. On his first journey, commemorated in his travel diary *Skeleton in the Fields* (*Nozarashi kikō*), Bashō traveled west, visiting the provinces of Owari (Aichi), Mino (Gifu), and Ōmi (Shiga)—especially the area south of Lake Biwa—and recruiting followers in all three areas before returning to Edo in the summer of 1685. At Nagoya, he composed linked verse with a local group led by Kakei that resulted in the *Withering Gusts* (*Kogarashi*) *kasen*, a thirty-six-verse haikai sequence, and in 1684 they compiled *Winter Days* (*Fuyu no hi*), the first major anthology of the Bashō circle and the beginning of what is now referred to as the Bashō style (Shōfū). In the early winter of 1687, in a journey later commemorated in *Backpack Notes* (*Oi no kobumi*), Bashō once again left Edo, returned to Iga Province, and then traveled to Yoshino, Nara, Suma, and Akashi, along the Inland Sea. At the end of the journey, in the fall of 1688, Bashō, accompanied by his disciple Etsujin, visited Obasuteyama (Abandoned Old Women Mountain) in Sarashina (Shinano), the site of the famous autumn moon, before returning to Edo at the end of the month—a journey commemorated in *Journey to Sarashina* (*Sarashina kikō*).

In the spring of 1689, Bashō departed once again, this time with his disciple Sora, for Mutsu, in the northeast, in an expedition later commemorated in *Narrow Road to the Deep North* (*Oku no hosomichi*). The arduous journey started in Fukagawa in mid-May 1689 and ended a little over five months and almost fifteen hundred miles later at Ōgaki in Mino. For the next two years, Bashō remained in the Kyoto-Osaka area. In September 1690, *Gourd* (*Hisago*) was published, an anthology of haikai compiled by his disciples at Ōmi (Lake Biwa) that embodied his new poetics of lightness (*karumi*). Together with Kyorai and Bonchō, two disciples in Kyoto, Bashō then edited *Monkey's Straw Coat* (*Sarumino*), the magnum opus of the Bashō school, which was published in the summer of 1691. He finally returned to Edo in December 1691, at the age of forty-seven. There he became involved with a new group of Edo poets, centered on another disciple, Yaba, with whom he pursued the poetic ideal of lightness and eventually produced *Charcoal Sack* (*Sumidawara*), which was published in 1694. Bashō died the same year on a journey to Osaka.

BASHŌ AND THE ART OF HAIKAI

As stated earlier, the art of haikai encompasses a series of related genres: hokku, linked verse, haibun, and haiga (haikai painting), the last usually combining a hokku and a visual image. All these genres embodied what Bashō called "haikai spirit" (*haii*). First of all, haikai spirit implied the interaction of diverse languages and subcultures, particularly between the new popular culture and the poetic tradition, and the humor and interest resulting from the sociolinguistic incongruity or difference between the two. Second, haikai spirit meant taking pleasure in recontextualization: defamiliarization, dislocating habitual, conventionalized perceptions, *and* their refamiliarization, recasting established poetic topics into contemporary language and culture. The haikai spirit was also marked by a constant search for novelty and new perspectives. Finally, the haikai imagination implied the ability to interact in a playful, lively dialogue that produced communal art.

Of particular interest here is the complex relationship between haikai and tradition, especially the refiguring of cultural memory. Bashō looked for poetic and spiritual inspiration to classical and medieval poets, especially Nōin (998–1050?), Saigyō (1118–1190), and Sōgi (1421–1502)—all of whom were travelers and poet-priests—and he was strongly influenced by Chinese poetry and poetics, especially those of the mid-Tang poets Li Bo and Du Fu. At the same time, Bashō was a poet of haikai, which, by its very nature, was parodic, oppositional, and immersed in popular culture. One result of this cohabitation of contrastive languages and subcultures was the emergence in the seventeenth century of a culture of *mitate* (literally, seeing by comparison), which moved back and forth between the two starkly different worlds, that of the Japanese and Chinese "classics" and that of the new popular literature and drama, each providing a lens or filter with which to view the other. In contrast to allusive variation (*honkadori*), the poetic technique of "borrowing" (*toru*) from a classical "foundation poem" (*honka*)—which assumed with classical poetry a common base of diction, tone, and subject matter—the Edo-period mitate was characterized by startling, dramatic, and often witty changes that it made in the target text. Artists such as Hishikawa Moronobu (1618–1694), a pioneer of ukiyo-e prints, used the technique of mitate in the visual arts, both alluding to and radically transforming the topics and imagery of the classical tradition into a contemporary, commoner form.

Bashō's haikai differed from the mitate found in Moronobu's ukiyo-e prints in that the popular culture in his poetry and prose was not that of the stylish men and women of the great urban centers' floating world but that of the mundane, everyday lives of farmers and fishermen in the provinces. The new popular literature and drama, including haikai, originated in urban society, especially that of the three major metropolises of Kyoto, Osaka, and Edo. Teitoku, the leader of Teimon haikai, was based in Kyoto; Sōin and Saikaku, the leaders of Danrin haikai, were from Osaka; but Bashō was a socially marginal figure. His poetry and prose are pervaded by liminal or marginal figures such as the beggar, the old man, the outcast, and the traveler, no doubt reflecting his own provincial origins. Likewise, his allusions are not to the Heian classical figures of Ariwara no Narihira, Ono no Komachi, and the shining Genji—the famous lovers so often referred to in contemporary ukiyo-e and by Ihara Saikaku—but to medieval traveler poets such as Saigyō and Sōgi or Chinese poets such as Li Bo and Du Fu. The difference is perhaps most evident in Bashō's treatment of nō drama. In contrast to the typical ukiyo-e mitate print, which alluded to the more erotic and elegant aspects of nō, especially the "women plays," Bashō focused on the muted image of the *waki*, or traveling monk, and the fate of the tragic heroes of the "warrior plays."

In the seventeenth century, as in previous centuries, a sharp distinction was maintained between the traditional genres—such as the thirty-one-syllable waka, Chinese poetry, and nō drama—and the new, popular genres—haikai, ukiyo-zōshi, jōruri, and kabuki. The popular genres such as Saikaku's ukiyo-zōshi frequently parodied their classical counterparts by borrowing the elegant, aristocratic forms of traditional literature and giving them a popular, vulgar, or erotic content. In a reverse movement, Bashō gave a popular genre (haikai) a spiritual or refined content, or, more accurately, he sought out the spiritual and poetic in commoner culture, giving to the contemporary language and subject matter, particularly that drawn from provincial life, the kind of nuances and sentiments hitherto found only in classical or Chinese poetry. In this way, Bashō was able to raise haikai—which until then had been considered a form of light entertainment—into a serious genre and vehicle for cultural transmission that, with the modern haiku, achieved a canonical status.

HOKKU

kareeda ni	Crows resting
karasu no tomarikeri	on a withered branch—
aki no kure	evening in autumn[1]

---

1. From *Arano*. The original version in *Diary of the East* (*Azuma nikki*) is *kareeda ni karasu no tomaritaru ya aki no kure*. Bashō first composed this hokku in the spring of 1681, during his late Danrin and Chinese-style period. *Aki no kure* can be read as either "end of autumn" or "autumn nightfall." In *Hakusen shū* (1698), a collection of Bashō's hokku, this hokku is preceded by the title "On Evening in Autumn" (*Aki no kure to wa*), indicating that the poem was written on a seasonal topic closely associated with Fujiwara Shunzei (d. 1204) and his medieval aesthetics of quiet, meditative loneliness. Because crows perched on a withered branch was a popular subject in Chinese ink painting, Bashō's hokku juxtaposes a medieval waka topic with a Chinese painting motif, causing the two to resonate in montage fashion.

A *haiga* (haikai sketch), on the Chinese painting theme of cold crows on a withered branch. The painting is by Morikawa Kyoriku (1656–1715), Bashō's disciple and his painting instructor, and the calligraphy and poem are by Bashō: "On a withered branch, a crow comes to rest—end of autumn" (*Kareeda ni / karasu no tomarikeri / aki no kure*). Probably done around 1692/1693 while Kyoriku, a samurai from Hikone, was in Edo. Signed "Bashō Tōsei." (42.1 in. × 12.2 in. Courtesy of Idemitsu Museum of Arts)

Going out on the beach while the light is still faint:

akebono ya—	Early dawn—
shirauo shiroki	whitefish, an inch
koto issun	of whiteness[2]

Having stayed once more at the residence of Master Tōyō, I was about to leave for the Eastern Provinces.

botan shibe fukaku	From deep within
wakeizuru hachi no—	the peony pistils, withdrawing
nagori kana	regretfully, the bee[3]

Spending a whole day on the beach:

umi kurete	The sea darkening—
kamo no koe	the voice of a wild duck
honoka ni shiroshi	faintly white[4]

furuike ya	An old pond—
kawazu tobikomu	a frog leaps in,
mizu no oto	the sound of water[5]

---

2. Bashō composed this hokku in the Eleventh Month of 1684 while visiting the Ise area during the *Skeleton in the Fields* (*Nozarashi kikō*) journey. Drawing on the phonic connotations of *shirauo* (literally, white fish), Bashō establishes a connotative correspondence between the semitranslucent "whiteness" (*shiroki koto*) of the tiny fish and the pale, faint light of early dawn (*akebono*). The poem has a melodic rhythm, resulting from the repeated "o" vowel mixed with the consonantal "s."

3. This is a good example of a semiallegorical poetic greeting. Bashō composed this hokku, which appears in *Skeleton in the Fields*, when he left the house of Tōyō (1653–1712), a friend in Atsuta (Nagoya), in the Fourth Month of 1685. The bee, representing Bashō, is resting peacefully in the peony, an elegant summer flower that symbolizes Tōyō's residence, joyfully imbibing the rich pollen of the pistils, but now, with much reluctance, it must leave. The hokku is an expression of gratitude and a farewell not only to Tōyō but to all the Nagoya-area poets who have hosted him on this journey.

4. The opening verse of a *kasen* sequence composed in Atsuta, in Nagoya, in 1685. The poet looks out toward the voice of the wild duck (*kamo*), which has disappeared with the approaching darkness, and sees only a faint whiteness (*shiroshi* implies a kind of translucency), which may be the waves or the reflection of the sea in the dusk. *Kamo* is a seasonal word for winter.

5. Written in 1686 and collected in *Spring Days* (*Haru no hi*). Since the ancient period, the frog had been admired for its singing and its beautiful voice. In the Heian period it became associated with spring, the *yamabuki*, the bright yellow globeflower (*Kerria japonica*), and limpid mountain streams. According to one source, Kikaku, one of Bashō's disciples, suggested that Bashō use *yamabuki* in the opening phrase. Instead, Bashō works against the classical associations

On the road:

kutabirete	Exhausted,
yado karu koro ya	time to find a lodging—
fuji no hana	hanging wisteria[6]

Lodging for the night at Akashi:

takotsubo ya	Octopus traps—
hakanaki yume o	fleeting dreams
natsu no tsuki	under the summer moon[7]

hototogisu	The cuckoo—
kieyuku kata ya	where it disappears
shima hitotsu	a single island[8]

---

of the frog. In place of the plaintive voice of the frog singing in the rapids or calling out for its lover, Bashō evokes the sound of the frog jumping into the water. And instead of the elegant image of a frog in a fresh mountain stream beneath the *yamabuki*, the hokku presents a stagnant pond. At the same time, the hokku offers a fresh twist to the seasonal association of the frog with spring: the sudden movement of the frog, which suggests rebirth and the awakening of life in spring, is contrasted with the implicit winter stillness of the old pond.

6. This hokku, which Bashō composed in 1688, appears in *Backpack Notes* (*Oi no kobumi*). The wisteria (*fuji no hana*), with its long drooping flowers, is blooming outside the lodge even as it functions as a metaphor for the traveler's heart.

7. Bashō composed this poem, which appears in *Backpack Notes*, in the Fourth Month of 1688. The octopus traps were lowered in the afternoon and raised the next morning, after the octopus had crawled inside. The octopus in the jars—and implicitly the troops of the Heike clan who were massacred on these shores at the end of the twelfth century and whose ghosts subsequently appear before the traveler in *Backpack Notes*—are having "fleeting dreams," not knowing that they are about to be harvested. Bashō juxtaposes the "summer moon" (*natsu no tsuki*), which the classical tradition deemed to be as brief as the summer night and thus associated with ephemerality, and the "octopus traps" (*takotsubo*), a vernacular word, giving new life to the theme of impermanence. The poem is intended to be humorous and sad at the same time.

8. Diverging from the classical poetic association of the cuckoo (*hototogisu*), which was its singing, Bashō focuses here on its arrowlike flight. In this poem, which Bashō wrote in 1688 during his *Backpack Notes* journey, the speaker implicitly hears the cuckoo, but by the time he looks up, it has disappeared, replaced by a single island, presumably Awajishima, the small island across the bay from Suma and Akashi, where the speaker stands. In haikai fashion, the hokku is also parodic, twisting a well-known classical poem in the *Senzaishū*: "When I gaze in the direction of the crying cuckoo, only the moon lingers in the dawn" (1188; Summer, no. 161). Another possible pretext is the following poem in the *Kokinshū*, attributed to Hitomaro: "Faintly, in the morning mist on Akashi Bay, it disappears behind an island, the boat I long for" (905, Travel, no. 409). In Bashō's hokku, the flight of the disappearing cuckoo, which the poet implicitly longs to see, becomes the path of the ship, which "disappears" behind (*shimagakureyuku*) Awajishima, a "single island."

While sleeping in a lodge in the capital and hearing each night the sorrowful chanting of the Kūya pilgrims:

karazake mo	Dried salmon
Kūya no yase mo	the gauntness of a Kūya pilgrim
kan no uchi	in the cold season[9]
kogarashi ya	Withering winds—
hohobare itamu	the face of a man
hito no kao	pained by swollen cheeks[10]
mugimeshi ni	A cat's wife—
yatsururu koi ka	grown thin from
neko no tsuma—	love and barley?[11]
hototogisu	A cuckoo—
koe yokotau ya	the voice lies stretched
mizu no ue	over the water[12]

---

9. Bashō composed this hokku while visiting Kyoto in the Twelfth Month of 1690 and later included it in *Monkey's Straw Coat* (*Sarumino*). Kūya were lay monks or pilgrims who commemorated the anniversary of the death of Priest Kūya by begging and chanting Buddhist songs in the streets of Kyoto for forty-eight days beginning in the middle of the Eleventh Month. *Kan* (cold season), a roughly thirty-day period from the Twelfth Month through the beginning of the First Month (February), was the coldest part of the year. The three parts—dried salmon (*karazake*), the gauntness of the Kūya pilgrim (*Kūya no yase*), and the cold season (*kan no uchi*)—each of which is accentuated by a hard beginning "k" consonant and by the repeated *mo* (also), suggest three dimensions (material, human, and seasonal) of the loneliness of a traveler on a distant journey.

10. Composed in the winter of 1691. The two parts of the hokku—separated by the cutting word *ya*—can be read together as one continuous scene or separately as two parts reverberating against each other. In the former, a person suffering from mumps (*hohobare*, literally, swollen cheeks) stands outside, his or her face contorted by the *kogarashi*, the strong winds that blow the leaves off the trees in the winter. In the latter, the person's face inflamed by and suffering from mumps echoes the cold, stinging wind. The expectations generated by withering winds, a classical seasonal topic associated with cold winter landscapes, are humorously undercut by the haikai phrase *hohobare itamu* (pained by swollen cheeks), which then leads to a double reversal: after the initial collision, the reader discovers a connotative fusion between the withering winds and the painfully swollen cheeks.

11. "Cat's love for its mate" (*neko no tsumagoi*), later simply called cat's love (*neko no koi*), was a haikai seasonal topic that became popular in the Edo period. Bashō composed this hokku in 1691 and included it in *Monkey's Straw Coat*. Bashō humorously depicts a female cat that has grown emaciated not only from being fed only barley—a situation that suggests a poor farmhouse—but from intense lovemaking. (*Yatsururu* modifies both *mugimeshi* and *koi*, implying "emaciating barley and love.")

12. Bashō apparently wrote this hokku in the Fourth Month of 1693 after being urged by his

hiyahiya to	Taking a midday nap
kabe o fumaete	feet planted
hirune kana	on a cool wall[13]

kiku no ka ya	Chrysanthemum scent—
Nara ni wa furuki	in Nara ancient statues
hotoketachi	of the Buddha[14]

aki fukaki	Autumn deepening—
tonari wa nani o	my neighbor
suru hito zo	how does he live, I wonder?[15]

kono michi ya	This road—
yuku hito nashi ni	no one goes down it
aki no kure	autumn's end[16]

---

disciples to compose on the topic of "cuckoos on the water's edge." As the cuckoo flies overhead, it makes a sharp penetrating cry, which "lies stretched" (*yokotō*), hanging over the quiet surface of the water, probably at dusk or night when it traditionally sings. The cuckoo quickly disappears, but the sound lingers, like an overtone.

13. This hokku, which appears in *Backpack Diary* (*Oi nikki*) and which Bashō composed in 1694 at the residence of Mokusetsu in Ōtsu (near Lake Biwa), uses *hiyahiya* (cool) as a seasonal word for autumn. The speaker, cooling the bottoms of his bare feet on the wall, has fallen asleep on a hot afternoon. The implied topic is lingering summer heat (*zansho*), which is captured from a haikai in a humorous angle, in the feet, through which the speaker feels the arrival of autumn.

14. Bashō composed this hokku in 1694, on Chrysanthemum Festival Day (Chōyō), which fell on the ninth day of the Ninth Month, while stopping at Nara on the way to Osaka on his last journey. Nara, the capital of Japan in the eighth century, is known for its many temples and buddha statues. The chrysanthemum, considered the aristocrat of flowers in classical poetry and a seasonal word for late autumn, possess a strong but refined fragrance. The many buddhas in the ancient capital of Nara evoke a similar sense of dignity, solemnity, and refinement as well as nostalgia for a bygone era.

15. Bashō composed this hokku, which appears in *Backpack Diary*, in the autumn of 1694, shortly before he died in Osaka. Bashō had been invited to a poem party at the home of one of his close followers, but he did not feel well enough to go and instead sent a poem that subtly expresses his deep regret at not being able to meet this friends. The poem (in highly colloquial language) suggests the loneliness of a traveler implicitly seeking companionship, the loneliness of those who live together and yet apart in urban society, or the loneliness of life itself, particularly in the face of death—all of which resonate with late autumn (*aki fukaki*), associated in classical poetry with loneliness and sorrow.

16. Bashō composed this poem in the late autumn of 1694, at the end of his life. The hokku, which was written at a large haikai gathering, can be read as an expression of disappointment that, at the end of his life, in the autumn of his career—*aki no kure* can mean either "autumn's end" or "autumn evening"—he is alone, and/or as an expression of disappointment at the lack of sympathetic poetic partners, as an expression of desire for those who can engage in the poetic dialogue necessary to continue on this difficult journey.

Composed while ill:

tabi ni yande	Sick on a journey
yume wa kareno o	dreams roam about
kakemeguru	on a withered moor[17]

[NKBZ 41: 61–282, translated by Haruo Shirane]

COMPOSING HAIKU

The successive verses in a linked-verse sequence were read both together and individually, as parts of a large scene and as a fragmentary collage. The same kind of tension existed in the seventeen-syllable hokku, which was both split and joined by the "cutting word" (*kireji*), generally marked by a dash in the English translation.

COMBINING

Morikawa Kyoriku (1656–1715), one of Bashō's foremost disciples, argued that the "combination poem" (*toriawase*), which brought together different topics in a single hokku, was the most important technique of the Bashō school and, furthermore, that it should leap beyond the established associations of a given topic. The end result was the unexpected "combination" of classical topics and popular subject matter, traditional and contemporary subcultures, classical diction and haikai words. The following is from Kyoriku's *Haikai Dialogue* (*Haikai mondō*, 1697).

The Master: "In composing a hokku, my students begin by searching within the topic. This will not yield anything. But if they begin by searching outside the topic, they will find a plethora of material."

I said, "I discovered this while reading *Desolate Field* and *Monkey's Straw Coat*. My approach can be compared to placing the topic in a box, climbing on top of that box, and viewing heaven and earth from that perspective."

The Master: "That is absolutely correct. That is why you were able to come up with verses like

kangiku no	Next to even
tonari mo ari ya	the winter chrysanthemums—
ikedaikon	fresh radish"[18]

---

17. Bashō's last poem, written four days before his death on the twelfth day of the Tenth Month of 1694, during a journey in Osaka, suggests a journey that remains unfinished.

18. Kyoriku composed this hokku in the winter of 1692 when he visited the Bashō hut at Fukagawa outside Edo. Using the metaphor of the box, Kyoriku argues that the poet must look

I then realized the following. If I search within the boundary of the topic, there will be nothing new. Even if, by some remote chance, something is left, if a neighbor decides to compose on the same topic on the same day, the neighbor will undoubtedly find it. Since the neighbor is following the same route, he or she is bound to come across it. This would be even truer if someone from a distant province or village were looking in a place with which I was not familiar. What would I find? On the other hand, if I leap beyond the boundary, it will be like a child who thinks differently from its parents or parents who conceive differently from their child.

The Master: "Ultimately, you should think of the hokku as something that combines. Those who are good at combining or bringing together two topics are superior poets."

[KHT 10: 147]

In *Three Booklets* (*Sanzōshi*), a treatise recording Bashō's teachings, Dohō (1657–1730), Bashō's most talented and faithful Iga disciple, argues that the hokku should have "the spirit of going and returning," a movement similar to that between a previous verse and an added verse in a linked-verse sequence. As the example suggests, Bashō's notion of the "combination poem" did not mean simply juxtaposing disparate elements but also finding some underlying connection between the seemingly disparate elements.

The hokku involves a spirit of the mind that moves in a specific direction and then returns. An example is

yamazato wa	In the mountain village
manzai ososhi	the New Year dancers are late—
ume no hana	plum blossoms[19]

---

beyond the "boundary" (*kuruwa*, originally meaning "castle wall"), that is, beyond the established associations of the topic. In classical renga, the added verse was typically linked to the previous verse by *yoriai*, established poetic and literary associations, which were conveniently listed in renga handbooks. In the example that Bashō praises, Kyoriku goes beyond the "boundary" of "winter chrysanthemums" (*kangiku*), a classical seasonal topic, by combining it with a vernacular word, *ikedaikon*, the large white radishes that farmers pulled out of the field and buried "alive" (*ike*) in the dirt, where they were stored until spring. The winter chrysanthemum was a flower (usually yellow, sometimes white) that bloomed in the winter after the other flowers had died and that was admired in classical poetry for its ability to endure the frost. The juxtaposed images, which at first glance seem antithetical, are unexpectedly joined by their implicit ability to endure the winter cold "alive." The hokku can also be read as a greeting from the guest, Kyoriku, who implicitly compares himself to the lowly radish lying at the feet of the elegant chrysanthemum, the master and host Bashō.

19. Bashō composed this hokku in the early spring of 1691, during his stay in the Kyoto-Osaka area following the journey to the Deep North. *Manzai*, a vernacular word, refers to the costumed, itinerant performers who went from house to house performing songs and dances in celebration

The poet first states that in the mountain village, the *manzai*, the New Year dancers, are late and then comes back to reveal that the plum trees are in bloom. This spirit of going and returning lies at the heart of the hokku. If the poem were simply "in the mountain village / the New Year dancers are late," it would have no more force than a single verse in a linked-verse sequence.[20]

[NKBZ 51: 592]

Many modern readers, perhaps influenced by mimetic notions of poetry, tend to read Bashō's hokku as the depiction or sketch of a single scene, but as the following passage in *Kyorai's Gleanings* (*Kyoraishō*) suggests, Bashō's hokku often started out as part of a "combination poem" with the poet trying to find the corresponding or matching part.

Shimogyō ya   Southern Kyoto—
yuki tsumu ue no   on top of the piled snow
yoru no ame   the evening rain

Initially, the first line was missing. Everyone, beginning with Bashō, tried his hand at capping the verse, and the Master finally decided on this version. Bonchō remained unconvinced. In response, the Master said, "Bonchō, cap this verse and reveal your talent. If you can find a better alternative, I will never discuss haikai again."[21]

[NKBZ 51: 434–435]

---

of the New Year. The manzai dancers make their rounds early in the New Year, at the beginning of the First Month (February). The plum trees usually bloom at the beginning of spring, in the First Month, but slightly later in the cold of the mountain village. The phrase "the New Year dancers are late" (*manzai ososhi*) implies that they arrived after finishing their rounds in the town, by which time the plum trees are already in bloom. The two parts of the hokku are thus joined by a seasonal congruence: the late blooming of the plum tree in the mountain village and the late arrival of the manzai combine to create a sense of delayed spring in the mountains. The original hokku probably served as a poetic greeting to Bashō's hosts at Iga, praising the beauty of the spring scene.

20. To borrow Dohō's metaphor, the reader first "goes" to part A, explores its connotations, and then "returns" by another route to part B, seeking to find a common path between A and B. The emotional or atmospheric flow first moves in one direction and then returns in a different direction, resulting in a mixing of the two currents.

21. The passage reveals that the poet did not begin with the place—Shimogyō, the southern part of Kyoto, from Third Avenue (Sanjō) south—and attempt to describe it. Instead, he started with an image of rain quietly falling on a blanket of snow, which in the Japanese context suggests warmth, and attempted to match its connotations. In contrast to the aristocratic northern half of Kyoto, southern Kyoto was a bustling, energetic area filled with merchants and craftsmen, which echoes the warm feeling of the accumulated snow.

INTERMEDIARIES

To bridge the gap between the two parts of the combination poem, Kyoriku urged the use of an "intermediary word" to bring together the incongruous elements, especially traditional seasonal topics and vernacular words. In *Haikai Dialogue*, Kyoriku notes that the "newness" (*atarashimi*) in the late Bashō-school anthologies lies entirely in the use of these intermediary words.

Recently, I thought that "scent of plum blossoms" would make a good combination with "blue lacquer bowl" and tried various middle phrases, but none of them felt right.

ume ga ka ya	Scent of plum blossoms—
shōjin-namasu ni	pickled vegetables and
asagiwan	a blue lacquer bowl
ume ga ka ya	Scent of plum blossoms—
sue-narabetaru	arranged in a row
asagiwan	blue lacquer bowls
ume ga ka no	Scent of plum blossoms
dokotomonashi ni	from somewhere or other
asagiwan	a blue lacquer bowl

I tried these various possibilities, but none of them was successful. When the subject matter and the combination are excellent but a good hokku does not materialize, it means that the necessary intermediary has yet to be found. After more searching, I came up with the following:

ume ga ka ya	Scent of plum blossoms—
kyaku no hana ni wa	beneath the guest's nose
asagiwan	a blue lacquer bowl[22]

[KHT 10: 147–148]

---

22. Kyoriku attempted to cross the gap between the plum blossom scent (*ume ga ka*), a classical topic, and the vernacular word *asagiwan*, a pale blue or aqua lacquer bowl painted with birds and flowers. He tried various intermediaries until he settled on "beneath the guest's nose" (*kyaku no hana ni wa*), an intermediary that brings together the plum blossom scent and the aqua bowl to suggest a larger banquet scene: the guest, smelling the fragrance of plum blossoms, raises the elegant bowl to his mouth. The fragrance of the plum blossoms resonates with the atmosphere of the exquisitely painted bowl. Here the poet "combines" by going outside the circle of established associations but needs an intermediary to do it.

SINGLE-OBJECT POETRY

In response to Kyoriku's emphasis on the combination poem and his claim that combining separate topics or images was Bashō's central technique, Kyorai (1651–1704), another of Bashō's disciples, argued that although combining was certainly important, it did not take precedence over other techniques and that Bashō also composed "single-object" poems, which focused on one topic and flowed smoothly from start to finish, without the leap or gap found in the combination poem. The following is from *Kyorai's Gleanings*, Kyorai's notes on Bashō's teachings.

The Master said, "A hokku that moves smoothly from the opening five syllables to the end is a superb verse."

Shadō [another disciple] remarked, "The master once told me, 'The hokku is not, as you believe, something that brings together two or three different things. Compose the hokku so that it flows like gold being hit and flattened by a hammer.'". . .

Kyorai: "If a poet composes by combining separate things, he can compose many verses and compose them quickly. Beginning poets should know this. But when one becomes an accomplished poet, it is no longer a question of combining or not combining."

[NKBZ 51: 498]

In *Travel Lodging Discussion* (*Tabineron*, 1699), Kyorai even went so far as to say that all hokku are single-object poems.

Generally speaking, all hokku focus on a single object. Allow me to explain and to provide some examples. First of all, the following verse is on a single object:

> kegoromo ni   Warmly wrapped
> tsutsumite nukushi   in its feathered robe—
> kamo no ashi   feet of the wild duck[23]

Bashō

They say that the Master took delight in this poem and told Shikō, "This hokku was deliberately composed on a single object." Other examples include

---

23. In the classical tradition, the wild duck (*kamo*) was often found floating on a winter pond or sea, and its figure and voice were associated with loneliness, longing for home, uncertainty, and, most of all, coldness. In a haikai reversal, this wild duck appears warm (*nukushi*), its feet tucked beneath its "feathered robe" (*kegoromo*).

iza saraba   Let's go
yukimi ni korobu   snow viewing
tokoro made   until we tumble over!

                                                        Bashō

utsukushiki kao   Scratching
kaku kiji no   its beautiful face—
kezume kana   the pheasant's spurs

                                                        Kikaku

. . . Someone might say that the "feet of the wild duck" and "the feathered robe" form a combination or that the poet combines "the pheasant's spurs" with "face," but what could they say "snow viewing" was combined with? When the late Master spoke about combining objects, he appeared to distinguish between those that worked inside the boundary and those that worked outside it. Kyoriku, it seems, defined the combination poem as something that went outside the boundary. But some poems, such as the following, combine inside the boundary, just as some combine outside the boundary:

haru mo yaya   Spring
keshiki totonou   gradually taking form—
tsuki to ume   moon and plum blossoms[24]

                                                        Bashō

[KHT 10: 206–207]

---

24. Kyorai argues that since the combination poem can be composed quickly and relatively easily, it is suitable for beginners, but that the more accomplished poet will not limit himself to this particular technique. Furthermore, a number of good combination poems, especially impromptu ones, remain within the "boundary" or circle of established poetic associations. Here Kyorai suggests that when beginners compose combination poems, they should go outside the established poetic associations, which makes it easier to find new material and avoid clichés. The rule, however, does not apply to accomplished poets, who can either discover new connections within the boundary of established associations or approach the traditional associations in new, haikai-esque ways. For example, "spring," "moon," and "plum blossoms," which appear together in Bashō's hokku, were closely associated in the classical poetry, especially as a result of *The Tale of Genji*, in which the fragrant plum blossoms in the light of the misty evening moon represent one of the beauties of spring. The haikai character of Bashō's hokku lay instead in the manner of the expression, especially in the rhythm. The middle phrase—which comes to a slow stop, ending on three drawn-out successive "o" sounds, the last sliding into the vowel "u"—suggests the gradual vernal movement that brings together the moon and the plum blossoms.

GREETINGS

Much of Bashō's prose and poetry, like that of his contemporaries, was dialogic and fulfilled socioreligious functions such as complimenting a host, expressing gratitude, bidding farewell, making an offering to the land, or consoling the spirit of a dead person. Almost half the roughly 250 hokku in Bashō's three most famous travel accounts originally were social addresses or replies of this sort.

> shiragiku no   White chrysanthemums—
> me ni tatete   not a speck of dust
> chiri mo nashi   to catch the eye

This hokku, which Bashō composed at the residence of Sonome, or Madame Sono (1664–1726), one of his disciples, is typical of Bashō's mature style in that at the same time it describes the purity and elegance of a white chrysanthemum, it compliments the host. As a greeting, a hokku could pay homage not only to the host or companion but also to the spirits of places, to ancient poets, and to religious figures. In the following excerpt from *Three Booklets*, Dohō comments on this technique.

> toginaosu   The holy mirror,
> kagami mo kiyoshi   repolished, is also pure—
> yuki no hana   blossoms of snow

> ume koite   Longing for the plum blossoms
> unohana ogamu   I pray to the white deutzia—
> namida kana   tearful eyes[25]

The first poem, on snow, was composed on the occasion of the reconstruction of the Atsuta Shrine. The first five syllables—"repolish" [*toginaosu*]—directly express the spirit of rebuilding and pay homage to the shrine. The second poem, on plum blossoms, was composed on the death of Bishop Daiten of the Engakuji temple. The poet pays tribute by comparing the deceased priest to

---

25. Dohō here selects two poems by Bashō, a celebration and a lament, in which the speaker's respect is expressed through an object that reflects the "status" (*kurai*) of the addressee. In the first hokku, from *Backpack Notes*, the purity (*kiyoshi*) of the repolished mirror, which resonates with the whiteness of the snowflakes, symbolizes the purity and holiness of the newly reconstructed shrine. In the second hokku, from *Skeleton in the Fields*, the elegant plum blossoms reflect the refinement and high status of the bishop, who died in the First Month (February), when the plum tree is in bloom. Bashō, who sent this hokku to his disciple Kikaku, did not hear of the bishop's death until the summer, the Fourth Month (May), the season of the deutzia, an ornamental shrub with white flower clusters that remind the poet of the whitish plum blossoms. The poet pays homage to the shrine and the bishop through the images of the holy mirror / snow, and the plum blossoms / white deutzia, respectively.

plum blossoms and then bowing before the white deutzia [*unohana*] which were in bloom when the poem was composed. In both cases, the poet's feelings are revealed indirectly through an object that captures the character and status of the person or place being addressed.

[NKBZ 51: 559]

OVERTONES

One of the characteristics of the landscape style, particularly that of Bashō's haikai, was that it often infused the external landscape (*kei*) with human emotion or sentiment (*jō*)—a fusion influenced by both the classical tradition and the Chinese poetry that came into fashion in the 1680s. In *Principles of Chinese Poetry for Beginners* (*Shogaku shihō*, 1680), Kaibara Ekiken notes: "In poetry, the scene is always in the emotion, and the emotion is always in the scene." In *Ten Discussions of Haikai* (*Haikai jūron*, 1719), Shikō, one of Bashō's late disciples, develops this notion into one of the central tenets of the Bashō style, using the famous frog poem, which was composed in 1686, as an example.

furuike ya	An old pond—
kawazu tobikomu	a frog leaps in,
mizu no oto	the sound of water

Truly, when it comes to what is called contemporary haikai, one is reminded of the poem on the frog in the old pond. Although it appears that the poem possesses absolutely no emotion, Bashō has managed to suggest the emotion of quiet loneliness.[26] This is what is called the overtones of poetry. Isn't this what haikai is all about?

[*Haisho taikei*, vol. 9, translated by Haruo Shirane]

THE ART OF LINKED VERSE

Before Bashō's time, the standard length for both renga and haikai was the hundred-verse sequence (*hyakuin*). From around 1678, however, when Bashō began to develop his own style, he turned to the much shorter thirty-six-verse sequence (*kasen*), which had rarely been used in classical renga. Haikai, like renga, could be composed by a single individual as a solo composition (*dokugin*). But for Bashō, haikai was a communal activity in which two or more participants took turns adding verses to create a sequence. Each added verse (*tsukeku*) was joined to the previous verse (*maeku*) to form a new poetic world

---

26. In other words, the poem implies that the observer is a recluse who appreciates the quiet loneliness, enough to hear the sound of the frog and to be sensitive to the approach of spring.

while pushing off from the poetic world that had been created by the combination of the previous verse and the penultimate verse (*uchikoshi*). Like classical linked verse, haikai depended on two simultaneous movements: the meeting (*tsukeai*), or the link to the previous verse (*maeku*), and the parting (*yukiyō*), or the separation from the verse before the previous verse (*uchikoshi*).

The manner in which the added verse reworked, transformed, and twisted, usually in humorous fashion, the world and language of the previous verse and the penultimate verse was directly related to the way in which haikai parodied classical texts and conventions: both involved pushing off and recontextualizing existing texts or established worlds so as to create new meanings and perspectives. At the same time, the complex rules of linked verse guaranteed a sense of continuity amid the constant change and movement and ensured that the cultural memory, particularly as embodied in the seasonal landscape, would be passed on, thereby providing the foundation for linkage and imaginative play. As a form of popular literature, haikai reflected the variegated social and economic worlds of the participants—who ranged from high-ranking samurai to merchants, farmers, doctors, and priests—but it also provided an important window onto "imagined worlds," onto the newly discovered "past" of China and Japan, giving the participants a sense of sharing both a history and a cultural tradition.

Bashō and his disciples distinguished three types of links, (1) the word link, based on lexical or classical associations, which was typical of earlier haikai; (2) the content link, based on scenic or narrative extension; and (3) the scent link, in which the added verse was joined to the previous verse by scent, mood, atmosphere, or other subtle connotations. Bashō's haikai are generally a mixture of content links and/or scent links. In turn, the scent links were divided into various subcategories such as reverberation (*hibiki*) and status (*kurai*).

REVERBERATION LINK

In a reverberation link, an excited, dramatic mood—an emotional intensity and tension—passes from one verse to the next. The following is from *Kyorai's Gleanings* (*Kyoraishō*).

kure'en ni	On a veranda
gin-kawarake	smashing to bits
o uchikudaki	a silver-glazed bowl
hihosoki tachi no	Watch out for
soru koto o miyo	the drawn saber![27]

---

27. In the first verse, someone smashes a decorative, silver-glazed bowl on a mansion veranda, suggesting an upper-class setting. This dramatic tension "reverberates" in the added verse, in

The Master gave this link as an example, his right hand pretending to smash a bowl and his left hand pretending to draw a saber.

[NKBZ 51: 504]

STATUS LINK

Another type of scent link is the status link, in which the two verses are joined by socioeconomic connotations, usually based on clothing, possessions, or other material signs. The following is from *Kyorai's Gleanings*.

Bonen asked, "What is a status link?" Kyorai answered, "A status link occurs when one grasps the social status of the content of the previous verse and adds a verse that matches that social status. Even if the added verse is superb, if it does not match the social status found in the previous verse, the result will be disharmony. Allow me to explain, using a love verse by the Master.

uwaoki no	Even while chopping
hoshina kizamu mo	the dried vegetables
uwa no sora	her heart was aflutter

| uma ni denu hi wa | When the horse stays in |
| uchi de koisuru | the groom makes love at home.[28] |

In the first verse, the woman is not the principal wife or a female attendant in the house of a samurai or that of a townsman. Instead, she is of lower social status, a maid working at a post station or a warehouse—a status matched by the content of the next verse, about a groom.

[NKBZ 51: 504–505]

WITHERING GUSTS (*KOGARASHI*, 1684)

The thirty-six-verse sequence called *Withering Gusts* is often thought to mark the beginning of the Bashō style, revealing the socioliterary dynamics of Bashō's communal art. In the fall of 1684, at the age of forty, Bashō left his home on the outskirts of Edo and began a journey that was later commemorated in *Skeleton in the Fields*

---

which a narrow-bodied saber, the type worn by aristocrats, is drawn, presumably in preparation for a violent confrontation.

28. Dried vegetables (*hoshina*)—probably dried radish leaves—were placed on top of a bowl of rice to make an inexpensive dinner. Realizing from the nature of the food that the character in the preceding verse was a woman of extremely low station, perhaps a maid working in a warehouse, Bashō matched her with a groom, a man of equally low social status.

(*Nozarashi kikō*). In the winter, he arrived in Nagoya, one of the major urban centers of that time, where he was invited to compose haikai with a group of local poets—Tokoku, Yasui, Jūgo, Shōhei, and Kakei—with whom he eventually produced *Winter Days* (*Fuyu no hi*), the first major haikai anthology of the Bashō school. With the exception of Kakei, a doctor of samurai origin and the local haikai leader, all the participants in *Withering Gusts* were young, well-educated, wealthy urban merchants. Yasui was an affluent dry-goods merchant; Jūgo, a well-to-do lumber dealer; and Tokoku, a successful rice merchant. As the honored guest and visiting haikai master, Bashō composed the hokku, or opening verse. Yasui, the host, wrote the second verse, and Kakei, the local haikai master, added the third verse. The following is the first half of the sequence:

kyōku	*Mad Verse*
kogarashi no	In the withering gusts
mi wa Chikusai ni	a wanderer—how like Chikusai
nitaru kana	I have become![29]

Bashō

taso ya tobashiru	Who's that?
kasa no sazanka	sasanqua spraying over a sedge hat[30]

Yasui

ariake no	Making
mondo ni sakaya	the Master of Early Dawn
tsukurasete	construct a brewery[31]

Kakei

---

29. Bashō, the guest of honor, greets his Nagoya hosts in self-deprecatory and humorous fashion, comparing himself with Chikusai, the eponymous antihero of a popular seventeenth-century comic novel (*kana-zōshi*) in which the protagonist, a poor, eccentric, quack doctor from Kyoto, embarks for Edo, composing comic waka (*kyōka*) along the way, and arrives in Nagoya, his clothes in tatters. Bashō has similarly arrived in Nagoya, blown about by the withering gusts, a seasonal word for winter and an implicit metaphor for the hardship of journey and his lowly position. The verse, particularly the opening word *kyōku* (mad verse), is an implicit invitation from Bashō to his hosts to join him in a new poetics of poetic madness (*fūkyō*) in which the poet's pursuit of poetic beauty—especially dark, cold, and impoverished images—is so extreme as to appear mad to the world.

30. The second verse, which is read together with the opening verse, must take up what is left unstated by the hokku, maintaining the same season and ending with a nominal. The white or crimson flowers of the sasanqua, a seasonal word for winter, scatter over or spray from the large traveler's hat, perhaps as a result of the withering gusts. Yasui, the host of the session, implies that although his guest may claim to be an impoverished, windblown traveler, his appearance is bright and colorful, thereby tacitly accepting Bashō's invitation to poetic madness.

31. Kakei, the local haikai master, shifts from winter to autumn. *Ariake* (early dawn) is a

kashira no tsuyu o   A red-haired horse
furuu akauma   shaking dew off its mane[32]

                                              Jūgo

Chōsen no   Korean grass
hosori-susuki no   the long thin blades
nioinaki   colorless[33]

                                              Tokoku

hi no chirichiri ni   In the scattered light
no ni kome o karu   harvesting rice plants in the fields[34]

                                              Shōhei

waga io wa   My grass hut—
sagi ni yado kasu   where I offer the heron
atari nite   a lodging[35]

                                              Yasui

kami hayasu ma o   Having to hide
shinobu mi no hodo   while the hair grows back[36]

                                              Bashō

---

seasonal word for autumn. The elegant nickname Master of Early Dawn suggests a colorful, elegant dandy, thus pushing off from the dark figure in the opening verse. The Master of Early Dawn, whose hat is decorated with sasanqua flowers, has been ordered to oversee the construction of a brewery.

32. The red-haired horse, which appears to be tied up in front of a brewery or a wine bar, is a packhorse and may be carrying a barrel of wine. In the fashion of a status link, the socioeconomic connotations of the red-haired horse, which belongs to the world of merchants and farmers, directly echo that of the wine bar or brewery. The horse is shaking dew—associated with autumn and early morning—off its mane.

33. The red-haired horse now stands in a large field of grass in Korea, which was thought at the time to be a kind of wild frontier with vast plains. Here the colorless grass, suggesting late autumn, echoes the packhorse's sense of impoverishment and coldness.

34. Shōhei, who was the scribe and whose participation is limited to this verse, moves from a close-up to a wider shot, establishing the time of the previous verse and adding a human element, that of the farmers harvesting rice in a field—probably poor farmers working on a small plot on the edge of a wild field of Korean grass. This verse, which is the sixth, marks the end of the overture (jo), or the first section of the sequence.

35. In Yasui's verse we look through the eyes of a recluse into the field where the farmers are harvesting rice. The action of giving lodging to a heron, a bird known to avoid humans, suggests a nature-loving recluse, which resonates with the implied loneliness of the autumn evening in the previous verse. The verse also can be read allegorically. Yasui, the host of the session, implicitly offers his humble residence to the visiting haikai master.

36. Bashō transforms the person in the grass hut into someone taking refuge and growing back his hair while in hiding—perhaps a monk who has taken the tonsure but is impatient to return to the secular world. The verse raises a number of intriguing questions: Why did the

itsuwari no	"The pain of deception"
tsurashi to chichi	she thought
shiborisute	squeezing dry her breasts[37]

Jūgo

| kienu sotoba ni | By an unfaded stupa |
| sugosugo to naku | sobbing with heavy heart[38] |

Kakei

kagebō no	A silhouette
akatsuki samuku	in the early dawn cold
hi o takite	lighting a fire[39]

Bashō

| aruji wa hin ni | An empty house |
| taeshi karaie | the owners died of poverty[40] |

Tokoku

tanaka naru	In a rice field
Koman ga yanagi	the Koman willow
otsuru koro	dropping its leaves[41]

Kakei

---

person take vows? What has caused the person to want to return to secular life? Is it related to a failed love affair?

37. This is a love verse, a requirement for a sequence. Jūgo transforms the secluded male figure into a woman who has recently given birth and is now nursing a child. A woman seems to have been betrayed or deceived by someone who has taken her child away, causing her pain and resentment. Whatever the reason, the love affair has caused the woman to escape to a place, perhaps a temple, where she is waiting for her hair to grow back, and in the process she has left behind a suckling infant, forcing her to "squeeze dry her [swollen] breasts," a startling haikai phrase.

38. Kakei transforms the previous "love" verse into a Buddhist verse on the topic of impermanence (mujō): the pain is no longer caused by betrayal or deception but by death, by the illusory nature of life. The woman squeezing milk out of her swollen breasts is now a mother whose child has just died and who weeps next to a newly marked grave, which stands as an unfading reminder of the illusory nature of all things.

39. Bashō turns the mother weeping in front of the stupa into someone who has spent the night at a wake: during the Edo period, relatives of the deceased customarily remained in a mourning hut all night and read sutras. Now, in the early dawn, it is so cold that someone has lit a fire, which casts a shadow. After four nonseasonal verses, the sequence returns to winter, indicated by the word "cold."

40. Tokoku transforms the person lighting the small fire into a vagrant or beggar living in an abandoned house whose owners have left or disappeared as a result of poverty. The implied desolation of the empty house and the poverty resonate with the hollow feeling of the silhouette in the previous verse. To some readers, the silhouette may even suggest the ghost of the dead owner.

41. After five consecutive verses on people, Kakei shifts to a landscape verse and a new lo-

| kiri ni fune hiku | A man pulling the boat |
| hito wa chinba ka | in the mist—is he lame?[42] |

Yasui

tasogare o	At dusk
yoko ni nagamuru	gazing sideways at
tsuki hososhi	the thin moon[43]

Tokoku

| tonari sakashiki | Retiring from court |
| machi ni oriiru | to a street of gossipy neighbors[44] |

Jūgo

ni no ama ni	Asking the Second Nun
konoe no hana no	about the cherry trees in full bloom
sakari kana	at the imperial palace[45]

Yasui

---

cale. Koman, a popular name for a provincial prostitute, suggests that the empty house is part of an abandoned post town, where prostitutes used to sell their favors to travelers. Or perhaps it was the presence of the prostitutes that caused the house to be abandoned. In either event, a willow named after a legendary prostitute now stands in a rice field. The dropping of the willow leaves transforms the previous nonseasonal verse into autumn. The sense of autumnal fading, including the implied death of a once-famous prostitute, reflects the mood of decay and emptiness in the abandoned house.

42. Yasui's verse, which continues the autumn season with the image of mist, places the willow tree next to a riverbank where a man is pulling a boat upstream. The boat puller appears to be lame, pulling in uneven, jerky movements.

43. This is a moon verse, which was required. "Gazing sideways" implies that the thin moon still lies low on the horizon. The person wondering about the boat puller now becomes a passenger in the boat, probably lying in bed and looking out sideways. Like a scent link, the awkwardness of the boat passenger, who must lean sideways to look at the moon, echoes the awkwardness of the lame man, who is pulling the boat unevenly. A connotative parallel also emerges between the thin dawn moon and the lameness of the boat puller.

44. Jūgo transforms the person gazing sideways at the moon into someone (a lady-in-waiting?) who has retreated from the imperial palace to a city block with gossipy neighbors. The classical verb *oriiru* (to retire from court service) creates a Heian, classical atmosphere, suggesting a fictional character, perhaps Evening Faces (Yūgao) in *The Tale of Genji*, whom the highborn hero discovers in a dusty corner of the capital. The gazing of the previous verse now suggests the boredom of an aristocratic lady living amid talkative commoners.

45. In composing the cherry blossom (*hana*) verse, a requirement for a sequence, Yasui deepens the Heian aristocratic atmosphere of the previous verse and transforms the person who retired to a city street into a Second Nun, a high-ranking female imperial attendant who took the tonsure after the death of an emperor. A woman or child from the local neighborhood is asking the Second Nun, who has recently retired from the palace, about a distant, imperial world. Or

PLUM BLOSSOM SCENT (*UME GA KA*, 1694)

The following is the opening of a two-poet haikai linked-verse sequence referred to as *Plum Blossom Scent*, which Bashō composed with Yaba in Edo in the early spring of 1694 and subsequently published in *Charcoal Sack* (*Sumidawara*, 1694). Bashō died in the early winter of the same year in Osaka, so this is one of his last sequences. It reveals the poetics of "lightness"—which stressed everyday commoner life, contemporary language, and rhythm and avoided heavy conceptualization or allusions to the past—that was characteristic of his last years.

ume ga ka ni	In the plum blossom scent
notto hi no deru	the sun pops up—
yamaji kana	a mountain path[46]

Bashō

tokorodokoro ni	Here there pheasants
kiji no nakitatsu	crying as they fly away[47]

Yaba

yabushin o	Beginning
haru no tesuki ni	house repairs in
toritsuite	spring's slow season[48]

Yaba

---

another nun, who has retired from the palace to a gossipy street, is asking the Second Nun about the cherry blossoms at the imperial palace.

46. In Bashō's opening verse, which is implicitly on the spring topic of lingering winter cold (*yokan*), the speaker is walking along a mountain path, smelling the fragrance of the plum blossoms (*ume ga ka*), a seasonal word for early spring. Then, perhaps when turning a corner, the sun suddenly "pops up" (*notto*), a colloquial adverb with a roundish, warm sound.

47. In the second verse by Yaba, which is read together with the first verse, the pheasants along the mountain path fly out from the grass, crying as they flee, apparently surprised at the sound of the footsteps. The primary function of the second verse was to expand on the content of the hokku, or opening verse, maintaining the same season and filling out and extending the setting. At the same time the two verses are linked by overtones, as in a scent link. Here the sharp cries of the pheasants connotatively echo the startling, bracing feeling of the sun as it suddenly appears in the early morning amid the scent of the plum blossoms.

48. In the third verse, which links with the second verse while turning away from the first verse, Yaba turns to the human world and describes the farmers' free time in the spring (*haru no tesuki*), which they use to build or repair their houses. The pheasants are outside the houses being repaired.

kami no tayori ni   From the city: news
agaru kome no ne   of a rise in the price of rice[49]

Bashō

[Translated by Haruo Shirane]

THE POETICS OF HAIKU

At first, haikai emphasized wordplay, parody, and satire, but by the middle of the 1680s, it had become a more orthodox form, a vernacular counterpart to waka and renga (classical linked verse). Bashō, who stood at this crossroads in haikai history, faced the difficult task of creating poetry and prose that had the spiritual, aesthetic, and social implications of traditional Japanese and Chinese poetry while retaining haikai's earlier popular character. Many of the poetic ideals of the Bashō school—expressed in slogans such as *kōga kizoku* (awakening to the high, returning to the low), *zōka zuijun* (following the Creative), *butsuga ichinyo* (object and self as one), and *fueki ryūkō* (the unchanging and the ever-changing)—reflect various attempts by Bashō and his disciples to bring together these two seemingly contradictory trajectories, to create poetry that was simultaneously orthodox and unorthodox.

AWAKENING TO THE HIGH, RETURNING TO THE LOW

If medieval haikai comically inverted the social and religious hierarchy by lowering gods, buddhas, and other figures of authority and power to vulgar or lesser beings, Bashō tended to work in the opposite direction, finding the subtle, the refined, and the spiritual in a regenerative process in everyday, commoner life. This transformative movement was reflected in the notion of *sabi/shiori*, which applied medieval, aesthetic overtones to vernacular language and scenes, and in the larger poetic ideal of *kōgo kizoku* (awakening to the high, returning to the low), which he developed toward the end of his career. The following is from Dohō's *Three Booklets* (*Sanzōshi*).

The Master taught, "You should awaken the spirit to the high and return to the low. You should constantly seek out the truth of poetic art and, with that high spirit, return to the haikai that you are practicing now."[50]

[NKBZ 51: 546]

---

49. In the fourth verse by Bashō, which links with the third and pushes off from the second verse, news has come from the Kyoto-Osaka (Kamigata) area that the price of rice has gone up. For farmers, such good news would be uplifting, renewing their energy as they set to work repairing the house.

50. "Awakening to the high" (*kōgo*) implied spiritual cultivation, a deepened awareness of

FOLLOWING THE CREATIVE

The poet's relationship to nature is revealed in the slogan "following the Creative" (zōka zuijun). Zōka (Ch. Zaohua), the Creator or the Creative, was not a transcendent, anthropomorphic deity but a creative spirit or force that gave birth to and constantly shaped nature, including human beings. According to the following passage from *Backpack Notes* (Oi no kobumi), which Bashō wrote around 1690, Saigyō, Sōgi, Sesshū (1420–1506), and Rikyū (1522–1591)—the great medieval masters of waka, classical renga, painting, and tea ceremony, respectively—are united by a common spirit, that of following the Creative. The way of art (*fūga*), the way of the inner spirit, and the way of the cosmos (of the Creative) have become inseparable.

The fundamental spirit that stands at the root of Saigyō's poetry, Sōgi's linked verse, Sesshū's paintings, and Rikyū's tea is one and the same. Those who practice such arts follow *zōka*, the Creative, and make the four seasons their friends. What one sees cannot but be cherry blossoms; what one thinks cannot but be the moon. When the shape is not the cherry blossoms, one is no more than a barbarian; when the heart is not the cherry blossom, one is no different from an animal. Leave the barbarians, depart from the animals, follow the Creative, return to the Creative![51]

[NKBZ 41: 311]

---

nature and the movement of the cosmos, and a pursuit of the "ancients," the noted poets of the past. "Returning to the low" (*kizoku*), by contrast, implied a return to the various languages and everyday, material world of seventeenth-century commoners and samurai, to those topics left out or overlooked by the traditional genres, a dimension that Bashō stressed in his later years, especially in the form of *karumi* (lightness).

51. If the artist follows the Creative and "makes a friend of the four seasons," a movement governed by the Creative, the artist will respond to the movement and rhythm of nature, especially of the seasons, which provide constant inspiration for poetry and art. When the poet follows the Creative, "what one sees," which represents the human senses, and "what one thinks," which represents human feeling and thoughts, become the "moon" and "cherry blossoms," which represent the beauties of nature. "Seeing" is as much an internal matter, of realizing the Creative within, as it is an external matter. The "cherry blossoms" do not exist by themselves in nature, nor do they exist solely as a figment of the poet's imagination. Instead, they come into being only when they are "seen" by and fuse with the Creative within the poet. The poet who "follows the Creative" implicitly engages in a process of spiritual cultivation that allows the Creative within to join the Creative of the cosmos. Here Bashō draws on Daoism, especially the chapter "All Things Are Equal" in the *Zhuangzi*. In contrast to the natural imagery found in classical poetry, which was refined, nuanced, and rich in associations, the nature that Bashō confronted was more uncultivated, variegated in character, and often vulgar and mundane. Without realizing the Creative within, what the poet "sees" in such a world cannot become the "moon" and "cherry blossoms"; the new material culture and its heterogeneous languages cannot be transformed into poetry. Instead, they remain vulgar, like an "animal." Without spiritual cultivation and the ability to enter into objects, the haikai poet will not have the power to discover the high in the low, to find beauty in the mundane.

OBJECT AND SELF AS ONE

Spiritual cultivation is also implied in Bashō's notion of "object and self as one" (*butsuga ichinyo*), which he explains in the following passage from Dohō's *Three Booklets*. Bashō argues that when composing poetry, the poet must be selfless—a state implied in "following the Creative"—in order to enter into the object and grasp its essence. If not, the spirit of the poet and that of the object will not be united, and the result will be verbal artifice.

When the Master said, "As for the pine, learn from the pine; as for the bamboo, learn from the bamboo," he meant casting aside personal desire or intention. Those who interpret this "learning" in their own way end up never learning.

The word "learn" means here to enter into the object, to be emotionally moved by the essence that emerges from that object and for that movement to become verse. Even if one clearly expresses the object, if the emotion does not emerge from the object naturally, the object and the self will be divided, and that emotion will not achieve poetic truth (*makoto*). The effect will be the verbal artifice that results from personal desire.[52]

[NKBZ 51: 547–548]

UNCHANGING AND EVER-CHANGING

The ideals of *fūga no makoto* (the truth of poetic art), *zōka zuijun* (following the Creative), and *kōga kizoku* (awakening to the high, returning to the low) were ultimately related to that of *fueki ryūkō* (the unchanging and the ever-changing), a notion that Bashō developed during his journey to the Deep North in 1689. In "Praise to Portraits of Three Saints" (Sanseizu no san, 1692–1693), Bashō wrote, "The ever-changing nature of poetic art [*fūga*] changes together with heaven and earth. One respects the fact that the changes are never exhausted" (NKBZ 41: 539). The *Three Booklets* records his remark that "the changes of heaven and earth are the seeds of poetry" (NKBZ 55: 551). The permanence of haikai is found here in its constant change (*ryūkō*), a paradox in which the "ever-changing" becomes the "unchanging" essence of haikai. Bashō's poetic career, too, was marked by constant change as he moved rapidly from one style or approach to another. At the same time, he held that "unchanging" poems move us as deeply now as they did audiences in the past. Haikai,

---

52. The phrase "learn from the pine" means that the poet must cast away personal, self-oriented desire and enter into the object and draw out its subtle essence, or *mono no bi* (literally, the faintness or depth of the thing). This "self" (*ga*) in *butsuga ichinyo* is not the modern notion of the "self" but a selfless state free of personal desire (*shii*). Only such a selfless "self"—one that "follows the Creative" (*zōka zuijun*)—can enter into the object. If the poet's feelings are not sincere, the heart of the subject and that of the object will not be united, and the result will be "verbal artifice" (*sakui*).

with its freedom and open expanse of language and topics, both encouraged and depended on this "unchanging" dimension, the result of constant change. As with many of his other poetic concepts, Bashō wrote little about fueki ryūkō. Instead, his disciples, especially Dohō, Kyorai, and Kyoriku, extensively debated the notion after his death, leaving us with conflicting interpretations. As the following passage from the *Three Booklets* (*Sanzōshi*) reveals, Dohō saw *fueki* (the unchanging) and *ryūkō* (the ever-changing) as two sides of the same poetic principle:

Bashō's poetry has both the eternal unchanging and the momentary ever-changing. These two aspects become one at the base, which is the truth of poetic art. If one does not understand the unchanging, one cannot truly understand Bashō's haikai. The unchanging does not depend on the new or the old and is unrelated to change or trends; it is firmly anchored in the truth of poetic art.

When one observes the poetry of successive generations of classical poets, one can see that it changes with each generation. And yet there are many poems that transcend the old and the new, that appear no different now than when they appeared in the past, and that are deeply moving. One should consider these poems the unchanging.

It is the law of nature that all things undergo infinite change. If one does not seek change, haikai cannot be renewed. When one does not seek change, one becomes content with the current fashion and does not pursue the truth of haikai. If one does not seek the truth or guide the spirit in that pursuit, one cannot know change based on truth. These people are only imitating others. Those who pursue truth, by contrast, will move one step ahead, not being content to tread on the same ground. No matter how much haikai may change in the future, if it is change based on truth, it will be the kind of haikai advocated by Bashō.

Bashō said, "One should never, even for a moment, lick the dregs of the ancients. Like the endless changes of the seasons, all things must change. The same is true of haikai."

As the Master lay dying, his disciples asked him about the future of haikai. The Master answered, "Since I have entered this path, haikai has changed a hundredfold. And yet of the three stages of calligraphy—the 'stopping' [*shin*], the 'walking' [*gyō*], and the 'running' [*sō*]—haikai has yet to move beyond the first and the second stages." While he was alive, the Master would occasionally say in jest, "My haikai has yet to untie the opening of the straw bag."[53]

[NKBZ 51: 545–546]

---

53. This view of the unchanging and the ever-changing suggests the cosmological view implicit in the Song Confucian cosmology: if "the ever-changing" suggests the material force (*ki*), "the unchanging" suggests the rational principle (*ri*), the metaphysical element that sustains the constant motion of the material force.

Perhaps Bashō's most famous statement related to the issue of the "unchanging and ever-changing" is the following brief statement in "On Sending Off Kyoriku," an essay written in 1693 in which Bashō alludes to a remark by Kūkai (d. 835), the founder of Shingon Buddhism.

Do not seek the traces of the ancients; seek what they sought.

[NKBZ 41: 542, translated by Haruo Shirane]

HAIBUN

Haibun, or haikai prose, was a new genre that combined Chinese prose genres, Japanese classical prototypes, and vernacular language and subject matter. Bashō wrote haikai prose throughout his literary career, but it was not until around 1690, shortly after his noted journey to Mutsu, the Deep North (Tō-hoku), that he consciously strove to develop prose with a haikai spirit as a new literary genre and that he began to use the word haibun. Haibun in the broad sense existed before Bashō in the form of prefaces, headnotes to hokku, and short essays written by haikai masters. Prominent early examples include Kigin's (1624–1705) Mountain Well (Yama no i, 1648), a haikai seasonal almanac whose prose style comes close to that of classical prose. Bashō's new notion of haibun, by contrast, is characterized by the prominent inclusion of "haikai words" (haigon), particularly vernacular Japanese (zokugo) and Chinese words (kango). In the preface to Prose Mirror of Japan (Honchō bunkan, 1717), an anthology of haibun edited by Shikō, one of Bashō's later disciples, the editor explains the significance of such prose:

> From long ago, there have been four poetic genres: Chinese poetry, classical poetry, renga, and haikai. If Chinese poetry and classical poetry have prose, so too should renga and haikai. . . . But an appropriate style for renga has yet to be established. Instead, renga has been subsumed by the house of classical poetry, and its prose is marked by the slipperiness of The Tale of Genji or The Tale of Sagoromo. Renga has yet to create a graceful prose style. Thanks to Bashō's brush, however, the principles of haikai prose have been created for the first time.

THE HUT OF THE PHANTOM DWELLING (GENJŪAN NO KI, 1690)

The Hut of the Phantom Dwelling, which Bashō rewrote a number of times in 1690, is considered the first outstanding example of haibun literature. Earlier haibun tended to be extremely short and to function primarily as salutations. But The Phantom Dwelling, which was closely modeled on Kamo no Chōmei's prose essay Ten-Foot Square Hut (Hōjōki, 1212), is an extended prose poem in a highly elliptical, hybrid style of vernacular, classical Japanese and classical Chinese, with Chinese-style parallel words and parallel phrases. Bashō probably first wrote *The Hut of the Phantom Dwelling* to express his gratitude to Kyokusui, a disciple and patron, who lent him this dwelling where he could rest after his arduous journey through the Deep North. The essay is known as a poetic statement of Bashō's ideal as a recluse.

Beyond Ishiyama, with its back to Mount Iwama, is a hill called Kokubuyama—the name, I think, derives from a *kokubunji*, or government temple of long ago. If you cross the narrow stream that runs at the foot and climb the slope for three turnings of the road, some two hundred paces each, you come to a shrine of the god Hachiman. The object of worship is a statue of the Buddha Amida. This is the sort of thing that is greatly abhorred by the Yuiitsu school, though I regard it as admirable that, as the Ryōbu assert, the buddhas should dim their lights and mingle with the dust in order to benefit the world. Ordinarily, few worshipers visit the shrine, and it's very solemn and still. Beside it is an abandoned hut with a rush door. Brambles and bamboo grass overgrow the eaves; the roof leaks; the plaster has fallen from the walls; and foxes and badgers make their den there. It is called the Genjūan, or Hut of the Phantom Dwelling. The owner was a monk, an uncle of the warrior Suganuma Kyokusui. It has been eight years since he lived there—nothing remains of him now but his name, Elder of the Phantom Dwelling.

I, too, gave up city life some ten years ago, and now I'm approaching fifty. I'm like a bagworm that's lost its bag, a snail without its shell. I've tanned my face in the hot sun of Kisagata in Dewa and bruised my heels on the rough beaches of the northern sea, where tall dunes make walking so hard. And now this year here I am drifting by the waves of Lake Biwa. The grebe attaches its floating nest to a single strand of reed to keep it from washing away in the current. With a similar thought, I mended the thatch on the eaves of the hut, patched up the gaps in the fence, and, at the beginning of the Fourth Month, the first month of summer, moved in for what I thought would be no more than a brief stay. Now, though, I'm beginning to wonder if I'll ever want to leave.

Spring is over, but I can tell it hasn't gone for long. Azaleas continue to bloom, wild wisteria hangs from the pine trees, and a cuckoo now and then passes by. I even have greetings from the jays and woodpeckers that peck at things, but I really don't mind—in fact, I rather enjoy them. I feel as though my spirit had raced off to China to view the scenery in Wu or Chu, as though I were standing beside the lovely Xiao and Xiang Rivers or Lake Dongting. The mountain rises behind me to the southwest, and the nearest houses are a good distance away. Fragrant southern breezes blow down from the mountaintops, and north winds, dampened by the lake, are cool. I have Mount Hie and the tall peak of Hira, and this side of them the pines of Karasaki veiled in mist, as well as a castle, a bridge, and boats fishing on the lake. I hear the voice of the woodsman making his way to Kasatori, and the songs of the seedling planters in the little rice paddies at the foot of the hill. Fireflies weave through the air in the dusk of evening, clapper rails tap out their notes—there's surely no lack of beautiful scenes. Among them is Mikamiyama, which is shaped rather like Mount Fuji and reminds me of my old house in Musashino, while Mount Tanakami sets me to counting all the poets of ancient times who are associated with it. Other mountains include Bamboo Grass Crest, Thousand Yard Summit, and Skirt Waist. There's Black Ford village, where the foliage is so dense and dark, and the men tend their fish weirs, looking exactly as they're described in the *Man'yōshū*. In order to get a better view all around, I've climbed up the height behind my hut, rigged a platform among the pines, and furnished it with a round straw mat. I call it Monkey's Perch. I'm not in a class with those Chinese eccentrics Xu Juan, who made himself a nest in a crab apple tree where he could do his drinking, or Old Man Wang, who built his retreat on Secretary Peak. I'm just a mountain dweller, sleepy by nature, who has returned his footsteps to the steep slopes and sits here in the empty hills catching lice and smashing them.

Sometimes when I'm in an energetic mood, I draw clear water from the valley and cook myself a meal. I have only the drip, drip of the spring to relieve my loneliness, but with my one little stove, things are anything but cluttered. The man who lived here before was truly lofty in mind and did not bother with any elaborate construction. Besides the one room where the Buddha image is kept, there is only a little place designed to store bedding.

An eminent monk of Mount Kōra in Tsukushi, the son of a certain Kai of the Kamo Shrine, recently journeyed to Kyoto, and I got someone to ask him if he would write a plaque for me. He readily agreed, dipped his brush, and wrote the three characters *Gen-jū-an*. He sent me the plaque, and I keep it as a memorial of my grass hut. Mountain home, traveler's rest—call it what you will, it's hardly the kind of place where you need any great store of belongings. A cypress-bark hat from Kiso, a sedge rain-cape from Koshi—that's all that hangs on the post above my pillow. In the daytime, I'm once in a while diverted by people who stop to visit. The old man who takes care of the shrine or the men from the village come and tell me about the wild boar that's been eating the rice plants, the rabbits that are getting at the bean patches, tales of farm matters that are all quite new to me. And when the sun has begun to sink behind the rim of the hills, I sit quietly in the evening waiting for the moon so I may have a shadow for company or light a lamp and discuss right and wrong with my silhouette.

But when all has been said, I am not really the kind who is so completely enamored of solitude that he must hide every trace of himself away in the mountains and wilds. It's just that, troubled by frequent illness and weary of dealing with people, I've come to dislike society. Again and again I think of the mistakes I've made in my clumsiness over the years. There was a time when I envied those who had government offices or impressive domains, and on another occasion I considered entering the precincts of the Buddha and the teaching room of the patriarchs. Instead, I've worn out my body in journeys that were as aimless as the winds and clouds and expended my feelings on flowers and birds. But somehow I've been able to make a living this way, and so in the end, unskilled and untalented as I am, I give myself wholly to this one concern, poetry. Bo Juyi worked so hard at it that he almost ruined his five vital organs, and Du Fu grew lean and emaciated because of it. As far as intelligence or the quality of our writings goes, I can never compare with such men. And yet in the end, we all live, do we not, in a phantom dwelling? But enough of that— I'm off to bed.

mazu tanomu Among these summer trees,
shii no ki mo ari a pasania—
natsu kodachi something to count on

[NKBZ 41: 500–504, translated by Burton Watson]

NARROW ROAD TO THE DEEP NORTH (OKU NO HOSOMICHI, 1694)

In the Third Month, in the spring of 1689, Bashō and his companion Sora departed for Mutsu, or Oku (Interior), the relatively unsettled area of northeastern Honshū. Bashō traveled north to present-day Sendai; crossed west over the mountains to Dewa (Akita and Yamagata) to the Japan Sea side; then moved south, down the coast, through Kanazawa; and arrived at Ōgaki in Mino Province (Gifu) in the Eighth Month. Although often read as a faithful travel account, Narrow Road to the Deep North is best regarded as a kind of fiction loosely based on the actual journey. Bashō depicts an ideal world in which the traveler devotes himself to poetic life in a manner that Bashō himself probably aspired to do but found impossible in the busy world of a haikai master.

The text, selections from which are translated here, consists of fifty or so separate sections strung together like a haikai linked-verse sequence. They describe a series of interrelated journeys: a search for *utamakura*, or noted poetic places, especially the traces of ancient poets such as Saigyō, the medieval waka poet-priest to whom this account pays special homage; a journey into the past to such historic places as the old battlefield at Hiraizumi; an ascetic journey and a pilgrimage to sacred places; and interesting encounters with individuals and poetic partners, to whom he composes or exchanges poetic greetings.

The interest of travel literature, at least in the Anglo-European tradition, generally lies in the unknown—new worlds, new knowledge, new perspectives, new experiences. But for medieval waka and renga poets, the object of travel was to confirm what already existed, to reinforce the roots of cultural memory. By visiting utamakura, the poet-traveler hoped to relive the experience of his or her literary predecessors, to be moved to compose poetry on the same landscape, thereby joining his or her cultural forebears—as Bashō does here in regard to Saigyō, his spiritual and poetic mentor. The travel diary itself became a link in a chain of poetic and literary transmission.

In contrast to medieval waka poets, however, who attempted to preserve the classical associations of the poetic topics, Bashō sought out new poetic associations in utama-kura and discovered new poetic places. In the passage on Muro-no-yashima, toward the beginning, Bashō suggests that *Narrow Road to the Deep North* will take a revisionary approach to utamakura. It will explore both the physical place and its historic and poetic roots in an effort to recast the landscape. A critical contrast is made between those utamakura in Mutsu or Michinoku in the first half of *Narrow Road*, which tend to be major utamakura—Shirakawa Barrier, Matsushima, Sue-no-matsuyama, Shinobu, and so on—and which bear the weight of the classical tradition, and those found along the Japan Sea side in the second half, such as Kisagata (Kisakata), which tend to be lesser utamakura or unknown in the classical tradition. Perhaps the best example of the latter is Sado Island, which appears on the Japan Sea side and which Bashō infuses with new poetic associations. In writing *Narrow Road*, Bashō sought a Chinese poetic ideal of "landscape in human emotion, and human emotion in landscape," in which the landscape becomes infused with cultural memory and a wide variety of human emotions and associations, from the sensual to the spiritual. Bashō achieved this poetic ideal most dramatically with lesser-known poetic places like Kisagata, Sado, and Iro-no-hama (Color Beach) in Echizen Province.

A number of the early sections—such as Kurokamiyama (Black Hair Mountain), Urami no taki (Back-View Falls), and Kurobane—imply that the journey also is a form of ascetic practice. Indeed, the title of *Narrow Road to the Deep North* (*Oku no hosomichi*) suggests not only the narrow and difficult roads (*hosomichi*) of Mutsu but the difficulty of the spiritual journey "within" (*oku*). Pilgrimages to sacred places, to temples and shrines, were popular from as early as the Heian period and formed an integral part of travel literature, particularly those accounts written by hermit-priests, a persona that Bashō adopts here. *Narrow Road*, in fact, has far more sections on this topic than usually found in medieval travel diaries. A typical passage begins with a description of the place and a history of the shrine or temple, usually giving some detail about the founder or the name. The climactic hokku, which may be a poetic greeting to the divine spirit or head of the temple/shrine, usually conveys a sense of the sacred quality or efficacy of the place. For example, in the passage on the Ryūshaku-ji temple in Dewa, that quality is embodied in the word "stillness" (*shizukasa*). Another climactic point, which suggests a rite of passage, a kind of death and rebirth, is the difficult climb over Feather Black Mountain (Hagurozan), Moon Mountain (Gassan), and Bathhouse Mountain (Yudono)—the three holy mountains of Dewa Province—in which the traveler almost dies from exhaustion and cold before coming to Yudono, a place of sexuality and fertility.

Bashō wrote the account a considerable time after the actual journey, probably in 1694 at the end of his life, when he was developing his new ideal of haibun. Indeed, *Narrow Road to the Deep North*, which is marked by a great variety of prose styles ranging from the allusive classical style in the Shirakawa section to the highly Chinese sections at Matsushima and Kisagata, may best be understood as an attempt to reveal the different possibilities of haibun in the form of travel literature. The resulting fusion of vernacular Japanese, classical Japanese, and classical Chinese, with its parallel and contrastive couplet-like phrases, had a profound impact on the development of Japanese prose. Of particular interest is the close fusion between the prose and the poetry, a salient characteristic of haibun, in which the prose creates a dramatic context for many of the best hokku that Bashō wrote.

> The months and days, the travelers of a hundred ages;
> the years that come and go, voyagers too.
> floating away their lives on boats,
> growing old as they lead horses by the bit,
> for them, each day a journey, travel their home.
> Many, too, are the ancients who perished on the road.
> Some years ago, seized by wanderlust, I wandered along the shores
>   of the sea.

Then, last autumn, I swept away the old cobwebs in my dilapidated dwelling on the river's edge. As the year gradually came to an end and spring arrived, filling the sky with mist, I longed to cross the Shirakawa Barrier, the most revered of poetic places. Somehow or other, I became possessed by a spirit, which crazed my soul. Unable to sit still, I accepted the summons of the Deity of the Road. No sooner had I repaired the holes in my trousers, attached a new cord to my rain hat, and cauterized my legs with moxa than my thoughts were on the famous moon at Matsushima. I turned my dwelling over to others and moved to Sanpū's villa.

> kusa no to mo   Time even for the grass hut
> sumikawaru yo zo   to change owners—
> hina no ie   house of dolls[54]

I left a sheet of eight linked verses on the pillar of the hermitage.

I started out on the twenty-seventh day of the Third Month.

The dawn sky was misting over; the moon lingered, giving off a pale light; the peak of Mount Fuji appeared faintly in the distance. I felt uncertain, won-

---

54. *Hina* (dolls), a new seasonal word for late spring, meant Hinamatsuri, the girls' festival on the third day of the Third Month, when families with daughters displayed dolls in their houses. The hokku suggests that dwellings, normally associated with a sense of home, are only temporary lodgings in life's journey; hence the time has come for even the "grass hut" (*kusa no to*) to become a domestic, secular dwelling, a "house of dolls" occupied by a new owner with a wife and daughter(s).

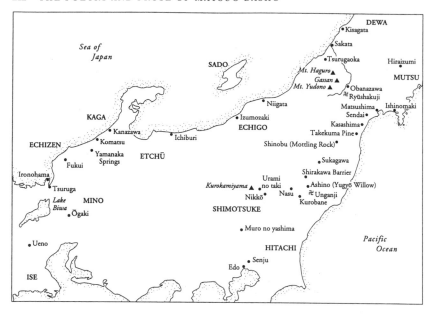

The places mentioned in Bashō's *Narrow Road to the Deep North*. (Courtesy of Stanford University Press)

dering whether I would see again the cherry blossoms on the boughs at Ueno and Yanaka. My friends had gathered the night before to see me off and joined me on the boat. When I disembarked at a place called Senju, my breast was overwhelmed by thoughts of the "three thousand leagues ahead," and standing at the crossroads of the illusory world, I wept at the parting.

> yuku haru ya   Spring going—
> tori naki uo no   birds crying and tears
> me wa namida   in the eyes of the fish[55]

Making this my first journal entry, we set off but made little progress. People lined the sides of the street, seeing us off, it seemed, as long as they could see our backs.

---

55. The birds—which cry out (*naku*) and/or weep (*naku*)—and fish mourn the passing of spring and, by implication, the departure of the travelers. Some commentators see the fish as the disciples left behind and the birds as the departing travelers (Bashō and Sora); others interpret the departing spring as the traveler. *Yuku*, a key word in *Narrow Road*, means both "to go" and "to pass time," thereby fusing temporal and spatial passage. The seasons thus become travelers.

Was it the second year of Genroku? On a mere whim, I had resolved that I would make a long journey to the Deep North. Although I knew I would probably suffer, my hair growing white under the distant skies of Wu, I wanted to view those places that I had heard of but never seen and placed my faith in an uncertain future, not knowing if I would return alive. We barely managed to reach the Sōka post station that night. The luggage that I carried over my bony shoulders began to cause me pain. I had departed on the journey thinking that I need bring only myself, but I ended up carrying a coat to keep me warm at night, a night robe, rain gear, inkstone, brush, and the like, as well as the farewell presents that I could not refuse. All these became a burden on the road.

We paid our respects to the shrine at Muro-no-yashima, Eight Islands of the Sealed Room. Sora, my travel companion, noted: "This deity is called the Goddess of the Blooming Cherry Tree and is the same as that worshiped at Mount Fuji. Since the goddess entered a sealed hut and burned herself giving birth to Hohodemi, the God of Emitting Fire, and proving her vow, they call the place Eight Islands of the Sealed Room. The custom of including smoke in poems on this place also derives from this story. It is forbidden to consume a fish called *konoshiro*, or shad, which is thought to smell like flesh when burned. The essence of this shrine history is already known to the world."[56]

On the thirtieth, stopped at the foot of Nikkō Mountain. The owner said, "My name is Buddha Gozaemon. People have given me this name because I make honesty my first concern in all matters. As a consequence, you can relax for one night on the road. Please stay here." I wondered what kind of buddha had manifested itself in this soiled world to help someone like me, traveling like a beggar priest on a pilgrimage. I observed the actions of the innkeeper carefully and saw that he was neither clever nor calculating. He was nothing but honesty—the type of person that Confucius referred to when he said, "Those who are strong in will and without pretension are close to humanity." I had nothing but respect for the purity of his character.

---

56. The following love poem by Fujiwara Sanekata, which draws on the homophonic association of fire (*hi*) with longing (*omohi*) and love (*kohi*) and uses smoke (*keburi*) as a metaphor for suppressed desire, is typical of the many classical poems on Muro-no-yashima. "How could I let you know of my longing were it not for the smoke of Muro-no-yashima?" (*Shikashū*, 1144; Love 1, no. 188). Classical poets believed that the steam from a stream in Muro-no-yashima looked like smoke or that the smoke came from an oven (*kamado*), an association suggested by the word *muro* (sealed room). However, Sora, who came from a family of Shintō priests, presents here a different explanation based on a close reading of the *Records of Japan* (*Nihon shoki*) and other early texts. Bashō suggests here that *Narrow Road*, with the help of a learned companion (Sora), will take a revisionary approach to utamakura, or poetic places. It will not simply follow the established poetic associations but explore both the physical place and the historical roots in an effort to renew and recast the cultural landscape.

On the first of the Fourth Month, we paid our respects to the holy mountain. In the distant past, the name of this sacred mountain was written with the characters Nikkōzan, Two Rough Mountain, but when Priest Kūkai established a temple here, he changed the name to Nikkō, Light of the Sun. Perhaps he was able to see a thousand years into the future. Now this venerable light shines throughout the land, and its benevolence flows to the eight corners of the earth, and the four classes—warrior, samurai, artisan, and merchant—all live in peace. Out of a sense of reverence and awe, I put my brush down here.

aratōto	Awe inspiring!
aoba wakaba no	on the green leaves, budding leaves
hi no hikari	light of the sun[57]

Black Hair Mountain, enshrouded in mist, the snow still white.

sorisutete	Shaving my head
Kurokamiyama ni	at Black Hair Mountain—
koromogae	time for summer clothes[58]

Sora

Sora's family name is Kawai; his personal name is Sōgoro. He lived near me, helping me gather wood and heat water, and was delighted at the thought of sharing with me the sights of Matsushima and Kisagata. At the same time, he wanted to help me overcome the hardships of travel. On the morning of the departure, he shaved his hair, changed to dark black robes, and took on the Buddhist name of Sōgo. That is why he wrote the Black Hair Mountain poem. I thought that the words "time for summer clothes" [koromogae] were particularly effective.

---

57. By incorporating the name of the place into the poem—hi no hikari (light of the sun) is the Japanese reading for Nikkō—the hokku becomes a salute to the spirit of the mountain, to the divine insight of Kūkai, and to the "venerable light" of the Tōshōgu (literally, Eastern Shining Shrine), which was dedicated to Tokugawa Ieyasu, the founder of the Tokugawa shōgunate, whose "light" implicitly brings peace to the land. The first version, which Bashō wrote during the journey, was "awe inspiring—reaching the darkness beneath the trees, light of the sun." In it, the "light of the sun" reaches down to the "darkness beneath the trees" (ko no shita yami), to the people. The revised version, by contrast, eliminates the overt allegory and symbolism, focusing instead on the poet's sense of awe before nature, on the sight of the sun shining on a rich mixture of dark evergreen leaves (aoba) and light green deciduous leaves (wakaba), with the divine presence emerging only in the overtones. The distinctive assonance and cadence that result from the repeated "a" and "i" vowels also make the revised version infinitely superior.

58. Embarking on a journey becomes synonymous with entering the Buddhist path: both imply a firm resolve and a new life, symbolized here by the seasonal word koromogae (change of clothes at the beginning of summer).

This painting depicts Bashō, followed presumably by Sora, both dressed in priestly attire, on the journey to the Deep North. Bashō carries a traveling hat and walking stick. Of the surviving portraits, this is considered the most reliable, since it was done in 1693 while Bashō was still alive, by Kyoriku, the best painter among Bashō's disciples. (34.4 in. × 11 in. Courtesy of Tenri Central Library)

Climbing more than a mile up a mountain, we came to a waterfall. From the top of the cavern, the water flew down a hundred feet, falling into a blue pool of a thousand rocks. I squeezed into a hole in the rocks and entered the cavern: they say that this is called Back-View Falls because you can see the waterfall from the back, from inside the cavern.

shibaraku wa   Secluded for a while
taki ni komoru ya   in a waterfall —
ge no hajime   beginning of summer austerities[59]

. . .

There is a mountain-priest temple called Kōmyōji. We were invited there and prayed at the Hall of Gyōja.

natsuyama ni   Summer mountains —
ashida o ogamu   praying to the tall clogs
kadode kana   at journey's start[60]

. . .

The willow that was the subject of Saigyō's poem, "Where a Crystal Stream Flows,"[61] still stood in the village of Ashino, on a footpath in a rice field. The lord of the manor of this village had repeatedly said, "I would like to show you this willow," and I had wondered where it was. Today I was able to stand in its very shade.

ta ichimai   Whole field of
uete tachisaru   rice seedlings planted — I part
yanagi kana   from the willow[62]

---

59. *Ge no hajime* refers both to the beginning (*hajime*) of summer (*ge* is the Sino-Japanese reading for *natsu*) and to the Buddhist austerities of summer (*ge* or *gegoromi*), in which Buddhist practitioners remained indoors from the sixteenth day of the Fourth Month to the sixteenth day of the Seventh Month, fasting, reciting sutras, and carrying out such ascetic and purification practices as standing under a waterfall. The traveler stands behind the waterfall, which gives him, at least for a while, the cool, pure feeling of being cleansed of the dirt of the world, as in a *gegomori*.

60. *Natsuyama* (summer mountains), a classical seasonal word for the thick, verdant mountains of summer, refers to both the mountains surrounding the temple and the many mountain peaks that lie before the traveler. At the beginning of the journey, the traveler bows before the high clogs, a prayer for the foot strength of En no Gyōja, the founder of a mountain priest sect (*shugendō*) and an "austerity man" (*gyōja*) believed to have acquired superhuman power from rigorous mountain training.

61. A poem by Saigyō: "I thought to pause on the roadside where a crystal stream flows beneath a willow and stood rooted to the spot" (*Shinkokinshū*, 1205; Summer, no. 262).

62. The entire passage is an allusive variation on *The Wandering Priest and the Willow* (*Yugyō yanagi*), a nō play based on Saigyō's poem in the *Shinkokinshū* (Summer, no. 262), in which an itinerant priest (the *waki*), retracing the steps of Saigyō through the Deep North (Michinoku), meets an old man (the *shite*) who shows him the withered willow about which Saigyō wrote his famous poem. The old man later turns out to be the spirit of that willow. At the end of the play the priest offers prayers to the spirit of the willow, thereby enabling it to achieve salvation. When the district officer offers to introduce Saigyō's willow to the traveler, the passage takes on the atmosphere of a nō dream play in which the traveler encounters the spirit of Saigyō, embodied

The days of uncertainty piled one on the other, and when we came upon the Shirakawa Barrier, I finally felt as if I had settled into the journey. I can understand why that poet had written, "Had I a messenger, I would send a missive to the capital!" One of three noted barriers, the Shirakawa Barrier captured the hearts of poets. With the sound of the autumn wind in my ears and the image of the autumn leaves in my mind, I was moved all the more by the tops of the green-leafed trees.[63] The flowering of the wild rose amid the white deutzia clusters made me feel as if I were crossing over snow. . . .

At the Sukagawa post station, we visited a man named Tōkyū. He insisted that we stay for four or five days and asked me how I had found the Shirakawa Barrier. I replied, "My body and spirit were tired from the pain of the long journey; my heart overwhelmed by the landscape. The thoughts of the distant past tore through me, and I couldn't think straight." But feeling it would be a pity to cross the barrier without producing a single verse, I wrote:

fūryū no   Beginnings of poetry—
hajime ya oku no   rice-planting songs
taue uta   of the Deep North[64]

---

in the willow. In contrast to Saigyō's classical poem, in which time passes as the traveler rests near a beautiful stream, in Bashō's hokku, time passes as the traveler journeys to meet Saigyō's spirit. Most modern commentators, finding it hard to believe that Bashō would plant rice seedlings himself, interpret the hokku as having two subjects: farm girls, who are planting the seedlings in the rice paddy in the summer, and Bashō, who stands under the willow. Filled with thoughts of Saigyō, who had stood by the same tree, the traveler loses track of time, and before he knows it, an entire field of rice has been planted by the farm girls. The context of the nō play and the grammar of the poem also suggest that Bashō, imagining himself as an itinerant monk, helps plant rice seedlings in the field as an offering or greeting to the spirit of Saigyō, his poetic host and patron. Bashō's entire journey can even be interpreted as an offering or tribute to the spirit of Saigyō (1118–1190) on the five-hundredth anniversary of his death.

63. The Shirakawa Barrier here exists almost entirely in the traveler's imagination as a circle of poetic associations. Taira Kanemori (d. 990), referred to as "that poet," was the first in a long line of classical waka poets to compose on the barrier: "Had I a messenger I would send a missive to the capital!" (*Shūishū*, 1005; Parting, no. 339). The following poem by Priest Nōin (998–1050), who first traveled to the Deep North in 1025, created the association of the Shirakawa Barrier with autumn wind (*akikaze*): "Though I left the capital together with the spring mists, autumn winds are blowing at the Shirakawa Barrier" (*Goshūishū*,1086; Travel, no. 518). At a poetry contest in 1170, Minamoto Yorimasa (1104–1180) composed an allusive variation on Nōin's poem that also linked the Shirakawa Barrier with bright autumn leaves: "In the capital the leaves were still green when I saw them, but bright autumn leaves now scatter at the Shirakawa Barrier" (*Senzaishū*, 1183; Autumn 2, no. 365). In a seemingly endless poetic transmission, Bashō follows the traces of Saigyō, Yorimasa, and others who had earlier sought the traces of Nōin, who in turn had followed the traces of Kanemori.

64. This hokku, which Bashō composed in the summer of 1689 and later placed in *Narrow Road*, is a greeting to his friend and host Tōkyū (1638–1715), a station master at Sukagawa, at the

This opening verse was followed by a second verse and then a third; before we knew it, three sequences. . . .

The next day we went to Shinobu Village and visited Shinobu Mottling Rock. The rock was in a small village, half buried, deep in the shade of the mountain. A child from the village came and told us, "In the distant past, the rock was on top of this mountain, but the villagers, angered by the visitors who had been tearing up the barley grass to test the rock, pushed it down into the valley, where it lies face down." Perhaps that was the way it had to be.

sanae toru   Planting rice seedlings
temoto ya mukashi   the hands—in the distant past pressing
shinobuzuri   the grass of longing[65]

. . .

The Courtyard Inscribed-Stone was in Taga Castle in the village of Ichikawa. More than six feet high and about three feet wide; the moss had eaten away the rock, and the letters were faint. On the memorial, which listed the number of miles to the four borders of the province: "This castle was built in 724 by

---

entrance to the Deep North (oku), the northeast region. Hearing the rice-planting songs in the fields (probably owned by Tōkyū), Bashō composes a poem that compliments the host on the elegance of his home and region, which he associates with the beginnings of fūryū (refinement, poetry). The poem also expresses Bashō's joy and gratitude at being able to compose linked verse for the first time in the Interior. Here Bashō leaves behind the web of classical associations— the white deutzia (unohana), autumn leaves, autumn wind, longing for the capital—to find fūryū in the rice-planting songs (taueuta) sung by the laborers in the fields, an ancient practice that had died out in the Kyoto and Kantō areas by the early Edo period. In a haikai twist, Michinoku, or the Interior, rather than the capital (miyako), becomes the beginnings of poetic and artistic sensibility. The Shirakawa Barrier, which stood at the entrance to the Deep North, marks not a turning back toward the capital, as the earlier classical poems on Shirakawa had, but an entry into the provinces as a poetic wellspring.

65. Shinobu, in present-day Fukushima Prefecture, was the most famous utamakura, or poetic place, in the Deep North. Shinobu mojizuri (Shinobu cloth mottling), the technique of rubbing the fronds of shinobugusa (hare's foot fern, literally, longing grass) onto woven cloth so as to create a wild pattern or design, became associated with uncontrolled longing (shinobu), owing to the following love poem by Minamoto Tōru, one of many classical poems that helped transform the Deep North from an area associated with barbarians (ezo) into a landscape for Heian courtly love. "I am not one to long uncontrollably like the wild Shinobu cloth mottling of the Deep North" (Kokinshū, Love 4, no. 724). The traveler in Narrow Road is disappointed to discover that an utamakura that had given birth to countless poems has been neglected and abused. The damaged utamakura, however, inspires the traveler, who sees in the hands of the nearby farm girls transplanting rice seedlings a glimpse of the hands of the young women who used to press "grass of longing" onto the Shinobu Mottling Rock. Time has obscured the literary utamakura, but the powerful memory of that poetic place enables the poet to find new poetry in the mundane,

Lord Oono Azumabito, the Provincial Governor and General of the Barbarian-Subduing Headquarters. In 762, on the first of the Twelfth Month, it was rebuilt by the Councillor and Military Commander of the Eastern Seaboard, Lord Emi Asakari." The memorial belonged to the era of the sovereign Shōmu.[66] Famous places in poetry have been collected and preserved; but mountains crumble, rivers shift, roads change, rock are buried in dirt; trees age, saplings replace them; times change, generations come and go. But here, without a doubt, was a memorial of a thousand years: I was peering into the heart of the ancients. The virtues of travel, the joys of life, forgetting the weariness of travel, I shed only tears. . . .

It was already close to noon when we borrowed a boat and crossed over to Matsushima. The distance was more than two leagues, and we landed on the shore of Ojima. It has been said many times, but Matsushima is the most beautiful place in all of Japan. First of all, it can hold its head up to Dongting Lake or West Lake. Letting in the sea from the southeast, it fills the bay, three leagues wide, with the tide of Zhejiang. Matsushima has gathered countless islands: the high ones point their fingers to heaven; those lying down crawl over the waves. Some are piled two deep; some, three deep. To the left, the islands are separated from one another; to the right, they are linked. Some seem to be carrying islands on their backs; others, to be embracing them like a person caressing a child. The green of the pine is dark and dense, the branches and leaves bent by the salty sea breeze — as if they were deliberately twisted. A soft, tranquil landscape, like a beautiful lady powdering her face. Did the god of the mountain create this long ago, in the age of the gods? Is this the work of the Creator? What words to describe this?

The rocky shore of Ojima extended out from the coast and became an island protruding into the sea. Here were the remains of Priest Ungo's dwelling and the rock on which he meditated. Again, one could see, scattered widely in the shadow of the pines, people who had turned their backs on the world. They lived quietly in grass huts, the smoke from burning rice ears and pinecones rising from the huts. I didn't know what kind of people they were, but I was drawn to them, and when I approached, the moon was reflected on the sea, and the scenery changed again, different from the afternoon landscape. When we returned to the shore and took lodgings, I opened the window. It was a two-story building, and I felt like a traveler sleeping amid the wind and the clouds: to a strange degree it was a good feeling.

---

in the everyday commoner life of the provinces. In a haikai movement, the refined and the mundane, the classical and the contemporary, merge momentarily in the women's hands.

66. Emperor Shōmu (r. 724–748). In actuality, Shōmu (701–756) was not alive at the time of this memorial.

Matsushima ya   Matsushima—
tsuru ni mi kare   borrow the body of a crane
hototogisu   cuckoo!!

Sora

I closed my mouth and tried to sleep but couldn't. When I left my old hermitage, Sodō had given me a Chinese poem on Matsushima, and Hara Anteki had sent me a waka on Matsugaurashima. Opening my knapsack, I made those poems my friends for the night. There also were hokku by Sanpū and Jokushi.

On the eleventh, made a pilgrimage to Zuiganji temple. Thirty-two generations ago, Makabe Heishirō took holy vows, went to China, returned, and founded this temple. Owing to his good works, the seven halls of the temple have been splendidly rebuilt, the gold-foiled walls and the grand decorations casting a light on everything. The temple, a realization of the land of the buddha in this world. Wondered where that temple of the famous Kenbutsu sage was.

On the twelfth we headed for Hiraizumi. We had heard of such places as the Pine at Anewa and the Thread-Broken Bridge, but there were few human traces, and finding it difficult to recognize the path normally used by the rabbit hunters and woodcutters, we ended up losing our way and came out at a harbor called Ishi no maki. Across the water we could see Kinkazan, the Golden Flower Mountain, where the "Blooming of the Golden Flower" poem had been composed as an offering to the emperor. Several hundred ferry boats gathered in the inlet; human dwellings fought for space on the shore; and the smoke from the ovens rose high. It never occurred to me that I would come across such a prosperous place. We attempted to find a lodging, but no one gave us a place for the night. Finally, we spent the night in an impoverished hovel and, at dawn, wandered off again onto an unknown road. Looking afar at Sode no watari, Obuchi no maki, Mano no kayahara, and other famous places, we made our way over a dike that extended into the distance. We followed the edge of a lonely and narrow marsh, lodged for the night at a place called Toima, and then arrived at Hiraizumi: a distance, I think, of more than twenty leagues.

The glory of three generations of Fujiwara vanished in the space of a dream; the remains of the Great Gate stood two miles in the distance. Hidehira's headquarters had turned into rice paddies and wild fields. Only Kinkeizan, Golden Fowl Hill, remained as it was. First, we climbed Takadachi, Castle-on-the-Heights, from where we could see the Kitakami, a broad river that flowed from the south. The Koromo River rounded Izumi Castle, and at a point beneath Castle-on-the-Heights, it dropped into the broad river. The ancient ruins of Yasuhira and others, lying behind Koromo Barrier, appear to close off the southern entrance and guard against the Ainu barbarians. Selecting his loyal retainers, Yoshitsune fortified himself in the castle, but his glory quickly turned to grass. "The state is destroyed; rivers and hills remain. The city walls turn to spring; grasses and trees are green." With these lines from Du Fu in my head, I lay down my bamboo hat, letting the time and tears flow.

natsugusa ya   Summer grasses—
tsuwamonodomo ga   the traces of dreams
yume no ato   of ancient warriors[67]

unohana ni   In the deutzia
Kanefusa miyuru   Kanefusa appears
shiraga kana   white haired[68]

Sora

---

67. The four successive heavy "o" syllables in *tsuwamonodomo* (plural for "warriors") suggest the ponderous march of soldiers or the thunder of battle. This hokku depends on polysemous words: *ato*, which can mean "site," "aftermath," "trace," or "track"; and *yume*, which can mean "dream," "ambition," or "glory." The summer grasses are the "site" of a former battlefield and of the dreams of glory of the many noted warriors who fought there in the distant past. *Ato* also refers to temporal passage: the summer grasses are the "aftermath" of the dreams of glory. All that is left of the once great ambitions are the "traces" or "tracks." The "dreams of the ancient warriors" (*tsuwamonodomo ga yume*) are the dreams of the three generations of Fujiwara who valiantly conquered the Ainu tribesmen and built a glorious civilization only to see it disappear, and of Yoshitsune's brave retainers, who died for their master. The ephemerality, the dreamlike nature of such "ambitions" (*yume*), is foreshadowed in the opening phrase of the prose passage ("in the space of a dream," *issui no yume*), a reference to the nō play *Kantan*, about a man (Rosei) who napped and dreamed about a lifetime of glory and defeat while waiting for dinner. These dreams of "glory" (*yume*) have turned to grass (*kusamura*), leaving only the site or traces of the dreams. The traveler here takes on the aura of the *waki* (traveling priest) in a nō warrior play (*shuramono*) who visits the site of a former battlefield and then, as if in a dream, watches the ghost of the slain warrior reenact his most tragic moments on the battlefield. A similar process occurs in the Chinese archetype in *Guwen zhenbao*: "Lamentation at an Ancient Battlefield" (Gu zhanchang diaowen, J. Ko senjō o tomurau bun) by Li Hua (ca. 715–ca. 774) in which the poet gazes down at an old battlefield, imagines the terrible carnage, and listens to the voices of the dead before returning to the present to ponder the meaning of the past. The "dreams" in Bashō's hokku, in short, are also the dreams of the visitors, who have had a fleeting glimpse of the past, of the dreams of others. *Natsugusa* (summer grasses), a classical seasonal word for summer, refers to the thick, deep grass resulting from the continuous summer rains (*samidare*), and was associated in the classical poetry with *shigeru* (to grow thick), *musubu* (to tie blades, bond), and *chigiru* (to tie, make a vow of love). Through the reference to Du Fu's noted Chinese poem on the impermanence of civilization—"The state is destroyed, rivers and hills remain / The city walls turn to spring, grasses and trees are green"—Bashō was able to transform these classical associations of eroticism and fertility into those of battle and the larger topos of the ephemerality of human ambitions. *Natsugusa*, in short, is both the rich, thick, replenished grass of the present *and* the blood-stained grass of the past, an image of both the constancy of nature and the impermanence of all things.

68. Sora's poem, which was probably written by Bashō himself, continues the nō-esque vi-

The two halls about which we had heard such wonderful things were open. The Sutra Hall held the statues of the three chieftains, and the Hall of Light contained the coffins of three generations, preserving three sacred images. The seven precious substances were scattered and lost; the doors of jewels, torn by the wind; the pillars of gold, rotted in the snow. The hall should have turned into a mound of empty, abandoned grass, but the four sides were enclosed, covering the roof with shingles, surviving the snow and rain. For a while, it became a memorial to a thousand years.

samidare no   Have the summer rains
furinokoshite ya   come and gone, sparing
hikaridō   the Hall of Light?[69]

Gazing afar at the road that extended to the south, we stopped at the village of Iwade. We passed Ogurazaki and Mizu no ojima, and from Narugo Hot Springs we proceeded to Passing-Water Barrier and attempted to cross into Dewa Province. Since there were few travelers on this road, we were regarded with suspicion by the barrier guards, and it was only after considerable effort that we were able to cross the barrier. We climbed a large mountain, and since it had already grown dark, we caught sight of a house of a border guard and asked for lodging. For three days, the wind and rain were severe, forcing us to stay in the middle of a boring mountain.

---

sion. The two hokku can in fact be read as linked verses: the white flowers of the *unohana* (deutzia), a kind of brier, appears in the midst of a field of summer grass, from which the figure of Kanefusa rises like a ghost, his white hair waving in the air. According to the *Record of Yoshitsune* (*Gikeiki*), Kanefusa, Yoshitsune's loyal retainer, helped Yoshitsune's wife and children commit suicide; saw his master to his end; set fire to the fort at Takadachi; slew Nagasaki Tarō, an enemy captain; grabbed Nagasaki's younger brother under his arm; and then leaped into the flames—a sense of frenzy captured in the image of the white hair.

69. Commentators are divided on whether the *samidare*, the long summer rains, are falling now, before the speaker's eyes, or whether *samidare* refers to past summer rains, which have spared the Hikaridō (Hall of Light) over the centuries. The latter interpretation is borne out by an earlier version of the poem: "Summer rains—falling year after year five hundred times" (*samidare ya toshidoshi furu mo gohyaku tabi*). In short, two landscapes coexist: the *samidare* falling immediately before the poet's eyes *and* the years and centuries of *samidare*, or monsoon seasons, which, while rotting houses and other buildings, have somehow, miraculously, spared the Hikaridō. The two visions are linked by the verb *furu*, which means both for the rain "to fall" and for time "to pass." In contrast to the earlier version, which highlights this pun, the revised version discreetly submerges the homonym, emphasizing the contrast between the somber, dark rains of summer and the implicit divine glow of the Hikaridō, the Hall of Light.

nomi shirami	Fleas, lice—
uma no shito suru	a horse passes water
makuramoto	by my pillow

. . .

I visited a person named Seifū at Obanazawa. Though wealthy, he had the spirit of a recluse. Having traveled repeatedly to the capital, he understood the tribulations of travel and gave me shelter for a number of days. He eased the pain of the long journey.

suzushisa o	Taking coolness
waga yado ni shite	for my lodging
nemaru nari	I relax[70]

. . .

In Yamagata there was a mountain temple, the Ryūshaku-ji, founded by the high priest Jikaku, an especially pure and tranquil place. People had urged us to see this place at least once, so we backtracked from Obanazawa, a distance of about seven leagues. It was still light when we arrived. We borrowed a room at a temple at the mountain foot and climbed to the Buddha hall at the top. Boulders were piled on boulders; the pines and cypress had grown old; the soil and rocks were aged, covered with smooth moss. The doors to the temple buildings at the top were closed, not a sound to be heard. I followed the edge of the cliff, crawling over the boulders, and then prayed at the Buddhist hall. It was a stunning scene wrapped in quiet—I felt my spirit being purified.

shizukasa ya	Stillness—
iwa ni shimiiru	sinking deep into the rocks
semi no koe	cries of the cicada[71]

The Mogami River originates in the Deep North; its upper reaches are in Yamagata. As we descended, we encountered frightening rapids with names like

---

70. Bashō, exhausted from a difficult journey, finds Seifū's residence and hospitality to be "coolness" itself and "relaxes" (*nemaru*)—a word in the local dialect—as if he were at home. In an age without air conditioners, the word "cool" (*suzushisa*), a seasonal word for summer, was the ultimate compliment that could be paid to the host of a summer's lodging.

71. In classical poetry, the cicada (*semi*) was associated with its cries, which were considered raucous and undesirable. In a paradoxical twist, the sharp, high-pitched cries of the cicada deepen the stillness by penetrating the rocks on top of the mountain. The first version appears to have been "Mountain temple—sticking to the rocks, cries of the cicada," and the second version, "Loneliness—seeping into the rocks, cries of the cicada." In contrast to the verbs *shimitsuku* (to

Scattered Go Stones and Flying Eagle. The river skirts the north side of Mount Itajiki and then finally pours into the sea at Sakata. As I descended, passing through the dense foliage, I felt as if the mountains were covering the river on both sides. When filled with rice, these boats are apparently called "rice boats." Through the green leaves, I could see the falling waters of White-Thread Cascade. Sennindō, Hall of the Wizard, stood on the banks, directly facing the water. The river was swollen with rain, making the boat journey perilous.

samidare wo	Gathering the rains
atsumete hayashi	of the wet season—swift
Mogamigawa	the Mogami River[72]

. . .

Haguroyama, Gassan, and Yudono are called the Three Mountains of Dewa.[73] At Haguroyama, Feather Black Mountain—which belongs to the Tōeizan Temple in Edo, in Musashi Province—the moon of Tendai concentration and contemplation shines, and the lamp of the Buddhist Law of instant enlightenment glows. The temple quarters stand side by side, and the ascetics devote themselves to their calling. The efficacy of the divine mountain, whose prosperity will last forever, fills people with awe and fear.

---

stick to) and *shimikomu* (to seep into), *shimiiru* (to penetrate, pass deep into) in the last version implies the nonphysicality of the voice, which passes as if untouched, deep into the rocks and, by implication, becomes stillness. As the last sentence of the prose passage suggests, the stillness (*shizukasa*) also passes deep into the poet, making his "heart grow pure" (*kokoro sumiyuku*). The penetrating screech of the cicadas is suggested by the repetitive vowel "i" in the middle *ku: iwa ni shi mi iru*. At the same time, a paradoxical sense of stillness is created by the slow succession of "a's" and the recurrent soft "s" consonants: *shi, sa, shi, se*.

72. The original version, which Bashō composed at the residence of Takano Ichiei, a wealthy shipping agent who owned a boathouse on the Mogami River, was "gathering the rains of the wet season—cool, the Mogami River," which was followed by the wakiku, "A wharf post, tying a firefly to the bank," by Ichiei. Bashō's hokku praised the view of the river from Ichiei's residence by commenting on the "cool" sight of the huge Mogami River gathering in *samidare* (Fifth-Month rains), the steady rains of the wet season. In the second verse, Ichiei compared himself to the wharf posts that restrain the beautiful firefly (Bashō), thereby thanking his distinguished guest for the opportunity to entertain him. The revised version in *Narrow Road*, which drops the word "cool" (*suzushi*), is no longer a greeting to a host. The Mogami River, the largest river in the province and the main artery for all the other tributaries and streams, is "gathering" (*atsumete*) or has been gathering over time—one interpretation is that the wet season (*samidare*) is already over—the rains of the entire province, resulting in a massively swollen river, the force of which is captured and condensed in the quick sound and meaning of the word *hayashi* (swift). Here Bashō gives a new "poetic essence" (*hon'i*), based on personal experience, to the Mogami River, an utamakura (poetic place) associated from the time of the *Kokinshū* (Azuma-uta, no. 1092) with rice-grain boats (*inabune*), which were thought to ply the river.

73. Feather Black Mountain (Haguroyama), Moon Mountain (Gassan), and Bathhouse Mountain (Yudono), are called the Three Mountains (Sanzan).

On the eighth, we climbed Gassan, Moon Mountain. With purification cords around our necks and white cloth wrapped around our heads, we were led up the mountain by a person called a strongman. Surrounded by clouds and mist, we walked over ice and snow and climbed for twenty miles. Wondering if we had passed Cloud Barrier, beyond which the sun and moon move back and forth, I ran out of breath, my body frozen. By the time we reached the top, the sun had set and the moon had come out. We spread bamboo grass on the ground and lay down, waiting for the dawn. When the sun emerged and the clouds cleared away, we descended to Yudono, Bathhouse Mountain.

On the side of the valley were the so-called Blacksmith Huts. Here blacksmiths collect divine water, purify their bodies and minds, forge swords admired by the world, and engrave them with "Moon Mountain." I hear that in China they harden swords in the sacred water at Dragon Spring, and I was reminded of the ancient story of Gan Jiang and Mo Ye,[74] the two Chinese who crafted famous swords. The devotion of these masters to the art was extraordinary. Sitting down on a large rock for a short rest, I saw a cherry tree about three feet high, its buds half open. The tough spirit of the late-blooming cherry tree, buried beneath the accumulated snow, remembering the spring, moved me.[75] It was as if I could smell the "plum blossom in the summer heat," and I remembered the pathos of the poem by Priest Gyōson.[76] Forbidden to speak of the details of this sacred mountain, I put down my brush.

When we returned to the temple quarters, at Priest Egaku's behest, we wrote down verses about our pilgrimage to the Three Mountains.

suzushisa ya	Coolness—
hono mikazuki no	faintly a crescent moon over
Haguroyama	Feather Black Mountain[77]

---

74. Kanshō and Bakuya.

75. Both the process of sword making and the cherry trees blossoming in the cold at the top of the mountain are implicit metaphors for Bashō's ascetic journey.

76. "Plum blossoms in summer heat" is a Zen phrase for the unusual ability to achieve enlightenment. The plum tree blooms in early spring and generally never lasts until the summer. The poem by the priest Gyōson (1055–1135) is "Think of us as feeling sympathy for each other! Mountain cherry blossoms! I know of no one beside you here" (Kinyōshū, 1127; Misc. 1, no. 521).

77. Greetings to the spirit of the land often employed complex wordplay, homophones, and associative words, which interweave the place-name into the physical description. In this hokku the prefix hono (faintly or barely) and mikazuki (third-day moon) create an implicit visual contrast between the thin light of the crescent moon and the blackness of the night, implied in the name Haguroyama, or Feather Black Mountain. The silver hook of the moon, which casts a thin ray of light through the darkness, brings a sense of "coolness" amid the summer heat, suggesting both the hospitality and the spiritual purity of the sacred mountain.

kumo no mine	Cloud peaks
ikutsu kuzurete	crumbling one after another—
tsuki no yama	Moon Mountain[78]

katararenu	Forbidden to speak—
yudono ni nurasu	wetting my sleeves
tamoto kana	at Bathhouse Mountain![79]

Left Haguro and at the castle town of Tsurugaoka were welcomed by the samurai Nagayama Shigeyuki. Composed a round of haikai. Sakichi accompanied us this far. Boarded a boat and went down to the port of Sakata. Stayed at the house of a doctor named En'an Fugyoku.

Atsumiyama ya	From Hot Springs Mountain
Fukuura kakete	to the Bay of Breezes,
yusuzumi	the evening cool[80]

---

78. *Kumo no mine* (literally, cloud peak) is a high, cumulonimbus cloud that results from intense moisture and heat. The mountain-shaped clouds, which have gathered during midday at the peak of Gassan, or Moon Mountain, crumble or collapse one after another until they are finally gone, leaving the moon shining over the mountain (*tsuki no yama*), a Japanese reading for Gassan. The word *ikutsu* (how many?) may be read either as doubt, as in "peaks of clouds, how many have collapsed?" or as "a considerable number," as in "peaks of clouds, a considerable number have collapsed." An earlier passage stating that "the moon of Tendai insight was clear" (*Tendai shikan no tsuki akiraka ni*) also suggests enlightenment, an "unclouded" state of mind. Movement, in short, occurs from midday, when the clouds block the view, to night, when the mountain stands unobscured; from the heat of midday to the cool of evening; from the ephemerality of the clouds, which disappear one after another, to the sacred mountain, which stands firm and awesome; and from mental obscurity to enlightenment.

79. In contrast to the first two mountains, Haguroyama and Gassan, which never appeared in classical poetry, Yudono (literally, Bathhouse) was an utamakura, referred to in classical poetry as Koi-no-yama, Mountain of Love. The body of the Yudono deity was a huge red rock that spouted hot water and was said to resemble sexual organs. "Forbidden to speak" (*katararenu*) refers to the rule that all visitors to Yudono, the holiest of the Three Mountains of Dewa, are forbidden to speak about the appearance of the mountain to others. The wetting of the sleeves echoes the erotic association with love and bathing and suggests the speaker's tears of awe at the holiness of the mountain. The journey over the Three Mountains, in which the traveler almost dies from exhaustion and cold before coming to Yudono, a place of sexuality and fertility, represents a rite of passage, a kind of death and rebirth.

80. This hokku is a greeting to the host Fugyoku, using the associations of the place names Atsumiyama (Hot Springs Mountain) and Fukuura (Blowing Bay) to indicate that the view from the host's house provides a feeling of "coolness" on a hot day—a theme further developed in the next hokku on the Mogami River.

atsuki hi o	Pouring the hot day
umi ni iretari	into the sea—
Mogamigawa	Mogami River[81]

Having seen all the beautiful landscapes—rivers, mountains, seas, and coasts—I now prepared my heart for Kisagata. From the port at Sakata moving northeast, we crossed over a mountain, followed the rocky shore, and walked across the sand—all for a distance of ten miles. The sun was on the verge of setting when we arrived. The sea wind blew sand into the air; the rain turned everything to mist, hiding Chōkai Mountain. I groped in the darkness. Having heard that the landscape was exceptional in the rain,[82] I decided that it must also be worth seeing after the rain, too, and squeezed into a fisherman's thatched hut to wait for the rain to pass.

By the next morning the skies had cleared, and with the morning sun shining brightly, we took a boat to Kisagata. Our first stop was Nōin Island, where we visited the place where Nōin had secluded himself for three years.[83] We docked our boat on the far shore and visited the old cherry tree on which Saigyō had written the poem about "a fisherman's boat rowing over the flowers."[84] On the shore of the river was an imperial mausoleum, the gravestone of Empress Jingū. The temple was called Kanmanju Temple. I wondered why I had yet to hear of an imperial procession to this place.

We sat down in the front room of the temple and raised the blinds, taking in the entire landscape at one glance. To the south, Chōkai Mountain held up the heavens, its shadow reflected on the bay of Kisagata; to the west, the road

---

81. The first version was composed by Bashō as part of a *kasen* at the residence of Terajima Hikosuke, a wealthy merchant at Sakata: "Coolness—pouring into the sea, Mogami River." The hokku, which is a salutation, praises the view from Hikosuke's house, which overlooks the Mogami River at the point where the giant river flows into the Japan Sea. In the revised version, the Mogami River is pouring the *atsuki hi*, which can be read either as "hot sun" or "hot day," suggesting both a setting sun washed by the waves at sea and a hot summer's day coming to a dramatic close in the sea. Bashō drops the word "coolness" (*suzushisa*) and the constraints of the greeting to create a more dramatic image, one that suggests coolness without using the word.

82. Here Bashō compares Kisagata to the famous West Lake in China, of which Su Dongpo (Su Shi, 1037–1101) wrote, "The sparkling, brimming waters are beautiful in sunshine; / The view when a misty rain veils the mountains is exceptional too. / West Lake can be compared to Xi Shi: / She is charming whether her makeup is light or elaborate" (translated by Helen McCullough).

83. Kisagata became associated with Nōin (d. 1050) as a result of the poem "I have spent my life making the thatched huts of the fishermen at Kisagata my lodging" (*Goshūishū*, 1096; Travel, no. 519).

84. The poem attributed to Saigyō is "The cherry trees at Kisakata are buried in waves—a fisherman's boat rowing over the flowers" (*Kisagata no sakura wa nami ni uzumorete hana no ue kogu ama no tsuribune*).

came to an end at Muyamuya Barrier; and to the east, there was a dike. The road to Akita stretched into the distance. To the north was the sea, the waves pounding into the bay at Shiogoshi, Tide-Crossing. The face of the bay, about two and a half miles in width and length, resembled Matsushima but with a different mood. If Matsushima was like someone laughing, Kisagata resembled a resentful person filled with sorrow and loneliness. The land was as if in a state of anguish.

Kisagata ya   Kisagata—
ame ni Seishi ga   Xi Shi asleep in the rain
nebu no hana   flowers of the silk tree[85]

shiogoshi ya   In the shallows—
tsuru hagi nurete   cranes wetting their legs
umi suzushi   coolness of the sea[86]

. . .

Reluctant to leave Sakata, the days piled up; now I turn my gaze to the far-off clouds of the northern provinces.[87] Thoughts of the distant road ahead fill me with anxiety; I hear it is more than 325 miles to the castle town in Kaga.[88] After we crossed Nezu-no-seki, Mouse Barrier, we hurried toward Echigo and came to Ichiburi, in Etchū Province. Over these nine days, I suffered from the extreme heat, fell ill, and did not record anything.

---

85. Kisagata was an utamakura associated, particularly as a result of the famous poem by Nōin (d. 1050), with wandering, the thatched huts of fisherfolk, lodgings, and a rocky shore. The traveler relives these classical associations, but in the end, he draws on Su Dongpo's poem "West Lake" (Xi Hu, J. Seiko), which compares the noted lake to Xi Shi (J. Seishi), a legendary Chinese beauty who was employed during the Zhou dynasty to debauch an enemy emperor and cause his defeat and who was thought to have a constant frown, her eyes half closed, as a result of her tragic fate. Echoing the Sino-Japanese mixed prose, Xi Shi is juxtaposed with the delicate flowers of the silk tree (nebu or nemu) whose slender hairlike stamen close up at night, suggesting that Xi Shi is "sleeping" (nemu) or that her eyes are half closed. Dampened and shriveled by the rain, the silk tree flower echoes the resentful Chinese consort: both in turn became a metaphor for the rain-enshrouded, emotionally dark bay.

86. Shiogoshi (Tide Crossing) was both a common noun, referring to the shallows at the mouth of a bay, and a proper name, designating such a place at Kisagata. Bashō here describes Kisagata after the rains, closing out a series of contrasts: between Matsushima and Kisagata, lightness and darkness, laughter and resentment, the dark brooding atmosphere of Kisagata during the rains and the cool, light atmosphere that follows.

87. Hokurokudō, or Hokurikudō. The seven provinces of Wakasa, Echizen, Kaga, Notō, Etchū, Echigo, and Sado (today, Fukui, Ishikawa, Toyama, and Niigata Prefectures) on the northwestern Japan Sea coast.

88. The distance 130 ri, about 322 miles or 520 kilometers. The city of Kanazawa, a castle town of the Maeda family.

fumizuki ya	The Seventh Month—
muika mo tsune no	the sixth day, too, is different
yo ni wa nizu	from the usual night[89]

araumi ya	A wild sea—
Sado ni yokotau	stretching to Sado Isle
Amanogawa	the River of Heaven[90]

Today, exhausted from crossing the most dangerous places in the north country—places with names like Children Forget Parents, Parents Forget Children, Dogs Turn Back, Horses Sent Back—I drew up my pillow and lay down to sleep, only to hear in the adjoining room the voices of two young women. An elderly man joined in the conversation, and I gathered that they were women of pleasure from a place called Niigata in Echigo Province. They were on a pilgrimage to Ise Shrine, and the man was seeing them off as far as the barrier here at Ichiburi. They seemed to be writing letters and giving him other trivial messages to take back to Niigata tomorrow. Like "the daughters of the fishermen, passing their lives on the shore where the white waves roll in,"[91] they had fallen low in this world, exchanging vows with every passerby. What terrible lives they must have had in their previous existence for this to occur. I fell asleep as I listened to them talk. The next morning, they came up to us as we departed. "The difficulties of road, not knowing our destination, the uncertainty and

---

89. The seventh night of the Seventh Month was Tanabata, when the legendary constellations, the Herd Boy and Weaver Girl, two separated lovers, cross over the Milky Way (Amanogawa) for their annual meeting. Even the night before is unusual.

90. Sado, an island across the water from Izumozaki (Izumo Point), was known for its long history of political exiles: Emperor Juntoku, Nichiren, Mongaku, Zeami, the mother of Zushiō, and others. As a consequence, the island, surrounded here by a "wild sea" (araumi) and standing under the vast Amanogawa (literally, River of Heaven), or Milky Way, comes to embody the feeling of loneliness, both of the exiles at Sado and of the traveler himself. The poem has a majestic, slow moving rhythm, especially the drawn-out "o" sounds in the middle line (Sado ni yokotau), which suggests the vastness and scale of the landscape. Bashō arrived at Izumo Point on the fourth day of the Seventh Month, but when he wrote Narrow Road many years later, he added the preceding hokku on the sixth day of the Seventh Month, thereby associating the Milky Way with Tanabata when the Herd Boy and the Weaver Girl cross over the River of Heaven for their annual meeting. In this larger context, the island surrounded by a "wild sea" also embodies the longing of the exiles (and implicitly that of the poet) for their distant loved ones. Bashō replaces what grammatically should be an intransitive verb yokotawaru (to be sideways) with a transitive verb yokotau (to lay or place sideways), implying that the Creative (zōka) lays the Milky Way sideways. As Andō Tsuguo argues, the Milky Way, laid down by the zōka, becomes like a boat or a bridge reaching out across the dark waters to the waiting exiles at Sado, that is, reaching out to the lonely soul of the poet.

91. From an anonymous poem: "Since I am the daughter of a fisherman, passing my life on the shore where the white waves roll in, I have no home" (Shinkokinshū, 1205; Misc. 2, no. 1701).

sorrow—it makes us want to follow your tracks. We'll be inconspicuous. Please bless us with your robes of compassion, link us to the Buddha," they said tearfully.

"We sympathize with you, but we have many stops on the way. Just follow the others. The gods will make sure that no harm occurs to you." Shaking them off with these remarks, we left, but the pathos of their situation lingered with us.

hitotsu ya ni	Under the same roof
yūjo mo netari	women of pleasure also sleep—
hagi to tsuki	bush clover and moon[92]

I dictated this to Sora, who wrote it down. . . .

We visited Tada Shrine where Sanemori's helmet and a piece of his brocade robe were stored. They say that long ago when Sanemori belonged to the Genji clan, Lord Yoshitomo offered him the helmet. Indeed, it was not the armor of a common soldier. A chrysanthemum and vine carved design inlaid with gold extended from the visor to the ear flaps, and a two-horn frontpiece was attached to the dragon head. After Sanemori died in battle, Kiso Yoshinaka attached a prayer sheet to the helmet and offered it to the shrine. Higuchi Jirō acted as Kiso's messenger. It was as if the past were appearing before my very eyes.

muzan ya na	"How pitiful!"
kabuto no shita no	beneath the warrior helmet
kirigirisu	cries of a cricket[93]
	. . .

---

92. The hokku suggests Bashō's surprise that two very different parties—the young prostitutes and the male priest-travelers—have something in common, implicitly the uncertainty of life and of travel. The bush clover (*hagi*), the object of love in classical poetry, suggests the prostitutes, while the moon, associated in poetry with enlightenment and clarity, implies Bashō and his priest friend, though it is not necessary to read a direct one-to-one correspondence here. The main point is that two natural images, while very different, are somehow unexpectedly linked, as the two sets of visitors to the lodge were.

93. In one of the more famous scenes in *The Tale of the Heike*, Saitō Sanemori (Saitō Bettō), not wanting other soldiers to realize his advanced age, dyed his white hair black and fought valiantly before being slain by the retainers of Kiso Yoshinaka (1154–1184). According to legend, Yoshinaka, who had been saved by Sanemori as a child, wept at seeing the washed head of the slain warrior and subsequently made an offering of the helmet and brocade to the Tada Shrine. In *Sanemori*, a warrior nō play by Zeami, a wandering priest travels to Shinohara Village in Kaga Province where he encounters an old man who turns out to be the spirit of Sanemori and who narrates the story of his death in battle. In a passage narrated by the ghost, Higuchi Jirō (d. 1184), one of Yoshinaka's retainers, is summoned to identify the washed, white-haired head of the slain warrior and exclaims, "Oh, how pitiful! It's Sanemori!" In Bashō's hokku, the traveler, presumably

The sixteenth. The skies had cleared, and we decided to gather little red shells at Iro-no-hama, Color Beach, seven leagues across the water.[94] A man named Ten'ya made elaborate preparations—lunch boxes, wine flasks, and the like—and ordered a number of servants to go with us on the boat. Enjoying a tailwind, we arrived quickly.[95] The beach was dotted with a few fisherman's huts and a dilapidated Lotus Flower temple. We drank tea, warmed up saké, and were overwhelmed by the loneliness of the evening.

sabishisa ya	Loneliness—
Suma ni kachitaru	an autumn beach judged
hama no aki	superior to Suma's[96]

nami no ma ya	Between the waves—
kogai ni majiru	mixed with small shells
hagi no chiri	petals of bush clover

I had Tōsai write down the main events of that day and left it at the temple.

---

reminded by Sanemori's helmet of the washed head of the slain warrior, utters Higuchi Jirō's words, and then awakening from these thoughts of the distant past, he hears a cricket beneath the warrior's helmet. The cricket, a seasonal word for autumn, was associated in the classical poetry with pathos and the loneliness that comes from inevitable decline, as in the following poem by Saigyō: "As the autumn nights grow old, the cricket seems to weaken, its voice fading into the distance" (*Shinkokinshū*, 1205; Autumn 2, no. 472). These associations of the cricket, particularly the pathos of old age, resonate with the image of the severed head of the white-haired warrior. As Sora's diary reveals, Bashō originally composed the hokku as a religious offering to the Tada Shrine, near Shinohara, the old battlefield where the head of Sanemori had been washed. Bashō drew on the dramatic structure of nō drama, particularly the two-part "dream play" (*mugen nō*), in which the *shite* (protagonist) encounters the spirits of the dead, listens to their stories of grief, and offers a prayer in a ritual of spirit pacification. In this context, the cries of the cricket in Bashō's hokku can also be taken as those of Sanemori's anguished soul, which the traveler, like the wandering priest in the nō play, pacifies with a poetic prayer.

94. Masuho are small red shells found at Iro no hama, Color Beach. Bashō is initially drawn to the beach because of Saigyō's poem on Iro no hama: "Is it because they gather crimson shells that dye the ocean tides that they call this Color Beach?" (*Sankashū*, no. 1194).

95. Echoes a passage in the "Suma" chapter of *The Tale of Genji* in which Genji takes a boat to the beach at Suma, which became associated with loneliness as a result of a famous passage in this chapter describing Suma.

96. In contrast to Saigyō, who was interested in Iro no hama, Color Beach, primarily for its lexical association with the word "color" (*iro*) and whose poem reflects Heian, aristocratic, court sensibility, Bashō saw the place as a toponym for autumnal loneliness (*sabishisa*), a medieval aesthetic that Bashō assimilated into haikai. Suma was an utamakura closely associated with the poetry of Ariwara no Yukihira (d. 893), who was exiled to Suma and, with the banishment of the eponymous hero of *The Tale of Genji*, was considered to be the embodiment of loneliness in the classical tradition. As Ogata Tsutomu has pointed out, the phrase "the loneliness of the evening" (*yūgure no sabishisa*) in the prose echoes the famous "three autumn evening poems"

Rotsū came as far as the Tsuruga harbor to greet me, and together we went to Mino Province. With the aid of horses, we traveled to Ōgaki. Sora joined us from Ise. Etsujin galloped in on horseback, and we gathered at the house of Jokō. Zensenshi, Keiko, Keiko's sons, and other intimate acquaintances visited day and night. For them, it was like meeting someone who had returned from the dead. They were both overjoyed and sympathetic. Although I had not yet recovered from the weariness of the journey, we set off again on the sixth of the Ninth Month. Thinking to pay our respects to the great shrine at Ise, we boarded a boat.

> hamaguri no   Autumn going—
> futami ni wakare   parting for Futami
> yuku aki zo   a clam pried from its shell[97]
>
> [NKBZ 41: 341–386, translated by Haruo Shirane]

(sanseki) in the Shinkokinshū (1205; Autumn 1, nos. 361–363), which include Priest Jakuren's "Loneliness is not any particular color—a mountain of black pines on an autumn evening." In contrast to the "front" of Japan, the eastern side of the Deep North, which appears bright, warm, and joyous in Oku no hosomichi, the "back" of Japan, extending from Kisagata in the north to Iro no hama to the south, is imbued with a monochromatic, mist-filled, white-ish, moonlit, lonely atmosphere. In a haikai twist, the quiet loneliness of Iro no hama, an obscure beach on the "back side" of Japan, is "judged superior" (kachitaru)—a phrase reminiscent of the judgments in waka poetry contests (utaawase)—to that of Suma as well as to the famed loneliness of the Shinkokin-shū. Instead of reaffirming the classical culture of the capital, the provinces have become a wellspring of poetic sensibility, a new carrier of cultural memory, that could match, if not supersede, that of the classical and medieval past.

97. Bashō's hokku turns on a series of homophones: wakaru means both "to depart for" and "to tear from," and Futami refers to a noted place on the coast of Ise Province (the traveler's next destination and a place known for clams) as well as the shell (futa) and body (mi) of the clam (hamaguri). The phrase "autumn going" (yuku aki) directly echoes the phrase "spring going" (yuku haru) in the poem at the beginning of the narrative. The passing of the season becomes an implicit metaphor for not only the sorrow of parting, which lies at the heart of travel, but also the ceaseless passage of time, the traveler's constant companion.

Chapter 6

CHIKAMATSU MONZAEMON AND

THE PUPPET THEATER

EARLY JŌRURI AND KABUKI

The art of *jōruri* (chanting), which lies at the heart of the puppet theater (*bunraku*), can be traced back to the late fifteenth century when blind minstrels chanted the story of Yoshitsune (Ushimakamaru) and his love affair with Lady Jōruri (Jōruri hime), whom he met while traveling in northern Japan. (Because the story was divided into twelve sections, it was also called the *Twelve-Section Book*, or *Jūnidan zōshi.*) Jōruri, the chanting of the story, was originally accompanied by a *biwa* (lute), probably similar to the Heike style. During the sixteenth century, however, the biwa was replaced by a *shamisen* (a three-stringed banjo-like instrument imported from China in the sixteenth century), which differed significantly in tone. Then, as early as the 1610s, puppets were added, transforming the combination into a theatrical genre.

Through the early seventeenth century, the puppets were relatively simple, each held by one puppeteer. Later, from about 1734, sophisticated three-man puppets, the type seen on the contemporary bunraku stage, were developed. Today a puppeteer begins his career as the operator of the doll's feet, an art that usually requires ten years to master; graduates to the manipulation of the left hand; and then, finally, after many years of experience, attains the position of head puppeteer, who controls both the head and the right arm. The main puppeteer usually wears a formal dress and has his face exposed, while the junior manipulators of the feet and left hand are dressed entirely in black with a hood covering their head and face. The bunraku dolls, whose heads are generally categorized by sex, age, and character (such as good, evil, or comic), range in size from two and a half to as much as five feet tall and may have movable eyes, eyebrows, mouths, and fingers.

A related genre was *sekkyōbushi*, sermon ballads, which date back to the Kamakura period and chanted, to the accompaniment of musical instruments, stories (such as *Karukaya*, *Sanshōdaiyū*, and *Oguri hangan*) about the power of gods or the origins of shrines and temples. Sekkyōbushi also began using the shamisen and then puppets in the Kanei era (1624–1644). This genre reached its height in the 1660s (during the Manji-Kanbun eras) and then, at least in the urban centers, was absorbed into the jōruri tradition.

Both kabuki and jōruri emerged in the early seventeenth century and flourished thereafter as popular entertainment. In contrast to nō and *kyōgen* (comic drama)—two medieval dramatic genres that continued to be staged but whose audience was largely samurai or merchant elite—kabuki and jōruri were aimed at a wide audience. Bunraku (puppet theater) consists of three elements: the puppets, music (shamisen), and chanting (jōruri) based on a text and performed by a *tayū* (chanter), who speaks or sings all the roles, including the third-person narration. Unlike kabuki, which originally emerged from dance, with the actor's body and voice as the center of attention, the art of jōruri focuses on the chanter, who sits conspicuously on the side of the stage and is the undisputed center of attention. The coordination among the three elements—the actors/puppets, music, and narration—is a key to both kabuki and jōruri, but in contrast to kabuki, in which the actors are given priority, in jōruri the chanter was originally ranked above the shamisen players and the puppet operators. Indeed, the jōruri (chanting) is so important that it often is performed alone, without the puppets.

The term *kabuki* is now written with three characters meaning "song" (*ka* or *uta*), "dance" (*bu* or *mai*), and "performance or skill" (*ki* or *gi*), representing the three central elements of this theatrical genre. In the Edo period the *ki* was usually written with the character meaning "courtesan," giving the term a more erotic flavor. The word originally came from the verb *kabuku* (to lean over, to violate the rules of behavior or dress, to act wildly)—that is, to work against the established social or moral order, to celebrate a liberated lifestyle and attitude. The creation of kabuki is attributed to Okuni, a female attendant at the Izumo Shrine, who led a female company that performed dance and comic sketches on the dry bed of the Kamo River in Kyoto in 1603. According to documents, Okuni dressed as a man, reflecting the kind of "wild" (*kabuki*) spirit that became the heart of kabuki. The Tenshō-Keichō eras (1573–1614), when kabuki dance began, were marked by this kabuki spirit, which was taken up by the *machishū*, Kyoto's new townspeople with commercial wealth, and which became one of the driving forces behind the early modern culture.

Okuni's kabuki dance attracted many imitators around the country and led to the rise of *onna* (women's) kabuki. The courtesans in the pleasure district in Kyoto, for example, frequently gave erotic performances at Shijōgawara, on the dry riverbed at Shijō Bridge. These female kabuki troupes—one of the most famous being the Sado Island kabuki group—were so popular that they were invited to the castle towns by various domain lords and traveled to give performances in mining and port towns. The performances of women's kabuki, mainly popular songs and dances, were mixed in with "teahouse entertainment" (*chaya asobi*) in which the courtesans played the shamisen, an instrument of the licensed quarters, and revealed other ways in which they entertained their customers at their teahouses or brothels. In a typical "teahouse" dramatic sketch, the female star of the troupe, dressed as a male customer and accompanied by a jester, would visit the madam of the teahouse, a male actor dressed as a woman. The cross-dressing and sex reversal gave the audience a highly erotic charge, much as Okuni had. The performances, however, were too provocative for the bakufu (government). In addition, they caused fights among the spectators for the personal favors of the female entertainers—for whom the kabuki was a means of luring customers—and resulted in the bakufu's banning women's kabuki in 1629.

With the abolition of women's kabuki, the spotlight shifted to *wakashu* (boys') kabuki, which had existed from as early as the medieval period. The popularity of these elegant dances was driven by the erotic fondness at this time for male youths, and as in women's kabuki, the young actors provided "teahouse entertainment" and played the role of women. Wakashu kabuki, however, differed from women's kabuki in that it incorporated aspects of other genres, especially the dances (*mai* and *komai*) from kyōgen and nō drama. This in turn led to the development of *buyō*, a distinct kabuki dance style that merged with the earlier popular dance (*odori*) that had been at the heart of kabuki. The lion's dance and other dynamic dances that revealed the physical agility of the young male actors were also incorporated into kabuki at this time. As did the performers in women's kabuki, the young actors in wakashu kabuki sold their favors to male customers. Indeed, Tokugawa Iemitsu (1604–1651), who became the third shōgun in 1623, was famous for his interest in the young actors and even had a kabuki troupe perform at Edo Castle. The association of this kind of kabuki with prostitution, however, proved to be too much, and in 1652, a year after Iemitsu's death, the bakufu banned wakashu kabuki as well.

Bowing to pressure from the theater people, the bakufu gave permission the following year to restore kabuki on the condition that the male actors shave off their forelocks (a sign of youth). The result was *yarō* (adult male) kabuki, which stressed realistic drama, mixed in humor, and went beyond song and dance. Nevertheless, the erotic dimension remained, and despite pressure from the authorities, kabuki continued under the guise of narrative drama to perform scenes that featured the buying of prostitutes. For example, Shimabara kyōgen—which became enormously popular and focused on a male customer, a high-ranking courtesan (tayū), and the owner of an *ageya* (where high-level courtesans entertained customers)—acted out on stage the customs of the licensed quarter in Shimabara in Kyoto, functioning as a kind of live guide to this area. Shimabara kyōgen created the "love scene" (*nuregoto*), the "prostitute scene" (*keiseigoto*), and the "dressed-down or in-disguise scene" (*yatsushigoto*), all of which became important conventions in kabuki. After Shimabara kyōgen was banned for the same reasons that onna kabuki and wakashu kabuki had been prohibited, the principal interest shifted to the performance of the older adult male actor (yarō) playing the role of a young female courtesan, thus refining the art of the woman's role (*onnagata*), which became a major part of kabuki performance. Another key development of yarō kabuki, which lasted from the 1650s through the 1680s, was the transition from a single act to multiple acts (*tsuzuki kyōgen*) in the Kanbun era (1661–1673), a development that occurred largely under the influence of nō drama and the puppet theater.

In contrast to the medieval performing arts, which were largely itinerant, jōruri and kabuki were usually performed at fixed locations, usually in the cities, where admission could be charged to the audience. From around the Genna era (1615–1624), the bakufu gave permission for the construction of particular licensed theaters, which led to the development of the two "bad places" (*akusho*): the theater district and the licensed pleasure quarters. The bakufu, whose first priority was to uphold the social order and public security, designated the "bad places" as spaces of controlled release (*nagusami*), where citizens' excess energy could be channeled and where it was understood that there would be no criticism of the existing order. Those who went into these "bad places" entered an intoxicating, out-of-the-ordinary, festival-like world where the line between reality and dream was blurred. Kabuki and jōruri explored this erotic, extraordinary space while absorbing as much as it could from nō and kyōgen.

The Genroku era was a golden time for kabuki, which played to large and enthusiastic audiences in Kyoto, Osaka, and Edo. Of the two main elements of kabuki, the *shosagoto* (the buyō dance pieces) and the *jigei* (speech and mime; drama), the latter underwent the greater transformation at this time, leading to the development of highly realistic dialogue and acting styles. The three most notable actors of Genroku kabuki were Ichikawa Danjurō (1660–1704), who made his debut on the stage of the Nakamura Theater in Edo in 1673, Sakata Tōjūrō (1647–1709), who came to fame in the Osaka-Kyoto region, and Yoshizawa Ayame (1653–1724), also from Kyoto, who established the art of the onnagata.

In the Kyoto-Osaka area, the center of Genroku culture, Sakata Tōjūrō perfected what later came to be called the *wagoto* (soft or gentle) style, in which a townsman falls in love with a courtesan or prostitute, is disowned, and falls into difficult straits. In Edo, Ichikawa Danjurō created the *aragoto* (rough) style, which originated in the city of the samurai and featured courageous heroes, bold, masculine characters who displayed superhuman powers in overcoming evildoers. In the kabuki version of Chikamatsu Monzaemon's *Battles of Coxinga*, Watōnai, the warrior hero of Japanese-Chinese parentage, is an example of an aragoto role, and in *The Love Suicides at Amijima*, Jihei, the weak paper merchant who falls tragically in love with the prostitute Koharu, became a noted wagoto role.

In both kabuki and the puppet theater, the status of the playwright originally was extremely low. The playwright's name did not appear in the puppet theater script or in the advertisement for the play. In fact, Chikamatsu Monzaemon was one of the first to have his name on the advertisement (*kanban*) and initially was criticized for it. In contrast to kabuki, however, whose texts were not published in full until the late nineteenth century, jōruri texts were published in their entirety with the first performance, thereby making them widely available.

CHIKAMATSU MONZAEMON

Chikamatsu Monzaemon (1653–1725) was born in Echizen Province, in what is now Fukui Prefecture, on the Japan Sea side of the country, where his father, Sugimori Nobuyoshi (1621–1687), was in personal service to the young daimyō of Echizen. His father's stipend of three hundred *koku* indicates that the family was upper-class samurai and relatively well off. His mother's father was the daimyō's doctor, with a large stipend of one thousand *koku*, and her family also had Kyoto connections. When Chikamatsu was fourteen or fifteen, his family moved to Kyoto, where he entered the service of several courtier families. One was that of Ichijō Ekan (1605–1672), the son of Emperor GoYōzei and the head of the Ichijō house, for which Chikamatsu worked until Ekan's death in 1672. Through Ekan, Chikamatsu participated in courtier cultural life in the late 1660s and early 1670s. When he was in his mid-twenties, Chikamatsu began writing plays for Uji Kaganojō (1635–1711), the foremost puppet chanter of the time in Kyoto, and sometime later he started to write kabuki plays as well. As one who came from a relatively well-off samurai family, served in the households of a member of the imperial family and other culturally active Kyoto aristocrats, and then went on to work for street performers and kabuki actors officially considered as outcasts (*kawara-kojiki*, riverbed beggars), Chikamatsu's experience was highly unusual in the strict social hierarchy of the day.

Chikamatsu's early jōruri and kabuki were written in collaboration with performers, and his later mature works were usually written in consultation with performers and managers. Chikamatsu learned his trade as a jōruri writer from Kaganojō who was almost twenty years his senior and, for unknown reasons, did not allow Chikamatsu's name to appear as the author or coauthor of his plays. The last performer in the oral tradition that held the chanter to be the undisputed source of the texts, Kaganojō was also a teacher and the employer of Takemoto Gidayū (1651–1714), the great chanter in Osaka and a crucial figure

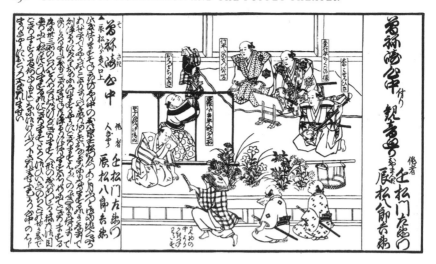

This woodblock print announces the 1703 production of *The Love Suicides at Sonezaki*, to be performed at the Takemoto Theater in Osaka. Tatsumatsu Hachirōbei (d. 1734), a noted puppeteer, is behind a transparent cloth single-handedly maneuvering Ohatsu in the opening pilgrimage scene. A special announcer sits in front of the screen advertising the play and exchanging notes with the audience. The three performers seated to the right in formal wide-shouldered attire are, from left to right, Takemoto Tanomo, the supporting chanter; Takemoto Gidayū (1651–1714), the lead chanter, holding a fan in his right hand; and the shamisen player. (From NKBZ 43, *Chikamatsu Monzaemon shū 1*, by permission of Shōgakukan)

in the development of jōruri theater. In his art treatise, Kaganojō claims nō drama as the parent of jōruri and describes jōruri as fundamentally a musical drama constructed of acts, each with a distinctive musical mood: auspicious (*shūgen*), elegant (*yūgen*), amorous (*renbo*), and tragic (*aishō*). Most of the plays thought to be the result of his and Chikamatsu's collaboration in the late 1670s and early 1680s borrowed from nō drama and other classical Japanese sources.

The earliest work that is definitely known to have been written by Chikamatsu is *The Soga Successor* (*Yotsugi Soga*, 1683), performed first by Kaganojō and then a year later by Gidayū. This pattern of composing plays—and often rewriting them slightly—for both chanters, one working in Kyoto and the other in Osaka, continued during the 1680s. But Chikamatsu's life changed after he began to write for Takemoto Gidayū, who was only two years his senior. Gidayū was initially an apprentice of Kaganojō and performed in Kyoto, where he probably met Chikamatsu. Gidayū then broke away from Kaganojō and established his own Takemoto Theater in Osaka in 1684. In 1685, Kaganojō provocatively moved his troupe from Kyoto to Osaka and competed for audiences alongside Gidayū. Around this time, Gidayū wooed Chikamatsu away from Kaganojō and took the decisive step of having Chikamatsu claim authorship for himself. The gap left by Chikamatsu was filled by the famous poet and novelist Ihara Saikaku (1642–1693), who in 1685 wrote two works for Kaganojō for the Osaka audience. The second work, at least, seems to have had some success, but Kaganojō's theater burned down, and Kaganojō returned to Kyoto, leaving Gidayū, now joined with Chikamatsu, the seemingly undisputed victor in Osaka. The collaboration of Chikamatsu and Gidayū, which continued on and off until Gidayū's death in 1714, produced a new age of jōruri writing and many of Chikamatsu's masterpieces.

By 1685, Chikamatsu was also writing for kabuki. In fact, his work for the kabuki theater dominated his creative energies from the mid-1690s until his final kabuki play of 1705, during which time most of his more than thirty surviving kabuki plays were produced. In this period, writers for kabuki were not highly regarded, and only a few theaters had playwrights on their staff. But Sakata Tōjūrō (1647–1709), who became a kabuki star actor in the 1690s, is known to have considered playwriting important to his success, and his relationship with Chikamatsu was one of mutual respect. From 1693 until 1702, Chikamatsu wrote almost exclusively for Tōjūrō, who became famous as the creator of the Kyoto-Osaka *wagoto* (soft) style of acting and focused on portraying young men of good background who have fallen on hard times. The showpiece was the *yatsushi* (disguise) section, in which the hero, formerly the heir of a samurai or high merchant house, is in disguise as a poor, destitute figure, having lost his position owing to either his own profligacy or the machinations of a younger brother or disloyal retainer. The climactic scene was often set in the pleasure quarter where Tōjūrō has an encounter with his courtesan lover. Sometime in the 1690s, Tōjūrō made Chikamatsu the staff playwright at his Miyako Theater in Kyoto, giving him financial security for perhaps the first time in his life. Chikamatsu's experience of writing five-act jōruri plays with integrated plots provided the framework for his kabuki plays, which were usually in three acts made up of different scenes.

Chikamatsu's involvement with kabuki was crucial to his later development as a jōruri playwright. The success of the topical, one-act *Love Suicides at Sonezaki* in 1703, Chikamatsu's earliest *sewamono* (contemporary-life) jōruri, obviously inspired by his experience in writing kabuki, was the first fruit of his maturity. In the last eighteen years of his career, he wrote about seventy-five jōruri, twenty-four of which were sewamono, in a tremendous burst of creativity after he had passed fifty. *The Love Suicides at Sonezaki* is a crucial landmark in both the history of Japanese theater and Chikamatsu's own career. Its success was unexpected and restored the Takemoto Theater to profit, and it spurred other changes in jōruri drama as it strove to compete with kabuki's live actors for audiences in theaters that sat side by side in the Dōtonbori entertainment district in south Osaka. Two changes made during this period were discontinuing the skits and interludes between acts and introducing the short one-act

sewamono made up of three scenes—under the influence of kabuki practice—
after a longer five-act history play.

Chikamatsu's twenty-four contemporary-life (sewamono) plays—conceived
as one-act dramas equivalent to the intense third act of a five-act history play
(jidaimono)—maintain a tight unity of place and time and are usually realistic,
without any of the fantastic elements of the period dramas. This temporal and
spatial unity, together with the realism, has earned praise in modern times for
sewamono. Chikamatsu's more than seventy history plays, by contrast, have
multiple plots and supernatural elements, often taking place over vast areas of
time and space. The climactic third act of the history play, however, which is
as long as many of the one-act, three-scene sewamono, is tightly structured and
realistically acted. In short, the two genres are built on entirely different premises and theatrical conventions. Whereas sewamono engage with contemporary
society directly through depictions of an actual incident of the time, jidaimono
use complex interaction and dialogue with an array of texts from both the
Japanese and Chinese traditions to portray contemporary politics. Whereas
contemporary-life plays usually focus on the private lives of average folk, history
pieces most often stress the individual's interaction with the public, political
sphere. Chikamatsu's history dramas from the latter half of his career in fact
present a tense balance between the private and public spheres of society, usually with the third act emphasizing the private consequences of conflict with
the public world of politics.

After the success of *The Love Suicides at Sonezaki*, Takemoto Gidayū expressed his desire to retire from the stage, exhausted by managing a theater
while being its star performer as well. This made way for the debut of Takeda
Izumo I (d. 1747) as the new manager, leaving Gidayū to concentrate solely on
performance. Izumo came from a different puppet tradition, the Takeda Ōmi
style of mechanical and trick puppets, which also competed with jōruri and
kabuki in Dōtonbori. Izumo took the decisive step of inviting Chikamatsu to
be the Takemoto Theater's staff playwright. After the actor Sakata Tōjūrō retired
in 1702 because of ill health, Chikamatsu left Kyoto early in 1706 to live the
last years of his life in Osaka writing solely for the Takemoto Theater.

Izumo himself brought a new element to the partnership of Gidayū and
Chikamatsu. With the production and tremendous success of the period play
Emperor Yōmei and the Mirror of Craftsmen (Yōmei tennō no shokunin kagami)
in the last month of 1705, the first play under Izumo as the manager of the
Takemoto, came increasingly elaborate stage props and more extravagant stage
tricks with puppets. It is from around this time that the puppeteer Tatsumatsu
Hachirōbei won fame for his depiction of female characters. Chikamatsu's work
with kabuki actors had involved him deeply in stage practice and the realistic
portrayal of characters. Izumo therefore encouraged him to turn to the potential
of puppets and to create scenes with spectacular stage action and sophisticated
props, thereby heightening the theatricality of his work.

Izumo's theatrical genius was credited for the unprecedented success of *The Battles of Coxinga* in 1715, suggesting that he collaborated closely with Chikamatsu in the play's production. The unprecedented seventeen-month run of *The Battles of Coxinga* in late 1715 ushered in a golden age of jōruri writing that lasted until the end of that century. The play was immediately performed in kabuki theaters around the country, and it has remained in the repertoires of both traditions. Its success also made it the classical model for later jidaimono. But while kabuki pushed Chikamatsu toward the increasingly realistic depiction of character in the contemporary-life plays, Izumo pulled him toward spectacular theatricality in acts 2 and 4 of the history plays. Thus Chikamatsu's mature-period plays thrive on the tension between fantastic spectacle and theatricality in acts 2 and 4 and the intensely realistic tragedy of act 3.

In *Souvenirs of Naniwa* (*Naniwa miyage*, 1738), which describes his conversations with his disciple Hozumi Ikan about his method of giving life to inanimate puppets, Chikamatsu frequently used the term *jō* (feeling or passion), which he considered the "basis of writing." The word *jō* is also fundamental to Confucian thought, which places human passions in conflict with the rules and morals of a civilized society. Many have commented that Chikamatsu's true genius was his masterful depiction of the passions, obsessions, and irrationality of the human heart. Perhaps because he wrote for puppet theater, Chikamatsu also emphasized the need for realism (*jitsuji*) in the depiction of characters; that is, their words must suit their station and rank. Chikamatsu also stressed pathos (*urei, awaré*), which refers to the tragic climactic moments in jōruri. He often dramatized a tragic conflict between *jō* and *giri* (rational behavior, principle), which is best regarded as a tension between desire and reason, between our natural, "animal-like" instincts and our rational, "civilized" mind with its rules, morals, and responsibilities inculcated by society. Chikamatsu's works are distinguished by a persistent view (perhaps unorthodox for the time but reflected in the views of the Kyoto philosopher Itō Jinsai) of human desires as natural and essentially good. Without the tempering of ethics, however, excessive passion inevitably leads to tragedy.

Jōruri must be understood in a musical context. One of Takemoto Gidayū's metaphors for jōruri was the stream with its "rapids and quiet pools"; that is, the action is propelled by different types of language and presentation. Gidayū saw the rapids as the dramatic moments in which the dialogue and action are quick and lively. By contrast, the quiet, deep pools are the songs, when the action stops and depth is achieved through lyrical and melodic power. The basic principle is having the chanter move between and among a relatively realistic declamatory "spoken" style with no musical accompaniment and various levels of "song" style accompanied by the three-string shamisen, in both the dialogue and narrative sections. This rhetorical technique of constantly shifting between lyrical and dramatic voices for emphasis and effect is the essence of jōruri chanting.

Even though Chikamatsu wrote for both jōruri chanters and kabuki actors, his thirty kabuki plays were printed only in illustrated summary editions (*e-iri kyōgenbon*). His more than ninety jōruri plays, however, were printed in full at the time of their first performance at Osaka's Takemoto Theater. Regardless of Chikamatsu's high stature as the preeminent writer in the theatrical traditions of both bunraku and kabuki, few of his plays were regularly performed after his death. In fact, many were rewritten, and it is clear that his plays were a model for playwrights and later fiction writers, particularly in the early-nineteenth-century popular fiction genres of *yomihon*, *gōkan*, and *ninjōbon*.

[Introduction to Chikamatsu by C. Andrew Gerstle]

THE LOVE SUICIDES AT SONEZAKI (*SONEZAKI SHINJŪ*, 1703)

The Love Suicides at Sonezaki was first performed in 1703 at the Takemoto Theater in Osaka by an all-star cast: Takemoto Gidayū and Tanomo as the chanters, Chikamatsu Monzaemon as the playwright, and Tatsumatsu Hachirōbei as the puppeteer. The result was a hit that revived the theater's fortunes. *The Love Suicides at Sonezaki* is based on an actual incident that had occurred just one month earlier. The largest soy sauce merchant in Osaka, with twelve clerks (*tedai*), including Tokubei, the son of the owner's brother, had decided to marry his adopted daughter to Tokubei and make him the head of his branch store in Edo, but Tokubei had fallen in love with Ohatsu, a prostitute in the Shimabara licensed quarter in Osaka who was about to be ransomed by another customer. Unable to remain together, Tokubei and Ohatsu committed double suicide in the Sonezaki Forest in Osaka. Chikamatsu's play follows the general outlines of the scandal, with which the contemporary audience was already familiar, and maintains the same names.

Kabuki in the Kyoto-Osaka area had already developed the contemporary-life (*sewamono*) genre which staged sensational current incidents such as double suicides and murders. Chikamatsu wrote *The Love Suicides at Sonezaki*, one of the earliest sewamono in puppet theater, in such a way that the audience deeply sympathized with the plight of the shop clerk and the low prostitute and placed the drama in the social and economic fabric of everyday urban commoner life in Osaka. Chikamatsu deepened the tragedy by adding the incident about the money that the owner offers for the dowry and that Tokubei's mother accepts (meaning that Tokubei must marry the owner's daughter or be dishonored) and adding the character of Kuheiji, the oil merchant, who swindles Tokubei out of this money and forces the issue.

Chikamatsu's contemporary-life plays do not glorify the kind of merchant values (such as prudence, thrift, ingenuity) found in Ihara Saikaku's *Japan's Eternal Storehouse*. Instead, Chikamatsu, who was originally from a samurai family, stresses samurai values (loyalty, devotion, self-sacrifice, honor), which urban commoners had absorbed into their own ethics. The double suicide thus becomes not simply a love suicide but the redemption of name and honor. The stress on samurai values deepens the tension within Tokubei between *giri* (his responsibility and duty to his shop master) and *ninjō* (human desire), with the tragedy arising from the fact that both giri and ninjō can be fulfilled only in death.

The double suicide has a simple three-part structure: the young townsman falls in love with a lowly prostitute; the young man then falls into financial difficulties, which prevent their union in society; and the young man joins the prostitute in death. Chikamatsu added the *michiyuki*, the poetic travel scene, which derives from medieval nō drama and transforms the final journey into a lyrical movement, as well as the suggestion that the dying protagonists will be reborn together and achieve buddha-hood, a convention found in medieval religious narratives. The michiyuki serves both to pacify the spirits of the dead (*chinkon*)—the ghosts of the dead lovers who have been recalled to the stage—and to give the star players (the chanter, the puppeteer, and the playwright) a chance to display their artistic skills, especially the music and the chanting, all of which transforms the double suicide into a sorrowful but beautiful moment.

The opening scene, which consists chiefly of an enumeration of the thirty-three temples of Kannon in the Osaka area and is no longer performed in jōruri and kabuki, has been omitted.

CHARACTERS

TOKUBEI, aged twenty-five, employee of a soy sauce dealer
KUHEIJI, an oil merchant
HOST of Tenma House, a brothel
CHŌZŌ, an apprentice
OHATSU, aged nineteen, a courtesan

The grounds of the Ikudama Shrine in Osaka.

CHANTER:
> This graceful young man has served many springs
> With the firm of Hirano in Uchihon Street;
> He hides the passion that burns in his breast
> Lest word escape and the scandal spread.
> He drinks peach wine, a cup at a time,
> And combs with care his elegant locks.
> "Toku" he is called, and famed for his taste,
> But now, his talents buried underground,
> He works as a clerk, his sleeves stained with oil,
> A slave to his sweet remembrances of love.
> Today he makes the rounds of his clients
> With a lad who carries a cask of soy:
> They have reached the shrine of Ikudama.
> A woman's voice calls from a bench inside a refreshment stand.

[OHATSU]¹: Tokubei—that's you, isn't it?²

CHANTER: She claps her hands, and Tokubei nods in recognition.

[TOKUBEI]: Chōzō, I'll be following later. Make the rounds of the temples in Tera Street and the uptown mansions and then return to the shop. Tell them that I'll be back soon. Don't forget to call on the dyer's in Azuchi Street and collect the money he owes us. And stay away from Dōtonbori.³

CHANTER: He watches as long as the boy remains in sight, then lifts the bamboo blinds.

[TOKUBEI]: Ohatsu—what's the matter?

CHANTER: He starts to remove his bamboo hat.

[OHATSU]: Please keep your hat on just now. I have a customer from the country today who's making a pilgrimage to all thirty-three temples of Kannon. He's been boasting that he intends to spend the whole day drinking. At the moment he's gone off to hear the impersonators' show,⁴ but if he returns and finds us together, there might be trouble. All the chair bearers know you. It's best you keep your face covered.

But to come back to us. Lately you haven't written me a word. I've been terribly worried, but not knowing what the situation might be in your shop, I couldn't very well write you. I must have called a hundred times at the Tanba House, but they hadn't had any news of you either. Somebody—yes, it was Taichi, the blind musician—asked his friends, and they said you'd gone back to the country. I couldn't believe it was true. You've really been too cruel. Didn't you even want to ask about me? Perhaps you hoped things would end that way, but I've been sick with worry. If you think I'm lying, feel this swelling!

CHANTER: She takes his hand and presses it to her breast, weeping reproachful and entreating tears, exactly as if they were husband and wife. Man though he is, he also weeps.

[TOKUBEI]: You're right, entirely right, but what good would it have done to tell you and make you suffer? I've been going through such misery that I couldn't be more distracted if Bon, New Year, the Ten Nights, and every other feast in the calendar came all at once. My mind's been in a turmoil, and my finances in chaos. To tell the truth, I went up to Kyoto to raise some money, among other things. It's a miracle I'm still alive. If they make my story into a three-act play, I'm sure the audiences will weep.

CHANTER: Words fail and he can only sigh.

---

1. Brackets have been placed around the names of the characters in the play to indicate that the chanter is narrating, or chanting, their speech.

2. His face is covered by a deep wicker hat, commonly worn by visitors to the licensed quarters.

3. A street in Osaka famed for its theaters and houses of pleasure.

4. Within the precincts of the Ikudama Shrine were booths where various types of entertainment were presented. The impersonators mimicked the speech and posture of popular actors.

[OHATSU]: And is this the comic relief of your tragedy? Why couldn't you have trusted me with your worries when you tell me even trivial little things? You must've had some reason for hiding. Why don't you take me into your confidence?

CHANTER: She leans over his knee. Bitter tears soak her handkerchief.

[TOKUBEI]: Please don't cry or be angry with me. I wasn't hiding anything, but it wouldn't have helped to involve you. At any rate, my troubles have largely been settled, and I can tell you the whole story now. My master has always treated me with particular kindness because I'm his nephew. For my part, I've served him with absolute honesty. There's never been a penny's discrepancy in the accounts. It's true that recently I used his name when I bought on credit a bolt of Kaga silk to make into a summer kimono, but that's the one and only time, and if I have to raise the money on the spot, I can always sell back the kimono without taking a loss. My master has been so impressed by my honesty that he proposed I marry his wife's niece with a dowry of two *kanme* and promised to set me up in business. That happened last year, but how could I shift my affections when I have you? I didn't give his suggestion a second thought, but in the meantime my mother—she's really my stepmother—conferred with my master, keeping it a secret from me. She went back to the country with the two *kanme* in her clutches. Fool that I am, I never dreamed what had happened. The trouble began last month when they tried to force me to marry. I got angry and said, "Master, you surprise me. You know how unwilling I am to get married, and yet you've tricked my old mother into giving her consent. You've gone too far, master. I can't understand the mistress's attitude either. If I took as my wife this young lady whom I've always treated with the utmost deference and accepted her dowry in the bargain, I'd spend my whole life dancing attendance on her. How could I ever assert myself? I've refused once, and even if my father were to return from his grave, the answer would still be no." The master was furious that I answered so bluntly. His voice shook with rage. "I know your real reasons. You've involved with Ohatsu, or whatever her name is, from the Tenma House in Dōjima. That's why you seem so against my wife's niece. Very well—after what's been said, I'm no longer willing to give you the girl, and since there's to be no wedding, return the money. Settle without fail by the twenty-second of the month and clear your business accounts. I'll chase you from Osaka and never let you set foot here again!" I, too, have my pride as a man. "Right you are!" I answered and rushed off to my village. But my so-called mother wouldn't let the money out of her hands, not if this world turned into the next. I went to Kyoto, hoping to borrow the money from the wholesale soy sauce dealers in the Fifth Ward. I've always been on good terms with them. But as luck would have it, they had no money to spare. I retraced my steps to the country, and this time, with the intercession of the whole village, I managed to get the money from my mother. I intended

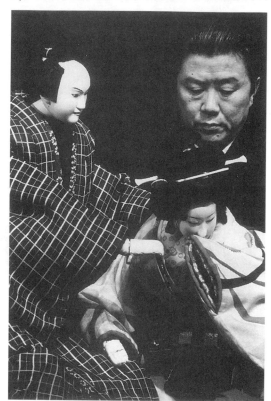

Tokubei and Ohatsu, who is weeping bitterly. (Photograph courtesy of Barbara Curtis Adachi Collection, C. V. Starr East Asian Library, Columbia University)

to return the dowry immediately and settle things for once and for all. But if I can't stay in Osaka, how will I be able to see you? My bones may be crushed to powder, my flesh be torn away, and I may sink, an empty shell, in the slime of Shijimi River. Let that happen if it must, but if I am parted from you, what shall I do?

CHANTER: He weeps, overcome by his grief. Ohatsu, holding back the welling tears of sympathy, strengthens and comforts him.

[OHATSU]: How you've suffered! And when I think that it's been because of me, I feel happy, sad, and most grateful all at once. But please, show more courage. Pull yourself together. Your uncle may have forbidden you to set foot in Osaka again, but you haven't committed robbery or arson. I'll think of some way to keep you here. And if the time should come when we can no longer meet, did our promises of love hold only for this world? Others before us have chosen reunion through death. To die is simple enough — none will hinder and none will be hindered on the journey to the Mountain of Death and the River of Three Ways.[5]

---

5. Places in the Japanese afterworld.

CHANTER: Ohatsu falters among these words of encouragement, choked by tears. She resumes.

[OHATSU]: The twenty-second is tomorrow. Return the money early, since you must return it anyway. Try to get in your master's good graces again.

[TOKUBEI]: I want to, and I'm impatient to return the money, but on the thirteenth of the month Kuheiji the oil merchant—I think you know him— begged me desperately for the money. He said he needed it for only one day and promised to return it by the morning of the eighteenth. I decided to lend him the money, since I didn't need it until the twenty-second, and it was for a friend close as a brother. He didn't get in touch with me on the eighteenth or nineteenth. Yesterday he was out and I couldn't see him. I intended to call on him this morning, but I've spent it making the rounds of my customers in order to wind up my business by tomorrow. I'll go to him this evening and settle everything. He's a man of honor, and he knows my predicament. I'm sure nothing will go wrong. Don't worry. Oh—look there, Ohatsu!

CHANTER:

"Hatsuse is far away,
Far too is Naniwa-dera:
So many temples are renowned
For the sound of their bells,
Voices of the Eternal Law.
If, on an evening in spring,
You visit a mountain temple
You will see . . ."[6]
At the head of a band of revelers

[TOKUBEI]: Kuheiji! That's a poor performance![7] You've no business running off on excursions when you haven't cleared up your debt with me. Today we'll settle our account.

CHANTER: He grasps Kuheiji's arm and restrains him. Kuheiji's expression is dubious.

[KUHEIJI]: What are you talking about, Tokubei? All these people with me are residents of the ward. We've had a meeting in Ueshio Street to raise funds for a pilgrimage to Ise. We've drunk a little saké, but we're on our way home now. What do you mean by grabbing my arm? Don't be so rough!

CHANTER: He removes his wicker hat and glares at Tokubei.

[TOKUBEI]: I'm not being rough. All I'm asking is that you return the two

---

6. A passage from the nō play *Miidera*, quoted here mainly because the first word Hatsuse, a place in Nara, echoes the name Ohatsu in the preceding line. The last words similarly point to the arrival of Kuheiji.

7. Tokubei, relieved to see Kuheiji, at first teases him about his singing of the nō passage, but his words have an undertone of criticism of Kuheiji's past behavior.

kanme of silver I lent you on the thirteenth, which you were supposed to repay on the eighteenth.

CHANTER: Before he can finish speaking, Kuheiji bursts out laughing.

[KUHEIJI]: Are you out of your mind, Tokubei? I can't remember having borrowed a penny from you in all the years I've known you. Don't make any accusations that you'll regret.

CHANTER: He shakes himself free. His companions also remove their hats.[8] Tokubei pales with astonishment.

[TOKUBEI]: Don't say that, Kuheiji! You came to me in tears, saying that you couldn't survive your monthly bills, and I thought that this was the kind of emergency for which we'd been friends all these years. I lent you the money as an act of generosity, though I needed it desperately myself. I told you that I didn't even require a receipt, but you insisted on putting your seal to one, for form's sake. You made me write out a promissory note and you sealed it. Don't try to deny it, Kuheiji!

CHANTER: Tokubei rebukes him heatedly.

[KUHEIJI]: What's that? I'd like to see the seal.

[TOKUBEI]: Do you think I'm afraid to show you?

CHANTER: He produces the paper from his wallet.

[TOKUBEI]: If these gentlemen are from the ward, I am sure that they will recognize your seal. Will you still dispute it?

CHANTER: When he unfolds the paper and displays it, Kuheiji claps his hands in recollection.

[KUHEIJI]: Yes, it's my seal all right. Oh, Tokubei, I never thought you'd do such a thing, not even if you were starving and forced to eat dirt. On the tenth of the month I lost a wallet containing the seal. I advertised for it everywhere, but without success, so as of the sixteenth of this month, as I've informed these gentlemen, I've changed my seal. Could I have put the seal I lost on the tenth on a document on the thirteenth? No—what happened was that you found my wallet, wrote the promissory note, and used my seal. Now you're trying to extort money from me—that makes you a worse criminal than a forger. You'd do better, Tokubei, to commit out-and-out robbery. You deserve to have your head cut off, but for old times' sake, I'll forgive you. Let's see if you can make any money out of this!

CHANTER: He throws the note in Tokubei's face and glares at him fiercely in an extraordinary display of feigned innocence. Tokubei, furious, cries aloud.

[TOKUBEI]: You've been damned clever. You've put one over on me. I'm dishonored. What am I to do? Must I let you just steal my money from me? You've planned everything so cleverly that even if I go to court, I'm sure to lose. I'll take back my money with my fists! See here! I'm Tokubei of the

---

8. Readying themselves to come to Kuheiji's defense.

Hirano-ya, a man of honor. Do you follow me? I'm not a man to trick a friend out of his money the way you have. Come on!

CHANTER: He falls on Kuheiji.

[KUHEIJI]: You impudent little apprentice! I'll knock the insolence out of you!

CHANTER: He seizes the front of Tokubei's kimono and they grapple, trading blows and shoves. Ohatsu rushes barefoot to them.[9]

[OHATSU] (to townsmen): Please everybody, stop the fight! He's a friend of mine. Where are the chair bearers? Why don't they do something? Tokubei's being beaten up!

CHANTER: She writhes in anguish but is helpless. Her customer, country bumpkin that he is, bundles her forcibly into a palanquin.

[CUSTOMER]: You don't want to get hurt.

[OHATSU]: Please wait just a moment! Oh, I'm so unhappy!

CHANTER: The palanquin is rushed off, leaving only the echoes of her weeping voice. Tokubei is alone; Kuheiji has five companions. Men rush out from the nearby booths and drive them all with sticks to the lotus pond. Who tramples Tokubei? Who beats him? There is no way to tell. His hair is disheveled, his sash undone. He stumbles and falls to this side and that.

[TOKUBEI]: Kuheiji, you swine! Do you think I'll let you escape alive?

CHANTER: He staggers about searching for Kuheiji, but he has fled and vanished. Tokubei falls heavily in his tracks, and weeping bitterly, he cries aloud.

[TOKUBEI] (to bystanders): I feel humiliated and ashamed that you've seen me this way. There was not a false word in my accusation. I've always treated Kuheiji like a brother, and when he begged me for the money, saying he'd never forget it as long as he lived, I lent it to him, sure that he'd do the same for me, though the money was precious as life, and I knew that without it tomorrow, the twenty-first, I'd have to kill myself. He made me write the note in my own hand, then put his seal on it. But it was a seal that he had already reported as lost, and now he's turned the accusations against me! It's mortifying, infuriating—to be kicked and beaten this way, dishonored and forced to my knees. It would've been better if I had died while smashing and biting him!

CHANTER: He strikes the ground and gnashes his teeth, clenches his fists and moans, a sight to stir compassion.

[TOKUBEI]: There's no point in my talking this way. Before three days have passed I, Tokubei, will make amends by showing all Osaka the purity at the bottom of my heart.

[CHANTER]: The meaning of these words is later known.

[TOKUBEI]: I'm sorry to have bothered you all. Please forgive me.

CHANTER: He gives his apologies, picks up his battered hat, and puts it on.

---

9. In her agitation, she fails to slip on her *geta* (clogs).

His face, downcast in the sinking rays of the sun, is clouded by tears that engulf him. Dejectedly he leaves, a sight too pitiful to behold.

Inside the Tenma House, the evening of the same day.

CHANTER:

 The breezes of love are all-pervasive
 By Shijimi River,[10] where love-drowned guests
 Like empty shells, bereft of their senses,
 Wander the dark ways of love
 Lit each night by burning lanterns,
 Fireflies that glow in the four seasons,
 Stars that shine on rainy nights.
 By Plum Bridge,[11] blossoms show even in summer.
 Rustics on a visit, city connoisseurs,
 All journey the varied roads of love,
 Where adepts wander and novices play:
 What a lively place this New Quarter is![12]
 But alas for Ohatsu of the Tenma House—even after she returns, the day's events still weigh on her. She cannot swallow her saké; she feels on edge. As she sits weeping, some courtesans from the neighboring houses and other friends come for a little chat.

[FIRST COURTESAN]: Have you heard, Ohatsu? They say that Toku was given a thrashing for something bad he did. Is it true?

[SECOND COURTESAN]: No, my customer told me that Toku was trampled to death.

CHANTER: They say he was tied up for fraud or trussed for counterfeiting a seal. Not one decent thing have they to report: every expression of sympathy makes their visit the more painful.

[OHATSU]: No, please, not another word. The more I hear, the worse my breast pains me. I'm sure I'll be the first to die. I wish I were dead already.

CHANTER: She can only weep. But amid her tears she happens to look outside and catches a glimpse of Tokubei, a pathetic figure wearing a wicker hat, even at night.[13] Her heart leaps, and she wants to run to him, but in the sitting room are the master and his wife, and by the entrance stands the cook, while in the kitchen a maid is hovering: with so many sharp eyes watching, she cannot do as she pleases.

---

10. The word *shijimi* means a "corbicula," a kind of small shellfish, suggesting shells.

11. Umeda Bridge, whose name literally means "plum field."

12. The Dōjima New Quarter in Osaka was opened in about 1700.

13. The wicker hat was worn for concealment, but at night this precaution was normally unnecessary.

[OHATSU]: I feel terribly depressed. I think I'll step outside for a moment.

CHANTER: She slips out softly.

[OHATSU]: What happened? I've heard rumors of every sort about you. They've driven me out of my mind with worry.

CHANTER: She thrusts her face under the brim of his wicker hat and weeps in secret, soundless, painful tears. He too is lost in tears.

[TOKUBEI]: I've been made the victim of a clever plot, as no doubt you've heard, and the more I struggle, the worse off I am. Everything has turned against me now. I can't survive this night. I've made up my mind to it.

CHANTER: As he whispers, voices are heard from within.

[VOICES]: Come inside, Ohatsu. There's enough gossip about you as it is.[14]

[OHATSU]: There—did you hear? We can't go on talking. Do as I show you.

CHANTER: She hides him under the train of her mantle. He crawls behind her to the garden door, where he slips beneath the porch at the step. Ohatsu sits by the entrance and, pulling the tobacco tray to her, lights her pipe. She assumes an air of unconcern. At this moment Kuheiji and a couple of his loudmouthed friends burst in, accompanied by a blind musician.

[KUHEIJI]: Hello, girls. You're looking lonesome. Would you like me for a customer? Hello there, host. I haven't seen you in ages.

CHANTER: He strides arrogantly into the room.

[HOST]: Bring a tobacco tray and some saké cups.

CHANTER: He makes the customary fuss over the guests.

[KUHEIJI]: No, don't bother about saké. We were drinking before we came. I have something to tell you. Tokubei, the number one customer of your Ohatsu, found a seal I'd lost and tried to cheat me out of two *kanme* in silver with a forged note. The facts were too much for him, and he finally met with some unpleasantness, from which he was lucky to escape alive. His reputation has been ruined. Be on your guard if he comes here again. Everybody will tell you that I speak the truth, so even if Tokubei tells you the exact opposite, don't believe him for a moment. You'd do best not to let him in at all. Sooner or later he's bound to end up on the gallows.[15]

CHANTER: He pours out his words convincingly. Tokubei, underneath the porch, gnashes his teeth and trembles with rage. Ohatsu, afraid that he may reveal himself, calms him with her foot, calms him gently. The host is loath to answer yes or no, for Tokubei is a customer of long standing.

[HOST]: Well, then, how about some soup?

CHANTER: Covering his confusion, he leaves the room. Ohatsu, weeping bitterly, exclaims.

---

14. Standing in the street outside the teahouse was likely to occasion gossip about secret lovers.

15. Literally, he is bound to end up at Noe or Tobita, execution grounds on the outskirts of Osaka.

[OHATSU]: You needn't try your clever words on me. Tokubei and I have been intimate for years. We've told each other our inmost secrets. He hasn't a particle of deceit in him, the poor boy. His generosity has been his undoing. He's been tricked, but he hasn't the evidence to prove it. After what has happened Tokubei has no choice but to kill himself. I wish I knew whether or not he had decided to die.

CHANTER: She pretends to be talking to herself, but with her foot she questions him. He nods and, taking her ankle, passes it across his throat, to let her know that he is bent on suicide.

[OHATSU]: I knew it. I knew it. No matter how long one lives, it comes to the same thing. Only death can wipe out the disgrace.

CHANTER: Kuheiji is startled by her words.

[KUHEIJI]: What is Ohatsu talking about? Why should Tokubei kill himself? Well, if he kills himself, I'll take good care of you after he's gone! I think you've fallen for me too!

[OHATSU]: That's most generous of you, I'm sure. But would you object if, by way of thanks for your kindness, I killed you? Could I go on living even a moment if separated from Toku? Kuheiji, you dirty thief! Anyone hearing your silly lies can only suspect you. I'm sure that Toku intends to die with me, as I with him.

CHANTER: She taps with her foot, and Tokubei, weeping, takes it in his hands and reverently touches it to his forehead. He embraces her knees and sheds tears of love. She too can hardly conceal her emotions. Though no word is spoken, answering each other heart to heart, they silently weep. That no one knows makes it sadder still. Kuheiji feels uncomfortable.

[KUHEIJI]: The wind's against us today. Let's get out of here. The whores in this place are certainly peculiar—they seem to have an aversion to customers like us with plenty of money to spend. Let's stop at the Asa House and have a drink there. We'll rattle around a couple of gold pieces, then go home to bed. Oh—my wallet is so heavy I can hardly walk.

CHANTER: Spewing forth all manner of abuse, they noisily depart. The host and his wife call the servants.

[HOST]: It's time to put out the lights for the night. Lay out beds for the guests who are staying on. Ohatsu, you sleep upstairs. Get to bed early.

[OHATSU] (to herself): Master, mistress, I shall probably never see you again. Farewell. Farewell to all the servants too.

CHANTER: Thus inwardly taking leave, she goes to her bedchamber. Later they will learn that this was a parting for life; how pitiful the foolish hearts of men who do not realize the truth in time!

[HOST]: See that the fire is out under the kettle. Don't let the mice get at the relishes.

CHANTER: They shut the place and bar the gate. Hardly have their heads touched their pillows than all are snoring merrily. So short is the night that before they've had a chance to dream, two o'clock in the morning has come. Ohatsu is dressed for death, a black cloak dark as the ways of love thrown over her kimono of spotless white. She tiptoes to the staircase and looks down. Tokubei shows his face from under the porch. He beckons, nods, points, communicating his intent without a word. Below the stairs a servant girl is sleeping. A hanging lantern brightly shines. Ohatsu in desperation attaches her fan to a palm-leaf broom and, from the second step of the staircase, attempts in vain to extinguish the flame. At last, by stretching every inch, she puts it out, only to tumble suddenly down the stairs. The lamp is out, and in the darkness the servant girl turns in her sleep. Trembling, the lovers grope for each other—a fearful moment. The host awakens in his room at the back.

[HOST]: What was that noise just now? Servants! The night lamp has gone out. Get up and light it!

CHANTER: The servant girl, aroused, sleepily rubs her eyes and gets up from bed stark naked.

[SERVANT]: I can't find the flint box.

CHANTER: She wanders about the room searching, and Ohatsu, faint with terror, dodges this way and that to avoid her. At last she catches Tokubei's hand, and softly they creep to the entranceway. They unfasten the latch, but the hinges creak, and frightened by the noise, they hesitate. Just then the maid begins to strike the flints; they time their actions to the rasping sound, and with each rasp open the door farther until, huddled together and their sleeves twisted round them, they go out the door one after the other, feeling as though they were treading on a tiger's tail. They exchange glances and cry out for joy, happy that they are to die—a painful, heartrending sight. The life left to them now is as brief as sparks that fly from blocks of flint.

The journey from Dōjima to the Sonezaki Shrine.

CHANTER:
> Farewell to this world, and to the night farewell.
> We who walk the road to death, to what should we be likened?
> To the frost by the road that leads to the graveyard,
> Vanishing with each step we take ahead:
> How sad is this dream of a dream!

[TOKUBEI]:
> Ah, did you count the bell? Of the seven strokes
> That mark the dawn, six have sounded.
> The remaining one will be the last echo
> We shall hear in this life.

[OHATSU]: It will echo the bliss of nirvana.

Tokubei, concealed by his hat, and Ohatsu, her face hidden by the white scarf. (Photograph courtesy of Barbara Curtis Adachi Collection, C. V. Starr East Asian Library, Columbia University)

CHANTER:

Farewell, and not to the bell alone—
They look a last time on the grass, the trees, the sky.
The clouds, the river go by unmindful of them;
The Dipper's bright reflection shines in the water.

[TOKUBEI]:

Let's pretend that Umeda Bridge
Is the bridge the magpies built[16]
Across the Milky Way, and make a vow
To be husband and wife stars for eternity.

[OHATSU]: I promise. I'll be your wife forever.

CHANTER:

They cling together—the river waters
Will surely swell with the tears they shed.
Across the river, in a teahouse upstairs,

---

16. Alludes to the Chinese legend, familiar also in Japan, that tells of two stars (known as the Herd Boy and the Weaver Girl) that meet once a year, crossing over a bridge in the sky built by magpies.

    Some revelers, still not gone to bed,
    Are loudly talking under blazing lamps—
    No doubt gossiping about the good or bad
    Of this year's crop of lovers' suicides;
    Their hearts sink to hear these voices.
[TOKUBEI]:
    How strange! but yesterday, even today,
    We spoke as if such things did not concern us.
    Tomorrow we shall figure in their gossip.
    If the world will sing about us, let it sing.
CHANTER:
    This is the song that now they hear.
    "I'm sure you'll never have me for your wife,
    I know my love means nothing to you . . ."
    Yes, for all our love, for all our grieving,
    Our lives, our lots, have not been as we wished.
    Never, until this very day, have we known
    A single night of heart's relaxation—
    Instead, the tortures of an ill-starred love.
    "What is this bond between us?
    I cannot forget you.
    But you would shake me off and go—
    I'll never let you!
    Kill me with your hands, then go.
    I'll never release you!"
    So she said in tears.[17]
[OHATSU]: Of all the many songs, that one, tonight!
[TOKUBEI]: Who is it singing? We who listen.
[BOTH]: Suffer the ordeal of those before us.
CHANTER:
    They cling to each other, weeping bitterly.
    Any other night would not matter
    If tonight were only a little longer,
    But the heartless summer night, as is its wont,
    Breaks as cockcrows hasten their last hour.
[TOKUBEI]: It will be worse if we wait for dawn. Let us die in the wood of
    Tenjin.[18]
CHANTER: He leads her by the hand. At Umeda Embankment, the night
    ravens.

---

17. The song overheard by Ohatsu and Tokubei is derived from a popular ballad of the time
that describes a love suicide.

18. The shrine of Sonezaki, sacred to Tenjin (the god of Sugawara no Michizane).

Tokubei and Ohatsu walking toward their death. (Photograph courtesy of Barbara Curtis Adachi Collection, C. V. Starr East Asian Library, Columbia University)

[TOKUBEI]: Tomorrow our bodies may be their meal.
[OHATSU]:

> It's strange, this is your unlucky year[19]
> Of twenty-five, and mine of nineteen.
> It's surely proof how deep are our ties
> That we who love each other are cursed alike.
> All the prayers I have made for this world
> To the gods and to the Buddha, I here and now
> Direct to the future: in the world to come
> May we be reborn on the same lotus!

CHANTER:

> One hundred eight the beads her fingers tell
> On her rosary;[20] tears increase the sum.
> No end to her grief, but the road has an end:
> Their minds are numbed, the sky is dark, the wind still,
> They have reached the thick wood of Sonezaki.
> Shall it be here, shall it be there? When they brush the grass, the falling

---

19. According to yin-yang divination, a man's twenty-fifth, forty-second, and sixtieth years are dangerous; for a woman, her nineteenth and thirty-third years.

20. The Buddhist prayer beads number 108, one for each of the sufferings occasioned by the passions.

dew vanishes even more quickly than their lives, in this uncertain world a lightning flash—or was it something else?

[OHATSU]: I'm afraid. What was that now?

[TOKUBEI]: That was a human spirit.[21] I thought we alone would die tonight, but someone else has preceded us. Whoever it may be, we'll have a companion on the journey to the Mountain of Death. *Namu Amida Butsu. Namu Amida Butsu.*[22]

CHANTER: She weeps helplessly.

[OHATSU]: To think that others are dying tonight too! How heartbreaking!

CHANTER: Man though he is, his tears fall freely.

[TOKUBEI]: Those two spirits flying together—do you suppose they belong to anyone else? They must be yours and mine!

[OHATSU]: Those two spirits? Then are we dead already?

[TOKUBEI]: Normally, if we saw a spirit, we'd knot our clothes and murmur prayers to keep our souls with us,[23] but now we hurry toward our end, hoping instead our two souls will find the same dwelling. Do not mistake the way, do not lose me!

CHANTER: They embrace, flesh to flesh, then fall to the ground and weep— how pitiful they are! Their strings of tears unite like entwining branches or the pine and palm that grow from a single trunk, a symbol of eternal love. Here the dew of their unhappy lives will at last settle.

[TOKUBEI]: Let this be the spot.

CHANTER: He unfastens the sash of his cloak. Ohatsu removes her tear-stained outer robe and throws it on the palm tree; the fronds might now serve as a broom to sweep away the sad world's dust. Ohatsu takes a razor from her sleeve.

[OHATSU]: I had this razor prepared in case we were overtaken on the way and separated. I was determined not to forfeit our name as lovers. How happy I am that we are to die together as we hoped!

[TOKUBEI]: How wonderful of you to have thought of that! I am so confident in our love that I have no fears even about death. And yet it would be unfortunate if because of the pain we are to suffer people said that we looked ugly in death. Let us secure our bodies to this twin-trunked tree and die immaculately! We will become an unparalleled example of a lovers' suicide.

[OHATSU]: Yes, let us do that.

CHANTER: Alas! She little thought she would use her light blue undersash in this way! She draws it tight and, with her razor, slashes it through.

[OHATSU]: The sash is cut, but you and I will never be torn apart.

---

21. *Hitodama*, a kind of will-o'-the-wisp believed to be a human soul.
22. The invocation of the name of the Amida Buddha, used in Pure Land Buddhism.
23. Exorcism practiced to prevent the soul from leaving the body.

CHANTER: She sits, and he binds her twice, thrice to the tree, firmly so that she will not stir.

[TOKUBEI]: Is it tight?

[OHATSU]: Very tight.

CHANTER: She looks at her husband, and he at her—they burst into tears.

[BOTH]: This is the end of our unhappy lives!

[TOKUBEI]: No I mustn't give way to grief.

CHANTER: He lifts his head and joins his hands in prayer.

[TOKUBEI]: My parents died when I was a boy, and I grew up thanks to the efforts of my uncle, who was my master. It disgraces me to die without repaying his kindness. Instead I shall cause him trouble that will last even after my death. Please forgive my sins. Soon I shall see my parents in the other world. Father, Mother, welcome me there!

CHANTER: He weeps. Ohatsu also joins her hands.

[OHATSU]: I envy you. You say you will meet your parents in the world of the dead. My father and mother are in this world and in good health. I wonder when I shall see them again. I heard from them this spring, but I haven't seen them since the beginning of last autumn. Tomorrow, when word reaches the village of our suicides, how unhappy they will be! Now I must bid farewell in this life to my parents, my brothers and sisters. If at least my thoughts can reach you, please appear before me, if only in dreams. Dear Mother, beloved Father!

CHANTER: She sobs and wails aloud. Her husband also cries out and sheds incessant tears in all too understandable emotion.

[OHATSU]: We could talk forever, but it serves no purpose. Kill me, kill me quickly!

CHANTER: She hastens the moment of death.

[TOKUBEI]: I'm ready.

CHANTER: He swiftly draws his dagger.

[TOKUBEI]: The moment has come. *Namu Amida. Namu Amida.*

CHANTER: But when he tries to bring the blade against the skin of the woman he's loved and held and slept with so many months and years, his eyes cloud over, his hand shakes. He tries to steady his weakening resolve, but still he trembles, and when he thrusts, the point misses. Twice or thrice the flashing blade deflects this way and that until a cry tells it has struck her throat.

[TOKUBEI]: *Namu Amida. Namu Amida. Namu Amida Butsu.*

CHANTER: He twists the blade deeper and deeper, but the strength has left his arm. When he sees her weaken, he stretches forth his hands. The last agonies of death are indescribable.

[TOKUBEI]: Must I lag behind you? Let's draw our last breaths together.

CHANTER: He thrusts and twists the razor in his throat, until it seems the handle or the blade must snap. His eyes grow dim, and his last painful breath is drawn away at its appointed hour.[24] No one is there to tell the tale, but the wind that blows through Sonezaki Wood transmits it, and high and low alike gather to pray for these lovers who beyond a doubt will in the future attain buddhahood. They have become models of true love.

[*Chikamatsu jōruri shū jō*, NKBT 49: 21–36, translated by Donald Keene]

THE DRUM OF THE WAVES OF HORIKAWA
(*HORIKAWA NAMI NO TSUTSUMI*, 1707)

The Drum of the Waves of Horikawa, a three-act contemporary-life play, was first performed at the Takemoto Theater in Osaka in the Second Month of 1707. Like *The Love Suicides at Sonezaki*, *Horikawa* draws on a contemporary scandal. In the Sixth Month of 1706, a vendetta was carried out in Kyoto during the Gion Festival by a samurai called Ōkura Hikohachirō, in the service of the lord of the Tottori Domain, who was assisted by his son Bunshichi, his younger sister Kura, and Fuu, the younger sister of his wife. In the Sixth Month of 1705, Hikohachirō had gone to Edo, following his lord on the alternate attendance system, and had stayed there until the Fifth Month of the following year. During his absence his wife, Tane, committed adultery with Miyai Den'emon, who was the domain drummer as well as the drum teacher of Hikohachirō's children. Rumors of the affair spread, and the younger sister Kura informed Hikohachirō in Edo. Deeply angered, Hikohachirō immediately took leave, returned to his domain, and questioned his wife, who confessed to the entire matter. On the sixteenth of the Fifth Month, Hikohachirō killed his wife, received permission to hunt down the adulterer, and, on the seventh of the Sixth Month, entered Den'emon's house and killed him.

Chikamatsu changed the names of the chief figures only slightly: Ōkura Hikohachirō became Ogura Hikokurō; the drum teacher Miyai Den'emon is Miyaji Gen'emon; Bunshichi became Bunroku; Kura takes the name Yura; and Fuu was changed to Ofuji. While preserving the outlines of the incident, Chikamatsu created a new drama by adding the villain Isobe Yukaemon and by focusing on the wife, Otane, whom he transformed into a sympathetic and tragic protagonist who, despite her weakness for alcohol, remains devoted to her husband. Although Chikamatsu's contemporary-life plays generally deal with the lives of urban commoners, this one describes the lives of the samurai, who normally were depicted in history plays, and ends with a vendetta (*katakiuchi*), which was standard fare for such history plays.

Adultery was a serious crime in samurai society, and the Tokugawa military government made every effort to maintain the special authority of the warrior class. Family succession was decided through the male line, from father to eldest son, and because

---

24. It was believed by practitioners of yin-yang divination that a person's hour of death was determined at his or her birth and could be foretold by an examination of the celestial stems governing the birth.

adultery jeopardized the authority of the family head, it was severely punished, with the samurai husband given the right to kill his wife and carry out a vendetta on the male adulterer. In this play, adultery takes the role that economic disaster (theft, embezzlement, and the like) does in Chikamatsu's *chōnin* (urban commoner) plays. Significantly, the three adultery plays written by Chikamatsu—*Gonza the Lancer* (*Yari no Gonza*, 1717), *The Drum of the Waves of Horikawa*, and *The Calendar Maker* (*Daikyōji mukashi goyomi*)—all concern privileged classes, particularly the samurai.

Some scholars have treated *Horikawa* as a samurai play because of the class of the protagonists. In contrast to samurai history plays, which uphold *giri* (duty/principle) over *ninjō* (emotion) at tragic human cost, the contemporary-life plays deal with the weakness of the individual for *ninjō*, with the ascendancy of *ninjō* over *giri* leading to tragic circumstances. Interestingly, *Horikawa* combines both dynamics, of succumbing to *ninjō* and upholding *giri*: Otane fails to maintain her obligations to her husband but commits suicide as a sign of her continued devotion to him, and Hikokurō puts aside his feelings for Otane to carry out his duty as a samurai in slaying the drum teacher. Significantly, the tragedy is almost as much on the side of the husband as the wife, with the end of the second act an implicit commentary on the harshness of samurai law.

Horikawa is of considerable interest for its exploration of female sexuality and its implicit critique of the life of lower-level samurai, who were separated from their wives for extremely long periods of time. The first act suggests—especially through its allusions to nō plays, particularly *Wind in the Pines* (*Matsukaze*)—a world of dream and illusion, a nightmare world of desire and intoxication. The second act takes place in the daytime and is a sober samurai view of public law in which crimes of passion are punished by death. The third act, which occurs during the Gion Festival, a time of daytime intoxication, echoes the first act but focuses on violence rather than sexuality. In the third act, which has been omitted here, Hikokurō and his entire family singlemindedly hunt down the drum teacher in Kyoto and kill him.

The interest that this play has had for modern readers is reflected in the production of the postwar film *Night Drum* (*Yoru no tsuzumi*), directed by Imai Tadashi and based on this play.

CHARACTERS

[OGURA] HIKOKURŌ, a samurai of low status in Inaba Province (present-day Tottori Prefecture)
[MIYAJI] GEN'EMON, a drum teacher from Kyoto
BUNROKU, Hikokurō's adopted son
[ISOBE] YUKAEMON, a samurai attracted to Otane
OTANE, wife of Hikokurō and daughter of Naruyama Chūdayū
OFUJI, younger sister of Otane in the service of a samurai mansion
YURA, younger sister of Hikokurō and wife of a samurai (Masayama Sangohei)
ORIN, Otane's maid

Act 1

Scene 1: The courtyard of a house in Tottori, the seat of the daimyō of Inaba. The house belongs to Chūdayū, the father of Otane and Ofuji. The sisters are hanging out the laundry while a lesson in the music of the nō play Matsukaze *is being taught inside the house.*

CHANTER (*chants in nō style*):
    And so three years of weary exile
    Yukihira whiled away aboard his boat,
    His heart illumined by the moon of Suma Bay.
    He chose two sisters as his maids in waiting,
    Fishergirls who dipped the evening tide,
    And named one Pine-Breeze and one Spring-Shower,[25]
    Names he thought well suited to the time of year.
    The sisters changed the clothes they wore,
    Fishergirls of Suma, familiars of the moon,
    When burning salt along the shore,
    For robes of damask burned with faint perfumes.

    Those were fishergirls' clothes, but here a matron is fulling her robes, her occupation during her husband's absence, in service at Edo. Her younger sister Ofuji fortunately happens to be at home today and offers to help, tying back her sleeves with a cotton cord. The sisters apply starch and wring out the clothes with dripping sleeves, so lovely a sight, it is clear why their charms are celebrated throughout the fief.

[OTANE]: It'd be best for you, Ofuji, to stay in service permanently. Remember always to keep your master pleased, and don't get married. I know that only too well from my own experience. Hikokurō and I were childhood sweethearts before our marriage, and I can't tell you how happy I was to become his bride. But it's hard being of low rank. Every other year Hikokurō must spend in Edo. Even when he's here, he must report every day at the castle, and ten nights each month it's his turn to stand guard duty. We've never spent a single relaxed night in conversation together like other couples. Hikokurō has the samurai spirit, and he encourages me by saying that unless he exerts himself as he does he'll never be able to make his mark in his profession. All the same, I can just see the expression on his face when he left for Edo last July. "I won't be seeing you again till I come back with his lordship next July," he said. "Take care of yourself and watch after the house."

---

25. Pine-Breeze (Matsukaze) and Spring-Shower (Murasame) are two sisters who fall in love with the nobleman Yukihira in the nō play *Matsukaze*.

Yes, I've never for a moment forgotten that look. It's as if I could see him now before my eyes. I wait here as though we were lovers who met every day, wondering when, when he'll return.

CHANTER: She stretches the silk with clothespins and ties it with cords to the pines; talking in this way has helped relieve her grief.[26] Her sister Ofuji bursts out laughing.

[OFUJI]: You're asking for too much, Otane! Look at the marvelous powers of endurance I have, with no husband whatsoever! And they're so strict about discipline at his lordship's mansion. It's forbidden for me to spend one single night away, even here, in my own family's house. I'm sure you'd die in such a place! Anyone hearing you complain would laugh!

[OTANE]: Listen—there's drum practice going on inside. You mustn't talk so loud. Hush!

CHANTER: She stretches the cloth on the clothesline and peers through a crack in the fence. Vague yearnings for her husband are stirred by the beat of the drum. As she hangs his robes on the pine to dry, the piece ends with a final cry.

(*Chants*) "This keepsake
Now is my enemy.
Without it
There might be a chance to forget."
The poet was right—
Keepsakes only deepen one's longing.[27]

[OTANE]: Oh I'm so happy! Look, my husband's returned! I must go welcome him!

CHANTER: She runs up to the tree.

[OFUJI]: Are you out of your mind, Otane? That's just a garden pine tree. Hikokurō's in Edo. Are you mad?

CHANTER: She reproaches her sister.

[OTANE]: Silly Ofuji! What makes you think I'm mad? The only solace for my boredom while Hikokurō's away is to pretend he's returned. Here we are in Inaba, just as in that piece they're playing. Listen to the words—"When I hear you're waiting, I'll come back again." Oh, that song and the beat of the drum give me hope again!

CHANTER (*chants*):

His song fills me with hope—
"Though I leave now I will return

---

26. Mention of the pines is dictated by the customary pun on *matsu* (to wait) and *matsu* (pine). Similarly, *yūte* is at once "tying" and "talking." Numerous other puns dot this section.

27. "This keepsake . . . to forget" derives from an anonymous poem in the *Kokinshū* (no. 746).

Otane, in work gear, hanging out the laundry. (Photograph courtesy of Barbara Curtis Adachi Collection, C. V. Starr East Asian Library, Columbia University)

If I hear you pine like the pines
Growing on Inaba Mountain's peak."[28]
He spoke of the pines of far-off Inaba,
But these are the pines of Suma's curving bay
Where once he lived, that dear prince.
If Yukihira returns, I will approach
The shade of that pine tree, tenderly.
Oh, that familiar pine on the beach, I love it!
The wind blows wild in the pines.
Now, when her loneliness is most intense
For the husband who is far away,
The drum has comforted her heart:
The drum brings rumors that her husband
Will presently return from the East.
The wind is cool as she washes and stretches
The thin raw silk of her husband's *hakama*;[29]
The mild spring sun will dry it soon.

---

28. The poem is by Yukihira, found in the *Kokinshū* (no. 365) and in the play *Matsukaze*. In the play, Inaba, a distant place, is contrasted with Suma, where the fishergirls live, but here Inaba is the scene of the action.

29. The trousers of a formal Japanese costume.

[OTANE]: I'm glad I've done something useful. And now I shall wait for my husband's return from Edo and listen to the wind in the pines.

CHANTER: She speaks in high spirits. Bunroku calls from inside.

[BUNROKU]: Mother! I've finished my drum practice. I'm sure you've heard me talk about my teacher, Miyaji Gen'emon. Wouldn't you like to come in and meet him?

[OTANE]: I would indeed. I was thinking of it a while ago, but I was so busy hanging up the clothes that the time went by before I knew it.

CHANTER: She unties the cords tucking up her sleeves and smoothes her clothes. When she enters the sitting room, Gen'emon at once changes to a formal sitting posture.

[GEN'EMON]: I live in Kyoto, at Horikawa near Shimotachiuri. I have the honor to teach the drum to the gentlemen of this fief, and I come here quite frequently now that my pupils are about to be permitted to serve in the palace. Sometimes I stay for three or four months or even a whole year at a time, but I have never had the pleasure of meeting your husband, Hikokurō. Recently your son Bunroku expressed a desire to learn the drum, and I agreed to take him as my pupil. He's quite exceptionally talented, and I can imagine how proud of him his mother must be.

CHANTER: He speaks very politely. Otane acknowledges his compliments with a bow of the head and a smile.

[OTANE]: Calling me Bunroku's mother makes Hikokurō and myself sound like old people. Actually, Bunroku is my younger brother. My husband adopted him as his son. We're people of very modest means, and for the time being we've put Bunroku under the protection of a certain gentleman in his lordship's household. His grandfather was anxious for Bunroku to learn—with your kind help—at least one drum piece well enough to appear personally before his lordship. That was why he decided, even though my husband's away, to ask you to teach him. I expect my husband to be returning with his lordship in July, and I'll be very grateful if Bunroku is able to perform a piece for his father then.

CHANTER: She has a graceful manner of receiving him. So gentle yet dignified are her appearance and actions that no one would object if she were introduced as the greatest lady of Kyoto. Who could guess that she was reared in the mountains of Inaba? Ofuji enters.

[OFUJI]: I'm Ofuji, Otane's younger sister. I'm in service in one of the households of the fief. Your kindness to Bunroku is very gratifying to us all. My sister's husband is away, and he draws only a small stipend. His house is so cramped that we must do the wash and everything else here, at my father's place. That's why we even have to ask you to give Bunroku his drum practice here, though I can imagine how inconvenient everything must be. I'm sure that Hikokurō will invite you to his house as soon as he returns. (To maid) Bring some saké cups, please. (Calls) Father, are you at home? (To

Gen'emon) We've just the one maid, fresh out of the country, and even with only a single guest everything is in complete chaos, as you can see. (*Laughs*) Really, it's quite embarrassing.

CHANTER: She bows in greeting. Her eyes are as lovely as Otane's.

[GEN'EMON]: Please don't go to any trouble on my account.

CHANTER: But even while they exchange these compliments, the maid, realizing what is needed, brings saké and relishes.

[OTANE]: Oh, what a good idea! (*To Gen'emon*) My father's only a rōnin, and we can't offer you anything to eat with the drinks, but have a cup—it'll cheer you.

[GEN'EMON]: I'm sure you must be busy, and I most appreciate your kindness. Please, you drink first.

[OTANE]: No, please, guests first. There's no need to stand on ceremony.

[GEN'EMON]: In that case, what about starting with Bunroku?

CHANTER: He offers the cup to Bunroku but tippler that she is, Otane's hand intercepts the cup.

[OTANE]: I'll play the part of a good mother and make sure first the saké's properly heated.

CHANTER: She accepts some saké and drains the cup. She offers it to Bunroku.[30]

[BUNROKU]: I've never drunk any saké before.

CHANTER: He swallows a little.

[BUNROKU]: Excuse me, master, for drinking first.

CHANTER: He bows. Gen'emon politely accepts the cup. He comes from a family of heavy drinkers, and his lips smack like a drum.

[GEN'EMON]: Ahhh, what marvelous saké! I don't drink very much as a rule, but I like a little saké now and then, and I've tried it all over the country. But not even the Kyoto saké can touch this. It has a good color, a fine bouquet, and the taste is excellent. I'm quite impressed by your husband's palate!

CHANTER: His praise of the saké and his company manners are a trifle too glib; how unfortunate that nobody recognizes this portent of later calamity!

[GEN'EMON]: Here, I'm returning the cup immediately to Bunroku.

[OTANE]: Let me, his mother, intervene here, and keep you company in drink!

CHANTER: She accepts some saké and again empties the cup.

[OTANE]: Please show you like the saké by having another drink.

CHANTER: He takes the cup from her hand without even letting her put it down.

[GEN'EMON]: I'll be delighted, of course.

---

30. It is a mark of friendship or intimacy in Japan to drink saké from the same cup as another person.

Bunroku (*left*) and Gen'emon, the drum teacher, drinking saké. (Photograph courtesy of Barbara Curtis Adachi Collection, C. V. Starr East Asian Library, Columbia University)

CHANTER: He accepts the brimming cupful and swallows it in one gulp. He returns the cup to Bunroku, who again merely touches it to his lips.

[BUNROKU]: Excuse me, but I'd like to offer my aunt some saké.

CHANTER: He is about to hand Ofuji the cup.

[OTANE]: You can't be so unsociable, no matter how unaccustomed you may be to drinking. Here, have a cup. I'll keep you company.

CHANTER: She lifts the flowing cup and empties it.

[OTANE]: It's a happy occasion when a mother drinks with her child. To make it all the happier, let's have an extra drink now for your father in Edo. Here, please join us.

CHANTER: She offers the cup once again to Gen'emon.

[GEN'EMON]: I see, madam, that you're partial to a little saké. Excuse my familiarity, but I'd like to see what kind of a drinker you are!

CHANTER: He returns the cup. Ofuji is dismayed.

[OFUJI]: No, Otane can't drink so much. Lately especially she's been under the weather and hasn't been feeling too well. Otane, I think you've had enough.

CHANTER: She stands beside Otane and tries to restrain her, but Otane, drinker that she is, becomes obstinate.

[OTANE]: What are you trying to tell me? We have nothing to eat with the saké, so the best entertainment I can offer our guest is to drink with him.

CHANTER: She speaks in haughty tones. Another bottle is brought from the kitchen. Her guest, beating a drum accompaniment with his hands, sings out.

[GEN'EMON]: Well, then, another for me too.

CHANTER: They pass the saké back and forth. Here indeed is a splendid (*chants*) gathering of champions,
a drinking party of bosom friends.[31]

They tilt their cups a number of times, and soon the sun is slanting in the evening sky. A servant comes from the mansion where Ofuji serves.

[SERVANT]: Miss Ofuji, I've come to escort you back. Please return with me. The gate will be closing soon.

[OFUJI]: Oh, is that you, Kakuzō? Sorry to have bothered you. Otane, I'll be leaving now. I must apologize to you, sir, for my rudeness, but a woman in service can't do as she pleases. I hope to see you again.

CHANTER: She takes her leave with these words and departs. Bunroku quietly speaks.

[BUNROKU]: I think I'll be going too. Tonight they're expecting guests at the house of the gentleman I wait on. Master, would you kindly remain here a bit longer, until my grandfather returns?

[GEN'EMON]: Well, if you say so. But how will it look if I'm found here with your mother, just the two of us? I'll go to the next room.

CHANTER: He leaves his seat in some embarrassment. Otane shows Bunroku to the door.

[OTANE]: Please stop by our house for a minute and ask your grandfather to return. I'm anxious to go home. Ask him to send Rin to fetch me.

[BUNROKU]: Yes, I will.

CHANTER: He departs for his master's house. This is the hour when gates are shut, here on the outskirts of town. The youthful mistress of the house, whose husband has been away for many months in Edo, is a trifle too fond of liquor—she thinks it will bolster her spirits. Her face has not lost its composure, but it is burning hot. In the mirror, when she combs her hair and strokes her heavy head, an indefinable seductiveness glows in her reflection. Tonight she seems to be awaiting her husband.

Isobe Yukaemon, though a fellow retainer of the same fief, was excused from accompanying his lordship to Edo, and remained in the country, claiming to be sick. Now he suddenly bursts into the house through the side door, all alone, without even a servant.

[YUKAEMON]: I've come to see how you're getting along.

CHANTER: Otane pushes away her mirror in alarm.

[OTANE]: Chūdayū isn't here. He's been out ever since morning.

[CHANTER]: She intends these words as a dismissal and starts to withdraw inside when Yukaemon catches her in his arms.

---

31. Quoted from the nō play *Rashōmon*.

[YUKAEMON]: I knew he was out. That's why I came. I haven't any business with your father. It's you I've been longing to see. I've felt like a boat, trapped by the shoals of other people's eyes, with the breakers pounding in on me.[32] I knew for a fact that if I spent this year serving in Edo, my stipend would be increased, but I gave up all thoughts of advancement as a samurai. I pretended to be sick, and I begged permission to remain here in the country. I want you to know that it's all been on account of you. My sickness was a ruse and yet not entirely so—I was suffering from the malady called love, and you were the cause, Otane. Please, I beg you, give me just one small dose of the medicine of your love. I implore you.

CHANTER: He holds her tightly in his arms. Otane is a little drunk from the saké.

[OTANE]: Stop it! You're acting outrageously. Leave me alone!

CHANTER: She shakes him off and gets away from him, but her hair bristles in terror, and she is trembling all over.

[OTANE]: Dog of a samurai! To think you're a close friend of Hikokurō! It goes against all the rules of human decency. The whole fief will point at you with scorn, and if his lordship hears about it, you'll be ruined. Don't you realize that? I'm Ogura Hikokurō's wife, a samurai wife! Don't do anything contemptible that will only make you hate me later on. I won't tell anyone what has happened. Now leave!

CHANTER: She forces out the words.

[YUKAEMON]: I've thought about how people would criticize me and the disgrace I would suffer. I've taken all that into account. I came here resolved that if by any chance you refused me, I would stab you first and then myself. Rumors would soon be flying throughout the province that we'd committed a lovers' suicide, the kind so popular in Osaka, and we would share a common disgrace.

CHANTER: He draws his sword and catches her by the front of the kimono.

[YUKAEMON]: What is your answer to that?

CHANTER: He threatens her. Otane supposes in her woman's heart that he speaks the truth, and she is mortified to think that she may die like a dog and be branded for a crime of which she is blameless. She decides that she will trick him.

[OTANE]: Are you really in love with me as you say?

[YUKAEMON]: If I'm not telling the truth, may I be dismissed by his lordship and have my head cut off by a common soldier!

[OTANE]: You delight me. Why should I treat you unkindly? But this is my father's house. Just supposing he were to return now! What would we do

---

32. The various sea images have for justification the name Isobe, which literally means "shore area."

then? If you will come secretly to my house tomorrow night, I'll throw off my reserve and chase away all your cares.

CHANTER: She taps him gently, with artful deceit. The ignorant, illiterate Yukaemon is tricked by one word and turns sentimental.

[YUKAEMON]: Oh, I'm so grateful for your kindness! I know that it's shameless to ask anything more, but I'd much rather if now, here, we might just—

CHANTER: He clutches her.

[OTANE]: You're unreasonable!

CHANTER: She runs from place to place trying to get away from him. On the other side of the partition Gen'emon beats his drum and raises his voice.

[GEN'EMON] (*chants*):
> The evil demon of lust
> Will attack and attack your flesh.
> Your beloved one will appear
> Over the Mountain of Swords.
> You'll cry in delight
> And grope your way up,
> Only for swords to pierce your flesh
> And great rocks crush your bones.
> What does this mean? What horror is this?[33]

[OTANE]: Somebody's heard! What am I to do?

CHANTER: She is terrified.

[YUKAEMON]: Everything I've been saying has all been a joke—not a word of truth in it.

CHANTER: With these parting words he dashes out and makes his escape. Otane, poor creature, is distraught with shame. Undoubtedly her guest from Kyoto has overheard the conversation without realizing that it was all a trick. Now he will despise her in his heart, and more than that, being a man with a wide acquaintance throughout the fief, he will soon spread the scandal. Then what will she do? Unable to control the agitation in her breast, she rouses the maid and orders her to heat some saké.

[OTANE]: You can shut the front gate while you're at it. It's time you went to bed.

CHANTER: She pours some saké and, drinking alone, forgets her grief and bitterness. The one thing she cannot forget is her husband in Edo. Her tears make the moonlight seem the mistier as it bathes the veranda where footsteps now are heard.

[OTANE]: Oh, it's you, Gen'emon.—Where are you going, sir?

[GEN'EMON]: I feel rather awkward being here in a house with only women. I'm leaving.

---

33. This description of a Buddhist hell is adapted from the nō play *Ominaeshi*.

CHANTER: He starts to go, but she catches his sleeve.

[OTANE]: Did you hear what happened just now? It was a perfect disgrace, a horrible experience. I'm sure you don't suppose for a moment that a woman with a husband like Hikokurō could actually have meant what I said. I talked to him that way only to deceive him, so that I might escape my predicament. Please don't tell anyone. I beg you most earnestly.

CHANTER: She joins her hands in supplication and weeps. Gen'emon is at a loss for words.

[GEN'EMON]: I wasn't listening—or not listening, for that matter. The conversation was exceedingly unpleasant for an outsider to overhear. I sang that piece to distract myself. What happened seems trivial enough, though it's quite a serious matter. I don't intend to tell anyone, but as they say, you can hide a gimlet in a bag but it'll soon show itself. I don't know what rumors other people may start.

CHANTER: He shakes himself loose, but she clings to him again.

[OTANE]: What a cruel thing to say! You are a young man and I am a young woman—even if what you heard was really true, it would be normal human kindness to hide it as best you could. I won't have any peace of mind if I let you go as things stand. Please exchange a cup with me as a promise that you won't tell.

CHANTER: She takes the saké jar and fills a large tea bowl to the brim. She empties the cup and, filling it again, drinks half, then offers the rest to him.

[GEN'EMON] (to himself): This is very strange, giving me the remains of the cup she drank from.

CHANTER: He accepts it politely and drinks. Otane by now is quite intoxicated. She presses Gen'emon's hand tightly.

[OTANE]: Now that you've shared a cup of saké with a married woman, your guilt is the same as mine. You mustn't ever tell anything.

CHANTER: She forces him into a hopeless dilemma.

[GEN'EMON]: Damn it! What a mess to put a man in!

CHANTER: He rushes for the door, but she throws her arms around him.

[OTANE]: You don't know anything about love, do you? What an infuriating man you are!

CHANTER: Her arms still around him, she undoes his obi, undoing his heart as well, for his mind is befuddled with drink and desire. Embracing and embraced, their love has become real before they knew it.

[OTANE]: Now do you agree never to tell what happened?

[GEN'EMON]: I thought it didn't concern me, but now that I'm involved, how could I fail to hide what's happened?

CHANTER: He opens the shōji, and they go into the next room. They share momentary dreams on one pillow, the beginning of a short-lived union, an evil alliance, a connection doomed from the start.

Otane clinging to Gen'emon. (Photograph courtesy of Barbara Curtis Adachi Collection, C. V. Starr East Asian Library, Columbia University)

Scene 2: Later that night.

CHANTER: The night is far advanced. Otane's father, Naruyama Chūdayū, returns alone, without a servant, and bangs furiously at the gate.[34] Otane, sober now, is awakened by the noise. She looks at herself. Her sash is undone, and the bed where she slept with a man is disordered.

[OTANE]: Good heavens! How unspeakable! I remember now deliberately enticing him, hoping to stop him from telling about Yukaemon's advances. Yes, I remember that. But afterward—I was so drunk I can't be sure what was only a dream and what really happened. My sister always warned me about my drinking, but I wouldn't listen to her. Now I have disgraced myself by touching another man's body—a perfect stranger! How depraved of me! I'm guilty of the worst sin a woman can commit, and I'll suffer for it, not only the torments of hell, but dishonor in this life. What shall I do, now that I've destroyed the reputations of even my father and brother? I feel utterly wretched. If only this would turn out to be a dream!

---

34. Chikamatsu, seemingly carried away by a pun on the name Naruyama, falsely identifies the person at the gate as Chūdayū, Otane's father. Most likely he intended to suggest here Otane's misapprehension of the person who later turns out to be Yukaemon.

CHANTER: She chokes in tears. Gen'emon, wakened by the sound of her sobbing, rises from bed. Drunkenness had so stupefied him, too, that he violated the code of a man of honor. Their eyes meet for an instant, then they look down in tears and embarrassment, ashamed to stand before each other. Chūdayū, his patience exhausted, pounds all the more violently at the gate.

[OTANE]: If my father discovers me, I'll have to kill myself. What am I to do?

CHANTER: She wanders around the room looking for somewhere to hide. By mischance she stumbles onto the sleeping place of the maid, who jumps up, stark naked.

[MAID]: Something awful's happened! A burglar's crawled into my bosom while I was sleeping, and now he's ravaging my snow white skin!

CHANTER: Carried away by her own shrieks and gyrations, she kicks over the standing lantern. "The darkness of the ways of love" they sing about—how could it be compared to this? Delusion springs even from inconsequential acts. At the gate someone shouts insistently, "Open up! Open up!" and pounds. Otane and the man, trembling with fear, whisper a plan: with her hand held behind her, she pulls his sleeve, shielding him with her body. She unfastens the latch and calls, "Is that you, Father?" But it is not her father. Yukaemon, his face averted, stretches out his hands, and tightly clasps their sleeves together.

[YUKAEMON]: Now, you adulteress, I've got proof of your crime!

CHANTER: At his shout, she slams the gate shut with a cry of dismay, but Yukaemon does not let the sleeves out of his grasp. Gen'emon, in desperation, unsheathes the dagger at his side, and slits off the ends of the sleeves. Opening a side door, he flees precipitously for home. Yukaemon stuffs the sleeves into the fold of his kimono. He forces his way in through the gate.

[YUKAEMON]: Well, madam, you've been unkind! Why were you so cold to me when you let someone else untie your girdle strings? If you want me to keep this a secret, I expect you'll show me some love tonight in return.

CHANTER: In the darkness he gropes for Otane, his arms spread wide, an object inspiring terror. As he wanders here and there, he bumps into the naked maid.

[YUKAEMON]: Now I have you! So this is where you were!

CHANTER: He throws his arms around her. The maid, knowing her way even in the dark, slips off to her bed.

[YUKAEMON]: This is wonderful! Thank you!

CHANTER: He pulls the bedclothes over him and flops down beside her. The maid dislikes his advances, and as she is fending him off, a voice calls from outside.

[SERVANT]: It's Rin. I've come to take Madam Otane home.

CHANTER: She enters with a lighted lantern. Yukaemon carefully examines the face caught in the light and sees that it is the maid.

[YUKAEMON]: How demeaning, and how disgusting! I was about to break my
fast to eat a sardine![35]

CHANTER: Without so much as looking back, he runs outside. The illusion in
the dark was lovely.

Act 2

Scene 1: Four months later, on the road from Edo to Tottori.

CHANTER (*song*):
>   "See the splendid horse
>   With a daimyō's wicker trunk,
>   Seven layers of cushions
>   And a riding seat above.
>   First we'll lay the cushions on,
>   Then we'll put the young lord on top."

This is the song the drivers cheerfully hum, leading their horses the hundred leagues of the Tōkaidō. The cherries are in blossom, and the soldiers
in the van of the brilliant procession carry lances—plain, single-pronged,
and cross-pointed; their helmets sport crimson-dyed yak tails from China;
their robes are magenta; and the fish that they eat is sea bream.[36] Needless
to say, these lancers are samurai. The lackeys carry spears with sheaths cy-
lindrical as the bowls from which they drank their saké this morning, or
round as a girl's braided head,[37] shaking, shaking, shaking white snow over
Fuji and Asama that they now leave behind. The road is as long as the shafts
of their many lances; the sheaths are festooned with rooster plumes.[38] Men
lead Mochizuki horses famous west of the Barrier.[39] The horses' bits jingle,
jingle, jangle, and now there come riding on pack steeds to the beat of the
same rhythm the night guards,[40] the inspectors, the samurai commanders,
and the master of ceremonies. Streams of pennants flap on their staffs before
and behind the chief of the ensigns. The world is at peace; the waves are
calm in the seas all around; the wind in the sky has abated.

---

35. After having remained continent in hopes of making love to Otane, Yukaemon has almost
lost his virtue for an unworthy object.

36. From a poem attributed to the priest Ikkyū in the miscellany *Mottomo no sōshi* (1634):
"Among men the samurai [is best]; among pillars, cypress wood; among fish, the sea bream;
among robes, magenta; and among cherry blossoms, those of Yoshino."

37. The *kaburo* (or *kamuro*) was a prostitute's maid. The word suggests *kaburu* (to put on
top), suggesting in turn that the lackeys have had one cup of saké on top of another.

38. Mention of "rooster plumes" is dictated by the word "barrier" (*seki*) following it. According
to ancient custom, rites were carried out in Kyoto during times of disturbance that involved tying
a rooster at the barriers around the city.

39. Mention of the "barrier" (Osaka Barrier, between Kyoto and Lake Biwa) leads to an
allusion to a poem by Ki no Tsurayuki about horses from Mochizuki (*Shūishū*, no. 170).

40. This and the following are English approximations of three samurai offices.

"—Look, there by the halberds you can see the doctors and philosophers!" Everybody, pundit and ignoramus alike, gapes at the endless procession of tent pegs, lacquered boxes on poles, rattan-wound bows and black-varnished bows, in numbers beyond reckoning, unpainted bows and half-blackened bows, quivers, arrow cases and arrow holders, cases of the commander's armor covered with double lids, and stands for his helmets.

It seems just yesterday they took the road to the East, but more than a year has passed since they left their province. All has gone smoothly; they have safely returned with the Seven Ceremonial Articles:[41] a wicker hat borne aloft on a pole, a long-handled umbrella in its case, an emblem to mark the general's horse (a ball of falcon feathers, true to the name of the clan, Tottori).[42] The horse the daimyō rides and the spare horse, too, neigh in high spirits at the northern wind of their native heaths. The rear of the procession is brought up by a pair of lancers.

His lordship has been away from his province for a long time, and his return brings joy to his deputy. When a prince acts in princely fashion, his subjects will be true subjects. New casks of saké are opened, and singing greets his lordship as he enters his province, where not even needles from the beach pines scatter,[43] in a land that will last ten thousand generations, a land that will last forever.

Men of the household, high and low alike, meet again their parents, wives, and children after a year's separation, and the happy tidings fly here and there. For everyone, down to the lowliest spear carriers, lackeys, and menials, this is a time of exchanging presents and souvenirs and of noisy celebration.

Among those returning is Ogura Hikokurō. At the moment of the departure from Edo, he was singled out for his service and achievements of the past few years and granted a special increase in stipend as well as a larger retinue of attendants and grooms. He and his family—his son Bunroku, Otane, and Ofuji—are overjoyed to be together again.

Masayama Sangohei, the daimyō's equerry and husband of Hikokurō's sister, is another in the returning party. He has sent a messenger to Otane.

Scene 2: Hikokurō's house.

[MESSENGER] (*speaking for Sangohei*): I am sure you must be delighted to see your husband again after the long separation and to learn that he has

---

41. Articles borne in a daimyō's procession, three of which are enumerated here.

42. The name Tottori is written with characters meaning "bird-take"—hence the design of feathers.

43. Alludes to the preface to the *Kokinshū*.

safely escorted his lordship here. I share these feelings. I had planned to offer you a souvenir from Edo, but nothing struck me as really unusual. For want of anything better, I am sending with this messenger some hemp thread.[44] It's a specialty of Edo—they call it Kantō hemp. I realize that it is not much of a gift, but while we were on the road, a rumor spread among his lordship's staff that during his absence you had taken to spinning hemp thread. I find now that I'm back that the rumor is in circulation here too. I am therefore taking the liberty of offering you this humble present.

CHANTER: Hardly has he finished speaking than other messengers arrive.

[MAN A]: Who sent you with this present?

[MAN B]: It's from a Mr. Something-or-other, a souvenir for Madam Otane.

CHANTER: Each present arriving strikes terror into Otane's heart. She wonders whether her husband too may not have heard the rumors, but looking at his face, she can detect no sign of suspicion.

[HIKOKURŌ]: Please help unpack the baggage. We must choose suitable presents for everybody and distribute them accordingly. Oh, I forgot—I should go immediately to pay my respects to my father-in-law. Bring me my *hakama*.

CHANTER: His wife answers yes and at once goes inside. Her sister Ofuji brushes past entering the room. Ofuji catches Hikokurō's sleeve.

[OFUJI]: You are certainly the most ungallant man. Why didn't you ever answer the two letters I sent you in Edo? Here, I've thought over everything very carefully, and I've written down exactly what I feel in this letter. I ask you please to take some notice of the contents, whether or not you welcome them.

CHANTER: She pushes a sealed letter into the fold of her brother-in-law's kimono. Hikokurō recoils with an expression of distaste.

[HIKOKURŌ]: Have you gone out of your mind? Yes, I know, when I was first considering marriage to your sister there was some talk of marrying you instead, but nothing ever came of it, and your sister and I are now husband and wife. All that took place more than ten years ago, and we're now rearing a son. I can't possibly divorce Otane to marry you, no matter how much you may care for me. I refuse even to hold such a letter in my hand.

CHANTER: He throws down the letter and goes to the gate. Otane, observing from the inside room what has happened, boldly marches out, snatches up the letter, and thrusts it into her kimono.

[OFUJI]: Wait! That letter is very important. I don't want anybody else to see it.

CHANTER: Ofuji clings fast to her sister, but Otane kicks her fiercely to the ground. She picks up a palm-leaf broom and hits her sister until Ofuji's shrieks of pain bring Bunroku and the maids running up.

---

44. A pun. *Mao* means both "hemp thread" and "paramour" (cuckold).

Ofuji catching Hikokurō's sleeve. (Photograph courtesy of Barbara Curtis Adachi Collection, C. V. Starr East Asian Library, Columbia University)

[BUNROKU]: I don't know what this is about, but please excuse me.

CHANTER: He grasps Otane's arm and wrenches away the broom. Otane snatches up a horsewhip tied to the baggage and lashes Ofuji again and again, as if determined to split her head and face. Ofuji's voice rises in a howl of pain.

[OFUJI]: You're hurting me! You'll kill me! Help!

CHANTER: She screams, in tears. Bunroku grabs the whip.

[BUNROKU]: Mother, I don't understand what's going on. If you have a quarrel with Aunt Ofuji, please let it be with words. She may lose consciousness if you continue beating her like that. Then what will be your excuse?

CHANTER: He speaks harshly.

[OTANE]: I don't care if I kill her. I've heard her say that she was in love with her sister's husband. She admitted sending him letters to Edo. Here, look what I've found.

CHANTER: She tears open the seal and unfolds the letter.

[OTANE]: Do you still think I'm lying? Or do you think it doesn't matter even if it's the truth? Here is what she writes in her letter: "Divorce my sister. Send her away and then we'll be married!" Look! She's even torn off her fingernail to the quick and enclosed it in the letter![45] Read it for yourself,

---

45. Fingernails torn to the quick were sent as pledges of love.

and see whether or not I'm making it up. How I loathe her! She makes me furious!

CHANTER: She flies at her sister. Seizing her hair, she twists it round and round in her hands, and pins the tresses under her knee.

[OTANE]: You hateful woman! I've been waiting for my husband for an eternity, the whole year he's been away, counting the months, watching the stars—my husband, my childhood sweetheart, for whom I wouldn't change my parents or a child. At last this morning I saw his face, and just when I was rejoicing that we'd be sleeping together until next year, you had the nerve to order him to send me away! You animal! It infuriates me to let you live!

CHANTER: Otane hits Ofuji, not caring whether her blows land on her sister's eyes or nose.

[OFUJI]: I have all the excuses in the world. Please, everybody, take her off me. I'm at my last gasp.

[BUNROKU]: First let's hear your excuses.

CHANTER: He restrains Otane forcibly.

[OTANE]: If your excuses aren't believable this time, I'll kill you. Let's hear them, if you have any.

CHANTER: She pulls Ofuji to her feet and pushes her away with understandable distaste. Her sister, breathing painfully, smoothes her hair, holding back her tears.

[OFUJI]: I can reveal my reasons, Otane, only when the two of us are alone together. Please leave the room, everybody.

CHANTER: At her request, all the others rise and withdraw.

[OTANE]: Now, no more innuendos—come out with your reasons plainly.

CHANTER: Ofuji sheds copious tears.

[OFUJI]: Otane. It was out of sisterly duty that I sent the letter to Hikokurō asking him to divorce you. I wanted to save your life. I'm sure you know what I mean without my having to say it. You've been rather friendly with that drum teacher Gen'emon, haven't you?

CHANTER: Otane flies at Ofuji and covers her mouth.

[OTANE]: Be still! You speak so casually, but it's no laughing matter. What have you seen that makes you say such a thing? Show me your proof!

[OFUJI]: I don't need any proof. You're four months pregnant. Whose child is it? And who's been taking that abortion medicine that your maid Orin's bought for you? You never guessed anybody knew, but the whole fief is gossiping about nothing else. I saw a minute ago how all those people brought you the same souvenir from Edo—hemp thread! I knew that they'd be coming to Hikokurō to tell him what was going on, to call his attention, as his friends, to the situation. You and you alone are responsible for destroying your family's honor and your husband's reputation as a samurai.

CHANTER: She weeps aloud. Otane is at a loss for words.

[OTANE]: I never listened when you urged me not to drink. The liquor was my enemy.

CHANTER: These are her only words; she can do nothing now but weep. Ofuji brushes away the welling tears.

[OFUJI]: Your repentance comes months too late. Now you know what I was worrying about. You are disgraced beyond redemption. I've wanted at least to save your life, and I've considered every possible scheme. I thought that if I could persuade Hikokurō to break with you and give you divorce papers, you could give birth to your baby in the middle of a public highway, and it still wouldn't be a crime. You couldn't be killed for it. So I tried, in my poor, feminine way, to help you. I made advances to my brother-in-law and acted like a loose woman. It wasn't only out of sisterly duty to you, however. I thought it was my duty to Mother. Poor Mother! I'm sure you can't have forgotten her last instructions when, just two days before she died, she called us to her pillow, one on either side. "I've taught you, ever since you were children, the proper conduct for women. You've learned to read, to sew, to spin thread and to stretch cotton wool.[46] Any girl who knows that much has nothing to be ashamed of. But the most important test of a woman's training comes after she's married. You must treat your parents-in-law with the same devotion you have shown to your own parents and your husband's brothers and sisters as if they were your own. When you are alone together with any other man, you are not so much as to lift your head and look at him. It doesn't matter who the man may be—a servant, a member of the household, a stranger, an old man, or a boy—when your husband's away, you must observe the proprieties. A woman who's doesn't do this may know the Four Books and the Five Classics by heart, but she won't be of any use to anybody. Remember your mother's dying words. Let them be your *Analects* and never forget them."

Those words have sunk into my bones and are engraved on my heart. I can't forget them. Then Mother went on, this time speaking to me, "Your sister has inherited her father's disposition. She's enjoyed drinking ever since she was in pinafores. Ofuji, you must act as her mother and reprimand her in my place." These were her last words. Every day, morning and night, I repeat those last instructions before her memorial tablet, just as if they were holy writing. Have you forgotten them so quickly? To think that you would want to bring grief to your sister in this world and suffering on Mother's dead body in the world of the hereafter!

---

46. Used in padding cotton garments. An ability to stretch cotton wool or silk wool evenly was considered a household art.

CHANTER: She utters words of bitter reproach and weeps aloud in her misery. Otane is speechless, choked by tears.

[OTANE]: I see now that the saké I enjoyed so much was a poisonous brew compounded of the sins of a previous existence. As soon as my drunkenness from the liquor had worn off, I decided to kill myself, but I wanted so badly to see my husband's face once again that I kept putting off my suicide from one day to the next. And now I have exposed my shame to the world. I wonder if I have been bewitched by some horrible demon.

CHANTER: At these repeated words of vain regret, the sisters, embracing, weep aloud with unrestrained voices, a pitiful sight in their utter helplessness. Just then a loud uproar is heard by the gate.

[OTANE]: It must be a fight. Let's leave for a while until it quiets down.

CHANTER: After they depart, Hikokurō's sister Yura enters, pursuing her brother with an outstretched lance.

[YURA]: I know I'm only your younger sister, Hikokurō, but I'm the wife of a samurai, Masayama Sangohei. Something has happened that goes against all decency, and I won't tolerate it, even though it involves my own brother. What do you say to that?

CHANTER: Hikokurō glares at her.

[HIKOKURŌ]: You impudent little hussy! What nerve you have to talk to me, your older brother, about decency or indecency! This is the height of impertinence! Out with your accusations! Out with them, or I'll twist your arms and that lance of yours, and break them both together!

CHANTER: The words are spoken in fury. Yura laughs at him mockingly.

[YURA]: Admirably said, Mr. Weak-Kneed! I'll tell you what's happened. Your wife has had a secret affair with Miyaji Gen'emon, a drum teacher from Kyoto, and the whole fief is buzzing with it now. That's why everybody gave her souvenirs of hemp thread—to call your attention to what was going on. But you pretend not to have heard anything because you're unable to avenge yourself on your wife's lover. My husband has ordered me out of his house. He said he couldn't go on living with the sister of Weak-Kneed Hikokurō. "You can return," he told me, "when your brother shows a little backbone. Then, and only then, will we be husband and wife again." We're separated now, and I've come to you. Well, my weak-kneed brother, are you going to reunite me with my husband or aren't you? It's up to you.

CHANTER: She holds out the lance and brandishes it, seemingly ready to run him through if he flinches. Hikokurō claps his hands in amazement.

[HIKOKURŌ]: This is incredible—I suspected nothing! I heard people talk about that Gen'emon, or whatever his name is, but I've never actually laid eyes on him. He's never set foot inside this house. What proof do you have?

[YURA]: Do you suppose that a man like Sangohei would make accusations without evidence? Your friend Isobe Yukaemon, suspecting that something was going on, used to come here, pretending it was merely to visit. He caught them one night in a secret rendezvous and cut off their sleeves. The affair has become a public scandal throughout the fief. It's impossible to hide it any longer, even with the best will in the world. But some things not even a close friend can tell a man to his face, so Yukaemon decided to tell my husband instead of going to you. Look!

CHANTER: She produces from her kimono the sleeves of the guilty pair, and throws them in front of Hikokurō.

[YURA]: Do you have any doubts now?

CHANTER: Her face is livid. Hikokurō picks up the sleeves and examines them.

[HIKOKURŌ]: I've never seen this man's sleeve before, but I remember the woman's sleeve very well. Yura, I promise you I shall lose no time in vindicating your honor. Come with me.

CHANTER: He leads her into the sitting room. Everyone in the house has heard their conversation, and a breathless silence has fallen. Hikokurō speaks quite calmly.

[HIKOKURŌ]: Otane, you and the other women come here. Bunroku, I want you too.

CHANTER: They all know that so curt a summons indicates some disaster. They slowly come before Hikokurō and bow their heads. Their bodies are chilled, their spirits faint, they can scarcely breathe. Among them, wretched creature, is Otane, fated on account of an evil deed, not of her intent or desire, yet blamable only on herself, to be impaled on a blade wielded by her husband, as she fully expects. All her long, patient waiting for her husband's return has been in vain. Never, until this very moment when she is about to be killed, did she imagine that the pillow she shared with her husband on the night before his departure in the previous year would be their last together. At this thought, she wants to look once more at her husband's face, but her eyes are too blinded with tears to see him. She weeps, her head hanging. Her husband throws the sleeves in front of her.

[HIKOKURŌ]: I'm sure you've all heard Yura's accusations. Well, woman, do you have an excuse? No? I didn't think so—you can't answer. Ofuji, I presume you know who brought them together. In crimes of immorality, the go-between shares the lovers' guilt.

[OFUJI]: You foolish man, Hikokurō! Had I known what was going on, do you suppose such a disgraceful thing would have happened?

CHANTER: She weeps bitterly again.

[HIKOKURŌ]: The servant must have been the go-between. Send for the wench.

CHANTER: At his summons the girl appears, trembling all over.

[ORIN]: Begging your pardon, sir, but I don't know anything about it. The other day Madam Otane asked me to buy some abortion medicine. She told me not to let anybody know. I bought three doses at seven *fun* each, which made two *monme*, one *fun*, all together. That's all I ever did. Even so, I was afraid, master, if you heard about it you might scold me for buying such expensive medicine. So I paid for it with bad coins.[47]

CHANTER: She prattles on in this inane fashion. Hikokurō is flabbergasted.

[HIKOKURŌ]: You say she's pregnant? Bunroku, I know you're still a boy, but why, when the whole fief's bursting with the scandal, didn't you kill Gen'emon and get rid of him long ago?

[BUNROKU]: I heard about it only this morning. I informed the household retainers, and they sent some men to Gen'emon's lodgings to kill him. But they discovered that he had gone back to Kyoto a couple of days ago.

[HIKOKURŌ]: It can't be helped, then. Somebody light a fire in front of the Buddhist altar. Stand up, woman. Come here before the altar.

CHANTER: His wife wipes away her tears.

[OTANE]: I expected you to hate me until the end of time. But I know now, when you tell me to stand before the Buddha, that something still remains of your old affection. How shall I forget it, even after death? My dear husband, I did not betray you intentionally, after knowing your goodness all those many months and years. My crime took place in a kind of nightmare. While I dreamed, a horrible man—but if I go on, it will only make my death mean and shameful. It may be wrong of me, I know, to kill myself before my husband's sword can strike, but let me vindicate myself in this way. Forgive me, please. This is my atonement.

CHANTER: She pulls open the front of her kimono and plunges the dagger to the hilt into her breast, a moving display of her resolve. Ofuji and Bunroku cry out in horror. The tears well in their hearts, but taken aback by Hikokurō's impassive expression, they clench their teeth in silent grief. Hikokurō unsheathes his sword and, jerking up Otane's body, deals her the death blow with a final thrust. He pushes away her body, wipes his sword, and deliberately sheathes it. He rises to his feet: this is the stern behavior expected of a samurai. Hikokurō picks up the traveling costume he had taken off only this morning—his wicker hat, straw sandals, and sword.

[HIKOKURŌ]: Bunroku, I'm going now to report to my superiors what has happened. I shall ask for leave, even though I can't wait until it is granted. I intend to go as quickly as possible to Kyoto. While I am busy disposing of my wife's lover, I want you to escort these women to a safe place with our relatives.

---

47. Literally, paying with the debased coinage of 1706 a debt that should have been paid in good Genroku money.

Hikokurō dealing Otane the death blow. (Photograph courtesy of Barbara Curtis Adachi Collection, C. V. Starr East Asian Library, Columbia University)

CHANTER: He starts to leave after these parting words. Ofuji, Bunroku, and Yura, all wishing to follow, vie in their eagerness to join him. Fury blazes in Hikokurō's dilated eyes.

[HIKOKURŌ]: Do you expect me to take along the lot of you just to kill one man, like some shopkeeper's vengeance? Are you trying to bring even more disgrace on me? If even one of you follows me, I'll never speak to you again.

CHANTER: He is outraged. The others burst into tears.

[OFUJI]: You are being too unkind. The man, as far as I am concerned, is my sister's enemy.

[BUNROKU]: For me, he's my mother's enemy.

[YURA]: And for me, my sister-in-law's enemy.

[ALL THREE]: Can we allow this villain to go unpunished? Please let us go with you.

CHANTER: The three together join their hands in supplication, weeping aloud. Hikokurō is unable to hide his grief any longer. His resolute expression gives way to despair.

[HIKOKURŌ]: If you think so much of your mother, sister, or sister-in-law, why didn't you beg me to spare her life? Why didn't you suggest that she put on Buddhist robes and become a nun?

CHANTER: Lifting the lifeless body in his arms, he shouts his grief, and the others are carried away by tears of sympathy. The misery of it! This is the heartbreaking conduct demanded of those born to be samurai.

[*Chikamatsu jōruri shū jō*, NKBT 49: 39–57, translated by Donald Keene]

THE BATTLES OF COXINGA (*KOKUSENYA KASSEN*, 1715)

Although now the contemporary-life (*sewamono*) puppet plays are the main focus of critical attention and the more frequently performed, the history plays (*jidaimono*) were the more important in Chikamatsu's time. Chikamatsu himself wrote three times as many jidaimono as sewamono, and *The Battles of Coxinga*, which was first performed in 1715, was his greatest success in this genre. This was the first play that Chikamatsu wrote after the death in 1714 of Takemoto Gidayū, the chief chanter of the Takemoto Theater with whom he had first established himself as a playwright. Chikamatsu wrote *The Battles of Coxinga* to maintain the life of the theater and ensure the success of Gidayū's successor, Masatayū. The play became a long-running hit and was quickly adapted by the kabuki theater. Indeed, until well into the nineteenth century, *The Battles of Coxinga* was performed more often than any other Chikamatsu play. The exoticism of the drama, the setting in China, and the incorporation of a number of foreign details contributed to its popularity, as did the many special puppet effects. Even so, the play was not performed in its entirety for long. The tendency toward fragmentation has left only the second half of act 2 (Bamboo Forest of a Thousand Leagues) and the two scenes of act 3, translated here, in regular production on the puppet and kabuki stages.

The *Battles of Coxinga* follows the five-act structure that Gidayū had advocated for jidaimono: the first act (love), second act (warriors and battle), third act (tragedy), fourth act (*michiyuki*/poetic journey), and fifth act (celebratory speech). In act 1, the Ming emperor is duped by Ri Tōten, one of his ministers, who gouges out one of his own eyes in what appears to be a show of loyalty but turns out to be a sign that he has joined the Tartars (Manchus), who are plotting to overthrow the Ming court. Go Sankei, a minister loyal to the Ming emperor, points out Ri Tōten's deception as well as the plight of Ikkan (Tei Shiryū), who was banished from the court and fled to Japan nineteen years earlier for similarly warning the emperor of treacherous courtiers. But the emperor refuses to believe Go Sankei. The emperor and the court are then attacked by the Tartar army, led by Bairoku, a Tartar prince. Bairoku also is intent on capturing Lady Kasei, the Ming emperor's consort, who is pregnant with the future crown prince. When the emperor and the pregnant empress are killed, Go Sankei takes the baby out of the womb and replaces it with his own child, whom he kills so that the Tartars will think that the imperial line has died. In the meantime, Go Sankei's wife manages to escape with Princess Sendan, the younger sister of the dead emperor, and the two set sail for Japan.

Act 2 opens in Japan some six months later and centers on Ikkan, now married to a lowly Japanese fisherwoman, and their grown son, Watōnai (*wa* stands for Japan and *tō* for Tang, his father's home), the future Coxinga. Watōnai and his wife discover the boat carrying Princess Sendan, who tells them that Ri Tōten has killed the emperor, allied with the Tartars, and taken over the empire. Watōnai and his parents then decide to sail for China to restore the Ming dynasty. Upon their arrival in China, Ikkan resolves to find Kinshōjo, his daughter by his previous wife. Kinshōjo's mother died giving birth, and Kinshōjo, who was only two years old when Ikkan fled to Japan, is now married to Gojōgun Kanki, an illustrious prince whose aid Ikkan hopes to enlist by appealing to Kinshōjo. Ikkan parts company with Watōnai and his mother, who enter the Bamboo Forest of a Thousand Leagues. In a scene long popular with audiences, they are attacked by a tiger, but Watōnai subdues it using a Japanese charm given to him by his mother.

In act 3, which is translated here, Watōnai and his mother rejoin Ikkan at Red Cliff Mountain and proceed to Kanki's castle only to learn that Kanki is away. With Kinshōjo's help, Ikkan and Watōnai manage to get the mother into the castle, as a hostage, to await Kanki's return. Upon his arrival home, the mother asks Kanki if he will join Watōnai to defeat the Tartars, whom Kanki has been serving. Although not related by blood, Kinshōjo acts as a filial daughter to Watōnai's mother, but she becomes an obstacle for Kanki, who wants to join Watōnai's cause but cannot because he would seen as a leader influenced by his wife and therefore a disgrace. Kinshōjo kills herself ostensibly out of shame over her inability to help Ikkan, Watōnai, and her stepmother, to whom she feels duty bound (*giri*); but implicitly, her reason is to free Kanki to join their cause. Watōnai's mother then joins Kinshōjo in death, taking her own life out of a sense of duty to Kinshōjo so that she will not be viewed as a "shame to Japan"—that is, as a cruel stepmother who forced her foreign stepdaughter to kill herself. Beneath the surface, however, the mother's suicide also reveals the purity and justice of their cause. The sacrifice of the two women allows Watōnai and Kanki—who play masculine *aragoto* (rough-style) roles and are about to fight each other to the death—to become allies. For both women, private and public conflicts are resolved through death. Their sacrifice is followed by a lament and praise for the dead, which function as a kind of catharsis.

The tragic third act of a jidaimono was considered especially important and thus was always performed by the chief chanter. By the early eighteenth century, it had become customary for the tragedy to involve the substitution of one person for another (*migawari*). This ill-fated substitute was a usually a secondary figure, such as a retainer to the main character or a relative, who was faced with the task of overcoming severe obstacles in order to help restore the social order. In the third act of Coxinga, Kinshōjo and Watōnai's mother, two relatively powerless women, are faced with just such a task, and it is their sacrificial death that finally resolves the major conflict between the two male figures, Watōnai and Kanki. Chikamatsu's humanism implies that such lesser people can, through self-sacrifice, make a major impact on the course of history, which, in Chikamatsu's jidaimono, means the return and triumph of the forces of good over evil.

While for the chōnin audience the history plays were a form of escape from the everyday world in which they lived, the jidaimono were also indirect commentary on the contemporary situation. As Uchiyama Michiko has pointed out, the danger in which the Ming court finds itself—particularly the corruption that comes from within in the form of Ri Tōten, the evil adviser—reflects the chaos that Japan found itself in following the corrupt administration of Shōgun Tokugawa Tsunayoshi (1646–1709).

Much like Tsunayoshi, the Ming emperor cannot discern between good (Go Sankei) and evil (Ri Tōten), thereby causing a crisis that requires the sacrifice of the innocent and weak to restore peace and stability.

CHARACTERS

WATŌNAI, later called Coxinga, son of a Chinese father (Ikkan) and a Japanese mother

[GOJŌGUN] IKKAN, Watōnai's father, also called Tei Shiryū, a former Chinese minister loyal to the Ming emperor, father of Kinshōjo by a previous Chinese wife, now married to a Japanese woman

[RŌ] KANKI, an illustrious Chinese prince, Ikkan's son-in-law

KINSHŌJO, wife of Kanki and daughter of Ikkan by his previous Chinese wife, the half sister of Coxinga

MOTHER, Japanese mother of Watōnai (Coxinga) and stepmother of Kinshōjo

Act 3

Scene 1: Outside the castle of Gojōgun Kanki.

CHANTER:
   The most benevolent ruler cannot keep a worthless minister,
   Nor can the kindest father love a shiftless son.[48]
   Thus with China and Japan: though their paths diverged by custom
      and tradition,
   They stray not from the Way of Sincerity.
   At the foot of Red Cliff Mountain, Ikkan joins his wife and son, and the three hurry on until they reach Lion's Keep, the stronghold of Gojōgun Kanki, knowing only that he is Ikkan's son-in-law. The castle looks more formidable than they had heard: far above the high stone walls, in the darkness of a spring night still bitterly cold, decorative dolphins arch their tails to the sky atop roof tiles glistening with frost. The waters of the moat, dark as indigo, uncoil like a long thick rope and flow toward the distant Yellow River. The tower gate is tightly bolted; a sentry's gong clangs noisily within. The loopholes in the castle wall bristle with crossbows, and cannons stand here and there ready to be fired: no fortress in Japan looked so mighty as this. Shocked by what he sees, Ikkan whispers to Watōnai.

[IKKAN]: I heard the country was at war, but such an imposing gate—it's enormous! If I knock on it in the middle of the night and tell them that I, Kanki's father-in-law, have arrived from Japan, no one will believe me—they've never

---

48. From a poem by Cao Zhi (192–232). By contrast, here Watōnai is the dutiful son, and Ikkan, the valuable minister.

even heard of me! If I could just speak to my daughter, I could offer all kinds of proof that I am the father who left her when she was two and went to Japan, but getting into that castle won't be easy. What'll we do now?

[WATŌNAI]: We shouldn't be surprised now. Ever since leaving Japan, I knew we wouldn't find any allies here. Sentimental appeals like "I am the father-in-law you never knew!" or "My son-in-law!" may fall on deaf ears. Better to ask him directly: "Can we count on you or not?" "No" means he is our enemy. The daughter you left here is also my half sister, but if she had cared for you at all, she would have wanted news from Japan and sent letters. Her feelings can't be trusted. If I made those brutes I defeated in the Bamboo Forest the core of an army and used them to win over others, then fifty or a hundred thousand men would join us in no time. But I don't need any help to kick down that gate, twist off the head of an unfilial sister, and fight it out with Kanki.

CHANTER: He leaps up to charge the gate, but his mother holds him back.

[MOTHER]: I don't know what her feelings are, but a woman's place is to obey her husband, not to do as she likes. Ikkan is her father, and you, Watōnai, are from the same seed. I am the outsider here, and although I've been separated from her by a thousand leagues of oceans and mountains, I cannot escape the title of stepmother. I am sure that her heart is filled with love for her family. If you fought your way in and then people blamed it on her Japanese stepmother's envy, it would bring shame not only to me but to Japan as well. Humble though your station may be, you are committed to a noble cause—to destroy the Tartars, a mighty foe, and restore the Ming dynasty. Don't think of my shame! Swallow your resentment!

The first rule of military strategy, they say, is to win over others to your side, even if it is just one from the lowest ranks. Far better still would be having Kanki on our side, the lord of a castle who controls the whole region! Do you think that is an easy task? Calm down and ask them to let you in!

CHANTER: Ikkan and Watōnai approach the gate, and Watōnai calls out.

[WATŌNAI]: We have something to discuss with Lord Kanki! Open the gate! Open the gate!

CHANTER: He pounds on the gate, but the sound only echoes back from within the walls. Then the sentries shout down, one by one: "Lord Kanki left yesterday by order of the Tartar king." "We don't know when he'll return." "Coming in the middle of the night while he's away is bad enough, whoever you are, but demanding to speak with him personally—what nerve! If you have something to say, then say it—we'll tell him when he returns!" Ikkan answers in a low voice.

[IKKAN]: A messenger won't do. If Lord Kanki is away, I would like to speak directly to his wife. Once you tell her that I've come from Japan, I'm sure she'll consent.

CHANTER: His words spark an outcry behind the wall even before he finishes speaking.

[SENTRY]: We've never even seen the lady's face, and you want to meet with her in private? Bold talk indeed—and from a Japanese! Keep your eyes on him, men!

CHANTER: In the light of the pole lanterns, the sentries bang their gongs and cymbals while a swarm of soldiers appear on top of the wall and take aim with their muskets. "Fire the cannons! Crush them!! Fuses! Bullets!" they shout, jostling against each other in alarm. Hearing the commotion from her rooms, Kinshōjo runs out and climbs the gate tower.

[KINSHŌJO]: Calm down! Calm down! I will listen to everything they have to say. Don't shoot until I give the order myself. Stand at ease!

You there, outside the gate! I am Kinshōjo, Lord Kanki's wife. The whole realm bows before the Tartar king. My husband, mindful of the times, also serves that king and has been entrusted with this castle. Why do you want to meet with me at a time like this, when he is away and the castle is under heavy guard? It makes no sense. And yet you mention Japan—tell me about those who are dear to me. How I long to hear news of them!

CHANTER: Even as she speaks, she wonders: "Could it be my father? Why would he have come here?" Though fearful of the danger, her yearning increases.

[KINSHŌJO]: You soldiers—Be careful! Do not fire your muskets by accident!

CHANTER: Her fears are understandable. Ikkan sees his daughter's face for the first time, like the hazy spring moon, and tears cloud his voice.

[IKKAN]: Pardon me for addressing you in this abrupt manner, but your father was Tei Shiryū of the Ming. Your mother died giving birth to you, and your father incurred the emperor's wrath. When he fled to Japan, you were only two years old, too young to understand his sorrow at leaving you behind, but you must have heard something about this, even from your nursemaid. I am your father, Tei Shiryū. I've passed the years at Hirado Bay in Hizen, a province in Japan, and my name now is Ikkan. This man is your brother, born in Japan, and this woman is your new mother. I come to you now, without hiding my shameful state, because I have something to ask of you, in private. Please have them open the gate.

CHANTER: His appeal, spoken so earnestly, stirs her memories. Thinking it might be her father, she wants to fly to him, cling to him, gaze into his face. Her heart is torn in a thousand pieces, but as the wife of Kanki, lord of the castle, she holds back her tears before the soldiers.

[KINSHŌJO]: I remember it all, but without some proof how can I be certain? If you have proof that you are my father, I would like to hear it.

CHANTER: Immediately the soldiers start shouting one after the other: "Prove it!" "Show us proof!" "He's just saying he's her father. " "He's a liar!" They all fix their gun sights on Ikkan. Watōnai runs up and stands in front of Ikkan, facing the soldiers.

[WATŌNAI]: If I hear so much as a pop from your silly guns, I'll cut you all down!

[SOLDIER]: Don't let that bastard escape!

CHANTER: They cock their muskets, covering them from all sides. "Proof!" "Proof!" they chant with growing menace, until they appear about to shoot. Ikkan raises his hands.

[IKKAN]: Wait!—You, my lady, have the proof yourself, I'm sure of it. The year before I fled from China, I had my portrait painted as a memento for you. I left it with your nursemaid. I've grown old, but my face must still bear some traces of the past. Compare it with the portrait—that should clear away any doubts!

[KINSHŌJO]: Your words are already proof.

CHANTER: She takes out the portrait that she has kept next to her heart over the years, and unfolds it on the railing. Then she takes out her mirror, holds it up so that she can see her father's face reflected by the moonlight, and carefully compares the two images. In the portrait, she sees the burnished skin and glossy sidelocks of youth; in the mirror, a face now ravaged by age. His hair has turned white as snow, but the eyes and mouth remain unchanged, closely resembling her own. The mole on her forehead, inherited from her father, is undeniable proof.

[KINSHŌJO]: Are you really my father? How I've longed to see you—my dear father! I was told only that my mother had died and that my father was in Japan. I knew no one who might have news. I knew that Japan lay to the east, at the edge of the world, so each dawn I bowed to the rising sun, and at dusk I spread out a map of the world and said to myself: "Here is China, there is Japan, where my father is!" Japan seemed so near on the map, but you were three thousand leagues away or more. I gave up all hope of seeing you in this life and looked forward to the next, hoping I might meet you in the underworld. For twenty years I've filled my days and nights with sighs and tears. It was so hard for me to bear, but you have stayed alive! Now I can bow to my father. I'm so grateful!

CHANTER: Her voice dissolves in sobs of joy as she loses all restraint. Ikkan, choking with emotion, clings to the gate tower and looks up as she looks down, their hearts too full to speak, their tears unending. Even the valiant Watōnai and his mother are overcome, and the tears of the brutish soldiers dampen their musket fuses. After a while Ikkan speaks.

[IKKAN]: We have come here on a very important matter. I wish to make a request of Kanki in secret. But I need to discuss this with you first, so please have the soldiers open the castle gate.

[KINSHŌJO]: I should, of course, invite you to enter without your even asking, but the country is still at war, and by order of the Tartar king, foreigners,

Kinshōjo, in Kanki's castle, holding up a portrait of Ikkan. (Photograph courtesy of Barbara Curtis Adachi Collection, C. V. Starr East Asian Library, Columbia University)

even close relatives, are strictly forbidden from entering. But this is a special case. Soldiers! What do you say?

CHANTER: The thickheaded Chinese cry out: "No! Impossible! Never! Go back to Japan! *Bin kan ta satsu bu on bu on!*"[49] The visitors are shocked, then dismayed as the soldiers again take aim with their muskets, but Watōnai's mother steps forward.

[MOTHER]: You are quite right, of course, quite right. Since it is the king's command, we are in no position to object. But you need not be concerned about an aged mother. I want only a few words with the lady. If you let me pass, it would truly be the greatest kindness I have ever known.

CHANTER: She presses her hands together in supplication, but they refuse to listen.

[SOLDIERS]: No! No! Nothing was said about allowing a woman to enter. If we let her in, she must be tied up with a rope. That way, even if the king hears of it, Lord Kanki will have an excuse and we would have done our duty. Quickly now—tie her up! If she doesn't like it, send her back to Japan! *Bin kan ta satsu Bu on bu on.. . .*

CHANTER: They glare down at the mother, and Watōnai's eyes suddenly widen with rage.

[WATŌNAI]: You dirty Chinese! Didn't you hear? She's the wife of Tei Shiryū

---

49. Meaningless words meant to sound like Chinese.

Ikkan and my mother. That makes her your lady's mother as well. To lead her in on a rope like a dog or a cat—no Japanese would tolerate such an insult. So what if we can't get into your damned castle—let's go!

CHANTER: He starts to lead his mother away, but she shakes him off.

[MOTHER]: Listen—have you forgotten what I just said? A person making a big request of another will suffer every kind of humiliation and bitterness. Even if I am bound hand and foot by shackles, much less ropes, as long as our request is granted, it will be like exchanging roof tiles for gold. Japan may be a small country, but its men and women do not forget their duty. Ikkan—please tie me up.

CHANTER: Watōnai feels ashamed, but he has no choice. Taking the rope he keeps at his waist for emergencies, he binds her arms to her torso and ties her wrists together. Mother and son acknowledge each other with a smile— a reflection of the bravery instilled in the Japanese. Although in almost unbearable anguish, Kinshōjo struggles to keep her composure.

[KINSHŌJO]: The times govern all things, and the law of the land must be obeyed. You need not worry so long as your mother is in my care. I don't know what she has to say, but I will listen to her request, convey her words to my husband Kanki, and beg him to grant her wishes. Now then, the waters of the moat surrounding this castle come through a conduit from a spring in the garden next to my dressing room and flow all the way to the Yellow River. If my husband grants your request, I will drop white makeup powder in the spring. So if you see the water in the moat turn white, it will be a sign of success, and you may enter the castle in high spirits. But if he does not grant your request, I will drop rouge powder into the water as a sign he has refused. Then you must come to the gate to take back your mother and be on your way. Success or failure will appear in the waters, pure white or deep red—keep your eyes on the moat! Farewell!

CHANTER: In the moonlight the doors of the gate swing open, and the mother is led through, across the threshold between life and death. This is not the Gateway to Enlightenment but the Gateway to the Darkness of Worldly Delusions. The doors close, and the heavy crossbar drops with a resounding boom. Kinshōjo's eyes cloud with tears, revealing the weakness of a Chinese woman. Neither Watōnai nor Ikkan sheds a tear—the way of the Japanese warrior. In the fashion of the Tartars, a cannon fires as the gates open and close. Crossbar and cannon boom together, the only sound heard as it fills the air and the distant reaches beyond.

Scene 2: Kinshōjo's rooms in the castle.

CHANTER:

Far-distant China, beyond the reach even of her dreams.
Having journeyed to a land she'd only heard about,

This woodblock illustration of *The Battles of Coxinga* is from a mid-eighteenth-century book entitled *Zashiki ayatsuri otogi gunki*. At the gate to Kanki's residence, Kinshōjo, on top of the tower, unrolls the portrait of her father, Tei Shiryū (Ikkan), over the railing and extends her hand toward him. Ikkan (*left*) stands next to his wife, now bound by rope. Two of Kanki's retainers (*center*) are speaking in Chinese and gesturing toward the gate to let in Ikkan's wife. Watōnai, with the shaved crown, stands vigilantly, grasping a long sword.

The mother finds the bonds of love between parent and child
As strong as the ropes that tightly bind her like a criminal.
Their meeting is as rare as plum blossoms in the snow,
but like two nightingales from different lands,
their songs harmonize and require no interpreter.

Kinshōjo brings the mother to her private rooms. With a deep sense of filial devotion, she comforts and honors her with heavenly splendor, providing her with layers of cushions and quilts, with fine wine and the best delicacies from the mountains and seas. But the ropes around the mother's wrists and arms make her look like a criminal guilty of the Ten Evils and the Five Sins,[50] a painful sight. Yet Kinshōjo attends to her in various ways with ad-

---

50. The Ten Evils are those of the body (murder, theft, adultery), the mouth (lying, thoughtless words, slander, causing strife through deception), and the mind (greed, anger, foolishness). The Five Sins are killing one's father, killing one's mother, killing an enlightened monk (arhat), killing a priest, and wounding the Buddha. Alternatively, the last three may be replaced by grandfather, grandmother, and sovereign.

mirable concern, treating her as if she were her real mother. Her maidservants gather around.

[MAID 1]: Have you ever seen a Japanese woman before? Her eyes and nose are like ours, but the way she ties up her hair is odd!

[MAID 2]: And her clothing are sewn so differently! I suppose the young women dress the same way, too. A gust of wind would raise the edges of that divided skirt and expose her thighs!

[MAID 1]: That would be embarrassing!

[MAID 3]: But if I'm reborn a woman, I'd rather be a Japanese. They say Japan is called Yamato, which means "land of great gentleness." For a woman, a country of great gentleness would be wonderful!

[MAID 1]: Yes, it must be a wonderful country!

CHANTER: They all narrow their eyes and nod in agreement. Kinshōjo approaches.

[KINSHŌJO]: What are you all chattering about so intently? This lady is not the mother who gave me life; yet for me, filial devotion and duty mean even more with her. But the law must be obeyed. It breaks my heart to see her bound like a common criminal, but what if the Tartar king heard about this and blamed my husband? I can't untie her, and that's my burden to bear.

Now then, I need your help. They say that Japanese food is different from our own; ask her what she would like and prepare something for her.

[MAIDSERVANT]: If I may speak, my lady, we have carefully prepared a meal that has everything—rice cooked with sweet longans, soup with duck and fried bean curd, pork in sweet sauce, steamed lamb, and beef-paste cakes. But when we served it, she said she couldn't possibly eat such things. She said that couldn't eat anyway with her arms and wrists tied up. So she asked us to make a simple *musubi*.[51] I haven't the faintest idea what sort of food a *musubi* might be, so we all gathered around to discuss it. One said that in Japan, a sumo wrestler is called a *musubi*. We asked around, but sumo must be out of season because we couldn't find any that she might like.

CHANTER: Just then a horse-drawn carriage thunders to a halt outside the castle wall to shouts of "Lord Kanki has returned!" One large chest after another is carried into the courtyard, followed by Kanki himself, walking beneath a stately silk parasol—an imposing procession befitting his noble name. Kinshōjo goes out to greet him.

[KINSHŌJO]: You've returned sooner that I expected. How do matters rest with you, my lord?

[KANKI]: Well, the Tartar king is deeply gratified with my efforts and has promoted me to a rank far greater than I deserve. I've been appointed a general with one hundred thousand cavalry, granted the hat and robes of a prince,

---

51. A *musubi* is both a cold rice ball and a rank in sumo wrestling.

Kanki, a Chinese prince and lord of the castle. (Photograph courtesy of Barbara Curtis Adachi Collection, C. V. Starr East Asian Library, Columbia University)

and directed to carry out important functions. There is no greater honor for our house.

[KINSHŌJO]: What a marvelous achievement—Congratulations! Our family's good fortune keeps growing. I have always told you how much I loved my father and longed to see him. He, the wife he married in Japan, and their son arrived at the gate today with a request, but I told them you were away. My father and his son, in deference to the strict laws of this country, have taken their leave, but I have kept the mother here. I feared the Tartar king might hear of this, so I had her bound with ropes. She is resting in one of my rooms. She may not be the mother who bore me, but imagine how she must feel being tied up like that—it's heartbreaking!

[KANKI]: Tying her with ropes was prudent—if word should reach those higher up, I will have an excuse. Treat her with the greatest courtesy, but first I will meet with her. Show me the way.

CHANTER: The mother must have overheard, for she calls out from behind the double doors.

[MOTHER]: Kinshōjo—has Lord Kanki returned? He is too exalted a person; I will go to him.

CHANTER: She emerges through the doorway and struggles, moving slowly toward them like an ancient pine tree tightly entwined by a wisteria vine. The painful sight fills Kanki with pity.

[KANKI]: It is true enough: a mother will do anything for her child, even journey ten thousand leagues over mountains and rivers to find her. To be rewarded with binding ropes—that I cannot change; it is the times we live in. Wife—be careful that the ropes aren't hurting her. We must see to every need of our precious guest. Whatever you may require, madam, I will provide it if I can. Do not hesitate to ask.

CHANTER: The mother's face brightens at the warmth of his reception.

[MOTHER]: I feel I can trust you; I am most grateful. After listening to you, how can I stand on ceremony? I wish to speak to you privately about an important request. Come closer, come closer.

CHANTER: She lowers her voice.

[MOTHER]: We did not come to China just because we longed to see our daughter. At the beginning of last winter, Princess Sendan, the younger sister of the Ming emperor, was blown ashore in a small boat at Matsura Beach in Hizen Province. She told us that China had been seized by the Tartars. Kinshōjo's father, as you know, was once a minister at the Ming court. Our son, Watōnai, though only a lowly fisherman, has studied the military writings of China and Japan. Once my husband and son heard her story, they resolved to destroy the Tartar king, to restore China to the Ming, and to put the princess on the throne. We left the princess in Japan and came to China, but we were shocked to find that everyone, even the plants and trees, bows to the Tartars. No one wishes to side with the Ming. The only person whom we can trust to be Watōnai's right arm is you, Lord Kanki. I beg you—please join us.

CHANTER: She struggles to bow at the waist, bringing her head to her knees. Her single-minded resolve is obvious to all, and Kanki is greatly surprised.

[KANKI]: I see . . . this Watōnai of Japan I've been hearing about must be Kinshōjo's brother and Ikkan's son! His bravery is no secret, even in China. I'm sure that he has a promising plan, one that we should follow. My forefathers were also ministers under the Ming. But after the death of the Ming emperor, I had nowhere to turn, so I've passed the months and days accepting favors from the Tartars. Now as fate would have it, your request coincides with my hopes. I would like to say I am your ally right now, but I need to give the matter some thought.

[MOTHER]: Coward! That's not what you said before! Once such an important matter is broached, the whole world knows about it. If word of this leaked out while you were mulling this over and we were defeated, there would be no going back no matter how much you regretted it. We won't bear a grudge. Yes or no, answer me—now!

[KANKI]: Well then, if you want an answer right away, that's easy enough: I, Kanki, will be Watōnai's ally.

CHANTER: In a flash, he grabs Kinshōjo by the front of her robe, pulls her toward him, draws his sword, and presses it to her throat. The old mother throws herself between them, kicking free Kanki's grip. With her back she pushes Kinshōjo down and lies on top of her, facing Kanki.

Drawing a sword, Kanki pins down Kinshōjo, causing her oval Chinese fan to fall to the floor. Although bound, the mother tries to intervene, coming between them. The checkered floor tiles symbolize Chinese architecture. Watōnai stands anxiously outside the gate, waiting for the water to change color. Bamboo and plum, also signifying China, adorn the garden.

[MOTHER]: You fiend! What are you doing? Is stabbing your wife when asked a favor a Chinese custom? Are you angry you had to listen to an offensive request from your wife's relative? Are you crazy? Are you so wicked that you'd kill your wife in front of her mother at their first meeting? If you don't want to side with us, then don't. (*To Kinshōjo*) My precious daughter, you have a mother now—don't be afraid. Hold me tight!

CHANTER: She covers Kinshōjo with her body like a protective wall. Kinshōjo does not understand her husband's intent but is grateful for her stepmother's love. "Don't hurt yourself!" she cries, her voice choking with tears. Kanki leaps back.

[KANKI]: Your suspicions are quite natural, but I am neither angry nor insane. Yesterday the Tartar king summoned me, saying, "Some no-account called Watōnai crossed over from Japan recently, intending to overthrow the king and restore the Ming. He is very resourceful, a born strategist, despite his humble origins. Who will lead a force against him?" He chose me from among all the nobles and gave me the rank of a general with command of ten thousand cavalry. Until this moment, I never dreamed that this Watōnai was my wife's brother. I told the king: "Watōnai may be endowed with the nerves of that Kusunoki what's-his-name, with the backbone of Asahina and Benkei's muscles, but I have probed the guts of Zhuge Liang. I'll borrow the bones of Fan Kuai and the marrow of Xiang Yu.[52] I'll hunt him down, defeat him in a single battle, and come back with his shaven head in my hands."[53] The Tartars know that I, Gojōgun Kanki, am not one to shrink in fear at tales of Japanese bravery. If I, having boasted in this way, become your ally without batting an eye, without once crossing swords, without firing even a single arrow, I am sure to be slandered: the Tartars will say that I lost my nerve and forgot that I was soldier because I was tied to a woman and influenced by her relatives. Then my sons and grandsons, and their sons after them, will be forever disgraced. I will stab my dear wife and sever all ties to her family so that I can join your side cleanly and with honor. Kinshōjo, your mother's words were filled with love, and the tip of your husband's sword is filled with his duty: give up your life for her love and for my duty!

CHANTER: These are the words of a brave warrior who does not varnish the truth.

[KINSHŌJO]: I understand. I can carry out such duty. Out of filial devotion, I will sacrifice this body that I received from my parents, and with no regrets.

CHANTER: Kinshōjo pushes aside her mother and approaches her husband. She opens the front of her robe and draws the icy blade to her chest as her mother looks on in horror.

[MOTHER]: No!!

CHANTER: The mother hurls herself between them, trying to separate the two, but it is hopeless: she cannot move her hands enough to drive them apart. She grabs her daughter's sleeve with her teeth and pulls her back, but Kanki closes in. Then she grabs Kanki's sleeve with her teeth and tries to drag him away, but Kinshōjo is set on death. The mother struggles, like a cat trying to move her kittens, until her strength dwindles, her eyes grow dim, and she collapses with a cry. Kinshōjo clings to her.

[KINSHŌJO]: All my life I've never known a parent. How can I repay my gratitude without ever once showing my filial devotion? Let me die in your place, Mother!

CHANTER: Kinshōjo bursts into tears.

[MOTHER]: What a sad thing to say! Especially when in this world and in that of the dead you have three parents. You owe a great debt to the father and mother who gave you life. Of your three parents, I alone have never had a chance to show you sympathy or even kindness. How cruel that I can never be rid of the title "stepmother"! If I let you die here and now, people will say that your Japanese stepmother let you be killed before her eyes out of

---

52. Kusunoki Masashige, Asahina Yoshihide, and Musashibō Benkei all were famous Japanese military heroes; Zhuge Liang, Fan Kuai, and Xiang Yu were equally famous in China.

53. Japanese men shaved the tops of their heads, originally to prevent enemies from grabbing them by the hair.

hatred for her Chinese stepdaughter. And the shame would not be mine alone but Japan's as well: people would say that the Japanese are a heartless people and point to me as an example. The sun that shines on China and the sun that shines on Japan are one and the same, but the Land of the Rising Sun is where the day begins. It is home to the Five Constant Virtues — and, above all, to sympathy.[54] How could I, born in the Land of the Gods where sympathy is everything, go on living after I watched my daughter be killed? Better that these ropes turn into the sacred ropes of the Japanese gods and strangle me. Then these ropes might lead my soul back to Japan even if my body remains in a foreign land!

CHANTER: Love, sympathy, and a sense of duty fill her tearful pleading. Kinshōjo clings to her mother's sleeves, now wet with both their tears. Even Kanki is moved to tears by the truth of her words. Pausing a while, he strikes his chair.

[KANKI]: Very well then, it is out of my hands. Since your mother insists on an answer now, Watōnai is my enemy from this day forth. But I do not intend to have people think I'm keeping your mother here as a hostage. Bring the carriage, ask her where she wants to go, and send her on her way.

[KINSHŌJO]: No, there is no need to send her away. I promised my father and brother that if I had good news I would drop white powder in the garden spring, and rouge if you refused. I shall put rouge into the water, and they will come and get her.

CHANTER: Kinshōjo goes into her sitting room as her mother sinks into dark despair at this unexpected turn of events. Worried about what she will have to tell her husband and son, the mother's tears of helplessness run red, like a Chinese brocade. Meanwhile, Kinshōjo prepares the rouge in an azure stone bowl.

[KINSHŌJO]: Father and daughter will never meet. The brocade will be cut in two; I will say my farewells — now![55]

CHANTER: The rouge slides into the moonlit waters of the spring and floats away, swirling like autumn leaves in a rapid stream. The red-stained bubbles carry the sad tidings along, through the conduit to the moat and beyond, toward the Yellow River. Downstream, Watōnai sits on the bank, his straw raincoat pulled over his shoulders, as he watches the water to see if it turns red or white.

[WATŌNAI]: Good Heavens — the water has turned red! Kanki has refused my request to join our cause. I can't leave my mother in the hands of that coward!

---

54. The Five Constant Virtues are benevolence, justice, courtesy, wisdom, and sincerity.

55. Based on an anonymous poem: "Tatsuta River — the autumn leaves flow by in disarray. If I should wade across, the brocade will be cut in two" (*Kokinshū*, Autumn 2, no. 283).

CHANTER: His feet churn through the rapids as he rushes to the moat and leaps across. He scales the wall, tramples down the garden fences, and arrives at the spring in the garden of Kanki's castle.

[WATŌNAI]: Well, thank goodness Mother is safe!

CHANTER: He leaps into the room, slashes through her ropes, and plants himself in front of Kanki.

[WATŌNAI]: So, you're that bearded Chinaman, Gojōgun Kanki, eh! I tied up my own mother—the only one I'll ever have in heaven or on earth—out of respect for who I thought you were. I wanted you to join our cause. And yet, when I treat you with respect it goes to your head.

You don't want to join us because I don't measure up as a general? I thought you would follow, above all, because your wife is my half sister. Now I, Watōnai, the greatest warrior in Japan, ask you man to man—answer me!

CHANTER: He grips the handle of his sword and stands ready to strike.

[KANKI]: Mentioning your relationship to my wife only makes your request more difficult. You may be the greatest warrior in Japan, but I am the one and only Kanki of China. I am not the sort who joins sides because of his wife, but I have no reason to divorce her, nor can I wait for her to die. Leave quickly now while you still can, or would you rather leave me your head as a memento?

[WATŌNAI]: Oh? I shall take yours back to Japan as a memento!

CHANTER: Both are about to draw their swords when Kinshōjo cries out. . . .

[KINSHŌJO]: No! No! You won't have to wait for me to die. Look! Here is the rouge I put in the water!

CHANTER: She opens her robe to reveal that she has slashed herself with her dagger diagonally from under her breast to her liver. At the sight of the bloody wound, the mother cries out and falls senseless. Watōnai is stunned, and even Kanki, although he had been ready to kill her, can only stare in disbelief. Kinshōjo's words come painfully.

[KINSHŌJO]: Mother would not let you kill me for fear of the shame it would bring to Japan, but if I cling to my life and don't help my parents and my brother, it will bring shame to China. Now that I have stabbed myself, no one will slander you, saying that your heart was moved by a woman. Kanki, please join my father and brother and lend your strength, and tell my father about this, too. Please, say no more—the pain!

CHANTER: With these words she collapses in a faint. Holding back his tears, Kanki speaks.

[KANKI]: How noble of you! Your sacrifice will not be in vain.

CHANTER: He bows his head before Watōnai.

[KANKI]: My ancestors served as ministers under the Ming. I was more than willing to join you, but I hesitated for fear that people would speak ill of me saying that I had been led astray by my wife's relatives. Now, by taking her

Watōnai arriving inside Kanki's castle. (Photograph courtesy of Barbara Curtis Adachi Collection, C. V. Starr East Asian Library, Columbia University)

own life, she has advanced the cause of justice, and I can join you with a clear conscience. I bow to you as my commanding general and confer upon you a princely name: Coxinga, lord of Enpei. Please honor me by putting on these robes.

CHANTER: Coxinga's future opens as Kanki opens a chest and hands him a double-layered scarlet court robe with sleeves of figured silk gauze, a black Confucian hat, slippers embossed with a floral pattern, a black leather belt set with coral and amber, and, finally, a ceremonial sword of polished gold. A silk parasol opens above Coxinga's head, and over a hundred thousand cavalrymen line up before him, arm band to arm band, holding shields and halberds, bows and muskets, and imperial flag poles topped with streamers, as if the king of Yue had come again to Mount Kuaiji. Coxinga's mother cries out in joy.

[MOTHER]: Oh, I'm so happy! My deepest wish has come true! Kinshōjo— do you see? By giving up your life, my husband and son have achieved their dream, and the dream of all China. Your dagger is less than a foot long, but your sacrifice will heal the land. For me to go on living now would make my earlier words a lie and again bring shame to Japan.

CHANTER: She grabs Kinshōjo's dagger and stabs herself in the throat. Kanki and Coxinga cry out in shock, but she glares back at them.

[MOTHER]: Stay back! Stay back! Kanki, Coxinga—don't lament my death, or Kinshōjo's. You mustn't grieve. If you think of the Tartar king as my enemy and as hers, it will give you added strength when you strike. My greatest concern was not allowing your resolve to weaken. Do not forget this, Coxinga; it is my dying request. Your father is still alive, so you will not lack a parent. Your mother exhorts you with her death; your father will live on to instruct you. Seeing you become the greatest of generals will be my fondest memory of this inconstant world; I want nothing more.

CHANTER: With that she deftly plunges the dagger into her liver.

[MOTHER]: Kinshōjo—have you no regrets at leaving this world?

[KINSHŌJO]: Why should I feel any regret?

CHANTER: And yet as a wife, Kinshōjo thinks of the husband she leaves behind. Mother and daughter take each other's hands and embrace. They look up at Coxinga, now dressed in his fine robes, as he looks down at their smiling faces, a remembrance of their final moment as they breath their last.

Coxinga, fierce enough to be mistaken for a demon, and Kanki, courageous as a dragon or tiger, blink back the tears that darken their eyes; one determined to obey his mother's last request, the other to honor his wife's sacrifice. Coxinga is ashamed to weep before Kanki, just as Kanki is ashamed to weep before Coxinga; they hide their pain-wracked faces.

The living and the dead travel one road: two bodies, mother and daughter, carried to their graves while an army led by Coxinga and Kanki sets out for battle. For Coxinga, his mother's last words are like the words of the Buddha; his father's teachings, like an iron bar given to a devil. When he strikes, he wins; when he attacks, he captures the field, a warrior of uncanny wisdom, benevolence, and bravery the likes of which will never be seen again.

The banks of a pool with a jewel in it will never crumble;
A pond where a dragon dwells will never dry up.[56]

A country that produces such a warrior is a well-governed country; its prince, a true prince.[57] People will say that this is a marvel of Japan, a hero who illuminates a foreign land with his fighting prowess.

[*Chikamatsu jōruri shū ge*, NKBT 50: 256–272, translated by
Michael Brownstein]

---

56. From the "Encouraging Learning" chapter of *Xunzi*: "When there are precious stones under the mountain, the grass and trees have a special sheen; where pearls grow in a pool, the banks are never parched" (translated by Burton Watson).

57. From the *Analects* of Confucius: "Let the prince be a prince, the minister a minister, the father a father, and the son a son" (translated by Arthur Waley).

THE HEIKE AND THE ISLAND OF WOMEN
(*HEIKE NYOGO NO SHIMA*, 1719)

"Devil's Island" (Kikaigashima) premiered in 1719 as the second scene of act 2 of the five-act *Heike and the Island of Women*, a jōruri play by Chikamatsu Monzaemon. Today, however, it is usually performed in jōruri and kabuki as a single play. In act 1, Chikamatsu focuses on the arrogant, insatiable, and lascivious Taira no Kiyomori, dictator of the land, presented as an example of the corruption and abuse of power. Kiyomori demands that Azumaya, Shunkan's wife, become his mistress, but she chooses to die by her own hand instead of submitting to him. Her lament at her suffering at the tyrant's hand is the climax of act 1. In act 2, the audience meets her husband Shunkan, who has been exiled to far-off Devil's Island as punishment for having led a rebellion against the despotic Kiyomori. The pregnancy of Kiyomori's daughter Kenreimon-in by Emperor Takakura brings about a general amnesty, but Kiyomori cruelly keeps Shunkan off the amnesty list because of Azumaya's refusal to submit to him. But Kiyomori's son Shigemori, the model of an honorable and compassionate samurai, adds Shunkan to the list.

"Devil's Island," which describes Shunkan's attempt to return home from his exile on Devil's Island, contains in microcosm two major themes of the entire play: the abuse of authority and the power of eros. Kiyomori is represented by Seno'o, who abuses his position of authority to taunt those weaker than himself, and the character of Shigemori is represented by Tanzaemon. "Devil's Island" is based on the story of Shunkan's exile, first told in the medieval *Tale of the Heike* and later in the nō play *Shunkan*. Chikamatsu adds a female character, the local fishergirl Chidori, and makes the scene more dramatic by revealing the death of Shunkan's wife, Azumaya, and by having Shunkan fight with the villain official Seno'o, who taunts him. Chidori is initially described by Chikamatsu as a fantastic metaphor for female erotic charm—a passage omitted in kabuki. The sexual attraction of Naritsune, one of the exiles on Devil's Island, to Chidori and the love that it leads to is presented as natural and an ideal, in contrast to Kiyomori's lust and his use of power to force women to submit to his will. Chidori's encounter with Kiyomori's abusive power in the guise of his representative, the bully Seno'o, leads to her song of lament, the first high point of the piece.

In 1772 "Devil's Island" was revived in the puppet theater as a play in itself, and during the nineteenth century it became part of the kabuki repertory as well. Takemoto Gidayū, the famous jōruri chanter for whom Chikamatsu wrote many of his plays, outlined a formula for the overall theme of each of the five acts. In this scheme, act 2 is set symbolically in the Buddhist realm Shura (Ashura), a sphere of never-ending fighting and revenge. For Chikamatsu, Devil's Island is clearly a kind of hell on earth.

A comparison with the medieval versions—the Shunkan scene (Ashizuri) in *The Tale of the Heike* and the nō play *Shunkan*—reveals Chikamatsu's method and the difference between medieval drama and early-eighteenth-century popular theater. Chikamatsu's most striking change is the addition of Chidori, the young fishergirl lover and lowly commoner who embodies love and eros, characteristics not found in the dark story of a celibate Shunkan in the medieval versions. First we see Shunkan as a reflective figure, alone and destitute; then we see him as the kind father to young Chidori and Naritsune, delighting in their happiness. Next we witness his devastation and despair at the news of his wife's death for refusing Kiyomori. This leads him to rise in rebellion against Seno'o, Kiyomori's agent. He convinces Chidori to board the boat and leave him behind because he is assured of a place on the boat that leads to Buddha's paradise in the next life. He tells her to think of him as a buddha, but the final image is of Shunkan the man, tragically alone, abandoned, desperately watching the departing ship as it disappears beyond the waves.

CHARACTERS

SHUNKAN, a high-level priest who plotted against Taira no Kiyomori and has been exiled to Devil's Island

NARITSUNE, Captain of Tanba who was exiled with Shunkan for the same crime and falls in love with Chidori

YASUYORI, Lord of Hei who was exiled with Shunkan for the same crime

TANZAEMON, an official from the capital who comes with Seno'o to pardon the exiles

SENO'O, an envoy for Kiyomori who comes with Tanzaemon to pardon the exiles

CHIDORI, a fishergirl and lover of Naritsune

Act 2

   Scene 2: Devil's Island (Kikaigashima).

CHANTER (*chants in nō style*):
     Known from ages long past
     as Devil's Island,
     a realm where demons roam,
     this lonely isle, a hell on earth.
     No matter how cruel the demon,
     has it no pity for my plight,
     abandoned far from home?
     Do even the birds and beasts cry out
     in sympathy for my suffering?[58]
     Tales of joyful times now silent,
     memories too, withered fragments.

---

58. These opening lines are from the nō play *Shunkan*. In the play they are Shunkan's lines

Only the light of the sun and moon coursing the sky
Stir thoughts of days and nights in the capital.
Few are the trees and grasses here;
no grains grow on this barren land.
We struggle just to live.
From mountain peaks flow molten lava.
Instead of fisherman' catches,
we have only kelp gathered from the rough waves,
or clams discarded by the tide.
The fragile figure before your eyes
is a broken man, bearded with snowy white hair.
A rough garment of leaves covers his shoulders,
its seams torn and tattered.
even the sound of chirping crickets has ceased.[59]
Leaning on a withered branch for a cane,
Wobbly, wobbly, like the Han warrior Sun Wu
captured fighting the Hu Di,[60]
who struggled on with but one good leg,
stands Shunkan, a shell of a man.

If one counts the days on this island, we see an almanac in the passing of snowy winters, summer breezes, spring and autumn—for three years no word has come save the lapping waves, mountain winds, and "chidori" plovers along the shore. All bring tears and thoughts of home; when will the wheels of fate carry me away? My grief is like that of a fish trapped in the puddle made by the tracks of a carriage.[61] Nothing to compare with my sad fate. To wait, the agony of eternal waiting.

---

as he reflects on his predicament after learning that he, the only one of the three exiles, has not been pardoned. Chikamatsu uses the lines at the opening of the scene to describe the horrible, uninhabited, prison island.

59. Alludes to the *Kokinshū*, no. 1020. The poem uses the verb *hokorobiru* in two senses: "the opening of a blossom" and "to tear the seam of a kimono." The "cricket" was said to make a noise that sounded like the word *tsuzurisase*, meaning "to sew." Even the crickets cannot help Shunkan. This also is quoted in *Matsumushi*, a nō play about the preciousness of friends (now departed) and their past delight in the autumn chirping of pine crickets. References in the play to drinking saké with friends and "chrysanthemum water" suggest associations with "Devil's Island."

60. Hu Di was the name for peoples on the north or west edges of China. This alludes to an incident from Chinese history described in *The Tale of the Heike* at the end of book 2 in the episode "Su Wu." Su Wu, wounded with one leg amputated and taken prisoner, sends a note on the wings of a goose to the Han emperor. Su Wu is an example of the loyal man who struggles on even when his situation is most dire.

61. This is a reference to the *Zhuangzi*, sec. 26, the story of a small fish trapped in a shrinking

Another of like mind with tattered clothes descends along a narrow, mossy path among the rocks.

[SHUNKAN]: Do I too look as worn and withered as that man? They say the Shura realm of revenge and never-ending fighting is along the shore of a great ocean; the sutras say the lower realms are in the mountain at the bottom of the sea. Have I fallen unwittingly into the Realm of Hungry Ghosts?[62]

CHANTER: Looking more carefully, he sees that it is Yasuyori, lord of Hei.

[SHUNKAN]: Ah, has everyone, like myself, fallen into this pitiful condition?

CHANTER: His heart flutters like the reeds along the shore as Captain Naritsune ambles aimlessly through them.

[SHUNKAN]: Is that you Naritsune? Yasuyori?

[YASUYORI]: Is that Shunkan?

CHANTER: Each calls out invitingly as they walk toward the other.

[SHUNKAN]: My friends, in the morning it is Yasuyori; in the evening, Naritsune. Besides us three, no others, all communication has ceased. Although I'm not a priest guarding over a lonely mountain rice field,[63] weary of this world, how sad I am.

CHANTER: They hold each other's hands and weep: their grief is all too real.

[YASUYORI]: I perform daily services without fail at the three island temples to Amida, Yakushi Kannon, and Senshu Kannon. Have you not heard, Shunkan, that the three companions have recently become four?

[SHUNKAN]: What, we're four now! There's another exile?

[YASUYORI]: No, nothing like that. Naritsune has fallen in love with a gentle fishergirl and taken her for his wife.

CHANTER: At this news, Shunkan's face brightens with joy.

[SHUNKAN]: How unusual, how strange! All these three years in exile, no one has spoken the word "love." This is the first time I've smiled. And especially to hear of love for a fishergirl—how romantic—like the tales told of Fujiwara no Kamatari[64] or Ariwara no Yukihira[65] who fell in love with fishergirls while in exile, dampened by the sea breezes, entangled in the flowing seaweed

---

puddle that asks a passing traveler for some water. The traveler promises to have his friend the nearby king divert a river to flood the road. The fish gets angry, saying that he will be dead by the time that happens. Chikamatsu often uses it as an image for loneliness.

62. From *The Tale of the Heike*, volume 3, "Ario." Ario was a favorite of Shunkan, and when Shunkan does not return with the others, he goes to the island to find his master Shunkan. These lines of Shunkan are Ario's description of meeting Shunkan on the island.

63. Alludes to *Shokukokinshū*, no. 1616, a poem that is also quoted in the nō play *Miwa*. The poem describes a priest who is lonely in the mountains where no one visits.

64. Kamatari vowed love for a fishergirl, as described in the old jōruri play and ballad drama *Taishokan*, and is taken up in Chikamatsu's own *Taishokan* (1711). In these plays the lover-fishergirl proves herself to be loyal and sacrifices herself to help others.

65. This is a reference to the nō play *Matsukaze*. Yukihira has relations with two sister fishergirls, Matsukaze and Murasame, at Suma where he is exiled for a period.

among the rocks. How delightful to hear of a love story! I, too, have a wife back home whom I love dearly. To speak of love or listen to its tales is to feel love. How wonderful! Let's hear your story, tell us of your passion.

CHANTER: Pressed to relate his tale, Naritsune blushes.[66]

[NARITSUNE]: Although we three have not tried to hide our existence here, many fishing boats come and go, bringing supplies; I am embarrassed to use the word "love." Who would have thought that anyone would have an affair here on this lonely, barren isle so far away from anywhere? She is the daughter of a fisherman from Kirishima Island. Her name is Chidori. Her task is to burn brine, collect it, and boil it on the shore. One day this young woman rose out of the evening waves, half naked, with a small bucket at her hip and a sickle in her hand. This nymph had emerged from the depths of the sea where the *mirume* seaweed grows, and *wakame* and *arame*.[67] On her gently curving body, supple and wet and glistening, sea eels and gray mullets clung; crabs, too, pinched her skin. A small bream, thinking it food, suckled at her breast. The wrap at her waist was transparent, dripping wet, showing her skin smooth and radiant. A tiny octopus, thinking it a jar, had settled in her navel. Her life floating and sinking, buffeted by the waves—a mermaid swimming must be like this! When the tide had receded, her waist was covered in sand. She stepped on a clam. At her loins clung a succulent ark shell.[68] She cast off an abalone from her finger; under her nails nestled ivory shells.

Resting after her diving, she quickly arranged her hair in a bun, curling it like a turban shell, not even a boxwood comb for ornament.[69] But in the eyes of a lover, her hair is jewel-like in its beauty. Was it a chance visit of cupid to this isle? She now lives happily in a small thatched hut with her husband whom she deeply loves. Gathering leaves from the trees, she has grown skillful at sewing them into robes. Waking in the night, she pulls her husband close to her sea-swept body and whispers love in the exotic tones of her Satsuma dialect.

"Someone simple like me never dreamed I'd meet a gentleman from the capital who enjoys poetry. But we met, fell in love, and slept together. How

---

66. This description weaves in an array of images from the sea to evoke the portrait of a beautiful and alluringly erotic nymph.

67. Like *mirume*, *wakame* and *arame* are kinds of seaweed. The *me* at the end of each of the three words can be written with the character for "woman" and has been an erotic image in poetry from earliest times.

68. The ark shell (*akagai*) is a symbol for a woman's private parts.

69. This is a reference to the Narihira poem in *The Tales of Ise*, sec. 87, set in Ashiya, and also in the *Shinkokinshū* and in the nō play *Nue*, again set in Ashiya, the locus of the poem. The poem evokes the severe life of fishergirls along a rough shore, burning brine, who have no time to care for their hair.

wonderful to receive his favor and be thought attractive. Since I have no parents, my husband's friends are my family; I want to consider Lord Yasuyori my elder brother and Priest Shunkan as my father. Ask them to call me 'sister,' 'daughter,' to do this and that, to serve them well, and let me come into their hearts."

[NARITSUNE]: The poor girl then broke down in tears. Her words, hoping to gain your favor, struck my heart deeply.

CHANTER: At Naritsune's words, Shunkan interjects.

[SHUNKAN]: What a fine, romantic tale! First of all let me meet your new wife. Shall I go to your hut?

[NARITSUNE]: No need; she came with me. Chidori, Chidori!

CHANTER: At his call she timidly answers yes and steps out from the reeds carrying a basket on a pole, a modest, pretty young woman, wearing a tattered but beautiful kimono with colorful brocade designs: her beauty bows to none. Why was she born to be wasted as a fishergirl? Shunkan offers his greetings.

[SHUNKAN]: You certainly match the description fondly told. I've heard that you've met Yasuyori, and that you want to consider me your father. The three of us are the same as relatives. Today I pledge us parent and child. You're my daughter, and I'll get a pardon so we all four can go to the capital. It's only a matter of time until you wear the formal silk robes as Naritsune's wife. How regrettable! Even if we were to drill into a boulder or dig a hole in the ground, we would have no saké. All I can do is offer congratulations nine times—with no saké.

[CHIDORI]: I'd surely meet a bad end if a poor, lowly fishergirl like me were to cover herself in fine silks. I'm happy to be marrying a man from the capital.

[SHUNKAN]: The medicine saké that seven-hundred-year-old immortals drank was from China's Ju Shui River.[70] Let's follow their lead and drink cold mountain water. If we think it is saké, it is saké. This abalone shell is our cup. From today we are parent and child.

CHANTER: Calling each other Father and Daughter, they drink a toast.

[CHIDORI]: Please accept me in your favor.

CHANTER: At this all laugh and agree: the mountain water is saké; the abalone shell, a jeweled cup. Back and forth the cup goes. Drinking, singing, the three now four celebrate, and like the Isle of Hōrai, their volcanic island has an endless supply of saké in its springs. Yasuyori looks off out to the sea.

[YASUYORI]: That ship's too big for a fishing boat. That's strange—it's coming toward our island. Look! Look!

---

70. From the nō play *Shunkan*. The Ju Shui (Chrysanthemum Water) River is in Hunan Province. This refers to a practice among Daoists of the feast of chrysanthemum and friendship. Chrysanthemum water is the elixir of life. In the nō play, Shunkan is presented initially as if he were an enlightened figure, a veritable Daoist immortal.

Shunkan reading the letter. (Photograph courtesy of Barbara Curtis Adachi Collection, C. V. Starr East Asian Library, Columbia University)

CHANTER: Before they know it, a ship bearing the colors of officers from the capital comes near shore, and two soldiers jump out onto the beach, setting up chairs in the shade of some pine trees.

[SENO'O]: Are the exiles Captain Naritsune, of Tanba, and Yasuyori, lord of Hei, present?

CHANTER: At the cry of this voice, wondering if it were a dream, they answer yes, and Shunkan and Yasuyori also answer "present." All three hurriedly run before the two men and fall on their knees, heads bowed to the ground. Seno'o takes out the letter of pardon.

[SENO'O]: Listen to the words of this pardon.

CHANTER: He opens the letters and reads:[71]

[SENO'O]: On the occasion of the imperial birth, a special amnesty has been granted. The two exiles of Devil's Island, Captain Naritsune of Tanba and Yasuyori, lord of Hei, have been given a pardon. They are to return immediately to the capital.

CHANTER: Before he finishes, the pair collapse with joy. But Shunkan says:

[SHUNKAN]: Have you somehow missed the name Shunkan?

[SENO'O]: How rude to suggest a man like Seno'o could possibly make a mistake. If you wish to check, here look for yourself.

---

71. The following until the line "saving net" in Shunkan's lament is based on the nō play *Shunkan.*

CHANTER: He hands over the letter. Both Naritsune and Yasuyori think it strange as he reads the letter—backward and forward, even checking the envelope.

[SHUNKAN]: There's no mention of Shunkan. Did Lord Kiyomori forget about me? Did the scribe make a mistake? We have the same crime, same punishment, and all the details were the same. The amnesty has pardoned two. Why have I alone slipped through the saving net? Has the bodhisattva singled me out to receive no pity, no mercy? If I had died earlier, I would not have to suffer this pain. How wretched to have lived so long!

CHANTER: He weeps tears of agony. Tanzaemon takes a letter out of his pocket:

[TANZAEMON]: You have heard the pardon, but to learn the full extent of Lord Shigemori's kind and benevolent heart, listen to the following: "The exile on Devil's Island. On the occasion of Lord Shigemori's compassion, the high priest Shunkan is allowed to go as far as Bizen in the Island Sea. Signed Lord Noritsune, Governor of Nōto."

[SHUNKAN]: Then are all three of us pardoned?

[TANZAEMON]: Yes.

CHANTER: Shunkan rubs his forehead in the sand, bowing three times in thanks and weeping tears of joy. Naritsune and Chidori and Yasuyori all dance about, wondering if it's all a dream. The sweet dew of Buddha has dampened the fires burning in this hell of hungry ghosts. Were one to sing of paradise it would surely be like this.

CHANTER: The two officials speak as one voice:

[SENO'O AND TANZAEMON]: We have no more business on this island. Fortunately the winds are good. Board the ship.

CHANTER: As the four start to board, Seno'o grabs Chidori and pulls her aside, fiercely shouting.

[SENO'O]: Wretched woman. If you're seeing them off, be gone.

[NARITSUNE]: No, it's fine. She is the woman whom I married while on this island, and we have pledged to live together when we return to the capital. Please let her travel as far as the first port of call. Please, my descendants and I shall never forget your kindness, please?

CHANTER: He bows to the ground, pleading. At this Seno'o replies angrily.

[SENO'O]: What a nuisance! I don't care who this woman is, away with her.

CHANTER: There is a scuffle.

[NARITSUNE]: Well if you won't allow this, then I won't return, I'll stay on this island. Shunkan and Yasuyori, board the boat.

[SHUNKAN]: No, no, it wouldn't be right to leave one behind.

CHANTER: All three exiles refuse to return. The three sit down resolutely on the beach—determination on their faces.

CHANTER: Tanzaemon has an idea.

[TANZAEMON]: Lord Seno'o, if they refuse, it's likely to have an effect on the

Seno'o holding a fan. (Photograph courtesy of Barbara Curtis Adachi Collection, C. V. Starr East Asian Library, Columbia University)

imperial birth. Even if we don't let the woman aboard, let's stay here for a day or two, explain the problem, and convince them to agree. Let's have this pardon completed in good faith, with all contented, as an offering for the imperial birth.

CHANTER: But before he finishes, Seno'o interrupts.

[SENO'O]: No, that's a bureaucrat's self-indulgence. My official letter of passage allows for only two passengers. You have permission to add one more. I can take three, but who has given permission for four? Until the exiles are handed over to the Heike headquarters in Rokuhara, they are my responsibility. Even if they refuse to board, do you think I won't force them? Shunkan's wife refused to obey Lord Kiyomori's order and was executed.[72] Ariō's treachery got him arrested. Men, get these three on board and into the hold of the ship.

CHANTER: The soldiers quickly thrust Chidori aside and forcibly drag the weakened exiles onto the boat. Like small birds forced into a hawk's cage, their arms are twisted, pulled. The severe Seno'o gives his order.

[SENO'O]: Set the sails! Launch the boat. Tanzaemon, all aboard. The exiles are in hand, is there any other business?

---

72. The modern kabuki version adds the line that on his return Shunkan is to be executed as a common criminal.

CHANTER: He has no reply to Seno'o's reasoning and boards the ship. Forlorn and despairing, Chidori is left friendless on the shore, a young bird weeping.

[CHIDORI]: It's all a lie, deceit. Who said that samurai understand human emotion and compassion? There are no demons on Devil's Island; all the demons are in the capital. From the day we fell in love, I prayed continuously to the dragon god of the sea, but not with the wish to live in glory and splendor in the capital. I wanted—if just for one night with him—to change these rags into flowery robes and experience the joy of being born a woman. This was my only wish. What a cruel demon, you devil! Would the weight of one slim girl sink your boat! Have you no eyes to see a poor creature's grief? No ears to hear my cries? Please let me come aboard, let me on!

CHANTER: Her voice rises in agony, her arms beg out, her feet stamp in frustration; she collapses, weeping unconcerned at peering eyes.

[CHIDORI]: Since I'm a diver, I have no fear of swimming two or three miles into the ocean, but I cannot swim eight hundred or nine hundred. I shall dash my head to pieces on this stone. Farewell, my love Naritsune, how I regret leaving you. Pray for me and remember me as your pitiful darling abandoned on this island.

CHANTER: She weeps and weeps as she heads for a large boulder.

[SHUNKAN]: Wait, wait there!

CHANTER: Shunkan yells as he clambers over the edge of the boat and runs to her.

[SHUNKAN]: You shall board the boat and go to the capital. You heard what Seno'o said. My wife refused Kiyomori and was killed. My wife, with whom I pledged to be for three lives, has died; what joy is left for me to return to the capital? I have no desire to view the moon or the cherry blossoms. Rather than face my grief all over again, I shall remain on this island, and you shall go in my place. The letter says three; there will be no problem at the barrier stations. Think of me as a buddha with no ties to this world. Leave me and board the boat. Hurry, get aboard.

CHANTER: As he weeps, he takes her hand and drags her forward to the boat.

[SHUNKAN]: Dear officials, both of you, let this woman come aboard.

CHANTER: As he stumbles toward the boat, Seno'o flies down from the boat in a fury.

[SENO'O]: Why you horned owl of a cleric! If we could be that free about the matter, there'd be no need for official letters of pardon or messengers. There's no way I'll let that woman board my ship!

CHANTER: To his fierce growls, Shunkan replies.

[SHUNKAN]: That's too cruel; please show some mercy.

CHANTER: He pleads, stealthily moving close to Seno'o. He suddenly grabs Seno'o's sword and like a flash of lightning thrusts at his left shoulder, leaving a cut of eight inches. Shunkan tries to finish him off, but the agile Seno'o unsheathes his short sword and stands up again to face Shunkan. He strikes

Shunkan reaching out to Chidori. (Photograph courtesy of Barbara Curtis Adachi Collection, C. V. Starr East Asian Library, Columbia University)

back but is now weakened, bending like a flowing willow. Shunkan, too, is frail like a withered pine; neither has any strength as they battle on the sandy shore. Back and forth they parry blows until exhaustion overtakes them; each thrusts wildly, seeking the final blow. Those on board begin to clamor, but Tanzaemon stands on the landing plank.

[TANZAEMON]: In this fight between the exile and the messenger, everyone shall stand back and let the fight take its course. No one shall interfere or help. Let no one approach.

CHANTER: He strikes a fierce pose, eyes glaring. Chidori, unable to stand back any longer, grabs a bamboo pole and thrusts it at Seno'o, but Shunkan calls out.

[SHUNKAN]: Don't come near! If you enter the brawl, you won't escape blame. If you strike him, I'll hate you for it.

CHANTER: At his anger, Chidori restrains herself; only her heart continues to fight. The bleeding Seno'o fends off the starved and exhausted Shunkan. Blows fly back and forth, back and forth, each time the arms growing weaker, locked in battle. Unable to beat the other, they fall back away from each other into the sand, panting with exhaustion. Seno'o, fearless as an eagle, tries to grab Shunkan, but Shunkan manages to trip him with his skinny, birdlike legs. Seno'o falls flat; Shunkan crawls over on top of him and raises his sword to give the final thrust. But Tanzaemon calls out from the boat to stop Shunkan from killing Seno'o.

Shunkan, on top of a hill, taking a last look at the disappearing boat. (Photograph courtesy of Barbara Curtis Adachi Collection, C. V. Starr East Asian Library, Columbia University)

[TANZAEMON]: I have seen clearly who the victor is. If you deliver the final thrust, your guilt will pile up on past crimes. It is useless to kill him.

[SHUNKAN]: Let my guilt pile higher and tie me to this island.

[TANZAEMON]: No, if you are left behind, all the concern that Lord Shigemori and Lord Nōto have shown will be wasted. If you go against orders, it will be blamed on me. Particularly, if we have fewer than the three exiles, it will be impossible to get past the barrier stations.

[SHUNKAN]: Then you can add this woman to Yasuyori and Naritsune to make three, and no one will give you trouble. Lord Shigemori's mercy has granted me freedom, but by killing the messenger, I am once again sentenced to exile on Devil's Island. The mercy is received with gratitude; the officials are not at fault. It is all my choice. Seno'o, prepare to receive your deathblow.

CHANTER: With his angry sword, once, twice, three times, again and again he strikes, finally cutting off Seno'o's head. All on board the ship cry out in tears. Naritsune and Yasuyori can only fold their hands in prayer. No words, all weep in silence. Witness to all this, Chidori alone feels lost.

[CHIDORI]: Husband and wife are married for two lives. Greed alone kept me from accepting my fate. I am the cause of this tragedy. How could I just board this boat as if nothing happened! You all are too good for me. Farewell.

CHANTER: She turns to leave, but Shunkan pulls her back.

[SHUNKAN]: Listen, since I shall stay on this island, I shall experience—in this life—the Realm of Hungry Ghosts, here where no grains grow. I have just lived in the Shura realm of never-ending fighting. On this smoldering volcano I live in hell. Do you think I won't be saved in my next life after experiencing the terrors of the three lower realms in this life? The ship I board will be the saving boat of Buddha. I have no desire for a boat to take me through this floating world. Now, hurry aboard!

CHANTER: He tugs and pulls at her sleeves until she is taken aboard. Ready to sail, the ropes are untied, the oars begin their task, pulling the boat out into the waves. Naritsune, Chidori, and Yasuyori call out their tearful farewell, pained to leave Shunkan behind. From the boat a fan waves; from the sand a hand is raised. "Again in the future, again we'll meet." The cruel winds carry the ship away. Faint grows the ship, blocked from view by the waves and islands, finally lost in the mist of the sea. Though determined in his path, Shunkan's heart is still human. He climbs up a hill to get a last look. On the tips of his toes he waves, only to stumble and fall onto the sand. No matter how his heart burns, how much he screams, no one shares his grief. All that is left are the gulls along the shore and the geese in the sky. His friends have flown like birds, leaving him alone; off they go to sea, traveling among the waves. Tears wet the many folds of his tattered robe.

[*Chikamatsu jōruri shū ge*, NKBT 50: 310–319, introduction and translation by C. Andrew Gerstle]

THE LOVE SUICIDES AT AMIJIMA
(*SHINJŪ TEN NO AMIJIMA*, 1721)

Chikamatsu Monzaemon's *Love Suicides at Amijima* is widely considered to be his best contemporary-life play. It was first performed at the Takemoto Theater in Osaka in 1721, during the Kyōhō era (1716–1736) when the restrictions on urban commoner society had become even more rigid than they had been in the Genroku era. The historical source for the play is unclear, but the incident inspired a number of later sewamono, and *The Love Suicides at Amijima* itself was subsequently revised. In the play, Kamiya (literally, paper merchant) Jihei, an Osaka paper merchant with a wife and children, falls in love with Koharu, a prostitute under contract to the Kinokuniya House in Sonezaki (a licensed quarter in Osaka). Forced into tragic circumstances, the two of them commit suicide at a temple in Amijima, in Osaka.

About half Chikamatsu's twenty-four contemporary-life plays focus on an incident concerning an Osaka urban commoner. Almost all the male protagonists are young and of low social station, either an adopted son or a shop clerk, and most of them become involved with a low-level prostitute. In that the lovers have already decided to commit double suicide at the beginning, *The Love Suicides at Amijima* differs from such double-suicide plays as *The Love Suicides at Sonezaki* which show the tragic chain of events that lead to death. Instead, the focus in *Amijima* is on those who attempt to prevent the suicide of the two lovers, with the climax coming in the middle of the famous second act when Osan sacrifices everything she can, including her dignity, in an attempt to save her husband's life. Chikamatsu places the tragedy in a tight web of urban commoner social relationships and obligations, particularly the hierarchical relations between master and apprentice, parent and child, and husband and wife, as well as in the context of the new monetary economy and commercial life of Osaka. *The Love Suicides at Amijima* follows the pattern established by *The Love Suicides at Sonezaki*, with Jihei and Koharu outwardly resembling Tokubei and Ohatsu in *Sonezaki*, but Jihei and Koharu bear a much greater social burden, particularly Jihei as a pillar of the family business (the owner of a paper shop, as opposed to Tokubei, a shop clerk), and the result is a greater tragedy, which pulls down not only the two lovers but others in the family—including Magoemon, Osan, the children, and Osan's parents. Here Chikamatsu develops one of the central themes of his contemporary-life plays: the conflict between those who try to preserve the family *and* the individual, driven by his or her own desires, who works against that social order.

Chikamatsu introduces a new kind of giri, that between women, between Osan and Koharu. Koharu breaks off her relationship with Jihei out of obligation to Osan, and Osan sacrifices herself and her property for Koharu. One result is that both Jihei and Koharu feel giri toward Osan, and as they prepare for death at the end, they remain apart out of obligation to Osan. Not only does Chikamatsu create complex conflicts between ninjō (desire/emotion) and giri (responsibility, obligation), but he also focuses on conflicts between giri and giri that result in extreme ninjō, or pathos. Osan, for example, is caught between her giri toward Koharu (whom she cannot let die) and her giri toward Jihei (as devoted wife). Ninjō and giri also are reflected in the settings: the first act occurs in the pleasure quarters, a world of desire, passion, and the individual; and the second act takes place in the paper shop, a world of responsibility, reason, and the family, with Jihei caught between the two. The third act focuses on a journey in which the lovers leave behind both these places and travel toward death. As critics have noted, there is a double movement in this poetic journey (*michiyuki*): a downward movement, the Buddhist cycle of *samsara*, of birth and death, of suffering, which leads to hell; and an upward movement, leading from hell to possible salvation. The fundamental assumption behind the two movements, which is symbolically mapped out, is that awakening is the result of some profound crisis or suffering. Accordingly, the lovers initially pass such places as Tenma Bridge and the River of the Three Fords—which represent places in hell—before they cross over Kyō (Sutra) Bridge and Onari (Becoming a Buddha) Bridge. The complexity of their fate is reflected in the *ten no ami* (net of heaven) of the play's title (*Shinjū ten no Amijima*), which alludes to both the place Amijima and a phrase in the *Laozi*, "The net of heaven is wide; coarse are the meshes, yet nothing slips through," which means that even though heaven is vast, it does not allow evil (here the destruction of the family and social order) to go unpunished. At the same time, the "net of heaven" is implicitly the generous vow of the Amida Buddha to save all. In Chikamatsu's double suicides, the final scene has the added function of praying for the spirits of the dead—that is, the play implicitly recalls to this world the spirits or ghosts of the two lovers, who have recently died a gruesome death, and now sends them off again to the world of the dead.

CHARACTERS

JIHEI, aged twenty-eight, a paper merchant
MAGOEMON, his brother, a flour merchant
GOZAEMON, Jihei's father-in-law
TAHEI, a rival for Koharu
DENBEI, proprietor of the Yamato House
SANGORŌ, Jihei's servant
KANTARŌ, aged six, Jihei's son
KOHARU, aged nineteen, a courtesan belonging to the Kinokuniya House in
    Sonezaki, a new licensed quarter in the north part of Osaka
OSAN, Jihei's wife
OSAN'S MOTHER (who is also Jihei's aunt), aged fifty-six
OSUE, aged four, Jihei's daughter

Act 1

In scene 1, which is rarely performed and is omitted here, Koharu makes her way to the Kawashō Teahouse in the Sonezaki licensed quarter to meet Tahei, a samurai customer. We learn that Koharu is in love with Jihei and that Tahei, a man that she dislikes immensely, is trying to buy out her contract. Koharu sees Tahei in the street and flees.

   The Kawashō, a teahouse in Sonezaki.

CHANTER: Koharu slips away, under cover of the crowd, and hurries into the
    Kawashō Teahouse.
[PROPRIETRESS]: Well, well, I hadn't expected you so soon—It's been ages
    since I've even heard your name mentioned. What a rare visitor you are,
    Koharu! And what a long time it's been!
CHANTER: The proprietress greets Koharu cheerfully.
[KOHARU]: Oh—you can be heard as far as the gate. Please don't call me
    Koharu in such a loud voice. That horrible Ri Tōten[73] is out there. I beg
    you, keep your voice down.
CHANTER: Were her words overheard? In bursts a party of three men.

---

73. The villain of the play *The Battles of Coxinga*.

[TAHEI]: I must thank you first of all, dear Koharu, for bestowing a new name on me, Ri Tōten. I never was called *that* before. Well, friends, this is the Koharu I've confided to you about—the good-hearted, good-natured, good-in-bed Koharu. Step up and meet the whore who's started all the rivalry! Will I soon be the lucky man and get Koharu for my wife? Or will Kamiya Jihei ransom her?

CHANTER: He swaggers up.

[KOHARU]: I don't want to hear another word. If you think it's such an achievement to start unfounded rumors about someone you don't even know, go ahead; say what you please. But I don't want to hear.

CHANTER: She steps away suddenly, but he sidles up again.

[TAHEI]: You may not want to hear me, but the clink of my gold coins will make you listen! What a lucky girl you are! Just think—of all the many men in Tenma and the rest of Osaka, you chose Jihei the paper dealer, the father of two children, with his cousin for his wife and his uncle for his father-in-law! A man whose business is so tight he's at his wits' end every sixty days merely to pay the wholesalers' bills! Do you think he'll be able to fork over nearly ten *kanme* to ransom you? That reminds me of the mantis who picked a fight with an oncoming vehicle![74] But look at me—I don't have a wife, a father-in-law, a father, or even an uncle, for that matter. Tahei the Lone Wolf—that's the name I'm known by. I admit that I'm no match for Jihei when it comes to bragging about myself in the Quarter, but when it comes to money, I'm an easy winner. If I pushed with all the strength of my money, who knows what I might conquer?—How about it, men?—Your customer tonight, I'm sure, is none other than Jihei, but I'm taking over. The Lone Wolf's taking over. Hostess! Bring on the saké! On with the saké!

[PROPRIETRESS]: What are you saying? Her customer tonight is a samurai, and he'll be here any moment. Please amuse yourself elsewhere.

CHANTER: But Tahei's look is playful.

[TAHEI]: A customer's a customer, whether he's a samurai or a townsman. The only difference is that one wears swords and the other doesn't. But even if this samurai wears his swords, he won't have five or six—there'll only be two, the broadsword and dirk. I'll take care of the samurai and borrow Koharu afterward. (*To Koharu*) You may try to avoid me all you please, but some special connection from a former life must have brought us together. I owe everything to that ballad-singing priest—what a wonderful thing the power of prayer is! I think I'll recite a prayer of my own. Here, this ashtray will be my bell, and my pipe the hammer. This is fun.

Chan Chan Cha Chan Chan.

---

74. A simile, derived from ancient Chinese texts, for someone who does not know his own limitations.

Ei Ei Ei Ei Ei.
Jihei the paper dealer—
Too much love for Koharu
Has made him a foolscap,
He wastepapers sheets of gold
Till his fortune's shredded to confetti
And Jihei himself is like scrap paper
You can't even blow your nose on!
Hail, Hail Amida Buddha!
Namaida Namaida Namaida.

CHANTER: As he prances wildly, roaring his song, a man appears at the gate, so anxious not to be recognized that he wears, even at night, a wicker hat.[75]

[TAHEI]: Well, Toilet Paper's showed up! That's quite a disguise! Why don't you come in, Toilet Paper? If my prayer's frightened you, say a Hail Amida![76] Here, I'll take off your hat!

CHANTER: He drags the man in and examines him: it is the genuine article, a two-sworded samurai, somber in dress and expression, who glares at Tahei through his woven hat, his eyeballs round as gongs. Tahei, unable to utter either a Hail or an Amida, gasps "Haaa!" in dismay, but his face is unflinching.

[TAHEI]: Koharu, I'm a townsman. I've never worn a sword, but I've lots of New Silver[77] at my place, and I think that the glint could twist a mere couple of swords out of joint. Imagine that wretch from the toilet paper shop, with a capital as thin as tissue, trying to compete with the Lone Wolf! That's the height of impertinence! I'll wander down now from Sakura Bridge to Middle Street, and if I meet that Wastepaper along the way, I'll trample him under foot. Come on, men.

CHANTER: Their gestures, at least, have a cavalier assurance as they swagger off, taking up the whole street. The samurai customer patiently endures the fool, indifferent to his remarks because of the surroundings, but every word of gossip about Jihei, whether for good or ill, affects Koharu. She is so depressed that she stands there blankly, unable even to greet her guest. Sugi, the maid from the Kinokuni House, runs up from home, looking annoyed.

[SUGI]: When I left you here a while ago, Miss Koharu, your guest hadn't appeared yet, and they gave me a terrible scolding when I got back for not having checked on him. I'm very sorry, sir, but please excuse me a minute.

---

75. Customers visiting the licensed quarter by day wear these deep wicker hats (which virtually conceal the face) in order to preserve the secrecy of their visits. But this customer wears a hat even at night, when the darkness normally is sufficient protection.

76. A play on words centering on the syllables *ami*, part of the name Amida, and on *amigasa*, meaning "woven hat."

77. Good-quality coinage of about 1720.

CHANTER: She lifts the woven hat and examines the face.

[SUGI]: Oh—it's not him! There's nothing to worry about, Koharu. Ask your guest to keep you for the whole night, and show him how sweet you can be. Give him a barrelful of nectar![78] Good-bye, madam, I'll see you later, honey.

CHANTER: She takes her leave with a cloying stream of puns. The extremely hard baked[79] samurai is furious.

[SAMURAI]: What's the meaning of this? You'd think from the way she appraised my face that I was a tea canister or a porcelain cup! I didn't come here to be trifled with. It's difficult enough for me to leave the residence even by day, and in order to spend the night away I had to ask the senior officer's permission and sign the register. You can see how complicated the regulations make things. But I'm in love, miss, just from hearing about you, and I wanted very badly to spend a night with you. I came here a while ago without an escort and made the arrangements with the teahouse. I had been looking forward to your kind reception, a memory to last me a lifetime, but you haven't so much as smiled at me or said a word of greeting. You keep your head down as if you were counting money in your lap. Aren't you afraid of getting a stiff neck? Madam—I've never heard the like. Here I come to a teahouse, and I must play the part of night nurse in a maternity room!

[PROPRIETRESS]: You're quite right, sir. Your surprise is entirely justified, considering that you don't know the reasons. This girl is deeply in love with a customer named Kamiji. It's been Kamiji today and Kamiji tomorrow, with nobody else allowed a chance at her. Her other customers have scattered in every direction, like leaves in a storm. When two people get so carried away with each other, it often leads to trouble, for both the customer and the girl. In the first place, it interferes with business, and the owner, whoever he may be, must prevent it. That's why all her guests are examined. Koharu is naturally depressed—it's only to be expected. You are annoyed, which is equally to be expected. But speaking as the proprietress here, it seems to me that the essential thing is for you to meet each other halfway and cheer up. Come, have a drink.—Act a little more lively, Koharu.

CHANTER: Koharu, without answering, lifts her tear-stained face.

[KOHARU]: Tell me, samurai, they say that if you're going to kill yourself anyway, people who die during the Ten Nights[80] are sure to become Buddhas. Is that really true?

[SAMURAI]: How should I know? Ask the priest at your family temple.

---

78. The imagery used by the maid has been altered from puns on saltiness (soy sauce, green vegetables, and so forth) to puns on sweetness.

79. A technical term of pottery making, meaning "hard-fired."

80. A period from the sixth to the sixteenth night of the Tenth Month when special Buddhist services were conducted in temples of the Pure Land (Jōdo) sect. It was believed that persons who died during this period immediately became Buddhas.

[KOHARU]: Yes, that's right. But there's something I'd like to ask a samurai. If you're committing suicide, it'd be a lot more painful, wouldn't it, to cut your throat rather than hang yourself?

[SAMURAI]: I've never tried cutting my throat to see whether or not it hurt. Please ask more sensible questions.—What an unpleasant girl!

CHANTER: Samurai though he is, he looks nonplussed.

[PROPRIETRESS]: Koharu, that's a shocking way to treat a guest the first time you meet him. I'll go and get my husband. We'll have some saké together. That ought to liven things up a bit.

CHANTER: The gate she leaves is lighted by the evening moon low in the sky; the clouds and the passers in the street have thinned.

For long years there has lived in Tenma, the seat of the mighty god,[81] though not a god himself, Kamiji,[82] a name often bruited by the gongs of worldly gossip, so deeply, hopelessly, is he tied to Koharu by the ropes[83] of an ill-starred love. Now is the tenth moon, the month when no gods will unite them;[84] they are thwarted in their love, unable to meet. They swore in the last letters they exchanged that if only they could meet, that day would be their last. Night after night Jihei, ready for death, trudges to the Quarter, distracted, as though his soul had left a body consumed by the fires of love.

At a roadside eating stand he hears people gossiping about Koharu. "She's at Kawashō with a samurai customer," someone says, and immediately Jihei decides, "It will be tonight!"

He peers through the latticework window and sees a guest in the inside room, his face obscured by a hood. Only the moving chin is visible, and Jihei cannot hear what is said.

[JIHEI]: Poor Koharu! How thin her face is! She keeps it turned away from the lamp. In her heart she's thinking only of me. I'll signal her that I'm here, and we'll run off together. Then which will it be—Umeda or Kitano?[85] Oh— I want to tell her I'm here. I want to call her.

CHANTER: He beckons with his heart, his spirit flies to her; but his body, like a cicada's cast-off shell, clings to the latticework. He weeps with impatience. The guest in the inside room gives a great yawn.

[SAMURAI]: What a bore, playing nursemaid to a prostitute with worries on

---

81. Tenma, one of the principal districts of Osaka, was the site of the Tenjin Shrine, to the memory of the deified Sugawara no Michizane (845–903).

82. The word *kami* (paper) is the homophone of *kami* (god). We have thus "Kami who is not a *kami*"—the paper dealer who is not a god.

83. The sacred ropes (*mishimenawa*) at a Shintō shrine. Here mentioned (like the gongs) as a word related to the imagery of Shintō.

84. The Tenth Month, called Kannazuki (literally, month of no gods), was a time when the gods were believed to gather at Izumo and thus were absent from the rest of Japan.

85. Both places had well-known cemeteries.

her mind!—The street seems quiet now. Let's go to the end room. We can at least distract ourselves by looking at the lanterns. Come with me.

CHANTER: They go together to the outer room. Jihei, alarmed, squeezes into the patch of shadow under the lattice window. Inside they do not realize that anyone is eavesdropping.

[SAMURAI]: I've been noticing your behavior and the little things you've said this evening. It's plain to me that you intend a love suicide with Kamiji, or whatever his name is—the man the hostess mentioned. I'm sure I'm right. I realize that no amount of advice or reasoning is likely to penetrate the ears of somebody bewitched by the god of death, but I must say that you're exceedingly foolish. The boy's family won't blame him for his recklessness, but they will blame and hate you. You'll be shamed by the public exposure of your body. Your parents may be dead, for all I know, but if they're alive, you'll be punished in hell as a wicked daughter. Do you think you'll become a buddha? You and your lover won't even be able to fall smoothly into hell together! What a pity—and what a tragedy! This is only our first meeting, but as a samurai, I can't let you die without trying to save you. No doubt money's the problem. I'd like to help, if five or ten *ryō* would be of service. I swear by the god Hachiman and by my good fortune as a samurai that I will never reveal to anyone what you tell me. Open your heart without fear.

CHANTER: He whispers these words. She joins her hands and bows.

[KOHARU]: I'm extremely grateful. Thank you for your kind words and for swearing an oath to me, someone you've never had for a lover or even a friend. I'm so grateful that I'm crying.—Yes, it's as they say, when you've something on your mind it shows on your face. You were right. I have promised Kamiji to die with him. But we've been completely prevented from meeting by my master, and Jihei, for various reasons, can't ransom me at once. My contracts with my former master[86] and my present one still have five years to run. If somebody else claimed me during that time, it would be a blow to me, of course, but a worse disgrace to Jihei's honor. He suggested that it would be better if we killed ourselves, and I agreed. I was caught by obligations from which I could not withdraw, and I promised him before I knew what I was doing. I said, "We'll watch for a chance, and I'll slip out when you give the signal." "Yes," he said, "slip out somehow." Ever since then I've been leading a life of uncertainty, never knowing from one day to the next when my last hour will come.

I have a mother living in a back alley south of here. She has no one but me to depend on, and she does piecework to eke out a living. I keep thinking that after I'm dead she'll become a beggar or an outcast, and maybe she'll die of starvation. That's the only sad part about dying. I have just this one

---

86. The master at the bathhouse where Koharu formerly worked.

Koharu attempting to persuade the samurai (Magoemon, in a hood, to hide his identity) to become her customer so that she and Jihei can avoid committing suicide. (Photograph courtesy of Barbara Curtis Adachi Collection, C. V. Starr East Asian Library, Columbia University)

life. I'm ashamed that you may think me a coldhearted woman, but I must endure the shame. The most important thing is that I don't want to die. I beg you, please help me stay alive.

CHANTER: As she speaks, the samurai nods thoughtfully. Jihei, crouching outside, hears her words with astonishment; they are so unexpected to his manly heart that he feels like a monkey who has tumbled from a tree. He is frantic with agitation.

[JIHEI] (to himself): Then was everything a lie? Ahhh—I'm furious! For two whole years I've been bewitched by that rotten she-fox! Shall I break in and kill her with one blow of my sword? Or shall I satisfy my anger by shaming her to her face?

CHANTER: He gnashes his teeth and weeps in chagrin. Inside the house Koharu speaks through her tears.

[KOHARU]: It's a curious thing to ask, but would you please show the kindness of a samurai and become my customer for the rest of this year and into next spring? Whenever Jihei comes, intent on death, please step in and force him to postpone his plan. In this way our relations can be broken quite naturally. He won't have to kill himself, and my life will also be saved.—What evil connection from a former existence made us promise to die? How I regret it now!

CHANTER: She weeps, leaning on the samurai's knee.

[SAMURAI]: Very well, I'll do as you ask. I think I can help you.—But I feel a breeze. Somebody may be watching.

CHANTER: He slams shut the latticework *shōji*. Jihei, listening outside, is in a frenzy.

[JIHEI]: Exactly what you'd expect from a whore, a cheap whore! I misjudged her foul nature. She robbed the soul from my body, the thieving harlot! Shall I slash her or run her through? What am I to do?

CHANTER: The shadows of two profiles fall on the *shōji*.

[JIHEI]: I'd like to give her a taste of my fist and trample her.—What are they chattering about? See how they nod to each other! Now she's bowing to him, whispering and sniveling. I've tried to control myself—I've pressed my chest, I've stroked it—but I can't stand any more. This is too much to endure!

CHANTER: His heart pounds wildly as he unsheathes his dirk, a Magoroku of Seki. "Koharu's side must be here," he judges, and stabs through an opening in the latticework. But Koharu is too far away for his thrust, and although she cries out in terror, she remains unharmed. Her guest instantly leaps at Jihei, grabs his hands, and jerks them through the latticework. With his sword knot he quickly and securely fastens Jihei's hands to the window upright.

[SAMURAI]: Don't scream, Koharu. Don't look at him.

CHANTER: At this moment the proprietor and his wife return. They exclaim in alarm.

[SAMURAI]: This needn't concern you. Some ruffian ran his sword through the *shōji*, and I've tied his arms to the latticework. I have my own way of dealing with him. Don't untie the cord. If you attract a crowd, the place is sure to be thrown in an uproar. Let's all go inside. Come with me, Koharu. We'll go to bed.

CHANTER: Koharu answers yes, but she recognizes the handle of the dirk, and the memory—if not the blade—transfixes her breast.

[KOHARU]: There're always people doing crazy things in the Quarter when they've had too much to drink. Why don't you let him go without making any trouble? I think that's best, don't you?

[SAMURAI]: Out of the question. Do as I say—inside, all of you. Koharu, come along.

CHANTER: Jihei can still see their shadows even after they enter the inner room, but he is bound to the spot, his hands held in fetters that grip him more tightly as he struggles, his body beset by suffering as he tastes a living shame worse than a dog's.[87] More determined than ever to die, he sheds tears of blood, a pitiful sight.

Tahei the Lone Wolf returns from his carousing.

---

87. A proverb of Buddhist origin, "Suffering follows one like a dog," is embedded in the text.

[TAHEI]: That's Jihei standing by Kawashō's window. I'll give him a thrashing.

CHANTER: He catches Jihei by the collar and starts to lift him over his back.

[JIHEI]: Owww!

[TAHEI]: Owww? What kind of weakling are you? Oh, I see—you're tied here. You must've been pulling off a robbery. You dirty pickpocket! You rotten pickpocket!

CHANTER: He beats Jihei mercilessly.

[TAHEI]: You burglar! You convict!

CHANTER: He kicks him wildly.

[TAHEI]: Kamiya Jihei's been caught burgling, and they've tied him up!

CHANTER: Passersby and people of the neighborhood, attracted by his shouts, quickly gather. The samurai rushes from the house.

[SAMURAI]: Who's calling him a burglar? You? Tell me what Jihei's stolen! Out with it!

CHANTER: He seizes Tahei and forces him into the dirt. Tahei rises to his feet, only for the samurai to kick him down again and again. He grabs Tahei.

[SAMURAI]: Jihei! Kick him to your heart's content!

CHANTER: He pushes Tahei under Jihei's feet. Bound though he is, Jihei stamps furiously on Tahei's face. Tahei, thoroughly kicked and covered with muck, gets to his feet and glares around him.

[TAHEI] (to bystanders): How could you fools just stand there and let him step on me? I know every one of your faces, and I intend to pay you back. Remember that!

CHANTER: He makes his escape, still determined to have the last word. The spectators burst out laughing.

[VOICES]: Listen to him brag, even after he's been beaten up! Let's throw him from the bridge and give him a drink of water! Don't let him get away!

CHANTER: They chase after him. When the crowd has dispersed, the samurai goes to Jihei and unfastens the knots. He shows his face with his hood removed.

[JIHEI]: Magoemon! My brother! How shameful!

CHANTER: He sinks to the ground and weeps, prostrating himself in the dirt.

[KOHARU]: Are you his brother, sir?

CHANTER: Koharu runs to them. Jihei, catching her by the front of the kimono, forces her to the ground.

[JIHEI]: Beast! She-fox! I'd sooner kick you than Tahei!

CHANTER: He raises his foot, but Magoemon calls out.

[MAGOEMON]: That's the kind of foolishness that's gotten you into all this trouble. A prostitute's business is to deceive men. Are you just realizing that? I could see to the bottom of her heart the very first time I met her, but you're so scatterbrained that in more than two years of sleeping with this woman you never figured out what she was thinking. Instead of kicking Koharu, why don't you use your feet on your own misguided disposition?—It's deplorable.

You may be my younger brother, but you're almost thirty, and you've got a six-year-old boy and a four-year-old girl, Kantarō and Osue. You run a shop with a thirty-six-foot frontage,[88] but you don't seem to realize that your whole fortune's collapsing. You shouldn't have to be lectured to by your brother. Your father-in-law is your aunt's husband, and your mother-in-law is your aunt. They've always been like real parents to you. Your wife, Osan, is my cousin, too. The ties of marriage are multiplied by those of blood. But when the family has a reunion, the only subject of discussion is our mortification over your incessant visits to Sonezaki. I feel sorry for our poor aunt. You know what a stiff-necked gentleman of the old school her husband, Gozaemon, is. He's forever flying into a rage and saying, "We've been tricked by your nephew. He's deserted our daughter. I'll take Osan back and ruin Jihei's reputation throughout Tenma." Our aunt, with all the heartache to bear herself, sometimes sides with him and sometimes with you. She's worried herself sick. What an ingrate not to appreciate how she's defended you in your shame! This one offense is enough to make you the target for Heaven's future punishment!

I realized that your marriage couldn't last much longer at this rate. So I decided, in the hopes of relieving our aunt's worries, that I'd see with my own eyes what kind of woman Koharu was and work out some sort of solution afterward. I consulted the proprietor here, then came myself to investigate the cause of your sickness. I see now how easy it was for you to desert your wife and children. What a faithful prostitute you discovered! I congratulate you!

And here I am, Magoemon the Miller,[89] known far and wide for my paragon of a brother, dressed up like a masquerader at a festival or maybe a lunatic! I put on swords for the first time in my life and announced myself, like a bit player in a costume piece, as an officer at a residence. I feel like an absolute idiot with these swords, but there's nowhere I can dispose of them now.—It's so infuriating—and ridiculous—that it's given me a pain in the chest.

CHANTER: He gnashes his teeth and grimaces, attempting to hide his tears. Koharu, choking all the while with emotion, can only say:

[KOHARU]: Yes, you're entirely right.

CHANTER: The rest is lost in tears. Jihei pounds the ground with his fist.

[JIHEI]: I was wrong. Forgive me, Magoemon. For three years I've been possessed by that witch. I've neglected my parents, relatives—even my wife and

---

88. It was customary to refer to the size of shops by giving their frontage on the street.

89. Magoemon is a dealer in flour (for noodles). His shop name, Konaya—"the flour merchant"—is used almost as a surname.

children—and wrecked my fortune, all because I was deceived by Koharu, that sneak thief! I'm utterly mortified. But I'm through with her now, and I'll never set foot here again. Weasel! Vixen! Sneak thief! Here's proof that I've broken with her!

CHANTER: He pulls out the amulet bag that has rested next to his skin.

[JIHEI]: Here are the written oaths we've exchanged, one at the beginning of each month, twenty-nine in all. I am returning them. This means our love and affection are over. Take them.

CHANTER: He flings the notes at her.

[JIHEI]: Magoemon, get my pledges from her. Please make sure you get them all. Then burn them with your own hands. (*To Koharu*) Give them to my brother.

[KOHARU]: As you wish.

CHANTER: In tears, she surrenders the amulet bag. Magoemon opens it.

[MAGOEMON]: One, two, three, four . . . ten . . . twenty-nine. They're all here. There's also a letter from a woman. What's this?

CHANTER: He starts to unfold it.

[KOHARU]: That's an important letter. I can't let you see it.

CHANTER: She clings to Magoemon's arm, but he pushes her away. He holds the letter to the lamplight and examines the address, "To Miss Koharu from Kamiya Osan." As soon as he reads the words, he casually thrusts the letter into his kimono.

[MAGOEMON]: Koharu. A while ago I swore by my good fortune as a samurai, but now Magoemon the Miller swears by his good fortune as a business-man that he will show this letter to no one, not even his wife. I alone will read it, then burn it with the oaths. You can trust me. I will not break this oath.

[KOHARU]: Thank you. You save my honor.

CHANTER: She bursts into tears again.

[JIHEI] (*laughs contemptuously*): Save your honor! You talk like a human be-ing! (*To Magoemon*) I don't want to see her cursed face another minute. Let's go. No—I can't hold so much resentment and bitterness! I'll kick her one in the face, a memory to treasure for the rest of my life. Excuse me, please.

CHANTER: He strides up to Koharu and stamps on the ground.

[JIHEI]: For three years I've loved you, delighted in you, longed for you, adored you; but today my foot will say my only farewells.

CHANTER: He kicks her sharply on the forehead and bursts into tears. The brothers leave, forlorn figures. Koharu, unhappy woman, raises her voice in lament as she watches them go. Is she faithful or unfaithful? Her true feelings are hidden in the words penned by Jihei's wife, a letter that no one has seen. Jihei goes his separate way without learning the truth.

Act 2

Scene 1: The house and shop of Kamiya Jihei. Time: Ten days later.

CHANTER: The busy street that runs straight to Tenjin Bridge,[90] named for the god of Tenma, bringer of good fortune, is known as the Street Before the Kami,[91] and here a paper shop does business under the name Kamiya Jihei. The paper is honestly sold, and the shop is well situated; it is a long-established firm, and customers come thick as raindrops.

Outside, crowds pass in the street, on their way to the Ten Nights service, while inside, the husband dozes in the kotatsu,[92] shielded from drafts by a screen at his pillow. His wife Osan keeps solitary, anxious watch over shop and house.

[OSAN]: The days are so short—it's dinnertime already, but Tama still hasn't returned from her errand to Ichinokawa.[93] I wonder what can be keeping her. That scamp Sangorō isn't back either. The wind is freezing. I'm sure both the children will be cold. He doesn't even realize that it's time for Osue to be nursed. Heaven preserve me from ever becoming such a fool! What an infuriating creature!

CHANTER: She speaks to herself.

[KANTARŌ]: Mama, I've come back all by myself.

CHANTER: Her son, the older child, runs up to the house.

[OSAN]: Kantarō—is that you? What's happened to Osue and Sangorō?

[KANTARŌ]: They're playing by the shrine. Osue wanted her milk, and she was bawling her head off.

[OSAN]: I was sure she would. Oh—your hands and feet are frozen stiff as nails! Go and warm yourself at the kotatsu. Your father's sleeping there.— What am I to do with that idiot?

CHANTER: She runs out impatiently to the shop just as Sangorō shuffles back, alone.

[OSAN]: Come here, you fool! Where have you left Osue?

[SANGORŌ]: You know, I must've lost her somewhere. Maybe somebody's picked her up. Should I go back for her?

[OSAN]: How could you! If any harm has come to my precious child, I'll beat you to death!

CHANTER: But while she is screaming at him, the maid Tama returns with Osue on her back.

[TAMA]: The poor child—I found her in tears at the corner. Sangorō, when you're supposed to look after the child, do it properly.

---

90. The reference is to Tenma Tenjin, a deified form of Sugawara no Michizane.
91. Again, a play on the words *kami* (god) and *kami* (paper).
92. A source of heat in which a charcoal burner is placed under a low, quilt-covered table.
93. Ichinokawa was the site of a large vegetable market near the north end of Tenjin Bridge.

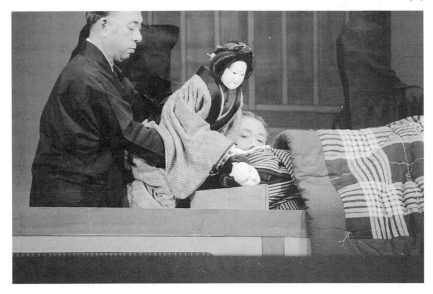

Osan trying to persuade Jihei to get up. (Photograph courtesy of Barbara Curtis Adachi Collection, C. V. Starr East Asian Library, Columbia University)

[OSAN]: You poor dear. You must want your milk.

CHANTER: She joins the others by the kotatsu and nurses the child.

[OSAN]: Tama—give that fool a taste of something that he'll remember![94]

CHANTER: Sangorō shakes his head.

[SANGORŌ]: No, thanks. I gave each of the children two tangerines just a while ago at the shrine, and I tasted five myself.

CHANTER: Fool though he is, bad puns come from him nimbly enough, and the others can only smile despite themselves.

[TAMA]: Oh—I've become so involved with this half-wit that I almost forgot to tell you, ma'am, that Mr. Magoemon and his aunt[95] are on their way here from the west.

[OSAN]: Oh dear! In that case, I'll have to wake Jihei. (*To Jihei*) Please get up. Mother and Magoemon are coming. They'll be upset again if you let them see you, a businessman, sleeping in the afternoon, with the day as short as it is.

[JIHEI]: All right.

CHANTER: He struggles to a sitting position and, with his abacus in one hand, pulls his account book to him with the other.

[JIHEI]: Two into ten goes five, three into nine goes three, three into six goes two, seven times eight is fifty-six.

---

94. A pun on the two meanings of *kurawasu*: "to cause to eat" and "to beat."

95. Magoemon's (and Jihei's) aunt but Osan's mother.

CHANTER: His fifty-six-year-old aunt enters with Magoemon.

[JIHEI]: Magoemon, aunt. How good of you. Please come in. I was in the midst of some urgent calculations. Four nines makes thirty-six *monme*. Three sixes make eighteen *fun*. That's two *monme* less two *fun*.[96] Kantarō! Osue! Granny and Uncle have come! Bring the tobacco tray! One times three makes three. Osan, serve the tea.[97]

CHANTER: He jabbers away.

[AUNT]: We haven't come for tea or tobacco. Osan, you're young, I know, but you're the mother of two children, and your excessive forbearance does you no credit. A man's dissipation can always be traced to his wife's carelessness. Remember, it's not only the man who's disgraced when he goes bankrupt and his marriage breaks up. You'd do well to take notice of what's going on and assert yourself a bit more.

[MAGOEMON]: It's foolish to hope for any results, aunt. The scoundrel deceives even me, his elder brother. Why should he take to heart criticism from his wife? Jihei—you played me for a fool. After showing me how you returned Koharu's pledges, here you are, not ten days later, redeeming her! What does this mean? I suppose your urgent calculations are of Koharu's debts! I've had enough!

CHANTER: He snatches away the abacus and flings it clattering into the hallway.

[JIHEI]: You're making an enormous fuss without any cause. I haven't left the house since the last time I saw you, except to go twice to the wholesalers in Imabashi and once to the Tenjin Shrine. I haven't even thought of Koharu, much less redeemed her.

[AUNT]: None of your evasions! Last evening at the Ten Nights service I heard the people in the congregation gossiping. Everybody was talking about the great patron from Tenma who'd fallen in love with a prostitute named Koharu from the Kinokuni House in Sonezaki. They said he'd driven away her other guests and was going to ransom her in the next couple of days. There was all kinds of gossip about the abundance of money and fools even in these days of high prices.

My husband, Gozaemon, has been hearing about Koharu constantly, and he's sure that her great patron from Tenma must be you, Jihei. He told me, "He's your nephew, but to me he's a stranger, and my daughter's happiness is my chief concern. Once he ransoms the prostitute he'll no doubt sell his wife to a brothel. I intend to take her back before he starts selling her clothes."

He was halfway out of the house before I could stop him. "Don't get so

---

96. Meaningless calculations. Twenty *fun* made two *monme*.
97. The name Osan echoes the word *san* (three).

excited. We can settle this calmly. First we must make sure whether or not the rumors are true."

That's why Magoemon and I are here now. He was telling me a while ago that the Jihei of today was not the Jihei of yesterday—that you'd broken all connections with Sonezaki and completely reformed. But now I hear that you've had a relapse. What disease can this be?

Your father was my brother. When the poor man was on his deathbed, he lifted his head from the pillow and begged me to look after you, as my son-in-law and nephew. I've never forgotten those last words, but your perversity has made a mockery of his request!

CHANTER: She collapses in tears of resentment. Jihei claps his hands in sudden recognition.

[JIHEI]: I have it! The Koharu everybody's gossiping about is the same Koharu, but the great patron who's to redeem her is a different man. The other day, as my brother can tell you, Tahei—they call him the Lone Wolf because he hasn't any family or relations—started a fight and was beaten up. He gets all the money he needs from his home town, and he's been trying for a long time to redeem Koharu. I've always prevented him, but I'm sure he's decided that now is his chance. I have nothing to do with it.

CHANTER: Osan brightens at his words.

[OSAN]: No matter how forbearing I might be—even if I were an angel—you don't suppose I'd encourage my husband to redeem a prostitute! In this instance at any rate there's not a word of untruth in what my husband has said. I'll be a witness to that, Mother.

CHANTER: Husband's and wife's words tally perfectly.

[AUNT]: Then it's true?

CHANTER: The aunt and nephew clap their hands with relief.

[MAGOEMON]: Well, I'm happy it's over, anyway. To make us feel doubly reassured, will you write an affidavit that will dispel any doubts your stubborn uncle may have?

[JIHEI]: Certainly. I'll write a thousand if you like.

[MAGOEMON]: Splendid! I happen to have bought this on the way here.

CHANTER: Magoemon takes from the fold of his kimono a sheet of oath-paper from Kumano, the sacred characters formed by flocks of crows.[98] Instead of vows of eternal love, Jihei now signs under penalty of Heaven's wrath an oath that he will sever all ties and affections with Koharu. "If I should lie, may Bonten and Taishaku above, and the Four Great Kings below, afflict me!"[99] So the text runs and to it is appended the names of many Buddhas

---

98. The charms issued by the Shintō shrine at Kumano were printed on the face with six Chinese characters, the strokes of which were in the shape of crows. The reverse side of these charms was used for writing oaths.

99. A formal oath. Bonten (Brahma) and Taishaku (Indra), though Hindu gods, were consid-

and gods. He signs his name, Kamiya Jihei, in bold characters, seals the oath with blood, and hands it over.

[OSAN]: It's a great relief to me too. Mother, I have you and Magoemon to thank. Jihei and I have had two children, but this is his firmest pledge of affection. I hope you share my joy.

[AUNT]: Indeed we do. I'm sure that Jihei will settle down and his business will improve, now that he's in this frame of mind. It's been entirely for his sake and for love of the grandchildren that we've intervened. Come, Magoemon, let's be on our way. I'm anxious to set my husband's mind at ease.—It's become chilly here. See that the children don't catch cold.— This, too, we owe to the Buddha of the Ten Nights. I'll say a prayer of thanks before I go. Hail, Amida Buddha!

CHANTER: She leaves, her heart innocent as Buddha's. Jihei is perfunctory even about seeing them to the door. Hardly have they crossed the threshold than he slumps down again at the kotatsu. He pulls the checked quilting over his head.

[OSAN]: You still haven't forgotten Sonezaki, have you?

CHANTER: She goes up to him in disgust and tears away the quilting. He is weeping; a waterfall of tears streams along the pillow, deep enough to bear him afloat. She tugs him upright and props his body against the kotatsu frame. She stares into his face.

[OSAN]: You're acting outrageously, Jihei. You shouldn't have signed that oath if you felt so reluctant to leave her. The year before last, on the middle day of the boar of the Tenth Month,[100] we lit the first fire in the kotatsu and celebrated by sleeping here together, pillow to pillow. Ever since then—did some demon or snake creep into my bosom that night?—for two whole years I've been condemned to keep watch over an empty nest. I thought that tonight at least, thanks to Mother and Magoemon, we'd share sweet words in bed as husbands and wives do, but my pleasure didn't last long. How cruel of you, how utterly heartless! Go ahead, cry your eyes out, if you're so attached to her. Your tears will flow into Shijimi River, and Koharu, no doubt, will ladle them out and drink them! You're ignoble, inhuman.

CHANTER: She embraces his knees and throws herself over him, moaning in supplication. Jihei wipes his eyes.

[JIHEI]: If tears of grief flowed from the eyes and tears of anger from the ears, I could show my heart without saying a word. But my tears all pour in the same way from my eyes, and there's no difference in their color. It's not surprising that you can't tell what's in my heart. I have not a shred of attach-

---

ered to be protective deities of the Buddhist law. The four Deva kings served under Indra and were also protectors of Buddhism.

100. It was customary to light the first fire of the winter on this day, which would generally be toward the end of November in the Western calendar.

ment left for that vampire in human skin, but I bear a grudge against Tahei. He has all the money he wants and no wife or children. He's schemed again and again to redeem her, but Koharu refused to give in, at least until I broke with her. She told me time and again, "You have nothing to worry about. I'll never let myself be redeemed by Tahei, not even if my ties with you are ended and I can no longer stay by your side. If my master is induced by Tahei's money to deliver me to him, I'll kill myself in a way that'll do you credit!" But think—not ten days have passed since I broke with her, and she's to be redeemed by Tahei! That rotten whore! That animal! No, I haven't a trace of affection left for her, but I can just hear how Tahei will be boasting. He'll spread the word around Osaka that my business has come to a standstill and I'm hard pressed for money. I'll meet with contemptuous stares from the wholesalers. I'll be dishonored. My heart is broken, and my body burns with shame. What a disgrace! How maddening! I've passed the stage of shedding hot tears, tears of blood, sticky tears—my tears now are of molten iron!

CHANTER: He collapses, weeping. Osan turns pale with alarm.

[OSAN]: If that's the situation, poor Koharu will surely kill herself.

[JIHEI]: You're too well bred, despite your intelligence, to understand someone like her! What makes you suppose that faithless creature would kill herself? Far from it—she's probably taking moxa treatments and medicine to prolong her life!

[OSAN]: No, that's not true. I was determined never to tell you so long as I lived, but I'm afraid of the crime I'd be committing if I concealed the facts and let her die with my knowledge. I will reveal my great secret. There is not a grain of deceit in Koharu. It was I who schemed to end the relations between you. I could see signs that you were drifting toward suicide. I felt so unhappy that I wrote a letter, begging her as one woman to another to break with you, even though I knew how painful it would be. I asked her to save your life. The letter must have moved her. She answered that she would give you up, even though you were more precious than life itself, because she could not shirk her duty to me. I've kept her letter with me ever since—it's been like a protective charm. Would such a noble-hearted woman break her promise and brazenly marry Tahei? When a woman—I no less than another—has given herself completely to a man, she does not change. I'm sure she'll kill herself. I'm sure of it. Ahhh—what a dreadful thing to have happened! Save her, please.

CHANTER: Her voice rises in agitation. Her husband is thrown into a turmoil.

[JIHEI]: There was a letter in an unknown woman's hand among the written oaths she surrendered to my brother. It must have been from you. If that's the case, Koharu will surely commit suicide.

[OSAN]: Alas! I'd be failing in the obligations I owe her as another woman if I allowed her to die. Please go to her at once. Don't let her kill herself.

CHANTER: Clinging to her husband, she melts in tears.

[JIHEI]: But what can I possibly do? It'd take half the amount of her ransom in earnest money merely to keep her out of Tahei's clutches. I can't save Koharu's life without administering a dose of 750 *monme* in New Silver.[101] How could I raise that much money in my present financial straits? Even if I crush my body to powder, where will the money come from?

[OSAN]: Don't exaggerate the difficulties. If that's all you need, it's simple enough.

CHANTER: She goes to the wardrobe, and opening a small drawer takes out a bag fastened with cords of twisted silk. She unhesitatingly tears it open and throws down a packet which Jihei retrieves.

[JIHEI]: What's this? Money? Four hundred *monme* in New Silver? How in the world—

CHANTER: He stares astonished at this money he never put there.

[OSAN]: I'll tell you later where this money came from. I've scraped it together to pay the bill for Iwakuni paper that falls due the day after tomorrow. We'll have to ask Magoemon to help us keep the business from going bankrupt. But Koharu comes first. The packet contains 400 *monme*. That leaves 350 *monme* to raise.

CHANTER: She unlocks a large drawer. From the wardrobe lightly fly kite-colored Hachijō silks; a Kyoto crepe kimono lined in pale brown, insubstantial as her husband's life, which flickers today and may vanish tomorrow; a padded kimono of Osue's, a flaming scarlet inside and out—Osan flushes with pain to part with it; Kantarō's sleeveless, unlined jacket—if she pawns this, he'll be cold this winter. Next comes a garment of striped Gunnai silk lined in pale blue and never worn, and then her best formal costume— heavy black silk dyed with her family crest, an ivy leaf in a ring. They say that those joined by marriage ties can even go naked at home, although outside the house clothes make the man: she snatches up even her husband's finery, a silken cloak, making fifteen articles in all.

[OSAN]: The very least the pawnshop can offer is 350 *monme* in New Silver.

CHANTER: Her face glows as though she already held the money she needs; she hides in the one bundle her husband's shame and her own obligation and puts her love in besides.

[OSAN]: It doesn't matter if the children and I have nothing to wear. My husband's reputation concerns me more. Ransom Koharu. Save her. Assert your honor before Tahei.

CHANTER: But Jihei's eyes remain downcast all the while, and he is silently weeping.

[JIHEI]: Yes, I can pay the earnest money and keep her out of Tahei's hands.

---

101. The medical images are occasioned by considering Koharu's plight as a sickness. If 750 *me* is half the sum needed to redeem Koharu, the total of 1,500 *me* (or 6,000 *me* in Old Silver) is considerably less than the 10 *kanme*, or 10,000 *me* in Old Silver, mentioned by Tahei.

But once I've redeemed her, I'll have to either maintain her in a separate establishment or bring her here. Then what will become of you?

CHANTER: Osan is at a loss to answer.

[OSAN]: Yes, what shall I do? Shall I become your children's nurse or the cook? Or perhaps the retired mistress of the house?

CHANTER: She falls to the floor with a cry of woe.

[JIHEI]: That would be too selfish. I'd be afraid to accept such generosity. Even if the punishment for my crimes against my parents, against Heaven, against the gods and the Buddhas fails to strike me, the punishment for my crimes against my wife alone will be sufficient to destroy all hope for the future life. Forgive me, I beg you.

CHANTER: He joins his hands in tearful entreaty.

[OSAN]: Why should you bow before me? I don't deserve it. I'd be glad to rip the nails from my fingers and toes, to do anything that might serve my husband. I've been pawning my clothes for some time in order to scrape together the money for the paper wholesalers' bills. My wardrobe is empty, but I don't regret it in the least. But it's too late now to talk of such things. Hurry, change your cloak and go to her with a smile.

CHANTER: He puts on an underkimono of Gunnai silk, a robe of heavy black silk, and a striped cloak. His sash of figured damask holds a dirk of middle length worked in gold: Buddha surely knows that tonight it will be stained with Koharu's blood.

[JIHEI]: Sangorō! Come here!

CHANTER: Jihei loads the bundle on the servant's back, intending to take him along. Then he firmly thrusts the wallet next to his skin and starts toward the gate.

[VOICE]: Is Jihei at home?

CHANTER: A man enters, removing his fur cap. They see—good heavens!—that it is Gozaemon.

[OSAN AND JIHEI]: Ahhh—how fortunate that you should come at this moment!

CHANTER: Husband and wife are upset and confused. Gozaemon snatches away Sangorō's bundle and sits heavily. His voice is sharp.

[GOZAEMON]: Stay where you are, harlot!—My esteemed son-in-law, what a rare pleasure to see you dressed in your finest attire, with a dirk and a silken cloak! Ahhh—that's how a gentleman of means spends his money! No one would take you for a paper dealer. Are you perchance on your way to the New Quarter? What commendable perseverance! You have no need for your wife, I take it.—Give her a divorce. I've come to take her home with me.

CHANTER: He speaks needles and his voice is bitter. Jihei has not a word to reply.

[OSAN]: How kind of you, Father, to walk here on such a cold day. Do have a cup of tea.

CHANTER: Offering the teacup serves as an excuse for edging closer.

[OSAN]: Mother and Magoemon came here a while ago, and they told my husband how much they disapproved of his visits to the New Quarter. Jihei was in tears and he wrote out an oath swearing he had reformed. He gave it to Mother. Haven't you seen it yet?

[GOZAEMON]: His written oath? Do you mean this?

CHANTER: He takes the paper from his kimono.

[GOZAEMON]: Libertines scatter vows and oaths wherever they go, as if they were monthly statements of accounts. I thought there was something peculiar about this oath, and now that I am here I can see I was right. Do you still swear to Bonten and Taishaku? Instead of such nonsense, write out a bill of divorcement!

CHANTER: He rips the oath to shreds and throws down the pieces. Husband and wife exchange looks of alarm, stunned into silence. Jihei touches his hands to the floor and bows his head.

[JIHEI]: Your anger is justified. If I were still my former self, I would try to offer explanations, but today I appeal entirely to your generosity. Please let me stay with Osan. I promise that even if I become a beggar or an outcast and must sustain life with the scraps that fall from other people's chopsticks, I will hold Osan in high honor and protect her from every harsh and bitter experience. I feel so deeply indebted to Osan that I cannot divorce her. You will understand that this is true as time passes and I show you how I apply myself to my work and restore my fortune. Until then please shut your eyes and allow us to remain together.

CHANTER: Tears of blood stream from his eyes, and his face is pressed to the matting in contrition.

[GOZAEMON]: The wife of an outcast! That's all the worse. Write the bill of divorcement at once! I will verify and seal the furniture and clothes Osan brought in her dowry.

CHANTER: He goes to the wardrobe. Osan is alarmed.

[OSAN]: All my clothes are here. There's no need to examine them.

CHANTER: She runs up to stop him, but Gozaemon pushes her aside and jerks open a drawer.

[GOZAEMON]: What does this mean?

CHANTER: He opens another drawer: it too is empty. He pulls out every last drawer, but not so much as a foot of patchwork cloth is to be seen. He tears open the wicker hampers, long boxes, and clothes chests.

[GOZAEMON]: Stripped bare, are they?

CHANTER: His eyes set in fury. Jihei and Osan huddle under the striped kotatsu quilts, ready to sink into the fire with humiliation.

[GOZAEMON]: This bundle looks suspicious.

CHANTER: He unties the knots and dumps out the contents.

[GOZAEMON]: As I thought! You were sending these to the pawnshop, I take it. Jihei—you'd strip the skin from your wife's and your children's bodies to

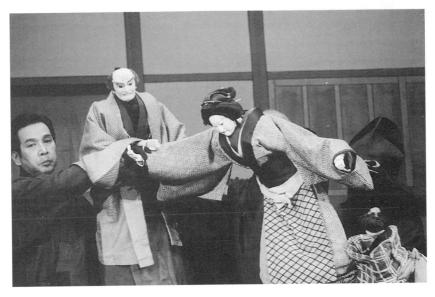

Gozaemon pulling away his daughter Osan while her child watches. (Photograph courtesy of Barbara Curtis Adachi Collection, C. V. Starr East Asian Library, Columbia University)

squander the money on your whore! Dirty thief! You're my wife's nephew, but an utter stranger to me, and I'm under no obligation to suffer for your sake. I'll explain to Magoemon what has happened and ask him to make good on whatever you've already stolen from Osan's belongings. But first, the bill of divorcement!

CHANTER: Even if Jihei could escape through seven padlocked doors, eight layers of chains, and a hundred retention walls, he could not escape so stringent a demand.

[JIHEI]: I won't use a brush to write the bill of divorcement. Here's what I'll do instead! Good-bye, Osan.

CHANTER: He lays his hand on his dirk, but Osan clings to him.

[OSAN]: Father—Jihei admits that he's done wrong, and he's apologized in every way. You press your advantage too hard. Jihei may be a stranger, but his children are your grandchildren. Have you no affection for them? I will not accept a bill of divorcement.

CHANTER: She embraces her husband and raises her voice in tears.

[GOZAEMON]: Very well. I won't insist on it. Come with me, woman.

CHANTER: He pulls her to her feet.

[OSAN]: No, I won't go. What bitterness makes you expose to such shame a man and wife who still love each other? I will not suffer it.

CHANTER: She pleads with him, weeping, but he pays her no heed.

[GOZAEMON]: Is there some greater shame? I'll shout it through the town!

CHANTER: He pulls her up, but she shakes free. Caught by the wrist she totters forward when—alas!—her toes brush against her sleeping children. They open their eyes.

[CHILDREN]: Mother dear, why is Grandfather, the bad man, taking you away? Whom will we sleep beside now?

CHANTER: They call out after her.

[OSAN]: My poor dears! You've never spent a night away from Mother's side since you were born. Sleep tonight beside your father. (*To Jihei*) Please don't forget to give the children their tonic before breakfast.—Oh, my heart is broken!

CHANTER: These are her parting words. She leaves her children behind, abandoned as in the woods; the twin-trunked bamboo of conjugal love is sundered forever.

Act 3

Scene 1: In Sonezaki, in front of the Yamato Teahouse.

CHANTER: This is Shijimi River, the haunt of love and affection. Its flowing water and the feet of passersby are stilled now at two in the morning, and the full moon shines clear in the sky. Here in the street a dim doorway lantern is marked "Yamatoya Denbei" in a single scrawl. The night watchman's clappers take on a sleepy cadence as he totters by on uncertain legs. The very thickness of his voice crying, "Beware of fire! Beware of fire!" tells how far advanced the night is. A serving woman from the upper town comes along, followed by a palanquin. "It's terribly late," she remarks to the bearers as she clatters open the side door of the Yamato Teahouse and steps inside.

[SERVANT]: I've come to take back Koharu of the Kinokuni House.

CHANTER: Her voice is faintly heard outside. A few moments later, after hardly time enough to exchange three or four words of greeting, she emerges.

[SERVANT]: Koharu is spending the night. Bearers, you may leave now and get some rest. (*To proprietress, inside the doorway*) Oh, I forgot to tell you, madam. Please keep an eye on Koharu. Now that the ransom to Tahei has been arranged and the money's been accepted, we're merely her custodians. Please don't let her drink too much saké.

CHANTER: She leaves, having scattered at the doorway the seeds that before morning will turn Jihei and Koharu to dust.

At night between two and four, even the teahouse kettle rests; the flame flickering in the low candle stand narrows; and the frost spreads in the cold river-wind of the deepening night. The master's voice breaks the stillness.

[DENBEI] (*to Jihei*): It's still the middle of the night. I'll send somebody with you. (*To the servants*) Mr. Jihei is leaving. Wake Koharu. Call her here.

CHANTER: Jihei slides open the side door.

[JIHEI]: No, Denbei, not a word to Koharu. I'll be trapped here until dawn if she hears I'm leaving. That's why I'm letting her sleep and slipping off this way. Wake her up after sunrise and send her back then. I'm returning home now and will leave for Kyoto immediately on business. I have so many engagements that I may not be able to return in time for the interim payment.[102] Please use the money I gave you earlier this evening to clear my account. I'd like you also to send 150 *me* of Old Silver to Kawashō for the moon-viewing party last month. Please get a receipt. Give Saietsubō[103] from Fukushima one piece of silver as a contribution to the Buddhist altar he's bought, and tell him to use it for a memorial service. Wasn't there something else? Oh yes—give Isoichi a tip of four silver coins. That's the lot. Now you can close up and get to bed. Good-bye. I'll see you when I return from Kyoto.

CHANTER: Hardly has he taken two or three steps than he turns back.

[JIHEI]: I forgot my dirk. Fetch it for me, won't you?—Yes, Denbei, this is one respect in which it's easier being a townsman. If I were a samurai and forgot my sword, I'd probably commit suicide on the spot!

[DENBEI]: I completely forgot that I was keeping it for you. Yes, here's the knife with it.

CHANTER: He gives the dirk to Jihei, who fastens it firmly into his sash.

[JIHEI]: I feel secure as long as I have this. Good night!

CHANTER: He goes off.

[DENBEI]: Please come back to Osaka soon! Thank you for your patronage!

CHANTER: With this hasty farewell Denbei rattles the door bolt shut; then not another sound is heard as the silence deepens. Jihei pretends to leave, only to creep back again with stealthy steps. He clings to the door of the Yamato Teahouse. As he peeps inside, he is startled by shadows moving toward him. He takes cover at the house across the way until the figures pass.

Magoemon the Miller, his heart pulverized with anxiety over his younger brother, comes first, followed by the apprentice Sangorō with Jihei's son Kantarō on his back. They hurry along until they see the lantern of the Yamato Teahouse. Magoemon pounds on the door.

[MAGOEMON]: Excuse me. Kamiya Jihei's here, isn't he? I'd like to see him a moment.

CHANTER: Jihei thinks, "It's my brother!" but dares not stir from his place of concealment. From inside a man's sleep-laden voice is heard.

[DENBEI]: Jihei left a while ago, saying he was going up to Kyoto. He's not here.

CHANTER: Not another sound is heard. Magoemon's tears fall unchecked.

[MAGOEMON] (*to himself*): I ought to have met him on the way if he'd been

---

102. On the last day of the Tenth Month (November 29, 1720). This day was one of the times during the year for making payments.

103. The name of a male entertainer in the quarter. Fukushima was west of Sonezaki.

going home. I can't understand what would take him to Kyoto. Ahhh—I'm shivering all over with worry. I wonder whether he took Koharu with him.

CHANTER: The thought pierces his heart; unable to bear the pain, he pounds again on the door.

[DENBEI]: Who is it, so late at night? We've gone to bed.

[MAGOEMON]: I'm sorry to disturb you, but I'd like to ask one more thing. Has Koharu of the Kinokuni House left? I was wondering whether she might have gone with Jihei.

[DENBEI]: What's that? Koharu's upstairs, sound asleep.

[MAGOEMON]: That's a relief, anyway. There's no fear of a lovers' suicide. But where is he hiding himself, causing me all this anxiety? He can't imagine the agony of suspense that the whole family is going through on his account. I'm afraid that bitterness toward his father-in-law may make him forget himself and do something rash. I brought Kantarō along, hoping he would help to dissuade Jihei, but the gesture was in vain. I wonder why I never saw him?

CHANTER: He murmurs to himself, his eyes wet with tears. Jihei's hiding place is close enough for him to hear every word. He chokes with emotion but can only swallow his tears.

[MAGOEMON]: Sangorō! Where does the fool go night after night? Don't you know anywhere else?

CHANTER: Sangorō imagines that he himself is the fool referred to.

[SANGORŌ]: I know a couple of places, but I'm too embarrassed to mention them.

[MAGOEMON]: You know them? Where are they? Tell me.

[SANGORŌ]: Please don't scold me when you've heard. Every night I wander down below the warehouses by the market.

[MAGOEMON]: Imbecile! Who's asking about that? Come on, let's search the back streets. Don't let Kantarō catch a chill. The poor kid's having a hard time of it, thanks to that useless father of his. Still, if the worst the boy experiences is the cold, I won't complain. I'm afraid that Jihei may cause him much greater pain. The scoundrel!

CHANTER: But beneath the rancor in his heart of hearts is profound pity.

[MAGOEMON]: Let's look at the back street!

CHANTER: They pass on. As soon as their figures have gone off a distance, Jihei runs from his hiding place. Standing on tiptoes he gazes with yearning after them and cries out in his heart.

[JIHEI]: He cannot leave me to my death, even though I am the worst of sinners! I remain to the last a burden to him! I'm unworthy of such kindness!

CHANTER: He joins his hands and kneels in prayer.

[JIHEI]: If I may make one further request of your mercy, look after my children!

CHANTER: These are his only words; for a while he chokes with tears.

[JIHEI]: At any rate, our decision's been made. Koharu must be waiting.

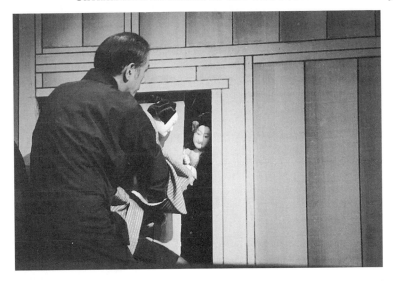

Jihei secretly meeting Koharu at the Yamato Teahouse. (Photograph courtesy of
Barbara Curtis Adachi Collection, C. V. Starr East Asian Library, Columbia
University)

CHANTER: He peers through a crack in the side door of the Yamato Teahouse
and glimpses a figure.

[JIHEI]: That's Koharu, isn't it? I'll let her know I'm here.

CHANTER: He clears his throat, their signal. "Ahem, ahem"—the sound blends
with the clack of wooden clappers as the watchman comes from the upper
street, coughing in the night wind. He hurries on his round of fire warning,
"Take care! Beware!" Even this cry has a dismal sound to one in hiding.
Jihei, concealing himself like the god of Katsuragi,[104] lets the watchman pass.
He sees his chance and rushes to the side door, which softly opens from
within.

[JIHEI]: Koharu?

[KOHARU]: Were you waiting? Jihei—I want to leave quickly.

CHANTER: She is all impatience, but the more quickly they open the door,
the more likely people will be to hear the casters turning. They lift the door;
it makes a moaning sound that thunders in their ears and in their hearts.
Jihei lends a hand from the outside, but his fingertips tremble with the
trembling of his heart. The door opens a quarter of an inch, a half, an inch—
an inch ahead are the tortures of hell, but more than hell itself they fear the
guardian-demon's eyes. At last the door opens, and with the joy of New Year's
morning[105] Koharu slips out. They catch each other's hands. Shall they go

104. The god was so ashamed of his ugliness that he ventured forth only at night.
105. Mention of New Year is connected with Koharu's name, in which *haru* means "spring."

north or south, west or east? Their pounding hearts urge them on, though they know not to what destination: turning their backs on the moon reflected in Shijimi River, they hurry eastward as fast as their legs will carry them.

Scene 2: The farewell journey of many bridges.

CHANTER:

The running hand in texts of nō is always Konoe style;
An actor in a woman's part is sure to wear a purple hat.
Does some teaching of the Buddha as rigidly decree
That men who spend their days in evil haunts must end like this?

Poor creatures, although they would discover today their destiny in the Sutra of Cause and Effect,[106] tomorrow the gossip of the world will scatter like blossoms the scandal of Kamiya Jihei's love suicide, and carved in cherry wood,[107] his story to the last detail will be printed in illustrated sheets.

Jihei, led on by the spirit of death—if such there be among the gods—is resigned to this punishment for neglect of his trade. But at times—who could blame him?—his heart is drawn to those he has left behind, and it is hard to keep walking on. Even in the full moon's light, this fifteenth night of the Tenth Month,[108] he cannot see his way ahead—a sign perhaps of the darkness in his heart? The frost now falling will melt by dawn, but even more quickly than this symbol of human frailty, the lovers themselves will melt away. What will become of the fragrance that lingered when he held her tenderly at night in their bedchamber?

This bridge, Tenjin Bridge, he has crossed every day, morning and night, gazing at Shijimi River to the west. Long ago, when Tenjin, then called Michizane,[109] was exiled to Tsukushi, his plum tree, following its master, flew in one bound to Dazaifu, and here is Plum-Field Bridge.[110] Green Bridge recalls the aged pine that followed later, and Cherry Bridge the tree

---

106. A sacred text of Buddhism (Karma Sutra). Here Chikamatsu alludes to a line from that text: "If you wish to know the past cause, look at the present effect; if you wish to know the future effect, look at the present cause."

107. The blocks from which illustrated books were printed were frequently made of cherry wood. The illustrated sheets mentioned here featured current scandals, such as lovers' suicides.

108. November 14, 1720. In the lunar calendar the full moon occurs on the fifteenth day of the month.

109. Sugawara no Michizane, unfairly abused at court, was exiled to Dazaifu in Kyūshū. When he was about to depart, he composed a poem of farewell to his favorite plum tree. The tree, moved by this honor, flew after him to Kyūshū. The cherry tree in his garden withered away in grief. Only the pine seemed indifferent, as Michizane complained in another poem. The pine thereupon also flew to Kyūshū.

110. Umeda Bridge. "Green Bridge" is Midori-bashi.

that withered away in grief over parting. Such are the tales still told, demonstrating the power of a single poem.[111]

[JIHEI]: Though born the parishioner of so holy and mighty a god, I shall kill you and then myself. If you ask the cause, it was that I lacked even the wisdom that might fill a tiny Shell Bridge.[112] Our stay in this world has been short as an autumn day. This evening will be the last of your nineteen, of my twenty-eight years. The time has come to cast away our lives. We promised we'd remain together faithfully until you were an old woman and I an old man, but before we knew each other three full years, we have met this disaster. Look, there is Ōe Bridge. We will follow the river from Little Naniwa Bridge to Funairi Bridge. The farther we journey, the closer we approach the road to death.

CHANTER: He laments. She clings to him.

[KOHARU]: Is this already the road to death?

CHANTER: Falling tears obscure from each the other's face and threaten to immerse even the Horikawa bridges.

[JIHEI]: A few steps north and I could glimpse my house, but I will not turn back. I will bury in my breast all thoughts of my children's future, all pity for my wife. We cross southward over the river. Why did they call a place with as many buildings as a bridge has piers "Eight Houses"? Hurry, we want to arrive before the downriver boat from Fushimi comes—with what happy couples sleeping aboard!

Next is Tenma Bridge, a frightening name[113] for us about to depart this world. Here the two streams Yodo and Yamato join in one great river, as fish with water, and as Koharu and I, dying on one blade, will cross together the River of Three Fords.[114] I would like this water for our tomb offering!

[KOHARU]: What have we to grieve about? Although in this world we could not stay together, in the next and through each successive world to come until the end of time we shall be husband and wife. Every summer for my devotions[115] I have copied the All Compassionate and All Merciful Chapter of the Lotus Sutra, in the hope that we may be reborn on one lotus.

---

111. The poem by Michizane bewailing the inconstancy of his pine tree.

112. Shijimi Bridge. Twelve bridges are mentioned in the michiyuki. The lovers' journey takes them along the north bank of Shijimi River to Shijimi Bridge, where they cross to Dōjima. At Little Naniwa Bridge they cross back again to Sonezaki. Continuing eastward, they cross Horikawa and then cross the Tenma Bridge over the Ōkawa. At "Eight Houses" (Hakkenya) they journey eastward along the south bank of the river as far as Kyō Bridge. They cross this bridge to the tip of land at Katamachi and then take the Onari Bridge to Amijima.

113. The characters used for Tenma literally mean "demon."

114. A river in the Buddhist underworld that had to be crossed to reach the world of the dead. Mention here is induced arithmetically: one blade plus two people equals three fords.

115. It was customary for Buddhist monks and some of the laity in Japan to observe a summer retreat from the sixteenth day of the Fourth Month to the fifteenth day of the Seventh Month, a

Sixteen Bridges of Naniwa (Osaka), looking south, from *Views of Naniwa* (*Naniwa no nagame*, 1777). Jihei and Koharu crossed twelve of these bridges to get to Amijima. The acclaimed Three Large Bridges of Naniwa—Naniwa Bridge, Tenjin Bridge, and Tenma Bridge—appear from the center to the left. Kyō Bridge (*far left*), was the eastern entrance to Osaka. Jihei's shop was near Tenjin Bridge. (Courtesy of Osaka Prefectural Nakanoshima Library)

CHANTER: They cross over Sutra Bridge and reach the opposite shore.[116]

[KOHARU]: If I can save living creatures at will when once I mount a lotus calyx in Paradise and become a Buddha, I want to protect women of my profession, so that never again will there be love suicides.

CHANTER: This unattainable prayer stems from worldly attachment, but it touchingly reveals her heart. They cross Onari Bridge.[117] The waters of Noda Creek are shrouded with morning haze; the mountain tips show faintly white.

[JIHEI]: Listen—the voices of the temple bells begin to boom. How much farther can we go on this way? We are not fated to live any longer—let us end it quickly. Come this way.

period of ninety days. During this time they practiced various austerities and copied out the holy books or wrote the Buddha's name over and over.

116. "Opposite shore" implies the Buddhist term *higan* (nirvana).

117. The name Onari is used here for the bridge more properly called Bizenjima because of a play on words meaning "to become a Buddha."

Jihei and Koharu pausing in the middle of a bridge and listening to the temple bells. (Photograph courtesy of Barbara Curtis Adachi Collection, C. V. Starr East Asian Library, Columbia University)

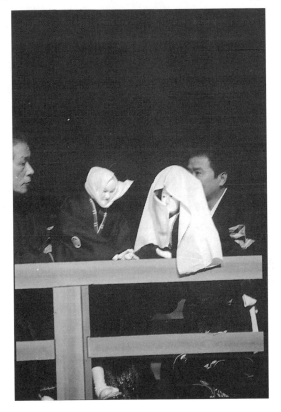

CHANTER: Tears are strung with the 108 prayer beads in their hands. They have come now to Amijima, to the Daichō Temple. The overflowing sluice gate of a little stream beside a bamboo thicket will be their place of death.

Scene 3: Amijima.

[JIHEI]: No matter how far we walk, there'll never be a spot marked "For Suicides." Let us kill ourselves here.

CHANTER: He takes her hand and sits on the ground.

[KOHARU]: Yes, that's true. One place is as good as another to die. But I've been thinking on the way that if they find our dead bodies together, people will say that Koharu and Jihei committed a lovers' suicide. Osan will think then that I treated as mere scrap paper the letter I sent promising her, when she asked me not to kill you, that I would not and vowing to break off all relations with you. She will be sure that I lured her precious husband into a lovers' suicide. She will despise me as a one-night prostitute, a false woman with no sense of decency. I fear her contempt more than the slander of a thousand or ten thousand strangers. I can imagine how she will resent and envy me. That is the greatest obstacle to my salvation. Kill me here, then choose another spot, far away, for yourself.

CHANTER: She leans against him. Jihei joins in her tears of pleading.

[JIHEI]: What foolish worries! Osan has been taken back by my father-in-law. I've divorced her. She and I are strangers now. Why should you feel obliged to a divorced woman? You were saying on the way that you and I will be husband and wife through each successive world until the end of time. Who can criticize us, who can be jealous if we die side by side?

[KOHARU]: But who is responsible for your divorce? You're even less reasonable than I. Do you suppose that our bodies will accompany us to the afterworld? We may die in different places, our bodies may be pecked by kites and crows, but what does it matter as long as our souls are twined together? Take me with you to heaven or to hell!

CHANTER: She sinks again in tears.

[JIHEI]: You're right. Our bodies are made of earth, water, fire, and wind, and when we die they revert to emptiness. But our souls will not decay, no matter how often they're reborn. And here's a guarantee that our souls will be married and never part!

CHANTER: He whips out his dirk and slashes off his black locks at the base of the topknot.

[JIHEI]: Look, Koharu. As long as I had this hair, I was Kamiya Jihei, Osan's husband, but cutting it has made me a monk. I have fled the burning house of the three worlds of delusion; I am a priest, unencumbered by wife, children, or worldly possessions. Now that I no longer have a wife named Osan, you owe her no obligations either.

CHANTER: In tears he flings away the hair.

[KOHARU]: I am happy.

CHANTER: Koharu takes up the dirk and ruthlessly, unhesitatingly, slices through her flowing Shimada coiffure. She casts aside the tresses she has so often washed and combed and stroked. How heartbreaking to see their locks tangled with the weeds and midnight frost of this desolate field!

[JIHEI]: We have escaped the inconstant world, a nun and a priest. Our duties as husband and wife belong to our profane past. It would be best to choose quite separate places for our deaths, a mountain for one, the river for the other. We will pretend that the ground above this sluice gate is a mountain. You will die there. I shall hang myself by this stream. The time of our deaths will be the same, but the method and place will differ. In this way we can honor to the end our duty to Osan. Give me your undersash.

CHANTER: Its fresh violet color and fragrance will be lost in the winds of impermanence; the crinkled silk long enough to wind twice round her body will bind two worlds, this and the next. He firmly fastens one end to the crosspiece of the sluice, then twists the other into a noose for his neck. He

will hang for love of his wife like the "pheasant in the hunting grounds."[118]
Koharu watches Jihei prepare for his death. Her eyes swim with tears, her
mind is distraught.

[KOHARU]: Is that how you're going to kill yourself? — If we are to die apart, I
have only a little while longer by your side. Come near me.

CHANTER: They take each other's hands.

[KOHARU]: It's over in a moment with a sword, but I'm sure you'll suffer. My
poor darling!

CHANTER: She cannot stop the silent tears.

[JIHEI]: Can suicide ever be pleasant, whether by hanging or cutting the
throat? You mustn't let worries over trifles disturb the prayers of your last
moments. Keep your eyes on the westward-moving moon, and worship it as
Amida himself.[119] Concentrate your thoughts on the Western Paradise. If
you have any regrets about leaving the world, tell me now, then die.

[KOHARU]: I have none at all, none at all. But I'm sure you must be worried
about your children.

[JIHEI]: You make me cry all over again by mentioning them. I can almost
see their faces, sleeping peacefully, unaware, poor dears, that their father is
about to kill himself. They're the one thing I can't forget.

CHANTER: He droops to the ground with weeping. The voices of the crows
leaving their nests at dawn rival his sobs. Are the crows mourning his fate?
The thought brings more tears.

[JIHEI]: Listen to them. The crows have come to guide us to the world of the
dead. There's an old saying that every time somebody writes an oath on the
back of a Kumano charm, three crows of Kumano die on the holy mountain.
The first words we've written each New Year have been vows of love, and
how often we've made oaths at the beginning of the month! If each oath has
killed three crows, what a multitude must have perished! Their cries have
always sounded like "beloved, beloved," but hatred for our crime of taking
life makes their voices ring tonight "revenge, revenge!"[120] Whose fault is
it they demand revenge? Because of me you will die a painful death. Forgive me!

CHANTER: He takes her in his arms.

[KOHARU]: No, it's my fault!

CHANTER: They cling to each other, face pressed to face; their sidelocks,

---

118. A reference to a poem by Ōtomo no Yakamochi (718–785): "The pheasant foraging in
the fields of spring reveals his whereabouts to man as he cries for his mate" (*Shūishū*, no. 121).

119. Amida's paradise lies in the west. The moon is also frequently used as a symbol of Buddhist
enlightenment.

120. The cries have always sounded like *kawai, kawai*, but now they sound like *mukui, mukui*.
These Japanese sounds seem more within the range of a crow's articulatory powers than "beloved"
and "revenge."

drenched with tears, freeze in the winds blowing over the fields. Behind them echoes the voice of the Daichō Temple.

[JIHEI]: Even the long winter night seems as short as our lives.

CHANTER: Dawn is already breaking, and matins can be heard. He draws her to him.

[JIHEI]: The moment has come for our glorious end. Let there be no tears on your face when they find you later.

[KOHARU]: There won't be any.

CHANTER: She smiles. His hands, numbed by the frost, tremble before the pale vision of her face, and his eyes are first to cloud. He is weeping so profusely that he cannot control the blade.

[KOHARU]: Compose yourself—but be quick!

CHANTER: Her encouragement lends him strength; the invocations to Amida carried by the wind urge a final prayer. *Namu Amida Butsu.* He thrusts in the savaging sword.[121] Stabbed, she falls backward, despite his staying hand, and struggles in terrible pain. The point of the blade has missed her windpipe, and these are the final tortures before she can die. He writhes with her in agony, then painfully summons his strength again. He draws her to him and plunges his dirk to the hilt. He twists the blade in the wound, and her life fades away like an unfinished dream at dawning.

He arranges her body with her head to the north, face to the west, lying on her right side,[122] and throws his cloak over her. He turns away at last, unable to exhaust with tears his grief over parting. He pulls the sash to him and fastens the noose around his neck. The service in the temple has reached the closing section, the prayers for the dead. "Believers and unbelievers will equally share in the divine grace," the voices proclaim, and at the final words Jihei jumps from the sluice gate.

[JIHEI]: May we be reborn on one lotus! Hail Amida Buddha!

CHANTER: For a few moments he writhes like a gourd swinging in the wind, but gradually the passage of his breath is blocked as the stream is dammed by the sluice gate, where his ties with this life are snapped. Fishermen out for the morning catch find the body in their net.[123]

[FISHERMEN]: A dead man! Look, a dead man! Come here, everybody!

---

121. The invocation of Amida's name freed one from spiritual obstacles, just as a sword freed one from physical obstacles. Here the two images are blended.

122. The dead were arranged in this manner because Shakyamuni Buddha chose this position when he died.

123. "Net" (*ami*) is mentioned because of the connection with fishermen. It is echoed a few lines later in the mention of the name Amijima. The vow of the Buddha to save all living creatures is likened to a net that catches people in its meshes.

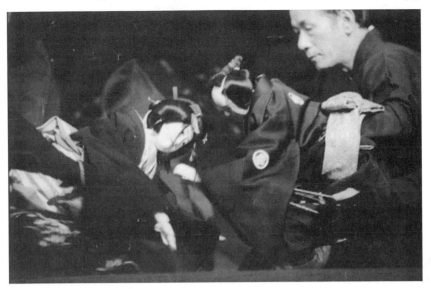

Jihei attempting to make the dying Koharu comfortable. (Photograph courtesy of Barbara Curtis Adachi Collection, C. V. Starr East Asian Library, Columbia University)

CHANTER: The tale is spread from mouth to mouth. People say that they who were caught in the net of Buddha's vow immediately gained salvation and deliverance, and all who hear the tale of the Love Suicides at Amijima are moved to tears.

[*Chikamatsu jōruri shū jō*, NKBT 49: 359–387, translated by Donald Keene]

HOZUMI IKAN

Little is known about Hozumi Ikan (1692–1769) other than that he was a Confucian scholar and devotee of jōruri (puppet theater). He became a consultant for the Takemoto Theater around 1717 and worked closely with Chikamatsu in his last years.

SOUVENIRS OF NANIWA (*NANIWA MIYAGE,* 1738)

Souvenirs of Naniwa was published in 1738, fourteen years after Chikamatsu's death. It is best remembered for the preface written by Hozumi Ikan, which is translated here and contains the only extended comments we have on jōruri in Chikamatsu's own words.

At the heart of Chikamatsu's understanding of the unique demands of jōruri is his conviction that the words of a play should be charged with the feelings of the characters and that those words must create movement in the puppets in order to make them come alive. In that respect, Chikamatsu is especially concerned with the use of language in jōruri, not only in describing a scene or in conveying differences between characters from different social classes, but, above all, in revealing their feelings. The word *jō*, translated here as "feelings," is important because it is the link between the play and the audience: the joys and sorrows of the characters should evoke a sympathetic response in the viewers. In Confucian thought, jō is usually contrasted with giri, which broadly referred to one's duties and obligations to others, and the conflict between giri and jō (or ninjō, human feelings) is fundamental to the plots of many jōruri and kabuki plays. Here, however, Chikamatsu uses giri in a different but related sense, "reason," in an important passage in which he discusses two other nearly synonymous terms: *urei* (sadness) and *awaré* (pathos). His point here is that as long as the sequence of events in a play is governed by reason, moments of pathos will seem natural and even more moving because of their inevitability. Here, then, Chikamatsu uses giri-as-reason in the service of the plot, which at another level, may driven by the conflict between giri-as-duty and human feelings.

Another important term is *gei*, or art. In several places Chikamatsu uses gei to refer to those aspects of a work of art that are not realistic, stating that it is precisely the unrealistic elements that make it art. When comparing jōruri with kabuki—for which he also wrote many plays—he argues for the necessity of such elements in the face of a growing demand for greater realism in the theater. In a key passage, however, he deploys two other critical terms, *uso* and *jitsu*, to discuss art in general. In this context, uso referred to the imaginary or the make-believe, in contrast to jitsu, the true or the real, but he characterizes uso and jitsu in terms of surface and depth as "skin and flesh" (*hiniku*). In Chikamatsu's words, art "lies between" the make-believe or artifice of the "skin"—what the viewer can hear or see on the surface—and an underlying reality, the "flesh." And because art "lies between" the two, it is both and neither: "Art is make-believe and not make-believe; it is real and not real." Chikamatsu offers by way of example in this passage the use of makeup in kabuki, but earlier in his comments he also cites as an instance of *gei* those women characters who say things that in Chikamatsu's day, a real woman would be expected to keep to herself. Although such artifices are not completely true to life as we know it on the surface, they serve to reveal the truth of an inner reality that might otherwise be inaccessible.

When I was visiting Chikamatsu at his home many years ago, he told me the following:

"Jōruri is a living thing: the most important consideration is that these are plays written for puppets, so jōruri differs from other kinds of fiction; the words must create movement. What's more, jōruri competes with the artistry of live actors at nearby kabuki theaters, but since jōruri tries to capture the sympathies of the audience by endowing inanimate puppets with a variety of feelings, the usual plays can hardly be called superb literary works.

"When I was young, I read a story about Heian court life describing how on the occasion of a festival, the snow had piled up rather deeply. An attendant was ordered to clear the snow off the branches of an orange tree, but when he did so, the branches of a nearby pine tree, also bent with snow, recoiled as if in resentment.[124] The stroke of a pen animated a soulless tree. That is because the pine tree, envious at seeing the snow cleared from the orange tree, recoiled its branches in resentment and dumped the snow that was weighing them down. Isn't that just how a living, moving thing would feel? With this model, I understood how to breathe life into the characters of my plays. It is essential, therefore, that even the words describing the scenery of the *michiyuki*, not to mention the narrative passages and the dialogue, be charged with feeling. If a writer does not bear that in mind, his plays will have little emotional impact.

"What poets call 'evocative imagery' is the same thing. For example, a poet may describe in a verse the marvelous scenery of Matsushima or Miyajima, but if it lacks the sense of wonder that comes from immersing oneself in the scene, it would be as if the poet were just looking idly at the portrait of a beautiful woman. A playwright, therefore, must keep in mind that his words should be based on feelings. . . .

"The old jōruri was the same as those tales sung by scandalmongers in the streets today; it had neither fruit nor flower. After I left Kaganojō and began writing plays for Takemoto Gidayū,[125] I took more care with my words, so my plays were a cut above those of the past.

"For example, my first principle is to distinguish between the social position of each and every character, from the nobility and the samurai on down, and to depict them accordingly, from their demeanor to the way they speak. By the same token, even among the samurai, there are daimyō, chief retainers, and others whose stipends vary according to their rank, so I distinguish one from the other based on their social position. This is because it is essential that readers sympathize with the feelings of each character.

"The words of jōruri depict reality as it is, but being a form of art it also contains elements that are not found in real life. Specifically, female characters often say things a real woman would not say, but such instances are examples of art. Since they speak openly of things that a real woman would not talk about, the character's true feelings are revealed. Thus, when a playwright models a female character on the feelings of a real woman and conceals such things, her deepest thoughts will not be revealed, and contrary to his hopes, the play will not be entertaining. It follows that when one watches a play without paying attention to the artistry, one will probably criticize it on the grounds that the female characters say many discomfiting things that are inappropriate for a woman to say. However, such instances should be regarded as art. There are, in addition, many other aspects that one should regard as art rather than reality,

---

124. The passage appears in "The Safflower" chapter of *The Tale of Genji*.

125. Kaganojō (1635–1711) and Chikugonojō (Takemoto Gidayū, 1651–1714) were important jōruri chanters (tayū). Chikamatsu wrote his first play for Takemoto Gidayū in 1686, after which he wrote only three more plays for Kaganojō, the last in 1699.

such as when a villain acts too cowardly or the humor is actually buffoonery. People should understand this when watching a play.

"Some playwrights, thinking that sadness is essential to a jōruri, often put in words like 'How sad it is!' or the lines are chant tearfully, as in the Bunyabushi style,[126] but that is not how I write plays. The sadness in all my plays is based entirely on reason [giri]. Since the audience will be moved when the logic [rikugi] of the dramatization is convincing [giri ni tsumarite], the more restrained the words and the chanting are, the more moving the play will be. Thus, when one says of a moment of pathos 'How sad it is!' the connotations are lost, and in the end, the feeling conveyed is weak. It is essential that the moment be filled with pathos in and of itself, without having to say 'How sad it is!' For example, when you praise a landscape such as Matsushima by saying 'Oh, what a beautiful scene!' you have said all you can about it in a few words but to no avail. If you wish to praise a scene, pointing out all its features objectively will reveal its intrinsic appeal naturally, without having to say 'it is a beautiful scene.' This applies to everything of this sort."

Someone said that in this day and age, people won't accept a play unless it is very realistic and logically convincing, so there are many things in the old stories that people will not stand for now. It is precisely for this reason that people are apt to think kabuki actors are skillful when their acting resembles real life. They think the most important thing is for the actor playing a chief retainer to imitate a real chief retainer and the actor playing a daimyō to imitate a real daimyō. They will not accept the sort of childish antics of the past.

Chikamatsu answered: "That argument seems quite reasonable, but it fails to grasp the true method of art. Art is something that lies between the skin and the flesh [hiniku], between the make-believe [uso] and the real [jitsu]. In today's world, of course, given the preference for realistic acting, an actor playing a chief retainer may imitate the speech and mannerisms of a real chief retainer, but if that's the case, would a real chief retainer of a daimyō wear makeup on his face like an actor? Or would it be entertaining if an actor, saying that a real chief retainer does not use makeup, appeared on stage and performed with his beard growing wild and his own bald head? This is what I mean by 'between the skin and the flesh.' Art is make-believe and not make-believe; it is real and not real; entertainment lies between the two.

"In this connection, a lady-in-waiting in the old imperial court was in love with a certain man. The two communicated their feelings for each other with passion, but the woman lived deep within the palace. The man was unable to visit her in the women's quarters, so she could see him only on rare occasions through the gaps of the hanging blinds at court. She longed for him so much

_____

126. A style of chanting used by Okamoto Bunya in the late seventeenth century. Chikamatsu preferred the style used by Takemoto Gidayū (Gidayūbushi), which became the standard.

that she had a wooden image carved in his likeness. It was unlike ordinary dolls in that its face was exactly like the man's down to the tiniest hair, even the color of his complexion. The pores of his skin, the holes for the ears and nose, and even the number of teeth in his mouth were reproduced exactly. Since the image was made with the man right next to it, the only difference between the man and the doll was the presence of a soul in the one but not the other. Even so, when the woman drew near and gazed at it, because the man's body had been duplicated exactly, her passion cooled; she found it somehow repulsive and frightening. Court lady that she was, her love for the man cooled as well. Just keeping the doll around became annoying, and it appears that she soon threw it away.

"With this example in mind, if we duplicate a living person exactly, even if it is Yang Gueifei,[127] we will become disgusted with it. For this reason, whether painting an image or carving it in wood, there will be places where the artist takes liberties, even while copying the original form, on the grounds that it is a fabrication; but in the end, this is what people love. It is the same with new plot situations: even though the story resembles the original version, there will be places where the artist takes liberties, but in the end, this is what makes it art and entertaining. There are many instances where the dialogue in a play should also be viewed with this in mind."

[*Chikamatsu jōruri shū ge*, NKBT 50: 356–359, introduction and translation by Michael Brownstein]

---

127. A concubine of the Tang dynasty's Emperor Xuanzong (r. 712–756), remembered for her great beauty.

Chapter 7

CONFUCIAN STUDIES AND

LITERARY PERSPECTIVES

In the early modern period, Confucianism, which had entered Japan together with Chinese culture and writing in the ancient period, emerged as the dominant mode of thought. Specifically, it was the Zhu Xi (1138–1200) school of Confucianism that was welcomed and supported by the samurai rulers, who used it to provide ideological support to the bakufu-domain system. Confucianism is a practical moral philosophy concerned with society and government and was absorbed in Japan primarily through the study of the Confucian classics, particularly the Four Books: Confucius's *Analects* (*Lunyu*, J. *Rongo*), *Mencius* (*Mengzi*, J. *Mōshi*), *The Doctrine of the Mean* (*Zhongyong*, J. *Chūyō*), and *The Great Learning* (*Daxue*, J. *Daigaku*).

Confucius (551–479 B.C.E.), a scholar-teacher who lived in the late Zhou period when the kingdom was in a state of decline and turmoil, addressed mainly the rulers (the princes and officials) concerning the restoration of social order and stability based on a moral and social code. The *Analects*, the collection of his most memorable pronouncements, focuses on the practicalities of interpersonal relationships and self-cultivation in the context of these relationships. Self-cultivation on the part of the rulers was in turn reflected in the conduct of government. Confucius stressed five cardinal relationships in the ethics of a family-centered society, those between lord and subject, father and son, husband and wife, elder brother and younger brother, and friend and friend. The most important of these relationships was that between father and son or parent and child, making filial piety (*xiao*, J. *kō*) the primary virtue. Since governance was modeled on the family, the practice of filial piety brought stability not only to the family but to society as a whole. Confucius also stressed humaneness (*ren*, J. *jin*), the notion of mutual feeling or reciprocity, with the expectation, for example, that the ruler ideally would treat the people as he himself would want to be treated. Another Confucian virtue was ritual decorum or propriety (*li*, J. *rei*), which provided a means of regulating and refining human desires so that they would remain within the proper bounds, giving order to one's personal life and providing a means for the ruler to express his virtue or moral power. One of the principal assumptions behind Confucius's thought was the concept of Heaven (*tian*, J. *ten*), a cosmic moral order possessing intelligence and will. Adherence to the Heavenly Way, which provided moral guidelines for the individual, made it possible to establish order in human society.

Mencius (385?–312? B.C.E.), the first great successor to Confucius, reaffirmed the Confucian confidence in the efficacy of morality in bringing stability to both the individual and society. His thoughts, gathered in the *Mencius*, expands on the Confucian idea of humaneness, the capacity for mutual respect based on the recognition of a common humanity. Mencius also stressed the complementary principle of rightness (*yi*, J. *gi*), an idea of justice and correct behavior in particular situations, and the human capacity for moral and social perfectibility through self-cultivation. He is especially noted for his discussion of the "four beginnings"—natural tendencies in all human beings that can be cultivated into the capacities for humaneness, rightness, ritual decorum, and wisdom. Significantly, both Confucius and Mencius looked back to the golden age of the Three Dynasties—Xia (ca. 2100–ca. 1600 B.C.E.), Shang, and Zhou (ca. 1027–256 B.C.E.)—and the ancient sage-kings—Yao, Shun, and Yu—whom they believed had governed according to the Heavenly Way.

SONG CONFUCIANISM

The Zhu Xi school of Confucianism, usually referred to as Confucianism of the Song period (960–1279), was introduced to Japan in the twelfth century. It became popular in the Tokugawa period as a philosophy of the new age and was eventually embraced by the bakufu as the country's official philosophy. In contrast to Buddhism, particularly Jōdo, or Pure Land, Buddhism, which had a negative, critical view of this phenomenal world, Song Confucianism affirmed both this world and human society. Song Confucianism covered issues ranging from cosmology to views of history and was broad enough to oppose both the worldviews represented by Buddhism and the folk beliefs associated with Shintō.

Scholars of the Zhu Xi school held that all things in nature are governed by a rational principle (*li*, J. *ri*) and material force (*qi*, J. *ki*). Rational principle exists within material force and gives it order. Human beings, too, are made up of material force and rational principle, with the differences in the material force accounting for the physical and moral variations among individuals. Rational principle was thought to be identical with "original human nature" (*xing*, J. *sei*). Consequently, the pursuit of rational principle was a means of developing the potential of one's inner nature to guide one in correct behavior. As a person begins to understand rational principle, he or she will be able to live in accordance with it and with the Heavenly Way. Human beings, then, originally are good, but their goodness has been blocked by material force, which makes them sink like jewels in dirty water. Song Confucianism was thus both a metaphysical system and a practical form of ethics based on rational principle, which gave order to the universe. Like earlier Confucians, the followers of the Zhu Xi school stressed the importance of the five cardinal relationships.

The first key figure in the spread of Song Confucianism in Japan was Fujiwara Seika (1561–1619), a former Buddhist priest who lectured on Confucian texts to Tokugawa Ieyasu and other daimyō. Many of those who studied with Seika later became teachers or prominent scholars. The most famous of them was Hayashi Razan (1583–1657), who gave a series of public lectures in Kyoto on the *Analects*, which was an attempt to extend the knowledge of this learning beyond the limited circle of aristocratic families and Zen priests, who until this time had monopolized Confucian studies. Razan entered the service of Tokugawa Ieyasu in 1607 and served four shōguns. Two prominent scholar-teachers who actually practiced the Zhu Xi school's Confucianism and whose works appear in the following sections were Nakae Tōju, who opened a school in Ōmi Province, and Yamazaki Ansai (1618–1682), who established a Confucian academy (the Kimon school) in Kyoto.

NAKAE TŌJU

Nakae Tōju (1608–1648), a samurai in the service of a feudal lord in Shikoku, resigned his post when he was twenty-seven to return to his native village in Ōmi Province, near Lake Biwa, to care for his aging mother and devote himself to scholarship. Around this time Tōju wrote *Dialogue with the Elder* (*Okina mondō*, revised in 1650), in which he explains the essential points of the Zhu Xi school and how they should be applied to actual situations. The book takes the form of a dialogue in which the Elder, a venerable master called Tenkun (Heavenly Ruler),[1] answers questions asked him by his disciple Taijū.[2] The

---

1. The name Tenkun comes from a passage in the ancient Chinese treatise *Xunzi* and refers to the human mind/heart (*shin/kokoro*).

2. The name Taijū, which literally means "fill the body" or "pervade the body," is used in the *Mencius* and refers to *ki*, or material force.

following is from the opening of the first volume, which focuses on the Confucian *Classic of Filial Piety* as a guide to human conduct. Here Tōju concentrates on filial piety (*kō*) as a treasure that exists within each person and permeates all existence. In Heaven it becomes the Heavenly Way; on Earth it becomes the Earthly Way; and for humans, it becomes the Human Way. For Tōju, filial piety embodies two fundamental virtues, "love" (*ai*) and "respect" (*kei*), found throughout the Five Relationships: between parent and child, ruler and minister, husband and wife, elder sibling and younger sibling, friend and friend. The key relationship was between parent and child, infused by love and respect, thus should support all the other social relationships and become the basis for all the other Confucian virtues. Tōju emphasizes that each person has an inherent good that must be cultivated and practiced. He goes on to argue that everyone—lord, retainer, or commoner—is endowed by nature with "luminous virtue" (*meitoku*), which, if one takes into account the "time, place, and one's status," enables one to act correctly in any situation.

DIALOGUE WITH THE ELDER
(*OKINA MONDŌ*, 1640–1641, REV. 1650)

On the Virtue of Filial Piety

TAIJŪ'S QUESTION: People's hearts appear in a variety of forms, so there is great diversity in their actions. When distinguishing between right and wrong in a particular situation, people often become confused and do not know which way to turn. Which way should we choose to govern the course of our lives?

ELDER'S RESPONSE: Each of us possesses a spiritual treasure unique under Heaven, called "the pinnacle of virtue, the essence of the Way."[3] You can make this treasure your guide, protecting it with your spirit and activating it with your body. This treasure is fully in accord with the Sun above us and is fully apparent to the Four Seas below us. Therefore, when you take part in the Five Relationships, they harmonize without discord.[4] When you apply this treasure to the wise deities, they accept it. When you order the realm under Heaven, all under Heaven are pacified; when you govern the state, the state is in order; when you organize your household, your household is regulated; when you apply it to yourself, you become single-minded; and when you follow it in your heart, your heart is clear. When you extend this treasure, it expands beyond Heaven and Earth, and when you put it away, it buries itself in the depths of your heart. It is truly a sublime and holy

---

3. The pinnacle of virtue here is "filial piety." This phrase is taken from the *Classic of Filial Piety*, sec. 1.

4. Also from the *Classic of Filial Piety*, sec. 1.

treasure. For these reasons, when people take good care of it, the ruler has a long, prosperous reign over the Four Seas; the various lords live in splendor in a unified realm; the houses of nobles and ministers flourish; the military make names for themselves and rise in rank; and the common people store up their goods and take pleasure in them.

Discarding this treasure means that the Human Way does not take hold. Not only does the Human Way not take hold, but the Heavenly Way and the Earthly Way do not take hold either. Not only do the Heavenly Way and the Earthly Way not take hold, but the mysterious changes of the Great Void cannot take place. Great Void, Three Realms,[5] Universe, Demons and Spirits, Creation and Transformation, Life and Death—this treasure encompasses them all. Seeking out and studying this treasure is known as the scholarship of Confucius. Those who embody this treasure from birth are known as sages; those who acquire it through learning and follow it conscientiously are recognized as wise. In order to shed light on the darkness of myriad generations, Confucius wrote the *Classic of Filial Piety* to serve as a mirror for seeking and studying this treasure. However, in the eighteen hundred or so years since the Qin dynasty,[6] few people have completely understood this treasure. Now in this age of the Great Ming, many have come to revere, trust, propagate, and elucidate this classic.[7] The Great Shun[8] embodied this treasure and rose from being a commoner to the rank of Son of Heaven. King Wen embodied this treasure and served at the side of the Heavenly Emperor.[9] Tongying preserved the treasure and thus made the Heavenly Weaving Maiden his wife.[10] Wuer preserved this treasure and was spared heavenly punishment for evil deeds committed in a former life.[11] It is impossible to enumerate all the wondrous examples that have been handed down to us from the past. You must redouble your faith and apply this treasure well!

TAIJŪ'S QUESTION: Such a treasure is truly something well worth discovering, but if the Way it comprises is so vast, then it may be impossible for people in our station to live up to it.

ELDER'S RESPONSE: That is not a good way of explaining this issue. It is

---

5. The Three Realms are Heaven, Earth, and Humanity.

6. Qin dynasty (221–207 B.C.E.), when the Confucian texts were burned.

7. When Tōju was writing in 1641, the Ming dynasty (1338–1644) still governed China.

8. Shun was believed to have been a sage ruler of the Xia dynasty.

9. First ruler of the Zhou dynasty. In the *Book of Songs*, no. 235 (King Wen), King Wen is declared to have governed the realm in direct communion with a supreme deity referred to as the "Heavenly Emperor."

10. The story of Tongying is found in the Yuan-dynasty (1206–1368) work *Twenty-four Exemplars of Filial Piety*, was translated into Japanese as *Nijūshi-kō*, a Muromachi-period *otogi-zōshi*; and was well known in Tōju's time.

11. Wuer is a paragon of filial piety featured in a Ming-dynasty collection.

precisely because it is a vast Way that ordinary people like us are able to grasp it. The light of the sun and the moon, for example, is great, so any creature with eyes can use that light. The very fact that this treasure is so vast means that without distinguishing between exalted and humble or male and female, all people, both young and old—provided they still have their original hearts—can follow the Way. When considering this treasure, we realize that in Heaven, it becomes the Heavenly Way; on Earth, it becomes the Earthly Way; and when it appears among people, it becomes the Human Way. Originally it had no name, but in order to teach sentient beings, sages in the distant past gave it an identity, calling it "filial piety." Since that time, it has come to be known to even the humblest of dense and deluded men and women. Its true nature, however, has rarely been fathomed, even by venerable scholars, learned Confucians, or others with extraordinary intellectual faculties. Because of this lack of awareness, people have generally held that if filial piety is just a simple matter of obeying one's parents, it is only a short-sighted principle of little value. Confucius lamented this state of affairs, so in order to clear the hearts of those for myriad ages to come, in the *Classic of Filial Piety* he explained that the virtue of filial piety, wondrous and incomprehensible, vast and deep, is a marvelous way without beginning or end.

If you wish to explain in simple words what runs through filial piety, it can be boiled down to the two terms, "love" [*ai*] and "reverence" [*kei*]. "Love" means to cherish. "Reverence" means to revere those above and to avoid treating lightly or contemptuously those below. For example, filial piety is like a bright mirror. Depending on the form and the color of whatever looks into this mirror, the images reflected will continue to change, but the shape of the brightly reflecting mirror itself will remain the same. In the same way, the human relationships between father and son or ruler and minister change in thousands and tens of thousands of ways, but not one of these relationships fails to contain these qualities of virtue, love, and reverence.

To further explain filial piety and its relationship to love and reverence, one needs first to address the notion of the Five Relationships. Since love and reverence for one's parents serve as the basis of all these relationships, we do not distinguish between the basic principle and its application but refer to it simply as "filial conduct" [*kōkō*]. Accordingly, because love and reverence are found in relationships in various manifestations, Confucius gave them names and described them in his teachings. To love and revere one's ruler with an undivided heart is referred to as "loyalty" [*chū*]. To love and revere one's ministers and subordinates according to the proper decorum is referred to as "humaneness" [*jin*]. To teach one's children well, loving and revering them, is referred to as "compassion" [*ji*]. To love and revere one's elder brother in accordance with harmony and order is referred to as "deference" [*tei*]. To strive toward goodness and to love and revere one's younger brother is referred to as "reverence" [*kei*]. To preserve the correct modes of conduct and to love and revere one's husband is referred to as "obedience" [*jun*]. To preserve righteousness and to love and revere one's wife is referred to as "harmony" [*wa*]. Finally, to love and revere one's friends without deception is referred to as "faithfulness" [*shin*].

When we discuss this principle from the perspective of the body, we realize that the clarity of our ears and eyes, the activity of our four limbs, and the laws governing motion, inertia, relaxation, and incumbency all are, without exception, present along with the virtue of filial piety and its corresponding love and respect. As we have seen, because this is a benign and morally based Way, no matter how dense and deluded men and women may be, anyone, even small children at our feet, can comprehend it and practice it well. At the same time, even renowned sages rarely understand filial piety completely. It is truly a singular Way of conduct and a precious treasure without equal. But when it is treated like Bian He's Jade Matrix and is incapable of illuminating the darkness of this vulgar world, the resulting state of affairs is truly lamentable.[12]

[*Nakae Tōju*, NST 29: 22–25, translated by Lawrence Marceau]

CONFUCIAN VIEWS OF LITERATURE

The modern scholar Nakamura Yukihiko identified three prominent Confucian-based views of literature in early modern Japan.[13] The first was the "transmitting the Way" (*saidō*) theory, which regarded literature as a means or vehicle for transmitting or teaching the Confucian way. This position assumed that literature was subordinate to or a tool for Confucianism. The second view was the "encouraging good, chastising evil" (*kanzen chōaku*) theory, which held that the purpose of literature was teaching moral behavior. According to this view, the purpose of the love poems in the *Book of Songs* (*Shijing*) was to encourage good and discourage evil by revealing the positive or negative consequences of human action and behavior. The third view assumed that because the function of Confucianism was to govern and aid society, there was no need for literature, which could be used as a vehicle for encouraging immoral behavior. To come into contact with such literature, to be seduced by its beauty, was to lose focus

---

12. Bian He repeatedly tried to present a jade matrix to the emperor, but the jade was not recognized for its true value, and Bian He was punished by having both his feet amputated. He was finally recognized and rewarded for his loyalty. The anecdote is found in the Legalist philosophical text *Han Feizi*.

13. Nakamura Yukihiko, *Kinsei bungei shichōkō* (Tokyo: Iwanami shoten, 1975), chap. 1.

and will, a position summarized by the phrase "playing with things, losing will" (*ganbutsu sōshi*).

These Confucian views of literature did not mean, however, that Japanese Confucian scholars were indifferent to or opposed to literature. On the contrary, Confucian scholars such as Fujiwara Seika and Hayashi Razan were avid practitioners and readers of literature, as evident in their collected writings: the voluminous *Prose Writings of Master Fujiwara* (*Fujiwara sensei bunshū*) and the *Collected Works of Master Hayashi Razan* (*Razan Hayashi sensei shū*). Seika also produced a collection of his waka and wrote a book on ancient theories of Chinese literature, while Razan wrote a commentary on *Essays in Idleness* (*Tsurezuregusa*) and edited collections of tales of the supernatural.

YAMAZAKI ANSAI

The scholar most responsible for making the Zhu Xi school of Confucianism the orthodoxy was Yamazaki Ansai (1618–1682), for whom the ultimate goal of this philosophy was preserving the correct social order. To achieve this, he stressed the attitude of "reverence" (Ch. *jing*, J. *kei*), which implied stability of mind and circumspect behavior.

JAPANESE LESSER LEARNING
(*YAMATO SHŌGAKU*, 1660)

In the following passage from the preface to *Japanese Lesser Learning*, Ansai reveals his views of vernacular fiction, condemning *The Tales of Ise* and *The Tale of Genji*, two Heian romances about the amorous heroes Narihira and Genji, respectively. The two texts, which recently had become available in woodblock-print editions to commoner audiences, were considered by many readers to be ideal vehicles for vicariously reliving the elegance of the Heian court. In *Japanese Lesser Learning* Ansai attacks the late medieval Confucian scholar Kiyohara Nobukata (1475–1550), who argued that even though these Heian classics included stories about love, they also taught respect and courtesy. Ansai urged his readers to focus on his own work instead of what he termed "licentiousness." This view, of "playing with things, losing will," was so widely accepted that even Emperor Kōmyō (r. 1643–1654), an avid student of Chinese poetry, would not go near classical Japanese poetry or *The Tale of Genji* because of the deleterious effect he thought these works had had on the court.

The fact that people today will frivolously walk down a road from which there is no return is due to the existence of *The Tale of Genji* and *The Tales of Ise*. It is said that *The Tale of Genji* was written as an admonishment for men and women. It is extremely doubtful, however, that such frivolity could serve to admonish anyone. Kiyohara no Nobukata asserted that although *The Tales of*

Ise deals with matters of lust, it also includes depictions of ritual decorum and humaneness and that Confucius and Mencius would have acted in the same way as Narihira did if they had been in his position. It is not worth discussing the merits or failings of such falsehoods!

[*Yamazaki Ansai zenshū, zokuhen ge,* translated by Lawrence Marceau]

ANDŌ TAMEAKIRA

A Confucian scholar samurai and commentator on the Japanese classics, Andō Tameakira (1659–1716) spent most of his career in the service of Tokugawa Mitsukuni (1628–1700), the lord of the Mito Domain who supported such scholarly projects as the *Great History of Japan* (*Dai Nihon shi*) and a commentary on the *Man'yōshū*, the ancient-period anthology of poetry, both of which Tameakira contributed to.

SEVEN ESSAYS ON MURASAKI SHIKIBU (*SHIKA SHICHIRON*, 1703)

The following selection from Andō Tameakira's *Seven Essays on Murasaki Shikibu* is a defense of *The Tale of Genji* from a Confucian standpoint. In the fifth essay, "The Intentions of the Author," Tameakira counters earlier Buddhist views of *The Tale of Genji* as "wild words and specious phrases" (*kyōgen kigo*), as senseless and deceiving fiction, as well as earlier Confucian views of the novel as causing moral depravity. He argues that fiction has a deeper Confucian purpose in "encouraging good and chastising evil."[14] For Tameakira, Murasaki Shikibu is the model of a virtuous woman, and her *Tale of Genji* teaches women proper values and social manners.

The Intentions of the Author

The Tale of Genji portrays human feelings [*ninjō*] and social conventions without passing judgment on such matters. By presenting the manners and mores of the upper, middle, and lower ranks of the aristocracy in the context of their romantic interests, the novel avoids didactic language. The reader is left to draw moral lessons from the story on his own. While the novel's greater purpose is to provide instruction for women, it also contains numerous lessons for men. A few illustrative examples follow:

In chapter 1, "The Paulownia Court," the Kiritsubo emperor has such a passionate nature that he lavishes excessive attention on a low-ranking consort, Lady Kiritsubo, completely disregarding the criticism of others. This self-

---

14. Tameakira was probably influenced here by the *gūgen* (allegorical) view of fiction, which assumes that the author's thought is not directly expressed but instead is embedded or couched in fictional form.

indulgent behavior is an affront to society and has become a cause for concern not simply among his highest-ranking councillors but among all his subjects as well. Disgraceful conduct of this sort certainly provides later emperors with an instructive example. In addition, the emperor's fondness for Genji, his son by Lady Kiritsubo, leads him to treat the child as if he were to become nothing less than a crown prince. He even acts as if Genji might take the place of the existing crown prince. Is this not conduct beneath the dignity of an emperor? Reading about the "arrogant and intractable behavior" of Lady Kokiden, the imperial consort and the mother of the crown prince, and her deliberate disregard for the emperor's bereavement following the death of his favorite consort should prompt more prudent behavior by an empress or a lady-in-waiting of lesser rank. Poor conduct of this sort inevitably leads to a bad reputation.

Chapter 2, "The Broom Tree," includes the scene in which Genji and his companions spend a rainy night comparing the attributes of various women. The novel's overarching goal is to provide moral instruction for women. Accordingly, this chapter is intended to appeal to the interests of a female readership.

In chapter 3, "The Shell of the Locust," the careless manner in which the character Nokiba no Ogi leaves her robes untied while playing a game of go and later remains fast asleep in the bedchamber as Genji approaches her is a clear example of moral laxity. As for Utsusemi, Nokiba no Ogi's companion, the author intended that because of her indifference to Genji's romantic advances, she would stand out as a model of chastity. . . .

In the remaining chapters the actions and emotions of the characters continue to be portrayed with all their good and bad features exposed before the eyes of the reader with the kind of verisimilitude one finds in looking at an image reflected in a mirror. The author's true intention is to offer the world a moral lesson. It is not her intention to deceive readers with fictional tales and falsehoods.

In chapter 25, "Fireflies" (Hotaru), Genji discusses earlier fiction:

> These works are not based on the actions of particular people who actually existed. Rather, they are inspired by the feeling that some events and people in this world are infinitely interesting to see and hear. Whether these things are good or bad, they should be passed on to later generations. Unable to keep such things bottled up inside, the authors take various details from things that they know and use them as the starting points for their works.

This commentary on fiction should be seen as nothing other than Murasaki Shikibu's own understanding and intentions concerning the novel. One should not call her novel a work of fabrications and falsehoods. In the way that it portrays the lives of people as they existed in this world, *The Tale of Genji* encourages good and punishes evil. Those who fail to appreciate the author's intention as such—instead calling the novel a guide to indecent behavior—are not even worthy of contempt.

[*Kinsei shintō ron, zenki kokugaku*, NST 39: 431–433, translated by Patrick Caddeau]

CHINESE STUDIES AND LITERARY PERSPECTIVES

Chinese studies (*kangaku*) in the seventeenth century tended to focus on the study of Confucianism, particularly that branch influenced by the Song Confucian philosopher Zhu Xi (1130–1200) and his followers. Two major Confucian scholars who opposed this school of Song Confucianism were Itō Jinsai (1627–1705) and Ogyū Sorai (1666–1728), who sought to return directly to the Confucian classics through a systematic philological and historical study of ancient Chinese texts. The views of these two scholar-philosophers on the function and effects of literary texts are critical to understanding the ways in which literature and literary studies were perceived and defended in the early modern period. Their writings also deeply influenced the perspective of the *kokugaku* (nativist learning) scholars who followed them.

ITŌ JINSAI

Itō Jinsai (1627–1705), the oldest son of a Kyoto merchant, started studying Chinese at a young age and became a devoted student of Zhu Xi, or Song Confucianism. After an illness when he was twenty-eight, he handed over the family business to his younger brother, became a recluse, and studied Buddhism and Daoism. It was at this time that he began to have doubts about Zhu Xi's philosophy. In 1662, with the help of his son Tōgai, Jinsai established a private school in Kyoto, the Kogidō (Hall of Ancient Meaning), where he is said to have attracted three thousand students from a wide variety of professions and classes. Jinsai's teachings were constructed around a sustained critique of Song Confucianism. Appropriately, his school stood on the east bank of the Horikawa River, directly across from Ansai's school, established in 1655 on the west bank, which firmly upheld Song Confucianism and rejected the value of poetry. Of the prominent Confucian scholars in the latter half of the seventeenth century—including Yamazaki Ansai—Jinsai was by far the most influential.

Jinsai believed that the speculative, metaphysical philosophy of Song Confucianism could not serve as a model for everyday practical ethics but, rather, that the way of the sages could be learned through a renewed understanding of the *Analects* and the *Mencius*. Jinsai pointed out that *The Great Learning* and *The Doctrine of the Mean*, two of the Four Books (along with the *Analects* and the *Mencius*) that had been the basis of Song Confucianism, contained theories added by later philosophers and in some ways were actually closer to Buddhism and Daoism. Accordingly, Jinsai argued that the later commentaries should be abandoned and instead recommended a careful rereading of the original *Analects* and *Mencius* based on a systematic linguistic reconstruction of the meaning of the texts' ancient words. (Today, Jinsai's approach is referred to as the "study of ancient meanings" [*kogigaku*] because his aim was clarifying the original meanings of the words of the Confucian classics. His approach in turn is considered part of the larger movement of *kogaku*, or "ancient learning," which Ogyū Sorai later took up.)

For Jinsai, human character was not inherently good, as the Zhu Xi school of Confucianism claimed. Instead, it held the potential for good, which had to be developed and expanded through everyday practice or action. Jinsai rejected the Song Confucian dualism of rational principle (*ri*) and material force (*ki*), contending that it was solely the movement of material force that had led to the creation and life of all things. In Song Confucianism, the Heavenly Way (*tendō*) was connected to the Human Way (*jindō*) through rational principle, which informed both. For Jinsai, the Way (*michi*) was not, as the Song Confucianists believed, a lofty state but was embedded in the low (*zoku*), the common and everyday. The world as material force was in constant flux, in Jinsai's view, and the key question was how to conduct oneself in everyday life. In contrast to the Song Confucian notion of "original human character" (*sei*), which was thought to be good and based on moral virtues, the Jinsai school stressed human emotions (*ninjō*), which were continually changing and rooted in everyday life. The value and function of poetry were its ability to express both everyday life and these human emotions. For Jinsai, poetry provided an expression of or release for human emotions, desires, and everyday needs. This humanistic conception of literature, which looked at both everyday life and human emotions in a positive light, was also the central assumption underlying the Genroku popular fiction of Ihara Saikaku and the jōruri puppet theater of Chikamatsu Monzaemon. This attitude toward poetry also began to attract students to the Kogidō who were more interested in composing Chinese poetry than in Confucian studies.

THE MEANING OF WORDS IN THE ANALECTS AND THE MENCIUS (GOMŌ JIGI, 1683)

In *The Meaning of Words in the Analects and the Mencius*, a major treatise written at the peak of his career, Itō Jinsai outlines his philosophy concerning such key issues as the Heavenly Way, rational principle (*ri*), and virtue (*toku*). In the following passage from the section on the *Book of Songs*, a Confucian classic, he reveals his views on poetry, which opposes the Song Confucian view that its function was to "encourage good and punish evil." Jinsai argues that the text took on a life of its own after it was composed.

In regard to a method for reading the *Book of Songs*, it is said that the poems dealing with virtue stimulate the virtue in one's heart, while those that deal with vice serve to correct one's tendency toward licentiousness. This is indeed true, but in their application, what matters for poetry is not the author's intent but, rather, the reader's reaction. The emotions found in these poems are of a thousand varieties and take myriad forms so they appear never to be exhausted. The lofty read the poems and through them rise higher, while the mean read the poetry and sink lower. Whether the shape is round or square, people will accept what they encounter. Be it great or small, people will follow what they see. [vol. 2, sec. 12]

[*Itō Jinsai, Itō Tōgai*, NST 33: 86, translated by Lawrence Marceau]

POSTSCRIPT TO *THE COLLECTED WORKS OF BO JUYI* (*HAKUSHIMONJŪ*, 1704)

In the following passage from his postscript to *The Collected Works of Bo Juyi*, Itō Jinsai quotes criticisms of various Tang-dynasty (618–906) poets, including that of Bo Juyi,[15] who is criticized for being "vulgar," "commonplace," or "mundane" (*zoku*). Jinsai then argues that the *Book of Songs* and, by implication, poetry in general commends the common and the everyday. That is, it is precisely because poetry is grounded in the everyday, vulgar world that it is valuable and effective.

Poetry, after all, values commonplace elements. The reason that the *Book of Songs* is considered one of the classics is that it deals with the commonplace. The essence of poetry is in the oral expression of inborn emotions. If a poem is based on the mundane world, it will encompass the full range of these emotions. If, however, the poem is overly polished, it will detract from the inborn emotions and destroy the poet's material force [*ki*].

[*Itō Jinsai, Itō Tōgai*, NST 33: 216, translated by Lawrence Marceau]

QUESTIONS FROM CHILDREN (*DŌJIMON*, 1693)

Although the Jinsai school generally distinguishes between the function of the *Book of Songs* as belles lettres and as an ethical text, Jinsai asserts in the passage translated here that poetry can serve a political function for rulers. He warns, however, that those in a position of responsibility should not overindulge in poetry.

---

15. Bo Juyi (772–846) was a Tang-dynasty poet who was popular in Japan, but his poetry was criticized in the Edo period for being low, common, and everyday (*zoku*).

Poetry serves as a guide to the emotions and character. Even though the number of people in the world is large and the procession of lives from the past to the present is endless, when you wish to know about those people's emotions, there is nothing that surpasses the *Book of Songs*. When you learn from these songs, things are ordered; when you refuse to learn from them, things are chaotic. This is why the former kings preserved them untouched and cherished them without change. . . . For this reason it is imperative to study the *Book of Songs*. . . . [vol. 3, sec. 5]

Chinese poetry is the chanted expression of emotions and thoughts in the mind.[16] Composing Chinese poetry is also truly beneficial, but not doing so is not harmful. Chinese poetry is the most elegant of the polite accomplishments, but becoming overly fond of it is not good. Poetry is fine for recluses in the wooded mountains, who have no pressing business. In their leisure, they can use it to vent their emotions, to sing nostalgically. They can express their feelings of despondence and boredom. But if aristocrats, generals and ministers, scholars, officials, and others in high position and office overindulge even once in poetic composition, they will lose direction, which will lead to their downfall. Beware! [vol. 3, sec. 39]

[*Kinsei shisōka bunshū*, NKBT 97: 154–155, 183, translated by Lawrence Marceau]

ITŌ TŌGAI

While Itō Jinsai enjoys a reputation as one of Japan's most creative and influential early modern philosophers, much of his thought would have been lost to posterity were it not for the efforts of his son Tōgai (1670–1736). Personally responsible for publishing the great portion of his father's writings, Tōgai himself broke new scholarly ground in his research on official ranks in both ancient China and ancient Japan. In contrast to Jinsai, who wrote almost exclusively in Chinese, Tōgai produced many essays and studies in Japanese, in an effort to promote learning among those who did not know Chinese. Under Tōgai, the Kogidō Academy flourished as a great center for ancient learning through the mid-eighteenth century.

ESSENTIALS FOR READING THE BOOK OF SONGS
(*DOKUSHI YŌRYŌ*, CA. 1730)

In the following passage from this commentary on the *Book of Songs*, Itō Tōgai, Itō Jinsai's eldest son and intellectual heir, further develops his father's views on the fundamental nature of poetry. The Jinsai school argued that "poetry reflects popular customs [*fūzoku*] and human emotions [*ninjō*]," a function that Tōgai sees as distinct from the political and ethical philosophy found in such Confucian classics as the *Book*

---

16. This phrase comes from the Great Preface to the *Book of Songs*.

of Documents (*Shujing*), the *Analects,* and the *Mencius.* At the same time, he contends that by confirming human feelings and allowing us to understand the emotions of others, poetry also serves a practical purpose in bringing about social order and harmonious human relations.

If you read the *Book of Songs* often and carefully, you will become familiar with the human emotions in society, and your mood will become mellow and peaceful. Then when you are interacting with others, if you are addressed in an outrageous manner or are treated badly, you will not respond in kind. Rather, in such a situation, you will be true to your father and your ruler and not be disloyal or unfilial. . . .

When stubborn or unsociable people interact with others, they often criticize them for trivial matters, thereby ruining such relationships. If you are familiar with human emotions, you can interact with large numbers of people and have pleasant relationships with them without argument or wrangling. . . .

The *Book of Documents* records matters of governance by the sage-emperors and illustrious kings, thereby explaining the Way for regulating the state and pacifying the realm. The *Analects* and *Mencius* clarify the distinctions between right and wrong and between proper and corrupt, thereby providing a means for cultivating the self and regulating others. The *Book of Documents* is the Way of the ruler; the *Analects* and *Mencius* are the Way of the teacher.

These kinds of functions do not apply to the *Book of Songs.* This book merely reflects popular customs and human emotions; it does not provide instruction about right and wrong or good and evil. Those who read the poems should recite and chant them aloud while thinking about human emotions and material appearances. In this way they will create a mellow and peaceful attitude. This is why the *Book of Songs* has been revered and is included among the classics, sharing the premier position with the *Book of Documents* so that the two are cited together as *Documents-Songs.*

[*Nihon shishi, Gozandō shiwa,* SNKBT 65: 13–15, translated by Lawrence Marceau]

OGYŪ SORAI

Ogyū Sorai (1666–1728), perhaps the most influential philosopher of the eighteenth century, was born in Edo. He was the second son of a samurai who served as the personal physician to Tokugawa Tsunayoshi, who became the fifth shōgun (r. 1680–1709). In 1690, Sorai, who had studied the Zhu Xi version of Song Confucianism, established himself as a private teacher of Chinese classics. In 1696 he entered into the service of Yanagisawa Yoshiyasu, the senior councillor (*rōjū*) to Tsunayoshi. After Tsunayoshi's death in 1709, Sorai retired from service with Yoshiyasu, turned away from the philosophy of Zhu Xi, and developed his own position and school, writing such influential texts as *Regulations for Study* (*Gakusoku*, 1715), *Distinguishing the Way* (*Bendō*, 1717), and *Master Sorai's Teachings* (*Sorai sensei tōmonsho*, 1724).

Sorai saw two fundamental weaknesses in Song Confucianism. First, in the early eighteenth century the bakufu-domain system was already in serious trouble. Thus he doubted that the bakufu's relying on the ideal of cultivating ethical good as a means of perfecting human character was sufficient. Rather, in Sorai's view, the political crisis demanded more than moral perfection, and he later argued that the Way (*michi*) of the ancient Chinese sage-kings had been concerned not just with morality but also with government, with bringing peace to the land. Second, Sorai feared that the heavy emphasis on morality would have the negative effect of repressing human nature, which was based on human emotion (*ninjō*). These fundamental deficiencies of Song Confucianism, according to Sorai, stemmed from a misreading of the Confucian classics, the Four Books and the Five Classics,[17] which in his view contained the original teachings of the ancient Confucian sages. The Song Confucians "did not know the old words." Sorai instead looked to history, to the ancient past, for deeper, more reliable knowledge, as noted in his famous dictum "The ultimate form of scholarly knowledge is history" (*Sorai sensei tōmonsho*). To Sorai, the historical text was the ultimate guide to the ever-changing present and could be authenticated through a systematic philological "study of ancient rhetoric" (*kobunjigaku*).

For Sorai, the study of philology should begin with a thorough study, and use, of the language. In this regard, he was heavily influenced by the Ming period's Ancient Rhetoric (*guwenci*, J. *kobunji*) school, led by Li Panlong (1514–1570) and Wang Shizhen (1526–1590)—a neoclassical movement that regarded the Qin (221–207 B.C.E.) and Han (202 B.C.E.–C.E. 220) periods as the models for prose and the middle Tang period as the model for poetry. Li Panlong is thought to have edited *Selections of Tang Poetry* (*Tangshi xuan*, J. *Tōshisen*), which the Sorai school introduced to Japan, where it became very popular. As a consequence, today Sorai's school is also called the Ancient Rhetoric (*kobunji*) school. Sorai's school differed from the Ming period's Ancient Rhetoric school in that he regarded the composition of Chinese poetry and prose primarily as a means of accessing the Five Classics, and he used poetry and prose composition in a pseudoarchaic Chinese style as a means of absorbing the heart of the ancients.

Sorai argued that the Way was not inherent in the cosmos, as was implied in the Song Confucian notion of rational principle (*ri*). Instead, he believed, the Way had been established by human beings, by the ancient sages, who had described their understanding of it in the Confucian classics. This Way was

---

17. The Five Classics are the *Book of Songs*, the *Book of Documents*, the *Classic of Rites* (*Yili*, later *Liji*), the *Classic of Changes*, and the *Spring and Autumn Annals*.

broadly divided into rites (*rei*) and music (*gaku*): the observation of rites pre-served the social order, while music or poetry inspired the heart. In Sorai's view, the Song Confucian emphasis on rational principle and moral training ignored and repressed the natural flow of human emotions, thereby demeaning them. The great achievement of the ancient sage-kings was that they had established a Way that responded to human emotions while allowing the land to be gov-erned peacefully. As Sorai argued in *Distinguishing the Way*, "The Way of the ancient kings was established through human emotions." To understand the Way of the ancient sage-kings, one must be familiar with, cultivate, and enrich human emotions. The most effective means of doing that was to read ancient Chinese poetry and prose, to use ancient words, and to compose poetry in the ancient style.

With its emphasis on literature as the expression of human emotion, Sorai's position had a revolutionary effect on the composition of Chinese poetry and prose, giving legitimacy to those intellectuals who wrote out of a need to express their emotions and desires. One result was that the Sorai school produced such outstanding men of letters as Hattori Nankaku (1683–1759), a major poet of Chinese poetry (*kanshi*) and a founder of the literatus (*bunjin*) movement in Japan who was not deeply interested in Confucianism but had a great talent for belles lettres. Chinese poetry and prose composition in Japan was thus trans-formed from a minor entertainment for Confucian scholars into a legitimate artistic pursuit.

MASTER SORAI'S TEACHINGS (SORAI SENSEI TŌMONSHO, 1727)

Master Sorai's Teachings, a record of Sorai's teachings edited by his students, is based on an actual exchange of questions and answers between Sorai and his disciples that is thought to have taken place around 1720. In the selection translated here, Sorai argues that poetry was not intended for either moral edification or instruction in gov-ernance. Instead, poetry or literature reveals human emotions through elevated, ele-gant language, thus allowing people of different status to understand one another's hearts. At the same time, however, poetry is in fact morally beneficial and also helpful in governance. Of particular significance here is Sorai's stress on courtly elegance and the elevating function of poetic language, a notion that underlay the eighteenth-century bunjin movement.

On the Study of Poetry and Prose

That you believe that the study of poetry and prose has no benefit is to be expected, given that you have been subject to the teachings of Song Confucian scholars on the transcription and recitation of words and passages.[18]

---

18. Song Confucian scholarship taught that the Way serves as the root, and literature serves

First, the *Book of Songs* is one of the Confucian Five Classics. Chinese poetry is just like the Japanese poetry of your own land. It teaches neither moral principles for regulating mind and body nor the Way for governing the state under heaven. These poems are the ones to which people of ancient times responded with joy and sorrow. From among these poems the sages collected and used as instruction for the people those that accord well with human emotions, that employ fine language, and that provide insight into the customs of a state at any given time.

The study of poetry does not offer you support in moral principles, but since it uses language skillfully and expresses human emotions effectively, from their power your heart will naturally mature, and your moral principles will be confirmed. Moreover, your heart will absorb those manners of the ages and customs of the state that are difficult to discern solely from the perspective of moral principle, so you will automatically understand human emotions. People of high rank become familiar with matters involving lower-class people; men become familiar with women's temperaments; and the wise come to know the workings of the hearts of the dim-witted. These are the benefits. Furthermore, since poetry uses language skillfully, it has the benefit of revealing one's heart to others without explicitly stating the matter at hand. Poetry has many other benefits in that it is used to instruct as well as to display one's discontent. Note that abstract theories are irrelevant here; the only way to understand the manners and customs of the rulers is through poetry. The poetry and prose of later ages all have the *Book of Songs* as their ancestral source. [Because] the age in which they were composed is closer to ours—and their meanings are thus easier to understand—if you study the *Book of Songs* knowing this, you will derive many benefits from it.

Since the sages are Chinese and the Confucian texts are written in the Chinese language, if you do not understand exactly the written characters of that language, you will have difficulty understanding the Way of the sages. In order to understand the written characters, it is necessary to understand the state of mind of the ancient sages when they composed their texts. Consequently, many matters will be incomprehensible unless you yourself compose poetry and prose. People who study only Confucian texts have trouble mastering written characters, and their reasoning becomes imprecise and limited. For this reason it is important that Japanese scholars become proficient in Chinese poetry and Chinese prose composition. Japanese scholars should also become familiar with the poetry of Japan, although the customs found in Japanese classical poetry reflect a kind of femininity that derives from the fact that Japan is a land without sages. I realize that as disciples you are not as badly trained

---

as the branches; in other words, literature is nothing more than a vehicle for transmitting the Way.

as the scholars that I have just described. As long as you are aware of that quality called courtly elegance [*fūga*], you will not lose touch with the ruler's state of mind; instead, you will find many benefits as you sit in authority over others. [vol. 2, sec. 19]

[*Kinsei bungakuron shū*, NKBT 94: 169–170, translated by Lawrence Marceau]

Chapter 8

CONFUCIANISM IN ACTION:

AN AUTOBIOGRAPHY OF A BAKUFU OFFICIAL

THE KYŌHŌ ERA (1716–1736)

The rapid development of both production and commerce in the late seventeenth century commodified society as a whole, in the large cities as well as the farming villages. The result was that farmers, who were supposed to be self-supporting, and samurai, who were dependent on the tribute collected from the farmers, became financially pressed, which in turn jeopardized the bakufu-domain system as a whole. Although the samurai's expenditures rose with the increase of commerce and the exchange of goods, the amount that they could squeeze from the farmers was limited. Accordingly, the bakufu and the domains (*han*) sought new forms of income, such as taxes on breweries, pawnshops, and other businesses run by wealthy farmers or urban commoners. But even this proved insufficient, and various han ordered large merchants to lend them money or sometimes even to sell them the rights to han industries (such as papermaking in Yamaguchi and Fukui, wax in Aizu, and salt in Kanazawa). Along with the han samurai, the Tokugawa direct retainers (*hatamoto*) and housemen (*gokenin*) were particularly hard hit, since their salaries had been either deferred or reduced while their expenses kept on rising. These samurai were thus forced to borrow from wealthy commoner merchants or to work on the side to support themselves. As the situation worsened in the late eighteenth century, it was not unusual for a samurai to become the adopted son of a wealthy urban commoner family. Rich urban merchants, by contrast, took advantage of the money-based economy to lend money to impoverished samurai, to develop new farmland, or to invest in new breweries or manual industries in farming villages. The samurai elite thus found themselves at the economic mercy of those below them on the social ladder.

Faced with the growing fiscal crisis in the bakufu-domain system, the eighth shōgun, Tokugawa Yoshimune (r. 1716–1745), initiated a series of measures — referred to today as the Kyōhō Reforms — in an attempt to restore its health. The main purpose of the reforms was to stabilize the fiscal sources necessary to pay the salaries of high-ranking samurai, particularly the hatamoto and goke-nin. Yoshimune issued an austerity directive requiring expenses to be reduced, ordered the daimyō to pay a fee to the bakufu in return for a shorter time in Edo in the alternate attendance system, and took various other measures, such as increasing income through the cultivation of special crops like ginseng and sweet potato. While Yoshimune's reforms were more effective than the subsequent Kansei and Tenpō Reforms and did bring some fiscal relief to the bakufu, the strategy of increasing the tribute caused hardship for the farmers, gradually leading to more agrarian riots (*hyakushō ikki*). The rise in rice production resulting from the development of new fields also had the unintended effect of lowering the price of rice, which in turn further hurt both the samurai and the farmers.

If the Genroku era (1688–1704) was a period of relative freedom and economic expansion, the Kyōhō era was marked by restriction and frugality. The shōguns who had ruled during the Genroku era — the fifth shōgun Tokugawa Tsunayoshi (r. 1680–1709); the sixth, Ienobu (r. 1709–1712); and the seventh, Ietsugu (r. 1713–1716) — had pushed for a policy of educated government. The eighth shōgun, Yoshimune, while not discouraging arts and letters, strove for a revival of military spirit. His extreme austerity measures, which were carried out to reverse the deficit spending that had begun with the third shōgun, Iemitsu (r. 1623–1651), created a more spartan atmosphere. In 1721, for example, Yoshimune issued an order regulating all new publications, which was followed the next year by a general restriction on all publications. The 1722 edict, which exempted "books on Confucianism, Buddhism, Shintō, medicine, and waka," banned pornographic books and those dealing with "sensuality" (*kōshoku*) or "matters not appropriate for society" and had a profound impact on the nature of literature, which moved in the direction of practical books.

At the same time, the interest in practical studies and foreign books grew. Chinese studies, which had focused on Confucian works, began to shift toward Chinese vernacular novels, which had been imported by Zen priests and traders through the port at Nagasaki during the Ming (1368–1644) and early Qing (1644–1911) periods. From literature and classical studies, which had been dominant in the Genroku era, Chinese studies spread into a number of subfields such as economics, medicine, and historical studies, as exemplified by the historiographical and anthropological studies by Arai Hakuseki (1657–1725). If writers in the Genroku era leaned toward sensation, those in the Kyōhō era—no doubt partly because of external pressures—moved toward rationality and intellect. Even in literature, the main accomplishments were in criticism and literary research.

The Kyōhō era was also a time of cultural expansion from Kyoto—which had been the focal point during the Genroku era—outward into the other two major cities, Osaka and Edo, and into the surrounding provinces. This expansion, both numerically and socially in terms of class, continued a trend that had begun in the Kan'ei era (1624–1644). During the eighteenth century, literature, art, and scholarship made their way into the provinces, with haikai becoming especially popular. After the death of Bashō, one of haikai's preeminent practitioners, his disciples split into two large groups, those who settled in the major cities (such as Kikaku in Edo) and those who went to the provinces and attracted large followings, particularly in Mino and Ise Provinces.

ARAI HAKUSEKI

Arai Hakuseki (1657–1725) was born in Edo, the son of a favored house retainer of Tsuchiya Toshinao, a daimyō in Kazusa (Chiba). Hakuseki was also favored by Toshinao, but when he was twenty-one, he was dismissed after a dispute. From 1682 to 1686 he served the high bakufu senior councillor (*tairō*) Hotta Masatoshi, after which he joined Kinoshita Jun'an's (1621–1698) Confucian academy and became friends with such influential men of letters as the linguist-diplomat Amenomori Hōshū (1668–1755), the poet-painter Gion Nankai (1666–1751), and the scholar Muro Kyūsō (1658–1734). Jun'an's recommendation led in 1693 to an appointment as a lecturer and adviser to the future shōgun Ienobu (1662–1712), to whom he taught history and the Confucian classics. After Ienobu (r. 1709–1712) became the sixth Tokugawa shōgun in 1709, Hakuseki was promoted to *hatamoto* (Tokugawa direct retainer), with a five-hundred-*koku* estate, and participated directly in the bakufu administration, helping dismantle the idiosyncratic policies of Ienobu's predecessor Tokugawa Tsunayoshi (r. 1680–1709).

Hakuseki was an innovative historian who wrote such noted works as *Genealogies of Domain Lords* (*Hankanfu*, 1702) and *Lessons from History* (*Tokushi yoron*, 1712), a history of Japan from a samurai perspective. His own autobiography, *Record of Breaking and Burning Brushwood* (*Oritaku shiba no ki*), can be read as a kind of contemporary history. Hakuseki also made significant contributions in geography, language study, poetry, anthropology, archaeology, military studies, and botany. His *Eastern Elegance* (*Tōga*), a dictionary of the Japanese language, provided the foundation for language studies by nativist scholars such as Mabuchi and Norinaga; and his books on the Ainu and Hokkaidō, *Record of the Ezo* (*Ezo-shi*), and on Okinawa, *Record of the Southern Islands* (*Nantō-shi*), became landmarks in anthropological folk studies. *Record of Things Heard About the Western Seas* (*Seiyō kibun*, 1715), an account based on interviews with the Italian Jesuit Giovanni Battista Sidotti, recognized Western technical superiority while maintaining Japanese spiritual superiority and greatly increased the bakufu's awareness of eighteenth-century European geography, international relations, and religion. His *Observations on Foreign Languages and Customs* (*Sairan igen*, 1725) similarly gathered information for the seventh shōgun, Ietsugu, about Africa, North America, Europe, and Asia.

RECORD OF BREAKING AND BURNING BRUSHWOOD
(*ORITAKU SHIBA NO KI*, 1717?)

After Tokugawa Yoshimune became the eighth shōgun in 1716, Hakuseki fell out of political favor and began to write his remarkable three-volume autobiography. The first volume begins with Hakuseki's grandparents and parents and then describes his own upbringing and early career before Ienobu's appointment as shōgun. The second and third volumes deal mainly with the family of the shōgun and bakufu matters. Hakuseki was motivated by at least two desires: to leave his descendants a record of his own life and accomplishments and to clarify the legacy and achievements of the two shōguns, Ienobu and Ietsugu, under whom he had served. In contrast to the works of Itō Jinsai and Ogyū Sorai, who were Confucian philosophers, Hakuseki's writings reveal the thinking of a prominent statesman-scholar, a Confucian in action. The first selection translated here, from volume 1, reveals some of Hakuseki's thoughts on his early education as the son of a samurai. The second selection, which describes Hakuseki's work as a Confucian adviser, deals with a woman caught between two Confucian legal principles: a woman's loyalty and her subordination to both her husband and her father. Hakuseki, who submits his opinion to the shōgun, handles the conflicting Confucian precedents in a manner that provides a compassionate outcome for the unfortunate woman while revealing the scholarly limitations of the arguments offered by the rival adviser Hayashi Hōkō, from the powerful Hayashi house of hereditary Confucian scholars.

Early Education

When I was very young, we had a book called *Tales of Ueno*.[1] This book depicted such things as crowds of people visiting Kan'ei-ji temple to view the cherry blossoms.[2] It must have been the spring of my third year, and I was stretched out on my stomach with my feet inside the kotatsu warmer looking

---

1. A kana-zōshi published in two volumes that no longer exists.
2. Kan'ei-ji was a Tendai temple in the Ueno district of Edo.

at that book. I asked for a brush and paper and began to trace. For every ten characters, I must have gotten one or two right, and my mother showed it to my father. Someone visiting my father then saw it, and word got around that I had done this. Later, in my sixteenth or seventeenth year, I went to the province of Kazusa and was able to see the copy that I had made.

At about the same time that I began to trace characters, I wrote my name on a folding screen. Two of the characters were legible, but the screen was later lost in a fire. Now I have nothing left from that time. After that, I constantly was taking up a brush and writing down things for fun, so eventually I came to recognize various characters on my own. Since I had never had a proper instructor for reading Chinese texts, I was left to read and learn from epistolary textbooks and other primers.

Among the minister's house retainers was a certain Tomita, who I hear came from Kaga Province and who was known for his lectures based on a critical edition of the *Record of Great Peace* [*Taiheiki*].[3] He was originally called Koemon-something and later Kakushin. Every night my father and others would gather together, and he would lecture to them. When I was in my fourth or fifth year I would always attend these sessions and, even though the hour grew quite late, would not leave until the lecture was over, after which I would then ask questions about various issues. People said they thought my actions were those of a prodigy.

In the summer of my sixth year, I met a man called Uematsu, who was somewhat familiar with Chinese characters. His name was Chūbei-something; he was a relative of Uematsu, a house retainer to the Imagawa of Suruga Province, and was a classical linked-verse aficionado and a proficient writer. He taught me a heptasyllabic quatrain in Chinese and explained its meaning to me. When I succeeded in reciting it on the spot, he taught me three more poems, which I then lectured on to others. One contained the line "Three times say, 'There is a tiger in the market,' and all will believe you." Another was the poem that a seven-year-old Korean child had recited to the retired regent Toyotomi Hideyoshi. The third one was composed by a priest known as Vice Abbot Jikyū on the occasion of his trip to Enoshima.

Uematsu remarked, "This boy has real literary talent. You should by all means find him a teacher so that he can receive instruction."

Obstinate people of the older generation discussed this issue among themselves, saying such things as "It has been noted since ancient times that 'without the three roots—intelligence, motivation, and wealth—it is impossible to become a scholar.' This child was born with intelligence, but since he is still young, we cannot yet determine whether he has any motivation. His family

---

3. Lectures on this fourteenth-century military chronicle were common during the Tokugawa period.

certainly does not seem prosperous, so there is little chance that he will inherit any money."

My father agreed. "Because of the minister's great beneficence, my son has been allowed to stay at his side. It will not do for him to become a scholar and follow the teachings of a particular master in another place. However, since even the minister has taken pride in him and spoken to others about his writing abilities, I believe that he should at least be given some training in this subject." Thus in the autumn of my eighth year, after the minister went to his domain in Kazusa Province, it was arranged that I would receive training in calligraphy. Midway through the Twelfth Month that winter, the minister returned, and I served at his side as before. In the autumn of the following year [1665], the minister again went off to his domain, and I was assigned the following curriculum: "During the day you should write out three thousand characters in the semicursive [gyō] and cursive [sō] forms, and at night you should write out another one thousand characters."

Because winter was approaching, the days were growing shorter, and often the sun would set before I was able to complete my assignment. Sometimes I even had to take my desk out to the bamboo veranda that faced west and finish writing there. It was difficult to stay awake during my writing practice at night, so I secretly planned with my attendant to have two buckets filled with water and placed on the bamboo veranda. When I got too sleepy, I would take off my clothes, toss them aside, and throw one bucketful over myself. Afterward I would put my clothes back on and continue writing. At first I would feel wide awake from the chill. Eventually, however, my body would warm up and I would once again get sleepy, so I then would throw the second bucketful over myself. After this, I usually could complete my assignment. I did this during the autumn and winter of my ninth year.

I soon was copying out in the prescribed manner my father's correspondence with others. In the autumn of my tenth year, I was given an assignment to practice the *Household-Precept Epistles* [*Teikin ōrai*] and, in the Eleventh Month, was ordered to make a clean copy within ten days.[4] I successfully completed the assignment as ordered, and my work was then bound and shown to the minister, who showered me with praise. After my thirteenth year I usually was the one who would copy out the minister's correspondence and replies.

In my eleventh year, I asked to learn the art of sword fighting from Seki, the son of a friend of my father's, who was training others. I was told that I was too young and that there would be time to learn such techniques later. I responded, "That may well be true, but without knowing sword-fighting techniques, doesn't it seem ridiculous for me to be dressed carrying a long and a short blade?"

---

4. The *Teikin ōrai*, attributed to Gen'e, a fourteenth-century Buddhist priest and Confucian scholar, is the best known of the language textbooks in the *ōraimono* format.

Replying, "You are absolutely right," Seki trained me so I would know at least one technique.

At that time a sixteen-year-old, the second son of a person named Kanbe, wanted to try out his skills on me. Using wooden swords we went for three bouts, and I won all three times. Various people took notice and found this extremely entertaining. I then became absorbed in the martial arts and lost interest in my writing practice. I still enjoyed reading, though, and there wasn't a single Japanese work of fiction that I hadn't read.

When I was seventeen I was visiting the quarters of a fellow young samurai by the name of Hasegawa, who also was in the minister's service, when I saw a book on his desk entitled *Dialogue with the Elder*.[5] I wondered what it was about, so I borrowed it and carried it home with me. This was the first time I became aware of the Way of the ancient Confucian sages.[6] From that time on I was determined to follow this Way with a single mind. . . .

Confucian Precedent and Justice for a Woman

During the last administration, after I had finished lecturing on the seventeenth day of the Eighth Month of the Year of the Hare [1711], I was made aware of a certain legal case that was under dispute.[7] The account is as follows:

A certain person from the town of Matsushiro in Mino Province who was in commerce was living here in Edo. His wife, Ume, is the daughter of a native of Komabayashi village in the town of Kawagoe, in Musashi Province. On the sixteenth day of the Seventh Month of this year, this wife's elder brother visited her and invited her to Kawagoe. Then on the twentieth, he again visited her and told his younger sister, "Your husband is returning to his home town on business. He shouldn't be back for some time. You ought to go to your father and wait there until your husband returns." On the twenty-first he took her to their father's house. Several days passed but the husband failed to return, so the wife asked her father about it, who told her, "He will definitely be back around the twenty-eighth of the month." But he did not appear even after the first of this month. The wife was worrying about what might have happened when she heard reports that a body had been found washed downstream in the river nearby. With much trepidation she rushed down to the river, but the body was floating face down in the water, and she could not identify it. She appealed to her father and brother to show her the body, but they refused, saying, "Why

---

5. *Okina mondō* (1640–1641), by Nakae Tōju (1608–1648).

6. *Seijin no michi*: the Confucian Way of scholarship, self-cultivation, social responsibility, and wise counsel to the ruler.

7. This was during the reign of the sixth shōgun, Ienobu (r. 1709–1712). The principals in this case were Jingobei (sixty-five), his son Shirōbei (forty-two), his daughter Ume (thirty-one), and her husband Ihei (thirty-nine).

would he ever end up like that?" Unable to bear it any longer, the next day she reported to the village headman, asking that the body be retrieved. When it was, it turned out in fact to be that of her husband.

Since this area is under the jurisdiction of Akimoto Takatomo, his officials interrogated the wife's father and brother, as well as everyone in the household.[8] Their testimonies were inconsistent so the officials searched the house and found the husband's clothes and other belongings there. The father and brother did not have an alibi, and it became apparent that on the nineteenth, they had strangled the husband and tossed his body in the river. There was no doubt that these two committed the crime of murdering the woman's husband. Given that the wife herself might be guilty of the crime of testifying against her own father, Lord Takatomo submitted the facts of the case to me.

I responded, "This particular case deals with a perversion of the tenet of the Three Bonds, and as such, we should not make rash decisions based on the usual practice.[9] My concern here is not limited to the father and child or to the husband and wife. This matter also concerns the ruler and the subject." To this Takatomo replied, "In that case, find out from the justice magistrates if there is an applicable precedent here. Have them look into it and report back to me."[10]

After I arrived back home, I discreetly discussed this matter with my friend Kyūsō, and the very next morning he sent me a letter in which he quoted the passage on hemp garments in the chapter "Mourning Clothes" in *Ceremony and Ritual* and concluded, "If you reach a judgment based on this passage, then there should be no question of her innocence."[11] When I first conferred with Kyūsō, we agreed, so it brought great satisfaction to have found a clear source of support from this text. . . .

On the twenty-fifth, I was summoned, given a copy of the counsel provided to the Council of Senior Councillors by Hayashi Hōkō [Nobuatsu], head of the Shōheikō Academy, and told to look at it.[12] His opinion was as follows: "'All

8. Akimoto Takatomo, governor of Tajima, served as a member of the bakufu Council of Senior Councillors from 1699 to 1714.

9. The Confucian Three Bonds were those between ruler and subject, father and child, and husband and wife.

10. The justice magistrates are the officials of the Hyōjōsho, or bakufu high court.

11. Murō Kyūsō (1658–1734), a renowned Confucian scholar, is the author of, among other works, the essay collection *Random Talks on Suruga Heights* (*Sundai zatsuwa*, 1732). *Ceremony and Ritual* (*Yi li*) is one of three Confucian classics dedicated to rituals.

12. The Council of Senior Councillors (Rōjū) was the main committee of advisers to the shogun. The text uses the name Nobuatsu for Hayashi Hōkō (1644–1732), adviser to the shogun and the first head of the Shōheikō Academy in Edo, which was supported by the bakufu and offered a Confucian curriculum. The scholars of the Hayashi school typically applied the Confucian texts conservatively, relying extensively on Song Confucian metaphysical teachings. Hakuseki generally held Hayashi Hōkō's opinions in low regard.

men can be your husband, but only one can be your father.'[13] This passage refers to what the daughter of Zhai Zhong of Zheng was told by her mother when she asked her whether she should be closer to her father or her husband. In this case the father's crime became apparent when his daughter notified the authorities. The *Analects* states, 'It is proper for you to hide your father's misdeeds.'[14] China's *Penal Code* states, 'Put to death one who reports the misdeeds of one's father or mother.'[15] Therefore, reporting one's father's misdeeds is a capital offense. But if the daughter did not know that her father had killed her husband, it would be another matter. Japan's *Penal Code*, furthermore, states, 'Exile one who reports the misdeeds of one's father or mother.' In the notes, though, 'exile' is replaced with 'hanging.'". . . The shōgun responded, "Must we really apply the words of Zhai Zhong's wife here? Also, this murder was not a crime committed in the heat of passion. Moreover, this case does not fit Confucius's statement that it is 'proper to cover up' for one's father. Put your opinions in writing and submit them to me."

On the twenty-sixth, I submitted the following opinion: ". . . The investigating officials have expressed concern that the wife may have committed the crime of reporting against her father. The justice magistrates have submitted the opinion that her property should be confiscated and she should be relegated to the position of maidservant. The Confucian minister has argued that she should be punished for testifying against her father.[16] . . . I humbly submit the following: This particular case is an unusual example of the Three Bonds, so one should not arrive at conclusions based on the usual principles. We must consider three factors in this case. The first is that one should judge fairly by applying the notion of the bonds of human relationships. The so-called Three Bonds refers to the ruler as the subject's bond, the father as his child's bond, and the husband as his wife's bond. With regard to these three bonds, the level of respect for ruler, father, and husband is the same from the perspective of the subordinate party.

"The second factor is that one should find an appropriate precedent in the regulations regarding mourning clothes. The writings of the ancient sage-kings stipulates that if a man's daughter is engaged to be married but is still living at home, or if she is already married but has returned home, then in the event of her father's death she should wear hemp mourning garb for a period of three

---

13. Hayashi Hōkō quotes a passage from the *Zuo zhuan* (*Tso chuan*), a hugely influential expansion of and commentary on the *Spring and Autumn Annals*. See Burton Watson, trans., *Tso Chuan: Selections from China's Oldest Narrative History* (New York: Columbia University Press, 1989), 11–12.

14. The *Analects* (13:18) does not include the term "misdeeds" but states that it is proper for fathers and sons to cover up for each other.

15. The Chinese *Penal Code* (*Lü shu*, J. *Rissho*) here refers to the Sui and Tang penal codes.

16. The Confucian minister (*jushin*) here refers to Hayashi Hōkō (Nobuatsu).

years. If she already is married and is subordinate to her husband, then if her father dies, she should wear a hemmed mourning garment for an unspecified period of time.[17] The issue is the inconsistency between when a daughter is living at home and when she has been married, which is clarified in the chapter 'Mourning Clothes' as follows: 'A woman is subject to the Three Subordinates. She may not follow her own way. Thus a woman before marriage is subordinate to her father. Once married, she is subordinate to her husband. Upon the death of her husband, she is subordinate to her child. In this way the father becomes heaven to his child. The husband becomes heaven to his wife. The reason that a woman does not wear the unhemmed mourning cloth twice is that she cannot exist under two heavens. A woman may not divide her respect between two men.' Thus based on this passage, 'a woman may not divide her respect between two men,' we can conclude that when a woman becomes a wife, she is subordinate to her husband and should no longer be subordinate to her father.

"The third factor is that we should consider in our decision the particular circumstances of the situation. Both normal and unusual elements exist in all matters. In practice, we use standard measures as well as expediencies. As an earlier Confucian wrote, 'Expediencies can serve as the ground for standard measures.'[18] When a daughter is living at home, she is subordinate to her father; when she goes off in marriage, she is subordinate to her husband. This is a fine division of duties based on one's situation and is what we call the 'righteous order of the ancient sage kings.'. . .

"Human relationships are disrupted when a woman's father murders her husband. . . . If she is to remain loyal to her husband, then she must be unfilial to her father. There is no greater tragedy for such a person than this. . . .

"According to the order of the ancient sage-kings, because a married woman treats her husband as heaven and may no longer treat her father as heaven, it is wrong to argue that the act of reporting to the authorities the murder of one's husband by one's father is subject to the laws against turning in one's father or mother to the authorities. Indeed, she found out that the body was that of her husband only after she had begged the village headman to retrieve it for identification. This state of events is different from what the justice magistrates have claimed, that the father and brother murdered the husband, and the wife, knowing that her own father and brother were the perpetrators, turned them in to the authorities. There is no reason whatsoever to find this woman guilty of a crime. If on the day of her father's and brother's arrest for her husband's murder, she had immediately taken her own life, she would have showed loyalty to her

---

17. An unhemmed hemp garment signifies the deepest degree of mourning, and a hemmed garment is one degree less severe. An unspecified period is also less severe than three full years.

18. This citation means that it is important to view each case on its own merits, because taking into account special circumstances may lead to new procedures. This particular quotation does not appear in canonical Chinese texts and so was probably taken from a commentary.

husband, filial piety to her father, and sororal piety to her elder brother. This would have been viewed as the ultimate act of integrity in the face of a great perversion in human relationships. She should by no means, however, be criticized for having failed to do so. . . .

"According to the ruling handed down by the justice magistrates, this woman should be sentenced to prison for one year, after which her property should be confiscated, and she should be relegated to the position of maidservant. The head of the Shōheikō Academy [Hayashi Hōkō] submitted the opinion that if this woman had knowingly reported her father's murder of her husband to the authorities, she should be condemned to death. But if she had acted out of ignorance, she should be sentenced to penal servitude.

"If, however, she is found not guilty of any crime, as I have just argued, I humbly wish to submit one more appeal. This pitiful, pitiful widow has already lost all means of support. At this point, it is not certain that the green color of the pines will not change when the bitter cold sets in.[19] But I would not regret only her loss of chastity as a widow. I would fear also the likelihood of the harm that her case would do to the status of official law. In many cases of common people in this land, a person who has lost a father or a husband becomes a priest or a nun. If this daughter were discreetly urged to become a nun for the sake of her father and her husband and she were admitted to a convent, had her head shaved, and were initiated into the holy precepts, her property could be donated to the convent with her, and she would be spared starvation and exposure to the elements. This would preserve both the official law and her chastity."

Ultimately my opinion was accepted, and what I had recommended was carried out. I later heard that through Lord Takatomo's good offices, the woman decided on her own to become a nun and that she entered the convent in Kamakura.[20]

[*Taion ki, Oritaku shiba no ki, Rantō kotohajime*, NKBT 95: 184–187, 336–343, introduction and translation by Lawrence Marceau]

---

19. This means that there is no guarantee that she can remain chaste as a widow under conditions of hardship. This metaphor comes from *Analects* 9:27.

20. Ume did in fact enter the Shōkōzan (Matsugaoka) Tōkeiji convent, a famous *kakekomi-dera*, or place of asylum for women, located in Kamakura.

Chapter 9

CHINESE POETRY AND THE LITERATUS IDEAL

During the Kyōhō era (1716–1736), such notable *kanshi* (Chinese-style) poets as Hattori Nankaku (1683–1759) and Gion Nankai (1677–1751) flourished. The Tokugawa bakufu encouraged learning and scholarship, and early scholars of Chinese studies like Hayashi Razan believed in learning as a means of governing. The reality, however, was that most scholars, even the most talented, were not given an opportunity to govern. Instead, they usually turned their attention to such areas of scholarship as historical investigation and phonology, which were not embraced by orthodox Confucian studies, or entered artistic fields that generally brought little income or worldly gain—Chinese poetry and prose, painting, calligraphy, seal engraving (*tenkoku*), the art of tea (*sencha*)—all of which became popular at this time.

Of particular interest at this time was the ideal of the *bunjin*, or literatus. These intellectuals devoted themselves to the arts, not as professionals who could profit from them materially or politically, but as serious devotees. The notion of the bunjin originated in the Chinese notion of the *wen-ren* (*bunjin*, literally, person of letters), although the Japanese bunjin were not born into a landed gentry class, as they were in China. In their youth, Gion Nankai, Hattori Nankaku, Yanagisawa Kien (1704–1758), and Sakaki Hyakusen (1697–1752)—who are now regarded as the pioneers of the bunjin movement—collided with society, became disillusioned with public service, and turned to the world of the arts.

The bunjin's disillusionment with contemporary society led also to a certain disdain for the vulgarity of the world. In reaction, they attempted to create or enter an alternative world of elegance and high taste, which would allow them a freedom of expression and imagination that they could not find in the vulgar, everyday world. They created this new world using their knowledge, particularly of Chinese culture, which gave them a sense of uniqueness. The subsequent Chinese influence was so great that even the study of the Chinese vernacular became part of the bunjin world. Imitating Chinese wen-ren, these bunjin lived a life of elegance and refinement (*fūga*), complete with the accoutrements of scrolls, flower vases, incense, and the like. This bunjin lifestyle and attitude eventually extended to non-kanshi writers and poets such as the haikai master Yosa Buson (1716–1783) and early *yomihon* writers like Ueda Akinari (1734–1809).

HATTORI NANKAKU

Hattori Nankaku (1683–1759), the second son of a wealthy urban commoner father, was born in Kyoto but moved to Edo after his father died. In 1700, at the age of seventeen, Nankaku was invited to become a samurai and waka poet in the service of Yanagisawa Yoshiyasu (1658–1714), a senior councillor and adviser to the fifth shōgun, Tokugawa Tsunayoshi (r. 1680–1709). Through Yoshiyasu, Nankaku came to know Ogyū Sorai and, around 1711, became one of Sorai's followers. After joining Sorai's Ancient Rhetoric school, Nankaku turned from waka to kanshi and put Sorai's philosophy—of actively affirming human emotions and the value of composing poetry as a means of expressing them—into practice, making the composition of Chinese poetry the equal of orthodox Chinese studies. This was a revolutionary move that had a lasting impact on later poets, who came to regard Nankaku's lifestyle and work as the ideal of the bunjin.

After Yoshiyasu died in 1714, Nankaku had a falling-out with Yoshiyasu's successor, and in 1718, at the age of thirty-five, he left the Yanagisawa house and spent the rest of his life out of samurai service, devoting himself to poetry, writing, and painting. Nankaku became an accomplished practitioner of the *nanga* (southern school) style of literati painting, which was closely connected to his poetic practice. After Sorai's death he kept alive Sorai's literary legacy while Dazai Shundai (1680–1747) carried on Sorai's work in political thought. As a representative of Sorai's Ancient Rhetoric school, Nankaku was a neoclassicist who looked to the middle Tang as an ideal, and in 1724 he printed an edition of the *Tangshi xuan* (*Tōshisen*), an anthology of Tang poetry said to have been compiled by Li Panlong, which popularized a certain version of Tang poetry in Japan. Nankaku also was interested in Daoism and wrote a number of Chinese poems about the ideals of the recluse.

TRAVELING DOWN THE SUMIDA RIVER AT NIGHT
(YORU BOKUSUI O KUDARU)

The following seven-word quatrain (*zekku*), a form popular in the middle Tang, is from the *Collected Prose and Poetry of Master Nankaku* (*Nankaku sensei bunshū*), first published in 1727. The poem transforms the Sumida River, a small river on the outskirts of Edo, into a grand river transporting the reader into another, fantastical, Chinese-like world. The watery reflection of Golden Dragon Hill (Kinryūsan), a local hill at Asakusa on the banks of the Sumida, creates the image of a golden dragon floating down the river. The reflection on the river also causes the moon to burst out of the water, a line that echoes Li Bo's poem "The Song of the Moon at Mount Emei" (Emeishan yue gi). In the last line, the poet arrives at the boundary between the "two provinces," Shimōsa and Musashi, in the present-day Ryōgoku area.

> On the banks of Golden Dragon Hill the moon floats over the river.
> The water sways back and forth, the moon bursts out,
>> the golden dragon moves forward.
> My little boat never stops; the sky is like the water.
> With the autumn winds blowing from both shores,
>> I pass between the two provinces.

[*Gozan bungaku, Edo kanshi shū*, NKBT 89: 214, translated by Haruo Shirane]

JOTTINGS OF MASTER NANKAKU UNDER THE LAMPLIGHT
(*NANKAKU SENSEI TŌKA NO SHO*, 1725)

In *Jottings of Master Nankaku Under the Lamplight*, written in the Japanese epistolary style (*sōrōbun*) around 1725, Nankaku insists in the passage translated here that the writer must strive to recapture the elegant (*ga*) language of the past, which he sees as having disappeared in a process of historical decline. He finds examples of this elegant language in a canon of classical Chinese texts that he regards as being influenced by such Ming-period Ancient Rhetoric school figures as Li Panlong (1514–1579) and Wang Shizhen (1526–1590), who discovered their model for prose in the *Record of History* (*Shiji*) from the Qin (221–207 B.C.E.) and Han periods (206 B.C.E.–C.E. 220) and their model for poetry in the middle Tang. Nankaku singles out for criticism the poetry of the Song dynasty (960–1279), for what he sees as its rational and discursive character. He argues that for Song Neo-Confucians—which the Sorai school attacked for their preoccupation with rational principle (*ri*)—the expression of anger and sorrow may appear to be a sign of weakness, characteristic of women and children, but in fact it is the "elegant emotions" (*fūga no jō*) of outstanding poets.

Beginning with the Six Classics, elegant [*ga*] language is beautiful and is not the language ordinarily used in the common [*zoku*] world. . . .

Writings such as the *Book of Songs* and the ancient-style *yuefu* ballads of the

Han and Wei and Six Dynasties are examples of elegant emotions. . . . For example, when parting from a friend, we recall the pleasures that we have had and lament the sorrows that will follow our parting, and together with our friend we shed tears and commiserate about our sadness. In the eyes of those of the Song and later, attuned only to the study of rational principle, these appear to be weaknesses of women and children, but in reality they are the emotions of elegant people. . . .

Poetry is something that is sung and is not, by nature, a means for exhaustively expressing rational principle. Things that can be manifested in rational principle are vulgar things.

> [*Nihon shiwa sōsho*, Bunkaidō shoten, 1920, 1: 49, 58–59, 60–61, translated
> by Peter Flueckiger]

RESPONDING TO THE LORD OF GOOSE LAKE
(GAKO-KŌ NI KOTAHU)

According to Nankaku, people of the present day can recapture the elegance of the past by imitating the proper models. As he explains in the following excerpt from his letter "Responding to the Lord of Goose Lake," elegant emotions do not simply pour out of the heart spontaneously; rather, they are found in and nourished by the textual tradition, which constructs and elevates the heart of the poet. At the same time, he emphasizes that this tradition must be internalized through a long period of study. The addressee of this letter was Suwa Tadatoki, daimyō of Takashima Domain in Shinano Province. Nantaku displays his bunjin consciousness by addressing Tadatoki as "Gako-kō," or the "Lord of Goose Lake." Gako, a reference to a place-name in China, is an elegant name for Lake Suwa, located in Tadatoki's domain.

The words I use have already been used by the ancients, and the conceptions I express have also been expressed by the ancients. When I try comparing my own poetry with the poetry of the ancients, they are so similar that it is difficult to tell them apart. It is like this not because I imitate the ancients but, rather, because my very self is a product of their writings. This is what makes poetry difficult.

> [*Sorai gakuha*, NST 35: 226–227, translated by Peter Flueckiger]

GION NANKAI

Gion Nankai (1677–1751), the son of a samurai doctor in Wakayama Domain, studied kanshi and Confucianism with Kinoshita Jun'an (1621–1698) and served as a Confucian official. Then in 1700, because of misbehavior, he lost his salary of two hundred *koku* and was imprisoned in a remote corner of the domain. In 1710, he was pardoned, returned to Wakayama Castle, and resumed his work as a Confucian official. His ten years of exile had a lasting effect on Nankai, particularly on his negative view of secular power, and it was through his poetry, painting, and calligraphy that he sought to liberate himself in an aesthetic world apart from contemporary society. In keeping with the style of his kanshi teacher, Kinoshita Jun'an (1621–1698), Nankai looked to Tang poetry as an ideal and became one of the "three [kanshi] masters" of the Shōtoku era (1711–1716), along with Arai Hakuseki and Yanada Zeigan.

Nankai came to embody the ideal of the bunjin in being able to distinguish himself not only in Chinese poetry but also in calligraphy and painting. Largely self-taught as an artist, Nankai became an outstanding Nanga painter and one of the founders of the Japanese *bunjinga* (literati painting) tradition. Many of his artworks were accompanied by poems, with the art, calligraphy, and text forming an organic whole in the bunjin manner. Nankai wrote in a kanshi poem entitled "Song on Poetry and Painting" (Shigaka), "What I cannot express through poetry, I express through painting, and what painting cannot describe, I explain through poetry. The voiceless poem and the formless painting can be said to give pleasure for an entire life." Painting, in other words, is a "voiceless poem" and poetry is a "formless painting," each complementing the other.

THE FISHERMAN (GYOFU)

Both the Daoist classic the *Zhuangzi* and the noted Chinese poetry collection *Soji* have sections on the "fisherman," who is depicted as an ideal, someone who forgets the cares of the everyday world and floats freely over lakes and seas. The fisherman fishing alone in the cold is also a common subject in Chinese painting. This poem similarly depicts the fisherman as a man free in the midst of nature and can be read as an allegorical reflection of Nankai's own ideal of a bunjin life. Both the horse carriage and the courtier headdress are signs of high social status. As the poet notes in the last two lines, the dangers of boating are not as bad as the dangers of surviving in human society. This poem, which appears in *Later Collection of Master Nankai* (*Nankai sensei goshū*), is a seven-word regulated poem (*risshi*) in eight lines, in which the third and fourth lines, and the fifth and sixth lines, form couplets.

> With only a straw hat, a cloak, and a fishing pole
> He never travels in a horse carriage, and no courtier hat rests on his head
> He spends his entire life simply riding the misty waves.
> While in his cups he never feels the chill of wind and snow.
> Roosting herons, sleeping seagulls: these are his companions.
> White and red floating weeds—where are the rapids?
> But stop talking about the dangers of boating on rivers and lakes!
> Look! The journey through this world is far more difficult.

[*Gozan bungaku Edo kanshi shū*, NKBT 89: 210, translated by Haruo Shirane]

Gion Nankai, *Eight Daoist Immortals of China.* This hanging scroll depicts a popular subject in literati painting—Daoist immortals, who were model recluses for the literati, occupying an imaginary mountain. Eight such immortals, in loose robes symbolizing their untrammeled existence, are engaged in elegant pastimes such as playing the flute and Chinese chess. Literati landscape motifs include mountain peaks, a waterfall, and a pine tree (*foreground*). In literati fashion, calligraphy, poetry, and painting are combined. In running script (*upper left*), Nankai transcribes part of a poem eulogizing the lifestyle of a recluse by the Chinese scholar-poet Tao Hongjing (452–536), an acclaimed Daoist master and calligrapher: "You asked what I have in these mountains? Many white clouds on the peaks." (42.5 in. × 16.3 in. Property of Mary Griggs Burke. Photograph: Otto E. Nelson)

ENCOUNTERING THE ORIGINS OF POETRY
(SHIGAKU HŌGEN, 1763)

Encountering the Origins of Poetry is Nankai's most systematic presentation of his views on Chinese poetry, particularly on the issue of elegance (*ga*) and vulgarity (*zoku*). In the passage translated here, Nankai argues that in all regards—content, diction, taste, spirit—Chinese poetry must be guided by the distinction between these two elements, with every attempt made to eliminate the commonplace and the vulgar and to stress the elegant. This view of elegance became one of the fundamental assumptions of bunjin culture with respect to not only poetry but also painting and calligraphy. The origin of this attitude can be found in a strain of Confucian thought that looked for the human ideal in the ancient sage-kings and saw history as a gradual decline leading up to the present. This translated into an emphasis on the elegant, which was associated with antiquity, and a denial of the vulgar, which became associated with the present. This perspective assumed that by mastering the language of the past through elegant poetry, one could elevate or transcend the present.

On Elegance and Vulgarity

Poetry [*shi*] is the vessel for elegance [*fūga*]. It is not something for vulgar use. If one needs to refer to things of vulgar use, one should not turn to poetry. One should be able to take care of such things with ordinary or low words. This applies not only to Chinese poetry but to Japanese poetry . . . as well as to music, chess [*shōgi*], calligraphy, and painting. All of these must be elegant activities. Earlier I spoke of painting. For example, when painting a mountain or a farmhouse in a landscape painting, no matter how realistic it may be, if one paints an outhouse, a pile of compost, or things like a stove, the result will be extremely shabby and vulgar. In depicting a human being, no matter what that person may be like, if one depicts the anus or the sexual organs, it will be rude and improper. . . . When it comes to elegant matters, one should avoid this kind of thing and paint those parts that are elegant and avoid those parts that are vulgar. . . . This distinction applies to things, words, and taste. . . . One must seek the elegant in things and avoid the vulgar.

[*Kinsei bungaku ron*, NKBT 88: 246–249, translated by Haruo Shirane]

Chapter 10

THE GOLDEN AGE OF PUPPET THEATER

The jōruri puppet theater reached a creative peak around 1715, beginning with the performance of Chikamatsu Monzaemon's *Battles of Coxinga* (*Kokusenya kassen*), through the rivalry of the Takemoto and Toyotake theaters, to the death of the playwright Namiki Sōsuke in 1751. It was a period when the puppet theater outshone the kabuki theater, particularly in the city of Osaka. In 1714, the popular kabuki actor Ikushima Shingorō, of the Yamamura Theater in Edo, was discovered having an affair with Ejima (1681–1741), a female attendant of the mother of the seventh shōgun, Tokugawa Ietsugu (r. 1713–1716). Ejima was exiled and the Yamamura Theater was shut down, a heavy blow to the Edo kabuki. Another reason for the puppet theater's popularity was the Kyōhō Reforms' 1722 ban on erotic literature and, in 1723, on the dramatization of double suicides, which affected popular fiction and literature more than it did puppet theater.

The puppet theater also thrived because of its location in Osaka, which had become the country's economic center. Most of Osaka's residents were urban commoners, and the city was away from the watchful eye of the bakufu in Edo. From about 1710, a great creative rivalry started in Osaka between two puppet theaters, the Takemoto Theater and the Toyotake Theater, located in Dōtonbori, the bakufu-licensed theater district. The competition between the two theaters, which produced one new jōruri play after another, overshadowed kabuki in the Kyoto-Osaka region, which had to rely on puppet scripts to attract audiences. The practice of multiple authorship, which was characteristic of the puppet theater after Chikamatsu—usually an older master playwright overseeing two or three younger playwrights—emerged out of the need to train successors and to meet the audience's increasing demands.

After the bakufu banned double-suicide plays, the contemporary-life (sewamono) genre faded from puppet theater, leaving the period drama or history play (jidaimono) as the central genre. The history plays, however, usually made a farmer or an urban commoner the hero of the climactic third act, enabling the playwright to incorporate contemporary manners, thought, and characters into a historical drama. In both jōruri and kabuki, history plays had a dual structure: the "world" (sekai), which was set in the past and drawn from a noted historical incident, legend, or classical tale; and the "innovation" (shukō), which was the fictional addition or contemporary twist on that "world." These "worlds" often came from medieval historical and military chronicles such as The Tale of the Heike, Record of Yoshitsune (Gikeiki), The Tale of the Soga Brothers, and Record of Great Peace (Taiheiki), each with an established cast of characters that was well known to the audience. The "innovation" provided this "world" with the new and the unexpected, which could take the form of contemporary events or figures injected into the past or new and unexpected combinations of two or more existing "worlds."

The puppet plays at this time also tended to be highly moralistic, reflecting a larger trend from the Kyōhō-Hōreki era (1716–1764). A similar tendency is apparent in the contemporary dangibon, the comic, didactic fiction that imitated the style of Buddhist sermons. A general trend was the fusion of the "Way of the warrior" (bushidō)—a samurai ethic of loyalty, self-sacrifice, and obligation—with Confucian virtues of filial piety, a wife's fidelity to her husband, or a subject's fidelity to his ruler. Even the social structure of the urban commoner family and business—specifically, the relationship between the employee (apprentice) and the employer—came to be governed by this samurai notion of loyalty and obligation. Of all samurai values, the one with the greatest weight was loyalty, which provided the moral foundation for the social and political order. Consequently, a number of the history plays, beginning with The Battles of Coxinga, are about loyalty to a lord, a ruler, or the imperial family, a theme explored in the context of war, struggle for succession of a prominent house (oie sōdō), and vendettas. Chūshingura, for example, describes the loyalty of the former retainers of the Ako fief to their slandered lord. The notion of loyalty, however, was taken to a new extreme in the mid-eighteenth century, with loyalty becoming tragically embodied in personal substitution (migawari), in which, for example, a retainer sacrifices his son for his lord's son or a woman sacrifices herself for her husband.

This interest in loyalty shifted in the 1740s, from an emphasis on the ties between man and woman to the ties between parent and child. The resulting conflict, particularly in the drama by Namiki Sōsuke and the Toyotake Theater, is not primarily—as it was in Chikamatsu's drama—between human desire (*ninjō*) and obligation/duty (*giri*) but between parental love and obligation/duty. In this dilemma, the parent's love and concern for the child is cruelly crushed in the face of larger social responsibilities and obligations that force the parent to sacrifice the life of the child. In contrast to the passion between the sexes, which directly violated feudal ethics, close ties between parent and child were central to the Confucian ethical system, which was based on the patriarchal family and filial piety. Even so, the puppet theater of the 1740s did not focus on filial piety but on the parent's love for the child, which conflicted with the higher Confucian virtues of loyalty and duty, which had to be observed even at the cost of the child.

Particularly important to the history plays is the fallen low-status figure. Each play is set in a historical "world" (*sekai*) with a cast of well-known, prominent figures. The crucial and climactic third act, however, centers on marginal low-status characters (such as Kanpei and Kumagai), who represent an "innovation." These marginal figures, who are fallen or weak and include women, become the exemplars of virtue inspired by the samurai code of honor, loyalty, and self-sacrifice. Kanpei and Kumagai (in *Chūshingura* and *Ichinotani*, respectively) each have made serious mistakes in the past and thereby atone for them through extreme self-sacrifice. For the puppet playwrights, who were not allowed to depict contemporary events, the medieval period became a means both to uphold samurai values and to comment indirectly on contemporary society and bakufu policy.

In the mid-eighteenth century, the bunraku history play usually had five acts, ten or more separate scenes (three or four of which were climactic), thirty to forty characters, multiple protagonists, and a performance time of about nine hours. Today, a performance of the bunraku version of *Chūshingura*, for example, has six chanters and six shamisen players, performing in succession, to present the protagonist Yuranosuke—an undertaking that no single kabuki actor could match. In 1733, puppets with movable fingers were introduced, and in the following year the Takemoto Theater invented the three-man puppet (one at the head and right arm, one at the left arm, and one at the feet), commandeered by the famous Yoshida Bunzaburō (d. 1760), who captivated the audience by making the movements of the puppets almost identical to those of living actors.

During Chikamatsu's time, the chanter always held the highest position, but beginning in the mid-1730s the puppeteer began taking the highest position. In the famous Chūshingura incident in 1748, Yoshida Bunzaburō, the puppeteer who was manipulating the protagonist Yuranosuke in the debut performance of *Chūshingura* by the Takemoto Theater, and Takemoto Konodayū (1700–1768), the chief chanter, had an argument, apparently over matters concerning the performance. The director of the Takemoto Theater, Takeda Izumo II, settled the matter in favor of Bunzaburō, who had become a superstar whom the theater could not afford to lose, and brought in a chanter from the Toyotake Theater. Konodayū moved to the Toyotake Theater and was followed there two years later by the playwright Namiki Sōsuke. Because the Chūshingura incident ended up mixing the distinctive styles of the two theaters, it is thought to foreshadow the end of the puppet theater's golden age. The Toyotake Theater (as a theater dedicated to puppet theater) closed in 1765, and the Takemoto Theater closed in 1767/1768.

TAKEDA IZUMO, NAMIKI SŌSUKE, AND MIYOSHI SHŌRAKU

At the Takemoto Theater, Takeda Izumo, the theater director and playwright, and his troupe—which included Takeda Izumo II (Koizumo, 1691–1756), Miyoshi Shōraku (1696?–1771?), and Namiki Sōsuke (Namiki Senryū, 1695–1751)— produced the so-called three great works of puppet theater, which were staged for a short time between 1745 and 1751 and continue to this day to be performed by both puppet theater and kabuki: *Sugawara and the Secrets of Calligraphy* (*Sugawara denju tenarai kagami*, 1746), *Yoshitsune and the Thousand Cherry Trees* (*Yoshitsune senbonazakura*, 1747), and *Chūshingura: The Storehouse of Loyal Retainers* (*Kanadehon Chūshingura*, 1748). In 1751, Namiki Sōsuke returned to the Toyotake Theater, where he wrote his final play: *Chronicle of the Battle of Ichinotani* (*Ichinotani futaba gunki*, 1751). Although some scholars consider Namiki Sōsuke to be the genius behind all these plays, others believe that the driving force was Takeda Izumo (both father and son).

CHŪSHINGURA: THE STOREHOUSE OF LOYAL RETAINERS
(*KANADEHON CHŪSHINGURA*, 1748)

Chūshingura: The Storehouse of Loyal Retainers was first performed in Osaka as a puppet play in 1748. It was and continues to be the most popular drama in the theatrical tradition, with later versions on film and television. It quickly became a staple in the kabuki theaters in Kyoto, Osaka, and Edo, where it remains the most frequently performed work in the repertory. *Chūshingura* was written as a collaboration by the same three authors—Takeda Izumo II, Namiki Sōsuke, and Miyoshi Shōraku—who had composed *Sugawara and the Secrets of Calligraphy*. There is some thought that it was Namiki Sōsuke who wrote act 6, which is translated here, but there is no direct evidence for this.

The attack by forty-seven former samurai of the Akō Domain on the Edo residence of Kira Yoshinaka in the Twelfth Month of 1702 to avenge the humiliation of their late lord, Asano Naganori, startled the military government and the public. More than a year and a half earlier, Asano had suddenly attacked Kira, a high bakufu official, in the palace of the fifth shōgun, Tokugawa Tsunayoshi (r. 1680–1709), during an important ceremony for representatives from the Kyoto Imperial Court. Although Kira was only wounded, Asano was ordered by the furious Tsunayoshi to commit *seppuku* (ritual suicide) immediately. The band of forty-seven thus were avenging what they saw as the wrong done to their lord, as they believed that Kira, too, should have been punished. The vendetta group went to the Asano family grave in Sengaku-ji temple to await judgment. After a period of deliberation by the government, they were condemned to commit seppuku, considered an honorable form of execution. The forty-seven loyal samurai instantly became popular heroes, but because the vendetta could also be interpreted as an affront to the bakufu, the plays based on the event were immediately banned. Soon after Tsunayoshi's death in 1709, however, a new administration began to change those bakufu policies deemed to be unpopular and publicly restored the Asano family's position. Then starting late in 1710, perhaps sensing a change in the official attitude toward popular tragic heroes, playwrights and fiction writers began to produce a string of plays and novels (ukiyo-zōshi) on the theme of the forty-seven rōnin but set the tale in the late-fourteenth-century world of the historical chronicle *Record of Great Peace* (*Taiheiki*), with actual or slightly altered names.

The final scenes of acts 2, 3, and 4, with the third as the most important, are considered to be the high points of the five-act history play. *Chūshingura* is different from other history plays of the time in having eleven acts (actually closer to scenes), but these eleven scenes can in fact be grouped into five (real) acts. Thus, the corresponding conventional high points of the play are act 4 (Lord Enya Hangan's suicide, equivalent to the last scene of act 2), act 6 (Kanpei's suicide, equivalent to the final scene of act 3), and act 9 (Honzō's suicide, equivalent to the last scene of act 4). In performances today, acts 6 and 9 are considered the most difficult and are performed by only the most experienced chanters in the troupe. Although Ōishi Kuranosuke, the leader of the forty-seven conspirators, who appears in the play as Ōboshi Yuranosuke, is the focus of those interested in the factual history of the vendetta, the core climactic scene in the play, the sixth act, which is translated here, centers on the lowest figure, Hayano Kanpei, whose indiscretions are thought to be one of the reasons for his lord's disgrace and who consequently has been kept out of the vendetta group. Hayano Kanpei's name is taken from the historical figure Kayano Sanpei, of the Akō Domain, who committed suicide before the vendetta, but the Hayano Kanpei in the play is essentially fictional. The same is true of two other lowly figures in the sixth act: Okaru, a farmer's daughter in the service of Lord Enya and the lover/wife of Kanpei, and her brother Teraoka Heiemon, named after the historical Terasaka Kichiemon, also of the Akō fief, who mysteriously disappeared after the vendetta attack. Significantly, the playwrights concentrated on two men, Kanpei and Heiemon, who were low foot soldiers (*ashigaru*) and who had to sacrifice themselves in order to regain their proper samurai status. Okaru and her two elderly parents also sacrifice themselves for the cause.

The nineteenth-century kabuki version, which is presented here, makes several changes in the original jōruri text, two of which alter the interpretation of the action. In the original jōruri, immediately after Kanpei stabs himself, he says that he intended to commit suicide if his request to join the vendetta were denied. The kabuki rendition, however, omits this line and creates the impression that Kanpei commits suicide to atone for the murder of his father-in-law, Yoichibei (Okaru's father). Also in contrast to the jōruri text, which presents a severe view of samurai honor as an absolute ideal, the kabuki version humanizes Kanpei. In both the jōruri and kabuki versions, the irony of Kanpei's death is that it was necessary for the restoration of his samurai position but also unnecessary, since he did not kill his father-in-law.

A review of Kanpei's actions earlier in the play is essential to understanding act 6. In act 3 Kanpei is on duty at the palace, the only attendant for his lord, Enya Hangan, representing the historical Asano. Okaru, in service to Lady Enya (Kaoyo) and in love with Kanpei, arranges for them to meet while on duty. Enya's attack on Kō no Moronao (representing the historical Kira) in the palace occurs while they are together. This lapse of duty is the cause of Kanpei's disgrace and of his exclusion from the vendetta group. In act 5 Kanpei, now a hunter trying to make a living, meets Senzaki Yagorō (a member of the vendetta group) at night and hears about the plan to raise money for a memorial to Lord Enya. He promises to raise money for the cause and asks to be allowed to join the vendetta. Then Yoichibei, father of Kanpei's wife, Okaru, returns along the same road at night from Kyoto to Yamazaki with fifty *ryō* in gold, half the agreed sale of Okaru to a Gion brothel for a five-year contract. Yoichibei has taken this initiative to help Kanpei raise money for his cause, though without Kanpei's knowledge but with the consent of his own wife and daughter. He encounters the thief Sadakurō, a former Enya retainer but now a villain, who kills Yoichibei and steals the money. A wild boar runs near by, and two shots fire out, instantly killing Sadakurō. Kanpei runs up, thinking that he has killed the boar, discovers in the dark that it is a man, finds the money, decides to accept it as a gift from heaven, and rushes off with the money to give it to Yagorō. Act 6 begins the next morning.[1]

CHARACTERS

HAYANO KANPEI, a former retainer of Enya Hangan, whose lapse on duty is considered a cause of his lord's tragedy; married to Okaru

YOICHIBEI, a poor farmer and father of Okaru

OKARU, wife of Kanpei and formerly in service to Lord Enya's wife, Kaoyo

OKAYA,[2] mother of Okaru

OSAI, female owner of the Ichimonjiya brothel in Kyoto (originally cast as Saibei, a male owner)

GENROKU,[3] agent for the Ichimonjiya brothel

YAHACHI, ROKU, KAKUHEI, local hunters

---

1. The text is from the modern Edo/Tokyo version. The modern Osaka kabuki version is closer to the original jōruri version.

2. This name was created in kabuki in the late Edo period.

3. Genroku does not appear in the original jōruri version.

SENZAKI YAGORŌ, a former retainer of Enya Hangan and one of the vendetta group

HARA GŌEMON, a former retainer of Enya Hangan and one of the vendetta group

Act 6, Kanpei's Suicide

The setting is a poor farmer's house in Yamazaki between Osaka and Kyoto. After the suicide of Lord Enya Hangan and the dissolution of the Enya fief, Kanpei has become a rōnin and taken refuge in the house of his wife Okaru's parents. The chanter, in full view and accompanied by a shamisen player, sings in bunraku musical style.

CHANTER (*singing*):
>The Misaki dance in full swing,
>your cue, old man,
>take Grandma's hand.
>
>The harvest song accompanies the farmers as they cut barley in Yamazaki, a hilly area, where the poor farmer Yoichibei lives in a weathered hut, now the hideaway of Hayano Kanpei, who has lost his position as a samurai. Kanpei's wife sits alone, facing a mirror, and combs her beautiful hair, disheveled by sleep—a beauty far too precious for rustic life.[4] Her mother, now old and needing a stick to walk, returns along a path through the fields.

OKAYA: My dear daughter, you've done up your hair? It looks beautiful! Everywhere you turn, people are busy harvesting the summer barley. All young folk are singing, "Your cue, old man, take Grandma's hand." Every time I hear it, I worry about father's being late. I went to the edge of the village, but there's no sign of him, no word at all.

OKARU: That's not good. What could be keeping him? Shall I run out and have a look?

OKAYA: No, no. A young woman can't just wander about the village. And you of all people, you hated to walk in the countryside even as a child. That's why we sent you into Lord Enya's service. But it seems that after all that, you're fated to be tied forever to the tall wild grass of the countryside. But you don't seem to mind—returning here with Kanpei.

OKARU: What are you talking about, mother? That's only natural. As long as I'm with the man I love, how can I complain, no matter how rustic the place or how hard the life? The Bon Festival will be here soon. Just as the song

---

4. Her hair is being fashioned for her trip to the Kyoto brothel. She has agreed to her father's plan for her to go into service to help Kanpei raise money to enable him to participate in the vendetta.

says, "Your cue, old man, take Grandma's hand." I want to go with Kanpei to the festival. You must still remember what it was like to be young.

OKAYA: What silly things you still say! Ha, ha, ha.

CHANTER: The mother laughs, embarrassed at such frank banter from her brash and lively daughter.

OKAYA: You sound so lively even when you know you have to leave soon.

OKARU: No, I'm resigned to the plan. As long as it's for Lord Enya, I'm ready and willing to go into service at Gion. But I can't help but worry about you and father.

OKAYA: Now, now, no talk of that. We're only simple folk. Your elder brother Heiemon also served Lord Enya. We have no one else to worry about.

CHANTER: Interrupting their intimate chat, a palanquin from the Ichimonjiya House in Gion arrives. (*Osai, Genroku, and two palanquin bearers enter along the hanamichi, or runway.*)

GENROKU: The house over there is the home of your new employee.

OSAI: Are we here already? My, it was hot on those winding paths in the rice fields. Not a spot of shade the whole way!

GENROKU: Didn't you know? That place is famous for being so exposed to the elements. (*He thinks a moment.*) Bearers, take the palanquin over to the next house and leave it there.

BEARERS: Yes, sir.

GENROKU: Take care of it. (*Turns to the house*) Is Yoichibei at home?

OKAYA: Yes, who is it? (*Realizing who it is*) Oh, you're the man from Kyoto who came before. You must be tired after such a long journey. Okaru, the man from Kyoto is here.

OKARU: We should be able to find out why father is late.

GENROKU: Sir, please come inside.

OSAI: Please excuse this intrusion. My, how hot it is today.

OKAYA: Daughter, aren't you serving tea to our guests?

OKARU: It's coming. (*Okaru sets out the tea and tobacco.*)

OSAI: No, please don't worry yourselves on our behalf. We don't need anything. By the way, wasn't the thunder and lightning terrible last night! (*Osai looks over at Okaru; Genroku tugs at Osai's sleeve.*)

GENROKU: Well, madam, what do you think?

OSAI: A fine specimen, one of the finest jewels I've ever seen. No problem here.

GENROKU: I knew you'd be impressed. Ha, ha. (*He pauses to think.*) By the way, it was a long, hot journey for Yoichibei yesterday. I presume that he returned safely.

OKAYA: You mean you didn't come with Yoichibei? He hasn't returned since leaving for Kyoto yesterday. He should be back by now!

GENROKU: How strange! (*He pauses to think.*) Perhaps he was bewitched by a fox near Fushimi Inari. (*Implying that he stopped off at the pleasure quarter*) No, that couldn't be it. He must've gone elsewhere.

OKAYA: No, he'd never do that.

GENROKU: No, you're right, Madam. The woman here is the owner of the house in Gion. Please come closer.

OKAYA: So, you're the madam of the house where my daughter will be in service? It's strange that we meet here in the countryside, in our humble home. Thank you for coming so far.

OSAI: So, you are the young lady's mother? Yes, I met your husband, Yoichibei, the other day, and I am pleased to meet you as well. I'm Osai of the Ichimonjiya House. You need not worry about your daughter.

OKAYA: Yes, thank you. I trust that you will look after her well.

GENROKU: By the way, madam, we finalized the negotiations we had the other day and agreed on the terms. Your daughter's contract is for exactly five years in exchange for a fee of one hundred gold ryō. Yoichibei said that he needed the money by tonight and asked to borrow the one hundred, begging us tearfully to give him all of it. We agreed to a promissory note and handed over half the money, promising to pay the remainder on delivery. Upon getting the fifty ryō, he set off immediately, happy as a lark, leaving us at about ten last night. We tried to stop him from traveling alone at night with so much money, but he refused to listen and left. Where has he gone?

OKARU: Mother, he wouldn't have gone anywhere else.

OKAYA: Yes, I'm sure he wouldn't stop somewhere else. Especially since he was so excited about showing us the money. He would have rushed home. I just don't understand it.

GENROKU: Now, now, I'm afraid this mystery is your problem. All we're expected to do is hand over the remainder and take the young lady back with us. Osai, give her the fifty ryō.

OSAI: Here's the balance of fifty ryō. Now we've paid the one hundred gold pieces that we agreed to. (*Osai takes out the purse made of a striped fabric and hands it to Genroku.*)

GENROKU: I hereby hand over fifty ryō to complete the deal.

OKAYA: Thank you, but only until father returns, right Okaru?

OKARU: I'm sure that he'll be back soon. Please let's wait until then.

GENROKU: No, if we stop now, we'll never get back. No matter what excuses you offer, Yoichibei's own seal on this contract states our case. Today we've bought this woman's body. We can't afford to lose even a day of her services. Osai, they seem reluctant to part with her. Let's be off.

OSAI: Yes, perhaps you're right. Genroku, could I ask you to escort the young lady?

GENROKU: Well, Miss, let's be off. It seems we'll have to use a little muscle here.

CHANTER: He forces her into the palanquin, pushing her all the way. Just as the bearers lift her up, Kanpei, rifle in hand, wearing a straw raincoat, returns home. (*Okaru is bustled forcibly into the palanquin. Okaya refuses to take the money, but Osai forces it on her. Osai and Genroku walk down the hana-*

michi, in front of the palanquin. Kanpei, coming from the other direction, sees Okaru.)

KANPEI: What, that's Okaru, isn't it?

OKARU: Is that you, Kanpei?

KANPEI: My, where're you going in a palanquin? A hunter's wife setting off in a palanquin! (*Stops to think*) Return it now please. (*Kanpei forces the group to back up along the hanamichi. Okaya notices and comes out.*)

OKAYA: Oh, is that Kanpei? You've returned just in time.

KANPEI: Yes, I just got back now.

OKARU: Mother, my husband has managed to get back in time. (*Osai shows her displeasure as Okaru goes back in the house. Kanpei sits down at the door and removes his sandals. Okaya brings a bucket for him to wash his feet.*)

KANPEI: Mother, wasn't the storm last night really loud? You don't like thunder at all. You must have been worried sick.

OKAYA: Yes, the lightning was terrifying. You must've gotten drenched.

KANPEI: The kimono you kindly washed for me is filthy now. (*Stops to reflect*) Mother, who are those people out front?

OKAYA: Those people . . . (*She hesitates, embarrassed.*)

KANPEI: Okaru, who are those people?

OKARU: Those people?

KANPEI: What's going on here? Here, take this kimono and hang it out to dry. (*Kanpei changes into his formal kimono, with the crest displayed. Okaya puts away his wet kimono.*) Okaru, bring me my two swords.

OKARU: You have no need for them.

KANPEI: I said bring them here! (*He pauses to think while Okaru goes to get the swords and returns. Kanpei puts the short sword into his obi and holds the long sword in his hand.*) Something important is going on here. Mother, dear wife, explain what this is all about.

CHANTER: He repeats his order and sits down in the middle of the room. The agent Genroku steps forward.

GENROKU: Well, then, you must be our new employee's husband. Whether you're her lord or master, not even Amida or the Buddha can interfere. The contract is legal and binding, with her father's name, signed and sealed. You can't do a thing about it. We handed over the gold and are taking her with us. We won't budge on this. You get what I mean?

KANPEI: Mother, I haven't a clue to what he's talking about. What's going on?

OKAYA: No surprise that you're confused. Remember that you told our daughter that you were in desperate need of money. We heard from her about it and wanted to help but didn't have a cent to our name. Father wondered if you had even considered selling your wife to get the money. He thought you were afraid to broach the idea in front of us. Father decided to sell Okaru without telling you, saying a masterless samurai is known to

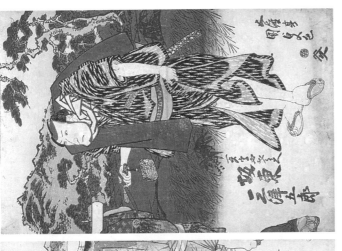

A woodblock triptych of act 6 of *Chūshingura* by Utagawa Kunisada (1786–1864), later known as Utagawa Toyokuni III. Kunisada, an extremely popular and prolific ukiyo-e artist acclaimed for the verisimilitude of his actor prints, made the original set for the 1833 production of *Chūshingura* at the Ichimura Theater. In 1835, for another production at the Morita Theater, Kunisada recycled the triptych, replacing the faces of at least two of the earlier actors. Kanpei (*left*), played in the 1835 production by Sawamura Tosshō I (1802–1853), whose name appears at the lower right, is in hunting clothes with a wicker rain hat, resting a rifle on his shoulder. He is wearing a specially patterned robe (with characters interwoven to form the name Kikugorō) made for Onoe Kikugorō III (1784–1849), who performed the role in 1833. Kanpei halts the palanquin that is about to take away Okaru (*center*), acted in 1835 by Bandō Tamasaburō (1813–1855), whose name appears on the palanquin roof. Ichimoniya Saibei (*right*), played in 1833 by Bandō Mitsugorō IV (1800–1863), whose name appears at the lower left, stands behind the palanquin, holding a pipe and a tobacco purse. Saibei, a male, was initially a female role, that of Osai. (Courtesy of the National Theatre of Japan)

kill and steal if the need arises. No shame in selling his wife as long as it raises money to serve his lord. He surely won't be angry with us, Father thought. So, yesterday he set off for Gion to settle the deal and should have returned by now. Just as we were worrying about him, this man and his agent arrived. They say that last night they gave Father fifty ryō, half the agreed sum, on condition that they would hand over the remaining half on the delivery of Okaru. We tried to stop them from taking Okaru away, but they wouldn't listen. Just as they were leaving, you arrived. What shall we do now?

KANPEI: Now it's clear. First, let me thank you and father for your thoughtfulness and my wife for her kindness. But there's no need now to sell Okaru. I've had a bit of luck myself.

OKAYA: A bit of luck—what good news!

OKARU: What's happened?

KANPEI: This bit of luck, it was strange the way it happened last night. (*He pauses to think and looks around, considering his words carefully.*) Let me tell you about it. In any case, we can't send Okaru away, at least not until father returns.

GENROKU: What's all this? How can you hold back an employee we've rightly paid for?

KANPEI: Mother, where are these people from?

OKAYA: They're the owners of the house where Okaru is to serve.

KANPEI: I see, then, you are the master of the Gion house?

OKAYA: No, the woman over there is the owner. The fellow here works for her.

KANPEI: I understand now. (*He pauses to think. Osai nods to him.*) I'm sorry to have been rude before. I didn't know the situation. Please forgive me. (*Pauses to think*) Of course you are within your rights and we cannot argue, but it was her father who made the deal, and it was to him that you supposedly paid the fifty ryō.

GENROKU: Sir, I am sorry to interrupt, but what do you mean by "supposedly paid"? That's not good enough. Though it may sound a bit immodest, "Genroku the Agent" is known throughout Kyoto and Osaka. My face is known as far as Edo and Nagasaki. Among my peers, I sit first at the table, respected by all. The madam here also runs the grandest pleasure house in all of Gion, virtually the fabled Isle of Women, with an unprecedented array of courtesans. We won't be taken in by any shenanigans. How dare you accuse us of lying about the money! There's surely a headman or an official in this village. Take us to him now! You're too afraid to take us there, are you? What? It seems you're wearing samurai swords. Um, I'm not afraid of samurai swords. If I were afraid of swords, how could I eat skewered tofu! What a joke! Hurry up, get the authorities. (*Genroku advances threateningly, but Osai intervenes.*)

OSAI: Now, now, Genroku. What are you yelling about? He understands well enough without your screaming.

GENROKU: I'm sorry that I've had to get involved in such a stupid argument.

OSAI: Not to worry. You should be ashamed of yourself. Yelling like that doesn't help anyone understand. It's much better to be calm and talk softly.

GENROKU: What you say is certainly true, but he just doesn't get it. (*Starts to threaten again.*)

OSAI: Shut up, will you! I'm telling you to stop. Won't you listen to me?

GENROKU: It's not that, but . . .

OSAI: All right, you step back over there. (*Genroku steps back, and Osai pauses to consider her words.*) So you're the husband of our employee.

KANPEI: Yes.

OSAI: I'm pleased to make your acquaintance.

KANPEI: We meet under strange circumstances. You've traveled far today. Thank you for coming all this way.

OSAI: Yes, yes. There's no need for such deep bows and formalities. Please lift up your head.

KANPEI: Yes, sir.

OSAI: Now, it seems that there has been some misunderstanding in your discussions with Genroku. He was afraid of embarrassing me and unfortunately began screaming to get his way. He's being too businesslike. I'm sure he has offended you, but please understand his position and try to forgive him.

KANPEI: You're being too polite. It was nothing.

OSAI: The gist of the matter is as Genroku has described it. Earlier the lady's father begged us several times to complete the deal. We were in fact planning to reduce the number of our women, and so I was reluctant to agree to his request. But since he was an elderly gentleman, I gave in to his pleas. (*She pauses to think.*) But better than talking, I can show you some proof. (*She takes out the contract.*) We kept this record of the contract. Her term is five years for one hundred gold *ryō*, with fifty on deposit and the remainder on delivery. (*Kanpei reflects on this.*)

KANPEI: Madam, would you let me see the contract, please.

OSAI: You mean this document?

KANPEI: Yes, I just want to check it.

OSAI: Yes, of course. (*She ponders a bit.*) There, have a look for yourself. (*Kanpei reads the contract and turns to Okaya.*)

KANPEI: Mother, this seal is definitely father's, isn't it?

OKAYA: Yes, no doubt about it.

KANPEI: Then, this is definitely father's seal. (*Thinking*) This seems to be father's seal all right. (*He returns the contract.*)

OSAI: There, as you can see, the seal is definitely Yoichibei's. (*Ponders*) Now let me explain what happened last night. We handed over the fifty gold pieces, and he was so delighted that he immediately wrapped them up in a towel and left. I told him that it was dangerous to carry the money like that and took a bit of material from an underkimono and made two purses, one for him to take the fifty in and one for the fifty that I would deliver. I had him put it around his neck on a string. He wanted to leave right away, but I told him to wait. It was already past eight in the evening, and it would be dangerous to travel at night alone. I suggested that he spend the night and leave the first thing in the morning, but he was determined and must have set off about ten last night. (*Kanpei sees the fabric of the purse and, after remembering something, drops his pipe.*)

KANPEI: What, you say that you lent Yoichibei that purse?

OSAI: Yes, I lent it to him.

KANPEI: That striped one. (*Ponders*) Let me see that please.

OSAI: Of course, here, take it.

KANPEI: Okaru, could you get me a cup of tea?

OKARU: Yes.

CHANTER: Kanpei glances cautiously around before he looks down to compare the purse with the one in his pocket. The fabric is exactly the same. "Oh, my god," he thinks. "Was the man I shot and killed last night my father-in-law?" A jolt of pain strikes his heart. (*Okaru serves him some tea. Kanpei tries to drink it but chokes and coughs.*)

OKARU: Did you choke on the tea?

KANPEI: It's OK.

CHANTER: Okaru, realizing nothing, presses him.

OKARU: Dear, what have you decided? Are you going to send me off or not? It's your decision.

KANPEI: Yes, of course. Since it must have been exactly as they've described it, you must go.

OKARU: Even without waiting to say good-bye to Father?

KANPEI: Oh, yes, I met Father this morning, but I don't know when he'll be back.

OKARU: What!? (*Ponders*) Mother, he met Father this morning.

OKAYA: Then, you met Father? What a relief! I'm so pleased! Okaru, he met Father.

OKARU: If you met him, you should have told us right away.

OKAYA: Sir, did you hear that? Our son-in-law met Father.

GENROKU: One should ask seven times before being suspicious, they say. You must be relieved to hear that Mr. Yoichibei is fine. I'm happy as well. If there're still any complaints, then they'll have to be taken up by the authorities. Your son-in-law met Yoichibei, so we all can celebrate.

OSAI: Madam, if you come to Hongan-ji temple to pray, be sure to drop by and see us. We're right in the middle of Gion. (*She pauses.*) The husband, too, is welcome to visit if he has time. I promise to let him see his wife. My, my, after all this talk, the shadows have grown long. We have at least ten miles to home. Genroku, let's get moving. Get everything ready.

GENROKU: Yes, ma'am. Young lady, let's be off. (*Okaru is reluctant to stand up.*)

OKARU: Yes, I'm coming, but let me have a moment more.

GENROKU: The farewells are always like this for the family. (*Pauses*) Madam, let's go out front. (*Osai and Genroku go outside. Okaru closes the door and moves close to Kanpei. Shamisen music plays in the background.*)

OKARU: Mother, I have to leave now. Listen, Kanpei, both Mother and Father are quite old. It's up to you to look after them. Take care especially of Father—he's got those painful ailments.

CHANTER: How sad that she pleads for the care of her father, unaware of his death. Her mother comforts her.

OKAYA: Oh, Kanpei, you must want to say farewell to your wife. Are you afraid that Okaru will regret her decision?

OKARU: No, no. No matter how long we're separated, as long as I'm selling myself in the service of my lord, I have no regrets at all. I'll leave bravely. But to leave without seeing father . . .

OKAYA: As soon as he returns, we'll send him right away to see you. Take moxa to keep strong. Come back with a healthy face. Wait, wait, there's something I want you to have. (*She thinks for a moment.*) Here, take this tissue and fan, you'll need them. Is there anything else you need? Make sure you don't stumble and fall and hurt yourself. Take this tea, it suits you well. Drink it morning and night. I must tell you about the pleasure quarter: women are often forced to prove their love by cutting a finger. If you get in that situation, don't cut your finger or even a strand of hair. Don't drink too much saké either. Even when pressed to drink, don't swallow too much. If you have to, just say that you dislike it and refuse. (*She pauses to think.*) What a cruel fate—to see my beautiful daughter suffer this way.

CHANTER: Teeth clenched, she finally breaks down in tears.

OKARU: Mother, don't say any more. The more you say, the harder it will be to leave. Dear Kanpei, I'm off now. (*Pauses*) Farewell. (*She begins to hurry out.*)

KANPEI: Okaru, wait.

OKARU: What is it? (*She rushes back to him.*)

CHANTER: Kanpei wants to tell her everything, but in front of the others he suffers in silence.

KANPEI: Take care of yourself.

OKARU: Yes . . . (*She breaks down crying. Genroku comes back inside.*)

GENROKU: Now, now, it's never good to have a tearful parting. Hurry. Get in the palanquin.

CHANTER: A pitiful sight: the bearers lift the palanquin and rush off. (*Okaya sees them off down the hanamichi.*)

OKAYA: Don't worry a bit about us. Remember what I told you. Don't do anything rash. Don't forget the moxa. Oh, show me your face once more! My, are you gone already? I talked too much. It won't do any good. Off to the mountains with me. Cranes and tortoises bring us luck. (*She continues talking as she returns and sees Kanpei.*) Um, now Kanpei, you can see how even her mother is reconciled to the situation. Don't you worry yourself sick over this. You're all the two of us have to depend on now. (*Pauses*) Speaking of Father, why hasn't he come back yet? You met him this morning, didn't you? Where was it you met? Tell me about it. (*She moves closer, urging him to speak.*)

KANPEI: Yes, I saw him all right.

OKAYA: Where did you meet him? Where did you leave him?

KANPEI: I left him at . . .

OKAYA: You left him where?

KANPEI: It was at Toba; no, at Fushimi.

CHANTER: Yodo, Takeda, he babbles on. At that moment three local hunters—Yahachi the Babbler, Roku the Musket, and Kakuhei the Badger—arrive, carrying Yoichibei's body. They set it down just inside the door and come inside.

YAHACHI: I was returning from hunting last night and found Yoichibei.

THREE HUNTERS: Members of the hunters' guild have brought him home.

OKAYA: What are you talking about? You mean that you've carried him home drunk again? No jokes, please. I was already worried sick. Enough of your teasing!

THREE HUNTERS: No, we're not joking. He's dead.

OKAYA: You're still fooling me. (*Pauses. Kanpei squirms in agony. The three lead Okaya over to the body. She lifts off the straw mat.*)

CHANTER: Okaya jumps back in shock at the sight.

OKAYA: No, who could have done this? Kanpei, who murdered him? You must avenge his death.

CHANTER: "Dear Yoichibei," she cries out in despair, but to no avail. The hunters try to comfort her.

YAHACHI: Madam, you must be devastated. It's only natural for you to weep. Madam, your son-in-law here, isn't he an upright fellow, a former samurai?

ROKU: If that's the case, then we will make a strong force. In any case, we must report this to the local office and have the murder avenged.

KAKUHEI: With a strong samurai leading us, we'll be glad to follow with our rifles.

YAHACHI: What a terrible thing to happen. Yoichibei was such a kindhearted man, always praying for salvation in the next life.

ROKU: It doesn't help to be a believer when facing a murderer. I feel bad for Okaya, who will be alone.

KAKUHEI: Yeah, with Yoichibei gone, it'll be like a lantern without a candle.

YAHACHI: What do you mean by that?

KAKUHEI: You know, she'll be alone at night.

TWO HUNTERS: How can you say that at a time like this!

THREE HUNTERS: It's a pity.

CHANTER: Offering their condolences, they depart for their homes.

OKAYA: Father's dead, killed! Who could have murdered him? My dear Yoichibei.

CHANTER: While the mother weeps, Kanpei moves closer to her.

OKAYA (*pauses*): Kanpei, I know that it couldn't be possible, but something worries me. No matter how much of a samurai you used to be, it seems strange that you're not at all surprised to see father dead. When you saw him this morning, did you get the money from him? What did he say when he saw you? Speak up! (*Pauses to think*) You don't seem to have an answer. The proof is right here.

CHANTER: She lunges at Kanpei and pulls the purse from his pocket.

OKAYA: I caught a glimpse of this purse earlier. Look, it has blood on it! You killed father! (*She grabs the lapels of his kimono.*)

KANPEI: No, that's . . .

OKAYA: Don't give me any excuses. No more babbling from you! Even if you try to hide it, heaven misses nothing. Killing Father and then stealing the money—who's it for? (*Pauses*) I get it. You plotted to sell the daughter of your destitute father-in-law. But instead of handing over the hundred ryō, you're keeping half for yourself. All this time, we took you to be an upright fellow. But we've been duped. Awful! Hateful man! A beast! I'm so shocked I can't even cry.

CHANTER: Pity my dear Yoichibei.

OKAYA: He had no idea that he had a beast for a son-in-law; he wanted so much to restore you as a samurai. Old as he was, he traveled at night to Gion in Kyoto, willing to give up everything to help you. But it was all for nothing, bitten by the dog that he fed, cruelly murdered. You demon! Bring my husband back to life!

CHANTER: Her anger rises and she attacks Kanpei, grabbing his hair and beating him on the head.

OKAYA: Even if I cut you to pieces, what good would it do, what peace would it give me?

CHANTER: Raging in anger and grief, she finally collapses in a flood of tears. Feeling the full weight of his crime, Kanpei too burns with fever, sweating all over. He claws the tatami floor, awaiting heaven's wrath. Just then, two samurai in large wicker rain hats arrive. (*Hara Gōemon and Senzaki Yagorō approach along the hanamichi.*) The pair walk slowly up to the house.

GŌEMON: Is this the house where Hayano Kanpei lives? I'm Hara Gōemon.

YAGORŌ: And I'm Senzaki Yagorō.

TOGETHER: We have come to see him.

CHANTER: Their timing is a disaster for Kanpei.

KANPEI: Mother, someone is at the door.

OKAYA: Are you going to flee?

KANPEI: I won't escape. Hold me tighter.

CHANTER: He takes out his short sword and puts it under his arm to greet the men. (*Kanpei, with Okaya at his side and his sword in hand, opens the door.*)

KANPEI: My, my, you've come a long way to this humble abode.

GŌEMON: It seems that we've arrived at an awkward moment.

KANPEI: No, no, it's just a little family matter. Don't worry. Please come inside.

GŌEMON AND YAGORŌ: Please excuse us.

CHANTER: Although there is no formal entrance hall, the samurai show deference to their hosts, awaiting permission to enter. Kanpei and Okaya bow to greet them.

KANPEI: Recently, with regard to the incident involving our lord's demise, I was negligent and absent from my post. No words can ever make up for this terrible error. I have requested a pardon and asked to join the others at the memorial on the anniversary of our master's death. I ask again for your consideration.

CHANTER: He speaks humbly, begging them to intercede. Gōemon responds.

GŌEMON: Yes, we know about your request, and despite being a rōnin of no means, you have raised a considerable sum for the memorial stone. Yuranosuke was duly impressed by your efforts, but since the memorial is for the salvation of our dead master, he has refused your offer. He said that money from someone who has committed such disloyalty and dishonor would not be acceptable to the spirit of Lord Enya. I return the money with the seal unbroken. Yagorō, hand it over.

YAGORŌ: Yes, sir.

CHANTER: He immediately takes the money from his pocket and places it before Kanpei.

KANPEI: Then this money could not be of service? (*Reflects*) Couldn't it be used . . . ?

CHANTER: He suddenly loses his senses, and Okaya bursts into tears.

OKAYA: What! Does this cruel villain still not know the wrath of his parents? Listen, Mr. Samurai. My husband was quite old, but ignoring his own welfare and going against his religion, he sold his daughter to a brothel. This man waited for him to return with the money and murdered him, stealing the money. Heaven's will has brought you here. How could he be worried about helping you out? Yes, yes, please, strike him down, beat him to death. I'm furious.

CHANTER: She collapses in tears. The samurai are shocked at this news, and both draw their swords and press Kanpei from both sides. Yagorō yells roughly.

YAGORŌ: Kanpei, how could you cleanse your past crime with money tainted by the vile murder of your father-in-law? Shall I make it clear for you? No one, as filthy and as inhuman as you are, could ever understand the way of the samurai. Killing your father-in-law is the same as murdering your father—to steal money. The vilest villain! I'll skewer you like meat on a spear.

CHANTER: Gōemon's eyes spit anger.

GŌEMON: Wait, Yagorō. Your words strike home, but wait, sit down. (*Thinks*) Listen, Kanpei. They say an honest man will not drink from a thieves' spring even when desperately thirsty.[5] Did you really think that money stolen from a father-in-law whom you murdered would serve the spirit of your dead lord? How perceptive Yuranosuke was to have refused your money, realizing that you were rotten to the core.

CHANTER (*for Kanpei*): Ah, forgive my crimes.

GŌEMON: The pity of it all is that news of this incident will get out and people will say, "Look at that Hayano Kanpei, a retainer of Enya Hangan; his disloyalty and crimes are notorious." Don't you see that the mud will soil not only you but also our dead lord? You idiot! Such wickedness could not be yours alone. What demon has entered your soul? What a twisted soul, a warped man! (*Pauses*) Yagorō, no matter what we say, it'll fall on deaf ears, like reading sutras to a cow. Just speaking with him will taint us. Let's leave at once.

YAGORŌ: Certainly. Let's be off. (*Kanpei tries to stop them leaving.*)

KANPEI: Wait a moment, both of you, please. Since you say I have shamed our master, let me explain. Please sit down and listen. (*Pauses*) Last night I saw Yagorō, and after we had parted, I was wondering how on earth I could raise the money needed for the memorial. I was lost in thought when I saw a wild boar on the mountain. I fired two shots and knew that I had hit it. But when I rushed to find it, I realized that it was a man, not a boar, that I had killed. I was desperate in the dark and checked his pockets for medicine and found instead a purse full of money. I knew it wasn't right, but I felt that the gods above had given me the money. Thankfully I accepted it. I set off immediately to hand over the money to you. Thinking that I might be allowed to join the vendetta, I returned home with hope, but I soon realized that the money was from the sale of my wife and that the man whom I had killed . . .

TWO SAMURAI: The man whom you killed was . . . (*Kanpei takes out his sword and stabs himself.*)

KANPEI: My father-in-law.

TWO SAMURAI: What!

KANPEI: (*A bamboo flute accompanies Kanpei's monologue.*) No matter what has happened since, I, Kanpei, was born the heir of Hayano Sanzaemon. At the age of fifteen I became a personal retainer of Lord Enya, receiving a stipend of 150 *koku*. My family received the beneficence of the Enya clan for generations, but I had a brief lapse: I forgot the gratitude that I owed my lord and let myself be overcome with carnal desire at a critical moment. I

---

5. From the Chinese collection *Wen xuan* and found in various earlier classical texts.

failed him at the palace when he needed me most. I felt the force of heaven's wrath for my crime and hoped to join the vendetta to clear my name. The gold did no more good than a stone tile. Like the crossbill's beak, everything I do goes the wrong way. I have no excuses, but please, both of you, witness my seppuku to the end.

CHANTER: Blood seems to run through his eyes, tears of shame and regret. Yagorō gets up after listening to his tale and goes to Yoichibei's body, checking the wound.

YAGORŌ: Look, here! It looks like a bullet wound, but it's from a sword.

GŌEMON: Where? (*Pauses and then checks the body*) You're right, Yagorō. You've made me remember something. Remember that on the way here, we saw a traveler dead from a bullet wound. Looking closer, we realized it was Ono Sadakurō, a treacherous villain, disowned even by his own father, the wicked Kudayū. We heard that he had turned into a highway robber who had joined roving gangs. No doubt, he's the one who murdered Kanpei's father-in-law. Kanpei, you've acted too soon.

CHANTER: At this revelation Kanpei is shocked; Okaya, too, is aghast.

OKAYA: Then, Father's murderer was not Kanpei?

TWO SAMURAI: That's right.

OKAYA: Listen, son. I beg with my hands folded in prayer. An old woman's stupid heart cursed you. It was all a mistake. Be strong, Kanpei. You mustn't die.

CHANTER: Her tears and warmth make Kanpei look up.

KANPEI: Mother, have your doubts been cleared? Are you both now sure of my innocence?

TWO SAMURAI: All doubts are gone.

KANPEI: Oh, how happy that makes me. My prayers have been answered. Mother, don't grieve. Father's death, my wife's service won't be wasted. The money will aid the cause. Hurry, hand it over!

CHANTER: At this, Okaya, still weeping, hands over the two packets of money, placing them in front of them.

OKAYA: This purse holds the spirit of Kanpei. Take it and think of it as Kanpei that goes with you on the vendetta.

GŌEMON: This gold is worth more than its weight.

YAGORŌ: Son and father-in-law, each presented fifty.

GŌEMON: Together, they make one hundred, a memorial for their spirits. The mother's duty is to pray for their salvation. (*Pauses*) May they achieve buddhahood.

TWO SAMURAI: Hayano Kanpei.

KANPEI: No, achieving buddhahood is defiling, not for me. I won't die. My spirit stays here on earth, to join you in avenging his death!

CHANTER: His voice grows weak as the torments of death grow fiercer. Mother still weeps.

This is one of a series of actor prints produced by Utagawa Toyokuni III (1786–1864) at the end of his career. Toyokuni made this print for the 1860 production of *Chūshingura* at the Nakamura Theater, starring Nakamura Fukusuke I (1830–1899) as Hayano Kanpei. This is a close-up portrait (*ōkubi-e*) of Kanpei committing suicide, graphically depicting his disheveled hair; the blood-smeared palm marks on his arm, chest, and face; and blood gushing from his stomach. (Courtesy of the Tsubouchi Memorial Theatre Museum, Waseda University)

OKAYA: Listen, Kanpei. I want to tell Okaru. Don't die now. Let me bring Okaru to see you.

KANPEI: No, no. You mustn't tell her about father's death or mine. She was sold to help the vendetta. If she hears about all this, she won't do her job as well and be disloyal to our master. Now that my honor is restored, I can help father across the Three Rivers of the netherworld.[6]

CHANTER: He pulls the sword across his stomach.

GŌEMON: No, Kanpei, don't. Stop! I have something to show you. Yagorō, bring it. (*Yagorō rises, opens the door, looks around, and returns.*)

CHANTER: From his pocket Yagorō takes out a scroll and rolls it open.

GŌEMON: Recently a group of us pledged to take revenge against our lord's enemy Kō no Moronao. Your sacrifice to get this money will impress Yuranosuke. This is the list of our league.

CHANTER: Before he can finish reading, Kanpei interrupts.

KANPEI: Then, who's on the list?

YAGORŌ: Ōboshi Yuranosuke is the first, followed by forty-four.

GŌEMON: Adding you to the list brings it to forty-six loyal retainers. Take this as a present with you to the other world.

KANPEI: Yes.

---

6. In order to reach the next world, departed souls must ford the Three Rivers seven days after they die. One's karma determines how difficult one's crossing will be.

CHANTER: He takes out a brush and writes his name.

TWO SAMURAI: Seal it with blood.

KANPEI: Yes sir.

CHANTER: He cuts further into his stomach, creating the shape of a cross, and grabs his entrails, pressing them to the oath.

GŌEMON: We witness the seal of blood.

TWO SAMURAI: We accept you into the league. (*After signing the vendetta conspiracy list with his blood, Kanpei slumps down for a moment. Yagorō gratefully accepts the money, and the samurai take their leave. They stand outside the house and respectfully bow farewell. Inside, Kanpei collapses again in pain. Okaya is desperate as she tries to hold up her son-in-law. She panics at the realization that she will be left alone, her husband dead, her daughter sold to a brothel, and her son-in-law dying before her eyes. She begs him not to die. She weeps behind Kanpei, who reaches out weakly to find his sword. He takes a kerchief, grabs the blade, and slits his own throat. He then struggles to sit up straight, puts his hands together in prayer, and strikes a defiant pose. His face shows the rising pain, and with one last attempt to hold on, he finally collapses. Yagorō and Gōemon bow from outside. Okaya weeps in despair, left alone.*)

CHANTER: Pity this life cut short. (*Memorial bells ring. Gōemon and Yagorō leave the house. Okaya clings to him weeping. Kanpei dies as Gōemon and Yagorō depart.*)

[Hattori Yukio, ed., *Kanadehon Chūshingura*, pp. 143–182, translated by C. Andrew Gerstle]

NAMIKI SŌSUKE

Namiki Sōsuke (1695–1751), the chief author of *Chronicle of the Battle of Ichinotani* (*Ichinotani futaba gunki*), had also collaborated a few years earlier in writing *Sugawara and the Secrets of Calligraphy*, *Chūshingura*, and *Yoshitsune and the Thousand Cherry Trees*. He had completed the third act of *Ichinotani* when he died in September 1751. Other writers completed the remaining two acts, and the full play opened two months after his death. However, since the premier production, only the "Atsumori's Camp" and "Suma Bay" scenes from the second act and "Kumagai's Battle Camp" scene, which is translated here, from the third act have been staged.

CHRONICLE OF THE BATTLE OF ICHINOTANI
(*ICHINOTANI FUTABA GUNKI*, 1751)

Chronicle of the Battle of Ichinotani is a five-act history play written for the Toyotake puppet theater in Osaka. The first performance was in 1751 and was followed the next year by a kabuki version in both Osaka and Edo. The story concerns the twelfth-century struggle between the Genji (Minamoto) clan, which was led by Yoshitsune and Yoritomo, and the Heike (Taira) clan, which had close ties to the emperor. In the thirteenth-century military epic *The Tale of the Heike*, which is the original source of this story, Atsumori, a young Heike warrior, is slain by Kumagai, an older Genji warrior who wants to spare the young man's life because Atsumori reminds him of his own son but is forced to slay him because his own troops are approaching. In the story's reincarnation in the late medieval nō play *Atsumori*, the ghost of the slain Atsumori, who is the protagonist (*shite*), recalls and relives his struggle with Kumagai, who has become a priest, taking the Buddhist name Renshō. In the end, Kumagai, once Atsumori's foe, becomes his spiritual ally and prays for his salvation. In *Chronicle of the Battle of Ichinotani* the story has been completely recast, adding, in the manner of Edo drama, love relationships with women and a complex web of hidden obligations and ties. Kumagai, the Genji warrior, has been ordered by his superior, the Genji general Yoshitsune, to kill Atsumori, a young Heike warrior and the son of the emperor by Lady Fuji. Kumagai is in a deep dilemma, for earlier both his life and that of his wife Sagami were saved by Atsumori's mother, Lady Fuji, who pardoned them for a serious transgression, but he must do his duty to his lord and the cause for which he is fighting. To satisfy both his commander Yoshitsune and his conscience, he substitutes the head of his own son Kojirō for that of Atsumori, whom he has taken prisoner. As it turns out, Yoshitsune also has hidden obligations to the Heike, specifically to Yaheibyoe Munekiyo, who saved him and his brother Yoritomo as children and who appears in disguise here as Midaroku, an old woodcutter. In the end Yoshitsune pays back Munekiyo by returning Atsumori to the Heike.

Before the "Kumagai's Battle Camp" scene, widely considered to be the most dramatic scene in *Chronicle of the Battle of Ichinotani*, Kumagai has already smuggled the real Atsumori off the battlefield and substituted his own son Kōjirō, whom he has disguised as Atsumori and decapitated. To carry the substitution (*migawari*) to its successful conclusion, however, Kumagai must deceive both his wife, Sagami, whom he wishes to console but cannot, and Lady Fuji, who thinks Kumagai has killed her son and wants to kill him for it. At the emotional climax of the scene, Yoshitsune inspects the severed head in a dramatic convention called *kubi jikken* (head viewing). The power of the drama derives in large part from the double roles that most of the main characters—Kumagai, Yoshitsune, Sagami, and Midaroku—must play simultaneously, resulting in considerable irony in the dialogue and in great tension between their outward behavior and inner feelings, appearance and fact. The tension and mixed emotions are intensified and complicated by the various obligations that the characters bear toward one another, particularly Kumagai toward Yoshitsune and Lady Fuji, Yoshitsune toward Midaroku, and Sagami toward Lady Fuji. The following is the kabuki version, which is very similar to the original jōruri text. It should be kept in mind that in the puppet theater, an evil character like Kajiwara is indicated by the puppet head, which cannot change, thereby making the distinction between good and evil characters absolute.

CHARACTERS

SAGAMI, Kumagai's wife, formerly in the service of Lady Fuji

GUNJI, Kumagai's family retainer

KOJIRŌ, the son of Sagami and Kumagai; the young warrior sacrificed to save Atsumori

LADY FUJI, a court lady, mother of Prince Atsumori, and consort of the emperor

ATSUMORI, a prince, the son of the emperor and Lady Fuji, who fought as a young Heike (Taira) warrior

KUMAGAI, Kumagai Jirō Naozane, a Genji (Minamoto) warrior in the service of Yoshitsune, father of Kōjirō, married to Sagami, and indebted to Lady Fuji

KAJIWARA, also known as Heiji Kagetaka, a retainer of Yoritomo, the Kamakura (Genji) shōgun; an evil man who threatens to reveal to Yoritomo Yoshitsune's kindness to Munekiyo/Midaroku (now a Heike warrior)

YOSHITSUNE, a Genji (Minamoto) general, the shōgun (Yoritomo)'s younger brother, and Kumagai's lord; saved by Yaheibyoe Munekiyo as a child

MIDAROKU, an old stonecutter in disguise, actually Yaheibyoe Munekiyo, a Heike (Taira) warrior who once saved the lives of the infant Yoshitsune and his brother Yoritomo

Act 3, scene 3: Kumagai's Battle Camp

The scene is Kumagai's battle camp in Ichinotani, at Suma. The main room, raised and with an open veranda fronting it, faces the audience. A cherry tree in full bloom grows to the right, next to an official notice board that reads, "Here stands a rare double-flowering cherry tree from the south. If anyone cuts off a branch, his punishment, following the ancient case of the Maple Tree, shall be to cut off one finger for each branch cut. Second Month, 1184."

CHANTER (*singing to shamisen accompaniment*): Even the heavens turn. Some day will the moon shine over Suma Bay through clear skies? The Heike drift on waves off Yashima Island in the bay, while among the prospering Genji host, the peerless Kumagai, has established his camp in Ichinotani by Suma Bay, encompassing in its impenetrable palisade of felled trees a youthful tree in full bloom, known as Kumagai's cherry tree. Passersby, of whom some can read and some cannot, crowd about staring at the notice board, which forbids the cutting of a single flower.

FIRST FARMER: That's a fine cherry tree, isn't it? Look at the blossoms.

SECOND FARMER: Not the tree, look at the notice. The priest Benkei wrote it, they say. But I can't read one character.

THIRD FARMER: The tree is protected by General Yoshitsune. (*Puzzled*) "Cut off a branch of flowers, cut off a finger," it seems to say.

FOURTH FARMER: That scares me. Instead of a flower, cut off a finger? Sounds like they want our heads.

FIRST FARMER (*wide-eyed*): Just standing here I feel like I'm stepping on a tiger's tail!

SECOND FARMER: Quick as a wink . . .

THIRD FARMER: . . . before we break a branch . . .

ALL: . . . we had better leave! (*They hurry off right to loud drum beats.*)

CHANTER (*singing to shamisen accompaniment*): Having traveled a long distance, Kumagai's wife, Sagami, approaches . . . (*Sagami, wearing a gold brocaded kimono and covered with a black traveling robe, enters, accompanied by a retainer and bearer.*) . . . immersed in thoughts of her son and her husband, she seeks out the palings of the battle camp and recognizes on the white curtains their family crest.

SAGAMI: We're here at last. (*To the retainer*) You may go ahead.

RETAINER: Attention inside!

CHANTER (*singing to shamisen accompaniment*): Hearing the noisy call, Gunji comes out. (*Gunji, the family retainer, enters, wearing a samurai's two swords.*)

GUNJI: Who approaches our master's gate? (*He is amazed to see Sagami.*) My lady, what are you doing at the battle camp?

SAGAMI: Ah, Gunji. You are looking well.

GUNJI (*bowing*): Thank you, Madam. But first you must come in. Please enter.

SAGAMI: If I may . . . (*The bearer helps Sagami remove her black traveling robe and replace it with another robe of gold brocaded silk.*) You may rest now.

RETAINER AND BEARER: Yes, my lady. (*Sagami climbs the short steps to the main room and sits in the place of honor to the left.*)

SAGAMI: Tell me, are my husband and son well?

GUNJI: Both are well, my lady.

SAGAMI: Please tell my husband I am here, Gunji.

GUNJI (*bowing*): Master has gone to the temple today, and Kojirō has not recently been seen with our lord. Aren't you tired from your long journey, my lady? Please lie down and rest. (*Sagami nods assent and is about to rise.*)

CHANTER (*singing to shamisen accompaniment*): As they are exchanging numerous greetings, Prince Atsumori's mother, the court lady Fuji . . . (*Alarm drums and cymbals sound. Lady Fuji runs onto the hanamichi, dressed in black and a straw hat low over her face. She carries a small dagger in her hand, ready for use. She looks anxiously behind her.*) . . . fleeing from the jaws of the tiger, hurries under falling blossoms toward the battle camp. (*She runs under the cherry tree and leans against the gate. She poses as cherry blossoms fall.*)

FUJI (*calling through the gate*): Pursuers are close behind. Please hide me!

GUNJI (*startled, answers stiffly*): This is a camp at war. You won't find a safe place here.

SAGAMI (*compassionately*): Wait, Gunji. A woman understands a woman's plight . . . (*She goes to the gate. Opening it, she takes one quick look at Fuji before she hides her face.*) Ahh! Isn't it Lady Fuji?

FUJI (*cautiously looking out*): Your voice . . . is it Sagami? (*They joyously recognize each other. Sagami kneels politely before Fuji, formerly her mistress at the imperial court.*)

SAGAMI: Imagine meeting again unexpectedly . . .

FUJI: . . . after so long. You are well I hope . . .

SAGAMI: . . . and you? My!

FUJI: My!

TOGETHER: My, my!

SAGAMI: Please enter, my lady.

FUJI: Forgive me. If I may. (*Sagami places her hands delicately before her and bows low. She gestures politely for Fuji to enter.*)

CHANTER (*singing*): She is welcomed with an open heart. (*Fuji loosens her robe, goes up the steps, and sits in the place of honor at the left. Sagami kneels opposite her. After closing the gate, Gunji kneels behind his mistress and bows low.*)

GUNJI: Clap if I can be of service, my ladies.

CHANTER (*singing*): Gunji then rises and leaves. (*The two women look fondly at each other. Sagami glances to each side to see that they are alone, then bows.*) Sagami, at last, bows. . . .

SAGAMI (*warmly*): Truly, an age has passed like a dream since the time you lived in the palace, an intimate of the emperor, and I, infatuated with the warrior Satake Jirō, then on duty at the palace too, was forced to flee with him to the east. You could not know it, but it pleased me to hear that after you had conceived by his Majesty, you became engaged to Lord Tsunemori, chief minister of the Heike clan, and shared in the time of Heike power and prosperity. Then, when this war between Heike and Genji scattered the Heike clan, I was worried for your safety. How relieved I am to see your ladyship's smiling face.

FUJI (*smiling*): Dearest Sagami, it is good to see you well. My, my. I heard you were carrying a child when you went away, and I do not even know if you gave birth to a girl or a boy. How is the child?

CHANTER (*singing*): Let two women meet even briefly and, happy in their tears, piled-up words tumble forth. Eyes glistening, Lady Fuji . . .

FUJI: Humans cannot escape adversity. The son I gave birth to and raised to become a handsome youth, dear Atsumori, has been slain in battle, while my husband, out at sea off Yashima Island, has left me alone to face I cannot imagine what future! Can you understand my despair?

CHANTER: As she laments plaintively . . . (*The two women dab their eyes with their kimono sleeves.*)

SAGAMI (*bowing sympathetically*): No wonder you are upset. I will consult with my husband. Out of consideration for the kindness you have shown us in the past, please entrust your welfare to us. While my husband was a member of the imperial Northern Guard he was called Satake Jirō; now his name is Kumagai Jirō Naozane. He is well known, the commander of all samurai forces in Musashi Province.

CHANTER (*singing*): Hearing this, Lady Fuji . . .

FUJI: The warrior you married as Satake Jirō is now Kumagai Jirō?

SAGAMI (*modestly*): He is.

FUJI: This Kumagai Jirō is . . . your husband? (*Fuji rises on her knees wide-eyed then slowly sinks back.*)

CHANTER: . . . calms her shocked heart.

FUJI (*deceptively quiet*): Do you remember, dear Sagami, when your adultery was discovered at the palace and the emperor sentenced you to prison? It was I who interceded and enabled you to escape with Satake Jirō through the great gate at night?

SAGAMI (*warmly*): How could I forget your kindness?

FUJI: If you have not forgotten, then you will return that favor by helping me slay an enemy.

SAGAMI: Kill someone? Who?

FUJI (*looks at Sagami piercingly*): Your husband. Kumagai. (*Sagami recoils.*)

SAGAMI: Ehh? You harbor such anger?

FUJI: I do! (*She weeps.*) The man who killed Prince Atsumori is . . . your husband, Kumagai! (*Fuji falls forward weeping.*)

SAGAMI: Can this be true?

FUJI: Haven't you heard?

SAGAMI: I have just arrived after the long journey from the east. Now to hear your story . . . it is unbelievable! (*Trying to mollify Fuji*) Allow me to ask my husband when he returns if this is true.

CHANTER (*singing*): Struggling to speak through their tears . . .

SENTRY (*off, at the rear of the hanamichi*): Announcing Lord Kajiwara!

FUJI: Why should he come here?

SAGAMI (*worried*): He must not see you. Quickly . . . (*They rise. Sagami directs Fuji toward the small room at the left.*)

FUJI: When Kumagai returns . . .

SAGAMI: . . . I will find out the truth . . .

FUJI: . . . and if he is my son's slayer . . .

SAGAMI: . . . even though he is my husband, he is your enemy.

FUJI (*intensely*): Kill him without fail.

SAGAMI (*weak and close to tears*): You may . . . trust me.

FUJI: Then, dear Sagami . . . !

SAGAMI: Lady Fuji . . . ! (*Fuji goes into the small room at the left. Sagami closes the sliding doors and stands alone, upset.*)

CHANTER (*singing*): Entering immediately, Kajiwara seats himself in the place of honor. (*Drums play, indicating the entrance of an evil person. Kajiwara strides onto the hanamichi. He wears dark-colored battle dress: armor, leggings, straw sandals, and a samurai's two swords. His face is dark and cruel. Without ceremony he enters the room and sits at the left.*)

GUNJI (*bowing politely*): What can I do, my lord?

KAJIWARA (*rudely*): Call your master.

GUNJI: Master Kumagai Naozane went to offer prayers at the temple today. Be so kind as to entrust any message to me.

KAJIWARA: What? Kumagai's left camp? Agh! (*Shouting off*) Hey! Soldier! Bring in the old stonecutter!

SOLDIERS (*off, at the rear of the hanamichi*): Yes, my lord!

CHANTER (*singing*): Saying yes, they drag before Kajiwara the innocent-looking stonecutter Midaroku. (*Two soldiers bring Midaroku, bound with ropes, down the hanamichi and force him to the ground by the veranda. He is an old man and is wearing work clothes.*)

KAJIWARA: Well, old man, who ordered you to make a monument for Atsumori? Since all the Heike have been driven into the western seas, a two-faced Genji samurai must be your benefactor. Confess it! I'll torture you with boiling lead, slice you down the back, and rub salt in your wounds if you lie! Well, you old fool?

MIDAROKU (*a bit ironically*): Your accusation is absurd. I told you, Atsumori's spirit requested the grave marker. He placed the order and vanished. I don't care whether he had any interest in buying a monument to the Five Roads to Virtue, but it's the principle of the thing, and he didn't pay me a penny, principal or interest. At least I'd have borrowed his soul-fire as a night-light to work by if I'd known what he was up to. Should I send a bill to the devil? I can't shake money from a ghost in hell, so, believe my story or not, the best one you'll get this side of nirvana is that I did a favor for Atsumori's ghost. *Namu Amida Butsu, Namu Amida Butsu.*

CHANTER (*singing*): His words are as slippery as eels.

GUNJI: You can see that talking to him is like pounding nails into rice paste. Please rest inside for a while, sir.

KAJIWARA (*though furious, bides his time*): It's obvious who ordered you to carve the marker. When Kumagai returns, the three of us will have this out face to face! Take this fellow in! Gunji, lead the way!

CHANTER (*singing*): The old stonecutter is forcibly led away. Kajiwara is ushered into the inner room. . . . The sun is setting in the west when Sagami slides open the center doors to wait for her husband's late return. (*Sagami enters and crosses slowly to the center of the room.*)

SENTRY (*off, at the rear of the hanamichi*): The master has returned!

CHANTER: Does Kumagai Jirō Naozane, slayer of Atsumori in the flower of youth, understand life's impermanence? (*Kumagai appears on the hanami-*

chi. He wears a formal kimono of white silk, covered by trousers and a vest made of royal brocade. A temple bell tolls. Deep in thought, head sunk on his chest, he slowly approaches the camp. Sagami, seeing him, kneels and bows very low.) Although he is a fierce warrior, he is capable of compassion, and returning home, his heart is full. (*He pauses and gazes at the Buddhist prayer beads grasped tightly in his hand. Slowly he crosses to the gate.*) He looks at his wife, Sagami . . . (*Angered that Sagami is there, he faces front, slaps his thigh, and strides up the steps into the room, where he immediately sits down.*) with stern displeasure and goes to sit without speaking. (*To distract his master, Gunji speaks immediately.*)

GUNJI (*bowing*): Lord Kajiwara arrived a short time ago, wishing to discuss with you his investigation of the stonecutter Midaroku, whom he has brought with him. He is waiting in the inner room, Master.

CHANTER (*singing*): He spins out the details.

KUMAGAI: What is he investigating, I wonder? In any case, see that he is offered saké. (*Still trying to protect his mistress, Gunji hesitates.*) Serve him saké, I say. What are you waiting for? Go!

CHANTER (*singing*): Severely scolded, he has no choice. . . . (*When Gunji rises to leave, Sagami pulls on his sleeve to hold him. Frightened, he politely frees himself and goes out to the center doors.*) . . . Sagami pleads with her eyes, and even though Gunji leaves, his heart remains behind. Watching him go, Kumagai speaks . . .

KUMAGAI (*harshly, to cover his grief*): You! Wife! What do you mean coming here? When I left home you were strictly warned not to disturb us, but you have paid no attention. You also know women are forbidden to enter a battle camp! Insolent, brazen woman!

CHANTER (*singing*): Before his angry display, Sagami hesitantly . . .

SAGAMI (*bowing politely*): Your rebuke is justified, dear husband, but I worried so much about Kojirō going into his first battle that I couldn't sleep. So, wondering whether I would walk only a mile and learn how he is or walk five miles and have word from him, I found I had traveled seven miles down the road, then ten, and, before I knew it, one hundred miles . . . until I was in the capital. (*Hoping to disarm him, she laughs.*) Ha, ha, ha, ha, ha! (*She covers her face with her partly open fan. Still unmoved, he looks stonily ahead.*) Arriving in the capital and hearing stories on every hand about the battle raging at Ichinotani, what parent would not be drawn to where her child was? Forgive me, I beg you. (*She bows, then looks up happily.*) Is Kojirō well?

CHANTER (*chanting*): The question draws a harsh reply from Kumagai!

KUMAGAI (*strongly*): Agh! When a warrior enters the battlefield, he abandons life! It looks cowardly to cling to affections, to ask if Kojirō is well. (*Pausing, he steals a glance.*) And if he had been killed, what would you do? Well?

SAGAMI (*slowly, with dignity*): You don't understand. If Kojirō died, even in his first battle, my heart would be at ease as long as the opponent who killed him was a worthy general.

CHANTER (*singing softly*): Her brave words match the thought in his heart. His face softens as he speaks . . .

KUMAGAI: Listen, then:

By wrestling from Hirayama Mushadokoro the honor of advancing to the head of our troops, Kojirō distinguished himself. Single-handed, he slashed his way into the Heike camp. Although he was slightly wounded in the struggle, he has brought eternal glory to our family.

SAGAMI (*startled*): What? It wasn't a fatal wound?

KUMAGAI: Ah. I see regret is written on your face. (*He poses strongly. His right hand rests on his closed fan. He glares at her.*) Answer me! If his wound were fatal, would you grieve?

SAGAMI (*with difficulty she lies*): It's not that. I was moved to ask out of joy whether his efforts were at least meritorious to the extent that he was slightly wounded. (*She pauses and looks closely at Kumagai.*) Were you with Kojirō then?

KUMAGAI (*gesturing with the closed fan*): I was. From the time of his first danger we were together in the battle. I took him, protesting, under my arm and carried him back to camp. Later, to my incomparable glory, I took the head of their rear-guard commander, Prince Atsumori! (*Kumagai poses. Sagami falls back with a gasp.*)

CHANTER (*rapidly to shamisen accompaniment*): At his words Sagami pales with shock while behind her, the emperor's intimate listens . . .

FUJI (*rushing from the room at the left*): My son's enemy! Kumagai!

CHANTER: Unsheathing her dagger, she cries "Kumagai!" He uses her scabbard . . . (*Fuji slashes at Kumagai several times to loud beats. He fends off the blows with the empty scabbard.*)

KUMAGAI: Who calls me an enemy?

CHANTER: . . . Pressing her to the floor. (*He does not see her face.*)

SAGAMI: Do not be hasty. She is our Lady Fuji.

KUMAGAI: What? Lady Fuji? (*He lifts her up enough to recognize her. He is aghast.*) Truly it is Lady Fuji!

CHANTER: Meeting so unexpectedly, he leaps back and bows in respect. (*He takes the dagger from her hand and starts to bow to her. Fuji seizes his long sword and is about to draw it out. To show his sincerity, he quickly removes the short sword from his sash and pushes it toward her, thus disarming himself. He looks Fuji directly in the eye, then prostrates himself before her. For the moment she is unable to kill him, but her desire for revenge is undiminished.*)

FUJI: How inhuman, Kumagai, to take the head of a mere child in combat. (*She weeps loudly. Recovering, she nods to Sagami.*) You have sworn to kill your husband.

SAGAMI: But I . . .

FUJI: Did you lie before?

SAGAMI: But . . .

FUJI: Will you help me?

SAGAMI: Well . . .

FUJI: Well?

BOTH (*alternately*): Well, well, well, well!

FUJI (*hand on hilt of Kumagai's long sword*): Well? Sagami! Will you?

SAGAMI (*weakly, after an anguished pause*): I . . . will!

CHANTER: "I will," she replies, although her breast feels paralyzed!

SAGAMI (*bowing, the words scarcely audible*): My Lord Naozane. Knowing all the while that Prince Atsumori was the noble seed of an emperor, you felt obliged to kill him. There must be some reason. If there is . . .

SAGAMI AND FUJI: . . . I pray . . .

CHANTER: They speak as if suffocating . . . (*Fuji seems ready to draw Kumagai's long sword, but Sagami gestures for her to stop. Fuji slowly sinks to the floor.*) . . . tears fall unrestrained.

KUMAGAI (*looking coldly ahead*): What nonsense. In this war all Heike warriors are enemies. Why should we forgive Atsumori, a Heike prince, or anyone else, when we're fighting for our very lives?

    (*He falls back on one hand and calms Fuji with a gesture.*) Listen to me, Lady Fuji, what happens on the battlefield is beyond human power. Resign yourself to it. I will tell you what happened that day and how Prince Atsumori died in battle.

CHANTER (*sings, with great emotion, to shamisen accompaniment*): He settles himself and begins to narrate the tale! (*Fuji sits reluctantly. He moves forward and poses on his knees, grasping the closed fan in his right hand.*)

KUMAGAI (*strongly*): Now then, it so happened that during the long night of the sixth, at the time the clouds in the east were beginning to brighten, among the throng of Heike warriors who assaulted our vanguard of two— Hirayama and Kumagai—one man stood out . . .

CHANTER: . . ."unsurpassed in scarlet-laced armor, forcing even Hirayama to cease fighting and flee to safety on the beach!" (*Kumagai lifts the closed fan, strikes his chest with it, and points into the distance, miming the action described in the narration.*)

KUMAGAI: What a fearless young samurai! "Come back," I shouted, "don't waste yourself on a fleeing enemy when I, Kumagai, am here! Come back! Come back!"

CHANTER: Holding the fan, he motioned him to return . . . until he turned his horse's head and strikes blows twice, three times, on the wave-struck shore. (*Kumagai closes the fan and, to block beats, strikes his thighs as if whipping a horse.*)

KUMAGAI: "Let us fight," I said; "Yes," he replied.

CHANTER: Casting away their long swords, they crash to the earth between their horses! (*He moves the fan back and forth as if the two were grappling over it, opens it, and suddenly presses it down to the floor.*)

FUJI (*trembling*): Ah! Then did you hold down the young warrior?

KUMAGAI: Looking closely at his face, I saw he was some sixteen years old, the same age as my son, a court child with blackened teeth and eyebrows delicately plucked, surely still living with his parents. Thinking of their deep agony and of my own affections for a son, I lifted him to his feet.

CHANTER (*slowly*): Brushing off the dust . . . (*Kumagai mimes brushing the dust from his sword.*)

KUMAGAI: "Quickly! Flee!"

FUJI: Did you urge him to go? Then you did not intend to kill him?

KUMAGAI: Although I urged him, "Quickly, flee," "No," he replied, "once thrown to the ground by the enemy, I am dishonored. Take my head quickly . . . Kumagai!"

FUJI: What? Did he say, "Take my head"? What a noble phrase! (*She collapses, weeping loudly.*)

KUMAGAI (*straining for control*): My lady, please! When I heard this, even more tears welled up in my breast. (*Forcing back tears, he presses the closed fan against his chest.*) Ahh, what if my son Kojirō had been thrown to the ground by the enemy and was about to lose his life in this same way? The way of the samurai is not so base! Even though I seized my long sword . . .

CHANTER (*singing loud*): "I hesitated! I could not draw! (*Kumagai seizes his long sword. Rising on his knees, he stamps one foot on the top step of the stairs and poses in an anguished pose to loud block beats. The chanter cries out Kumagai's agony.*) Then I heard! From the mountaintop behind me, the routed Hirayama cried out!!"

KUMAGAI (*chants powerfully*): "Kumagai! You are a traitor! He is at your mercy, yet you dream of helping Atsumori," he called out to me! Ahhhh!! (*With a prolonged cry, Kumagai falls forward. He steadies himself by leaning on the upright closed fan*). "There is nothing I can do. Have you any final words? If so, speak and I will . . ." (*He breaks off and puts his hands to his eyes.*)

CHANTER: Eyes brimming with teardrops . . .

KUMAGAI: "Father is safely at sea, but Mother's welfare weighs on my heart. In this unsettled world, yesterday's clear skies have clouded. My single request, Kumagai, is that you help my mother in the difficult life to come." There was nothing else to do but . . . strike off the child's head! (*Screaming*) Thus I fulfilled the custom of the battlefield! (*The two women rise on their knees in horror, then sink back weeping loudly. Kumagai's face twists in agony; he rises on one knee, holds the open fan before his chest, and poses. He throws the closed fan to the floor in a gesture of revulsion. His chest heaves with sobs, and he prostrates himself on the floor. The three weep together.*)

CHANTER (*singing*): In the midst of this narrative, Lady Fuji . . .

FUJI: Had he truly loved his mother, couldn't he have hidden in the capital as his father urged . . .

CHANTER (*speaking for Fuji*): ". . . instead of setting out for Ichinotani? Ah, how I bitterly regret that when you bravely dressed in armor . . ." (*Rising on her knees, Fuji mimes bidding Atsumori farewell.*)

FUJI: . . . I urged you, joyfully, to go!

CHANTER (*for Fuji*): "Although I was resolved, my heart bursts with anguish!" (*Sagami and Fuji look comfortingly at each other, then fall forward, weeping loudly and wiping their eyes. In her grief Fuji turns away. Kumagai sits impassively.*) Thinking, "how natural her grief," Sagami deliberately raises her lamenting voice.

SAGAMI: No, my dear lady. Among all the soldiers who fled by ship to Yashima Harbor, only one, Prince Atsumori, remained behind to earn through death a greater fame than that of a hundred thousand mounted warriors. Would you be happy if he quaked in hiding, the object of people's jibes and laughter? How disgraceful that would be.

CHANTER (*singing*): As she is admonished, Kumagai . . .

KUMAGAI (*turns to Sagami, soberly*): Excellent, Wife. It will not do for a lady of the court to remain here. Go with Lady Fuji at once, anywhere she wishes. (*He faces Fuji gravely.*) Resign yourself, my lady. I must prepare for Lord Yoshitsune's inspection of Prince Atsumori's head. Gunji, are you there? Gunji? Gunji! (*The two women bow very low. Kumagai replaces the short sword in his sash and takes the long sword in his hand. He rises and looks intently at Fuji.*)

CHANTER: Calling, he goes out of the room. (*Kumagai gestures to Fuji to be restrained, then strides out through the doors at the center, which automatically open and close for him. A time bell tolls in the distance. Sagami rises and helps Fuji put on her outer robe. Plaintive poetic narration.*) As the sunset bell tolls time's uncertain passing, the lights of the battle camp light up more and more[7] (*The bells toll again. Two boy servants bring out small glowing lanterns.*) . . . the grief of stricken Lady Fuji. (*Sagami sheathes the small dagger and hands it respectfully to Fuji. She kneels and bows. The bell tolls.*)

FUJI (*sadly, to quiet shamisen accompaniment*): When I think of him, pity overwhelms me. He carried an object next to his flesh, from which, until his death, he was never parted:

This flute called Green Leaves. (*She takes out a small flute wrapped in cloth.*) It proves how strong the bond between mother and son is, that this flute, which Atsumori gave the stonecutter as payment to raise a marker over

---

7. "More and more" (*itodo*) is a "pivot word" (*kakekotoba*). In translation the line may be read either "light up more and more" or "more and more the grief."

his grave, should mysteriously come into my hands. (*She gazes wonderingly at the flute.*)

CHANTER (*singing slowly for Fuji*): "If the soul still remains on earth, why do you not appear before me?"[8]

FUJI: You do not hear my voice, my son. Ahh! What memories are contained in this flute! (*She folds back the cloth and gazes longingly at the polished bamboo tube.*)

CHANTER: Pressing it inconsolably to her breast, she laments. (*Fuji presses the flute to first one cheek and then the other. She cradles it tenderly in long kimono sleeves and holds it tightly to her breast. She sinks to the floor, weeping loudly.*)

SAGAMI (*drying her tears*): The flute should be a consoling memento, its notes, even more than a chanted dharani prayer, leading his soul through all obstacles to repose. Dearest mistress, let its sound be Prince Atsumori's voice. (*Sagami looks inquiringly at Fuji.*)

CHANTER: In accordance with her urgings, Lady Fuji plays. . . . Although her tears flow into the holes of the flute and her fingers tremble, the notes rise clear. . . . (*Two boy servants enter from the inside room. One carries a black lacquered pitcher of water and matching basin; the other, an incense tray. The first servant pours water over Fuji's hands, then moves back respectfully. The second servant passes a small white towel to Sagami, who in turn passes it to Fuji, who carefully dries her hands. Fuji takes the flute from inside her kimono, unwraps it, and holds it before her reverently. Sagami places a pitch of incense on the coals and clasps her hands in a silent prayer. Fuji raises the flute to her lips.*) Bound by ties of love between mother and son . . . (*Gentle notes of "Tsukuebue," flute accompaniment. The shadow of a man appears on the translucent paper doors.*) She catches one fleeting glimpse of a form, vague as shadows of a heat wave, cast on the sliding paper doors. "Surely it is Atsumori!"

FUJI: My child! My beloved!

CHANTER: Rushing forward, she is stopped and calmed by Sagami.

SAGAMI: Dear lady, please listen. The spirit of the dead may appear in the smoke of incense.[9] When Fujiwara Sanekata died in exile, his soul's longing for the capital was so great that he returned in the form of a sparrow. While this form you see may be such a spirit, it is said that the ties of parent and child last but one lifetime. If you approach, his spirit will surely vanish.

FUJI: No, no! Isn't it said that souls of the dead wander on earth for forty-nine days before their incarnation? At least a single word . . . !

---

8. According to Buddhist belief, the soul remains on earth for forty-nine days after death.

9. According to Chinese legend, the spirit of Emperor Li appeared in the smoke of incense offered in his memory.

Lady Fuji (*left*) and Sagami, in white, in the jōruri version of *Chronicle of the Battle of Ichinotani*. (Photograph courtesy of Barbara Curtis Adachi Collection, C. V. Starr East Asian Library, Columbia University)

CHANTER: Shaking loose, breaking loose . . . ! (*Three times Sagami tries to prevent Fuji from reaching the doors, but in the end Fuji forces Sagami to the floor and rushes to the doors.*) When the sliding doors rattle open, there is no figure to be seen, only a suit of scarlet-laced armor standing in its place. (*Both women fall back in surprise.*)

FUJI (*tremulously*): Was the shadow only this?

SAGAMI (*on her knees, gently*): Did you imagine this form in the longing of your heart?

FUJI: Oh, Sagami!

SAGAMI: Dearest lady!

CHANTER: Bound in yearning, unheedingly . . . they cry out their weeping lament. (*Both women wipe their eyes as they cry out rhythmically in unison.*) Time slips by. Then Kumagai Jirō Naozane enters carrying the head box. Sagami pulls her husband's sleeve. (*Kumagai, a deeply melancholy expression on his face, slowly enters. He wears formal dress and carries under his left arm a round case, made of plain wood, used to contain a head taken in battle or execution. Sagami politely holds his sleeve so that he cannot move.*)

SAGAMI (*modestly*): Dear Naozane, the life of mother and child together ends here. Allow them to take final leave of each other at least.

CHANTER (*singing to shamisen accompaniment*): Lady Fuji, still in tears . . .

Lady Fuji, Kumagai holding the head box, and Sagami. (Photograph courtesy of Barbara Curtis Adachi Collection, C. V. Starr East Asian Library, Columbia University)

FUJI (*weeping*): Kumagai, don't you have a child, too? Understand what is in a parent's heart. Even wild beasts grieve for their children. Have pity, allow me one last glimpse.

CHANTER: Although wretchedly imploring him . . . ! (*She sinks to her knees and pulls on his other sleeve.*)

KUMAGAI (*severely*): No! Until the head has been identified, permission cannot be given to view it!

CHANTER: As he pulls free and moves between them, about to go . . . (*He pulls first one sleeve free, then the other, and deliberately walks down the steps. Suddenly the clear, refined voice of Yoshitsune is heard offstage. Kumagai stops and looks back.*)

YOSHITSUNE (*offstage*): Kumagai! Kumagai, don't leave with Atsumori's head! Give it to Yoshitsune! I shall verify it immediately!

CHANTER: With the call of "I shall verify it immediately," the door flies open to reveal . . . General of the Army Yoshitsune! (*Nō drums play a military piece. The center doors slide open to reveal Yoshitsune, the shōgun's younger brother. He wears armor threaded with gold, black leggings, and red shoes. His handsome face is powdered a delicate white.*) Jirō Naozane, his wife, and Lady Fuji fall prostrate. Yoshitsune takes his seat. . . . (*Yoshitsune holds a large war fan firmly in his right hand. Kumagai quickly mounts the steps and kneels at center stage while Sagami and Fuji bow flat to the floor. Four samurai squat on their heels behind Yoshitsune, keeping guard. The music stops.*)

YOSHITSUNE (*elegantly, yet with great inner strength*): Kumagai, to delay in presenting the head for verification and to request leave in the midst of battle cast doubt on your intentions. Concealed in the inner room, I have heard your conversation from beginning to end. I command you: This instant, produce Atsumori's head!

CHANTER (*singing slowly to the shamisen*): Hearing his words, Kumagai strongly answers yes and moves quickly to the young cherry tree, where a notice board has been stuck in the ground, which he pulls out and places, unafraid, before Lord Yoshitsune.

KUMAGAI (*strongly composed*): A short time ago at Horikawa Palace, my Lord Yoshitsune made known his will to one of his vassals by means of a poem fastened to a mountain cherry. In the same way here, Priest Benkei has written on this notice board your command to take Atsumori's head. In obedience to my lord's decree, as written here, the head has been taken! Now, then, confirm it!

CHANTER (*ponderously singing to the shamisen*): When he lifts open the lid . . . ! (*Sagami recognizes Kojirō.*)

SAGAMI: Ahh! That head is . . . !

CHANTER (*singing rapidly*): Struck by the truth, the wife rushes forward; Lady Fuji strains to see! (*With lightning speed, Kumagai claps the lid back over the head. Sagami rushes forward, but he forces her down the steps with the notice board. Fuji, straining to see, is prevented from approaching by Kumagai, who presses her back, using the notice board as a pole.*)

KUMAGAI (*harshly*): Stop! You may see the head after our lord has verified it! You will be silent now! Silence! (*The last word is drawn out in an agonized cry. They pose in a tableau.*)

CHANTER (*emotionally*): Kumagai's admonition . . . (*Both women try to move forward. Kumagai shakes his head fiercely and pushes Fuji back with the board.*) . . . calls them to shame . . . wanting to approach but unable to . . . (*Kumagai raises the notice board over his head. Fuji, suddenly released, plunges headlong down the steps.*) . . . racked by unendurable anxiety! (*To loud beats they pose: Kumagai flicks a long trouser leg forward, plants his foot loudly on the top step, presses the notice board upside down against his shoulder, and glares at the women; Sagami and Fuji, kneeling, face Kumagai, hold up their hands to protect themselves, then fall forward, sobbing bitterly.*) Circumspectly, Kumagai Jirō Naozane proceeds.

KUMAGAI (*gripping the board emotionally*): Prince Atsumori is the emperor's offspring, living in the emperor's Southern Palace. (*Glances significantly at the notice board*) "Rare double-flowering cherry tree from the south: if any person strikes off the flower of one branch, he must strike off the flower of

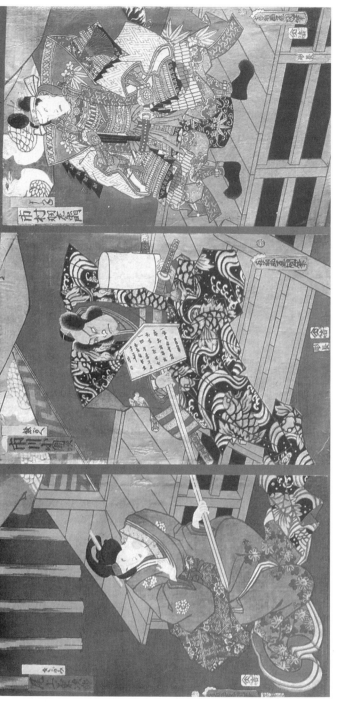

This triptych by Utagawa Toyokuni III (1786–1864) depicts "Kumagai's Battle Camp" with the actors who starred in the 1863 performance of *Chronicle of the Battle of Ichinotani* at the Ichimura Theater in Edo. Yoshitsune (*right*), played by the kabuki actor Ichimura Uzaemon XIII (1844–1903), is dressed in elegant battle armor and seated on a brocade stool. On the stairs, Kumagai, acted by Ichikawa Kodanji IV (1812–1866), holds off with a notice board his wife, Sagami, performed by Onoe Kikujirō II (1814–1875), while secretly holding the head of their son Kojirō. The vertical cartouches note each actor's name and role. (Courtesy of the Tsubouchi Memorial Theatre Museum, Waseda University)

the other."[10] Inferring what your intentions might be, I have cut off his head to correspond to the flower of your command! (*His words are a strangled scream. His body trembles violently.*) Has my lord's will been fulfilled? Or has Kumagai misunderstood? Pronounce judgment!

CHANTER: He cries out! . . . (*The chanter's voice quivers with emotion. His face contorted, Kumagai throws down the notice board and, with a single gesture, takes the lid from the case and thrusts the head of Kojirō before Yoshitsune. The chanter's voice becomes hushed.*) Yoshitsune smiles and initiates the inspection. (*Yoshitsune opens his fan in a languid movement, holds it before his face, turns toward the head, and then slowly lowers the fan. Kumagai looks intently into Yoshitsune's eyes, trying to read his lord's expression. Yoshitsune nods slightly as he recognizes Kojirō. He continues to gaze at the pale face of the dead boy as he speaks delicately, yet he is deeply moved.*)

YOSHITSUNE: Ahh. You have read Yoshitsune's heart to spare the flower. The head was well taken. Now, let those relatives present pay final honor to this dead person, who unmistakably . . . is Atsumori.

CHANTER (*sings slowly*): After hearing these words . . . (*Kumagai bows and moves, on his knees, to the veranda.*)

KUMAGAI (*scarcely audible*): Here, Wife. (*He places the head before her on the veranda.*) Show Prince Atsumori's head to Lady Fuji. (*He looks at her with a look of warning. She slowly raises her eyes to meet his. A look of understanding passes between them. He retires upstage.*)

SAGAMI (*bowing*): Yes.

CHANTER: Saying no more than yes, the wife . . . (*Sagami rises, anguished, unable to look at the head of her son. She sinks to her knees weeping.*) . . . lifts the pitiful head in her hands . . . (*At last, she turns and looks but cannot bring herself yet to touch it. She takes folded paper from her breast, bites down hard on it to gain control of herself, turns away, and stands in a grief-stricken pose, head rhythmically bobbing up and down like a puppet to express her conflicting emotions.*) . . . with brimming eyes she gazes at the changed face of her dead son . . . her breast, choked with bitter grief, her body quaking . . . (*She staggers, catches herself, then sinks to the floor. Holding the head*

---

10. Kumagai's interpretation of the order contains several complicated puns. The word for "bud," *futaba*, is written with the character meaning "youth," but audiences would be reminded of the more common way of writing futaba, with the characters meaning "two" and "leaf," referring to the double leaf that accompanies a budding flower, thus suggesting Atsumori and Kojirō, who are budding or flowering youths of the same age. Being the emperor's son, Atsumori is "rare" or precious; it is "rare" or fortunate that Kojirō, so like Atsumori, would be available for substitution; and a double-flowering cherry tree itself is a rarity. The order (*isshi o kiraba, isshi o kiru beshi*), previously read "if you cut one branch, you must cut one branch [or finger]," is read here, "if you cut one child, you must cut one child," because "one branch" and "one child" are written with characters having the same pronunciation (*isshi*).

out at arm's length, at last she gazes at it, lovingly, as she rocks from side to side.) ahhh! . . . the head in her trembling hands . . . *(Taking the paper from between her teeth, she cradles the head in the crook of her arm and wipes Kojirō's face. Her hands and body tremble.)* . . . seems to be nodding . . .

SAGAMI: . . . as he did, when turning back at the gate, he smiled at me! When I recall his features . . . *(She clutches the head to her breast and presses her cheek against Kojirō's.)*

CHANTER *(emotionally)*: . . . how tragic . . .

SAGAMI: . . . how pathetic!

CHANTER: Her voice stops in her throat!

SAGAMI *(tearfully)*: Dear Lady Fuji. Look. Lamented Prince Atsumori's . . . head! *(Putting a piece of clean paper beneath it, Sagami places the head on the floor facing Fuji. Seeing the head of Kojirō, Fuji turns to Sagami in wonder.)*

FUJI: What? That head is . . . ?

SAGAMI: Yes, it is! *(Sagami quickly covers the head with the trailing of her robe as if to protect it and cries anew. She looks meaningfully at Fuji and partially uncovers the head.)* Look carefully upon this head. May it dispel your rancor. You should, indeed, pay homage . . . pay homage to it! . . . *(Covering the head again, she cries softly in time to the rhythm of the shamisen.)* Ahh, this head . . . at the time I was secretly pregnant by Kumagai at the palace and forced to flee to the east to give birth . . . this head . . . you, too, gave birth to a child who became . . . Prince Atsumori! Together we carried a child in our wombs when we left our homes.

CHANTER: That, after sixteen years of separation, a maid-in-waiting could be of service to her lady . . . *(Sagami looks down at the head under the robe. She waves her hands in the air distractedly.)* . . . surely is an act of karma!

SAGAMI *(frantically)*: At least, in death were his . . .

CHANTER: . . . last moments brave? she asks in tormented fear. *(She lifts the robe to peer at her son's face, then drops the robe with an agonized expression on her face. Tearfully she hugs the head in the robe to her breast.)* The husband does not even blink before his lord, but tears stream from his eyes. . . . *(Kumagai grips his fan tightly, his lips tremble, but he does not speak.)* Were he to speak a word of consolation, he would choke on tears, he would spit blood! *(Sagami falls to the floor, leans back first on one hand and then on the other. Suddenly she rises and runs to embrace Kojirō's head once more, but Kumagai firmly gestures for her to go back. She collapses on the floor weeping.)* Lady Fuji, in tremulous voice . . .

FUJI: Ah, dear Sagami, it had not crossed my mind until now that Kumagai had compassionately sacrificed your son for mine. With what words can I thank you? As to how he could play his flute and show his shadow on the doors—now I understand. *(She faces Yoshitsune and bows deeply, indicating that she knows he has arranged these events. Suddenly battle alarms—a conch shell and drums and cymbals—sound offstage.)*

CHANTER (*rapidly*): Carried by the wind, the conch shell's battle cry clamorously pierces the ear! Roused by its sound, Yoshitsune . . .

YOSHITSUNE (*briskly*): Kumagai. The conch shell sounds assembly. Prepare yourself. Prepare for battle!

CHANTER (*singing rapidly to shamisen accompaniment*): Obedient to his words, Kumagai hurries from the room. Kajiwara, who has been listening all the while, runs in from the garden gate!

KAJIWARA: I heard you, I heard you! (*Laughs harshly*) I expected something like this, so on the excuse of investigating the stonecutter, I've done some spying! (*He runs to the hanamichi.*) The Kamakura shōgunate will be pleased to hear that Yoshitsune and Kumagai want to save Atsumori! Ha, ha! Just wait!

CHANTER: He shouts over his shoulders as he rushes off, when from behind, a stonemason's steel chisel pierces his back as cleanly as a dagger's blow! With a single cry, breath and life expire! As the general is thinking, "Who has done this?" the old stonecutter enters. (*Midaroku, holding a stone chisel in his hand, runs on stage from the left. Seeing Yoshitsune, he assumes a pose of innocent old age.*)

MIDAROKU: Well, well. A piece of worthless trash blocking your way has been removed, and a recent conversation has set my mind at ease. I will take my leave.

CHANTER: . . . he says, turning to go.

YOSHITSUNE: Wait, old man.

MIDAROKU: What is it you wish, my lord?

YOSHITSUNE: Identify yourself.

MIDAROKU: I have nothing to conceal. I am an old stonecutter: Midaroku from Mikage Village.

YOSHITSUNE: Then stand. You may go. (*Relieved, Midaroku bows and crosses onto the hanamichi with the small slow steps of an elderly person. Yoshitsune suddenly glares at him.*) Munekiyo, wait! Yaheibyoe Munekiyo! Wait!

CHANTER: Surprised at Yoshitsune's words, he gasps but shows an innocent face.

MIDAROKU: Hey, Yahei! Our commander is calling you! Hey there, Yahei! (*He enters and bows contritely to Yoshitsune.*) No person called Yahei is here, your lordship.

YOSHITSUNE: The saying is true: "When a man is touched by extreme hatred, sorrow, or joy, these are not forgotten through a lifetime." I recall with joy how, long ago, when my mother, Tokiwa, was nursing me at her breast, your kindness saved her, my brothers, and me from freezing in the snows of Fushimi outside the capital. Although I was only three years old, I remember your face and can clearly picture, whether or not you conceal it, the mole between your eyes. You disappeared soon after Councillor Shigemori died. It is good to see you well, Grandfather.

CHANTER (*singing*): Hearing this, Midaroku briskly returns, staring at Yoshitsune's face as if to bore a hole through it!

MIDAROKU: Your insight is monstrous! They say Laozi was born wise,[11] that by the age of three Zhuangzi could read a man's face! But you, Yoshitsune! (*A stage assistant helps him drop his kimono top, showing a samurai's white underkimono beneath it, and take off his cap, revealing a thatch of snow white hair. No longer acting as the devious commoner, we see him as he really is: a proud samurai.*) Had I not overlooked you that time, long ago, there would have been no general to breach the cliffs at Tekkai and at Hiyodorigoe and to reduce the Heike force at Suma Bay. Had I not saved Yoritomo's life, the Heike would be ascendant now. Aghh! The greatest error of my life was helping you! Because of you, Lord Shigemori knew the Heike faced a perilous future. At the time of his death, he advised me to renounce the warrior's life, go into hiding, and offer masses in memory of all the Taira who might fall. I took under my care the only remaining princess of the Taira family[12] and retired to Mikage Village with three thousand gold *ryō*, which was intended for memorial services at the Heike ancestral temple at Iozan. Throughout Harima Province, at Nachi and Mount Kōya—at Heike mausoleums everywhere—I erected gravestones for those already departed, each memorial, each one, sprung from the bitter tears of its unknown donor . . . Yaheibyoe Munekiyo!! (*He points to himself and screams his name as if it were a curse.*) Although I had not seen Atsumori since he was an infant and could not possibly remember his face, without knowing why, I somehow felt the man who came to order Atsumori's marker was a noble of the vanquished Heike, so I accepted his commission happily, never dreaming that he was ordering a stone memorial on this shore for the salvation of Kojirō's soul, whose fate had changed his! Agh! The will of heaven is beyond man's understanding, but for the two infants whom I saved from death—Yoritomo and Yoshitsune—to become leaders who would utterly annihilate the greatest Taira nobility . . . !

CHANTER: ". . . is fate too cruel to bear!" (*Midaroku clasps his hands supplicating heaven.*)

MIDAROKU: I am the traitor among the Heike who betrayed their trust! How the spirits of dead Taira lords and warriors will vent their hatred on me! Ahhh! Munekiyo! Wretched man!! (*Like one demented, he tears his hair. He strikes his chest and arms.*)

CHANTER: First raging, then contrite, his tears . . . challenge a waterfall! Ahhhhh! (*Midaroku tumbles down the steps and collapses, weeping bitterly.*) Wise since birth, General Yoshitsune says . . .

YOSHITSUNE (*sensing Kumagai's presence offstage*): Ah, it is you, Kumagai. Bring the box of armor from the small room.

---

11. Said to have been born an old man with white hair.
12. Shigemori's daughter, Princess Koyuki.

Midaroku revealed as a proud samurai with a white underkimono. (Photograph courtesy of Barbara Curtis Adachi Collection, C. V. Starr East Asian Library, Columbia University)

CHANTER: Kumagai Jirō Naozane enters from within. Bearers place an armor box before their lord. (*Kumagai wears battle dress: dark armor, gloves, leggings, and helmet. Bearers bring out a large wicker box and place it in front of Yoshitsune.*)

YOSHITSUNE: Old man, take this box of armor to the princess. Do it . . . Midaroku!

MIDAROKU (*surprised*): Midaroku, did you say? Ah, I see. A Genji general can't ask Munekiyo, friend of the Heike, for a favor! Ha, ha! Isn't this an interesting situation? (*He chuckles and assumes his previous guise of innocent old age.*) I could do what you request, but armor for a girl? It seems inappropriate. I'll just peek inside . . .

CHANTER (*sings*): When he lifts the lid and looks inside . . . ! (*Opening the lid, he sees Atsumori. Fuji rushes forward.*)

FUJI: Ahh! Is it . . . ? (*Midaroku claps the lid on the box. She tries to open it. He holds the lid tightly with one hand and pushes her back with the other.*)

MIDAROKU (*seeing Atsumori inside the box*): There is . . . nothing . . . inside. (*He pushes Fuji gently back and shakes his head. He looks at her meaningfully.*) Even a traitor would be satisfied. Give thanks to Kumagai for . . . (*He picks up the notice board and looks at it with tears in his eyes.*) . . . strike off the flower of one branch, strike off the flower of the other. Ahh! How grateful we are! (*He bows to Kumagai and Yoshitsune, weeping quietly in gratitude.*)

CHANTER (*sings*): Hearing this, Sagami turns to her husband . . .

SAGAMI (*dabbing her eyes*): Although I am resigned knowing my child's death was an act of loyalty, still, how could Kojirō and Atsumori, opponents in the battle, be exchanged?

KUMAGAI (*gruffly*): I have told you: I carried Atsumori from the field, pretending he was wounded. Obviously, it was Kojirō whom Hirayama challenged and Kojirō's head I took!

CHANTER: She weeps at his harsh words.

SAGAMI: You are inhuman, Kumagai! He was not your child alone. After I have come one hundred, two hundred miles hoping anxiously to see his face, how can you scold me, saying nothing of what you have done except "obviously it was Kojirō's head I took"?

CHANTER: She has reason to weep bitter tears and raise her voice. The general understands her feelings.

YOSHITSUNE: Kumagai. The time has come to depart for battle in the west. Prepare yourself.

KUMAGAI: My Lord, please grant the leave I have requested.

YOSHITSUNE: I understand. From time immemorial, the samurai has fought for fame in life in order to pass on glory to his heir. Should one's son die before him, the will to battle dies, too. I grant your request, Kumagai. Enter monkhood in good spirits and offer services for the repose of my parents' souls, I pray.

CHANTER (*sings*): This compassionate command is heard gratefully as he loosens his sash and slips off his armor. . . . (*Beneath his helmet his head is shaven, and beneath his armor he wears a monk's black cloak and plain gray kimono.*) Seeing this, Sagami says . . .

SAGAMI (*amazed*): But . . . Kumagai . . . !

KUMAGAI (*calmly, holding Buddhist prayer beads in his hands*): I am doing nothing strange. In the midst of strife the general has generously granted my deep desire to renounce the world. From this moment, let me take the monk's name Renshō and turn my steps toward Amida Buddha's Western Paradise, where Kojirō—embarked before me on the Nine Stages of Bliss— and I shall one day sit together on the same lotus. Buddha Merciful All Hail. *Namu Amida Butsu, Namu Amida Butsu, Namu Amida Butsu.*

CHANTER (*singing*): Commendable . . . and . . . heartbreaking! (*Kumagai lifts the prayer beads to his forehead and prays.*) Thinking "a long stay brings misfortune," Midaroku plans to conclude the affair and quickly leave. (*Midaroku kneels in front of the armor box and tries to tie it onto his back.*)

MIDAROKU: Yo, ho! Yo, ho! Yo, ho! (*Panting, he tucks one leg under him, plants the notice board firmly in the ground and, to accelerating shamisen music, manages at last to rise to his feet. He staggers left, then right, and finally stands straight.*) Lord Yoshitsune! What if Prince Atsumori gathers once again remnants of the Heike clan and returns evil for good?

Kumagai as a monk, his head shaven, in a black cloak. (Photograph courtesy of Barbara Curtis Adachi Collection, C. V. Starr East Asian Library, Columbia University)

YOSHITSUNE: It would be no more than heaven's just retribution, for when Yoshitsune and his brother Yoritomo were saved, they rewarded with evil the kindness done to them.

KUMAGAI: Truly, when that time comes, the vanity of this world abandoned, unfettered to any man, Kumagai will stand apart from the bloody carnage and help equally the tortured souls of both Genji and Heike dead . . .

CHANTER: . . . offering prayers for their salvation. (*Kumagai raises the prayer beads to his forehead and eyes. Midaroku looks at Kumagai and laughs wryly.*)

MIDAROKU: When that time comes, Midaroku will abandon this world and return as Munekiyo!

KUMAGAI: Thoughts of a monk's black robes fill my heart. I shall become a disciple of Priest Hōnen, submitting to his teaching in Kurodani, Black Valley. (*Turns to Yoshitsune*) May your good fortune increase, my lord.

CHANTER (*singing*): Saying this, wife joins husband . . . the stonecutter, together with Lady Fuji, stand beneath the eaves of the encampment. (*Fuji kneels by Midaroku and looks questioningly at the box. Midaroku indicates with a reassuring nod that Atsumori is safe in his care.*)

SAGAMI AND FUJI (*slowly in unison*): If destiny allows . . .

CHANTER: . . . say the women . . .

KUMAGAI AND MIDAROKU: . . . we shall meet again . . .

CHANTER: . . . say the men.

YOSHITSUNE: Live your lives in good health!

CHANTER (*singing*): Hearing their lord's will, with tears of gratitude, tears of sad remembrance . . . (*Kumagai looks at Yoshitsune with an expression of gratitude. He bursts into tears and bows down to the ground. After a moment he rises, and Sagami puts over his shoulder a monk's alms bag and gives him a plain straw hat and walking staff.*) . . . reminded, the general takes into his own hands Kojirō's head.

YOSHITSUNE: This shall be consecrated at Suma Temple, so that the unblemished name of . . . Atsumori, inscribed in gold shall live for generations to come. (*They pose for a moment in silence, then express their unbearable anguish in a linked dialogue of alternating phrases.*)

MIDAROKU: Though we pity the flower, mentioned on the sign . . .

FUJI: . . . of Musashibō Benkei, we must pity more . . .

SAGAMI: . . . the forsaken samurai . . .

RETAINER: . . . the pride of a warrior thrown aside . . .

KUMAGAI: . . . a traveler whose place of rest will never be known . . .

YOSHITSUNE: . . . in this transient and mutable . . .

ALL: . . . world of man!

CHANTER: Tears cloud their voices!

YOSHITSUNE: Kumagai! (*Slowly Kumagai turns back. Although he has renounced the world, he cannot help wishing for a final view of his son.*)

KUMAGAI (*anguished*): Now that I am entering Buddha's blessed land . . . all cares have vanished! (*He turns away from Kojirō to gain control over himself, trying to forget the ties of earthly affections, but he cannot. Again he turns to look at his son.*) Ahh! Sixteen years have passed, like a single day! Ahh! It is a dream, a dream! (*Numbly he lifts his hand to wipe away a single tear. He turns his back on Kojirō.*)

CHANTER (*quietly singing*): A single teardrop of dew, splashing to the ground; from a holly leaf sprinkled, by winter's first snow; melted in the sun's clear light[13] . . . how like Kumagai! (*Kumagai, Fuji, Midaroku, Sagami, and Yoshitsune stand in a strong group pose. The curtain is slowly closed to loud, accelerating ki clacks. Drawn once again by the memory of the son he killed, Kumagai slowly pivots to look back. His shoulders are slumped, the hat and staff hang loosely in his hands. The music stops. He stands motionless, silently recalling the past. Hesitantly, as if worldly ties were holding him back, he begins to leave, each deliberate footstep accented by drum and cymbals and shamisen music. He pauses, looks up once more, and, then with an expression of agonized resolve, pulls down his hat sharply in a gesture of humility and runs faster and faster down the hanamichi and off to accelerating music and loud bata-bata tsuke breaks.*)

[Toita Yasuji, ed., *Kabuki meisakusen* 2: 71–86, adapted from a translation by James Brandon]

---

13. Alluding to the light of Buddha's salvation.

SUGA SENSUKE

Suga Sensuke (ca. 1767–1791), the son of a doctor, began his career as a professional jōruri chanter. In 1767 he wrote his first play, *Dyed Pattern Lovers New Year Pine* (*Some moyō imose no kadomatsu*), which was a tremendous success. He continued to perform as Toyotake Kōtayū for another three years and then became a full-time playwright. Thirty-three plays, many of which are revisions of the works of Chikamatsu Monzaemon and other playwrights, bear his name, ten as the sole author and the rest as a coauthor. His best works were contemporary-life pieces (*sewamono*) rather than period plays (*jidaimono*). Together with Chikamatsu Hanji (1725–1783), Sensuke created the last flourish of playwriting for jōruri puppet theater. Many of his plays are performed today in both bunraku and kabuki.

GAPPŌ AT THE CROSSROADS (SESSHŪ GAPPŌ GA TSUJI, 1773)

Written by Suga Sensuke (ca. 1767–1791) and Wakatake Fuemi (ca. 1759–1799), *Gappō at the Crossroads* was first performed in Osaka in 1773, in the last decades of a century-long period of playwriting that had given bunraku and kabuki the core of its current repertoire. The climactic scene from act 2, which is translated here and is performed today as a separate play, was written by Sensuke, the senior playwright of the pair.

Gappō at the Crossroads is a historical play set in the age of Hōjō Takatoki (1303–1333), the leader of the Kamakura military government, but it has the tone and content of a contemporary-life play (*sewamono*). Sensuke blends two distinct "worlds" (*sekai*) to produce something totally new yet abundantly familiar. Two stepmother legends are woven together: one from the Aigonowaka "world" in which an upright, handsome young man (Aigonowaka) is desired and ultimately destroyed by his stepmother (Kumoi no mae), and the other from the Shuntoku/Shintoku "world" in which an equally handsome and well-born fellow is driven to blindness and suffering by the slandering of an evil stepmother who wishes to make her own son the heir to the household. The main strand of the Aigonowaka "world" can be found in the seventeenth-century miracle (*sekkyō*) play *Aigonowaka*; that of Shuntoku/Shintoku, in the miracle play *Young Shintoku* (*Shintoku-maru*), the nō play *Unsteady Beggar Priest* (*Yoroboshi*), and Namiki Sōsuke's *Young Musicians and Model Wives* (*Futaba reijin azuma no hinagata*, 1733).

In the miracle play *Young Shintoku*, Shintoku, a young man of good family, is cursed, slandered, and driven out of his home by his stepmother but is saved in the end by his childhood fiancée (Otohime). In the nō play, Takayasu Michitoshi, deceived by someone's slanderous words, has driven out his only son, Shuntoku, and is praying at Tennō-ji temple when his son (the *shite*, or protagonist), now a blind beggar, appears on the temple grounds and is recognized by and eventually reconciled with his father. In Sōsuke's *Young Musicians and Model Wives*, a rival tricks Shuntoku into drinking poisoned saké, but it is Shuntoku's lover (Hatsuhana) who saves him by offering her own blood, since she was born on the day, month, and year of the tiger, a condition necessary for the antidote. In *Gappō at the Crossroads*, Suga Sensuke created the character Tamate from both the Aigonowaka and the Shuntoku/Shintoku "worlds": Tamate is both the stepmother who causes the stepson's blindness and the lover who sacrifices herself to restore his health. This innovative twist produced a complex character whose dramatic potential and implications are deepened by a knowledge of these preexisting "worlds."

The main characters in Suga Sensuke's jōruri version are Tamate Gozen, formerly Otsuji (her name is the "Crossroads" of the title), now the wife of Lord Takayasu, an old and sick samurai; Tamate's father, Gappō, a former samurai turned poor priest; Gappō's wife; Shuntoku, the handsome heir of Lord Takayasu and stepson of Tamate; and Shuntoku's fiancée, Lady Asaka. In the first act, Tamate, originally a lady-in-waiting but now the principal wife of Lord Takayasu, discovers that Shuntoku's half brother Jirō (by a concubine) is plotting to kill Shuntoku in order to become the family heir. During a pilgrimage to Sumiyoshi Shrine, Tamate takes the opportunity to share some saké with Shuntoku and confesses her love for him. At the same time she poisons his saké, which causes him to fall ill and become blind. Shuntoku, pained by the forbidden desires of his stepmother, subsequently flees, and Tamate pursues him. In the second act, while gathering funds for a Buddhist hall at the Western Gate of the Tennō-ji temple, Gappō, Tamate's father, comes across the blind and disfigured Shuntoku and his fiancée, Asaka, and takes them to his own house. That evening, Gappō and his wife, thinking that their daughter, having committed an unspeakable act, has been killed, carry out services for her soul. In the scene that follows, Tamate, seeking out Shuntoku, unexpectedly appears at her parents' house.

Like the Phaedra character of Euripides, Seneca, and Racine, Tamate sees death as the only escape from her illicit love. After she is stabbed, she begins a long explanation of her actions, particularly about finding a poison with the well-known folk antidote of blood from the liver of a woman born at the particular moment of Tamate's own birth: the year, month, day, and hour of the tiger. As her audience begins to believe that her actions were a scheme to save both her stepsons from death, all her wanton passion is transformed into virtue. And yet Suga Sensuke has her seek death almost too passionately, and so her remarks create an atmosphere of ambiguity by echoing an earlier moment in act 1 when Tamate first tried to seduce Shuntoku. When he protests that she is intoxicated with the saké they have exchanged, she replies:

> No, I'm neither drunk nor crazy. From when I first came to serve your mother, I was entranced by your beauty and always wanted to confess my love but feared a letter would fall into the wrong hands. Although I didn't care about myself, I didn't want your name to be ruined. But what happened while I was still holding back is all too cruel. After your mother died, I was asked to become your father's

The blind Shuntoku. (Photograph courtesy of Barbara Curtis Adachi Collection, C. V. Starr East Asian Library, Columbia University)

wife. I could hardly refuse such a request, as that would mean I couldn't live near you any longer. I had no choice but to become a parent and bear the pain of being your mother. Hidden away much longer, my love would have smoldered and burned until I died.

Later in the same scene in act 1, Tamate confesses, "I'm the servant of the former mistress. I'm not your parent; you're not my child. I'll follow you anywhere. I can't live any longer if we're not married. Even though I may be thought to be like a bitch in heat, I'll follow you everywhere. I'm a hawk; I'll never let you free."

The portrayal of a woman's passion is not unusual in the Japanese tradition, and many of the best nō and bunraku plays depict women who are willing to die or suffer in hell for love. The genius of Suga Sensuke's character Tamate is that she does not appear to be entirely innocent. The technique of having a character appear as one thing (usually evil or, at least, unpleasant) and then at a crucial moment reveal his or her true intentions is a common motif in bunraku and kabuki. The tension created between the surface action and the "true" feelings is exploited by performers who developed histrionic techniques to present characters at two levels, an important element in all traditional Japanese acting. Since women made up a large proportion of both the bunraku and kabuki audiences and the amateur performers, one can well imagine an author subtly probing the audiences' latent and forbidden desires. In the end Tamate dies a virtuous woman, her desires transformed, at least on the surface, into motherly devotion.

CHARACTERS

GAPPŌ, a former samurai of good lineage, now a poor priest

WIFE, Gappō's wife and mother of Tamate

TAMATE, Tamate Gozen, Gappō's daughter, whose original name was Otsuji (Crossroads), or Tsuji, originally a maidservant to Lord Takayasu's wife, but after his wife's early death, Lord Takayasu's principal wife and the stepmother of Shuntoku

SHUNTOKU, Shuntoku-maru, the handsome heir of Lord Takayasu and stepson of Tamate, one or two years younger than Tamate; now a blind leper and engaged to Princess Asaka

LADY ASAKA, daughter of a wealthy lord from Izumi Province, engaged to Shuntoku

LORD TAKAYASU, Takayasu Michitoshi, the lord of Kawachi Province (in present-day Osaka) and the father of Shuntoku, now elderly and in ill health

IRIHEI, Lord Takayasu's servant

Act 2, Climactic Scene

CHANTER (*sings*): Dark is the path at night. Bright should be the way of love, but dark like a black opal is the heart of Tamate Gozen, the Jewel Princess. Unable to find her lover Shuntoku, she has come to her parents' home, her face veiled but unable to hide the shame of her flaming cheeks. She kept their relationship a secret, but she now returns to her childhood home seeking refuge. Behind her is Irihei, Lord Takayasu's servant, who has heard that Shuntoku and Lady Asaka have come to this area. Catching sight of Lady Tamate, he hides in order to watch what will happen. Unaware of his presence, Tamate calls out in a high-pitched, strained voice.

[TAMATE]: Mother, Mother!

CHANTER: Gappō recognizes the voice instantly but says to himself:

[GAPPŌ]: What . . . aren't you dead? Weren't you killed?

CHANTER: He jumps up but has an idea. He looks around and sees that his wife hasn't heard anything because of the bell and her chanting. "That's lucky!" he says and ignores the visitor.

[TAMATE]: Mother, Mother, open the door!

CHANTER: The sound of the knocking reaches the wife.

[WIFE]: Gappō, dear, did you say something?

[GAPPŌ]: No, no, I didn't say anything. You must have ringing in your ears.

[WIFE]: I may have imagined it, but I'd swear I heard our daughter's voice.

CHANTER: She stands up.

[TAMATE]: Is that Mother's voice? Please open the door. It's Tsuji. I'm home.

CHANTER: The wife is shocked.

[WIFE]: Is it a dream, are you really home? How wonderful that you're still alive.

Tamate, her face veiled, returns to her parents' house. (Photograph courtesy of Barbara Curtis Adachi Collection, C. V. Starr East Asian Library, Columbia University)

CHANTER: But as she goes toward Tamate, Gappō grabs her sleeve.

[GAPPŌ]: No, no, no. Don't be foolish. Even if she's our flesh and blood, she's an adulterous beast. Lord Takayasu would never let her escape here. How did you make it this far? What have you come stumbling in here for? There's no way you can hide from him; you'll be discovered. You told him you had no parents, but he must know the truth. From time to time when you sent money to help us, it was Lord Takayasu's benevolence. How could you deceive a husband like that! I can't let a lecherous daughter through the door. My daughter is dead. It's the voice of a ghost. Doesn't that frighten you? The closer a person is, the more frightening it is. Don't you dare open the door.

CHANTER: And yet his wife replies.

[WIFE]: No, no. It's ridiculous to say it's a ghost. Even if it's a badger or fox in disguise, I want to see my daughter's face once more. Even if I see a frightening demon and fall into a frenzy and die, I'll still be happy. I'd rather die in front of my daughter than continue to live a life of shame. Just a quick look.

CHANTER: She tries to break loose, but he holds onto her even more tightly.

[GAPPŌ]: Think again, dear! It's not so bad if it's a fox or badger or even a ghost. What if it's really our daughter? I'll have to use these hands again to wield a sword—to take her life. It's my duty to Lord Takayasu. That's why I'm holding you back.

CHANTER (sings): Although he does not weep, his wife and daughter feel the compassion in his heart; they grieve face to face, heart to heart—despite being separated by the door. Tamate wipes away her tears and leans against the door.

[TAMATE]: I can understand why Father is angry and bitter. But I have a reason for doing this, and I must keep out of sight. Please open the door.

CHANTER (*sings*): In tears, she pleads.

[WIFE]: Gappō did you hear that? She has a reason. Please, you must listen to her story. If you consider her your daughter, you have a duty. But if we let in a ghost, we have no responsibility.

[GAPPŌ]: Yes, I guess you're right. If it's a spirit from the lower world, then we have no need to worry about the eyes of the world. Call her in and offer the ghost a bite to eat. The poor thing has no place to rest; even ghosts get hungry.

CHANTER (*sings*): Duty forces him to look away, an action a hundred times more painful than weeping. His wife is delighted and hurriedly opens the door.

[TAMATE]: How long it's been! How good it is to see you again!

CHANTER: The mother touches Tamate's skin, confirming that it is indeed her daughter.

[WIFE]: How wonderful to see you healthy. It was awful to carry out a funeral service, thinking that you were dead. It seems like a dream that you should appear unharmed on the very night we were praying for your soul.

CHANTER: The mother hugs her, weeping tears of joy. Her father, too, turns around unwittingly to look at the face he hasn't seen for years, but thoughts of duty restrain him. He fidgets about, not knowing what to do with himself. His wife finally calms him down.

[WIFE]: There are rumors that you fell in love with Shuntoku and left your husband's home. They say you're an adulterer. But *you* could never do anything like that. It can't be right. It must be all a lie. It *is* a lie, isn't it? Surely it's a lie.

CHANTER (*sings*): A mother's love leads her daughter on, like spoon-feeding a child. Tamate seems embarrassed.

[TAMATE] (*in an aria-like song*): Even though you say the rumor's a lie, it must be karma from a past life. I fell in love with young Shuntoku, and waking or sleeping I could think of nothing but him. Finally, I had to open my heart to him. His response was cold—saying it wasn't proper, since I was his step-mother. But his refusal inflamed my love all the more. The deeper I fell into the abyss, the more determined I became to follow him anywhere. Barefoot, I chased him to the Bay of Naniwa. Take pity on my heart; it's exhausted by love. For love of your own child, help me find him and make us husband and wife.

CHANTER: She begs with folded hands, but her mother, more shocked than ever, can only stare dumbfoundedly at her child's face. For a moment her father is silent. Then from the storage room he takes out his old sword.

[GAPPŌ]: You lecherous beast. I've never told you, but my father was Aoto Saemon Fujitsuna. He was chosen by Shōgun Tokiyori to run his government, and he was praised as a model samurai. Thanks to his fame, I was made a provincial lord. But under Lord Takatoki's reign, I was slandered by sycophants, and twenty years ago, I became a rōnin. Now I'm a priest who has been forgotten by the world, but within me is the firm integrity of my father. When I think of my reckless, wanton daughter—a disgrace to womanhood, to all humanity—the anger crushes my bones. Yet I see that Lord Takayasu's compassion has allowed you to live on until now. At first you were a maidservant to the former lady of the house. When he offered to make you his official wife, I tried to have you leave his service, but he insisted, out of sense of righteousness and love, that you become his wife. If he hadn't been so kind and showered you with favors, it wouldn't have come to this! You can see for yourself why I must kill you. I'm happy that Lord Takayasu has spared you out of regard for us. If you felt even a bit of shame, no matter how much you loved Lord Shuntoku, you would be able to give him up. But this . . . you've been allowed to go free, and even then you come begging to us to help you marry him! Such nerve! How could you say such things? My duty to Lord Takayasu demands that I save you. I could never stand on my honor if I let you continue to live. Prepare yourself for the end.

CHANTER (sings): He unsheathes the sword, but his wife grabs the handle.

[WIFE]: Now, now, Gappō, you've got it all wrong. Does your honor really demand her death, even though she's been forgiven by her husband? Let's try to talk some sense into her, make her forget Lord Shuntoku. Let's have her become a nun. No matter what the crime, it's a priest's duty to save a criminal. If she abandons the world, it's the same as death, and your honor will remain unblemished.

CHANTER: She points to the back room; trying to calm Gappō, she moves close to Tamate.

[WIFE] (to Tamate): I understand your feelings, but no matter how much you love him, it'll never work. You must give him up and become a nun. You're barely twenty, a young girl, bright and pretty. I want to save you. That's all. That's why I want you to enter a convent, to leave the world in the blossom of youth. Your fate—to think that the beautiful black hair that I once combed, that should be cherished all your life. . . .

CHANTER: She breaks down in tears, hugging her daughter. Tamate jumps back, her expression changed.

[TAMATE]: What ridiculous talk! I'll never become a nun, never! Do you think I'd cut off the hair that I've spent so much time combing into a fine sheen? No, I'm going to get rid of my samurai coiffure and dress fashionably like the ladies of the pleasure quarters. Then when I meet Shuntoku, he'll fall for me. Don't you dare mention nuns or monks to me.

CHANTER (sings): Determined as ever in love.

[GAPPŌ]: She'll never change. I can't bear it any longer!

CHANTER: But again his wife intervenes.

[WIFE]: You have every right to be angry, but just let me have her for an hour or two. I'll get her to turn over a new leaf and forget him. All these years of our marriage—it's my only request. Please, let me have this one chance.

CHANTER (sings): Gappō can hardly refuse her earnest plea and leaves the room without looking back. His wife takes the stubborn Tamate by the hand and forcefully leads her into the backroom.

 Poor Shuntoku, a blind bird in flight, is unable to see even the light of the moon. His constant guide is Lady Asaka, who quietly leads him out from the next room.

[ASAKA] (to Shuntoku): Hearing all this has convinced me that you can't stay here even a moment longer. We must leave immediately.

CHANTER: Shuntoku replies.

[SHUNTOKU]: I haven't been able to escape the sins of my past lives. My mother's feelings, now so extreme, also must be due to karma. If she were to see me now, blind and disfigured, her infatuation would surely end. Take me to her. Then when Irihei gets here, we'll escape with him.

CHANTER: Irihei listens from outside the door.

[IRIHEI]: Yes sir, your servant has heard everything. If the villagers find out that you're here, word may get out to your enemies. You must leave immediately to avoid danger.

CHANTER: But as he tries to hurry the couple out, Tamate rushes in.

[TAMATE]: Oh, how wonderful to see you, dear Shuntoku! I've struggled through every imaginable trouble, with every thought of finding you. My effort has finally been rewarded. I'm happy to see that you're well.

CHANTER: She hugs him, but he pushes her aside.

[SHUNTOKU]: Mother, please control yourself. You know that it's against the law for members of the same family to marry. Even more when it's parent and child! If I were to agree, I would be adding more sins to those from my past. Can't you see this wretched body, disfigured and blind in both eyes? Is this what you call caring for me? Don't you know what shame means?

CHANTER: Bitter tears have no effect on Tamate.

[TAMATE]: Ahh . . . what foolish things you say. Your miserable condition is all my doing. I'm not the least bothered by your awful figure. Since I was responsible for that, the more I think of your suffering, the deeper my love grows. I want you more than ever.

[SHUNTOKU]: Wha . . . what do you mean my misfortune is your responsibility?

[TAMATE]: About that . . . last winter at the Sumiyoshi Shrine, when I had you drink saké from this abalone shell—it was really poison to disfigure you. The saké that I drank was all right, but yours wasn't. I was jealous. I hated your face because you had eyes only for Lady Asaka and none for me. After you fled the castle saying you'd choose a life of suffering as penance for past sins, I was delighted and followed you. Seeking you along unknown roads, I've held this shell next to my heart to remember you. How heartless of you not to return my love, not to be the other half of this shell!

CHANTER (*sings*): She throws herself at his knees, weeping. Although he is angry, Shuntoku is constrained by filial duty. He does not show any bitterness; he only weeps, accepting everything as fate. But Lady Asaka, without a tear, bursts out angrily:

[ASAKA]: The more I hear, the more awful it seems. How horrid! Too horrible! How could you destroy his jewel-like face? You've gone too far, lusting after your child. There's is a limit to depravity. Restore his face!

CHANTER (*sings*): Anger shatters her reserve. Tamate jumps up in fury.

[TAMATE]: Lost in the dark depths of love, I have no ears for morality or reason. Do you think I'd let Shuntoku run away with you? I'll never let you block my love. Get in my way, and I'll kick you to death!

CHANTER: She grasps Shuntoku's hand. (*Tamate seductively cuddles up to Shuntoku, her hand on his lap, directly in front of Asaka.*)

[SHUNTOKU]: How disgusting! (*Asaka rushes to push Tamate away from Shuntoku. Tamate erupts into a mad fury, her hair hanging loose and her outer kimono falling off her shoulders. She throws Asaka aside and grabs Shuntoku. The shamisen music is forceful as the two women fight. Tamate pins Asaka down and then drags her around the room.*)

CHANTER: Shuntoku tries to throw off Tamate, but she prevents him from escaping. Lady Asaka tries to intervene, but Tamate kicks her aside, her angry eyes now fiery plums. Her disheveled hair flies about like willow branches in the wind. Jealousy drives her to the edge of madness as she pummels Asaka. Irihei waits outside in a cold sweat. Gappō, unable to restrain himself any longer, rushes in with his sword in hand, grabs her hair, and stabs her in the side with an icy blade. As Tamate cries out in pain, Irihei comes running in. Both Shuntoku and Asaka are in shock.

[SHUNTOKU]: For him to kill my mother—what a cruel fate! He weeps as Gappō's wife holds Tamate in her arms.

[WIFE] (*to Tamate*): This was all your own doing—the pain must be awful!

CHANTER: They all join in lamenting her death. Gappō's face shows his anger, his body taut with emotion. (*Angry and accusatory, Gappō keeps the blade in Tamate's side.*)

[GAPPŌ] (*to his wife*): Dear, what are you wailing about? You should be weeping that we've neglected our duty to Tamate's husband and to Lord Shuntoku and Lady Asaka. How can you still think of her as your child—this evil woman, this lustful woman? I was so angry I couldn't bear it any longer. (*Gappō regrets his action, realizing that he has broken his priestly vow against violence. The shamisen rhythms bring the emotion of the scene to a crescendo.*) For ten years this hand hasn't harmed a flea—and then for it to kill my own child! How, how could a priest do such a thing, even out of duty to the world! You devil—not only have you violated Buddha's teachings, but you're dragging me to hell with you. Fiend!

CHANTER: His fists tighten with anger. Tamate pushes him back.

[TAMATE]: You're right, Father, you're right. You should hate me. But there's a reason for all this. Don't pull out the sword. I want to speak.

CHANTER: She gasps, trying to catch her breath. (*Tamate, in a long emotional appeal, struggles to convince the others of the hidden truth behind her actions.*)

[TAMATE]: It's because of Jirō, Shuntoku's half brother. He's older than Shuntoku and couldn't accept Shuntoku as the rightful heir to my husband. His anger led him to join with Tsuboi Heima in a plan to kill his brother. My suspicions were confirmed when I overheard their plot. I felt it was my duty as stepmother to save him. I thought that if Shuntoku did not succeed his father, then Jirō's anger would eventually subside, and Shuntoku's life would be spared. So I decided to feign a lecherous infatuation. I got Shuntoku to drink the poisoned saké and tried to get him to run off with me. I thought if he were sick and disfigured, he wouldn't be killed. It was all a ploy; it wasn't passion. Proof of my intentions is in the abalone shell that I used for a saké cup when pledging my love. Although Shuntoku couldn't know the maternal love hidden in my heart, I fulfilled my duty as stepmother. But my husband Takayasu's scorn for me as a low, beastly woman will keep me from salvation in the afterlife.

CHANTER: Gappō continues to sneer at her words.

[GAPPŌ]: If you were so sure of Jirō's plot, why didn't you just tell Lord Takayasu? One word would have stopped the need for poison or lechery. A good story, but don't expect your father to believe that now! (*Tamate begs her father to forgive her. His acceptance of her pleas is emotionally brought to a peak through the singing and shamisen accompaniment.*)

[TAMATE]: No, no, Father, you've got me wrong. If I had told my husband, an honest man, his anger would surely have forced Jirō to commit seppuku, or he would have simply killed him. Both Jirō and Shuntoku are my stepsons. If I took sides and informed on one of them, causing his death, it would bring me shame in society. Furthermore, what would Takayasu think of his children? Considering everything, I decided to save both lives and give up my own, becoming an evil adulterer and dying. I hoped to repay my husband's love by saving his children.

CHANTER: Her explanation begins to make some sense, but Gappō is still not convinced.

[GAPPŌ] (*to Tamate*): But dear, if those were your true intentions, why did you leave home and follow Lord Shuntoku? I don't understand that!

[TAMATE]: Your doubts are reasonable, but if I didn't chase after him, his horrible condition would never be cured.

CHANTER: Irihei, finding her words strange, interrupts.

[IRIHEI]: Wha . . . what are you saying? If you stayed with him, he'd be healed?

Tamate and her father, Gappō. (Photograph courtesy of Barbara Curtis Adachi Collection, C. V. Starr East Asian Library, Columbia University)

[TAMATE]: Yes. I told the pharmacist about my plans when I went to buy some poison. I asked how any disfiguring effect could be reversed. He said that since it would not be a birth defect, there was an antidote for the poison. The blood taken from the liver of a living woman born in the year, month, day, and hour of the tiger and served to the person in the same cup as the poison would instantly restore his health. How happy I was to find that I could save him! That's why I've carried this shell with me, to fulfill my plan. Dear Father, do you still doubt me?

[GAPPŌ]: No, no, no more. Since your birth was exactly at the times of the tiger, you had him drink the poison, knowing that you could save him later by giving up your life?

[TAMATE]: Yes, yes.

[GAPPŌ]: Such bravery! Such deeds! Daughter, say no more. Please forgive me, forgive me. In all of China, India, or Japan there's no woman as virtuous as you are. And yet I called you an evil beast and cruelly killed you. I'm a stubborn idiot. Forgive, please forgive me.

CHANTER: He collapses, weeping tears of regret. Having listened to Tamate's tale, Shuntoku seeks out and grasps her hand in gratitude.

[SHUNTOKU]: You have gone far beyond the duty of a stepmother to her son. Your compassion makes you my real parent, the savior of my life. I will never be able to express enough gratitude. I could never repay you even if my body were torn into a hundred, a thousand, pieces. Thank you, thank you.

CHANTER: He bows his head to the floor.

[ASAKA]: I never dreamed that you had such intentions. How awful to have called you such terrible names. Please forgive me.

CHANTER: She clasps her hands in apology.

[IRIHEI]: A virtuous woman! How harsh, pitiful that you had to suffer such abuse to the end.

CHANTER: He joins the others in weeping. Tamate's mother wails uncontrollably.

[WIFE]: It's true that my child was born in the year, month, day, and hour of the tiger. Since they say that one should never tell anyone of such a birth, we never dared to mention it to anyone outside the family. Pressed by duty, my child turned against herself and became the tiger of her own destruction. Was it her misfortune to be born at such a fateful moment?

CHANTER: All sympathize with her grief. Tears flow like the famous springs of Ausaka and Masui. The wounded Tamate lifts her head.

[TAMATE]: I've been ready to die for a long time, but your grief at my passing will only cause my spirit to wander after death. Shuntoku, I want you to report all this to my husband. If he knows and understands the real reasons for my wantonness, I will have no more regrets. As a reward for sacrificing my life, please beg your father to pardon Jirō. You must promise me that.

[SHUNTOKU]: No, no, you must recover and live on. Your words are too kind. If you die for your child, I will fear heaven's wrath.

[TAMATE]: Your words are kind; thank you, but this deep wound will be my end. I've wanted to die for some time. If you believe you've caused your parent's death, it will weigh down my soul in the next life. I am not your mother. I am the maidservant Tamate and am giving up my life for my lord. It will bring fame to this samurai house. Don't grieve over me. Father, cut here below my breast bone and take some blood from my liver. Hurry and put it into the shell, quick!

CHANTER: She gasps in pain.

[GAPPŌ]: I was able to stab you in a fit of anger, but how can I cut my precious daughter's flesh now! No . . . this is a task for a younger, steadier hand. Irihei, can you do it?

[IRIHEI]: An awful request. I'd do anything to save my master Lord Shuntoku, but how can I stab Lady Tamate? Don't make me do it . . . please.

[TAMATE]: You are too kind. I won't ask anyone.

CHANTER: She readies her dagger, but Gappō intercedes.

[GAPPŌ]: Now, please wait, a moment, dear. While you're still alive, please pray to be reborn on the lotus. May the power of Buddha lead you to rebirth in paradise, carried along by our prayers. Let's form a circle, holding the prayer beads. (*Tamate and Shuntoku are encircled by a large string of prayer beads, which the others hold up. Tamate prepares to extract the blood from her liver. Tamate slides up to Shuntoku's lap just as before, but this time to offer farewell.*)

Tamate and Shuntoku. (Photograph courtesy of Barbara Curtis Adachi Collection, C. V. Starr East Asian Library, Columbia University)

CHANTER: Tamate sits up in the middle of the circle, Shuntoku near her knees, the sword in her right hand, the shell in her left. Off to the side her father chants a Buddhist sutra while ringing a prayer bell. Her mother's tearful eyes remain shut. Earlier they had thought their child was dead and had held a memorial service; now after discovering that she was alive and well, she must disappear with their prayers, like the morning dew. (*Tamate strikes a grand pose, with dagger in hand. Gappō strikes the prayer bell. Tamate weakens and collapses, but then, riding the rhythms of the shamisen, she stands again and hugs her father in an emotional farewell. Tamate's mother holds up Tamate's funeral tablet and then embraces her daughter. Tamate and her mother strike a pose during a dancelike sequence. Tamate hugs Shuntoku in a final farewell.*)

[ALL] (*sing*): Hail Amida Buddha, hail Amida Buddha.

CHANTER (*sings*): Tamate stabs herself, letting the blood flow into the cup. Her hand shaking, she passes it to Shuntoku. (*To the quick rhythms of shamisen music, Tamate drains blood into the shell for Shuntoku to drink.*)

[SHUNTOKU]: I take this gift of a mother's incomparable love.

CHANTER: In one gulp he drains the cup. Remarkably, both his eyes open, and in an instant, the disfigurements disappear; his face blossoms like a flower. Tamate smiles painfully to see his face.

[TAMATE]: It's worked. (*Tamate rejoices to see Shuntoku's beautiful face restored.*)

CHANTER: All rejoice. Tamate suffers the four pains and the eight sufferings as she approaches her end. The prayer bell rings louder. (*Tamate collapses. Her parents weep over her body, and the others break down into tears.*)

[ALL] (*sing*): Praise to Amida . . .

CHANTER (*sings*): They chant loudly that her virtue will bring her rebirth in paradise, clinging to her body, wailing tears of grief and gratitude, which flow like waves into the garden. Tamate's mother, restraining her tears, flings back her white hair. She cuts a lock of her daughter's hair, making the dead woman a nun. Lord Shuntoku holds back his tears.

[SHUNTOKU]: My stepmother's compassion was as wide and deep as that of the Buddha. To repay her, if only in part, I'll build a temple in this area after I succeed my father. I will have a nun become the head of the temple. And since my stepmother was a model of womanly virtue, with an unclouded heart, her virtue will live on, reflected in the moonlight on the clear waters of the bay. I'll call it Gekkō-ji, Temple of the Moonlit Bay!

CHANTER (*sings*): Shuntoku's words have come true, and the temple still stands today. In the sound of its bell and sutra chanting can still be heard the echoes of sorrows long past. Gappō, dedicating his life to the spread of Buddhism, says:

[GAPPŌ]: With the help of Buddha and others, I'll rebuild this house into a temple to commemorate my daughter. It will be called the Tsujidō, Temple at the Crossroads. May all souls receive its blessings; may my daughter pass through the gates of paradise.

CHANTER (*sings*): Gappō's prayers are for the afterlife, a farewell to this life. Tamate has awakened from the dream of one hundred and eight desires and now floats on her way to the shores of Nirvana. The shell cup remains, a memory of how a crooked path can lead to the knowledge of good. Here outside Tennō-ji, the oldest Buddhist temple, on the road near the Western Gate, there still remain Tamate Spring and Gappō's Temple at the Crossroads.

[*Bunraku jōruri shū*, NKBT 99: 309–327, with stage descriptions from a recent production, introduction and translation by C. Andrew Gerstle]

Chapter 11

DANGIBON AND THE BIRTH OF
EDO POPULAR LITERATURE

Popular literature and culture flourished between two sets of reforms by the Tokugawa shōgunate, the Kyōhō Reforms and the Kansei Reforms. The Kyōhō Reforms (1716–1736) were carried out by the eighth shōgun, Tokugawa Yoshimune (r. 1716–1745), and the Kansei Reforms (1789–1801) were executed by Matsudaira Sadanobu, who became senior councillor in 1787. The Kyōhō Reforms were intended to resolve the financial crisis facing the shōgunate and the samurai caused by the increasing disparity between the samurai's elite sociopolitical status and economic reality. The initial stage of the reforms (1716–1722) concentrated on curbing expenditures and restoring the currency, but it proved to be inadequate, and the shōgunate was unable to pay its retainers' stipends in full. It was not until the last stage of the reforms (1736–1745), when the shōgunate adopted an expansionary financial policy that increased tax revenues while allowing greater penetration of urban merchant capital into the countryside, that many of these problems were surmounted. These measures laid the groundwork for the commercial development and close shōgunate–merchant ties that marked the so-called Tanuma era (1768–1786) when Tanuma Okitsugu (1719–1788), the bakufu's senior councillor (*rōjū*), exerted his greatest influence on its policy.

These reforms also had a far-reaching effect on the culture of this period. One characteristic of the literature of the latter half of the eighteenth century is the deep interest in other cultures, particularly China's. The neoclassical

Chinese poetry and prose that had been encouraged by the Ancient Rhetoric (*kobunji*) school of Ogyū Sorai (1666–1728) stimulated the literati (*bunjin*) movement, which looked to China for its cultural models. At the same time, Hiraga Gennai (1728–1779) and scholar-artists like him became interested in Dutch studies (*rangaku*) and European culture and literature. Ironically, during a period of national seclusion and under the policies of Tanuma Okitsugu, Japan gave birth to an internationally oriented culture. At the same time, interest was growing in another "other," Japan's ancient past, which was idealized by such nativist learning (*kokugaku*) scholars and poets as Kamo no Mabuchi (1697–1769) and Motoori Norinaga (1730–1801) and became the source of inspiration and material for much of the period's fiction, poetry, and drama.

Although the center for kabuki and jōruri remained in Osaka and eminent writers like Ueda Akinari and Yosa Buson remained in the Kyoto-Osaka area, from the middle of the eighteenth century the locus of cultural production and consumption began to shift from the Kamigata (Kyoto-Osaka) region to Edo. Not surprisingly, the literature of the rulers, or the samurai—such as the Chinese studies of Ogyū Sorai, who worked in Edo—had begun to appear in Edo, the seat of political power and the center of samurai society. By the middle of the century, the literature of the ruled also started to move east. Until the mid-eighteenth century, economically and culturally Edo had been a colony of Osaka and Kyoto. In its first century, Edo had been a city of strangers coming from all parts of the country, mainly on the alternate attendance system, with no common customs or dialect. But by the mid-eighteenth century, a distinct Edo language had developed, and Edo had become home for many people. The establishment of a distinctive Edo culture and the economic growth came together to create a socioeconomic sphere that competed directly with the Kyoto-Osaka region, which had been the cultural capital for many centuries.

After the Hōreki era (1751–1764), Edo's popular literature showed spectacular energy and creativity. The *ukiyo-zōshi* (books of the floating world), which had emerged and flourished in the Kyoto-Osaka region—published by the Hachimonjiya and other publishers and eagerly awaited by the Edo townspeople—disappeared by the mid-eighteenth century. In their place, new *gesaku* (vernacular playful writing) emerged: *sharebon* (books of wit), *ninjōbon* (books of sentiment), *yomihon* (reading books), *kusa-zōshi* (text-picture books, particularly *kibyōshi*), and *kokkeibon* (humor books), which included *dangibon* (satiric teachings). The publishers in Edo were, for the most part, branches of Kyoto-Osaka firms. They were small-scale merchants who sought new talent and marketed their goods to samurai. Because their sphere of activity was limited, they produced an urban literature whose main locus was the city of Edo itself.

The notion of *ugachi* (hole digging), or satirically viewing and commenting on the flaws in contemporary manners and mores, was central to the new gesaku genres—senryū, kyōka, kyōshi, sharebon, kibyōshi, and kokkeibon—that came to the fore in the latter half of the eighteenth century. In a society under military control where free expression was not encouraged, ideas had to be expressed in roundabout ways. One way was through satire, to point to various defects, weaknesses, and bad tendencies in society that were normally hidden or covered over. Making these kinds of satirical observations brought intellectual pleasure to both the writer and the reader. The person who practiced ugachi, however, was not a social critic or reformer; instead, he was a bystander, someone on the outskirts of society who did not assume responsibility for further action or change. It was sufficient merely to expose the "hole." In a kind of twisted or inverted pride, gesaku writers referred to their work as "useless" (*muda*).

Interestingly, each major period of literary humor followed a period of extreme political, social, and economic repression. Rather than succumbing to these repressive measures, urban culture thrived after the reforms had passed. The Hōreki (1751–1764)-Tenmei era (1781–1789) and the Bunka-Bunsei era (1804–1830) proved to be great creative periods for urban commoner culture, especially comic fiction. Reflecting the nature of the times, moralistic and didactic books came into vogue during the Kyōhō Reforms, which enforced frugality, restraint, and moral rectitude. Then the death in 1751 of the shōgun, Tokugawa Yoshimune, marked a return to greater freedom and prosperity for urban commoners. One result was the flowering of kabuki, prosperity in the pleasure quarters, the return of jōruri singing (such as Tokiwazu, Tomimoto, Kiyomoto, and Shinnai), and the emergence of new comic genres like senryū and kyōka in poetry; dangibon, sharebon, and kibyōshi in prose fiction; and rakugo in storytelling.

JŌKANBŌ KŌA

The life of the mid-eighteenth-century writer Jōkanbō Kōa remains a mystery. In his youth, Kōa was a monk of the Jōdo (Pure Land Buddhism) sect in Kyoto, but he left the temple and went to Osaka where he became a doctor. After traveling around the country, he settled in Edo during the Genbun era (1736–1741) and became a writer but returned to Kyoto in the mid-Hōreki era. While in Edo he published *Modern-Style Lousy Sermons* (*Imayō heta dangi*, 1752), seven tales criticizing various aspects of contemporary Edo culture, which quickly captured the interest of the townspeople and became a sensational bestseller. Within a year, Kōa published a sequel, *Teachings: Sequel to Lousy Sermons* (*Kyōkun zoku heta dangi*, 1753), and not long afterward, several works imitating Kōa's works in tone, style, and format appeared in Edo. Although the *dangibon* (satiric sermon) genre, characterized by its didactic tone and critique of contemporary society, had begun developing in the first half of the eighteenth century, it was Kōa's *Lousy Sermons* that made it popular.

MODERN-STYLE LOUSY SERMONS (IMAYŌ HETA DANGI, 1752)

Jōkanbō Kōa's work stands between the conservatism of the Kyōhō Reforms, a highly conservative and repressive period during which the bakufu clamped down on those cultural activities that it believed encouraged moral depravity and social disorder, and the Hōreki era, during which the popular culture, particularly in Edo, was reborn. This period was noted for the prosperity of Edo kabuki, led by the actor Ichikawa Danjurō II and featuring the spring performances of the Soga brothers' story, in which Danjurō always starred. In addition, popular forms of haikai poetry such as *maeku-zuke* (verse capping) flourished, as did senryū. The *bungo* songs—jōruri songs that became fashionable during the 1730s but were prohibited in 1741—also regained popularity at this time.

One basis for the satire in *Modern-Style Lousy Sermons* appears to have been the "mind study" (*shingaku*) thought of Ishida Baigan (1685–1744). This new thinking had emerged in Kyoto in the 1720s and soon spread to Osaka at a time when the Kyoto-Osaka economy was suffering. It provided a new ethics for urban commoners in reaction to what appeared to be the material and carnal excesses of chōnin life. Apparently influenced by shingaku thought, Kōa criticized contemporary kabuki, the extravagance of funerals, the commercialization of the *kaichō* (the display of Buddhist images in temples), and other ostentatious, decadent practices. In "The Spirit of Kudō Suketsune Criticizes the Theater," the first of the seven stories in *Lousy Sermons*, Suketsune, the protagonist, criticizes the double-suicide plays, the bungo songs, and the immorality of the Edo kabuki plays in general. There is, however, a seeming contradiction between the popularity of *Lousy Sermons* as a work embodying the new Edo culture and dialect and its didacticism, which reinforced the frugality and conservative morals of the Kyōhō Reforms. The key to understanding this seeming contradiction is Kōa's ironic humor. In "The Spirit of Kudō Suketsune," the spirit of Suketsune complains in a self-serving manner about how he is depicted in contemporary Soga drama, thereby undermining the credibility of his claims. This humorous depiction produces an ironic distance between Kōa, who seems to wink at the audience and implicitly parody the dangibon genre, and Suketsune, who embodies the conservative values of the Kyōhō Reforms. Suketsune's conservative stance may in fact have been a means for Kōa to avoid the censors, who plagued other writers of the time.

As subsequent dangibon influenced by *Modern-Style Lousy Sermons* suggest, this literary genre became a combination of didactic tone and ironic humor rather than simply a conservative vehicle for upholding public morality. In this sense, Kōa's *Lousy Sermons* stood on a middle ground between the old and the new tendencies of the dangibon genre. The dangibon remained at the forefront throughout the Hōreki and Meiwa (1764–1772) eras, climaxing with the publication of Hiraga Gennai's *Rootless Weeds* (*Nenashigusa*, 1763) and *The Modern Life of Shidōken* (*Fūryū Shidōken*). The dangibon gradually shifted its emphasis from its didactic and ironic character to its humor, and by the Kansei period (1789–1801), it had all but disappeared, replaced by the new *kokkeibon* (humor books) such as Jippensha Ikku's *Travels on the Eastern*

Seaboard (*Tōkaidōchū hizakurige*, 1802), which had almost no traces of social and moral didacticism.

The Spirit of Kudō Suketsune Criticizes the Theater

Understanding Jōkanbō Kōa's satire of the Soga plays in "The Spirit of Kudō Suketsune Criticizes the Theater" requires some knowledge of its history and dramatic tradition. Kudō Suketsune was the lord of the Itō Manor on the Izu Peninsula in the twelfth century. When his cousin Itō Sukechika attempted to take control of the manor in 1176, Suketsune fought back, injuring Sukechika and killing his son, Itō Sukeyasu. Kudō Suketsune later served the shōgun, Minamoto Yoritomo, in Kamakura, but in 1192 he was killed by Sukeyasu's sons Soga Jūrō Sukenari (1172–1193) and Soga Gorō Tokimune (1174–1193), who were later captured and executed for their offense. The Soga brothers, Jūrō and Gorō, had been only children at the time of their father's death, which they finally avenged almost sixteen years later. The Soga brothers' story of revenge, the principal source of which was the late-Kamakura-period *Tale of the Soga Brothers* (*Soga monogatari*), was frequently dramatized in nō, jōruri, and kabuki. Chikamatsu Monzaemon wrote numerous plays on the topic. By the 1730s, the Soga brothers' story of revenge had become the customary topic of New Year's plays in Edo, and by the mid-eighteenth century the brothers were cultural icons and theatrical archetypes.

According to Sengaku's commentary on the *Man'yōshū*,[1] in ancient times there was a path called Crossing Run that started at Mount Ashigara,[2] crossed the foot of Mount Fuji, and ended at the Kiyomi Barrier, between Mount Fuji and Mount Ashitaka.[3] Only since the Heian period had it become customary to pass through Kiyomi Point and exit onto Tago Shore.[4] In the ancient period, the foot of Mount Fuji had also been part of the main road between Kyoto and the eastern provinces. In any event, during a storm last autumn, the roads and bridges of the Tōkaidō, the Eastern Seaboard Highway, around the Yoshiwara Plains[5] were severely damaged, and all travelers had to put up with the inconvenience of passing through this rather desolate path at the foot of Mount Fuji.

Meanwhile, at Hell's Crossroads, around Saihō-ji temple in the Kitano area of Kyoto, there lived an arrogant man named Chikushōdō Bagyū. Although he

---

1. Priest Sengaku (b. 1203) was the first significant scholar of the *Man'yōshū* (ca. 759), the first major collection of Japanese poetry.

2. Mount Ashigara is in Kanagawa Prefecture, near present-day Yokohama City.

3. Mount Ashitaka was a volcano on the south side of Mount Fuji.

4. Tago Shore, on the Pacific coast, faces the south side of Mount Fuji.

5. The Yoshiwara Plains, one of the fifty-three stations on the Tōkaidō, is in eastern Shizuoka Prefecture.

was only a judge of verse capping and line capping,[6] he looked down on even the noted masters of haikai poetry and strutted down the main street, putting on airs. A few years earlier, he had been a mediocre actor named Fujita Turtle's Tail who played at the Arashi San'emon Theater in Osaka the role of handsome young men. However, when the bones around his eyes began to protrude and his cheekbones became more prominent with age, he gradually sank to minor roles and finally ended up playing the role of a horse and making a living by occasionally striking the drums at the end of the play.

One year, a man called Ōtani Hiroji, a fat actor who played leading male roles, arrived from Edo.[7] Bagyū, playing the role of a horse, was mounted by this very large man and caused him to fall off six times between the dressing room and the stage bridge, not unlike what happened to Prince Takakura in *The Tale of the Heike*.[8] As a result, the actor was paralyzed, making the promoter absolutely furious. "It's an unspeakable act—injuring a prominent actor!"—the words were spoken like the wise person in a kabuki play.[9] This is how Bagyū sadly left the theater business and became a verse-capping teacher. But the number of such teachers was growing, and at the present time not even a lowly blacksmith's apprentice would bring his five-syllable linked verse to Bagyū.[10] He felt hopeless and disgusted, thinking he would die from ever-growing hunger if this situation continued. What a turn of events! It would be better to be in a profession with which he was already familiar, he thought, and knowing numerous actors in Sakaichō and Kobikichō,[11] he decided to go to Edo and request the role of the horse again. The consolation of a single man is that he does not have a wife who cannot part with him or crying children who will chase after him. His only concern was his landlord, since he had not paid his rent. But Bagyū conveniently got away while the landlord was asleep, and looking back, he amused himself with the thought that the phrase "horse's basket trick" matched his circumstances.[12]

---

6. In verse capping (*maekuzuke*), one person, normally a judge or a marker, presents a short verse (*maeku*) normally consisting of fourteen syllables (7–7), to which another person adds a seventeen-syllable (5–7–5) verse (*tsukeku*). In line capping (*kamuritsuke*), a participant adds a twelve-syllable (7–5) verse (*tsukeku*) to a five-syllable line (*kamuri*) presented by a judge to create a seventeen-syllable hokku or haiku.

7. Ōtani Hiroji (1695–1747), an Edo actor, went to Osaka in 1723 to perform for one year at the Arashi Theater.

8. In *The Tale of the Heike* (chap. 4, sec. 11) Prince Takakura (1151–1180) fell off his horse six times between Miidera Temple in Shiga Prefecture and Uji in Kyoto.

9. *Jitsugotoshi*, a male role in kabuki, was a person who maintained dignity, composure, and wisdom in tragic circumstances.

10. In five-syllable linked verse (*gomojitsuke*), a person adds a five-syllable line to a five-syllable line presented by the judge or marker.

11. Two theater districts in Edo.

12. *Kagonuke* (basket trick) was an acrobatic trick in which a person jumped through a bot-

Eventually, he reached the foot of Mount Fuji, and when he looked around, he heard a sound and saw a rather dark cave, which he thought might be the famous Human Cave.[13] In the past, in the third year of Ken'nin (1203), Nitta Tadatsune had entered this cave, following the orders of his lord Yoritomo in Kamakura.[14] "What a foolish search that had been!" he thought. "Even if one entered this cave and discovered the room of soybean paste in Hell, the bathroom of Paradise, or whatever, it would hardly be a feat to which a warrior aspired. If a warrior became ill from the humidity in the cave and was bitten by poisonous snakes and bugs, it would, regrettably, mean his end. What silly things they did back then!"

As soon as Bagyū had muttered these words to himself, a respectable-looking samurai appeared, around forty years old, his forehead unshaven, his hair knotted, and wearing a robe with vertical stripes and black sleeves and decorated at five points with a family crest in a hermitage-and-flower design.[15] The samurai, startling Bagyū, blocked his way, saying, "I have a minor favor to ask you. Would you wait, please?"

For a bandit, he has a courteous appearance, Bagyū thought. His tight-fitting robe was in the best old-fashioned style. Come to think of it, his appearance was splendid. Bagyū thought that the man might be a samurai from a respectable clan, but he noticed that he did not even have a sandal servant with him. The man might be a masterless samurai, but Bagyū saw that the man wore white silk sleeves.[16] Maybe he had strayed from group following a Shintō priest in the Ōyama Mountains.[17]

He found the stranger suspicious, like the cloudy skies hovering overhead. In a hurry to get to Edo, Bagyū said, "I am heading to Edo on urgent business. I found the road impassable and was forced to make a detour, which has taken a toll on both my legs and my funds. I would like to be on my way as quickly as possible. The travelers behind me do not appear to be busy, so if you have a request, please ask them." With this, he quickly went by, but the samurai grabbed his sleeve.

"Well, what an impatient fellow! Of course, it makes sense for you to hurry, but the nature of my business is such that I cannot ask others. When a samurai

---

tomless basket. Since a horse cannot perform such a nimble trick, "horse's basket trick" (*uma no kagonuke*) became a proverb for doing something thought to be impossible. The word *kagonuke* is also used to describe the act of entering through one door and escaping through another.

13. Hitoana (Human Cave), at the northwest foot of Mount Fuji, was considered a spiritual place where it was believed the Great Bodhisattva of Asama had resided.

14. Nitta Tadatsune (d. 1203), or Nitan no Shiro, was a warrior who served Minamoto no Yoritomo (1147–1199) and is known for defeating Soga Jūrō Sukenari at Mount Fuji.

15. The crest of the Kudō clan indicates that the dress is official attire.

16. Only warriors of high rank, monks, and ladies were allowed to wear white silk sleeves.

17. From the Hōreki era (1751–1764), it was popular to make summer pilgrimages to a Shintō shrine on Ōyama Mountain, in Sagami, present-day Kangawa Prefecture.

The spirit of Kudō Suketsune (*left*) speaks on a rock at the foot of Mount Fuji while Bagyū listens. Suketsune is dressed in official samurai attire, and Bagyū wears commoner travel clothes. From the 1752 edition.

asks for a favor, you must listen without fail. But this is no place to talk. Please come this way."

Bagyū was taken by the hand, and his fear increased greatly when it occurred to him that even though the samurai did not appear to be a bandit, he might be taking him to a place where he could test his new blade. His legs wobbling and his teeth chattering, Bagyū shuddered violently and flinched. Seeing this, the samurai laughed loudly, "You seem to be frightened, but there's no need to be so wary."

The samurai took him along to the mouth of the cave, sat down on the edge of a smooth rock, pulled out a flint, and began stuffing a short-stemmed pipe with tobacco. Although it seemed a bit vulgar, he appeared to be a great lover of tobacco, and Bagyū thought the smell of smoke was surely that of Maidome.[18] "It's a fine tobacco, with a pleasant smell." When Bagyū, out of fear, made these trivial comments, the samurai, perhaps out of vanity, quickly handed him the prepared pipe.

"It's not very good, but why don't you smoke a bit? It's more enjoyable to smoke in a place like this than to smoke lying on the floor indoors. See, it's not

---

18. Maidome was a type of tobacco produced near Kyoto.

bad to smoke using tinder," the samurai said, appearing to have no other designs.

"Why, I love unusual things! To smoke with a match rope is my favorite thing."

"Indeed, it's nice to smoke with a match rope, but it saddens me, since it reminds me of the theater,"[19] the samurai said and began crying profusely.

"What a strange spectacle this is! I can't understand why you should cry about the theater."

Seeing Bagyū's disturbed expression, the samurai said, "Your reaction to my suspicious behavior is understandable. For a start, you're currently going to Edo to see your actor friends in Sakaichō and Kobikichō, aren't you?"

"Indeed, that's true, but how did you know what was on my mind?"

As Bagyū became increasingly uneasy, the samurai smiled and said, "You're right to be suspicious, but there is nothing to be surprised about. I'm the spirit of Kudō Suketsune. For a long time, I have remained at the foot of Mount Fuji, waiting to express my thoughts. But because this area is no longer on the main road for inns, there have been no travelers, and I haven't had a chance to speak my mind. Fortunately, because of the recent storm, travelers have been coming and going in unexpected numbers, but ordinary people will not do for my business. I want this letter delivered without fail to the playwrights in Edo. It is not a request for money.

"As you are well aware, for a long time, the Soga brothers and I have been the central topic of the auspicious kabuki plays performed at the beginning of the spring, in the First Month, in the Edo theaters.[20] Even a three-year-old child knows about the Soga brothers—they've become the custom of the land. Nothing else—not even a play that tries to devise something new—ever becomes popular. New ideas are wasted, and such new plays do not even last past the First Month. At the end of the year, at the busiest time of the season, townspeople—whether young or old, master or apprentice—holding red sardines in one hand, argue with head clerks about the kabuki cast:[21] 'Shichizō should play Soga Jūrō at the Kanzō Theater.'[22] 'No way! It should be Utagawa.'[23] They argue

---

19. Match rope was commonly used in theaters and ships because it lasted longer than tinder.

20. From 1709 it was the custom to perform a Soga play as part of the auspicious spring performances (*haru kyōgen*) of kabuki at the beginning of the year, in the First Month.

21. On the day before the beginning of spring (the last day of the lunar calendar year), a salt-cured red sardine was customarily placed on a holly tree branch at one's gate to ward off evil spirits.

22. Shichizō refers to the actor Nakamura Shichisaburō II (1703–1774). Every year from 1745 to 1749, Shichisaburō played Sukenari's role in Soga plays at the Nakamura Kanzaburō (Kanzō) Theater in Edo. The Nakamura Theater was one of the three major kabuki theaters of Edo, along with the Ichimura Theater and the Morita Theater.

23. Utagawa refers to the kabuki actor Sawamura Sōjurō II (1713–1770), also known as Utagawa Shirōgorō, who played the role of Sukenari at the Nakamura Theater in 1743.

so vehemently that they almost poke each other's eyes out with their New Year's holly branch. The minds of the people are so tied to the Soga brothers that the clerks lose their heads and mark inventory books that they don't even keep. Because hundreds and thousands of people—from the actors to those in the teahouses and bookstores—make their living in the shadow of the Soga brothers, every year there is the so-called Soga Festival on the twenty-eighth of the Fifth Month when people make offerings to the spirit of the Soga brothers. On that day, people can see the play for free.[24] But from what I have heard, not one cup of bitter tea has been offered to me.

"This was before your time, but it's because I died in pain that I am treated so poorly. If I had lived a careful and steadfast life, the Soga brothers would never have killed me. Since I wasn't careful and let them defeat me, the reputation of the brothers is now as high as the lofty peak of Mount Fuji and has even become the source of new kabuki plays. By contrast, my reputation doesn't even reach the Hōei knoll on the side of Mount Fuji,[25] and many people hate me; nobody loves me. Even that Moriya minister who destroyed Buddhist temples is favored by Shintō believers,[26] and in the nō play A Quiver of Arrows, even Kajiwara Kagesue is spoken of highly.[27] It's hard for me and completely unfair.

"What's more, they often represent me, Kudō Suketsune, in a very vulgar manner, rudely addressing my relatives in a manner not befitting a daimyō. 'Hey Tokimune!' 'Hey there, Suke!' What cruel treatment! I'm embarrassed to be taken lightly by samurai spectators, but there's no way to clear up these deep-seated delusions about me. It just makes me sad. Some time ago, the actor Mizuki Takejūrō played me at the Ichimura Theater in Edo and recited the line 'Lord Tokimune, you should not treat the wounds in such an exaggerated manner.'[28] This line stuck in my ears, and I was delighted. Famous actors after him have played me several times, but in the end no one learned from Mizuki. His performance was truly befitting a feudal lord. I was satisfied, and the spectators liked it, too.

---

24. The twenty-eighth day of the Fifth Month is the day on which the Soga brothers defeated Kudō Suketsune. The three major kabuki theaters of Edo deemed this Soga Festival day, and normally it marked the last performance of spring plays.

25. Mount Hōei, a bump on the side of Mount Fuji, is said to have been created by the eruption of Fuji in 1707.

26. Mononobe no Moriya (d. 587), who destroyed Buddhist temples and acted against Prince Shōtoku's desire to protect Buddhism, was admired by eighteenth-century Shintō followers who wanted to get rid of Buddhism.

27. Kajiwara Kagesue (1162–1200), a servant of the shōgun Minamoto Yoritomo, is depicted unfavorably in most kabuki plays, but in the nō play A Quiver of Arrows (Ebira), he is depicted favorably.

28. Mizuki Takejūrō (1674–1721) played Kudō Suketsune at the Ichimura Theater in the spring of 1721. One of the reviews at the time states that Mizuki's Suketsune was sympathetic and well mannered.

"It all depends on the playwright's lines. Things can be said in any number of ways. Also, illiterate actors who play villain's roles would learn a thing or two if the star actors in each troupe did not ignore them but gave them instructions. These things may be considered unimportant, but they shouldn't be. It is annoying to think that a future samurai will take me for a boor and a country bumpkin. Everywhere I look, Kudō Suketsune's reputation is sinking. This is completely the fault of the playwrights. I thought about taking revenge by becoming a vengeful demon, but this would require a loincloth made of a tiger's skin,[29] and I would have to get my hands on drums to create thunder. Instead, I have devised a plan that requires no such things. Dressed in a paper robe, I will become a god of poverty and bring down the playwrights who distress me, and for this purpose, I have even bought a dark red fan.[30]

"And this is not all. In recent years, the playwrights have introduced a person completely unrelated to me, Oshichi, the grocer's daughter.[31] We have been mixed together like seven-herb rice gruel.[32] It's disgraceful for spring kabuki plays to perform stories about criminals. To urge the young girls in the audience to imitate the kind of depraved act that Oshichi committed is outrageous. Oshichi may be young, but she is a monstrosity. If it were made clear why Oshichi was punished, then innocent young girls who don't know right from wrong would become fearful of the consequences and behave themselves. But the plays are rewritten and freely rearranged every year, adding fools who die in double suicides. In recent years this illness—of committing double suicides—has returned, and I've heard of double suicides here and there.

"Generally speaking, since commoner audiences and young girls learn by directly mimicking the theater, the theater should not be a place for senseless things. No doubt there have been a number of instances in which a silly wife, desperate for money when the seasonal payments didn't come in and reluctant to sell her hair for money, breaks the wash basin with a bamboo ladle in the hopes of receiving money, because she has seen this act performed on the stage.[33] Why don't the playwrights distinguish right from wrong and devise stories that will serve as medicine for the audience? The actors of the past were masters a

---

29. It is said that in order for one to become a demon (*oni*), one had to make a loincloth from a tiger's skin.

30. A paper robe and dark red marked the god of poverty.

31. Oshichi was a daughter of a grocer in Edo who was executed for having started a fire because she wanted to meet her lover. This story, which may be apocryphal, was first described by Ihara Saikaku's *Five Sensuous Women* (*Kōshoku gonin onna*, 1686) and then taken up in popular songs and the kabuki theater.

32. Seven-herb rice gruel, served on the seventh day of the New Year, is made by mixing together seven different chopped herbs with rice.

33. One legend states that when a hand basin is struck with a bamboo ladle, one gains wealth in the present life but spends his or her next life in hell. From the Genroku era (1688–1704), plays based on this legend were occasionally performed, one of which became a hit in 1739.

hundred times superior. The stars of today find everything to be difficult. If the theater became a means of teaching the masses, it would be divinely protected.

"And there is another thing—when one looks at the plots of the chivalrous commoner plays in Edo,[34] they differ from those in Kyoto and Osaka in that they generally find fault with a samurai and show him being pushed around and stepped on. As a result, all the commoner playboys in town imitate this behavior and show no restraint in bad-mouthing and abusing the maidservants of the samurai houses and being rude and insolent to the samurai. Even when the weather is sunny, they wear those wooden clogs that those chivalrous heroes wear, raising their shoulders and sticking out their elbows and causing trouble in liquor stores and noodle shops. They learn all this from the theater and end up tearing families apart and destroying lives. That's why strict fathers fear the theater more than dangerous blowfish soup.[35] If the playwrights understood right from wrong and wrote stories that could serve as medicine for the people, then even narrow-minded parents would take care of their young daughter's lunch and buy the best seats in the house with their retirement savings, and brothers would do the same. This should be the basis for the theater's prosperity and its eternal goal.

"But what is the state of affairs now? The playwrights introduce unnecessary things into their plays like those good-for-nothing bungo songs[36] that tempt young girls and maidservants, giving them a bad name and destroying their lives. Simply wicked! To make Osan, the almanac maker's wife who committed adultery with her husband's employee, appear to be a good person is the biggest mistake made by Chikamatsu Monzaemon.[37] Only by representing an immoral criminal clearly as an evil person can a play be called a lesson in justice. What's more, the play should also be a confession of guilt. Obviously, no playwright should be illiterate. How could they cause people harm if they thought honestly about the ways of Heaven with a benevolent heart and kept in mind the world and its people? To think that it is fine as long as people fill the theater, even though the play may corrupt public morals, is the same as making vulgar

---

34. In a chivalrous commoner (*otokodate*) play, the protagonist is ready to fight the strong and help the weak for the sake of honor. For example, Sukeroku, the swashbuckling hero of *Sukeroku and the Flowering Edo Cherry*, is a chivalrous commoner who defeats a brutal samurai villain who is his rival for the favors of Agemaki, a Yoshiwara courtesan.

35. Blowfish (*fugu*) contains a venom that can cause paralysis and death when prepared incorrectly.

36. Bungo was a genre of jōruri songs that became extremely popular among Edo youth at the end of the Kyōhō era (1716–1736) and was known for its erotic quality. It was officially banned from Edo theaters in 1739.

37. Osan was executed in 1683 for having had an affair. Her story was first made famous by Ihara Saikaku in *Five Sensuous Women* (1686). In his jōruri play *The Calendar Maker* (*Daikyōji mukashi goyomi*), which was first performed at Osaka's Takemoto Theater in 1715, Chikamatsu Monzaemon (1653–1724) used the story of Osan's adultery but changed the plot so that she is saved at the end—a change that Kudō Suketsune objects to.

jokes at a street performance. For talented playwrights, this should never happen. . . .

"From now on, be very prudent and careful not to portray in amusing and comical ways the idiots who commit double suicides, the adulterers, the arsonists, and the rest. No doubt some people will say that these stories are not worth making a fuss about. But this is the favorite phrase of someone who does not think about the world and its people. Everyone knows the proverb 'A levee of three thousand meters crumbles from an ant hole and leads to a flood that washes away houses.' So one should be careful about even the smallest things. Please show me the ways of a loyal retainer, a filial son, a benevolent aunt, and a chaste wife. I bring these things up only because if I keep my silence, then the clouds of deep-seated delusion will become the source of many more tears, more than the endless rains of the Fifth Month.

"When you get to Edo, please make sure you communicate these matters in detail and tell them to immediately shut down the plays about double suicides and about Oshichi, the grocer's daughter."

Saying this, Kudō Suketsune cleared his pipe, and with the smoke that rose from the ashes, his spirit disappeared without a trace.

"What a strange exchange!" thought Bagyū. Lord Kudō was of exceptionally good character compared with the Kudō who appears in the theater, but what a cheapskate! Because he asked for a big favor, you would think that he would at least have left some money for wine. But he just made the request and disappeared. What a cunning perversion of Kannon's wisdom![38] Thinking what a thick envelope it was, Bagyū looked at it carefully and realized that it was just a leaf marked with insect bites. Oh, dear, could he also have been tricked earlier? Could the rice cakes that he ate at the teahouse have been made of horse manure? In retaliation for such treatment, he decided not to deliver the message. Bagyū resigned himself with the thought, "Since I am an actor who plays a horse, horse manure and I go hand in hand." With that, he headed off for Edo.

[*Inaka sōshi, Imayō heta dangi, Imayō anasagashi*, SNKBT 81: 110–119, introduction and translation by Satoru Saitō]

HIRAGA GENNAI

Hiraga Gennai (1728–1779) was born in Sanuki Province (Kagawa), in Shikoku. His father was Shiroishi Mozaemon, a low-ranking foot soldier in the service

---

38. Kannon, the bodhisattva or goddess of mercy, manifests herself in various forms to save people in need. Bagyū here compares the spirit of Kūdo Suketsune—who manifests himself before Bagyū for selfish reasons without offering anything in return—as a perverted form of the Kannon.

of the lord of Takamatsu Domain. His elder brother died young, and when his father died, Gennai inherited the house and changed the family name to Hiraga. In 1744 he was employed as an herbalist by the Takamatsu daimyō Matsudaira Yoritaka and in 1752 was sent to Nagasaki, where he studied plants, minerals, and animals that could be used for medicinal purposes. Two years later he turned over his house to his younger sister's husband and moved to Edo to study herbal medicine under the eminent botanist Tamura Ransui (1718–1776) and became acquainted with Sugita Genpaku (1733–1817), a scholar of Western learning. From his study of new medical products and resources came Gennai's great work, the six-volume *Classification of Various Materials* (*Butsurui hinshitsu*), which he published in 1763. By this time, he had resigned the minor samurai post given to him by Takamatsu Domain and had become a rōnin in Edo.

Gennai was a polymath. He was interested in Dutch studies (*rangaku*); invented the magnetic compass needle, the thermometer, the electric generator, and other scientific machines; practiced Western-style painting; discovered his own pottery-making technique (called Gennai-yaki); and studied under the kokugaku scholar Kamo no Mabuchi (1697–1769). In 1763, at the request of a neighborhood library publisher and apparently in need of a change, he published two satiric novels under the pen name Fūrai Sanjin: *Rootless Weeds* (*Nenashigusa*, 1763) and *The Modern Life of Shidōken* (*Fūryū Shidōken*, 1763), both of which are now considered dangibon, or satiric sermons. These works attack contemporary society, specific individuals, and venerable institutions. They also reveal his own strong personality and are humorous, matching the mood of the time. In 1777 he finished "A Theory of Farting" (Hōhi-ron), a self-satirical comic essay. Toward the end of his life, frustrated by a lack of recognition and success, Gennai began to show signs of psychological deterioration. In 1779, during a fit of madness, he killed a disciple with a sword and died in prison later that year.

ROOTLESS WEEDS (NENASHIGUSA, 1763)

In 1763 the popular *onnagata* (woman's role) kabuki actor Ogino Yaegiri drowned while pleasure boating on the Sumida River. In Gennai's *Rootless Weeds*, which gives a comic twist to this incident, Enma, the king of hell, falls in love with a picture of Segawa Kikunojō II (d. 1773), an onnagata kabuki actor, and tries to summon him to hell—a satire of the scandalous infatuation by Mizoguchi Naonori, a castle lord from Echigo, with the real Kikunojō. Following orders from the dragon god, who has been asked by Enma to find Kikunojō, a *kappa* (water spirit) takes the shape of a young samurai and manages to become intimate with Kikunojō while he is pleasure boating, but in the end Ogino Yaegiri jumps into the water, sacrificing himself for Kikunojō.

Gennai was influenced here by witty *mitate* (superimposition) narratives such as

Tales of the Outrageous (*Furachi monogatari*, 1755) in which hell bears the features of contemporary urban life, including a new licensed quarter. In *Tales of the Outrageous*, news of these excesses in hell reaches the Pure Land, causing Shakyamuni, the buddha, to subdue this world. Gennai used the hell narrative found in works like *Tales of the Outrageous*, wove in satiric sermons and debates, and provided a completely uninhibited description of society—all of which revolutionized the dangibon genre. *Rootless Weeds* offered readers not only an elegy to a stage star but also a vivid depiction of the diversity of contemporary urban life in Edo.

The passage, translated here, that describes contemporary life on the bridge at Ryōgoku on the Sumida River became a famous example of *haibun* (haikai poetic prose), a kind of *fu* (rhyme-prose) about a noted place. Gennai was a great satirist who believed that fiction ("lies") should be used to reveal truth. *Rootless Weeds*, a metaphor for "books without foundation," is a book of such "lies," revealing the truth about contemporary Buddhist priests and bakufu-domain officials. It appeared during the period (1764–1787) dominated by Tanuma Okitsugu (1719–1788), a powerful official in the Tokugawa shōgunate who was known for his corrupt ways and for his lack of interest in censoring the various arts, including Gennai's books. The corruption and hypocrisy of the bakufu and daimyō are reflected in the behavior of Enma and the other officials of hell. *Rootless Weeds* was so popular that it was followed by *A Sequel to Rootless Weeds* (*Nenashigusa kōhen*) in 1769, generating debate about whether *Rootless Weeds* or Jōkanbō Kōa's *Modern-Style Lousy Sermons* was superior. In later years, *Rootless Weeds* had two important influences: it spawned narratives describing hell, and it inspired imitations of the "Hiraga style" (Hiragaburi), with its sharp satiric observations.

In Hell (chapter 1)

In ancient China, which none of us has ever seen, the wife of a drowned man expressed her unbearable grief in a poem[39] we still read:

> Husband, don't cross that river!
> But at last you wade out.
> In the current you fall and die.
> Ah, you, what shall I do?

And then in the Sixth Month of 1763, a kabuki actor of women's roles, Ogino Yaegiri, also went into a river and died. Conflicting rumors abound, and no one knows anything for certain about his drowning.

---

39. A Han-period yuefu ballad-poem reportedly sung to a harp by a Korean woman who had tried to stop her drunk husband from trying to cross a river. After she finished the song, she threw herself into the river.

This woodblock print (ca. 1757) portrays Segawa Kikunojō II (1741–1773), a noted kabuki female impersonator, popularly known by his haikai name Rokō (written to the right). Kikunojō appears here as a courtesan, holding a long tobacco pipe and wearing a kimono marked with the Segawa family crest and tied with a sash in front. The chrysanthemum and butterfly patterns on the robe allude to Kikunojō's alternative crest. Kikunojō became so popular that his style of tying a sash came to be known as the "Rokō knot" and was imitated by the women of Edo. A hokku, "Weary of a blizzard, the sight of a plum blossom in the cold" (*kanbai no / fubuki wo itou / sugata kana*), which praises Kikunojō, appears to the left, next to his name. The name of the ukiyo-e artist Ishikawa Toyonobu (1711–1785), known for his prints of beautiful women, appears next to Kikunojō's right foot. (Courtesy of the Tobacco and Salt Museum, Tokyo)

Careful inquiry shows, however, that Yaegiri was no Qu Yuan,[40] who indignantly wrote, "Could I let my pure whiteness be soiled by the world's dirt?" and then jumped in the Miluo River. Neither was he like the diver in the nō play *Fisherwoman* who lost her life retrieving a jewel from the Dragon Palace on the ocean floor. It all began in the other world, halfway between paradise and hell, at the court of the most august king Enma, supreme judge of newly dead souls. This great king rules over three thousand worlds, together with nine lesser kings and countless retainers who oversee numerous agencies and departments.

In the human world, warriors, farmers, artisans, and merchants all were very busy pursuing the separate occupations appropriate to each class. Enma's palace had once been a place of leisure, but now it, too, was bustling. In recent years human minds had been growing more and more twisted, and people were

---

40. A Chinese poet from Chu who lived in the second century B.C.E. In "The Fisher" a sage urges Qu Yuan, slandered and exiled, to be more flexible, while Qu Yuan righteously insists on his innocence. The poet committed suicide by jumping into the Miluo River.

committing all sorts of crimes. The number of offenders Enma had to condemn to hell was rising daily, with no limit in sight, and the great king faced a crisis. There was no longer enough land left in hell as we had known it.

Profiteering developers and shady contractors took advantage of the land shortage and fought with one another to be first to present their petitions, privately meeting the officials in charge and gaining approval for their projects through flattery, fraud, and bribery. They searched along all the roads through the trillion buddha lands this side of paradise to find desolate, unused wasteland, and they cleared land at the very edge of hell, extending to the eggplant fields in the merciful bodhisattva Jizō's territory. Some contractors dug lakes hundreds of miles wide and boiled redwood dye in them to make the water look like the steaming blood in the traditional hell, while others constructed artificial mountains and planted sharp seedlings on them to make them resemble the old Mountain of Swords which dead souls had to cross. Since there no longer were enough rank-and-file hell guards to pound and mash all the convicts in mortars, contractors built waterwheel devices to do the job, and in the Hell of Burning Heat they installed a large bellows.

To supplement the Hell of Shrieks, the Hell of Great Wailing, the Hell of Continual Dismemberment and Rememberment, the Hell of Hot Cables, the Hell of Unending Pain, and other traditional properties, the developers opened various new areas that they called Hells of Unlicensed Hookers.[41] Claiming that the old woman by the River Between Worlds who strips newly dead souls of their last belongings couldn't possibly oversee all the new hells herself, the developers got officials to pardon and recall the old woman in Asakusa who cracked open visitors' heads, the old female demon who ate passersby in Adachigahara, the old woman moneylender in the Sakaichō theater district in Edo who rented out boys and female prostitutes dressed like traveling nuns, and all the other old women who had abused their sons' brides or hated their stepchildren.

As hell gradually expanded, the shady developers came to officials with still more petitions. "I would like to become a landlord in one of the new hell blocks," proposed one. "But the payments[42] I get for manure from the houses of the hungry ghosts aren't going up at all. Those famished ghosts just aren't allowed to eat anything. So I beg you to raise the special seasonal tenant fees to two hundred coppers per festival." Another sought contracts to procure tongue-pulling tongs, iron cudgels, and fiery wagons. "And you won't need to order new cauldrons," he stated. "I can collect all the old abandoned cauldrons without bottoms in traditional hell and have them recast for you. I can also

---

41. Unlicensed prostitutes worked in various parts of Edo, many in newly developed areas known as "hells."

42. Produce given by farmers to Edo landlords in return for shipments of human manure.

provide you with the wicks you force your convicts to use to try to dig up bamboo roots. If you let me buy up odd pieces from candle makers, your savings will be dramatic." The speculators knew even a very small project would eventually grow like a piece of dust into a whole mountain during the minimum of a million eons that hell would be around.

One entrepreneur asked to be granted a monopoly on handling clothes taken from the newly dead before they crossed the River Between Worlds. In return, he guaranteed, whenever hell guards lost at dice, he would give them very low interest rates on the tiger-skin loincloths they pawned with him. "If implemented," said petition after petition, "your benevolence will spread downward for the betterment of all hell"—as if the profits were for others. Even in hell, they say, money talks. It's a very canny place.

King Enma was so busy making the final decisions on all these projects and other official matters that he no longer had any free time. One day some devil magistrates, preceded by guards holding up lanterns marked with the first character for "hell," came to him with still another criminal. Gazing down from a distance, Enma could see the man was a Buddhist monk of about twenty. Pale and thin, he was in handcuffs and an iron collar. Tied to his waist was something wrapped in fine crepe.

"And what is his crime?" Enma asked.

The registrar god standing beside the throne walked out before the king. "This monk," he said, "was an acolyte in a temple in Edo in the land of Japan

An official wearing double samurai swords and a developer inspect a newly installed apparatus in hell for mashing condemned souls. In Gennai's time, similar devices had actually been developed for hulling rice and crushing herbs. From the 1763 edition.

A dead acolyte monk is led directly to King Enma's court for judgment. Since it is a complex case, the acolyte is not being tried by the three magistrates sitting in the building (*upper right*).

in the southern sector of the universe. He fell helplessly in love with Segawa Kikunojō, a beautiful actor who plays young women's roles in kabuki plays in Sakaichō, one of their theater districts. In order to buy private meetings and sleep with this actor, the monk stole money from his own master. Then he took all the scarlet brocade curtains from the sacred halls and statues. They ended up fluttering in a secondhand market! And then he caused the precious image of Amida Buddha carved by the holy man Gyōki[43] to manifest itself, surrounded by bodhisattvas and purple clouds, in the storehouse of a pawnshop. The monk loved the young actor much too much. He couldn't keep his hips shut, things came out, and the situation went from bad to worse. Finally the other monks locked him in a room in the temple. The monk realized he could never meet Kikunojō again, and the actor's soul didn't come visit him in his dreams, so he fell very ill. His longing was too strong for his body, and he left the other world and came here. But even in his death throes he never forgot the actor's picture. He still refuses to let go of it. That thing at his waist is a portrait of Kikunojō done by one of their leading artists, Torii Kiyonobu.

"Just because the monk was young and hot-blooded doesn't excuse his crime of deceiving his master, who was like a father to him. Each of his crimes is

---

43. A noted eighth-century Buddhist monk. The ancient statue would be priceless.

written right here on this iron plate. On the other hand, all monks these days pretend to be pious but spend most of their time chasing women. Or eating duck meat, which they refer to as a 'god,' and onions, which they call 'Shintō priests.'[44] Compared with that, loving a young actor seems like a lesser crime. How about giving him an easier route over the Mountain of Swords? And he likes young men, so he must like pots.[45] How about letting him off with a soak in a boiling cauldron?"

Enma, outraged, answered in anger: "Most definitely not. His crime may look minor, but don't be deceived! I'm told something called 'male homosexuality' can be found all across the human world, and I absolutely cannot allow this kind of thing. The Way of the husband and wife is the natural harmonizing of yin and yang. This is as it should be. A man should never violate another man. It has long been so since the days of ancient China. The *Book of Documents* clearly warns, 'Do not keep company with loose boys.' After King Mu of Zhou loved the Chrysanthemum Boy Sage, people began to talk about the Chrysanthemum Seat.[46] There were others of that ilk as well, like Mi Zixia, loved by the duke of Wei, or Dong Xian, the favorite of a Han emperor, or the poet Meng Dongye, who loved another poet, Han Yu.[47]

"They also appeared in Japan. While Saint Kōbō[48] was on a pilgrimage to India in the ninth century, he stopped along the Upper Liusha River in China and exchanged vows of love with Manjusri, the beautiful boy bodhisattva of wisdom. After that encounter, Manjusri became known in Japan as Rear End Monjushiri,[49] and Kōbō's name lives on in shame as the founder of the Way of Loving Young Men in Japan. And a well-known legend claims that the famous warrior Kumagai[50] pulled down his enemy, the fetching young Atsumori, and took him right there on the beach at Suma. As a boy, Yoshitsune[51] was embraced by a mountain goblin. The ancient Buddhist holy man Zōga loved the young

---

44. Ducks (*kamo*) are homophonous with the famous Kamo god. "Shintō priest" (*negi*) is homophonous with "onion" (*negi*). These words became euphemisms for forbidden food.

45. Slang for "young male homosexuals."

46. According to a legend dramatized in the nō play *Chrysanthemum Boy*, the Chrysanthemum Boy Sage was loved by a king until he was banished at sixteen; in exile he drank dew from chrysanthemums and gained immortality. "Chrysanthemum Seat" implies anus.

47. Young man loved by the duke of Wei in the Zhou period. Dong Xian, loved by the Han emperor Ai, became a powerful official. Meng Dongye (Meng Jiang) is a Tang-period poet reputed to have loved the poet Han Yu.

48. Kūkai (774–835), who founded the Shingon Buddhist sect in Japan.

49. "Master of Beauty" and guardian of Buddhist wisdom. In Japanese, *srii* (Master) becomes *shiri* (rear end).

50. Fighting for the Minamoto at the battle of Ichinotani in 1184, Kumagai unhorsed the Taira hero Atsumori on the beach and beheaded him. Enma is referring to a homoerotic version of the confrontation.

51. Younger brother of the shōgun, Minamoto Yoritomo.

poet Narihira; Emperor Go Daigo had the boy Kumawaka; and the great war-
lord Nobunaga loved his page Ranmaru. The famous monk Mongaku, who
rebuilt the Jingo-ji temple in Takao, lost his head over the boy Rokudai. Later
he was rebuked by the shōgun, Yoritomo, for suggesting that the shōgun replace
the emperor, but he kept on plotting. Finally he was exiled, and his boy lover
was executed. After that, whenever a human was punished for a bad deed that
came to light later, people spoke of 'the tail end arriving.'

"The reason so many men go to heal themselves in the hot springs at Ki-
nosaki and Sokokura is obvious. They're almost all homosexuals. The Chinese
character for 'hemorrhoids' combines one part meaning 'ailment' with another
meaning 'temple.' Perhaps that is because in ancient times, homosexuality was
practiced only by Buddhist monks. But recently it's been spreading beyond the
temples. All kinds of men have begun to like it. It's outrageous and the height
of wickedness. Issue an order strictly forbidding homosexuality in the human
world!"

Councillors repeated "Certainly, your Majesty" to this awesome command.
All except Tenrin, the tenth of the ten kings and the manifestation of the merciful Amida Buddha. He walked out in front of Enma's throne. "It is with the
greatest trepidation," he said, "that I ask Your Majesty to revoke a royal edict,
yet if I did not speak my mind I would fill to bursting with my thoughts. As
Your Highness has most excellently said, homosexuality is not harmless. Nevertheless, the harm it does is much less than that done by the love between
men and women. These two different kinds of love should not even be discussed
on the same day. Heterosexual love has a sweet taste to it, resembling honey,
while homosexual love is light and uncloying, like water. It has a taste without
taste[52] that is hard to appreciate unless you experience it and enter into an
extremely interesting state yourself. Your Majesty doesn't know anything about
loving young men, so he is like a connoisseur of saké who wishes to prevent
others from entering rice-cake shops. Moreover, although it is only a rumor
from the human world, there has been talk for some time about this Kikunojō's
being unbearably attractive. It would be a memorable experience just to see
what he looks like, even if only in a portrait. For this proposal," he pleaded, "I
ask Your Majesty's most generous understanding."

"'Different people,'" Enma began, obviously displeased, "'like different
things.' Whoever coined that phrase must have had you in mind. Yet your
petition is earnest and impossible to refuse. Go ahead, look at the picture if you
want. But I dislike looking at young men, so I'm going to close my eyes for as
long as you have the picture out. Hurry. Quickly, quickly!"

After Enma had closed his eyes, they hung the portrait on one of the palace
pillars. The young actor was as fresh as the early moon rising through willow

---

52. A Taoist mystical phrase used in *Laozi* (sec. 55).

branches in spring, as voluptuous as peach blossoms touched by morning haze. Everyone stood transfixed before his indescribably graceful form. The sounds of exclamations continued for some time.

In the human world, they say the most beautiful sight of all is a celestial woman descending through the sky, but that is only because the most distant things seem most attractive. In paradise, sky-flying women are as common as kites, and their fluttering robes might as well be squid legs. Heavenly women are so common that no one considers them beautiful. To compare Kikunojō with one would be to liken Enma's crown to a hungry ghost's loincloth. The actor was even more beautiful than he was reputed to be, beyond anything the kings or anyone else in the palace had ever seen. The eyes of the seeing-head demon glistened; the sniffing-head demon began to breathe hard;[53] and even the ordinary bull-headed guards and ox-headed torturers wagged the horns on their foreheads and exclaimed in wonder.

When the commotion did not subside, Enma opened his eyes in spite of himself and looked. He was overwhelmed by the actor's beauty. He had intended to laugh, but now he was staring as if in a trance, unmoving, the mere empty shell of himself. Suddenly he tumbled from his throne. His shocked attendants lifted him up again, and when he had finally returned to consciousness, he sighed deeply.

"Now, well, how embarrassing to have that happen in front of you all," he said. "When I saw the actor just now in the picture, he was so very refined, I was simply overcome. I lost my way, like the monk Henjō[54] when he saw a maiden flower. My, my, my. There have been some very famous beautiful women over the centuries, but none compares with this Kikunojō. He has Xi Shi's eyes, Komachi's eyebrows, Yang Guifei's lips, Kaguya-hime's nose, Feiyan's supple waist, and Sotoori-hime's elegant way of dressing—all in one. People in Japan sing about shōguns' daughters who are like empress trees or young women being like mountain lilies or wild pinks, but next to this actor they're all just ordinary. Even cherry blossoms and full moons and graceful bodhisattvas can't equal this young man. No one like him will ever be born again, in either China or Japan. Therefore I hereby resign as supreme ruler of the afterworld. What's a precious throne worth when I can go to the human world and share a pillow with him?"

Enma's eyes were glazed, and light-footed with love, he began to leave the palace. Sōtei, third of the ten kings, ran out and grabbed Enma's sleeve. "Your

---

53. On a pole that Enma held were two demons with heads but no bodies. One saw through newly dead souls brought before Enma; the other sniffed out their true characters.

54. Ninth-century Buddhist priest. Enma is referring to the poem: "I plucked you, woman-flower, charmed only by your name—Do not tell others I fell and broke my vows" (*Kokinshū*, Autumn 1, no. 226). "Fall" also means "to break a vow of chastity."

Majesty's conduct," he said scowling, "is most unbecoming. If you abandon your position as supreme ruler of the afterworld and cohabit with humans simply because you feel attracted to one of them, there will be no one to oversee the governance of hell and paradise. And if there is no place where good and evil actions are judged, what doctrine can we use to rule the beings in the three thousand worlds?

"If Your Highness stoops to buying young men, the gold dust covering paradise will soon belong to the Sakaichō theater district in Edo. No matter how much gold we had, it would never be enough. Later Your Majesty would come to regret what you'd done and be reduced to singing children's songs about money trees. We would have to sell everything, even the golden skin of Shakyamuni Buddha, the don of all paradise, to scrap-metal dealers. And Jizō, the gentle bodhisattva who cares for dead infants, would become the laughingstock of children in the street, just like the monk Chōtarō in Edo. The sweet-singing heavenly kalavinka birds, why, they would end up in cages in freak shows beside Ryōgoku Bridge. The celestial flying women would be sold off to prostitution brokers; the old woman guarding the River Between Worlds would be reduced to hawking homemade laundry glue; and the guardian demons of Buddhism would have to use their muscles to carry riders in cheap palanquins. Hell and paradise would collapse in no time at all. Your Majesty is not too old to realize that.

"And supposing Your Highness does copy their latest styles and wears a short bat cloak and long dagger, ties your hair in a long topknot, smokes a silver pipe, and acts in a way that shows you're looking for young men—no human man would ever agree to meet you, not with that face of yours. When Ichikawa Danjūrō II played Your Majesty in the kabuki play about Kagekiyo several years ago, the humans who saw him shuddered with fear. If Your Majesty tries to go out into the streets dressed like that, you will immediately arouse suspicion and be taken into custody. When the authorities question the local landlords about you, they could say Your Grace is Shakyamuni himself, and the block leaders could swear your Highness is the Great Sun Buddha Dainichi—but unless Your Highness has someone to vouch for him, they will surely put him in among the outcasts. It would be a miserable experience. If that prospect does not deter Your Majesty, then I, King Sōtei, will cut myself open right here before him. I await Your Majesty's reply." In the heat of his admonition, Sōtei struck the throne.

Then Byōdō, the eighth king, stood up quietly and came before the throne. "King Sōtei's warning," he began, "rivals that of Bi Gan, who reproached a Yin king and had his chest split open, or Wu Zixu, who had his eyes gouged out for cautioning the king of Wu, or Kiso no Chūta, who reprimanded his lord Yoshinaka and then cut himself open. Recently Your Highness has become very stubborn. Once he makes a proclamation, he refuses to consider changing it.

Counseling him is, as Mencius put it, like pouring a cup of water on a wagon-load of burning firewood. No matter how much advice we give, it has no more effect than wind on a horse's ear or a bee sting on a cow's horn. It would not show Your Majesty's wisdom as supreme ruler of all hell and paradise to abandon his position like a reckless young human male simply for the sake of this beautiful Kikunojō, who looks like a man and a woman in one body. If Your Highness absolutely must see him, then send a royal messenger to fetch him for you and bring him here. Could there be anything wrong with that? What do you all think?"

Everyone agreed that King Byōdō's counsel made excellent sense and was worth heeding. Unable to resist any longer, Enma reluctantly approved the plan. And so the deliberations turned to choosing who would abduct Kikunojō. . . .

In the remainder of the chapter, other kings offer various badly thought-out plans. Finally it is decided that Kikunojō should be kidnapped while he is boating. The head dragon god, who rules over the element of water, is made responsible for capturing Kikunojō and is called before Enma, who sheepishly asks the dragon to bring him the young man. Then Enma declares an amnesty and decrees the legality of all the male entertainment and prostitution districts in Edo, although it is made a crime for anyone but Enma to go near Kikunojō.

The second chapter reconstructs the history of kabuki, presenting its origins in the performances of the gods. The society of the gods is thrown into chaos and darkness when the sun goddess goes into a cave and stays there. At last she is lured out by her desire to see a superb kabuki performance in which women's roles are played by female gods. "After kabuki became all male, the first male actors who played women's roles grew up thinking and speaking like women, even believing they suffered women's ailments. Acting women's roles is the most difficult kabuki art, and actors do not measure up to the earlier high level. Only Segawa Kikunojō II has both the artistry and the physical beauty to play young women on the stage as they should be played."

The third chapter takes place at the bottom of the sea, in the palace of the head dragon god, one of eight described in the Lotus Sutra. The dragon is presented as a daimyō ruling over the water domain who has received a supreme order from the shōgun-like king, Enma. "When the dragon lord asks for volunteers to fetch Kikunojō, numerous sea creatures, resembling domain elders, advisers, and administrators, offer various in-genious and learned excuses for avoiding the responsibility and not going. The dragon lord grows very angry until finally a lowly kappa water spirit, who works in the palace guardhouse, volunteers." The spirits, who have the ability to capture humans, have hollows in the tops of their heads in which they carry water, allowing them to live out of the water for short periods, and they are known in legends for stealing humans' intestines. But the king also knows this reputation comes from their fondness for loving human males, making the water spirit a dangerous choice. The spirit, however, swears his absolute loyalty to his dragon lord and is given the honor of capturing Kikunojō, who has been persuaded by another actor, Ogino Yaegiri, to take an all-day pleasure boat ride on the Sumida River in Edo.

Ryōgoku Bridge (chapter 4)

The river flows ceaselessly, yet its water is never the same. So wrote Kamo no Chōmei[55] centuries ago. His brush and inkstone left behind deep thoughts that continue to be read. The pure water of the Sumida River, too, has from antiquity flowed between Musashi Province, which now includes Edo, and Shimōsa Province farther east. Ryōgoku, the Bridge Between Two Realms, is so named because it spans this border. A thousand years ago, when the area was rough frontier, the poet Narihira addressed a gull on the Sumida as "capital bird"[56] and wept remembering Kyoto. But today boats pass each other constantly, numerous as floating autumn leaves, and Ryōgoku Bridge lies long across the water like a sleeping dragon.

On one bank of the Sumida the large drum of an acrobat show echoes up to the clouds so loudly that even the thunder god runs away in shame. In a riverside restaurant, cool thin white noodles are shaken dry[57] and heaped high as a snowy Mount Fuji on the Island of Tiny People. A mother with children holds up her wide, hanging sleeve so her children won't see as they pass a sign advertising Long Life Ointment for lengthening men's lovemaking. A cautious country samurai notices a man wearing a wide sedge hat suspiciously far down over his face and moves out of the man's way, gripping the front of his robe and the purse inside. A smooth-talking juggler sends beans and saké bottles spinning up into the air, and a watermelon seller on the street curses a red shop-lantern nearby for stealing the fresh color from his slices.

The cries of insects! A salesman brings autumn early to the city in cages hanging from both ends of his shoulder pole. "Cup of water? Cold water!" A water seller calls from the shade of a willow, which, unlike the country willows that poets praise, has no clear stream running beneath it. A low voice chanting a puppet play in an impromptu reed-screen shed is drowned out by "Repent! Repent!" as passing pilgrims pour purifying water over their heads. A fragrance comes from Igarashi's Hair-Oil store, followed by the smell of spitted eels broiled in soy sauce. People peep into boxes at moving stereoscopic prints, imagining they're in other worlds, and the crowd around a glassblower wonders whether

---

55. Kamo no Chōmei (1155–1216), the poet and author of *An Account of My Hut* (*Hōjōki*), whose opening is quoted here. In the following lines, allusions to ancient poems overlap with contemporary scenes.

56. *Kokinshū*, Travel, no. 411, also sec. 9 of *The Tales of Ise*, by Ariwara no Narihira.

57. *Furitsutsu*, homophonous with "snows continuously," a line from a poem about Mount Fuji by the ancient poet Akahito (*Shinkokinshū*, no. 675).

icicles have formed in summer. Potted trees revive and suddenly look fresh when a florist sprinkles water on them, while papier-mâché turtles hanging out for sale move in the wind and take on souls.

The soft tofu is salty; the jam-covered rice cakes are very sweet. The waitresses at the Kanbayashi restaurant have pinch marks on them, and the big second-floor room at the Wakamori hums with sounds of eating and entertainment. It won't be long until the Feast of Souls, and the sellers of lanterns for greeting returning souls are doing a brisk business, amid shouts for more saké to go with shad sushi. Colorful crests cover the sliding door of a hairdresser's shop, and the kettle in a riverside teahouse has been scrubbed until it shines. From a makeshift hut comes the high voice of a man reading and commenting on classical tales; from the street, a sharp "Eggs! Eggs!" and a candy seller's voice even sweeter than his wares and then the country accents of a man peddling nutmeg throat lozenges. Coral formations decorate a toy shop selling dyed shell noisemakers. Nearby, large kernels of baking corn bulge like sharkskin.

The booming of the evening bell at the temple for the nameless abandoned dead reminds people of their mortality, and profligates finally feel the sting in the writings of the raconteur Buddhist preacher Jōkanbō. Horses neigh in the water, taking stunt riders across the river, while in teahouses nearer the temple unlicensed hookers called "wildcats" go discreetly upstairs with monks and pilgrims. For a copper you can buy a turtle and set it free: grateful, it will grant you long life, and your chances in the next world will improve, too. Hired monks, legs moving for coins, trek to the temple to the bodhisattva Kannon to say others' prayers. A father buys a fishing pole, his face as contented as the ancient sage Taigong Wang, while his daughter compares herself with a famous beauty depicted in a woodblock print and frowns as deeply as the unlucky Han court woman Wang Zhaojun when she studied a portrait of her that the painter hadn't touched up. Bats forage the sky for mosquitoes, and on Earth, streetwalkers try to stop men. "Need a boat?" "Need a boat?" Calls from boatmen cross the water. On the bank, palanquin carriers wait for riders.

Monks mix with ordinary people and men with women, while gawking country samurai serving at the Edo mansions of domain lords mingle with stylish commoners wearing the latest long combs and short capes. The attendant of a lord's son carries a glass goldfish bowl, and a woman-in-waiting follows a lord's wife, dangling a brocade pipe sheath. A chambermaid's thighs rub as she pulls her behind after her, and a low-ranking samurai who hires himself out to big mansions looks like he's stabbing himself as he walks awkwardly with pretentiously long swords. The man over there seems to be a popular doctor, and that man trying to look very elegant must be a haikai linked-verse master. The amorous-looking woman pulling her sleeves stiffly away from the men who tug on them looks like a professional dancer who already has a lover, and that other stiff woman with an amorous look on her face must be a maid looking for love

On the left in this two-part view of the Sumida River, Ryōgoku Bridge is crossed by commoners and a lord with a spear carrier, while on the right, a full moon rises above the Sumida River at a quieter location downstream, described later.

on a rare day off from the women's quarters in Edo Castle. And over there are the smooth body motions of a master swordsman; the steady movements of the bearers of a large palanquin; the relaxed humming of a blind masseuse who knows exactly where he's going; the two-colored formal robes of a merchant who sells to great lords; the old, ripped divided skirts of an unemployed samurai; the loose, light cape of a retired man; the leisurely strides of kabuki actors; the clipped motions of artisans; the long topknots of construction workers; the loose sidelocks of farmers, hunters coming, and woodcutters going.

So many different styles and customs, and such diverse faces, in crowds too dense to push through—has Edo emptied the houses of the provinces? Dirt and dust rise, filling the air as if the world's clouds formed here. They say you can always see at least three minor lords with spear bearers crossing the bridge, but that must refer to ordinary times. From the middle of summer until early fall, when people come to the Sumida River to cool off, there are always at least five to ten minor lords with spear bearers crossing the bridge. The banks of the Kamo River in Kyoto by Fourth Avenue are also famous as a place to cool off and are very lively, but compared with Ryōgoku, they're like one of those young men with thin sidelocks you hire as an attendant.

Amid all the Ryōgoku sounds, a samurai footman listens, enraptured, to an outcast woman playing her shamisen and chanting a puppet play for coppers in the street. He's fallen in love with her and forgets gate-closing time at his lord's mansion. A man follows a woman's backside, works his way ahead through the crowd, turns, and glimpses her face—to his regret. Another man praises a pretty woman, but her friend behind her smiles sweetly back at him. Fireworks shoot up from tubes on the Tamaya boats into marvelous patterns, while the Kagiya crew, on other boats, tries to steal the night with an ingenious new program. People look up and exclaim, and when a shooting star cluster bursts and hangs above the river, the crowd on the far bank surges noisily onto the bridge, trying to get closer. From vending boats below come "Baked bean curd saké!" "High-class saké!" The drooling man in that boat looks like the Tang drunk Ru Yang, and over there's the poet Li Bo throwing up. Liu Ling, a hard-drinking sage of the bamboo grove, empties his purse completely, and the red-cheeked elf Xing-xing throws up even the hot wine-absorbing stone in his stomach.

There are tea-vending boats, flat-bottomed ferries, fast one-passenger boats, boats with awnings, and, here and there, large, roofed pleasure boats. The elegant *Yoshino* is decorated with a cherry blossom design; the *Takao* flutters with the scarlet sleeves of dancers; and the *Ebisu* rocks with the laughter of merchants. On the *Daikoku*, monks rendezvous with mistresses, and the *Hyōgo* carries a whole island of fish in a sea of saké. Kotos mingle with shamisens, stately kabuki music with lively pieces, finger counting with *shōgi* chess, imitations of actors' gestures with vocal impersonations. From one boat comes quiet, soulful kabuki background chanting. On another, people are singing so loudly to shamisens and drums that even the boatman quickens his oar to the rhythm. Elsewhere people hit hanging gongs and large drums to the music of the Gion Festival or bang without reverence on Buddhist hand gongs and cymbals. Every kind of boat and raft is here, even foul-smelling freighters taking human manure from the city to farmers in the north and east. Such prosperity can surely be found only in Edo.

One of these large pleasure boats had been rented for the day by Kikunojō. With him rode Ogino Yaegiri, Kamakura Heikurō, and Nakamura Yosahachi, and other kabuki actors, who were drinking and performing and generally making a great commotion on board. Actors play the shamisen and chant passages from puppet plays as naturally as scholars give lectures, retired people chant sutras, rice pounders shoulder pestles, or carpenters carry adzes in their belts, and other boats gathered around to watch and listen. It resembled cherry blossom viewing, when even those who drink quietly have a nice time just wandering around, watching other people sing and dance. Reserve was as pointless as a lantern under a full moon. The actors weren't performing for the boats around them, and the onlookers felt relaxed and free.

The group of boats anchored first in one place, then another. Finally the actors decided to go somewhere quiet, and they had their boat row downstream to Mitsumata. To the south, they could see the Sumida entering the bay and then the sea, although it was hard to tell exactly where the clouds met the sea at the horizon. In the middle distance, sails were gliding like butterflies, and farther away, ships dotted the mouth of the bay between Awa and Sagami as if brushed in ink in a single flowing stroke. To the west, the actors could barely make out Hakone, Ōyama, and other low mountains, but above them the peak of Mount Fuji was clearly visible. It was the hottest time of year, and Fuji had been bare at noon, but summer snow lay on it now, just as in an ancient poem.[58] Closer by, the actors saw nothing but houses and early evening smoke trailing up from the people's cooking stoves. Once the wide Musashino plain had been covered with high grass, but now it was covered with human dwellings, and the moon rose and set beyond house eaves. People making their way along streets and roads looked like ants on their errands, and the actors felt as if they'd entered the realm of Daoist sages. Suddenly they found themselves beating for joy on the sides of the boat.[59] Then they began to sing very softly. Someone said dust was scattering in delight from the boat's roof beams and clouds were wavering in the sky,[60] and everyone felt extremely good. Incense was lit, and they enjoyed it in silence. Then they decided to get into dinghies and go look for small freshwater clams on the shore of Nakazu.

"I'm writing a hokku now," Kikunojō told the others. "I want to finish it here. I'll catch up with you later."

It was the fifteenth of the Sixth Month, and the full moon appeared in the east while the sun was still going down over the mountains to the west. Small waves rose on the surface of the river, and the air grew cool. It was hard to believe now that the day had been so hot. Kikunojō felt he had entered another world. He pulled close a brush and inkstone and wrote:

> Changing the color
> of late sunlight on the waves —
> summer moon

He smiled to himself, feeling he'd done justice to the subtle changes brought by the cool moonlight to the sunset color of the waves, and he read the verse out loud. Then he heard a faint voice:

> From darkening cloud peaks,
> the booming of a temple bell.

---

58. *Man'yōshū*, no. 320.

59. The man recalls a poem by the Chinese poet Su Dongpo (Su Shi, 1037–1101), "Prose Poem at the Red Cliff," in which a lone poet hits the sides of a boat. Gennai is describing a kind of group ecstasy.

60. A reference to Ki no Tsurayuki's *Tosa Diary* and that text's allusion to two legendary Chinese singers.

Amazed, Kikunojō wondered who could have written this sensitive second verse and linked it to his hokku to form the opening of a sequence.

Searching the water nearby, he found a young samurai alone in a small boat without a boatman. Absorbed in fishing, he wore his wide hat far down over his face. Kikunojō realized that this must be the man who had linked the second verse to his hokku, and he wanted to know who he was. He went to the edge of the pleasure boat and gazed at the man. When the man raised his head and looked up, Kikunojō could see he was twenty-four or twenty-five, fair skinned, and beautiful. His smiling face revealed a love too strong to be kept inside, but the feelings obviously rising inside him kept him from looking directly at Kikunojō. He gazed instead at Kikunojō's clear reflection on the water. I'm not an unfeeling rock or tree, Kikunojō thought. If he loves me, I can't ignore him. Kikunojō gazed back, full of longing. For some time, neither man was able to speak. Then a soft breeze began to blow, and the young samurai looked up and made a third verse:

> My body—
> would it were wind in
> your summer robe.

Kikunojō replied immediately, linking a fourth:

> My fan has stopped moving—
> I watch you through its slats.

Both men grew less reserved, and the young samurai poled closer. He tied his small boat to the pleasure craft and climbed on board. He spoke about how cool it had become after sundown and concealed his feelings with other small talk, so Kikunojō brought over a saké holder and a cup.

"My hokku was very clumsy," Kikunojō told the man. "After you replied with that wonderful second verse, I realized you were no ordinary person. Perhaps a relationship in one of our previous lives has brought us together like this. Where are you from? And please tell me your name."

"I live in Hamamachi along the river," the man said. "To escape the heat I like to go out poling alone. The view from here is really quite nice. But today I caught sight of you. The sky suddenly clouded over with my desire, and my fishing boat rocked back and forth. My heart is a deep ocean with wild shores. If we could only spend a night of love together on the waves and share our deepest secrets . . . it would be the greatest wish of my whole life." The man took Kikunojō's hand and moved closer to him. He was sophisticated, but his feelings for Kikunojō were obviously quite real. Kikunojō was also attracted to him and felt awkward.

Unable to speak, Kikunojō held the saké dipper and offered the man the cup. The man took it and politely placed it under the dipper mouth to be filled. He emptied the cup and offered it to Kikunojō. Again and again, each drank and then offered the cup to the other. Alone, they could dispense with formalities. The cup moving directly back and forth between them seemed—like their own meeting—the work of the god who brings lovers together.

It was already past eight o'clock, and they were quite intimate. Then they decided that one would become clouds and one a dragon rising toward heaven.[61] When crows cried out, mistaking the bright moonlight for dawn, the two men swore by the Kumano crow god that they loved each other from the bottoms of their hearts. Their pledges were not shallow ones, and they did not simply go to the floor of the boat or immediately sleep together. They untied each other's sashes very gently. What they whispered on their touching pillows and what dreams they saw are beyond anyone's knowing.

The Lover Reveals His True Form (chapter 5)

The world has long been called changeable and unreliable. But it is people's minds, not the world, that are changeable and unreliable. The poet Su Dongpo said a moment of evening in spring is worth a thousand pieces of gold, while another man says the whole floating world is worth only three and a half coppers.[62] But nobody's ever paid a thousand gold coins for a moment of spring evening, and no one's ever remaindered off the floating world for three and a half coppers, either. Talk never paid the rent, yet in the floating world good and bad are determined by the way we speak. The mutability of the world is the mutability of people's minds.

Even the sage Confucius hitched up his robes and left his native land of Lu. It was a big place, but he never met anyone there who could really understand him. The very first time he met Chengzi, however, both men understood each other immediately. Confucius had his attendant hold his big parasol over Chengzi, and they talked so long that Confucius got leg cramps. Without such understanding, even parent and child and brother and brother become bitter enemies. With understanding, every man in the world can become your older or younger brother.[63] These are the words of someone who has looked long and hard at both sides of the world.

---

61. Dragons traditionally rise into the sky, entering clouds and causing rain. This is an allusion to a legend that the Chinese poet Han Yu loved another poet, Meng Dongye, with Han Yu becoming the clouds and Meng, the older poet, becoming the dragon. The samurai, a lowly water spirit, symbolically represents his lord, the dragon.

62. Gennai himself, in the preface to *The Modern Life of Shidōken*.

63. Terms for older and younger male lovers in a relationship, a parody of the *Analects* (12:5): "If the virtuous man is circumspect, blameless, and courteous, then every man in the world will be his brother."

Kikunojō was considered the consummate young actor of female roles, and there was no one who didn't desire him. Men became very excited at just seeing his beautiful face at a distance or catching a glimpse of the entwined cotton-cord crest on his robe, and although a few wealthy men had slept with him, no one had actually become his lover. Yet somehow an unknown man had suddenly come and met directly with Kikunojō, and Kikunojō had fallen in love with him and pledged himself to the man forever. The man was truly the supreme lover among all those following the way of male love.

Later the two men sat up again and washed their hands gracefully and nonchalantly in the river as if nothing had happened. Then they went back to where they had been sitting before and sat facing each other. But the way they exchanged cups of saké now was perceptibly more intimate. The full moon continued to rise and shone down on the boat so brightly that now it seemed to be noon. A cool breeze ruffled the surface of the river, making both men realize that fall was coming soon, even while summer lingered.

As they were enjoying the magnificent night, the samurai began to gaze soulfully into Kikunojō's eyes. He looked very lonely, and then a feeling he could no longer hide showed itself on his face, and tears streaked his cheeks.

Kikunojō, concerned, moved closer to him. "What is it that's bothering you?" he asked very gently.

But the man looked down even more sadly, still crying and unable to speak.

Kikunojō felt uneasy. "Do you find something lacking in my love for you?" he asked. "Please tell me. Why should we hide anything from each other when we've come this far?"

Hearing a sulking tone of soft reproach in Kikunojō's voice, the man brushed away his tears. "Despite your deep feelings for me," he said, "I ignored you and said nothing. It is very, very hard for me to say anything. If I speak, you'll dislike me, and if I don't speak, you'll be angry with me. Though I love you more than I can express, I made you feel that I disliked something about you. When I heard what you said just now, your words went through me and shook my whole body. I realize now that I have to tell you everything. But please don't be shocked by what I have to say. Please. I'm not actually human. I'm a kappa water spirit. I live down on the ocean floor, and I spend my time swimming through very rough waves."

Kikunojō was astonished, but he tried to keep calm and waited to hear more. Then he realized he felt afraid. He was cold all over and was looking around nervously in every direction. After a while he managed to control the pounding in his chest. He said some charms and prayers silently to himself and went on listening.

"I'll explain to you why I came in this human shape," the man said, wiping away more tears. "It's very hard to explain completely, but King Enma in the other world has fallen deeply in love with you and wants you very much. So Enma ordered the seven-headed dragon god, who's the lord of all the oceans,

Beyond the pleasure boat, the samurai lover appears in his true form as a kappa, who stands near the shore of Nakazu, a landfill area at the confluence of the Sumida and Hakozaki Rivers. It was an area of teahouses and restaurants (*right*).

to bring you to his palace. A lot of discussions about how to capture you went on at the dragon palace at the bottom of the sea, where I live, and I said I would do it even at the risk of my life. Finally the dragon god agreed, and I was given the mission of bringing you back to his palace in any way I could. Out of loyalty to my lord, I devised a plan to capture you. Tonight, following my plan, I stole a small boat that someone had left on the shore and changed myself into the shape of a human samurai. I then used my divine powers to link haikai verses with you. That allowed me to row near you. After I got close enough, I planned to grab you and jump back down into the water with you.

"But I was overcome by your beauty. I lost control of myself, and I told you of my love for you, even though I knew it was completely impossible. But then you responded with deep feeling, and I began to feel that I wanted to be with you forever. My heart wrapped hopelessly around and around you like vines around a tree. Together we took off our sashes and put on a single robe of love. And the things we said to each other then, I can never forget them. Most of all, I'll never forget our promise to meet again.

"My mind's completely different now from what it was when I came here earlier. Everything's changed, just the way the Asuka River shifts, with its depths suddenly becoming shallow pools.[64] For me, too, there are no more depths I could take you to. Now there are only shallows.

---

64. Kikunojō's family name, Segawa, means "River of Shallow Pools."

"So I've decided to give up my life. If I went back to the dragon palace and told the dragon god that even using all my powers, I couldn't capture you, he'd punish me terribly. He's done it before. Once long ago, when the dragon god's daughter Otohime was very sick, he asked a jellyfish to get hold of a live monkey liver for her to eat as a cure. The jellyfish went up, tricked a monkey, and came back down with him, but then the jellyfish stupidly mentioned his plan and the monkey realized what was happening and escaped. The dragon god was so furious he ripped out every one of the jellyfish's muscles and bones. That's why jellyfish are in the pitiful formless shape they're in today. They can hardly live down the shame.

"But I, well, I didn't just let out a secret. I went up in front of endless rows of every kind of sea creature and shot off my big mouth about what I was going to do. I won't be able to face any of them again. So I've decided to commit suicide instead. I'll throw myself into a deep forest on some mountain and die from lack of water. I've been able to help you, though, so now I don't mind dying. But there is one thing. When I'm dead, my body will turn back into its true shape, and you'll find me disgusting. And not only that. Ordinary lovers can promise to meet again on a lotus in the Pure Land paradise after they die, but in our case, well, King Enma is going to keep you for himself, and I'll surely be reborn as an animal. So we'll never be able to meet again, ever. When I think about our karma, how we'll never be together again in all eternity, my heart turns into a slab of ice. Please, after I'm dead, if you say even one Buddhist requiem for me, I'll be able to escape the worst suffering. Even so, I'll never be able to go near any river or seashore again. There are some pretty mean characters down there in the water who know a lot of tricks." Then the man began to weep again.

Kikunojō also was crying. "I'm overwhelmed by your story," he said, "and I'm completely amazed. But don't give up hope like that. It's not impossible for animals to be reborn as humans, you know. In China they say the spirit of a plum tree became a beautiful woman and loved a man. And in Japan, Abe no Yasuna lived with a female fox, and their child was human. He became the famous diviner Abe no Seimei. We've been together only a short time, but we've vowed always to be true to each other. I simply can't allow someone I love to die instead of me. It goes completely against the way of true love between men. And I won't live much longer, anyway. If King Enma desires me, then his order's bound to catch up with me. Please, please, don't die! Take me with you down into the ocean." Kikunojō got up and stood by the railing, preparing to jump.

The man grabbed Kikunojō and stopped him. "Your wish to die for my sake makes me very happy," he said. "But even if I were to take your life and go back with you, rumors would start. People would say that after all I really was just a lowly creature who betrayed a human who'd showed him love and killed him in return. And the shame wouldn't be mine only. My parents and brothers and all my relatives would be completely disgraced. And besides, I couldn't bear to see your beautiful face on the ocean bottom after you drowned. Stop, please. Reconsider. Let me die, and everything will be all right."

"Never! You're my lover. Men never cause their true loves to die."

As the two men argued about who would die, they heard a loud "Hey, wait!" It was the actor Ogino Yaegiri. Surprised, Kikunojō and the samurai tried to jump, but Yaegiri grabbed them both and held them.

"Calm down," he said. "Don't lose your heads. I went with the others to catch clams on Nakazu, but I was just too drunk, so I came back in a small boat. I thought something strange was going on when I saw you sleeping together, but I didn't want to bother you, and I decided to wait and see what happened. I hid on the other side of the boat, and I heard everything you've been saying. Mayflies, as they say, die at nightfall, and summer cicadas live only one season. They value every moment they live, yet you two are arguing over who should kill himself. Each of you wants to die for your lover. That's admirable, very admirable. But if Enma's fallen in love with you, Kikunojō, and issued a royal edict, then there's no way you'll get out of it. Remember, though, Enma's never seen you in person. So let me go instead. That way you won't have to die.

"You both must wonder why I want to die instead of Kikunojō. But there's nothing strange about my motives. Kikunojō, you know well enough about my family line. It began with Ogino Umesaburō and came down to my father, Yaegiri. They all played women's roles using the stage name Ogino Yaegiri. They were well known in Kyoto, Osaka, and Edo, and in Kyoto my father served as head of a theater company, so the family's quite famous. But my father, Yaegiri, died young, when I was only three. My mother took me with her, and we managed to survive with some family friends. But when I was five my mother died, too, and I became an orphan. I would have become an outcast beggar, but Kikunojō, your father, who was a friend of my father's, pitied me and took me in. He brought me up very carefully, as if I were his own son. He even had a nurse and a helper look after me. And when I was old enough, he taught me singing, shamisen, dancing, body movement, and how to speak in women's voices. He made me into the professional actor I am. He said he wanted to give his own stage name to me and have me become the next member of his line, but he felt strongly I should take my father's name and honor my ancestors' souls in that way. So I took the name Yaegiri, and he adopted you and gave the name Kikunojō to you. Remember how he always used to tell us to think of ourselves as brothers?

"I'm nowhere as good as my father was, but I've managed to appear in major theaters in Kyoto, Osaka, and Edo. I feel very grateful to my father, but I'm even more grateful to my stepfather for helping me become what I am today. As both a father and a teacher, his great love for me is something I'll never forget. When he was about to die, he called me to him and told me he didn't mind dying, since he'd been able to gain fame and respect for the name Kikunojō, and his younger brother Kikujirō would also keep the family name famous. But he was worried about you, Kikunojō. He asked me to be your guardian and to teach you his art until you could act well enough to become the second Kikunojō. He was crying when he said that. Those were his last words.

"I was deeply moved, and I vowed to your father that the most important thing in my life from then on would be to look after you and help you become worthy of the title Kikunojō II. I assured him that he didn't have to worry about anything. When he heard that, your father smiled, and then he died. I can't help crying every time I remember it. You were still young then, and your father was also my stepfather and had done so much for me, and I was glad to help you in turn. Then, five years ago, I taught you all the acting secrets your father taught me, and you started out on your own. After that, you became more and more famous, and it made me much happier than if I myself were becoming so famous. Every time you achieve a new success, you know, I go and sit in front of your father's memorial tablet and pray to him proudly, telling him all about it. His deathbed wish is always in my mind, and I want very much to see it fulfilled.

"Just now I stopped you from jumping, because if I let you die, I could never explain it to your father's soul. And not only that. I don't want the name Segawa to disappear. Even if I die, I have a son, so the name Ogino will continue. Now, after all these years, I want to repay all the great kindness your father showed me ever since I was five. But there is one thing I want to ask you. Please look after my wife and family after I'm gone. Don't ever forget them. That's the only thing I worry about. When I go to Enma's palace, my beauty will be nothing compared with yours. But that's a minor problem. Turning ink into snow and crows into white herons is something I've been trained to do. Kikunojō, please live the way you should, and don't drink too much and ruin your reputation. Concentrate on your art, practice hard, and become an actor whom people will consider even greater than your father and uncle. If you do that, I'll feel very content over there in the other world."

Yaegiri spoke with such deep emotion that Kikunojō and the samurai were in tears. Kikunojō clung to him. "After my father died," he said, "you took care of me and taught me everything, and you did it all with loving care. Your offer to die for me is something truly precious. I'll never forget it, no matter how many times I'm reborn. But I owe too much to you. I could never go on living knowing I'd caused your death. Please, please let me die."

"Never," Yaegiri said. "Let me."

"No! I will," the samurai said.

The three men argued on and on about who would die until suddenly they heard the loud sounds of Heikurō, Yosahachi who was acting as captain, and the others coming back with their clams. The three men panicked and didn't know what to do. Then the two actors realized the samurai had disappeared as silently as a shadow.

"Wait! Don't go yet!" Kikunojō wanted to shout, but the others were too close now and would hear. While Kikunojō was searching the surface of the river for a trace of the samurai, Yaegiri made up his mind. He climbed to the roof of the cabin and jumped into the water with a loud splash, sending up spray in all directions. He disappeared beneath the water and left nothing behind to remember him by but the bubbles briefly on the river's surface.

Suddenly everyone on board was in an uproar, shouting that Yaegiri had jumped into the river and committed suicide. But the only reply was the sound of the stiffening wind. They looked frantically here and there among the waves but found no sign of Yaegiri anywhere.

Kikunojō, tears running down his face, refused to explain anything. He felt he would never be able to face other people now and go on living, and he made up his mind to jump in the river together with Yaegiri, to whom he owed so much. Heikurō didn't know what was happening, but he saw Kikunojō edging toward the side of the boat and held him back.

"Don't worry," Yosahachi told Kikunojō. "You were the one who hired the boat for the cruise, but we'll say Yaegiri fell in the water by accident. We'll never tell anyone you were alone with him. We'll say we were all here on the boat the whole time. Nobody will ever think of blaming you. And when we report it to the authorities, we'll stick together and swear we were all together here on the boat, no matter how they threaten us or punish us." He and the others said many different things, and finally Kikunojō agreed not to jump.

Kikunojō didn't even try to explain what had happened. He kept it in his heart, crying again and again, and those who saw him also cried as they went on looking everywhere among the rising waves for Yaegiri. They strained to see anything resembling a body, but they found nothing at all. Yaegiri had been carried away, pitifully, forever. Then suddenly, rain began to fall, making their search even harder. They prayed fervently to many gods, but nothing helped. At last they gave up hope and made the journey back.

On land, the roads seemed visited by souls as the actors walked to the house of Yaegiri's young widow, who was as radiant and filled with life as new spring grass. When they told her what had happened, her soul almost left her. After she had recovered, she realized how alone she was and how helpless to do anything. The man she loved so dearly had disappeared without a trace under the waves. She would never even see his body again.

"I feel," she told them, "like the woman in that ancient poem:

> How inconsolable
> the woman who waits
> each day to see
> her husband lying
> at the bay's bottom.[65]

---

65. *Man'yōshū*, no. 3342.

It must have been written about me." Her grief was as endless as the sands of the shore. No sea of ink in a human inkstone is deep enough to record it, and no one who heard her had dry eyes.

[*Fūrai Sanjin shū*, NKBT 55: 37–93, translated by Chris Drake]

THE MODERN LIFE OF SHIDŌKEN (*FŪRYŪ SHIDŌKEN DEN*, 1763)

Under the pen name Fūrai Sanjin, Hiraga Gennai published *The Modern Life of Shidōken* in 1763, the same year he published *Rootless Weeds*. The protagonist is modeled on another star of popular culture, the lecturer and showman Fukai Shidōken (ca. 1680–1765), who performed on a street corner in Asakusa in Edo, but the content is almost entirely fictional. The first chapter describes the divine birth of Asanoshin (as the son of the Kannon bodhisattva at Asakusa), his entry into a Buddhist order, and his encounter with a beautiful woman who takes him to a utopian place. When he awakens from this dream, a Daoist hermit, a pedagogically inclined sage-wizard called Fūrai Sanjin (whose name deliberately echoes the author's), instructs him to leave the order and to teach the masses through humor and the vulgar, and gives Asanoshin a feather fan that enables him to fly.

The *Modern Life of Shidōken* has been compared with Jonathan Swift's *Gulliver's Travels* (1726) and other imaginary travel literature that became popular in Europe during the eighteenth century. In this period of *sakoku* (the bakufu policy of national seclusion), Gennai drew his views of other lands from a variety of sources, including the Muromachi-period (*otogi-zōshi*) tale *Yoshitsune's Visits to Various Islands* (*Onzōshi shima watari*), in which the legendary Yoshitsune wanders to various foreign lands; Chinese-based encyclopedias like Terajima Ryōan's *Illustrated Encyclopedia of China and Japan* (*Wakan sansai zue*, 1713), which describes strange peoples from the Chinese tradition; and information about the West derived from Chinese translations. In *The Modern Life of Shidōken*, Gennai transposes various contemporary circumstances onto the landscape of other lands. In "pointing out the holes" (*ugachi*) in contemporary society, showing the backside of the bakufu-domain system, and condemning, among others, Confucian scholars, Buddhist priests, and the ignorance of the populace, he creates a sharp and humorous satire. The story about the Land of the Chest Holes, for example, is a satire of the bakufu-domain system in which a man without samurai blood (a man without a chest hole) could not be recognized for his abilities. The *dangi* (satiric sermon) element, which appears in the form of interwoven debates and lectures, is stronger than it was in *Rootless Weeds* and moves the dangibon genre in a new direction by taking the form of a biography and a travel narrative through many countries.

Asanoshin Meets the Sage (chapter 1)

In the precincts of the Asakusa Kannon Temple in Edo, there is an utterly unique and fearless man named Shidōken. He advertises himself as a reciter of old warrior tales together with commentary, but he holds a strange wooden object shaped like a mushroom and beats it on his low desk to the rhythm of his tales. His bawdy, humorous stories are so zany and impossible they're like trying to wipe your rear with your ear, and he makes people laugh so hard they dislocate their navels. Sometimes he clenches his toothless gums; sometimes he shakes his head with its waves of cascading wrinkles; and sometimes he stares coldly down at his fellow humans and denounces them in whatever scathing terms come into his mind. Then, though he's a thin, haggard man of almost ninety, he's suddenly making the movements and speaking the words of young kabuki actors of women's roles. He captures them so intricately he is truly a marvel to behold.

The message he preaches is a mixed Shintō, Confucian, and Buddhist broth served with a spicy Daoist fish salad, ice soup, and deep-fried lightning. His groundless, nonsensical stories make the most unhappy babies laugh, and even hired men who carry sandals around for their employers know that "Idiot Monk" refers to Shidōken. There's no other Buddhist monk like him, and there never has been.

Once Edo had two human monuments: the kabuki actor Ichikawa Danjūrō II[66] and old man Shidōken. But when Danjūrō died, it left Shidōken the most famous person in all Edo. You see him depicted everywhere—woodblock prints of him, clay dolls of him, and illustrations of him even on festival lanterns and hairdressers' paper-covered sliding doors. He's admired so intensely that people now think of him and laugh whenever they see a mullet's wrinkled head or a large mushroom.

How was Shidōken able to achieve all he did? The story begins many years ago. His father was a trusted administrator in a daimyō lord's Edo mansion. Loyal, trustworthy, and of good lineage, his name was Fukai Jingoemon. Even though he had reached forty, Jingoemon still had no male heir, and so he grieved. Together he and his wife made a pilgrimage to the temple of the merciful bodhisattva Kannon in Asakusa, and there they remained, showing reverence for twenty-one days and offering a fervent prayer on the final night. At dawn on the twenty-first night, they saw a dream in which a golden mushroom came flying through the air from the south and entered the navel of Jingoemon's wife. Soon she discovered she was pregnant, and later she bore the baby boy who would come to be known as Shidōken. Since their son was a special blessing from the Asakusa Kannon, the elated parents took the first two syllables of Asakusa and named the child Asanoshin.

---

66. Ichikawa Danjūrō II (1688–1758), admired for his mixture of rough, exaggerated acting and refined feeling.

Asanoshin's parents brought him up with the greatest care and love. At his first New Year's, they gave him a small magical arrow set to protect him against demons and disease. With the prayer that he continue the family line eternally into the future, they placed sacred green leaves beside the rice cakes they put before their home altar to the gods. They conscientiously prayed at every other festival during the year. On the Children's Festival on the fifth of the Fifth Month, for example, they put up a streamer painted with two pine tree gods, an old man and an old woman, as a prayer that their son live a very long life. It was the same blind love that parents everywhere show for their children.

When Asanoshin was three, his parents carried him to the Asakusa Temple to show him to Kannon and give their thanks to her. After that, they let his hair grow long. Then when he was five, he put on his first tiny formal clothes. Time passes like a bullet, and Asanoshin was soon seven and then eight, so he entered a private school and began studying calligraphy. Parents always lose their objectivity when they look at their own children, and when Asanoshin's parents saw the letters bent like cow horns that their son had drawn in black ink on his dirty practice papers, they were effusive in their praise. Soon Asanoshin had progressed to reading out loud, *"The Great Learning* is a book bequeathed by Confucius. It is the gate to virtue through which all beginners pass," and then he was reading the whole book. His concerned parents had someone go with their son as far as the school gate and then meet him there when he was finished. The boy received a far from ordinary education.

Asanoshin was very bright, and when he began to understand what was happening in the world, he displayed the cleanliness, responsiveness, and good

Shidōken gives a performance. From the 1763 edition.

Shidōken's parents see a miraculous dream at the Kannon Temple in Asakusa in which a mushroom-like object enters Shidōken's mother. They sit below a pillar on which worshipers have pasted small posters as prayers. The large hanging lantern is dedicated to the temple by the Yoshiwara courtesan Chōzan.

behavior required by Confucius in the *Analects* in ways that showed he was quite mature for his age. He studied the martial arts, and he also received a thorough training in flower arrangement, tea ceremony, kickball, indoor archery, Chinese poetry, waka poetry, renga and haikai linked verse, and all the other arts.

When Asanoshin turned fifteen, however, his parents began to worry about him. They were sure a child this intelligent, especially one given them by a bodhisattva, was bound to die young. Miraculously, they had also been blessed with two younger sons, so they decided to ask Asanoshin give up the world and become a Buddhist monk. That way he would surely live a long life, and he would also be able to pray for his ancestors' souls and help them reach the Pure Land paradise. When Asanoshin's parents told their son of their wish, he said he felt bound to honor it, even though he personally had no desire to become a monk. And so Asanoshin went off to live in the Kōmyōin, the temple where his ancestors had worshiped for generations.[67]

The youthful Asanoshin thought hard about his situation. He had not wanted to become a monk, but he believed his parents had surely been led by the

---

67. The name of the temple is apparently Gennai's creation.

Buddha to make their request, so he made up his mind to master the intricacies of Buddhist doctrine, become an outstanding monk, and help people all over the country escape their suffering and achieve enlightenment. Every day from morning till night Asanoshin studied the sutras and meditated, whether he was moving, standing still, sitting, or lying down. He let nothing interfere with his studies, and even if someone invited him to go see the summer fireworks over the Sumida River, he refused, since he had already realized that worldly pleasures were as fleeting and unsubstantial as any fireworks. And when people were thronging noisily to see the cherry blossoms at Asukayama in Ōji, Asanoshin merely recited Saigyō's poem:

> The cherries'
> only fault:
> the crowds
> that gather
> when they bloom.[68]

Asanoshin remembered how diligent scholars in ancient China, having no lamp oil, read by the reflected luminescence of snow or by the light of fireflies they'd caught, and he, too, sat each day below the window in his room, with bamboos rising just outside, copying out sutras on his desk and becoming friends with authors of the past.[69]

One bright spring day Asanoshin was gazing at some peach trees in the temple garden, which were now in full bloom. As he gazed on and on, absorbed in the blossoms, he remembered a poem about a man who entered a peach grove and reached a timeless realm of Daoist immortals.[70] Just then, a swallow that had built its nest in the eaves flew in through the window and landed on Asanoshin's desk. Not wanting to startle the bird, Asanoshin sat motionless, watching it. As he stared, the bird laid an egg on the desk and then flew off. Asanoshin decided to try to put the egg in the bird's nest if he could find it, but when he picked it up, it cracked in two, and out came a tiny person. It looked like a woman. Asanoshin wondered whether she wasn't a divine being like the tiny woman Kaguya-hime, whom an old bamboo cutter found inside a bamboo trunk in the *Tale of the Bamboo Cutter*. As Asanoshin stared at the woman, she grew larger and larger and was soon human size. Surely, Asanoshin thought, she must be the most beautiful woman in the world. Her face was radiant, her eyebrows deep black, and every feature was perfect. When she looked at

---

68. *Gyokuyō wakashū*, vol. 1, no. 144.

69. That is, reading literature from earlier ages. Evokes section 13 of Yoshida Kenkō's *Essays in Idleness (Tsurezuregusa)*.

70. Reference to Tao Qian's (365–427) "Peach Blossom Spring," in which the poet discovers a utopian community in a peach grove but is unable to return to it.

Asanoshin and smiled at him, his mind seemed to melt, and he felt as if he
were drunk.

The woman stepped softly out into the garden. Then she turned around and
gestured to Asanoshin to follow her. When he did, she took his hand and gently
led him to a small hill. There, between some rocks under the blossoming peach
trees, was a small cave. Asanoshin followed the woman into the narrow passage.
From above, the cave had looked only five or six inches wide, but once they
had gone inside it, he saw it was wide enough to let a person through. When
they had gone about sixty feet inside it, they began to walk across level ground,
and Asanoshin could faintly hear dogs barking and roosters crowing. Then he
saw many kinds of trees and plants growing everywhere. Nearby he saw plum
trees blooming in spring and heard warblers in their branches, while farther on
he saw early summer bellflowers blooming white on a hedge beneath the cries
of a nightingale in the sky. Then he saw a lonely male deer crying out for his
mate among bright autumn leaves. And then, as a cold winter wind blew, a
flock of plovers cried out amid snow flurries. Flowers and fruits of every season
appeared together. The sand was a different color in this land, and water in a
stream made unbelievably pure sounds.

Asanoshin followed the woman for some time. Then he detected an indescribably delicate scent and the sounds of wind and stringed instruments, and
soon they had reached a great jeweled palace. The ground around it was covered with grains of gold and silver, the stairs were of lapis lazuli, and the railings
were of agate. Asanoshin hesitated, but the woman told him to follow her. She
walked down a hall past many, many rooms, finally ushering Asanoshin into
one of them. After he went inside, beautiful women appeared, bringing him
tea and various cakes. They were even more elegant than the woman who had
appeared from the egg. Wearing intricately embroidered robes, they entered
and left continually, serving fine wine and rare dishes. They gave Asanoshin a
very warm welcome, playing and singing recent popular songs, taking his hand,
and rubbing his feet. Asanoshin began to enjoy himself, and before he knew it
he had drunk too much wine. Soon he drifted off to sleep on the lap of one of
the women.

When Asanoshin awoke, he found no trace of the beautiful women, the
feast, or the palace. He wondered if he had been dreaming and looked around
him. He saw nothing but evergreen trees and heard only a rushing stream. He
obviously wasn't in the temple garden. Perhaps, he thought, he'd been possessed
by the spirit of a fox or badger. As the dazed Asanoshin looked around, one of
the clouds above him dropped down, and out of it came a mysterious shape. It
seemed to be a man. He wore a robe of leaves and had a cap on his head. In
his left hand was a staff of goosefoot wood, and in his right he held a feather fan.

"Excellent!" the figure said, beckoning to Asanoshin. "I need to teach you
something, so I used my ascetic powers to bring you here. There's no need to
be suspicious."

When the figure came closer, Asanoshin saw that although he looked like an old man, his face was radiant. He couldn't have been more than thirty. His black hair, long beard, and clear eyes made him look dignified yet not over-bearing. Asanoshin got down on his knees and bowed respectfully.

"As a child," the sage said, "because you showed much talent, your parents, infatuated with Buddhism, forced you to become a monk. What a waste! Like throwing away gold into the mud. I felt I had to save you, so I brought you here. Buddhists talk about paradise and hell in order to teach ignorant old women and wives about nirvana, but they have nothing to teach the wise. Humans are made up of yin and yang, and life comes into being the same way a spark does when stone and metal are rubbed together. Life continues as long as the firewood burns, but when the fire goes out, nothing is left but burned-up charcoal — yes, that's right, your body. Yet Buddhists claim that after the fire goes out, it goes on to hell or to paradise. If you think you know where fire goes when it goes out, then please, by all means, believe in hell and paradise!"

Enlightened, Asanoshin clapped his hands together. "Your wise teaching," he said, "has stripped away my delusions in a single moment. I feel as though I've just woken from a dream. As of now, I renounce my Buddhist vows. I will go to live in the world. But I don't want simply to rot away there. Please teach me what I should do for a living."

The sage raised his feather fan. "You have trusted me and understood well," he said. "Now I, for my part, will tell you who I am and how you will live your life. I was born many years ago, at the end of the twelfth century. When I was young I heard all about the battles between the Heike and the Minamoto clans. After a few years the Minamoto shōgun in Kamakura came to rule the country, and people could enjoy peace once more.[71] I myself grew up in the country, but I observed things closely and thought about what was happening. In China, the first Han emperor carried nothing but a three-foot sword, and yet he estab-lished a dynasty that lasted four centuries, and Zhen She of Zhu said that "you don't need a good lineage to be a minister of state or a general." When I looked at all the large and small lords here in Japan, I, too, saw that a lot of them were ordinary servants who started famous clans by grabbing onto the tails of the horses of the shōgun, Yoritomo, and his brother, Yoshitsune.

"But I grew up in an age of peace. It would have been a crime against heaven if I'd tried to make a career out of fighting, so I decided to establish a clan of my own by mastering an art. First I studied tea ceremony. People in the world call tea ceremony an art, but it's actually a form of business in which rich tea masters and collectors spend thousands of gold pieces for old cups and bamboo spatulas for spooning out powdered tea. And the tea houses make you feel cramped. You have to drink the tea in a small, cramped room, and to get there you have to crawl through a door only two feet high and straighten out your

---

71. Suggests the Tokugawa shōgunate and the Edo period.

Asanoshin bows to the sage, who stands on a cloud.

shoes after you go in. It's not something any active, self-respecting man can do. Then there's flower arrangement. Its proponents say you can capture the feeling of thousands of plants and trees in a single flower pot, yet the way they nail stalks and limbs in place and change their shapes with wires looks very unnatural.

"Masters of the game of *go* spend their time continually lining up and scattering little round stones. Their wisdom never goes beyond the 360 small squares on the board, and after they die and their souls reach the river on the border to the other world, they're reduced to piling up stone prayer mounds in the riverbed and clinging to the sleeves of the bodhisattva Jizō, begging him for protection from the club-swinging guards from hell. Masters of Chinese chess, meanwhile, claim the game is basically military strategy, but famous generals like Han Xin or Kong Ming never played chess. If you gave a commander's rod to one these chess masters and had him lead an actual army into battle, he'd be trampled to death by enemy horses, and his knights would jump too far ahead and be killed by enemy pawns.

"Those who practice the way of incense frown significantly and act as if they ruled the whole universe with their noses. They say they've reached an exalted state of peacefulness and spiritual bliss, and they boast that distinguishing subtly different scents increases all their powers of perception and thinking, but it's actually nothing more than a worthless amusement. And when famous incense masters claim that the names of the six main kinds of incense are the names of the countries from which they came, well, their ignorance of the fact that these countries don't even exist is truly laughable. Practitioners of indoor archery who get five hundred hits out of a hundred shooting at a standing target can't get near a moving mouse. And then there's kickball. But even if you become an expert, all you'll get are an empty stomach and, if you pay enough money to a master, a permit to wear aristocratic robes in elegant colors.

"Shakuhachi flute masters produce sounds even more delicate than a courtesan's farts. But they lose their teeth early, and the only work they can get is as spies in vendettas dressed as wandering flute-playing monks. Drummers cry out sharply as they hit their small hand drums or beat out long series of deep sounds on larger drums. Some of them are very skilled, and drumming gives great pleasure, but sounds last only as long as you hear them. No one ever remembers drummers after they die. As for the other activities people usually call arts, they're all children's games.

"The only things you really need to study are the Chinese classics, poetry, and painting. But even these are sometimes badly taught by narrow-minded Confucian scholars who only study books and know nothing about the real world. One scholar, for example, is so inflexible and attached to politeness he wears starched formal clothes even to clean out his well.[72] And another, knowing nothing about farming, claims the way to save the country is by spreading sweet potato cultivation; but his plan is so unrealistic, it's like trying to cook sweet potatoes in a tinderbox.[73] These men have wrapped themselves so tightly in wastepaper from ancient China they've lost their own freedom. They're as rigid and solemn as sets of old armor placed out on racks for airing. But even with this pose, they can't hide their ignorance of the world. They know less about it than ordinary people. That's why they're called 'rotten scholars' or 'farting Confucianists.' They stink as badly as ripe bean paste.

"Some Confucian scholars have seen through this pose and instead follow the Song Confucianist Zhu Xi even to the point of wearing ancient Confucian caps.[74] But their marginal criticisms and tinkering cause even worse problems. They try to straighten the horns and end up killing the cow. The minor followers of this philosophical school play on ancient Chinese flutes as they go to the Yoshiwara licensed quarter in small boats on the Sumida River[75] or sing songs in contemporary Chinese pronunciation to a shamisen. The worst of them,

---

72. Refers to Itō Jinsai (1627–1705), a Confucian philosopher who established the Ancient Studies (*kogigaku*) school.

73. Refers to Aoki Kon'yō (1698–1769), a scholar of Confucianism and Dutch studies (*rangaku*) who gave advice to the bakufu on agricultural policy.

74. Refers to Ogyū Sorai (1666–1728), an influential scholar of Confucian studies, and his followers. Zhu Xi (1130–1200) was a Song Confucian scholar who had a large impact on Japanese Confucian philosophy.

75. Dazai Shundai (1680–1747), a follower of Ogyū Sorai.

incredibly, go around gambling with six-sided tops and doing whatever else they want. Their arrogance has prevented them from knowing anything about the Doctrine of the Mean. China is China, and Japan is Japan. The past is the past, and the present is the present."

Continuing to overlap the medieval and Edo periods, the sage describes how corrupt and incompetent the administration of the Kamakura period (1185–1333) was and how only flatterers or those offering bribes were employed, while those with skill and wisdom were ignored.

"The most influential people then were Buddhist monks, millionaires, women, shamisen players, puppet-play chanters, and jesters. No one knew any longer how to tell what was of great value from what wasn't, so finally I decided to leave the world behind, and I went to a forest on a mountain, where I managed to survive on nuts and berries. After a while I discovered I had strange new powers. I found I could move in the air and fly here and there wherever the wind took me, so I began using the name Vagabond Sage.[76] I've been living like this for more than five hundred years now. I don't know anything about the world these days, but I do know, Asanoshin, that after you give up being a monk, you must never, never become so arrogant as to call yourself a professional artist. On the other hand, if you teach lofty truths, people won't gather to listen to you. If you aim too high, eventually you'll have to abandon the world—or it will abandon you. So follow the example of Dongfang Shuo of Han, who had much learning but wrote amusing poems. Appeal to people with lightness and humor, and they will gather around you. Take your images from things near at hand and give people guidance."

Asanoshin moved closer to the sage and spoke. "Hearing your teaching," he said, "I am filled with reverence. But I am still young and know little about human feelings and emotions. What should I do?"

The sage then handed Asanoshin the feather fan he was holding. "This fan," he said, "bears within it my most secret powers. Use it. In summer you will feel a cool breeze, and in winter you will be warmed by its wind. If you wish to fly, this fan will become your wings, and if you want to cross a river or sea , it will be your boat. You can learn much about places near and far, and you will be able to see even the tiniest things. If you want to hide yourself, this fan will make you invisible. It is a marvelous and mysterious treasure. Please use it to travel between heaven and earth and learn about the feelings of people in many areas and countries. But remember, people in the world consider physical love to be the highest form of human feeling, so while you're in a country, be sure to visit the places where people make love. As you travel around to all these

---

76. Literally, Sage Who Comes and Goes with the Wind, similar to Gennai's pen name, Vagabond Mountain Man.

countries, you will have many experiences that are interesting and many that are very sad. But never, never consider them simply painful. We will meet again after you have completed your training and returned here once more. Well, until then! Until then!"

Was it a voice? Wind blowing the sliding doors? Asanoshin sat dazed, somewhere between sleeping and waking, in a room of the Kōmyōin Temple He found himself leaning against his desk, and he sat up straight again. He looked around and saw nothing. But there beside him was the feather fan he had received in the dream.

In the second chapter Asanoshin looks closely at and is shocked by the decadence of the Kōmyōin Temple, which exists to generate money for the monks, who spend it on sexual, gustatory, and other pleasures. He leaves and rents a hut on Surugadai Heights, from where he watches the customs and activities of all four seasons in Edo. The fan gives Asanoshin great powers of vision, and he describes in detail Edo life throughout a whole year. Fascinating as it is, Edo life finally teaches Asanoshin that everything in the world moves only according to money and desire.

Land of the Giants (chapter 3)

Asanoshin sets off for the Yoshiwara licensed quarter and then goes to see kabuki actors in a theater district, call boys working in teahouses, and female hookers and streetwalkers of many sorts all over Edo. Then he wanders up and down Japan, visiting almost every kind of licensed quarter and brothel district.

. . . After seeing professional women in every part of Japan, Asanoshin decided he wanted to go to learn about love in other countries as well. So he went to the shore and waded out into the ocean. The feather fan floated just like a ship, and when he sat on it, it took him rapidly over the blue water, which spread out endlessly before him. White-capped waves raced more wildly than white horses, yet amazingly, the fan kept him dry. He never became hungry, and for several days he traveled on in this way. When at last he reached an island, he had no idea where he was.

Asanoshin got off the fan and carried it ashore with him. He walked here and there until he saw some very large houses. As he went toward them, the people inside saw him, and a large number came outside to watch him. All of them were at least twenty feet tall, and even the children they carried on their backs were larger than Japanese adults. Asanoshin realized this must be the famous Land of the Giants. But he didn't understand their language at all, nor they his. He and they both improvised and tried to explain themselves, making many different gestures and expressions, but none worked. Finally Asanoshin got the idea of putting his fan to his ear. When he did, he was able to understand the giants' speech. And when he put his fan to his mouth, they seemed to be able to understand him.

After that, Asanoshin and the giants were able to converse. Asanoshin explained that he was from a country called "Japan," and the giants brought him many kinds of delicious food. After a couple of days of feasting, they suggested that he go out for a nice trip, and they put him in one of their palanquins. The destination, however, turned out to be a rough, temporary shed covered on all sides by reed screens. It was obviously located in the middle of a very busy area. After Asanoshin got out, the giants put him on a stage in the shed and then, to the rhythm of strange flutes and drums, they began calling out in high, loud voices, "Come right in, now! Take a good look! See a real live Japanese! A handsome man so small you can put him on the palm of your hand and watch him crawl! He's no imitation. He's no fake. We'll show him to you live and in the flesh. Come right in! He's what everybody's talking about!" At that, a dense crowd of men and women of all ages thronged toward the shed. They pushed and shoved their way inside, and when they saw Asanoshin, they pointed at him and laughed.

Asanoshin tried to think of a way to escape. He knew that all he had to rely on was the feather fan, so he looked up in the direction of the sky and bowed to the sage. Then he got on the fan, and it began to fly upward. He broke through the roof of the shed and continued to climb until he reached a high altitude. The giants were dumbfounded and disappointed at losing their amusing visitor. None of them had ever heard of a Japanese being able to fly before, and some concluded that he must be one of the mountain goblins[77] that were said to be so common in Japan. Others pointed out that although he carried a fan in the way that Japanese goblins do in pictures, his nose was too small for him to be a goblin. Still others felt he was indeed a goblin who'd been around to many countries, contracted syphilis somewhere, and lost his nose. A conference was held and many theories proposed, but none was accepted.

Asanoshin sat on the fan without trying to steer it, letting it fly where it would. When he saw the faint outlines of another island ahead, he decided to land there. It turned out to be the Land of the Tiny People, and its inhabitants were only fifteen or sixteen inches high. They never went outside alone but always walked in groups of four or five so they wouldn't be snatched up and eaten alive by cranes, and when they saw Asanoshin they began shaking with fear. They all went inside their houses, locked the doors, and refused to come out again. Unable to communicate with them, Asanoshin headed inland, and the farther he went, the smaller the people got. Already they were only about five or six inches high. When he reached the center of the country, the people were the size of tiny dolls.

In this land, as in Japan, there were various different lords. Near one superbly built castle, Asanoshin saw a large procession of well-dressed tiny people head-

---

77. Also a term for self-conceited egotists.

Asanoshin, smoking a pipe, watches two processions of tiny people outside a castle. The palanquin containing the princess is at the far right.

ing toward the castle and another that had just come out of it. The procession leaving the castle went forward with great ceremony, and there, surrounded by vigilant guards, Asanoshin saw the tiny palanquin of a very high-ranking young woman who must be a princess. He picked up the palanquin with the princess in it very delicately with two fingers and placed it into the upper section of the small pillbox hanging from the sash at his waist. When he did, the guards and attendants immediately made a big commotion and began racing off in every direction, looking for the princess. One old gentleman, apparently the minister in charge of the women's quarters in the castle, was wandering around completely disoriented, so Asanoshin picked him up carefully between his fingers and put him into the lower section of the pillbox.

Several hours later, Asanoshin opened his pillbox and took out the minister again, but all he found was the man's body. The minister, apparently overcome by his feeling of responsibility for losing the princess, had placed himself in the middle of the square black throat lozenge, and there he had committed ritual suicide by cutting himself open. Now he slumped forward on the lozenge, motionless. Asanoshin began to cry when saw that even these tiny people suffer because of their deep feelings of loyalty and obligation to their lord, so he took the princess out of the top section of the pillbox and carefully placed her back in the same place from which he had taken her. He had already caused enough suffering in this land, so he got on his feather fan and flew off again, toward where he could not guess.

Land of the Chest Holes (chapter 4)

Asanoshin rode farther on his feather fan, letting it fly wherever it would through the sky. Presently it came down beside a great river running from north to south. Most of the plants and trees here had fascinating shapes Asanoshin had never seen before, and the river water was a reddish color. People back home, he thought, would certainly be very interested in hearing about this.

Asanoshin wanted to cross the river and explore the area, but he had no idea how deep rivers were in this country, so he sat down on a pine root and waited to see where the local people crossed. Then, in the distance, he saw four or five people fording the river. They were about halfway across, but the water didn't reach their waists. The river certainly didn't look shallow enough to walk across, but Asanoshin pulled up his robe and stepped into the water. It quickly became more than ten feet deep, and he was swept away by the strong current. Again and again, he was dragged below the surface, barely managing to come up each time. Almost drowning, he gripped his feather fan and pushed aside the surging water. Spraying water in every direction, he opened a path for himself and walked across the river bottom to the other side.

When he'd climbed up the far bank, Asanoshin looked around, wondering what had happened to the people who were crossing the river. He discovered he was in the legendary Land of the Long Legged People. The torsos of the people he'd seen were the same size as those of people in Japan, but their legs were fourteen or fifteen feet long, and they'd crossed the river with ease.

These people had also seen Asanoshin. After watching his feat with his fan, they'd decided to take it for themselves, and now they stood deliberating about how they should do it. The fan, they concluded, wouldn't be an easy capture, and they decided to ask the aid of people in the neighboring Land of the Long Armed People. These people had arms fourteen or fifteen feet long and worked as professional thieves.

Asanoshin, completely unaware of what was being planned, stopped at a teahouse for travelers beside the road. He was exhausted from his struggle to keep from drowning, so he rented part of a room, separated off his portion with a standing screen, and fell fast asleep—only to be awakened by strange sounds. Looking around, he saw a thin but very long arm. It had come down through the open skylight window and was now lifting up his feather fan.

"Well now," he exclaimed, "if it isn't a burglar! You know, you look just like the demon Ibaragi Dōji in a Toba comic print. You're going to keep your arm about as long as he did, too. This instrument here's just as sharp as the one Watanabe no Tsuna used when he sliced off the demon's arm at Rashōmon Gate." Asanoshin's short sword passed completely through the arm.

Suddenly there was shouting and commotion in every direction. All heaven and earth shook with attack drums and battle cries. Prepared for the worst, Asanoshin ran outside and found himself surrounded by hundreds of thousands

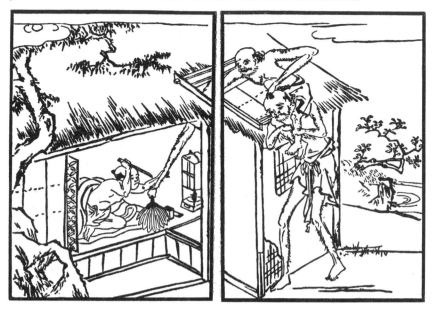

At an inn, Asanoshin stabs a long-armed person who is attempting to steal his fan.

of long-legged people carrying long-armed people on their shoulders. Each pair must have been thirty feet high. The attackers spread out around all him like a vast expanse of tangled trees and vines.

Asanoshin knew that even his feather fan might not be able to save him unless he flew with the utmost skill beyond the long reach of the attackers' arms. He remembered the Vagabond Sage who had sent him on this journey, and silently he prayed to him for guidance. Then he charged the attackers, hitting their long shins again and again with the fan and quickly pulling back. With long-armed people on their shoulders, the long-legged people were even less stable than they normally were, and those in front fell backward and struck those behind. They toppled in long rows like poles, one after another. Those who remained standing reached out and grasped wildly at Asanoshin, but their long arms moved clumsily, and Asanoshin swerved right and left, under and between them, finally knocking down every single pair.

Asanoshin then rode up into the clouds on his fan. Looking down, he saw long-armed people crawling off in all directions, escaping with hips held high. But the long-legged people were having a harder time. Unable to stand up by themselves, these people always carried drums tied to their waists. If one of them fell down, the unfortunate would beat the drum, calling for others to come hoist him or her up with pulleys, like a ship mast being raised. But today all the long-legged people had fallen down together, and they now lay writhing on the ground, unable to get up. Asanoshin knew that if he left these many thousands of long-legged people the way they were, they would starve to death, so he took the feather fan and fanned them so hard they all were blown up onto their feet again.

Asanoshin left while the long-legged people were still standing around dazed. Then, after flying eleven thousand or twelve thousand miles, he arrived in another large country. It was the Land of the Chest Holes, where everyone has a hole in the middle of his or her chest. When the aristocrats here go out, they don't ride in palanquins but have their carriers pass a pole through their chests and carry them around on the poles. It's completely painless. Commoners holding poles stand waiting on street corners shouting "Get poled! Get poled!" just the way they call out "Ride our palanquin!" in Japan.

Asanoshin wanted very much to try this form of transportation, but since he had no hole in his chest, he couldn't ask to be carried. As he walked on farther into the heartland of the country, he saw more houses, and crowds bustled here and there. It was an undeveloped country, and the people didn't dress very stylishly. Everyone who saw Asanoshin, aristocrat or commoner, man or woman, stopped to look at him.

"He certainly has a unique look."

"Have you ever seen such an attractive man?"

The crowd of people around him refused to stop gaping.

In the days that followed, Asanoshin became known throughout the whole country. The ruler, Emperor Great Hole, heard about him and had some of his officials bring Asanoshin into his presence. When the assembled courtiers saw the visitor, they were quickly captivated by his beauty. Although the emperor had no son, he had a daughter, a princess, who was then sixteen. After seeing Asanoshin's good looks, both daughter and father decided that the visitor would be the right husband for her. So the emperor called his ministers together and proposed adopting Asanoshin into the royal family as his heir and turning over the country to him. The ministers deliberated for some time, but since it was a royal request, and in view of the fact that the princess was in love with the man, they concluded that it was a splendid idea and offered their most enthusiastic congratulations.

A large group of court women quickly gathered to help Asanoshin change his clothes in preparation for assuming his new role. They took him to a room where, on a pedestal, they placed imperial robes of figured silk decorated with gold and jade. Then they gathered around Asanoshin and untied his sash. But when they removed his robes, they discovered he had no hole in his chest. In shock, they dropped the robes and ran away. Then Asanoshin heard many people talking excitedly in a room nearby. "He certainly is handsome," someone was saying above the noise. "He has such a fine face and features you'd never know he was deformed."

"An emperor without a hole? Ridiculous!"

"We must tell the emperor and the princess about this."

When Asanoshin heard what people were saying about him, he was as shocked as they were. Soon the prime minister came into the room and addressed him. "The emperor," he began, "decreed that you become his adopted son. He did this because he liked your looks. But now the ladies in waiting report you are deformed. In this country, it is without exception the case that intelligent people have large holes and fools smaller holes in proportion to their lesser intelligence. That is the reason why it is very difficult for people with small holes to attain a high rank. As for those who have no hole at all, well, it would be more than just out of the question for one to become emperor. The wedding, therefore, has been canceled. Moreover, his majesty orders you to leave the country immediately. You are not to stay in the Land of the Chest Holes even a single day longer. Say nothing and leave now."

Palace guards beat loudly on the floor with sharp split-bamboo poles, making threatening noises all around Asanoshin until he finally realized that the proposed marriage, which had made him so happy, was actually not to be. Desperately, he searched his chest once more and was bitterly disappointed to find absolutely no hole in it anywhere—and no trace of there ever having been one. So he rode off once more on his feather fan to the northern islands of the Ainu, to the Ryukyus, to the Mogul kingdom, to Annam, to Sumatra, to Borneo, to Persia, to Moscow, to Pegu and Arakan in Burma, to Armenia, to India, to Holland, and beyond.

After visiting several countries that satirize aspects of Japan, Asanoshin travels to Korea and then to China, where he uses his fan to become invisible and enter the women's quarters of the imperial palace. He loves various women there until his footprints give him away, and his fan is burned during his capture. He escapes punishment by telling the emperor about everything he has seen and receives a commission to lead a fleet to Japan to make a full-scale papier-mâché replica of Mount Fuji to be used as a model for reconstructing the mountain in China.

Island of Women (chapter 5)

The great goddess of Mount Fuji is worshiped at the Sengen Shrine in Udo in Suruga Province. Her name is Konohana-sakuya-hime, the daughter of the god Ōyama-tsu-mi-no-mikoto. With her mysterious powers transcending human understanding, she immediately realized that plans were being made in a faraway place to build a gigantic papier-mâché model of Mount Fuji. It would be unbearably shameful if the sacred mountain she protected were copied and the model taken to China, so she consulted privately with her assistant, the god of nearby Mount Ashitaka, and sent the swift god of the Soga Brothers Hachiman Shrine, located near her slopes, to notify the Ise Shrine and the Iwashimizu Hachiman Shrine of the impending danger. From there, warnings were sent out to every province, and in no time all the myriad gods of Japan had gathered for a conference on the peak of Mount Fuji.

The gods discussed every aspect of the matter. Finally they decided to follow the venerable plan they'd used to sink the invading Mongol ships centuries before. They ordered the wind and rain gods from the Ise Shrine to promptly station themselves over the open waters at the border between China and Japan. As soon as the gods saw the Chinese fleet, they were to descend on it until nothing remained.

But the wind god protested. "If I and my whole clan go out there," he said, "no one in Japan will catch cold any more, and if no one catches cold, the doctors of Japan will have a very hard time making ends meet. I propose we leave a few of my relatives behind in Japan."

The assembled gods exploded in anger. "If Asanoshin and the Chinese succeed in copying Mount Fuji with papier-mâché," they exclaimed, "Japan will never outlive the shame, never in all eternity. How can you dare compare such humiliation to the economic hardship of a few doctors? Anyway, most people who become doctors these days don't really want to be physicians. They're swindlers who know virtually nothing about curing people. A vegetable peddler opens a practice named Pickled Radish Hermitage; a fish seller changes his name to Mullet Anglerfish Clinic; a rice-cake dealer suddenly advertises Satō's Sugared Treatments; a candy salesman turns into the Sage of Sweet Syrup; and a very suspicious character calls himself Mysterious Azabu Hermitage. Don't worry about any of them starving. Earthenware returns to earth, as they say, and if people stop coming, these doctors can go back to doing what they've always done. Forget all your petty calculations. When the Chinese fleet enters Japanese waters, you, wind and rain gods, will use all your divine powers, and you, sleet and hail gods, will help them. Blow long and hard against the planks of their ships until the whole fleet is destroyed." The other gods spoke so strongly that the wind, rain, sleet, and hail gods promptly raised billowing clouds and set off in a raging storm.

Unaware of what lay in store for it, the huge Chinese fleet set out through the white-capped waves with a fair wind in its sails. When the fleet neared Japan, however, the waiting gods packed every quadrant of the sky with black clouds. The ships' navigators no longer knew where they were, and as the millions of confused Chinese sailors and paper workers began to sail around in different directions, a tremendous storm burst over them. All thirty thousand ships were blown together, battering and splintering against one another until they were one great pulverized mass.

Tens of thousands of the sailors managed to leap into the ocean. They were well trained and used many secret swimming techniques, but thirty thousand shiploads of paste and paper had been dumped into the ocean all at once, and the open sea was now as thick and sticky as water in a papermaking tub. The sailors stuck to the substance like flies in lime and were carried beneath the high waves. How pitiful it was. Sailor after sailor turned into what looked like white bean curd and drowned.

Miraculously, the ship on which Asanoshin rode—was it because he was Japanese?—escaped damage from the storm. Where it had been blown, however, no one on board knew. The great ship drifted wherever the wind and the waves took it. Somehow the days passed, and the food and water began to run out. No one on board expected to live much longer. But then, in the distance, beyond the surging waves, lookouts saw an island. The excited sailors used all the life left in them to row toward it.

It was the Island of Women, a country inhabited only by women. There wasn't a single man on the entire island. When the women here wanted to have a child, they opened their robes and faced in the direction of Japan. Wind blew on their bodies and made them pregnant, and later they bore girl babies. They had a ruler, but it was always a woman.

Island law required that if a ship from outside were blown here, the women had to go greet any person who came ashore. The women had to place their straw sandals on the beach facing toward the sea, and the law stipulated that if a man put on a pair he had to marry the woman whose sandals he happened to use. But the island was so far from anywhere that no one from outside had ever landed here before. When the drifting Chinese ship appeared, the women took it to be a gift from heaven. They gathered on the beach, took off their sandals, and placed them down on the sand as quickly as they could.

Asanoshin stepped ashore with more than a hundred Chinese sailors, and they all put on the sandals they found there and began to walk around on dry land for the first time in a long while. The happy women whose sandals they'd put on soon came and placed their arms around the men, speaking to them easily and intimately, saying things like "I'll bet women don't get husbands this way in China." But the numerous women whose sandals hadn't been chosen felt left out, and while they were making a great commotion, messengers from the empress arrived and announced that all the men, without exception, were to appear before her. The men were put in palanquins and carried off to the castle.

The large crowd of women stood there stunned. They felt as if they they'd just awakened in the morning and found their navels had been pulled out while they were sleeping. How stupid they'd been. After they realized what had happened, they began to discuss the situation.

"Every woman living on this island wants a man in the same way," one declared, "whether she's an aristocrat or a commoner."

"Just because those aristocrats have power doesn't mean they can take away every single man for themselves."

"What sheer cruelty!"

"How can we go on living like this?"

All the women there signed their names to a pledge of solidarity, and soon every woman on the whole island had come to join them. In a great crowd they besieged the castle walls from all sides, shouting out their various demands.

"Give us back the men!"

"If you don't, we'll attack the castle and tear it apart!"

"We may not be warrior women like Tomoe and Hangaku, who are so famous for bravery over in Japan. But a woman's will can go through solid rock!"

The women's indignation filled heaven and earth. The empress had no idea
what to do, and her ministers conferred desperately. Asanoshin felt he must
speak.

"The whole country is in turmoil because of only a hundred men," he said.
"If you aristocrats take us, the commoners will never be satisfied. And if we go
back among the commoners, then you will never be satisfied. The country will
be plunged into civil war. Please allow me, therefore, to make a suggestion. In
China and Japan there are special houses where women perform various arts
for men. My plan is this. I and the other men will work together, put up
performance houses, and make our living by entertaining women. Then all the
women in your country, high or low, aristocrats or commoners, can come,
without distinction, to hire us, as long as they have the money. In this situation,
there would surely be no grudges or jealousy among them. What do you think
of this proposal?"

The empress considered it an excellent idea, and soon the plan was publicly
announced. The women surrounding the castle agreed to try the plan, and they
ended the siege and returned to their villages across the island.

The women had the men find a suitable spot in the northern part of the
capital and dig a moat around it. Inside the moat, the men built everything
from teahouses and performance houses to shops for the merchants who would
do business there. They raised a single great gate to serve as the entrance and
exit and placed guards there to watch everyone who passed through and to
ensure that none of the men left the quarters. Then the women divided the
sailors, including Asanoshin, into groups of five to ten men and placed them
in various houses.

If they had been women, they would have been called "courtesans" or "professional women," but since they were men, they were referred to as "performer
men" or "professional men." The older sailors went to work as matrons, overseeing the younger ones, but because they were men, they were called "police."
The whole place was modeled after the Yoshiwara licensed quarter in Edo. The
top-ranking men were called "great performers," and those of the second rank,
"men behind the latticework." These men never performed in the houses where
they lived but met women customers at elegant performance houses for considerable sums. Below them came the "powdered-tea men," who met customers
for a lesser fee right in the houses where they lived. The lowest-ranking men
were sent to live in small houses by the moat around the quarter, and some
had to stand by their doors and pull in customers for a few coins.

The men displayed themselves in various fashions in front of the women.
The Japanese styles turned out to be the most popular, so the Chinese sailors

shaved the tops of their heads and tied topknots in back, combed their sidelocks upward and curled them around, and wore long cloaks like kabuki actors. They also made themselves up with lipstick and white face powder. Every evening, when it began to grow dark, a small bell would ring at each house, and women would come and stand along the front. Then when the lanterns went on inside, the waiting women would excitedly press their faces against the latticework at the front of the house, trying to decide which man inside to ask for.

Soon some of the women were going directly to second-floor rooms with the lower-ranking men. Other women went to teahouses to negotiate with the owners to obtain meetings with the higher-ranking performer men. These women waited at performance houses while the men paraded through the streets to the same houses, each escorted by two young assistants, one of whom held a high parasol high above his head. The men's collars curved seductively down in back, and they held up the hems of their robes as they walked with wide, dramatic strides. The sides and corners of the streets were packed with women trying to get a better look at the men as they passed by. No one had ever seen anything like it, and nothing in the island's legends compared with it.

Crowds of women jostled and competed for a chance to hire the man they wanted for the night. Some couples became intimate even at their first meeting,[78] while other women had to pay to have men take time out from another performance and visit them. Women with enough money made promises to meet men on prestigious holidays, when the men's fees were highest, and some women made regular visits and became more and more sophisticated in the way of love. There also were rivalries, displays of pride, graceful separations, and well-timed breakups. The only way that these performer men differed from courtesans in the outside world was in not going through women's coming-of-age ceremonies when they debuted at their houses.

At first, the men enjoyed their jobs so much they felt they must be in heaven, and they forgot all about their homelands. But as time passed, they felt less satisfied. When the winds of autumn began to blow, the men disliked what they were doing as much as the cold winds, and they complained and grumbled about how they really didn't want to meet customers on rainy or snowy nights. Later, they didn't even want to look at customers. But they found they couldn't easily reject customers they didn't like in the way that courtesans in Japan could. The women here weren't restrained by a sense of decorum or concern for their reputations the way men in Japan were. Refusing to leave, snubbed customers grabbed hold of the men and poured out their bitterness on them all through the night.

The men had to take customers day and night, and before six months had passed they were pale and thin. Their coughs grew rasping, and all of the more

---

78. Customarily, high-ranking courtesans never slept with men before the third meeting.

Asanoshin, a high-ranking performer man, walks with dramatic steps and displays himself on his way to an assignation teahouse in the pleasure quarter, where he will meet a woman customer. Two assistants walk beside him, and an old male "matron" stands at right. Outside the quarter gate stands a tub of water for use in case of fire. The dark banner behind the open gate says "Edo-chō," the name of a busy section near the main gate of Yoshiwara.

than a hundred men eventually succumbed to fevers and died, called to the other world by beckoning winds of desire. After they died, their contracts were transferred to new managers in Amida Buddha's Pure Land paradise. How pitiful it was. But as the Buddha taught, all living things must also die. Human life lasts only as long as a drop of dew—or a stroke of lightning.

Women across the land wept, and their grief was deep and intense. They remembered the performer men's pledges of everlasting love, even into the next life, and still filled with longing, the women stumbled blindly onward along the dark road of love. They lit special incense reputed to have the power to bring back the dead and to show their spectral forms in its smoke, but incense was lit at so many gates around the island that the confused souls of the dead sailors didn't know where to go and couldn't appear at all.

Somehow Asanoshin managed to stay not only alive but vigorous. Since he was the only male performer left, the former customers of the other men also began negotiating to see him, and soon his schedule was divided up into short segments so that he could meet fifty women a day. But even then his energy wasn't exhausted. He seemed to be made of iron. The women were amazed, as was Asanoshin. When he analyzed the situation, though, he realized he didn't have much to look forward to. As the only man left, he'd have to keep on doing this for the rest of his life. They'd never allow any woman to buy out his contract and let him go into retirement. He liked entertaining and making love with all the women who came to enjoy him, but if this became a settled way of life, he knew it would turn into something rather unpleasant.

While Asanoshin was thinking about what it really meant to be a performer and how tiresome the world was, he began to doze off. Suddenly, from out of nowhere, the Vagabond Sage appeared. Indignantly he struck Asanoshin with his goosefoot staff and knocked him over. When Asanoshin realized who it was, he prostrated himself before the sage and begged his forgiveness.

"In spring and summer," the sage said in a resounding voice, "trees and grasses flourish. In fall and winter, they wither. In the human world, success and fame mean it is time to withdraw. This is the Way of heaven. Fan Li counseled a king superbly and retired to the Five Lakes. Zhang Liang advised an emperor on strategy, then left to follow a Daoist immortal, Master Red Pine. These exemplary men knew when to enter the world and when to withdraw. They are models of wisdom for all time. Even a horse that can run a thousand leagues a day won't go anywhere unless it's noticed by a good judge of horses. Trying to will your way to success is like looking for ice on a summer day. You may actually achieve something small, but it will be as unattractive as a hot-house plum tree. And as short-lived.

"And suppose you do find a lord who employs you. You have the ability of a hawk, but they feed you ground rice and fish paste and throw millet seeds for you on the ground. It's only a matter of time until you get out of the cage and fly away. If you're strong enough to fly up to the clouds but you serve a lord in some low position for a pittance just to make a living, you're actually weaker than seed-eating sparrows and larks. A hawk never eats seeds, even when it's starving. And it does not deceive its lord and pretend to be loyal in order to fill its stomach. Instead, it quickly leaves the world behind.

"But retiring to mountains or forests isn't the only way to withdraw. The greatest withdrawal of all is to the heart of the city. There is no single way to achieve this. People withdraw by doing many things—being professional diviners or practicing herbal medicine or writing Chinese or Japanese poetry. The poet Dongfang Shuo had so much wit he could admonish the emperor, but he withdrew to serve at the palace gate.

"I have tried to teach you to experience and understand all there is to know about human feelings all over the world and, at the same time, to live beyond the world in the realm of humor. But look at you. You let yourself become attached to things and have been carried away by your emotions toward them. You've gotten yourself in trouble again and again. Go to the world the way you go to a public bath. There's a lot of dirt there, but you don't go there to get dirtier. Wash away dirt with dirt! After you come out of the bath and rinse yourself a final time, you're always clean, aren't you?

"If you remember this when you mix with the world, you'll never get dirty, even if the grimy people next to you are stark naked. It's the same with the lotus. Swamp mud and dirty water never stain it. You can't blacken what isn't black. But people grow attached to things and become infatuated with them, hurting themselves and destroying their families. I'm not talking only about men losing their heads over courtesans. Clinging to anything always causes harm. You've been all over the world. Surely you saw this for yourself.

"Humans everywhere recognize the Five Relationships between ruler and subject, parent and child, husband and wife, older and younger brother, and friend and friend. And not only humans. Ruler and subject bees fly separately; grown crows feed their parents to show their gratitude; and young doves honor their parents by perching three limbs below them. Roosters lower their wings and love hens, and even freely mating cats follow the way of conjugality. And in pictures, younger mice even climb up on abacuses with their older brothers and sisters. Dogs wag their tails and socialize. Sardines and young mullet swim in schools. All these follow the way of comradeship. Nothing between heaven and earth compares with the teaching of the sages.

"Itō Jinsai in Japan therefore quite justifiably wrote that the Confucian *Analects* is the greatest book in the universe. And the *Analects* say one should act in accordance with how evident the Way is in the world at any particular time. For example, Confucius warned those who followed his teachings not to drink wine or eat dried meat from the market. But in Japan the situation is different. Japanese scholars eat Echigo salted salmon, Suō salted mackerel, dried ear shells, dried sea slugs, and similar plain food, and they drink sweet saké brewed for festivals and do not insist on brewing their own. This is because Chinese drink wine and not saké, like that brewed in Ikeda and Itami in Japan. And China is mainly an inland country, so most people don't eat dried fish or shellfish. In China people eat dog and pork, so Confucius's teaching takes on a different meaning there. The *Analects* also say the virtuous man always includes ginger in his meals, yet in Japan it's not the custom to flavor raw fish or shellfish with ginger.

"Many Japanese Confucian scholars are truly frogs who know nothing outside their own small wells. They slavishly copy everything Chinese and refer to Japan as a nation of 'Eastern Barbarians.'[79] Or they make forced comparisons and propose that the sun goddess Amaterasu was actually Count Tai of Wu. They advertise that they teach the double way of literary and martial arts and fart out all sorts of nonsense, but if they actually had to receive their rice stipends calculated in the small measures of the Zhou period, when the sages lived, they would surely hate the sages.

"Someone once remarked that you could tell a badly governed country by its large number of laws and rules. Likewise, teachings appeared because the

---

79. Refers to Ogyū Sorai (1666–1728), a Japanese Confucian scholar.

world was in disorder, just as herbal cures are discovered after diseases appear. Unlike in Japan, the Chinese emperor is basically nothing more than temporary hired help. If they don't like him, they change him. They freely argue that the realm does not belong to any one ruler, but to the whole people, and they take the emperor's realm from him right away. It was only after the country had fallen into lawlessness that the sages appeared and disseminated their teachings. But in Japan, benevolence and righteousness have been spontaneously followed. Peace has prevailed even without sages.

"China preoccupied itself with culture and was invaded by the Mongols, and now, under the Manchus, when the whole country is wearing pigtails, the submissive fools still try to pretend they are the Great Qing. Japan has always had its share of evil men, such as Taira no Kiyomori or Hōjō Takatoki, but none ever tried to become emperor himself. In Japan loyalty is fierce, and even young children speak out rudely against their elders if they hear them slighting the emperor. This is why Japan, unlike other countries, has an unbroken imperial line. Please understand me. I am not saying that Chinese ways and methods are bad. Rather, the teachings of the sages must be modified to suit local customs in order that they not cause harm.

"Japanese think the people living on the Island of Tiny People are like bugs, and the giants put Japanese in freak shows. The Chest Hole People think holeless people are deformed, and various countries have different ideas about the proper proportion of arms to legs is. In India people show respect by baring their right shoulders and placing their palms together, while in Japan people follow Ogasawara-style decorum. Both Indians and Japanese act courteously, even though their behavior differs.

"The principles of the sages are like carpenters' measures. All carpenters use the same measuring rods, but they build their houses in many lengths and sizes, according to the number of people who will live in them. Likewise, the Way of economics responds flexibly to the times, correcting customs, making up for scarcities, and reducing surpluses. You can't play a koto if the bridges are glued down and won't move. And you can't use a ladle as a ruler.

"In recent years, however, some Confucianists have published economic theories that are as useless as trying to practice swimming in a dry field. Among ordinary people, these ridiculous theories produce only astonishment. Ignoring Confucius's warning against trying to govern when you aren't in a position to do it, these forgetful scholars expound on the Way of the sages like sumo wrestlers climbing into the ring without wearing their loincloths. Other scholars teach the Way in order to make a living, and they reach shallow, distorted conclusions. They gaze at heaven through narrow tubes and attempt to cast great iron bells with bamboo blowpipes. Many reach momentous conclusions with whatever they happen to have at hand and believe they are suddenly turning into sages, as if two or three inches of the tail end of a yam were miraculously turning into a magnificent eel. They are so proud of themselves that they believe their coming will be announced to the world if not quite by fiery horses and phoenixes then at least by stained or chipped versions. In the hands of these farting Confucianists who substitute an attachment to the Way for an understanding of it, even the teachings of the sages often cause confusion.

"Clinging and sticking to anything results in great harm. While you were traveling to many countries to learn more about human feelings, you visited the imperial Chinese palace and soon forgot about everything except making love with the court women there. That certainly got you into big trouble. Finally your fan was burned, but even that didn't stop you from believing that sexual love was the highest form of human happiness. That's why I sent you to the Island of Women. As a performer man there, you saw with your own eyes that sexual pleasure can lose its glamour and even become fatal.

"Life in the floating world really is like a dream. Look at yourself. You still believe you're young. Yet while you were out there wandering around in all those countries, seventy years passed. Here, let me show you." The sage took out a mirror and held it up. Moments before, Asanoshin had been a young man, but the figure he saw in the mirror had changed, as suddenly as the legendary Urashima Tarō, into a man in his eighties. He was thin; his face was covered with wrinkles; his jaw jutted out; his sidelocks and beard had fallen out; and his head was shaved like a monk.

Astonished and confused, Asanoshin looked around him. The air in every direction was filled with music and a radiance so pervading that it could belong only to a buddha. Then he saw something descending toward him on a purple cloud. A few moments later it stopped in his right hand. When Asanoshin examined it, he found it was a wooden object carved in the shape of a large mushroom.

"What you have in your hand," the sage said, smiling at Asanoshin, "is the merciful bodhisattva Kannon. Once the life of the condemned warrior Kagekiyo was spared when the Kannon manifestation of Kiyomizu Temple in Kyoto miraculously appeared at the execution ground in Kagekiyo's place. And on the Island of Women, the Kannon of Asakusa Temple in Edo changed herself into a wooden mushroom and stood in your place, saving you from dying, as you surely would have, with all the other men.[80] Repay the bodhisattva now for her kindness. Hurry back to your country and change your name to Shidōken, using characters that mean 'Seeker of the Way.'

"Then go to Asakusa and gather audiences in the precincts of the Kannon Temple there by telling humorous stories, all the while pointing out the many holes and gaps and hidden backsides in the world and sternly warn people against falling into these faults and habits themselves. If women are present while you tell all your suggestive stories, your listeners will get very excited. And

---

80. The statue of Kannon is in the shape of a dildo.

Asanoshin, suddenly old, holds onto the staff of the sage above him and flies to Asakusa. He looks back in the direction of a seven-star constellation (part of Hydra) marking the southern sky, the direction of the Island of Women.

Buddhist monks are proud and conceited. So criticize monks and women and get them to leave as soon as you can. All right then. Please come along with me."

As the sage began to fly off, Shidōken grabbed hold of his staff. He seemed to be flying behind the sage, but the next thing he knew he was sitting dazed on a low platform in a simple shed walled with hanging reed screens in a corner of the large Asakusa Kannon Temple compound. People of all ages were coming inside. As soon as they were seated on their stools, Shidōken took his wooden mushroom and began beating with it rhythmically on his low desk. *Ton-ton ton-ton ton-ton, tototon-ton tototon-ton.* "It's time," he began, "to hold on and ride on a high-flying story you'll never believe."

[*Fūrai Sanjin*, NKBT 55: 155–220, translated by Chris Drake]

A THEORY OF FARTING (HŌHI-RON, 1774)

This comic allegorical essay, which Gennai wrote toward the end of his career, belongs to the dangibon genre in that it includes a humorous debate between a believer in the artistic achievements of the Farting Man and a samurai who condemns that activity as immoral and dishonorable. "A Theory of Farting" is also considered to be an outstanding example of *kyōbun* (literally, crazy prose), or comic prose, the prose equivalent of *kyōka* (literally, crazy Japanese poetry), or comic waka. This genre, which was pioneered by Hiraga Gennai, Yomono Akara (1749–1823), and other kyōka poets, used vernacular prose for satirical and comic purposes. Of particular interest is the degree to which the Farting Man reflects Gennai's own position as a partial outsider who constantly pointed out the limitations and contradictions of the samurai class and sought out new frontiers and new "ways" (professions). For mid-eighteenth-century audiences, Gennai's achievements in botany generally were little more than a curiosity, but in his view, this profession had value precisely because he pursued it to perfection and did not rely on traditional authority or historical precedent, which tended to corrupt most artistic and scholarly "ways." In this regard, "A Theory of Farting" is a satire of both contemporary samurai and Confucian values and the system of artistic houses and strictly codified traditions.

Some fools survive a serious illness by taking ginseng and then go hang themselves when they can't pay for it. Other men love potentially poisonous blowfish soup yet manage to reach old age. Some housemaids get pregnant their very first time, while some hired men buy streetwalkers every night, never get syphilis, and still have noses. Ah, to put it a bit grandiosely, ah, is it all simply the will of heaven? And whether something interests people and becomes popular—is it due only to the luck of the moment? Surely it also depends on how imaginative your basic concepts are.

When the kabuki actor Ichikawa Danjūrō II[81] was alive, he invented striking new makeup, costumes, staging, and interpretations for the roles his father had created. Nakamura Tomijūrō, on the other hand, develops novel dances for his women's roles; Nakamura Nakazō constantly discovers new ways of acting men's parts; and Yamashita Kinsaku II plays women realistically and with great charm. Ōtani Hiroji III articulates well and projects his powerful voice, and Arashi Sangorō II gets far inside the characters he plays and expresses their emotions. Onoe Kikugorō went from Edo to Osaka and captivated the city, while Segawa Tomisaburō left Osaka, changed his name to Kikunojō III, and awed Edo.

Places, too, change and thrive as new concepts appear. Pilgrims now throng to the Zenkō-ji temple in Kawaguchi, just north of Edo, to see public unveilings of its secret buddha image.[82] In the city, people fill the Asakusa Kannon Temple and the small theaters around it, crowd into the Hachiman Shrine in Fukagawa to see sumō wrestling, and visit the Yoshiwara licensed quarter to watch male and female geisha improvise new farces in the street every fall. In the Kobikichō theater district, Masumi Katō V is now appearing at kabuki performances, demonstrating Katō-style puppet-play chanting there, while in the theaters in Fukiyachō the jōruri chanter Takemoto Sumidayū[83] is setting new stan-

---

81. Ichikawa Danjūrō (1688–1758). The other actors mentioned are contemporaries.

82. An especially popular unveiling was held from the Second to the Fourth Month of 1774, when a large number of Edo residents traveled up the Ara River on boats to worship. The temple raised a tremendous amount of money, and gamblers lined the road outside the gate.

83. Chanted Gennai's puppet play *Epiphany at Yaguchi Crossing* (1770).

dards for the Gidayū style. And then there are puppet variety shows, all-boy kabuki plays, mime shows, voice impersonations of famous actors, and Buddhist street preachers. Edo has prospered for some time now and has more kinds of shows than you can count, but reports and rumors about a "farting man" performing near Ryōgoku Bridge were causing heated discussions throughout the city.

Careful reflection shows that humans are microcosms of the universe. Heaven and earth thunder; humans fart. Yin and yang collide and chafe, sometimes reverberating deeply, sometimes releasing small, high sounds. But somehow the Farting Man was said to go far beyond the traditionally transmitted ladder method of crescendo farting and the prayer-bead technique of continuous farting. People said he produced the lonely cloth-fulling beat made by a kabuki drum, slow kabuki shamisen strumming for scenes in the licensed quarter, music for a felicitous nō dance performed before kabuki plays, three-beat percussive phrases, a koto ensemble version of the song "Seven Plants," drums, flutes, and gongs from the Gion Festival in Kyoto, dogs howling, cocks crowing, fireworks bursting above Ryōgoku Bridge, and a waterwheel creaking beside the Yodo River above Osaka. The man could perform long shamisen pieces from the kabuki dance plays *Young Woman at Dōjōji Temple* and *Wizard-Child Jidō*, short love songs, quiet background shamisen music from kabuki plays, an antiphonal folk song from Ise, and puppet-play chants in the Itchū, Hanchū, Bungo, Tosa, Bun'ya, Handayū, Geki, Katō, and Ōzatsuma styles. He would even do long Gidayū-style puppet plays. On request he would perform *Chūshingura* or *Epiphany at Yaguchi Crossing*, one act at a time, both the shamisen and the chanting. Word was that an incomparable master had appeared on the scene.

When I heard about the man, I knew I had to see him for myself, and I persuaded a couple of friends to go with me to the entertainment district at the west end of Ryōgoku Bridge. Just before we got to the bridge, we turned right and followed the wide avenue to a small theater with a high banner you couldn't miss: "Old Tale Comes True — Man Makes Blossoms Bloom."[84] From the midst of the pushing, jostling crowd of Buddhist monks and lay men and women, we looked up at the sign above the entrance. It showed a strange man with rear end lifted high, behind which were depicted, in various tints of ink, a group of unrelated objects, including the bell from *Young Woman at Dōjōji Temple* and

---

84. Refers to the folktale "The Old Man Who Made Blossoms Bloom," in which an honest man is helped by the gods and all his acts have good results; even ashes sprinkled on a tree turn to blossoms in front of a lord, and he is rewarded. However, when his neighbor imitates him, hoping for the same rewards, the neighbor fails. Similarly, in the Muromachi-period otogi-zōshi popular tale *The Tale of Fukutomi*, the protagonist, Fukutomi, has an almost divine ability to fart artistically, and he is rewarded by a lord. However, when his covetous neighbor asks for instruction, receives pills, and performs before the lord, his farting turns to diarrhea and soils the lord's garden.

At the entrance to the Farting Man's show at Asakusa, people discuss the show and look at the sign, which shows the man farting visual icons—such as the ladder and fulling mallet—representing the styles and pieces he performs. The bottom part of the banner says, "Man Makes Blossoms Bloom." From the 1780 edition.

the black mask from the auspicious Sanbasō dance. The sign seemed to be trying to depict a dream. An innocent person from the country who happened to stroll by and saw the sign would surely imagine the man was dreaming with his rear end. Still muttering, we went inside and saw a narrow red and white striped curtain stretched across the top of the stage. Below, on a low stage, sat the Farting Man and the musicians. He was of medium build and light-skinned, with sidelocks curving rakishly up like crescent moons. Beneath his deep blue summer robe he wore an undergarment of scarlet crepe silk.

The man's greetings to the audience were clear and unaffected. His opening number, together with the musicians, was a fart version of the Sanbasō blessing dance.[85] He progressed rhythmically with nō drums and flutes, *toppa hyoro-hyoro, hiih-hiih-hiih*. Then he gave off a rooster's cry at the ruddy eastern sky, *bu-bu-buuu-buu*. Next came a waterwheel. He loosed a sloshing *buu-buu-buu* as he did cartwheels and made the exact sounds of water filling the buckets and then pouring out as it pushed the wheel around.

"Move on. Next show! Next show!"

We left the place to the beating of the large, show-ending drum. On the way back we dropped in on some friends, and when we told them we'd seen the Farting Man, they all began to debate about him. Opinion was divided between those who asserted the man was using medicine and those who argued he had some sort of hidden device. No conclusion was in sight.

---

85. The Sanbasō, the felicitous dance from the "god" nō play *Old Man* (*Okina*), was performed early in the morning on kabuki stages before the day's performance began.

"Gentlemen," I finally said, "won't you please stop and listen? Yes, there is in fact a farting medicine on the market. A man in Osaka, Seiemon, who owns the Chigusaya Publishing House, also sells unusual herbal remedies. His sign-board advertises both Argument Laxatives and Fart Starters. But when I asked about the ingredients of the farting formula, I discovered it's only for nudging out stubborn farts, not for producing the artistic releases we saw today. As for a secret device, yes, it certainly sounds reasonable enough. But the man's not using a Takeda trick puppet stage with curtains and hidden strings and wheels. His stage is open on all sides. Besides, you can't control when farts come. There doesn't seem to be a device anywhere on him. If he does have one, he's been able to hide it from tens of thousands of people looking on only a few feet away, so it's virtually the same as if he were actually farting. If everyone calls them real farts, then it's better to go along with them and, as one sage put it, eat their dregs and stir up their mud. Just regard the man's deliveries as farts.

"It's very hard to get along in the world, and people rack their brains thinking of ways to separate other people from their money. They come up with all sorts of slightly novel designs and plans, but basically they're all the same. Yesterday's new seems old today, and the old gets even older. But the Farting Man is different. True, you can find gifted fictional farters in old tales. But what that Farting Man actually does right in front of your eyes can't be found in any old record or legend—in all the 2,436 years Japan's supposed to have existed, from the first year of Emperor Jinmu's reign all the way up until 1774. And you won't find anyone like him in China, Korea, India, Holland, or any country on earth. What brilliant conception! And what execution!"

Everyone there seemed impressed by my praise. Then, from the back of the room, came a voice: "Sir, your theory is completely wrong. Allow me to reply."

When I looked, I saw a samurai fresh from the country, head hard as rock. He was walking to the front of the room, and his expression showed outrage. "What we have just heard," he said, "is truly shameless. The authorities permit plays and other public performances only as a means of harmonizing people and revealing the proper Way of ruler and ruled, father and child, husband and wife, older and younger brother, friend and friend. For example, the total faith-fulness that Ōboshi Yuranosuke shows to his lord in the puppet play *Chūshin-gura* makes him a model retainer. Or take the puppet play *Hiragana Tales of Glory and Decline,* in which Umegae vows to get money for her husband even if she herself has to go to hell for it. When she does that, why, she's actually encouraging all women to be chaste and true. Even freak shows teach audiences that their own children will be punished if they commit bad deeds. The strangely shaped hunter's child on the stage, well, he was born that way because of his father's sinful hunting. Freak shows urge constant vigilance and demon-strate the chilling truth that retribution for bad deeds comes swiftly and without mercy. In the last few years, however, the people who put on these shows have completely abandoned morality. All they care about these days is making money. And now a 'farting man' is on exhibit! It's outrageous!

"One must absolutely never fart in public. For a warrior to fart during a formal meeting is an act so dishonorable it calls for suicide. And not only warriors. A rumor is going around about a high-class courtesan in Shinagawa who farted during an audience with some customers. Two well-known men happened to be there, a fish wholesaler from Odawarachō who uses the title Ridō[86] and a kabuki actor from Sakaichō he'd brought along with him, a man calling himself Mii. When these sophisticated celebrities laughed at the woman's fart, she couldn't bear it and promptly went into another room and prepared to kill herself.

"Some of the other women in the house saw what she was doing and tried to talk her out of it. 'They're both proud, experienced men who get around,' the woman retorted, 'and people listen to what they say. I know perfectly well they're going to spread nasty rumors. Pretty soon everybody in Edo is going to know about it. I'd rather kill myself than become famous for farting.' The two men said all sorts of things to calm the woman and swore they would never mention what had happened to anyone. 'No,' she protested, 'even if you promise now, later you'll tell people, and I couldn't live with that kind of shame. Please let me die.'

"She was in no mood to change her mind, and the two men were at their wits' ends. Finally, after they'd signed a formal pledge to keep the matter secret, the woman relented. It might seem strange to some, but the woman was actually prepared to kill herself. She knew that by doing something as disgraceful as farting she'd already committed professional suicide. And seeing her deep sense of shame, the two refined gentlemen who had gone too far swallowed their pride, felt compassion for her, and wrote an amateurish pledge in order to save her life. It is all very touching, is it not?

"Such people know what shame is. But for someone to put up a sign beside a main street and fart right in front of people's eyes, why, it's vulgar and impudent beyond words! The man and his manager are willing to do anything at all for money. And those who watch him are dimwits. Yet you, sir, do nothing but mimic their adulation. I find your groveling praise of the man nothing short of disgusting. In China, wise people loathe even hearing immoral names like Well of Thieves or Mother-Conquering Village. Confucius was very clear. We must never to listen to what is improper. And never look at it, either!" Blue veins stood out on the samurai's temples.

"Your words," I replied, "are perfectly correct. Nevertheless, you still lack deeper understanding of the Way. Confucius valued even children's songs, and I, too, have good reasons for praising the Farting Man. Everything between heaven and earth is naturally noble or base, high or low. At the farthest extreme of the low are usually placed urine and feces. In China, people show they

---

86. Ridō was one of the famous "Eighteen Great Connoisseur Playboys" (Dai-tsū) of the 1770s.

despise something by calling it 'dung earth.' In Japan they say something is 'like shit.' Nevertheless, though dirty, shit and piss fertilize the various grains and feed the people. But simply to fart and momentarily feel good, why, that is completely useless and requires no talent. According to the *Book of Songs*, in heaven there is neither sound nor smell. In contrast, farts make sounds, although, unlike the sounds of large or small drums, they're hardly listened to and enjoyed. And farts have smell, yet they can't be used for incense like aloes wood or musk. Instead, they make you stink. When people say 'onions, garlic, and a fistful of fart in your nose,' they mean something smells pretty awful. Farts rise up from nothing and disappear into nothing. They're completely useless, even as fertilizer. So it was only natural that the mad Buddhist preacher Shidōken began calling rotten, worthless Confucian scholars 'farting Confucianists.'

"Until now farts have been completely rejected everywhere for being without value or significance. But the Farting Man is inspired. He's hit on idea after idea and mastered numerous releases. And now he's drawing such crowds that none of the other small theaters will be in business very long. Tomisaburō became a great kabuki star only after he began using the prestigious stage name Kikunojō II. But farts have no hereditary titles, no fans to sleep with, and no rich patrons. They have only themselves, plainly, as they actually are. They ask to be judged for that alone. Using nothing but a two-inch hole, the Farting Man is blowing away all the other shows. Triumfartly, if I may put it that way, he's left the competition flatulented on their backs.

"How different he is from our professional musicians who go to a certified master to receive secret instruction on the proper way to articulate and chant so they themselves can later charge high fees to their own students. A good voice, however, is something you're born with. These musicians caw and croak like crows or night herons, imitating old pieces without putting any feeling into the phrases. They're ignorant of tempo changes in the prelude, main section, and finale and know nothing about vocalization or interpreting notation marks. They simply slaughter the words of the new puppet plays. The profession as a whole is in decline. But look at the Farting Man. He's invented everything by himself, without master or secret oral transmission. With an unspeaking rear end and uncomprehending farts, he's learned articulation and rhythmic breathing, he has a natural sense of timbre and pitch at all five tones and twelve semitones, and he's able to make so many clearly distinct sounds that his rear end is clearly superior to the voice of a second-rate puppet-play chanter. Call him one of a kind, call him a wonder. Truly he is the founder of the Way of Farting.

"But musicians aren't the only ones these days who are, as they say, 'shit-bad.' Scholars stare at thousand-year-old wastepaper from China, and writers who use classical Chinese collect stray shavings from the works of Han Yu, Liu Zongyuan, and the middle-Tang poets, heaping them into what they think are great pillars. Waka poets just sit around, but rice grains manage to stick to the bottoms of their feet, and they make a good living. Herbal doctors follow the Old Method or the Later Method and dispute loudly among themselves, but they can't cure ordinary ailments, while epidemics kill thousands. The people who call themselves haikai linked-verse masters suck up the drool of Bashō and Kikaku,[87] and tea ceremony masters try to look genteel and elegant as they lick the two-centuries-old turds of Sen no Rikyū and Sōtan.[88] The other arts are also atrophied. Artists don't use their own minds, so they can't invent or create, and their efforts fall far short of the achievements of the past, on which they themselves rely so completely. But the Farting Man, he's using his rear end in a totally unknown way and making music that people of the past never heard. He's captured the imagination of the whole country.

"Chen Ping of Han once cooked some meat and took great care to give equal portions to all his guests. 'If I become an imperial minister,' he said, 'this is how I will govern.' Now what I say is this. It would be an incomparable service if some brilliant people were to show as much creativity as the Farting Man and invent new ways to help the people of this land. That man uses his mind and pursues things deeply, and look, even farting has reached a very high level.

"Ah, if those who wish to save the world and those who learn the various arts would exert themselves using all of their minds, their fame would resound through the land even more loudly than farts. If I were to say I've borrowed the sounds of farts in order to wake the despairing, the inexperienced, and the idle from their dreamlike torpor, that would smell of pure theory. Go ahead, call my argument empty as a fart. That objection, I say, is of less consequence than a fart."

[*Fūrai sanjin shū*, NKBT 55: 229–236, translated by Chris Drake]

---

87. Matsuo Bashō (1644–1694) and his Edo disciple Kikaku (1661–1707) were virtually worshiped by later-eighteenth-century Edo poets.

88. Sen no Rikyū (1522–1591), one of the great masters of the art of tea and the pioneer of *wabicha*, and his grandson Sen Sōtan (1578–1658), who systematized and popularized it. By Gennai's time, the art of tea had become highly codified.

Chapter 12

COMIC AND SATIRIC POETRY

SENRYŪ

In the 1750s, the seventeen-syllable *senryū*, or comic haiku, became popular. The senryū has the same 5–7–5 syllabic structure as haiku, but unlike haiku, which focuses primarily on the natural world, the senryū uses humor, satire, and wit to comment on contemporary society and the human condition. Historically, senryū derived from a particular type of linked verse, *maeku-zuke* (verse capping), which can be traced back to linked verse in the medieval period. In verse capping, the judge (*tenja*) presents an initial or "earlier verse" (*maeku*) to which the participants respond with an "added verse" (*tsukeku*), which is then judged and scored. The initial verse usually is fourteen syllables long, and the added verse is seventeen syllables.

Unlike haiku, which stresses overtones and tries to create a subtle, elegant mood, senryū focuses on popular and lowbrow subjects and are intended to surprise and amuse the reader. In contrast to haiku's relatively circumscribed topical range, that of the senryū is broad, encompassing a range of topics of interest to eighteenth-century audiences, particularly in Edo. Examples are everyday domestic life, various occupations (from that of doctor to laundryman to thief), relations between the sexes, the Yoshiwara licensed quarter, recent incidents, and noted historical events and literary figures. As a popular new genre, senryū took up subjects that haiku avoided, such as love and sexuality. Indeed, senryū's heavy reliance on vulgar topics, including highly erotic and pornographic material, has often prevented it from being considered literature or serious poetry.

The fundamental differences between haiku and senryū can be traced to their historical origins. Haiku, the modern word for *hokku* (literally, opening verse), was originally the opening verse in a linked-verse sequence, and senryū was an offshoot of the added verse. Consequently, senryū, unlike haiku, does not require a seasonal word (*kigo*), which connects the haiku to nature and the larger poetic tradition. In addition, unlike the hokku, senryū does not require a cutting word (*kireji*), which splits the verse into two syntactic parts. Instead, the senryū usually consists of a single grammatical unit. The haiku also usually ends in a noun or a sentence-ending declension, which gives the verse a sense of closure, whereas the senryū often closes with the continuative verb form (*renyōkei*), suggesting further action. Generally, the senryū abbreviates the key word or topic, forcing readers to fill in the blank space and creating a sense of surprise and excitement when they realize what has been left out.

The humor of senryū frequently stems from deflating or inverting objects or persons of high status, authority, or elegance. Senryū parodies figures and incidents in classical literature as well as famous poetic phrases and well-known aphorisms (*kotowaza*). Senryū frequently uses wordplay, such as puns and word associations (often impossible to translate), and makes surprising metaphors or comparisons (*mitate*). But beyond parody and wordplay, senryū examines the world with a sharp and satirical eye. Indeed, senryū's greatest strength is revealing human weaknesses and failings and pointing out the contradictions and paradoxes of contemporary society.

Senryū, *kyōka* (comic waka), *kyōshi* (comic Chinese poetry), and *kyōbun* (comic prose) appeared at the same time as such comic or satirical fictional forms as *dangibon* (satiric sermons), *kokkeibon* (books of humor), *sharebon* (books of wit and fashion), and *kibyōshi* (comic illustrated books). The simultaneous emergence and growth of "wild" (*kyō*) or comic literature at this time, in the An'ei-Tenmei era (1772–1789), has been at least partly attributed to the lax rule of Senior Councillor Tanuma Okitsugu (r. 1772–1786), who neglected to enforce the restraints placed on society during the Kyōhō Reforms.

KARAI SENRYŪ

Karai Senryū (1718–1790) was a town official in the Asakusa district of Edo. But he also was a noted judge of verse capping and was known for his judgments on *manku awase* (ten-thousand-verse contests) in which a judge presented an earlier verse and the participants submitted added verses. Prizes were awarded to those people whose added verses were selected by the judge as superior. In 1765 Senryū's disciple published *Willow Barrel* (*Haifū yanagidaru*, commonly called *Yanagidaru*), a collection of 756 prize-winning verses from earlier *manku awase* (dating from 1757 to 1765). Significantly, this was one of the first such collections to leave out the earlier verse and to treat the added verses as independent poems. In this way, a new genre was created, named after Senryū himself. Indeed, *Willow Barrel* proved to be so popular that it was expanded, and by the time it ceased publication, in 1838, it numbered 167 volumes.

Most of the following selections are from the first twenty-three volumes of *Willow Barrel*, which were published while Karai Senryū was alive. Some of the verses are from *Additional Gatherings for the Willow Barrel* (*Yanagidaru shūi*, 1796), which was published thirty years later and organizes the poems by topic. Other sources are *Willow Along the River* (*Kawazoi yanagi*, 1780–1783) and *Safflower* (*Suetsumuhana*, 1776–1801), a collection devoted to erotica. Today about 200,000 senryū from the middle to the end of the Tokugawa period survive, but almost all of them are anonymous (unlike the *kyōka*, which were signed and whose authors made a name for themselves). Even Karai Senryū, the founder of Edo senryū, is known primarily as a judge rather than a poet. The practice of writing senryū, which extended into the Meiji period, continues to be popular today.

Various Occupations

ohanage wo	All he does at work:
kazoete iru ga	count the number of hairs
tsutome nari	in his lord's nostrils[1]

        [*Yanagidaru*, vol. 24, translated by Makoto Ueda]

yakunin no	The official's little son—
ko wa niginigi wo	how fast he's learned to open
yoku oboe	and close his fist![2]

        [*Yanagidaru*, vol. 1, translated by Makoto Ueda]

yoi goke ga	"There'll soon be
dekiru to hanasu	a charming widow"—that's the talk
isha nakama	among the doctors[3]

        [*Yanagidaru*, vol. 5, translated by Makoto Ueda]

---

1. "To count the number of hairs in one's nostrils" meant "to fawn on a superior." This was a satirical comment on the state of the samurai in the Tokugawa period, when ordinary samurai were no longer engaged in combat but had to concentrate on attending their lord.

2. One of the best-known premodern senryū. This little son has learned to open and close his fist at a very early age because he watches his father receiving bribes day in and day out.

3. Although doctors are usually not moved by the death of a patient, if the patient's wife is beautiful, they may have a special interest.

hen to iu	The doctor has prepared
nigemichi isha wa	a way out—
akete oku	"A sudden change for the worse."

[*Yanagidaru*, vol. 23, translated by Haruo Shirane]

yoku shimete	Off to work,
nero to ihi ihi	the burglar to his wife:
nusumi ni de	"Lock up tight when you go to bed!"[4]

[*Yanagidaru shūi*, vol. 10, translated by Burton Watson]

sentakuya	The laundryman:
kinjo no hito no	a fellow who feeds on the filth
aka de kuhi	of his neighbors

[*Yanagidaru*, vol. 36, translated by Makoto Ueda]

sekitori no	The sumo wrestler—
chichi no atari no	a crowd of fans swarming
hitodakari	below his chest

[*Yanagidaru*, vol. 1, translated by Makoto Ueda]

kiku hito mo	Whatever he says
kokoro de gowari	is discounted 50 percent
hiite oki	by anyone who listens

[*Yanagidaru shūi*, vol. 9, translated by Makoto Ueda]

The Human Condition

kamiyo ni mo	Even in the time of gods
damasu kumen wa	they needed wine
sake ga iri	to deceive others[5]

[*Yanagidaru*, vol. 1, translated by Haruo Shirane]

gakumon to	Learning and a ladder—
hashigo wa tonde	you can climb neither
noborarezu	if you skip a step[6]

[*Yanagidaru shūi*, vol. 10, translated by Makoto Ueda]

---

4. The paradox of the robber, too, being afraid of being robbed. The same paradoxical phrase was used by men to their wives before they set off for the licensed quarter.

5. In a noted episode in the ancient chronicles, the god Susanoō used wine to intoxicate and slay a dangerous serpent, a practice that seems to continue today.

6. The choice of a ladder to explain the process of serious study and scholarship reflects commoner sensibilities.

e de mite wa   Judging by the pictures
jigoku no hō ga   hell looks like a more
omoshiroshi   exciting place[7]

          [*Yanagidaru*, vol. 71, translated by Makoto Ueda]

he wo hitte   Laying a fart—
okashiku mo nai   no humor in it
hitorimono   when you live alone[8]

          [*Yanagidaru*, vol. 3, translated by Burton Watson]

nete tokeba   How long it seems
obi hodo nagaki   when you undo a woman's sash
mono wa nashi   while lying in bed![9]

          [*Yanagidaru*, vol. 3, translated by Makoto Ueda]

gokezakari   "You're in the prime
da to homeyō mo   of widowhood"—what a way
arō no ni   to compliment a woman!

          [*Yanagidaru shūi*, vol. 2, translated by Makoto Ueda]

Domestic Life

nyōbo ga   His wife away from home
rusu de ichinichi   he spends the entire day
sagashigoto   looking for things

          [*Kawazoi yanagi*, vol. 5, translated by Makoto Ueda]

meshitaki ni   For a housemaid
babā wo oite   she's hired an old woman—
hana akase   a nice surprise for him!

          [*Yanagidaru*, vol. 1, translated by Makoto Ueda]

---

7. The comparison is between pictures of heaven, with its buddhas and lotus flowers, and those of the Eight Great Hells, including the Lake of Blood and the Mountain of Needles.

8. Edo, where people gathered from the provinces, was a city with a large number of inhabitants living alone. The senryū humorously captures the dreary side of solitary life.

9. A scene so passionate that there is no time to stand and undo the sash. The *maeku* (previous verse) was "Things good from beginning to end" or "Things that come out well." From 1765.

chōnai de
shiranu wa teishu
bakari nari

The whole town
knows of it, except
the husband

[*Suetsumuhana*, vol. 4, translated by Makoto Ueda]

wakadanna
yoru wa ogande
hiru shikari

The young master
who scolds the maid in the daytime
worships her at night

[*Senryū hyō manku awase*, translated by Makoto Ueda]

nyōbō o
kowagaru yatsu wa
kane ga dekiru

The guy
who fears his wife
makes money[10]

[*Yanagidaru*, vol. 3, translated by Haruo Shirane]

haha no na wa
oyaji no ude ni
shinabite i

A tattoo of
the mother's name shriveled
in the father's arm[11]

[*Yanagidaru*, vol. 2, translated by Haruo Shirane]

ko wo motte
kinjo no inu no
na wo oboe

Now that he has a child
he knows all the local dogs
by name

[*Yanagidaru shūi*, vol. 9, translated by Makoto Ueda]

soeji shite
tana ni iwashi ga
gozariyasu

Baby at her breast
she tells him, "There're sardines
on the shelf"[12]

[*Yanagidaru*, vol. 14, translated by Makoto Ueda]

---

10. When invited to go out, he declines, saying that his wife will object. It is precisely these types who accumulate money, though implicitly at the cost of not appreciating the finer things in life.

11. The tattoo of a lover's name, barely visible in the wrinkled skin, reveals a time long past when the father had fallen head over heels for the mother.

12. The master of the house is expecting a meal when he comes home, but the baby gets priority.

```
ashioto ga                Each time footsteps
suru to Rongo no          approach, he puts it under
shita e ire               the Analects[13]
```

> [*Kawazoi yanagi*, vol. 2, translated by Makoto Ueda]

Yoshiwara, the Licensed Quarter

```
Yoshiwara e               Yoshiwara—
otoko no chie wo          that's where a man goes to dump
sute ni yuki              all his better judgment
```

> [*Yanagidaru shūi*, vol. 7, translated by Makoto Ueda]

```
yo no naka wa             When the night falls
kurete kuruwa wa          the day starts to break
hiru ni nari              on the brothels
```

> [*Yanagidaru shūi*, vol. 6, translated by Makoto Ueda]

```
waraigao                  Even her smile
made keisei wa            is carefully made up—
koshiraeru                the courtesan
```

> [*Yanagidaru*, vol. 13, translated by Makoto Ueda]

```
yubi no nai               As he smiles
ama wo waraeba            at the nun without a finger
warau nomi                she only smiles[14]
```

> [*Yanagidaru*, vol. 1, translated by Makoto Ueda]

Noted Historical Events and Literary Figures

```
Narihira no               What a miracle
kasa wo kakanu mo         that disease never caught up
fushigi nari              with Narihira[15]
```

> [*Yanagidaru*, vol. 4, translated by Makoto Ueda]

---

13. A student appears to be studying Confucius's *Analects* but is in fact looking at a more interesting, unapproved book, which is hidden when a parent approaches.

14. Courtesans sometimes cut off the tip of a finger as a gesture of loyalty to a customer, suggesting that the nun may have been a courtesan. To the man who has noticed this, she responds with only a smile, creating a sense of mystery.

15. A reference to the numerous amorous adventures of Ariwara no Narihira (820–880), the protagonist of *The Tales of Ise*.

shirami nado	Sitting idly
sotoba no ue de	and crushing lice on a stupa
tsubushite i	Lady Komachi[16]

[*Yanagidaru shūi*, vol. 4, translated by Makoto Ueda]

mata fumi ka	"Another letter?
sokora e oke to	Put it down somewhere over there,"
hikaru kimi	says the Shining Genji[17]

[*Yanagidaru*, vol. 17, translated by Haruo Shirane]

Kiyomori no	The doctor disrobed
isha wa hadaka de	before he went in to take
myaku wo tori	Kiyomori's pulse[18]

[*Yanagidaru*, vol. 1, translated by Makoto Ueda]

Tsugunobu mo	That Tsugunobu—
tō ga kokonotsu	he too thought nine times out of ten
ataranu ki	the arrow would miss him[19]

[*Yanagidaru*, vol. 8, translated by Makoto Ueda]

sono toki no	The priest in charge
oshō wa goke no	saw more widows than even he
miaki wo shi	ever wanted to see![20]

[*Yanagidaru shūi*, vol. 5, translated by Makoto Ueda]

---

16. In the nō play *Komachi on the Stupa* (*Sotoba Komachi*), Komachi, a former passionate lover and now an old woman, is seen sitting on a stupa, the holy image of the Buddha's incarnation.

17. The standard image of Genji in the Edo period was that he was so beautiful that women were always chasing after him.

18. In the famous death scene in *The Tale of the Heike*, Kiyomori, the leader of the Heike, dies of an extremely high fever, so hot that his body causes water to boil.

19. At the battle of Yashima, moments before Minamoto Yoshitsune, the Genji leader, was shot at by the enemy general Noritsune, governor of Noto, Yoshitsune's loyal retainer Satō Tsugunobu (1158–1185) stepped in front of him and was killed, thus becoming a model of self-sacrifice. The senryū suggests that Tsugunobu did not really expect the shot to be so accurate.

20. Forty-six of the forty-seven rōnin in the Chūshingura incident died by committing ritual suicide at Sengaku-ji temple in Edo a couple of months after their successful vendetta. Hinted at here is the alleged penchant of Buddhist priests for seducing young widows.

KYŌKA

Waka poets wrote *kyōka*, a parodic and popular form of the thirty-one-syllable waka, as a form of amusement or diversion, in the same way that Japanese *kanshi* (Chinese poetry) poets composed *kyōshi* (comic Chinese poetry) or haiku poets composed *senryū*. In the Tokugawa period, kyōka split into two types. One began in the sixteenth century in Kyoto and was practiced by aristocratic poets such as Matsunaga Teitoku (1671–1653) before it gradually spread to commoner devotees and then to Osaka, where it became known as Naniwa (Osaka) kyōka. The other type, which peaked in the Tenmei era (1781–1789) and is represented here, began in the mid-eighteenth century among the Edo samurai before spreading to the Edo commoners and then throughout the country. In the 1770s a coterie of samurai in Edo—Yomono Akara (1749–1823), Akera Kankō (1740–1800), Karakoromo Kishū (1743–1802), and others—gathered for kyōka meetings and contests, and in the Tenmei era they began publishing their comic waka. The first and largest of these Edo kyōka anthologies was *Wild Poems of Ten Thousand Generations* (*Manzai kyōka shū*, 1783), edited by Akara, which spurred what literary historians have called the Tenmei "kyōka boom" in Edo. This kyōka movement was encouraged by the atmosphere created by the bakufu administration of Senior Councillor Tanuma Okitsugu (r. 1772–1786), whose pro-commerce policies generated a sense of liberation among Edo samurai and contributed to the flowering of new Edo genres such as senryū, sharebon, and kibyōshi.

The humor of kyōka essentially derives from placing something vulgar, low, or mundane in an elegant Japanese form or context. Typically, a kyōka poet treated a classical topic using popular language and attitudes or, conversely, approached a popular, mundane topic (such as theater, licensed quarters, or farting) using classical diction or a classical perspective. The fundamental form of kyōka is the *honkadori*, or allusive variation on a specific "foundation poem" (*honka*), in which the kyōka poet transforms the meaning of part of a classical poem (or part of a well-known song or proverb), thereby bringing the foundation text into the vulgar or popular world. Wordplay also is a central element of kyōka, particularly puns (*kakekotoba*) and word associations (*engo*). Both rhetorical devices make kyōka very difficult to translate. Jippensha Ikku's *Travels on the Eastern Seaboard* (*Tōkaidō hizakurige*, 1802–1809), one of the most popular comic narratives (*kokkeibon*) of the early nineteenth century, includes numerous kyōka, many of which rely on homophonic play for their humor.

In contrast to senryū, which flourished at the same time as kyōka and remains popular today, kyōka as a genre did not last into the modern period. Although in the late eighteenth century it eventually spread beyond the sphere of educated samurai and aristocrats to commoners, it still required a knowledge of the classical poetic tradition, which made it difficult for commoner audiences to appreciate.

YOMONO AKARA

Yomono Akara (1749–1823) was the kyōka pen name for Ōta Nanpō, a writer of kyōshi, sharebon, and kibyōshi. Akara was recognized at an early age by Hiraga Gennai (1728–1779) and published *Master Groggy Literary Collection* (*Neboke sensei bunshū*), an anthology of kyōshi and kyōbun, in 1767, when he was just eighteen. His greatest talent, however, was writing kyōka. In the early 1780s, the style of two of the leading kyōka poets diverged. Karakoromo Kishū, the more conservative poet, stressed allusive variation and wordplay, whereas Akara (and his followers such as Kankō) saw kyōka as a means of describing everyday emotions, particularly those of the Edo townspeople. In 1783, when Akara edited *Wild Poems of Ten Thousand Generations* (*Manzai kyōka shū*), the most influential of the Tenmei kyōka anthologies, he attracted his own following. A Tokugawa houseman (*gokenin*) in the Edo bakufu, Akara was careful not to write anything that would endanger his relatively high position as a samurai and did not express subversive or critical thoughts in the way that Gennai did. But then, as a result of the Kansei Reforms (1787–1805), led by Senior Councillor Matsudaira Sadanobu, which cracked down on the liberties of the Okitsugu era, Akara left the literary world and concentrated on his responsibilities as a bakufu official. In his last years he returned to poetry, took the pen name of Shokusanjin, and became a highly influential figure in the world of letters.

Composed at the beginning of the year

> namayoi no
> reisha wo mireba
> daidō wo
> yokosujikai ni
> haru wa kinikeri

> The season greeter,
> tipsy with toasts,
> weaves unsteadily
> down the avenue—
> lo, the New Year has come![21]

> [*Kyōka saizō shū*, vol. 1, translated by Burton Watson]

On the blossoms of Yoshiwara

> Yoshiwara no
> yomise o haru no
> yūgure wa

> In Yoshiwara
> the women are showing their wares
> this evening—

---

21. Here the season greeter (*reisha*) began his rounds of the neighborhood in formal dress, but with each reception of celebratory wine, he becomes more tipsy. The kyōka celebrates the arrival of spring (which coincides with the arrival of the New Year under the lunar calendar), not, in the classical fashion, by referring to an aspect of nature but by capturing an aspect of contemporary social life.

iriai no kane ni
hana ya sakuran

blossoms glowing in the echoes
of the vesper bells.[22]

[*Manzai kyōka shū*, vol. 2, Spring 2, translated by Steven Carter]

AKERA KANKŌ

Akera Kankō (1740–1800), a low-ranking bakufu retainer and one of the leading kyōka poets during the Tenmei boom, was a contemporary and colleague of Akara and became one of his followers after Akara broke from Karakoromo Kishū.

On the year's end

shakkin mo
ima wa tsutsumu ni
tsutsumarezu
yaburekabure no
fundoshi no kure

Under a ragged loincloth
some things can't be hid—
my debts, too,
protrude through
the frayed end of the year.[23]

[*Manzai kyōka shū*, vol. 6, Winter, translated by Burton Watson]

On the autumn wind

sato no ko ni
oikakerarete
igaguri no chi o
nigemawaru
kaze no hageshisa

Chased round and round
by village urchins,
the chestnut burrs
escape over the ground—
so strong is the wind.[24]

[*Kyōka saizō shū*, vol. 5, Autumn 2, translated by Haruo Shirane]

---

22. This kyōka, written in praise of the Yoshiwara, the bakufu licensed quarter in Edo, is an allusive variation on a famous waka by Priest Nōin: "Coming upon a mountain village at nightfall on a spring day, I saw blossoms scattering in the echoes of the vesper bells." Akara transforms the image of the sound of the vespers in the evening, which had become associated in the classical tradition with the quiet loneliness of the mountain village and with the impermanence of this world, into a bright celebration of the pleasures offered by the women at Yoshiwara at night. Nōin's cherry blossoms become the beautiful female "flowers" of Yoshiwara.

23. As in many kyōka, humor is generated through the treatment of vulgar subject matter and homophonic wordplay: the word "loan" (*shakkin*) suggests "balls" (*kintama*), whose exposure is implicitly as embarrassing as that of debts, and *fundoshi* (loincloth) is a homophone for "year" (*toshi*). Particularly striking is the rhythmic, musical quality of the poem, resulting from the repetitive sounds of "u" and "a."

24. In this poem, the humor lies in the personification of the fallen chestnuts, which are fleeing the children.

HEZUTSU TŌSAKU

Hezutsu Tōsaku (1726–1789), the owner of a tobacco shop in Edo, is known mostly for his discovery of Akara (Ōta Nanpō) and for being one of the founding members of Edo kyōka, along with Akara and Kishū. He became a priest at the age of fifty-four.

On dawn cherry blossoms

yama no ha ni	On the crest of the hills,
hana ja kumo ja	"Cherry blossoms!" "No, clouds!"
to arasoi no	till the dawn sun rose up
naka e deru hi ya	to squelch the argument.
rachi wo akebono[25]	

[*Kyōka saizō shū*, vol. 2, Spring 2, translated by Burton Watson]

fūki to wa	Affluence—define it as:
kore wo nazuke ni	pickled greens,
kome no meshi	rice for supper,
sake mo kototaru	wine, one container,
kotaru hito taru	modest but never empty.[26]

[*Manzai kyōka shū*, vol. 14, Misc. 1, translated by Burton Watson]

YADOYA NO MESHIMORI

Yadoya no Meshimori (1753–1830), who ran a post station at Nihonbashi, studied kyōka with Akara (Ōta Nanpō) from the early 1780s and later became known as one of the "four kings" of kyōka. He helped edit *Wild Poems of Ten Thousand Generations* (*Manzai kyōka shū*) and became a noted kokugaku scholar under the name of Masamochi.

utayomi wa	When it comes to poets,
heta koso yokere	the clumsier the better—
ametsuchi no	what a mess

---

25. One of the well-known conventions of classical Japanese poetry was to visually mistake the white petals of the cherry blossoms for snowflakes. In this kyōka, this elegant confusion is turned into a debate that is finally resolved by the rise of the dawn sun, which makes clear that these are cherry blossoms.

26. After beginning with a small pun on *nazuke*, which means both "pickled greens" and "to name/define," the kyōka rides on a series of buoyant rhymes with *taru*, used to mean "to suffice" (*kototaru*), "a small container" (*kotaru*), "a wine barrel" (*taru*), and finally, "to be enough" (*taru*). This poem on knowing "sufficiency" (*taru*) reflects Tōsaku's own modest life.

ugokiidashite
tamaru mono kawa

if heaven and earth
really started to move![27]

[*Kyōka saizō shū*, vol. 12, Misc. 2, translated by Burton Watson]

KI NO SADAMARU

Ki no Sadamaru (1760–1841), a nephew of Akara and a bakufu retainer in Edo who eventually became a Tokugawa bannerman (*hatamoto*), began writing kyōka at an early age and was recognized by Kisshū.

On comparing impermanence to a fart

Sukashihe no
kieyasuki
koso aware nare
mi wa naki mono to
omoinagaramo

Though this body, I know,
is a thing of no substance,
must it fade, alas,
so swiftly,
like a soundless fart?[28]

[*Toku waka gomanzai shū*, vol. 6, Lament, translated by Burton Watson]

KYŌSHI

Pioneers of the early-eighteenth-century literatus (*bunjin*) movement, such as Gion Nankai (1677–1751) and Hattori Nankaku (1683–1759), turned away from the contemporary society that had disappointed them and entered instead the elegant and largely imaginary world of Chinese poetry and culture. These bunjin kanshi poets did not criticize the society around them so much as ignore and transcend it. Indeed, those following the Ogyū Sorai school, like Hattori Nankaku, had little opportunity to express their social or political dissatisfaction except through elegant Chinese poetry. It was in this context that an alternative consciousness, that of the "mad person" (*kyōsha*), emerged.

Not only did the "mad person" criticize and mock the society that deprived the individual of opportunity and freedom, but he also criticized and laughed at himself. This persona has a long history in Japan, going back to the notion of the *fūkyō* (wild poetry) of the Buddhist and Confucian traditions. Particularly

---

27. This kyōka, one of Meshimori's most famous, is typical of Tenmei-style kyōka in the manner that it destroys authority. The kyōka begins with a surprising inversion—"that poor poets are better"—and then proceeds to prove it by twisting a famous phrase in Ki no Tsurayuki's kana preface to the *Kokinshū*, which assumes that great poetry can move "heaven and earth."

28. Ki no Sadamaru gives a comic twist to a classical and Buddhist theme, the impermanence of all things. The solemnity of the last line (*aware nare*, or the sadness of it all) stands in comic contrast to the risqué metaphor.

influential in the eighteenth century, however, was the philosophy of the Wang Yang-ming school (Yōmeigaku), particularly that of Li Zhi (Ri Shi, 1527–1602), who wrote a commentary on the *Water Margin* (*Suikoden*), a noted Chinese vernacular novel, arguing that it was an expression of anger or protest against society. In turn, this view had an impact on the Kyoto school of Confucianism, which had become the main base for anti-Sorai thought. In the latter half of the eighteenth century, samurai intellectuals who considered themselves "mad" turned not to the elegant forms of expression advocated by the Sorai school but to a comic, antiestablishment form, that of *kyōbun* (mad or comic Chinese prose) and *kyōshi* (mad or comic Chinese poetry), two genres that, despite their roots in Chinese literature, became an integral part of popular *gesaku* (playful) literature.

"Mad" poet-intellectuals used the "mad" genres to express their frustration with and rage at society. The two pioneers of the genre were Ōta Nanpo (1749–1823), whose kyōka pen name was Akara and whose kyōshi pen name was Neboke Sensei (Master Groggy), and Dōmyaku Sensei (1752–1801), or Master Artery. Nanpo, from Edo, became famous for his humor and literary parodies, while Dōmyaku Sensei, a noted kibyōshi and kyōka writer from Kyoto, became known for his social criticism and satire. The publication of Nanpo's *Master Groggy's Literary Collection* (*Neboke sensei bunshū*), in 1767 and Dōmyaku Sensei's *Ballads for the Age of Great Peace* (*Taihei gafu*) in 1769 firmly established the reputations of both writers, who were still in their teens, and made them masters of the new genre in the Edo and Kyoto regions, respectively.

By the middle of the eighteenth century, the Japanese had naturalized the medium of Chinese poetry (kanshi), adapting it to their own tastes and needs. In the process, kyōshi—which concentrated on social satire, wordplay, and such low topics as farting, fleas, and itching—emerged as an anti-genre, standing in the same relationship to kanshi as the seventeen-syllable senryū did to haiku or the kyōka did to the classical waka. Kyōshi had a long history, which can be traced to Chinese poetry and medieval Gozan (Five Mountains) Zen kanshi, such as the kyōshi of the medieval "mad" monk-poet Ikkyū (1394–1481). Kyōshi, however, reached its high point in the twenty years between 1770 and 1790, especially in the Tenmei era (1781–1788), precisely when senryū, kyōka, and kibyōshi blossomed. Like senryū, which used humor as a weapon, kyōshi parodied high literature and humorously explored low topics that lay outside the bounds of orthodox literature.

DŌMYAKU SENSEI, MASTER ARTERY

Dōmyaku Sensei (1752–1801) was a low-ranking samurai from the Hatakenaka family, which served the Shōgoin Temple residence in the imperial palace in Kyoto. The Hatakenaka were *sangoku-san* (Mr. Three Koku)—an ironic, derisive nickname for low-class retainers with minuscule stipends. In the kyōshi

"Kyoto Minor Retainer" Dōmyaku mocks members of his own class for being arrogant while hiding their extreme poverty. In another kyōshi, "To Master Groggy, from Afar," published in 1790 under the title "Elegant Compositions by Two Masters" (Nitaika fūga), Dōmyaku describes his social upbringing and the life of dissipation that caused him to be thrown out of his house.

In "The Housemaid's Ballad" (Hijo kō), a poem in seven-character lines in the old style (koshi) included in Ballads for the Age of Great Peace (Taihei gafu, 1769), Dōmyaku describes the life of a young woman who has come from the provinces and, while working as a maid, gradually and increasingly visits the dangerous regions of the city. The poem is a sharp and humorous description of contemporary mores and urban social dangers, but it also has, like contemporary sharebon and kibyōshi, a satiric dimension, revealing the underside of society and implicitly criticizing those elements of it that have caused the housemaid to fall to these depths.

KYOTO MINOR RETAINER

Most of these minor samurai draw a stipend of three koku—
So how come they act so big?
From head to toe, they're a mass of unmitigated gall.
At the theater, they always get in—for free.

TO MASTER GROGGY, FROM AFAR

Priests make a brothel's flushest clients;
Among buddhas, Zuigu is foremost.
But I get a chilly reception at all the teahouses;
My bills have piled up into mountains.
Pleasures and reprimands jointly accumulate;
Relatives hold solemn family council to debate my case.
But I head straight for the brothels, make the long nights fly by—
Even by breakfast time, I'm still not home.
The day I'm disowned, whenever that may be,
I'll make my way to the East.
Just as I've reached the last word in looniness
I've happened to make the acquaintance of Master Groggy.

THE HOUSEMAID'S BALLAD

A green girl from the back country—employment was my quest.
I came up to the capital—not knowing east from west.

I only knew my dear auntie, who lives in Senbon, north.[29]
And thanks to her I found a job; she was my guarantor.[30]
A hundred coppers moving costs! My budget's lost, for sure!
My valise had one single quilted robe in it—no more.[31]
Sprout green it was, embroidered all with cranes and baby pines;
the sleeve mouths and sleeve linings were a scarlet rich and fine.
I'm honest and a healthy lass—the master's true delight!
On three days' bush-leave holiday I toured all the sights:[32]
to Gion, Kiyomizu, and Hongan-ji temple so blessed,[33]
to Atago, the Great Buddha, and Sanjō Bridge, no less.
The next day, then, I'm off again with Auntie for some fun:
I've heard so much about theaters—now I'm seeing one!
Those fellows grab and hurl themselves about—such dangerous spills!
They slash and hack away, one at another—gives me chills![34]
The fox Tadanobu is played by Onoe Baikō,
and the sushi maker's daughter—she's Nakamura Richō.
This Richō and this Baikō—both these actors are top-drawer;[35]
at next season's attraction each will show his stuff and more.
While heading home we rest a spell at Shijō riverbed;[36]

---

29. Senbon is a general designation for the area northeast of Kitano Tenmangu Shrine in Kyoto.

30. Her aunt provides a temporary place to stay and personally supervises her efforts to find a position—thus freeing the young woman from having to rely on temporary but costly lodgings or to pay exorbitant placement fees to unscrupulous job brokers. The young newcomer's aunt serves as her guarantor and negotiates the "warranty" to establish responsibility in the case of unsatisfactory performance, damage, or absconding.

31. Presumably, the quilted garment is hopelessly countrified in its color and decoration.

32. "Bush-leave" (yabuiri) holidays, usually granted for a few days in the middle of the First and Seventh Months, immediately after the busy New Year's and Bon holidays, were among the rare free days for a domestic servant.

33. Gion and Kiyomizu are still standard highlights of a tour of Kyoto.

34. Theater violence. It is possible that the heroine does not understand, at first, the nature of stage representation—it may be a stock comic situation.

35. In the kabuki play Yoshitsune and the Thousand Cherry Trees (Yoshitsune senbonazakura, 1747)—a title that echoes the Senbon residence of the newcomer's aunt—after the defeat of the Taira, Minamoto no Yoshitsune entrusts his beloved mistress, Shizuka, to the care of his valiant retainer Satō Tadanobu—who is in reality a fox drawn by the enchanted sound of a drum manufactured from its parent's hide. In the "Sushi Shop" scene, a humble sushi maker's son sacrifices his wife and child to ensure the safe escape of the hunted Taira general, Koremori. The sushi maker's daughter, O-Sato, is a character of secondary importance in the scene. Onoe Kikugorō (1717–1783), known as Onoe Baikō, was one of the most celebrated kabuki actors in the 1750s and 1760s. The kabuki actor Nakamura Kumetarō (1724–1777), known as Nakamura Richō, made his debut in Kyoto in 1735 and became famous for his portrayals of young women.

36. The Shijō riverbank. The location was famous for gaudy attractions and as a location for escaping the worst of the summer heat.

I'm in a daze! Kyoto's as posh, as swanky as they said!
From that day on, I scrubbed my face each morning as a start;
I want to wash away all country clay that's in my heart.
I try on eight-penny powder—makes your skin so nice and white.
"Plum Blossom" scented hair pomade—six ounces seems about right.
It's been some time now since I've had wheat rice or *miso* stews;
whenever I spot tea porridge it just gives me the blues.[37]
I've learned to smoke, can even handle little sips of wine—
invite me to your party, and you'll have the best of times!
Now I can chirp, "Oh, not *my* way!" and "Clown, go hike a mile!"[38]
I hum the puppet dying scenes in Kunidayū style.[39]
I flatten down the best I can my Kinshōjo coiffure,[40]
then tease out both my "lantern flares" as much as they'll endure.
I sport eight-inch-long hairpins—ones with tortoiseshell inlay.
What's that? Brass earwax scrapers? Oh, my dear, they're quite passé!
That plain white smock I took apart, retailored it, and dyed it:
now half of it's a darling "mouse" and half bellflower violet;
right in the middle is *his* crest—the crest of Ogawa Eishi.[41]
I wear the highest platform clogs with thongs so slim and lacy.
Nearby there lives a fellow, name of Chūshichi "the card";[42]
I asked him first for little loans—you know, when things were hard.
Sometimes he'd take me for a date, and where is it we'd go?

---

37. "Wheat rice" (*mugimeshi*) and salty "*miso* stews" (*zosui*) are robust, though unrefined, country dishes. "Tea porridge" (*chagayu*) is a sort of gruel flavored with tea dregs—a dish more suggestive of economy than specifically rustic.

38. These are fashionable expressions. *Sukan* is a prostitute's expression of distaste. *O, shoshi* is an exclamation of irritation at a patent absurdity.

39. The Kunidayū chanting style ultimately derives from the jōruri chanting style pioneered by Miyakodayu Itchū (1650–1724) in the 1660s. The sensual, inflammatory nature of the style— often known as *Bungo-bushi*—made it the ideal accompaniment for *michiyuki*, or lovers' suicide scenes. Restrictions—either instigated by moral indignation or sponsored by commercial rivals— finally culminated in a ban on Bungo-bushi in 1739. The implication here may be that the housemaid, inspired by extravagant theatrical productions, is daydreaming about a sensational, passionate double suicide.

40. Kinshōjo is the patriotic heroine of Chikamatsu's *Battles of Coxinga* (1715), the wife of Watōnai's Chinese ally, Kanki. The Kinshōjo "bun" inspired by this role and popular in the licensed quarters in the 1750s featured a thin protruding spindle of hair rising from the back of the head and an elongated "duck tail" at the nape. "Lantern flares" (*tōrōbin*), or flaring sidelocks, also become popular in the 1750s.

41. Ogawa Kichitarō (1737–1781), known as Ogawa Eishi, was a noted kabuki actor who became known from 1761 for his adolescent and male hero roles, particularly the down and out lover (*yatsushigata*).

42. Chūshichi was an epithet in the Kyoto-Osaka dialects for a glib or comical talker.

Off to the Nijō New Quarter or behind old Goryō.[43]
Two hundred coppers paid the rent, three hundred went for wine;
right after our night's tippling was the time to say my "lines."
The lines I fed him! Most of them were just my little scams.
But then Chūshichi ran out on me; the boy went on the lam.
Now since I've come to have a little money, just for me,
I wear crepe when I'm on the town; for casual wear, pongee.
The crepe and pongee range of silks seems easiest to wear.
Those Madras plaids from Ōme—oh, they're far too coarse to bear!
"But have you not heard?[44]
Your old dad in the country—long he's dwelt in poverty!
How can you prance with lofty airs, your days a boundless spree?
Miss, tell us this! We know your wage, precisely what you earn:
just thirty *monme*—yes, that's all—each semiannual term!"[45]

[*Taihei gafu, hoka*, pp. 18–20, 26–30, 67–68, translated by Andrew Markus]

---

43. Nijō New Quarter was an unlicensed pleasure district in Kyoto, immediately east of the Kamo River and south of Nijō. Goryō, located just west of Ponto-chō, on the west bank of the Kamo, was, like the Nijō New Quarter, notorious for its many cheap, unregistered prostitutes.

44. From this line, the poet or the spectator intrudes to criticize the housemaid directly for ignoring the welfare of her parents in the country.

45. The thirty *monme*, a relatively small sum for a half year's income, implies that the housemaid is living far beyond her modest income and probably is indulging in illicit side activities to subsidize her costly urban indulgences.

Chapter 13

LITERATI MEDITATIONS

The *bunjin* ideal was the Chinese-inspired scholar-artist literatus ideal which first emerged in Japan in the early eighteenth century. Because the bakufu system allowed for only a limited or restricted expression of talent, the bunjin sought liberation in the arts, particularly Chinese poetry, painting, and calligraphy. For well-educated clan officials like Gion Nankai (1677–1751) and Yanagisawa Kien (1706–1758), who resigned from their posts because they were unwilling to conform, the literati mode was an alternative lifestyle. But for commoners like Yosa Buson (1716–1783) and Ike Taiga (1723–1776), who came from more humble backgrounds, the literati mode also reflected a yearning for the cultural cachet embodied at the time in the Chinese tradition.

A *bunjin* (literatus) was someone who worked in several art forms as an avocation instead of a livelihood. A haikai master like Buson was a professional, although as someone who first turned to Chinese poetry and painting as an amateur, Buson could also be considered a bunjin. The bunjin also aimed for an ideal in which the various genres came together as one. For example, the objective of the bunjin painters was not realistically depicting objects or landscape but, rather, as in the Chinese tradition, capturing the elegance of nature and its constantly moving life force. Buson's media were haikai and the three Chinese bunjin arts: poetry, calligraphy, and painting. He also became a master of a genre called *haiga*, or haikai painting, a pictorial style that used minimal brushwork and light colors to create a visual effect analogous to the seventeen-syllable haiku in its economy and stress on the moment.

YOSA BUSON

Yosa Buson (1716–1783), a noted painter, literatus, and haikai poet, was born in Settsu Province (Hyōgo) in Kema, a farming village in present-day Osaka, where his father probably was the village head. Buson lost both his parents at an early age, but little is known about the rest of his childhood. Apparently he showed an early interest in painting and received instruction from a Kanō school painter. Then, at around the age of twenty, Buson moved to Edo and became a disciple of Hajin (1676–1742), a haikai poet who had established the Yahantei circle in Nihonbashi. Hajin had been a student of Kikaku, a disciple of Bashō and the founder of the Edo-za school to which Buson later had close ties. After Hajin's death in 1742, Buson left Edo and for the next ten years lived in various places in northeastern Honshū, working with Hajin's disciples and working on his painting. Buson—who assumed the pen name Buson in 1744—traveled to the Tōhoku region and occasionally returned to Edo where he probably met with Hattori Nankaku (1683–1759), a major kanshi and bunjin poet-artist. In 1751 Buson moved to Kyoto and then shortly thereafter, in 1754, to Tango Province (north Kyoto), where he spent the next three years practicing *bunjinga* (literati painting), also known as *nanga* (southern painting), and produced both historical and landscape paintings. In 1757, he returned to Kyoto, married, and changed his family name from Taniguchi to Yosa, the area from which his mother had come. By the 1760s, his talent as a bunjin painter had been recognized, and he eventually became, along with Ike Taiga, one of most famous bunjin painters of the Edo period.

In 1766, Buson formed, together with Taigi (1709–1771), Shōha (1727–1771), and others, the Sankasha haikai circle. In 1770, at the age of fifty-four, he became the head of the Yahantei school, succeeding his teacher Hajin, and became a haikai master in Kyoto. In 1771 Taigi and Shōha, who had long been his poetic partners, died in quick succession, but Buson was joined by such new, talented disciples as Kitō (1741–1789), Gekkei (1752–1811), and Chora (1729–1780). Beginning in 1772, the Yahantei group produced a series of notable poems and linked-verse collections; Kitō edited both *Dawn Crow (Akegarasu,* 1773) and *Sequel to Dawn Crow (Zoku Akegarasu,* 1773). Buson reached the peak of his poetic powers in 1777 when he composed "Spring Breeze on the Kema Embankment" (Shunpū bateikyoku), a new genre that combined Japanese and Chinese poetry. "Spring Breeze on the Kema Embankment," his masterpiece, focused on his longing for Kema, his birthplace. In the same year, he began writing *New Flower Gathering (Shinhanatsumi)*, which he initially intended as a memorial to his mother but which became a loosely connected prose and poetry collection. In 1783, Buson participated in the events com-memorating the hundredth anniversary of Bashō's death but fell ill soon after-ward and died at the end of that year at the age of sixty-seven.

The period in which Buson was active—from the 1750s to the 1780s—was the heyday of the bunjin ideal. Hiraga Gennai (1728–1779), Takebe Ayatari (1719–1774), Tsuga Teishō (1718?–1794?), Ueda Akinari (1734–1809), and Ōta Nanpo (1749–1823) all can be considered bunjin. But of these poet-intellectuals, only Buson was closely associated with the Bashō haikai revival, which took place in the latter half of the eighteenth century. The result, for Buson, was a signifi-cant cross-fertilization between the kanshi literati tradition and haikai—that is, between the Chinese and Japanese artistic cultures. One of the ideals of Buson's poetry and painting was the notion of *rizoku*, or "departure from the common," which was closely related to his awareness of himself as a bunjin. Although Buson was a great admirer of Bashō's poetry, his viewpoint differed from Bashō's in important respects. Unlike Bashō, who advocated "awakening to the high, returning to the low" (*kōga kizoku*) and sought "lightness" (*karumi*), or the poetics of everyday life, Buson advocated "departing from the common," an exploration of other worlds through Chinese literature and painting as well as the Japanese classics, wandering freely in a world of elegance and imagination that he found far superior to the life immediately around him. The difference between Bashō's "return" to the common or low, which was an acknowledg-ment of everyday life, and Buson's "departure," which was a rejection of con-temporary society, reflects a fundamental difference between the culture of the Genroku era, at the end of the seventeenth century, and the attitude of many late-eighteenth-century intellectuals.

Buson wrote in a variety of haikai styles. Some of the most striking elements are his realistic portraits of people, reflecting the influence of the Edo-za school; his fictional narratives; his ability to conjure up the atmosphere of a children's story or fairy tale; his playfulness and sense of humor; his painterly eye; his construction of imaginary, romantic worlds; and his heavy use of Chinese and Japanese classical sources as a means of drawing the reader into another world. More than half of Buson's hokku were composed at *kukai*—hokku meetings or parties where the topic was fixed or given in advance—leading to considerable richness in the use of seasonal words and topics. In contrast to Bashō, who frequently returned to his home in Iga, Buson was the poet of the lost home (never returning to his home village of Kema) whose poetry is pervaded by nostalgia, which is evident in "Spring Breeze on the Kema Embankment."

HOKKU

At the beginning of the Tenth Month, I went on a pilgrimage to Shimotsuke Province and described the scene before my eyes, in the shade of an old willow called the Yugyō yanagi.

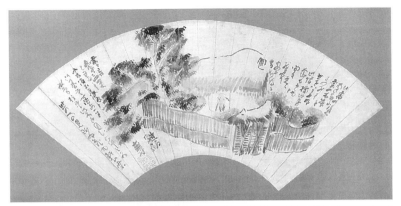

A *haiga* (haikai sketch), with the calligraphy and painting by Buson. The text, in flowing cursive script, is from Matsuo Bashō's *Narrow Road to the Deep North*, in which Bashō visits Kashin, who reminds him of the monk-poet Saigyō (1118–1190) and the prominent Buddhist monk Gyōki (668–749): "Under a great chestnut tree in the corner of the town, there lived a hermit monk. It seemed to me that his cottage, with its aura of lonely tranquillity, resembled that place deep in the mountains where Saigyō had gathered horse chestnuts. I set down a few words: 'To form the character "chestnut," one combines the graphs for "tree" and "west."' I have heard that the holy monk Gyōki perceived an affinity between this tree and the Western Paradise and used the wood of the chestnut for staffs and pillars throughout his life: 'Chestnut at the eaves—blossoms undiscovered by people of the world' [*yo no hito no / mitsukenu hana ya / noki no kuri*]." The recluse monk Kashin, compared by Bashō to the undiscovered blossoms of the chestnut tree, is in his hut facing the huge chestnut tree to the left. The soft colors, the abbreviated calligraphic strokes, the light humor, and the haikai text are characteristic of haiga. The painting was once part of a folding fan, as indicated by the folding marks. (Courtesy of the Mary and Jackson Burke Foundation. Photograph: Christopher Burke.)

yanagi chiri	Willow leaves fallen,
shimizu kare ishi	the clear stream gone —
tokorodokoro	stones here and there[1]

At a place called Kaya in Tanba:

natsugawa o kosu	Crossing a summer
ureshisa yo	stream — what fun!
te ni zōri	sandals in hand[2]

sararetaru mi o	The divorced woman
fungomude	stomps into the field —
taue kana	seedling planting time[3]

haru no umi	The spring sea —
hinemosu notari	all day long the waves
notari kana	rising and falling, rising and falling[4]

---

1. This hokku was composed around 1743 when Buson visited Tōhoku, the northeast region of Honshū. It is both a description of a natural scene and a haikai variation on a famous classical poem by Saigyō (1118–1190): "By the side of the road, alongside a stream of clear water, in the shade of a willow tree, I paused for what I thought would be just a moment" (*Shinkokinshū*, Summer, no. 262). Matsuo Bashō wrote about the same willow tree in his *Narrow Road to the Deep North*: "A whole field of rice seedlings planted — I part from the willow" (*ta ichimai uete tachisaru yanagi kana*). Having come to the place where Saigyō had written this poem, Bashō relives those emotions, and before he knows it, a whole field of rice has been planted. In contrast to Bashō's poem, which recaptures the past, Buson's poem is implicitly about loss and the passage of time, contrasting the situation now, in autumn, when the stream has dried up and the willow leaves have fallen, with the past, when the clear stream beckoned to Saigyō and the willow tree gave him, as it did Bashō, shelter from the hot summer sun.

2. This poem was composed between 1754 and 1757, when Buson was living in Kyoto. Summer river (*natsugawa*) can refer to either a river swollen from the rainy season or a cool brook. Here it is the latter, a stream shallow enough to walk across and delightfully cold on a hot summer day. Nakamura Kusatao and other modern haiku poets have praised this hokku for capturing a sense of youth in its purity. Kaya is a village near Kyoto.

3. Rice seedlings were transplanted into the wet fields (*taue*) by young women in a communal effort. Here a woman has been abandoned or divorced by her husband, probably against her will, and now, to her shame and embarrassment, she must appear in front of everyone and join in the seedling planting, perhaps even in her former husband's field. This poem, which was published in 1758 and is typical of Buson's narrative or fictional style, captures the emotions of the woman by noting that she "stomps into the field."

4. The "spring sea" (*haru no umi*) suggests a relatively calm, open surface. The light waves gently rise and fall, either out at sea or against the shore. The onomatopoeic phrase *notari notari* suggests a gentle swelling and subsiding, whereas the phrase *hinemosu* (all day long) implies a sense of time stretching out forever. This poem was published in 1762.

ayu kurete	You brought sweetfish
yorade sugiyuku	but didn't drop in—
yowa no mon	the gate at midnight[5]

inazuma ya	Flash of lightning—
nami moteyueru	girdled by waves
Akitsushima	the islands of Japan[6]

kusu no ne o	Roots of the camphor tree
shizuka ni nurasu	quietly moistened
shigure kana	by the winter showers[7]

yuku haru ya	The passing spring—
senja o uramu	resenting the anthology editor,
uta no nushi	a poet[8]

komabune no	The Korean ship
yorade sugiyuku	not stopping, passing back
kasumi kana	into the mist[9]

---

5. Buson composed this hokku in 1768 on the topic of "sweetfish" (*ayu*), a seasonal word for summer. It is a light, trim, clean fish with a subtle aroma and is prized as a delicacy. On a summer midnight, there is an unexpected knock at the gate: a friend leaves sweetfish, caught that day, and departs without stopping to talk. The poem captures the nature of the friendship— one in which the friend brings a perfect gift but does not stay to brag about or savor it—a friendship that harmonizes with the delicate, light nature of the sweetfish.

6. Buson composed this poem in 1768 on the topic of "lightning," a seasonal word for autumn. Lightning was associated in the ancient period with the rice harvest (*ina*). It enables the viewer to see—as if from far above the earth—the waves surrounding all the islands of Akitsushima, an ancient epithet for Yamato, or Japan. This poem is an implicit paean to the country's fertility and beauty.

7. This poem was composed in 1768 on the topic of "sudden winter showers" (*shigure*). The camphor (*kusu*) is a large tree with large branches protecting the trunk from the showers and causing the roots at the bottom to turn moist only after a long time, that is, "quietly" (*shizuka ni*). The hokku captures the passage of time, as the showers gradually dampen the camphor tree, which implicitly gives off a scent that matches the quiet atmosphere.

8. Buson composed this hokku on the topic of "spring's end" in 1769. "The passing spring" (*yuku haru*) was a classical subject that implied regret and sorrow at the slipping away of a beautiful season. The poet resents a poetry anthology editor (*senja*)—probably in the Heian or Kamakura period, when inclusion in an imperial anthology could mean immortality—who has failed to include a poem by the poet. The poet's feelings are embodied in the passage of spring, which is implicitly passing the poet by.

9. *Komabune* were the large Korean ships that sailed to Japan in the ancient period, bringing cargo and precious goods from the continent, a practice that had long been discontinued by Buson's time. Viewed from the land, the Korean ship appears at first to be heading for the port but then gradually disappears into the "mist" (*kasumi*), a seasonal word for spring. The mist covers the water, blurring the boundaries between the real and the unreal, the present and the

Tobadono e   Toward Toba Palace
gorokki isogu   five or six armed horsemen hurry—
nowaki kana   an autumn storm[10]

Fuji hitotsu   Only Mount Fuji
uzumi nokoshite   has been left uncovered—
wakaba kana   the lush young leaves[11]

botan chirite   The peony petals scatter
uchikasanarinu   falling on top of one another
ni san pen   two, then three[12]

ono irete   My ax sinks in—
ka ni odoroku ya   surprising scent
fuyukodachi   from the winter tree[13]

yuku haru ya   Spring passing
omotaki biwa no   the lute lies heavier
dakigokoro   in my hands[14]

---

past. The key middle line, "not stopping, passing back" (*yorade sugiyuku*), suggests a long passage of time, a sense of growing anticipation and then of disappointment. This poem was published in *Haikai shinsen* in 1773.

10. Buson composed this hokku on the topic of "autumn storms" (*nowaki*) in 1768. Toba Palace, which appears in medieval military tales as the site of political intrigues and conflicts, was an imperial villa that the retired emperor Shirakawa (1053–1129) constructed at Toba, south of Kyoto, in the eleventh century. The hokku, which has been compared to a scene from a picture scroll (*e-maki*), is representative of Buson's narrative style. The word *nowaki*, like the armed horsemen, suggests a sense of both turmoil and urgency.

11. This poem was published in 1776. The *wakaba* (young leaves) are the early-summer leaves that have reached maturity but still retain the freshness and vitality of spring. They seem to cover the whole earth, leaving only Mount Fuji, which is implicitly so massive that even the *wakaba* cannot cover it. This may be an aerial view.

12. Buson probably composed this hokku in 1771. *Botan* (peony), a seasonal word for summer, is a large, colorful flower that was highly admired by Chinese poets and painters and was imported to Japan in the Genroku era. The sound of the phrase *uchikasanarinu ni san pen* suggests the slow dropping of the large, heavy petals. Some readers believe that the peonies are in a flower vase, with the petals dropping on a table; others, that they are in a garden, dropping on the dark ground.

13. The speaker, thinking that the tree is dead, sinks his ax into the trunk several times, only to be surprised by its scent, which reveals life beneath its lifeless exterior. This poem was published in 1772.

14. In the poetic tradition, the passing of spring (*yuku haru*) brings regret. The speaker (probably an elegant Heian courtier) picks up a lute (*biwa*), perhaps starting to play a piece on the passing of spring, and feels that the instrument is heavier than usual, a heaviness that echoes the sense of spring (life) passing. Some readers have interpreted the lute in the courtier's hands as a phantom woman. Buson composed this hokku in 1774/1775.

ikanobori	A paper kite—
kinō no sora no	exactly where it was
aridokoro	in yesterday's sky[15]

Longing for the past:

osoki hi no	The long, slow days of spring
tsumorite tōki	piling up—
mukashi kana	so far away, the past![16]

samidare ya	The rainy season—
taiga no mae ni	before the great river
ie niken	two houses[17]

mi ni shimu ya	Piercing chill—
naki tsuma no kushi o	stepping on my dead wife's comb
neya ni fumu	in the bedroom[18]

kindachi ni	The fox disguised
kitsune baketari	as a dashing prince—
yoi no haru	spring evening[19]

---

15. Kites were flown by children on New Year's Day, and "kite" is a seasonal word for spring. The sky around the kite is not the sky of today but that of the past; that is, the kite or, rather, the sky around the kite takes the speaker into the past, not just of yesterday, but of many yesterdays, perhaps nostalgically back to childhood days. For Hagiwara Sakutarō (1886–1942), the poem implies that while time and space (represented by the sky) change, the kite, a kind of bearer of memory, remains unchanged, alone in the sky. This poem was probably composed in 1769.

16. "Long day" (osoki hi) is a late-spring day when the sun sets late and the day seems to last forever, reminding the poet both of the past, of youth, which seems so far away, and of the many springs and years that have come and gone since that time. This poem was composed in 1775.

17. Samidare, the continuous rains of the summer rainy season, have caused the river to swell, leaving the two houses on the bank in a precarious position, seemingly with only each other for protection. One modern commentator and poet (Andō Tsuguo) sees the two houses as Buson and his only daughter, who was recently divorced, leaving both in a precarious position. This poem was composed in 1777.

18. The widower, sleeping alone, accidentally steps on a comb in the dark, bringing back memories of his relationship with his wife. Mi ni shimu (piercing chill), a seasonal phrase for autumn, refers to the sense of loneliness that sinks into the body with the arrival of the autumn cold. This poem is fictional. Buson composed it while his wife was alive; in fact, she outlived him by thirty-one years. Buson composed the poem in 1777.

19. Yoi no haru is a warm, hazy spring evening, evocative of romantic or mysterious things, a mood matched by the mysterious behavior of the fox. Buson was fascinated by the strange nocturnal movements of foxes and badgers, as evident in his many verses on this topic and in his stories in New Flower Gathering (Shinhanatsumi). Buson composed this hokku in 1777.

shiraume ya	White plum blossoms—
dare ga mukashi yori	who from long ago stands
kaki no soto	outside the brushwood fence?[20]

Early spring:

shiraume ni	Amid white plum blossoms
akuru yo bakari	night turns to dawn—
to narikeri	the time has come[21]

[*Buson zenshū*, Kōdansha, 1992, vol. 1, translated by Haruo Shirane]

BUSON'S POETICS

PREFACE TO SHŌHA'S HAIKU COLLECTION
(SHUNDEI KUSHŪ, 1777)

As Buson states in his preface to *Shōha's Haiku Collection*, Chinese poetry was critical to achieving his haikai ideal of the "departure from the common" (*rizoku*). At that time, Chinese poetry and haikai were considered to be two separate genres. The former was high and refined, dealing only with elegant topics (particularly as defined by the Sorai and Nankaku schools of Chinese poetry), and the latter was low or popular, treating the commonplace and using contemporary language. Here, however, Buson argues that Chinese poetry and haikai are unified in spirit, that haikai should aspire to the ideals of Chinese poetry, and that through Chinese poetry, haikai can turn to common (*zoku*) or contemporary language while departing from the common in terms of spirit and content. The author of the poems in this collection, Kuroyanagi Shōha (1727–1771), was a wealthy merchant who had studied Chinese poetry with Hattori

---

20. This poem is deliberately ambiguous about time so that the second half can also be translated as "who long ago stood outside the brushwood fence?" The poem suggests that someone (perhaps a lover) once waited for the subject of the poem (probably a woman, in the poetic tradition of the waiting woman) outside the fence where the plum tree now blooms, who even now feels that someone is waiting there. The "white plum blossoms," a seasonal word for spring, conjure up memories of the distant past. Other interpreters have treated the white plum blossoms as a lover who is waiting outside the fence. The word *shiraume* (white plum) suggests the word *shiranu* (don't know), implying there is no answer to the questions posed. Buson composed the hokku in 1776.

21. Buson composed this poem, a death poem, in 1783, when he was sixty-eight. Plum blossoms, which are admired for their light fragrance, appear at the beginning of spring when the weather is still cold. The darkness of the cold night turns into the dim light of dawn amid the faint whiteness of the plum blossoms, which seem to embody Buson's spirit as it disappears into the light of dawn. The poem is also about the transition from winter to spring. Buson died on the twenty-fifth day of the Twelfth Month, the last month of winter, just before the arrival of spring on the first day of the First Month.

Nankaku in Edo, where he met Buson. Shōha (whose real name was Shundei) eventually became a follower of Buson's Yahantei school of haikai in Kyoto. The conversation recounted in the portion translated here from the preface to the collection of Shōha's poems is thought to have taken place some time before 1766.

I once met with Shōha at his villa in western Kyoto. When Shōha asked me about haikai, I said, "Although haikai greatly values the use of common language, it nonetheless departs from the common.[22] That is, haikai departs from the common while using the common. The doctrine of departure from the common [rizoku] is most difficult to understand. It is like the famous Zen master who said, 'Listen to the sound of one hand clapping.'[23] The principle of departure from the common is the zen of haikai." Shōha was immediately enlightened.

He asked again, "Your explanation of departure from the common is, in its essence, profound and mysterious. Doesn't it mean finding a way to accomplish the deed by oneself? Isn't there another way? Isn't there a quicker way to change naturally, to depart from the common without others knowing it, without knowing it oneself?" I answered, "There is: Chinese poetry. From the beginning you've been very skilled at Chinese poetry. You needn't look elsewhere."

Shōha had doubts and asked again, "Now Chinese poetry and haikai differ in character. And yet you tell me to disregard haikai and discuss Chinese poetry—isn't this a roundabout approach?" I answered, "Painters assume that there is only one method for departing from the common, that if one reads many books, one's literary inclinations will increase and one's common or vulgar inclinations will decrease. Students must pay attention to this. To depart from the common in painting, they must throw away their brushes and read books. In this case, how can there be a distance between Chinese poetry and haikai?" Shōha immediately understood.

[Translated by Jack Stoneman]

JAPANESE-CHINESE POETRY

One important result of Buson's interest in Chinese poetry and the bunjin ideal was the creation of an experimental poetic form that combined elements of haikai and kanshi. The three main works are "Mourning the Old Sage Hokuju" (Hokuju rosen o itamu), "Spring Breeze on the Kema Embankment" (Shunpū batei kyoku), and "Yodo River Songs" (Denga ka). These also can be regarded

---

22. Zoku is translated here as "common," but it also can refer to the vulgar or popular, as opposed to the refined and elegant.

23. Hakuin Ekaku (1685–1768), a Zen master, painter, and calligrapher.

as linked-poetry sequences in which verses (in the case of "Spring Breeze," eighteen separate poems) are linked to make one poetic sequence, as in haikai linked verse (but without its constrictive form). To later, modern poets, the Japanese-Chinese form seems to have foreshadowed the *shintaishi* (new-form verse) that appeared in the early Meiji period.

MOURNING THE OLD SAGE HOKUJU (HOKUJU RŌSEN WO ITAMU)

Although it was first believed that Buson wrote "Mourning the Old Sage Hokuju" soon after the death of Hokuju (1671–1745), when Buson was around thirty years old, scholars now believe that he wrote it in 1775, when he was fifty-nine, at the same time that he wrote "Spring Breeze on the Kema Embankment." The sequence, which was published posthumously in 1793, is told from the point of view of the narrator, who climbs a hill and listens to a pheasant mournfully tell of its experience, describing how the pheasant's close friend suddenly died (probably from a gun, the source of the smoke), an experience that echoes that of the speaker, who also has suddenly lost a friend. The pheasant's narration can also be read as a first-person narration by the deceased pheasant, which, like a ghost in a nō play, relives the moment of its own death.

> You left in the morning. In the evening, my heart in a thousand shards
> How far you have gone!

> Thinking of you, I wander in the hills.
> Why are the hills so sad?

> Among the yellow dandelions, shepherd's purse blooms white.
> But you are not here to see this.

> Is the pheasant here? I hear its mournful voice:

> "I had a friend. He lived on the other side of the stream.

> Eerie smoke rose and scattered, a strong west wind
> swept over the bamboo field, over the sedge moor,
> leaving nowhere to hide.

> I had a friend. He lived on the other side of the stream; today
> There's no sound at all."

> You left in the morning. In the evening, my heart in a thousand shards
> How far you have gone!

In my hut, I have no strength to offer a light to the Amida Buddha, have given no flowers. In the twilight, lingering in sorrow, a sense of awe.

Buson, Buddha's disciple, with great respect.

[*Buson shū, Issa shū*, NKBT 58: 258–260, translated by Haruo Shirane]

SPRING BREEZE ON THE KEMA EMBANKMENT
(SHUNPŪ BATEI KYOKU, 1777)

"Spring Breeze on the Kema Embankment," Buson's most famous long poem, consists of eighteen separate poems or songs that are linked to make one poetic sequence. The short introduction, which appears to be fictional and part of the poem itself, introduces the male traveler, the narrator who frames the whole poem. The poems are written in three styles, traditional hokku, Sino-Japanese prose, and metered lines of Chinese poetry, a mixture so innovative that the sequence was regarded by many twentieth-century readers as a precursor to modernist poetry. The separate songs are linked by association, as they are in haikai linked verse, of which Buson was a master, but they are also loosely unified by the narrative of a young woman's journey home, which Buson compared in a letter with a *michiyuki* journey on stage.

One day I set out to see some elders in the village where I was born. After I crossed the Yodo River and began walking along the high riverbank at Kema, I happened to meet a young woman who also was returning to her village. For several miles we walked near each other, and sometimes we turned and talked together. She was cute, already becoming very attractive. To commemorate our meeting, I composed eighteen songs that express her feelings and called them "Spring Breeze on the Kema Embankment."

> Three whole days off,
> she leaves Osaka, reaches
> the Nagara River
>
> Spring breeze—
> the bank goes on and on,
> her home still far[24]

---

24. The sequence begins with two panoramic hokku in the third person evoking a young woman returning to her village during a three-day break granted by her employers beginning on or around the sixteenth day of the First Month, in late February, a time when the weather is growing milder. The opening hokku is a wide view of the young woman leaving Osaka, while the second hokku is a closer view of a specific location north of the city. The young woman crosses the Yodo River eastward at the point where the Nagara River branches off from the larger Yodo, and when she climbs to the high bank on the east side of the Yodo, she feels a fresh breeze.

I went down the bank to pick fragrant plants,
but everywhere brambles blocked the way.
How jealous those thorns are!
They've ripped my robe and scratched my thighs.[25]

Rocks rising from the rushing water—
stepping on some, I picked fragrant parsley.
Thank you, rocks, thank you so much.
You've kept my robe completely dry.

The willow
by the lone teahouse
older now[26]

The old woman at the teahouse
looks me over, says very politely
how glad she is I'm looking so well.
She also likes my fancy robe.

Two men drink wine at the only table,
talking in the south Osaka way.
They pay with three whole strings of coppers
and, as they leave, invite me to sit down.[27]

---

25. The series now shifts to a verse in literary Chinese spoken in the first person, a form that continues in the next verse, also in Chinese. As the young woman nears the area where she grew up, the wind brings the scent of early herbs, and she remembers pleasures of picking them years ago, although she feels that the thorns are jealous—presumably of her great happiness at going home at last. She speaks to natural objects now with the same intimacy she once did as a girl.

26. The form shifts again to a laconic, scenic hokku in which the narrator suggests her feeling that a willow has changed since she last saw it.

27. The form shifts to Sino-Japanese prose in which the owner of a teahouse for travelers remembers the young woman and praises her for the stylish woman she has now become. The old woman's praise probably comes from sympathy, since she has known the young woman for years and is aware of the hard life she leads as a servant in Osaka. The young woman must wait at the small teahouse until two men from Osaka leave. They may be apprentices or, like herself, servants returning home on a short leave from the commercial district in south Osaka where they live and work. They speak in the language of south Osaka merchants (or perhaps the licensed quarter there), and they are feeling a bit rich at the moment, since it was the custom to give male servants monetary gifts before they went home. The men either know the young woman or salute her as a fellow returnee. Once a regular stopping place for travelers, there is little money or lively city conversation in the place now, only a few old houses that double as inns.

Old post town, two or three houses—
a male cat moans out for a mate,
no female comes[28]

From outside a hedge, a hen calls her chicks.
The ground outside is covered with grass.
The chicks try to fly up and over:
hedge too high, they fall—a third, a fourth.[29]

The road becomes three,
branching through spring grass—
the short way invites me[30]

Dandelions blooming in fives and threes,
the larger groups yellow, the smaller white,
just as they did three years ago
when I left along this path.

Softly she breaks off
a dandelion—from its short stem
white liquid[31]

Long, long ago . . .
my mother fills my mind.
Inside her robe,
at her breast, was another
very special spring.[32]

---

28. The form shifts to a hokku with very long lines of the type influenced by the Sino-Japanese phrasing that Matsuo Bashō, Onitsura, and others experimented with in the 1680s. The number of men and the number of strings of coins are linked to the number of houses, and the lonely cry of the tomcat echoes the conversation of the two, no doubt single, young men.

29. Outside the hedge of one of the houses, a hen calls in a very different way to her chicks, in Chinese verse. The mother hen's warm, loving call marks a turning point in the poem, and the young woman begins to yearn even more strongly for home. She has left behind the fast-moving, fashion-conscious world of Osaka, just as the female cat has left the male cat to his own yowling.

30. In this Sino-Japanese style hokku, an inaudible voice comes from the woman's memory: her mother is calling her to take the best path, a choice that brings back further memories of walking and picking dandelions and of leaving the area three years earlier to go to Osaka to work.

31. The white liquid that oozes from the dandelion stem is, in Japanese, homophonous with the word for mother's milk, and the form returns to a hokku, although one with long lines. The white liquid initiates another series of verses linked by new spring images.

32. The first and most basic spring images are the young woman's strong memories of spending

> Springs passed—
> older now, I work
> in Osaka
>
> White plum blossoms
> in a rich merchant's garden
> near Naniwa Bridge
>
> I've learned how
> men and women love
> Osaka style[33]
>
> I set out from my village three springs ago,
> leaving behind my little brother—
> I'm a tree that's forgotten its root,
> a plum branch grafted on another trunk.[34]
>
> As I near my village, spring deepens.
> I walk on and on, then even farther
> on the long, willow-lined embankment.
> At last I stop and start downward.[35]

---

several springs at her mother's breast. The image is probably to be taken literally, since children often were nursed for several years. Her mother's warm breast is a kind of utopian season unequaled by later seasonal springs. Here the traditional waka form (or perhaps a hokku plus a linked second verse, or wakiku) resonates with the young woman's early experiences. Eventually she had to leave her mother and go to work in Osaka in the house of a rich merchant. As she learned Osaka city life and its styles, she has also experienced physical love—literally, spring feelings—perhaps with a male servant in the large house where she lives and works.

33. In this song, consisting of three hokku, she compares love to a plum tree that is newly blooming in the middle of the First Month, in the garden of the house where she works.

34. In Osaka she has matured and learned to look attractive and has nearly forgotten her mother and brother, but as she nears home she suddenly feels she is a plum tree that has been taken away and grafted onto a distant trunk in Osaka. Something about her newfound sophistication and beauty now makes her feel artificial. In this song, two forms—a passage of Sino-Japanese prose and two hokku—have been grafted together to give the reader the sensation of moving back and forth between the two.

35. As the young woman comes even closer to her village, spring takes on psychological tones in this song in Sino-Japanese and feels to her even further advanced. In her mind the plums give way to more modest rows of budding willows planted along the high riverbank to prevent erosion. Their long limbs are no doubt swaying in the breeze, and their beauty will continue long after the plum blossoms have fallen. Since she feels spring has deepened, she may already be feeling again the warmth she once felt at her mother's breast. Her village is not very far from Osaka in

Raising my head, I make out my house in the twilight.
She must be leaning against the front door,
her hair white now, holding my little brother,
thinking, "This spring, surely she'll come again this spring."

Perhaps you know this hokku by Taigi, now dead:

Home for three days,
she sleeps again beside
her widowed mother[36]

[*Buson shū, Issa shū*, NKBT 58: 261–265, translated by Chris Drake]

HAIBUN

NEW FLOWER GATHERING
(*SHINHANATSUMI*, 1784, PUBLISHED 1797)

New Flower Gathering consists of a series of hokku and a prose section of short passages on a variety of topics. The prose section begins with Buson's discussion of poetry and then makes some comments on collecting art objects, followed by several accounts of the strange doings of foxes and badgers, such as the one translated here, continuing an interest found in his hokku.

The Badger

Jōū of Yūki acquired a second house and had an old man stay there as a caretaker. Even though it was in the middle of town, it was surrounded by trees and luxuriant with plants, and because it was a place where one could escape the hustle and bustle of the world, I myself stayed there for quite some time.

---

terms of physical distance, but her longing for home makes her journey seem endless. Both time and spring deepen, and finally at dusk she reaches the place where a path goes down the embankment to the village. In the following Chinese verse, she can almost see her mother and brother again, yet they are not quite visible.

36. The sequence shifts from the fictional narrator's songs to a hokku by Buson's late friend and fellow poet Taigi (1707–1771). The direct address to the reader breaks the fiction of a single forward-moving journey: the hokku is said to come from another poet now in the world of the dead. The shift indicates a movement from the daughter's acute visual imagination in the first seventeen songs to a tactile, bodily, and emotional level at which the daughter can sleep again like a child within her mother's dark, enveloping, loving "special spring." The Sino-Japanese address generalizes this experience to all readers. It has been suggested that Buson is also expressing his own prayer here for the soul of his mother and for the success of his daughter's marriage.

The old man had nothing to do there other than keep the place clean. One time he spent the long autumn night praying over his beads in the light of a single lamp while I stayed in the back room, working on my haikai and my Chinese poetry. Eventually I grew tired, and I spread out the blankets and pulled them over my head. But just as I was drifting off to sleep, there was a tapping sound on the shutters by the veranda. There must have been some twenty or thirty taps. My heart beat faster, and I thought, "How strange!" But when I got out of bed and quietly slid open the shutter to take a look, there was nothing. When I went back to bed and pretended to be asleep, there was the same tapping sound. Once again I got out of bed and looked outside, but found nothing. "How very strange," I thought, and consulted the old caretaker: "What should we do?" The caretaker responded, "It's that badger again. The next time it starts tapping like that, quickly open the shutter and chase after it. I'll come around from the back door, and it will probably be hiding under the fence." I saw that he was holding a switch.

I went back to bed and once more pretended to be asleep. Again there was the sound of tapping. When I shouted, "Aha!" opened the shutter, and ran out, the old man came out too, yelling, "Gotcha!" But there was nothing there, so we both got very angry. Even though we looked in every corner of the property, we couldn't find a thing.

This went on for some five nights running. Wearied by it all, I finally came to the conclusion that I could no longer stay there. But then a servant of Jōu's house came and said, "You will not be disturbed tonight, sir. This morning one of the villagers shot an old badger in a place called Yabushita. I know for sure that all that fuss and trouble was the work of this badger. Rest well tonight."

And indeed, from that night on, all the noises ceased. I began to think sadly that the animal that I had thought of as a nuisance had really offered me some comfort from the loneliness of my lodging. I felt pity for the badger's soul and wondered whether we had formed a karmic bond. For that reason I called on a cleric named Priest Zenku, made a donation, and for one night chanted the *nenbutsu* in order that the badger might eventually achieve buddhahood.

aki no kure	Late in autumn
hotoke ni bakeru	transformed into a buddha
tanuki kana	—the badger

A badger had come to the door to visit, and people said he made tapping sounds with his tail, but that was not the case. In fact, he had pressed his back against the door.

[*Buson shū, Issa shū*, NKBT 58: 279–280, translated by Cheryl Crowley]

TAKEBE AYATARI

Takebe Ayatari (1719–1774) was a noted haikai poet, kokugaku scholar, novelist, and bunjin painter. He was the second son of a powerful house elder (karō) in Hirosaki Domain (Aomori) and was probably groomed for a political and military career as a domain administrator. But a great scandal—apparently an affair with his sister-in-law—resulted in Ayatari's banishment from the province and the removal of his samurai status. For the next thirty-five years he traveled—teaching, writing, and painting. He first pursued a career as a haikai poet and teacher, began to study painting, and then, around the age of forty-five, turned to kokugaku (nativist learning), becoming a student of Kamo no Mabuchi (1697–1769). His involvement with nativist learning led him to press for the revival of the archaic katauta (5–7–7 syllable poem), as opposed to the 5–7–5 hokku. Besides Chinese vernacular fiction, kokugaku also inspired Ayatari to write two major novels, Tale of the Western Hills (Nishiyama monogatari, 1768) and Japanese Water Margin (Honchō suikoden, the first part published in 1773), in which he created romantic, imaginary worlds using a neoclassical style. Ayatari was later considered by Takizawa Bakin, the nineteenth-century master of the yomihon, to be the founder of the yomihon (reading books) genre. As a painter, Ayatari traveled to Nagasaki and studied under Chinese émigré painters, excelling in both bird-and-flower and ink landscape paintings. He also strove to expand his style of painting through the publication of several painting manuals (gafu), including Painting Manual of the Cold-Leaf Studio (Kan'yōsai gafu, 1762).

Although not as well known today as his talented contemporaries Hiraga Gennai (1728–1779), Yosa Buson (1716–1783), and Ueda Akinari (1734–1809), Ayatari was considered by observers at the time to be one of the best painters and writer-poets of his day. During the final decade of his life, Ayatari deliberately abandoned a lucrative career as a professional haikai master to devote his many talents to achieving the bunjin (literatus) ideal of scholarly and artistic detachment, of someone who refused to join the established sociopolitical order and instead pursued a life of painting, music, and poetry and interacted with like-minded friends. While traveling, Ayatari died at the age of fifty-five.

TALES FROM THIS TIME AND THAT (ORIORIGUSA, 1773)

Tales from This Time and That (completed in 1771 but not published in Ayatari's lifetime) is a collection of thirty-six short vignettes organized according to the four seasons. Ayatari wrote the vignettes in an archaic style that used the genre of Heian-period miscellanies (zuihitsu), such as Sei Shōnagon's Pillow Book, in a contemporary setting. Someone later edited the manuscript and in 1798 published seventeen of the vignettes with illustrations under the title *Random Stories on the Road* (*Man'yūki*). In his introduction to the first printed version of *Tales from This Time and That*, written in 1908, the noted Meiji novelist Kōda Rohan (1867–1947) praised the work as an unusually compelling collection of short stories with realistic scenic representations.

Walking the Neighborhoods of Negishi in Search of a Woman

"Walking the Neighborhoods of Negishi in Search of a Woman," from the "Spring" section of the collection, is an enigmatic look into one physician's efforts to find a mysterious woman he had been called on to treat for an animal bite. The vignette shares more with the work of such modern writers as Kawabata Yasunari and his depictions of male obsession than it does with eighteenth-century Edo fiction. Ayatari casts his story in an intriguing blend of contemporary language and an archaic, neoclassical style reconstructed from his study of ancient Japanese texts. It is this combination of a strikingly modern scene described in a hybrid written style that identifies this work as a prime example of bunjin prose narrative.

The New Year and the arrival of spring are so delightful in Edo, in the province of Musashi. The pine-and-bamboo decorations found throughout the city are unlike those of any other place. Whether they are great houses or small, their gates have truly become forests of greenery. On the expanses of the rivers, boats crossing back and forth show off their spring adornments, each according to its own means, providing the onlooker with a sense of serenity. Negishi lies to the northeast, away from bustling districts, and since it is a hamlet like a mountain's droplets, its water is pure in essence, and its dwellings are comfortable. The homes depend only on bamboo and brushwood hedges for protection and put up only rough-hewn woven gates as barriers.[37]

On the second day of spring in the new year, my friend invited me to accompany him and led me around the neighborhood composing poems as we walked. The day was gentle and pleasant, with a mist hanging among a grove of tall trees, while at the low riverbank, the willows were budding. Warblers also were singing. As we curved around a winding path, we reached a rustic-looking woven gate that opened onto the garden of a distinguished-looking residence. In the garden we were struck by a camellia tree in full bloom and stopped to look at the vibrant colors of the blossoms.

My friend stood there for a moment. "It must have been next door to this house," he said as he peered across but shook his head and muttered to himself, "It's not here either. This is really strange."

---

37. Negishi was north of the Kan'ei-ji monastic compound in Ueno, northwest of Asakusa's Sensō-ji, and west of the New Yoshiwara licensed quarter.

A hermit's residence in the idyllic hamlet of Negishi, from *Guide to Famous Places in the Edo Area* (*Edo meisho zue*, 1834–1836), edited by Saitō Yukio and his son Yukitaka and published by his grandson Gesshin (1804–1878), with illustrations by Hasegawa Settan (1778–1843). A hedge made of bound *kuretake* bamboo encloses the hamlet. A well-to-do retired man wearing a hemmed cap and a pair of black-rimmed glasses is playing *go* with someone smoking a pipe. A female servant greets a vendor at the thatched gate. The text (*upper right*) reads: "Perhaps because of its refined location in the shadows of Ueno, many cultured men of the city come to live in seclusion at the village of Negishi, known for its *kuretake* bamboo. Both the bush warblers that sing among the flowers and the frogs that live in the waters of Negishi carry a melody that is widely admired."

"What are you talking about?" I asked.

"It's a very mysterious thing. Let me tell you about it." Walking quietly along, he began explaining. "It happened last year on the twenty-third day of the Eleventh Month. There was a certain woman, not of this neighborhood, I had been seeing and in whom I had come to lose interest. That evening I was on my way to see her and to provoke her into a senseless quarrel, thereby gaining an excuse for breaking off our relationship. So I was hurrying along this road when as it grew darker, it started to snow heavily, and I could find no place to go for shelter. I am quite familiar with this neighborhood and was definitely next door to the house we see before us now. An elderly woman of great refinement came out and said, 'Where on earth could you be going? How do you expect to travel in this weather without a broad-rimmed sedge hat? Let me lend you a straw cape. Please come in for a moment.' Overjoyed at this offer, and since she did not seem at all like the mountain hag Yamauba, I followed her inside.[38]

"The house turned out to be swept and cleaned to a sheen, more than I had imagined from having seen it from the outside. She then said, 'Come this way.' This was totally unexpected, so I merely sat at the edge of the veranda and explained, 'I am in a hurry to be someplace right now, so I shall just stay here. Please lend me the straw cape.' She replied, 'Actually I have a favor to ask of you; please don't stay there. I beg you to come in.' An attractive young girl then appeared, took hold of my sleeve, and gave it a tug. I followed her without resisting and came to a room that I took to be the parlor. It gave off a very pleasant fragrance, and the walls were covered with skilled drawings of autumn pastoral landscapes.

"In the room I could vaguely see the form of a woman reclining behind some screens that had been set up. She seemed to be about twenty years of age, and with her pillow drawn up a bit, she was engaged in thoughtful conversation. Her manner of speech indicated high birth and refinement, and her voice sounded lovely. I could tell immediately that she was not like any ordinary person. I mulled over in my mind why someone of such apparent rank might be hidden away in this place but could not come up with a satisfactory explanation. I was about to inquire, but at that moment the elderly woman who had first led me in appeared, saying, 'The person you see before you is my mistress whom I have raised from childhood. It is not important at this point to explain to you just why we happen to be here now. I asked you to come in here because as my mistress was on her way for dawn prayers yesterday, she was attacked by a miserable cur. Although the people with her were able to chase the dog away, it bit one of her legs. She lost a great amount of blood and, from the shock of her ordeal, also fell into a faint. In that state of distress, she was finally placed on something and brought to this place. According to what people say, if someone gets sick from being bitten by a dog, it's almost always hopeless. For this reason, perhaps, she has a fever, and nothing we give her helps. She is just lying here as you see her. It is obvious that you are a physician, so please give her some medicine and some immediate relief for her distress.' She begged me fervently, and looking at the woman, I could see that her face was indeed flushed and that she was in some distress.

"I responded, 'This is certainly unexpected! Today of all days I am out alone without an assistant and without my bag. However, in case of an emergency, I always have with me in my breast pocket a small amount of medicine, which should be of some use here. How is her leg? I need to examine it.' 'By all means,' she said.

---

38. Yamauba, or Yamamba, is a well-known figure in Japanese legend, believed both to devour children and to wreak havoc on those traveling in the mountains, as well as to provide good fortune to those in need.

"She had the young people around the woman move away and began to raise up the bedding. The young woman's quilt was of Chinese silk on whose surface were overlapping patterns of cherry blossoms and maple leaves woven with gold thread in overlapping patterns, and on the underside was a layer of deep crimson. She rolled up the thick cotton batting at the edge and said, 'Please show him your leg.' With some embarrassment, the woman exposed her slender gam, which was pale with a translucent sheen. I saw that she was uncommonly beautiful, but since I could not detect any sign of a wound, I asked, 'Where did the dog bite you?' The elderly woman smiled and replied, 'She is shy about such matters. I shall raise the covers for you a bit more.' She then folded over the soft white-patterned fabric and pulled it up so I could see the full extent of the woman's thighs. I could clearly see the bite marks in the badly swollen flesh. 'This would have been a hopeless matter, just as you said, madam, if the bite had been from a diseased dog. This one, though, does not look like that, and it seems as though the bite was not too deep. Put on the medicine I have brought, and wrap up the wound. It should heal quickly. I would like to come back later and examine it again.' At this, everyone smiled. The woman then said, 'I hope we can depend on you from now on as well. This place is very inconvenient, so in two days we shall be moving to the home of my mistress's cousin in the Yanagigahara district of Kamita.'[39] She brought out an inkstone box with a richly lacquered design painted on it, and, rubbing a hard stick of fine ink into the stone's inkwell, pushed the box over to me. She then untied a long, deeply dyed, tasseled cord tied around another, similarly lacquered box, from which she took a sheet of thick *michinoku* paper, placed it before me, and withdrew. Watching the elderly woman go through even these simple motions made me regret the waste it would be to defile this ink and paper with my unsightly bird scratchings, but I swallowed my pride and wrote as boldly as I could. I announced to the people around me, 'I'd like to come back and look in on you again,' and prepared to take my leave, but they suddenly began to rush around, offering me something to eat. Part of me was tempted to stay, but the snow had let up, and so I rushed off without even borrowing the straw cape. Even so, as I was walking on the stones and through the snow, I found myself thinking about how fascinating the woman was. At the third hour of the cock [about 6:00 P.M.], I finally arrived with some difficulty at my lover's place.

"At that, she and I entered into a heated and unrestrained discussion, and

---

39. According to the *Edo meisho zue* (1:115, 119, 120–121), the Yanagihara (field of willows, referred to as "Yanagigahara" in the text) dike extended along the Kanda River from the Sujikai to the Asakusa Bridge. Centrally located here was the Yanagi-no-mori (willow grove) Inari Shrine. Foxes figure prominently in Inari lore. Kamita is an archaic form of Kanda. This area was only a few blocks from the neighborhood near Benkei Bridge where the author Ayatari lived for a time.

In this woodblock illustration from *Random Stories on the Road*, an edited version of *Tales from This Time and That*, the doctor, dressed formally in a crested black kimono and *hakama* (divided overskirt), discusses the condition of the mistress's leg while sitting in the parlor, which is lit by an oil lantern. A serving woman, offering him a large lacquered writing box, asks him to write down his instructions. The ailing mistress looks on from the adjacent room, reclining on an armrest. The sliding door, with an autumn landscape on gold leaf, decorative handles, and lacquered borders, suggests the resident's wealth, as does the patterned curtain stand (*kichō*).

the hour grew late, so I curled up and slept there that night. I returned home at dawn the next morning, and even though I now had a cold, the memory of that evening when I took shelter from the snow stuck in my mind. I waited for someone to come calling for me, but day after day passed, until finally the year ended without any word at all from the household. I found myself so fascinated with the young mistress that I finally decided to look for the house myself. That is why we are now here. Things were so confused that evening that I don't have any memory of her house. I do remember, though, the bright blossoms of the camellia tree in the garden next door and the fact that the roughly woven gate had a roof over it made of bark-covered wood. This house is clear in my memory, but the one next door is gone without a trace. I'm sure it's been only about a month since I saw it. How could a house disappear in that period of time — how could a hedge? That's what was on my mind as I stood here just now staring at this place. I couldn't have been elsewhere. If I had known this would happen, I would have made it a point to learn the name of the household or to find out more about its occupants. Damn!" He spoke with heartfelt regret.

I commented, "If you are so certain that this is the place, then why don't you go and inquire at that house with the camellias in bloom? If the house has been torn down and the people there have moved, then you should be able to find out where they've gone."

He agreed and, approaching the house, cleared his throat and called out, "There is something I wish to ask you." There was no response, however. He muttered to me, "Somebody should be home even on an ordinary day, and here it is New Year's when a person might come calling!"

"Maybe the master of the house is taking a nap. Speak a bit more loudly," I suggested.

He cleared his throat again and called out, "I have something to ask." Since still no one answered, and because the sliding door was partly open, he rattled it open the rest of the way, poked his face in the doorway, and yet again called out, "I've come with a request."

Suddenly an old lady's face appeared, and placing her fingers behind both ears, she shouted, "Speak up!" She was practically deaf.

Responding with "We beg your pardon" so loudly that it echoed everywhere, my friend inquired in detail about the house next door.

The old lady listened and said, "Today they went out, saying that they were going to call on the mansion for a New Year's visit. Since they took both of the other servants, only this old lady before you is left to look after things here." Deducing from this exchange that they had not yet moved, he repeated his question even more clearly.

She replied, "The master of this house is a lower official in the Bureau of the Storehouses. He has now left his house and his name behind to his heir and lives quietly here, as you see." She just could not hear him!

Figuring that he might get her to hear in spite of everything, he raised his voice to a high "A" in the *banjiki* mode and asked, "When was the house next door demolished? And the occupants—when did they leave, and where have they moved to?"

She gave the impression that she caught a little of what was said and started to flap her ancient tongue in reply. "That's why I shaved my head in the spring the year before last. And then I came here last fall."

This response frustrated us all the more; knowing that we could get nowhere with her, we just nodded over and over. My friend muttered, "Old coon dog, senile old woman!" but did not ask her any more questions.

Cracking a broad, unsightly smile, she exclaimed, "Why don't I bring you a cup of tea?" and stood, but since the entire situation seemed so ludicrous, we laughed as we took our leave.

At this point my friend decided that it must indeed have been the wrong place, so we searched about here and there looking for a garden in which a camellia would be in full bloom, and where the gate would be crowned with a bark-covered wooden arch, but however much we looked, we found nothing. In fact, we were scouring the neighborhood so thoroughly that people started to glare at us as though they suspected we might be burglars. I tried to put a bright face on this unfortunate situation by laughing and suggesting, "Just forget about it now. I'm so famished that instead of walking around looking for camellias, we should go to a place where they sell camellia cakes!"[40] We thus started out on our way back home.

"Having searched for it this much, it is so strange that we can't find the house. Since she was bitten by a dog, wouldn't it be more likely that her leg was covered with fur?"[41]

He insisted, "No, no, she had a human pulse; there's no doubt about that!" Since that time he has continued to live in longing for this person he now meets only in his dreams.

[*Honchō suikoden, Kiko, Mino nikki, Oriorigusa,* SNKBT 79: 460–465, introduction and translation by Lawrence Marceau]

---

40. *Tsubaki mochi* are rice cakes filled with bean paste jam and wrapped in two camellia leaves. They seem to have been a specialty of Edo and appear regularly in poems and anecdotes written around this time.

41. In other words, "Might you not have been tricked by foxes?"

Chapter 14

EARLY YOMIHON: HISTORY, ROMANCE,
AND THE SUPERNATURAL

With the advent of the Kyōhō era (1716–1736), the popularity of the *ukiyo-zōshi* (books of the floating world), a fictional genre developed by Ihara Saikaku, gradually began to decline, partly because of the increasing difficulties of urban commoner life and partly because of the scarcity of good writers. In addition, the Hachimonjiya, the central publishing house for ukiyo-zōshi, was publishing more and more historical fiction that borrowed heavily from drama and lacked the freshness of Saikaku's work. By the middle of the eighteenth century, the ukiyo-zōshi had been displaced by a new prose fiction genre, the *yomihon* (literally, reading books), which first appeared in the Kyoto-Osaka region. The term *yomihon* originally referred to books "to be read," as opposed to books "to be viewed" for their pictures, or *katarimono* (narrated or chanted texts), such as jōruri. Eventually, however, the word came to refer to a specific fictional genre that reached its first major peak with the work of Ueda Akinari, the author of *Tales of Moonlight and Rain* (*Ugetsu monogatari*). Written by bunjin writers in a unique Japanese-Chinese (*wakan-konkō*) style that merged classical and vernacular diction, these works were noted for their elegant, intellectual, rhythmic style and their allusions to Chinese and Japanese texts.

In contrast to the ukiyo-zōshi, which drew its material from contemporary society and current events, the yomihon looked to another world, that of either China or Japan's past, using history and classical scholarship, devising complex plots and characters, and laying the foundation for a new kind of extended

narrative. Early yomihon writers such as Tsuga Teishō (active 1748–1772), Takebe Ayatari (1719–1774), and Ueda Akinari (1734–1809) were particularly interested in Chinese vernacular literature. The Confucian scholars belonging to
Ogyū Sorai's school in Edo were especially enthusiastic about this newly popular study of the Chinese spoken language, as were the students of Itō Tōgai's
Kogidō school in Kyoto. Indeed, from the Kyōhō era onward, the Kyoto-Osaka
region became the center for the study of Chinese vernacular novels. Tsuga
Teishō, a doctor and Confucian scholar in Osaka, is generally regarded as the
grandfather of the yomihon. In A *Garland of Heroes* (*Hanabusa sōshi*, 1749),
he adapted the plots of Chinese vernacular stories to Japanese history or legends.
But he used a mixed Japanese-Chinese style that retained the style of the Chinese original, thus making for some awkward reading in Japanese. In 1757, the
first volume of a Japanese translation of the great Chinese vernacular novel
Water Margin (*Suikoden*) appeared; the entire novel was completed in 1790.
Scholars translated other works of Ming- and Qing-period vernacular fiction,
and Japanese readers also became interested in Chinese tales of the miraculous
from the Tang period. Ghost stories such as "The Peony Lantern" from Asai
Ryōi's *Hand Puppets* (*Otogi bōko*), which had been a minor genre within kana-
zōshi, suddenly became popular again, together with stories of the strange and
miraculous.

Before long, yomihon began to be written by scholars of *kokugaku*, or nativist
learning, rather than by scholars of Chinese studies. The result was a twofold
change: a rethinking of philosophical, religious, and ethical issues in these
narratives, and a new neoclassical, elegant style (*gabuntai*), which differed significantly from the mixed Chinese-Japanese translation style that Tsuga Teishō
used. Examples of this new kind of yomihon are *Tales of Nishiyama* (*Nishiyama
monogatari*, 1768) and *Japanese Water Margin* (*Honchō suikoden*, 1773) by Takebe Ayatari, who studied kokugaku with Kamo no Mabuchi. Both are written
in an elegant, neoclassical style. *Japanese Water Margin* led to a new kind of
extended narrative and inspired many imitations, including *Women's Water
Margin* (*Onna suikoden*, 1783), in which the hero is transformed into a female
hero in the late medieval period. These *Water Margin* variations, which were
written in the Kyoto-Osaka region, had a profound influence on later Edo-
based, early-nineteenth-century yomihon authors such as Takizawa Bakin and
Santō Kyōden.

UEDA AKINARI

Ueda Akinari (1734–1809), a waka and haikai poet, kokugaku scholar, novelist,
and man of tea, was born in Osaka. An illegitimate child, he was abandoned
by his mother when he was four and adopted by Ueda Mosuke, an Osaka
merchant. Even though his hands were crippled from the polio he had con-

tracted at an early age, he began his literary career as a haikai poet. He gradually began to write fiction in the Hachimonjiya format, depicting the lives of contemporary urban commoners in *Characters of Worldly Mistresses* (*Seken tekake katagi*, 1767) and other ukiyo-zōshi. At about this time, he met two literary figures who changed the course of his career. The first was Katō Umaki (1721–1777), a kokugaku scholar and a disciple of Kamo no Mabuchi, who introduced Akinari to classical Japanese scholarship and the complex beauty of classical Japanese literature. The other was Tsuga Teishō, who taught him the excitement of the Chinese vernacular novel.

As a consequence of his association with Umaki and Teishō, Akinari moved into a world of fantasy and history that resulted in *Tales of Moonlight and Rain* (*Ugetsu monogatari*, 1768 preface, published 1776), which transformed Chinese vernacular fiction into Japanese short fiction that had deep roots in both Japanese history and Japanese literary classics such as the *Man'yōshū*, *The Tale of Genji*, and nō drama. Writing in the kind of elegant, neoclassical (*gabun*) style developed by Ayatari, Akinari created an interior, psychological dimension that elevated the novel of the strange and mysterious to a new artistic height, creating a new kind of yomihon.

The heavy allusive use of both Chinese and Japanese classical sources in the fiction of Akinari and other early yomihon writers was aimed at highly educated readers. These writers also considered themselves to be literati (bunjin) and wrote for pleasure rather than for money, as the earlier ukiyo-zōshi writers had done. Akinari, who was also a waka and haikai poet, shared many characteristics with Yosa Buson, whom he knew. Both sought elegance (*ga*) in distant, imaginary worlds—especially China and the classical and medieval Japanese past—as opposed to the vulgar (*zoku*) world that they saw around them. This bunjin consciousness largely disappeared in the Bunka-Bunsei era (1804–1830) with the late yomihon writers Takizawa Bakin and Santō Kyōden, professional authors who wrote to attract a mass audience and sell to publishers.

In 1771, Akinari lost his property and home in a fire and decided to become a doctor. Five years later, at the age of forty-two, he returned to Osaka, established a medical practice, and published *Tales of Moonlight and Rain*. In the following years he published studies of *The Tale of Genji* and other Japanese classical literature and began a fierce debate with Motoori Norinaga (1730–1801), a leading kokugaku scholar from Ise. At the age of fifty-four, because of illness, Akinari retired from his medical practice and moved to Kyoto, where he often met with Ozawa Roan (1723–1801), a noted waka poet, and others. Akinari's last years were marked by a stream of publications on the study of Japanese language, Japanese literary texts, and historical issues. Today, however, he is better known for his fiction, especially *Tales of Moonlight and Rain* and *Tales of Spring Rain* (*Harusame monogatari*, 1808?), the latter written at the end of his career. Both have had a profound influence on modern writers such as Satō Haruo and Mishima Yukio. Akinari died in Kyoto in 1809.

TALES OF MOONLIGHT AND RAIN (*UGETSU MONOGATARI*, 1776)

Tales of Moonlight and Rain, which was published under the name Senshi Kijin, consists of nine stories, each of which draws from Chinese and Japanese sources, particularly *New Tales of Lamplight* (*Jiandeng xinhua*, J. *Sentō shinwa*, ca. 1378), a Ming collection of classical short stories of the supernatural, and *San yan* (J. *Sangen*), three late-Ming (early seventeenth century) anthologies of Chinese vernacular short stories. "The Chrysanthemum Vow" (Kikuka no chigiri), the first story included here, is partly adapted from "Fan Juqing's Eternal Friendship," a vernacular tale in *Old and New Stories* (*Gujin xiaoshuo*, J. *Kokin shōsetsu*, 1620–1621), one of the *San yan*.[1] "The Reed-Choked House" (Asaji ga yado), which follows, is based on a tale in *New Tales for Lamplight*.[2] The model for "A Serpent's Lust" (Jasei no in), the third story, is "Madame White Forever Buried at Thunder Peak Pagoda," a vernacular tale in *Warning Words to Penetrate the Age* (*Jingshi tongyan*, J. *Keisei tsūgon*, 1625), one of the *San yan* anthologies.[3] To some modern readers, these three short stories may appear to be no more than Chinese adaptations with minor alterations in name and setting. Edo readers, however, did not regard imitation to be a lesser art. In fact, stories had more value if they were old or came from China, so imitation was encouraged and accepted as a form of creativity. Accordingly, these stories are thought to be particularly interesting for the subtle manner in which Akinari weaves Japanese images, texts, and history into the original Chinese narrative. In "The Chrysanthemum Vow," for example, Akinari transforms a Chinese tale of the supernatural into a samurai tale of loyalty, love, and revenge.

Akinari sets each tale in the historical past. "The Chrysanthemum Vow" takes place in the late fifteenth century, after the Ōnin Wars (1467–1477), when strong local leaders challenged the authority of distant lords. The setting of "The Reed-Choked House" is the mid-fifteenth century, when Uesugi Noritada drove Ashikaga Shigeuji (1438–1497) from Kamakura and created chaos in the east. Finally, "A Serpent's Lust" is a story about the aristocratic Heian period. But instead of simply placing the Chinese story in a historically accurate Japanese setting, as Tsuga Teishō had done, Akinari took great care to use locales with rich historical and literary associations, such as Kumano and Yoshino in "A Serpent's Lust." "The Reed-Choked House," for example, ends with a reference to the *Man'yōshū*, to the story of Tenkona of Mama, where the story takes place. In this manner, Akinari was able to generate a highly romantic mood for the

---

1. For an English translation of "Fan Juqing's Eternal Friendship," see John Lyman Bishop, *The Colloquial Short Story in China: A Study of the San Yen Collections* (Cambridge, Mass.: Harvard University Press, 1956).

2. A Japanese adaptation (Yūjo miyagino) of the Chinese source also appears in Asai Ryōi's seventeenth-century *Hand Puppets* (*Otogi bōko*, 1666).

3. For an English translation of "Bai niangzi," the Chinese source for "A Serpent's Lust," see Diana Yu, trans., "Eternal Prisoner Under the Thunder Peak Pagoda" in *Traditional Chinese Stories: Themes and Variations*, ed. Y. W. Ma and Joseph S. M. Lau (New York: Columbia University Press, 1978), pp. 355–378.

unexpected encounter with the supernatural, which in turn allowed him to express his own deeper desires, fears, and sense of defeat and victimization.

Akinari also used the structure of medieval nō drama to create similar effects. The structure of "The Chrysanthemum Vow," for example, is like that of a warrior play (*shuramono*) in which the dead warrior returns as a ghost to tell of his past. "The Reed-Choked House," which focuses on the poetic motif of the waiting woman, is similar to a woman play like *Wind in the Pines* (*Matsukaze*) or *Well Curb* (*Izutsu*), in which a woman waits in vain for a man who has promised to return, or like *Fulling Block* (*Kinuta*), in which a woman dies from illness and longing and her husband hurries home, only to encounter the spirit of his dead wife. "A Serpent's Lust" resembles a demon play such as *Lady Aoi* (*Aoi no ue*) or *Dōjōji Temple* (*Dōjōji*) in which a traveler-priest meets a person of the village who later appears in her true form as a serpent or an evil spirit, which must be pacified by the traveler-priest. The modern film director Mizoguchi Kenji (1898–1956) borrowed from "The Reed-Choked House" and "A Serpent's Lust" as well as this nō framework to create a film masterpiece entitled *Ugetsu monogatari* (1953).

The Chrysanthemum Vow

Lush and green is the willow in spring; do not plant it in your garden. In friendship, do not bond with a shallow man. Although the willow comes into leaf early, will it withstand the first winds of autumn? The shallow man is quick to make friends and as quick to part. Year after year the willow brightens in the spring, but a shallow man will not visit again.

In the province of Harima, in the post town of Kako,[4] lived a Confucian scholar named Hasebe Samon. Content with an upright life of poverty, he abhorred the encumbrance of possessions, except for the books that he made his companions. With him was his elderly mother, as virtuous as the mother of Mencius. She worked steadily, twisting and spinning thread to support Samon's desire for learning. He had a younger sister, too, who was provided for by the Sayo clan, of the same town. The Sayos had great wealth. Admiring the sagacity of the Hasebe mother and son, they took the sister as a bride, thus becoming family, and often would send goods to Samon and his mother. Insisting that they could not trouble others for their own sustenance, Samon and his mother never accepted the gifts.

One day Samon was visiting a man of the same town, talking with him of matters ancient and contemporary, when just as the conversation was gaining momentum, he heard a sad moaning from the other side of the wall. He questioned his host, who replied, "The man seems to be from someplace west of

---

4. Kako (on the Inland Sea in Hyōgo Prefecture) is about sixty-five miles west of Kyoto, on the San'yō Highway.

here. He asked for a night's lodging, saying that he had fallen behind his traveling companions. He appeared to me to be a man of quality, a fine samurai, and so I allowed him to stay. That night he was seized by a violent fever that made it difficult for him even to rise by himself, and so taking pity on him, I have let him stay these three or four days. I am not sure where he is from, however, and think I might have made a terrible mistake. I do not know what to do." Samon said, "A sad story indeed. Your misgivings are understandable, of course, but a fever must be especially distressing to a man who takes ill on a journey, far from everyone he knows. I should like to have a look at him." His host restrained him: "I have heard that such diseases can spread and afflict others, and so I have forbidden everyone in my household to go in there. You must not put yourself in danger by going to him." With a smile, Samon replied, "Life and death are a matter of Destiny.[5] What disease will spread to another person? It is the ignorant who say such things; I do not believe them." With this he opened the door and went in. Looking at the man, he saw that his host had not been mistaken—this was no ordinary person, and the illness appeared to be grave: his face was yellow; his skin was dark and gaunt; and he lay in agony on an old quilt. Looking affably at Samon he said, "Give me a cup of hot water, if you would." Samon went to his side. "Have no fear, sir, I shall help you," he said. Consulting his host, he selected some medicines and, by himself, determined the dosage and prepared a decoction, which he gave to the man to drink. He also had him eat some rice porridge. In short, he cared for the man with extraordinary kindness, as though he were nursing his own brother.

The samurai was moved to tears by Samon's warm compassion. "That you should be so kind to me, a complete stranger. . . . Even if I die, I will show my gratitude," he said. Samon comforted him: "You must not use fainthearted words. Generally this disease has a certain term; once it has run its course, your life will no longer be in danger. I shall come every day to look after you," he vowed with all sincerity. Samon cared for the man devotedly, and the illness gradually abated. Feeling quite refreshed, the man thanked his host warmly and, esteeming Samon for his unobtrusive kindness, inquired into his vocation and then related his own circumstances: "I am from the village of Matsue, in the province of Izumo, and my name is Akana Sōemon. Since I have some slight understanding of military texts, the master of Tomita Castle, En'ya Kamonnosuke, employed me as his tutor.[6] During that time, I was sent as a secret

---

5. Confucius, *Analects* (12:5): "Sima Niu appeared worried, saying, 'All men have brothers. I alone have none.' Zi Xia said, 'I have heard it said: life and death are a matter of Destiny; wealth and honor depend on Heaven. The gentleman is reverent and does nothing amiss, is respectful towards others and observant of the rites, and all within the Four Seas are his brothers. What need is there for the gentleman to worry about not having any brothers?'" (*The Analects*, trans. D. C. Lau [Harmondsworth: Penguin Books, 1979], p. 113).

6. Matsue, Izumo, in Shimane Prefecture, is on the Japan Sea coast about 125 miles west-

The surprise attack on Tomita Castle. From the 1776 edition. (From NKBZ 48, *Hanabusa sōshi, Nishiyama monogatari, Ugetsu monogatari, Harusame monogatari*, by permission of Shōgakukan)

envoy to Sasaki Ujitsuna, in Ōmi. While I was staying there, the former master of Tomita Castle, Amako Tsunehisa, enlisting the support of the Nakayamas, launched a surprise New Year's Eve attack and captured the castle. Lord Kamonnosuke was among those killed.[7] Since Izumo was, properly speaking, a Sasaki domain, and En'ya the administrator, I urged Ujitsuna to join the Mizawa and Mitoya clans and overthrow Tsunehisa. Despite his formidable appearance, Ujitsuna was in fact a coward and a fool—far from carrying out my proposal, he ordered me to stay in his domain. Seeing no point in remaining there, I slipped away by myself and started for home, only to be stricken by this disease and forced against my will to impose on you, sir. Your kindness is more than I deserve. I shall devote the rest of my life to repaying you." Samon responded, "It is only human nature to help someone in distress.[8] I have done

---

northwest of Kakogawa. "Akana" survives as a place- and family name in the region, but the chronicles make no mention of an Akana Sōemon. The impressive ruins of Toda ("Tomita" is Akinari's unorthodox reading) Castle can still be seen in Shimane Prefecture.

7. En'ya Kamonnosuke, Sasaki Ujitsuna, and Amako Tsunehisa all lived in the fifteenth century. The attack on Toda Castle began on the last day of the Twelfth Month of 1485. Ōmi today is in Shiga Prefecture.

8. This sentiment derives from one of the most famous passages in the *Mencius* (2.A.6.): "Mencius said, 'No man is devoid of a heart sensitive to the suffering of others. . . . Suppose a

nothing to earn your very gracious thanks. Please stay longer and recuperate." Taking strength from the sincerity of Samon's words, Akana stayed for some days, and his health returned almost to normal.

During this time, thinking what a good friend he had found, Samon spent his days and nights with Akana. As they talked together, Akana began to speak hesitantly of various Chinese thinkers, regarding whom his questions and understanding were exceptional, and on military theory he spoke with authority. Finding that their thoughts and feelings were in harmony on every subject, the two were filled with mutual admiration and joy, and finally they pledged their brotherhood. Being the elder by five years, Akana, in the role of older brother, accepted Samon's expressions of respect and said to him, "Many years have passed since I lost my father and mother. Your aged mother is now my mother, and I should like to pay my respects to her anew. I wonder if she will take pity on me and agree to my childish wish." Samon was overjoyed. "My mother has always lamented that I was alone. Your heartfelt words will give her a new lease on life when I convey them to her." With this he took Akana to his house, where his mother greeted them joyfully: "My son lacks talent, his studies are out of step with the times, and so he has missed his chance to advance in the world. I pray that you do not abandon him but guide him as his elder brother." Akana bowed deeply and said, "A man of character values what is right. Fame and fortune are not worthy of mention. Blessed with my honored mother's love, and receiving the respect of my wise younger brother—what more could I desire?" Rejoicing, he stayed for some time.

Although they had flowered, it seemed, only yesterday or today, the cherry blossoms at Onoe had scattered, and waves rising with a refreshing breeze proclaimed that early summer had arrived.[9] Akana said to Samon and his mother, "Since it was to see how things stand in Izumo that I escaped from Ōmi, I should like to go down there briefly and then come back to repay your kindness humbly as a servant living on bean gruel and water.[10] Please allow me

---

man were, all of a sudden, to see a young child on the verge of falling into a well. He would certainly be moved to compassion, not because he wanted to get in the good graces of the parents, nor because he wished to win the praise of his fellow villagers or friends, nor yet because he disliked the cry of the child. From this it can be seen that whoever is devoid of the heart of compassion is not human, whoever is devoid of the heart of shame is not human, whoever is devoid of the heart of courtesy and modesty is not human, and whoever is devoid of the heart of right and wrong is not human'" (*Mencius*, trans. D. C. Lau [Harmondsworth: Penguin Books, 1970], pp. 82–83).

9. Alludes to a poem composed in 1171 by Priest Gen'yū: "The blossoms at Onoe will have scattered in the spring breeze—waves lap at the row of cherries here on Takasago shore" (*Fuboku wakashō*, vol. 25, no. 94).

10. This hyperbolic expression of filial devotion derives from a line attributed to Confucius in the *Li Ji* (Book of Rites): "To sip bean gruel and drink water, and to do so joyfully—this is what I call filial devotion."

to take my leave for a time." Samon said, "If it must be so, my brother, when will you return?" Akana said, "The months and days will pass quickly. At the latest, I shall return before the end of this autumn." Samon said, "On what day of autumn shall I expect you? I beg you to appoint the time." Akana said, "Let us decide, then, that the Chrysanthemum Festival, the ninth day of the Ninth Month, shall be the day of my return." Samon said, "Please be certain not to mistake the day. I shall await you with a sprig of blossoming chrysanthemum and poor wine."[11] Mutually they pledged their reunion and lamented their separation, and Akana returned to the west.

The ever-renewing months and days sped by; the berries colored on the lower branches of the oleaster; and the wild chrysanthemum in the hedge put out brilliant blossoms as the Ninth Month arrived. On the ninth day, Samon rose earlier than usual, swept the mats of his grass hut,[12] placed two or three sprigs of yellow and white chrysanthemums in a small vase, and emptied his purse to provide wine and food. His aged mother said, "I have heard that Izumo, the Land of Eight Clouds, lies far to the north of the mountains, more than one hundred *ri* from here, and so we cannot be sure that he will arrive today. It would not be too late if you made your preparations when you see that he has come." Samon said, "Being a samurai of honor, Akana certainly will not break his vow. I am ashamed at what he would think if he should find me rushing to get ready only after I had seen him." Buying fine wine and cooking some fish, he prepared them in the kitchen.

On this day, the sky was clear and cloudless in every direction, and many groups of travelers appeared, talking as they went: "So-and-so enjoys good weather today as he enters the capital, an omen that our merchandise will fetch a good profit," said one as he passed. A samurai in his fifties said to his companion, a man in his twenties and wearing the same attire: "The weather is so good, the sea so calm. If we had hired a boat at Akashi and set out at dawn,[13] we would now be approaching the harbor at Ushimado Straits. You youngsters waste money with your timidity." The other soothed him, saying, "I should think anyone would hesitate to cross here. Our lord had a terrible time, according to his attendants, crossing from Azukijima to Murozu on his way up to the capital. Do not be angry. I shall treat you to some *soba* noodles when we reach Uogahashi." They moved on out of sight. A packhorse man said angrily, "Are you dead, you nag? Open your eyes." Pushing the packsaddle back into place, he drove the horse on. Noon passed, too, but the one awaited had not come. As the sun sank in the west, the travelers' steps quickened in their search

---

11. "Poor wine" is an expression of humility.

12. "Grass hut" signifies a humble dwelling and is not to be taken literally.

13. Alludes to a poem by Mansei: "To what shall I compare the world? Like a ship that rows out at dawn and vanishes, leaving no wake" (*Man'yōshū*, no. 351).

for lodging. Samon saw them, but his gaze was fixed on the distance, and he felt something like intoxication.

Samon's aged mother called to him: "Although the man's heart be not fickle like autumn, is it only today that the hue of the chrysanthemum is rich and warm?[14] If he is sincere about returning here, what reason have you to reproach him, even though the gentle rains of early winter fall? Come inside, lie down, and wait again tomorrow." Unable to disobey, Samon reassured his mother and asked her to retire first, and then just in case, he stepped out through the door and looked again. The Milky Way shone faintly; the solitary moon cast its light on him alone; a watchdog's bark reached him clearly from the distance; and the waves on the shore seemed to crash at his very feet. As the moon set behind the hills and its light faded from the sky, he thought it time to go inside and was about to shut the door behind him when he glimpsed a figure in the shadows, moving toward him with the wind. Doubting his eyes, he looked again. It was Akana Sōemon.

Samon's heart leapt with joy. "I have been waiting for you since early this morning. How delighted I am that you have kept your pledge! Here, please come in," he said, but Akana merely nodded and did not speak. Samon led him to the south window and seated him there. "Since you were so late, my brother, Mother grew weary of waiting. 'He will come tomorrow,' she said, and went into her bedroom. I shall go to waken her." Akana stopped him with a shake of the head. Still he said nothing. Samon said, "You have traveled day and night; your heart must be weary and your legs tired. Please have a cup of saké and rest." He warmed the saké, arranged some dishes of food, and served them; but Akana covered his face with his sleeve, as if to avoid a foul smell. Samon said, "This is simple, homemade fare, inadequate to welcome you properly, but I prepared it with all my heart. Please do not refuse it." Akana still did not reply. Heaving a long sigh, he paused, then finally spoke. "My brother, what reason could I have to decline your heartfelt hospitality? I lack the words to deceive you, and so I shall tell the truth. You must not be startled. I am not a man of this world. A filthy ghost has taken this form briefly to appear before you."

Samon was astounded. "What makes you say this monstrous thing, my brother? I am certain that I have not been dreaming." Akana said, "Parting with you, I returned to my native place. Most of the people there had submitted to Tsunehisa's authority; no one remembered En'ya's kindness. I called on my cousin, Akana Tanji, at Tomita Castle. He explained the advantages and disadvantages and arranged for me to have an audience with Tsunehisa. Tentatively accepting my cousin's advice, I observed Tsunehisa's conduct closely and found that even though he is a man of great courage who trains his troops well,

---

14. Alludes to a poem by Sagami: "When I saw the bush clover's lower leaves change color, I knew before all else the fickle heart of man in autumn" (*Shinkokinshū*, no. 1352).

he is jealous and suspicious in his dealings with men of learning and as a consequence confides in no one and has no retainers willing to give their lives for him. I saw no point in lingering there, and so explaining my chrysanthemum vow with you, asked for leave to go. But Tsunehisa looked displeased and ordered Tanji not to let me out of the castle. This state of affairs continued until today. Imagining how you would regard me if I broke my pledge, I pondered my options but found no way to escape. As the ancients said, although a man cannot travel a thousand *ri* in one day, a spirit can easily do so. Recalling this, I fell on my sword and tonight rode the dark wind from afar to arrive in time for our chrysanthemum tryst. Please understand my feelings and take pity on me." As he finished speaking, his eyes seemed to fill with tears. "Now we part forever. Please serve our mother faithfully." With this, he rose from his seat and faded from sight.

In a panic, Samon tried to stop him, but blinded by the dark wind, he could not tell where Akana had gone. Falling to his knees and then on his face, he began to wail loudly. His mother, startled from sleep, came to look and found Samon lying on the floor among the saké flasks and plates of fish that he had arranged by the seat of honor. Hurrying to help him rise, she asked, "What is wrong?" But he only sobbed quietly, saying nothing. His mother spoke again: "If you resent your brother Akana now for breaking his pledge, you will have nothing to say if he comes tomorrow. Are you such a child that you can be so foolish?" Thus she admonished and encouraged him. Finally Samon replied: "My brother came tonight to fulfill our chrysanthemum pledge. When I welcomed him with saké and food, he refused them again and again and said, 'For this and that reason, I was about to break our pledge, and so I fell on my sword and came these one hundred *ri* as a ghost.' Then he vanished. As a result, I have roused you from your sleep. Please forgive me," he said and began to weep, the tears streaming down his face, whereupon his mother said, "I have heard that a man in prison dreams that he has been pardoned, and a thirsty man drinks water in his dreams. You must be like them. Calm yourself." But Samon shook his head. "Truly, it was nothing like an empty dream. My brother was here." Again he cried out in grief and threw himself down, weeping. His mother no longer doubted him, and together they passed the night raising their voices in lamentation.

The next day, Samon bowed in supplication to his mother and said, "Since childhood I have devoted myself to the writing brush and ink, but I have neither made a name for myself in public service nor been able to discharge my filial duty to my family; I have merely dwelt here uselessly between heaven and earth.[15] My brother Akana gave his life for loyalty. Today I shall set out for Izumo, where I intend at least to bury his remains and fulfill his trust. Please

---

15. In other words, he has not been a good Confucian, in either his public or his private life, except insofar as he loves learning.

take good care of yourself and give me leave to be away for a time." His mother said, "Go, my son, but come back soon and comfort me in my old age. Do not stay there so long that you make today our final day of parting." Samon said, "Our lives are like foam on the water—we cannot know whether they might fade away, morning or evening, but I shall come back soon." Brushing away his tears, he left the house, went to beg the Sayos to look after his mother, and started down the road to Izumo. Even though he was hungry, he did not think of food; even though he was cold, he forgot about clothing; and when he dozed off, he lamented all night in his dreams. After ten days he reached Tomita Castle.

He went directly to Akana Tanji's house and sent in his name, whereupon Tanji came to greet him and led him inside. Questioning Samon closely, he said, "Unless you heard of Sōemon's death from some winged creature, how could you know? It does not seem possible." Samon said, "A samurai does not concern himself with the vicissitudes of rank and fortune; he values only loyalty. Valuing his pledge, my brother Sōemon came one hundred *ri* as a ghost. I, in return, have traveled day and night to come down here. I should like to ask you, sir, about something I learned in my studies. Please answer clearly. In ancient times, when Gongshu Zuo of Wei lay ill in bed, the king of Wei himself came and, holding Zuo's hand, said, 'If the unavoidable should happen, whom shall I appoint to protect the country? Give me your guidance.' Zuo replied warmly, saying, 'Even though Shang Yang is young, he has rare ability. If your highness does not employ him, do not let him cross the border, even if you must kill him. If you allow him to go to another country, calamity will surely result.' Then Zuo secretly summoned Shang Yang and told him, 'I recommended you, but the king appeared not to accept my advice, and so I told him to kill you if he does not employ you. This is putting the lord first and the retainer after. You must go quickly to another country and escape harm,' he said.[16] How would you compare this case, sir, with that of you and Sōemon?" Tanji hung his head and said nothing. Samon moved closer. "My brother Sōemon was a loyal retainer for remembering En'ya's former kindness and not serving Amako. You, sir, having abandoned En'ya, your former master, and submitted to Amako, lack the righteousness of a samurai. My brother, cherishing his chrysanthemum pledge, gave up his life and traveled one hundred *ri*:

---

16. Akinari based this account on chapter 68, "Biography of Lord Shang," of the *Records of the Grand Historian (Shi Ji)* by Sima Qian (145?–190? B.C.E.). Gongshu Zuo was prime minister of the fourth-century B.C.E. kingdom of Wei. Shang Yang, or Lord Shang (d. 338 B.C.E.), one of the fathers of the Legalist school of Chinese thought, left Wei and eventually reorganized the state of Qin, paving the way for the unification of the Chinese empire about a century later by the first Qin emperor (259–210 B.C.E.).

this is the ultimate sincerity. You, sir, seeking favor with Amako, have tormented your own kin and caused his unnatural death: this is not the sincerity of a friend. Tsunehisa forced him to stay here, but if you had remembered your long-standing friendship, you would secretly have shown the utter sincerity of Zuo with Shang Yang. Instead you were driven by wealth and fame—this differs from the way of a samurai house and must be the way of the House of Amako as well. No wonder my brother had no wish to linger here. Now I, valuing loyalty, have come. Leave behind you a name stained by unrighteousness!" He had not finished speaking when he drew his sword and struck in one motion; Tanji fell with a single blow. Before the retainers could raise an alarm, Samon escaped without a trace. It is said that Amako Tsunehisa heard the story and, moved by the warmth of the brother's loyalty, chose not to pursue Samon. Truly, one must not form bonds of friendship with a shallow man.

The Reed-Choked House[17]

In the province of Shimōsa, Katsushika District, in the village of Mama, lived a man named Katsushirō.[18] Since his grandfather's time his family had lived here in comfort, holding many paddies and fields; but being by nature indifferent to details, Katsushirō came to dislike farming as he grew up, finding it irksome, so that finally the family grew poor. Mortified to see that he had lost favor with many of his relatives, he considered various schemes to revive the family fortunes. In those days a man named Sōji of Sasabe came down from the capital every year to stock up on dyed silk from Ashikaga.[19] Having distant relatives in the village, he often came to visit and had been on familiar terms with Katsushirō for some time. Katsushirō pleaded that he, too, wanted to become a merchant and go up to the capital. Sasabe agreed immediately: "Let me see, when will the next trip be?" he said. Delighted that he could now rely on Sasabe, Katsushirō sold his remaining paddies, used the gold to buy a large supply of plain silk, and prepared for his journey to the capital.

Katsushirō's wife, Miyagi, was a woman of arresting beauty, intelligence, and

---

17. The title of "The Reed-Choked House" alludes to chapter 137 of Yoshida Kenkō's *Tsurezuregusa*: "Does the love between men and women refer only to the moments when they are in each other's arms? The man who grieves over a love affair broken off before it was fulfilled, who bewails empty vows, who spends long autumn nights alone, who lets his thoughts wander to distant skies, who yearns for the past in a dilapidated house [*asaji ga yado*]—such a man truly knows what love means" (Donald Keene, trans., *Essays in Idleness* [New York: Columbia University Press, 1967], pp. 117–118).

18. Mama is now part of the city of Ichikawa, just east of Tokyo, in Chiba Prefecture.

19. Sasabe was a village northwest of Kyoto, later incorporated into the city of Fukuchiyama. Ashikaga, in Ibaraki Prefecture north of Tokyo, was noted for its dyed silk.

steady disposition. Dismayed to hear that he had bought merchandise and was going to the capital, she used every argument she could think of to dissuade him; but she was helpless against his obstinacy, now worse than ever, and so despite her misgivings about how she would fare in the future,[20] she busied herself with his preparations. As they talked together that night about the painful separation to come, she said, "With no one to depend on, my woman's heart will know the extremities of sadness, wandering as if lost in the fields and mountains.[21] Please do not forget me, morning or night, and come back soon. If only I live long enough, I tell myself,[22] but in this life we cannot depend on the morrow, and so take pity on me in your stalwart heart." He replied, "How could I linger in a strange land, riding on a floating log?[23] I shall return this autumn, when the arrowroot leaf turns over in the wind.[24] Be confident and wait for me." Thus he reassured her; the night sky brightened with dawn; and leaving the East Country where the roosters crow, he hurried toward the capital.[25]

In the summer of 1455, the shōgun's deputy in Kamakura, Lord Ashikaga Shigeuji, had a falling out with the family of Uesugi, his own deputy, and so when troops burned his palace to the ground, he took refuge with an ally in Shimōsa. From that moment, the lands east of the Hakone Barrier were thrown into chaos, and each man did just as he pleased. The aged fled to the mountains and hid; the young were conscripted; women and children, hearing the rumors—"They will burn this place today! The enemy will attack tomorrow!"— fled weeping, now east, now west. Katsushirō's wife Miyagi, too, wanted to escape, but relying on her husband's words—"Wait for me this fall"—she lived on, anxiously counting the days. Autumn came, but there was no word, not even in the wind. Sad and resentful that the heart of man proved to be as unreliable as this world itself, she composed in her despondency: *No one will*

---

20. Alludes to an anonymous poem: "Though I know not how I will fare in the future, my heart is with you" (*Man'yōshū*, no. 2985).

21. Alludes to a poem by Sosei: "Where shall I loathe this world? Whether in fields or in mountains my heart will surely wander" (*Kokinshū*, no. 947).

22. Alludes to a poem by Shirome, composed when parting from Minamoto no Sane at Yamazaki, as he set out for the hot springs of Tsukushi: "If only life obeyed the wishes of our hearts what pain would we feel in our partings?" (*Kokinshū*, no. 387).

23. Riding on a floating log signifies rootlessness and anxiety, as seen in "The Wind in the Pines" chapter in *The Tale of Genji*: "How many autumns have come and gone as I was dwelling here—why now should I return, riding on a floating log?"

24. There is a pun on *kaeru*, which means "to return" and "to turn over." Arrowroot, being one of the "seven autumn grasses," signifies autumn.

25. *Tori ga naku* (rooster's crow) is a pillow word for Azuma, the East Country, an old name for the region now called Kantō, or greater Tokyo. The image is further enriched by the truism that roosters crow at dawn and by the fact that Azuma is often written with characters signifying "my wife."

report my misery, I fear—Oh decorated cock of Meeting Hill, tell him autumn too has passed.[26] Yet she had no way to communicate with him since many provinces separated them. Men's hearts grew more villainous in the turbulence of the world. Passersby, noting Miyagi's beauty, tried to seduce her with comforting words, but firmly guarding her chastity she would treat them distantly, close the door, and refuse to meet them. Her maidservant departed; her meager savings melted away; and that year, too, came to a close. The new year brought no peace. What is more, in the autumn of the old year the shōgun had commissioned Tō no Tsuneyori, governor of Shimotsuke and lord of Gujō, Mino Province, who went down to the domain of Shimōsa, made plans with his kinsman Chiba no Sanetane, and attacked. Shigeuji's forces defended their position resolutely, however, and so there was no end in sight. Bandits threw up strongholds here and there, set fires, and pillaged. No haven remained in the Eight Provinces; the losses were appalling.

Katsushirō accompanied Sasabe to Kyoto and sold all his silk. Because it was an age when the capital delighted in luxury, he made a good profit. As he prepared to return to the East Country, word spread that Uesugi troops had toppled the shōgun's deputy and then had pursued and attacked him. Katsushirō's home village would be the battlefield of Zhuo Lu, bristling with shields and halberds.[27] But even rumors close at hand are frequently untrue; Katsushirō's home was in a distant land beyond myriad layers of white clouds.[28] Anxiously he left the capital at the start of the Eighth Month. Crossing the pass at Misaka in Kiso, he found that robbers had blocked the road, and to them he lost all his baggage. Furthermore, he heard reports that new barrier stations had been established here and there to the east, where even travelers were not allowed to pass. In that case, there would be no way to send any message at all. His house had surely been leveled by the fires of battle. His wife would no longer be alive. His village would have become a den of ogres, he told himself, and so he turned back toward the capital. When he entered the province of Ōmi, however, he suddenly felt unwell and came down with a fever. In a place called Musa lived a wealthy man named Kodama Yoshibei. Because this was the birthplace of Sasabe's wife, Katsushirō pleaded for help. Kodama did not turn him away but summoned a physician and devoted himself to Katsushirō's

---

26. Cocks decorated with mulberry-cloth ribbons were occasionally sent to the barrier stations around Kyoto, including the Osaka Barrier, as part of a purification ritual. The Osaka Barrier, not to be confused with the city of Osaka, was in the mountains east of Kyoto. Since this "Osaka" means "meeting hill," poets frequently used the name in a double sense.

27. Zhuo Lu, in the present Hebei Province, China, was the scene of an ancient battle involving the legendary Yellow Emperor.

28. Alludes to a poem by Ki no Tsurayuki: "Composed for a person who was going to Michinokuni: Even far away where white clouds pile in myriad layers let not your heart grow distant from him who thinks of you" (*Kokinshū*, no. 380).

care. Feeling well again at last, Katsushirō thanked Kodama deeply for his great kindness. He was still unsteady on his feet, however, and so he found himself still there when they greeted the New Year. Presently he made new friends in the town, where he was admired for his unaffected honesty, and formed close ties with Kodama and many others. Thereafter, he would call on Sasabe in the capital, then return to stay with Kodama in Ōmi. Seven years passed like a dream.

In 1461 the struggle between the Hatakeyama brothers in the province of Kawachi showed no sign of ending, and the turmoil approached the capital. Moreover, corpses piled up in the streets as an epidemic swept through the city in the spring. Thinking that a cosmic epoch must be coming to an end, the people lamented the impermanence of all things.[29] Katsushirō pondered his situation: "Reduced to this pointless existence, how long should I drag out my life, and for what, lingering in this distant land, depending on the generosity of people with whom I have no ties of blood? It is my own faithless heart that has let me pass long years and months in a field overgrown with the grass of forgetfulness, unmindful even of the fate of her I left at home.[30] Even if she is no longer of this world and has gone to the land of the dead, I would seek out her remains and construct a burial mound." Thus he related his thoughts to those around him and, during a break in the rains of the Fifth Month, said farewell. Traveling for more than ten days, he arrived at his village.

Although the sun had already sunk in the west and the rain clouds were so dark they seemed about to burst, he doubted he could lose his way, having lived so long in the village, and so he pushed through the fields of summer. But the jointed bridge of old had fallen into the rapids, so that there could be no sound of a horse's hoofs;[31] he could not find the old paths because the farmland had been abandoned to grow wild, and the houses that used to stand there were gone. Scattered here and there, a few remaining houses appeared to be inhabited, but they bore no resemblance to those in earlier days. "Which is the house I lived in?" he wondered, standing in confusion, when about forty yards away, he saw, by the light of stars peeking through the clouds, a towering pine that had been split by lightning. "The tree that marks the eaves of my house!" he

---

29. "Cosmic epoch" (kō): kalpa, a Sanskrit term for an almost unimaginably long period of time. Here the reference is to the second kalpa, during which there is life on earth. Epidemics and famines did occur throughout the country in the 1450s. This sentence echoes Kamo no Chōmei's description of Kyoto in 1182, in An Account of my Ten-Foot-Square Hut (Hōjōki).

30. "Grass of forgetfulness" (wasuregusa) is a kind of day lily (Hemerocallis aurantiaca) mentioned in The Tales of Ise, sec. 100: "Long ago, as a man was passing by the Kōrōden, a high-ranking lady sent a message out to him, saying, Do you refer to the grass of forgetfulness as grass of remembrance? to which he replied, This may look to be a field overgrown with grass of forgetfulness, but it is remembrance, and I shall continue to depend on you."

31. Alludes to a poem in the Man'yōshū: "I wish for a horse whose hoofs would make no sound. Across the jointed bridge of Mama in Katsushika would I always go to her" (no. 3387).

cried and joyfully moved forward. The house was unchanged and appeared to be occupied, for lamplight glimmered through a gap in the old door. "Does someone else live here now? Or is she still alive?" His heart pounding, he approached the entrance and cleared his throat. Someone inside heard immediately and asked, "Who is there?" He recognized his wife's voice, though greatly aged. Terrified that he might be dreaming, he said, "I have come back. How strange that you should still be living here alone, unchanged, in this reed-choked moor!"[32] Recognizing his voice, she quickly opened the door. Her skin was dark with grime, her eyes were sunken, and long strands of hair fell loose down her back. He could not believe she was the same person. Seeing her husband, she burst into wordless tears.

Stunned, Katsushirō could say nothing for a time. Finally he spoke: "I would never have let the years and months slip by had I thought you were still living here like this. One day years ago, when I was in the capital, I heard of fighting in Kamakura—the shōgun's deputy had been defeated and taken refuge in Shimōsa. The Uesugi were in eager pursuit, people said. The next day I took my leave from Sasabe and, at the beginning of the Eighth Month, left the capital. As I came along the Kiso road, I was surrounded by a large band of robbers, who took my clothing and all my money. I barely escaped with my life. Then the villagers said that travelers were being stopped at new barriers on the Tōkaidō and Tōsandō Highways. They also said that a general had gone down from the capital the day before, joined forces with the Uesugi, and set out for battle in Shimōsa. Our province had long since been razed by fire, and every inch trampled under horses' hoofs, they said, and so I could only think that you had been reduced to ashes and dust or had sunk into the sea. Returning to the capital, I lived on the generosity of others for these seven years. Seized in recent days with constant longing, I returned, hoping at least to find your remains, but I never dreamed that you would still be living in this world. I wonder if you might not be the Cloud of Shaman Mountain or the Apparition in the Han Palace."[33] Thus he rambled on, tediously repeating himself. When she stopped crying, his wife said, "After I bid you farewell, the world took a dreadful turn, even before the arrival of the autumn I relied on, and the villagers abandoned their houses and set out to sea or hid in the mountains. Most of the few who remained had hearts of tigers or wolves and sought, I suppose, to take advantage of me now that I was alone. They tempted me with clever words,

---

32. This paragraph contains several echoes of "The Wormwood Patch," chapter 15 of *The Tale of Genji*.

33. "The Cloud of Shaman Hill" refers to a story in the *Wen Xuan* (sixth century), in which King Xiang of Chu dreams that he has slept with a woman at Shaman Hill (Wu Shan, in Sichuan), who turns out to have been a cloud. "The Apparition in the Han Palace" derives from a story in the *Han shu*, in which the Han emperor, Wu, grieving the death of a beloved lady, commands a sorcerer to summon her spirit. Both episodes bespeak a confusion of illusion and reality.

but even if I had been crushed like a piece of jade, I would not imitate the perfection of the tile,[34] and so I endured many bitter experiences. The brilliance of the Milky Way heralded the autumn, but you did not return. I waited through the winter, I greeted the New Year, and still there was no word. Now I wanted to go to you in the capital, but I knew a woman could not hope to pass the sealed barrier gates where even men were turned away; and so with the pine at the eaves I waited vainly in this house, foxes and owls my companions, until today. I am happy now that my long resentment has been dispelled. No one else can know the resentment of one who dies of longing, waiting for another to come."[35] With this she began to sob again. "The night is short," he said, comforting her, and they lay down together.

He slept soundly, weary from his long journey and cooled through the night as the paper in the window sipped the pine breeze. When the sky brightened in the early morning, he felt chilly, though still in the world of dreams, and groped for the quilt that must have slipped off. A rustling sound wakened him. Feeling something cold dripping on his face, he opened his eyes, thinking that rain was seeping in: the roof had been torn off by the wind, and he could see the waning moon, lingering in the sky. The house had lost its shutters. Reeds and plumed grasses grew tall through gaps in the decaying floorboards, and the morning dew dripped from them, saturating his sleeves. The walls were draped with ivy and arrowroot; the garden was buried in creepers—even though fall had not come yet, the house was a wild autumn moor.[36] And where, come to think of it, had his wife gone, who had been lying with him? She was nowhere in sight. Perhaps this was the doing of a fox? But the house, though extremely dilapidated, was certainly the one he used to live in. From the spacious inner rooms to the rice storehouse beyond, it still retained the form that he had favored. Dumbfounded, he felt as though he had lost his footing. Then he considered carefully: since the house had become the dwelling place of foxes and badgers, a wild moor, perhaps a spirit, had appeared before him in the form of his wife. Or had her ghost, longing for him, come back and communed with him? It was just as he had feared. He could not even weep. I alone am as I was before, he thought as he walked around.[37] In the space that was her bedroom, someone had taken up the floor, piled soil into a mound, and pro-

---

34. That is, "I would not prolong my life [the perfect tile] by being unfaithful, even though death [crushing of the jade] might be the consequence."

35. Alludes to a poem by Taira no Kanemori: "If unknown to him I die of longing while I wait for him to come, for what shall I say I have exchanged my life?" (*Goshūishū*, no. 656).

36. Alludes to a poem by Priest Henjō: "The house is ruined, the people are grown old—both garden and brushwood-fence have become a wild autumn moor" (*Kokinshū*, no. 248).

37. Alludes to a poem by Ariwara no Narihira: "The moon is not that moon nor the spring the spring of old, I alone am as I was before" (*The Tales of Ise*, sec. 4, and *Kokinshū*, no. 747).

tected the mound from rain and dew. The ghost last night had come from here—the thought frightened him and also made him long for her. In a receptacle for water offerings stood a stick with a sharpened end, and to this was attached a weathered piece of Nasuno paper, the writing faded and in places hard to make out, but certainly in his wife's hand. Without inscribing a dharma name or date, she had, in the form of a waka, movingly stated her feelings at the end: *Nevertheless, I thought, and so deceived I have lived on until today!*[38] Realizing now for the first time that his wife was dead, he cried out and collapsed. It added to his misery that he did not even know what year, what month and day, she had met her end. Someone must know, he thought, and so drying his tears, he stepped outside. The sun had climbed high in the sky. He went first to the nearest house and met the master, a man he had never seen before. On the contrary, the man asked him what province he had come from. Katsushirō addressed him respectfully: "I was the master of the house next door, but to make my living I spent seven years in the capital. When I came back last night, I found the house had fallen into ruins and no one was living there. Apparently my wife has left this world, for I found a burial mound, but there is no date, which makes my grief all the more intense. If you know, sir, please tell me." The man said, "A sad story indeed. I came to live here only about one year ago and know nothing of the time when she was living there. It would seem that she lost her life long before that. All the people who used to live in this village fled when the fighting began; most of those who live here now moved in from somewhere else. There is one old man who seems to have lived here a long time. Occasionally he goes to that house and performs a service to comfort the spirit of the departed. This old man must know the date." Katsushirō said, "And where does the old man live?" The man told him, "He owns a field thickly planted with hemp, about two hundred yards from here, toward the beach, and there he lives in a small hut." Rejoicing, Katsushirō went to the house, where he found an old man of about seventy, terribly bent at the waist, seated in front of a hearth on a round, wicker cushion, sipping tea. Recognizing Katsushirō, the old man said, "Why have you come back so late, my boy?" Katsushirō saw that he was the old man called Uruma, who had lived in the village for a long time.

Katsushirō congratulated the old man on his longevity, then related everything in detail, from going to the capital and remaining there against his true desires, to the strange events of the night before. He expressed his deep gratitude to the old man for making a burial mound and performing services there. He could not stop his tears. The old man said, "After you went far away, soldiers began to brandish shields and halberds in the summer; the villagers ran off; the

---

38. Miyagi's waka is borrowed from *Gon Chūnagon Atsutada kyō shū* (*Gunsho ruijū*, no. 235), the collection of the courtier and poet Fujiwara no Atsutada (905?–943).

Katsushirō and the old man Uruma return to the reed-choked house to pray for Miyagi's soul. (From SNKBZ 78, *Hanabusa sōshi, Nishiyama monogatari, Ugetsu monogatari, Harusame monogatari,* by permission of Shōgakukan)

young were conscripted; and as a result the mulberry fields turned quickly into grasslands for foxes and rabbits. Only your virtuous wife, honoring your pledge to return in the fall, would not leave home. I, too, stayed inside and hid because my legs had grown weak and I found it hard to walk two hundred yards. I have seen many things in my years, but I was deeply moved by the courage of that young woman, even when the land had become the home of tree spirits and other ghastly monsters. Autumn passed, the New Year came, and on the tenth day of the Eighth Month of that year she departed. In my pity for her, I carried soil with my own hands, buried the coffin, and, using as a grave marker the brush marks she left at the end, performed a humble service with offerings of water; but I could not inscribe the date, not knowing how to write, and I had no way to seek a posthumous name, as the temple is far away. Five years have passed. Hearing your story now, I am sure that the ghost of your virtuous wife came and told you of her long-held resentment. Go there again and carefully perform a memorial service." Leaning on his staff, he led the way. Together they prostrated themselves before the mound, raised their voices in lamentation, and passed the night invoking the Buddha's name.

Because they could not sleep, the old man told a story: "Long, long ago, even before my grandfather's grandfather was born, there lived in this village a beautiful girl named Tegona of Mama.[39] Since her family was poor, she wore a hempen robe with a blue collar; her hair was uncombed; and she wore no shoes. But with a face like the full moon and a smile like a lovely blossom, she surpassed the fine ladies in the capital, wrapped in their silk brocades woven with threads of gold. Men in the village, of course, and even officials from the capital and men in the next province, everyone came courting and longed for her. This caused great pain for Tegona, who sank deep in thought and, the better to requite the love of many men, threw herself into the waves of the inlet here. People in ancient times sang of her in their poems and passed down her story as an example of the sadness of the world. When I was a child my mother told the story charmingly, and I found it very moving; but how much sadder is the heart of this departed one than the young heart of Tegona of old!" He wept as he spoke, for the aged cannot control their tears. Katsushirō's grief needs no description. Hearing this tale, he expressed his feelings in the clumsy words of a rustic: *Tegona of Mama, in the distant past—this much they must have longed for her, Tegona of Mama.* It can be said that an inability to express even a fragment of one's thoughts is more moving than the feelings of one skilled with words.

This is a tale passed down by merchants who traveled often to that province and heard the story there.

A Serpent's Lust

Once—what era was it?—there was a man named Oya no Takesuke, of Cape Miwa in the province of Kii.[40] Enjoying the luck of the sea, he employed many fishermen, caught fish of every kind and size, and prospered with his family. He had two sons and a daughter. Tarō, the eldest, had an unaffected, honest nature and managed the family business well. The second child, the daughter, had been welcomed as a bride by a man of Yamato and gone to live with him.[41] Then there was the third child, Toyoo. A gentle boy, he favored the courtly, refined ways of the capital and had no heart for making a living. Distressed by this, his father deliberated: If he left part of the family fortune to Toyoo, it would soon find its way into the hands of others. Or he could marry Toyoo into another family; but the bad news, which surely would come sooner or later, would be too painful. No, he would simply rear Toyoo as the boy wished, eventually to become a scholar or a monk, and let him be Tarō's dependent for the rest of his life. Having reached this conclusion, he did not go out of his way to discipline his younger son.

---

39. The old man's narrative is based on a long poem by Takahashi Mushimaro: "Of the Maiden of Mama of Katsushika" (*Man'yōshū*, no. 1807).

40. Cape Miwa (Miwagasaki) is in the present city of Shingū, Wakayama Prefecture, on the southeast shore of the Kii Peninsula.

41. Yamato is now Nara Prefecture, south of Kyoto.

Toyoo traveled back and forth to study with Abe no Yumimaro, a priest at the Shingū Shrine. One day late in the Ninth Month, the sea was remarkably calm, with no trace of wind or wave, when suddenly clouds appeared from the southeast—the direction of the dragon and the snake—and a gentle rain began to fall. Borrowing an umbrella at his mentor's house, Toyoo started toward home, but just as the Asuka Shrine came into view in the distance, the rain fell harder, and so he stopped at a fisherman's hut that happened to be nearby. The old man of the house scrambled out to meet him: "Well, well, the master's younger son. I am honored that you have come to such a shabby place. Here, please sit on this." He brushed the filth off a round wicker cushion and presented it. "I shall stay for only a moment," Toyoo said, "Anything will do. Please do not go to any trouble." He settled down to rest. A lovely voice came from outside, saying, "Please be kind enough to let me rest under your eaves." Curious, Toyoo turned to look, and saw a woman of about twenty, resplendently beautiful in face, figure, and coiffure, wearing a kimono printed in fine colors in the distant-mountain pattern, and accompanied by a lovely servant girl of fourteen or fifteen to whom she had entrusted a package of some kind. Drenched to the skin, she appeared to be at her wit's end, but her face flushed with embarrassment when she saw Toyoo. His heart leaped at her elegance, and he thought: "If such a noble beauty lived in these parts, I would surely have heard of her before this. No doubt she is from the capital, here for a look at the sea on her return from a pilgrimage to the Three Shrines of Kumano.[42] But how careless of her not to have a male attendant," he thought. Moving back a little, he said, "Do come in. The rain will soon end." The woman: "Just for a moment, then; please excuse me." The hut was small, and when she sat directly in front of him, he saw that her beauty at close range was scarcely that of a person of this world. His heart soaring, he said to her, "You appear to be of noble family. Have you been on a pilgrimage to the Three Shrines? Or perhaps you have gone to the hot springs at Yunomine? What could there be for you to see on this desolate strand? Someone wrote of this place in ancient times: *How distressing this sudden fall of rain—and there is no shelter at Sano Crossing of Cape Miwa.*[43] Truly, the verse expresses the mood of today. This is a shabby house, but my father looks out for the man here. Please relax and wait for the rain to clear. And where are you lodging on your travels? It would be impertinent for me to escort you there, but please take this umbrella when you go." The woman said, "Your words cheer me, and I am most grateful. My clothing

---

42. The Three Mountains (shrines) of Kumano—the Hongū, Shingū, and Kumano Nachi Shrines—together constituted a popular destination for pilgrimages in the Heian period. The retired emperor Go Shirakawa is said to have made the pilgrimage, a round trip requiring nearly a month, as often as thirty-four times.

43. Toyoo is showing off his learning. The poem is by Naga Okimaro and is in the *Man'yōshū*, no. 265.

will surely dry in the warmth of your kindness. I do not come from the capital but have been living near here for many years. Thinking today would be fair, I made a pilgrimage to the Nachi Shrine, but frightened by the sudden rain, I came bursting into this house, not knowing that you had already taken shelter here. I do not have far to go; I shall start now, during this lull in the rain." "Do take the umbrella, please," Toyoo urged; "I will come for it sometime later. The rain shows no sign of letting up. Where is your home? I shall send someone for the umbrella." She replied: "Ask at Shingū for the house of Agata no Manago. Soon the sun will set. I shall be on my way, then, shielded by your kindness." With this, she took the umbrella and left. He watched her go, then borrowed a straw hat and raincoat from his host and returned home. Her dew-like figure lingered in his mind, and when at dawn he finally dozed off, he dreamed of going to Manago's house, where he found an imposing gate and mansion, with shutters and blinds lowered and the lady residing gracefully inside. Manago came out to welcome him. "Unable to forget your kindness, I have longed for you to visit," she said. "Please come inside." Leading him in, she entertained him elaborately with wine and small dishes of food. Enraptured, he finally shared her pillow, but then day broke and his dream faded. "How I wish it had been true," he thought. In his excitement, he forgot breakfast and left the house in high spirits.

Arriving at Shingū, Toyoo asked for the house of Agata no Manago, but no one had heard of it. He continued his inquiries wearily into the afternoon, when the servant girl approached him from the east. Overjoyed to see her, he said, "Where is your house? I have come for the umbrella." The girl smiled and said, "You were good to come; please follow me." She led the way and in no time said, "Here it is." He saw a high gate and a large house. Everything, even the shutters and the lowered blinds, was exactly as he had seen in his dream. Marvelous, he thought as he went through the gate. Running ahead, the servant girl said, "The gentleman has come for his umbrella, and I have led him here." Manago came out, saying, "Where is he? Show him this way." Toyoo: "There is a Master Abe in Shingū with whom I have been studying for some years. I am on my way to see him and thought I would stop here for the umbrella. It was rude of me to call unexpectedly. Now that I know where you live, I shall come again." Manago detained him: "Maroya, do not allow him to leave," she said. The servant girl stood in his way, saying, "You forced us to take the umbrella, did you not? In return, we shall force you to stay." Pushing him from behind, she guided him to a south-facing room. Woven mats had been placed on the wooden floor; the curtain stands, the decorated cabinet, and the illustrated draperies—all were fine antiques. This was not the home of any ordinary person. Manago entered and said, "For certain reasons this has become a house without a master, and so we cannot entertain you properly. Let me just offer you a cup of poor wine." Maroya spread delicacies from the mountains and the seas on immaculate stands and trays, presented a flask and an unglazed cup, and poured for him. Toyoo thought he was dreaming again and must awaken. That everything was real made it all the more wonderful for him.

When both guest and host were feeling the effects of drink, Manago raised her cup to Toyoo. Her face was like the surface of a pond that warmly greets the spring breeze and reflects the limbs of the cherry, laden with luscious pink blossoms; and her voice was as bewitching as the song of the warbler, fluttering from treetop to treetop, as she said: "If I keep my shameful thoughts to myself and fall ill as a result, which god will carry the undeserved blame?[44] Do not imagine that I speak flippantly. I was born in the capital but lost my parents early and was reared by my nurse. Already three years have passed since I married a man named Agata, an assistant to the governor of this province, and came down here with him. This spring, before completing his term, my husband died of some trifling disease, leaving me with no one to rely on. When I learned that my nurse, back in the capital, had become a nun and set out on ascetic wanderings, that place, too, became for me an unknown land. Take pity on me. From your kindness yesterday as we took shelter from the rain, I know that you are a truehearted man, and so I ask that I may devote the rest of my life to serving you. If you do not dismiss me in disgust, let us initiate, with this cup, a vow of one thousand years." Since in his agitated longing for her he had hoped for exactly this, Toyoo felt his heart leap with joy, like a bird soaring from its roost, but then he remembered that he was not yet on his own and did not have permission from his father and brother. Now joyous, now afraid, he could not find words with which to reply right away. Seeing his hesitation, Manago looked forlorn and said, "I am ashamed at having spoken, from a woman's shallow heart, foolish words that I cannot take back. Miserable creature that I am, it was a grave sin for me to trouble you instead of sinking beneath the waves. Although I did not speak flippantly, please take my words as a drunken jest and cast them into the sea." Toyoo: "From the first I thought that you were a high-ranking lady from the capital, and I was right. How often can someone who has grown up on this whale-haunted shore expect to hear such joyful words? I did not answer straight away because I still serve my father and my brother and have nothing to call my own but my nails and hair. I can only lament my lack of fortune, for I have no betrothal gift with which to welcome you as my bride. If you are willing to put up with all adversity, then I will do anything to become your husband, forgetting filial obedience and my status for the sake of the mountain of love, where even Confucius stumbled." "What joyful words I hear," she said. "In that case, do please come and stay from time

---

44. That is, "If I died without saying anything, some god would be blamed unfairly for my death, and so I shall tell you." Manago's speech tends to be flowery and decorated with poetic allusions. In this case, the allusion is to a poem by Ariwara no Narihira: "If I died of love unknown to others, pointlessly, which god would carry the unfounded blame?" (*The Tales of Ise*, sec. 89, and *Shinzokukokinshū*, no. 1157).

to time.[45] Here is a sword that my late husband cherished as his greatest treasure. Wear it always at your waist." She handed it to him. Decorated with gold and silver, it was a wonderfully tempered antique. To refuse a gift at the start of their relationship would be inauspicious, he thought, and so he accepted it. "Stay here tonight," she said, eager to detain him, but he replied, "My father would punish me if I slept away from home without his leave. I shall make some clever excuse tomorrow night and come." With this he departed. That night, too, he lay awake until dawn.

Tarō rose early to assemble the net boys.[46] Glancing into the bedroom through a gap in the door, he saw Toyoo in bed and, beside the pillow, a sword glittering in the lingering lamplight. Strange, where did he get that? Suspicious, he opened the door roughly, and Toyoo awoke to the sound. Seeing Tarō there, he said, "Do you need me for something?" Tarō said, "What is that glittery thing beside your pillow? Valuables have no place in a fisherman's house. How Father would scold you if he saw it." Toyoo: "I did not spend money to buy it. Someone gave it to me yesterday, and I have placed it here." Tarō: "Who in these parts would give you such a treasure? If you ask me, even these bothersome Chinese writings that you collect are a terrible waste of money, but I have held my tongue until now because Father has said nothing about it. I suppose you plan to wear that sword in the procession at the Great Shrine Festival. Have you lost your mind?" He spoke so loudly that his father heard him. "What has that useless boy done? Bring him here, Tarō," he called. Tarō replied, "Where could he have gotten it? Buying a glittery thing such as a general should wear—it is not right. Please call him and ask him about it. As for me, the net boys are probably loafing." With this he went out. The mother summoned Toyoo. "Why did you buy such a thing? Both rice and cash belong to Tarō. What can you call your own? We have always let you do as you please, but if Tarō were to turn against you over something like this, where in the world would you live? How can one who studies the wisdom of the past fail to understand a matter as simple as this?" Toyoo: "Truly, I did not buy it. Someone gave it to me for a good reason, but Brother was suspicious when he saw it and said what he said." The father: "And what have you done to deserve such a gift? I am even more suspicious now. Tell us the whole story this moment," he shouted. Toyoo: "I am too embarrassed. I shall explain through someone else." His father said roughly, "To whom can you speak if not to your parents and brother?" Tarō's wife, the mistress of the house, was seated to one side. She said, "Inadequate though I am, I shall listen to his story. Come with me." Thus making peace

---

45. In Heian court society, it was customary for the husband and wife to live separately and for the husband to spend the night with his wife from time to time.

46. Alludes to a poem by Naga Okimaro: "Even in the palace it can be heard—the cry of a fisherman assembling the net boys to pull in the nets" (*Man'yōshū*, no. 238).

among them, she stood and led Toyoo out of the room. "I had planned to tell you secretly, even if Brother had not seen the sword and questioned me, but I was scolded before I could. A certain man's wife,[47] now left defenseless, asked me to care for her and gave me the sword. For me to proceed without permission, when I am not on my own, could bring the heavy penalty of disinheritance, and so I regret all the more what I have done. Please, Sister, take pity on me." The mistress of the house smiled. "For some time I have felt sorry that you sleep alone. This is very good news. Inadequate though I am, I shall put in a good word for you." That night she explained the situation to Tarō. "Don't you think it very fortunate?" she said. "Please speak with Father and work things out." Tarō knitted his brows. "Strange. I have never heard of an assistant to the governor named Agata. Since our family is the village head, we could hardly have failed to hear of such a person's death. Anyway, bring the sword here." She returned immediately with the sword, and Tarō examined it closely. Heaving a great sigh, he said, "This is terrible. Recently a court minister presented a great many treasures to the avatar when his prayer was fulfilled, but the sacred objects quickly vanished from the shrine treasury, whereupon the head priest appealed to the provincial governor. In order to find the thief, the governor sent the vice governor, Fun'ya no Hiroyuki, to the head priest's mansion; and I have heard that he is now devoting all his attention to this matter. However you look at it, this is not a sword that a mere provincial official would have worn. I shall show it to Father." Taking it to him, he explained the dreadful circumstances. "What should we do?" he asked. His father blanched. "This is a wretched business indeed. What retribution from a former life could have aroused such evil thoughts in a boy who, until now, never stole so much as a hair? If this matter is exposed by someone else, our family could be wiped out. For the sake of our ancestors and descendants, I shall harbor no regrets over one unfilial child. Turn him in tomorrow morning," he said. Tarō waited for dawn, then went to the head priest's mansion, where he explained matters and displayed the sword. Astonished, the head priest said, "This sword was indeed an offering from the minister." The vice governor heard and said, "We must find the other missing objects. Arrest him." Ten soldiers set out with Tarō in the lead. Toyoo knew nothing of this and was reading when the soldiers rushed in and arrested him. "What is my crime?" he asked, but they paid no attention and tied him up. Now that it had come to this, father, mother, Tarō, and his wife all were lost in grief. "A summons from the government office! Hurry up!" the soldiers cried as they surrounded Toyoo and pushed him along to the mansion. The vice governor glared at him. "Your theft of sacred treasures is an unprecedented crime against the state. Where have you hidden the various other treasures?

---

47. Here and later the text uses stock expressions to indicate, without repeating them, that all the details are being provided.

Tell me everything." Finally understanding, Toyoo began to weep and said, "I have stolen nothing. For this and that reason, the wife of a certain Agata gave the sword to me, saying her late husband had worn it. Please summon this woman, right away, and you will understand my innocence." "We have never had an assistant named Agata. Such lies will only make your crimes greater." "Why would I lie, when I have already been arrested like this? I beg of you, please find that woman and question her." The vice governor turned to the soldiers and said, "Where is the house of Agata no Manago? Take him with you, arrest her, and bring them back here."

The soldiers bowed respectfully and, pushing Toyoo along once more, went to the house. The posts of the imposing gate were rotting, and most of the roof tiles had fallen off and shattered; ferns had taken root and were trailing from the eaves.[48] The place did not appear to be occupied. Toyoo was dumbfounded. Soldiers went around and assembled the neighbors. Old woodcutters, rice huskers, and the like knelt in terror. A soldier said to them, "Who lived in this house? Is it true that the wife of a man named Agata lives here?" An elderly blacksmith came forward and said, "I have never heard of a person by that name. Until three years ago, a man named Suguri lived here, and a lively, prosperous place it was, but then he sailed for Tsukushi with a load of merchandise and the ship was lost. After that, the remaining people scattered, and no one has lived here since. But the old lacquer maker here says he was surprised to see this boy go inside yesterday and then leave a little while later." "Let us take a good look, in any case, and report to our lord," said the soldiers. They pushed open the gates and went in. The house was even more dilapidated than the exterior. They moved farther inside. In the spacious landscape garden, the pond had dried up, and even the water weeds had withered. A giant pine, blown over in the wind, lay ominously in the drooping thicket on the wild moor. When they opened the shutters of the guest hall, a reeking gust of air came at them, and everyone fell back in terror. Toyoo was speechless with fear and sorrow.

Among the soldiers was a bold one named Kose no Kumagashi. "Follow me," he said as he went in, stomping roughly on the floorboards. An inch of dust had piled up. Amid the rat droppings, beside an old curtain stand, sat a blossom-like woman. Addressing her, Kumagashi said, "The governor summons you. Come quickly." When she did not reply, he approached and tried to grasp her. Suddenly there was a clap of thunder as violent as though the ground itself were splitting open. They had no time to escape; everyone toppled over. When they finally looked up, the woman had vanished without a trace. Something glittered on the floor. Creeping forward, they found Korean brocades, Chinese

---

48. The description of the house and grounds echoes "The Evening Faces," chapter 4 of *The Tale of Genji*.

damasks, *shizuri* weavings, *katori* weavings, shields, halberds, quivers, hoes, and the like—the lost sacred treasures.[49] Gathering up these objects and carrying them back, the soldiers recounted the strange events in detail. The vice governor and the head priest, recognizing the work of an evil spirit, relaxed their investigation of Toyoo. Nevertheless, he could not escape his obvious offense, possession of a stolen sword. He was sent to the governor's mansion and confined in jail. The Oya family made large payments in an attempt to redeem him and were able to obtain a pardon after about one hundred days. Toyoo said, "Under the circumstances, I would be ashamed to mingle in society. I would like to visit my sister in Yamato and live there for a while." His family replied, "Truly, one is likely to fall gravely ill after such a dreadful experience. Go and spend some months there." They sent him off with attendants.

Toyoo's elder sister, the Oyas' second child, lived in a place called Tsubaichi with her husband, a merchant named Tanabe no Kanetada. They were delighted to have Toyoo visit them and, taking pity on him for the events of the past few months, consoled him warmly, saying, "Stay here just as long as you like." Tsubaichi was near Hatsuse Temple.[50] Among the many Buddhas, that of Hatsuse in particular was known as far away as China for its wonderful effectiveness and so drew many pilgrims from the capital and from the countryside, especially in the spring. Since the pilgrims always stayed here, travelers' lodgings lined the streets. The Tanabe family dealt in lamp wicks and other goods for the sacred flames. Into the crowd of customers came a beautiful, aristocratic lady with a servant girl, apparently on an incognito pilgrimage from the capital, asking for incense. Seeing Toyoo, the servant girl said, "The master is here!" Startled, he looked up—it was Manago and Maroya. Crying out in terror, he fled to the back. "What is going on?" asked Kanetada and his wife. "That demon has followed me here. Do not go near it," said Toyoo, desperately looking for a place to hide. "Where? Where?" cried the other customers. Manago went among them and said, "Do not be startled, people. My husband, do not be afraid. In my sorrow at having incriminated you through my own imprudence, I wanted to seek out your home, explain the circumstances, and put your heart at rest. I am overjoyed that I could find this place and meet with you again. Shopmaster, please listen carefully and decide for yourself. If I were some kind of monster, could I appear among this crowd of people and, moreover, at noon on such a tranquil day as this? My robes have seams; when I face

---

49. Hoes (*kuwa*, here perhaps plows), symbolic of agriculture, are often found among a shrine's treasures.

50. Tsubaichi (Tsuba Market), now part of Miwa-chō, Sakurai City, at the foot of Mount Miwa, in Nara Prefecture, was a market town on the approach to Hasedera, the celebrated Buddhist temple at Hatsuse (now Hase, in Sakurai). Since ancient times, Mount Miwa has been associated with a snake cult.

the sun, I cast a shadow.[51] Please consider the truth of what I say and throw off your doubts." Feeling more like himself again, Toyoo said, "It is clear that you are not human, for when I was arrested and went with the soldiers, we found the place in a shambles, utterly unlike it was on the day before, and there, in a house befitting a demon, you sat alone. When the soldiers tried to capture you, you caused a clear sky suddenly to shake with thunder, and then you disappeared without a trace. All this I saw with my own eyes. Why have you come chasing after me again? Go away at once." Weeping, Manago said, "Truly, it is no wonder that you think this way, but listen now a little longer to my words. Hearing that you had been taken to the government office, I approached the old man next door, to whom I had shown some kindness in the past, and persuaded him to transform the place quickly into a house in the wilderness. Maroya contrived to have thunder sound when they tried to arrest me. After that we hired a boat and fled to Naniwa.[52] In my desire to learn what had become of you, I prayed to the Buddha here. It is through his great compassion that with the sacred sign of the twin cedars we have flowed again together on the rapids of joy.[53] How could a woman have stolen those many sacred treasures? That was the doing of my late husband's evil heart. Please consider carefully and try to grasp even a dewdrop of the love I feel." The tears streamed down her face. Now suspicious, now sympathetic, Toyoo could find nothing more to say. Kanetada and his wife, seeing Manago's reasonableness and feminine demeanor, no longer harbored the slightest doubt. "We were terrified by Toyoo's account, but surely such things could not occur in this day and age. We are deeply moved by the feeling you have shown in your long search and shall let you stay here, even if Toyoo does not agree." They showed her to a room. Ingratiating herself to them during the next day or two, she entreated them, and they, moved by the depth of her determination, prevailed on Toyoo and finally arranged a wedding ceremony. Toyoo's heart melted day by day; he had always rejoiced in her beauty, and as he exchanged thousand-year vows with her, clouds rose by night on Mount Takama of Kazuraki, and the rains subsided at dawn with the bell of Hatsuse Temple.[54] Toyoo regretted only that their reunion had been so long delayed.

---

51. A popular belief held that ghosts and other supernatural beings cast no shadows, nor did their clothing have seams, however cunningly they might disguise themselves as humans.

52. Naniwa is the present-day city of Osaka.

53. Twin cedars standing on the banks of the Hatsuse River and associated with the sun goddess, Amaterasu, were celebrated in poetry as a sign of meeting or reuniting. In "The Jeweled Chaplet," chapter 23 of *The Tale of Genji*, Ukon, overjoyed to find Tamakazura at Hasedera, recites: "Had I not come to the spot where twin cedars stand would I have met you on this ancient river bank?" Ukon adds, "on the rapids of joy" (*ureshiki se ni mo*), in which *se* (rapids) also denotes an occasion or opportunity and echoes the *se* in Hatsuse.

54. The image of clouds rising at night and producing rain, which then abates at dawn,

The Third Month came. Kanetada said to Toyoo and his wife, "Of course it does not compare with the capital, but it surpasses Kii: Yoshino, fair of name, is a lovely place in spring. Mount Mifune, Natsumi River—one would never tire of the views even if one saw them every day, and how fascinating they will be right now. Let us set off." Manago smiled and said, "People of the capital, too, say that they regret not seeing the place that good people consider good,[55] but since childhood I have suffered from an ailment that causes blood to rush to my head when I go among a crowd or walk a long distance, and so to my deep regret I cannot go with you. I eagerly await the souvenir that you will surely bring me from the mountains." Kanetada and his wife encouraged her, saying, "Yes, walking would no doubt be painful. We do not have a carriage, but one way or another we shall not let your feet touch the ground. Think how worried Toyoo would be if you stayed behind." Toyoo said, "Since they have spoken so reassuringly, you cannot refuse to go, even if you collapse on the way." And so reluctantly, she went. Everyone dressed gaily, but none could compare with Manago's beauty and elegance. They stopped at a certain temple with which they had long been on friendly terms. The head priest welcomed them: "You have come late this spring. Half the blossoms have fallen, and the warbler's song has grown a bit wild, but I shall show you where to find the good spots that remain." He served them a beautifully simple and refreshing evening meal. The sky at dawn was thick with haze, but as it cleared they looked out from the temple's high vantage point and could clearly see monks' residences here and there below. Mountain birds were chirping everywhere; trees and grasses blossomed in a profusion of color.[56] Although it was a mountain village like any other, they felt as though their eyes had been opened anew. Thinking that the falls offered the most for a first-time visitor, they employed a guide familiar with that area and set out. They wound their way down the valley. At the site of the ancient detached palace, the rapids crashing along the boulders, and tiny sweetfish struggling against the current delighted their eyes. They spread out their cypress boxes and reveled in the outing as they dined.

---

suggests lovemaking. There is perhaps an echo here of the legend of King Xiang of Chu, who dreamed that he had slept with a woman at Shaman Hill who turned out to have been a rain cloud. Mount Takama is the highest peak in the Katsuragi (formerly Kazuraki) Range, southwest of Hatsuse. The bell at Hatsuse Temple anticipates that of Dōjōji, the temple that figures in the ending of the story.

55. Alludes to a poem by Emperor Tenmu: "On the occasion of a visit to the Yoshino palace: Yoshino, which good people could well see was good, and said is good—look well, good people, look well" (Man'yōshū, no. 27).

56. Much of this description derives from "Lavender," chapter 5 of The Tale of Genji: "Stepping outside, he looked out from the high vantage point and could clearly see monks' residences here and there below." "The sky at dawn was very thick with haze, and mountain birds were chirping everywhere. The blossoms of trees and grasses whose names he did not know scattered in a profusion of color."

The two women, Manago and Maroya, plunge into the falls. (From SNKBZ 78, *Hanabusa sōshi, Nishiyama monogatari, Ugetsu monogatari, Harusame monogatari*, by permission of Shōgakukan)

Someone approached them, stepping from boulder to boulder. It was an old man with hair like a bundle of hemp threads but with sturdy-looking limbs. He came alongside the falls. Seeing the group, he eyed them suspiciously, where-upon Manago and Maroya turned their backs and pretended not to see him. Glaring at them, the old man muttered, "Disgraceful demons. Why do you go on deceiving people? Do you think that you can get away with this before my very eyes?" Hearing him, the two sprang to their feet and plunged into the falls. Water boiled up to the sky, and they vanished from sight.

Just then, as if the clouds had overturned a pot of ink, rain began to fall so hard that it might have crushed dwarf bamboo. The old man calmed the pan-icky group and led them down to the village where they cowered together under the eaves of a shabby house, feeling more dead than alive. The old man said to Toyoo, "Looking closely at your face, I see that you are tormented by that demon. If I do not help you, you will surely lose your life. Be very careful from now on." Pressing his forehead to the ground, Toyoo related the affair from the beginning. "Please help me keep my life," he pleaded fearfully and respectfully. The old man said, "It was just as I expected. That demon is a giant snake and very old. Having a lascivious nature, it is said to bear unicorns when it couples with a bull and dragon steeds when it couples with a stallion. It appears that out of lust, inspired by your beauty, it has attached itself to you and led you astray. If you do not take special care with one so tenacious as this, you will surely lose your life." When the old man had finished, they were more terrified than ever and began to pay reverence to him as if he were a god in human form. The old man smiled. "I am not a god. I am an old man named Tagima no Kibito who serves at Yamato Shrine. I shall see you on your way. Let us go." He started out, and they followed him until they reached home.

The next day, Toyoo went to the village of Yamato, thanked the old man, and gave him three bolts of Mino silk and twenty pounds of Tsukushi cotton. "Please perform a purification rite to protect me from the monster," he asked respectfully. The old man accepted the gifts and divided them among the priests under him, keeping not a single measure for himself. Then he turned to Toyoo: "The beast has attached itself to you out of lust for your beauty. You, for your part, have been bewitched by the shape it took and have lost your manly spirit. If henceforth you summon your courage and calm your restless heart, you will not need to borrow an old man's powers to repel these demons. You must quiet your heart." Feeling as though he had awakened from a dream, Toyoo thanked the old man profusely and returned. To Kanetada he said, "It is because of the unrighteousness of my heart that I have been deceived by the beast these years and months. There is no reason for me to presume on your family, neglecting my duty to my parents and elder brother. I am deeply grateful for your kindness, and I shall come again." So saying, he returned to the province of Kii.

When they heard of these dreadful events, Toyoo's parents, Tarō, and Tarō's wife felt even greater pity for him in his blamelessness and also feared the demon's tenacity. "It is because he is single," they said, and discussed finding a wife for him. In the village of Shiba lived a man known as the steward of Shiba. He had sent his daughter into service at the sovereign's palace, but his request that she be relieved had been granted and, thinking that Toyoo would make a fine son-in-law, he approached the Oya family through a go-between. The talks went well, and in no time the two were engaged. An escort was sent to the capital for her, and so the palace lady, whose name was Tomiko, happily came back home. Having grown accustomed to her years in service at the palace, she surpassed other women in the beauty of her manners and appearance. When Toyoo was received in Shiba, he saw that Tomiko was a great beauty. Satisfied in every respect, he could barely remember the giant snake that had been in love with him. Nothing unusual occurred the first night, and so I shall not write about it. The second night, Toyoo was feeling pleasantly tipsy: "Considering your years of living in the palace, I suppose you have grown to dislike us rustics. I wonder which captains and councillors you slept with there. It is too late now, but I am quite provoked by you," he said playfully. Tomiko looked up quickly: "And I am all the more provoked by you, who have forgotten your old vows and bestowed your favors on this undistinguished person."[57] The voice was unmistakably Manago's, although her form had changed.

---

57. She echoes the spirit that possesses the lady in "Evening Faces," chapter 4 of *The Tale of*

Appalled, Toyoo felt his hair stand on end and was speechless with horror. The woman smiled: "Do not be startled, my husband. Even though you have quickly forgotten our vows of the sea and of the mountains,[58] a bond from a former life ensured that I would meet you again. But if you believe what others say and try to avoid me, I shall hate you and take revenge. However tall the mountains of Kii may be, I shall pour your blood from the peaks into the valleys. Do not throw your precious life away." He trembled with fear and felt faint, thinking he was about to be taken. Someone emerged from behind a folding screen, saying, "Master, why do you fret so? This is such an auspicious match." It was Maroya. Aghast, Toyoo shut his eyes and fell face down. Manago and Maroya spoke to him by turns, now soothing, now threatening, but he remained unconscious until dawn.

Then Toyoo slipped out of the bedroom, went to the steward, and described to him these frightening events. "How can I escape? Please help me find an answer," he said, keeping his voice low in case someone was listening behind him. The steward and his wife blanched at the news and were grief stricken. "What shall we do? There is a monk from Kurama Temple in the capital who goes on a pilgrimage to Kumano every year. Yesterday he took up lodgings at a temple atop the hill across the way. He is a wonderfully efficacious dharma master, revered by everyone in the village for his skill in exorcising plagues, evil spirits, and locusts. Let us call on him for help." They sent for him quickly and, when he finally came, explained the situation. With his nose in the air, the monk said, "It should not be difficult to capture these fiends. You need not worry." He spoke as if nothing could be easier, and everyone felt relieved. First he asked for some orpiment, which he mixed with water and poured into a small flask. Then he turned toward the bedroom. When everyone ran to hide, the monk said with a sneer, "All of you stay there, young and old. I shall capture this giant snake now and show it to you." He advanced toward the bedroom. The moment he opened the door, a giant snake thrust out its head and confronted him. And what a head this was! Filling the door frame, gleaming whiter than a pile of snow, its eyes like mirrors, its horns like leafless trees, its gaping mouth three feet across with a crimson tongue protruding, it seemed about to swallow him in a single furious gulp. He screamed and threw down the flask. Since his legs would not support him, he rolled about, then crawled and stumbled away, barely making his escape. To the others he said, "Terrible! It is a calamitous deity; how can a monk like me exorcise it? Were it not for these hands and feet, I would have lost my life." Even as he spoke, he lost conscious-

---

Genji: "Though I admire you so much, you do not think of visiting me, but instead keep company with this undistinguished person and bestow your favors on her. I am mortified and hurt."

58. In addition to reminding the reader of the cliché that vows are "deeper than the seas and higher than the mountains," this phrase refers to the seas around the province of Kii and the mountains in the province of Yamato.

Toyoo becomes slightly intoxicated and discovers that the serpent's jealous spirit has entered Tomiko's body. (From SNKBZ 78, *Hanabusa sōshi, Nishiyama monogatari, Ugetsu monogatari, Harusame monogatari*, by permission of Shōgakukan)

ness. They held him up, but his face and skin looked as though they had been dyed black and red, and he was so hot that touching him was like holding one's hand to a fire. He appeared to have been struck by poisonous vapors, for after he came to himself he could move only his eyes, and although he seemed to want to speak he could not produce a sound. They poured water over him, but finally he died. Seeing this, they felt as though their spirits had fled their bodies, and they could only weep in terror.

Composing himself, Toyoo said, "Since it pursues me so tenaciously and cannot be exorcised by even such an efficacious monk, it will track me down and catch me as long as I am here between the heavens and the earth. It is false hearted of me to let others suffer for the sake of my own life. I shall not ask for help any longer. Please set your minds at ease." With this he started toward the bedroom. The steward and his wife cried, "Have you lost your senses?" but he paid no attention and kept going. When he opened the door gently, all inside was calm and quiet. The two were seated facing each other. Tomiko turned to Toyoo: "What enmity has led you to enlist another to capture me? If you continue to treat me like an enemy, I shall not only take your life but also torment the people of this village. Be glad that I am faithful to you; forget your fickle thoughts." As she spoke she put on coquettish airs, moving him to disgust. Toyoo replied, "It is as the proverb says: *Although a man means no harm to the tiger, the tiger will hurt the man.* Your inhuman feelings have led you to pursue me and even to torment me time and time again, and what is more, you answer my playful words by speaking of a horrible revenge. You terrify me. Nevertheless, your love for me is in the end no different from the love that humans feel. It is cruel for me to stay here and cause these people to grieve. If only you will spare Tomiko's life, you may take me anywhere you wish." She nodded joyfully in agreement.

Toyoo went again to the steward and said, "Since I have been possessed by this wretched demon, it would be wrong for me to stay on here and torment everyone. If I may have your permission to depart right now, I am sure your daughter's life will be spared." The steward refused, saying, "I know one end of the bow from another, and the Oyas' view of such an unavailing notion would put me to shame. Let us think some more. There is a priest named Hōkai at the Dōjōji in Komatsubara, a venerable prayer master.[59] He is very old now and I have heard that he does not leave his room, but surely he will not reject an appeal from me." He galloped off on horseback. Since the way was long, he reached the temple at midnight. The old priest crept out of his bedroom and listened to the story. "Indeed, you must be perplexed. Having grown so old and foolish I doubt that I will be of any use, but I cannot ignore a calamity in your family. You go ahead; I shall follow soon." He took out a stole scented with the smoke of poppy seeds from previous exorcism rituals and gave it to the steward. "Trick the monster into coming close, throw this over its head, and press down with all your might. If you falter, it will probably escape. Pray well and do your best," the priest instructed him carefully. Rejoicing, the steward galloped back.

He quietly summoned Toyoo, exhorted him to carry out the priest's instructions carefully, and handed him the stole. Toyoo hid it inside his robes and returned to the bedroom. "The steward has just given me permission to go. Let us be on our way." She was delighted. Pulling out the stole, he quickly threw it over her and pressed down with all his strength. "Oh! You're hurting me! How can you be so heartless? Take your hands off me!" she cried, but he pressed down ever harder. Priest Hōkai's palanquin arrived right away. Helped inside by the steward's people, he mumbled incantations as he pushed Toyoo away and lifted the stole. Tomiko was lying prone, unconscious, and on top of her a white serpent, more than three feet long, lay coiled, perfectly motionless. The old priest picked it up and placed it in an iron bowl that one of his disciples

59. The Buddhist temple Dōjōji, about twenty-five miles from Shiba, is remembered particularly for the legend of the monk Anchin, from Kurama, and Kiyohime, the daughter of the steward of Masago in the village of Shiba. According to the legend, Kiyohime fell in love with the handsome young Anchin when he spent the night at her father's house on a pilgrimage to Kumano. When he failed to return to her, as he had promised, her jealous anger turned her into a serpent and she pursued him to Dōjōji, where he had taken refuge inside the temple bell. She coiled around the bell and roasted him to death. The story is familiar through many versions, including the nō play Dōjōji.

held up to him. As he renewed his incantations, a little snake, about one foot long, came slithering out from behind the folding screen. He picked it up, placed it in the bowl, covered the bowl tightly with the stole, and entered his palanquin with it. The people of the household, tears streaming down their faces, held their hands together and paid reverence to him. Returning to the temple, he had a deep hole dug in front of the main hall, had the bowl buried there with all its contents, and forbade them ever to appear in this world again. It is said that a serpent mound stands there to this day. The steward's daughter eventually fell ill and died. Toyoo's life was spared. So the story has been handed down.

[*Hanabusa soshi, Nishiyama monogatari, Ugetsu monogatari, Harusame monogatari*
NKBZ 48: 345–359, 360–375, 411–441, translated by Anthony Chambers]

Chapter 15

EIGHTEENTH-CENTURY WAKA AND

NATIVIST STUDY

By the mid-eighteenth century, the center of poetic activity for the thirty-one-syllable waka had shifted from the *dōjō*, or court aristocrats, who had monopolized waka in the medieval period, to the *jige*, or commoner poets, who revolutionized the genre. The court poets had belonged to various aristocratic poetic houses such as the Nijō, Reizei, Kyōgoku, and Asukai, which formed exclusive societies in which poetry was read, composed, and taught. These poets based their poetry on that of the *Kokinshū*, the *Shinkokinshū*, and other imperial waka anthologies of the Heian and early medieval periods, with guidelines for the interpretation and composition of poetry passed on from master to disciple in the form of closely guarded *hiden*, or secret transmissions.

In the seventeenth century, a number of commoner scholars challenged the authority of the court poets, charging that their blind acceptance of the traditions of their poetic houses, as imparted in the secret transmissions, drove them to perpetuate errors in textual interpretation and imposed arbitrary restrictions on poetic composition. Such scholars as Shimokōbe Chōryū (1627–1686), Toda Mosui (1629–1706), and, most notably, the Buddhist priest Keichū (1640–1701) responded to the weaknesses they found in court poetics by developing a philological mode of scholarship in which they interpreted texts not by relying on the authority of previous commentaries but by searching for evidence within the texts themselves. This methodological break with the court poets was accompanied by a shift in emphasis to the eighth-century *Man'yōshū*, which generally lay outside the purview of court poetics. Chōryū and Keichū produced groundbreaking studies of this anthology, which were followed in the eighteenth century by a revival of poetry in the *Man'yōshū* style, a movement led by the scholar and poet Kamo no Mabuchi (1697–1769).

Kokugaku, or nativist learning, is a term used to refer to a number of tendencies in Tokugawa literary, religious, and political thought, all concerned in some way with recovering native Japanese traditions and cultural forms. Although in the nineteenth century, kokugaku developed into a form of religious-political activism aimed at overthrowing the Tokugawa bakufu and restoring imperial rule, during the eighteenth century it was primarily a scholarly movement directed toward the study of native literary texts and Shintō. Important early figures in kokugaku include Keichū, who is often considered its founder, and Kada no Azumamaro (1669–1736), who was a Shintō priest at the Fushimi Inari Shrine in Kyoto and a scholar of Shintō and waka. In turn, Keichū and Azumamaro were important influences on Kamo no Mabuchi and Motoori Norinaga (1730–1801), both of whom wrote commentaries on Japanese texts and helped systematize kokugaku as a scholarly methodology.

As a form of scholarship, kokugaku can refer broadly to scholarship centered on native Japanese texts, but the term is usually used more narrowly to indicate a certain attitude toward these texts, one that tries to find in them a uniquely Japanese spirit or tradition. The study of the Japanese classics had taken the form of commentaries as early as the Nara period (710–794), when scholars began to comment on the *Nihon shoki* (*Chronicle of Japan*) not long after it was written. Such major works of the Heian period as *The Tale of Genji, The Tales of Ise,* and the *Kokinshū* became the object of extensive commentaries from around the twelfth century onward. The development of kokugaku in the Tokugawa period involved a repudiation of many of these earlier commentaries, in part because of their philological inaccuracies, but also because they interpreted Japanese texts through the lens of foreign value systems like Buddhism.

Kokugaku scholars leveled similar charges against contemporary Tokugawa-period attempts to view Japanese texts through a Song Confucian conceptual framework, especially the application to Japanese texts of the notion that literature should serve to "encourage good and chastise evil" (*kanzen chōaku*). By liberating native texts from what they saw as the constrictive moralism of foreign forms of thought, kokugaku scholars could read these texts as the product of a native emotionality that expressed human nature on a more elemental level, irreducible to the rigid good and evil of Confucianism and Buddhism (although as many scholars have pointed out, the supposedly purely native values of kokugaku in fact owed much to various strains of continental thought). Indeed, the development of kokugaku represents one response to the growing sense of social fragmentation in the eighteenth century, and in this context the discovery of a native emotionality was related to the imagining of a distinctly Japanese social structure in which people lived in a state of harmony, their relations governed by mutual empathy rather than by oppressive moral codes.

As scholars became concerned with identifying purely Japanese forms of literary expression, waka—which had been the orthodox literary form from as early as the Heian period—acquired greater ideological significance. Kokugaku scholars such as Mabuchi and Norinaga regarded Japanese history as a process of decline from an ideal past, a decline brought about by the infiltration of foreign (particularly Chinese) institutions and forms of thought. These scholars were attracted to waka because both its language, which eschewed Chinese loanwords, and its subject matter, whose emotional character was contrasted with Chinese rationalist thought, were considered to be purely native. Also, many kokugaku scholars were preoccupied with the supposedly corruptive effects of the introduction of Chinese characters (*kanji*) to Japan and saw waka as preserving an ancient oral culture uncontaminated by the continental writing system. In this way, even though the composition and study of waka retained their importance as literary endeavors, they also became a way to access an idealized native language and culture.

DEBATE ON THE *EIGHT POINTS OF JAPANESE POETRY*

The debate on the *Eight Points of Japanese Poetry* (*Kokka hachiron*), which centered on the question of the relationship of poetry to politics and morality, was probably the most important literary controversy of the eighteenth century. It began in 1742 when Tayasu Munetake requested that Kada no Arimaro (1706–1751), who was in his service at the time as a classical studies assistant, give his views on waka. Arimaro, the nephew and adopted son of the kokugaku scholar Kada no Azumamaro, responded with an essay entitled *Eight Points of Japanese Poetry* (*Kokka hachiron*), made up of eight short sections, each dealing with a specific aspect of waka, such as poetic diction, the origins of waka, and the relative merits of various periods in the history of waka.

The section that sparked the greatest disagreement was the one entitled "On Poetry as Amusement," in which Arimaro argued that although waka was a source of pleasure and a means for scholars to appreciate the purity of the Japanese language, it had no ethical or political value. This view collided with that of Munetake, who, in a rebuttal entitled *My Views on the Eight Points of Japanese Poetry* (*Kokka hachiron yogen*, 1742), upheld the political and moral functions of poetry from a Confucian perspective. Both Arimaro and Munetake saw poetry as having undergone a process of historical change in which it had become separated from its original character as orally performed song and developed into a form of linguistic artifice. But whereas Arimaro celebrated this transformation of poetry into artifice or rhetoric (*waza*), praising the *Shinkokinshū* for its refined expression and criticizing ancient poetry as crude and unsophisticated, Munetake deplored what he regarded as the trivialization and decadence of poetry and tried to recover its moral function by returning to the poetry of the *Man'yōshū*.

In time, Munetake asked Kamo no Mabuchi (1697–1769) for his opinion on the matter. Mabuchi agreed that poetry should have a role in governance and, like Munetake, found his poetic ideal in the *Man'yōshū*. But he criticized Munetake for locating the political function of poetry in its ability to serve as a vehicle for rational principle (*ri*). In the passage included here from *Another Reply to Tayasu Munetake* (*Futatabi kingo no kimi ni kotaematsuru no sho*, 1744), Mabuchi argues that the political benefits of poetry come instead from its ability to express people's deepest emotions, thereby allowing rulers to know the true nature of their subjects (a view that itself can be seen as very Confucian, although Confucian in a different way from the position taken by Munetake). Within Munetake's framework the depiction of immorality in poetry was tolerated to the extent that it showed the negative consequences of such behavior, thus serving as an admonition. For Mabuchi, however, this immorality was admissible because it represented genuine emotion, a view that appeared again and was developed further in Motoori Norinaga's theory of literature as an expression of *mono no awaré*, or the pathos of things.

While Munetake and Mabuchi did not agree completely, the series of responses to Arimaro's essay made it apparent that Mabuchi had more in common with Munetake than Arimaro did, and eventually Arimaro resigned from his position with Munetake and recommended Mabuchi as his replacement. Mabuchi served Munetake from 1746 to 1760, a period in which both cultivated their *Man'yōshū*-style poetry and became two of the most influential poets of their day. The debate over the *Eight Points of Japanese Poetry* marked a watershed in the history of early modern waka. All the participants were united in rejecting the authority of medieval court poetics and so clearly belonged to a new age in waka, while their differences of opinion brought to the forefront key issues regarding the value, function, and content of poetry. The debate was revived in the 1760s with a new set of participants, when Norinaga, Ban Kōkei (1733–1806), and others offered responses to the *Eight Points of Japanese Poetry*, in this way developing their own ideas through a dialogue with Arimaro's essay and demonstrating its continued relevance.

KADA NO ARIMARO

EIGHT POINTS OF JAPANESE POETRY (KOKKA HACHIRON, 1742)

On Poetry as Amusement

Poetry [*uta*] does not belong among the six arts,[1] and so by nature it is of no use in governing the realm, nor is it of any benefit to everyday life. The state-

---

1. *Rikugei* refers to the six arts to be mastered by the Confucian gentleman: etiquette, music, archery, charioteering, calligraphy, and mathematics.

ments in the preface to the *Kokinshū* about how poetry "moves heaven and earth" and "arouses feeling in gods and demons" come from believing in baseless theories.[2] To a certain extent, poetry may console the hearts of brave warriors, but how could it do this as well as music does? Poetry may facilitate the relations between men and women, but doesn't it also encourage licentiousness? Poetry is therefore not something to be venerated. Rather, when we see poems that are elegant in expression or deep in meaning, with their words skillfully connected or depicting a scene as if before our very eyes, we also want to achieve this. And if we can manage to compose even a single poem that satisfies our heart, it will never fail to bring pleasure. This is the same feeling as, for example, that of a painter who successfully completes a picture or a *go* player who wins a game.

Still, it is not without reason that scholars devote themselves to poetry. I say this because even though Japan has been the country of countless generations of our ancestors, it was late in developing a culture and thus used Chinese characters for writing. Japan has nothing, from ceremonies and laws down to court dress and utensils, that did not originate in a foreign country. Only poetry uses the natural sounds of our country, without mixing in Chinese words at all. Furthermore, epithets,[3] phrases in which words shift in meaning,[4] and other such devices cannot be expressed in the Chinese language. Scholars simply take joy in the fact that poetry is something purely of our country. But the court nobles, who have been idle since governance of the realm passed to military families in the medieval period, devote themselves entirely to poetry and end up calling it the "Way of Japan" [*waga shikishima no michi*]. Not only does this fail to recognize the nature of poetry, but it is an absurdity that comes from not understanding the meaning of the term "Way."[5] This is not even worth refuting.

ON CHOOSING WORDS

If, as I just said, scholars take pleasure in poetry because it is something purely of our country, then what should we think of those who disregard the fact that the style of poetry has changed greatly as the times have changed, ignoring what

---

2. These quotations, as well as the following comments on the effect of poetry on warriors and on relations between the sexes, are from the *kana* (Japanese) and *mana* (Chinese) prefaces to the *Kokinshū*. The comment on "believing in baseless theories" refers to the fact that the two prefaces to the *Kokinshū* draw heavily on the Great Preface to the *Book of Songs*.

3. Another term for *makurakotoba*, or pillow words, a type of poetic epithet that modifies the following word.

4. Arimaro appears to be referring here to the use of *kakekotoba*, or pivot words, a punning technique in waka.

5. The implication is that the term "Way" (*michi*) properly refers to teachings that provide a normative standard for behavior, a function that, according to Arimaro, poetry does not serve.

others do and instead composing poetry using the words of antiquity? If they did this, then we could perhaps say that the ancient words would be passed on forever and would not die out, and this does make a certain amount of sense. But poetry was originally meant to be sung. In the past, adults could sing and clear their hearts, but today only children can take pleasure in singing. Even if we composed the words of a song ourselves, what kind of melody could we use to sing these words, from among the many types of elegant and vulgar music that please the ear today, that would be sufficient to clear our heart? It is best, then, to set aside for the moment the original nature of poetry and instead take pleasure, as everyone else does, in refined expression. And in regard to refined expression, we must take care with both the expression of the entire poem and the continuity of the lines. But ancient words are simple and unsophisticated, so they include words that do not go well together, words that are strained and words that are choppy. Therefore, if we use ancient words indiscriminately, our poetry will not be refined, and thus since the time of Emperor Tenji [r. 668–671] and Emperor Jitō [r. 690–697], they gradually changed these words and moved toward elegance [ga].

[Karonshū, NKBZ 50: 540–543, introduction and translation by Peter Flueckiger]

TAYASU MUNETAKE

MY VIEWS ON THE EIGHT POINTS OF JAPANESE POETRY
(KOKKA HACHIRON YOGEN, 1742)

It is truly the Way of poetry [uta]⁶ that placates the heart. For this reason, in the reigns of the ancient sage-kings⁷ they valued rites and music. Song [uta], dance, string instruments, wind instruments, and percussion instruments all are part of music. Noble poetry aids people, and base poetry harms people. Still, when one recognizes base poetry as bad, it can serve as an admonition. Even after the decline of proper music, the sage Confucius compiled the Book of Songs in order to guide people. He did this because even though this poetry was not sung in later ages, it was superior to ordinary language [tsune no kotoba] in placating people's hearts. By the Tang dynasty [618–907], poetry had not entirely lost this purpose, but in many ways it had become only decorative and did not help the people at all. The poetry of our country does not have as deep a meaning as that of other countries, but it is gentle and appeals to people's

---

6. In this section the term uta is translated alternately as "song" and "poetry," depending on the context. Both English terms are relevant, as Munetake's argument is based on the idea that poetry, as something that was originally sung, belongs by nature among the "rites and music" used by the ancient sage-kings to govern.

7. The legendary sage-kings of ancient China.

hearts. It should not be expected to be equal to that of other countries, but now, when it is composed without any meaning at all, with people simply taking pleasure in composing something unusual or decorative, it cannot be used as a basis for matters of good and evil and even encourages licentiousness. Therefore we should follow the manner of ancient poetry and learn from that of other countries, so that it can become something that truly helps people.

[NKT 7: 99–100, translated by Peter Flueckiger]

KAMO NO MABUCHI

ANOTHER REPLY TO TAYASU MUNETAKE
(*FUTATABI KINGO NO KIMI NI KOTAEMATSURU NO SHO*, 1744)

It is difficult for the ruler to govern if he does not understand human emotions. In general, it is hard for people of high position to understand human emotions, and even more so for the one at the very top. It is poetry that allows us to know of human emotions and the customs of a country. . . .

The Song Confucians discussed poetry only in terms of rational principle [*ri*] and claimed that the sole purpose of poetry was to encourage good and punish evil.[8] Although rational principle may generally apply in the world, one cannot govern solely by reason. Poetry expresses the true nature of people, and true emotions expressed just as they are felt do not necessarily follow reason. In Japanese we refer to those unbearable emotions that go above and beyond reason as "irrepressible yearnings.". . . But if such irrepressible feelings are just flatly declared, then who would sympathize? It is by singing, using gentle words and with pathos [*aware*] in our voice, that we express those human emotions that exist outside the realm of reason. This is why in the *Book of Songs* the songs of Zheng and Wei are not discarded, nor are the songs of maidens among the mulberry bushes edited out.[9]

[NKT 7: 154–155, translated by Peter Flueckiger]

KAMO NO MABUCHI

Kamo no Mabuchi (1697–1769) was one of the most prominent figures of eighteenth-century Japanese literary culture, revolutionizing the waka genre with his *Man'yōshū*-style poetry and producing interpretations of ancient

---

8. Refers to the views of Zhu Xi (1130–1200) and his followers.

9. Zheng and Wei were feudal states of the Spring and Autumn period (722–482 B.C.E.) known for their lewd songs. Mulberry bushes have an erotic connotation in Chinese poetry as a site for illicit liaisons.

Japanese texts that formed the basis for much of the later *kokugaku* (nativist learning) scholarship. Mabuchi was born in Hamamatsu into a collateral branch of the family that served as hereditary priests at the Kamo Shrine in Kyoto, so he had an early association with Shintō. In his youth he studied waka under Sugiura Kuniakira (1678–1740), a disciple of the kokugaku scholar Kada no Azumamaro, and was introduced to the teachings of Ogyū Sorai's Ancient Rhetoric school through his Chinese studies teacher Watanabe Mōan (1687–1776). Mabuchi had met Azumamaro when he stopped in Hamamatsu en route from Kyoto to Edo on the Tōkaidō, and in 1728 he registered in Azumamaro's school, eventually moving to Kyoto to study with him more intensively. After Azumamaro's death in 1736, Mabuchi moved to Edo and joined an intellectual circle that included Kada no Arimaro, Azumamaro's nephew and adopted son, and Tayasu Munetake. In Edo, Mabuchi established his Agatai waka school, which cultivated many of the most important poets and scholars of the late eighteenth century. Between 1746 and 1760 he served Munetake as a classical studies assistant, during which time he was active as a waka poet and produced some of his best scholarly work. After his retirement from official service, Mabuchi continued to write commentaries and treatises until his death in 1769.

Mabuchi's thought centered on the notion of the ancient Way (*kodō*), a term he used to refer to an all-encompassing principle underlying ancient Japanese religion, government, and literature. In the medieval period, Shintō (Way of the gods), the study of poetry (*kagaku*), and the study of ancient court practices (*yūshiki*) had been separate fields of study, but for Mabuchi they were inseparable, as each offered a different manifestation of the "ancient Way." He believed that this ancient Way had been lost over time, obscured by the corruptive influence of foreign thought. In *Thoughts on the Nation* (*Kokui kō*, 1765), for example, he describes how even though such Confucian virtues as benevolence (*jin*) and righteousness (*gi*) appear to bring moral order to the world, they in fact are evidence of a decline in society, because in ancient Japan such virtues were practiced so automatically that there was no need even to give them names.

Despite his negative view of contemporary society, Mabuchi was ultimately optimistic about the ability of the people of his own time to recover the ancient Way. He believed that it could be reached by assimilating the spirit of the ancients, or the "ancient heart" (*inishie no kokoro*). Following a methodology similar to that of Sorai's Ancient Rhetoric school, he also saw ancient language as the means by which the ancient heart and the ancient Way could be conveyed. This concern for ancient language, specifically the ancient Japanese language, is reflected in Mabuchi's linguistic philosophy, as presented in *Thoughts on Language* (*Goi kō*, 1769) and in a number of studies he wrote about the Japanese language and literature of the ancient period, such as his commentaries on the *Man'yōshū* (*Man'yō kai*, 1749, and *Man'yōshū kō*, 1768), on *makurakotoba*, or poetic epithets (*Kanji kō*, 1757), and on *norito*, or Shintō prayers (*Norito kō*, 1768).

Mabuchi especially valued the composition of poetry and prose in the ancient style, viewing this literary practice as a means of embodying ancient language and thus recovering the ancient heart and the ancient Way. In texts like *Thoughts on Poetry* (*Ka'i kō*, 1764), selections from which are translated here, and *New Learning* (*Niimanabi*, 1765), he advocates learning waka by imitating the *Man'yōshū* (*Collection of Ten Thousand Leaves*, 759), the ancient-period Japanese poetry anthology, stressing its "sincerity" (*makoto*), "rhythm" (*shirabe*), and "masculine style" (*masuraoburi*). By contrast, he criticizes the waka from the Heian-period *Kokinshū* (*Collection of Old and New Japanese Poems*, 905) onward as weak, artificial, and in the "feminine style" (*taoyameburi*). Mabuchi's ideological concern with ancient literature is reflected in how he actually tried to compose poetry in the style of the *Man'yōshū*, going beyond earlier Tokugawa-period scholars who had taken up the *Man'yōshū* as an object of study while continuing to compose their own poetry in later styles.

The following poem, composed on the topic of "storm" (*arashi*), has a rich melody and a sweeping vista typical of Mabuchi's mature style. Here Mabuchi combines a series of "strong" images: the eagles (*washi*), the wild fields at Suga, and the strong winds. Like Munetake, Mabuchi draws on the *Man'yōshū*, specifically number 3352: *When I hear the calls of the cuckoos crying out on the rugged moor of Suga in Shinano, I realize time has passed.* The poem also is reminiscent of the *Man'yōshū* in focusing on a single image rather than, as was the tendency in Heian poetry, contrasting two or more separate images.

shinano naru	A storm rages,
suga no arano o	straining even the wings
tobu washi no	of the eagles that soar
tsubasa mo tawani	over the rugged moor
fuku arashi kana	of Suga in Shinano[10]

THOUGHTS ON POETRY (*KA'I KŌ*, 1764)

In ancient times, people's hearts were direct and straightforward. Because their hearts were direct, their actions were simple, and because things were simple, the words they spoke also were uncomplicated. When emotions rose up in their hearts, they would put them into words and would sing, and they called this "poetry" [*uta*]. When they sang, they did so directly and with a single heart. Their words were in ordinary, straightforward language, so they flowed and were well ordered without any conscious effort to make them so. Poetry was simply the expression of a single heart, so in the past there was no particular differentiation between those who were poets and those who were not. The august

---

10. Shinano Province is in present-day Nagano Prefecture.

reigns of those distant gods, our emperors, continued without end, and they governed for countless generations.

But then the ideas and words of babbling China and of India were blended together and introduced into our country, where they were mixed in with our own ideas and words. Things became complex, so the hearts of those here who used to be straightforward were blown by a wind from the shadows and turned wicked. Their words became disordered like dust on the road and grew extremely diverse. Thus in recent times, the feelings and words of poetry have become different from ordinary feelings and words. In poetry, people distort their proper heart and seek words to describe this distortion. They use worn-out methods[11] and now compose with a heart that is not their own. Just as a reflection in a dusty mirror[12] always is clouded and the pistils of flowers[13] that grow among rubbish always are filthy, how could the words chosen and uttered by the clouded and filthy hearts of people of later times fail to be soiled?

Still, this does not mean we should just complain and give up. We have forgotten that the form of the mirror made by Ishikoritobe[14] and the flowers of the trees planted by Itakeru no Mikoto[15] have been passed down to this day.[16] Because people have become accustomed to dirt and rubbish, they do not even recognize them as filth, and they do not realize that it is possible for things to be otherwise.

When we remember that heaven and earth are unchanging and that all the birds, beasts, plants, and trees are the same as in they were the past, why should only humans be different now from how they used to be? Well, when people's hearts became more clever, they began to quarrel with one another, so naturally they learned wicked ways, causing society to decline as well. Why would a person who realized this was bad not want to return to the better ways of the past? We should create in ourselves a desire to return to the past, each morning face the sacred mirror of old, combine with it a thousand treasured flowers, and strive to compose poetry and prose in a way reminiscent of their earlier form

---

11. That is, they imitate old poetry. Mabuchi advocates imitating the *Man'yōshū*, so he is not necessarily against all imitation of old poetry, but here he is criticizing people who, instead of composing based on what they actually feel, simply express conventional sentiments in imitation of the *Kokinshū* and other later poetry.

12. A metaphor for *kokoro* (heart).

13. A metaphor for *kotoba* (words).

14. In the *Nihon shoki*, Ishikoritobe is the goddess who crafted the mirror used to lure out Amaterasu when she hid in a cave. In the *Kojiki* this goddess appears under the name Ishikoridome no mikoto. The mirror she created is said to have later become one of the three imperial regalia.

15. In the *Nihon shoki*, Itakeru no Mikoto is the god who sowed the seeds of trees throughout Japan.

16. Continuing the earlier metaphor, these represent the ideal heart and words of ancient Japan, which, according to Mabuchi, have been passed down in the ancient texts that he values.

and beauty. Because the people of today are by nature the same as the people of the past, when they carry out such practices their hearts become polished mirrors and their words move past the overgrown moor to become flawless mountain flowers. The return to the past in all matters is valued even in China, where the rulers constantly change. But in this country, governed by an unbroken line from heaven, why should we cling to times that have fallen like a mountain stream rather than return to the style of reigns as lofty as the clouds in heaven, ruled over by the glorious imperial ancestors?

Those who say that poetry should be composed in the style of later times have extremely small hearts. Despite their decline, the ways of our country from the time of the awesome distant gods are still evident, and those who long for the past are not few. Still, when we read the writings of ages as lofty as the skies, sometimes it seems as if the perilous road of the high mountain is cut off, the awesome depths of the blue sea cannot be known, the spring moon is obscured by haze, and the autumn wind mixes in leaves from other trees.[17] Many people of later ages have been confused by this haze and go in the wrong direction or are captured by the ways of babbling foreign lands and forget the original ways of their own land.

In ancient poetry, though, the feelings and words composed by people a thousand years ago remain completely unchanged with the passage of time, just as autumn leaves and cherry blossoms are the same now as in the past. If we follow the courtly style [*miyaburi*] of the renowned Fujiwara[18] of the deep purple[19] and of Nara, leave behind the inferior acorn-dyed gray of the woodsman,[20] and strive over time to compose poetry, the ancient style will naturally be absorbed into our hearts. Then we will surely grasp the lofty and manly spirit of the ancients, whose straightforward hearts and courtly words had not a speck of filth or dust. When we go on to read various ancient texts, it will be as if having crossed over the deep mountains we came out into a village, or having traversed the distant sea we arrived at our country of destination. We will realize that the world was originally without human artifice and recognize the vanity of a heart that pursues such artifice. We will learn about the reigns of the gods, who with the ancient and tranquil great Way of this peaceful country governed in accordance with heaven and earth and without regulation, fabrication, force,

---

17. "Leaves from other trees" is a metaphor for foreign ideas; the rest of the sentence refers to the general difficulty of interpreting ancient texts.

18. Mabuchi is referring to the capital at Fujiwara (694–710, when it was moved to Nara), not to the aristocratic clan of the same name.

19. *Komurasaki* (deep purple) is associated with Fujiwara because of the purple color of *fuji* (wisteria). Because it was the color worn by high-ranking members of the nobility, it also connotes courtliness.

20. The rusticity of the woodsman is meant to represent the opposite of courtliness and functions as a metaphor for inferior poetry.

or instruction. The poetry of the ancients makes this clear, and our own poetry should be the same. . . .

. . . We should be careful, though, about poetry by women. The anonymous poems in the *Kokinshū*[21] include some that begin with those Nara-period poets who came after the *Man'yōshū* and continue until the early years of the present capital.[22] If we recite these poems and compare them with those of the Engi period [901–923],[23] we will see that the former imitate the *Man'yōshū* in that they have a wide range of subject matter and a rich and courtly spirit. They also are smooth and refined, though, so they are truly poems appropriate to women. In ancient times men were brave and manly, and so was poetry. But by the time of the *Kokinshū*, even men were composing in an effeminate style, so women's and men's poems were indistinguishable. So while one could say that it is enough for women to study the *Kokinshū*, this collection is from an age that had declined somewhat. People's hearts were full of artifice; their words no longer were sincere [*makoto*]; and their poems were crafted deliberately, so their poetry was naturally poor and cumbersome in conception.

We should grasp the ancients' straightforward, lofty-minded, and courtly qualities from the *Man'yōshū* and, only after that, study the *Kokinshū*. Generations of people have forgotten this principle and have studied the *Kokinshū* as the basis for poetic composition, so no one is able to compose poems like those in the *Kokinshū*.[24] And no one really understands the spirit of the *Kokinshū*. When we look up at things from below, they are blocked by clouds and haze and are unclear. But if we find a ladder, we can immediately climb up it, see what is at the top, and then look at what is below. As I have said before, we can see everything in a single glance, as when we look out across the land from on top of a high mountain. It is the same with people's hearts. Although it is difficult for those below to fathom the hearts of those above, it is easy for those above to know the hearts of those below.[25] For this reason the Chinese, also, have said that we should study by beginning at the top and climbing down from there.

[*Karonshū*, NKBZ 50: 569–573, 579–580, introduction and translation
by Peter Flueckiger]

---

21. *Kokinshū*, the first imperial anthology of waka, was edited in the early tenth century.

22. That is, the early Heian period. The capital was moved to Heian (present-day Kyoto) in 794.

23. This is the period during which the *Kokinshū* was compiled.

24. The idea here is that poets can compose properly in the *Kokinshū* style only if they have a thorough knowledge of the *Man'yōshū*. Mabuchi continues this line of reasoning in the following section, in which he explains the methodology of learning the *Man'yōshū* before the *Kokinshū* in terms of the perspective one gains by climbing to a vantage point in order to view what lies below.

25. Those "above" and "below" refer here to the rulers and the ruled.

MOTOORI NORINAGA

Motoori Norinaga (1730–1801) was born in Matsusaka in Ise Province (Mie), the second son of Ozu Sadatoshi, a wholesale cotton-goods merchant. When Norinaga was eleven his father died, and when he was nineteen he went to Yamada in the same province to be adopted as the son of a paper merchant. But things did not go well there, and he returned to his original family. A year later, in 1751, his elder brother died, and Norinaga became the head of the Ozu house. He found, however, that he was not suited to be a merchant, and in 1752 he moved to Kyoto at his mother's urging to study medicine. At that time he changed his surname to Motoori. In Kyoto he read the Chinese classics under Hori Keizan (1688–1757), a Confucian scholar and a friend of Ogyū Sorai (1666–1728), the founder of the Ancient Rhetoric school. Keizan then introduced Norinaga to the commentaries of Keichū (1640–1701), whose philological methodology was a cornerstone of much of Norinaga's own work.

In 1757 Norinaga returned to Matsusaka to practice medicine, and around this time he produced his first treatise, "A Small Boat Punting Through the Reeds" (Ashiwake obune), an essay on waka. In the following year he began giving lectures on *The Tale of Genji* and wrote "Defense of Aware" (Aware ben), a short piece in which he introduced his theory that *aware* (pathos) is the underlying theme of Japanese literature and transcends differences of genre. He followed these preliminary studies with two major works, both written in 1763, that present his literary thought in a form that remained largely unchanged for the rest of his life. The first of these, *My Personal View of Poetry* (*Isonokami no sasamegoto*), is a treatise on waka, and the other, *The Essence of The Tale of Genji* (*Shibun yōryō*), deals with the *monogatari* (tale/novel), specifically *The Tale of Genji*.

Norinaga's literary thought is centered on the notion of *mono no aware*, or the pathos of things. He used this term to imply a certain emotional sensitivity to and capacity for empathy, as opposed to rational thinking or rigid morality, and regarded it as a key to understanding both literature and human nature. Norinaga describes human nature as fundamentally weak and emotionally susceptible and sees the strict moral self-control demanded by Confucianism and Buddhism as suppressing natural human emotions. On one level, Norinaga's view that literature is an outgrowth of *mono no aware* can be read as a kind of expressive theory, but he was ultimately concerned with intersubjectivity, with grasping the emotional essence (*aware*) of others. For Norinaga, the objective of emotional self-expression was not only the release of pent-up emotions but also the process of understanding others, of becoming the object of emotional empathy. Modern scholars have argued that Norinaga's idea of *aware*, particularly his deep sympathy for the emotional plight of others, grew out of the sense of alienation experienced at the time by urban commoners (*chōnin*). They have also pointed out that his theory has much in common with the idea of *ninjō* (human emotion), which was the basis of contemporary kabuki and jōruri, and was also developed in the early nineteenth century in Tamenaga Shunsui's (1790–1843) *ninjōbon*.

After his early studies of Heian literature, Norinaga's scholarship developed in a new direction when he turned his attention to Shintō and the earliest Japanese texts. He was interested particularly in the eighth-century *Kojiki* (*Record of Ancient Matters*), a mythohistory that describes the creation of Japan by the gods and the descent of the imperial line from its divine ancestors. It is said that Norinaga was urged to study the *Kojiki* by Kamo no Mabuchi, who was the foremost kokugaku scholar of the time. The two met in a famous one-night meeting in Matsusaka in 1763, soon after which Norinaga officially registered as a student in Mabuchi's school and began corresponding with him, discussing poetry and scholarly matters. In 1771 he wrote the first draft of *The Spirit of the Gods* (*Naobi no mitama*), which encapsulates his view of the Way of the gods, or the ancient Way, and which later became the general introduction to the *Kojikiden*, his vast commentary on the *Kojiki*, which he completed in 1798. Norinaga valued the *Kojiki* as a pure example of the ancient Japanese language, and in the *Kojikiden* he tried to recover the original oral text that he believed lay underneath the obscuring layer of Chinese characters in which the *Kojiki* had been recorded. Other important late works of Norinaga include *A Jeweled Basket* (*Tamakatsuma*), a series of essays covering a wide variety of topics begun in 1793 and written over a period of several years; *The Tale of Genji, a Small Jeweled Comb* (*Genji monogatari tama no ogushi*), a revision of the earlier *The Essence of The Tale of Genji* (*Shibun yōryō*), completed in 1796; and *First Steps in the Mountains* (*Uiyamabumi*), a guide to studying the Japanese classics, written in 1798.

In his writings on Shintō and the ancient Way, Norinaga argued against the position of Ogyū Sorai, who believed that before the appearance of the Confucian sages in ancient China, the world had no ethical order. Instead, in Norinaga's view, the true Way was a creation of the Japanese gods, not of human sages, and allowed both the individual and the state to be governed without the need for the explicit rules and rigid moral codes that he saw as characteristic of Confucianism. In his commentaries on the Japanese classics, Norinaga, like Mabuchi, believed that Japanese texts provided not only pleasure but also ethical, aesthetic, social, and political norms—that is, a "Way" (*michi*), which he regarded as a superior alternative to the Confucian and Buddhist "Ways." After coming under the influence of Mabuchi, Norinaga began to attack the notion of the "Chinese spirit" (*karagokoro*), a term that he used not only to refer to the adulation of Chinese cultural artifacts, such as the Chinese writing system and Chinese texts, but also to indicate the infiltration of a foreign mode of thought, an ethical rationalism that divides all things into good and bad. Norinaga argued that before the importation of such external artifacts, the Japanese had expressed tender, honest emotions, as depicted in the thirty-one-syllable waka and monogatari of the early periods. Today, however, owing to the influence of the "Chinese spirit," the Japanese have lost touch with their "real emotions" (*jitsujō*) or "sincerity" (*makoto*) and have no choice but to seek them again in ancient and classical Japanese literature.

Norinaga's work was continued by his disciples, who at first were clustered in the Ise, Mino, and Owari Provinces, with Matsusaka, Norinaga's birthplace, at the center, but gradually spread throughout the country. Norinaga's son Motoori Haruniwa (1763–1828), Suzuki Akira (1764–1837), and Ishizuka Tatsumaro (1764–1823) continued his linguistic studies, and Ishihara Masaakira (1760–1821) and Fujii Takanao (1764–1840) carried on his literary studies. Norinaga's philosophy of the ancient Way was further developed by Hirata Atsutane (1776–1843), who molded it into a religious-political ideology that had a powerful influence on the movement that culminated in the Meiji Restoration. The following is Norinaga's most famous waka.

shikishima no	If I were asked
yamatogokoro o	to explain the Japanese spirit,
hito towaba	I would say it is
asahi ni niou	wild cherry blossoms
yamazakura hana	glowing in the morning sun![26]

A SMALL BOAT PUNTING THROUGH THE REEDS
(ASHIWAKE OBUNE, 1757)

In the following selection from the opening of "A Small Boat," Norinaga advocates an autonomous role for waka poetry by declaring that it should be subordinated to neither politics nor personal moral cultivation but should simply be an expression of authentic human emotion. As one example, he challenges the view that Buddhist monks should not compose love poetry, arguing that even though their religious practices may demand that they suppress such emotions as love, in the realm of poetry

---

26. Norinaga affixed this poem to a self-portrait dating from 1790. It represents his ideal of seeking out an essentially Japanese spirit. Cherry blossoms are a conventional image in the Japanese poetic tradition, and the morning sun is associated with Japan, which, as the country farthest to the east, is described (in both Norinaga's time and today) as the "land of the rising sun." *Shikishima no* is a *makurakotoba*, an epithet for Yamato (Japan).

these emotions are accepted unconditionally in their natural state. While at first Norinaga may appear to be advocating nothing more than the direct expression of raw emotion, he reveals a more complex view when he introduces the idea that historical decline has also degraded people's emotions, leading to a somewhat paradoxical state in which natural emotions no longer arise naturally. For people of his own age to compose poetry, he then argues, they must recapture the elegance of the past by immersing themselves in the world of classical texts.

The essence of poetry is not to aid in governance, nor is it for personal cultivation. Rather, it consists of nothing but simply expressing what is felt in the heart. . . .

Poetry is something that properly expresses feelings. It expresses the feelings in the heart, regardless of whether they are good or evil. So what problem is there with expressing the amorous desire that is felt in the heart? If the poem comes out well, then why should it not be praised? If it is an excellent poem, we should not be concerned whether it was composed by a monk or a layman. The judgment of a person's conduct and the correctness or incorrectness and good or evil of his heart should be critiqued and discussed according to the Ways that are appropriate to this.[27] In the Way of poetry, though, one should not argue such matters; in this Way, one should determine only whether a poem is good or bad. Why should one make baseless arguments about why monks should not compose love poems? People seem to think that just because someone takes the tonsure, his heart becomes completely like that of a buddha or bodhisattva. They show greatly different attitudes toward monks and laymen in the way they severely reprimand a monk if he shows even the slightest amorousness, treating it as a great evil. It is true that amorousness is what the Buddha warned against most strongly and that nothing else binds people more to transmigration and delusion, so it is of course something that monks should despise and avoid. Still, monks are no different from laymen in nature. At bottom, they also are ordinary humans [bonbu], so we should not expect their human emotions [ninjō] to be any different. . . .

Poetry is a Way that uses language and that properly expresses feelings. If we were to say what we felt, without artifice, it would not be a poem. Even if it did result in a poem, it would be a bad poem unworthy of consideration. Therefore we should carefully consider our language. As long as our words are beautiful, even if the conception underlying our poetry is not deep, it will naturally be carried along by the beauty of the words and become deeper. Conversely, even deep emotions will sound shallow when poorly expressed in words.

---

27. That is, Confucianism and Buddhism. See the discussion of this issue in the selections from *The Essence of The Tale of Genji.*

Ancient poetry used beautiful language and was moving even when it expressed real emotions just as they were. The reason is, first of all, that in the past, even ordinary language had ancient elegance. Also, when people of that time composed poetry, the poetry was proper and well ordered, so it was naturally beautiful. Furthermore, their hearts were genuine and their human emotions were deep, so without even trying, their words were beautiful, their hearts were deep and meaningful, and they naturally achieved an indescribable effect in their poetry.

But as the world changed, we entered an age in which ordinary language greatly changed, becoming filthy, and human emotions have naturally turned shallow. Therefore if we composed poetry that expressed what we felt, without refining our language, it would surely be extremely bad poetry. If we composed poetry that expressed the emotions of the present age in the language of the present age, it would no doubt be very unseemly. . . .

The expression of human emotions reveals weakness like that of a woman or child. Manly and proper steadfastness does not represent human emotion. . . . For example, on the battlefield it is the custom of the loyal warrior to die honorably for his lord and country, throwing away his life without the slightest regret. But at the moment of death does he not think sadly of the wife and children he has left behind at home? Does he not wish to see his aged parents just one last time? When on the verge of death, how could even the most demoniac ruffian not feel sad? To think of one's family at such a moment, to be moved by sorrowful pathos [*aware*], and to feel mournful are natural human emotions shared by all people and do not differ between sages and ordinary humans. . . .

As another example, when a dearly beloved child dies, the parents are extremely saddened, and both father and mother surely must feel the same sadness. But while the father appears little affected, the mother is overcome by grief and lost in tears. The reason is that the mother does not suppress her true emotions and expresses them just as they are, while the father is concerned about how he appears to others. Lest they think him weak he brings his heart under control and keeps himself from shedding a single tear. The sorrow welling up in his breast is not revealed on his face, and he puts on the appearance of brave resignation. The mother, on the other hand, appears frantic and disorderly and improper, but this is the state of emotions just as they are. The appearance of the father is truly manly and steadfast, and it is admirable that he does not lose control at all, but these are not his true emotions. If he were really like this from the depths of his heart, he would be extremely cruel, like a tree or a stone. . . .

If we constantly devote ourselves to the Way of poetry and constantly read *The Tales of Ise*, *The Tale of Genji*, *The Pillow Book*, *The Tale of Sagoromo*, and other works of pathos [*aware*], our heart will naturally become polished and gentle and will become one with the heart of the ancients. We will be captivated by the flowers and birds, and our eyes will be delighted by the moon and the snow. Our heart will naturally be captivated by the appearance of the changing of the seasons and by the other joyful and sorrowful things of this impermanent world and will come to be refined, so that the poetry we compose will also come to embody natural emotions. The virtue of poetry, then, is not just to express emotions and give vent to feelings but also to assimilate the ancient elegance, to come to possess the heart of the ancients, and to compose poetry like the ancients.

[MNZ 2: 3, 28–29, 31–32, 35–37, 42, introduction and translation by Peter Flueckiger]

MY PERSONAL VIEW OF POETRY
(ISONOKAMI NO SASAMEGOTO, 1763)

In My Personal View of Poetry Norinaga further develops many of his ideas about waka poetry that he had first presented six years earlier in "A Small Boat Punting Through the Reeds." In My Personal View of Poetry he describes poetry as the product of the emotional experience he refers to as mono no awaré, or the pathos of things. For Norinaga, one who "knows mono no awaré" has the capacity to be deeply moved personally, as well as to sympathize with the sufferings of others. One of the most important ideas in My Personal View of Poetry is the notion that by making our deepest emotions known to others, poetry serves to establish feelings of mutual empathy that form the basis for our relations with others. Norinaga argues that deep emotions can be communicated only through language that possesses aya, or design, a term he uses for an elevated form of language associated with the oral recitation of poetry. He then discusses the mutual understanding achieved through poetry as having certain political and social benefits. While this may seem to contradict Norinaga's earlier statement in "A Small Boat" that the essence of poetry is not to aid in governance, he is careful to point out that these political and social benefits are a secondary effect of poetry and are not part of its essential nature, which is simply to express human emotions. Another key point presented in the selections translated here is the idea that poetry is the repository of an essentially Japanese spirit, a view that has much in common with Norinaga's later writings on Shintō.

Poetry is not just something that we compose when we are unable to bear mono no awaré [the pathos of things] and that naturally relaxes the heart. When we feel awaré [pathos] very deeply, composing alone will not satisfy our heart, so we have a person listen to us and are comforted. When another hears what we have composed and sympathizes, it greatly clears the heart. Moreover, this is something natural. For example, if a person feels something strongly about something that is difficult to keep bottled up in his heart, even if he talks to himself about it in great detail, his heart will not be cleared. So he tells someone else and has him listen, and then his heart is cleared. And if the person who hears agrees with what he says and sympathizes, the poet's heart will be cleared even more. Therefore it is difficult not to tell others about the things that we feel deeply in our heart. When we see and hear things that are unusual, frightening, or amusing, we always want to tell others about them, and it is difficult to keep them bottled up in our heart. Although it is of no use to ourselves or others when we tell them about such things, it is natural that we cannot help but do so. This is the nature of poetry, so having someone listen is truly the essence of poetry and not an accidental aspect of it. Those who fail to understand this principle say that true poetry consists simply of saying what we feel, just as we feel it, whether well or poorly, and that the aspect that relates to the listener is not true poetry. Although this seems reasonable at first glance, it fails to grasp the true principle of poetry. . . . It is important that poetry be heard by another who sympathizes, so it is the essential nature of poetry that we create design [aya] in our words and sing in a drawn-out and well-modulated voice, and it has been this way since the age of the gods. . . .

Ordinary language can explain the meaning of things in great detail, and its logic sounds precise, but without poetry it is difficult to express the indescribable emotions of aware. The reason that such deep indescribable aware can be expressed through poetry is because poetry has design in its words. Because of this design, even limitless aware can be expressed. . . .

Our august[28] country is the august country of the sun goddess Amaterasu Ōmikami. It is the beautiful and magnificent august country superior to all other countries, so people's hearts and actions, as well as the words they speak, are straightforward and elegant. In the past, the realm was governed peacefully without incident, so unlike in other countries there was not the least trace of anything bothersome or troubling. But then writings came over from China, and people began to read and study them. When people saw things written about other countries in these writings, they were impressed that everything appeared to be wise and profound, and they came to think of these writings as splendid. Soon they came to do nothing but emulate their spirit, and in the Nara period everything was as it was in China. But even at this time, poetry, alone, was different from all other things, as both its spirit and its language remained in accordance with the natural spirit of our august country from the age of the gods. . . .

Now I will speak about the benefits for people who are sensitive to aware. First, those who govern the people and the country must have a detailed knowl-

---

28. The term "august," which is meant to convey somewhat the sense of Norinaga's self-consciously archaic style in this passage, is used as a translation for various honorific terms pertaining to gods and emperors. This kind of deliberate archaism is particularly prominent in *The Spirit of the Gods*.

edge of the condition of the hearts of the ordinary people and know *mono no aware*. Yet those of high rank usually are ignorant of such detailed knowledge of the hearts of those who are lowly and beneath them. In general those who are prosperous and powerful have all their needs met, so they do not understand what it is to be troubled, and thus they have little sympathy. They do not understand that lowly and poor people always have many sorrows, so they feel no compassion.

Even though they may have a general knowledge of such matters from reading Japanese and Chinese writings or from things they are told, the fact that they do not share these experiences themselves means that even though they may read or hear of them, they think of them as something pertaining to others, and thus they do not sink deeply into their hearts. Poetry, though, sings of various deeply felt joys and sorrows just as they are, so even if we have not experienced them at all ourselves, when we hear the poetry, it sinks into our heart and we can understand these feelings. We can know in great detail how such and such a person upon encountering such and such circumstances will feel such and such emotions and how this will make them joyful or resentful. The hearts of the people of the realm will appear more perfectly than a reflection in a clear mirror, so this will naturally bring about feelings of sympathy, which will make the rulers not want to do things that harm the people. This is a benefit of making people sensitive to *mono no aware*.

This does not pertain only to those who govern, though. In people's everyday dealings with one another as well, those who do not know *mono no aware* have no sympathy for anything and are often hard-hearted and cruel. Because they have no encounters with various matters, they do not understand them. The rich do not know the hearts of the poor; the young do not know the hearts of the aged; and men do not know the hearts of women. . . . But when people deeply understand the hearts of others, they naturally act so as not to harm society or other people. This is another benefit of making people sensitive to *mono no aware*.

> [MNZ 2: 112–113, 154, 166–168; *Motoori Norinaga shū*, SNKS 60: 312–315,
> 414, 441–446, introduction and translation by Peter Flueckiger]

THE ESSENCE OF THE TALE OF GENJI (*SHIBUN YŌRYŌ*, 1763)

Norinaga is considered the first major Japanese theorist of prose fiction and is noted for fitting Japanese waka poetics into the theory of the monogatari (tale/novel), which had been traditionally treated on either Confucian or Buddhist grounds, usually negatively, as immoral or deceptive, but sometimes positively, as a means of leading to virtue or enlightenment. In the passage translated here from *The Essence of The Tale of Genji*, Norinaga argues that the monogatari needs to be judged according to its own value system, rather than those of Confucianism and Buddhism. This value system, which monogatari share with waka poetry, is governed by the emotional sensitivity that Norinaga refers to as *mono no aware* or the pathos of things, a sensitivity to both phenomena in the natural world, such as cherry blossoms and other traditional objects of poetic beauty, and events in the human world, particularly those that cause sorrow and suffering. He argues that in *The Tale of Genji* those characters who are presented as "good" are not those who obey rigid moral strictures but those who "know *mono no aware*," or those who are emotionally sensitive and compassionate toward others. Norinaga does not go so far as to maintain that *mono no aware* is a reversal of Confucian and Buddhist values but contends that when reading monogatari, we should simply suspend such moral judgments and instead focus on the depth of emotion, or *mono no aware*, displayed by the characters.

All judgments of good and evil differ depending on the relevant Way. They also differ depending on time, place, and circumstance. Some things are considered good according to the Way of Buddhism but evil by Confucian scholars, and some things are considered good according to the Way of Confucianism but evil by Buddhist priests. In this manner, good and evil differ. Poetry and monogatari, unlike the Ways of Buddhism and Confucianism, are not a Way for freeing ourselves from delusions and entering enlightenment, nor are they a Way for cultivating ourselves, managing our household, and governing our country. Still, they naturally contain their own good and evil.

When we investigate what is good and evil in a monogatari, we find that even though it is not explicitly different from what is good and evil in both the Ways of Confucianism and Buddhism, it is nonetheless different. First, Confucianism and Buddhism are Ways that instruct and guide people, so sometimes they conflict with human emotions and severely reprimand people. According to these Ways, it often is evil to act in accordance with our natural emotions, and so it is good to try to suppress these emotions. But monogatari are not didactic writings, so they have no relation to the good and evil of Confucianism and Buddhism. Instead, what they consider good or evil is simply the distinction between what is in keeping with human emotions and what is not. . . .

Until now, all commentaries have emulated the theories of moralistic Confucian and Buddhist writings, so they also tried to force monogatari to become didactic. They comment on what this monogatari speaks of as good as if it were evil and claim that it is this or that admonition or teaching. Commenting in this way, they often mislead the heart of the reader and lose sight of the true intentions of the author. The reason is that when they try to force the monogatari into being an admonition and view it in terms of punishing evil, they also dilute the *mono no aware* [pathos of things]. Although perceptive people are not led astray by the commentary, most people use it as a guide and accept things just as the commentary says to, so they are greatly misled by it. We should not read this monogatari as an admonition at all, as this is not the true intention of the author. Proof that monogatari are not moralistic can be found clearly in the "Fireflies" chapter of *The Tale of Genji*, which I cited earlier.[29] One should always read monogatari with an emphasis on *mono no aware*.

The fifty-four chapters of *The Tale of Genji* can be exhausted in the single phrase "to know *mono no aware*." I have already spoken of the general meaning of *mono no aware*, but now I will go into it in more detail. Upon seeing, hearing, and encountering various events in the world, to savor the heart of these many events, and to discern the heart of them with our own heart is to know the heart of events. It is to know the heart of things and to know *mono no aware*.

When we make further distinctions, we find that *mono no aware* involves knowing the heart of things and knowing the heart of events. To discover their hearts and to be moved in accordance with their different qualities is to know *mono no aware*. For example, when seeing splendid and beautiful cherry blossoms in full bloom, to appreciate the blossoms as beautiful is to know the heart of the thing. When discovering the beauty of the blossoms, we are moved by their beauty. This is *mono no aware*. But not to be moved by the beauty of the blossoms, no matter how beautiful they may be, is to fail to know the heart of the thing. Such a person is not affected by the beauty of the blossoms at all. This is to fail to know *mono no aware*.

Also, when encountering the deep grief of another and witnessing his or her great sorrow, it is because we know about the events that ought to make us sad that we realize that he or she must be sad. This is to know the heart of events. To know the heart of events that ought to make us sad and to be moved in our own heart by the realization of how sad something must be is *mono no aware*. When we know why something ought to be sad, even if we try to ignore it and not be moved, we will naturally find it hard to bear and will not be able to help but sympathize. This is human emotion. The person who does not know *mono no aware* does not feel anything and does not discern the heart of the event that ought to make him sad. Therefore no matter how much he witnesses another's sorrow, he does not relate to it at all, so his heart is entirely unmoved.

I have just presented these as one or two examples, but we should know the *mono no aware* of all events in a similar manner. Events vary in that some move us lightly and others move us strongly, but each event in the world has its own *mono no aware*. Although there are differences in the good or evil and correctness or incorrectness of the events that are moving, we are moved by something that arises spontaneously and is difficult to bear, so even though our heart may be our own, it is not under our own control, and even events that are evil and

---

29. The "Fireflies" chapter of *The Tale of Genji* includes a scene in which monogatari are defended against the charge that they are a frivolous diversion and full of falsehoods. In an earlier section of *The Essence of The Tale of Genji*, Norinaga provides an extensive commentary on the defense of the monogatari in the "Fireflies" chapter and uses the ideas presented in this chapter to develop his own theory of the monogatari. Norinaga includes a similar discussion in his later work *The Tale of Genji, a Small Jeweled Comb.*

incorrect can be moving. Although we may try to not be moved by them because they are evil, we are moved nevertheless because our emotions arise spontaneously and are difficult to hold back. This is why the common Ways of Confucianism and Buddhism caution against being moved by such evil events and teach us not to be moved by evil. Poetry and monogatari, however, consider it good in such cases to be moved by knowing the heart of things and the heart of events and set aside the issue of whether these events are good or evil and correct or incorrect. Instead they refer to everything that is moving as *mono no awaré* and consider this something wonderful. . . .

The Way of the Buddha is a Way that cannot be practiced by someone who is weakhearted and knows *mono no awaré*. It is a Way, then, that is practiced by trying to become a person who does not know *mono no awaré*. First, we must break our ties of affection to our beloved family and take the tonsure. This is something very difficult to bear from the standpoint of human emotions. It is the Way of the Buddha to be resolute in separating from human emotions. If we know *mono no awaré* at such a time, we will be unable to take the tonsure. We must also change our appearance, renounce wealth, retire to the forest, not eat fish or meat, and forsake the pleasures of song and women. All these things are difficult to bear from the standpoint of human emotions. But it is the Way of the Buddha to endure this in carrying out religious practices, so we cannot adhere to such practices if we know *mono no awaré*. Furthermore, when urging others and leading them to the Way of the Buddha and helping them to escape the cycle of life and death and transmigration, it is difficult to save them if we know *mono no awaré*. Unless we become someone who does not know *mono no awaré* and urges people resolutely, we cannot lead them to salvation. . . .

In general, the true emotions of a human being are weak and foolish, like those of a woman or a child. To be manly and resolute and wise is a superficial display and does not represent true emotions. When we look into the depths of the true heart, we find that even the wisest people are no different from women and children. The only difference is whether or not they are ashamed and conceal their emotions. . . .

Poetry emerges from a knowledge of *mono no awaré*, and we come to know *mono no awaré* by reading poetry. This monogatari was written based on a knowledge of *mono no awaré*, and so we will come to know *mono no awaré* well through reading this monogatari. Therefore poetry and monogatari are identical in nature. . . .

Confucianism has the basis of Confucianism as its essence; Buddhism has the basis of Buddhism as its essence; and monogatari have the basis of monogatari as their essence. To discuss these by straining to compare them is to argue by using forced analogies. It is correct to discuss poetry and monogatari according to the essence of what they are based on, but it is erroneous to use forced analogies to discuss poetry and monogatari by applying the essence of other kinds of writings, no matter how good this essence may be. . . .

To view this monogatari from a didactic perspective is, for example, like cutting down and using for firewood a cherry tree that had been planted in order to view its blossoms. Firewood is indispensable to everyday life, so I do not despise it as something evil, but it is hateful to make into firewood a tree that was not meant for that purpose. Many other good trees are suitable for firewood, so there surely will be no lack of firewood, even without cutting down cherry trees. Cherry trees are originally planted in order to view their blossoms, so to cut them down would go against the heart of the person who planted them. Would it not be heartless to cut them down, pointlessly, for firewood? The essence of cherry trees is simply always to appreciate the *mono no aware* of the blossoms.

[MNZ 4: 37, 56–58, 61–62, 94, 100, 111–112; *Motoori Norinaga shū*, SNKS 60: 82–83, 124–127, 134–135, 202, 215, 240–241, introduction and translation by Peter Flueckiger]

THE TALE OF GENJI, A SMALL JEWELED COMB
(GENJI MONOGATARI TAMA NO OGUSHI, 1796)

The Tale of Genji, a Small Jeweled Comb is a revision of *The Essence of The Tale of Genji (Shibun yōryō)* and contains many of the same themes. In the passages translated here, Norinaga continues with his idea that monogatari should operate according to a value system different from that of Confucian and Buddhist views of morality, and he supports his theory by citing Murasaki Shikibu's own views on the monogatari as presented in the "Fireflies" (Hotaru) chapter of *The Tale of Genji*.

The Intentions of the Monogatari

Over the years there have been various interpretations of the purpose of this monogatari. All of them, however, have neglected to take into account the basic nature of these books we call monogatari. They discuss *The Tale of Genji* only in the terms of Confucian and Buddhist writing, which was contrary to the author's intent. Although it has random resemblances to Confucian and Buddhist writings, we cannot point to them as characterizing the whole work. Its overall meaning differs sharply from other works of that sort. . . .

Since monogatari generally depict events of this world and the thoughts and deeds of human beings, by reading them we naturally gain a knowledge of life and better understand the actions of human beings and the workings of their emotions. This is the main object of those who read monogatari. . . .

This more or less is the reason why monogatari are read. The reader puts herself into a situation from the past and assumes the emotions that moved the people of the past. The reader likens her own circumstances to those of the past and thus comes to understand these emotions. In this way the reader finds some solace for her melancholy.

From these examples we can see that the attitude of those who read the old monogatari—which is to say the present-day readers of *The Tale of Genji* as well—is quite different from that of the readers of most Confucian and Buddhist works.

Now in the "Fireflies" chapter Murasaki Shikibu makes quite clear her intentions in writing *The Tale of Genji*. . . . This monogatari, she says, is indeed a complete fiction, but it is not groundless nonsense. She does not state actual names or describe events as they actually happened. They are events such as one sees or hears of every day in this world—events that so intrigue us that we wish to pass them on to ages to come. As Murasaki Shikibu could not bear to shut these up in her heart, she wrote them out in the form of a monogatari. You must realize, therefore, that she would say that fiction though it is, false it is not. You may wonder, then, whether all these are events that Murasaki Shikibu herself saw or heard of in her own time and wrote down, concealing only the names. But such was not the case. They represent no particular persons or events, but merely such things as one sees or hears of every day in this world, things by which she was deeply moved and which she could not let pass. She thus would create a certain person or event, commit her thoughts to that person, and so express what was in her heart. . . .

Good and evil as found in this monogatari are not the same as the good and evil described in Confucian and Buddhist works. Thus in many passages, it would be a mistake to interpret the good and evil in the monogatari strictly in a Confucian or Buddhist sense.

First, good and evil extend to all kinds of concerns. Even with regard to people, they need not apply only to thoughts and deeds. There are good and bad people in rank and social position, the noble being good and the lowly being bad. In the monogatari, those of high rank are called the "good people," while in our everyday speech we speak of "good family" or of "good or bad standing." Needless to say, we speak also of good and bad appearance. Again, long life, wealth, prosperity, and the acquisition of property all are good things; whereas short life, poverty, failure, loss of property, as well as illness, disaster, and the like all are bad things.

Nor is this so only in human affairs. Clothing, furniture, houses, and countless other such things all have their good and their bad. The good and bad are by no means limited to the realm of human thoughts and deeds. Moreover, good and evil change with the time and the situation. For example, an arrow is good if it penetrates its mark, while armor is good if it is impenetrable. On a hot summer day, what is cold is good, and in the cold of winter, what is hot is good. One traveling at night considers darkness bad, but one seeking to conceal himself considers moonlight bad. And so it is in all matters.

Thus too, there is good and evil in men's thoughts and deeds. The contrast is not as complete, and the good and evil differ depending on doctrine. What Confucianism considers good, Buddhism may consider bad; whereas what Buddhism considers good, Confucianism may consider bad. There is no absolute agreement. Likewise, what is considered good or evil in the monogatari may at times differ from Confucian and Buddhist concepts of good and evil.

What sorts of thoughts and deeds, then, are considered good and evil in the monogatari? Generally speaking, those who know what it means to be moved by things, who have compassion, and who are alive to the feelings of others are regarded as good; whereas those who do not know what it means to be moved by things are regarded as bad. Having said this much, there may appear to be no great difference from the good and evil of Confucianism and Buddhism. But if we state the case more precisely, we will find that sensitivity and insensitivity to the feelings of others do not correspond to Confucian and Buddhist concepts of good and evil. Moreover, even when it deals with good and evil, the monogatari does so in gentle and moderate terms, rather than in the overbearing manner of a Confucian disputation.

The main object of the monogatari, then, is understanding what it means to be moved by things, and hence it often opposes the teachings of Confucianism and Buddhism. When a man is moved by something, whether for good or bad, right or wrong, his feelings may contradict reason. Although it is improper thus to be moved, man's emotions do not always follow the dictates of his mind. They have a power of their own and are difficult to suppress. For instance, Genji's attraction to Utsusemi, Oborozukiyo, and Fujitsubo and his affairs with these ladies are, from the Buddhist and Confucian points of view, the most sinful and immoral acts imaginable. However good Genji might be in other respects, Buddhists and Confucianists would find it difficult to call him a "good person." But in the monogatari, his sinfulness and immorality are given no particular prominence; rather, his great depth of feeling is described again and again. Genji is depicted as the very model of the "good person," possessing every good quality imaginable. This, then, is the main intent of the monogatari, and the good and evil it depicts is different from that in Confucian and Buddhist works.

Yet the monogatari does not present such immorality as good. The evil in Genji's deeds would be plain to see even if it were never mentioned. Because there are enough books discussing such sins, there is no need to go so far afield as to a monogatari for information of this sort. The monogatari is not so inflexible a thing as the Confucian and Buddhist Ways; it does not require that man leave behind earthly lust in order to achieve enlightenment or that he "regulate his country, his family, and his person." It is simply a story of life in this world and so leaves aside questions of good and evil. Rather than concern itself with such matters as these, it depicts the virtues of knowing what it is to be moved by things.

In this respect, the monogatari may be likened to the man who wishes to enjoy the lotus flower and so must keep a store of muddy water, foul and filthy though it may be. It is not the mud—the illicit love depicted in the monogatari—that we admire; it is the flower that it nurtures—the flower of the emotions [mono no aware] it arouses. Genji's conduct is like the lotus flower that grows in muddy water yet blooms with a beauty and fragrance unlike any other in the world. Nothing is said about the water's filth; the monogatari concentrates instead on Genji's deep compassion and his awareness of what it means to be moved by things and holds him up as the model of the good man.

[*Kinsei bungaku ron shū*, NKBT 94: 93–94, 96–97, 99–103; MNZ 4: 183–186, 191, 197–199, translated by Thomas Harper]

THE SPIRIT OF THE GODS (*NAOBI NO MITAMA*, 1771)

The Spirit of the Gods, consisting of a main text interspersed with extensive notes, occupies a prominent place among Norinaga's writings as the general introduction to the *Commentary on the Record of Ancient Matters* (*Kojikiden*), his lifework. In the following excerpt from *The Spirit of the Gods*, Norinaga argues that the true Way—the normative system governing the world—is a product of the gods of Japan, whose deeds are recorded in the *Kojiki* (*Record of Ancient Matters*). He conceives of these gods as existing on a plane that transcends the limited powers of human understanding. They are the source of bad as well as good things in the world, but as humans we cannot pass judgment on them or seek the reasons for what they do but must simply submit to them with an attitude of passive resignation. For Norinaga, a proper recognition of divine authority serves to guarantee social and political harmony. He attributes the stability of Japan's single imperial line to the absolute legitimacy that the emperors had from being descended from the gods, specifically from the sun goddess Amaterasu Ōmikami. He argues that because China lacks such a divine source of authority, power is simply held by whoever can succeed as a master of realpolitik at any given moment, a situation that invariably leads to constant strife and usurpation. Norinaga recognizes that Chinese political thought also invokes a higher source of legitimacy, in the form of the notion that a ruler is granted a "mandate from heaven" to rule, but he sees this theory as nothing more than a fiction designed to conceal the exercise of power. He furthermore attacks this and other foreign theories, such as the Buddhist idea of karmic retribution, for their attempts to impose a rational framework on all events, with the bad always being punished and the good always being rewarded. Norinaga's view of Chinese history is similar to that expressed by Kamo no Mabuchi in *Thoughts on the Nation* (*Kokui kō*, 1765), and his theory of the Way as a creation of the Japanese gods challenges Ogyū Sorai's view that the Way is an invention of the human sage-kings of ancient China.

What follows is a discussion of the Way:

The august imperial country is the august country in which the awesome august divine ancestor Amaterasu Ōmikami[30] came into being.

---

30. According to the *Kojiki*, Amaterasu, the sun goddess, was the ancestor of the imperial line.

The reason this country is superior to all other countries is, first and foremost, apparent from this fact. Of all countries, not one fails to receive the august beneficence of this august goddess.

The august goddess held up the heavenly symbols in her august hands.[31]

These are the three divine treasures that have been transmitted as symbols of the throne through the many imperial reigns.

She decreed that the country be ruled eternally by her own august descendants.

That the succession of the lofty throne of the heavenly sun would be as immutable as heaven and earth was established at this point.

It was established that as far as the heavenly clouds trail and as far as the toad ranges,[32] this would be the country under the august governance of the imperial descendants of Amaterasu Ōmikami. Within the realm there were no disruptive gods nor any disobedient humans.

What lowly person would turn against the emperor, however many reigns may pass? Alas, during the numerous imperial reigns, there was occasionally a despicable one who did rebel, but in accordance with the precedent of the age of the gods, the emperor would instantly destroy him with a brilliant display of his august might.

Until the last of countless imperial reigns, the emperors will be the august descendants of the august goddess.

The emperors of the many imperial reigns are, in other words, the august descendants of Amaterasu Ōmikami. Therefore they are called the august descendants of the heavenly goddess, or the august descendants of the sun. . . .

To refer to how there must be a principle underlying things, or to various teachings, as this "Way" or that "Way," is a practice of foreign countries.

---

31. The heavenly symbols (or the three divine treasures) are the mirror, beads, and sword that constitute the imperial regalia. Norinaga is referring here to a passage in the *Kojiki* in which Amaterasu Ōmikami bestows these on her grandson Ninigi no Mikoto, ordering him to descend from the heavens to rule Japan. Ninigi no Mikoto is the great-grandfather of Emperor Jinmu, the founder of the Japanese imperial line and the first human ruler in the *Kojiki*.

32. *Man'yōshū*, no. 800, a *chōka*, contains the lines ". . . as far as the heavenly clouds trail, and as far as the toad ranges, he reigns."

Foreign countries are not the august country of Amaterasu Ōmikami, so they do not have stable rulers. Gods proliferate there like flies in summer and cause disruption, so people's hearts are wicked and customs are disordered. Even a lowly servant can instantly become a ruler if he seizes the country, so those above are wary of being overthrown by those below, and those below watch for those above to be off guard and plot to seize power. They regard each other with hostility, so since ancient times it has been difficult to govern. In those countries some displayed authority and intelligence, won over the people, seized countries held by others, took successful measures to avoid being overthrown themselves, governed well for some time, and served as models for later ages. In China they refer to such people as "sages." In times of chaos, people become practiced at war, and therefore it is only natural that many great generals emerge. In the same way, when people make great efforts to govern a country that has wicked customs and is difficult to govern, in each generation they devise various methods and become practiced in them, leading to the emergence of clever rulers. But it is mistaken to imagine these so-called sages to be as superior as the gods and to naturally possess miraculous powers. And yet they call what is created and established by these sages a "Way." When one considers the essence of what is called a "Way" in China, one finds that it consists of nothing more than the two elements of trying to seize others' countries and trying to keep one's own country from being seized. . . .

All things in heaven and earth are in accordance with the august will of the gods.

All things in this world, such as the changing of the seasons, the falling of the rain, and the gusting of the wind, as well as the various good and bad things that happen to countries and people, all are entirely the august works of the gods. Among the gods there are good ones and bad ones. Their actions are in accordance with their different natures, so they cannot be understood with ordinary reason. But all the people of the world, whether wise or foolish, are completely deluded by the theories of the Ways of foreign countries, so they are unable to understand this. This surely ought to be comprehended by scholars of matters of the imperial country from their reading of the ancient writings. Why is it that even these people are not able to understand? In foreign countries all the good and bad things that happen are either attributed to karmic retribution according to the Way of the Buddha or else thought to be, according to the various Ways of China, acts of heaven that are referred to as the "mandate of heaven."[33] All these theories are mistaken. The theories of

---

33. *Tenmei* (Ch. *tianming*) has a variety of meanings, but Norinaga is specifically dealing with

the Way of the Buddha are well understood by many scholars, so I will not discuss them now. But even intelligent people are deluded by the Chinese theory of the mandate of heaven, and none realizes its error, so I will clarify it here. The mandate of heaven is a pretext concocted by the sages of ancient China in order to be absolved of their crime of killing rulers and seizing countries. . . .

There is nothing to be done about the violence of the august hearts of the Magatsubi[34] gods, and this is extremely sad.

It is entirely due to the august will of these gods that there is harm in the world, that everything cannot be proper and in accordance with reason, and that there are many wicked things. When they are extremely violent, sometimes they cannot be contained even by the august power of Amaterasu Ōmikami and Takaki no Ōkami,[35] so even less can be done with the power of humans. The fact that many things go against ordinary reason, such as good people meeting misfortune and bad people prospering, is all because of the deeds of these gods. In foreign countries, though, there is no correct transmission of the age of the gods, so they do not understand this. Instead, they offer the theory of the mandate of heaven and believe that everything is established through proper reason. This is very foolish. . . .

When we inquire about what kind of a Way this Way is, it is not the natural Way of heaven and earth.

Understand this well, and do not mistakenly think it to be the same as the ideas of those such as Lao Zi and Zhuang Zi in China.

---

the theory that a ruler's legitimacy derives from having been granted a mandate from heaven to rule, a mandate that could be withdrawn if the ruler failed to govern properly. In Chinese historiography, the transfer of power from one dynasty to the next was explained in this way as a withdrawal of the mandate to rule from the old dynasty and its handover to the new dynasty, but here Norinaga argues that this kind of explanation is merely a pretense designed to grant moral authority to new rulers by covering up the fact that their power derived from an exercise of force.

34. An alternative reading of Magatsuhi. The two Magatsuhi gods are Yaso Magatsuhi no Kami and Ō Magatsuhi no Kami. According to the *Kojiki*, these gods have their source in the pollution to which the god Izanagi was exposed when he traveled to the underworld to visit his dead wife, Izanami. After returning from the underworld, Izanagi undergoes a process of purification by bathing in a stream, and the Magatsuhi gods are born from the impurities that he washes away from his body.

35. Another name for Takamimusubi, one of three gods described in the opening section of the *Kojiki* as coming into being at the beginning of heaven and earth.

Nor is it a Way created by humans.[36] Rather, this Way was created by the august spirit of the awesome god Takamimusubi.

All occurrences and things in the world came into being through the august spirit of this great god.

The divine ancestors Izanagi and Izanami initiated this Way.[37]

All occurrences and things in the world began with these two gods.

It is the Way that Amaterasu Ōmikami inherited, preserved, and passed on. For this reason it is called the Way of the gods. . . .

The meaning of this Way will become clear if one studies well the *Kojiki* and then the various other ancient writings. But the hearts of many generations of scholars have been bewitched by the Magatsubi gods, so they are deluded by Chinese writings. All their thoughts and words follow the spirit of Buddhism or of China, and they are unable to awaken to the spirit of the true Way.

. . . The teachings of this august country have been transmitted un-changed since the age of the gods, without the slightest trace of human cleverness, so they may sound shallow on the surface. But in truth they are limitless and are imbued with a deep and mysterious principle that cannot be understood by the human intellect. The failure to understand this comes from being deluded by Chinese writings. As long as one is unable to escape from these writings, even if one exhausts one's energy in study for a hundred or a thousand years, it will be a vain effort providing no clarification of the Way. All the ancient books have been written in Chinese, though, so one should also have a general knowledge of matters of that country, and in order to learn characters and the like, one should study Chinese books if one has spare time. As long as one is steadfast and unwavering in one's grasp of the spirit of the imperial country, this will cause no harm.

[MNZ 9: 49–55, 57–59, 61, introduction and translation by Peter Flueckiger]

FIRST STEPS IN THE MOUNTAINS (*UIYAMABUMI*, 1798)

Norinaga wrote *First Steps in the Mountains* near the end of his life, after completing his monumental *Commentary on the Record of Ancient Matters*. Consisting of a main

---

36. Here Norinaga is specifically targeting Ogyū Sorai's theory that the Way is a creation of the human rulers of ancient China.

37. Izanagi and Izanami are described in the *Kojiki* as giving birth to the islands of Japan as well as to a large number of other gods.

text with notes, it gives students guidelines to studying the Japanese classics, offering advice on not only the texts to study but also the methodologies and attitudes necessary to make scholarship a lifetime pursuit. In the passage translated here, Norinaga discusses the relationship between the two main divisions of his scholarship: literary studies and the study of the ancient Way. He puts his primary emphasis on the ancient Way but sees poetry and monogatari as indispensable to assimilating the ancient elegance that lies at the core of this Way. For this reason he criticizes those scholars who regard poetry as irrelevant to the Way, as well as those who ignore the Way and simply pursue poetry for the sake of pleasure.

By composing one's own poetry and constantly reading *monogatari*, one comes to know the elegant style of the ancients. This is, of course, useful for learning poetry, but it is also very helpful for carrying out scholarship that clarifies the ancient Way.

All people should know the elegant style. Those who do not know it do not know *mono no aware* and are heartless people. Such knowledge of the elegant style comes from composing poetry and reading *monogatari*. Knowledge of the elegant sentiments of the ancients and of everything about the elegance of the world in ancient times is a stepping-stone to knowing the ancient Way.

When we look at scholars today, though, those who concentrate on studying the Way are, as I said earlier, mostly just entangled in the Chinese type of argumentation and reasoning. They dismiss the composition of poetry, considering it a mere frivolity, and do not see poetic anthologies as worth opening and reading. They know nothing of the elegant sentiments of the ancients, so they are unable to know anything about the ancient Way that they purport to study. This is the Way of the gods in name only and is in fact just the thought of foreign countries, so in reality it is not the study of the Way.

Conversely, some people compose poetry and prose and have a fondness for the past but are simply caught up in surface elegance while neglecting the Way and paying no attention to it. So while they long for the past in all matters, enjoying ancient clothing and furnishings and becoming engrossed in ancient writings, these all are nothing more than elegant pastimes for them.

[MNZ 1: 6–7, 29; NST 40: 516, 539–540, introduction and translation by Peter Flueckiger]

Chapter 16

SHAREBON: BOOKS OF WIT AND FASHION

The *sharebon*, which flourished in the late eighteenth century at the same time as *senryū, kyōka, kyōshi,* and *kibyōshi*, was a short-story form that satirized the life of the sophisticate in the licensed quarters, particularly Yoshiwara in Edo. The sharebon was preceded by the *ukiyo-zōshi*, which became popular in the late seventeenth century, and was followed by the *ninjōbon*, which emerged in the early nineteenth century. The sharebon differed from the ukiyo-zōshi in having been influenced by *enshi*, Chinese courtesan literature. Very early sharebon such as *Words on the Wine Cup of the Pleasure Quarters* (*Ryōha shigen*, 1728), which was a narrative description of the Yoshiwara and its customs, were written in *kanbun* (Chinese prose), were similar in size to Chinese books, bore Chinese titles, and had a preface and an afterword. By the Kyōhō era (1716–1736), Chinese studies was no longer confined to ethics and politics but had come to embrace poetry and belles lettres, which were pursuits of both samurai and urban commoners. These scholars considered themselves Chinese-style literati (bunjin), detached literary dilettantes, for whom Chinese courtesan literature was a form of escape and entertainment. In their experimentation with Japanese versions, they produced the early sharebon. The form became popular and spread from Edo to Kyoto and Osaka, where it incorporated a dialogue-libretto style derived from drama.

Sharebon acquired a definitive shape during the Meiwa era (1764–1772), particularly after the publication of *The Playboy Dialect* (*Yūshi hōgen*) in 1770, and took the generic name of sharebon in the An'ei era (1772–1781). The Edo-based sharebon, beginning with *The Playboy Dialect*, blended two fundamental dimensions. The first was satirical humor, which it shared with the Edo-based *dangibon* (satiric sermons), and the second was an interest in the manners of the pleasure quarters. Licensed quarters such as the Yoshiwara in Edo were a world run by money and separate from everyday life and society. To understand this special culture with its complex rules and customs and to know how to conduct oneself in this world was to be a *tsūjin* (man of *tsū*), a sophisticate or connoisseur. Accordingly, the Edo-based sharebon satirized customs of the pleasure quarters, and the main target became the half-sophisticate, the fake *tsū* or half-*tsū*, whom the contemporary reader both laughed at and empathized with. That is, instead of describing a person of *tsū*, the sharebon humorously described those who failed to achieve this aesthetic and social ideal.

THE PLAYBOY DIALECT (*YŪSHI HŌGEN*, 1770)

The first true sharebon was *The Playboy Dialect*, written by an anonymous author who called himself Inaka Rōjin Tada no Jijii (Justa Geezer the Old Hayseed). The title *Yūshi hōgen* is a comic twist on *Master Yang's Sayings* (*Yōshi hōgen*), a noted Chinese imitation of Confucius's *Analects* by Yang Xiong (53 B.C.E.–C.E. 18), a Han Confucian scholar. On the surface, *The Playboy Dialect* resembles the early sharebon *Words on the Wine Cup of the Pleasure Quarters* (*Ryōha shigen*, 1728) with its Chinese-style cover, Chinese title, and Chinese preface. The body of *The Playboy Dialect*, however, combined dramatic dialogue with the satire of the Edo-based dangibon to create a new form that flourished throughout the An'ei-Tenmei era (1772–1789). The title *Playboy Dialect* refers to the highly specialized, modish jargon used only in the licensed quarters, the mastery of which was a mark of a *tsū*. In the manner of the sharebon, the main character (the Man-About-Town), a half-baked sophisticate, takes a young man (the Youth) on a trip to the Yoshiwara, where the Man-About-Town tries to show off his "knowledge" of the quarter. The Youth, who is well dressed and has an attendant, appears to be from a prosperous merchant family, while the Man-About-Town is a middle- or lower-level samurai—as are almost all the half-*tsū* characters in other sharebon—and is not affluent, even appearing to have run up debts around town. Hira, another important male character, is a high-ranking samurai, probably from the provinces, with more resources. Like the Man-About-Town, Hira has pretensions but is in fact largely ignorant of the subtleties of Yoshiwara. The Man-About-Town boasts to the Youth that he is engaging in a *tsū* activity called *shinzō-kai* (literally, buying an apprentice courtesan) in which the favored (and usually young and less affluent) lover of a high-ranking courtesan hires an apprentice courtesan in the same establishment at a much lower price, and the high-ranking courtesan then finds an opportunity to slip away from her paying client and surreptitiously spend time with her lover. In a somewhat similar fashion, Hira mistakes the custom of myōdai (substitution) for shinzō-kai. Myōdai was a common practice in which an apprentice courtesan was sent to fetch and then to entertain (but not sleep with) a client as he waited for his assigned courtesan while she was occupied with another customer.

The Playboy Dialect set the pattern for all subsequent sharebon, with its pseudo-dramaturgical format, its description of a journey to the pleasure quarters, an implicit comparison of the *tsū* and the half-*tsū*, and the temporal span of one afternoon and one night. In *The Playboy Dialect* the implicit desire of the protagonist—the half-baked sophisticate—is to be liked and admired by the courtesan or to create the appearance of being attractive to the courtesan. Note here that the women maintain firm control over the men, whom they skillfully manipulate, stroking their egos, keeping them in line, and extracting from them as much money as possible. The exception here is the Youth, whom the women find genuinely attractive for his good looks, youth, and lack of pretension. While the Man-About-Town's and Hira's bungled attempts to be admired by the top courtesans are satirized and the reader laughs at their struggles, the contemporary reader and the author at the same time empathized and identified with the half-*tsū*'s desire to be admired by the courtesan—a desire that lay at the heart of this genre but was never explicitly stated.

Preface

There are many blossoms of great beauty—many indeed. But they cannot compare with the beauty of the blossoms of blossom town,[1] for these blossoms also have human feelings. The blossoms of the peach and plum may be beautiful, but they can neither speak nor recite verse. Peony and crabapple blossoms may be splendid, but they can neither laugh nor sing. But as for *these* blossoms, not only can they speak and recite, but glance once at their hues and instantly they will snatch away your spirit and bemuse your soul; let their fragrance once touch your nostrils, and instantly it will cause your heart to soar and your guts to twist. And what is more, they do not droop beneath the frosts and dews, nor are they crushed by the winds and rains. To possess them is not forbidden; to use them is not to exhaust them. Spring or fall, day or night, we never need be without their fragrant loveliness. How can we equate their flowering and decline with the blossoms of mere shrubs and grasses? We sing the praises of flowers that bloom on plants—but what, then, of *these*

---

1. Hanamachi, a conventional epithet for the licensed quarters.

blossoms? Ah, what a delight it is to roam at will throughout the Northern Continent![2] And thus concludes my preface.

Justa Geezer the Old Hayseed

Live for Pleasure Alone![3]

BEGINNING

On an unseasonably warm day in early winter, a man some thirty-four or thirty-five years of age can be seen near Weeping Willow Bridge.[4] He is balding slightly, and his hair is shaven far back from his forehead on top and plucked back above the temples in an outsize broad-forehead Honda hairstyle.[5] He wears an outer coat of fine black- and yellow-striped figured silk, with a narrow striped sash wound high about the midriff, into which is thrust a rather slender short sword, its haft somewhat stained. The family crests on his kimono[6] of fine, glossy black silk are slightly soiled, and he appears to have exchanged one of the sleeves of his finely patterned silk undercoat for that of a lover's garment. He wears an underrobe of faded scarlet silk crepe, and his feet are in wide, low, uncomfortable-looking geta. In one hand he holds a pointed Yamaoka cloth hood. He has no tissue case; some leaves of kogiku tissue paper, folded in four, can just be seen protruding from under his lapel.[7] He gazes about him with glittering eyes as if to say, "No man can hope to rival me in love."

As he ambles along with no apparent destination, from the opposite direc-

---

2. In Buddhist cosmology, Hoku-shū (Skt. Uttarakuru), the Northern Continent, stands far to the north of Sumeru, the central continent that we of this world are said to inhabit. Here it is a humorous reference to the New Yoshiwara licensed quarter, a walled area of some twenty acres to the north of Edo proper, which was rebuilt here after a fire destroyed the original Yoshiwara in 1657. Yoshiwara in this story refers to the rebuilt licensed quarter.

3. Two signets, one engraved with the two Chinese characters *jin sei* (human life) and the other with the two characters *ichi raku* (only pleasure), are imprinted next to the author's pseudonym to form this four-character motto.

4. The Yanagibashi (Weeping Willow Bridge) area in Edo, where the Kanda River empties into the Sumida River, was the site of numerous boathouses whose boats could be hired to convey customers up the Sumida to the vicinity of Yoshiwara.

5. The Honda hairstyle, a very popular men's hairstyle of this period, involved shaving the middle third of the head in a U-shape from the forehead back to the crown and sweeping the remaining hair back from the sides and up from the back into a short ponytail, which was then doubled over forward to form a loose topknot lying on top of the head, near the crown. In a *hirobitai*, or broad-forehead Honda, the shaved area was wider than usual.

6. The *kosode*, rendered here simply as "kimono," was a full-length robe with very generous sleeves. It was the basic garment for both men and women during the Edo period. It was worn either with or without the trouser-like divided skirts known as *hakama*.

7. Ordinarily a gentleman would carry a "nasal-tissue case," which was a sort of paper billfold in which to hold money, documents, and *kogiku*: smallish squares of paper for various uses. The fashion was to fold one's tissues in thirds.

The Honda hairstyle.

tion comes a young man of barely twenty. He looks to have a mild and con-
genial disposition. He is wearing a splendid short sword and a cotton-padded
outer coat of black crepe marked with five pure white family crests,[8] *a kimono*
patterned in brown stripes on a dark background, an olive-color crepe under-
robe, glossy striped hakama trousers of fine kohaku *silk, and straw sandals,*
their thongs intertwined with white paper. He is accompanied by an attendant
carrying a bunch of flowers and a parcel wrapped in an unfigured silk cloth,
and he shades his face with a fan as he walks.

MAN-ABOUT-TOWN: Hey, there, lover boy, lover boy!

YOUTH: Well, hello—how goes it? I was just talking about you with our teacher[9] the other day.

MAN-ABOUT-TOWN: Teacher? Never mind all that, never mind all that! Where are you off to?

YOUTH: I'm headed up toward Honjo.

MAN-ABOUT-TOWN: Do you have to go? What is it you're going there for?

YOUTH: My uncle is sick, and I'm going over to visit him.

MAN-ABOUT-TOWN: If your uncle is sick, then I'd say just to let it slide.[10]

YOUTH: Why is that?

MAN-ABOUT-TOWN: It's such splendid weather; I was hoping to get you to come view the autumn leaves with me at Shōtō-ji temple.

YOUTH: I see. I'd like to visit Shōtō-ji too. I wonder if I could go there and still make it back in time to get to Honjo.

MAN-ABOUT-TOWN: Oh, you'll make it, you'll make it! Or you could always just let Honjo slide entirely.

YOUTH: Anyhow, I believe I *will* go.

MAN-ABOUT-TOWN: In that case, it's best if you send your attendant home. If he did come, the autumn leaves would be no fun for him at all; he'd be

---

8. That is, a single crest reproduced in five places: one in the center of the back, one on each side of the chest, and one on each sleeve.

9. Apparently the two men study some art together—very likely Chinese literature, which was much in vogue among gentlemen of the time. This is perhaps the source of their acquaintance.

10. The Man-About-Town uses the verb *nagasu* (literally, let flow), in the then-fashionable colloquial meaning of "let it go" and so forth.

better off just staying home. You, Kakuhei!—some man about town you are! And as for you, lover boy, off with those hakama, off with them![11]

ATTENDANT KAKUHEI: Or if you think you'll need me, should I come along?

YOUTH: No, there's no need for you to come. Go home and tell them that I ran into this gentleman and have gone with him to Shōtō-ji temple, so I'm sending you home, and be sure not to worry.[12] (*The attendant departs.*)

MAN-ABOUT-TOWN: Ah, good, this is much better! I have a lot to tell you on the boat as we make our way there. Our would-be lover boy could easily end up as a "buried tree,"[13] so I'm going to have to initiate you by transmitting to you the secret instructions that will transform you from a Zenjibō-type lover boy into one like Agemaki's Sukeroku.[14] Ah, here we are at the Izu House, the boathouse inn where everyone embarks. I myself embark here every day. We'll get a boat from here. Mistress! Just snip us off a skiffy in a jiffy—we want to be on our way without delay![15]

---

11. It would seem that the Man-About-Town is chiding Kakuhei, the Youth's attendant, because he feels that Kakuhei should have immediately recognized Shōtō-ji (a Buddhist temple located near the licensed quarter) as sophisticates' code for Yoshiwara and should have tactfully offered to withdraw. (The name Kakuhei, the first character of which means "corner," or "angle," suggests someone rather straitlaced and rigid, a "square.") The Man-About-Town urges the Youth to remove his hakama because entering Yoshiwara without this more formal attire was considered sophisticated Yoshiwara etiquette.

12. Judging by their physical description and manner of speaking, the Man-About-Town appears to be a member of the samurai class, while the Youth is probably the son of a well-to-do merchant family. Thus the Man-About-Town condescends to the Youth, who speaks deferentially to him. Since it was considered a mark of the fashionable Yoshiwara sophisticate to dress in clothing that was just comfortably worn, the Youth's crisp new clothing identifies him as a neophyte in such matters. The Man-About-Town's attire, however, is beyond fashionably worn and closer to scruffy. Thus, as was very common during this period, the Youth is the Man-About-Town's nominal social inferior yet far surpasses him in affluence.

13. *Umore-gi*, a cherry tree that sinks into oblivion without ever having had a chance to blossom, implying that unless someone takes him in hand, the Youth will never get the chance to become a Yoshiwara sophisticate.

14. All three are characters from popular kabuki plays. Zenjibō is the straitlaced but spineless younger brother of the two samurai heroes Jūrō and Gorō in the filial-revenge drama *The Soga Confrontation* (*Soga no taimen*), which at this time was put on in Edo each year at New Year's. Sukeroku, the swashbuckling hero of *Sukeroku and the Flowering Edo Cherry* (*Sukeroku yukari no Edo-zakura*), is a chivalrous commoner (actually the same Gorō in disguise) who protects the weak from the strong, defeating a brutal samurai villain who is his rival for the favors of Agemaki, a Yoshiwara courtesan. The sobriquet given here for Sukeroku derives from a jeering self-introduction in the play in which he identifies himself as "Sukeroku of Hanakawado, in cherry-blossom-scented Nakano-chō—also known as Agemaki's Sukeroku." He was seen as the epitome of the dashing Yoshiwara sophisticate.

15. The Man-About-Town's words (*Choki-bune chokkiri gui-zukuri, hayaku dashi to shitai wai*) are a pun on *choki-bune* (skiff), *chokkiri* (a bit; snip off), and *Choki!* (an exclamation shouted when choosing "scissors" in the popular "rock/scissors/paper" game). He also uses the expression *gui-zukuri* (go ahead and get it ready)—another pun on "*Gū!*" the exclamation shouted when

BOATHOUSE INN PROPRIETRESS: Yes sir, good day, gentlemen, and welcome to our establishment. We do have skiffs, sir, but I'm afraid we haven't got any of these other whatchamacallem boats you mention.

MAN-ABOUT-TOWN: Yes, well . . . just any skiff will do fine.

PROPRIETRESS: And where will you be going, gentlemen?

MAN-ABOUT-TOWN: What do you mean, where? To the Moat—to the Moat, of course![16] (*The proprietress goes down to the riverbank. A boatman has just returned and, intending to take a break, has moored his boat at the riverbank.*)

PROPRIETRESS: Gorō! I hate to ask you, but could you row out one more time? . . . Hey, hey, now, what's wrong?

GORŌ: Nothing's wrong, I'm just hungry! And I oughta be hungry! I've rowed out to Matsusaki and back twice and taken two boatloads over to the Moat, and I'm starving!

PROPRIETRESS: OK, then, just have a quick bowl of *chazuke*,[17] then get going. They're in a hurry. (*The Man-About-Town and the Youth emerge from the boathouse inn, pipes dangling from their mouths, to see whether their boat is ready yet.*)

PROPRIETRESS (*apologetically*): Please wait just a moment longer. All the boatmen were out; now one of them's finally gotten back in, but he says he's famished. He'll just have a bowl of *chazuke*, and then he'll be right along.

MAN-ABOUT-TOWN: Well, dammit all!

PROPRIETRESS: Yes sir, but the tide is favorable right now, so the boat should get you there in no time.

MAN-ABOUT-TOWN: Well, in that case, let's have us a smoke. (*With these words, he goes down to the boathouse to wait. A roofed boat arrives with two or three dancing girls on it. Three or four men embark, whereupon the Man-About-Town, smoking his pipe, strikes a pose suggesting that he knows them and expects them to address him. The older man in the group bows silently and moves away.*)

MAN-ABOUT-TOWN: Don't know any of those fellows. There are only two of them whose faces I've even seen before.

YOUTH: That vigorous-looking old man who just bowed to you—I've seen him around here from time to time.

MAN-ABOUT-TOWN: That's an old acquaintance of mine, an uncouth old

---

choosing "rock." The boathouse proprietress, who understands perfectly well what he is asking for but is evidently irritated by his affected and overfamiliar tone, snubs him by feigning incomprehension.

16. *Hori*, short for Sanya-bori, the Sanya Moat, where visitors to Yoshiwara got off the boat and climbed up to the embankment along which they walked to reach the walled enclosure of the licensed quarter itself.

17. *Chazuke* is a sort of soupy rice snack made by pouring hot water or tea over leftover rice, usually eaten together with pickled vegetables.

geezer named old Kamachi-ya Honjirō. The debonair-looking one behind him, with the loose Nitayama Honda hairstyle,[18] is named Yokosuke. When he walked by, he put on a look as if he knew me, though I've never even met him. You know, seeing someone getting out of a boat who tries to act as if he knew me always makes me just want to hurry up and go. How about it?

BOATMAN (*from the riverbank*): Climb aboard, gentlemen! (*The two men climb briskly into the boat.*)

BOATMAN: Shove us off, please! (*The proprietress sends two people down to shove them off.*)

PROPRIETRESS: Enjoy the ride!

BOATMAN: Please sit flat, gentlemen.

MAN-ABOUT-TOWN: Here, now, lover boy, let's begin your initiation with the secret transmission on how to ride in a skiff. The way a skiff works, if you don't sit cross-legged, leaning back on your elbows with your head hanging down, puffing away at your pipe, the boat will be hard to row. So doing that will please the boatman. Look, look, on the other side of that hill over there is the home of the famous Ippyō, who can mimic every kind of performing art. But with all this talk of this and that, I was forgetting that we have something important to discuss. You see, we won't be able to go to Shōtō-ji temple after all. Did you really think we were going to Shōtō-ji?

YOUTH: Yes, well, it's a bit too late for going to Shōtō-ji now, isn't it?

MAN-ABOUT-TOWN: My thoughts exactly! The truth of the matter is, Shōtō-ji was actually just camouflage; what I was scheming at[19] all along was really a trip to Yoshiwara. I don't suppose you mind if we go to Yoshiwara?

YOUTH: No, as long as I get home early, that's all right.

MAN-ABOUT-TOWN: If you're going to come along, it's no time to be talking about early and late. Since you're going with me, there's no way you'll be getting home early. Unlike going with certain uncouth boors, you'll find that going with me will be an extraordinarily enjoyable experience. And so it should be. When I say that I'm going, all the sophisticated playboy brothel-owners in Yoshiwara come running—to say nothing of all the jesters.[20] Last time—get this—the son of the owner of the Tsurube noodle shop,[21] of all

---

18. A popular, somewhat looser variation on the Honda hairstyle.

19. He uses the word *hara* (literally, belly), an expression then in vogue with Yoshiwara sophisticates, meaning "ulterior motive," "real intention."

20. A *taiko-mochi* (literally, drum holder) was a professional entertainer who acted as a sort of master of ceremonies, comedian, and companion to customers drinking and disporting themselves in the licensed quarters. His function was to keep the party going and everyone in high spirits.

21. A Yoshiwara landmark that served *soba*, or buckwheat noodles.

people, tagged along to party with us. Lord, this boat is slow! Look, we've only just made it to Outcome Pines![22]

BOATMAN: We left Outcome Pines behind us quite a ways back.

MAN-ABOUT-TOWN: Um-hm . . . well, you see, we've come quite some distance. Ah, here we are at the Konokimi-Yamabushi riverbank.

YOUTH: Who are Konokimi and the Yamabushi?

MAN-ABOUT-TOWN: Ah, now there hangs a tale! In Yoshiwara, you see, sometimes a man's looks are not as important as his style. On this bank lives a combed-back fellow[23] some eighty years old. He's been carrying on a great love affair with one Konokimi. This man has such style that every last one of Konokimi's clients has been driven away and been cut off by her. I myself have taken him on and made love to her any number of times, but it looks like this time even I may not prevail.

The Man-About-Town goes on to give the Youth advice on a variety of topics—including how he should style his hair, how he ought to dress, and what shops the gentleman visitor to the licensed quarters should frequent to acquire the most fashionable accoutrements (such as a tissue case and a tobacco pouch)—nonchalantly revealing, in the process, how knowledgeable and well connected he is.

MAN-ABOUT-TOWN: I'm always calling over the owner of Sumiyoshi-ya[24] for one thing or another—look, just come out to my place anytime you want. It's a bit difficult for me to send you a letter: it might look like I was trying to corrupt a young fellow—for a person with my reputation, it's a bit difficult. Do you have a nom de plume?[25]

YOUTH: Perhaps you would be so kind as to choose one for me using one of the Chinese characters from your own.

MAN-ABOUT-TOWN: In that case, take the *ban* from my pseudonym Banchō and call yourself Bankei. From now on, you'll be just like me: everywhere

---

22. The Shubi no matsu (literally, The-Outcome-Awaits Pines) a well-known landmark to regular Yoshiwara visitors, was a stand of large pine trees just past Yanagibashi whose branches reached out over the river. They derived their whimsical appellation from a pun on *matsu*, meaning "pine trees," and *matsu*, meaning "waiting," and from the conceit that a passenger on his way to or from Yoshiwara would, from about this point onward, be waiting to see how things would turn out in the licensed quarter or back home.

23. That is, a man who wears his hair combed straight back instead of shaven and allows it to hang down in back instead of gathering it into a ponytail. This hairstyle resembled that favored by Buddhist *yamabushi* (mountain ascetics), hence the sobriquet.

24. A well-known shop that specialized in made-to-order tobacco pipes. The Man-About-Town would be summoning the shop owner to his house in order to view his wares and order pipes.

25. It was customary for people to adopt a nom de plume when engaged in such fashionable pursuits as haikai poetry and painting. But even someone not engaged in such pursuits would use a pseudonym when visiting Yoshiwara.

you go they'll call you "Mr. Bankei," "Mr. Bankei."[26] And that reminds me of a story. The other evening I was in the Matsu-ya in Nakano-chō, dressed to the nines and puffing on a thick pipe, when the jōruri reciter Tōjū[27] comes over and sits down next to me and we get to talking. So the courtesan from the inner suite[28] comes over and starts coming on to Tōjū. She really wanted to come on to me, but she felt intimidated, so she did various things to let me know how willing she was. Then she asks Tōjū in a low voice, "What's his name?" So Tōjū says, "What, you don't know his name? He's called Mr. Banchō." I could tell by her expression that she wanted to say "Mr. Banchō," but instead she merely tossed her head archly and said, "You gentlemen enjoy your stay here this evening," and stood up and left the room (it seems a client had just arrived). So this very night I'm going to go back to that house, and under the pretext of hiring an apprentice courtesan,[29] I'll wait until it gets very late and everyone has settled in for the night; and then I'll sneak into this courtesan's chambers, see, and without even romancing her, right away—considering the way she acted earlier—right away I'll make it with her. Now, when I say "make it," I'm talking about sleeping on three layers of futon[30] instead of with the original apprentice courtesan; about secretly being served *chazuke* and whatnot;[31] about knocking that courtesan's socks off to my heart's content until daybreak;[32] and about staying on late,

---

26. The Man-About-Town's licensed-quarters pseudonym, Banchō, was the name of an up-scale Edo neighborhood, populated mostly by respectable samurai. Presumably the Man-About-Town either lives in that part of town or wants people to think he does. The character *kei* in Bankei has various meanings, including "to look up to"; possibly the Man-About-Town's intent is to name the Youth, roughly, "Looks up to Banchō."

27. Masumi Tōjū, a reciter of the Katō-bushi school of jōruri and reportedly the son of a Yoshiwara brothel owner. The Katō-bushi school was currently in vogue among Yoshiwara sophisticates.

28. *Oku-zashiki no jorō* designates a courtesan of sufficient rank to be entitled to two or more private upstairs rooms. She would be the highest-ranking (and most sought-after and expensive) courtesan in the establishment.

29. The term used is *shinzō-kai* (literally, apprentice courtesan buying). This was a subterfuge whereby an expensive, high-ranking courtesan would arrange for a lover to enter her brothel by hiring a much less expensive apprentice courtesan (typically a girl in her early teens) to pretend to be with him for the night. The high-ranking courtesan would then arrange to slip away and secretly meet with her lover during the wee hours. The one expected to propose this stratagem was, of course, the courtesan herself.

30. One of the status symbols denoting high rank in a courtesan was a softer, more luxurious bed made up of three futon mattresses instead of the usual one or two.

31. *Chazuru*, a fashionable Yoshiwara sophisticates' neologism, makes a verb out of the noun *chazuke* and so means "to eat *chazuke*" or "to be served *chazuke*" (a soupy rice snack). For a courtesan to offer a client a bowl of *chazuke* before he left in the morning meant favoring him with a mark of special intimacy and esteem.

32. Literally, a bellyful by daybreak of beating the courtesan to death, that is, making her hopelessly enamored of him.

until full daylight, and *then* going home. Now how's *that* for the perfect lover-boy plot, eh? That's how they all turn out in *my* Yoshiwara. This boat is getting nowhere! No, no, it looks like we're getting there at last.

BOATMAN: Where would you like to get off?

MAN-ABOUT-TOWN: OK, let's see, now . . . at Ichigawa-ya I owe money, of course, and at Yoshino-ya they're so snooty I can't stand them. Where shall we go?—I know! How about that Yamamoto-ya fellow I met just recently? There's still one boathouse inn that takes me for a big shot!

BOATMAN: Where shall I tie up, then? Uh, . . . sir?

MAN-ABOUT-TOWN: Right, tie up at the Yamamoto dock.

BOATMAN: Yamamoto-ya! Yamamoto-ya!

YAMAMOTO-YA PROPRIETOR: Hey! Somebody's arriving! (*He comes out to the dock to welcome them.*) Well, what a surprise! Welcome—come on up! Yes, you can just tie up right over there.

MAN-ABOUT-TOWN and YOUTH: No, no, right here will be fine, right here will be fine. (*They climb lightly out of the boat.*)

YAMAMOTO-YA PROPRIETOR: Please feel free to have a quick smoke, if you like.[33] (*The Man-About-Town and the Youth both sit down.*)

YAMAMOTO-YA PROPRIETRESS: Why, it's Mr. Banchō, the client who rode up to Suidōbashi Bridge yesterday morning![34]

MAN-ABOUT-TOWN: In future, I hope to be dropping by now and again. Mistress, look and see if my hair is coming undone.

YAMAMOTO-YA PROPRIETRESS: Not a bit of it.

MAN-ABOUT-TOWN: May I please have a hand towel moistened in hot water and wrung out?

YAMAMOTO-YA PROPRIETRESS: Certainly, sir.

MAN-ABOUT-TOWN: Here, I'll supply my own hand towel.[35] (*He pulls out a pale blue hand towel, takes it back moistened with hot water, wrings it out, and runs it over his face, wiping his shaven hairline with great care.*)

MAN-ABOUT-TOWN: This gives you such a good, brisk feeling! Like to wipe off your face? You do look a trifle uncouth.

YOUTH: Come on, let's get going. (*The two men depart.*)

MAN-ABOUT-TOWN: Come on, come on, let's hurry, let's hurry!

YAMAMOTO-YA PROPRIETOR AND PROPRIETRESS: Please stop by again in the morning!

MAN-ABOUT-TOWN: All right, now, here we are at the embankment.[36] Come,

---

33. It was customary to smoke a pipeful and spruce up oneself a bit at the boathouse before proceeding to Yoshiwara.

34. The Banchō neighborhood was not far from the Suidōbashi Bridge area.

35. The Man-About-Town is apparently taking the opportunity to flaunt his own hand towel, which the others are to understand is a memento from a famous kabuki actor or another performing artist, handed out to particularly favored fans and patrons at special performances.

36. That is, having stepped out of the boathouse inn and walked uphill for a short distance.

come, this way! Now here, too, there is the adept's way and the amateur's way. If you go this way it's much closer. Hmm, the embankment certainly does seem rather desolate. OK, now dab some saliva on the end of your nose, like this.

YOUTH: What for?

MAN-ABOUT-TOWN: Never mind what for, just dab it on. You'll find out why in a moment. . . . There, there—there it is!

YOUTH: It's true, there's a very odd smell here.

MAN-ABOUT-TOWN: That's the smell of burning corpses.[37] But even a corpse smells good when you smell it at the embankment. The embankment seems awfully long tonight![38] (*He chants in jōruri dramatic recital style, with professional-sounding flourishes.*) "Smartly holding up the hem of her robe, and wearing, not a phoenix helmet, but . . ."[39] I have some more advice for you. I hear you're taking *uta* singing lessons. If you really want to study singing, forget that stuff. Nowadays it's only uncouth samurai who sing *uta*. Study Katō-school chanting![40] Everyone from Gajū to Danji and Fudejirō is always coming over to my house, so you may study with whomever you please. And as for Katō, his voice has been failing of late, so he's taken to sleeping over at my place. And Fudejirō's changed his name to Benshirō, and naturally he needs to plan his recital, so now he's coming over every day, too. I tell you, once you become a man about town, even just these recitals can be such a bother! The printed programs alone can really pile up! Well, we've been talking so much we're already at Emonzaka.[41] They still follow old-fashioned ways here, so we'd better straighten our clothes properly at this point. Now, this time, let's move along quietly from here on.

The New Yoshiwara licensed quarter was situated on reclaimed land buttressed by an embankment. Having arrived at the embankment, they are still a short distance from Yoshiwara. They must now walk down the road along the top of the embankment to reach the great gate that was the sole entrance to the quarter.

37. There was a crematorium not far from the New Yoshiwara licensed quarter. Folk belief held that dabbing saliva on one's nose helped ward off foul odors.

38. Because he is so impatient to get to Yoshiwara.

39. A line from the jōruri verse "Midaregami yoru no amigasa" (On a Night of Disheveled Hair, a Braided-Sedge Hat).

40. All the names that follow are those of prominent disciples of the Katō-bushi chanting style, which was established by Masumi Katō (1684–1725). The Masumi Katō referred to here, however, is not the founder himself but Dennosuke (d. 1771), the fourth-generation holder of his Katō-bushi lineage. It appears that the Youth is studying not jōruri but a different genre of poetic recital: either *kouta* (short songs) or, more likely, *nagauta* (long songs).

41. The famous Emonzaka (Attire Slope or Lapel Slope) was the short, gently curving road on which Yoshiwara patrons descended from the road along the top of the embankment to the single great gateway into the walled enclosure of the licensed quarter. It is said to have been so named because it was here that visitors adjusted their attire to make themselves presentable before entering Yoshiwara.

If anybody catches sight of me, they'll all flock around and kick up a fuss! Tonight I'd like us to amuse ourselves quietly, just the two of us. (*They arrive at and enter the grand gateway to the Yoshiwara district.*) My, the place is deserted tonight! What teahouse[42] shall we go to? I know so many places that wherever I go, my eye always wanders to some other place. Besides, I hate deciding on a teahouse beforehand. What's that one called? See what it says on the *noren* curtains.

YOUTH: It's called the Odawara-ya.

MAN-ABOUT-TOWN: Oh, Mata's place. Yes, I imagine they'd appreciate a visit from me. Come, let's go in, let's go in. (*They stride right in and see the teahouse proprietress seated alone in the sitting room.*) Mistress, how goes it?

TEAHOUSE PROPRIETRESS: Welcome to our establishment. Please come on up[43] and sit down.

MAN-ABOUT-TOWN: Let's go on up, let's go on up! (*He climbs right up and sits down, sprawling cross-legged in the middle of the teahouse.*) It's awfully slow tonight, isn't it?

PROPRIETRESS: No, actually we have more guests upstairs.

MAN-ABOUT-TOWN: It's good to hear that you're always so busy. It's been quite a while since I've been here. (*The proprietress, however, does not seem to take his meaning at all.*)

PROPRIETRESS: It's very rude of me, but I seem to have forgotten your face — could you remind me who you are?

MAN-ABOUT-TOWN: How could this be? My goodness gracious! However long it may have been since I've been here, don't try to tell me that you've forgotten my face! But of course, it has been a long time. I do run into your husband now and again in the course of my wanderings, but it's true that it's been quite some time since I came to your place. And where has your husband gone off to?

PROPRIETRESS: He's gone into Edo today.

MAN-ABOUT-TOWN: Ah — and the man who just left here, who was that?

PROPRIETRESS: That was Mr. Fudejirō.

MAN-ABOUT-TOWN: Ah, old Fude, was it? I wonder why he pretended not to see me. Ah, of course: he was supposed to come over last night but didn't — *that's* why he acted as if he didn't see me!

PROPRIETRESS: What, he was supposed to go to your house last night?

---

42. A *hikite-jaya*, or guiding teahouse, was an eating-and-drinking establishment in the licensed quarter that functioned as a sort of lounge or salon where clients went to request courtesans' services and where they were asked to wait before being escorted to the brothels themselves. According to Yoshiwara custom, anyone wanting to visit such an establishment first had to be introduced by an existing patron; a teahouse would generally balk at serving any newcomer who lacked the proper introduction.

43. The floor of the sitting room is raised a foot or two higher than the entrance level.

MAN-ABOUT-TOWN: Katō's been staying at my place lately, so Fude said he'd be coming by for a chat. But since he didn't show up, Ryūsen[44] came over, and we spent the night composing haiku. (*Meanwhile, saké cups, snacks, and saké have been brought out, and the proprietress is directing the serving of the soup.*) Katō slept over at the house again last night, too, so I told him I was off for Yoshiwara and didn't he want to come along, but he's such a lazy so-and-so—said he'd rather sleep than come to Yoshiwara, or some such nonsense.

PROPRIETRESS: Mr. Katō has been here since yesterday evening.

MAN-ABOUT-TOWN (*blanching, and looking pathetically uncomfortable*): Who, Katō? My goodness, this is just too strange—it must have been a ghost! (*The proprietress, abruptly losing patience with him, departs for the kitchen, her nose in the air, declining to dignify this with an answer. The men in the kitchen comment.*)

KITCHEN MAN: Mistress, I tell you that is one odd individual. You'd better just humor him and send him on his way.

PROPRIETRESS: Yes, I think so, too. Anyhow, the master will deal with him when he gets back. So until then, just try not to engage him at all. And if there's any question of vouching for his payment to the pleasure house, absolutely do not. I'm going up to attend to the upstairs guests. If Mr. Hira and Mr. Kawa come in, put these two in the parlor and let me know right away. (*She goes up to the second floor.*)

YOUTH: The proprietress here's not very friendly, is she?

MAN-ABOUT-TOWN: Now that you mention it, that's true. All in all, they don't treat their customers well at all here. Even when they know what's going on, they act as if they had no idea. I do wish some nice girls would get here soon. We'll entertain them with a little high-toned give-and-take while we're here. (*Puffing away at his pipe, he goes on in this vein, putting on all manner of airs. Hira,[45] a customer, arrives. A physically large man, he is dignified in appearance, his hair in the* awase-bin *style—pulled back and tied with a thick paper cord—and dressed in a new kimono of finely woven glossy black silk, an outer coat of black silk crepe adorned in five places with a pure white family crest, and an elegant silk crepe underrobe. He calls out in a clear, booming voice.*)

HIRA: Is the master back yet? (*A male employee comes running out from the kitchen. As he hurries out, paying no attention to the Man-About-Town and the Youth, he knocks his leg against that of the Man-About-Town.*)

---

44. A renowned haikai poet of the day.

45. Hira would be a licensed-quarter nickname, probably an abbreviation of the client's actual family name.

MAN-ABOUT-TOWN: Mannerless oaf! (*The male employee, not even troubling to apologize, addresses Hira.*)

MALE EMPLOYEE: Welcome to our house, sir.

HIRA: Listen, should I go on upstairs?

MALE EMPLOYEE: Please wait a moment. (*Turning to the Man-About-Town and the Youth*) Would you please step into the parlor?

MAN-ABOUT-TOWN (*punning*): Anywhere's fine—as a Yoshino cherry tree, a Yoshino cherry tree.[46] Come along, lover boy, step this way, *entrez*—an herb-and-miso entrée![47]

MALE EMPLOYEE (*bringing Hira a cup of saké*): You're quite late this evening.

HIRA: The master's not in yet, eh? How about the lady of the house?[48]

MALE EMPLOYEE: She's upstairs at the moment. She's been expecting you. I'll let her know right away that you're here.

HIRA: You seem awfully busy tonight.

MAN-ABOUT-TOWN: Here, lover boy, take a look at this place's clientele. If that type wasn't born to get dumped by the ladies, I don't know who was. Looking at us after looking at a guy like that, even a whore couldn't help but fall in love. (*This boasting aside is aimed at impressing the Youth.*)

PROPRIETRESS (*coming downstairs and into the serving area*): You're quite late this evening.

HIRA: I suppose I am. Today a bit of a celebration was held at a colleague's house, and we got to drinking, and then your husband came by.

PROPRIETRESS: I thought as much. He said that since his errand today was an urgent letter and since an underling might botch the job, he'd deliver it himself. So I'm glad to hear you saw him. Is Mr. Kawa not coming?[49]

HIRA: Oh, he should be along any minute, and your husband should also be getting back any time now. Of course, he did mention that he'd be stopping by Tora-no-mon.[50]

PROPRIETRESS: Yes, that's right. He does take a long time whenever he stops by Tora-no-mon. Not long ago he stopped by there, and even though the Tora-no-mon client came out here, instead of coming back he went from

---

46. There is a dreadful pun here in the original that turns on *yoshi* (good, fine) and *Yoshino-gi* (cherry trees of Yoshino). The cherry blossoms of Yoshino, in western Japan, had for centuries been extolled in classical literature for their exceptional beauty.

47. A rough approximation of a still more inept pun on *kinasai* (come along) and *kinome dengaku* (herb-and-miso entrée), a dish consisting of tofu, konnyaku, or eggplant, cooked with a glaze of miso mixed with *kinome*, the tiny leaf buds of the Japanese pepper plant (*sanshō*).

48. Hira's use of the samurai expression *go-naishō* (the lady of the house) marks him as a member of the warrior class.

49. This probably is the Yoshiwara nickname of the samurai colleague whose home Hira was visiting when the urgent letter—presumably to Hira from his Yoshiwara mistress—was delivered.

50. An Edo neighborhood where many warrior clan mansions were located.

there to Shinagawa[51] and leisurely made his way home the next morning. And because he hadn't come home even though that night was a very busy one for us, when he did get back you'd better believe I gave him the old cold shoulder.[52]

HIRA: Oh, you're good, you're good! I sure wish I could find me a courtesan who's the genuine article, like you.[53]

PROPRIETRESS: Why, your Yama is as genuine as can be—so why talk like that?

HIRA: That's just the thing: I can't tell what her true feelings are. She seems so sincere, and yet somehow there's something funny about her.[54] But let's not talk about such things—how about a drink?

PROPRIETRESS (*offering him a cup of saké*): Yes, by all means have one.

HIRA: This cup sure is petite, though. Of course, I've been drinking all day, but a cup this petite feels like a bit of a tease. Bring me my regular Biggie— my regular Biggie![55]

PROPRIETRESS: Shall I? (*She gets up, goes to the kitchen to get the cup, and orders soup to be brought out. Hira, quite drunk, repeatedly snaps his fan open and closed.*)

MAN-ABOUT-TOWN (*whispering to the Youth and taking something out from inside his sleeve*): I say, Mistress! Mistress! Could I see you a moment?

PROPRIETRESS: Yes, what can I do for you? We've gotten quite busy, and I'm afraid I can't pay proper attention to you.

MAN-ABOUT-TOWN: If not, that's fine—as Yoshino arrowroot.[56] Here—there may be nothing you can do, oh do accept this trifle as a memento of my

---

51. Shinagawa, in southern Edo, was an unlicensed district inhabited by lower-ranking prostitutes.

52. The term rendered by "gave him the old cold shoulder" is delivered in a stylish turn of phrase characteristic of Yoshiwara prostitutes' slang.

53. Hira's speech has a non-Edo, countrified sound to it. This and the description given of him suggest that he is a *rusu-i*, that is, the official government representative in Edo of one of the provincial feudal domains. This was an important position rather resembling that of a diplomat dispatched from the distant feudal domain to the central shōgunal government in Edo.

54. Hira's unsureness of his ability to accurately read his Yoshiwara mistress's feelings about him indicates that even though he is a frequent visitor to the licensed quarter and is well-heeled and very high in status, he is a provincial samurai, not entirely at home with the urban ways of Edo in general and the subtle intricacies of Yoshiwara etiquette in particular. Therefore he feels at somewhat of a disadvantage in his dealings with a courtesan of such high rank and refinement.

55. Hira, a regular customer, evidently keeps a regular saké cup at the teahouse. The term that he uses, *taibutsu* (literally, big one, indicating a person or thing that is large, expensive, or illustrious), seems to be intended as a double-entendre.

56. The Yoshino region was also famous for the high quality of its *kuzu*, or arrowroot, pulverized to a very fine powder and used in cooking as a thickener. This is the same pun on *yoshi* (good) and Yoshino as the earlier one about Yoshino cherry trees.

long overdue visit here, or whatever. Call it a chrysanthemum seed for your flower garden—tuck it away, and mum's the word.[57]

PROPRIETRESS: Yes, well, that's very . . . (*Without further comment, she rises to go.*)[58]

MAN-ABOUT-TOWN: Now, now, there's still one more matter to discuss. Would you please send someone to inquire about Some-no-suke, at Matsuba-ya?

PROPRIETRESS (*with an incredulous expression*): Yes, sir. (*She thinks for a moment.*) Yes, sir, Some-no-suke is not available at present. She left a short while ago for the teahouse down the way.[59]

MAN-ABOUT-TOWN: Well, then, where shall we go? Shall we make it Chōji-ya?

PROPRIETRESS: There's a new establishment in Sumi-chō—wouldn't you like to try going there?[60]

MAN-ABOUT-TOWN: Sumi-chō's just not *with* it, you know—it's just not *with* it, you know! (*Turning to the Youth*) Shall we go to the love-affair place I was telling you about? Ah, but the thought of hiring an apprentice courtesan brings me down.

PROPRIETRESS: Well, you two just talk it over and decide where it is you want to go.

MAN-ABOUT-TOWN: Anyway, just get someone with a lantern to escort us.

PROPRIETRESS: Yes, sir. Somebody come as an escort! (*Meanwhile, her other client is still waiting for his saké cup.*)

HIRA: How about that Biggie, that Biggie?

PROPRIETRESS: Yes, sir, I'll be right there with it. (*She brings him a large cup.*)

HIRA: All right, now that's more like it—that's more like it! (*He drinks it in one gulp.*)

---

57. The word *senzaemon*, which sounds like a person's name, is probably intended as a pun on *sezu tomo*, meaning "even if (you) do nothing," and on *senzai*, meaning "garden flowers and shrubbery." This picks up from the previous "arrowroot" pun a vegetative motif that is continued by the ensuing pun: *Sotchi ni shimatte okina* means "Go ahead and tuck it away for yourself," to which the Man-About-Town adds *-gusa* (flower, plant), to form a gratuitous pun on *okinagusa*, an alternative name for chrysanthemum. The overall result is a ludicrous mélange of painfully heavy-handed badinage.

58. The coin that the Man-About-Town has dug out of his sleeve to tip her with has apparently left the proprietress less than overwhelmed by his largesse.

59. Meeting their clients in a teahouse and escorting them back to their own establishment was a common practice among courtesans in the licensed quarters.

60. The Man-About-Town is asking the proprietress to send for famous, very high level courtesans at extremely high class establishments, courtesans completely out of the league of anyone but a very wealthy and important Yoshiwara patron. She of course deflects these importunate requests and suggests instead Sumi-chō, a less glamorous Yoshiwara street whose brothels are considerably less illustrious than Matsuba-ya and Chōji-ya.

MAN-ABOUT-TOWN: Let's be off, let's be off! (*With the Youth in tow, he descends to the entryway floor.*)

PROPRIETRESS: Do stop in tomorrow morning.

MAN-ABOUT-TOWN: Yes, well, tomorrow, if it rains, we may just stay on there for a while—it's been quite some time since I've done that. It's all up to tonight's girl![61] (*So saying, he departs, ushering the Youth ahead of him. Hira, who has been looking on throughout this exchange, now turns to the proprietress.*)

HIRA: Well—that was quite a hairstyle! Would that be what they call the Honda style?

PROPRIETRESS: Um-hmm, that's right. He kept talking such tommyrot, I hardly knew how to respond.

HIRA: Well. . . . You know, tonight I thought I'd just try a little something new.

PROPRIETRESS: How so?

HIRA: Oh, a little number over in Shin-chō sort of caught my eye, and I thought it might be rather amusing to go over there tonight—give her a little something to worry about, don't you know.[62]

PROPRIETRESS: Hey, now—stop talking like that! You know that would get us in all kinds of trouble! Why, even that time your friend took you to that place in Edo-chō a while back, you know we caught hell for it![63] Well, well— while we've been jawing about this, it seems the apprentice courtesan has arrived to escort you over.[64]

HIRA: I'm gonna hide, I'm gonna hide!

APPRENTICE COURTESAN: Say! Why were you trying to sneak out when you saw me coming?

HIRA: No, I wasn't trying to sneak out; I was just on my way out to meet you, that's all.

APPRENTICE COURTESAN: Whew! They do keep me running! (*She perches herself precariously on the edge of the raised floor area.*) Mama! My mistress says to tell you what a pleasure it was to come over and have that leisurely chat with you this afternoon[65] and asks why, since Mr. Hira was here, you

---

61. Literally, it's all in the belly of tonight's whore; that is, all will depend on what she decides to do.

62. By spending the night with another courtesan, in violation of Yoshiwara etiquette, Hira is trying to pique the jealousy of his *najimi*, or "regular" courtesan mistress. Shin-chō is another section of Yoshiwara.

63. According to Yoshiwara custom, the brothel held the teahouse responsible if a client visited a courtesan other than his "regular" one. Some leeway was normally granted, however, if the client was perceived to have strayed not of his own volition but at the invitation of a drinking companion who had brought him to his own favorite brothel.

64. It was traditional for a high-ranking courtesan to come in person to collect a regular client from the teahouse where he was waiting for her. If she was busy with another client, however, she would generally send a *shinzō*, or apprentice courtesan, in her place.

65. Presumably when she stopped into the teahouse to escort a waiting customer. Among

didn't send him right over? (*Having delivered her message, she continues.*) Why didn't you send a messenger?

PROPRIETRESS: Yes, well, I knew you were busy over there, so I thought, well, I'll take my time about letting her know. Speaking of which, I have something to tell you. Mr. Hira here was just telling me that . . . (*Shifting her gaze to Hira's face, she acts as though she was going to continue. Hira, who by now is quite tipsy and feeling ebullient, sonorously intones the next line.*)

HIRA: "Such a thing must never be said aboard a ship!"[66]

APPRENTICE COURTESAN: My goodness, what a huge voice!

HIRA: Is my voice huge? (*Intones*) When you have a thing so huge, to hire an apprentice courtesan is . . . ha, ha, ha, ha! Oops! That's an improper ending, an improper ending! Instead of sitting here gossiping, let's get going, shall we? Tonight is a "substitute" night,[67] so I want to hurry up and go!

APPRENTICE COURTESAN: You've certainly cheered up, haven't you?

HIRA: Ah, there's a deep meaning to "substitution"![68] Hurry up, let's go, let's go!

PROPRIETRESS: Please have some soup before you leave. We've already set everything out on the table.

HIRA: No, I really don't feel like eating at the moment. I want to hurry up and get going. (*He puts on two mismatched sandals and hastily sets out, a large tissue case spilling out of his robe, the family crest on the back of his kimono now skewed around to one shoulder, and stuffing in the ends of his sash, which has been tucked in instead of properly knotted and is now coming unwound. The apprentice courtesan seizes his sleeve to restrain him.*)

Yoshiwara denizens, "Mama" (Oka-san) was a typical way of addressing a teahouse or brothel proprietress.

66. Hira is quoting from the libretto of *Benkei Aboard Ship* (*Funa Benkei*), a famous nō play by Kanze Nobumitsu (1434–1516). This line is a rebuke delivered by the legendary warrior Benkei when a sudden storm blows up at sea and one of the ship's passengers inauspiciously blurts out that the ship has been possessed by an evil spirit. The proprietress has called Hira's bluff: it seems he does not in fact want Yama to learn of his threat to visit another courtesan.

67. *Myōdai*, or substitution, refers to a practice in which a primary courtesan who was currently busy with a customer would assign an apprentice courtesan to escort a second customer to the brothel and keep him company until she was available. Sexual relations between the substitute and the customer were strictly prohibited. In such situations, it was common practice for the primary courtesan to find an opportunity at some point to excuse herself and briefly look in on the waiting gentleman before returning to her present customer.

68. Hira, the unsophisticated provincial samurai, is confusing two similar-appearing but utterly different practices of the Yoshiwara world: *shinzō-kai* (apprentice courtesan buying) and *myōdai* (substitution). Myōdai was the routine practice of keeping a second, overlapping customer on hold while entertaining a client who arrived earlier. But in *shinzō-kai*, the common practice of dropping in on the waiting client was used as a cover for visiting a lover on the sly, and this is what Hira imagines is being planned for him. Hira probably has heard of shinzō-kai and fatuously believes that Yama's routine "substitution" gesture of sending an apprentice courtesan to escort him from the teahouse to her place and keep him company while he waits his turn is tantamount to a romantic declaration of love on her part.

APPRENTICE COURTESAN: The moment you say you're going to do something, you're always in such a rush! Now, wait a moment!

PROPRIETRESS: Hurry up and light a lantern! I say—aren't your sandals mismatched?

HIRA: Sandals be damned! I want to get going! (*He rushes out pell-mell.*)

APPRENTICE COURTESAN: Wait, please! Wait, please! (*She leaves with him.*)

MALE EMPLOYEE: There's something wrong with this lantern. (*He begins taking the lantern he has brought out back toward the rear of the teahouse.*)

PROPRIETRESS (*angrily*): Just hurry up and get going!

The ensuing section contains a thumbnail sketch of the licensed quarter, a lyrical evocation of the overall sights and sounds of a brief evening stroll through Yoshiwara. This is followed by a description of a Yoshiwara party scene centering on an unnamed, rather inebriated customer—presumably Hira—being entertained by a group of apprentice courtesans, jesters, and so forth on the first floor of his usual brothel while he waits for his "regular" courtesan mistress to become free to receive him in her second-floor room.

IN THE WEE HOURS

Because two of the courtesan's customers have overlapped, one is in a waiting room being kept company by a "substitute."

HIRA: Damn! So I end up getting stuffed into a cramped little room like this yet again! I may as well go ahead and get some sleep. Damn! The drink's wearing off, and I'm in the mood. (*He half dons a sleeved quilt, lies down, and pretends to fall asleep. The apprentice courtesan plucks fitfully at the strings of a plain shamisen. Her customer pretends to awaken.*)

HIRA: Unnh . . . Hey, hey—stop playing the shamisen and crawl in here and lie down, by all means.

APPRENTICE COURTESAN: No. Just let me be. You'll get me bawled out again.

HIRA: The problem is you say it in such a loud voice. Just slip in here for a minute. (*He takes her by the hand and pulls.*)

APPRENTICE COURTESAN: Your pardon, if you pleeeease, sir![69] (*She speaks now in serious tones, leaving Hira little choice but to release her. He sulks for a time, then suddenly rises, reties his sash, and stands in an earnest, upright posture, deliberating.*)

HIRA: Listen, you put away my tissue case and outer coat somewhere; bring them to me now.

---

69. The expression she uses, *ogaminsu* (literally, I join my hands in prayer), was a set phrase used by Yoshiwara prostitutes when repulsing a customer's advances. Her addition of the final particle *e*, drawn out into a prolonged *e-e-e-e*, seems intended as a slight coquettish softening of this rejection, presumably to avoid unduly alienating her mistress's client.

APPRENTICE COURTESAN: What is it you want to do?

HIRA: I'm going home.

APPRENTICE COURTESAN: You've never gone home before—why go home?

HIRA: Well, it's already five o'clock in the morning, so . . .

APPRENTICE COURTESAN: No, it's not that late yet. My mistress will be here any moment now. She told me not to allow you to budge from here, no matter what, so I mustn't allow you to budge. Stay right where you are, sir.

HIRA: She'll be here any moment?

APPRENTICE COURTESAN: She'll be here any time now. Don't be so impatient; just stay put for a bit. Stay right there. Lie down.

HIRA: Yeah, but . . . this is no fun at all. She'll be here any moment? (*He lies down again. In the room next door, the customer is a blind man*[70] *from the provinces. His prostitute, an apprentice courtesan, is sleeping peacefully. He claps his hands together to summon her, but no one comes. He sighs and mutters to himself.*)

BLIND MAN: This is no fun! (*He begins fiddling with the tobacco tray.*)[71] It's long since struck four A.M.; I keep trying to wake her, but whatever I do, I get nowhere. (*Snapping the back of his fingernail against her wooden pillow, he calls out.*)[72] Hey, hey, wake up, wake up! Emergency, emergency! I've spilled an ember next to my pillow! Wake up, wake up!

APPRENTICE COURTESAN (*groggily*): Yeah, what is it?

BLIND MAN: Never mind, just wake up for a minute!

APPRENTICE COURTESAN (*sitting up*): You've got your nerve, harassing me like this.

BLIND MAN: How many times do you think I've tried to wake you tonight? It must be five o'clock!

APPRENTICE COURTESAN (*pushing open the folding screen and pretending to peer about in all directions*): It seems to be morning already.

BLIND MAN: No, no, it's not morning yet. It's only been an hour since it struck four.

APPRENTICE COURTESAN: That's because you can't see. The sun's been up for some time already.

BLIND MAN: But the crows haven't started cawing yet.

APPRENTICE COURTESAN (*pretending to hit the blind man on the head, mutters under her breath*): Ooh, I hate—!

BLIND MAN (*catching what she said*): What is it you hate?

---

70. The word *zatō* (literally, head of a guild) was by this time a generic term for blind men with shaven heads and monks' robes who made their living as entertainers (raconteurs, musicians, and so forth), masseurs, or acupuncturists.

71. The *tabako-bon*, or tobacco tray, was a lacquered dish or tray on which were laid out the paraphernalia for pipe smoking: pipes, tobacco case, charcoal holder (for lighting one's pipe), and ash receptacle.

72. The hollow wooden pillow resounds when he flicks it with the back of his fingernail.

APPRENTICE COURTESAN: The client in the next room. He tries so hard to sound witty and sophisticated—I just can't stand him!

MAN-ABOUT-TOWN (*in the next room*): Hey, girlie![73] Where has she gotten to? Hey, girlie! Hey, girlie!

APPRENTICE COURTESAN: What is it? And stop talking to me in that patronizing way!

MAN-ABOUT-TOWN: Listen, I want you to wake up that young man I was with earlier.

APPRENTICE COURTESAN: He'll be here in a moment. (*The Youth appears, looking sleepy.*)

MAN-ABOUT-TOWN: What's the matter, lover boy? You don't look so sharp at all!

YOUTH (*sheepishly*): She wouldn't let me get any sleep, so I'm kind of sleepy.

MAN-ABOUT-TOWN: You're so lucky! Now, this girlie here hardly poked out her little mug the entire night.[74] I'm never coming to Yoshiwara again— never again!

YOUTH: You want to come back day after tomorrow?

MAN-ABOUT-TOWN: What for?

YOUTH: I've made a date[75] for the day after tomorrow.

MAN-ABOUT-TOWN: You're joking! This is appalling—appalling! This house is a horrible house! (*The Youth's courtesan, a very attractive "bedroom courtesan,"*[76] *sleepily comes out to stand beside the apprentice courtesan.*)

BEDROOM COURTESAN AND APPRENTICE COURTESAN (*glowering at the Man-About-Town*): I hate him!

MAN-ABOUT-TOWN: Say, girlie, let me have a little *chazuke!*

APPRENTICE COURTESAN: What's that? Let you tipple the *chazuke?*[77]

MAN-ABOUT-TOWN: Come on, now, don't crack jokes like that—just hurry up and bring it, will you? What say, lover boy—don't you want a little *chazuke* before we go?

---

73. He addresses her as *shin*, an overly familiar, cavalier-sounding abbreviation of *shinzō* (apprentice courtesan).

74. In ostentatiously larding his speech with such Yoshiwara slang expressions as *chokkiri* (a bit, hardly) and *tsundashita* (poked out), the Man-About-Town gives the impression of trying very hard to be "with it."

75. *Yakusoku* (appointment, promise), that is, an assignation with the courtesan with whom he spent the night. This is a Yoshiwara-ism.

76. A *heya-mochi* (literally, room holder) was a courtesan one rank below the *zashiki-mochi* or suite holder, who had two or more private rooms of her own. A *heya-mochi* was entitled to a single private room, whereas courtesans of lower rank than this were obliged to move from room to room to serve their customers.

77. The apprentice courtesan mocks him by pretending to mishear *chazurasero* (give me some chazuke) as *kezurasero*, another Yoshiwara sophisticates' expression meaning "give me a drink."

YOUTH: Sure, that sounds fine.

BEDROOM COURTESAN: Are you going home already?

YOUTH: Yes.

BEDROOM COURTESAN: Stay just a little longer! It's early yet.

MAN-ABOUT-TOWN: Say, why don't you try to stop *me* from leaving?

BEDROOM COURTESAN: *She's* the one who should stop *you* from leaving, so there's no need for *me* to!

APPRENTICE COURTESAN: What? I can't *stand* you! You think you're the type I'd try to keep from leaving? Hurry up and get out of here! The night is over.

MAN-ABOUT-TOWN: Girlie here doesn't seem to think I'm even human.

APPRENTICE COURTESAN: It's this "girlie"-ing that I've been unable to abide the entire night!

MAN-ABOUT-TOWN: That may be, but did you give my message to the lady of the inner suite?[78]

APPRENTICE COURTESAN: Yes, and when I told her what you said, my mistress said she'd never heard of anyone by that name.

MAN-ABOUT-TOWN: Dear me, how cruel! Still, I'm sure the courtesan in the suite down the hall[79] won't have forgotten me!

APPRENTICE COURTESAN: Yes, I told her earlier that you'd said so, so when you went off to relieve your bladder, she took a look at you from behind and said she had no recollection of you whatsoever.

MAN-ABOUT-TOWN: Have I aged so very much, then? I've lost all interest— lost all interest in any of this. I'm just going to go on home, just go on home.

APPRENTICE COURTESAN: For pity's sake, stay just a tiny bit longer! I'll simply *die* if you go home! (*With these words, she ushers him out into the hallway. The Youth and the bedroom courtesan remain behind, immersed in intimate conversation.*)

MAN-ABOUT-TOWN: Lover boy, that's bad form—bad form, I tell you!

APPRENTICE COURTESAN: Don't you bother about other people—just get on down those stairs, just get on down those stairs!

AROUND DAYBREAK

HIRA (*next door*): Lord, what a racket! Sounds like the one who's been shooting his mouth off all night has finally gone. And the noise of the wicket gate opening for the past hour or so has been driving me crazy.[80]

---

78. Probably the highest-ranking courtesan of the establishment. This would be the lady about whom the Man-About-Town was boasting, in the boat, that she had found him irresistible.

79. The next-highest-ranking courtesan of the establishment.

80. The sound of its opening and closing as one customer after another leaves the brothel in the early morning.

HIRA'S REGULAR COURTESAN MISTRESS[81] (*who has replaced the "substitute"
  apprentice courtesan*): Don't worry, when I move to the inner suite, all this
  racket will be no problem. The only real hardship is getting to that point.[82]

HIRA: Come, now, I've been telling you this all night—what are you so concerned about? I'll put up the cost of your attendants' debuts as apprentice
  courtesans, however much it comes to. So it's merely a matter of funding
  this move to the inner suite. And even this I'll take care of, if it should come
  to that.[83]

COURTESAN: That makes me so happy! (*She begins to embrace and fondle
  him.*) If I just had one more client like you, everything would be perfect!

HIRA: Oh, you're a fickle one, you are! (*He cuddles close, in an amorous mood.*)

COURTESAN: The truth is, I've been having trouble sleeping, night or day. But
  last night, after the night's client left and I came in here with you, my cares
  melted away and I slept like a baby. Still, last night when you got in such a
  bad mood, you were really scaring me. From now on, please don't lose your
  temper like that.

HIRA: I won't, I won't. Forgive me—forgive me, please. Well, I must be getting
  along now, I must be getting along.

COURTESAN: Oh, stay just a little while longer!

HIRA: No, the day is dawning. Open the blinds a bit, will you? (*The courtesan
  opens the lattice window. The sun has fully risen. Hira blanches.*) Blessed
  Three Jewels![84] The crows must have been cawing for some time now, but
  somehow I was totally unaware of it. (*He calls loudly.*) Boy! Boy! Quickly,
  put out my sandals! The teahouse said they'd send someone to pick me up
  at four o'clock; but look how late it is already, and they still haven't sent
  anyone!

---

81. That is, Yama.

82. That is, raising the considerable funds necessary to move up to the status of "inner-suite
courtesan," the highest-ranking courtesan in the establishment. She may also be hinting at her
own "hardship" in giving the royal treatment to her previous customer, the one who just left, in
order to induce him to promise her his financial assistance with this move. The purpose of such
a hint would be to prod Hira into offering such support himself by making him see a serious
competitor in this potentially more generous customer, whom Yama seems to have been favoring
over Hira all evening.

83. Moving up in rank had to be done with the proper pomp and ceremony and involved
various expenses such as giving elaborate gifts to everyone in the brothel, as well as to those in
its affiliated teahouse, boathouse inns, and others. The courtesan's young attendants would also
move up at this time, to apprentice-courtesan rank. The considerable cost of these ceremonial
preparations would typically be borne by one of the courtesan's regular clients.

84. *Namu sanbō* (literally, Homage to the Three Jewels!) expresses surprise and consternation,
much like "Good God in heaven!"

BROTHEL'S MALE EMPLOYEE: He's been here for some time, sir.

HIRA: Oh my, oh my, this is just . . . (*As he is tying his sash, the crows all begin cawing again in unison.*)

COURTESAN: Be sure and come this afternoon, now—I'll be waiting for you.[85]

HIRA: Well, since I'll be getting back so late, I can't promise absolutely, but I'll do my best to get here somehow.

COURTESAN: In that case, I won't walk you back to Nakano-chō.[86]

HIRA: Don't worry about that. Damn! It's so late, it's so late!

COURTESAN: You be sure and come, now. (*The crows begin cawing again.*) "All unfeeling, the dawn bell."[87]

> [*Kibyōshi sharebon shū*, NKBT 59: 272–293, translated by Herschel Miller]

SANTŌ KYŌDEN

Santō Kyōden (1761–1816) was one of the leading writers of his day. The eldest son of Iwase Densaemon, a pawnbroker in Fukagawa in Edo, he was the author of kibyōshi, gōkan, sharebon, yomihon, and kyōka, as well as being a ukiyo-e artist. When he was thirteen, his family moved to Ginza in Kyōbashi, from which he took his pen name (Kyō from Kyōbashi, and Santō, or "east of the hills," from the location of Kyōbashi) and where he remained the rest of his life. At the age of fourteen or fifteen Kyōden became the student of the ukiyo-e master Kitao Shigemasa and took the painter name of Kitao Masanobu. In 1778,

---

85. That is, having refused all requests from other clients for the afternoon.

86. That is, I won't escort you back to Nakano-chō, since I'll be seeing you anyway later today. It was customary for a high-ranking courtesan, at the end of a "regular" customer's visit, to escort him back as far as the intersection of her brothel's street and Nakano-chō, Yoshiwara's central boulevard. If she held him in particularly high regard, she might escort him all the way back down Nakano-chō to Yoshiwara's main gate. This exchange would appear to indicate that their intimacy is now such that they can occasionally forgo this formality. However, it can also be read as indicating that having obtained Hira's pledge of financial support, the courtesan calculates that her hold on him is now secure enough that she can safely dispense with such niceties.

87. The last line is a slight alteration of the last line of a *nagauta* (long song), "Love's Crimson Cherry Blossoms" (Omoi no hizakura, 1742), a courtesan's love-plaint, which ends: "To me alone he is true—believing thus, we slip so easily into the abyss of *sui*. As one who is sinking, how clearly now I see: it is better by far not to be *sui*! All unfeeling, the dawn sky." (*Sui* was an aesthetic ideal that was supposed to combine a proclivity for sensuality, warmth, and genuine sympathy for others with an unerring sense of taste and a capacity for cool nonattachment.) The courtesan alters the final word from "sky" to "bell," thus elegantly protesting the heartless "dawn bell" that tolls the hour of the lovers' parting. Owing to certain puns, the last line can also be read as the courtesan's patting herself on the back for having hooked such an easily manipulated dupe as Hira, whose ready money will ring in the dawn of a new day for her as an inner-suite courtesan.

he began to draw illustrations for kibyōshi, and by 1782, he had made a name for himself as the author of *Things for Sale You Know About* (*Gozonji no shō-baimono*), joining the samurai authors Koikawa Harumachi and Hōseidō Kisanji as one of the foremost writers of kibyōshi in the Tenmei and Kansei eras (1781–1801). In 1791, Kyōden wrote a three-part sharebon, beginning with *Behind the Brocade* (*Nishiki no ura*), which resulted in his being handcuffed for fifty days for having violated the bakufu's publication restrictions under the Kansei Reforms. After that, he abandoned the sharebon genre and turned to yomihon, with which he broke new ground. During the early nineteenth century, he was the only writer to rival Kyokutei Bakin in this genre. Kyōden's best-known works include *Grilled and Basted Edo-Born Playboy* (*Edo umare uwaki no kabayaki*, 1785) and *Shingaku: Quick-Staining Dye, Worker of Wonders* (*Shingaku haya-somegusa*, 1790) in the kibyōshi genre; *Forty-Eight Techniques for Success with Courtesans* (*Keiseikai shijū hatte*, 1790) in the sharebon genre; and *Chūshingura Water Margin* (*Chūshingura suikoden*, 1801) in the yomihon genre. As a painter, he is known for such works as *New Beauties Contest Self-Penned Mirror* (*Shinbijin awase jihitsu kagami*, 1784), a multicolored picture book. Of Kyōden's many students, Kyokutei Bakin was his best; Kyōden also had a significant impact on later writers such as Jippensha Ikku, Shikitei Sanba, and Tamenaga Shunsui.

FORTY-EIGHT TECHNIQUES FOR SUCCESS WITH COURTESANS (*KEISEIKAI SHIJŪ HATTE*, 1790)

By the An'ei-Tenmei era (1772–1789), sharebon and kibyōshi had become the central genres of Edo vernacular fiction. In 1790, at the end of this period, Santō Kyōden wrote *Forty-Eight Techniques for Success with Courtesans*, a sharebon divided into five sections, "The Tender-Loving Technique" (Shipporitoshita te), "The Cheap Technique" (Yasui te), "The Revealed-as-Fake Technique" (Minukareta te), "The Unsettled-Feeling Technique" (Sowasowa suru te), and "The True-Feeling Technique" (Shin no te), each of which describes a distinct type of courtesan and a specific type of customer relationship. Following the format of the sharebon, the text resembles a play script centered on dialogue, with only occasional prose descriptions. In its shift of focus away from the pursuit of *tsū* to the emotional consequences of male–female relationships in the licensed quarter, *Forty-Eight Techniques* had a profound influence on such later sharebon as *Two Ways of Approaching a Courtesan* (*Keiseikai futasuji*, 1797) and foreshadowed the nineteenth-century ninjōbon.

"The Tender-Loving Technique," the first of the two sections translated here, is interesting in that both the customer and the high-ranking courtesan (*chūsan*) are new to the ways of the quarter and lack the pretensions of the experienced older courtesans and long-time customers. As in *The Playboy Dialect*, a contrast is established between a youth figure, who is clearly of considerable means, and an older, apparently more experienced male client, who is Santō Kyōden's version of the half-baked sophisticate, the half-*tsū*. In contrast to *The Playboy Dialect*, in which we seem to be looking at the women from the outside, Santō Kyōden gives a more sympathetic and affectionate inside view of the courtesan, who comes across as a vivacious, charming, and warm-hearted young lady. The comments of the intrusive narrator are likewise sympathetic to the courtesan, explaining her difficulties in dealing with the demands of the brothel's hierarchy and describing the youth's appeal from her point of view. This kind of perspective is developed more fully in "The True-Feeling Technique," the second selection and the last section in *Forty-Eight Techniques*, which sensitively depicts a relationship between a high-ranking courtesan and a customer that has gone beyond the usual play, resulting in a genuine love affair. The pathos of this impossible rela-tionship is viewed with a certain amount of sympathy by the narrator, who, at the end, ironically offers commonsense criticisms (no doubt in part to ward off the censors). Of particular interest here is the notion that true love seriously conflicts with the economic situation of both the man and the woman. If the man were rich, he would be able to buy out the woman's contract, and the two could consummate their love. In fact, Kyōden himself married a lower-ranking licensed-quarter woman, and after her death he married yet another. The man in "The True-Feeling Technique," how-ever, is living off his parents' income and so does not have this option.

The Tender-Loving Technique

The client is a youth, and his companion for the evening is a high-ranking courtesan[88] *who has only recently made her debut. This is their first meeting.*[89] *The courtesan is sixteen years old but seems well developed and is exceedingly beautiful. She has on Shimomura face powder, sparingly applied. Her dis-position is warmhearted, and her face overflows with sweetness. Her hair, done up in the* shinobu *style, emits an alluring fragrance of Momosuke matrimony-vine oil.*[90] *She is dressed for bed in a scarlet crepe kimono with a lavender satin border in a rugged-strand motif fashioned with gold and silver threads and secured with a crenellated silk obi adorned with the large-paulownia pattern,*[91] *custom-made by Echigawa. In the same hand with which she is holding up the hem of her robe, she holds several sheets of fine, soft tissue paper. She is in the hallway.*

---

88. After the 1750s, *chūsan* was the highest rank of courtesan in Yoshiwara.

89. By Yoshiwara custom, no sexual intercourse was permitted on a first visit to a high-ranking prostitute.

90. Shimaya momosuke was a top Edo cosmetics boutique. The seeds of the *kuko* (Chinese matrimony vine) yielded an aromatic oil commonly used for dressing hair.

91. A heraldic pattern consisting of three paulownia leaves surmounted by three vertical paulownia blooms: two five-petaled flowers to left and right, with one, seven-petaled flower be-tween them.

In the frontispiece for *Forty-Eight Techniques for Success with Courtesans*, the text on the right reads, "Picture by Kyōden," and that on the left, "Capital of Celestial Beings in the World of Desire, Country of Pleasure in Prosperity and Peace," which refers to the licensed quarters. Kinkō Sennin (Sage of the Koto), a master of the koto instrument in Song China, was frequently pictured skillfully riding on a carp, a symbol of good fortune. In a *mitate* (double vision) allusion to the Chinese Sage of the Koto, Kyōden depicts an elegant courtesan reading a letter from a customer as she rides a gigantic carp. From the 1790 edition. (From SNKBZ 80, *Sharebon, kokkeibon, ninjōbon*, by permission of Shōgakukan)

COURTESAN: Hey, Kotoji!

CHILD ATTENDANT[92] (*carefully turning her head, with her heavy-looking coiffure held in place by a long, flat hairpin, thrust through sideways and adorned with flower ornaments at both ends*): Yes miss?

COURTESAN: You haven't forgotten what I told you earlier, have you?

CHILD ATTENDANT: I already told them! (*That is, to lay out the bedding in a different place than usual, out of consideration for the client now waiting alone in the adjoining room, so that he will not be able to hear the intimate exchanges taking place next door. Tonight's client is about eighteen and looks as though he would be very popular with the ladies. Well-built, handsome, and sparing of speech, he looks every inch the scion of a well-to-do family. He has come with one companion. Still wearing his haori jacket and reclining on top of a bed made up of five futon mattresses, he is now doodling in the ashes of the hand-warming brazier with the tip of a long metal charcoal-handling chopstick.*)

---

92. *Kamuro*, or preteenage attendant to a high-ranking courtesan.

COURTESAN (*entering and bashfully kneeling in a dim part of the room*): Won't you take off your jacket?

YOUTH: OK. (*Without further comment, he removes it.*)

COURTESAN (*folding it and placing it in the room's small alcove*): You're making me awfully nervous.

YOUTH: How come?

COURTESAN: Well, because you're not saying anything.

YOUTH: I don't know what I'm supposed to say.

COURTESAN: That's right, lie! You've obviously got a sure hand with the ladies.

YOUTH: The only hands I've got are these two right here.

COURTESAN: Oh, cute! (*She seems on the point of pinching him but stops herself. She puffs on a pipe, trying to light it, but the pipe-lighting ember has gone out. She claps her hands in summons. The child attendant enters.*)

COURTESAN: Put some charcoal in here. Make sure it's properly banked, now.

CHILD ATTENDANT: Yes, miss. (*She takes away the charcoal holder.*)

FELLOW COURTESAN (*from the other side of the wall, next door*): My, aren't *we* having fun!

COURTESAN (*deliberately, though in fact she heard*): What did you say? I can't hear a thing! (*She beams delightedly. Presently the child attendant returns carrying the charcoal holder, blowing on the ember inside it.*)

COURTESAN: Hey! What have you done to your finger?

CHILD ATTENDANT: I got bit by a dog last night in Nakano-chō.

COURTESAN: You see? What did I tell you? Now, let that be a lesson to you; that'll teach you not to trifle with dogs and whatnot! (*Her chiding is childlike and without rancor. The Youth smiles, and the Child Attendant hangs her head.*)

COURTESAN: Here, now put these away, then change your clothes and go on to bed. (*She pulls out her ornamental combs and hairpins, wraps them up in tissue paper, and hands them to her.*)

CHILD ATTENDANT: Yes, miss. Well, good night, then. (*As she rises to go, her sleeve brushes against a koto leaning against the wall, and the instrument sounds discordantly:* Plonk-twang!)

COURTESAN: Softly! (*She pulls the tobacco tray over next to the head of the bed and lights a pipe. The flame flares up, and by its light she carefully, surreptitiously, examines the Youth's face. After puffing briefly on the pipe to get it going, she offers it to the Youth.*)

YOUTH: No, I don't care for tobacco.

COURTESAN: You won't have any? Say, are you from the same part of town as Hanagiku's customer?[93]

---

93. Hanagiku is probably the name of the courtesan now entertaining the man with whom the Youth has come to the establishment.

YOUTH: No, I'm not.

COURTESAN: From where, then?

YOUTH: From Hatchō-bori, in Kanda.[94]

COURTESAN: You liar! How dare you try to fool me?

YOUTH: I'll tell you where later.

COURTESAN: How come? This is really bugging me now. Come on, tell me! If you don't tell me, I'll tickle you!

YOUTH: Why should you care if I tell you or not? Anyhow, it's a long way from here.

COURTESAN: Really?

YOUTH: See if you can guess.

COURTESAN: OK, tell me what syllable it starts with.

YOUTH: It starts with *ni*.

COURTESAN: OK, hold on. *Ni*, right? Let's see, now . . . OK—Nihonbashi?

YOUTH (*laughing*): Wrong!

COURTESAN (*thinks again for a bit*): OK, then, how about Nikawa-chō or whatever it is?[95]

YOUTH: Nope.

COURTESAN (*scratching her hair in front with an ornamental hairpin*): Damn! So where is it?

YOUTH: Actually it *is* near Nihonbashi: it's Nishigashi.

COURTESAN: There, you see? Pretty good guess, huh? Say, if you're from Nihonbashi, then I guess you pass by the Asakusa Kannon Temple on your way, huh?[96]

YOUTH: Of course!

COURTESAN: I suppose you have a wife at home, right?

YOUTH: What? Not yet—no way!

COURTESAN: Then you must be seeing a courtesan somewhere, right?

YOUTH: My family is very strict, and I can't get out of the house, so there was no way I could ever visit here before. Last year on the way home from the Tori-no-machi festival, I did go along with somebody to a different establishment. But instead of talking only about me, tell me about *your* love affairs!

---

94. A neighborhood commonly claimed as a spurious address. The Youth is teasing her by giving her an address that is patently false.

95. She is mispronouncing Mikawa-chō, a place-name she must have half-heard somewhere.

96. Nishigashi was a neighborhood of prosperous merchant families, suggesting that the Youth comes from a well-to-do household. Asakusa Temple, which enshrines the Buddhist deity Kannon, is near Yoshiwara and would be one of the very few parts of Edo with which this inexperienced young woman, having spent the past few years in the closed world of Yoshiwara, would be familiar. She is apparently unsure of the exact location of Nihonbashi, a very well known section of Edo. Her unsophisticated observation, like her earlier mispronunciation of Mikawa-chō, betrays her ignorance of the world outside Yoshiwara.

COURTESAN: How could I have any such thing? Up until the end of last year I was in the dormitory[97] at Minowa; I debuted only this spring. Even supposing if I wanted to have a love affair, nobody would take a person like me.

YOUTH: You do lie well. I'm going to name you Liar.

COURTESAN: It's true!

YOUTH: OK, well, have you ever fallen in love with a customer?

COURTESAN: No, I don't like to fall in love.

YOUTH: Well, then, that would be all the more true in regard to me, I suppose.

COURTESAN: You? (*She looks into his face, smiling.*) I'd better not say any more. (*As she speaks, she is twisting the "binding monkey" attached to the corner of her mattress.*)[98]

YOUTH: You do like to tease, don't you?

COURTESAN: You know, I have only one wish.

YOUTH: What wish is that?

COURTESAN: That the customer I love would come.

YOUTH: Didn't you just say you weren't in love with anybody?

COURTESAN: There is just one person.

YOUTH: I envy him. Who is it? (*The courtesan says nothing.*)

YOUTH: Come on, who is it?

COURTESAN (*gathering her courage and coming out with it*): It's you!

YOUTH (*his heart racing*): You sure are one smooth talker!

COURTESAN: It's the truth. But considering the kind of person I am, I suppose this is the last time you'll be coming here, right?

YOUTH: You deserve better—a beautiful courtesan like you!

COURTESAN: Oh, sure, that's right, make fun of me all you want!

YOUTH: But seriously—if you'd really be willing to make me a regular patron, I *would* like to come calling on you.

COURTESAN: What a lie!.

YOUTH: Suppose I did come?

COURTESAN: You mean it?

YOUTH: Of course!

COURTESAN: Ah, well, I'm glad, even if it *is* a lie!

YOUTH: Now *that's* a lie!

COURTESAN: No, it's true.

YOUTH (*taking her in his arms and slipping between her legs*): Which is it— the truth or a lie?

COURTESAN: Whoops, my feet are cold—I hope you don't mind. (*She wraps*

---

97. A house in the Minowa area of Edo where young prospective courtesans were sequestered and given education and training in various arts and skills related to their profession.

98. This was a piece of cloth stuffed with cotton batting and stitched into the shape of a monkey. It was a charm that, attached to a corner of the mattress, was said to bind a prostitute's customer so that he could not leave her.

her legs tightly around him. Just as they are about to really get into it, another
customer, holding in one hand a tobacco pouch with a pipe sticking out of it,
enters the room.)

COMPANION CUSTOMER: It's freezing tonight! (*Belches*) Mind if I come in?
(*This customer is fortyish and appears to be a long-standing patron. He pre-*
sents himself as a man of the world, knowledgeable in every respect, but is in
fact a great humbug.)

COURTESAN (*though resenting the interruption at just the wrong moment*):
How good of you to drop in on us! Do, please, come on in.

COMPANION CUSTOMER (*kneeling down*): Well, then, perhaps I *will* have just
a token pipeful.[99]

COURTESAN (*lighting a pipe and handing it to him*): Why don't you come on
up here?[100]

COMPANION CUSTOMER: No, here is fine—as Yoshino arrowroot powder.[101]

YOUTH (*out of a sense of polite obligation*): Please, come on in.

COMPANION CUSTOMER: Now, lady, this one's like a kid brother to me, so
you take good care of him.

COURTESAN: He's been teasing me something terrible all evening.

YOUTH: What? *I'm* the one who's been getting led by the nose the whole time!

COURTESAN: There he goes again! He's hateful! (*She pretends to strike at him*
with the pipe.) But you are his teacher, so of course he *would* know all the
tricks.

COMPANION CUSTOMER: Look, Ei,[102] you've got it all to look forward to, so
do all the wenching you can—knock yourself out! As for me, I'm getting on
in years. My vitality's sapped—one little drink just knocks me right out—so
there's no way a high-ranking beauty's going to fall for me now!

COURTESAN: Oh, come, now, I'd say you've done pretty well, getting Hanagiku
to fall for you as hard as she has.

COMPANION CUSTOMER: Oh, please! No, that high-ranker's[103] not the type
of girl I'd want to plant in *my* field! I won't be coming to visit her again.

COURTESAN: The poor thing!—don't say that! I'm gonna tell on you!

COMPANION CUSTOMER: It's fine with me if she *does* hear. If I do say so

---

99. There is a gratuitous pun on the phonetic similarity between *nome* (smoke!) and *nobe*
(meadow).

100. That is, up onto the futon.

101. This uninspired pun turns on *yoshi* (good) and the place-name Yoshino, a region famous
for the high quality of its *kuzu*, or arrowroot, which was pulverized and used in cooking as a
thickener.

102. Probably an abbreviation of the Youth's family name. It was customary to avoid using
real names in the licensed quarters.

103. He refers to her as *kei*, a Yoshiwara slang abbreviation of *keisei*, or city toppler (rendered
earlier as "high-ranking beauty"), that is, a woman whose charms were enough to inspire the
razing of a fortified city. *Keisei*, a term borrowed from Chinese literature, was commonly used
to refer to a beautiful, talented, high-ranking courtesan.

myself, I'm a man who's come to this quarter for three hundred sixty-odd days straight, a man with palanquin calluses on his behind, a man who can't fall asleep unless he feels velvet against his face. . . . [104] (*Warming to his topic, he fails to notice that the ember has dropped out of his pipe onto his lap; his brand-new pongee kimono, of striped Ueda silk, begins to smolder.*)

COURTESAN (*noticing*): Look—your ember's dropped out!

COMPANION CUSTOMER: Uh-huh. (*He merely rubs it out. Hoping to save face in front of the courtesan, he shows no concern but continues.*) That's the kind of guy I am, so when a woman so much as twitches her left eye, I know exactly what's up with her—I know every trick in the book—so even for a high-ranking beauty, I suppose it's not so easy to entertain a guy like me. (*Thus, having been poorly treated this evening, he comes over here and blows off steam. The courtesan, fed up, says nothing but looks bored and fiddles, twisting tissue paper into little strings and tossing them against the arrangement of irises in the alcove.*)

COMPANION CUSTOMER: Well, I've ended up talking for quite some time. To overstay one's welcome is the height of boorishness, you know.[105] Lady, good night. (*He gets to his feet.*)

YOUTH: Hey, stay awhile.

COMPANION CUSTOMER: Naw—I'm getting awfully sleepy. It's OK once in a while for me—but I imagine you've got to get up pretty early, so. . . .

YOUTH: That's right—the earlier the better.

COURTESAN (*though overjoyed that at last he is leaving*): Oh, do stay just a little bit longer. But we'd better not keep you. Hanagiku will be cross with you, no doubt.

COMPANION CUSTOMER: We're beyond that point. (*Moving into the adjoining room*) What do you know, everyone's drifted off to dreamland, even the head apprentice courtesan.[106] This is a situation made to order for stealing into a lady's bedchamber. (*He goes over by the wood-and-paper lantern, pokes an exploratory finger into the fresh burn-hole in his robe, and departs, greatly crestfallen. Behind him, the couple heave a sigh of relief. The clock in the office downstairs chimes the seventh hour.*)[107]

TEAHOUSE MAN: Gentlemen, I've come to escort you back![108]

---

104. He is proudly claiming to have palanquin calluses from riding to and from Yoshiwara every day. "Velvet" is a reference to the velvet-lapeled sleeping robes used in Yoshiwara houses.

105. He speaks in a preachy tone, suggesting that he is greatly impressed with his own considerateness.

106. A head apprentice courtesan (*bantō shinzō*) attended a high-ranking courtesan but was older (generally over twenty) than the other *shinzō*. She typically also served as a sort of chaperon and kept the brothel management informed of the courtesan's activities.

107. Around 5:00 A.M.

108. As was the custom, an employee of the "guiding teahouse" has come at the appointed hour to collect the customers and escort them back to the teahouse. He is announcing his arrival from outside the room.

NARRATOR: The use by the courtesan of the flame from the pipe tobacco to examine the Youth's face harks back to the "Fireflies" chapter of the *Tale of Genji* and is very refined.[109] At this stage of her career, she is still intimidated by the madam and the head apprentice courtesan, so even though she may be in love, her love will remain no more than a feeling locked inside her heart. And it will often happen that the head apprentice courtesan will instruct her, "Tonight, say thus-and-such to the customer and urge him to come on the seasonal festival day";[110] yet the girl will end up missing the chance to ask him, and the head courtesan will lie stewing in the next room, eavesdropping on it all from start to finish and fuming, "Ah! Why doesn't she latch on to what he just said and make him agree to do it!" But since she is a courtesan with a promising future, she will not be dependent on her brothel owner for long and will soon clear the hurdle of launching her apprentice courtesans' careers.[111] And again, these little youths nowadays do tend to get carried away with trying to be the very height of style and sophistication, yet there is none of that about this customer—he is exactly the type a courtesan will fall in love with. Truly, a match like this is an enviable amusement. Someone once described as priceless the words of one high-ranking courtesan who, when staying in temporary quarters at Nakazu,[112] remarked, "Now, I like the quarter, because there the weather's good—but my, how it rains in Nakazu!"[113] In any case, when it comes to high-ranking beauties, innocence is to be greatly prized.

[*Sharebon, kokkeibon, ninjōbon*, SNKBZ 80, translated by Herschel Miller]

---

109. In this chapter, Genji's half brother Prince Hotaru comes calling one evening on Genji's ward Tamakazura, and Genji releases a bag of fireflies into Tamakazura's room so that Hotaru can catch a glimpse of her face in the darkness.

110. Several times a year, festivals were held in the licensed quarters. The occasion might be seasonal gatherings for flower viewing or moon viewing or special licensed-quarter holidays. On these days, fees were doubled, and each courtesan was expected to persuade customers to visit her. Any courtesan who failed to bring in a customer was required by her brothel to pay his fees herself. Thus there was enormous pressure on courtesans to persuade their regular customers to visit on these days.

111. Apprentice courtesans (*shinzō*) must, by long-standing Yoshiwara tradition, debut in proper ceremonial fashion. This cost a great deal of money, and the courtesan whom the apprentice courtesans served was responsible for raising it. She did so by obtaining commitments from her regular customers.

112. After the original New Yoshiwara licensed quarter was destroyed in a fire in 1787, its inhabitants were moved to various temporary locations, including a section of newly reclaimed land known as Nakazu.

113. Nakazu was, in fact, quite near Yoshiwara (the quarter) and, of course, had exactly the same weather; but to this ingenuous courtesan, for whom Yoshiwara was the center of the world, Nakazu (which was actually somewhat closer to central Edo than was Yoshiwara) seemed like the middle of nowhere.

The True-Feeling Technique

The setting: A large house in the Yoshiwara quarter. The woman wants to marry the man, and he wants to marry her.

A man wipes the floorboards of a second-floor hall. Another walks up and down calling out, "Bath's closing! Bath's closing!" Although the weather is good, a male customer has stayed the night in one room on the second floor and still hasn't gone home. It's already past noon. The courtesan is high ranking, a chūsan of twenty-two or twenty-three. She's not feeling well and lies under a quilt with a torn strip of white silk around her head. She hasn't bothered to put on makeup or fix her mussed hair. The man is thirty-three or thirty-four. His face is taut and somber, but he's unaffected in his behavior and quite attractive. He's wearing only his inner robe and sits beside the woman with one leg up, bent at the knee.

GEISHA MUSICIAN (*plays her shamisen and softly finishes her song*): ". . . in the quarter they drift and float day after day, pretending they're wife and husband."

JESTER: Well done!

CUSTOMER (*holding out a saké cup to the musician*): Here, have one.

GEISHA MUSICIAN: I'd like you to have it.

CUSTOMER: Please.

GEISHA MUSICIAN: Well, all right then. (*She accepts the cup with one hand, holding her shamisen in the other.*)

TEAHOUSE MAN:[114] Let me pour.

GEISHA MUSICIAN (*to the teahouse man*): Hey, where were you headed this morning? On the way back from Bishamon Temple, I saw you going somewhere. (*As those familiar with the licensed quarter know, women musicians often go in the morning to pray to the Buddhist demon god Bishamon at the temple dedicated to him in San'ya.*)

TEAHOUSE MAN: Just on an errand. To a customer's house.

GEISHA MUSICIAN: Hmm. Is that all? (*The jester takes the musician's plectrum, which she's rested on a decorated saké stand, and he mimes playing the shamisen.*)

JESTER: Wonderful wood. (*He uses the quarter's word for ivory.*)

GEISHA MUSICIAN: Not really. It's not quite right. It's made for Katō-style playing. (*The geisha musician has been there for some time already, and*

---

114. Teahouses in the quarters served as intermediary agents who introduced customers to houses and handled their accounts; they also managed musicians' performances. Teahouse employees came with the customers and later returned with them to the quarter gate. They also ran errands for them.

someone in the house calls the teahouse man out into the hall. He comes back in and says the musician's time here is up and she's wanted at a party somewhere else in the quarter. She pretends not to hear.)

TEAHOUSE MAN (*whispers to the customer*): Shall I have the musician leave now?

CUSTOMER (*under his breath*): All right. She can leave now.

TEAHOUSE MAN: Well then, let's ask her to put her shamisen back in the case.

JESTER: I think we're all about finished. (*Just then, the thinnest of the three strings on the shamisen, now lying beside the musician, snaps with a sharp twang.*)

GEISHA MUSICIAN: What style that string has. Perfect sense of timing. (*She loosens the other two strings and puts her shamisen back into its case, which she pushes out into the hall. She then makes five or six gracious remarks.*)

JESTER AND GEISHA MUSICIAN: Well, good-bye for now. (*They leave. Soon the jester comes back in.*)

JESTER (*to the woman*): Please take care of yourself!

TEAHOUSE MAN: Here are some radishes. They've been pickled perfectly. (*He's talking about some lightly pickled long white Hadana radishes from the south of Edo.*) Here, I'll give you some.

MAIN COURTESAN: Thanks.

CUSTOMER: Well, thank you all for coming over. (*He taps his pipe to clean it.*)

JESTER: You know, I could swear I left my shoes at the entrance downstairs.

TEAHOUSE MAN: Sorry. I put them in the shoe box with all the others.

JESTER: Much obliged. (*Everyone leaves. The maids bring up trays of food and place them just outside the standing screen at the head of the high-ranking courtesan's bed. Her two young female assistants come into the room. One has her hair twisted up and held in place with an ordinary comb. She's wearing the short cotton robe that the house sent her. It's so dirty it looks deep-fried, and the long, hanging parts of her sleeves are tucked into her sash. She's kidding around with the other girl, whose head is shaved.*)

YOUNG FEMALE ASSISTANT: Never mind. It's all right. I'll do it for you.

CUSTOMER: Matsuno, you got here just in time. Pour me some, will you? (*He holds out a large cup.*)

MAIN COURTESAN: Hey, no more saké. You've been at it long enough.

CUSTOMER: Don't worry about me. I feel like another drink, so I'm going to have one. Matsuno, be a good girl and pour me some, quick.

YOUNG FEMALE ASSISTANT: You've had enough already. (*She watches the high-ranking courtesan and doesn't pick up the saké server.*)

CUSTOMER: Pour me some, will you?

MAIN COURTESAN: Well, all right. Hold out your cup. (*She picks up the long-handled saké server herself and pours so hard that some of the saké splashes out of the cup. When the man tries to drink what's left, she knocks the cup out of his hand with her long pipe. The saké spills onto the hand-warming brazier.*)

CUSTOMER: I give up. You're crazy! (*He fans the fire in the hand warmer with his wide sleeve, trying to revive it. Then he takes out four or five pieces of tissue paper.*)

YOUNG FEMALE ASSISTANT: Oh, look at that! (*She wipes up the saké with the paper. Just then another high-ranking courtesan drops by, opening the sliding door halfway and looking in. She's wearing only an inner robe made of many pieces of the same color. She's just beginning to prepare herself for a performance and has white makeup on her neck, but she hasn't made up her face yet.*)

VISITING COURTESAN: Hi there. I hear your guest stayed over and is still here. Please enjoy yourself. I really envy you, you know. (*She comes in and hunkers down beside her courtesan friend, who's still lying under a quilt.*)

CUSTOMER: The weather's wonderful outside. I must be crazy. I've been here since last night.

VISITING COURTESAN: It just shows how true your feelings are. (*She lights a pipe and gives it to her courtesan friend.*)

MAIN COURTESAN (*one hand reaching out from her robe*): Thanks. (*To the visiting courtesan*) You're visiting me, so I should be the one entertaining you. But here you are doing what I should be doing. Are you going down to wait for customers on the first floor this afternoon?

VISITING COURTESAN: No. Some clerk who has the day off is coming to see me this afternoon.

MAIN COURTESAN: Turn around and let me see your hair. Hey, you look stunning.

VISITING COURTESAN: It's a shame I had to have it done today. (*Tomorrow is the twenty-seventh, when the women in the house wash their hair.*)

CUSTOMER: How about a cup of saké?

VISITING COURTESAN (*frowning slightly and shaking her head*): No. (*She turns to her courtesan friend.*) The only reason I came is to see you. Honest. I heard you were here, so I threw on a few things and came right over. Well, please make lots of love. (*She starts to get up, but the man pulls at the skirt of her robe.*)

CUSTOMER: Won't you stay a little longer? If you go, all the beautiful blossoms will scatter.

VISITING COURTESAN: Do you think pretty words can fool me? I'll have to watch out for you. (*She leaves. A young apprentice passes her on her way in. Her hair's done up well, but she has on too much white makeup. She wears a dirty dark green wadded cotton robe.*)

APPRENTICE COURTESAN: Excuse me. I'm here to see the high-ranking courtesan. (*The woman doesn't answer.*)

APPRENTICE COURTESAN: Excuse me. I need to see the courtesan.

MAIN COURTESAN: Well, what is it? You sure know how to make a racket.

APPRENTICE COURTESAN: It's Hatsuyama. She wants you to let her have some of the radishes.

MAIN COURTESAN: All right, take what you need. (*The young woman picks up some of the pickled radishes that the teahouse gave her. Just as she's leaving, another apprentice comes into the room.*)

SECOND APPRENTICE COURTESAN: I'm very sorry to bother you, but could you spare a sheet of thick paper?

MAIN COURTESAN: You're such a dear! You come and ask for so many different things. Well, go ahead, take it.

SECOND APPRENTICE COURTESAN: Thank you so much. (*She goes out.*)

THIRD APPRENTICE COURTESAN (*from the hall*): Hey, Hanazaki wants to know where the robe she lent you is.

SECOND APPRENTICE COURTESAN: I hung it out to dry on the latticework in the hall. (*Suddenly a bell rings, surprising some of the more casual courtesans. The house is about to open for afternoon business,[115] and all but the high-ranking women rush around and go down to the first floor and sit in the parlor, where they can be seen from the street through latticed windows. Their apprentices begin to play background music on their shamisens. Afternoons are even lonelier than midnight on the second floors of these houses. A special sadness pervades the place. The room where the customer has stayed overnight is so empty it seems hushed. He and the high-ranking courtesan now are alone behind the standing screen.*)

CUSTOMER (*referring to the man from the teahouse*): That Sensuke, today he was being super-nice to you. He's trying to persuade you to get me to give him a nice cloak.

MAIN COURTESAN: That's just like him. I can't stand any of the people who work for that teahouse. Just because you're hard up right now and can't give them any big tips or presents doesn't give them the right to treat you that way—to be so demanding. All they care about is money. It makes me furious.

CUSTOMER: That's not the way they think. You're just imagining things.

MAIN COURTESAN: Listen, will you? When I'm over at that teahouse, they completely ignore my apprentices. They treat them as if they didn't even exist. So these days I'm really careful to tip those teahouse people well. Recently, I got angry twice while performing on the second floor over there. They have an attitude problem.

CUSTOMER: Just ignore them. You don't really listen to them, and then you lose your temper. If I could just pay the teahouse the rest of the money I owe, then all your problems would disappear just like that.

MAIN COURTESAN: They sure would. How much do you still owe them?

CUSTOMER: More than thirty gold *ryō*. I never go upstairs with women at the other houses. They wouldn't let me stay over, anyway. But if I can't come up with at least twenty or thirty gold *ryō*, you know what that means? I'm wiped out. (*He looks fairly depressed.*)

MAIN COURTESAN (*looks down without saying anything. Finally she speaks*): I

---

115. From about 2:00 until 4:00 P.M.

think about your situation a lot. I know how unhappy you must be. It's because you kept coming to see me for so long and spent so much. It was all because of me. I guess you must really dislike me now. Have you stopped loving me?

CUSTOMER: Of course not. When my parents disinherit me for this, I'd be very happy to beg in the streets as long as we're together. But a high-class courtesan like you might not want to . . .

MAIN COURTESAN: Do you still think of me only as a courtesan? I think of myself as your wife, you know. How about showing a little sympathy? If you really feel that way about me, though, I have an idea. I'll pawn my second-best bedding. I can get seven gold *ryō* for that. And I think I'll be able to get three out of my other steady customer. I should be able to get another three more from my other customers. I'll give it all to you. So you do something too. At least take care of the other half. I don't care what happens to me. Even if I have to borrow on my contract and stay here longer, I'll do it—as long as it's for you.

CUSTOMER: I didn't realize you loved me that much. Really, I'll never forget your offer as long as I live. But let me try to handle it by myself. If I can't, let's talk about it some more. How about that?

MAIN COURTESAN: Well, take care of it as soon as you can. The other day the matron called me over and yelled at me again. But the criticism can't stop me from thinking about you. If it could, I wouldn't have kept on like this and gotten you into debt. Even my own mother couldn't stop me from seeing you. Actually, a little while ago my mother came to see me again. She said I looked really thin and then started crying. And the managers of the house, they've given up on me completely. But if they stop you from coming up to the second floor to see me, I'll refuse to work, and they'll have to sell my contract to another house. I'll refuse to work, I really will. I haven't sold my soul to them, after all! (*Discouraged, the man is unable to say anything.*)

MAIN COURTESAN: Oh, I hate this. These days, everything is going wrong. I just want to leave this place as soon as I can. I guess we're really bad for each other. They won't let us be together, and we can't bear to be apart. So how's your mother doing? I've been so upset by all this, I haven't asked how she is. Please give her this Buddhist charm. Make sure she gets it. I asked someone to go all the way to Nichiren Temple in Horinouchi to get it for her. It's supposed to be really effective. I've also offered a prayer for her at Kishimojin Earth Mother Shrine in Iriya. The day before yesterday I gave up eating everything but vegetables. It's not easy. But I've made a big vow, and I'm praying very hard.

CUSTOMER: I've been very bad to my parents, I really have. The reason my mother's sick is because she's so worried about me. She gets even worse when I stay here like this. I'm surprised some god hasn't punished me yet.

MAIN COURTESAN: There are so many things to worry about. Really, I'd like to die as soon as I can. (*She rubs her cold forelocks against the man's face*

*and wets his face with her tears. An afternoon performance is getting under
way in one of the rooms at the back of the second floor, and they can hear
someone singing a soft, soulful song. It's about the lovers Sankatsu and Han-
shichi making their journey toward a love suicide: "Make up your mind, there's
no more need for tears—I'm not crying, and you, now, too . . . ")*

CUSTOMER: You know, I'm getting very depressed. Let's talk about something
else. We've said everything there is to say about this.

MAIN COURTESAN: Really. I agree. If we're not alive, we haven't got anything.
Listen, let me take care of that cloak Sensuke's been pestering you for.

CUSTOMER: Well, if you could. Yes, that would be very nice.

MAIN COURTESAN: I'd better do it soon. Before he starts spreading more bad
rumors about you. (*The man doesn't answer. The woman stares at him.*)

MAIN COURTESAN: Hey, are you asleep? Wake up! (*She blows smoke in his
face, and he wakes up coughing.*)

CUSTOMER: I didn't sleep at all last night. (*He goes back to sleep.*)

MAIN COURTESAN: Hey, don't do that. Don't sleep now. Sleep at night. Open
your eyes!

CUSTOMER: Please. I'm begging you. Let me sleep just a little.

MAIN COURTESAN: Well, then, do whatever you want. It's none of my business. (*She turns her head and looks the other way.*)

CUSTOMER: All right, I'm sorry. If you dislike it that much, I won't. I really
won't. But hey, how come you made me fall for you like this? I'll never
forgive you for it, you know. (*He pulls the woman close.*)

MAIN COURTESAN (*smiling*): Why did you make me fall for you? (*They're
lying together now. She puts her arm under the man's head and kisses him
hard on the lips.*) My period didn't come last month. So you're making things
pretty hard for me. (*She puts her arm around him.*) Hey, you dirty old man!
Untie your sash first! (*She loosens the man's sash and tosses it beyond the
bedding. Then she unties her own sash and holds her body tightly against his.
Outside the big bell tolls at sunset.*)

THE AUTHOR KYŌDEN: Damn! They're really getting it on!

COMMENTARY:

> If the courtesan
> has a true heart
> the man's finished[116]

---

116. Kyōden begins by improvising a senryū, playing ironically on a popular saying, "Courtesans don't have true hearts" (*keisei ni makoto nashi*), and on a humorous senryū in *Mutamagawa*
(vol. 1), "In Yoshiwara, if the woman has a true heart, the man's finished" (*Yoshiwara ni makoto
ga atte un no tsuki*). "If the courtesan has a true heart, the man's finished" because he would
have to pay a large amount to buy out the woman's contract.

If you fall in love the way this man has, your assets will hollow out like a bad tooth that hurts everywhere at once and nowhere in particular. You'll have nothing left at all. The man's gotten used to expensive performances, and even now he hires a jester and musician on credit. The teahouse that handles his account must be getting quite nervous. By now both the woman and the man have begun to act natural and no longer try to impress each other. They stop using nice stationery and write to each other on any coarse, recycled paper they happened to have, and they don't bother to use polished phrases. Instead, they say directly what's on their minds. Before the woman knows it, she finds she likes the same food the man likes, and she even picks up some of his mannerisms. She stops appearing at performances for other customers, and more and more of them give up on her. Finally she and the man are left with only each other and have nowhere to turn. When the woman's matron and the other courtesans drop by to warn her about what she's doing, it only makes her love the man all the more. The two lovers begin to feel as if they're the only ones in the world. They talk nonsense and resent it when people try to give them advice. People grow cold toward them, and then nothing seems interesting any more.

Finally the woman tells the man not to come and to stay at home for a while. The man tells her she ought to have many different men pay for her performances, and he gives her advice on how to control some of the men he knows. After the woman finally says good-bye to the man and sends him home, she's so depressed the next day she can't even eat, and she refuses to sit in the downstairs parlor with the other women. Back at home, the man sees the woman's face everywhere, even on the statue of Amida Buddha in his living room. To others, both lovers look like complete fools, but if you asked them, they probably could tell you why their feelings are perfectly natural. How hard it is to give up the delusion-filled way of love between men and women! Didn't the old hand Yoshida Kenkō[117] write so himself?

[*Sharebon, kokkeibon, ninjōbon*, SNKBZ 80, translated by Chris Drake]

---

117. In section 9 of his *Essays in Idleness* (*Tsurezuregusa*), Yoshida Kenkō (1283–1352) describes how passionately women love men and how attractive women are to men. From a Buddhist point of view, he warns that the intense desire men feel for women is the most dangerous form of sensory attachment and must be resisted. Like many other Edo-period writers, Kyōden here adds irony to his allusion, suggesting the strength of the love between men and women.

Chapter 17

KIBYŌSHI: SATIRIC AND DIDACTIC PICTURE BOOKS

Kibyōshi (literally, yellow booklets), picture books in which the image and text are intended to be enjoyed together, flourished in the thirty-one years between 1775 and 1806. The kibyōshi shared the humor and wit of kyōka, senryū, kyōshi, and sharebon, which also prospered at this time. Although initially its subject matter was largely limited to the pleasure quarter, by the time the kibyōshi reached its creative peak in the 1780s, virtually no segment of society was spared its satiric treatment.

The kibyōshi fell under the rubric of *kusa-zōshi* (literally, grass books), "middle-size" books with ten pages in a volume, with a large picture on each page. The text, which was written primarily in kana and included descriptive prose and dialogue, filled the blank spaces in the picture. Many kibyōshi consisted of two or three volumes and were, on average, about thirty pages in length. Other fictional genres were accompanied by pictures as well, but the images were secondary to the text. By contrast, the kusa-zōshi, particularly the kibyōshi, were noted for their harmonious balance and close interaction between image and text.

The early kusa-zōshi, dating from the late seventeenth century through 1750, were unsigned and appreciated primarily for their pictures. They began mainly as children's stories or as books for adults with little education, featuring such familiar tales as "Peach Boy" (Momotarō), "Tongue-Cut Sparrow" (Shitakiri suzume), and "Kachikachi Mountain" (Kachichiyama), and had bright red covers, giving them the name of "red books" (*akahon*). As the kusa-zōshi matured, they began taking stories from kabuki, jōruri, war tales, ghost stories, and love romances. Because the covers of these more adult kusa-zōshi were black or blue, they were called "black booklets" (*kurohon*) or "blue booklets" (*aohon*). Despite the more adult subject matter, these early kusa-zōshi remained essentially picture books for telling stories (*etokihon*). Koikawa Harumachi's *Mr Glitter 'n' Gold's Dream of Splendor* (*Kinkin sensei eiga no yume*, 1775), considered to be the first major kibyōshi, dramatically and fundamentally changed the nature of this kusa-zōshi genre.

KOIKAWA HARUMACHI

Koikawa Harumachi (1744–1789) was a low-level samurai from Suruga Province (Shizuoka) who was stationed in Edo. He took his pen name from the location of his lord's mansion (Koishikawa Kasuga-chō) and from his painting teacher, Katsukawa Shunshō (1726–1792), a popular ukiyo-e artist who had become known for his pictures of kabuki actors, warriors, sumo wrestlers, and beautiful women. Harumachi was so impoverished in the mid-1770s that he probably turned to working as a painter to earn some extra income. In addition to writing more than thirty kibyōshi, he composed kyōka under another pen name, Sake-no-ue Furachi, and became one of the leading samurai men of letters in the 1780s. He died at the age of forty-five.

MR GLITTER 'N' GOLD'S DREAM OF SPLENDOR
(KINKIN SENSEI EIGA NO YUME, 1775)

The success of *Mr Glitter 'n' Gold's Dream of Splendor* can be attributed to several factors. First, Harumachi was the first to use the content of the sharebon (books of wit and fashion in the pleasure quarters) in the kusa-zōshi picture-text format. He added a kanbun-style preface which gave the text an intellectual, urban style, reminiscent of the kanbun prefaces found in sharebon such as *The Playboy Dialect* (*Yūshi hōgen*, 1770). Equally important, Harumachi, a serious aspiring artist, incorporated into his kibyōshi the visual style of his painting teacher and captured the latest fashion and lifestyle of contemporary youth.

    Mr Glitter 'n' Gold is based on a Tang story, which also was dramatized in the nō play *Kantan*, about a young man who goes from the country to the city in hopes of seeking a fortune, takes a nap at an inn while waiting for dinner, dreams of rising and then falling from the peak of glory, wakes up to find his dinner ready, and realizes the transience of glory. In kyōka fashion, Harumachi transforms this classic tale into a contemporary story of a young man's rise and dissolution in the pleasure quarter. More important, the kibyōshi becomes a means of describing the life of the sophisticate. The term *kinkin* (literally, gold gold, but implying something like "Mr Glitter and

Glitz"), a popular phrase at the time, referring to being in fashion, stylish, with an erotic allure. The "splendor" or "glory" (*eiga*) achieved by Master Kinkin (Kinbei) is not merely worldly glory but success with certain women in the licensed quarter, which appealed to the pleasure-seeking youth of the time.

Harumachi did not depict the sophisticate (*tsūjin*) directly but revealed this ideal by its comic failure, the kind of *hanka-tsū* (half-sophisticate or pretender) found in such sharebon as *The Playboy Dialect*. The protagonist is transformed from a country bumpkin into a suave, urbane man and then is revealed to be a pretender. He is, in other words, both the object of laughter and someone with whom almost every male reader could identify. Contemporary readers of *Mr Glitter 'n' Gold* appreciated both the images in the Katsukawa Shunshō style, which revealed the latest fashions, and the satiric "hole poking" (*ugachi*). Both media appealed to the tastes of urban, intellectual audiences and stimulated the growth of the new genre.

Like Mr Glitter 'n' Gold, the characters are cleverly named. The crafty shop hand is Genshirō, an epithet for slick swindlers. Guichi (literally, five-plus-one, the equivalent of boxcars in crapshooting), the blind bard, implies Luckless-Guichi. The professional jester is Manpachi, a byname for liars. Kakeno, the Yoshiwara courtesan, suggests *kakeru* (to defraud). Likewise, the name of Omazu, the artless prostitute, evokes the adjective *mazui* (tasteless, inept).

A major characteristic of *Mr Glitter 'n' Gold* and subsequent kibyōshi was the attention given to minute and often allusive visual detail. For this reason, a commentary is provided after each image.

Preface

As stated in literature, "Life, in its uncertainty, is like a dream; how much of it is given to happiness?"[1] Surely the line rings true. Mr Glitter 'n' Gold's dream of splendor, like the dream inspired by the pillow at Kantan, was of no greater duration than the time it takes to cook millet. We do not know the identity of this Mr Glitter 'n' Gold. The mystery is as deep as that surrounding the Three-Bird Secrets of the *Kokinshū*.[2] Those with money become the Mr Glitter 'n' Golds of this world, while those without it become the blockheaded nobodies. Thus, Mr Glitter 'n' Gold is someone's name and yet belongs exclusively to no one person. . . .

A frivolous story by the painter Koikawa Harumachi

---

1. This line, by the eighth-century Chinese poet Li Bo, is from his poetic essay *A Prelude to a Banquet on a Spring Eve for My Clan in the Garden of Peaches and Plums* (*Chunye yan zhuzongdi taoliyuan xu*), which is in the *Tang wen cui* (*juan* 97) and other anthologies.

2. One of the secret transmissions of the *Kokinshū* (905), concerning the identity of three birds that appear in the poetry.

1. Kinbei, wearing a traveling overcoat and holding a woven traveling hat in his right hand, arrives at the millet-cake shop and points to a road sign that says "From here to the right, Meguro Street." The broad topknot on the crown of his head and his disheveled side hair emphasize that he is a boorish man (*yabo*) from the suburbs. The standing sign notes "Famous Specialty—Genuine Millet Cakes," and the shop awning gives the shop name: Musashiya. Two people are preparing steamed millet. The woman, with her hair wrapped in a *tenugui* (patterned washcloth), flips the millet in the mortar while the man pounds it with a pestle. From the 1775 edition. (From SNKBZ 79, *Kibyōshi, senryū, kyōka*, by permission of Shōgakukan)

Book 1

1. Long ago there lived in the backwoods a man by the name of Kanemuraya Kinbei. By nature he was elegant in mind and heart. Although he wished to savor all the delights of the floating world, he was poor and could not realize his wish. Having given the matter much thought, however, he decided to seek work in the bustling metropolis, attain a high station in life, and enjoy every conceivable pleasure in the floating world. And so he set out for Edo.

[KINBEI]: Once I get to Edo, I'll work my way up to chief clerk. I'll make my money by picking up whatever slips past the accounting beads on the abacus, and then I'll have the time of my life.

Because the famed Exalted Fudō of Meguro was a god of fortune, he worshiped at the temple and prayed for good fortune.[3] It was near dusk by then, and

---

3. At this time, Meguro was on the outskirts of Edo. Fudō (Acala) is a ferocious Buddhist guardian deity.

2. Kinbei falls asleep on a bench with a pillow pulled to his side. Behind him a pestle rests in the mortar, and in front of him are his tobacco set and travel sandals. He holds a tattered fan, similar to the fan of the god of poverty, suggesting his current state. The dark black line on the bench suggests a prop used to represent bridges and palaces in nō drama, thus evoking the nō play *Kantan*. In his dream, a man with a sword in ceremonial attire bows before Kinbei, leading the group of people accompanying the palanquin. The servant at the back holds a lacquered traveling box, which contains slippers and a change of clothes for an outing. (From SNKBZ 79, *Kibyōshi, senryū, kyōka*, by permission of Shōgakukan)

being famished, he stopped to eat some of the millet cakes for which the area was famous. Now, the Exalted Fudō of Meguro has produced many miracles; this is known to everyone. The principal icon of the temple was sculptured by the Great Teacher Ennin.[4] The monastery is named Ryūsen-ji temple. Specialties of this area include the millet cakes and something called "rice-cake blossom," which is made by slitting a section of a length of bamboo, tying the filaments together to form a floral ring, and then attaching red, white, and yellow rice cakes—like petals on a blossom. Hence, the name "rice-cake blossoms."

[KINBEI]: Hello! I wonder what time it is? May I have a dish of millet cakes?
[WOMAN]: It must be past midafternoon. Do go into the inner guest-room.

2. The famished Kinbei went into the inner guest-room of the millet-cake shop, but the cakes had not yet been made. During the short while he was kept waiting, he became a bit drowsy—perhaps as a result of the tiring journey—so

---

4. Ennin (794–864), one of the founders of the Tendai sect, who wrote a diary about his travels in China between 838 and 847.

he grabbed a pillow that lay nearby and was soon lulled into peaceful slumber and dream.

Seemingly out of nowhere, an elderly man appeared. He was accompanied by men bearing a specially licensed Hōsenji palanquin,[5] a slipper bearer dressed all in black, a shop boy in his early teens, and a great many shop hands and clerks besides.

The man straightened the folds in his ceremonial vest, made himself formally presentable, and said, "Now, we are in the service of Izumiya-Seiza, maker of clear saké, who has resided for many long years in Hatchōbori in the Kanda District. Seiza, our master, has become old and infirm and still has no children. This year he became a Buddhist monk and adopted the clerical name Bunzui. He has been searching for an heir and had the good fortune to be blessed with a revelation by the Great Bodhisattva Hachiman, the deity he has worshiped devoutly these many years. He has learned that you would be here on your journey in quest of a high station in life, and so we came here. We hope you will accede to the wish of our master, Bunzui."

Kinbei was forced into the palanquin and didn't know where they were taking him. Strange, indeed! Kinbei was quite mystified, for he had been taken completely by surprise. But he recalled such proverbs as "The Good God of Fortune smiles but once every three years" and "Cakes plop into mouths held wide open," and he felt a buoyancy that could float him up to the heavens. He let himself be borne on the palanquin, though to where he didn't know.

[CLERK]: Good! Good! We've finally found the young master.

[SHOP BOY]: This is probably what they mean when they say, "Why search for something when it's bound to turn up during spring housecleaning?"

3. The men carried Kinbei along, and they soon arrived at the gate of Izumi-ya, where he was allowed out of the palanquin. The clerks and shop hands led him through the house, and Kinbei gazed at its magnificence with amazement. Indeed, "staircase of jade" and "curtains of emerald" would be apt epithets for what greeted his eyes. The folding screens and sliding partitions were speckled with gold and silver dust. The portable partition was adorned with solar disks of gold, and the sliding screen-door was graced with lunar disks of silver.

Shortly there appeared the venerable master of the household, Seiza, a maker of clear saké, his brows no longer furrowed with care. He bestowed his own name on Kinbei, who would be known thereafter as Izumi-ya Seiza, maker of clear saké. He relinquished to him possession of the seven rarities and myriad treasures and then brought out saké so fine as to warrant the label "nectar of

---

5. A type of palanquin that townspeople of means or those in specialized professions were sometimes allowed to own privately.

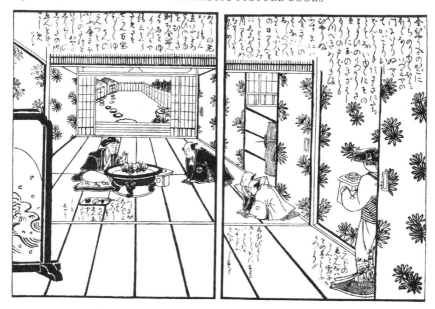

3. The residence of Izumi-ya Seiza, or Bunzui. Three contiguous rooms are depicted in
the style of a "perspective print" (uki-e), a novel effect created by the adaptation of the linear
perspective found in Western painting, which heightens the sense of grandeur and provides
a view as far away as the two storehouses in the garden—all symbolizing Bunzui's wealth.
Bunzui, wearing a flat black cap with a round crown (daikoku zukin), best known as the
cap worn by Daikoku, the god of wealth, sits in front of an extremely large metal brazier
with lion faces on the legs. Kinbei, his hands to the floor, bows to Bunzui, and the other
clerks dressed in ceremonial dress sit respectfully behind him. A maid carrying a wooden
stand with saké cups (for a celebratory banquet) enters from the right. A single-panel screen
depicting the rising sun among the waves stands to the left. All the sliding-door panels are
covered with a chrysanthemum pattern, alluding to a similar celebratory scene in the nō
play Kantan. (From SNKBZ 79, Kibyōshi, senryū, kyōka, by permission of Shōgakukan)

heaven." Thus began the feast to celebrate the new ties between father and son,
master and servants.

[BUNZUI]: We were brought together by an odd fate. You must take exceptionally good care of yourself from now on.

[CLERKS]: The succession of the mastership came off very well. We offer you
our heartiest congratulations.

[MAID]: Our new master looks exactly like Raishi in the role of Lazy Tarō.[6]

---

6. Raishi was the haikai name of the actor Arashi Sangorō, who played the role of Lazy Tarō
(Monokusa-tarō) on the Edo stage in 1773.

4. Because Kinbei, as head of the household, had everything he wanted, he gave himself up more and more to extravagance and began devoting all his time, night and day, to carousing. In contrast to his earlier appearance, the crown of his head is now shaved stylishly, right down to the sidelocks, and the remaining lock—about the size of a rat's tail—is done up in a Honda topknot. Notable was the lavish use of heavy black silk in his clothes; and he sported sashes of velvet, Hakata silk, or Mogul weave. He was modish in every possible way.

As usually happens, birds of a similar feather came flocking to him. Genshirō, the shop hand, acted in collusion with Manpachi, the professional jester, and Guichi, the blind minstrel; and the three did their best to urge Kinbei along a path of profligacy.

Taking his former name of Kanemura-ya Kinbei, someone coined the nickname Mr Glitter 'n' Gold, and everyone addressed him this way, pandering to his vanity. The shop hand Genshirō called in a few geishas to get him excited.

4. Kinbei, dressed as a dandy, wears a black double-layer jacket over a striped robe. Genshirō (with the "gen" on his sleeve) holds a saké container, urging Kinbei to have more to drink. Manpachi (with the "hachi" on his back), the professional jester, urges him on with a fan. The blind Guichi (with the "go" on his sleeve) massages Kinbei as he leans on an armrest. The geisha sings a parody of the Itako-bushi boatman's song on her shamisen while the men drink saké and eat broiled sea bream (*tai*), an auspicious fish. The surrounding walls evoke the fishing port of Itako, in Ibaragi Prefecture. (From SNKBZ 79, *Kibyōshi, senryū, kyōka*, by permission of Shōgakukan)

5. Kinbei and his entourage set out for Yoshiwara, seen in the far distance, marked by rain barrels on the rooftops (for fighting fires). Customers approached the licensed quarter by boat from the Sumida River and then walked along the Nihonzutsumi embankment to Yoshiwara or went by carriage. Kinbei wears a black hood, a black cloak, and a striped silk robe. Genshirō is on the left, and Manpachi, without a cloak (indicating his lower status), is on the right. The blind bard Guichi, behind the group, wears wooden clogs (*geta*), indicating his even lower status. (From SNKBZ 79, *Kibyōshi, senryū, kyōka*, by permission of Shōgakukan)

[GEISHA]:

> Yo-tsu-yaa,-yaa, Shinjuku . . .
> Never did I dream of finding
> Courtesans, flowering with such beauty,
> Amid heaps of horse manure.
> He comes, he comes, he comes—
> Konpira, deity of Sanuki.[7]

[MANPACHI] (*mimicking a kabuki actor*): Who should make an appearance this very moment but Arashi Raishi! Without mistake, this is what he said . . .

[GENSHIRŌ]: There's just one thing, sir. It's not all that fun just staying home and making all this racket. Tomorrow, why don't you go up to the North Country.[8]

5. Egged on in this way, Mr Glitter 'n' Gold tried going to the Yoshiwara quarter and, from that time on, became intimate with a prostitute named Kakeno. Turning a deaf ear to admonitions from his adoptive parents, he fre-

---

7. Yotsuya and Shinjuku were stopping points for travelers and horses on the highway leading westward out of Edo. The brothels of Shinjuku, closed down earlier by the government, were reopened the year this story was published. The song parodies the lines from a popular boatman's song, "How lovely to see an iris blooming amid wild rice at Itako Dejima." The last two lines are from "Konpira-bushi," a type of folk song that was in vogue in cities around this time.

8. The Yoshiwara licensed pleasure quarter in Edo.

6. On the night before the beginning of spring (*setsubun*), Kinbei scatters from a measuring box gold and silver coins instead of the customary roasted beans. Manpachi and Guichi ecstatically gather up the money, but the courtesan Kakeno looks the other way in disinterest, smoking her pipe. This is one of the first suggestions that Kinbei, while fashionable in dress, is lacking in inner sophistication (*tsū*). Seasonal decorations, above the alcove, include a straw festoon decorated with paper strips and *yuzuriha* evergreen leaves. (From SNKBZ 79, *Kibyōshi, sen-ryū, kyōka*, by permission of Shōgakukan)

quented the pleasure quarter in the company of the shop hand Genshirō and Manpachi even on nights so dim that the next step would lead into a world of complete darkness.[9]

The attire of Mr Glitter 'n' Gold: a *haori* cloak made of figured silk from Hachijō Island, a padded kimono of striped crepe silk, and an underrobe embellished with patterns favored by kabuki stars. He went about deeply hooded, with only his eyes Mr Glittering—the better to be somewhat inconspicuous. [MANPACHI]: The figure you cut is too much for words. A fantastic getup!

Book 2

6. Mr Glitter 'n' Gold was carried away by the courtesan Kakeno. The year drew quickly to a close, and it was the night before the New Year. At the urging of Genshirō, who suggested that roasted beans were passé, Mr Glitter 'n' Gold filled a boxed tray with gold and silver coins—his gift to celebrate the change of seasons.[10]

---

9. There is a pun on the word *yo*, which means both "night" and "world." The vicissitudes of life in "a world where darkness enshrouds everything more than an inch beyond one's nose" is proverbial in Japan.

10. Spring began in the First Month of the New Year. The custom was to scatter roasted beans at that time of the year to chase out evil forces. Kinokuniya Bunzaemon (1666–1734), a well-known tycoon, is said to have been the first to scatter gold coins instead of beans.

7. Kinbei visits an elegantly appointed teahouse with the sign "Miyamoto," an actual tea-house that stood in the large precincts of the Tomioka Hachiman Shrine in Fukagawa, the unlicensed pleasure quarter on the east side of the Sumida River. It is very early spring, and everything is covered in snow. Manpachi waits at the entrance as Kinbei appears in the dandy style for bad weather, wearing a straw hat and a Kaga straw rain cape and holding a cane. A young attendant accompanies him, holding a *furoshiki* that contains his spare clothes, a practice of wealthy commoners at the time. (From SNKBZ 79, *Kibyōshi, senryū, kyōka,* by permission of Shōgakukan)

[MR GLITTER 'N' GOLD]: In with the good fortune and out with the devil! In with the good fortune and out with the devil!

[GUICHI]: What a crow-bird mountain of luck! With this money, I'll be on my way to achieving the rank of Master Bard.[11]

[MANPACHI]: This is wild! Just like Satsuma-ya Gengobei. It's a takeoff on Umegae.[12]

7. Having exhausted the many pleasures of the North Country, Mr Glitter 'n' Gold next went to the Dragon-Serpent Quarter and had all the fun there

---

11. "Crow-bird mountain of luck" is a rendering of the nonsense phrase *arigata-yama no tonbi-garasu,* which contains the words "grateful," "mountain," "kite," and "crow." The practice of buying a higher rank as a blind minstrel was not uncommon.

12. Gengobei, the hero of the fifth story in Ihara Saikaku's *Five Sensuous Women* (*Kōshoku gonin onna,* 1686), inherits a fortune at the end of the tale. Umegae, the heroine in the puppet drama *Hiragana Tales of Glory and Decline* (*Hiragana seisuiki,* 1739) is, in a climactic scene, the recipient of a shower of gold coins.

8. Lying in bed, Kinbei enjoys his time with Omazu, drinking saké and eating fish. The tall folding screen, adorned with plovers flying above the waves (a winter motif), gives the two a sense of privacy, and the robe placed over the screen indicates, as was the custom in the Fukagawa pleasure quarter, that the space is occupied. A teahouse hostess approaches Omazu to tell her that Omazu's true love, Genshirō, is expecting her. (From SNKBZ 79, *Kibyōshi, senryū, kyōka*, by permission of Shōgakukan)

was to have there.[13] But his suave manners were put on and were not well received. The blessings dispensed by the Amida Buddha are in direct proportion to the amount of gold one gives the priest. Because he scattered the yellow stuff about liberally, everyone called him Mr Glitter 'n' Gold and played up to his vanity.

[MR GLITTER 'N' GOLD]: My, how it has snowed! And how cold it must be for those without status in this world. Snowflakes swirl about like goose down, and a man clothed in a paper robe is about to leap into the river . . . oh, the hell with it all.[14]

[MANPACHI]: There you stand, clad in a straw coat from Kaga, forgoing the palanquin despite the snowstorm. I'm reminded of the line—how did it go now?—"Though skiffs are to be had in the Dragon-Serpent village, it is only because I love you that I've come barefooted."[15] You're terrific! Simply terrific!

8. Mr Glitter 'n' Gold fell deep in the clutches of a courtesan named Omazu in the Dragon-Serpent Quarters. He went to see her daily and spent a tidy sum

---

13. The "Dragon-Serpent" (southeast) sector of Edo was the site of the unlicensed pleasure quarter at Fukagawa.

14. A parody of a passage from the nō drama *The Potted Tree* (*Hachi no ki*): "Ah, such snow! How it must delight those who have station in life. Snowflakes swirl about like goose down. Cloaked in a mantle of crane feathers, a man aspires to roving." The nō passage is, in turn, modeled on a verse by the Tang poet Bo Ju-yi.

15. An allusion to, and a parody of, a passage from the nō drama *The Commuting Courtier of Komachi* (*Kayoi Komachi*): "Though steeds are available in the hamlet of Kohata in Yamashiro

9. The wavy line on the right border indicates the passing of time and a change of scene. Genshirō and Manpachi try to calm the angered Kinbei while the teahouse hostess protects Omazu. The agitation is expressed through the overturned saké container. (From SNKBZ 79, *Kibyōshi, senryū, kyōka*, by permission of Shōgakukan)

on her. So far as Omazu was concerned, however, she was merely performing her duty. Outwardly she behaved as if she had fallen deeply in love with him, all the while carrying on behind his back and having fun with Genshirō.

Here is how the girls at the teahouse would speak to one another in make-believe Chinese whenever they ridiculed Mr Glitter 'n' Gold.

[TEAHOUSE HOSTESS]: *Geken-shiki-rokō sakaiid tokoo yokoo tokoo cokome.*[16]

[OMAZU]: *Tekell hikim tokoo wakait akand akaill bekee thekere sokoon.* Be sure to tell him now.

9. Until then, Mr Glitter 'n' Gold knew nothing of what went on. He had believed that Omazu was completely sincere, and he had fallen for her. But he sensed something suspicious in Omazu's behavior that night, and he raised a big fuss and broke off their relationship.

[MANPACHI]: Come now, sir. Take it easy. What went wrong?

[MR GLITTER 'N' GOLD]: It's not important; let's forget the whole thing. It'll turn up during spring housecleaning.

[TEAHOUSE HOSTESS]: Don't bother with him, Omazu. You don't have to stay around. He's such a nincompoop!

Province, it is only because I love you that I came barefooted [spoken by Captain Fukakusa]. And you were attired [spoken by Komachi] . . . in a platter hat and a straw coat [spoken by the captain]."

16. The first line, "Genshirō said to tell you to come," approximates the Japanese, in which extra syllables, all beginning with "k," are injected into words. The next line is "Tell him to wait and I'll be there soon."

10. Near the great southern gate to Edo, at Takanawa, with the ocean to the left, two boats are tied to the embankment, and boat sails appear far out at sea. Kinbei comes across a palanquin being carried energetically by two men. A professional male entertainer accompanies the palanquin, carrying a *furoshiki* full of spare clothes. Kinbei looks on bitterly as he reflects on his reduced state. A rural samurai emerges from the stone wall at the right, with two swords, a towel cap on his head, and an Ichimatsu- (checkered) design dress, which was out of fashion at the time. Priests and low-ranking samurai, serving in the nearby domain residences, were frequent visitors to the unlicensed pleasure quarter in Shinagawa, which was cheaper and lower in status than that in Fukagawa. (From SNKBZ 79, *Kibyōshi, senryū, kyōka,* by permission of Shōgakukan)

10. Having been royally fleeced at various places, Mr Glitter 'n' Gold lost his sheen. Those who used to bow and scrape before him would pretend not to know him and would avoid him. Although he felt bitter to the core, there was nothing he could do. He was without the resources to ride even a plain rattan palanquin. He cut a pitiful figure—the pair of plain wooden clogs clinging to his feet. He appeared quite forlorn as he ventured nightly, alone, to Shinagawa.[17]

[MR GLITTER 'N' GOLD]: Only yesterday everyone was calling me Mr Glitter 'n' Gold and making a fuss over me. I was able to ride in skiffs and rattan palanquins. Here I am today wearing a *patchi* underwear and fair-weather clogs. What an uncertain world we live in. Dammit all!

[PASSERBY]: Come on, boys! Let's hear you shout. And move a little faster.

[COUNTRY SAMURAI]: Edo is one rip-roarin' town.

---

17. Shinagawa is the location of lower-class brothels, south of the center of Edo.

11. Kinbei, disowned and weeping, leaves Bunzui's house. Even though he still has his Honda hairstyle, Kinbei now wears the traveling clothes that he originally had when he appeared at the millet store. Genshirō, on the right, points at him contemptuously. Bunzui holds a robe (with the "kin" on the sleeve) that he has just stripped off Kinbei. (From SNKBZ 79, *Kibyōshi, senryū, kyōka,* by permission of Shōgakukan)

12. The wavy line on the right border indicates a change of scene. Kinbei, his hair disheveled, yawns and stretches, waking from his dream. The tattered fan is nowhere to be seen, and the line on the low platform has disappeared, indicating that Kinbei has truly awakened from his dream. (From SNKBZ 79, *Kibyōshi, senryū, kyōka,* by permission of Shōgakukan)

11. Because the family fortune seemed to be tottering with Mr Glitter 'n' Gold's indulging daily in wanton extravagances, his adoptive father, Bunzei, became furious. At the urging of the shop hand Genshirō, he stripped Mr Glitter 'n' Gold of his finery and drove him out dressed as he was when he first came.

[GENSHIRŌ]: Serves you right.

12. Having been driven out, Mr Glitter 'n' Gold had no place to go. He was

sobbing with grief, not knowing what to do or where to go, when he was startled by the thud of millet being pounded. He arose and realized that he had been dreaming while the millet was being cooked. The millet cakes he had ordered were not yet done. Kinbei clapped his hands to register the amazing discovery. "In a dream I became the son of Bunzui," he thought to himself, "and thirty years passed while I enjoyed the ultimate in splendor. I can only conclude that a lifetime of pleasure is as brief as the time it takes to grind a mortarful of millet." [WOMAN]: Your millet cakes are done, sir!

[*Kibyōshi, sharebon shū*, NKBT 59: 34–46, translated by James Araki]

SANTŌ KYŌDEN

Unlike Koikawa Harumachi and other first-generation kibyōshi writers, who were low-level samurai serving in Edo, Santō Kyōden (1761–1816) was an urban commoner, was much younger, and exhibited an unrestrained sensibility and humor not found in the works of his samurai predecessors. Kyōden first made a name for himself when he was twenty-one, with the publication of *Things for Sale You Know About* (*Gozonji no shōbai mono*, 1782). But it was *Grilled and Basted Edo-Born Playboy* (*Edo umare uwaki no kabayaki*, 1785), with his own illustrations under his painter name Kitao Masanobu, that is considered one of the masterpieces that brought him lasting fame. Kyōden's comic depiction of a conceited, spoiled youth in contemporary Edo was so successful that the word Enjirō became synonymous with conceit, and the image of Enjirō, with his pug nose, became a Kyōden trademark.

GRILLED AND BASTED EDO-BORN PLAYBOY
(EDO UMARE UWAKI NO KABAYAKI, 1785)

Grilled and Basted Edo-Born Playboy appeared in three volumes, each with a cover illustrated by Kyōden himself. The title contains puns on the word *kabayaki*, or basted eel, a famous Edo dish. Relying on money to make up for what he lacks in physical charm, Enjirō, the son of a wealthy merchant, sets about to acquire a reputation through a series of publicity stunts: he tattoos the names of fictitious lovers on his arm, pays a courtesan to beg his parents for permission to marry their son, employs newspaper boys to distribute tabloid sheets about his exploits, hires a mistress to act jealous, and finally commits a fake double suicide with a courtesan from Yoshiwara, but each ruse is exposed and he is shown to be a fool. The two friends whom he hires to help him seem to profit from his repeated failures. Like Koikawa Harumachi's *Mr Glitter 'n' Gold's Dream of Splendor*, this kibyōshi draws on the conventions of such sharebon as *The Playboy Dialect* (*Yūshi hōgen*), which humorously reveals the protagonist to be a fake and not the sophisticate (*tsū*) he claims to be. But in *Edo-Born Playboy* this

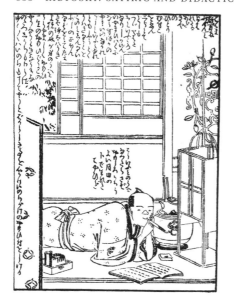

1. Lying on his stomach with a large lamp on the right, Enjirō smokes a pipe while reading a *shinnai* libretto. The curtain leading out to the shop area bears the crest of the Dutch United East Indian Company, suggesting that his father has made his fortune selling exotic imported goods. Enjirō's tobacco tray, on the left, holds a jar for the charcoal fire and a tall bamboo tube for pipe ashes. To the right lies a tobacco pouch. Water is heating in the kettle on the brazier. Enjirō has a pug nose that became known as the Enjirō Nose or Kyōden Nose because Kyōden depicted himself with the same nose. From the 1785 edition. (From SNKBZ 79, *Kibyōshi, senryū, kyōka*, by permission of Shōgakukan)

narrative convention becomes more complex and unrestrained, turning into a series of deliberately planned performances in which the protagonist is consumed by the heroes and images found in various popular performing arts: shinnai-bushi (romantic ballads), kabuki, and jōruri. Enjirō attempts to play all these imagined roles, with each increasingly radical act bringing more mockery to the unbowed and indefatigable protagonist. The high point of the narrative is an elaborate parody of the *michiyuki*, the poetic and lyrical travel scene that forms the climax of the love suicides found in jōruri and kabuki. *Edo-Born Playboy* thus provides a metacommentary on the function and effect of performance, including, implicitly, that of the tsū as the ultimate performer.

1. Enjirō is the only son of the noted millionaire Adakiya, who owns the Wanton Shop.[18] Now nineteen and feeling frisky, he's never suffered from the disease of poverty, and as the ballad says, he doesn't plan to catch any other. He was born amorous, and he likes to read romantic *shinnai* ballads. He especially envies heroes like Tamakiya Itahachi and Ukiyo Inosuke, who become the lovers of famous courtesans in the licensed quarters and decide to commit love suicide with them. He feels he must become a lover hero himself and have an affair with a courtesan so scandalous he'll remember it for his whole life, even if he has to die with the woman. His mind fills with idiotic thoughts, and he contemplates giving up his life for love and fame.

---

18. Enjirō means "Sexy Son," and Adakiya means "Wanton Shop."

2. In the parlor, Enjirō sits facing Kitari Kinosuke and Warui Shian (who, like many herbal doctors, has shaved his head). Behind Enjirō, in the alcove, is a book box containing *The Tale of Genji* and *The Tales of Ise*, two Heian classics about famous lovers. By contrast, Kinosuke and Shian sit in front of a standing screen of Enma, the king of hell, who judged newly dead souls. The screen bears the signature of Hanabusa Itchō (1652–1724), a noted painter of contemporary manners. Although Kinosuke speaks of Yoshiwara as if he were a connoisseur, the image of Enma suggests otherwise. Kinosuke and Shian are attired with the black scarves worn by pleasure seekers, but Enjirō is bare necked, implying that he is still a neophyte. The composition of the three figures sitting together alludes to a passage in book 16 of the *Analects* in which Confucius warns of bad friendships: "To make friends with the ingratiating in action, the pleasant in appearance and the plausible in speech is to lose" (*The Analects*, trans. D.C. Lau [Harmondsworth: Penguin Books, 1979]). (From SNKBZ 79, *Kibyōshi, senryū, kyōka,* by permission of Shōgakukan)

[ENJIRŌ]: Utterly fantastic! Those guys must have been born on really lucky days.

2. Enjirō is good friends with Kitari Kinosuke, a suave young playboy who lives nearby, and Warui Shian, an herbal doctor and amateur jester who often entertains his rich patients.[19] One day they begin to discuss ways that Enjirō could become a great playboy.

[ENJIRŌ]: There must be some way I can make an incredible name for myself as a great lover.

---

19. Kitari Kinosuke means "Fond of the Yoshiwara," and Warui Shian means "Bad Idea."

3. Kinosuke tattoos Enjirō's arm by pricking the skin with a needle and filling the wound with ink from the inkstone at his knee. Enjirō's tobacco set lies in front of him. (From SNKBZ 79, *Kibyōshi, senryū, kyōka*, by permission of Shōgakukan)

[KINOSUKE]: First of all, to be a killer playboy, you have to be able to sing some of those emotional solo kabuki songs that everybody knows and hums. Start with "Pheasants Crying," "Bell Tolling in Hell," "Drinking While the Bell Tolls," "Moon of Our Love," "Three Kinds of Birds," "Woman Who Sleeps on Three Mattresses," "Linked Lovers' Crests," "Two Lovers, Four Sleeves," "Raised in the Quarters," "Hidden Underwater Rock of Love," "Clouds of Cherry Blossoms," "Morning Glory," "Six Great Poets," "Komachi," "Henjō," "Kuronushi," "Narihira," "Yasuhide," "White Thread Undyed by Love," "Love Suicide—Alone," "Cutting off My Finger to Prove My Love," "Tattooing Her Name," "Pledge of Unchanging Love," "Tangerine Memories," "Eternal Flower," "The Requiem Bell Tolls Thirteen," "Water Mirror," "River Boat," "Waiting for Night," "Parting," "Last Autumn Leaves," "A Short Sleep," "Summer Robe," "Spring Night," "Autumn Night," "Clear Mirror," "Bell at Midnight," "Hazy Moon," "Spring Mist," "Birds Flying up at Dawn," "River of Desire," "The Third Princess," "Rite of Manhood," "Chrysanthemums," "Mosquito Net in Fall," "Yoshino Cherries," "Summer Moon," "Crows at Daybreak," "Flock of Crows," "Fan," "Flower Fragrance," "Cherry Blossom–Viewing Party," "Lingering Summer Heat," "Comb Holding Her Hair," "Mountain Between Us," "Tied Forever," "Love-Dyed Thread," "Nightingale from the Other World," "Love Cherries," "Seven Autumn Plants," "Syllabary Letter Written with Two Strokes," "Letter in Reverse," "My Heart," "Edo Robe," "Floor Mat Divination," "A Single Ditch," and "Love Talk." Whew! My jaw won't move. These are just a few, but they're a good beginning.

And there are lots of secrets to writing and reading letters. If a courtesan doesn't seal the envelope, it means she's ending the relationship. But if she signs with her personal name, you're in trouble. It means she really wants you.

[SHIAN]: If you see lipstick on the letter, well, ordinary women never tear off letter paper from the roll with their mouths. And here's another way you can tell if a woman was once a professional, no matter how plain she looks. She'll have a callus behind her ear from her wooden pillow.

3. The first step to getting a romantic reputation is to get tattooed, so Kisuke tattoos the names of almost thirty women on both of Enjirō's arms and even between his fingers. All the names are imaginary, but Enjirō wants to look as though he's exchanged vows of eternal love with each of them, so he endures the terrible pain with manly pride.

[KINOSUKE]: You want to look like you've been around. Some of the names ought to be partly rubbed out and illegible. I'll burn some moxa grass on them.

[ENJIRŌ]: Becoming an attractive man's very painful.

4. Enjirō envies the spectacular way kabuki actors are chased by pretty young women who run right into the actors' houses. So he asks Warui Shian to visit the popular geisha musician Oen, who lives in the neighborhood, and offer her fifty gold coins to run right into his house in front of everyone.

[SHIAN]: That's his offer. It's a great opportunity. If you only will accept, I'll make a bit off it myself.

[OEN]: If you're sure that's all there is to it, I'd be very glad to.

4. Shian visits Oen, a noted geisha performer. A shamisen case, containing the instrument of her trade, sits above, on a shelf. Holding a cloth in his mouth and emulating a kabuki actor who specializes in female roles, Shian demonstrates to Oen how she should perform her act. Freelance geisha, who lived outside Yoshiwara, were professional musicians and dancers. Oen, who holds a long pipe, is dressed like a town girl with a black half-collar and a sash tied in the back. (From SNKBZ 79, *Kibyōshi, senryū, kyōka,* by permission of Shōgakukan)

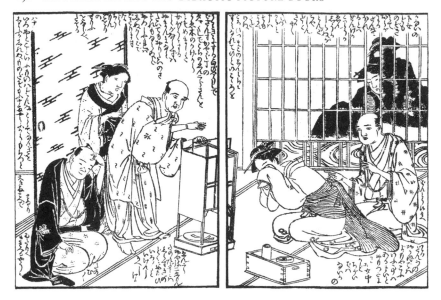

5. At Enjirō's house Oen weeps, claiming that she spotted Enjirō at the Yakushi Temple in Kayabachō, in Edo, which many people visited on the eighth and twelfth of the month. Enjirō's parents, standing flustered, try to console her. The tilted lantern provides a silhouette of the maidservants peeping through the rice-paper shades. The incredulous head clerk, on the right, reaches out to Oen. Enjirō, acting abashed, is in fact telling Oen to raise her voice. (From SNKBZ 79, *Kibyōshi, senryū, kyōka*, by permission of Shōgakukan)

5. The women servants in the house peep in at their employer's son and whisper.

[SERVING WOMAN]: She really has weird taste. Maybe she's one of those eccentric tea masters.

[OEN]: I'm just a poor wandering geisha who's failed as a musician. Recently I've been living on a small alley near here, seducing men for their money. Then one night, beyond some potted trees at the night market at the Yakushi Temple in Kayabachō, I caught sight of your son. If you won't let me be his wife, then please, I beg you, allow me to cook in your kitchen. If you refuse me even that, I'll kill myself.

She's memorized her lines perfectly.

[ENJIRŌ]: Sexy men never know what kind of trouble they're going to get into. (*To the woman*) Listen, I'll give you ten more gold pieces, so shout, please. Loud enough so the neighbors will hear.

[SOROBEI, THE HEAD CLERK]: I never thought that a lady would fall for someone with a face like our master's. Young woman, are you sure you're in the right house?

Enjirō's father, Yajiemon, is unaware the woman has been hired. He pities her and tries hard to dissuade her from committing suicide. Finally she agrees to leave.

6. Tabloid vendors (*yomiuri*) walked around as a team, reading out and selling broadsheets (*kawaraban*) that announce the latest news. This vendor, whom Enjirō has hired to go all over Edo and spread the news for free, has traveled to the residential area of the daimyō mansions, indicated by the white plaster walls and the protruding window. (From SNKBZ 79, *Kibyōshi, senryū, kyōka*, by permission of Shōgakukan)

6. Instead of rumors spreading like wildfire, even the neighbors haven't heard what's happened. Disappointed, Enjirō pays to have the affair written up on a broadsheet. He gives a gold piece each to hawkers to advertise it all over Edo.

[HAWKER]: Extra! Extra! Read all about it! A beautiful geisha's fallen in love with Enjirō, the handsome son of millionaire Adakiya. She forced her way right into his house. It's unbelievable. But the details are all here. It's so hot we're giving the issue away. Get yours free!

[MAID][20] (*inside a daimyō's mansion*): Give me a break, will you? Nothing in there's true. It's all just made up. Even for free, who'd want to waste time reading that?

7. Believing the superstition that sneezing means someone's talking about you, Enjirō is sure that each sneeze he hears is due to his widening fame. But no one even on the same block has heard about the incident. So Enjirō changes course and decides to make a name for himself by visiting the Yoshiwara licensed quarter and going to expensive private performances led by a famous high-ranking courtesan at one of the houses there. Now he's at the Wanton Pines Teahouse, on the main street of the Yoshiwara. Warui Shian and Kitari Kinosuke are with him, acting as his jesters for the night. They both use exactly the right words and sound very sophisticated.

[FEMALE OWNER]: I've sent someone to ask whether Segawa or Utahime's

---

20. Educated maids were an important part of the readership of kibyōshi picture books and later gōkan picture books. They loved romantic plots and were considered to be naïve. But even they could see through the broadsheet.

7. Enjirō, Kinosuke, and Shian visit the Wanton Pines Teahouse (Uwaki Matsuya), on the Naka-no-chō, the main street in Yoshiwara. Wealthy customers first gathered at a teahouse, drank and ate, conversed with the host or hostess, and made arrangements to meet a courtesan. The hostess here is serving saké with a light meal. The Uwaki Matsuya did not exist, but the single-panel screen on the right, bearing the signature of the Rinpa school painter Tawaraya Sōri (act. ca. 1764–1781), the altar with Buddhist reverse-swastika designs, and the letter rack above Enjirō no doubt suggest an existing teahouse. (From SNKBZ 79, *Kibyōshi, senryū, kyōka*, by permission of Shōgakukan)

8. Enjirō meets Ukina, a high-ranking courtesan, for an evening at the Ukinaya. Ukina sits with her child attendant (*kamuro*) by her side. Enjirō quietly straightens out his collar in the manner of a playboy. Kinosuke and Shian are busy flattering Ukina, who covers her mouth in a pose of embarrassment. An elaborate gold-leaf screen, by the lamp, adds brilliance to the room. (From SNKBZ 79, *Kibyōshi, senryū, kyōka*, by permission of Shōgakukan)

free tonight. Just now I saw Konomo, one of Utahime's girl assistants, over at the Low Pines Teahouse, so Utahime's probably tied up over there.
[FEMALE OWNER]: Did you hear? Kōshirō's going to play Bokuga at the Moritaza theater downtown in Kobikichō.[21]

---

21. Yoshiwara insider talk. Bokuga was the haikai name of Ōgiya Uemon, the owner of the

9. Enjirō interviews a prospective mistress at home. Some mistresses escaped from their contracts by wetting their beds. The pillar tablet behind Enjirō, on which "Bed-Wetting Forbidden" is written in a formal seal script, reflects Enjirō's thoughts and alludes to a famous hokku by the haikai poet Kikaku (1661–1707): "No pissing in this place—flower-covered mountain." The signature in the corner of the tablet "Brushed by Kazan (Mountain of Flowers)" adds the last phrase of the haiku, confirming the allusion. (From SNKBZ 79, *Kibyōshi, senryū, kyōka,* by permission of Shōgakukan)

8. Enjirō decides on a top-ranking courtesan named Ukina[22] of the Ukinaya, the House of Floating Fame, who is very experienced and knows all the techniques there are for controlling and manipulating customers. He's confident that he'll get quite a reputation after a woman like that falls for him. He tries very hard to look suave and constantly straightens the neckpiece of his underrobe as nonchalantly as he can. He wonders, though, why attractive men have to worry about such small details.

[SHIAN]: People say you're incredibly good at stringing men along.

[KINOSUKE]: You're the boss of all the courtesans, and you must know every trick in the book.

[UKINA]: Please, can't we dispense with the tasteless jokes?

9. Enjirō can't put all of himself into visiting the Yoshiwara because he doesn't feel the excitement of having a wife at home to be jealous about his visits. So he asks an agent to find him a mistress who knows how to show her jealousy. Looks are no concern. When the agent appears with a woman almost forty, Enjirō hires her as his mistress and gives her a down payment of two hundred gold pieces.

[ENJIRŌ]: Aren't you the old hooker I bought on Nakazu Island last spring? I must warn you, I won't hire you if you're planning to start wetting your bed

---

Ōgiya House in Yoshiwara, which is alluded to later in the text. In the first month of 1784, the famous kabuki actor Matsumoto Kōshirō IV actually played a character named Ōgiya Izaemon in a play at the Morita Theater. Sophisticated visitors to Yoshiwara would have recognized that the character Izaemon was based on the actual Uemon.

22. The name Ukina (literally, floating name) means "Hot Reputation."

10. Enjirō decides "to play with an apprentice courtesan," considered a most sophisticated (*tsū*) activity at the time. This was a ploy in which a male lover of a high-ranking courtesan pretended to spend time with her apprentice to fool the owner of the house and later met secretly with the high-ranking courtesan so that he could save money. In this scene, Enjirō has set up Shian as Ukina's affluent customer while he plays the role of the secret lover. Shian, resting on five layers of *futon*, covered by a brocade robe, and with an elaborate tobacco tray by his pillow, looks into Enjirō's room through the open sliding doors. The single-layered *futon* in a cramped room adjacent to the washing room indicates Enjirō's "low" status. The double-flower crest on the tobacco tray in front of Enjirō is an allusion to Hanaōgi, a famous courtesan in Yoshiwara. Next to the pair of clogs, a poem for repelling insects is pasted upside down for magical effect. Near the hand-washing bowl is a notice of the washing room rules: "Be vigilant against fire. No overnight guests. Don't throw garbage on the street from the second floor." To an informed reader, these details would have suggested the Ōgiya House where Hanaōgi lived. (From SNKBZ 79, *Kibyōshi, senryū, kyōka*, by permission of Shōgakukan)

and doing other things to make me send you away after you've gotten your down payment.

[WOMAN]: I certainly hope you won't hire me if you're planning to ignore me and spend most of your time going to Yoshiwara or having affairs.

She's already demonstrating her ability.

10. Enjirō is a born playboy, and he's bought women in unlicensed areas like Fukagawa, Shinagawa, Shinjuku, and all the other nooks and crannies of Edo. But none of them knew how to control men the way Ukina does. Still, Enjirō is soon bored with paying to meet her directly. It's too easy. He wants to be Ukina's secret lover. But she'll never agree to that. So Enjirō pays to have Warui Shian reserve meetings with Ukina for several days straight while he

11. Near the entrance to Yoshiwara, two child assistants (*kamuro*) seize Enjirō from the side while a teenage apprentice (*shinzō*) stops him from behind. Enjirō has his head wrapped in the manner of Sukeroku, the kabuki hero. The sign at the bottom right corner reads "Naka-no-chō," the main street of Yoshiwara. A man with a parcel wrapped around his shoulder has a lantern marked "Naka," indicating that he is a clerk at the Nakaya, a kimono store that sold robes to high-ranking courtesans in Yoshiwara. (From SNKBZ 79, *Kibyōshi, senryū, kyōka*, by permission of Shōgakukan)

hires Ukina's teenage apprentice to perform music for him in a room nearby. It all costs him a fortune, but it's very exciting to have to go to the trouble of meeting Ukina secretly while another customer is paying for her time.

[ENJIRŌ]: Right about now that rich customer of yours is getting jealous and complaining to your matron and the house employees. Just imagining his jealousy feels so good it's worth five or six hundred gold pieces at least.

[UKINA]: You have really eccentric tastes.

[SHIAN] (*under the covers*): My role's really tough. In the performance room out front I'm a big spender playboy, but in the bedroom back here there's only me and a beautiful gilt smoking tray. It's just a job, though, so I can't complain. But here I am, sleeping with a brocade quilt and five soft mattresses. I'd say the deal's not quite equal.

11. Enjirō remembers a passage from a jōruri chant about the playboy Sukeroku in Yoshiwara:

> Cherry trees and dogs bark,
> announcing the departure of male customers.
> The buds of a love quarrel begin to bloom
> and the girl attendants tug at the man's sleeves.
> He's pulled back as if pulled by the hair,
> his heart unable to cut off his love.

The words make Enjirō envy the way the young attendants of high-ranking courtesans catch any man who tries to visit another high-ranking courtesan

12. Enjirō is greeted by his "jealous" mistress, who sits in front of a clothes cabinet framed with decorative metal fittings, visually echoing her request for new robes. On the wall hangs a special letter holder for love letters exchanged between a courtesan and a customer, a mark of a playboy. Enjirō wears a black scarf, showing that he, too, is now a pleasure seeker. (From SNKBZ 79, *Kibyōshi, senryū, kyōka*, by permission of Shōgakukan)

while he's still seeing their mistress.[23] Wanting to be in the same dilemma, he hires Ukina's two child attendants and her teenage apprentice to ambush him at the quarters gate and pull him through the main street as though they were forcing him to go back to Ukina again. He asks them to rip his cloak as they pull him along.

The girls are doing it only because Enjirō's promised each a doll, and they chat about all sorts of things as they go.

[ENJIRŌ] (*his hood deliberately half off so people can see his face*): Hey, let go, will you! (*Lowers his voice*) Getting dragged along like this will really make my reputation.

12. When Enjirō comes back after five or six days to the house he's rented for his mistress, she shows she's worth her pay. Going on and on, she remembers every line she's practiced and displays fierce jealousy.

[MISTRESS]: How can men be so cruel? Tell me! How can you be so cold-hearted? If you don't want to be adored so much, you shouldn't have been born so handsome. That courtesan's shameless. She knows perfectly well she's keeping you away from the woman who loves you. And it's your fault, too. All right, go ahead and stay with her! Well, that's a good stopping place for today. I really need a striped silk robe, you know, and a striped crepe one, too.

---

23. A man caught two-timing a high-ranking courtesan was taken back to the first woman's house where, as punishment, his topknot was cut off and he was forced to dress in women's clothes.

13. Kinosuke visits a lantern maker in Tamachi, his shop marked by a sign at the far left. An apprentice offers some tea to Kinosuke while the master, bald-headed with a pair of glasses dangling from his ear, reads the order. Materials for lantern making—glue bowl, brushes, inkstone case, and bamboo—surround the man. Three completed lanterns, hung on the right, are for the famous night cherry viewing held in Yoshiwara in the Third Month. The lantern next to Kinosuke has the crest of Matsubaya, a courtesan house in Yoshiwara, and says "Utahime of the Matsubaya," indicating that she has ordered it. The lantern on the bottom right bears the name "Minoya," suggesting that it was ordered by the Minoya House. (From SNKBZ 79, *Kibyōshi, senryū, kyōka*, by permission of Shōgakukan)

[ENJIRŌ]: I hate to admit it, but this is the first time anyone's ever gotten jealous over me. It feels so nice I can't describe it.

If you'll just be jealous a little longer, I promise I'll buy you both the silk robe and the crepe one that you've been craving. Just a little more. Please.

[MISTRESS]: After I get my striped silk and striped crepe robes, I'll really let you have it.

13. In the fashion of kabuki actors and high-ranking courtesans, Enjirō decides to make a large offering to the Ekōin Pure Land Temple near Ryōgoku Bridge during the services for Saint Dōryō.[24] He asks Kitari Kinosuke to go to a lantern shop in Tamachi in Asakusa with his order for lanterns designed with his and Ukina's double crests. Kinosuke then goes to the Nakaya clothing store near the Yoshiwara and orders special handkerchiefs marked with their double crests to be prominently hung at the holy washing basins at various popular

---

24. The image of the Zen saint Dōryō had been shown at this temple the previous year, in the spring of 1784. Kyōden's own grave is located there.

14. A street sign is placed against a rain barrel (*right*), giving the reader a view from the side alley of the toughs beating up Enjirō. (From SNKBZ 79, *Kibyōshi, senryū, kyōka,* by permission of Shōgakukan)

shrines and temples around Edo. These also cost a great deal, and Enjirō's contributions to the shrines and temples are substantial. Yet he has no prayer to make. His offerings are intended only to create a reputation for himself as a famous lover.

[KINOSUKE]: He's in a real hurry. And put a lot of ribs and folds in them. The round caps at the top and bottom should be the standard lacquer with brass fittings. Make them as fancy as you can. Money's no concern.

[LANTERN MAKER]: Sorry, but it'll take a little time. We've got a huge backlog of orders. They're hanging lanterns on the cherry trees in the Yoshiwara every night now.

14. Enjirō goes to see some kabuki plays and concludes that sexy men get roughed up a lot.[25] After that he's consumed by the desire to get beaten up, and he gives three gold pieces each to four or five toughs who hang around outside the quarter and asks them to attack him on the main street of the Yoshiwara. He carefully prepares for the beating. He hires the jester Tōbei to wait on the second floor of a teahouse nearby and sing a sad, soulful passage from a kabuki play while Ukina combs his mussed hair for him, just the way Tora does for Soga Jūrō in the play. He brushes blue actor's paint all over the shaved part of his head, and he doesn't put oil on his hair. He uses only water so his hair will all fall wildly down as soon as anyone touches his topknot. The toughs are on time and begin to punch Enjirō as planned, but they beat him so well that he

---

25. Kabuki plays that feature an erotic male protagonist usually include a scene in which he gets beaten up.

falls unconscious and gasps for breath. No one even notices his messy hair as they shout for strong medicine and an acupuncturist to try to bring him back to life. At last he regains consciousness, and he gains a little notoriety as a complete fool.

[TOUGH] (*on the left*): When a sexy dude like you starts hanging out around here, it's serious trouble, see? The women used to meet us in their spare time, but now they won't even look at us. I'm getting a bit jealous, understand?

All their words have been written by Enjirō.

[TOUGH] (*on the right*): This is where the audience in the theater shouts "Villains! You'll be punished for that!"

[ENJIRŌ]: It's three-quarters of a gold coin for each punch. I can handle the pain. Just make it look real.

15. Enjirō listens hard for rumors, but all he hears is talk that people are doing whatever he asks them to because he's rich and they want his money. Suddenly he hates being rich, and he asks his parents to disown him. But he's an only son, so his father adamantly refuses. Then his mother intervenes and calms his angry father. Finally a temporary disinheritance of seventy-five days is arranged, since rumors, as the saying goes, last only seventy-five days. When the time is up, Enjirō will be taken back into the family.

[FATHER]: This is what you want, son, so I can't refuse. Hurry up, get out!

[SOROBEI, THE HEAD CLERK]: I cannot believe that what the young master desires is really for the good.

[ENJIRŌ]: So I've actually been disowned. You'll never know how grateful I feel. Being rich is more painful than any of the 404 diseases the Buddha

15. Enjirō's heavyset father sits in front of a screen, exuding authority. The head clerk, Sorobei, sitting on the right, quietly watches Enjirō as he hears himself being disowned. (From SNKBZ 79, *Kibyōshi, senryū, kyōka*, by permission of Shōgakukan)

16. Each of the three geisha holds straw tally slips, one of which they drop after each barefoot pilgrimage. A sign reading "Yanagiya Sugubei's Toothpick Shop," indicating a vendor of various toothpicks for brushing teeth, and a placard advertising an archery range on a reed screen appear in the upper-right-hand corner. The fallen ginko leaves, which indicate that it is now autumn, and the placard suggest that the geisha are standing by a ginko tree in Oku-yama inside the large precincts of the Asakusa Kannon Temple (Sensōji), an area known for archery ranges and tooth-pick shops, each with a beautiful woman employee (*kanban musume*). (From SNKBZ 79, *Kibyōshi, senryū, kyōka*, by permission of Shōgakukan)

talked about. Why in the world do popular songs always talk about attractive men being rich?

16. Enjirō hires seven or eight famous geisha musicians who live near Nihonbashi to pretend they're distressed by his disinheritance. He pays them to make a hundred barefoot pilgrimages each to the merciful bodhisattva Kannon in Asakusa and fervently pray that his father forgive him and take him back. Barefoot pilgrimages are a good way to get publicity, since everyone knows they're usually made to pray for success in love affairs.

[FIRST GEISHA]: Let's skip a few trips and go home early.

[SECOND GEISHA]: A few? Ten's enough.

17. Enjirō has succeeded in being disowned, but his mother secretly sends him money for everything he needs. Still, he's supposed to be banished, so he really ought to take up a disreputable trade. He wants to work at something unusual that will make people notice him, and he thinks selling fan paper in the street is the sexiest job there is. So even though summer's a long way off, he sets out and walks around with boxes of curved fan paper on his shoulder. At the end of the first day he has big blisters on his feet, and that, he decides, is the end of that. But he's gained a considerable reputation as a crackpot.

[WAITRESS IN A TEAHOUSE]: Hey, everybody, come quick. A Toba comic picture's walking down the street. What a face!

[ENJIRŌ]: Outside like this, I'm really getting a bad tan. Oh no! Another woman's whispering. She's fallen in love with me, too. Handsome men really have a hard time.

18. Enjirō is just getting used to being disinherited when the seventy-fifth day comes. The people at home send him messages every day asking him to come back, but there's still something sensational that he wants to do. He asks

17. Enjirō, dressed as a fan-paper vendor, passes by a café covered with a reed screen to shield it from the sun and provide privacy. The waitress holds a saucer in front of her mouth to hide her laughter, since Enjirō reminds her of a popular Toba cartoon figure, with dots for eyes. Disinherited sons often became vendors because the job required no training, and fan-paper vending was particularly attractive to playboys who wanted to walk around in dandy style. Enjirō is dressed in a flamboyant kimono with a large maple-leaf pattern and a scarf with the crest—the *mimasu*, or triple-rice measure—of the famous kabuki actor Ichikawa Danjūrō. The placard placed against the counter reads "Lottery tickets sold here," a side business for the café. (From SNKBZ 79, *Kibyōshi, senryū, kyōka*, by permission of Shōgakukan)

some relatives to intervene, and through their good offices he's granted a twenty-day extension. He feels he must do the most scandalous thing of all—commit double love suicide with a high-ranking courtesan. If he succeeds, Enjirō's sure he'll get the ultimate reputation as playboy. He makes up his mind to throw away his life, but he's unable to persuade Ukina to die with him. So he decides on a fake love suicide. He'll ask Kinosuke and Shian to go ahead to the suicide site and wait there. As soon as they hear Enjirō and Ukina chanting for Amida Buddha to come and take their souls to the Pure Land paradise, the men will appear and force the couple to stop. It'll be expensive, though. Enjirō will have to pay fifteen hundred gold coins to Ukina's manager to buy out the remainder of her contract, and he also has to buy a lot of props and implements. He wants to imitate a famous old song that goes

> If you find some money
> let's dye our summer robes
> with a crowbar at the shoulders
> and an anchor at the knees—
> and if we have to pawn them
> we'll always pay the interest
> and never let them float away.

So Enjirō orders matching outer robes for himself and Ukina dyed with heavy crowbar designs over their shoulders and anchor designs at the knees.[26] The

---

26. People will see that their resolve to die together is as firm as that of the couple in the song.

18. In a scene that resembles a kabuki dressing room, Kinosuke, list in hand, instructs Shian to make sure that all the props are ready for the fake double suicide. They include a stack of folded *surimono* (privately commissioned prints for special occasions) with Enjirō and Ukina's farewell hokku, an umbrella with a bull's-eye design (a prop used in kabuki to indicate that they are lovers), a collapsible Odawara lantern, a string of Buddhist prayer beads (for the final moments), a sword, and a branch of Japanese star anise (*shikimi*) to purify the suicide site. A roll of felt carpet stands beside Kinosuke, alluding to Chikamatsu's puppet play *Double Suicide During the Kōshin Vigil* (*Shinjū yoi gōshin*), in which the main characters, Ochiyo and Hanbei, commit love suicide on top of a red felt carpet. Enjirō, having his hair prepared, and Ukina, on the right, wear matching robes with the crowbar-at-the-shoulders, anchor-at-the-knees design, which was inspired by a popular song about indivisible love. Ukina's mirror table, on the right, is decorated with a cherry blossom design, emphasizing a link to the real-life courtesan Hanaōgi of the Ōgiya House: the third Hanaōgi actually committed a double suicide with a retainer. Ukina's two child assistants, in matching kimono, watch the busy preparation. (From SNKBZ 79, *Kibyōshi, senryū, kyōka*, by permission of Shōgakukan)

Nakaya clothing store makes still more money off the pair, and the Yamazaki store also makes a nice profit.

Enjirō and Ukina write final parting hokku verses and have them printed on fine, thick paper together with a picture to go with the verses. Then they have the prints distributed to all the main teahouses in Yoshiwara.

[SHIAN] (*referring to the envelopes on the floor*): What a superb idea you had, asking Kitao Shigemasa[27] to do the picture of them sitting together on a lotus

---

27. Shigemasa was a famous Edo painter and Kyōden's teacher. Privately distributing poems on sheets with paintings was an important literary activity at the time.

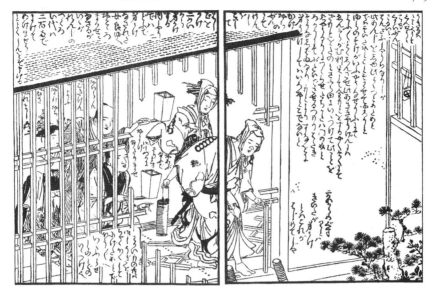

19. Two house employees hold lamps so that Enjirō and Ukina can see their way down a ladder in the dark. Both have their heads wrapped in cloth as if they needed to hide their identities. Actual double suicides were far more secretive. (From SNKBZ 79, *Kibyōshi, senryū, kyōka,* by permission of Shōgakukan)

in the Pure Land paradise. He didn't use any ink at all. It's perfect, pure white and completely embossed.

[KINOSUKE]: I ordered a short wooden sword with silver leaf on the blade.

19. Ukina is strongly opposed to even a fake love suicide, since she'll get a reputation as a woman with bad judgment who can't choose good customers, and would-be suicides who fail, if caught, are publicly punished and made outcastes. But Enjirō doesn't give up. He offers to buy out the rest of her contract and help her get together later with the man she loves if she'll only play her part in his scheme. He imitates the ploy that Yuranosuke uses in *Chūshingura* to persuade Okaru to leave the quarters with him, and finally Ukina gives in. Enjirō also negotiates with the head of a kabuki troupe to have the love suicide made into a play in time for the fall season. In return for providing a no-interest loan to the troupe, Enjirō has the right to tell the playwright Sakurada Jisuke how the plot should be written. He'll be played by Ichikawa Monnosuke II, and Ukina, by Segawa Kikunojō III, both great stars, but it's one of those plays that don't have a chance in the world of succeeding.

Sexy men, Enjirō is sure, never simply buy out the contracts of high-ranking courtesans. So he decides to run away from the house with Ukina, breaking the lattice along the second-floor hall and escaping down a ladder. "You've bought out her contract," the house manager tells him, "so you can leave any way you want. But I'll have to have the lattice repaired. I'll tell you what. I'll give you a

20. Attacked by two masked highwaymen, who have their leggings pulled up, exposing their thighs, Enjirō and Ukina beg for mercy. Ukina holds a purificatory sprig. In this deserted area, they cannot expect anyone to help them. (From SNKBZ 79, *Kibyōshi, senryū, kyōka,* by permission of Shōgakukan)

special discount price on that of two hundred gold coins." The manager is a greedy man, so Enjirō pays ten times the normal repair cost. Then Enjirō lets a couple of house employees pocket some of the large tip he hands them to give to the manager, and in return they agree to spread news of the daring escape all over Edo.

[ENJIRŌ]: You all know the saying about trying to apply eye ointment from the second floor to somebody on the first floor. It's very difficult. But now, for the first time, someone's actually ransomed a courtesan from the second floor.

[EMPLOYEE] (*in front*): It's dangerous, sir. Gently now.

[EMPLOYEE] (*in back*): Ukina, please have a pleasant escape.

20. Enjirō wants a stylish, eye-catching spot for the fake suicide attempt. So he chooses the dike on the far bank of the Sumida River near the famous Mimeguri Shrine. He's afraid to walk through the area late at night, so they set out early in the evening. Representatives from the teahouses in the quarter and the Sumida River boat companies Enjirō has patronized also come along, together with amateur and professional jesters and male geisha comedians who have performed for him. They all wear formal cloaks and skirts and say farewell to the couple with as much ceremony as a Shintō group sending off specially chosen members on a pilgrimage to the Ise Grand Shrine. They make a big procession east across the Ōkawa Bridge at Asakusa, and on the far side the good-byes continue along the embankment near the Tada Yakushi Temple.

21. The upper bars of the shrine gate (*torii*) of the Mimeguri Shrine, a symbol of Mukōjima, appear to the right. The high dike hides the shrine itself. Enjirō drags his scarlet loincloth, and the fake tattoos on his left arm are exposed. (From SNKBZ 79, *Kibyōshi, senryū, kyōka*, by permission of Shōgakukan)

Alone now, Enjirō feels elated. At last he's about to achieve his great wish, and he sets out with Ukina north along the embankment on their journey toward death. When they reach a spot that looks right for their final moments, Enjirō unsheathes his silver-leaf wooden short sword. Then the moment comes when two must do the act. Just as Enjirō is calling out to Amida Buddha to come for their souls and guide them to paradise, two highwaymen with black scarves over their faces jump out from some stacks of newly cut rice. They take everything the couple has except their underwear.

[ROBBER]: You're going to cut yourselves up anyway. We'll stand beside you and disconnect your heads for you.

[ENJIRŌ]: Hey, wait a minute! We're not committing suicide in order to kill ourselves. Right now, some people are supposed to appear and stop us. I wonder why they screwed up. We've given you our clothes, so spare our lives. Spare us, please! I've learned my lesson. I swear I'll never commit love suicide again.

[ROBBER]: You won't even think about it? Are you sure?

21. LOVE-SUICIDE PASSION COOLS TO GOOSE BUMPS

Adakiya Enjirō journeys with Ukina of the House of Floating Fame.

> Make love in the morning
> and in the evening die fulfilled —
> not quite your vintage Confucius,

but hot enough to teach the Way
to those in the floating world
and sung in soft tones and phrases
of a bungo-bushi ballad
about lovers naked to the skin
who've made a solemn promise
never to untie alone
the sashes they've tied for each other.
But now they doubt each other's pledge.
Will each be loyal to the end?
Full of suspicion, they pass
along a dike under construction
beside the Sumida River
wondering whether if they jump
they'll really gain enduring fame
the way the famous ballad claims.
The god of love and marriage
who brings men and women together
and ties them as tightly
as reliable, chemically treated
Nabeya lice-repellant sashes
worn by high-ranking courtesans
looks away from these two now,
abandons them, swelling with anger.
And the passionate quarrels between the two,
she angry as a curling slice of cooking squid,
his face as contorted as if he'd drunk
a swig of spiced soy sauce—
their lovers' spats are a thing long gone.
Once she walked proudly with wide steps
through the main street of Yoshiwara
but now she stumbles, toes pointed inward.
And as they cry, the lovers' noses run.
They have no sleeves to wipe their snot
so they wring and wring again
their wet loincloths. An east wind
chills them now, and their skin
is completely covered with goose bumps.
The man's dim, grimy face looks like
a maze of strangely written words
as if he sought to send a message
by way of some returning geese,

like letters written
in thin ink across the misty sky.
Simple cursive characters
describe a crowbar on the shoulders
and an anchor at the knees
dyed in dark purple on two Edo robes
now entered in a pawnshop book
beside the famous Sumida,
its waters running dark as ink.
As they pass Iozaki Point
they complain about small things
and then the big Chōmei-ji temple bell
booms out ten o'clock,
reminding Enjirō of the shop
that sells Chōmei-ji ointment for men
for lengthening their performance.
All through the night
Enjirō bares his chest to Ukina
and tells her what is in his heart.
And when dawn comes they are revealed,
he with his brand-new scarlet loincloth
loose and dragging on the ground,
and she in a musty scarlet petticoat.
And as the sun now rises high
they're nowhere near
the famous Hidaka Temple
where a woman turned into a fiery snake
and burned her man to death,[28]
yet both, naked, press on. (*Shamisen flourish and exeunt.*)

Cows, they say, ask to have rings put through their noses. And Enjirō? His botched fake love suicide is in such bad taste that great fame comes to him at last. He's depicted everywhere, even on cheap fans.

[ENJIRŌ]: I just did it for thrills. It's my own fault, so I can't complain. But you must be really cold. Everything's backward now, isn't it? In a self-respecting love suicide we'd be making our final journey with our clothes on. But here we are making a journey home—with nothing on. It's ridiculous. Just ridiculous. Everyone will stare at us. We're very conspicuous in scarlet.

[UKINA]: I really got wrapped up good in someone else's underwear.

---

28. Alludes to the nō play *Dōjōji Temple*.

22. Back at home, Enjirō discovers that the highwaymen were in fact his father, Yajiemon, and Sorobei. The stolen robes now hang on a kimono rack. Enjirō, at bottom, is now almost completely wrapped in a felt rug, a visual pun on the saying "to be covered by a felt rug," meaning "to fail" or "to be disowned." Enjirō, it is implied, has failed in all his attempts to become a playboy. (From SNKBZ 79, *Kibyōshi, senryū, kyōka*, by permission of Shōgakukan)

    22. It's the day the extension on Enjirō's disinheritance runs out, and he returns home humbled and chastened. There, on a clothes rack in his room, he's amazed to see the robe that had been robbed from him at the Mimeguri Shrine. Just then, his father, Yajiemon, and the head clerk, Sorobei, come into the room and begin to lecture him. Thanks to them, Enjirō at last understands what the real world is all about and becomes a mature, serious man. Ukina decides she can put up with his bad looks and, since she doesn't have any other candidates in line at the moment, agrees to marry him. The family is rich, and under Enjirō, the business prospers even more for many long years. As a final sensational gesture to show he's separating himself forever from his scandalous reputation as a monger of scandalous reputations, Enjirō decides to have his life depicted in a kibyōshi picture book so others can learn from it. He asks Kyōden to write it and teach all the floating-head would-be playboys in the world a good lesson.

[FATHER]: Son, haven't you read Confucius? He says very clearly that young men are full of untamed vitality and must guard against lust in any form. Ideas that exceed proper bounds always fail, so it was natural your plan ended the way it did. We went to a lot of trouble, you know, to dress up and put on our little robber play just to scare the shit out of you. It was all for your sake, so from now on be very careful. I'm confident you'll never hang out with that Kinosuke again, or Warui Shian, either. Don't worry. You're not the first one who's acted like this. The world's full of idiots like you.

[ENJIRŌ]: I've got to let my mistress go. I'll really be in trouble if she gets jealous now.

[UKINA]: Because of you, I've got a terrible cold.

     [*Kibyōshi, senryū, kyōka*, SNKBZ 79: 86–108, translated by Chris Drake]

FAST-DYEING MIND STUDY (*SHINGAKU HAYASOMEGUSA*, 1790)

In an attempt to crack down on what the bakufu considered the excesses and moral dissipation of the times, in 1787 Senior Councillor Matsudaira Sadanobu instituted the Kansei Reforms (1787–1793), a series of large-scale political, economic, and moral reforms. The following year, Koikawa Harumachi and Santō Kyōden, among others, produced notable kibyōshi satirizing the reforms; but even though they were set in the past, they did not escape the bakufu's censure. Many writers, illustrators, and publishers were punished, and those who were samurai, like Harumachi, stopped writing popular fiction.

The result of the bakufu's pressure was that after 1790 the nature and content of the kibyōshi quickly changed. The obvious political and social satire of the earlier works was replaced with a thick layer of ethical didacticism, as evidenced in Santō Kyōden's *Fast-Dyeing Mind Study*. By the mid-eighteenth century, Shingaku (Mind Study, or Heart Learning), the school established by Ishida Baigan (1685–1744), had become extremely popular in the Kyoto-Osaka area. Baigan's teachings, a unique combination of Confucianism, Shintō, and Buddhism, were specifically aimed at the urban commoner and insisted that the merchant—who officially ranked lowest among the four classes—was the equal of the samurai with regard to moral practices. Baigan, who stressed the Way of the merchant, emphasized moral practice, particularly virtues such as filial piety, diligence, frugality, and honesty. The Shingaku school, whose leaders included Nakazawa Dōni (1725–1803), experienced a revival and spread to Edo in the late eighteenth century, partly as a result of the Kansei Reforms, whose ideology closely matched that of the Shingaku school. Nakazawa Dōni, who went to Edo, was so popular that he ended up speaking around the country to commoners of all backgrounds and was repeatedly invited to lecture to the highest samurai.

These teachings are dealt with in Santō Kyōden's *Fast-Dyeing Mind Study*, which was published in Edo in 1790 in three volumes. In it, the dangers of straying from the fundamental virtues are dramatized through the conflict between the "good souls" (*zendama*) and the "bad souls" (*akudama*) over the body of Ritarō, the son of the merchant Rihei. With the aid of Master Dōri, whose name echoes that of the noted Shingaku master Nakazawa Dōni, the good souls are able to regain control of Ritarō's body. As it evolved in the late eighteenth century, Shingaku stressed "knowing the original mind" (*honshin o shiru*), a notion originally found in the *Mencius* (6A:10), which asserted that if one ignored the good impulses that arose naturally in one's mind, one would "lose" the true or original mind.[29] *Fast-Dyeing Mind Study*[30] had a

---

29. In several passages, Kyōden draws on the writings of Nakazawa Dōni, specifically, *Old Man Dōni's Lectures on the Way* (*Dōni ō dōwa*, 1791) and *Old Man Dōni's Lessons for the Young* (*Dōni ō zenkun*). But Kyōden also saturates this work, like most of his kibyōshi, with irony and humor.

30. The title *Fast-Dyeing Mind Study* (*Shingaku hayasomegusa*) parodies the name of a popular Edo clothes dye called "fast-dyeing grass" (*hayasomegusa*). The comparison of Mind Study

considerable influence on subsequent kibyōshi, showing that a morally conscious, commonsense style could draw far more readers than had the earlier, pre–Kansei Reforms kibyōshi. The book became the subject of *nishikie* (brocade) prints, and the phrase "good souls, bad souls" (*zendama, akudama*) became very popular, with the vigorous, humorous bad souls being widely depicted. The comic depiction of half-naked good and bad souls was made even more famous by a kabuki dance called Sanja matsuri (Three-Shrine Festival, first performed in 1832). Kitao Masayoshi, later and better known as Kuwagata Keisai (1764–1824), was the ukiyo-e artist. Particularly eye-catching was the simultaneous presentation of the human and the spiritual realms and the struggle between the good and bad souls that exteriorize human inner conflict.

Preface

People say picture books aren't suited to theory, but the conception underlying the present book is a theoretical one, presented in three volumes for the instruction of children.[31] If Big Daddy Buddha in India grasps the truth of this book, he'll put all his expedient means for teaching in his breast pocket and retire, and Old Man Confucius from Lu will stuff the Will of Heaven in his sleeve and exit gracefully. Even Japan's own Boss Woman, the sun goddess Amaterasu, and other women readers may well praise it as pure and clean.[32]

1. Humans have souls. The souls of men are swords. The souls of women, according to Shunkan in the puppet play *White Pines*,[33] are definitely mirrors. And the souls moving across kabuki stages are said to be copper, wrapped in red paper. But these theories aren't worth listening to. Swords and mirrors are just comparisons. Likewise, a jingle in the back of a popular chronicle claims the soul is made from five elements:[34]

> Hearing from nine woods
> of a three-fire secret mountain:
> one is earth, seven are metal,
> five waters are a guess.

(Shingaku) to a fast-working product suggests that Mind Study aims at immediate, effective "mind dyeing." "Grass" also means "book," as if the kibyōshi were an easy guide to understanding Mind Study.

31. This is a parody of a stock phrase in earlier kusa-zōshi picture books, which allows Kyōden to treat Mind Study on a simplistic, childish level without contradiction. That is, he can present Mind Study with apparent moral seriousness and, at the same time, maintain an ironic distance.

32. This phrase refers to the Mind Study doctrine of the "six virtues of women," one of which was to be "pure and clean."

33. *White Pines* (Hime-komatsu ne no hi no asobi) was first performed in 1757.

34. The energy of the five elements—wood, fire, earth, metal, and water—are combined with yin and yang in this traditional Chinese theory to constitute all the forms of the cosmos.

1. Standing among clouds, the Heavenly Emperor blows out new souls from his bamboo tube. With a halo behind his head, signifying his divinity, and wearing an ancient courtier's robe, as Shintō deities were depicted in paintings, the Heavenly Emperor appears as a distinctly Japanese god. The Heavenly Emperor comically resembles a child playing with bubbles. The bubbles close to the tube are round and perfect, while those carried into the distance by "winds of delusions and dishonesty" change into misshapen ovals. From the 1790 edition. (From SNKBZ 79, *Kibyōshi, senryū, kyōka*, by permission of Shōgakukan)

But this is sophistry. The soul is only one thing. Alive, the soul is called "energy"; dead, it's called "ghost." It's also called "mind" or "spirit," and nothing's more important to humans. Where does it come from? It's granted by heaven.[35]

In heaven dwells an august deity named Heavenly Emperor.[36] He spends his time dipping a bamboo tube into what looks like a wide teacup. This bowl contains water into which something resembling elm-berry skins have been dissolved. Using the tube, the deity blows out souls. The principle is the same as for children blowing soap bubbles. When the souls are first blown, they are round and perfect, but carried by winds of delusion and dishonesty, some change into ovals, triangles, or squares.

[HEAVENLY EMPEROR]: The illustrators are going to have a lot of trouble depicting me. For today only, I'll appear as a Japanese god. Don't let any other countries know about this!

Gather round, it's the Bubble Man! Everyone buys my bubbles. Everyone!

---

35. This view is a basic Mind Study belief.
36. The Heavenly Emperor is not a standard Mind Study belief.

2. The sliding door and a low two-panel screen demarcate the area of childbirth. This is a sitting-style delivery with the wife sitting up against a panel, covered with a *futon*. The midwife holds the newborn baby above a tub of water for the first bath while another maid waits with a towel. The good soul, on the left, is about to enter the boy's body while the Heavenly Emperor prevents the bad soul from doing the same by twisting its arm. The Chinese characters for "good" (*zen*) and "bad" (*aku*) are written on their faces. (From SNKBZ 79, *Kibyōshi, senryū, kyōka*, by permission of Shōgakukan)

2. Near Nihonbashi in downtown Edo lived a merchant named Rihei. He was the owner of the Quick and Easy Shop and dedicated himself to turning a fast profit.[37] Rihei's wife became pregnant, and nine months later she gave birth to a gem of a baby boy.[38] Everyone in the house offered their congratulations and made quite a commotion.

An infant is truly a white thread waiting to be dyed life's various colors. As soon as Rihei's son was born, a distorted bad soul attempted to enter the child by slipping under its skin. The Heavenly Emperor appeared, however, and firmly twisted the bad soul's arm. He sent in a completely round good soul instead. The deity showed Rihei special mercy because he always kept his mind in good order. Unfortunately ordinary people were unable to see this at all.[39]

37. The Quick and Easy Shop, or Right in Front of Your Eyes Shop, suggests his narrow interests and focus on quick profits.

38. The term "gem" (*tama*) is homophonous here and elsewhere with "soul" as well as with "circle" or "sphere."

39. "Ordinary people" was a commonly used term in Mind Study.

3. Rihei and his wife (*right*) admire Ritarō's calligraphy. Throughout the text, the Chinese character *ri* (profit/use) appears on Rihei's robe, as it does here, while a different *ri* (reason/ principle) appears on Ritarō's robe. Behind Ritarō (*left*) is a single-panel screen with round and square paintings of bamboo and a piece of calligraphy in intaglio with a Chinese saying, "Green bamboo grows straight as the virtuous man." The screen and the way in which the good soul points directly to Ritarō show that he is expected to become such a character. The sliding doors behind the standing screen also depict a Chinese-style landscape, indicating that Rihei has pretensions to learning. The scene suggests the kind of children's lessons for which Nakazawa Dōni was famous. (From SNKBZ 79, *Kibyōshi, senryū, kyōka*, by permission of Shōgakukan)

[HEAVENLY EMPEROR]: Go in right here.

[GOOD SOUL]: Yes, Majesty! (*The curtain closes to the rapid beating of wooden kabuki clappers offstage.*)

   3. Rihei named his son Ritarō.[40] The good soul stayed with the boy constantly and protected him, so as Ritarō grew he revealed intelligence and was well behaved and skillful at everything. His parents could tell he was different from other children. He was their precious jewel, and they raised him with the greatest care. Once a soul is three years old, it never changes until it's a hundred.[41] The child's future looked very bright.

[RIHEI]: What superb calligraphy! He's my own child, but I'm already in awe of what he could be.

---

40. Ritarō means "Greatest Truth or Principle."
41. A proverb, not from Mind Study doctrine.

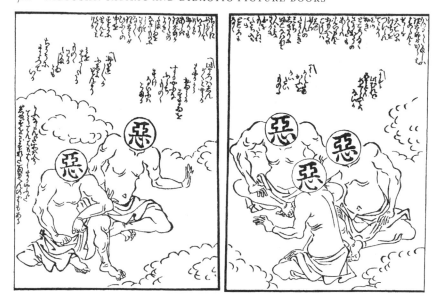

4. With nowhere to go, five bad souls sit in a circle in the sky, plotting to find suitable bodies. (From SNKBZ 79, *Kibyōshi, senryū, kyōka,* by permission of Shōgakukan)

[RIHEI'S WIFE]: It's miraculous. Shouldn't we get someone famous to teach him?

[NURSE]: He certainly is a clever child.

[GOOD SOUL] (*proudly stroking its beard*): But surely you exaggerate. . . .

[RITARŌ]: My teacher says he's going to write out samples of province names for me to copy.

[RITARŌ AND GOOD SOUL]: My dad and mom are very important to me. I'll never gamble or toss coins into holes. Or pull strings for prizes.

[STANDING SCREEN]: "Green bamboo grows straight as the virtuous man."

4. After the bad soul got chewed out by the Heavenly Emperor, it had nowhere to live. It looked for another suitable body, but in those days people had pure hearts and earnestly practiced the venerable ways of Confucianism, Buddhism, and Shintō. The bad soul found nobody it could break into. It just dangled in space and plotted, waiting for a chance to get rid of the good soul in Ritarō's body and live there instead.

[FIRST BAD SOUL] (*far right*): What do you say to fifty rounds of cards?

[SECOND] (*upper right*): I'd really like to buy stock in a nice body.[42]

[THIRD] (*middle left*): Ever hear of Mind Study? It's the rage now. Almost nobody's doing any wrong these days. I can't find anyone bad to live inside.

---

42. Satirizes the contemporary practice of buying and selling official positions and names.

5. Ritarō comes of age. With a razor in hand, the clerk (*left*) is about to shave Ritarō's forehead and give him an adult hairstyle. In the An'ei-Tenmei period (1772–1789), plucking the hairline at the temples to make the forehead look wider was fashionable, a practice that Ritarō declines and that the Kansei Reforms discouraged. A figure of a standing crane, a symbol of longevity, adorns the screen behind Rihei. The good soul, sitting next to the clerk, admires Ritarō. (From SNKBZ 79, *Kibyōshi, senryū, kyōka*, by permission of Shōgakukan)

[Fourth] (*far right*): Sitting together like this, hey, we look like gamblers without dice. Or maybe we're Buddhists who forgot to bring our communal prayer beads.[43]

Each was once the soul of someone who died badly, by suicide or execution. Still attached to their former lives, these bad souls wander, lost between life and death.[44]

5. When Ritarō turned sixteen, his parents cut off his long hair and dressed him in men's clothes. He also had a good character to go with his good looks. His father turned over most of the shop business to him, and he proved a model of conscientiousness and honesty. He woke up early and went to bed late, paid close attention to details, and was thoroughly frugal. He honored his parents, showed kindness to the employees, never put down his abacus, and protected the shop both while he was in it and while he was out. Soon he was the talk of the neighborhood.

[Rihei]: Son, don't pluck the hairs on your temples trying to look sexy. People will think you're a bad person.

[Ritarō]: Never!

[Clerk]: You look perfect.

---

43. Here and elsewhere the bad souls compare themselves with many kinds of ordinary people living in the world.

44. The bad souls suggest the large number of unemployed or minimally employed laborers gathering in Edo at the time. These people were a major problem for the bakufu, which asked Nakazawa Dōni to preach to them and reform them.

6. Ritarō takes a short nap under a thick night robe, as was the custom at the time. His tobacco set is near his pillow. Above him, three bad souls tie up the good soul as it steps out of Ritarō's body. (From SNKBZ 79, *Kibyōshi, senryū, kyōka,* by permission of Shōgakukan)

6. While people sleep, it's certain their souls leave their bodies and have a little fun. One day, when Ritarō was eighteen, he felt tired after doing inventory and took a nap. His soul, worn out from keeping the bad soul away day after day, went out and relaxed nearby. The bad soul noticed this and called his comrades. Together they tied up the good soul and entered Ritarō's vacant body.

[GOOD SOUL]: Aagh. This can't be happening.

[BAD SOULS]: What a great feeling!

7. When Ritarō woke, he decided he'd make a pilgrimage that very day to the Kannon Temple in Asakusa. After making his prayers to the bodhisattva Kannon, he turned to go home. Then he started thinking. He'd never had any interest in seeing the Yoshiwara licensed quarter before, and just looking around wouldn't cost anything. Surely there wouldn't be anything wrong with seeing it just once. His steps felt light as he began walking the half-mile stretch of river embankment between Asakusa and the quarter. This all happened because the bad souls had gotten inside him.

[RITARŌ]: No, I won't go after all. People at home will worry about me. Still, I've come this far. Maybe I should just take a look. But then again, maybe I'll go home.

Again and again he set out along the bank, then turned back. This was the work of the bad souls.

[FIRST BAD SOUL] (*on Ritarō's right*): Stop dithering. I'll tell you exactly how to act when we get there. Don't worry. Why not take a look at a few of the

7. Urged on by the bad souls, Ritarō hesitantly walks along Nihonzutsumi, the embankment leading to Yoshiwara, which appears in the far distance. Ritarō is wearing a fashionable long coat over his kimono. Many of the roofs hold rain barrels for use in case of fire. The two notice boards advertise the unveiling of sacred Buddhist treasures at the Fudō Temple and the thousand-sutra chantings at the Yūten-ji temple. Both events were held in Kansei 1 (1789), the year before this kibyōshi's publication. The bad soul in front of Ritarō likens himself to a barker for an inn, while the two bad souls pushing Ritarō yell phrases as if he were a parade float. (From SNKBZ 79, *Kibyōshi, senryū, kyōka*, by permission of Shōga-kukan)

stylish places? Rice cakes in soybean flour, young man, come on! I look like I'm pulling in customers for an inn—and got stripped by bandits!

[SECOND AND THIRD BAD SOULS] (*behind*): Uh-huh, uh-huh, uh-huh, you've got it, you've got it. Uh-huh, uh-huh, uh-huh. Hey, now. We look like we're pushing a festival float with someone on it.

[SIGN TO FAR RIGHT]: "Chikubu Island, Designated Imperial Prayer Place. Greatest of Only Three Manifestation Sites of the Female Fortune God Benzaiten. Thirtieth of Thirty-three Kannon Pilgrimage Temples in the Kyoto Area. Secret Kannon Image Officially on Limited Display at Fudō Temple in Mejiro: Seventeenth of Intercalary Sixth Month to Eighteenth of Eighth Month."

[NEXT SIGN]: "Thousand-Sutra Chantings Daily: Seventeenth to Twenty-Fifth of Seventh Month. Yūtenji Temple, Meguro."

8. At the Miuraya House, Ritarō is entertained in an upstairs parlor. A single candle in the center lights the room. With a fan in hand, Ritarō dances to the shamisen music while keeping the beat with his tobacco pipe and a teacup. As partial exteriorizations of Ritarō's feelings, the bad souls dance, too. Ayashino, whose name suggests *ayashi* (suspicious), a character that appears on her robe, sits next to Ritarō, who sits in front of the alcove (*to-konoma*), where a hanging scroll is displayed, indicating that he is the main guest. To the far right, a teenage apprentice (*shinzō*), marked by the long sleeves of her robe (*furisode*), converses with a male jester, who provides entertainment. To her right sits a child attendant (*kamuro*), wearing elaborate hairpins and assuming a pose very similar to that of Ayashino. The shamisen player (*bottom right*) is singing a verse from a popular song called "Wankyū of the Four Seasons," about a man of extreme dissipation. (From SNKBZ 79, *Kibyōshi, senryū, kyōka*, by permission of Shōgakukan)

8. Led by the bad souls, Ritarō arrived at the Yoshiwara. He thought he'd just take a quick look around and go home, but as he walked around watching the evening sights along the main street of the quarter, he gradually fell under the full control of the bad souls and finally asked the owner of a teahouse to arrange a meeting with a courtesan named Ayashino[45] at the Miuraya House. The bad souls flew straight up to heaven and forgot about ever going home again. Ritarō had completely lost his mind.

The souls jump into the air and dance.

[FIRST BAD SOUL] (*singing*): Do it!

[SECOND] (*singing*): Yeah, yeah.

[THIRD] (*singing*): That's it! That's it!

---

45. Ayashino means "Suspicious Field."

9. Elaborate bedding with three layers of *futon*, a custom at Yoshiwara, is prepared for Ritarō. Two bad souls help Ayashino and Ritarō undress each other. The bad soul sitting on top of the *futon* cover addresses the reader as if it were the end of a kabuki act, a technique used to close the scene humorously, avoiding erotic details. The folding screen depicts the branches of a plum tree in bloom, an image that often appears in erotic ukiyo-e prints. (From SNKBZ 79, *Kibyōshi, senryū, kyōka,* by permission of Shōgakukan)

[RITARŌ]: Ah, what a nice fragrance. It's Okamoto's Hair Oil for Young Ladies.
[GEISHA] (*singing with shamisens*):
    Each night he drank till dawn.
    On and on, until he reached—insanity.
[RITARŌ]: Hey, this is fun. Really fun. Where have I been all my life?

9. After the performance, Ritarō was shown to a bedroom. Soon Ayashino appeared, and the bad souls took her by the hand and had her untie Ritarō's loincloth. Then they had the two hold each other tight and led Ritarō's hand far down underneath her open collar. Ritarō's whole body felt as if it were melting.

[AYASHINO]: Over this way. Oh, your hand's so cold!
[FIRST BAD SOUL]: All right! Perfect!
[SECOND]: Even if your parents punish you, so what?
[THIRD]: That's all for tonight, folks. (*Kabuki drumbeats mark the end of the act just in time.*)

10. The good soul, who'd loyally lived so many years inside Ritarō, remained tied up where the bad souls had left it. The good soul worried about Ritarō, but no one came to release it, and it agonized alone. A superb chanter like Chūgorō or Isaburō[46] would have been there to express the good soul's suffering by singing softly to the shamisens in the background.

---

46. Two famous Edo kabuki narrators, neither of whom is there to accompany the main actor's silent travails with background singing. The good soul is tied to a large character meaning "disaster," a reflection of the Mind Study practice of showing large characters during sermons.

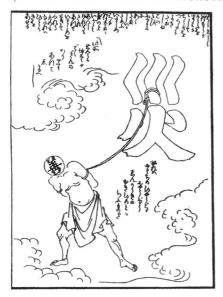

10. Ousted from Ritarō's body, the good soul, which is tied to a giant Sino-Japanese character for *wazawai* (disaster) in the sky, compares itself with characters in two puppet plays who experience similar difficulties. (From SNKBZ 79, *Kibyōshi, senryū, kyōka*, by permission of Shōgakukan)

[GOOD SOUL]: I'm Hyōgo's brave wife tied to a post in the puppet play *Epiphany at Yaguchi Crossing*. I'm the loyal daughter Yukihime tied to a tree in *Gion Festival Record*.[47]

11. The bad souls, exhausted from a night of dancing, went inside the front of Ayashino's robe. Just when they were falling asleep, Ritarō began thinking uneasily about home. Why had he ever come here? What had made him do this? He felt as if he were waking from a dream and got up to leave without even saying good-bye, but that woke the bad souls. Determined not to let him go, they immediately jumped inside him again. Ritarō quickly changed his mind and told the house he would stay on. Just then the good soul, who'd finally escaped, came running in. He grabbed Ritarō's hand and tried to pull him outside. The bad souls, determined, pulled the other way.

"I'd really like to stay on," Ritarō said, pulled to the left. Then, tugged to the right, "No, I need to be going right now." He kept walking up and down the hall.

Souls are completely invisible to ordinary human eyes. "What a weird customer," exclaims the teahouse guide who has come to see Ritarō off.

[AYASHINO]: Either you go home or you stay. Stop acting like an idiot.

[THIRD BAD SOUL]: Come on boys, let's get this well clean. Hey, no farting!

[FIRST AND SECOND]: Heave ho! Heave ho!

---

47. In Hiraga Gennai's puppet play *Epiphany at Yaguchi Crossing* (*Shinrei Yaguchi no watashi*, 1770), the wife of the warrior lord Hyōgonosuke reprimands him for planning to surrender his castle, so he ties her to a pillar. In the puppet play *Gion Festival Record* (1757), Yukihime attacks an enemy of her father and is tied to a cherry tree.

11. Ritarō stands confused, torn between the good and bad souls in a corridor. This is the second floor, where the courtesan's parlor and rooms are located. Note that it takes three bad souls to compete against one good soul. The way in which the bad souls are pulling Ritarō is similar to the way in which workers and tools, attached to a rope, were pulled from wells that the workers had fixed and cleaned. The teahouse guide, holding Ritarō's slippers and a lantern with the teahouse's crest, comes for him. (From SNKBZ 79, *Kibyōshi, senryū, kyōka*, by permission of Shōgakukan)

12. The good soul returned inside, and Ritarō's experience in the quarter now seemed like a distant dream. Ritarō felt disgusted even to remember it and busied himself with the shop accounts. Then one day a messenger from the teahouse arrived with the standard follow-up letter from Ayashino. When Ritarō innocently opened the letter, the bad soul entered it and struggled to possess him again.

[MESSENGER]: A letter after only one meeting! It's unheard of, even in the age of the gods.

The good soul anxiously tried to keep Ritarō from looking at it.

13. After reading Ayashino's skillfully worded letter, Ritarō's mind began to waver again. With the fortune I've got, he thought, I can easily afford to spend three hundred or four hundred pieces of gold a year. I'm not going to live ten thousand or even a thousand years. And when I'm dead, all I can take with me are six coppers to pay to cross the river to the other world. I've really been wasting my time scrimping and saving. Doesn't the old Chinese poem say "Take a lamp and go where pleasure is"?[48] He interpreted the line willfully, as though it referred to his own desire, and bad thoughts appeared.

---

48. From the sixth-century Chinese poetry anthology *Wen xuan*.

12. At the shop, Ritarō reads a letter from Ayashino delivered by the teahouse guide. An account book box, on which is written *chōbako* (account book box), functions as a desk. The good soul takes Ritarō's arm and tries to redirect his attention to the thick account book opened before him. However, the bad soul once again gains entry to Ritarō's body through the letter. (From SNKBZ 79, *Kibyōshi, senryū, kyōka,* by permission of Shōgakukan)

13. With Ayashino's letter before him, Ritarō sits perplexed. The picture on the low two-panel *furosaki* screen echoes the phrase that Ritarō utters, "six coppers to pay to cross the river to the other world," by depicting two men pulling a boat across a river. Above him, the bad soul slays the good soul. (From SNKBZ 79, *Kibyōshi, senryū, kyōka,* by permission of Shōgakukan)

While Ritarō was having many bad thoughts, the bad soul got its chance. Finally it cut down the good soul and got revenge.

[BAD SOUL]: Resign yourself.

[GOOD SOUL]: This can't be happening!

14. The bad soul and his comrades at last entered all the way into Ritarō's body and drove out the good soul's wife and two sons with a sharp split-bamboo

14. Ritarō is again with Ayashino (*right*), with a bad soul straddling his shoulders and another sitting in front of him, while, with a split-bamboo cane, a bad soul expels the wife and two sons of the good soul (*left*). The folding screen depicts a bamboo thicket and a pheasant, serving as a reminder of the faithful son that Ritarō was once expected to become. On the left, Ritarō's head clerk begs Ritarō to come to his senses, as the teenage apprentice (*shinzō*) behind him appears to be laughing at the ridiculous situation. (From SNKBZ 79, *Kibyōshi, senryū, kyōka*, by permission of Shōgakukan)

cane. How pitiful the three looked, holding hands as they left the body that had been their home for many years. Ritarō then began a life of dissipation, staying with Ayashino four or five days at a time.

[BAD SOUL WITH CANE]: Hurry up. Faster. Out!

[GOOD SOUL'S WIFE]: Just wait. You'll pay for this.

[FIRST SON]: I feel really sad.

[SECOND SON]: Mommy, let's leave!

[BAD SOUL ON RITARŌ'S SHOULDERS]: Wait'll you see what I can do!

[BAD SOUL SITTING]: Serves you right!

Ritarō's head clerk comes for him and rebukes him in the manner of the kabuki villain actor Okuyama.[49]

[CLERK]: You weren't always like this. What happened to your brain? An evil spirit must have gotten into you. You're completely hopeless.

[RITARŌ]: Please, old boy. Don't be tasteless. Whatever happens, I simply refuse to go. Shad sushi to that!

---

49. Asao Tamejūrō III. The clerk's face actually resembles that of the kabuki actor in contemporary actor prints.

15. Shingaku instruction books typically taught that an imprudent person would be reduced to a robber who broke into homes by cutting holes in the foundation. Ritarō, his head covered like that of a robber, is confronted by his own dog as he breaks into his family storehouse. A throng of bad souls behind him urge Ritarō on, and more bad souls line up to enter his body. (From SNKBZ 79, *Kibyōshi, senryū, kyōka*, by permission of Shōgakukan)

Ayashino also feels that Ritarō has stayed too long, but she speaks indirectly: "Your papa and mama must be concerned about you. I don't want to tell you to go home, but well, I don't know what to say."

15. More and more bad souls entered Ritarō. He not only went to the quarter but drank heavily, started fights, gambled, and swindled. His behavior was so disrespectful to his parents that finally they disowned him. He had nowhere at all to go. Then one night he cut a hole in the back wall of his own family storehouse and robbed it. A large group of bad souls gathered around Ritarō, urging him to commit one wrong after another. It was shocking, totally reckless.

[DOG]: Old Master, you've become a thief! You're like the old master in Yamashina in that puppet play—the one who gets covered with mud repairing a storehouse.[50] But hey, he was repairing the wall, not breaking in. If I didn't bark, I wouldn't be doing my duty. (*Barks*)

[RITARŌ]: Spot, boy! It's me! Don't bark! Say, listen to this. "Kitchen god pictures," don't you bark! Did you like that one?[51]

---

50. In the puppet play *Commentary on the Taiheiki Loyal Retainers* (*Taiheiki Chūshingura kōshaku*, 1776), a former warrior master repairing a storehouse wall in Yamashina, near Kyoto, is covered with mud (*doro*), which, to the dog, suggests a robber (*dorobō*).

51. Ritarō exchanges puns with his dog. The phrase "kitchen god pictures" (*oenma*), shouted

16. On a deserted road with wild grass growing through a dilapidated fence and a crescent moon lighting an open field, Master Dōri (the character "dō," or the Way, appears on his robe), echoing the Shingaku master Nakazawa Dōni, forcefully throws Ritarō to the ground after being attacked by him. (From SNKBZ 79, *Kibyōshi, senryū, kyōka*, by permission of Shōgakukan)

16. Finally Ritarō became a vagrant. The bad souls grew even bolder, and Ritarō began robbing travelers on deserted roads. Pitiful!

Now there was a widely revered man of great learning and insight named Dōri, Master of Truth, who naturally felt deep compassion and love and had the ability to act on his beliefs.[52] One night, returning from a lecture, he was attacked by Ritarō. But Master Dōri, a strong man, grabbed Ritarō and threw him to the ground. He felt only pity for his assailant. Hoping to reform the young man, he forgave him and took him back to his lodgings.

[MASTER DŌRI]: What a disgrace!

The bad souls, who were responsible for Ritarō's actions, pointed at Ritarō and roared with laughter.

17. The good soul's widow and sons had been watching the movements of the bad soul, waiting for a chance to take revenge. But there were too many other bad souls, so their days and months were bitter. Now that Ritarō had

---

out by street vendors, is nearly homophonous with "don't bark!" (*hoeru na*). From the perspective of Mind Study, Ritarō's frivolity indicates that he has strayed from his "original mind."

52. Like Ritarō, Master Dōri (Master Truth) has *ri* (truth/reason/principle) in his name. He suggests the famous Kyoto proselytizer Nakazawa Dōni (1725–1803), who went to Edo in 1779 and helped spread Mind Study there.

17. Ritarō listens humbly to Master Dōri's teachings and regains his original mind. Master Dōri sits at a Chinese desk, with a writing box, in front of a bookcase labeled "Chinese and Japanese texts," indicating that he is a man of learning. The wife and two sons of the good soul return to drive away the bad souls. (From SNKBZ 79, *Kibyōshi, senryū, kyōka*, by permission of Shōgakukan)

returned to his original mind, however, they had little trouble realizing their long-cherished desire. To their great joy, the other bad souls abandoned their comrade and fled.

[GOOD SOUL'S WIDOW]: Revenge for my husband! Put up your sword!

[FIRST SON]: This will teach you!

[SECOND SON]: This is for my father! Prepare to die!

Ritarō was indebted to Master Dōri for his life, and he listened intently to his explanations of the virtues common to Confucianism, Buddhism, and Shintō. He deeply regretted his former misconduct and returned to his original mind.[53]

[MASTER DŌRI]: In everything humans do, only the mind is important. Without intending to, people inflict great pain on themselves with their own minds. The mind is the soul. This is a truth you must firmly grasp.

[RITARŌ]: I alone ignore the truth.[54] I gave money to that woman just so she

---

53. As conceived by Shingaku, "original mind" (*honshin*) is the mind (*kokoro*) with which people are born and that is at one with Heaven. Dōni noted that his objective was to teach the recovery of the "selfless original mind" (*ware nashi no honshin*).

54. Citation from a solo *meriyasu* song called "Blossom Banquet," in which a woman admits

18. Ritarō, dressed in formal robes, bows to
his parents, both hands touching the floor.
The saké cup placed on a small wooden
stand and the saké container on the side
show that Ritarō has exchanged sips of saké
with his father and has been formally accepted back into the family. Text on right:
"Written by Kyōden." On left: "Pictures by
Masayoshi." (From SNKBZ 79, *Kibyōshi,
senryū, kyōka,* by permission of Shōgakukan)

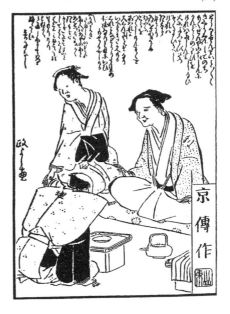

would say she loved me. I even gave her special tips on holidays. Now all
that money seems unclean. Very unclean.

[MASTER DŌRI]: Next I've got to put it to the author of this book.[55] He sounds
like a mighty scoundrel who has ignored the Way.

18. After Master Dōri had carefully taught Ritarō, the young man went to
see his parents at the Quick and Easy Store and begged their forgiveness. Overjoyed, they took him back immediately. From then on, Ritarō discerned the
Way clearly. He honored his parents, treated his relatives and employees with
kindness, and became a living example of a virtuous man. The house and its
business prospered greatly. Near and far, people praised Master Dōri's deep
compassion and high character, which, they said, had made it all possible.

The good soul's sons inherited their father's house and duties and lived for
many years in Ritarō's body, taking good care of their mother and diligently
protecting Ritarō. From then on, the good souls stayed right where they were
and never got restless again.

[*Kibyōshi, senryū, kyōka,* SNKBZ 79: 171–193, translated by Chris Drake]

---

that she foolishly ignores the truth (*dōri*) in the criticisms around her, but in spite of them and
the solemn warning of the evening bell, she continues to love and wait for a man who no longer
loves her. Like the woman, Ritarō admits to ignoring the truth, but the song also suggests that
he continues to love Ayashino.

55. Kyōden, the text suggests, still hasn't seen the truth of Mind Study. In fact, a little more
than a year after the publication of this kibyōshi, he was punished by the Edo authorities for
writing about "bad places."

Chapter 18

KOKKEIBON: COMIC FICTION FOR COMMONERS

Kokkeibon (literally, humor books) were a new type of comic fiction that emerged in Edo during the Hōreki era (1751–1764) and became a major fictional genre. Comic fiction in the wider sense had existed from the beginning of the seventeenth century, in kana-zōshi such as *Fake Tales* (*Nise monogatari*) and *Today's Tales of Yesterday* (*Kinō wa kyō no monogatari*), which today are categorized as comic stories (*shōwa*). Although humorous fiction also appeared in the form of sharebon and kibyōshi in the late eighteenth century, kokkeibon was a distinct genre that arose in the mid-eighteenth century and continued into the Meiji period (1868–1911), thus lasting more than a hundred years.

The Kansei Reforms (1787–1793) had a profoundly negative effect on the popular literature of the time, particularly on the sharebon, the books of wit and fashion, a genre that was banned by an edict in 1790 and forced to change form. It was in this context that *Country Theater* (*Inaka shibai*, 1787), which until now had not been regarded as a real sharebon, received attention. *Country Theater* was written by Manzōtei (1756–1810), a Dutch studies (*rangaku*) scholar who had studied with Hiraga Gennai. Instead of describing the pleasure quarters, as the early sharebon had, *Country Theater* comically depicted the life of a provincial theater in a village in Echigo Province, using the same kind of dialogue-based narrative as found in the sharebon. Significantly, *Country Theater* referred to itself as a *yabobon* (boorish book) instead of a *sharebon* (suave book). Modern scholars have regarded this book as the beginning of a new kind of humor book (*kokkeibon*) and the immediate predecessor to Jippensha Ikku's *Travels on the Eastern Seaboard* (*Tōkaidōchū hizakurige*).

The kokkeibon genre can be roughly divided into early and late. The early kokkeibon, which flourished in the latter half of the eighteenth century, centered on *dangibon*, or satiric sermons, which made fun of contemporary mores. The best examples are Jōkanbō Kōa's *Modern-Style Lousy Sermons* (*Imayō heta dangi*, 1752) and Hiraga Gennai's *Rootless Weeds* (*Nenashigusa*, 1763) and *Modern Life of Shidōken* (*Fūryū Shidōkenden*, 1763). The late kokkeibon, which appeared in the early nineteenth century, began with Jippensha Ikku's *Travels on the Eastern Seaboard* and Shikitei Sanba's *Floating-World Bathhouse* (*Ukiyoburo*) and *Floating-World Barbershop* (*Ukiyodoko*) and continued into the Meiji period with the works of Kanagaki Robun (1829–1894) and others.

The early kokkeibon, as exemplified by Gennai's dangibon, had a didactic purpose in which humor served the higher ends of social, religious, or political critique. By contrast, the later kokkeibon of Jippensha Ikku and Shikitei Sanba (1776–1822), while satiric in part, had no overt moralistic or didactic motives and were fundamentally sympathetic to rather than critical of the object of laughter. The later kokkeibon poked fun at everyday life in a fashion that almost all readers could share in. Storytellers who entertained Edo audiences with amusing tales had, as early as the Tenmei era (1781–1789), cultivated and incorporated this kind of humor in their work, and the kokkeibon of the early nineteenth century can be seen as an outgrowth of that storytelling tradition.

Physically, the early kokkeibon were the same size as the yomihon (about 10 inches by 14 inches), while the nineteenth-century kokkeibon were slightly smaller middle-size books (*chūbon*). In contrast to the early kokkeibon, which retained the monogatari (tale) format of the ukiyo-zōshi, the later kokkeibon were an extension of the sharebon genre in typographically resembling a dramatic script.

JIPPENSHA IKKU

Jippensha Ikku (1765–1831) was not born and raised in Edo. Rather, he was the son of a samurai in Sunpu, in Suruga Province (Shizuoka), served in the house of a daimyō for a short time, and had another unsuccessful stint of service in Osaka before embarking on a career as a jōruri playwright and a sharebon and kibyōshi writer. In 1802, Ikku wrote *Travels in the Floating World* (*Ukiyo dōchū hizakurige*), which, by the third volume, had become *Travels on the Eastern Seaboard* (*Tōkaidōchū hizakurige*). In addition to writing the text, Ikku drew many of the illustrations.

TRAVELS ON THE EASTERN SEABOARD
(*TŌKAIDŌCHŪ HIZAKURIGE*, 1802–1809)

The narrative of *Travels on the Eastern Seaboard* centers on two protagonists, Yajirobei and Kitahachi (Yaji and Kita), who travel west from Edo, on the Tōkaidō, the Eastern Seaboard Highway, visiting the Ise Shrine, Kyoto, and Osaka. *Travels* developed elements found earlier in *Country Theater* (*Inaka shibai*): the middle-size book format, the description of local dialect and provincial customs, the focus on a pair of male characters, and, most of all, humor based on "boorishness" (*yabo*) rather than on the "suaveness" (*tsū*) found in the sharebon.

In short, the audience for *Travels* was not the kind of refined urban readers who would appreciate the sharp social critique of the earlier sharebon. Instead, it aimed at a broad range of readers. Its protagonists, Kita and Yaji, have no particular social status; instead, they are characters with whom readers of all classes could identify. *Travels* also had an easy-to-read style. Even though the sharebon were written in the vernacular in a dialogue format, the content was often difficult, while late yomihon such as Kyokutei Bakin's *Eight Dog Chronicles* (*Nansō Satomi hakkenden*, 1814–1842) used a highly literary, mixed Japanese-Chinese style. *Travels*, by contrast, was written largely in the form of a dialogue in a local dialect, supplemented by descriptive prose that is very close to colloquial Japanese.

Travels contains fundamentally two types of humor. One is realistic, deriving from the sharebon tradition and describing, as objectively as possible, the local customs and dialects of different locales. The other type comes from the comic behavior of the two central characters, Yajirobei and Kita. The two types of humor are evident in subsequent kokkeibon. Shikitei Sanba's *Floating-World Bathhouse* (*Ukiyoburo*) exemplifies the first type, while the humor in *Cherry Blossom Calendar, Eight Laughing People* (*Hanagoyomi hasshōjin*) by the rakugo entertainer and writer Ryūtei Rijō (d. 1841)— which describes eight comic characters failing at one silly stunt after another—is of the second type. *Travels* also reflects the intense interest in travel on the Tōkaidō, the Eastern Seaboard Highway, which linked fifteen provinces from west to east. The Tōkaidō had been an important route since the seventeenth century, but the expansion of commerce, the alternate attendance system, the pilgrimages to Ise, and the popularity of sightseeing trips to Kyoto and Osaka, all increased both traffic on the road and curiosity about the sites along it, as evidenced by the publication of *Famous Places on the Eastern Seaboard Illustrated* (*Tōkaidō meisho zue*, 1797), which became the definitive guide. Indeed, *Travels* also functioned as a guidebook that offered realistic descriptions of the customs and special products of each noted locale, including a taste of the local dialect. Kita and Yaji captured the hearts of the readers who had traveled or who looked forward to traveling, particularly as an escape from the restrictions of provincial society.

The various literary sources for *Travels* include two early kana-zōshi, Tomiyama Dōya's *Tale of Chikusai* (*Chikusai monogatari*, 1621–1623) and Asai Ryōi's *Famous Places on the Eastern Seaboard* (*Tōkaidō meishoki*, 1659), both comic tales of travel in which a pair of characters travel between Edo and Kyoto composing kyōka, or comic waka.

One of the features of *Travels* is in fact the kyōka, which come at the conclusion of each scene as a way of bringing the reader back down to earth, preparing the way for the next scene, and giving the narrative a special rhythm. Ikku also used the same kinds of puns and verbal jokes found in the humorous stories (*hanashibon*) performed by Edo storytellers.

Another important source of inspiration was kyōgen, or medieval comic drama, with Yajirobei and Kita often acting like the comic protagonist (Tarōkaja) and his sidekick (Jirōkaja) in kyōgen. *Travels*, however, differed from kyōgen in its focus on food and sex. The repeated failures on the road are often related to the search for good food (especially local delicacies) or for women, two of the common pleasures of travel for men at this time, which elude them time and again. The two protagonists' low intelligence and their ignorance of the local customs and goods cause them to lurch humorously from one embarrassing mistake to the next. But while the two characters repeatedly fail, they are quickly resuscitated and never seriously threatened.

Travels on the Eastern Seaboard was finally completed in 1822, twelve years after the initial episode. Its success was such that it continued for eight volumes and was followed by a sequel called *More Travels* (*Zoku hizakurige*), in which Yaji and Kita travel to the Konpira, Miyajima, Kiso, and Zenkōji temple. The popular narrative was imitated even before it was finished and long afterward. In the Meiji period, for example, Kanagaki Robun (1829–1894) even wrote *Travels to the West* (*Seiyō dōchū hizakurige*, 1870).

Following a short introduction, the first episode comes from book 4, which describes the journey from Arai, in present-day Shizuoka Prefecture, to Kuwana, on the northeast coast of what is now Mie Prefecture. The episode, which may have been inspired by the kyōgen play *Fox Grave* (*Kitsunezuka*), in which the Tarōkaja mistakes his master for a fox, takes place at Goyu, near present-day Nagoya City. The reader should remember that in Japan it was widely believed that foxes have the power to change their shape and deceive gullible human beings. The next episode, concerning the fake Ikku, is from book 5, on the way from Kuwana to Ise.

Journey's Start (from the beginning of book 1)

. . . Now is the time to visit all the celebrated places in the country and fill our heads with what we have seen, so that when we become old and bald, we shall have something to talk about over our teacups. Let us accept the invitation of these bosom friends and go with them on their long, long journey. Let us join this dissipated Yajirobei and his hanger-on Kitahachi, with their money kept warm in the loincloths around their navels; with their light footgear and their many layers of ointment, which will keep their feet from getting sore for thousands of miles; and their cotton robes dappled like the flesh of a clam. Let us go with them through foot-worn Yamato, welcomed by the divine wind that blows from the Grand Shrine of Ise, with the flowers of the capital and the plum blossoms of Naniwa at the end of our journey.

Portraits of Yaji (*right*) and Kita (*left*), with their travel gear and luggage, from the preface to the 1814 edition of *Travels on the Eastern Seaboard*. A Chinese-style description of each character by a disciple of Jippensha Ikku is given at the top, coupled with a complementary haiku encircling the face. Text for Yaji: "From the beginning, a lazy good-for-nothing; he has the face of a clown; his heart is like that of a sexy kabuki actor, and he speaks a lot, but he's always off the mark," by Gohensha Hanku. "A man overblown at the waist carrying a blowfish!" by Ikka. Text for Kita: "First he was a boy actor selling sexual favors, but he couldn't get many customers because of his short height and vulgar looks; no matter what he tries his hand at, he ends up with nothing; impetuous and thinking only of the moment, he dives into things," by Gusha Ittoku. "The willow bending lithely in the wind, as if to say the pine and the bamboo are too upright," by Ittō. (From SNKBZ 81, *Tōkaidōchū hizakurige*, by permission of Shōgakukan)

Changed into a Fox (from the first part of book 4)

The sun was now reaching the horizon, and it would soon be twilight. They quickened their pace, but their feet were getting tired.

"How slow you are, Yaji," said Kita.

"I'm awfully tired," replied Yaji.

"I'll tell you what," said Kita. "We stopped at a dreadful place last night, so I'll go on ahead to Akasaka and look for a good inn. As you're tired, you can come on slowly behind, and I'll send someone from the inn to meet you."

"That's a good idea," said Yaji, "but mind you pick out a good inn—one where there's a nice girl."

"Trust me," said Kita. Leaving Yaji, he went on ahead.

Yaji trudged on, but by the time he got to Goyu, night had already fallen. The inn girls, with their faces painted up as though they were wearing masks, caught hold of his sleeves and tried to stop him, but he pulled himself away. At the end of the town he went into a small teahouse to take a short rest. The old woman who kept the teahouse welcomed him.

"It's only a little way to Akasaka, isn't it?" he asked.

"It's about a mile," said the old woman. "But if you're traveling alone, you'd better stop here, as there's a wicked old fox lives in the pinewood you have to pass, and he's bewitched a lot of travelers."

"That's bad," said Yaji, "but I can't stop here. My friend's gone on ahead and he'll be waiting for me. I'll be all right."

He paid the old woman and started off again. When he left the teahouse it was already dark, and soon it got darker and darker and he began to feel nervous. Still he went on, though taking the precaution to rub some spit on his eyebrows.[1] Just then he heard the bark of a fox a long way off. "There it's barking," he thought. "Come over here and show yourself, you beast. I'll soon beat you to death." Boasting to keep up his courage, he went on.

Meanwhile, Kita had gone on ahead as fast as he could until he came to the very place where he had been told a wicked fox lived and, afraid that the fox would bewitch him, he decided to wait there for Yaji so that they could go on together. He was sitting by the side of the road enjoying a smoke when Yaji came along.

"Hallo, is that you Yaji?" he called.

"Hallo!" replied Yaji. "What are you doing here?"

"I was going on ahead to arrange rooms at an inn," said Kita, "but I heard that a wicked old fox lived here, so I thought I would wait for you so that we could go on together."

Now Yaji got the idea that the fox had changed itself into Kita to deceive him. "Don't talk nonsense," he said boldly. "That's not the reason at all."

"What are you talking about?" asked Kita. "I brought some rice cakes, as I thought we might get hungry. Have some?"

"Hold your tongue," said Yaji. "Do you think I'm going to eat that filth?"

"Ha-ha-ha!" laughed Kita. "Don't you know me?"

"Know you, indeed!" replied Yaji. "You're just like Kita, just his shape, you devil." He struck Kita with his stick and made him howl.

"Ow! Ow! That hurts," yelled Kita. "What are you doing?"

"What am I doing? I'm going to beat you to death." Catching Kita off his guard, Yaji then knocked him down and began to jump on him.

"Oh, oh, oh!" roared Kita.

---

1. Said to be effective in warding off foxes.

A scenic view, with the Kabuto Mountains of Goyu in the distance (*right*) and the main street of Akasaka in the foreground, in present-day Aichi Prefecture. The distance between Goyu and Akasaka was among the shortest between major stops on the Eastern Seaboard Highway, and the two places became acclaimed amusement centers. Text: "Goyu Kabutoyama: Behind my head, the mist shrouds Kabutoyama like the neck plates dangling from my helmet," by Tatsunami Shizumaru of Suifu. "The Sleeve Port of Akasaka: Mist on the sleeves of Goddess Saohime look like the lavender patterns of spring," by Hon'ya Yasune of Oku Aizu. From the 1805 edition. (From SNKBZ 81, *Tōkaidōchū hizakurige*, by permission of Shōgakukan)

"Well, if it hurts," said Yaji, "why don't you change into your proper form?"

"What are you feeling my behind for?" roared Kita.

"Put out your tail," replied Yaji. "If you don't, this is what I'll do." He seized Kita's hands and, twisting them behind his back, tied them with a towel. Kita was so surprised that he let himself be tied up.

"Now," said Yaji, "get up and walk." He pushed Kita along until they came to Akasaka. As it was late, there were no innkeepers in the road to greet the travelers and no girls waiting at the doors of the inns. Yaji wandered about in the hope that he would meet the inn servant that was to be sent to meet him.

"Yaji," pleaded Kita, "do let me loose. Think how bad it would look if anyone saw me."

"Shut up, you beast," said Yaji. "I wonder where the inn is?"

"How could anybody take a room for us at an inn if I'm here?" asked Kita.

"Are you still talking, you beast?" said Yaji.

Just then they met an inn servant. "Are you gentlemen stopping at this stage?" he inquired.

"Have you come to meet us?" asked Yaji.

"Yes," said the man.

"There," said Yaji. "What do you think of that, you cheat?" Here he gave Kita a whack with his stick.

"Ow!" yelled Kita. "What are you doing?"

"Are there any others with you?" inquired the man, looking surprised.

"No, no," said Yaji. "I'm alone."

"Oh, then it's a mistake," said the servant. "I understand that I am to meet a party of ten."

He went off hurriedly. Then an innkeeper called to them from the front of his inn. "Won't you stop at my house tonight, gentlemen?" he asked, as he came running out and caught hold of them.

"No, no," said Yaji. "My companion went on ahead, and he must be here somewhere."

"That's me," said Kita.

"What an obstinate brute you are," scolded Yaji. "Put out your tail. Wait a bit. There's a dog. Here, doggie, doggie, get him, get him. Aha, the dog doesn't seem to mind. Perhaps he isn't a fox after all. Are you really Kita?"

"Of course I am," said Kita. "I call it a cruel joke you've had with me."

"Ha-ha-ha!" laughed Yaji. "Then we'll stop at your place after all," he added, turning to the innkeeper. Feeling sorry for Kita, he then untied him.

"Please come in," said the landlord. "Here, bring some hot water. Is the room ready?"

"What a time I've had," groaned Kita as he washed his feet.

The maid took their baggage and ushered them into a room.

"I'm very sorry, Kita," said Yaji. "I really took you for a fox."

"You made a fool of me, all right," growled Kita. "I'm pretty sore."

"Ha-ha-ha!" laughed Yaji. "But I don't know; he may be a fox after all. Somehow I've got kind of a strange feeling. Here, landlord, landlord." He started bawling for the landlord and clapping his hands.

"Did you call, sir?" asked the landlord.

"Look here, there's something strange about this," said Yaji. "Where am I?"

"At Akasaka, sir," replied the landlord.

"Ha-ha-ha!" laughed Kita. "What's the matter with you, Yaji?"

"Are you still trying to bewitch me?" said Yaji, beginning to wet his eyebrows again. "Landlord, isn't this a graveyard?"

"Eh?" said the landlord. "What did you say, sir?"

"Ho-ho-ho!" laughed Kita. "How funny you are."

Just then the maid came in from the kitchen. "Would you like to take a bath, sirs?" she inquired.

"There, Yaji," said Kita. "You go and take a bath. It'll calm you down."

"I suppose you think you'll lead me into some dirty water, you beast," replied Yaji. "You can't catch me that way."

"No, no," said the landlord. "The bath is filled with pure springwater and is quite clean, sir. Please try it."

The landlord went off to the kitchen, and the maid brought in some tea. "If you feel lonely," she said, "I'll call some courtesans."

"Fool!" said Yaji. "Do you think you're going to catch me embracing a stone image?"

"Ha-ha-ha!" laughed the girl. "What strange things you say!"

"Well, I'll go first then," said Kita. He went off to the bathroom, and while he was gone, the landlord came in again.

"I've got something to tell you, sir," he said. "I'm having a little celebration in my house tonight, and it would please me if you would join us in a bottle of wine." As he spoke, a dish of savories and a bottle of saké were brought in from the kitchen.

"Oh, please don't go to any trouble for us," said Yaji. "What's the occasion?"

"Well," said the landlord. "The truth is that my young nephew is getting married tonight. We're just going to hold the marriage ceremony, so I'm afraid it'll be a bit noisy."

He went off busily to the kitchen just as Kita came back from the bath. "What's that he said?" asked Kita.

"There's a marriage ceremony here tonight," said Yaji. "I'm getting more bewitched every minute. I'm not going to any of your springwater baths."

"Try and control yourself, and don't be so nervous," said Kita.

"No, no," said Yaji. "You won't catch me off my guard. For all I know, this food they've brought in may be dirt, although it looks so nice."

"Yes," said Kita. "I wouldn't touch it if I were you. Just watch me while I eat. I won't be angry. Excuse me for not standing on ceremony." He helped himself to the saké and gulped it down.

"It makes me feel quite bad to see you," said Yaji, with a look of disgust on his face.

"Don't be so nervous," said Kita. "Try a cup."

"No, no," said Yaji. "I know it's some filth—horse's piss or something. Let's smell it. It smells all right. I can't stand this; I must have some." He poured himself a cup and drank it down.

"Yes, it's saké all right," he said, smacking his lips. "What have they got to eat? I don't like the look of those eggs. I'll try a prawn. Yes, it's a prawn all right," he added after he had bitten into it. Thus he began to eat and drink.

Meanwhile there were sounds of preparations from the kitchen, where there was great bustle and confusion. It appeared that the wedding feast was already beginning. Now they could hear the sound of chanting:

> Still are the waves on the four seas;
> The world is at peace. The soft winds blow,

Not rustling the branches. In such an age
Blessed are the pines that meet to grow old together.[2]

"Yan-ya!" cried Kita joining in the chant.

"What a noise!" said Yaji.

"They can be as noisy as they like, as far as I'm concerned," said Kita. "Aren't you going to let go of that wine cup? Just hand it to me, would you? If you think it's horse dung or piss, I'll take the risk and drink it all myself. Ha-ha-ha!"

"I really thought I was bewitched," said Yaji, "but now I know I wasn't. What a time I've had!"

"It doesn't compare with my being tied up and beaten," said Kita.

Just then the supper was brought in, and as the door opened, they could hear the sound of another chant:

Through ages unchanging, from generation to generation,
Like pine tree and plum, may they flourish together;
Like two tender seedlings may they grow both together,
Until old age shall find them happily joined. Rejoice! Rejoice!
He has taken a bride from the best in the world.

This was followed by the clapping of hands and the sound of talking and laughing. Soon the maid came in and asked whether she should lay out the beds.

"You might as well," said Yaji.

"Is the marriage ceremony over?" asked Kita. "I suppose the bride is very beautiful."

"Yes," said the maid. "The bridegroom's a handsome fellow, and the bride's very beautiful too. Unfortunately, they have to sleep in the next room, where everybody will be able to hear their love talk."

"What a nuisance!" said Yaji.

"Awful!" said Kita.

"Have a good rest," said the maid.

She went off, leaving them to get into bed, and soon they heard the sound of the door being opened in the next room. Apparently the bride and bridegroom were going to bed. Then they heard whispers and other movements, from which they judged it was not the first time that the couple had tasted the delights of love. The sounds kept Yaji and Kita from going to sleep.

"This is awful," said Yaji.

"We've come to the wrong inn again," said Kita. "They don't mind us. How loving she is, the little beast."

---

2. From the celebratory nō play *Takasago*.

"They've stopped talking," said Yaji. "Now's the time." He crawled softly out of bed and listened to what they were doing. Then he stood up and peeped through the cracks in the sliding door. Kita also crawled out of bed.

"I say, Yaji," he whispered. "Is the bride beautiful? Just let me have a peep."

"Don't make a noise," said Yaji. "It's the critical moment."

"Eh?" said Kita. "Just let me look. Move away a little."

But Yaji was peeping through the crack like a man in a dream, and what with Kita shoving him and his own obstinacy, they managed between them to push the sliding door out of its grooves, and it fell suddenly forward into the next room with Yaji and Kita on top of it. This startled the newly married couple.

"Oh, oh!" shouted the bridegroom. "What's that? The door's fallen out of its grooves." Jumping up, he overturned the lamp and plunged the room into darkness. Yaji had already fled back into his own room and jumped into bed, but Kita was not quite so quick and got caught by the bridegroom.

"Excuse me," said Kita. "I was going out to do something and mistook the door of my room. Really the maid is very careless, putting the lamp in the middle of the floor. I'm sorry you tripped over it. But I really must go if you'd just let go of me."

"Such outrageous conduct!" said the bridegroom. "Everything's covered with oil. Here, San, San, get up."

The maid came out of the kitchen with a lamp and put things to rights, and Kita, looking exceedingly foolish, put the door back into its grooves and went very dejectedly to bed. Then as the night deepened, all was still in the inn except for the snores of the travelers.

The False Ikku (from the second part of book 4)

Thus joking and laughing, they went on until they reached Ueno, where they were accosted by a man in a cloak, who was accompanied by an apprentice.

"Excuse me, gentlemen," he said. "Are you from Edo?"

"Yes," said Yaji.

"I've been following you since Shiroko," said the man, "listening to your poems, and although I am only an amateur in such matters, I must say I was quite impressed."

"Oh, that's nothing," said Yaji. "I made them all up on the spur of the moment."

"Really," said the stranger. "I'm surprised. The other day I had a visit from Shunman Shōsadō and others from Edo."

"Did you really?" said Yaji. "Aha!"

"May I ask under what name you write?" continued the stranger.

"Oh, I'm Jippensha Ikku," said Yaji.

"Indeed," said the man. "That's a very celebrated name. Are you really Jippensha Ikku? I'm very glad to meet you. My name is Kabocha Gomajiru.[3] Are you going to Ise on this journey?"

"Yes," said Yaji. "I came on this journey especially to write *Travels on the Eastern Seaboard.*"[4]

"Dear me," said Gomajiru. "That's a strange way of writing a book. I suppose your friends in Nagoya, Yoshida, and Okazaki will come and meet you."

"Well, you see," said Yaji, "as I have to call at every place on the Eastern Seaboard and as the entertainments offered to me naturally delay my journey, I thought it would be a bother to them to have to wait for me. That's the reason why I'm traveling in common clothes just like an ordinary person, so that I can take my time and do just as I please."

"That must be very enjoyable," said Gomajiru. "My house is at Kumotsu. I would be very pleased if you paid me a visit."

"Thank you very much," said Yaji.

"Truly you would be a most welcome guest," continued Gomajiru. "I would like to introduce you to some people in the neighborhood. In any case I would like to accompany you for the next stage. How extremely fortunate it was that I met you just when I did. But here is Ogawa, which is famous for its cakes. Shall we stop?"

"No, no," said Yaji. "I've had enough cakes. Let's go straight on."

Proceeding on their way, they soon reached Tsu. This is the place where the road from Kyoto meets the road to Yamada, and as a consequence the streets are very lively with people from the capital, all dressed in the same kind of clothes, riding on horses, and singing:

Oh come, and I will show you the famous sights, the temples high,
The hill of Otowa and where Kiyomizu and Gion tell of days gone by.
In a pearly haze lie the cherry blossoms in full flower;
So dark one would think it was the evening hour.

"Look, Kita," said Yaji. "How beautiful the girls all look."

"They're Kyoto people," said Gomajiru. "But although they all look so grand, they don't waste their money."

Just then one of the men stopped Gomajiru and asked him for a light.

"Take it from here," said Gomajiru, and he held out the pipe that he was smoking. The Kyoto man put his pipe to it and puffed.

"Can't you get it?" asked Gomajiru. Still the stranger went on puffing without saying a word.

---

3. Kabocha Gomajiru literally means "Pumpkin Sesame-Sauce."

4. Since *Travels on the Eastern Seaboard* was written over a number of years in several volumes, it certainly was possible that the real Ikku was doing research for the next installment.

"What's this?" said Gomajiru. "Why, you haven't got any tobacco in your pipe. I've heard of this before. You pretend you want a light, and all the time you go on smoking other people's tobacco. That's enough, that's enough. There," he added, turning to Yaji. "That's how stingy Kyoto people are. Ha-ha-ha! Would you oblige me with another pinch of your tobacco?"

"Well, I don't know about Kyoto people being stingy," said Yaji, "but I notice you're very fond of smoking my tobacco."

"I didn't bring my tobacco pouch with me," said Gomajiru.

"Did you forget it when you came out?" asked Yaji.

"No, no, I didn't forget it," said Gomajiru. "The fact is I haven't got a pouch, the reason being that I'm such an inveterate smoker that I found I was spending too much money on tobacco. So I gave up carrying a pouch and carry only a pipe."

"Is that so you can smoke other people's tobacco?" asked Yaji.

"Yes, certainly," said Gomajiru.

"So while you call Kyoto people stingy, you're stingy yourself."

"Ha-ha-ha!" laughed Gomajiru. "That's so, that's so. But hadn't we better walk a little faster, as it's getting late."

Quickening their pace, they soon arrived at Tsukimoto, from where, they learned, there is a road to Karasu-no-miya. Then they came to Kumotsu, where Gomajiru led them to his house. This appeared to be an inn, although there were no other guests there just then. They were shown into a back room and treated with great respect, evidently because Yaji had told a lie about his name. Both he and Kita thought it all very amusing, and after taking a bath, they relaxed. Then Gomajiru came in.

"You must be very tired," he said. "Please make yourselves comfortable. Unfortunately, there is no fish today, so I won't be able to give you much of a feast, but since the *konnyaku* here is very good, I thought you would like to try that."

"Please don't go to any trouble for us," said Yaji. "But landlord, I'd like to introduce my friend."

"Oh really," said the landlord. "To whom have I the pleasure of speaking?"

"I'm Jippensha's best pupil," said Kita, "by name, Ippensha Nanryo. This is my only excuse for troubling you."

"Not at all, not at all," said Gomajiru. "Please make yourself at home."

The maid announced that the meal was ready.

"Then you'd better have it at once," said Gomajiru. "Please take your time." He hurried off to the kitchen, and the maid brought in a tray and put it before Yaji.

"Not bad, is it?" said Yaji looking at the tray.

"Fine girl," said Kita. "But now that you're a poet, you've got to be good."

Then a small girl of eleven or twelve brought in another tray and put it before Kita, and they both took up their chopsticks to eat. On both their trays was a black thing, about the size of a bean cake, put on a flat saucer beside the *konnyaku,* which was heaped up in a bowl, and some bean paste on a small plate.

"Whatever's this?" said Yaji in a low voice to Kita, "this round thing on the saucer?"

"I'm sure I don't know," said Kita. He felt it with his chopsticks, but it was so hard that he couldn't make a dent in it. Examining it more closely, he saw that it was a stone.

"It's a stone," he said.

"What, a stone?" said Yaji. "Here, waitress, what's this?"

"It's a stone, sir," said the maid.

"Dear me," said Kita. "Just give me a little more soup."

He gave his soup bowl to the girl and waited until she had gone out.

"What a swindle!" said Yaji. "How can we eat stones?"

"Wait a bit," said Kita. "There must be some way of eating it since they've served it to us. He said he'd give us some of the things this place is noted for, and I suppose this must be one of them."

"I never heard of such a thing," said Yaji.

"Wait a bit," said Kita. "You know they call dumplings stones in Edo. Perhaps it's a dumpling."

"Aha!" said Yaji. "That's it, that's it. It can't be a real stone."

He poked it with his chopsticks, but still it appeared to be a real stone. Then he struck it with the bowl of his pipe, and it sounded like a stone.

"It's a stone all right," he said. "I suppose it would make him angry if we asked him how we're supposed to eat it, but it's very strange."

Then Gomajiru came in.

"Really I'm ashamed of the poor fare I have to offer you," he said, "but please eat heartily. I'm afraid the stones have got cold. Let me change them for some hot ones."

At this the two travelers became more and more puzzled as to how the stones were to be eaten, but still they didn't like to ask for fear of offending the landlord.

"Don't trouble, don't trouble," said Yaji, trying to look as if he had been eating the stone. "One stone will be enough, although they're very nice. In Edo, you know, they serve gravel pickled in hot pepper sauce or with boiled beans, and we also give stones to troublesome mothers-in-law as a kind of medicine. They're my favorite food. Why, when I was living in Fuchū, we used to have stones stewed like turtles. Really, when I had eaten four or five my stomach used to get so heavy that I couldn't stand up. I had to be tied to a stick and carried along like a suitcase when I wanted to go anywhere. Your stones are especially delicious, but I'm afraid of eating too many for fear I should inconvenience you."

"What's that?" said Gomajiru. "Have you been eating the stones?"

"What of it?" said Yaji.

"It's incredible," said Gomajiru. "Why, to eat stones you would have to have terribly strong teeth. Besides, you'd burn yourself."

"Why?" asked Yaji.

"Those stones are red hot," replied Gomajiru. "They're to put the *konnyaku* on so as to take out the water and improve the flavor. That is why they're hot. They aren't to eat."

"Aha! I see, I see," said Yaji. "Now I understand."

"You shall see for yourselves," said Gomajiru. He ordered the maid to change the stones for hot ones. Then Yaji and Kita put the *konnyaku* on the stones as he had told them, which made the *konnyaku* hiss, and then they ate it with the bean sauce and found it exceptionally light and well flavored. They were greatly impressed.

"I never saw such a strange way of cooking before," said Yaji. "The stones are all so much alike."

"I have a store of them," said Gomajiru. "Shall I show you?" He went into the kitchen and brought in a box like that for soup bowls.

"Look," he said. "I have enough here for twenty guests." Sure enough there were the stones inside, and written on the box was "*Konnyaku* stones for twenty people."

By this time all the poets in the neighborhood had begun to assemble at the door. "Excuse us," they cried.

"Dear me!" said Gomajiru. "Is that you, Master Baldhead? Please all come this way."

"Are you Jippensha Ikku?" said the first to enter. "This is the first time I have had the honor of meeting you. I am Awfully Funnyman. The gentleman next to me is Master Gaptooth, then comes Master Snottyface, and the one farthest away is Master Scratchy. Please give us all the honor of your acquaintance."

"By the way, Master," said Gomajiru, "if it is not too much trouble, would you be so kind as to write one of your poems on a fan or a scroll?" He brought out a fan and a scroll as he said this.

Yaji was greatly perplexed as to what he should do. Should he boldly carry out his joke? But then he had no poems of his own, and he couldn't think of one on the spur of the moment. He decided that he would write a poem by somebody else, and he wrote one.

"Thank you, thank you," said Gomajiru. "The poem reads:

> Where can I hear the cuckoo sing?
> Far from the wineshop's roistering;
> Far from the cookshop's guzzling throng,
> There can you hear the cuckoo's song.

"Dear me!" said Gomajiru. "I seem to have heard that poem before." Then he read another:

Would you know of lovers' sorrow?
Ring the dawn bell once again;
For it brings the fatal morrow
Tells them they must part in pain.

"But isn't this poem by Senshuan?" asked Gomajiru.

"What are you talking about?" said Yaji. "That's one of my best poems. It's a very well known poem in Edo. Everyone knows it."

"Yes, but when I was up in Edo last year," said Gomajiru, "I saw Sandara and Shakuyakutei Ushi and others, and I brought back that very poem and pasted it on the screen behind you. It is in the poet's own handwriting."

Yaji turned round and saw on the screen the very poem that he had written.

"My master's very careless," put in Kita, "and can't tell the difference between his own poems and those of others. Look here, Yaji—I mean Master—write one of the poems you made up on the road."

Yaji, although he was rather flustered, put on his usual bold face and commenced to write another poem, one of those he had made up on the road.

Meanwhile Kita, who had nothing to do, fixed his eyes on a screen.

"Aha!" he said. "That's a picture of Koikawa Harumachi. What's that phrase [san] written above it?"

"That's a poem [shi]," said Gomajiru.

"And that poem [shi] above the god of good luck," asked Kita, "who did that?"

A maid brings out a new heated stone for Yaji, who sits at his low dining table and scratches his head in embarrassment. Poem: "A sedge hat hanging from the eves of an inn, waiting for the late ones—early evening at the inn of Kumotsu," by Sankōsha Yoneya of Toro, Sanshū (Mikawa Province). From the 1806 edition. (From SNKBZ 81, *Tōkai dōchū hizakurige*, by permission of Shōgakukan)

"No, that's a religious maxim [go] written by the priest Takuan," said Gomajiru.

"What a chap this is," thought Kita. "When I say it's *san* [three] he says it's *shi* [four], and when I say it's *shi* [four] he says it's *go* [five]. Whatever I say, he always goes one more. I'll catch him yet."

"I say," he said aloud, after he had looked round, "that written on top of that hanging scroll—I suppose that's *roku* [six]."

"I don't know whether it's six or what it is," said Gomajiru. "It was taken as a pledge of seven [*shichi*]."

Just then the maidservant came in. "A letter has come from Master Hige-tsuru," she said.

"Dear me!" said Gomajiru. "I wonder what it is about." He opened it and read it aloud: "This is to inform you that Jippensha Ikku has just arrived at my house from Edo and has brought letters of introduction from his friends in Nagoya. I hasten to inform you at once of the news and shall later take the liberty of accompanying him to your house. This in the meantime."

"What can be the meaning of this?" said Gomajiru. "I can't understand it at all. You hear what my friend says, master. It seems that this man is taking your name. Luckily he will soon be here, and you will be able to confront him. Don't you think we should have some fun with him?"

"I never heard of such impudence," said Yaji. "But still I don't think I'd care to meet him."

"Why not?" asked Gomajiru.

"Well, just a minute ago," said Yaji, "I felt a touch of my old complaint, the colic. If it weren't for that, I'd like to show him up. It's a great nuisance."

This unexpected coincidence made Yaji feel very miserable, and his behavior increased the suspicions of the landlord and his guests that he was trying to deceive them. They now began to press him with questions.

"Look here, Master," said Master Funnyman, "this is a very strange thing that's happened. Even if you don't feel well, I think you certainly ought to meet the false Jippensha."

"Don't ask me, don't ask me," said Yaji.

"By the way, Master," said Master Snottyface, "where is your house in Edo?"

"Let's see," said Yaji. "Where is it? Is it in Toba or Fushimi or Yodotake?"

"Oh yes," said Master Scratchy, "you cross the ferry at Yamazaki and ask for Master Yoichibei. Get out. Ha-ha-ha!"

"But I see you have written on your hat Yajirobei, Hachō-bōri, Kanda, Edo," said Gomajiru. "Who is this Yajirobei?"

"Aha!" said Yaji. "Where have I heard that name before? Oh yes, of course. My real name is Yajirobei."

"Oh, you're one of the Yajirobeis that go round begging with the dolls, I suppose," said Gomajiru.

"That's it, that's it," said Yaji.

"Well, Master Yajirobei," said Funnyman, "shall I bring the false Ikku?"

"No, no," said Yaji. "No, no. I'm just going."

"Why, what time do you think it is?" said Gomajiru. "It's ten o'clock."

"Maybe, maybe," said Yaji. "It's my colic. If I sit like this it gets worse and worse. When I go out in the cool night air and walk a bit, it soon gets better."

"So you're going to start now," said Gomajiru. "Well, I'm agreeable. At any rate you can't stop here—taking other persons' names like that and deceiving everybody. Get out."

"How have I been deceiving you?" asked Yaji.

"How have you deceived us? Didn't the real Jippensha bring letters from his friends in Nagoya?" said Gomajiru. "There's no getting around that."

"I thought they were cheats from the first," said another. "Get out before we throw you out."

"Throw us out?" said Yaji. "Don't be ridiculous."

"Look here, Yaji," said Kita. "Let's not have a fight. We're in the wrong. Let's go somewhere else and stop, even at a cheap lodging house. We're very sorry if we've done anything wrong."

Kita thus went on repeating apologies to the landlord, who was half angry and half amused.

While they were getting ready to start, all the people in the house came to see them off and jeered and laughed and clapped their hands. Yaji, with a very angry face and a dignified air, walked out followed by Kita.

It was now past ten, and everybody had gone to bed. Yaji and Kita walked on, but they could not see any inn, or anybody in the street to ask. The only things that were awake were the dogs under the eaves of the houses, and they only barked at them.

"These curs!" said Yaji. "I'll show them," and he picked up a stone and threw it at the dogs. This only made them more angry, and they ran after the travelers, barking furiously.

"Don't take any notice of them," said Kita. "Even the dogs despise us. What are you making those strange signs for?"

"When you're attacked by dogs," said Yaji, "if you make the character for tiger in the air and show it to them, they'll run away. They don't seem to run away here, though. Perhaps the dogs in this town can't read. Here, shoo, shoo!"

Somehow they managed to get rid of the dogs and then went on. Very soon they unexpectedly came to the end of the town.

[*Tōkaidōchū hizakurige*, NKBZ 49: 75–76, 221–226, 285–292, adapted from *Shank's Mare*, a translation by Thomas Satchell]

SHIKITEI SANBA

Shikitei Sanba (1776–1822) was born and raised in Edo, the third son of a wood-block cutter in Asakasa. He worked in a bookstore as a youth and was adopted as the son-in-law of the owner but eventually ran his own business in Nihon-bashi. Sanba became familiar with popular literature at an early age and pub-lished his first kibyōshi at the age of eighteen, in 1794. Sanba also wrote shar-ebon, and in the aftermath of the Kansei Reforms (1787–1793), when the sharebon genre fell into disfavor, he turned to gōkan (extended illustrated books) and kokkeibon (books of humor).

Sanba's kokkeibon were inspired by Jippensha Ikku's best-selling *Travels on the Eastern Seaboard* and by the realistic, detailed description and dialogue of Santō Kyōden's sharebon. In 1809, Sanba published *Floating-World Bathhouse* (*Ukiyoburo*), his first major kokkeibon, which consisted of two volumes, "Women's Bath" and "Men's Bath." In the same year, for financial security, Sanba established a pharmacy, which became quite profitable. Then, in 1810, in response to popular demand, he wrote a sequel, which became the second half of *Floating-World Bathhouse*. In 1813, he published the first volume of *Floating-World Barber* (*Ukiyodoko*), another kokkeibon in the same socially oriented vein as his earlier work. Even though Sanba used the realistic dialogue and format of the sharebon (supplying *furigana*, or *kana*, for all the Chinese graphs and compounds), he deliberately parted from the sharebon in not de-scribing the licensed quarters in either *Floating-World Bathhouse* or *Floating-World Barber*. Although he continued to write in other genres, he is best re-membered for these two kokkeibon. Together with Jippensha Ikku, Sanba, who died at the age of forty-six, became one of the two leading writers of the kok-keibon genre, thus achieving success as both a merchant and a writer.

FLOATING-WORLD BATHHOUSE (*UKIYOBURO,* 1809)

In the preface to *Floating-World Bathhouse*, Sanba notes that he got the idea for his book from listening to Sanshōtei Karaku (1777–1833), a noted performer of rakugo (the art of comic storytelling), describe a public bathhouse scene. In the Tenmei era (1781–1789), urban commoners began to meet in small halls to hear professional storytellers relate humorous stories that were drawn from their own everyday lives and that were not intended for moralistic or educational purposes. This kind of oral storytelling, which included military, religious, and other genres, achieved its greatest popularity in the Bunka-Bunsei era (1804–1829). In 1815, Edo alone had seventy-five storytelling halls. The humorous stories performed there—a tradition that can be traced back as far as the kana-zōshi collections of such humorous tales as *Today's Tales of Yesterday* (*Kinō wa kyō no monogatari,* ca. 1620)—were recorded and published as books (*hana-shibon,* literally, talk books), which became the foundation for the kokkeibon. In many respects, *Floating-World Bathhouse* can be considered a kind of written *rakugo,* in which the storyteller evokes in slightly exaggerated form the gestures and speech of different social types. The reader of *Floating-World Bathhouse* is transported to another world mainly through the dialogue, which creates a sense of intimacy, as if the reader were overhearing a conversation.

One of the features of *Floating-World Bathhouse* and *Floating-World Barbershop* was that they focused on places where people commonly gathered, such as the public bath (*sentō*) and the barbershop. These places differed from the theater in that people from every walk of life came together there to engage in everyday conversation. Sanba subtly exaggerated this dialogue to allow the reader to realize the humor it often contained. He also created a sense of intimacy, which allowed the audience to become the butt of the humor itself. In contrast to *Travels on the Eastern Seaboard*, which moves from one place to another, the setting of *Floating-World Bathhouse* and *Floating-World Barbershop* does not change, although it moves in time, from morning through evening or through the different seasons. There is no narrative or plot. Instead, Sanba presents a constantly rotating array of characters from different sexes, social classes, age groups, occupations, and birthplaces and goes to great lengths to depict minute differences in speech, behavior, and thought. In the first volume, "Men's Bath," Sanba describes an apoplectic man, a father with children, a doctor, a blind man, a Gidayū chanter, and others, with the humor deriving primarily from small incidents and the characters' actions (such as the blind man being teased and having his bucket stolen), similar to the situational comedy found in *Travels on the Eastern Seaboard*. But in the second volume, "Women's Bath," the approach changes significantly. Instead of concentrating on physical behavior, Sanba engages in a social critique, humorously revealing the weaknesses and contradictions of contemporary social types. His humor is also evident in the tongue-in-cheek manner in which he stresses the didactic function of baths in *Floating-World Bathhouse*.

In the Edo period, except for those of the upper-rank samurai or extremely wealthy merchant families, houses did not have baths; almost all people used public bathhouses. Even in those mansions with baths, the maids and servants usually had to go to a public bathhouse after work. In the Bunka era (1804–1818), Edo alone had more than six hundred public bathhouses. When they first appeared in the middle of the sixteenth century, the same baths were used by both men and women, but gradually more and more urban bathhouses constructed separate facilities for men and women, as is the case in *Floating-World Bathhouse*.

The Larger Meaning

Public baths are the shortest route there is to moral and spiritual enlightenment. Careful reflection shows this. It is a truth of Heaven, Earth, and all nature that everyone, wise or foolish, righteous or evil, rich or poor, high or low, goes naked into the bath. Shakyamuni Buddha and Confucius, Osan the maid and Gonsuke the hired man, all return to the shapes with which they were born. They take off the things they've desired and cherished and leave them as far behind as the mythical Western Sea to which beggars send impure spirits in their chants. Bathers enter the water freely, without a trace of desire. Both master and servant stand naked after they've washed away the grime of greed and worldly wants and rinsed themselves with fresh water—and you can't tell which is which! From the time people are washed at birth until their corpses are rinsed a final time, in the bath they're all equal and reveal their true forms. And just as the red-faced drunk of the night before sobers up fast in steaming bathwater the next morning, public baths show each of us that our death is separated from our life by no more than the thickness of the paper on the bathhouse sliding door.

Once they begin to soak, even old people who dislike Buddhism forget themselves and intone Amida Buddha's holy name. Naked, the lustiest young bathers feel bashful and hold towels over their private parts. Fierce warriors, washing themselves off before bathing, endure the hot water splashed by others onto their heads and resign themselves to the ways of crowded places. Even irritable toughs with spirits and gods tattooed on their arms say "Pardon please" as they stoop and go through the low door leading from the washing room to the bathing room. Where else but in a public bath can such virtues be found?

People have individual minds and private feelings, but in a public bath there are no individual minds, and nothing is private. If a bather secretly farts, the water makes sounds, and a moment later bubbles rise to the surface. When we were young, we all heard about how little Yajirō farted off in the bushes and then lied about it, but a member of the public bath community who thinks about acting secretly also has to consider what the impartial water is thinking and will feel ashamed.

All five Confucian paths of virtuous conduct are continually followed at public baths. Hot water warms the body, loosens dirt, cures diseases, relieves fatigue, and otherwise shows the path of benevolence. When the people washing off before entering the bath ask, "Is there a pail no one's using?" or when they refrain from using pails placed on reserve by others, or when they finish quickly and give their pails and places to others who are waiting, then they are following the path of righteousness. The path of courtesy is evident whenever a new bather entering the tub says "Pardon me, I'm a rough country person," or, in winter, says "Forgive my cold body," or simply "Excuse me," or when people say "Leaving already?" to someone getting out, or when those leaving say "Pardon me for going first" or "Please take your time" to those who remain. The path of wisdom is followed whenever bathers use small bags of rice bran, powder, soft pumice stone, or vegetable sponges to scrub off dirt or when they use a pair of sharp stones to trim their pubic hairs. And the path of mutual trust can be seen whenever someone says "It's too hot" and someone else pours in cold water, or when another person says, "It's cooling down" and someone else pours in hot water, or when people pour water on each other's backs.

Celebrated by all, the public bath is an imposing place. Inside, bathers come to see that water follows the contours of different containers—from the square cups at the cold-water basin to the round buckets for pouring clean hot water after the bath—and they come to understand that the mind flows into different shapes with different human relationships. Thus they realize they must con-

In the men's bath, customers first took off their clogs and sandals near the entrance (*lower-right corner*), placed them in the cubbyholes, and then changed their clothes near the entrance. They cleaned themselves in the large washing area (*left*) before entering the bath. The low entrance to the bathing room is visible at the upper left. Refreshments were served in the upstairs parlor. The paper notices near the ceiling stated the rules of the bathhouse. From the 1809 edition.

stantly scrub their minds and keep them as clean as the floorboards in the bathhouse washing room.

The sign at the bathhouse entrance tells bathers "Full payment each time, even twice a day" and helps them realize that life is short and comes only once. On the walls are advertisements for products you can buy. Cure-All Skin Cream reminds people that learning techniques are less important than sincerity and devotion. There's no cure for a fool, but Thousand-League Ointment will give spring to your legs, and Peerless Chapped-Skin Cream stings and urges you on like your best friend. Toothache Powder, pronounced while you hold it with your tongue against a bad tooth, sounds like Loyalty-and-Filial-Piety Powder, and Spirit-Calming Pills for dizziness will put bathers' elderly parents at ease.

"Look Out for Fire!" The sign reminds bathers of the Buddhist caution against flames of desire, while "Early Closings in Case of Strong Winds" warns that bursts of wild spending will destroy a household in no time at all. The human body is a precious combination of five elements borrowed from the universe, and if you ignore the sign that says "Keep Your Valuables with You" and lose yourself in drinking or sensuality, well, then "We Disclaim Any Responsibility." You bring such harm on yourself alone: "Absolutely No Articles Kept at Front Desk." As the bathhouse clearly states, there must be "No Fights or Arguments," for pride or for profit. And "Never Raise Your Voice" from joy, anger, sadness, or pleasure. If you ignore these rules, you'll make the mistake of your life and miss the bath altogether. When you finally get to the tub late at night, they'll tell you, "Sorry, we've just pulled the plug." By then you're old, and regret is as helpful as biting your washcloth.

People's minds jump between good and bad the way lice travel between clothes in the bathhouse dressing room, leaping from Gonbei's work pants to Hachibei's soft silk robe, from a country-born maid's underskirt to the fine clothes of a wealthy young merchant wife. Just as yesterday's underwear was taken off and tossed on the bathhouse floor and today's set of nice clothes is arranged on a rented shelf, wealth and position depend on the will of heaven. But good or bad, straight or crooked—these are a matter of choice. If you truly comprehend what this means, you'll listen to others' opinions and let even smarting words seep into you like hot morning bath water.

Finally, and above all, be especially vigilant your whole life about the following points: Just as you place your clothes inside your rented private wardrobe and close the latch, be careful to act only in ways proper to your social class, and always keep your mind safely locked. As for your six emotions, keep them separate and clearly marked, never putting on the wrong one at the wrong time. This will be strictly adhered to by all parties, declares the General Manager of the Association of Shinto, Confucian, and Buddhist Baths as he presses down on the agreement with his big official seal.[5]

Women's Bath

AFTERWORD TO THE PREFACE

Both bitter pills and sweet syrup are useful in raising children. Likewise, the Three Histories and Five Classics[6] are bitter medicine, while fictions and popular histories are sweet syrup. There are numerous books, such as the *Greater Learning for Women* or the *Women's Imagawa*,[7] that preach to women about how they should act, but they taste bitter, and women rarely savor them in their minds.

The present fiction about the women's bath is a frivolous, humorous work. If readers use their minds while they read it, however, they will easily taste its

---

5. Suggests the Association of Bathhouses, membership in which was a requirement for bathhouse operation. The wording parodies an actual document.

6. The Three Histories (Sanshi) are the three noted histories of ancient China: *Record of History* (Shiki), *History of Early Han* (Kanjo), and *History of Later Han* (Gokanjo). The Five Classics (Gokyō) are the five Confucian classics: *Book of Changes, Book of History, Book of Songs, Book of Rites,* and *Spring and Autumn Annals.* These two sets of texts represent orthodox learning.

7. *Onna daigaku* (1716–1736) and *Onna imagawa* (1700) were two widely read textbooks in kana that gave instructions to women on conduct and etiquette.

sweetness and, without even trying, realize the difference between good and bad or between straight and crooked conduct. As the saying goes, if watching others is a remedy for mending your own ways, then this book will no doubt provide a shortcut to true moral learning. Even young people who ignore criticism are willing to consider teachings if they're humorously presented, and they remember them naturally. If you pay close attention and savor this trifling, playful book, you will discover small-seeming gains that are actually very large.

EARLY MORNING AND MORNING

The streets are filled with the chants of beggars, each one pretending to have phrases more effective than the next. "This all-purpose purification really works," cries one beggar dressed as a Shintō priest. "Filth won't gather, and you'll never get dirty. The gleaming shrine fences are really clean and pure!" Nearby a Buddhist beggar sings, "Heaven and all the seas return to the marvelous dharma. Praise Saint Nichiren, great founder, great bodhisattva. Praise the miraculous Lotus Sutra." And then the voice of another Buddhist beggar from the rival Pure Land sect: "May Amida's great benevolence spread virtue to all living creatures. Praise Amida Buddha, praise Amida Buddha." But inside the public bathhouse, women of every religion and sect gather together without distinction.

"Ho, it's really cold this morning!" says a shivering woman as she slides open the paper-covered door at the bathhouse entrance and comes inside. Eighteen or nineteen, obviously unmarried, she looks like a singer and shamisen player with an impressive professional title. The design on her robe has pictures of three objects that, pronounced together, mean "I've heard good news." The crest of her favorite kabuki actor over one arm, she carries a bathrobe dyed with a fashionable new picture-pun design.[8]

"Otai! Why, good morning," the woman says. "You're really up early. Last night the party I was performing at must have made quite a racket."

"Yeah. No kidding," says Otai, a young woman who looks like she works at a restaurant. She's finished her bath and is about to leave. "How did you keep from falling asleep, Osami? That lush never gives up until the middle of the night, does he?"

"Yeah, well," says Osami. "Still, he's gentle and well behaved. And he buys lots of drinks and knows how to hold his liquor. He doesn't lose control the way that Kasubei does. Later, he said he wanted to see me home. He slipped while we were turning into the alleyway, and he had a hard time walking for a while, but he did finally see me to my front gate."

"How sweet of him," Otai says. "He sounds like a well-meaning old guy. Not

---

8. The old rebus, consisting of a hatchet, koto (zither), and chrysanthemum, was used by Onoe Kikugorō III, a famous actor of both women's and men's roles.

Outside the women's bath (*top*), a sign reads "Women's Bath." In the entrance to the bath (*right*), where customers paid the attendant, was the changing area with the cubbyholes for clothes. The rinsing area appears to the left. From the 1810 edition.

like that clumsy Donsuke who tries to do hand games, or Inroku, with all his gibes and nasty jokes. I can't stand either of them."

"Really," says Osami. "Or that Shukō. His noisy country songs are a bit much, aren't they?"

"And then he always ends up snoring. Hey, it looks like you've had your hair done!"

"Yeah," says Osami. "Okushi came over to my place and did my hair before she went anywhere else. Who does your hair?"

"Osuji."

"It's nice. Very nice."

"Really?" says Otai. "This morning a new person did it. It's not the same. It feels funny."

"When someone you're not used to does your hair, it never feels right. No matter how good she is. Turn your head. Let me have a look at it. Well, well. It looks perfect to me."

"Isn't the back part tied up a little too high?"

"Not at all. It's perfect."

"Well," says Otai, "Enjoy yourself." She gets out her wooden clogs, puts them on, and walks toward the door.

"Drop by sometime," Osami urges, going inside. "My manager's staying at my place right now, and she loves visitors. Bye!"

(*Later that morning, in the washing room, outside the bathing room*) Near one end of the cold-water rinsing basin, two old women talk through the gaps in their teeth as they scrub themselves with small, porous bags of rice bran.

"Are you finished, too, Auntie?" asks Saru.

"Why Auntie," says Tori, "you're certainly here early! When did you come in?"

They both look about the same age, and they're not related, but each politely calls the other "Auntie." You can't tell who's actually older.

"You know," says Saru, "we've really been out of touch."

"Really," says Tori. "You haven't been sick, have you?"

"You guessed it," says Saru. "All these problems I have, it must be my age. My eyes are bad, and my legs and hips are stiff. It's just ridiculous. The only one who's happy is my daughter-in-law."

"What are you talking about?" says Tori. "You're not old enough to be talking that way."

"How old do you think I am?"

"Since you ask," says Tori, "I guess you must be older than I am."

"Older?" says Saru. "I must be twelve years older. I'm at that age."

"Eighty?" asks Tori, grinning.

"Now, now, Auntie," says Saru. "What a heartless thing to say. I'm seventy."

"Well, actually," says Tori. "until the end of last year I was fifty-nine. This year I turned sixty. And you know what? People are going around spreading rumors that next year I'm going to be celebrating my sixty-first!"

"Auntie, you say the silliest things," says Saru. "Really. You always look so young and spry."

"If only I were!" says Tori. "In children's songs aunts can still get married up in the Shinano Mountains when they're forty-nine. But at sixty, well, this aunt's ready to kick the bucket. Ha-ha-ha-ha."

"Don't you worry," says Saru. "You're always so cheerful about things. You've got white hair, but your mind's still young."

"Well," says Tori, "feeling down all the time doesn't get a person anywhere, does it? I just don't let the little things bother me. You know what? I'd really like to dye my hair and look nice again. Know any eligible men? You be my go-between, and I'll get myself a new husband. They say even demons are good-looking when they're in their prime. And sixty's my prime. I'm in the prime of being an old woman. Ah-ha-ha-ha-ha-ha."

"Ha-ha-ha-ha-ha. You're going to have a good life in the next world, I can tell."

"Please," says Tori. "Who cares three cups of rice about the next world? While we're alive, we ought to do what we want and not worry about what happens afterward. We never know what's going to happen in this world, anyway. How can we know what happens after we're dead? I'll tell you what heaven is. It's drinking a cup of saké before going to bed and getting a good sleep."

"That's what I mean," says Saru. "You can drink, so you can feel good. I just don't have any way of getting myself in a good mood. From morning till night I'm always getting angry or depressed. I've forgotten what it feels like to be cheerful. I'm really fed up. Tired. Tired of living in this world."

"Mercy, Auntie," says Tori. "Don't get tired of the world yet. You don't know what you'll get yourself into after you die. At least you know a few things about this world. Stick around to be a hundred."

"What a dreadful thought! Really, that would be awful. I'm just waiting for Amida Buddha to find time to come for my soul."

"Really, that's such claptrap. All those people saying they want to die and not one of them really wanting to! When Amida Buddha comes for you, you'll be begging him to wait just a little bit longer."

"No," Saru answers. "I really won't."

"Once you see what it's like to be dead," says Tori, "you'll want to be alive again. But it'll be too late then. Like praising your son's first wife and complaining about his second after you've forced the first one to leave. In summer, people say they like winter. In winter, they say they like summer. Humans, why, all they ever say is what they feel like at the moment! That's what I'm always telling my son and his wife. 'Listen,' I say to them, 'you'd better feed me a lot of nice things while I'm still alive. If you don't, you're going to regret it when I'm gone. Who cares how many offerings of bean paste soup and potatoes you put in front of the altar to my soul? When people die and become buddhas, who knows if they eat or not? You talk about filial piety. Well, be real good to your mother right now. Give me in-season bonito and saké anytime. That's a lot more virtuous than putting fried tofu on the altar on my memorial day when you're supposed to offer it fresh. Or piling up rice cakes and crackers on the Feast of Souls Day.' Isn't that the way it is, Auntie?

"That son of mine, he takes good care of me and works real hard at his job. Every day on his way back from his business he buys me food wrapped up in dried bamboo skin. 'Eat this, Mama,' he says. And he also gives me a little bottle of saké to drink before I sleep." Tears of happiness appear in Tori's eyes. "You know," she says, "he used to be a bit of a playboy. But these days, he seems to have learned how hard it is to get along, and what do you know, he does just what he should now, and he's a real hard worker. Losing his father early like that made him a lot more responsible. But I had to bring him up all by myself. That wasn't easy, believe me. Even now I don't know how I did it. Still, if that boy'd been born bad, he'd have spent all his time carousing and he'd still be a good-for-nothing. But he has a good head on his shoulders, and he learns fast. Things have been going well for him. And for me, too.

"That wife of his, you know, she does everything. And she looks after me day and night. You don't know what a comfort that is. That go-between Ashiemu who lives on Dragonshit Alley suddenly mentioned her one day, and after that things just seemed to happen by themselves. They've been married three years already. I'd really love to have a grandchild, but those two aren't, well, they're not making much progress yet. It's something that just comes if it comes. If you don't have the stuff, then you just don't.'"

"You're right," says Saru. "There's not a thing you can do. Over at my house, we've had two babies in two years. My body won't move the way I want it to anymore, so I can't baby-sit for one, much less two! I'd almost like to give one of them to you. I really would. My son's first wife left us three children when she went, and his second wife's already had two. And now, can you believe it, she's going to have another one! It wouldn't be so bad if my son would at least work hard, but he loves saké, you know. Sometimes he'll lie around for four or five days on end and won't even touch the little crafts that he sells. And his wife, well, the other people in the tenement, they call her a lazy tart, you know. She doesn't care a thing for her babies and spends all her time doing up her hair. She gives her husband rags to wear, and she never washes a single diaper, though they're all covered with piss and shit. And after meals, well, she just puts the trays on the kitchen door and then ties her latest baby onto her back and takes a nice stroll. There's no one at all to clean up after meals, so I always end up doing it. That woman uses the fact she has to care for a lot of kids as an excuse to get out of doing any housework at all. Whoever asked her to have so many babies, anyway? They had them because they enjoyed making them, didn't they? And they actually act proud of it!

"I'm so amazed I can't even get amazed any more. You should see the mess they're in. That woman will show up at your place sooner or later. Take a look for yourself. She goes around in real fancy hairdos, and she wears her only fine robe every single day. It's almost worn out. If she'd take care of her clothes properly, she could wear neat, clean things instead of that grubby robe. But it's not just that she doesn't wash her things. She doesn't know the first thing about sewing. She used to be a geisha; so I thought, well, she probably can't have children, and if I teach her little by little, she can learn how to sew. But can she sew? All she can do is make babies nobody asked her for! She can hardly even make a dust cloth! If you put a needle in her hand, well, she stabs away like she's sewing the edges of a straw floor mat. But she's a smooth talker, and she goes on and on. And she talks back, telling you ten things for every thing you tell her. She really knows how to get me upset.

"And listen to this. That woman grates dried mackerel flakes onto the food right on the serving trays. And she knocks the ashes out of her pipe onto the doorsill. She's not even ashamed to lie down and sleep in broad daylight whenever she feels like it. She just puts her head down on whatever dirty thing she finds nearby. And she spits into the charcoal brazier, and then she rolls the gobs around in the ashes with the tongs. She makes all these little round things, you know, and I have to come over and dig them out and throw them away. So then she goes and spits into the oven just to annoy me. And at night she stays up until who knows when and then gets up late, and she has lots of people over in the middle of the night talking hour after hour about completely boring theater things. And at last she says she's cold and wants some hot buckwheat noodle soup. She bolts down the noodles as if she were starving, drops onto the floor, and immediately starts snoring. My son talks in his sleep, and whenever he stops, she starts grinding her teeth. It's so noisy I can't go to sleep. And whenever there's a lull, one of the kids wakes up and starts bawling, and pretty soon the rest are, too. But even with all those kids screaming, I still can't get her up. She doesn't wake up at all. So that's the situation I'm in, Auntie. All night! It's so noisy I just don't know what to do."

"Where's your problem?" says Tori. "It sounds all right to me. You have no way of knowing what's going on between a husband and wife. Just let them be. You're meddling too much."

"Well, actually I don't really care," says Saru. "If they were getting along well, though, they wouldn't be fighting, would they? Every time they stop yelling at the children, you know, they start fighting with each other. Eventually my son tells his wife to get out of the house, but he doesn't really mean it, and she knows it. That woman looks down on him, and she sulks, too. Later she'll take out her anger on the poor standing lamp, saying it's too dim. It's perfectly bright with one wick, you know, but she yells at it for not giving her enough light and for everything else she can think of. Then she puts in extra wicks and burns them all just out of spite. Do you have any idea how expensive lamp oil is? She acts like it was free. And my son, being how he is, he gets furious and breaks any pots or bowls he can find. He does it every time. We must be the best customers the crockery mender and the lacquerware dealer have. And those two aren't satisfied even with that. Really, I never have a moment's peace."

"Well," says Tori, "you're not doing yourself any good worrying about things like that. You get too involved, and you keep yourself from having any peace. Stop praying for happiness in the next life and just think of this world as paradise. If you get all hot and angry like a Buddhist demon, your family's going to get all upset, too, and before you know it, you'll be suffering in hell. I try my best not to interfere, but even so, my daughter-in-law usually says I talk too much. Listen, fifty years ago you were twenty, too, weren't you? Try to remember what it was like fifty years ago. Imagine you're the new wife and she's the mother-in-law, and listen to everything she says. Things will be a lot easier that way. If a mother-in-law really wants to have a peaceful family, she'll find a nice bride for her son and then stay out of the way. Once a mother-in-law opens her mouth, there's no end to it. You talk so much about how you want to die—just tell yourself you're already dead and none of this will bother you."

"So," says Saru. "Even you're taking my daughter-in-law's side."

"Gracious," answers Tori, "who's taking sides? You know, you're complaining. I'm a woman, but I think like a man, and I don't like griping and grumbling. If you have time to complain, you're better off spending your time raising money for the temple. You feel bad because you stay at home all the time. Get outside and walk around, beat your gong, and raise some money. Call out, 'Each day I chant Amida Buddha's name!' and then your partner will shout, 'Yes, that's what I do!' You'll feel so much better you'll be amazed. We never know how much longer we're going to live, after all. Forget all those complaints. They're not doing you any good at all. Oh, it's really getting cold in here! Are you finished? Please drop over during the Ten Nights ceremonies to the Amida,[9] will you? Somebody from the temple's going to stop by your house anyway for a donation."

"Yeah," says Saru. "Of course I'm planning to go, no matter what."

"Planning to go? Hurry up and get out of that house of yours," says Tori, going off into the bathing room.

[*Ukiyoburo*, NKBT 63: 47–49, 111, 112–130, translated by Chris Drake]

---

9. Buddhist service held by the Pure Land (Jōdo) sect for ten nights, from the fifth to the fourteenth day of the Tenth Month.

Chapter 19

NINJŌBON: SENTIMENTAL FICTION

Ninjōbon (literally, books of pathos or emotion) first appeared in the Bunsei era (1818–1830), reached their peak in the Tenpō era (1830–1844), but lasted into the Meiji period (1868–1911). By the 1820s, readers had grown tired of the satire, cynicism, and mannerisms of the *sharebon* (books of wit and fashion), which were gradually supplanted by popular novels called *sewa-yomihon* (literally, books about contemporary life), and *shinnai* ballads, specializing in sad tales and suicides, both which were highly sentimental in content. The sewa-yomihon were appropriately also termed *nakibon* (books to cry by), a genre that Tamenaga Shunsui (1790–1834), the first writer of ninjōbon, unsuccessfully experimented with before 1830. Then, in 1833 in *Spring-Color Plum Calendar* (*Shunshoku umegoyomi*), he found the right combination, successfully fitting earlier sharebon elements into a nakibon framework to create a narrative about contemporary life that emphasized *ninjō*, or emotion, sentiment, and romantic love, particularly from a woman's perspective.

Unlike the earlier sharebon, which confined their focus to the licensed quarters, the ninjōbon described various additional aspects of contemporary life in the city of Edo. Structurally, the sharebon are essentially short stories or sketches, with little plot. By contrast, the ninjōbon, which combines elements of the sentimental novel and the romance, depends on plot and dramatic conflict and developed an extended, serial structure. Typically, a man and a woman fall in love; are thwarted by various negative forces, particularly an unwanted rival, that result in a sorrowful situation; but in the end the man and the woman (or women) manage to overcome these obstacles. The principal narrative feature of both the sharebon and the ninjōbon is dialogue, but in *Plum Calendar*, Shunsui also adds his own commentary, which is set apart from the dialogue and is directly addressed to the reader.

Sharebon such as *The Playboy Dialect* (*Yūshi hōgen*) described and made fun of the half-*tsū* and boor (*yabo*) in order to establish an implicit contrast with the true tsū, or sophisticate of the pleasure quarter. Ninjōbon, however, depict the love and suffering of the professional woman, who, though realizing that the man may be incompetent, falls in love and cannot leave him. The leading male characters like Tanjirō in *Plum Calendar* are in fact fallen protagonists who have to be saved by a woman. If the sharebon focuses on the male sophisticate's knowledge of and behavior in the licensed quarters and scoffs at displays of tender emotion, the ninjōbon celebrates the depths of human emotions—joy, suffering, and intense jealousy, particularly as a consequence of falling in love—and is unabashedly sentimental.

In the sharebon, the attitude toward the characters tends to be critical and detached, with the humor coming from their ironic dissection, although later sharebon such as Santō Kyōden's *Forty-Eight Techniques for Success with Courtesans* (*Keiseikai shijū hatte*) sometimes describe genuine emotions. In the ninjōbon, however, particularly those by Tamenaga Shunsui, the attitude toward the central characters is one of sympathy, understanding, and even indulgence. This applies especially to courtesans, geisha musicians, and their female colleagues, for the reader realizes that however glamorous their external or professional life may seem, they probably are suffering silently. (In fact, some critics have pointed to the close resemblance between Motoori Norinaga's late-eighteenth-century notion of *mono no aware*, a kind of poetics of sympathy and pathos, and the presentation of ninjō found in Tamenga Shunsui's ninjōbon.)

Most important, in contrast to the sharebon, which were intended mainly for male readers, the ninjōbon were written primarily for female readers, both those who worked at various professions and young women living at home. The emergence of a genre aimed specifically at women was an epochal moment in the history of early modern fiction, which until the early nineteenth century had been written largely for men or a mixed audience. Generally living in a smaller social and physical space than men and having less formal education, women closely identified with the world of the theater and of romantic love. Women of means had always read fiction, but in the eighteenth century, women became avid readers of jōruri texts as well as kusa-zōshi picture books and kibyōshi. The *gōkan* genre, also popular at the time of the ninjōbon, was addressed to female readers as well and used a combination of pictures and printed text to draw its readers into a kabuki-like world. Unlike yomihon and gōkan, which looked to the past in the form of historical drama (*jidaimono*) and generally emphasized duty (*giri*), the ninjōbon focused on love affairs in the contemporary world.

The appeal to different genders is apparent in the titles. Unlike the titles of sharebon, which were concise, Chinese, and masculine in style, using Sino-Japanese *on*-readings like *Yūshi hōgen* (*The Playboy Dialect*), the titles of ninjōbon like *Shunshoku umegoyomi* (*Spring-Color Plum Calendar*) were softer, longer, and more elegant, frequently using terms such as *shunshoku* (spring colors / spring love) and romantic Japanese words like *hana* (plum or cherry blossoms), *tsuki* (moon), *kasumi* (mist), and *koi* (love). Indeed, Tamenaga Shunsui was aided by Kiyomoto Nobutsuga, a female writer and master of Kiyomoto-style singing and shamisen playing, who wrote the first drafts of the women's dialogue for *Spring-Color Plum Calendar* and for Shunsui's other ninjōbon, as well as helping him with passages dealing with songs and music.

TAMENAGA SHUNSUI

Not much is known about the first half of Tamenaga Shunsui's (1790–1843) life, except that he was born in Edo. Toward the end of the Bunka era (1804–1818), he managed a bookstore called the Seirindō, which operated as a lending library. It was at this time that he became interested in writing fiction and worked with such writers as Ryūtei Tanehiko (1783–1842) and Shikitei Sanba (1776–1822). In 1819 Shunsui published his first work of fiction, which was followed by a series of novels, most of which were written with friends and students. He also became a professional storyteller who performed *sewamono*, or stories of contemporary life, rather than *rakugo*, or comic stories. In 1829 a fire destroyed his bookstore/publishing house, and thereafter he devoted himself solely to writing, taking the pen name Tamenaga Shunsui, by which he became widely known. In 1832 he published the first two installments of *Spring-Color Plum Calendar*, which became the model for later ninjōbon. In response to his publisher's demand, Shunsui wrote *Spring-Color Southeast Garden* (*Shunshoku tatsumi no sono*), about Fukagawa, and other sequels to *Plum Calendar*, creating a distinctive "Tamenaga style."

Shunsui's indebtedness to Shikitei Sanba's kokkeibon is apparent in his interest in contemporary manners and realistic dialogue, an interest no doubt enforced by his experience as a professional storyteller. Shunsui's vivid descriptions of Edo commoner life and his narrative format had a large impact on Meiji literature, particularly the Kenyūsha (Society of Friends of the Inkpot) novelists. In 1842, during the repressive Tenpō Reforms (1830–1844), Shunsui was found guilty of writing pornography and was imprisoned for fifty days. He died a year later at the age of fifty-three.

SPRING-COLOR PLUM CALENDAR (*SHUNSHOKU UMEGOYOMI*, 1833)

The plot of *Spring-Color Plum Calendar* revolves around the efforts of four women—Yonehachi, Ochō, Oyoshi, and Konoito—to become independent, support themselves, and find happiness with the men whom they love. All four women are in difficult situations, and two, Ochō and Yonehachi, are in love with the same man, Tanjirō. The first half of the book focuses mainly on Ochō and Yonehachi, who are at first jealous of each other but come to trust each other by the end of the book. Ochō is the daughter of the managers, now dead, of the Karakotoya House in the licensed quarter in Kamakura, a code word for Yoshiwara in Edo. While Ochō is still in her early teens, her parents adopt a man named Tanjirō into the family and tell Ochō that he is her future husband and will help her run the Karakotoya. Before the action begins, Ochō's parents die, and the head clerk, Kihei, usurps Ochō's place as manager, claiming that she is too young, and tricks her fiancé, Tanjirō, into being adopted by another family with large debts to Kihei, debts for which Tanjirō becomes responsible. The impoverished Tanjirō goes into hiding and is discovered by Yonehachi, a geisha musician at the Karakotoya, who works to help him.

Kihei tries to seduce Ochō and force her to marry him so that he will have a legal right to the house. But Ochō loves Tanjirō and adamantly refuses, so Kihei harasses her. Konoito, the highest-ranking courtesan in the house, is a motherly figure who does her best to help Ochō. She begins by helping Ochō escape from the Karakotoya to an area south of Edo where she can begin a new life and find Tanjirō. During her escape, Ochō is saved from a difficult situation by Oyoshi, a female gang leader who works as a hairdresser just east of Edo. The fearless Oyoshi adopts Ochō as her sister and encourages her to support herself by becoming a Gidayū performer of jōruri librettos.

Meanwhile, Konoito strives with almost sisterly affection to help Yonehachi, who also loves Tanjirō. First she concocts a scheme to allow Yonehachi to break her contract and become an independent geisha performer outside the quarter, and then she has her special customer and lover, Tōbei, test Yonehachi in order to find out whether her love for Tanjirō is true. Finally convinced that it is, Tōbei and Konoito do their best in the second half of the book to help both Ochō and Yonehachi. Through Tōbei's efforts, Konoito and Oyoshi discover that they are sisters, and both are united with their lovers. Tōbei also discovers that Tanjirō is actually the son of the head of a prominent warrior clan, and Tanjirō, after a brief fling with a geisha named Adakichi, becomes the new clan leader, marries Ochō, and makes Yonehachi his official mistress. Ochō and Yonehachi are reconciled and become good friends, sharing Tanjirō equally.

Tanjirō is an erotic male figure, the disinherited young man often found in *wagoto* (soft-style) kabuki, the young man from a good family without money or power for whom women fall head over heels. In Yanagawa Shigenobu's original illustrations for *Plum Calendar*, Tanjirō has the face of Onoe Kikugorō III, the popular actor noted for his erotic young male roles. In the late Edo period, the name Tanjirō, along with those of Genji and Narihira, became synonymous with the erotic man. Like the sensuous protagonist of *The Tale of Genji*, Tanjirō has a number of affairs with different women, but he is a kind of Genji in reverse, since the loving care, support, and protection are provided not by the man Tanjirō but by the dynamic women who love him. The focus of the narrative is clearly on Ochō and Yonehachi, working women who support Tanjirō, as well as their sisterly comrades Konoito and Oyoshi. All are capable of deep feeling but remain tough, bravely facing every adversity.

As critics have noted, Shunsui was interested in the woman of *iki* (having spirit), which meant being passionate without being promiscuous, tough without being callous, practical without being vulgar, polished without being affected, and a good loser without being weak. A woman with spirit could flirt with a man—a necessary tool of survival in the Fukugawa world of entertainment—but she also had a strong will, professional consciousness, pride, compassion, and an inner drive that distinguished her from other, inexperienced, women. In a world in which women had to compete for men, they had to be soft and polished to attract a man's attention but tough and determined enough to overcome rivals and other difficulties. Since men generally could not be relied on, this kind of attitude—being both proud and accepting—was probably a useful psychological tool for survival and social harmony. Yonehachi, for example, is flirtatious and yet has immense compassion: she saves Tanjirō from his wretched circumstances and sympathizes with the plight of other women. She also is able to tolerate difficult circumstances and eventually share Tanjirō with Ochō and other women. There are also "tough" women like Oyoshi, who, in a kind of gender reversal, rescues Ochō from male thugs and also represents an equally important form of female iki.

Most important, Shunsui recognized the difficult fate of women in nineteenth-century Japan: their low social status, the dangers and difficulties of becoming self-supporting and independent, and the sacrifices that society forced them to make. At the same time, he seems to have understood the fantasies of young women of that time and gave them heroines with whom they could identify in terms of their accomplishments, their sensitivity, and their suffering. Shunsui's descriptions and the illustrations of the physical appearance of the women of iki in *Plum Calendar*—their clothes, hairstyles, and makeup—were so popular that women all over Japan tried to achieve the so-called iki look.

In an apparent effort to attract female readers, Shunsui deliberately tried in *Plum Calendar* to include as many love scenes as possible. They are presented not as the kinds of verbal and sexual encounters with courtesans found in the male-centered sharebon but as romantic episodes of faithful love and mutual affection. Each of *Plum Calendar*'s four volumes has at least one climactic love scene. Perhaps in an attempt to protect himself from Confucian condemnation and charges of pornography, Shunsui has his narrator, who directly addresses the reader, argue that compassion and fidelity are the essence of ninjō. In addition, Shunsui often defends the faults of his female characters, pointing out redeeming qualities that the reader may have missed. Indeed, an interesting aspect of *Spring-Color Plum Calendar* is the tension between the author's comments and the world of the characters. As long as his love scenes could be interpreted as portrayals of fidelity and devotion, young female readers did not need to feel guilty reading about forbidden topics, and Shunsui could avoid criticism. In the end, however, his worst fears were realized when he was arrested for violating public morals.

CHARACTERS

TANJIRŌ, the adopted son of the former managers of the Karakotoya House; having been wrongfully disinherited and adopted by another family, he has been placed in debt and has gone into hiding; loved by Yonehachi and Ochō

YONEHACHI, a geisha musician at the Karakotoya; later lives as a freelance geisha in Futagawa (Fukagawa), on the outskirts of Edo, to be closer to Tanjirō, whom she loves and supports; eventually becomes Tanjirō's official mistress and reconciles with Ochō

OCHŌ, the only daughter of the former managers of the Karakotoya; Tanjirō's fiancée; harassed by Kihei and befriended by Oyoshi; becomes a gidayū chanter under the professional name of Take Chōkichi; eventually marries Tanjirō

KONOITO, a resourceful high-ranking courtesan at the Karakotoya who constantly helps Ochō and Yonehachi

OYOSHI, a tough "boss woman" who works as a women's hairdresser, rescues Ochō from an attack; Konoito's lost sister

KIHEI, the male head clerk who takes over the Karakotoya after the death of the managers and drives out Tanjirō

TŌBEI, a special customer and lover of Konoito who shows great sympathy and aids all four women characters

Book 1

CHAPTER 1

Torn paper umbrella
thrown away in a field—
now protecting daffodils.

The dilapidated tenement was nothing to look at, and it provided little more protection from the early winter frost than a torn oil-paper umbrella. There were many gaps in the spindle-tree hedge surrounding it, and beyond that spread rice fields sparsely covered with rice. But for those who lived together in the tenement, it was a warm, intimate place they would never exchange for anywhere else. It was one of five or six such houses in this nearly deserted part of Nakanogō,[1] and the people living in it trusted one another and said what they truly felt.

A new tenant had moved into the old house recently, and he was still trying to get used to his cramped living quarters, which lacked everything he was used to. He looked to be eighteen or nineteen and seemed quite gentle. He'd obvi-

---

1. A thinly settled area east of the Sumida River in southern Koume.

Yonehachi, wearing a hood, appears at the entrance to Tanjirō's tenement. The illustration is by Yanagawa Shigenobu I (d. 1832). From the 1832 edition.

ously had some bad luck and was now extremely poor. And in the last few days he'd fallen sick and was lying in bed, thin and haggard. Something had surely happened to him to bring him to this wretched condition. This morning a strong, bitterly cold wind was blowing, chilling his whole body, and his face was full of bitterness and anger as he lay alone, thinking.

"Excuse me!" a woman was saying at the door. "May I come in?"

"Yeah, who is it?"

"It *is* your voice. It's you, isn't it, Tanjirō!" the woman cried, pulling hard at the badly fitted, paper-covered sliding door. It bumped and banged in the frame, but she finally she got it open and rushed inside. She was a stylishly dressed woman wearing a thick silk outer robe with wide gray vertical stripes and a sash of purple striped and figured silk with black satin on the inside. Her inner robe was dark blue and green figured crepe, as was the long kerchief she held in her hand. Her hair was tied in a high bun in back in the style of a professional geisha musician, but her sidelocks were coming loose. She had on no makeup. Either she was proud of her natural face or she'd just gotten up. But her face was beautiful just as it was, and she looked even more attractive when she smiled. Yet there was sadness in her eyes.

Tanjirō, amazed, stared at her. "Yonehachi!" he said. "Why are you here? And how in the world did you find me when I'm trying to hide from everybody? Well, come in, come in. Are you real, or am I just dreaming?" He raised himself and sat up.

"I was afraid you wouldn't recognize me any more," Yonehachi said. "I was so worried my heart was really pounding. And I walked as fast as I could, the whole way. Ah, it hurts. Let me have a minute to catch my breath!" She pounded her chest several times. "My throat's so dry it's practically stuck together," she added, sitting down next to Tanjirō. She examined his face closely. "Are you sick with something? You've really lost a lot of weight. Ah, look at that, you've got no color in your face at all. You're completely pale. How long have you been like this?"

"It's nothing. It started about fifteen or sixteen days ago. It's really not much of anything. I just can't shake this depressed feeling, that's all. But let's not talk about that. How in the world did you ever know I was here? You know, there are so many things I really want to hear about." A few tears came to his eyes. He truly seemed to be suffering.

"Well," Yonehachi said, "this morning when I left the house I was planning to make a pilgrimage to the Myōken bodhisattva near here at Hōshō-ji temple. But now . . . it's just amazing, isn't it! I had absolutely no idea you were living in a place like this. But the other day, you know, a girl came to live in the house for a while to try out as an apprentice musician. When I asked her her address, she said she lived east of the Sumida. Later, when we all were relaxing, she began talking about her home and her neighborhood, and one of the people she mentioned sounded exactly like you. So that night, when we were talking in bed before we fell asleep, I asked her some more about the man in the place where she lived. But the girl said he had a very stylish, attractive wife, so, well, I decided the girl must not be talking about you. I asked some more, though, and the girl said the man's wife looks older than you are, and she also said his wife doesn't stay home all the time. The more I heard, the more I felt like the man must be you. After that I was so worried I just couldn't stand it. So I talked to the girl and made her promise never to tell anyone I'd asked her all those questions. After that I could hardly wait for the fifteenth to come so I could go pray to Myōken early in the morning and go see everything for myself on my way back. So that's why I came way out here this morning. Recently I've been praying very, very hard to find you, but I never expected to learn where you were just like that! It's got to be Myōken. She must have helped me. I'm very happy to find you like this, but now, you know, now I'm also very worried. What's this about your having a wife? Where's she gone today?"

"What are you talking about? Don't be ridiculous. How could I possibly have a wife in this place? And who was the girl who told you that, anyway? Where does she live?"

"I think she said something about her parents being grocers. Well, but who cares, anyway? The important thing is, right now you, well, you hardly even remember me or what went on between us, do you? So you don't need to hide anything. Come on, who's the wife that people are talking about?"

"Please. How could I be hiding a wife when I'm this poor? Use your eyes and look around, will you? She's just a little girl. She doesn't know anything about me. Well, let's just leave it at that. So, how are things back in the quarter?"

"At the house? Everything's just terrible. That head clerk Kihei's really getting out of control. Ever since the old managers died, he's been strutting around trying to get everyone to call him 'Boss.' It was bad enough after the old man died and Kihei wanted us to treat him like the manager even while the old woman was still alive. Well, nobody thought he was the manager then, and they're not about to start thinking it now, either. So he tries to show he's boss by complaining all the time and giving people orders about one little thing after another. He's yelling at someone about something practically all the time. You know, ever since you went away to be readopted, I got real worried and started thinking about leaving and getting my contract changed to somewhere else. But Kihei's got a really twisted personality. I was sure he'd refuse to let me get out of my contract just so he could refuse me, so I've just been putting up with it all. But now I know where you are, and, well. . . . " As Yonehachi sat looking around the room, tears began falling onto her lap. "After seeing you like this, how could I possibly stay in that house any longer? I couldn't even imagine you were in a place like this. When I get back today, I'm going to tell the house I want to work somewhere else. I'll go outside the quarter completely, down to Futagawa.[2] It'll be hard at first, but after a while I'll be able to help you out a little so you won't have to live like this any more."

Tanjirō could see Yonehachi's heart was true and her love deep and unchanging. But he felt powerless do anything about the situation and was too depressed to reply.

"Listen," Yonehachi said. "Tell me about the new family you got yourself adopted into. How come it suddenly went completely bankrupt?"

"Yeah, it sure did. When I look back on it, I'm sure Kihei sent me right out for adoption before anybody could check things out. He's really tight with Matsubei, the head clerk at the family I was adopted into. They must have planned everything together. They both knew the family was about to declare bankruptcy, and that's why Kihei did everything so fast. I had no idea at all what was going on. But as soon as I became a member of my new family, I discovered it had huge debts. Well, by then I was already the legal family head. I was part of the family, so I wanted to do something to help out. So I took all the hundred gold coins I'd borrowed from Kihei as my adoption dowry and used them to start paying off some of the debts. But it was all a complete loss. I'll never be able to pay any of it back to Kihei. Ever. After that, Kihei refused to let me come back to the house. He wouldn't even let me near it, and he wouldn't let me contact you or anyone else there. It was all my own fault. I really messed everything up.

---

2. Shunsui uses Futagawa to suggest Fukagawa, an unlicensed pleasure quarter in southeast Edo.

"And then that clerk Matsubei told me they'd auctioned off all the family belongings to pay off its debts. But he also said there were a hundred gold coins left over that the creditors didn't know about. And he said he needed some cash right away and wanted to make a deal. He told me the family had lent five hundred gold coins to Lord Hatakeyama,[3] and he said he'd give me the loan document if I'd give him the hundred gold coins. I agreed, and he took seventy coins for himself and said he'd give the other thirty to some of his friends. Then he said he had to go to Kyoto and Osaka and just disappeared. I haven't seen him since. The second clerk, Kyūhachi, is very kind and honest. He went to see Lord Hatakeyama for me, and they told him they'd try their best to pay back the five hundred gold coins. But they also said they hadn't received any payment yet for a very famous tea canister called Moon at Dawn they'd recently left with Matsubei, who'd promised to find a customer for them. They were very puzzled, because they'd heard Lord Kajiwara had already bought the canister for fifteen hundred gold coins. They said they'd be glad to deduct the five hundred coins in the loan document, which was made out to Natsui Tanjirō— that's my new name—but they demanded I deliver the remaining thousand coins immediately.

"Kyūhachi could hardly believe it. After he got back to his house, we started planning how we could pay back the money. But we'd hardly started talking when some of the lord's officials showed up at his house. They said they'd been very busy recently, since the lord was getting ready to leave Edo and go back to his domain, and they hadn't realized that the Natsui house had declared bankruptcy. Since it had, they very strictly ordered Matsubei and the new Natsui family head—me—to appear without fail at the lord's mansion with the thousand coins we owed for selling the canister. When Kyūhachi heard that, he arranged for me to quickly disappear from sight for a while. I hear Matsubei never came back, and Kyūhachi's getting into worse and worse trouble himself. But he's not the only one who got himself into trouble. I feel pretty angry, too. Why should I get stuck with all those debts? Do I really deserve it?"

"Of course not. Just hearing about it makes me angry, too. And who's taking care of you while you're sick like this?"

"There's nobody here to take care of me. The other people in the tenement help out when they can. But mainly, well, Kyūhachi, the clerk I just mentioned, his wife has a younger sister who works as a hairdresser. She lives near here, so sometimes she drops in and does a few things."

"Oh really? And what about this woman?"

"What do you mean, what about this woman?"

---

3. To avoid censorship, Shunsui uses the name of a warrior clan prominent in the Kamakura period.

"You mean there's nothing special between you two? It makes me a little worried."

"Don't be silly. We don't make love or anything like that. Not at all. I'm really very lonely here like this, you know." Tears began to streak his face.

"Tanjirō, why do you say such sad things? Now that I know where you are, I'm going to do my best, no matter what happens, to see that you live a lot better than this. So get hold of yourself. And get well as soon as you can, understand? In a lonely place like this, alone at night, it must get pretty . . ." Yonehachi turned away and put her sleeve over her eyes. Tanjirō had changed so terribly in such a short time. Until recently he'd been the young manager of a small, prestigious house on the main street of Yoshiwara, even if the house hadn't been making that much money, and he'd been surrounded by gorgeous things in the latest style. Yet here he was now in an old, tiny room only three floor mats wide. Yonehachi could imagine how ashamed he must feel at being suddenly seen like this in such a pitiful place. She had many, many worries of her own, too, but she loved Tanjirō and wanted to comfort him, so she didn't mention any of them.

"Don't worry," Tanjirō said, wiping away his tears. "I'm hiding out from everyone, so it's natural that I'm poor and can't do what I want. I guess I was just meant to be poor."

"That's exactly why I don't want to leave here and go home."

"Hey, don't talk like that. Go on back and come and see me again, will you? It's pretty late already, so you'd better go now. All right?"

"There's nothing to worry about. I knew I might come back late today, so I took care of everything already. The top courtesan Konoito, she asked me to take a letter for her to Toku, and I brought it with me. I was planning to take it to him in Uramae[4] myself. But I can ask someone else to deliver it for me. It'll still get to him today. And I told everyone I was going to do a hundred prayers each to Kannon and the goddess Awashima at Asakusa Temple. Everybody knows that'll take a long time, so they aren't expecting me back right away. Hey, you don't have a single live coal in this place." Yonehachi got up, looked for the tinderbox, and finally started a fire. "Let me boil your medicine for you. Which pot should I use?"

"The one over there next to the charcoal brazier." Tanjirō got out a bag of ground herbs from near where he was lying. "Put in a little ginger, too. I think there's some right above that tray."

"Ah, yes. It's right here. My goodness, you don't mean this pot with the broken spout, do you?" Suddenly Yonehachi began laughing—until she remembered how poor Tanjirō was. Then she stopped, sad once again. "Where's your doctor?"

---

4. Oblique reference to Kuramae, an area along the west bank of the Sumida River near Asakusa, associated with rich merchant playboys.

"I don't have one. Ohama brought it."

"Ohama?"

"The younger sister of Kyūhachi's wife. I told you about her just now. You know, I think that girl who's trying out with you might have thought Ohama was my wife. That's all right, but if people find out where I am, I'm in big trouble."

"Don't worry. Nobody around here can possibly figure out who you are. Listen, do you have any food?"

"Yeah. Last night a middle-aged woman from the other end of the building came and cooked something for me, so I'm fine. But you must be hungry. There don't seem to be any places around here that deliver food, though. We're just too far from everything out here."

"I'm fine. As part of my prayer to find you, I vowed not to eat anything with salt in it before noon, and it's still pretty early. But I sure would like to cook something delicious for you. I'll put something or other together. And while I'm here, try to think of something you'd especially like." Then Yonehachi took a small packet out of her purse. "Well, buy some things you need with this. And get yourself some food that'll give you some strength, understand? This morning I was just going out to pray, and I didn't even know whether I'd meet you. So this is all I have right now. It's not much at all. But I'll get hold of some more and bring it the next time I come."

Tanjirō took the folded packet with a pained expression on his face. "Well, thanks very much. I'm sorry to put you out. Are you going now, Yonehachi?"

"Of course not. I don't need to be back yet. I told you, everybody thinks I'll be back late. Well, you know, Tanjirō, your hair looks really messy. Shall I comb it up a little and retie the topknot for you? I'm sure that would make you feel a little better."

"That's for sure," Tanjirō said. "If you think you can stay a little longer, please comb it for me. But do it gently."

"All right, well, all I have is my long hairpin comb, but it should work fine," Yonehachi said happily as she went around behind Tanjirō. "Oh ho, your hair's an incredible mess!" Like other women, Yonehachi was quickly overcome by her emotions, and as she remembered what she and Tanjirō had shared together in the past, she began to cry. Her tears were already cold by the time they fell on Tanjirō's neck, and he turned around.

"Yonehachi, why are you crying?"

"But . . ."

"But what?"

"How can you possibly, well, be like this now? There's nothing here at all." She clung to his shoulder and began to cry again.

Tanjirō looked around at Yonehachi, took her hand, and pulled her to him. "Forgive me," he said.

"For what? Why are you apologizing?"

"Because now I've made you sad, too."

Yonehachi leans against Tanjirō. Yonehachi's gold coin lies on the floor unwrapped.

"Really?" Yonehachi said. "Are you really worried about me?"

"I don't want you to feel sad like me," Tanjirō said. He put his arms around Yonehachi and pulled her to him. She lay naturally and without hesitation against his lap and looked into his eyes.

"I'm really happy now, you know," she said. "Let's."

"What do you mean 'Let's'?"

"I mean let's stay like this forever."

Tanjirō began to gaze deeply back at Yonehachi. He realized how attractive Yonehachi was and completely forgot about everything else. "What about right now?" he said, holding her close against him.

"Hey, that tickles!" Yonehachi said.

"Sorry."

As they lay down on the floor, they heard the distant booming of the 10:00 A.M. bell at the temple to Kannon in Asakusa.

In the second chapter, Yonehachi and Tanjirō converse again after their lovemaking. Yonehachi tries to determine whether Tanjirō loves her deeply, and he claims that he has never forgotten her. But she becomes jealous when he asks about Ochō, his fiancée and the daughter of the now-dead manager of the house in the quarter. As Yonehachi leaves, she begs Tanjirō to be faithful to her, although Tanjirō replies only vaguely. She is so distracted by the anxiety of leaving Tanjirō that she forgets her hood and must come back for it. Shunsui comments to his readers:

Ah, how completely foolish they look. But for the lovers themselves, it is a feeling that no one else could understand. Individual men and women have different feelings of love, yet all are equally true. Love can't be judged by common sense, as the saying goes, and through love one comes to learn great sympathy and sensitivity to others' feelings. Learning this will surely help soften the hearts of even us ordinary people who hold such distorted views about love.

Chapter 3 opens on the third day of the new year. Konoito, the leading courtesan of the Katakotoya House, is in her apartment on the second floor secretly conferring with Yonehachi. To help Yonehachi, Konoito has devised a plan that will allow her to escape from her contract and the quarter. Konoito asks Yonehachi to pretend that she is sleeping with Tōbei, Konoito's most intimate customer and lover. According to Konoito's plan, she will discover what is happening and severely criticize Yonehachi in front of everyone. Having broken one of the fundamental rules of the house, the manager will then be forced to release Yonehachi from her contract and send her away. Once Yonehachi leaves the quarter, she will be free to visit and help Tanjirō, now hiding on the outskirts of the city in Nakanogō. Then Ochō also confides in Konoito about her difficulties with Kihei, the new manager of the Karakotoya, who is harassing the young and orphaned Ochō in her own house. With Konoito's assistance, Ochō decides to flee the Karakotoya and the city— a journey that is described in the next chapter. The chapter ends with a disclaimer from the narrator-author:

This book seeks only to present the feelings of Yonehachi, Ochō, and the other characters and is not an exposé of what goes on in the licensed quarter. I myself do not even know very much about the houses of pleasure. This book deals with them only briefly and generally, so I ask readers not to judge this book as if it were a sharebon, a book of wit and fashion about the licensed quarter. Furthermore, as readers read about Ochō's anger at the suffering she must endure after losing her parents, I hope they will realize how important their own parents are and always listen to what they say. Ochō is hardly unique. Many children lose their parents early, and they are forced by strangers into very shameful situations and are abused even more badly than Ochō. Readers should realize how lucky they are if their parents remain alive until they become adults. It is a gift more precious than any treasure.

> While they lived
> I took them for granted
> and neglected them—
> now, gone forever,
> how dear they grow.[5]

---

5. Variation on a requiem waka poem for the dead Kiritsubo lady in "The Paulownia Court," the opening chapter of *The Tale of Genji*. The poem appears in Fujiwara Teika's *Okuiri* commentary on *Genji*.

CHAPTER 4

Four or five toughs stood around a small bamboo palanquin, which hung from a long carrying beam. The palanquin had been put down beside the road and its beam propped up in front and back on two sticks. "Hey, young lady," one tough was saying. "It's time to get out now. Hurry up!"

From inside the hanging straw mats that formed the sides of the palanquin came a young woman's voice. "All right," she said. "Thanks very much for bringing me such a long way. You must be completely worn out. I suppose this must be Kanazawa."[6]

"Well," one of the toughs said, "it's still two and a half miles to Kanazawa. But there's more money here than in Kanazawa.[7] You're so good looking, you know—the carriers and us, well, all our poles are propping up your palanquin beam.[8] We're so excited we've come all the way here without even stopping to rest."

"We're all good buddies," one of the carriers said, "and we're all real kind. Luckily there's an old deserted Buddhist temple right over there. The Temple of Mutual Bliss. There's no priest around any more, so we want you, young lady, to sit right up front, and we'll all sit next to you and pray to Amida Buddha in one big group. You won't mind it."

"Come on now," the tough said again, "you'd better get out." He threw up the flap on one side of the palanquin.

"All right then," the young woman said uneasily. "Is this a temple? You say you want me to lead a ceremony to Amida Buddha? In this deserted graveyard? As you can see, I'm not a Buddhist nun. Why do you want me to sit in front and lead the chanting?"

"You mean you don't know the chant?" said the tough. "My, my, you certainly are an unsophisticated young lady, aren't you. In this day and age it's hard to find anyone as naive and ignorant as you. We're the ones who are going to pray. You'll be our buddha, and we're going to call out your name again and again, one after the other, and go to paradise. Hurry up and get out." He pulled the young woman out of the palanquin.

"Hey," she said, sounding as if she were about to cry. "It's very dark out here. It's so dark it gives me the creeps. If you want to do a long group prayer, do it after you take me to my relatives in Kanazawa. You'll have all the time you want then."

"No matter how you look at it," one carrier told her, "there's not a single one of us here you'd ever consider sexy or want to sleep with."

---

6. In present-day Yokohama.

7. Kanazawa (literally, Gold Marsh) is money in name only. The men evidently plan to sell Ochō later as a prostitute or an indentured servant.

8. The carrying beam was placed on vertical poles while the carriers rested.

"You said it," one of the toughs said, "you said it. Anyway, let's hurry. We'd better make her cry now before someone comes by."

"If you're going to make her cry," a carrier said, "you'd better take her over to the main hall."

"Pick her up and carry her," someone else said.

Four or five men grabbed the trembling arms of young woman, whose whole body was now shaking. "Hey," she shouted. "Please let go of me! You may think I'm too conceited for my age, but I'm engaged, you know. I pray to the gods for my fiancé, and I fast and pray to Benten,[9] too. I never even hold hands with other men. To show Benten how serious I am, I vowed I'd never go near any man for three whole years. Absolutely never. Even if I meet up with my fiancé again before that, I won't stay with him until my vow is up. You men look like you want to force yourselves on me. Stop it, please! Let me go!"

"I feel sorry for you," one of the toughs said. "You really are in a bad situation. You couldn't be more than fourteen or fifteen. This must be your very first time. You know, you're making me even more excited."

"Damn right," said another. "Even the waitresses in the inns down on the highway won't give us anything. If we don't do it this way, no ripe young virgin . . ."

". . . this delicious is ever going to come our way again," said another. "Come on, haul her up to the main hall."

When the men tried to lift her up, she tensed her whole body. "Listen!" she said, her teeth chattering. "If any of you has any feelings, let me go. I'm begging you. My hands are together. I'm praying, can't you see? Help! Somebody! Somebody, please, come quick!" Tears ran down her face. Just then the clouds overhead broke, and bright moonlight streamed through, revealing a road stretching out through fields as far as she could see. There was no town anywhere in sight, and the deserted temple was now even more terrifying.

"Hey, young lady, if we were just here to pray, we could do the praying ourselves. There's no way in the world you're going to escape from here in the middle of all these fields. Just do what we say and let us sleep with you, and it'll all be over in no time at all."

"He's right, you know. You won't mind it at all."

The young woman pulled her sleeves away from the men and began dodging them in every direction. "Hey!" she yelled. "Don't touch me! I'll give you five big gold coins. A famous courtesan gave them to me. But I'll give them all to you. And my robe, too. It's a very nice one. She also gave that to me. Just let me keep this dappled crimson inner robe. I'll give you everything else. As long as you don't make me. . . . Hey, let go. Stop it! Please!"

---

9. Benten means Benzaiten, goddess of music, eloquence, intelligence, and wealth worshiped by Buddhists.

She ran this way and that, but the men caught and picked her up by the arms and legs and carried her toward the main hall of the temple, which was so rundown that moonlight fell through the roof in patches on the floor. The young woman screamed as the men forced her forward.

The young woman was Ochō, daughter of the former managers of the Karakotoya House. She ended up in this deserted place because of a plan conceived by Konoito, the leading courtesan in the house, who took care of Ochō after her parents died and acted as her older sister. When Ochō's parents died, the head clerk Kihei, her guardian, tried to make her feel obliged to him because he'd taken on the debts of the house and was acting as its new manager. Then he tried to seduce Ochō, and when she refused, he made life miserable for her. Konoito saw it was an impossible situation and decided to help Ochō escape from the house. She knew that Chūbei, who'd once worked as head clerk at the house, was now a merchant in Kanazawa and that her own family also lived there, so she wrote letters of introduction to both and gave them to Ochō. Then she went with Ochō to pray to Saint Nichiren's soul[10] in the southern outskirts of the city. On the way, Konoito secretly sent off Ochō in a palanquin for Kanazawa. But Konoito hadn't thought about the dangers of the road. She was very bright, but she was a courtesan who'd grown up inside the quarter and didn't realize how careful people had to be when they traveled outside. And Ochō was still too young and inexperienced to grasp the situation. Please consider this and do not judge them harshly.

The sounds of a far-off eight o'clock bell were already echoing through distant towns and fields, and the temple seemed even lonelier than before. As she was carried inside, Ochō was like a small bird in the claws of an eagle. The unfeeling men pulled off the broken doors of the temple hall and pushed Ochō down onto the floor inside.

"Hey, gents," said one thug. "Control yourselves! We've got to take turns. Let's draw lots."

Ochō felt as if she were being tortured in hell as the men stood there shouting and counting straws. Suddenly she realized that someone was behind her in the dark. Then a mouth was whispering in her ear. "Come this way," it said. It was a woman's voice. Ochō, shaking, moved slowly backward in the direction the person was pulling her. The toughs were too busy fighting over lots to notice. Then, with a loud shout, five or six men with sticks and poles rushed into the room and began beating the toughs.

"Kidnappers! Thieves!"

"Tie every one of them up!"

"Hey, don't let any get away!"

---

10. Nichiren's memorial day was the thirteenth day of the Tenth Month.

Thugs force Ochō into a room in a deserted temple while tissue paper scatters. A kyōka by Hakkyōsha Chō (*bottom left*) reads: "Their sleeves already scented with plum blossoms, yet they seek to break off the branch—until a wind drives them away."

The men shouted and ran here and there after the toughs, who were so depraved that each thought only of escaping by himself.

The woman who had pulled Ochō by the hand was dashing and brave, and everything about her showed style. She was in her twenties and wore no makeup, and in the moonlight her face was so beautiful it made Ochō shiver. The woman also wore a large hairpin in her hair, but it was a rough, sturdy wood one instead of the ornate tortoiseshell hairpins women usually wore. Her clothes were for traveling, but they all were very attractive.

"All right, boys," she called out. "Isn't it about time to let up? They've all escaped by now."

"Scum of Edo!" one of the men was shouting. "Morons! Get out while you can!"

"Don't you criminals know who you're dealing with?" another shouted.

"Hey! Clean out your ears and listen up," another called after them. "I'm Ryōkichi, honored and privileged to be a follower of Oyoshi, the boss woman of Koume.[11] The tattoo on my back's in the tried-and-true style of the dragon Kurikara!"

---

11. Literally, Small Plums. A thinly settled area east of the Sumida River (on the eastern outskirts of Edo) near Tanjirō's hiding place.

"Anybody who's anybody knows me already," shouted another man. "I was born and bred in Koume, and I'm black with soot from all the tile kilns. My parents prayed at the Narihira Temple there, and then I was born. So people call me Playboy Gonpachi.[12] My color's purple. My boss is Oyoshi of the Plums,[13] and I'm her right-hand man."

"Hey, hey, hey," Oyoshi said. "You boys never cease to amaze me. We're in the middle of a tight situation, and you start improvising a farce."

"It's true," one said. "But we just wanted to show you some dramatic-looking action."

Oyoshi turned to Ochō. "You must have been pretty scared. Everything's all right now, though, so don't worry. My name's Oyoshi, and I'm a hairdresser in Koume. I'm an unmannered, rambunctious woman who does what she wants. These days I've been praying to Benten for something very important, and I go on a pilgrimage every month to her shrine at Enoshima down the coast here. I have no talent, and I'm rather forward and don't know how to hold back anything. But these young men, here, well, for some reason they seem to like it, and they go around calling me 'boss woman.' I'm a bit conceited, I admit, so I can't really say I hate it when they call me that. These days I'm getting a bit famous, you know, and I almost never yield to anyone. I'm one of those loud-mouthed women they call 'chivalrous' who does anything a man can.

"Right now we're on our way back from Enoshima. We were fooling around a lot and didn't pay attention, and we ended up taking the wrong road. That sure was good luck for you! We walked through some fields and then between some rice paddies and then into some woods. We were going through low brush when suddenly we came to this temple here. We decided to go in and then we saw you. In big trouble! I talked things over with the boys real fast and then we acted. You were in a very serious situation, weren't you?"

As Ochō listened, she gradually forgot her fear and calmed down. She felt so happy she began sobbing and couldn't even thank the woman who had saved her.

"Really," Ochō finally said, "really, I feel like I just died and came back to life again. And, well, actually, I hate to ask you, but there's one more thing, if it isn't too much. . . ."

"Are you asking me to go with you to wherever it is you're going?" Oyoshi asked.

"Yes. Could you, please?"

"Of course. Don't worry about it at all. And all the boys will be glad to come

---

12. The ancient poet Narihira was commonly regarded as a divine lover. The man takes his name from the seventeenth-century outlaw Hirai Gonpachi, who loved the tayū Komurasaki, or Deep Purple, her name being a reference to Murasaki Shikibu.

13. Reverses the gender of Yoshibei of the Plums, a famous male outlaw.

along, too. As soon as you tell me who you are, then I'll take you wherever it is you're going. If there's any trouble going on at the place where you're headed, then my place is your place, understand? I don't care who shows up there or how much they try to threaten me, I'll do everything I can to take care of you myself. Of course, that's assuming it's not the authorities who're after you. As long as you're involved in a clean fight, then I'll stand behind you all the way. But hey, it's getting pretty late. If we don't hurry, all the inns will be closed. Well, boys, what do you say we get moving? Let's make a circle around this young woman here as we walk. And look out for an ambush!"

"Don't worry," one of the young men said. "Those thugs'll never be back. But if you want, I can carry her on my back."

"Uh-uh," said Oyoshi. "Not you, Kane, and not Gen, either. Let Ei or Kinta or maybe Jirō do it. I can't let you two anywhere near her!" As Oyoshi laughed, thin clouds covered the moon again, but the travelers made their way safely through the dim light and finally reached the nearest town.

In chapter 5, Yonehachi, who has moved to the entertainment district in Futagawa, on the southeastern outskirts of the city, meets with Tōbei, Konoito's intimate customer and lover, who has helped her leave the Karakotoya and become an independent banquet entertainer. Tōbei has been asked by Konoito to attempt to seduce Yonehachi, to test her love for Tanjirō. Yonehachi remains faithful to Tanjirō and skillfully evades Tōbei's continued advances. Chapter 6 takes place on a day in early spring, a few months after Ochō's escape in the Tenth Month of the previous year. Ochō, who has been adopted as a younger sister by Oyoshi, the women's hairdresser who saved her, is now living with Oyoshi and learning shamisen and jōruri chanting in order to make a career for herself as a performer at parties and private concerts.

CHAPTER 6

Ochō walked home from her chanting lessons completely absorbed in the jōruri text she was now learning. Over and over she sang the lines, "Moving water and human life, who knows where they will flow? And Minosaku, too . . . "[14] She was now fifteen, and her face was as radiant as a full moon. The red lipstick on her lips made them look even more attractive, and she wore a fashionable robe striped with the triple-box crests of her favorite kabuki actor, the wild, flamboyant Ichikawa Danjūrō. The striking satin sash around her waist was in the latest style.

Coming the other way down the street was an attractive man of nineteen or twenty. His head was tilted a bit, and he looked down as if he were deeply

---

14. The famous climax of act 4 of the puppet play *Twenty-four Filial Exemplars in Japan* (*Honchō nijūshikō*, 1766).

Tanjirō and Ochō talk in the street in front of a shop.

worried about something. Suddenly he and Ochō found themselves about to walk into each other. Then their eyes met.

"Aren't you Ochō?"

"Tanjirō! What in the world are you doing here?"

"Really! This is amazing. I mean, meeting you here like this. I'd like to hear all about how you've been. But we can't do that here in the middle of the street. Let's go somewhere."

He looked around. "Hey, over there's a grilled eel restaurant. Meeting you like this after such a long time calls for a celebration. Why don't we go have something to eat?"

Ochō felt so happy and embarrassed at the same time that she began to blush. But she hid her face with her wide, flat handbag. "Sure," was all she could say. They walked into the restaurant together.

"Come right on in," the amiable woman who ran the restaurant was saying. "Go on up to the second floor." Then she asked the waitress to bring up a tobacco tray set for them. Tanjirō and Ochō climbed the stairs to the room on the second floor, where they found a spot looking out over the busy Takabashi area[15] outside. Spring made the view even finer.

"This is incredible," Tanjirō said. "I've been thinking about you all the time,

---

15. At the time there was a noted female jōruri chanter called Take Miyashiba. The location of Ichihara is unknown.

Ochō, shamisen in hand, is portrayed as if she were the popular kabuki actor Iwai Hanshirō VI (1799–1836). She sits below a fan, one of his emblems, and beside a box filled with books of fiction. Text: "Take Chōkichi, chanter and musician, who works for Okuma in Ryōbōmachi." In the fan (*upper left*): "Seeing the returning geese, her heart, true to her distant lover, feels even sadder: / The line of geese / blurs and bends / through tears of longing /—Tamenaga Kikujo."

you know. But I never dreamed I'd see you anytime soon like this. Why are you walking around a place like this? Did you leave the quarter?"

"Well, actually I haven't lived there for quite a while."

"So where are you living right now? You're carrying around a handbag for jōruri texts, so I guess you must live somewhere around here, right? You're taking chanting lessons somewhere."

"Not around here," Ochō said. "I'm living out in Koume."

"Then you're coming here to take lessons?"

"No. I'm studying with Miyashiba, a really famous jōruri chanter who lives in Ginza.[16] Six times a month she comes out to a big mansion near where I live, and I go there to study with her. She's good at teaching me the difficult points. On other days, I go to study with a teacher in Ichihara."

"All right. Finally I get it," said Tanjirō. "You're lucky to be able to study with a master like Miyashiba. She'll make you perfect. And where did you say you were going today after you left Ichihara?"

"My older sister in Koume's busy today, so I promised her I'd drop by Jōsen-ji temple[17] on the way home and say some prayers in her name there."

"Older sister in Koume? Who are you talking about?"

Just then the waitress brought up some tea. "What'll you have?" she asked.

"Yeah, well, grill us three plates of medium-size ones," Tanjirō said.

---

16. East of the Sumida River, not far from Fukagawa, on the eastern edge of Edo.

17. Probably the Nichiren-sect Jōshin-ji temple, near the restaurant.

"What about some saké?"

"No," said Tanjirō. "We'll stick to food. Good old food. Or, Ochō, what do you say to having a little to drink?"

"No thanks," Ochō said, grinning.

The waitress, sensing something between them, picked up a small standing screen leaning against the stairs railing and stood it near them to give them some privacy. Then she went down the stairs noisily.

"It's amazing!" said Ochō. "You had no way at all of knowing I'm living in Koume and you don't know anything about my older sister."

Ochō went on to tell Tanjirō about Konoito's kindness and how Konoito had helped her escape Kihei's harassment and how she'd gotten into trouble on the way to Kanazawa and how Oyoshi of the Plums had saved her and then negotiated very forcefully with the house and persuaded them to formally let Oyoshi take Ochō into her own family and how Oyoshi cared for her as if she were her real younger sister. As Ochō went over the whole story in detail, she became very sad, and tears came to her eyes. Tanjirō, too, couldn't help crying, and he pulled Ochō closer to him. Ochō responded and put her arms around Tanjirō.

"I've really been worried about you," Ochō said. "I was so afraid and sad I went and prayed very hard to Benten and Saint Nichiren. I always miss you and think about you, you know. But you don't really think about me at all, do you?"

Just then the waitress brought up the eels grilled in soy sauce.

"Look at all that!" Tanjirō said. "Eat it while it's still hot." He reached for the wooden paddle to dish out some rice for Ochō.

"No you don't. Let me do that," she said, moving the bowls closer to her.

"It's really been a long time since we've eaten together, hasn't it." Tanjirō began pulling out the wooden grilling spits from the delicious back sections of the eels and giving them to Ochō.

"Well, thank you," Ochō said and began to eat. "Tanjirō, where are you living these days?"

"My house? Well, you can hardly call it a house. It's pretty bad. In fact, it's too embarrassing to even talk about."

"Hey, that's not fair! Tell me about it right now. Everything, Tanjirō." Her sweet way of taking liberties attracted him even more.

"It's nothing really. It's just a temporary place I'm renting for a little while."

"Well then, are you living just east of Asakusa? Or south by the river?

"Nowhere like that," said Tanjirō. "That's where the quarter moves if there's a fire. But I'm not in the quarter at all any more. I'm living in a place called Nakanogō."

"Oh really?" said Ochō. "Then you're living very close to where I am. Very. That's the best thing you've said yet. I'll come see you every day from now on."

"Hey, don't talk like that. I really don't want you to see me in the hole where I am right now."

"Why not?" Ochō asked.

"Why not? Well, you know."

"Did you get married?"

"Cut it out, will you?" Tanjirō answered. "How could I even think of having a wife in that place? It's so small, it's smaller than the bathing room at the Karakotoya House."

"Come on," said Ochō. "If you're living alone, you don't need to feel embarrassed about living in a small place."

Just then the waitress brought another plate of eel slices. "Here's the rest of your order."

"Hey, grill us one more plate, will you?" Tanjirō said. "Big ones this time."

"Right." Her footsteps disappeared down the stairs.

"Well," Ochō asked, "so who's cooking for you and taking care of you?"

"An old woman in the same tenement helps me out."

"Then I definitely think I'd better drop over and take care of things myself."

"You never learned to cook or keep house," Tanjirō said. "How do you expect to suddenly be able to do all that? And do you have any idea what the other tenants would say if a young woman started visiting a single man in the building?"

"Are you telling me not to visit you?"

"No, there's nothing wrong with visiting."

"Then if it's all right, I'll drop in tomorrow," Ochō said.

"Tomorrow I'm going out."

"That's all right. Just don't leave before I get there. I'm really excited about dropping in, so please. Stay home until I get there."

"You ask me to stay home, even though I say I'm going out. You know, you're really intelligent, but this time you just don't get it. Eat, will you? It's getting cold."

"I'm already full," Ochō said.

"But you've hardly eaten any at all. Put the eel on your rice and pour some tea over it. Try a little at least. It's delicious."

"Tanjirō, you haven't eaten much, either. Please have some more yourself. And from now on, please be kind to me and think about me a lot."

"Of course."

"Well, but you forgot all about me until we met just now. You didn't even know I'd been having a really hard time."

"Please." Tanjirō said. "How could I possibly forget you even a little? I even got into an argument because of you."[18]

"Argument? With whom?"

"Well," Tanjirō said, falling silent for a moment. "Actually, I saw Kihei in a dream and really had it out with him."

---

18. That is, with Yonehachi in chapter 2.

"Do you expect me to believe that?" Ochō said. "Listen, there's something I've been meaning to tell you when I saw you. Yes, yes, it's about that Yonehachi, who's such a big fan of yours. She did something really outrageous."

"Why? What did she do?" Tanjirō asked without showing any emotion.

"She was having an affair with Tōbei, the man who belongs to Konoito. People found out, and then finally she had to leave the house. Everybody was really upset about it." Ochō was very bright, but even she didn't realize that the real reason Yonehachi had gone to work somewhere else was because she wanted to look for Tanjirō.

"Really?" Tanjirō said, pretending not to know. "Konoito must have been very angry at her. And she had every right to be. By the way, the smoke from downstairs is getting pretty bad, isn't it? They must be cooking a lot of delivery orders. I hate the smell of broiled fish. The place where we used to go in San'ya was a lot better, wasn't it."

"Yeah, I agree. The first floor's bigger, so you don't need to go upstairs. And you can sit in the back where there's no smoke."

"I'll open another window," Tanjirō said and pushed open a rice-paper sliding screen in the front window of the room. Resting his hands on the railing, he gazed down for a moment at people passing in the street. Suddenly he saw Yonehachi coming by with her friend Umeji. They were on their way back from a party and were walking behind their customers, seeing them off.

Yonehachi saw Tanjirō almost immediately. "Hey, Tan!" she called up. "You still haven't gone home yet? I'll be back in just a minute with Umeji, so wait for me, will you?" She smiled and then turned her attention toward a drunk customer.

Tanjirō, amazed, could only stand there watching Yonehachi's back as she walked on past the restaurant toward Takabashi.

Ochō rushed to the window. "Hey, isn't that Yonehachi?"

"Are you kidding? That's not Yonehachi." Words came out of Tanjirō's mouth, but inside he was in a state of shock. He knew Yonehachi would be back soon from wherever she was going, and he began to feel nervous.

"If you've had enough," he said, "why don't we go?"

"All right, let's go. But I'm sure that was Yonehachi. You shouldn't hide it from me, you know." Ochō looked down as she spoke, and tears fell on her lap. She put her sleeve in her mouth and bit on it as hard as she could, trying not to let out any sound, and her body began to shake. Her silence was sadder than any words she could have said.

To Tanjirō, the stray hairs that fell across her cheek were very attractive. "Hey now," he said. "There's no need to cry."

"I'm not crying."

"But something's wrong. I can see it. Here, wipe your face." He gave her a small hand towel.

Ochō wiped her eyes and looked at Tanjirō resentfully, but there was still something of the young woman about the way she glared at him. They'd been engaged for several years but hadn't slept together, and Ochō worried that if she spoke too strongly, Tanjirō might stop loving her. So she suffered silently.

"Well, it's getting pretty late," Tanjirō said. "You ought to be getting back home. Remember what happened the last time you were out late."

"I don't need to go yet. But if I'm in the way, I guess I'd better leave."

"It's been a long time since we saw each other," Tanjirō said. "It would be a shame spend the time sulking."

"I know. I'm not sulking. I'll go to your place for sure tomorrow."

"Well, all right, but if you're going to come, please come in the afternoon. I'll be out all morning." The next day was the fifteenth, and Tanjirō was afraid Yonehachi might drop by on her way back from her early-morning prayer to the bodhisattva Myōken at a nearby temple. It was natural for him to worry, since Yonehachi was supporting him, and it was thanks to her help that he'd recovered from his illness and now had enough money for the things he needed.

"Bring the bill," Tanjirō shouted, clapping his hands loudly. There was no one else in the small restaurant, so the waitress came right up, and he paid the bill. Just as he and Ochō started downstairs, Yonehachi came into the restaurant. She'd rushed right back after seeing off her customers. A geisha musician like Yonehachi, in the prime of her career, didn't even look at the rare, expensive food that was served at the parties at which she performed. She'd wait until later and buy exactly the food she liked with her own money and talk about love affairs with her friends.

"Well, even if Tan's gone already," Yonehachi was saying, "we can just sit back and have a good old time by ourselves. After you, Umeji."

"Please," Umeji said, "you go first."

"Why not, do you want to go to the bathroom? Maybe I should go, too." Tanjirō is coming down the stairs with Ochō right behind him. What will they feel when they run into Yonehachi? Even the author doesn't know. At a time like this, an attractive man suffers more than others realize. How should the story continue? If readers have any good ideas, the author begs them to contact him as soon as they can.

> As you read on
> and find the first plum blossoms,
> telling of spring's coming,
> may their fragrance drift far
> on the breeze of your kind opinion.
>
> Kiyomoto Nobutsuga[19]

---

19. Kiyomoto Nobutsuga, a writer and master of Kiyomoto-style singing and shamisen playing, helped Shunsui, who was a close friend, to write *Plum Calendar* and other ninjōbon. She appears as a minor character in *Plum Calendar*.

Book 2

PREFACE

People now, as in the past, value gentleness of mind far above thousands of gold coins. Women, especially, should be gentle in every sort of situation. With enough money and no need to worry, everyone has a pure, noble mind and never looks resentful or uses words in rough ways. But in hard times, when each day brings only deeper poverty, a person's true mind shows itself.

This is especially true of the love between married couples. When they first sleep together in their beautiful new bedroom, they vow to grow old together and share the same grave. They are so intimate that they pledge to marry in the next life as well and are drawn to each other with feelings of great love. After the couple has exchanged such deep promises, it is too sad for words and very wrong when, if the man's fortunes decline, the woman's love changes color like the fall leaves and becomes as sparse as withered plants by the wayside.

In ancient China there lived a woman named Mengguang. Her father was rich, but her husband, Ling Baichun, gradually lost his wealth and finally had to leave the world behind and go away to a place called Baling. Although they were now extremely poor, Mengguang cheerfully left together with her husband, tilling the soil and cutting wild grasses. She also wove cloth herself and did menial jobs for people nearby. She always remembered what marriage was and remained devoted to her husband without ever envying the wealth of others.

Unfortunately, modern young women are incapable of even half of what Mengguang did. And some, without any sense or feeling, forget about all obligations and the Way and think they're a great success if they can show off in pretty clothes. Yet their beauty will pass, as it does for all things, and surely they will end up very unhappy. But if your mind is pure, you will be esteemed and respected even if you wear rags. Recall the poem by Fujiwara no Naoko:

> Like the tiny shrimp
> living on seaweed strands
> cut by fisherfolk,
> I will cry, "It is my own fault"
> and not blame my lover.[20]

Young women readers may feel that the author of this book, Kinryū Sanjin,[21] writes like an overly kind old woman and has the tiresome habit of of-

---

20. *Kokinshū*, Misc. 2, no. 807.

21. Hermit of Asakusa Kannon Temple, a title that Shunsui began to use after he moved to the precincts of the temple. At the end of chapter 2, he also uses the title Person with the Heart of an Old Woman (Rōbashinjin).

fering unnecessary opinions. I beg these readers to please persevere and read closely.

Kyōkuntei,[22] Tamenaga Shunsui

CHAPTER 7

Tanjirō was coming down the stairs from the second floor. Umeji and Yonehachi, at the bottom, were climbing up. Startled, Tanjirō turned around and looked at Ochō. Her attractive face was flushed red with anger, and her eyes filled with jealousy. The tears were tears of resentment toward Tanjirō. Yonehachi stared coldly at Ochō and finally calmed herself.

"Tan," she said, "I asked you to wait for me, but you seem to be going already." Then she turned to Ochō. "Well now, if it isn't Ochō. It's been a long time, hasn't it! My, you've gotten quite pretty. And you're a lot taller, too. How nice! It looks like you're almost ready to go off and get married." As Yonehachi spoke, she glanced sharply toward Tanjirō.

"She really has grown while we weren't looking, hasn't she," Tanjirō said without changing his expression. "Just now we ran into each other outside in the street, and I almost didn't recognize her."

"Really?" Yonehachi said. "How could you possibly not recognize her? Ochō, you have to be very careful about men. They seem to be dependable, but they're actually unreliable. Don't you agree, Umeji?"

"You know, you're right about that," Umeji said. "It all depends on how strong a woman's mind is. If a man's attractive enough to fall in love with, then other women are also going to fall in love with him, too, so you can never relax and stop being careful."

Ochō had not yet learned how to ignore her emotions and act graciously on the surface. Her feelings showed directly on her face. She said nothing until she had finally calmed herself.

"Yonehachi," she said, smiling, "please excuse me for just standing here like this. Whenever I meet someone I haven't seen for a while, I suddenly feel very emotional and don't know what to say. So I didn't say anything." Ochō didn't know how to flatter and pretend, and this was the politest thing she could think of to say.

"You have nothing to apologize for, Ochō," Yonehachi said. "And how are things at the Karakotoya?"

"Yes, well," Tanjirō said, cutting in. "I'll tell you all about it later. You'd better pour some saké for Umeji pretty soon. She's waiting."

"Not really," Umeji said. "I'm just fine."

---

22. Kyōkuntei, literally, Pavilion of Crazy Teachings, another of Shunsui's pen names.

"You already ordered another plate, didn't you?" Yonehachi said. "Even before we started up the stairs."

"Oh yes," Tanjirō said, "yes, I guess I did."

Just then the waitress brought up another plate of grilled eels and some saké. The four went upstairs after her, and soon the saké was passing back and forth.

"So," Yonehachi was saying, "how is it Ochō was having dinner with you just now?"

"It's all quite amazing," Tanjirō said, and he went on to relate in detail everything that Ochō had told him.

Yonehachi had a big heart, and she sympathized with Ochō. "You've really suffered and gone through a lot, haven't you," she said. "But look at it on the good side. At least you're out of that house, so you don't have to watch Kihei lording it up all the time." As Yonehachi talked, she analyzed the situation and realized that Tanjirō and Ochō were, after all, engaged and that it was natural for Ochō to be with her fiancé. If she wasn't careful, Ochō might take Tanjirō completely away from her. And Tanjirō liked Ochō, so Yonehachi knew she had to be very careful. Her only option, she decided, was to talk very frankly and make Tanjirō and Ochō feel indebted to her. She could keep Ochō from outmaneuvering her if she didn't hide anything, no matter what Ochō thought. Balancing defensiveness with calculation, she offered Ochō a cup of saké.

"If I may," she said. "Please have a few sips, won't you?"

"Well, all right," Ochō said. "Pour me a little."

"Umeji," Yonehachi said, "Would you?"

"All right."

"Ochō, I hope you'll pardon me for speaking so freely when we've just met again after so long. Somehow or other I've managed to become an independent geisha, and I perform at the restaurants in Futagawa. I guess it sounds conceited and ridiculous of me to say this, but actually I wouldn't have been able to do it without all the friendly help I've gotten from Umeji and the other musicians there. I can live as I want now, and don't need to depend on anyone. But Tanjirō, he's had all kinds of bad luck. And I . . . well . . . this is really hard for me to say." Yonehachi stopped for a moment and then made up her mind to go on. "Well, you know, Tanjirō and I started talking one day when we were in the Karakotoya, and after that we became very intimate. And after I set up on my own, and now, too, of course, we do everything but live together. I never stop thinking of him, even while I'm giving a performance. In my mind we're married already." Yonehachi spoke aggressively in the hope that she could force Ochō to give up her love for Tanjirō, which had yet to develop into something deep. "I'm sorry to speak so bluntly like this," she continued, "but I intend to help Tanjirō out as far as I'm able. I can't really say I'm supporting him, but I help him make ends meet, you might say. And after hearing about you, Ochō, it sounds like you're also having a harder time now than you admit. But please don't hold back in front of me. I'll come up with something for you, too, although I'm sure it won't be enough."

"I'm very moved by your kindness," Ochō said, cutting Yonehachi off. She was still young, but her love made her very determined. "Both the musicians in my parents' house used to help me out quite a bit. I was quite a burden on them for a while. But I'm on my own now. And I also intend to find a way to help out Tanjirō a little from now on."

Yonehachi laughed sarcastically. "Oh really?" she said. "Then Tanjirō's very lucky, isn't he!" She turned to Tanjirō and said, "Ah, there's something I've been meaning to tell you, but I keep forgetting. I found a cozy little house for you in Wakaura.[23] So please move in as soon as you can. It takes a long time for me to go all the way out to Nakanogō and then come back again, you know. And anyway, it's not safe out there,[24] so I always have to worry. You really ought to move. When I go home today, I'll buy some furnishings for you and a cabinet and things."

Umeji could see that Yonehachi had suddenly lost her temper, and she felt she'd better smooth things over. "Yonehachi," she said, "your words are getting a bit sharp, aren't they? I know you're not just being unprofessional and jealous, but don't you think the air in here's getting a bit thick? Tanjirō, why don't you make a nice exit now with this young woman?"

"Good idea. Ochō's out alone, so they'll be worried about her if she doesn't come back soon. I'll see her off right away. Well, Yonehachi, pardon me for leaving first. Please enjoy yourself with Umeji."

"Yes, well, good-bye," Yonehachi said. "You'd better get going. Ochō, I'll see you again, too." She spoke amicably, but in her heart she wondered whether the man she loved had been grabbed away from her right in front of her eyes. It may seem to be an unsophisticated worry, but she was in love, and it was quite understandable.

"Good-bye then," Ochō said to both Yonehachi and Umeji, and then she went downstairs. Tanjirō followed after her, and when he reached the top of the stairs, Yonehachi gave him a hard lover's pinch on the back. Arching her eyebrows in anger, she kept glaring at him as she walked back into the room and sat down again. "Hurry up and leave, will you?" she said. "You're disgusting."

"Stop it," Umeji said. "You're talking like a child now."

"I can't deal with you at all," Tanjirō said, forcing a smile. "You're crazy."

"Ah, yes, I'm crazy," Yonehachi said, throwing away the toothpick in her teeth. Then lowering her voice, she said, "Hold Ochō's hand very tight so she won't get lost."

"Stop talking like an idiot, will you?" Tanjirō said. He walked over and whispered something to Umeji and then went downstairs.

"Damn him," Yonehachi said.

---

23. In Fukagawa, on the eastern edge of Edo.
24. Because it is thinly settled and Ochō lives nearby.

Yonehachi and Tanjirō stare at each other on the second floor of the Yanagawa eel restaurant.

"Stop being so dumb," Umeji said. "Who in the world would feel jealous about an immature little twit like that? Yonehachi, you're really not yourself. When you talk about Tanjirō, you really do sound like an idiot. Stop it, will you?"

"I know, but, well, you know."

"That's just stupid. Tanjirō's not going to do anything to humiliate you or hurt your reputation. You know he won't."

"No, of course not. But Ochō's smart. I have to be very careful."

"You're hopeless." Umeji gave a saké cup to Yonehachi. "Here, let me pour the rest of this for you. Then let's go. You're not letting me have any fun at all today."

"Nope, none at all. But try to forgive me, will you? I really am shameless. How could I let myself get so involved?"

"Listen," Umeji said. "I refuse to talk about love with you any longer. Understand? I've had it!" She was smiling. "I don't sell myself any more than you do, but I've known a lot of different men, you know. I understand just about every kind of love there is, and I take it in stride. Still, if I really do fall in love with a man, I act just as foolish as anyone else. We all do."

"I used to laugh at other people for letting themselves fall in love," Yonehachi said with deep feeling. "But now I . . . I can't control myself at all." Umeji spread a hand towel on Yonehachi's lap. "Hey, what are you doing?" Yonehachi asked.

"You keep going on and on about this man," Umeji said. "I'm afraid you'll start drooling."

"Oh, what a wicked woman you are! I didn't even realize you were making fun of me."

"If you realize it now, then let's go, shall we?"

"Yes, let's," said Yonehachi. "No more saké for me!" A man from the tea-house where they'd been performing was waiting to escort them home, and they had him pay the bill. As they walked down the street, they whispered to each other. Who could have known that one of them was deeply worried? She was so attractive that people called out as she went by, comparing her with a kabuki star who played beautiful women.[25] Looking at her, no one could have guessed she was being torn by her emotions, suffering more than most people ever do.

Once, at a party, the author wrote the following poem about geisha musicians:

> The women singers
> look easy to pluck,
> yet their strong hearts,
> always true to their lovers,
> bend without breaking.

Meanwhile, after Ochō left the grilled-eel restaurant, she had been thinking so deeply she could hardly move her feet forward along the street. Yonehachi and Tanjirō had a much closer relationship than she'd imagined, and Yonehachi had all but come out and said that Tanjirō belonged to her because she was supporting him. And Tanjirō. Ochō analyzed the situation and realized he would probably never be able to separate himself from Yonehachi now.

Tanjirō walked slowly beside Ochō. As he watched her lost in thought, she looked very attractive, with a beauty that was just beginning to show itself.

They were in the neighborhood of samurai mansions, and the street was almost empty. "Ochō," Tanjirō finally said, "Why are you crying like that? Hey, how about trying to cheer up?"

After looking around to see if anyone was coming, Ochō looked into Tanjirō's eyes. Then she put both arms around his left arm and clung tightly to him.

"Tanjirō!"

"Yes?"

"You know, I really hate you."

"Why?"

"Do you need to ask? When I saw Yonehachi in the street, you pretended you didn't even know who she was. And now suddenly you're married to her!"

"No, no. You don't understand. I was in trouble and I didn't have any way

---

25. She is compared with the popular female-role actor Segawa Kikunojō V.

to survive, and then I got sick. Then she suddenly showed up and did a lot of things for me, and we ended up, well, you know, doing it."

"Did you end up getting married?"

"How could we possibly be married?"

"Maybe not yet, but later. You've promised to marry her, haven't you?"

"No, no, no. We're never going to be married."

"Then who are you planning to marry?"

"I know a young woman who's ten times prettier and more irresistible than Yonehachi."

"Oh really? Where is she?"

"Hey, she's right here," Tanjirō said, putting his arm around Ochō and holding her tightly as they walked.

Happily, Ochō held onto Tanjirō. Then she reached up and softly pinched the upper part of Tanjirō's arm. A smile came to her face, and she grew flushed around the eyes. To Tanjirō she looked even more attractive. Luckily no one else came down the street, because after that the two said some very foolish things that only lovers could ever understand.

Suddenly a loud voice burst out of a side street: "Pans! Pots! I fix everything!"

Surprised, Ochō and Tanjirō ran across the stone bridge spanning a drainage canal, vowing never to part. It was spring and the thin ice below was melting, much as they melted into each other. By the time they passed through Naka-nogō, where Tanjirō lived, they were sure they were already wife and husband, and then they reached the plums of Koume, heading for the secluded stylish house where Ochō was staying. Afraid someone might see them, they let go of each other and held hands in their minds as they went by houses surrounded by spindle-tree hedges and bushes. As they passed a public well with a hanging bucket, they walked farther apart, sure someone was watching. Even a warbler in the eaves made them feel shy. Was it laughing at them? Unsure any longer of where they were really going, they made their way back toward Ochō's house.

> Blossoming plum branches,
> whip-like, urge warblers to come,
> "Quickly! Quickly!"
>
> Hakei

One night, sleeping beside Oyoshi, Ochō has a vivid dream in which debt collectors come to the house while Oyoshi is away and threaten her, trying to force her to tell them where Tanjirō is hiding. Alarmed, the next morning Ochō visits Tanjirō in his squalid room, and just as they are becoming intimate, blackmailers come and threaten Tanjirō. Then a high official of the Hatakeyama clan who is investigating the theft of the tea canister arrives and reduces the amount Tanjirō must repay. Tanjirō, however, has noth-

ing except what Yonehachi has given him, so Ochō decides to contract herself to a woman
who runs an entertainment agency that sends out jōruri chanters and singers to parties,
and she gives the contract money to Tanjirō, who uses it to pay off his debt. Ochō, who
does jōruri singing and chanting under the professional name of Chōkichi, is skilled and
popular and is invited to perform at many mansions. Meanwhile, Yonehachi remains
true to Tanjirō despite Tōbei's repeated, strenuous attempts to seduce her and test her
love for Tanjirō. At the same time, Tōbei has completely stopped visiting Konoito, and
Konoito suspects Yonehachi of actually having an affair with Tōbei, although he is
simply trying to test Yonehachi. After Yonehachi swears she loves only Tanjirō, Konoito
reveals that her true lover is actually Hanbei, now far away. Yonehachi becomes very
successful as an independent musician and is in great demand. Then one day both Ochō
and Yonehachi are invited to perform at the same mansion.

CHAPTER 13

Although he'd been reduced to being a lowly luggage carrier for Yonehachi,
Tanjirō's love for her is as true as hers is for him. Today Yonehachi has been
asked to perform at Lord Kajiwara's country mansion in Kamedo,[26] a farming
area east of Edo. A number of guests have gathered there for a tea ceremony,
and at the party afterward, professional comedians serve saké while music is
provided by many different women performers. Tanjirō, however, sits in a small
waiting room for visitors' hired help and has nothing to do. As the mere carrier
of Yonehachi's shamisen, he keeps out of the way, ashamed to be seen by
anyone.

Tired of sitting, Tanjirō went into the kitchen and gazed out the door at the
wide field of autumn grasses and flowers that spread out beyond the mansion
garden. Excited and drawn by the moonlight, he found himself going outside
and then climbing a low hill at the back of the garden. At the top he found a
stylishly designed one-room pavilion surrounded by a low veranda. He stepped
up onto the veranda and gazed down. Beyond a carefully landscaped pond he
could see part of the mansion's largest room. From inside came music and
animated voices. The drinking had been going on all day, and guests and hosts
mingled intimately. At this point, no one cared any longer about rank or ceremony. Tanjirō could see all the excited people so clearly that he felt as if he
could reach out and touch them.

As Tanjirō gazed, he began to feel drowsy. Suddenly he saw someone running through the garden, breathing hard. Strangely, the person was running
barefoot. The figure came up the hill, threw open the wicker gate, and ran

---

26. Suggests Kameido, a place east of Edo.

right toward the spot where Tanjirō was standing. Surprised, Tanjirō and the figure stared hard at each other in the moonlight.

"Tanjirō?"

"Is that you? Ochō? What are you doing here?"

Ochō started sobbing and was unable to answer. Tanjirō held her and pushed open one of the sliding doors of the pavilion. He helped Ochō inside, had her sit down, and tried to comfort her.

"You know, your heart's really thumping!" he said. He rubbed Ochō's chest for a while until her heart finally slowed and she calmed down.

"Oh! I was really afraid," she said finally. "What are you doing here, Tan?"

"Me, well, no reason, really."

"Did you come all the way out to this mansion with Yonehachi because you're worried about her?"

"No, that's not it at all. I came because I had to ask her for something.[27] But who cares about that? Tell me why you came running up here so fast."

Ochō rested her head against Tanjirō's lap. "All right. I'll tell you. The steward of the mansion is Banba no Chūda. He has a son named Chūkichi, and Chūkichi's always saying fresh things to me whenever I come here to perform. He wants me to go with him and do whatever he asks. It's disgusting. I can't stand it. Well, today the guests are completely drunk, as is everybody else, and nobody can tell what's going on, so Chūkichi grabbed me. Luckily they decided just then to play hide-and-seek. I went and hid in the bath, but he came and hid in the same place. He told me that this time he absolutely wasn't going to be refused. He stood there staring at me, his hand on his short sword. So I ran at him as hard as I could and knocked him over and ran outside. He'll be here any second. I don't know where to go now."

"You're in a real fix, aren't you," Tanjirō said. "Then again, if he's the son of the steward, it's in your interest to be on his good side. You really ought to go back and fix things up."

"Tanjirō!" Ochō said, her eyes flashing. "You, too? Do you want me to do whatever party guests or other men ask me to? You sound just like my manager. Whenever I go back to my manager's house after a party and explain what's happened, that heartless old woman tells me to agree with what the men say and to do what they ask. But she just wants me to make more money so she can get her hands on it. She's always telling me to find a patron and become his mistress. A lot of men drop by her house, and she's always pointing out the rich ones to me. And she tells me to greet them pleasantly and make them feel good. She just wants me to think of ways of getting their money, that's all. I have to hear disgusting things like that every single day, from morning till night.

---

27. Tanjirō is embarrassed that he has become Yonehachi's shamisen carrier and does not want to talk with Ōchō about it.

I know I'm not able to support you yet, but still, I'm true to you, and I always think of you. It makes me want to cry whenever I have to play in front of those kinds of men. Show me a little sympathy."

"Yeah, well . . ." Tanjirō said. "Actually, I never stop thinking of you, either, even for a minute. But I can't see you at your place the way I can drop in on Yonehachi. But you know, not being able to see you makes me love you even more. But there's nothing I can do right now. . . . "

"That's fine," Ochō said. "Just fine. Please be good friends with Yonehachi, because pretty soon I'm going to be dead anyway."

"How come you're so angry?"

"Why? You never come to see me, Tanjirō, so you have no way of knowing this, but my manager's the same woman who used to call herself Okuma. Remember, she was a matron at the Karakotoya. She still resents the fact that she had to do whatever my parents told her, so she's extra mean to me now. Really mean. She keeps talking to me, saying every unpleasant thing you can imagine. The only way I can stand it is by thinking about how maybe you and I'll be together someday. I can't be sure of it, but it helps me endure each day. Meanwhile all you're really thinking about is Yonehachi. You even come all the way out to these country mansions with her and then wait to go home with her. Why should I want to live and suffer like this? There's no reason for me to go on living. So I won't, that's all."

"Stop talking nonsense, will you?" Tanjirō said. "I'm working for Yonehachi. I carry her things so I can save a little money and get you back to Oyoshi as soon as I can. How can I act like a self-respecting man if I don't? At least that's what I tell other people. Actually, your being like this really worries me. I don't like it at all."

"What are you so worried about?"

"It's pretty obvious, isn't it? You're getting more attractive and desirable every day. And while you're far away from me, you're surrounded by all those other men. It bothers me a lot. When I imagine how those men aren't going to want to leave you alone, I get really upset. Especially at night. Some nights I dream about them doing something to you, and I can't stand it."

"Tanjirō, I really don't like you when you lie to me."

"Why am I lying? Just look at what happened tonight. You have to be very careful."

"What are you talking about? It's Yonehachi you're worried about. That's why you go with her when she goes out to perform."

"No, really, that's not why. Listen, I'm not the one. . . . You, didn't you, you must have come up here because you've promised to meet some man in this nice secluded little house. And I'm in the way. All right, I understand. I'll go back down to the mansion and wait in the servants' room."

Tanjirō stood up, but Ochō held onto him. "How? How could you say such a cruel thing?" She was crying again, and her body shook.

In the dim light of the room, Tanjirō thought he could see redness around Ochō's eyes, although he wasn't quite sure. He pulled Ochō to him. "I was just joking," he said. "Will you forgive me? Really, we've never had a good heart-to-heart talk alone until now. You're suffering all this because of me and . . . and I know how hard it is for you. But be patient just a little longer, please. Pretty soon I'll get together enough money to buy out your contract and get you out of there."

"Listen, I realize I can't be with you right away. But you've got to come see me for a little while every two or three days. Just long enough so I can see your face." Ochō held Tanjirō as hard as she could, her arms twining around him like the vines turning crimson on the autumn slope outside. Cries of insects filled the deepening night.

From the great room in the mansion came the sounds of superbly played shamisens and two women singing. It was an old song, but people still liked to hear it.

> Before I met you I heard you were stylish
> and when we met you were oh so refined
> even down to your clothes—so full of wit and grace,
> so direct and self-possessed, you're such a handsome man
> I've fallen in love with you—is there karma between us?

"Hey," Tanjirō said, "isn't that Masakichi and Daikichi from Futagawa?"[28]
"Yes, you're right. It's them."
"What did you chant tonight?"
"Well, I performed with Imasuke from Nakachō,[29] and we sang the duet from the scene where Chichibu Shigetada has the geisha Akoya play her koto while he asks her about Kagekiyo.[30] That's all we did. Tonight everyone was so wild and noisy, it felt funny to be playing a jōruri piece. I got impatient and kept wanting to play too fast."

Ochō and Tanjirō were so happy that they felt they as if they were floating. They forgot everything and looked deeply into each other's eyes, silently understanding each other. Then came the sounds of shamisens playing a lively song in a typical geisha tempo with strong, expressive pauses:

> I fell in love, I'm burning up,
> but all, all for nothing—tonight we met

---

28. Two male geisha musicians from Fukagawa.

29. Another geisha from Fukagawa. Nakachō was in Fukagawa.

30. The popular third act of the jōruri puppet play *Dannoura Battle Helmet* (*Dannoura kabuto gunki*, 1732), in which a Minamoto ally questions the woman Akoya, the former lover of a Taira enemy, Kagekiyo.

and only talked of this and that
and didn't do a thing.

And then came the sounds of a different song:

> I worry that he doesn't think of me
> the way I think of him—when we're apart
> I act just like a fool and let it get me angry.

"Listen to that," Ochō said. "They talk about it even in songs. You have Yonehachi, so you never remember me."

"You still don't understand, do you? If you have to remember someone, it means that sometimes you're thinking about somebody else. It means that you've forgotten them for a while. So no, I don't remember you. I think about you all the time."

"Hey, Tanjirō, now you're lying again. Yonehachi's the one you never forget." As Ochō spoke, she tickled Tanjirō's side below the armpit.

"What are you doing? That tickles. Stop it, or I'll tickle you back." As they lay there holding each other, Tanjirō reached up Ochō's wide sleeve and began lightly touching her breast.

"Hey, that really tickles!" Ochō's face flushed, and she stared into Tanjirō's eyes.

"Well," Tanjirō said, "everything's quiet down there now. I can't hear a single shamisen, but people are sure laughing a lot. I wonder if one of those Sakura-gawa comic storytellers is putting on a show."

"No, it's another one, Ryūchō. He's telling one of his funny stories now. This afternoon Yūchō told one and started chanting part of a romantic puppet play[31] right in the middle. It was really interesting."

"Hmm. Really? I guess pretty soon Yūchō's going to be the best of all the young comic storytellers."

"Yes, he's not stiff at all. He's really relaxed and smooth."

"Hey," Tanjirō said, "I thought you were praising his stories. But no, you're praising him. I see. I guess I'd better pay more attention. Now you're telling me how much you love him. And I didn't even notice."

"There you go again, you liar. Why would I fall in love with Yūchō? One of the women I work with, Okiku, she's completely crazy about him. They're so close it makes even me feel jealous."

"Have you ever slept with him?"

"Tanjirō! Stop it, will you? If I liked him that much, I'd never go through all this just for you. You're horrible!"

---

31. *Shinnai-bushi.*

Ochō and Tanjirō meet unexpectedly at a hilltop pavilion overlooking a pond and, beyond it, a mansion. The pavilion door is still partly open, suggestively showing a pillow, and the lovers wipe their hands with tissue paper, much as in an erotic print. The two are now preparing to leave, so the time is later than that mentioned in the text.

"And I think you're charming. Hey, prove you're not in love with Yūchō." Tanjirō pulled Ochō tightly against him and lay down on the floor.

"Let go a minute, will you?" Ochō said, turning around. She pushed open one of the sliding paper doors and looked down at the party room in the mansion. Then she banged the door shut again.

Inside the room, Ochō and Tanjirō loved each other again and again. They spoke to each other of all the difficult things that had happened to them and revealed their innermost secrets. The people in the mansion never realized they were there, and luckily no one thought to search as far as the hill at the back of the garden.

The author is aware that some people hate such scenes and believe that publishing them in a book amounts to teaching women and girls to become loose and immoral. Some even loathe my books intensely. Surely they are wrong! Confucius said that if you are with two people, you should make the good one your teacher and avoid the bad one.[32] And a venerable proverb says, "Watch

---

32. *Analects* 7:21. Shunsui is arguing that his main characters are good "teachers" for his readers.

others' actions; change your own." Since my books are meant mainly for women readers, they are of course unsophisticated and hardly high literature. But while the women characters may look lascivious, the love they feel is deep, and they are always true to their lovers and to their principles. They never have sexual relations with different men at the same time, do indecent things for the sake of money, or stray from the Way and act in a manner improper for women. Many amorous words are exchanged, yet the affections shared by the lovers, both men and women, are pure and beyond reproach. In this book, Konoito, Ochō, Oyoshi, and Yonehachi all differ in style and appearance, but each remains true to her lover, showing as much bravery as any man. Please read on to the very end and see for yourself how things finally turn out well for these virtuous women and how they act faultlessly and protect the men they love.

[*Shunshoku umegoyomi*, NKBT 64: 47–149, translated by Chris Drake]

Chapter 20

GŌKAN: EXTENDED PICTURE BOOKS

Gōkan (literally, bound books), bound picture books, was the last of the kusa-zōshi, or picture books, to appear. Gōkan were the direct successor of the ki-byōshi, the satiric picture books that were in vogue from 1775 to 1805. After the Kansei Reforms, the kibyōshi shifted to vendetta narratives, which eventually could not be contained in the short kibyōshi format. Consequently, from around 1803/1804, writers such as Jippensha Ikku and Kyokutei Bakin began to bind together several kibyōshi booklets to form what came to be called *gōkan*. An important characteristic of the gōkan was the inclusion of the calligraphic text (which was primarily kana) in the illustration wrapped around the central images, as in the kibyōshi. Gōkan had even more text packed on the page than did kibyōshi, a ratio of about 60 percent text to 40 percent image, which was the opposite of kibyōshi. The artists, who came from the Utagawa family or school, appeared on the cover alongside the author of the gōkan.

One of the first successful writers of the bound picture book, Santō Kyōden adapted kabuki plays to this format, intended to appeal to young women who were enamored of the world of kabuki. The 1810s were the age of the kabuki playwright Tsuruya Nanboku, and Kyōden made Ichikawa Danjurō VII (the most popular kabuki actor in Nanboku's plays) the hero of a gōkan that included illustrations of the handsome actor and his costumes by the renowned ukiyo-e artist Utagawa Toyokuni. The female audience thus had a chance to see the actor on the covers (which were in color by the end of the 1810s) and follow the action through both words and pictures. The gōkan, which specialized in kabuki-type vendettas (*katakiuchi*) and struggles for house succession (*oie sōdō*), brought the world of the theater into the hands of the average reader. This art of transforming the stage onto paper was perfected by Ryūtei Tanehiko, who also understood the importance of the prints. The gōkan peaked with Tanehiko's *A Country Genji by a Commoner Murasaki* (*Nise Murasaki inaka Genji*, 1829–1842) before fading in the 1860s and finally being replaced by the newspaper novel in the 1880s.

RYŪTEI TANEHIKO

Ryūtei Tanehiko (1783–1842), whose real name was Takaya Hikoshirō, was born in Edo into a family of lower-level samurai. The family received an annual hereditary stipend of four hundred bushels of rice, which enabled Tanehiko to get an education and live without undue financial pressure. Tanehiko made a name as both a kyōka and senryū poet and a writer of yomihon and gōkan. The first chapter (four volumes) of *A Country Genji by a Commoner Murasaki* was published in 1829 and was followed by another thirty-eight chapters (152 volumes) over the next fourteen years. *A Country Genji* became one of the most popular books in the Edo period, selling more than ten thousand copies. But in 1842, during the Tenpō Reforms, Tanehiko was summoned by the bakufu and told to cease publication of the book. The blocks were confiscated, thereby preventing any reprints. Shortly thereafter, Tanehiko died.

A COUNTRY GENJI BY A COMMONER MURASAKI
(*NISE MURASAKI INAKA GENJI*, 1829–1842)

Apparently inspired by Kyokutei Bakin's success with the extended gōkan adaptations of Chinese novels such as *Courtesan Water Margin* (*Keisei suikoden*, with illustrations by Utagawa Toyokuni, 1825), in which the genders of the protagonists of the *Water Margin* were reversed, Tanehiko adapted *The Tale of Genji* to the gōkan format and placed it in a kabuki world, that of the tumultuous period of the Ōnin Wars (1467–1477), at the Higashiyama Palace of the Ashikaga shōgun. Genji was likewise transformed into a handsome warrior named Ashikaga Mitsuuji, who was skilled in both sword and the arts. Mitsuuji's many love affairs differ significantly from those of the original Genji in that they fall into a framework of feudal morality in which the man pursues a woman in order to recapture a lost treasure or hostages or to effect a political marriage. Tanehiko also depicted characters who acted and spoke like contemporary urban commoners; he dressed the characters, particularly the women, in contemporary fashion, and replaced the original waka with original haiku. By the Edo period, commentaries on *The Tale of Genji* as well as simplified digests of *Genji* for women and young people had been published, but these texts remained difficult to obtain, and

This ukiyo-e woodblock print by Hishikawa Ryūkoku (act. 1804–1818) reveals the influence of Kitagawa Utamaro (1753–1806). The fan-shape cartouche reads: "Elegant Pastimes of the Five Seasonal Festivals" (*Fūryū gosekku asobi*). This print celebrates the first of these festivals, on the seventh day of the First Month. Together with her infant son, in a lozenge-pattern robe, a *chōnin* mother, absentmindedly adjusting her hairpin, reads a gōkan (extended picture book) describing warriors. (Gōkan were originally sold in the early spring and thus considered auspicious.) The young daughter, in a plover-pattern kimono with a cloud-design sash, is holding a wooden paddle (decorated with the red and white plum blossoms of spring) used for *hanetsuki*, a type of badminton and a traditional New Year's girl's game. Signed "From the brush of Ryūkoku." (Courtesy of Museo d'Arte Orientale in Genoa, Italy)

the original still was very hard to read. The title *Nise Murasaki inaka Genji* (literally, *Imitation Murasaki, Country Genji*) suggests a new Genji described in the local or country (*inaka*) language of Edo and eastern Honshū. In the preface, Tanehiko claims that the author is the Edo-born commoner woman O-Fuji, whose work is like "imitation lavender" (*nise murasaki*), an inexpensive synthetic dye that was very popular with Edo commoners but faded over time, unlike the "genuine" lavender dye.

A *Country Genji* appeared at a time when the gōkan was shifting from stories of vendettas to stories of romantic love. The story of the shining Genji and his many splendid women proved to be perfect material for illustrated books aimed at women and young people and for the new trend toward romantic love. Furthermore, the author's special talent for mixing kabuki and jōruri materials into the gōkan worked well with the material of *The Tale of Genji*, which was given the kinds of unexpected plot twists and multiple identities that gōkan and kabuki audiences expected. By setting the narrative in the medieval period and adding kabuki plot devices such as the struggle for succession of a house and the search for treasure, Tanehiko evoked a feudal, military world in which he was able to combine the mood and romance of the ninjōbon with the kinds of fantastic elements found in the yomihon. Tanehiko, like many late-Edo *gesaku* (playful writing, usually in the vernacular) fiction writers, wrote to please his audiences, especially women readers, whose number had grown, owing to the spread of education, but who still had few sources of entertainment. The gōkan, particularly A *Country Genji*, opened up a colorful world to which they could escape, if only temporarily. For more learned readers, A *Country Genji* could also be enjoyed as a fascinating kabuki variation on a Heian classic. One of its main attractions was the dazzling illustrations by Utagawa Kunisada (1786–1864), a leading ukiyo-e artist, who followed Tanehiko's initial sketches and gave the characters the faces and costumes of famous kabuki actors. The combination of pictures and calligraphic text in the illustration was extremely effective, a technique that continued into the Meiji period with illustrated and serialized newspaper novels. Indeed, Tanehiko's *Country Genji* was so popular that it led to the introduction of such products as Genji rice crackers and Genji noodles and also was adapted for the kabuki stage, where it became a huge hit.

The main plot of A *Country Genji* resembles that of a mystery novel with constant echoes of *The Tale of Genji*. A beautiful, intelligent boy named Mitsuuji (suggesting Prince Genji) is born to the Ashikaga shōgun Yoshimasa (suggesting the Kiritsubo emperor) and his favorite, Hanagiri (suggesting Kiritsubo). As the boy grows, Yoshimasa loves him more than the boy's older brother (suggesting the Suzaku emperor), his son by his official wife, Toyoshi (suggesting Kokiden), and so Yoshimasa goes against convention by planning to make his second son the next shōgun. Mitsuuji's mother is tormented by the jealous Toyoshi, falls sick, leaves the shōgunal palace, and dies. Feeling sorry for his father, Mitsuuji arranges to have a woman who looks like his mother come to take his mother's place at the palace, where she calls herself Lady Fuji (suggesting Fujitsubo). Mitsuuji then learns of a plot between Toyoshi and Yamana Sōzen—a powerful lord who officially supports the shōgun but is actually hoping to become shōgun himself—to smuggle Sōzen into Lady Fuji's quarters in a large chest. To foil the plot, Mitsuuji enters Lady Fuji's bedroom when the chest is delivered and asks to sleep with her. Before the act can be consummated, Sōzen bursts out of the chest, accuses Mitsuuji and Lady Fuji of a bestial act, and then gives up his interest in Lady Fuji. Exposed, Mitsuuji and Lady Fuji attempt suicide but are stopped by the shōgun, who warns Mitsuuji that his action is unworthy of a future shōgun.

The motives of Mitsuuji and the other major characters are rarely simple. In addition to symbolically satisfying his desire for his mother and stopping Sōzen, the intelligent Mitsuuji understands politics well and knows that if his father tries to make him shōgun, the succession will be challenged and the stability of shōgunate threatened. Moreover, he remains loyal to his older brother. Thus, although people call him the "shining prince" (*hikaru kimi*)—the name Mitsuuji means Shining Clan—he devotes his life to love affairs, thereby ruining his reputation for the sake of his older brother, his clan, and the shōgunate. Even when his father has him marry Lady Futaba, the daughter of one of his supporters, Mitsuuji rarely visits her. A playboy reputation, Mitsuuji hopes, will keep him from becoming shōgun, thus allowing him freedom of movement and the ability to act unnoticed behind the scenes.

One night, however, a thief breaks into the shōgunal storehouse and steals a precious sword, one of the three treasures that must be passed down to each new shōgun. This incident causes Mitsuuji to begin to live a dual life as both a prolific lover and an investigator. Running throughout the text is the constant tension between these different sides of Mitsuuji—on the one hand are his rational calculations and desire for knowledge and understanding and, on the other, are his sensitivity and capacity for deep feeling. His double personality is dramatically apparent in the following sections, from books 4 and 5, an allusive variation on the "Evening Faces" (Yūgao) chapter of *The Tale of Genji*, which combines its gothic and romantic elements with a plot and characters from kabuki and jōruri dramas.

CHARACTERS

AKOGI, a high-ranking courtesan who lives on Sixth Avenue (Rokujō), suggesting Lady Rokujō in *The Tale of Genji*

DOROZŌ, husband of Shinonome, father of Tasogare, and elder brother of Karukaya/Kikyō

FUTABA, wife of Mitsuuji and daughter of Akamatsu Masanori, the minister of the left, suggesting Lady Aoi, Genji's principal wife in *The Tale of Genji*

HANAGIRI, Yoshimasa's favorite concubine and mother of Mitsuuji, suggesting the Kiritsubo consort in *The Tale of Genji*

HIRUGAO, Ashikaga Yoshimasa's concubine

KARAGINU, Kiyonosuke's young wife, suggesting Utsusemi in *The Tale of Genji*

KIKYŌ/KARUKAYA, Kikyō, maidservant to Hirugao, referred to as Karukaya after becoming a nun, and sister of Dorozō

KIYONOSUKE (NIKKI KIYONOSUKE), Mitsuuji's retainer from Iyo Province, suggesting the vice governor of Iyo in *The Tale of Genji*, married to Karaginu

KOREKICHI, Mitsuuji's retainer, suggesting Koremitsu, Genji's retainer

MITSUUJI (ASHIKAGA MITSUUJI), the second son (Jirō) of the Ashikaga shōgun Yoshimasa by Hanagiri, suggesting the Shining Genji

MURAOGI, Kiyonosuke's daughter, suggesting Nokiba no Ogi in *The Tale of Genji*.

SHINONOME, mother of Tasogare

SŌZEN (YAMANA SŌZEN), a powerful lord who wants to displace the Ashikaga shōgun Yoshimasa

TAKANAO (AKAMATSU TAKANAO), son of the minister of the left, brother of Lady Futaba, and Mitsuuji's brother-in-law, suggesting Tō no Chūjō in *The Tale of Genji*

TASOGARE, daughter of Shinonome and mother of Tamakuzu who lives on Fifth Avenue (Gojō), suggesting Evening Faces in *The Tale of Genji*

YOSHIMASA, Ashikaga shōgun, father of Mitsuuji, and husband of Toyoshi, suggesting the Kiritsubo emperor

Book 4 (concluding part)

Mitsuuji spent all his time and energy pretending to be a great lover while secretly searching for the stolen sword. But no matter how hard he thought, he was unable to come up with a good plan for retrieving it. Still, he couldn't carry on his investigation in public, crowded places, so he went on discreet visits to the licensed quarter near Sixth Avenue[1] and listened for the latest rumors and talk. When he learned that the mother of his retainer Korekichi[2] had fallen very ill, he decided to visit her, and he set out for her house on Fifth Avenue. When the palanquin reached the house gate, he had the carriers put it down and had one man go inside to tell Korekichi why he had come. Soon Korekichi came rushing out to welcome him.

"I haven't been able to visit you recently," Korekichi said, "because my mother is very ill. I'm quite surprised to see you here." He bowed so low his forehead touched the ground.

"There's no need to worry," Mitsuuji said. "I came to see your mother. She was like a mother to me, too, and she fed me her own milk. When I heard she was sick, how could I possibly not come? Where is she?"

"Very good," Korekichi told the carriers, "take the palanquin inside." He went through the small side door and tried to open the gate from the inside, but the bolt was locked, so he rushed off to get the key. Mitsuuji lifted the

---

1. Rokujō, actually the location of the licensed quarter in the early seventeenth century, suggests Lady Rokujō in *The Tale of Genji*.

2. Korekichi and his sick mother suggest Koremitsu and his mother in *The Tale of Genji*.

Tasogare, appearing through a gate entwined with crow gourd vines, holds out a round paper fan. Korekichi (*center*), having picked a flower from the gourd vines, takes the fan on behalf of Mitsuuji, who stands and fans himself near the palanquin. The crow gourd flower and the round fan allude to the *yūgao* (evening faces) flower and the folding fan in the "Evening Faces" chapter of *The Tale of Genji*. A gourd motif and the characters for Yūgao appear just above the palanquin carrier's head, further accentuating the allusion. A Genji incense symbol (to represent *The Tale of Genji* chapters in one method of incense appreciation) for the "Evening Faces" chapter also marks the wall and the paper lantern. Parts of an old summer robe, patterned with unfolded cypress fans, are stretched on two sliding shutter boards. From the 1831 edition.

hanging screen on one side of the palanquin and gazed at the avenue and the commoner area around him. Through gaps in the wooden fence surrounding the next house he could see that the sliding paper doors above the low veranda had been thrown completely open. Only a semitransparent white reed blind hung down, giving room inside a feeling of coolness. Mitsuuji made out women's shapes through the blind and heard laughing voices. He wondered who the women could be. He knew he had never seen them before, so he got out of the palanquin to get a better look. The house was nothing to look at. It had two floors, but neither was very large. In front two boards leaned against each other, and on them pieces of an old summer robe had been stretched out to dry.

Deep green vines extended gracefully over the fence and gate. On them bloomed strikingly beautiful white flowers.

"What are those?" Mitsuuji asked.

"They're 'crow gourds,'"[3] one of the carriers replied. "From their name, you'd think they were black as crows, but they have white flowers and red fruit. They bloom only on poor, run-down fences like this one."

"Yes," Mitsuuji said, "most of the houses here certainly are very small. And their roofs look like they're about to collapse. Those flowers certainly have bad luck blossoming in a place like this. Pick a few. I'll take them back with me."

The man walked over to the house and through its wicker gate. When he did, a young woman surely not yet twenty came out of the house wearing an apron of thin, yellow silk. She had an attractive face, and her skin was even whiter than the blossoms. She beckoned to the man with her round white fan.

"Put the flowers on this," she said. "They're wet with evening dew, and the thorns on the vine will hurt your beautiful hands." She came forward very bashfully.

Korekichi had finally managed to open his gate, and when he did, he saw the woman and went over to her. He accepted the fan for Mitsuuji and took it to him.

"I apologize," Korekichi said. "I forgot where I put the gate key and made you wait out in this noisy street. But no one around here will know who you are. Come along with me now." Even after Mitsuuji's palanquin had disappeared inside the gate, the young woman continued to stand where she was, gazing after it with a deep, wistful look.

12

When Mitsuuji went inside, Korekichi's mother, worn out from her sickness, managed to get up slowly and greet him. "I cut off my hair," she said, "and I've become a nun. I hesitated to visit you and haven't been able to see your face at all. But I've followed the five precepts faithfully, and now I've been blessed by a visit from you in this poor house of mine. You're my Amida Buddha, and this is the most memorable moment of my life. Now I'm ready to go away to paradise in the next world."

The woman's voice was filled with such joy that tears came to Mitsuuji's eyes. "But your condition," he assured her, "isn't really that serious. Please think only about recovering, get some treatment, and be healthy again. Korekichi's still young. Please take care of him until he's able to get a proper position as a retainer. If you die while you're still worried about his future, your anxious soul will have a hard time reaching the Pure Land. Don't worry. I'll have some monks at a temple I know chant sutras and pray for your recovery." He went on at length, encouraging her and showing her great kindness.

After leaving the sick woman's bedside, Mitsuuji asked Korekichi to light a rolled paper torch so he could read the fan from the young woman next door.

---

3. A climbing variety of wild melon with round red fruit; it flowers in the evening in mid-summer.

Mitsuuji reads the writing on the round paper fan under the light held by Korekichi. Shinonome, Tasogare's mother, approaches Mitsuuji from behind, holding a paper lantern.

He picked it up and saw that on it were written, most attractively, the words of a short commoner song:

> Mistaking your light
> for the bright full moon,
> gourds float on their vines
> and crows fly up cawing.

Mitsuuji was unprepared for the beauty of the flowing brushwork, and he was deeply moved. "Who lives in that house just to the west?" he asked.

"As you know," Korekichi answered, "I came back here to take care of my mother. It's the first time I've been home in a long while, and I've been so busy with Mother I don't really know anything about the neighbors. Sometimes young women go in and out of that house, but I think the young woman who gave you the fan is the owner's daughter."

Mitsuuji listened closely, nodding and gazing fondly at the fan, from which came the scent of the incense the woman wore in her robes. He seemed to be longing for her already. "There's something about this fan," he said, "that I must know more about. Quickly, find someone who knows the neighborhood."

It was a small room, so Mitsuuji's voice must have traveled beyond the walls of the house, because a woman of about forty then entered the room without the slightest pretense of reserve. "With your kindest permission," she said to

Korekichi, "let me tell you all about your neighbors. My name is Shinonome,[4] and I moved into the house next door in the Fourth Month. I have one daughter, Tasogare.[5] She's the one who gave you the fan. She's extremely happy you've noticed the song she scribbled on it. I've heard your name before, but tonight's the first time I've had the honor of meeting you in person. I make my living by teaching dancing to young women. My daughter teaches the shamisen, an instrument that recently came here from the Ryukyus.[6] She's not very good yet, but for people like you who move in high places, it would be something new and entertaining, I'm sure. My husband's dead, so I'm a widow now, and there's no one you need to worry about. Both my daughter and I hope very much that you and your visitor will come visit our house, though it's a very shabby place."

Mitsuuji smiled. "It sounds like a wonderful idea," he said, getting up. "We'll go over right now. Well, Shinonome, lead the way." Korekichi thought Mitsuuji was being very imprudent, but he remembered his young age and said nothing.

Mitsuuji followed the woman through the gate he had seen earlier and entered her house. All the reed screens on the second floor were hanging down at full length, and the light that came through here and there was more deeply moving than the light of fireflies.[7] Tasogare came out to greet him and invite him to come inside the hanging screens. Both mother and daughter treated him cordially, and he was fascinated by this commoner house, which was so new to him that he gazed all around.

13

"Earlier," Mitsuuji asked, "when I was resting out in front, I saw two boards leaning against each other and pieces of a robe stretched out on them. Look, they're still there. What are they?"

Shinonome looked through the screen in the front window. "It looks like Tasogare got very excited after she saw you," she said, smiling. "She forgot about the laundry and left it outside. Fall's coming soon, and there's a lot of dew at night now. That robe's going to get all wet. It must be a mess already. It's one of my old summer robes, you know. Ordinary people like us don't have special stretching frames, so we dry our robes on boards."

---

4. Shinonome means Dawn.

5. The name Tasogare (Twilight) suggests the woman Yūgao, named after the evening-blooming moonflower in *The Tale of Genji*.

6. The shamisen was brought from the Ryukyu Islands to Osaka in the late sixteenth century. Tanehiko continues to overlap imagery from the early Edo period, when the three-string instrument had become popular, with the medieval setting.

7. Alludes to a love poem in the *Kokinshū*: "When darkness comes, I burn hotter than any firefly—does he not come because he cannot see my light?" (no. 562). The allusion suggests that the house is lit by Tasogare's love and that Mitsuuji has seen that light.

Shamisen in hand, young Tasogare stands and looks shyly at Mitsuuji, who is enjoying saké and refreshments. A red and white dandara-pattern steel cane, representing a stylized rein, is hooked behind the head of a "spring horse" (*harugoma*), which is hanging on the wall above Mitsuuji. Both are props used for dances and appropriate to the house of a dance teacher, Shinonome's profession.

Keeping time with his fan, Mitsuuji sang, "My house has curtains between rooms and hangings in the rooms. . . ."[8]

"Yes, that's the old saibara song," Shinonome said. "The word 'curtain' in it sounds the same as those boards outside, but it's a different word. The long hanging silk curtains in the song were made from damask and brocade. But the house in the song, well, it's also my house, so let me change some of the words and sing the whole song:

> My house has clothes drying
> on a stretcher made of boards
> while I wait for a great lord to come
> so I can make him my son-in-law—
> What shall I give him with his wine?
> Abalone, wreath shell, and sea urchin

---

8. A saibara song contemporaneous with the historical *Tale of Genji*. Mitsuuji recalls elegant "curtains" (*tobari*) used in upper-class houses, because they are homophonous with "clothes-drying boards."

"When I sing it, it turns into a short commoner song. 'Make him my son-in-law' sounds like a sign of good fortune to come, though the only delicious food I can 'give him' are the abalone, wreath shell, and sea urchin in the noisy songs of ordinary fisherpeople that my daughter sings to her shamisen. But tonight, please stay with us. Don't you agree, Tasogare?"

"Well, yes," Tasogare said. "But my bedding isn't fit for a great man like this." She spoke rather awkwardly and didn't seem to know much about the world yet, but she was glowing with youth and quite charming.

14

Just then a man coughed at the front door. "My lord, it's me, Kiyonosuke," he said. "I've just returned to the capital, and I heard you were here."

When the man came up to the second floor, Shinonome's manner suddenly became more formal, and she carefully watched Kiyonosuke out of the corner of her eye to see who he was. "I can see that he's here on urgent business," she said to Mitsuuji, "and I'm sure you'll want to talk with him alone. Tasogare, bring in the robe and put the boards away. I'll go get some good saké." Both women left the room.

Kiyonosuke, kneeling, moved closer to Mitsuuji. "As you requested," he said, "I told everyone I was going to go to a hot springs for a while, and I've traveled all the back roads around Kyoto. But I couldn't find anything at all. Finally I couldn't think of anything else to do, so today I came back. I went directly to your house, where I heard about Korekichi's mother and your visit. I hurried to the house next door and then came all the way to this place and troubled you here. As you asked, I've retired using the pretense of illness. And at last I've found a good husband for Muraogi.[9] Munekiyo, Yamana Sōzen's only son, has asked to marry her. But my wife, Karaginu,[10] has no relatives I can leave her with. Her father, Tsuchihashi Masanaga, died, and her clan no longer exists, so I'm going to take her with me back to my home in Iyo Province. Then I'll be free to search the whole country for the sword."

Mitsuuji motioned to Kiyonosuke with his fan, asking him to stop. Then he whispered to his retainer, who showed great surprise at what he was hearing.

"There's no doubt about it," Kiyonosuke said. "I'll have them arrested right away."

But Mitsuuji stopped him from getting up and looked around carefully. "If we rush, we'll make mistakes. Listen, here's what we'll do." Then his voice dropped even further.

---

9. Kiyonosuke's daughter, who suggests Nokiba no Ogi in *The Tale of Genji*.

10. Karaginu suggests Utsusemi, and Kiyonosuke, the vice governor of Iyo on Shikoku in *The Tale of Genji*.

Mitsuuji converses with Kiyonosuke on the second floor. Tasogare appears anxious as she folds the robe. Two pillows lie in front of a folding screen, which is adorned with images of the *yūgao* flower, foreshadowing Tasogare's relationship with Mitsuuji.

"Very good, my lord, you stay here alone tonight."

"Until dawn comes," Mitsuuji said, "stay at the house next door."

"Certainly. But there's one other thing I would like to talk to you about. It has nothing to do with all this. I heard that while I was away, you were forced to stay at my house to avoid traveling in an unlucky direction. That night you asked that Muraogi be sent to serve your food, but unfortunately she was staying overnight at Kiyomizu Temple, offering an important prayer. So my wife Karaginu lied and said she was my daughter and went instead. She told me other people had heard about it, and now she feels so ashamed about deceiving you that she has decided to commit suicide. But I can't allow a small thing like that disturb our important business, and I absolutely refused to let her kill herself. Still, I'd like to know what actually happened."

"It was all just a trifling one-time thing," Mitsuuji said in a faltering voice. "There's no real reason to blame your wife. I don't care about it at all." He repeated the same words over and over again.[11] "Please tell Karaginu she doesn't

---

11. Mitsuuji is embarrassed because on the night he stayed at Kiyonosuke's house, he later went into the bedroom of Kiyonosuke's young wife, Karaginu, and tried to seduce her, thinking that she was Kiyonosuke's daughter Muraogi. Later, with the aid of Karaginu's younger brother,

need to worry, but never mention any of this to anyone. Well, what are you waiting for?" Kiyonosuke left quickly for Korekichi's house.

15

Even unrefined mountain people feel the desire to rest for a while beneath beautiful cherry blossoms.[12] Although everyone in the world has that wish, Tasogare could never have expected the high-ranking Mitsuuji to show any interest in her, but that night she slept beneath his love. The two exchanged vows as deep as those made by the lovers who compressed a thousand nights of love into a single night,[13] and their desire to exchange even more vows ended only when roosters crowed at dawn. Soon the people in the houses in the neighborhood were up and busy at their business. Noisy conversations could be heard from many houses, and the grinding sound of a mortar and its foot pestle sounded to Mitsuuji like roaring thunder. He didn't know what it was, but unable to sleep, he finally got up. He had never slept in such a small house before, and he was interested in seeing what it was like, so he helped Tasogare roll up the reed blinds, and together they looked outside. Bamboo had been planted in the tiny garden, but he was saddened to see that the white flowers on the fence had closed and were now drooping. From where he was, he could make out everyone who walked along the wide street in front. Then he saw a nun in black robes walking closer and closer. A young disciple, also in black robes, followed her, carrying her bundle. As Mitsuuji casually watched the nun pass the front gate, he realized it was Karukaya, whom he hadn't seen for some time.

He wondered where she could be returning from. "Get her attention before she goes by!" he said to Tasogare, who stood up and clapped her hands from the second floor. Then she waved to the nun, inviting her in. The nun waved back and walked closer with an uncomprehending look on her face. When she saw Mitsuuji, she was extremely surprised. She went into the living room while Mitsuuji and Tasogare were coming down from the second floor.

"Ah, Karukaya!" Mitsuuji said, "It's been all too long. Don't sit so far away."

At that, Karukaya, showing great respect, politely came closer to him, pushing herself along the floor as she knelt. "I'm very surprised to see you around

---

he entered the house secretly, spied on Karaginu, and again tried to seduce her but discovered she was only pretending to be Muraogi. Karaginu escaped, but Mitsuuji did not find consolation with her younger brother, as Genji did in *The Tale of Genji*. Meanwhile, Muraogi is angry that her desire for Mitsuuji has been thwarted.

12. Alludes to the kana preface of the *Kokinshū*, which describes the unpolished poet Kuronushi as a woodsman resting under a blossoming cherry tree.

13. Alludes to the poems exchanged by a woman and Narihira in *The Tales of Ise*, sec. 22. In the Edo period, "exchange vows" also meant lovemaking.

Having just awakened and with her sash still half tied, Tasogare beckons to the nun Karukaya and her apprentice from upstairs.

here," she said. "People of your stature are usually more careful about where they stay."

Mitsuuji stopped her before she could go on. "That's enough about me," he said. "What about you? Last night you stayed somewhere. Did you have some interesting dreams[14] there?"

Karukaya continued to stare at Mitsuuji. "Night after night you go prowling around," she said, "and you don't even know your own wife is sick. You even joke that no man should marry an older woman like Lady Futaba,[15] who gets jealous so easily. You can be sure that those who want to criticize you have heard those remarks, and you soon will be blamed for them. Everything Futaba says is true, after all. She asked me to come chant sutras for her the day before yesterday, and this morning she felt better and said I could leave. Just now I was on my way back to my hermitage. Futaba gave me one of her beautiful outer robes and told me I could resew it into cloths for my altar. My disciple there is carrying it for me. Futaba was so kind as to suggest that I ride home in a palanquin. I was grateful for her offer, but I told her that for an ordinary

---

14. A common euphemism for lovemaking. Mitsuuji assumes that Karukaya also has spent the night with a lover.

15. Lady Futaba, Mitsuuji's wife, suggests Lady Aoi, Genji's first wife in *The Tale of Genji*.

person like me, with my upbringing, it was easier to walk. That's why I was passing by with my disciple. The only reason I sometimes go to Futaba's house is because she asks me to come, but I must say, she's a very gentle person who was born with a marvelous personality. And yet you treat her as if you hated her." She wept as she spoke.

Unable either to sit or leave, Tasogare felt very uncomfortable and moved her hands restlessly. But Mitsuuji laughed.

"Futaba would never tell you what she's really thinking," he said. "You've seen her only when you were chanting sutras for her. She looks like a beautiful person, but she's always burning with jealousy inside. A while ago, at dawn, a strange woman appeared above my pillow. I can still see her staring fiercely at me, as if to say how bitterly she resented my ignoring her and visiting a common woman with no lineage. When I woke up, my body was covered with cold sweat. I thought about it carefully, and I'm sure it was Futaba. She's utterly consumed by jealousy. I'm afraid of seeing her real face, you know, but if she's sick I can't just ignore her. Well, I'm off for the Akamatsu mansion."[16] Mitsuuji retied his sash and stood up.

Karukaya seemed to find something suspicious. "None of your men is out front," she said.

"Don't worry. My palanquin carriers are waiting for me at Korekichi's house next door. Well, Tasogare, until next time."

When Mitsuuji got up to leave, Shinonome, who had been listening to everything behind a sliding paper-covered door, stood up and came into the room. Bowing very politely with both hands on the floor, she said, "Please at least have a cup of tea before you go. My daughter's not very good, but she will make a cup for you." As Shinonome spoke, she looked at Karukaya's face and was amazed. "Why, you're Kikyō, aren't you!"

The nun, too, was surprised at suddenly hearing her old name. "Then you must be Shinonome," she said. "Well, what a surprise!" The two women took each other by the hand and began to cry together.

Mitsuuji could see that their relationship was very close, but he did not ask about it and left directly for the Akamatsu mansion. When he got there he found that Futaba's sickness was not serious, and so his wanderings began again. Whenever he went out, he also stopped at the house on Fifth Avenue, and Tasogare fell more and more deeply in love with him. Time passed, and autumn[17] came. The many small intimacies they shared have been omitted here.

Yamana Munekiyo, son of the scheming Yamana Sōzen, pays for many performances by the top-ranking courtesan Akogi,[18] *but she never appears. Finally she tells him that while*

16. Owned by Futaba's father, Akamatsu Masanori, minister of the left.
17. Autumn begins with the Seventh Month, in early or middle August.
18. Akogi suggests Lady Rokujō in *The Tale of Genji.*

Karukaya (*bottom left*) and Mitsuuji reunite in the living room as Tasogare watches nearby, holding a toothpaste case and brushing her teeth with a toothpick. The incense symbol in the "Yūgao" chapter of *The Tale of Genji* once again adorns the reed curtain beside her. Shinonome (*top left*) is surprised to see Karukaya.

her mother was alive, Yamana's father was one of her vassals and that she cannot stand him. Meanwhile, Mitsuuji visits the same licensed quarter on Sixth Avenue, the big avenue immediately south of the one on which Tasogare lives. He rarely buys performances by the women there, and when he occasionally goes as far as the bedroom, he then sends the women away and invites the house staff to drink with him. He and Akogi love each other but only exchange hokku.

Book 5

1

Mitsuuji did not forget the white flowers blooming forlornly on the ramshackle fence, and tonight he returned to the house on Fifth Avenue still another time, but Tasogare sat looking down at the floor, lost in thought. She was unable to say what she felt, and tears filled her eyes. Mitsuuji had come here many times, and the two had talked without reserve about their most intimate thoughts, so he could not understand why Tasogare was treating him in this way, but he kept his thoughts to himself.

Mitsuuji shows a sleeve patterned with folding fans to Shinonome (*right*). The pattern matches that of the faded piece beside her knee. Shinonome is wearing a robe with a crow-flock pattern, suggesting the prized sword Kogarasumaru (Small Crow), which Mitsuuji is looking for. Tasogare (*left*), wearing a *yūgao*-pattern robe, prepares the pillow in front of a vase of pampas grass and two containers of saké offerings for harvest moon viewing. The back of a folding screen appears on the upper left, with the bed on the far side.

Shinonome spoke as pleasantly as always, and now she asked her daughter to get her bed ready. In the light of a lamp nearby, Shinonome was sewing together some scraps into a lined nightgown for herself.[19] Tonight was the fifteenth of the Eighth Month, and light from the full moon fell into the house between the rough boards that formed its walls. The cries of crickets in the walls, which had sounded so far away, now seemed to Mitsuuji to come from beside his pillow. Unable to sleep, he broke the silence and spoke to Shinonome.

"Those pieces of thin robe beside you," he said, "aren't they the same pieces I saw stretched out to dry the first night I stayed here?"

Shinonome laughed. "When I was young," she said casually, "I had a small job in an upper-class mansion. This was something they gave me. Back then it was a respectable formal robe, but many years have gone by, and neither it nor

---

19. It was customary to change into lined sleeping robes at the beginning of the Ninth Month.

I am any the better for it. One sleeve ripped off, so I had my daughter unstitch the other pieces and wash them so I could use them to line a nightgown."

Mitsuuji got up and went over to her. "The sleeve that came off that nice thin robe," he said, reaching into the front of his robe, "didn't it have large folding fans on it in gold leaf? This must be it." He threw a sleeve down in front of Shinonome.

Suspicious, Shinonome picked up the sleeve and examined it. "Yes, this is it," she said. "But something's written on one of the fan designs." She held the sleeve close to the lamp and read out a hokku:

> Coming close
> you can make it out—
> a crow gourd

Startled momentarily, she regained her composure, laughing as if nothing had happened. "The sleeve came apart long ago," she said, "so I couldn't wash it. But this sleeve you've given me looks a lot like it. If I sewed it onto the old pieces I have and called the robe a 'rare historical item,'[20] I could probably get several gold pieces for it. Gold. Yes. Ah, I forgot! Tonight I've promised to go to a meeting to pray to Maitreya on the Golden Peak.[21] I'll be back late, so please make yourself at home. *Praise be to Maitreya*," she chanted as she went out, "*Master of the Future*."

Tasogare, tears streaking her cheeks, watched until her mother had gone. Very gently Mitsuuji came to her. "Just now," he said, "your mother was chanting the name of the buddha who lives on the Golden Peak south of Nara. Our love, too, isn't only for this world. Let's promise to be true to each other forever, until Maitreya appears at the end of time. I've never loved anyone as deeply as I love you. We must have been brought together by some very strong karma. That night we first met, when I was traveling secretly, I felt uneasy when I lay down and couldn't sleep. But tonight no one's watching us. I want to take you away from here and go to a place I know well, a place where we can live peacefully together. I've made the arrangements already. You won't regret it. Why are you crying?"

Finally Tasogare looked up. "You would never tell me your name," she said, "so we had someone follow after you, trying to discover where you live. But you skillfully hid the way you came. You think I don't know where you live. But even my fingers told me about you, and long ago I guessed you were no ordinary

---

20. In the Edo period, montage-design robes sewn from patches of fabrics from different periods were considered very fashionable.

21. Mount Ōmine. On this sacred mountain, climbed by mountain monks, such as the one who appears later, the bodhisattva Maitreya was believed to wait until he came to save the world, eons in the future.

person. I saw Karukaya only when I was young, so I didn't even recognize her, but she's related to my mother, and she told her you were Mitsuuji. My mother never talks about the past, so recently I asked next door, but you had asked Korekichi not to say anything. I had no idea you were the younger son of the shōgun. I was very surprised when I heard who you were. Very. Each time you stopped at our rundown house, though, I realized your feelings for me had not changed, and you became more and more dear to me. But there's something else. Mother's involved in some very bad things. I couldn't possibly betray her and tell you about them, but the thought of your staying in this house with her knowing who you are—it frightens me." Tasogare began to weep again.

Mitsuuji understood why she was crying, and he smiled.

3

"I'm an old fox," Mitsuuji joked. "Please allow me to show you a few tricks." He pulled some standing screens in front of their bed, and soon their voices could be heard no more. After a while, Shinonome made her way stealthily back to her house together with two well-known toughs in the area with whom she'd been negotiating. Once inside, she whispered into their ears, and they both nodded back. But when the toughs kicked over the standing screens, Tasogare wasn't there. Instead they found a calm young samurai snoring soundly.

"Ah!" Shinonome cried. "Tasogare's gone, and that Mitsuuji, he's disappeared, too. Look, there's a hole in the back wall. Tasogare's fallen under his spell, and she's told him all about my plan. It makes me so angry I can't stand it." She stood clenching her fists.

The thugs were also shocked. "I was really looking forward to the money we'd get for catching the man alive," one said, "and my muscles are popping out, just waiting for a good fight. We can't give up now."

"Let's rough up this young guy a bit," the other said, "and force him to tell us where Mitsuuji's run off to. He's got a lot of nerve, lying there snoring as if nothing's happened. Let's remodel his face for him."

Just as the toughs attacked, the young samurai leaped up, dodged them, and, as they passed by him, sent them flying head over heels. Then he stood straight up and said in a resounding voice, "You must be Shinonome. Well, listen carefully. I serve the Ashikaga, and my name is Akamatsu Takanao.[22] Do you really think Mitsuuji would be so careless as to come here alone? His retainers have quietly placed themselves all around the house, and they've been keeping watch all night. Mitsuuji suspects you, and he asked me to question you, so I came here with a large company of men. We have the house surrounded, so there's no way you can escape. And your daughter Tasogare, well, Mitsuuji's

---

22. Son of a famous general, minister of the left, and brother of Lady Futaba, thus Mitsuuji's brother-in-law. He suggests Tō no Chūjō in *The Tale of Genji*.

Shinonome (*left*) and two very muscular toughs, each with a stick in hand, are ready to attack Mitsuuji and Tasogare. One of the toughs has removed the ceremonial paper streamers from the sacred saké container and is drinking the saké.

taken her away. She's his hostage now. There's nothing you can do any more, so tell me about yourself. Everything."

While Takanao was talking, the two toughs got up and rushed at him again with all their might. He could easily have driven them off, but he needed them as evidence, so he grabbed their thrusting hands and twisted them until the men went down to the floor. Then he sat on them; neither was able to move.

Shinonome's face showed her anger. "Just now, when I was coming back," she said to herself, "I saw two people walking along, hiding their faces. I thought it was very strange, but the moon went behind some clouds, so when I passed them I couldn't see who they were. That must have been my daughter and Mitsuuji. They were headed for a narrow path between rice paddies, and I know where it goes. It's that old temple out in the fields. Yes, yes!" She ran into a closet and came out with a bundle under her arm. She left the room so quickly she seemed to fly.

4

While Shinonome was away, Mitsuuji had broken a hole in the back wall of the bedroom, but once outside he realized that even though he had carefully

Akamatsu Takanao beats the toughs and throws one against the folded screen (*right*). The large hole through which Mitsuuji and Tasogare escaped appears behind the bed (*top right*). To the left, Shinonome escapes with a *hannya* (female demon) mask in her mouth and a small bundle under her arm. The way she tucks her sash and steps out with one foot up resembles the *okkake* (chase) pose in kabuki performances.

disguised himself, the gold ornaments on his fine sword glinted conspicuously in the bright moonlight. So he pulled down one of the reed screens hanging from the eaves and quickly wrapped it around himself and Tasogare. For a while, he pushed between the low limbs of some pine trees, carrying Tasogare. He then put her down lightly, and they walked hand in hand, unsure of their way. In the other direction they saw Shinonome coming toward them with two gruesome-looking men. But before Shinonome caught sight of them, clouds covered the moon, and they moved to the side of the road to let her and the thugs pass by.

Then they began walking along a narrow path through deserted fields, pushing through long wild grass until they no longer knew where they were. They could hear the sounds of women fulling their white cotton robes, and in the distance wild geese cried out to one another high in the sky.

5

Although the pure white moon shone brilliantly, a breeze began to blow, and they found themselves in a sudden rain shower. And there, beside the path,

Mitsuuji and Tasogare, wrapping themselves in a reed screen, walk barefoot through the wild grass. Caught in a sudden rain shower, Mitsuuji looks enviously at the sedge hat on a stone statue of a Jizō bodhisattva. A stone bridge leads to the entrance of an old temple on the far left.

stood a stone statue of the gentle bodhisattva Jizō.[23] Regarding this as a sign of good karma, Mitsuuji took the wide sedge hat that a pilgrim had placed on the statue and held it above their heads.

"Look," he said, "someone wrote 'Paradise in the next life' and 'We two traveling together'[24] on it. That means we'll both go to the Pure Land paradise after we die and live together happily in the next life, too. Please don't lose hope." Mitsuuji tried to encourage Tasogare as much as he could, but he had never been on this path before, and he himself felt uneasy and didn't know what to do next. Tasogare felt anxious about many things, but above all she worried about how far she had come with Mitsuuji and what might happen between them in the future, and she stood still, unable to go on, her sleeves more wet from her own tears than from the rain.

Then Mitsuuji made out the faint flame of a lamp flickering up ahead. "Ah!" he said, "there's a big temple up there. I used to know the head monk very well, but he died, and no one lives there any more. I heard it was abandoned, but

---

23. Famous for guiding dead souls safely to the other world.

24. A phrase used by tantric Shingon-sect believers, who believed that Saint Kōbō (Kūkai) walked every step with them.

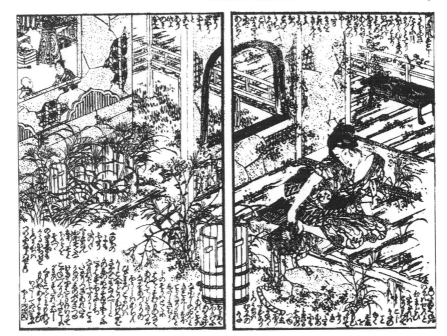

Tasogare sits in a sensuous pose and wipes her feet with her apron as Mitsuuji and the caretaker monk converse in the other room. The exposed walls and the overgrown wild grass reveal a temple going to ruin.

there must be a monk still living in it. Let's stay there for the night. When it gets light, I'll take you the rest of the way to Saga." Mitsuuji and Tasogare kept following the path, which led to the temple that Shinonome had predicted they would reach. They went through the desolate front gate and pushed through the dew-wet grass in the temple garden. Mitsuuji wrapped his two swords in the hanging screen.

"Hello!" he called out. "Is there a caretaker here?" When a monk appeared, Mitsuuji told him, "I'm a merchant who often goes up to Muromachi Avenue.[25] But I'm having trouble paying back a loan, and the collectors are coming to my house, so my older sister and I, well, we have to stay away tonight. I remembered the head monk of this temple. We used to be good friends while he was alive, so I came here, hoping we could stay the night."

Mitsuuji made up a very smooth excuse, but the monk had been to the Muromachi shōgunal palace the year before with the former head monk, and he soon recognized Mitsuuji. He moved back and bowed very respectfully. "I am honored by your visit," he said, "but it is most unexpected. I would like to invite you to the reception room, but the roof leaks. It looked like we'd have a

---

25. Many textile wholesalers were located on Muromachi Avenue, as was the shōgunal palace.

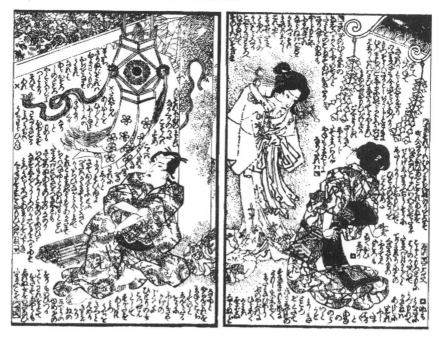

An unknown female figure appears before Tasogare (*right*) while a large paper hanging lantern swings ominously. Mitsuuji watches the lantern, his sword wrapped in reed blinds to his right.

hard rain, so I took out all the straw floor mats and put them in a dry place. But it's cleared up again already, so I'll go put the room in order. Please wait here for a while until it's ready." The monk led them to a small, dark room beside the main prayer hall and then ran off.

Tasogare was timid and easily became afraid. The place terrified her, and suddenly she put her body against Mitsuuji's. "Listen," she said, "you can hear someone's loud footsteps behind us. They're coming closer and closer." She seemed to be in a daze and began shaking all over.

Mitsuuji smiled. "You're worrying too much," he said. "There's someone in the kitchen, but who would come over here? Hold on tight to me. I have a question for you. We've told each other everything without holding anything back, but you've never mentioned anything about your family. Tell me, what was your father's name?"

Tasogare sighed. "My father was an ordinary fisherman," she said faintly, "who spent his life wandering here and there. I'm ashamed to tell you this, but he was just a commoner. We don't even have a family name." She looked behind her again and again as she spoke. Mitsuuji stood up and opened the wooden doors between the room and the porch outside.

"If the darkness frightens you, come over here," he said, walking with her to the porch. The moon shone down even more brightly than before. The grass and trees in the old garden grew wildly, without any hint of beauty. Water weeds filled the pond, and the fence had been blown down by the wind. Autumn fields stretched for as far as they could see. There was something eerie about the temple. Mitsuuji closed the paper-covered sliding doors, but wind came in between the cracks, causing the lamp to flicker repeatedly. A strip of paper dangling from a ripped standing screen swayed back and forth like a tuft of long grass, and Tasogare felt it was calling to her. The room became completely quiet, and then suddenly—was it a shadow?—a woman's shape appeared. It glared at Mitsuuji.

"You saw me in a dream," she said, "when you stayed overnight at Fifth Avenue. As I said then, I am deeply offended that you have abandoned me for a woman who doesn't even come from a good family. And now you have brought her all the way here." Then she disappeared as quickly as she had come.

7

Mitsuuji had heard about this kind of thing happening in old tales, but it was very odd and even suspicious to see something like this in front of his eyes. When he turned around to see if Tasogare was all right, he found her lying face down on the floor beside him. Anxiously he tried to raise her up, but her body lay limp on the floor. She didn't seem to be breathing. Tasogare must have seen the strange shape, too, and fainted. Mitsuuji was frantic but didn't know what to do. The flame in the lantern that hung from the eaves had gone out, and he couldn't see where anything was.

"Someone! Bring a lamp!" he said, clapping his hands loudly. But all he could hear were echoes, so he kicked open the inner and outer sliding doors. Moonlight fell into the room, and he groped around and found a bowl of tea placed as an offering in front of a mortuary tablet. He splashed the tea on Tasogare's face and said her name again and again, trying to call her soul back to her body.

At last, Tasogare regained consciousness. "Are you Mitsuuji?" she asked. "I saw a vision of some woman I'd never seen before. She stared at me in a very threatening way. Her face was so horrible I couldn't stand it. After that I don't remember anything." Her body shook as she lay there.

Trying to encourage her, Mitsuuji spoke loudly and firmly. "In old abandoned buildings like this," he said, "foxes and other wild animals are known to take mysterious shapes and frighten humans. But as long as I'm here with you, I won't let anything harm you. Look, I can see a lamp coming in our direction along that passageway from the building over there. It must be the monk. He recognizes me, so please don't act helpless in front of him, or he'll laugh at both of us."

Strengthened by Mitsuuji's words, Tasogare calmed down by the time the monk arrived.

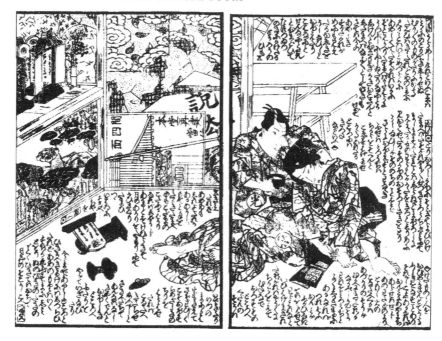

Mitsuuji takes from the altar a bowl filled with tea to revive Tasogare. Mortuary tablets and a stand for tea bowls lie scattered on the floor. Beneath the altar, parts of the lotus painting have come off. Various announcements for prayers and the building of new temple compounds hold together the adjacent wall, further accentuating the temple's desolate state.

"I didn't realize your lamp was out," the monk said. "You must have felt pretty miserable out here. I've put the reception room back together, so please come with me." He led them to what looked like the visitors' hall. Unlike the previous room, this one was beautifully decorated and furnished, but rain had leaked through the roof and formed streaks like long strands of the Nunobiki Waterfall down the pictures painted on the sliding doors. The handles of the doors had come off, and moonlight fell here and there onto the floor, making the room resemble the famous moonlit paddies on the lower slopes of Mount Obasute. Soon the monk brought them some rice gruel and fruit he had prepared.

"Which door did you come in by?" the monk asked. "I can't find your shoes." The monk looked here and there, but Mitsuuji knew his reputation would be damaged if he let on that they had rushed off without even putting on shoes, and he made only vague replies. The monk, however, tried even harder to please him. "Well," he said, "first of all, let me put your hat over here." But as he lifted the hat, he saw what was written on it and stared at the words with a puzzled expression. Then he gathered up their other things, even the apron Tasogare had tossed away after she had wiped off the mud on her feet with it. Then the monk placed a standing screen around the couple to give them some

Guided by the monk's lantern, Mitsuuji and Tasogare walk down a dilapidated corridor. Mitsuuji holds his sword under his arm and leads Tasogare by the hand while she loosens her sash and tries to calm herself. The large text to the right reads: "Drawings by Kunisada, Text by Tanehiko."

privacy. Mitsuuji could see that the monk thought he had come here secretly with a commoner lover, and he felt so ashamed that sweat soon covered his forehead.

"I'm extremely tired tonight," Mitsuuji finally said to Tasogare. "We don't need to leave until late in the morning. Let's take our time and get some rest." Only then was he able to get the monk to leave.

9

After they were alone again, Mitsuuji continued to comfort and encourage Tasogare in the abandoned guest room. It must have been past midnight. A strong wind was blowing, and they could hear the rough soughing of many pines. The weak, low voice of an owl made them feel even lonelier. Then the woman's shape appeared again. She was a demon woman now, and she kicked her way through the sliding doors, which were painted with an aristocrat's oxcart.[26] She waved her horns, which were like gnarled old branches, and in one hand she held an iron pole. Her eyes bore down on the two.

"Other people," she said, "have listened to Buddhist preachings and ridden

---

26. Suggests Lady Aoi's oxcart in the "Heartvine" chapter of *The Tale of Genji*, where Aoi's oxcart and entourage come into conflict with Lady Rokujō's oxcart and entourage at the Kamo Festival. The oxcart wheel is also the wheel of the Buddhist law and of karma.

At a house in the Sixth Avenue licensed quarter, the courtesan Akogi sleeps, resting against her long pipe. The ornamental scent bag hanging above her and the pattern on her robe reveal that her spirit has left her body and has gone to haunt Mitsuuji and Tasogare.

on the cart of the Buddhist law, escaping from the burning house of existence.[27] Yet I—have I not destroyed the cart painted on those doors? I am one of those who will never escape. Ah, how unbearable this sadness is. The spring blossoms we watched, the autumn full moons we enjoyed together, the vows we made to become one for all time—they were all, all empty. My heart has grown bitter like dew on fern sprouts no one comes to pick, and I have come all the way here to take revenge. Who am I? The angry soul of Lady Futaba, whom you once loved but now neglect." The woman shook out her hair until it fell the length of her body, and she stood there motionless.

Mitsuuji laughed loudly. "There is one known case in ancient times of an aristocrat seeing a demon at the palace and driving it away. But something's very suspicious. True, your outer robe is one that Lady Futaba likes to wear. I remember its design. So you must be someone with a grudge against her. You managed to get hold of one of her robes, and now you pretend to be a demon— to shock me with a display of jealousy and make me leave her completely. And do you also hold a grudge against me? Confess everything."

27. The image of Akogi at Sixth Avenue and the words of the spirit suggest the angry spirit of Lady Rokujō, Genji's neglected lover, who tries to kill Aoi, Genji's wife, in the nō play *Lady Aoi* (*Aoi no ue*). Tanehiko overlaps Lady Rokujō and Akogi, a leading courtesan in the Rokujō (Sixth Avenue) licensed quarter. In the picture, Akogi's spirit is shown leaving her body while she naps, while in the text the spirit is said to be that of Futaba, Mitsuuji's wife. The demon woman wears Lady Rokujō's demon mask from the nō play.

A demon woman appears, tearing a hole through the rain-streaked sliding door panels. Her underrobe with the crow-flock pattern and the red and white dandara-pattern cane she holds in her right hand reveal that she is Shinonome in disguise. The large painting in the back of an ox carriage, which was used by Heian aristocrats, alludes to the nō play *Lady Aoi* and the "Aoi" chapter of *The Tale of Genji*.

"How dare you speak like that?" the strange woman said, shaking her head. "Time keeps passing, and your unfaithfulness has made me more miserable than the morning glory that shrivels in the early sun. So soon. Oh so soon! Yesterday I was beautiful, but today—only a dream.

11

"It is always hard for women to achieve salvation," she said, "but know this. Your acts, too, have consequences in the bitter floating world of human existence. The cartwheel of karma never stops turning, and retribution for your own acts is now coming back to you." She tossed aside her iron pole and in an instant unsheathed a dagger, pointed it at Mitsuuji, and lunged at him.

Earlier in the evening, Tasogare had fainted when she saw the strange shape, but now she showed no fear. Grabbing the wide sedge hat, which lay near her on the floor, she placed herself between the shape and Mitsuuji and shielded him with the hat.

The demon woman was furious. "Move," she said, pulling Tasogare out of her way. As she did, a mountain monk pushed his way up through the floor mats and appeared beside her. He had done austerities on Mount Ōmine, where the Diamond World and Womb Word mandalas interpene-

Tasogare fearlessly grabs the sedge hat and stands between the demon woman (*center*) and Mitsuuji. Kiyonosuke (*right*) appears in the guise of the mountain monk who repels the demon woman in the nō play *Lady Aoi*.

trate,[28] and his linen cloak had brushed against the dew of the Pure Land paradise that manifests itself on the sacred mountain. Over his shoulders he wore the surplice that had helped him endure his many austerities and protected him from impurity, and in his hands he held large prayer beads made of red quince wood. These he fingered as he came closer to the demon woman. Suddenly he grabbed her firmly around the waist.

"Life," he said, "is as fleeting as a flash of lightning. Humans should not hold grudges, and no one ever needs to grieve. Realize this and be enlightened!" As he spoke, he tried to force the demon woman down onto the floor.

But the woman quickly pushed his arm away. "Enough," she said. "I suffer so much I will never be saved, and my bitterness is very deep. Tonight I will take revenge for something I can never, never forget. This man is the offspring of the man who destroyed my father. What I do now I do for my father's anguished soul. May it now leave this world, liberated at last!" She ran once more at Mitsuuji.

"Stop!" Tasogare said, stepping in the demon woman's way again, with no regard for her own life.

---

28. Suggests the mountain monk who soothes the angry spirit of Lady Rokujō in the nō play *Lady Aoi*.

To everyone's horror, Tasogare slits her throat. Shinonome rushes toward Tasogare, flinging her demon woman mask to the floor. Both Mitsuuji and Kiyonosuke (*left*) gasp at the sight.

The mountain monk quickly came up behind the demon woman. "Malicious being, out!" he said. "You pretend to attack my lord's lover, then suddenly want to harm my lord."

Very slowly the three circled one another, the demon woman determined to stab Mitsuuji, and the other two equally determined to stop her. Mitsuuji stood calmly nearby, watching with no hint of surprise on his face. The mountain monk waited, and when he saw a chance, he grabbed the demon woman's forearm, twisting it until she was on the floor. Then he sat on her, not allowing her the slightest movement.

"Ah, is there no pity anywhere?" Tasogare said. She seemed ready to go to the demon woman but didn't. Shocked, she uttered only "Oh!" and collapsed forward onto the floor.

"She must be afraid again," Mitsuuji said, going toward her. "That demon's not even very frightening. She certainly is fainthearted." But when Mitsuuji reached Tasogare, he was shaken. "Ah!" he exclaimed. "She's cut her throat with a razor. She's hardly breathing."

"Of all the things!" the mountain monk said. "Now we've lost our valuable hostage." His grip on the demon woman loosened momentarily, and she pushed him away and flung off her demon mask. It was Shinonome. She went to her daughter and lifted her in her arms.

"I did all those horrible things just for you," Shinonome said, overcome with grief. "So you could find a good place for yourself in the world. Do you really hate me so much you've killed yourself? What a shame, what a terrible shame!"

Impatient, Mitsuuji came up to her. "Listen, Shinonome, listen carefully. You dressed yourself up as a demon woman, but I could see it was you by the way your feet moved—just like a dance master's.

12

"It's fortunate you've come," Mitsuuji said. "Just now I was about to capture you and question you, but then Tasogare committed suicide. I want to ask you about many things, but first, let me tell you we know it was you who broke into the shōgunal storehouse and stole the Kogarasumaru sword.[29] Your thin robe with the folding fan designs is missing a sleeve—that's clear evidence. I noticed the robe stretched out to dry when I visited Korekichi's house to see his sick mother, and I wanted to know more about it. Then, fortunately, you invited us in, and I became intimate with your daughter. Every time I've visited, including tonight, I've looked for the sword, but it was nowhere in the house. You've given it to someone else. And now you're going to tell me who you gave it to." He came up and stood beside Shinonome.

The mountain monk also came up to her. "My name is Nikki Kiyonosuke," he said, "and I was in charge of guarding the shōgunal treasure house. It was a cloudy night in the Fifth Month. I saw a shape escaping, but it was so dark I couldn't really make out anything. While we were struggling, the moon came out from behind the clouds, but the light was very dim. I could see that the thief was a woman, but she had a towel over her face, so I couldn't see her face. I used my pronged pole, though, and ripped off one sleeve of her robe as she got away. I presented the sleeve as evidence, and then I myself went searching everywhere for the sword. When I came to your house, I had no idea you were the thief, but Lord Mitsuuji quietly pointed out to me that the cypress-blade folding fan design on the torn sleeve matched the design on the robe pieces that were stretched out to dry, and he ordered me to watch you. So I've paid close attention to you in your different disguises. I didn't see the thief's face, but there's definitely something about your appearance that reminds me of her. And now you've plotted to kill my lord Mitsuuji. There must be a reason for it. It's time to confess."

Caught between Mitsuuji and his retainer, Shinonome suddenly raised her dagger and plunged it deep into her own stomach. Then she gave out a great sigh. "Now that I've come this far," she said, "why should I hide anything? I'll

---

29. Small Crow (Kogarasu-maru), a sword believed to have been brought from heaven by a shamanic crow and given to Emperor Kanmu (r. 781–806).

Placing one foot on the table, Shinonome commits *seppuku* as she tells her story, and Mitsuuji and Kiyonosuke listen attentively. The sedge hat is smeared with Tasogare's bloody handprints.

tell you now how karma worked itself out in my life. It's a long story, but please listen to it all. I once was named Yokogumo.

13

"My father was Itabatake Noritomo, the former governor of Ise Province. He led a rebellion against the shōgun, but he was surrounded at Kontaiji Castle and destroyed by Yoshimasa.[30] I am the only member of the clan who survived. I escaped with my wet nurse, and she helped me get a job serving in the palace. When I was twenty, it must have been, I had a secret affair with a low-ranking young samurai named Shigesaka Hamon. Soon I found I was pregnant. It was Tasogare. Then people began to notice my condition, so we had to run away. We found a small house near Tadasu,[31] and my husband hid the fact that he was a samurai with a family name and pretended to be a commoner named Dorozō. At that time Yoshimasa's favorite was Lady Hirugao, and one of her

---

30. The eighth Ashikaga shōgun (r. 1443–1473), during the period of the Ōnin Wars; here, Mitsuuji's father, Yoshimasa.

31. A wooded area in the Lower Kamo Shrine in Kyoto.

A scene from seventeen years earlier. Hitting the floor with her long pipe, Shinonome admonishes her husband Dorozō, who holds a handscroll containing the secrets of stealth. Tasogare (*left*), still a child, plays by a small two-panel screen.

ladies-in-waiting was Dorozō's younger sister Kikyō.[32] Through his sister, Dorozō got a job as a servant running errands for Hirugao outside the palace, and eventually Hirugao came to treat him just like one of her regular retainers.

"One day when Tasogare was three, Dorozō told me he'd heard that the Itabatake clan possessed very rare techniques for achieving virtual invisibility. And he asked me to teach the techniques to him if they'd been transmitted to me. Well, my wet nurse had given me a keepsake sword from my father as well as an amulet dedicated to our clan god. She also passed on to me a scroll describing the clan's secret stealth techniques. When I got it out and showed it to Dorozō, he read right through it and then told me very happily that at last his hopes were going to be realized. I thought this was very strange and asked him why anyone would want to use those techniques when the country was at peace.

"'Yoshimasa loves many women,' he answered, lowering his voice, 'but one of them, Hanagiri,[33] is more beautiful than all the rest, and she's caused Hirugao to lose her place as the shōgun's favorite. These days he almost never visits

---

32. Kikyō, Dorozō's sister, is now the nun Karukaya.

33. Mitsuuji's mother, who suggests Kiritsubo in *The Tale of Genji*.

Hirugao. So she asked me to get rid of Hanagiri for her. But I didn't know how to get into the women's quarters unseen, and I had to keep putting it off. Then I remembered that your clan was supposed to have some special techniques. Now I've read the scroll, and I'm finally ready. I'll do the job tonight.'

"I was astounded. 'Has poverty brought your spirit down so low,' I asked, 'that you're willing to do a thing like this? Why in the world are you going to kill a woman who's never done a thing to harm you? And Hanagiri's pregnant now, so you'd be taking two lives. Don't even think of doing it.'

"But he refused to listen. 'Kikyō owes a lot to Hirugao,' he said, 'and so do I. Hirugao's enemy is my enemy.' That same night he managed to get into the women's quarters, but he was careless and killed Hirugao by mistake. He knew he could never raise his head in front of me again, so he never came home. He became a monk and went around the country praying for the dead woman's soul. After five years, though, he was killed accidentally by Kikyō.[34] But you know about that already, Mitsuuji. While Dorozō was dying, he didn't mention he had a wife and child. I'd already taken Tasogare and gone somewhere else, and when Dorozō heard about it later he thought I'd remarried and was extremely bitter.

14

"After I left Dorozō, I made a living teaching dancing and managed to remain a widow, but we were very poor, and in the summer of the year Tasogare was fifteen, a man said he wanted her for his mistress. It was a miserable situation. She didn't like the man, but I made her sleep with him anyway. After Tasogare had a baby girl, the man's wife became very jealous and forced him to break off the relationship. I had a granddaughter, but after the man stopped coming we couldn't take care of her and gave her away.

"We were having a very hard time getting along, and then one day someone came and told me he'd heard I knew some powerful stealth techniques. He promised to give me a very nice reward if I could get inside the shōgunal treasure house, steal a short sword called Karasumaru, and deliver it to him. Then he held some gold pieces out in front of me. Ah! As soon as I saw that gold, I started thinking about how I could buy my daughter the clothes she wanted. And instead of making her suffer, I could help her find a man she loved. I loved Tasogare so much I couldn't see straight. Years before, I'd tried to stop Dorozō, but now I was the one who made a bad mistake. I stole the sword and turned it right over to

---

34. At the end of book 1, Kikyō changes her name to Karukaya and goes to work for Hanagiri, her mistress's rival, in order to kill Hanagiri's son, Mitsuuji. After Hanagiri dies, Kikyō's brother Dorozō, now a wandering monk, stops at the mansion, and in the dark Kikyō stabs her brother, thinking that he is Mitsuuji. She then becomes a wandering nun and prays for the souls of Hanagiri and her brother.

the man. Then I remodeled the house on Fifth Avenue and got us new things and clothes—all with the money he gave me.

"And then you came to visit Korekichi and saw the blossoms on the crow gourd vines and asked a man to pick some. I could see Tasogare had fallen in love with you and was longing to meet you, so I went next door and invited you over. I still didn't know you were Mitsuuji, but you obviously weren't an ordinary person, so I thought you would be a good match for Tasogare. While we were entertaining you, this man here, Nikki Kiyonosuke, came to the door wanting to see you. Well, I was sure I'd seen him before, and then I remembered. He was the one who ripped off my sleeve after I'd stolen the sword. My face was hidden, so he couldn't have seen it, but in the dim moonlight I'd seen his face clearly. I was afraid to be in the same room with him, so I left, pretending I was going to get some saké. And the next morning, when I saw the face of the nun whom Tasogare had invited in, it was Kikyō, my husband's sister. It had been a long time, but we both remembered each other. After you left, we began talking about the old days, and we both got carried away and cried a lot. Kikyō also told me about you, and I learned who you were. Before she left, she gave me the robe Lady Futaba had given her and told me to use it for Tasogare if she got lucky and began to appear in high places.

15

"Then, at the beginning of this month, the same man who asked me to steal the sword came to my house again. 'I hear Mitsuuji is coming to see Tasogare,' he said. 'He's still young, but he's very intelligent and sees things. He's blocking a very important plan. If you can dispose of him, I'll give you twice as much as I did before. If you refuse, well, then I'll come here with a lot of other men, and we'll put you and your daughter away along with Mitsuuji.' Then he disappeared. I thought about how Tasogare was the daughter of a man who tried to kill your mother, Hanagiri, and I knew if you ever heard about that from Kikyō, you would never stay with her. That would be the end of it. You're the son of the shōgun Yoshimasa, who destroyed my father, Noritomo. You were the closest I could get to my real enemy, so why shouldn't I take revenge for my father and use the money to help my daughter find someone else to marry? I'm sure Tasogare told you how I spent all my time coming up with a good plan.

"And then earlier tonight you shocked me with the hokku about the crow gourds that you wrote on the torn sleeve of my robe. You already knew I'd stolen the Kogarasumaru sword. I remembered that when you were describing your dream to Kikyō, you said that Lady Futaba was extremely jealous. So I turned Futaba's padded robe into this long outer cloak and dressed up the way I am now. I was going to stab you while you were confused. But then my daughter committed suicide. After that I just couldn't go on. I have nothing left to hope for, so I decided to commit suicide too." Shinonome talked to the very end without giving in to her pain.

Tasogare, also in great pain, was still breathing. "I never imagined," she said to Mitsuuji, "all the things that were on your mind. I thought you were coming to see me only because you loved me, even though I was a poor commoner, and I found myself loving you more and more. I had discovered the terrible thing Mother was planning to do, so I left and came all the way here to this temple with you. Earlier tonight, I was frightened by the strange woman's shape, and after I fainted, you held me in your arms. Later, when the demon woman's shape burst through the sliding doors, I was afraid at first, but when I looked closely, I recognized the embroidery on her robe. It's the one the nun gave her. And her voice sounded exactly like Mother's, so I realized she'd come here to kill you. What utter sadness I felt then! It was the end of everything. But if I killed myself, I thought she might relent, so I used the razor I brought with me. But it was all for nothing. Now Mother's killed herself, too. The words written on the hat you held over us when it started raining, 'We two traveling together,' I think they must have been saying mother and daughter would soon be setting out together for the other world. But how could we possibly go together to the Pure Land paradise? Mother's demon costume shows well enough where she's going—she's already being tortured in hell. Ah, sadness beyond sadness!" She began to cry uncontrollably.

Mitsuuji's eyes, too, were moist, and he blinked. "Our relationship was very special," he said. "We must have been brought together by some karma in our previous lives. We've known each other only a short time, but you loved me truly with your whole heart.

16

"And you cared very deeply for me. How could I ever forget your great kindness? Your mother has confessed her crimes, and she is no longer bound to them. Both of you will surely be reborn in the Pure Land and sit on lotuses there. Please save a space on your lotus and wait for me to come."

At that Tasogare smiled a wide smile. "You are my priest," she said softly, barely able to breathe, "and you have spoken the final words for us that will lead us to paradise. I am happy now. I will gladly become a buddha."

Mitsuuji turned to Shinonome and said, "When I saw Karukaya and asked Tasogare to invite her in, you used Karukaya's old name, Kikyō, and were very surprised to see her. That made me suspicious for the reason you mentioned, and I was planning to ask her later about what had happened between you. But many years ago she tried to kill me. She's unreliable, and I decided not to ask her. I was afraid she might mention to someone that I was making secret trips to look for the sword. So I never knew that you were married to Dorozō or that Tasogare was Dorozō's daughter. Your father was killed and his clan destroyed because he was disloyal and led a rebellion against the shōgun. His death was his own doing. You don't seem to have a grudge against me personally, and it was natural for you, as a woman, to think of my clan as the enemy of yours.

But you have committed suicide,[35] and I have no more bitter feelings toward you at all. Your daughter hardly knew what was happening. She loved me with a true love, and she was so overwhelmed by it she killed herself. It is sorrowful beyond words. The least I can do for her is take care of her child. Where is the girl now?"

"Ah, Mother," Tasogare said, "you've gone and told him something very strange. My hair isn't tied up yet, and my teeth aren't blackened. I'm not married, so how could I possibly have a child? Don't say things like that." She was almost dead, but she still felt deeply ashamed of the child. She was so upset that blood spurted from her throat as she spoke. Choking, she collapsed onto the floor. She crawled about until finally she lay silent.

Slowly Shinonome pulled herself over to Tasogare's body. When she reached it, she took her daughter's hand and began sobbing. "My husband and I were your enemies," she said to Mitsuuji, "but our daughter loved you so much she was willing to die for you. It all must have been her karma from a previous life. Soon everyone, even children, will be talking and spreading rumors about us. It is too shameful even to think about. Ah, daughter, let me hear your voice again!" She began weeping uncontrollably.

Nikki Kiyonosuke went into the next room, and now, in privacy, Mitsuuji gently came and held Tasogare in his arms. He looked at her. She was cold now, and her breathing had stopped. "We had such a short time together," he said to her and then put one sleeve over his face to hide his tears. Soon Kiyonosuke reappeared. He had changed back into his ordinary clothes and had on his long and short swords, which he had hidden earlier. When he came in, Mitsuuji stepped back from the body and pretended to have his emotions completely under control.

Kiyonosuke placed his fingertips on the floor and bowed deeply to his lord. "Talking with Shinonome is surely a waste of time," he said. "Why not ask her about the man she gave the sword to?"

"Her spirit is stronger than any man's," Mitsuuji said, laughing. "If she's vowed never to tell the man's name, do you think she'd ever give a clear answer?

17

"Asking her whom she gave it to would truly be a waste of time," Mutsuuji said. "Well now, Shinonome, I understand you, and I sympathize with you. So how about telling me something very indirectly? That way, I won't have asked you and you won't have told me anything."

---

35. True to her samurai upbringing, Shinonome has committed ritual suicide (the first step of which is cutting open her stomach) in order to take responsibility for her actions and atone for them.

The blood-smeared dagger drops from the hand of the dying Tasogare. Shinonome holds the reed blind with the Mount Fuji design upside down.

The suffering woman smiled. "I am moved," she said, "by your kindness toward my daughter. You even wish to raise my granddaughter and asked where she lives. I would like to tell you many, many things, but as you say, I've made a vow of secrecy. The man's money allowed me and my daughter to survive, and I owe a debt to him. I could never tell you his name. Try to understand with this." She unrolled the see-through reed screen with its Mount Fuji design and lifted it upside down.

Mitsuuji stared at the hanging screen, his head at an angle, lost in thought. "Fuji is the most famous mountain in the world," he said, "but if you read 'famous mountain' upside down. . . . Yes, of course, of course."[36] As Mitsuuji was speaking, Shinonome slit her throat and finally died. It was a painful death, and Mitsuuji pitied her. He picked up the rush hat and paid his last respects to her by placing it over her face. Then he looked over at Tasogare's face. She seemed to be sleeping. Once when they had been saying gentle things all night, Tasogare had given him her underrobe as a symbol of her heart and her true wish to sleep with him. He had given her his own underrobe then, and it was

---

36. When the character for "famous mountain" (*meizan*) is read in reverse order, the Japanese reading is "Yamana," suggesting Yamana Sōzen, the powerful lord who wants to displace the Ashikaga shōgun Yoshimasa.

Mitsuuji stands and weeps beside Shinonome, whose head is now covered with the sedge hat. Her dagger lies beside a pool of blood. Kiyonosuke (*left*) wraps Tasogare in the reed blind. The Mount Fuji cutout reveals the *yūgao* design of her robe.

still wrapped around her body. But now it was covered with blood stains as bright as wet red autumn leaves floating on the Akuta River.[37] He had taken Tasogare away from her home, only for this to happen. Mitsuuji stood as if in a trance, staring at Tasogare's body and remembering their time together.

Seeing Mitsuuji's expression, Kiyonosuke wrapped the reed blind around Tasogare's body where it lay. But Mitsuuji could still see her attractive hairline and her lustrous hair spreading across the floor. Mount Fuji was fabled to have an elixir of eternal life, but the Fuji on the reed screen had done nothing to help Tasogare, who was dead at only nineteen or twenty. The smoke rising from its peak suggested to him the smoke that would soon rise from Tasogare's body while it was being cremated.[38] Mitsuuji found himself overcome by tears. For some time he stood, unable to move.

Then Mitsuuji heard the sounds of a gong and drum and turned his head to see where they were coming from. Near the board-roofed building facing the visitors' quarters was a hall of worship. Some lamps in front of a buddha

---

37. An allusion to *The Tales of Ise*, sec. 6, in which Narihira takes a woman away from her home and crosses the Akuta River with her, only to have her killed by a demon in the middle of the night.

38. Tasogare's graceful hairline with sharp angles at the temples resembles the peak of Mount Fuji.

Kiyonosuke strikes the fish-shaped wooden block to announce the departure of Mitsuuji, who now wears clogs and has two swords at his side. The moon lights the paths of Mitsuuji's men as they emerge from the fields in the upper-left corner.

image were barely visible inside, and the caretaker monk seemed to be chanting Amida Buddha's name over and over in a muted voice so as not to bother his visitors. Mitsuuji called the monk over and asked him to take great care in praying for the two bodies and having them cremated. While he spoke, a rooster crowed in the distance.

Kiyonosuke bowed to Mitsuuji. "Dawn has come already," he said. "You need to be going home now."

Mitsuuji nodded. "I was planning to capture Shinonome last night and question her," he said, "so I had the temple surrounded. My men are all ready, just waiting for someone to beat on that fish-shaped wooden block over there.[39] That's the signal. It's time to leave now." He stepped calmly down from the temple porch onto the ground. "Well, what are you waiting for?"

Kiyonosuke finally understood and went over to the hollow wooden fish hanging from the eaves and began beating on it. At its sharp sound, Akamatsu and Otokawa[40] warriors appeared in the distance, bringing Mitsuuji's glittering, decorated horse and leading a large number of men. With the moon setting

---

39. Used in temples at certain hours to mark the time.

40. Suggests the Hosokawa clan headed by Katsumoto, a main supporter of shōgun Ashikaga Yoshimasa.

behind them, the warriors pushed their way through the long grass, and the moonlight glinting on their armor made them look like stars as they lined up in the temple garden. Kiyonosuke told the men they were going back to Mitsuuji's mansion, and Mitsuuji stepped lightly up into his saddle and began to ride off through the dew-wet grass. Early morning mist rose everywhere, and he wandered here and there, his mind lost and troubled by his deep karmic ties to Tasogare, which bound both of them as tightly together as the reins he held in his hands. Only when the sky grew light was he able to turn away from his sorrow and spur his horse quickly on toward his mansion in Saga.

[*Nise Murasaki inaka Genji*, SNKBT 88: 150–174, translated by Chris Drake]

Chapter 21

GHOSTS AND NINETEENTH-CENTURY KABUKI

Kabuki's focus on evil was one of its characteristics in the nineteenth century, especially in the work of Tsuruya Nanboku, who—along with Chikamatsu, Namiki Sōsuke (Senryū), and Mokuami—was one of the leading kabuki-jōruri playwrights of the early modern period. In contrast to earlier plays in which the evil male character is the opposite of the good male character and thus basically a foil for the hero, in Nanboku's plays the evil male character is the protagonist and is simultaneously attractive and repulsive, erotic and loathsome. During this period as well, two new evil characters were created in kabuki, the "poisonous wife" (*dokufu*) and the "evil woman" (*akuba*), both *onnagata* roles (a male actor playing a female part), which traditionally had been that of the elegant, highly feminine, younger woman. Kabuki was also moving away from the speech-based drama that had dominated the genre to one that emphasized the actor's physical expressiveness in the *henge buyō* (transformation dance), in which he moved swiftly from one character to another within a single dance; in the *tachimawari* (fight scene); and, most of all, in the *hayagawari* (quick change), in which the same actor played several different roles in a single play.

Nanboku's plays transformed the nature of kabuki by depicting a world in which the sociopolitical order was crumbling, causing a profound sense of material loss or decay and leaving little foundation for spiritual order. It is not surprising, therefore, that Nanboku also was one of the pioneers of the ghost-story genre (*kaidan mono*) in kabuki. Value, it seems, could be found only in an individual's life force or energy, which was embodied in the "quick change" and other physical aspects of the acting, as well as in the strong, tenacious characters, who are often evil or horrifying. Nanboku was noted, as well, for his *kizewa* (literally, raw contemporary life) plays, which realistically depicted the lives of people at the bottom of society, thus capturing a dark side of late Tokugawa society that the printed literature often overlooked. The term "realistic," however, is not entirely satisfactory. As some modern critics have pointed out, Nanboku's *Ghost Stories at Yotsuya* (*Yotsuya kaidan*, 1825), for example, is not "realistic" in that it depends heavily on ghosts and the supernatural. Rather, the word is better understood to mean that even though Nanboku uses the "world" (*sekai*) of history plays and of powerful samurai houses, he fills this world with outcasts or "nonhumans" (*hinin*) from the lower classes, such as masterless samurai (*rōnin*), beggars, grave diggers, and tobacco sellers. Into this drama, Nanboku intersperses erotic love scenes, brutal murders, and frightening ghost stories—all of which made for immensely popular and effective theater.

TSURUYA NANBOKU

Little is known about Tsuruya Nanboku IV (1755–1829) except that he was born in Edo and was the son of a dyer. In 1776 he became an apprentice to Sakurada Jisuke I (d. 1806), one of the leading kabuki playwrights of the day, who specialized in drama depicting contemporary life. In the following year Nanboku began working at the Nakamura Theater under the pen name Sakurada Heizō. In 1780, at the age of twenty-five, he married Oyoshi, the daughter of Tsuruya Nanboku III, the third in a succession of kabuki comic actors. It took another twenty years, however, before he produced his first hit, *Indian Tokubei, a Story of a Foreign Country* (*Tenjiku Tokubei Ikokubanashi*, 1804), starring Onoe Matsusuke, an actor with a tremendous range of roles who specialized in the kind of ghost plays and stage tricks that Nanboku was to make his own. Then, after taking the name Tsuruya Nanboku IV in 1811, he wrote more than 120 plays, the most famous today being *Scarlet Princess of Edo* (*Sakurahime azuma no bunshō*, 1817)[1] and *Ghost Stories at Yotsuya* (*Yotsuya kaidan*, 1825).

GHOST STORIES AT YOTSUYA (YOTSUYA KAIDAN, 1825)

In his *Eastern Seaboard Highway Yotsuya Ghost Stories* (*Tōkaidō yotsuya kaidan*), better known as *Ghost Stories at Yotsuya*, Nanboku, who was considered a master of innovation (*shukō*), weaves recent events in Edo—such as a samurai's murder of his wife and a servant's murder of his master—into the historical "world" of *Chūshingura*:

---

1. A translation of *Scarlet Princess* appears in James Brandon, ed. and trans., *Kabuki: Five Classic Plays* (1975; reprint, Honolulu: University of Hawai'i Press, 1992).

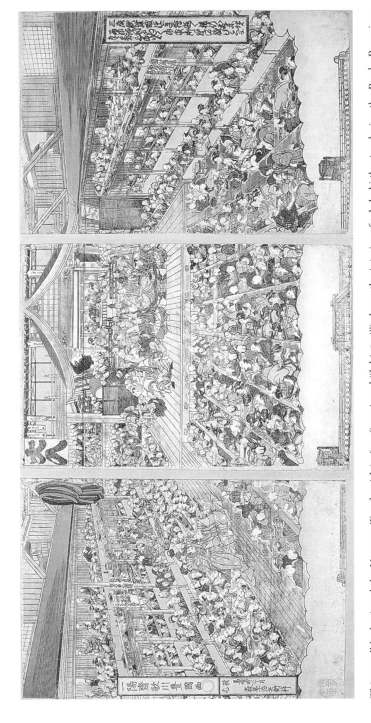

This woodblock triptych by Utagawa Toyokuni I (1769–1825; signed "Ichiyōsai") shows the interior of a kabuki theater during the Bunka-Bunsei era (1804–1829) depicted in the "perspective print" (*uki-e*) mode, with Western linear perspective. On stage is a scene from *Confrontation with the Soga*. The actors on center stage are Matsumoto Kōshirō V (1764–1838) playing Kudō, Bandō Mitsugorō III (1775–1831) playing Asahina, and Iwai Hanshirō V (1776–1847) playing Ōiso no Tora. The two actors on the runway (*hanamichi*), which functioned as another stage space, are Ichikawa Danjūrō VII (1791–1859) and Onoe Matsusuke II (1784–1849, later Kikugorō III), performing as the Soga brothers Gorō and Jūrō. The simultaneous appearance of the most popular kabuki actors of the time suggests an imaginary production. Light enters from two large windows (*ryōmado*) near the ceiling flanking the stage roof (*hafu*). The "full house" (*ōiri*) sign hangs next to the tricolor curtain (*upper left*). The square earthen-floor pit (*doma*) stands directly in front of the stage. On the two sides are the galleries (*sajiki*) for more affluent audiences. (Courtesy of the Tsubouchi Memorial Theatre Museum, Waseda University)

The Storehouse of Loyal Retainers (*Kanadehon Chūshingura,* 1748). Accordingly, in *Chūshingura,* Lord Enya, provoked by Lord Kō no Moronao, injures him with a sword and is forced to commit suicide, leading to the destruction of Enya's family and the dispersal of his retainers, who eventually take revenge on Moronao as their master's enemy. On the first day of the debut performance, the first three acts of *Ghost Stories at Yotsuya* were preceded by the first six acts of *Chūshingura,* and on the second day the remaining acts of both plays were woven together. Act 3 became pivotal and was performed twice, once at the end of the first day and once at the beginning of the second day.

If *Chūshingura* reflected the popular uplifting view of the famous vendetta, *Ghost Stories at Yotsuya* revealed the negative, dark, hidden side of the same world, of those at the bottom of society who wanted to participate in the vendetta but could not. Instead of rising up like the exemplary heroes of *Chūshingura,* these men fall down a hole of self-destruction. When we juxtapose the two plays, one from the mid-eighteenth century and the other from the early nineteenth century, we can see the immense difference in the attitudes toward and of the samurai, whose circumstances deteriorated precipitously during the eighteenth and nineteenth centuries. The warrior values of loyalty, obligation, self-sacrifice, and patience, which are extolled and dramatized in *Chūshingura,* are replaced in *Ghost Stories* by acts of betrayal and murder for the sake of sex and money.

Nanboku originally wrote *Ghost Stories at Yotsuya* for two actors, Onoe Kikugorō III (the young son of his mentor Onoe Matsusuke), who simultaneously played three roles, Oiwa, Kohei, and Satō Yomoshichi; and Ichikawa Danjurō VII, who performed the role of Tamiya Iemon, the archetype of the "erotic evil character" (*iroaku*). When the bodies of Oiwa and Kohei are fished out of the river by Iemon at the end of act 3, Kikugorō played both Oiwa and Kohei in a "quick change" (*hayagawari*).

In *Ghost Stories at Yotsuya,* the life force exemplified in the "quick change" can be found in the seemingly inexhaustible energy of the two protagonists, the ghost Oiwa and the villain Iemon, who collide with stunning force in a world that seems to have been stripped of all moral sense and justice. Equally important is the delicate mixture of comedy and tragedy, humor and horror, bantering and gruesome murder, with the drama rapidly and constantly shifting from one to the other. An essential part of this ironic mixture is the "erotic evil character" of Iemon, who is both repulsive and attractive. Of particular interest is the transformation of Oiwa from a vulnerable young woman into a vengeful ghost.

Of the original five acts, acts 2 and 3, which are translated here, are the most frequently performed today.

Main Characters

Tamiya Iemon, a masterless samurai (rōnin) and a former retainer of Lord Enya

Oiwa, Iemon's wife

Kohei, Iemon's servant, loyal to Lord Enya

From the frontispiece of the gōkan edition of *Ghost Stories at Yotsuya*, called *Head Start on an Eastern Seaboard Journey: Ghost Stories at Yotsuya* (*Tōkaidōchū kadode no sakigake Yotsuya kaidan*, 1826), "written" by Onoe Baikō (Onoe Kikugorō III, 1784–1849), who performed in the first production in 1825, but in fact written by the playwright Hanagasa Bunkyō (1785–1860) and illustrated by Ippitsuan Eisen (Keisai Eisen, 1791–1848). Oiwa's ghastly face—swollen forehead and enlarged mouth—looms large above a wheel of fire. The character for "heart" (*kokoro*) is placed above Tamiya Iemon, and eerie images of gourds on the border echo Oiwa's disfigured face. Text: "Autumn grasses also change in this way—a withered field" (*aki no chigusa / kō mo kawaru ka / kare nohara*). Ippitsuan."

Bᴀɴsᴜᴋᴇ, Kanzō's retainer
Cʜōʙᴇɪ, a rōnin, Iemon's crony
Iᴛō Kɪʜᴇɪ, a rich samurai doctor in the service of Lord Kō no Moronao, father of Oyumi and grandfather of Oume
Kᴀɴᴢō, a rōnin, Iemon's crony
Mᴀɢᴏʙᴇɪ, the father of Kohei
Mᴏsᴜᴋᴇ, a pawnbroker
Oᴍᴀᴋɪ, a nurse in the Itō household
Oᴜᴍᴇ, Oyumi's daughter and Kihei's granddaughter, wants to marry Iemon
Oʏᴜᴍɪ, widowed daughter of Itō Kihei and mother of Oume
Tᴀᴋᴜᴇᴛsᴜ, a masseur, working for Iemon

Act 2, Tamiya Iemon's House

Tamiya Iemon's Residence
   Tamiya Iemon, a rōnin, lives in a shabby tenement in Yotsuya, a neighborhood in Edo occupied by poor people and rōnin. Swallowing their pride,

many must do craftwork at home to make ends meet. The set has gray walls with cracked and peeling plaster and a sliding, freestanding lattice door to the outside. There are a few sparse furnishings: a square paper floor lamp, a dirty white standing screen, and a small brazier with a teapot on it. Lively shamisen and percussion music suggests the bustle of commoner life. Iemon sits on the floor of the main room gluing triangles of paper onto the partially covered bamboo frame of an umbrella. His clothing is that of a commoner, but his bearing reveals that he once was a samurai. He listens coldly, not interrupting his work, as Magobei, the father of Iemon's servant Kohei, and Takuetsu, a masseur, bow apologetically at his right. Magobei wears a plain cotton ki-mono, and his wig is flecked with gray. He crouches on all fours. Takuetsu has the shaved head of a masseur and sits between Iemon and Magobei, trying to mediate their dispute.

TAKUETSU: Master Iemon, please listen! You are quite right, but please try to be a bit more understanding. It's all my fault. I made the mistake of intro-ducing Kohei to you when you needed some help. I take full responsibility, so please give me a day or two to try to settle the matter.

IEMON: No, no, this is a matter that can't wait. Kohei is an embezzler and a thief. When he's caught, my samurai spirit won't be satisfied until I execute him. Ever since I lost my master, I've had to make umbrellas just to get by. Me, a samurai! Look at this! Do you think I do this for fun? (*To Magobei*) You there! You're his father. Everything depends on what you have to say. Stop acting like a senile old fool. (*He rises and threatens Magobei.*)

MAGOBEI: Oh, no, no, you are quite right. There is nothing I could possibly say to defend what my son has done. You said that Kohei stole something. If I may, I would like to ask what he took.

IEMON: It's nothing someone like you would know anything about. He stole a packet of rare Chinese medicine called *sōkisei* that has been passed down in the Tamiya house for generations. It's priceless; you won't find it anywhere else. The medicine is so potent that if someone lost the use of his legs, this drug will enable him to walk right before your eyes. My stipend was cut off when my master's household was disbanded, and I haven't received a cent since then. Even so, I have never let that medicine out of my hands. That's what Kohei stole. Look at this thing. (*Picks up a short, badly made sword*) This is all that Kohei left behind. He took my family's greatest treasure and left me with a rusty penknife. My friends are furious at what happened and left early this morning to try to track down Kohei. I'd be out there too, but I can't leave my wife, since she just had a baby and is still weak. That's why I needed help around here and took Kohei into my service. He's certainly been more trouble than he's worth! Just thinking about it makes me furious. When I get my hands on him, I'll take care of him once and for all. Takuetsu, you're his guarantor. You're responsible for what he's done. Do you under-stand what I'm going to do?

At his residence, Iemon, in a black kimono with a tobacco set before him and tools and materials for making umbrellas, reprimands Magobei (*left*) and Takuetsu (*center*) with his tobacco pipe. Oiwa, wearing a headband and looking ill, looks on from the next room as she reclines on the bedding. A mosquito net hangs behind her. Omaki, a maid from the Itō household, reaches into her robe to give the special medicine to Oiwa.

TAKUETSU: You are only right to feel that way. You accepted the introduction of this humble masseur and took Kohei into your service, only to have him steal from you and flee. And what a time to run off, just when poor Oiwa has given birth and has not yet recovered her health. How could Kohei abandon you at such a time? I can find nothing to say to apologize. Magobei, Magobei! What do you think?

MAGOBEI: I don't quite know what to say. Kohei has never amounted to much, but I always thought he was honest. I'm shocked that he stole something. A family heirloom? A priceless packet of medicine?

TAKUETSU: That is strange, isn't it? Stealing cash is normal, but who steals medicine?

MAGOBEI (*to himself*): Hmm, now that his real master is so sick, maybe he thought this was his only hope.[2]

IEMON: What?

---

2. Kohei's former master, Matanojo, is another retainer of Lord Enya of the Chūshingura story. Matanojo is extremely ill, and Kohei is desperate to get the medicine so that Matanojo can recover enough to participate in the vendetta.

MAGOBEI: I mean, what Kohei did was unforgivable.

IEMON: Listen, old man. That medicine may not look like much, but it's very rare. A druggist would pay at least a dozen gold pieces on the spot. My medicine is even more valuable because it has a certificate guaranteeing its authenticity. The medicine and the certificate have been handed down through my family for generations. There's nothing like it anywhere else. However, I'll give you a chance. You can have a couple of days to try to find Kohei yourself. If you don't find him by then, you can give me what the medicine is really worth—fifteen gold pieces. Got it? That's fifteen gold pieces. Find him or you owe me a fortune.

MAGOBEI: Thank you. I'll find him, and I'm sorry for what my son has done. (*To Takuetsu*) Forgive me for having caused you so much trouble.

TAKUETSU: It's not your fault. It's troublesome, but I got us into this situation in the first place. This is just one of those things that happens when you try to help someone. No wonder more people aren't helpful. (*Magobei puts on his straw sandals and gets ready to leave.*)

IEMON: Remember, two days. Come here the instant you hear anything about Kohei. I can make things difficult for you if you try to hide anything.

MAGOBEI: I understand. (*To Takuetsu*) Doctor, thank you for everything. Good-bye. (*Magobei departs down the runway, muttering as he goes. Takuetsu prepares medicine for Oiwa and takes it into an enclosed room.*)

IEMON: No cash, not even enough to keep up appearances, yet she's dumb enough to go and have a kid. If you want sweet innocence, that's what you'll get. (*Lively lion dance music is played by the shamisen and percussion in the music room to the side of the stage. Chōbei, dressed in tattered clothing but wearing the two swords that indicate his samurai status, comes racing down the runway to the front door.*)

CHŌBEI: Iemon, are you there? We found Kohei!

IEMON: Chōbei! You saw him?

CHŌBEI: Yes. I knew he lived somewhere across town, maybe on the other side of the river. I captured him just before he reached the bridge. Here's the packet of drugs he stole.

IEMON: Thank you. Where is that damn Kohei?

CHŌBEI: He's with Kanzō. Ah, it sounds like they're here. (*The lion dance music begins again. Kanzō, his retainer Bansuke, and Kohei enter down the runway. Kohei's hands are tied with a coarse rope, his hair is disheveled, and his clothing is torn. He apologizes profusely, but Kanzō and Bansuke tell him that he won't get away with it.*)

IEMON: Kanzō, thank you for all your trouble. I heard the details from Chōbei. I greatly appreciated your work. Ah, Bansuke, is it? Thank you for your efforts.

BANSUKE: Thank you, sir. You should be feeling better now. (*He removes the rope from Kohei.*)

TAKUETSU (*to Kohei, who sits, his head hanging in shame*): Here, here.

For your sake I've also gone to a lot of trouble, too. Even your old father had to be called in. What got into you?

KOHEI: I owe everything to your kindness in finding me this position. Instead of showing the proper gratitude, I've made things difficult for you, all because I was seized by a sudden impulse. And now my father has been drawn in, too. I guess he must have gone home already. I'm sorry to hear that. He must be worried sick about me. Master, since Chōbei took back the medicine, and I didn't touch anything else, please have mercy and forgive me. I beg you.

IEMON: That's ridiculous. When a servant disobeys his master, it can't be overlooked. A dishonest and insubordinate servant has to be punished properly. We'll have to find just the right treatment for you.

KANZŌ: Iemon, I've been thinking about some of the things he said. I hear that his old master was a samurai in Lord Enya's house, where you also served. Remember Oshioda Matanojo, the most loyal samurai in the whole house? Kohei's entire family was in his service. You'd never guess that someone who used to work for such an honest person would go so bad, would you?

IEMON: Do you mean the same Matanojo I knew in Lord Enya's mansion? Kohei used to serve him? Is that true?

KOHEI: Yes, everything you say is true. My father's family has served Matanojo's family for generations. When Lord Enya's house was disbanded, Matanojo became a rōnin. Then recently he became very ill. I entered your service to help support him. My wife, my father, and even my little boy have gone to work also. We all want to do whatever we can to help him now that he's facing hard times, but we're so poor that we can't do very much. I wanted desperately to cure him, so I attempted to steal the medicine. I did it for the best possible reason: I stole out of loyalty to my master. I thought there could be no higher cause. Even so, the fact that you found me out must be heaven's punishment. Please forgive me.

IEMON: You mean you stole my family heirloom for your master's sake? Did Matanojo order you to do that?

KOHEI: No, no. He knows nothing about it. I did it myself, thinking that it was the only loyal thing to do.

IEMON: It doesn't matter whether loyalty or insanity made you do it. If you steal, you're a thief. Is there some law saying thieves can get off if they're properly loyal? What a ridiculous idea! At least I have the medicine back now. I might have spared you if you had paid me something for it. But you didn't give me a cent. For the theft of the medicine, I will break all your fingers, one by one.

CHŌBEI: That sounds like fun. Can we start right now?

KANZŌ: Ten fingers instead of taking his life? That's letting him off too easy.

BANSUKE: Since I'm an apprentice, let me try breaking one too—for the practice.

IEMON: Come on, help me.

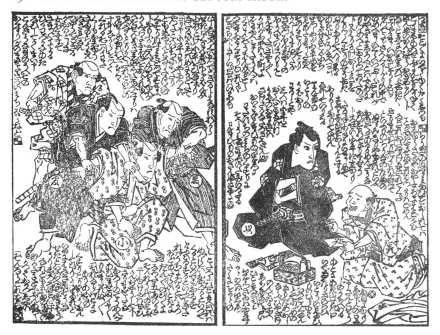

Kohei (*left*) is restrained by Kanzō and others. The medicine is placed in front of Iemon (*right*), in a black robe, next to the tobacco tray. The pawnbroker (*far right*) happily holds the paper-wrapped bundle containing the cash given to him by Omaki.

KOHEI: Stop it! I have to take care of my parents. What can I do if my hands are useless?

ALL THREE (KANZŌ, BANSUKE, AND CHŌBEI):[3] What do we care?

KOHEI: Mercy! Show some kindness. Please, I returned the medicine.

IEMON: Shut up! Gag him!

ALL THREE: OK, OK. (*The three surround him, and Bansuke takes a hand-kerchief and ties it over Kohei's mouth.*)

BANSUKE: That should keep him quiet.

KANZŌ: After we finish with the fingers, how about pulling his hair out?

CHŌBEI: That's a good idea. (*They mime kicking and beating him. Music announces the appearance on the runway of Omaki, a wet nurse serving in the neighboring household of the rich Dr. Itō Kihei. She is accompanied by a servant bearing a red lacquered ceremonial barrel of saké and a stack of lacquered boxes filled with food—expensive ceremonial gifts celebrating the birth of a child. She carries a gray cloth bundle that we later learn contains a baby's yellow- and black-checked kimono. She comes to the front door.*)

---

3. The lines attributed to these three are not spoken entirely in unison. Usually one or another of them speaks, with the others joining in for the last few words or for a laugh together at the end of the line.

OMAKI: Is anyone home? May I come in?

ALL THREE: Who could that be?

IEMON: Someone's here. Stick Kohei in the closet.

ALL THREE: OK, OK. Get in there. (*They drag Kohei to the closet, slide the door open, throw him in, and close the door. Omaki presents the gifts and a packet of medicine she claims will cure Oiwa. She goes into the room at left to attend the mother and child. Mosuke, a pawnbroker, enters and demands the repayment of five gold pieces plus the rental for mosquito netting, bedding, and a padded nightgown. Iemon is forced to give the pawnbroker his precious medicine and the accompanying document.*)

MOSUKE: Well, now that's cleared up. Now the rentals. I'll just take the mosquito net and the bedding. Excuse me.

IEMON: What are you doing? You're still taking the other things?

MOSUKE: Yup. If you don't pay another gold piece, I can't clear the account. Excuse me. (*He heads toward the room at stage left, but Omaki comes out and stops him.*)

OMAKI: Pray wait a moment. Don't force your way into a sickroom. If I heard correctly, it's a matter of money, isn't it? Here, this will probably do. Go away and leave the things here. (*She hands Mosuke a paper-wrapped bundle, somewhat more than the amount that is owed. Iemon is surprised and wonders what he will have to do in exchange.*)

MOSUKE (*examining the packet*): Hey, this is too much.

OMAKI: Shh, there's no need to wake up the mother. Well, sir?

MOSUKE: Uh, well, I'm speechless. This is truly a great favor, ma'am.

IEMON: After all this help, there is no way to show my thanks.

OMAKI: Please, there is no need to worry about it. Well, I must take my leave now.

MOSUKE: I'll walk you to the street.

IEMON: Nurse, thanks. You've been a great help.

OMAKI: My best wishes to all of you. Well, Mosuke?

MOSUKE: After you. (*Omaki and Mosuke exit to lively music. The rest are silent for a moment, impressed with the generosity of Itō Kihei and his household.*)

CHŌBEI: Well, Iemon, we've been getting a lot of help from the Itō mansion. You probably should go over there and say a few words of thanks.

IEMON: Maybe I should, but I can't do it.

CHŌBEI AND KANZŌ: What do you mean?

IEMON: Itō Kihei is a retainer of our enemy, Lord Kō no Moronao. Our master is dead, and his retainers have been expelled from his mansion and scattered. Meanwhile, Kō no Moronao lives in the best part of town in a rich mansion. I was once a retainer of Lord Enya, a victim of Lord Moronao's evil plots. Even after all they've given us, I can't go to my enemy's house.

CHŌBEI AND KANZŌ: You're right, that's a problem. (*During this time the baby starts crying in the room at stage left.*)

TAKUETSU: Oh, no. That child again.

IEMON: That brat cries a lot. Maybe the fleas are getting to him. (*The music becomes languid, suggesting the atmosphere of a sickroom. Iemon pushes open the sliding screens to reveal his wife, Oiwa, sitting on the cotton bedding and looking sick and weak. A large mosquito net hangs from the ceiling, and a small folding screen protects the bed from drafts. An amulet for safe birth hangs around Oiwa's neck, and she is holding her baby and patting him on the back.*)

IEMON: Oiwa, are you better today? How do you feel?

CHŌBEI AND KANZŌ: We came to visit you.

OIWA: You are very kind. Please excuse me. They say one always feels ill after giving birth. But perhaps because of the strange weather we've been having lately, I feel even worse than usual. (*Takuetsu helps her into the main room. She puts the baby on a cushion and covers him with a robe.*)

IEMON: Oiwa, I've never seen that kimono before. Did you make it?

OIWA: This came a moment ago from the Itō mansion with the warm wishes of the widow Oyumi. Dear, please go and thank them.

IEMON: Is that so? They've been so generous it's embarrassing. I don't understand why.

CHŌBEI: Look here, it's like I always say. What's past is past. Tamiya Iemon, now you're a rōnin. Forget about ideas like duty and avenging former masters and go to the enemy's mansion.

OIWA: He's right. You really must go to the mansion and thank them.

IEMON: You're right, Oiwa, I have to go, but I shouldn't go alone, without you.

OIWA: If you have to go with someone, take those two along.

CHŌBEI: Yeah, we'll go—

IEMON: Well, as they say, the sooner the better. Let's go.

TAKUETSU: And I'll look after things while you're gone. It's best for you to go and express your gratitude.

IEMON (*puts on his two swords and an old short formal jacket*): I'm going, but I haven't fixed anything to eat yet. Could you do it?

TAKUETSU: Yes, yes. I'll take care of everything.

IEMON: Remember, keep your eye on the closet. (*Points to Kohei's sword*) He thinks that thing makes him look important. (*To Oiwa*) This medicine for your blood circulation came from the Itō mansion. You'd better take it. They said it was an old family secret. (*He hands over the packet of powdered medicine.*)

OIWA: Oh? A little while ago the nurse said something about some medicine. Please give it to me. I'll take it when the water is ready. (*Slips the medicine into her kimono*) Come back quickly.

IEMON: I'll come right back. Let's go. (*To Takuetsu*) Remember to make dinner.

TAKUETSU: OK.

IEMON: I'm going now, Oiwa.

OIWA: Please come back as soon as you can.

IEMON: What would keep me there? Let's go. (*Moderately lively music plays as the men depart. The sound of a temple bell increases the feeling of loneliness and creates a foreboding mood. The shamisen music begins again, slowly and pensively, as Oiwa stares after the men.*)

OIWA: Iemon has been mean to me from the moment we were married. He didn't even look pleased when I told him his baby was a boy. Every day, from dawn to dusk, he calls the boy a brat, saying he is nothing but a nuisance. He grumbles that the baby is just another mouth to feed. He says things like that even when he knows I can hear him. Living in this house is constant torture, with little wounds that never heal. But I must remember that Iemon promised to help me attack my father's murderer.[4] (*She stops and weeps, then continues to speak while crying.*) If I can just endure this a little while longer, I'll be able to leave this evil man. Please, let us avenge my father's murder soon. (*She pauses in fervent prayer. A decorative tortoiseshell comb in her hair drops to the floor. She picks it up.*) This tortoiseshell comb was my mother's. Look at the cheerful swirl of chrysanthemums and the beautiful old-fashioned silver work. Even though we need money desperately, I'll never give up this comb. But since I had my baby, I've been so sick—I feel so weak I'm not sure I can live. If I die, I want my sister Osode to have it to remember our mother. It's the only thing from our mother that I still have left. (*She gazes at the comb. The baby starts crying. She comforts him and returns him to his cushion.*) Oh, I'm dizzy again. It must be my bad circulation. I hope that the powder will help. (*To slow background music, she picks up the packet of medicine with a prayer of thanks. Ominously, the action is emphasized by the boom of a temple bell. She lays down the package and picks the comb up off the floor and puts it back in her hair. She pours the medicine directly onto her hand, happily lifts both hands to her forehead in a gesture of gratitude and takes the medicine.*) I'm sure I'll feel better now. Here, my precious little boy. (*She dangles the new kimono in front of the baby.*). You got something nice today, didn't you? I wonder who made it, little Oume? The nurse? (*She drops the kimono unknowingly and continues to wave her hands. After a moment she notices the kimono on the floor, picks it up, dangles it in front of the baby, but drops it again. She notices that her fingers are numb and begins to rub them. Suddenly she gasps as she feels a sharp pain in her chest and starts to moan as her face begins to burn with fever.*) Oh, oh! The medicine has made me feel worse. Oh! My face is burning. It's never felt like this before. The pain. (*She huddles on the floor in pain. Just then, there is a sharp pounding on the door of the closet where Kohei is tied up.*)

---

4. In act 1, Oiwa's father, Yotsuya Samon, learned that Iemon had stolen from his master and demanded that Iemon give up Oiwa. Wanting to keep her, Iemon killed her father without her knowing and then cynically promised to avenge his death if Oiwa remained with him.

TAKUETSU (*enters from the back and, since Oiwa is hunched over, is totally unaware of what has happened to her*): Oh Oiwa, shall I fix some soup? (*She lifts her head, and he can see that she has changed, but the room is too dark to see clearly.*) This is awful. What happened to you? You're pale, your face looks different.

OIWA: I took the powder and right away—Oh, it hurts.

TAKUETSU: It started to hurt after you took the medicine? The draft is bad for you, come here. (*He bends over her and screams at the sight of her face, but quickly recovers and rubs her back, being careful not to look directly at her face, which the audience still cannot see. The baby begins to cry, and Takuetsu goes to comfort him, but then Oiwa cries out in pain, and he runs back to her. Just as he is running back and forth between them, the closet door slides open and Kohei tries to get out.*) Hey! Don't try to escape! (*Slides the closet door shut and tries to decide what to do*) If I take care of one thing, the other two will get away from me. What a time to be house-sitting. (*Oiwa is in pain. Takuetsu puts the baby in the room at left and closes the door. He tries to comfort Oiwa, patting and massaging her back. The action is punctuated by the sound of the temple bell as the stage revolves.*)

Itō Kihei's Mansion

Lively folk music sounds as the stage revolves to reveal the grand and luxurious home of the rich doctor Itō Kihei. The interior is surrounded by a veranda with a step down into the garden. The alcove at stage left contains a precious scroll and a flower arrangement. Iemon is seated in the center with Chōbei and Kanzō to his right. Behind them sit Oyumi, Kihei's widowed daughter and Oume's mother, wearing a somber kimono befitting a widow; and Omaki, Oume's nurse. Chōbei and Kanzō enjoy the banquet while Bansuke performs a folk dance in the garden below. Kihei is dressed in the restrained colors of a prosperous retired man and wears glasses with round black frames. He is carefully washing gold coins in a large copper basin and putting them away in a small wooden box. When the stage stops turning, Bansuke tumbles and everyone laughs. Bansuke joins the banquet, and the scene begins with some improvised light conversation about the private lives of the actors on stage. Servants in formal divided skirts bring in three covered soup bowls on trays, which they set in front of Chōbei, Kanzō, and Bansuke.

IEMON (*observing Kihei's actions*): Sir, are those sword ornaments you are cleaning?

KIHEI: No, nothing so important. These are just some old coins I inherited from my father. If I don't wash them from time to time, the gold and silver gets all tarnished. This is about all an old retired man can do anymore. Ha, ha, ha.

IEMON: Not a bad job to have.

At the Itō residence, Kanzō and Chōbei gasp in awe at the gold coins in their soup bowls. Behind them stand Oyumi and her daughter, Oume (*far left*), in a long-sleeved robe. Kihei (*far right*), the master of the house, stands behind Iemon.

ALL THREE (KANZŌ, BANSUKE, AND CHŌBEI): Let us give you a hand. Ha, ha, ha.

OYUMI: It's not much, but please have some soup and a cup of saké.

OMAKI: Please do have a drink.

ALL THREE: You're going to too much trouble. But Iemon doesn't have a tray.

BANSUKE: Here, let me. (*He tries to pass his tray to Iemon.*)

OYUMI: Oh no. We have something very special for Master Iemon. Please, it's not much, but go ahead and eat.

CHŌBEI: Let's eat then. (*They lift the lids of their soup bowls. To their astonishment, the bowls are filled with gold coins.*) This is a real delicacy.

KANZŌ AND BANSUKE: We're much obliged.

OYUMI: We've invited Master Iemon so many times. Now that he has graciously accepted our invitation and you have been kind enough to come along with him, please have as much as you like. We are happy that you like our humble meal. Omaki, give them another helping if they want more.

OMAKI: As you wish. Please don't hesitate to ask.

ALL THREE: What a great banquet. (*They put the money away in the breasts of their kimono.*)

KIHEI: Now that we've taken care of your companions, what shall we serve you, Iemon, our eminent guest of honor?

IEMON: It must be something special. (*The music stops.*)

OYUMI: If you are ready, we can serve you, but—if you will excuse us for a few moments.

KANZŌ AND CHŌBEI: We understand. Let's give them some time alone.

OYUMI (*to Omaki*): Please take care of our guests.

OMAKI: Let me show you around the grounds. (*Omaki leads Chōbei, Kanzō, and Bansuke through the curtained door at the rear. Oyumi exits. Kihei puts the coins he has been washing on the lid of the box, which he slides over in front of Iemon.*)

KIHEI: Please be kind enough to accept these, Iemon.

IEMON: Why are you giving me all this money? (*Looks pointedly at Kihei*)

OYUMI (*from behind the curtained door*): Let me explain the matter to you. (*She leads her daughter, Oume, through the doorway. Oume is wearing a kimono with long flowing sleeves, the dress of a young, unmarried girl.*) This girl is Oume, my daughter by my late husband Mataichi.

KIHEI: Oume is my dearest granddaughter. By some mysterious fate, she fell in love with you the first time she saw you and began to suffer from love sickness. One day we thought it would do her good to get outside, and so we all went to the Asakusa Temple. There she miraculously—

OYUMI: Saw you again. She was happy for the first time in so long. (*To her daughter*) Well, dear, now you can finally say what you've kept hidden in your heart for so long. (*She leads Oume to Iemon's side.*)

OUME: After having worried my dear mother so much, how can I hide anything? One day, shortly after you moved into this neighborhood, Master Tamiya, I caught a glimpse of you, and from that moment—I have done nothing but dream of you.

OYUMI: She was so consumed with love that she would not leave her bed. Every day her face and body grew thinner. When I questioned her, she told me about you, the man she could not forget.

OUME: But you're married. I couldn't hope to have my wish granted; I tried to be firm and put you out of my mind. But when two people are linked by fate, it's impossible to forget. Let me be your servant or even your scullery maid. I don't mind. Anything to let me stay by your side. (*Bows to Iemon*)

KIHEI: It's just as you have heard. I would like to have you as my son-in-law. Please grant Oume her wish.

OYUMI: My daughter has become obsessed with you. Listen to her, she says she would even condescend to live as a commoner. She would be Oiwa's servant or your mistress. But this is a samurai household, and such a breach of class could not be kept secret. (*To Oume*) Now that my husband is dead, you are all I have left. How can I allow you to do such a thing?

IEMON: Your daughter's feelings leave me quite speechless. I was adopted as the heir to the Tamiya family, and duty binds me to my wife, Oiwa. It's all heartbreaking, but unfortunately—

KIHEI: So you deny my granddaughter's request?

OYUMI: It is only right that you refuse her. And now, Oume, we must be resigned to forgetting about Iemon.

OUME: Yes, I'm resigned to it. I've made my decision, and I will prove it to you now. (*Takes a razor from her sash*) Hail Amida Buddha! (*She bends over and tries to cut her own throat, but they stop her.*)

KIHEI: You have acted virtuously. Your heart's desire was not granted. . . .

OYUMI: So you have decided to die with honor. My daughter's spirit is worthy of a samurai. How sad that your prayers could not be granted.

CHŌBEI: Hey, Iemon, you're making a big mistake. Look, Oiwa's going to die sooner or later. After she's gone, you're going to need a wife anyway. So why don't you make these two nice people happy and go ahead and change your nest? That's what you should do.

IEMON: No, no. Even if it makes me rich, it's not right for me to abandon Oiwa. That's the one thing I couldn't do.

KIHEI (*takes all the gold from the box and presents it to Iemon*): Please, kill me. Please kill this poor old man.

IEMON: What are you talking about? I know that it must be a shock for Oume to be refused, but why are you asking me to kill you?

KIHEI: There is something else I must tell you. I found my granddaughter's suffering pitiful, but I knew that because you already had a wife, getting you to marry her would be difficult. I considered all kinds of plans, and finally, without telling Oyumi anything, I sent a disfiguring poison to Oiwa, falsely claiming it was medicine. I thought that the problem would solve itself as soon as her beauty disappeared. Your love for your wife would vanish, so you would divorce her and marry my granddaughter. I kept this evil plan to myself and sent the medicine by way of the nurse. I knew that it would ruin her face but leave her life untouched. It would leave her alive! I clung to that fact, telling myself that it wouldn't be such a great crime. However, matters have not worked out as I hoped. I am responsible for a great tragedy. That's why I want you to kill me.

OYUMI: You thought up this evil plan all for the sake of my poor young child?

OUME: This is how I am being punished for my sinful desires.

KIHEI: If you're able to forgive me, all my family's gold is yours.

CHŌBEI: It would be a big mistake not to take what's on your plate.

KIHEI: Get rid of your anger by killing me!

OYUMI: No! Not here in your own house.

OUME: It's better for me to die. (*She tries again to kill herself, but Oyumi stops her.*)

KIHEI: Will you forgive me?

IEMON: I, I—

OYUMI: If you die, how can I protect this child all by myself?

IEMON: Well—

KIHEI: Then kill me!

IEMON: I, well . . .

KIHEI: I've done a monstrous thing.

OYUMI (*forcefully*): Please, give us your answer.

IEMON: I've made my decision. I'll leave Oiwa and take your granddaughter's hand.

KIHEI: Then you give your consent?

OYUMI: You're granting—

CHŌBEI: This child's wishes?

IEMON: In exchange, I have a request myself.

KIHEI: And that is?

IEMON: Recommend me to Lord Moronao as a retainer.[5]

KIHEI: Done. I would have done that even if you hadn't asked, now that we all are one family.

IEMON: If I take your granddaughter, we will be father and son-in-law. From this moment, I will change my name from Tamiya to Itō.[6]

OYUMI: As they say, the sooner, the better.

KIHEI: We'll have the wedding ceremony tonight. Do you agree?

IEMON: Certainly. (*To himself*) Hmm, maybe I can put the blame on that masseur who comes to see Oiwa.

KIHEI: What?

IEMON: Oh, nothing. I suppose we can discuss the details later.

CHŌBEI: First things first. Now you should exchange wedding cups. I'll be your go-between.

OUME: This is embarrassing.

OYUMI: She's still a bit shy.

OUME (*bashfully*): Oh.

KIHEI: Well, son-in-law? (*Takes out a marriage cup. Oume bashfully clings to Iemon.*)

IEMON (*changing his tone and putting his hand on Oume's shoulder*): Now that you are my wife, I'll swear an oath on my sword.

OYUMI AND KIHEI: A blessing on you both. (*They clasp their hands in prayerful thanks. The temple bell sounds. The music increases in volume and tempo as the stage revolves. The actors continue to celebrate the marriage as they are carried out of sight.*)

---

5. Many rōnin dearly wished to find service in a samurai household so that they could serve in a position befitting their social rank and receive a stipend. For Iemon, this is perhaps the most attractive aspect of marrying Oume, even though Moronao was responsible for his former master's death.

6. Iemon announces that he will be adopted into the Itō clan and serve Lord Kō no Moronao, the enemy of his own master, Lord Enya. It was a common practice to adopt a son-in-law as one's heir.

Tamiya Iemon's Residence

To heighten the tension, the large drum plays wind patterns, which derive from the sound of wind rattling the wooden sliding doors and shutters of the commoners' houses. Takuetsu lights a lamp, sees how horribly Oiwa's face has become disfigured, and staggers out to buy some lamp oil. He collapses in fear at center stage and finally makes it out the front door. He collapses again on the runway and tries to stand several times, but his legs keep collapsing under him. Finally he runs off. Oiwa takes the baby into the room at left; the audience still has not seen her face. A popular song is played, and the temple bell sounds. Iemon staggers down the runway, tipsy from drink. He stops outside the gate.

IEMON: Kihei claimed the drug wouldn't kill her, only change her appearance. If she's—I'll look for myself first. (*He enters the house. Languid music plays, evoking the heat of summer.*)

OIWA (*calling from inside the room*): Takuetsu, are you back with the oil already?

IEMON: What oil? It's me.

OIWA: Is that you, Iemon? (*Iemon opens the sliding paper screens in front of the room at stage left. Oiwa is still hidden by the mosquito netting, which is almost opaque.*)

IEMON: How are you feeling? Did the medicine help your circulation?

OIWA: It helped my circulation, but as soon as I took it, I broke into a terrible fever. My face felt like it was on fire.

IEMON: The fever felt the worst in your face?

OIWA: Yes, it's all numb now. (*She comes out of the mosquito netting. Iemon sees her and is shocked.*)

IEMON: Oh, it's changed so quickly.

OIWA: What's changed?

IEMON: What I was saying was that—that while I was at Kihei's, your face has changed, the color has come back into your cheeks. It must be the effect of the drug. Yes, you look like you're getting better.

OIWA: I don't know if my face looks better or worse. I feel just the same. It's been like this day after day without a break. Iemon, if I died now, I would leave this world with no regrets—except for my child. It's only pity for my child that keeps me tied to this wretched life. If I die, please don't marry again, at least for a while.

IEMON: I'll marry if I feel like it.

OIWA: What?

IEMON: I'll find a new wife right away. I'll get a better wife. So what? There are plenty of people who get married again.

OIWA: Iemon, you're cruel! You were born heartless. I always knew what you were like. I married you because—

IEMON: You needed help to avenge your father's murder. Well, I don't feel like getting involved. Avenging murder is old-fashioned. Leave me out of it. We got married because you wanted a swordsman, but I'm not interested.

OIWA: What? So now—but you—

IEMON: So I don't feel like it anymore. What are you going to do about it? If you don't like it, leave. Go find someone else who has the time to waste on vendettas. Vendettas make me sick.

OIWA: If you refuse, I have no one else to turn to. I suppose I should have expected you to fail me. If you want me to go, I will. But what about the child? Will you have your new wife take care of our baby?

IEMON: If you don't want a stepmother to have him, take the brat with you. I'm not giving up a chance for a good new wife for the sake of a stupid baby. But I need some cash; something came up. Do you have something you can lend me? Is there anything around here we can pawn? (*Looks around and sees the ornamental comb on the floor*) Why don't I take this? (*Picks it up*)

OIWA (*grabbing it from him*): That's the comb my mother left me. I'll never let that out of my sight.

IEMON: You won't, will you? Well, my new woman doesn't have a nice dress comb, so she keeps asking me to buy her one. What's wrong with giving her this one?

OIWA: This is the one thing I can never give up.

IEMON: Then give me something I can buy a comb with. Also, I need to dress up tonight, so I need to get my good clothes out of hock. Lend me something! Come on, make it quick. (*Shoves her. The languid music begins again.*)

OIWA: There's nothing left to speak of, but perhaps this? (*She takes off her outer kimono, leaving herself dressed only in a thin, pale gray underkimono, which makes her look more ghostlike.*) I'm sick, but since you asked for something, I'll give you this. (*She hands the kimono to Iemon.*)

IEMON (*examining the clothing*): This won't bring enough. I need more. Isn't there anything else? How about the mosquito netting? (*He takes it down and starts to go. She clutches at the net.*)

OIWA: Wait! Without a mosquito net, my baby will be eaten alive by mosquitoes as soon as it gets dark. (*She takes back the net.*)

IEMON: If the mosquitoes start eating him, your job as a parent is to chase them away. Let go! I said, let go! (*He tugs roughly. Oiwa is dragged along the floor with the net. Finally he kicks her and pulls the net away, her fingernails caught in the net. Oiwa lets out a cry and holds up her hands; her fingertips are covered with blood, showing that the nails have been torn away.*)

IEMON: This still isn't enough, you stingy bitch! (*A popular song and a temple bell are heard as Iemon goes up the runway, stops, and looks up as he calculates how much he can pawn the items for. Then he exits.*)

OIWA: Iemon! I can't let you have the mosquito net. (*Goes to the door*) He's already gone. He took the only thing I couldn't give up. Even though I'm weak and sick, I hung on to it for dear life for the sake of my child. The net's torn my fingernails away. (*Stares at her blood-covered fingers*) Iemon,

Iemon takes Oiwa's clothing and the mosquito net and drags her across the floor. Oiwa, her face half swollen, is left wearing only a single underkimono. A brazier burns pine needles.

you're so cruel. I feel sorry for my poor baby when I think that he's your flesh and blood. (*She broods. The baby cries. Oiwa stands unsteadily, looking around. She finally pulls out a small brazier and wearily starts burning incense to drive away the mosquitoes. Iemon reappears on the runway with the kimono and mosquito netting slung over his shoulder. He has Takuetsu in tow.*)

TAKUETSU: Master, you're going too far. If you do that, everyone will talk about me and Oiwa.

IEMON: I'll fix it all if you do your part right. (*He whispers his plan in Takuetsu's ear.*)

TAKUETSU: Then you're going to have the wedding tonight?

IEMON: Keep it quiet. Here. (*He shows him a small gold coin wrapped in paper.*)[7]

TAKUETSU: You're giving me this gold coin? To make me—

IEMON: Do it right, and it's yours. (*He gestures with his sword to show what will happen if Takuetsu refuses.*)

TAKUETSU: Yes, I understand. (*After Iemon has exited*) What a mess I'm in

---

7. Iemon has the gold coins he received from Kihei, but he is pawning Oiwa's possessions to get her to leave him of her own volition or at least to throw her into Takuetsu's arms.

now! Oiwa, I'm sorry to have kept you waiting so long. Here's the oil. (*He picks up the lantern.*)

OIWA (*resignedly fanning the incense burner*): You're back? So soon? After you left, Iemon came and took away the mosquito net.

TAKUETSU: Back to the pawnshop, eh? Tsk, tsk, how very thoughtless of him. What will happen to you and the baby without it? Well now, look at you. My, how thin your kimono is.

OIWA: Even though I'm sick and shouldn't get chilled, Iemon forced me to give him my kimono.

TAKUETSU: Really? How unfortunate. What hard times you've been through. Instead of all that trouble, wouldn't it be better to find another man? Think about it. I used to read palms. Let me look. (*Goes to Oiwa, takes her hand, and looks intently at the palm, looking for an excuse to try to seduce her*) Look at this, there's an unlucky line running through your palm. According to this, your husband will cause you endless pain. It says here that you should cut off this line, cut off all ties with that man. (*As he says this, Oiwa looks at Takuetsu. He sees her face, gasps, and turns away.*)

OIWA (*jumping up in surprise*): What are you trying to do? Remember, I'm the wife of a samurai. If you try anything like that again, I won't forgive you next time.

TAKUETSU: Wait! Your faithfulness will only hurt you, Iemon lost his love for you long ago. If you insist on staying with him, it will lead to nothing but more misfortune. I'm the man for you.

OIWA: What? Rather than patiently enduring hardships with my rightful husband, I should turn to you? Explain yourself. Are you trying to lure me into adultery? You insolent creature! Even though I'm only a woman, I am the wife and the daughter of samurai. Do you think you can get away with talking that way to me? (*Picks up Kohei's sword, deftly unsheathes it, and confronts Takuetsu*) There must be a reason you're doing this, tell me!

TAKUETSU (*shaking*): Put that down, it's dangerous! You'll get hurt! (*He tries to grab Oiwa's hand. They struggle back and forth. Finally he grabs the sword, tosses it into the room at left, and holds her down in a seated position. The sword lands against the pillar of the room, with the tip sticking out.*) Listen. It was all a lie. What I said just now was all a lie. Really, calm down! Even a poor wretch like me wouldn't want a woman with your awful face. I don't know why this was fated to happen, but on top of your sickness, now your face. It breaks my heart.

OIWA: My face? Along with the fever there was a sudden pain, could that have—?

TAKUETSU: It is a woman's fate to be deceived. That miracle drug for your circulation that you got from Kihei was all a trick. It was a poison meant to change a person's face, an extraordinary poison. When you took it, your face changed and now you look like an ugly, evil woman. Don't you know that?

How pitiful. (*He goes to the back of the room and takes her mirror off its stand.*) Here, if you want to know, look at this. Look at your face in this. (*He stands behind her and forces her to look in the mirror.*)

OIWA: Ahh, my face is gray, gray as my kimono. What's happened to my face? Is this my face? Have I really changed into a demon? (*She holds the mirror at various angles, hoping that the image will change. She huddles on the floor and cries, leaving the mirror on the floor beside her.*)

TAKUETSU: This play had another author, Kihei's granddaughter Oume. She wanted Iemon to be her husband, but her family knew that Iemon already had a wife. Kihei has gold to spare and thought he could buy Iemon, but he worried that perhaps Iemon had some feeling of loyalty to you. To make absolutely sure he wouldn't be refused, Kihei tricked you with this medicine. He thought that if your faced changed, your husband's love would run out. Poor Oiwa, you innocently took the medicine, not knowing a thing. What a sad situation. (*Her face has been gradually revealing her growing fury as she looks intently at the mirror.*)

OIWA (*spoken with great deliberateness*):
I never guessed the
truth these gifts concealed,
sent day after day by our good neighbor Itō Kihei.
My heart swelled with thanks.
Even when the wet nurse came, the destructive poison in her hand,
to cause my ruin, I clapped my hands in gratitude.
Now each time I think of it, my heart fills with shame.
They must laugh and laugh at me.
Bitter, oh how bitter, is this humiliation. (*She lies on the floor sobbing.*)

TAKUETSU (*drawing near*):
Iemon has run out of love for you.
As bridegroom of the house of Itō, he plotted to rid himself of you.
"Play my wife's lover," he ordered.
I replied, "Never!" and up came his sword.
So we have no choice but to play out our little comedy.
He stripped you of your robe, cruelly tearing it away.
But now the truth is revealed.
Tonight! The wedding is tonight.
By pawning your things,
money for the preparations fell into the bridegroom's hands.
He ordered me to seduce you and to flee with you as lovers do,
so that when he leads his bride here, you won't be an obstacle for
them.
I was to be the made-to-order lover,
but that terrible face of yours keeps tender passion down.
Forgive me, please forgive me.

OIWA (*strengthening her resolve*): Now all that is left to me is suffering and death. But while I still have breath, I must go and thank Master Kihei properly. (*She stands unsteadily and begins to stagger to the front door.*)

TAKUETSU: No, no! If you go out looking like that, people will think you're a madwoman. (*Pushes her back*) Your clothing is torn and—your—face—(*He stops and inadvertently looks up at her face, shrieks, and looks down. They are just at the spot where the mirror is still lying on the floor. Takuetsu and Oiwa are transfixed by the horrible image in the mirror.*)

OIWA (*takes the mirror and looks carefully*):

> How frightful—the hair of the woman in the mirror.
> I must blacken my teeth as married women do.
> Then I must dress my hair.
> I must look proper to give Kihei and Oume, parent and child,
> one small word of thanks.
> (*Quietly*) Bring me my tooth blackening.

TAKUETSU: But you're still sick and weak. You've just given birth. It's not safe for you to go out.

OIWA: It's quite all right. Bring my tooth blackening quickly.

TAKUETSU: But—

OIWA (*firmly*): I said, bring it right now.

TAKUETSU (*startled by her firmness*): Yes. (*A singer accompanied by a shamisen begins singing a plaintive song. Takuetsu brings the lantern, a large metal container, and a stick of blackening. Oiwa sets up the mirror on a stand and sits down in the center of the main room. She rinses her mouth, wipes her teeth dry, and then applies the blackening.[8] She messily covers the corners of her mouth, which makes it look as though her mouth is monstrously wide. The baby, who has been sleeping in the other room, starts to cry. Takuetsu tries to comfort him and put him to sleep. Takuetsu clears away the utensils while Oiwa spreads some paper on the floor and takes her comb from her kimono.*)

OIWA (*singing*):

> My precious comb, all that is left from my mother.
> After my death, this comb must go to my sister, Osode.
> This is my one remaining wish.
> My father, my husband, my sister, and I
> all are tied together by bonds thousandfold.
> As I dream of the one thing I can do for my sister,
> let the teeth of this comb pass through my hair
> and straighten out its tangled strands.

(*Oiwa has Takuetsu cut the cord holding her hair in place. She sweeps her hair forward over her head and begins combing it. Hair comes out in great*

---

8. It was customary for married women to blacken their teeth, but Oiwa has not done this since giving birth.

Oiwa stands in front of a dressing table, her hair disheveled and her swollen face fully exposed, tying her sash with a determined look. She has turned away from her dressing table, where she has just blackened her teeth using the mirror and ceramic bowl at her feet. The end of Kohei's sword sticks out from the pillar behind her. The small cartouche (*upper left*) shows the next scene, in which Iemon slays Kohei.

handfuls.[9] The hair piles up on the floor. When Oiwa sweeps her hair back, her hairline has receded considerably, leaving the grotesque swelling above her right eye totally exposed. This action is emphasized by doro-doro drum patterns, which suggest strange occurrences. She drops the comb on the pile of hair.)

Every moment is uncertain, as the end comes for Oiwa.
But one thing is sure, the moment I die he will marry that girl.
I can see the scene right before my eyes.
Now I have nothing but hatred for you, Iemon,
and hate for the house of Kihei, hatred for the Itō family.
None of you shall ever escape to a life of peace.
The more I think about it
the more my heart is filled with bitter, bitter hatred.

9. This is a grotesque parody of a kabuki tradition in which scenes of combing hair (*kamisuki*), often with a woman dressing her lover's hair, are intimate and erotic moments.

(*She picks up the pile of hair and tries to go to the door, but Takuetsu stops her, pushing her back with the standing screen. Oiwa's face twists with fury, and she begins to wring her bundle of hair. Blood drips from the hair onto the white screen in front of her. Clappers strike to emphasize the dripping of blood.*)

TAKUETSU (*seeing the blood and shaking*): Ahh, ah, ah, ahh. She's squeezing blood from her hair.

OIWA: My fury will not rest until it reaches its goal!

TAKUETSU: Oiwa, please, please! (*He grabs Oiwa and tries to stop her, unintentionally letting go of her and sending her tottering into the room at stage left. Oiwa tries to reenter the main room and accidentally cuts her throat on Kohei's sword stuck in a pillar. She gestures with painful spasms, emphasized by the sharp clanging of a prayer bell. Finally, she collapses on the floor and dies.*)

TAKUETSU (*shaking*): Oh no, no. Kohei's sword was there. I wanted to stop her, but not like this. Oh, oh, how awful, awful. (*Doro-doro drum patterns and the nō flute played breathlessly produce an eerie effect. A rat appears and tries to tug at the baby.*[10] *Takuetsu shoos it away. A green spirit flame floats near Oiwa's body.*) I can't stay here any longer! (*The terrified Takuetsu runs out the front door, continually slipping and falling in his haste. Iemon enters the runway dressed in a magnificent formal costume and runs into Takuetsu.*)

IEMON: It's my good masseur. How did it go? Did you run away with Oiwa? Did things go according to plan?

TAKUETSU: Uh, uh. You ordered me to do that, but it just didn't work.

IEMON: Then she hasn't gone away yet? What a useless old fool you are. I just came from the marriage ceremony at the Itō mansion. I was sure you would have taken her away by now. Tonight they are bringing over the new bride. If Oiwa is still in there, it will be a problem. This is awful!

TAKUETSU: It was awful, awful. That rat was awful! (*He shivers and exits.*)

IEMON (*looking after him*): That idiot went off just babbling about some rat without telling me what happened. Who can I use in his place as an excuse for chasing Oiwa out? Wait, I know. I'll turn my servant Kohei into her lover and drive the two of them out. In any case, tonight Oume will be coming. (*Reaches the front door*) Oiwa, where are you? Oiwa, Oiwa. (*Notices the crying baby on the floor and jumps in surprise*)[11] One more step and I would have crushed him. Oiwa, Oiwa! (*Picks up the crying baby*) Hey, Oiwa. (*Sees

---

10. The rat represents Oiwa's spirit, since she was born in the year of the rat. In the original version, this was a more elaborate scene with a cat, thought to be able to raise the spirits of the dead, appearing and then being pursued and killed by a huge rat.

11. In early performances, several puppet rats would enter. The first one would grab the baby's clothing and tug, and the others would line up, each grabbing the tail of the one in front. They would attempt to carry off the baby, but Iemon would chase them away.

her body) Oh, oh. This is Oiwa with Kohei's rusty old sword in her throat. Did he kill her? But he was in the closet. (*He puts the baby down, opens the closet, and pulls out Kohei.*) He's still tied up just as before, then he didn't. . . . In any case, he'll get the blame for killing Oiwa. (*He unties Kohei.*)

KOHEI: Master, you're a real monster.

IEMON: What the hell are you talking about?

KOHEI: You may have bound my hands and gagged me, but I know that hounding Oiwa to death in that miserable way was all your doing. Takuetsu told Oiwa everything about the plot between you and your neighbor Kihei. He told her about the poison that disfigured her. How could you drive out your wife at a time like this, all for your own advancement? Do you really think you can get ahead that way? You're the lowest scum!

IEMON: Shut up! Peasant! Oiwa was killed with your sword. You killed her. You killed your master's wife. You killed her!

KOHEI: That's insane! I was tied and gagged. How could I?

IEMON (*shouting*): But look! Your hands are moving now. You must have killed Oiwa! Murderer! (*Iemon refuses to listen to Kohei. They continue to argue. Kohei suggests that he be given the medicine in return for being labeled a murderer. Iemon refuses.*)

IEMON: I have no choice. You're Oiwa's enemy, and I must avenge her death. You killed her, so you're a murderer. Anyway, how could I let you live after you heard about our plot? Here, go on to the next world, with the help of my sword. (*Strikes him. They struggle in a stylized, dancelike manner. Lively music plays as they fight, posing dramatically from time to time. Kohei defends himself desperately, throwing everything he can get his hands on, including umbrellas. Finally, wounded in several places, Kohei clings to Iemon.*).

KOHEI: I guess even during just one night's employ, if one fights with one's master—

IEMON: Justice strikes you with your master's sword. That's why I'm killing you, slowly. You are Oiwa's enemy! Die! (*After a struggle, Kohei collapses to the sounds of a Buddhist wooden gong. Chōbei, Kanzō, and, later, Bansuke enter down the runway. After being told what has happened, they carry the bodies out the back door. Stately entrance music is played for a grand procession up the runway. Kihei, dressed in a formal coat and divided skirts, leads Oume by the hand. Behind them, Omaki is accompanied by two servants bearing silk bedding and a six-section folding screen. They arrive at the front door.*)

KIHEI (*slightly tipsy from the wedding saké*): Master Iemon, Master Iemon. It's Kihei.

IEMON: Well, well, good sir. You're here already with Oume. Come in, come in.

OUME: Oh please, wait. We have been married as you promised, but I feel funny moving right into your house so soon.

KIHEI: Don't worry. Iemon made a mistake by not having anyone to look after Oiwa, but fortunately, we're all one family. Even if it does go a little against samurai practice to bring everything over before we've had a public ceremony, we brought the screen and the bedding anyway. Don't worry.

OMAKI: You are undoubtedly right, but remember how young the girl is. She hasn't come of age yet.

KIHEI: I say not to worry! (*He pulls Oume into the house, and they all sit down.*) By the way, Iemon, is it true about Oiwa and you know who?

IEMON: When I told you about it at the wedding, I had the wrong man. It was actually my servant Kohei who was having an affair with her. When the two were discovered, she ran off with her lover, leaving her baby behind. Oume, tonight, if my new father-in-law will allow it, I would like you to stay here.

KIHEI: Ah, so she did have another man? Among samurai, that sort of thing just will not do. But as far as we are concerned, the timing was perfect. Congratulations!

OMAKI: I'm sure you are right, but I'm surprised that she left the house when she was still so sick. Well, I guess that certainly is a marvel. But what are you going to do about the little boy?

IEMON: That really is a problem.

KIHEI: Well, for that very reason, I'll stay here starting tonight and help you out. Early tomorrow morning, the nurse will come and help too. Omaki, spread out my bed.

OMAKI: As you wish. (*She spreads out the bedding at stage right and puts the large folding screen around it.*) Master, I've prepared your bed over here.

KIHEI: Then where will the young couple sleep?

IEMON: Let's use my old bed. It will serve that faithless old wife of mine right.

KIHEI: Of course, what a fine idea. Here Oume, this is your good luck charm. Take care to keep it around your neck. (*He hands her a red charm.*)

OUME: I'll never let go of it. I'm scared of Oiwa.

OMAKI: I know you are, but put her out of your head, at least while you are in your wedding bed.

IEMON: Don't worry about it. Who would dare to say anything against people as important as we are?

OMAKI: No, no. Of course, no one could object. Now here you go. (*Takes Oume by the hand and leads her to the bed in the room at stage left*) Tonight your wishes will come true at last.

OUME: I know you're right, but when I remember that for my sake, poor Oiwa . . .

OMAKI: Now hush or your wishes won't come true. (*She closes the sliding doors. The baby starts to cry.*)

IEMON: What a time for the kid to . . .

KIHEI: Ah ha. I may not be able to give any milk, but tonight I'll be the child's wet nurse. I'll keep him with me tonight. (*He picks up the baby, cradles him, and retires to the bed at stage right.*)

IEMON: Father-in-law, thank you for everything.

OMAKI: What shall I do?

KIHEI: Go and tell my daughter that everything is all right here.

OMAKI: As you wish. Well, my deepest congratulations.

IEMON: Good night, nurse.

OMAKI: Enjoy your wedding night. (*To a lively song and the tolling of the temple bell, Omaki, preceded by the servants carrying the lanterns, exits. Kihei closes the screen around his bed. Iemon, left alone, is pleased with the turn of events.*)

IEMON: Now it's off to the bridal bed with an innocent girl who's never done anything. Well, let's start her out right. (*Eerie flute music plays, and the temple bell tolls. Iemon enters the room at left and slides open the doors so the interior is visible to the audience.*) Oume, I'm sorry I've kept you waiting. Listen, my bride, there's no reason to stare at the floor. Even if you feel bashful, come, lift up your face. Tonight is the night that all your dreams come true. Here, look happy. Look at me, smile, and say, "Now you're my husband." (*He draws closer.*)

OUME: Yes, Iemon, you are my husband. (*She lifts up her face. The red charm is around her neck, but the face is that of Oiwa. She glares with hatred at Iemon and cackles. Iemon picks up a sword from nearby, draws it, and strikes her, immediately closing the screen door behind him. The decapitated head of Oume falls to the floor. Rats come onstage and surround the head, accompanied by the sound of light doro-doro drum patterns.*)

IEMON (*looks closely at the face*): Oh no, no. That was really Oume, I acted too quickly! (*Still holding the sword, he runs over to the screen at right and pulls it aside. Inside, Kihei is sitting up, his face turned away from the audience. He is wearing a thick padded jacket and is holding the baby, his mouth stained from eating the baby. Iemon goes over to him.*) Father-in law! Father-in law! Something terrible has happened. By mistake . . . (*Kihei turns his head: it is Kohei who is eating the baby. Kohei glares at Iemon.*)

KOHEI: Master, give me the medicine.

IEMON: Oh no! You're Kohei! And now you're killing the baby! (*Iemon cuts off Kohei's head. The blood-stained head of Kihei falls on the floor. A snake emerges from Kihei's hips, crawling toward the head and coiling around it.[12] Iemon looks closely.*) That was really my father-in-law. I can't stay in this cursed place! (*He runs to the front door. With one hand, he grabs his collar as though pushing away some unseen force that is tugging him back. With the other hand, he reaches forward desperately in the direction he wants to go. This movement is punctuated by a doro-doro drum pattern. He pushes away whatever it is and starts running again, only to be stopped. The forward and backward movements alternate with increasing rapidity until Iemon is stand-*

---

12. The snake is an incarnation of the spirit of Kohei, who was born in the year of the snake.

Iemon is caught between the vengeful spirits of Kohei (*left*) and Oiwa (*right*), both of whom are legless and wear white robes, a characteristic depiction of Japanese ghosts in the Edo period. The dead bodies of Kihei and Oume lie face down in pools of blood at Iemon's feet.

ing in one place, desperately trying to move. Finally, he is pulled back into the house, spins in a circle, and sits down hard in the middle of the floor. Green spirit flames float in the air in front of Iemon as he stiffens and shouts.) You spiteful spirits! *(The clacking of the wooden clappers begins to mark the end of the act.)* Hail Amida Buddha, Hail Amida Buddha, Hail Amida Buddha . . . *(Two green spirit flames hover in the air. Iemon clasps his hands together, praying fervently as the curtain is pulled shut.)*

Act 3, Deadman's Ditch

MAIN CHARACTERS

CHŌBEI (AKIYAMA), a rōnin, Iemon's crony

IEMON (TAMIYA), a masterless samurai, marries into Kihei's family

KIHEI (ITŌ), samurai in service of Kō no Moronao, grandfather of Oume, mistakenly killed by Iemon

KOHEI, Iemon's servant, killed by Iemon

MAGOBEI, the father of Kohei

NAOSUKE, a masterless samurai married to Osode, Oiwa's sister; calls himself Gonbei, now an eel fisherman

OIWA, Iemon's wife, accidentally kills herself after being disfigured

OKUMA, Iemon's mother

OMAKI, a nurse in the Kihei's household

OUME, Oyumi's daughter and Kihei's granddaughter, married to Iemon, mistakenly killed by Iemon

OYUMI, Kihei's widowed daughter and mother of Oume

Onbōbori, or Deadman's Ditch, a river near a temple crematorium in the Fukagawa district of Edo. The river flows in front of a steep grassy dike with a dry riverbed on the left and right sides. The scene opens to shamisen music called "Zen no tsutome," which is used for scenes with a funereal, Buddhist atmosphere. A prayer bell is also striking. Oyumi, the widowed daughter of Kihei and the mother of the recently deceased Oume, and Omaki, the wet nurse of the Itō family, have been reduced to the status of beggars and are in ragged clothing, though retaining some air of their previous status. Omaki has a bag of rice around her neck. Even though her mistress is now a penniless beggar, Omaki continues to serve her faithfully. They are on the dry land in front of the dike to the left. A small tripod holds a pot over a fire. Oyumi is ill, and Omaki rubs her back to comfort her.

OMAKI: Oyumi-sama, how are you feeling today?

OYUMI: Please don't worry about me. Today I feel much better. The only thing that worries me is that we still don't know where Tamiya Iemon is. What could have made him kill my father and daughter? To return all our generosity with murder is inhuman. It's an outrage, Omaki.

OMAKI: You're right. All because the Itō clan tried to welcome a worthless man as son-in-law, the family has been destroyed and the mansion repossessed by Lord Moronao. Even though we've been reduced to being outcasts, we're searching for Iemon to avenge the destruction of our family. I am only one person, but I'm pleased to serve you faithfully. Oyumi-sama, please take heart and don't despair.

OYUMI: You haven't forgotten the past and are so kind that for me you're not a servant, you're part of my family. (*She takes out an amulet.*) My daughter Oume kept this amulet next to her heart all the time. That she forgot the amulet when she went to Iemon's house was perhaps a sign that she would die so horribly. The more I think about it, the more I'm determined that Iemon be punished properly for his evil acts.

OMAKI: Please don't dwell on it. Why don't you pray for your father and daughter, and I'll start boiling the rice for dinner. (*The shamisen music continues and is joined by the pounding of a wooden gong. The steady pounding of a large drum suggests the flow of the river. Omaki scoops up water from the river and washes the rice and then puts it in the pot to boil. Meanwhile, Oyumi hangs the amulet bag from the tripod and prays fervently to it. Magobei, the father of the deceased Kohei, appears on the runway. He carries a sotoba, long, thin wooden plaque that was a kind of grave marker. He seems to be gazing at the river looking for something. He sees the two women.*)

MAGOBEI (*to himself*): There are some beggars who look like they come from much better circumstances. (*Calls to them*) Excuse me. Are you living here next to the river? By any chance have you seen a wooden door float by with the bodies of a man and a woman attached to it?

OYUMI: I don't believe that there have been any bodies like that, have there?

OMAKI: No, there haven't been. Why do you ask?

MAGOBEI: Please listen to my story. My son Kohei served in a samurai mansion, but he ran away and disappeared. I heard today that a door with the bodies of a man and a woman was spotted floating in the river. I was afraid that might be my son. But if I go home and tell his wife and son, they would just start to grieve again. The only thing I could do was to go to the Reigan Temple and ask for funeral prayers to be said for my son and to have this funeral plaque made. If he is still alive, all is well, but if he is already dead, this plaque will help to ease his spirit.

OYUMI (*hearing Magobei's story, Oyumi becomes emotional*): How terribly sad. Everywhere it's the same tragedy.

OMAKI: Oyumi-sama, you've been praying to this amulet in memory of Kihei and Oume, but perhaps this makes it impossible for you to forget unpleasant events. Why don't I do this. (*She takes the amulet.*) Tomorrow, I'll go to the Reigan Temple and give the amulet to the priests and have them pray for your father and daughter.

OYUMI: Perhaps you're right. As long as I have this amulet, I can't forget Oume. Please go and dedicate this amulet to the temple.

OMAKI: I will. As soon as evening comes, let us go visit the temple. (*Omaki puts down the amulet. The pounding of the drum suggests the rattling of wooden shutters in the wind. There is a rustling in the grass, and a rat appears and takes the amulet. The two women cry out in shock.*)

OYUMI: That rat ran away with the amulet.

OMAKI: Where did that rat come from!? (*They chase after the rat, and it jumps into the river.*) It took the amulet into the river. (*Omaki tries to recover the amulet, but the ground is soft and slippery.*)

OYUMI: Watch out! (*Oyumi tries to hold onto Omaki and grabs her obi sash, but the obi rips apart in her hands and Omaki falls into the river, accompanied by a loud boom of the drum suggesting a splash. Oyumi falls on the ground holding the torn-off section of the obi, and she passes out from the shock. Magobei rushes to her and tries to help her.*)

MAGOBEI: Madam! Madam! Are you all right? (*Muses on what he has just seen*) I never thought that a single rat could pull a human being into a river, but that maid fell in and drowned. Now the other woman has passed out. What a terrible thing. (*He is torn between staying to help and wanting to go on with his search.*) But I don't want to get involved in the troubles of a couple of beggars. All the same, I don't want to abandon them either. (*He decides to go.*) I do not know who you are, but I hope you recover. (*He sees a red raincoat on the ground and covers Oyumi with it. He picks up the sotoba again and, mumbling prayers for Oyumi's well-being, leaves. Lively shamisen music called "Tsukuda bushi" suggests boats on the Sumida River, while the pounding of the drum suggests the flow of the river.)*

Naosuke, a *rōnin* married to Osode, appears. In act 1, Naosuke fell in love with Osode, Oiwa's sister, and to make her his own, he killed a man whom he thought was Sato Yomoshichi, her lover. At the same time, Tamiya Iemon, who was pursuing Oiwa, killed Oiwa's father, Samon Yotsuya. Naosuke and Iemon subsequently work together. Iemon promised Oiwa to find and kill the murderer of her father, while Naosuke promised Osode to avenge the deaths of her father and her lover. There is also a connection to the story of *Chūshingura*, since Oiwa and Osode's father, Samon, was a member of Lord Enya's clan, and Sato Yomoshichi is also one of the loyal retainers hoping to find an opportunity to attack Lord Kō no Moronao and avenge their lord's death.

Now Naosuke calls himself Gonbei, a name that in the Edo period meant "a person not worthy of note," also suggesting Naosuke Gonbei, the name of a retainer-servant who became notorious for betraying and killing his lord. Naosuke is currently an eel fisherman and wears tight-fitting dark blue trousers and a long, persimmon-colored coat. There is a basket for his catch at his waist, and he carries a three-pronged rake with a long handle used for catching eels. Even though Naosuke wears common work clothes, the cut and color of his costume make him look sharp and stylish, the epitome of Tsuruya Nanboku's villainous heroes.[13]

NAOSUKE (*stops and speaks on the runway*): There's never been a year for fishing that's been as bad as this one. The water seems good and muddy over here, just right for eels. Well, let's start fishing. (*He wades into the river and starts fishing for eels. Finally he fishes up a clump of hair tangled around Oiwa's comb.*) Ugh. My rake fished up a clump of hair. (*He's about to throw it away but looks more closely and sees the comb.*) This comb is tortoiseshell. Let's wash it. (*He climbs back onto the riverbank and wipes the mud and hair off of the comb with some dry grass. He sits on a rock on the riverbed, gets out his pipe, and has a smoke. Meanwhile, to the accompaniment of quiet shamisen music, Iemon and his mother, Okuma, appear on the runway. Okuma, an old woman in a plain kimono, carries a sotoba. Iemon, in a black silk–crested kimono, wears a large basket-like straw hat that completely conceals his face. He carries a fishing pole and tackle. The two go to the middle of the dike.*)

IEMON: Mother, I'm glad to see that you're safe and healthy.

---

13. At the time of the first performance, there had been a sensational incident in which an eel fisherman had discovered the bodies of a man and a woman floating in the Onbōbori River.

OKUMA: Iemon, after hearing all these rumors, I've been worried about you. I couldn't be happier to have met you here. As you know, I left your foster father Genshiro and then went to serve as a maid in the mansion of Lord Moronao. I helped the lord seduce Lady Kaoyo, but that stubborn woman ruined everything and her silly husband attacked Lord Moronao. At the time Lord Moronao was thankful for everything that I did and said that if I ever needed anything, I should just come to him. (*She takes out a document wrapped carefully in a cloth, unwraps it, and gives it to Iemon.*) This document is from Lord Moronao. I knew that you had become a masterless samurai, so I asked for this to get you out of trouble. But I couldn't do anything with it, since my current husband is a servant of a retainer of the Enya household, Lord Moronao's enemy. Then I heard that a masterless samurai named Iemon killed his wife and the people next door. So I thought up this trick to protect you. (*Holds out the sotoba*) If I had a Buddhist name put on this grave marker, no one would know that it was you. So I had the priest write, "In life, his name was Tamiya Iemon." This way, everyone will think that you're dead. How about that! It still takes a lot to outsmart your old mother.

IEMON: Mother, I'm extremely grateful for all your kindness. But I've already made sure that my fellow samurai Kanzō and his retainer take the blame for the killings. Nothing is likely to touch me. But if it will make you feel better, let's just put up this grave marker here. (*He sticks it into a clump of grass on top of the dike.*)

OKUMA: Let's do that. This dike is the perfect place for it. If you want to see me, I'm living near all the temples in Fukagawa, with a poor man named Hotoke Magobei. Be sure to visit.

IEMON: Mother, I'll be sure to visit you soon. (*Shamisen music with the dull thumping of a wooden Buddhist gong. Okuma exits. Naosuke has been listening from below. From the top of the dike, Iemon looks at the river.*) This looks like a good place to fish. (*He gets out his fishing pole, drops the line into the river, and plants the pole in the ground so that it sticks out over the edge of the dike. He gets out his pipe, but then realizes that he doesn't have anything to light it with. He notices Naosuke smoking on the riverbank below.*) Excuse me, could you give me a light?

NAOSUKE: Here you are. (*He takes Iemon's pipe and puts the bowls of the two pipes together. As the two pose, one above, the other below, it creates a handsome image. Naosuke peeks under Iemon's hat and speaks in a light but somewhat menacing tone.*) Hey Iemon, it's been a while, hasn't it?

IEMON (*warily*): Is that you, Naosuke?

NAOSUKE: Yeah, I'm Naosuke, but I go by the name Gonbei now. Iemon, you're the murderer of my sister-in-law.

IEMON (*startled*): Are you joking? What are you talking about?

NAOSUKE (*in the grand tones of heroes in a kabuki history play*): Iemon,

Iemon and Naosuke smoke pipes and fish at the embankment next to a wooden water gate. Iemon, in a black silk–crested kimono and armed with two swords, sits on a straw mat and holds a fishing rod. A large, basket-shaped straw hat conceals his identity. Naosuke, dressed as an eel fisherman with a cotton cloth (*tenugui*) around his head, crouches beside him. A straw basket for Naosuke's catch sits on the upper dike.

how could you forget! My wife's older sister is Oiwa. My wife is her younger sister Osode. That means that we are enemies and that I must avenge the death of my wife's sister. How fortunate to meet here. Prepare for your death, Tamiya Iemon. Stand and we'll fight it out here. (*Switches to a conversational tone*) That's what I should say, but I'm not going to. But I overheard you talking about that document from Kō no Moronao. When you find success, I'll pay you a little visit to take my share. When I come, don't say that you're not at home.

IEMON: Of course not. That'll be perfect for me. The moment I find success . . .

NAOSUKE: If you plant the seeds, then Gonbei will dig them up. I'll be by to see you soon.[14]

IEMON: I understand. How fortunate for things to be settled this way. (*There is a tug on the fishing line, and Iemon pulls up a small fish.*)

---

14. This is a play on the popular saying that "If Gonbei plants seeds, the crows will dig them up."

NAOSUKE: You caught something. (*Iemon throws the line in again and almost immediately catches a large fish. He pulls it onto the dike, where it flops vigorously.*) It's getting away. (*Naosuke grabs the sotoba with Iemon's name on it and uses it to hold the fish down. After Iemon has the fish, Naosuke tosses the sotoba toward the river, but it falls right by Oyumi and revives her. She picks up the sotoba and is shocked when she reads the name on it.*)

OYUMI: Oh no! Tamiya Iemon's grave marker! That means that the killer of my father and daughter must already be dead. (*Hearing her voice, Iemon tries to make himself inconspicuous. He tugs at Naosuke's sleeve and signals for him to speak for him.*)

OYUMI: Excuse me, I wish to ask you something.

NAOSUKE: What is it?

OYUMI: The name on this grave marker is Tamiya Iemon. Do you know whether he died of illness?

NAOSUKE (*without thinking, answers carelessly*): What? Tamiya Iemon? He's not dead, he's right . . . (*Iemon tugs at his sleeve and urgently signals for him to say that Iemon is dead. Immediately Naosuke changes his tone.*) I mean, he's dead. Of course he's dead. Look, because he's dead, his family put up this grave marker. Nobody goes around putting up grave markers for living people. He's dead. (*In a burst of enthusiasm*) Dead, dead, dead!

OYUMI: When did he die?

NAOSUKE: When? Um . . . today, er, that is, today marks forty-nine days since his death.

OYUMI: What, forty-nine days have already passed since he died. Oh no! (*Weeps bitterly*)

NAOSUKE: To be crying and carrying on like that, you must be family or something.

OYUMI: No, Tamiya Iemon killed my father and daughter. Even though I am only a woman, I've been searching for him to avenge the deaths in my family. But now there is no hope left for me, since the murderer has died peacefully. (*Iemon writes instructions to Naosuke on how to respond.*)

NAOSUKE: But listen, even if by some chance Tamiya Iemon were alive, he is not the one that killed your father and daughter.

OYUMI: What? Who is it?

NAOSUKE: The real killers are Chōbei, Kanzō, and his retainer Bansuke. These three men are the real killers.

OYUMI: But those are the three men that served as go-betweens when Iemon married my daughter Oume. Why did they turn on us like that? Those ingrates. Outrageous! (*She speaks passionately. Meanwhile, Iemon sneaks up behind her and unceremoniously kicks her into the river. There is the boom of a drum, suggesting the splash as she falls in. Iemon takes off his hat and poses, staring at the water. This is the first time the audience sees his face in this scene.*)

NAOSUKE (*impressed with the casual way that Iemon killed Oyumi*): Iemon, you're a real villain indeed.

IEMON: I learned it all from you.

NAOSUKE: I'm ashamed to hear it. But now I'm nothing more than a crooked eel fisherman. In the end, my body will be split lengthwise, just like that of an eel.

IEMON: Even if my head is cut off, I'll keep moving anyway.

NAOSUKE: Nice! (*As Naosuke leaves, he keeps an eye on Iemon. As the music fades, there is the gloomy sound of a temple bell, indicating that night is approaching. Iemon is left alone on stage.*)

IEMON: Just because that woman showed up where she had no business being, I was forced to take a life needlessly. (*There is a tug on his fishing pole, and he pulls up the line immediately, but there is nothing on it.*) Damn, the fish swam away with the bait. (*Iemon puts some more bait on the line and drops it into the river again. To shamisen music, Chōbei comes rushing along the runway, in the somewhat ragged robes of a masterless samurai. But now his hair is rather messed up, and he wears a light blue cloth tied as a hood to hide his face. He sees Iemon and shouts at him.*)

CHŌBEI: There you are Iemon, I've found you!

IEMON: Shh.

CHŌBEI (*in a quieter voice*): You killed Oiwa and Kohei and then killed Itō Kihei and his granddaughter. But you put all the blame on the three of us. You have made three innocent men into murderers. The only way that we can clear our names is to go to the authorities and report your crimes. The real murderer is Tamiya Iemon. This is the only way we can escape. You can't complain about that. I've explained our situation, and now I am leaving.

IEMON: Listen, how could you forget all that I've done for you in the past? Don't worry about all that. As they say, gossip lasts for only seventy-five days. If you just stay put, things will clear up eventually.

CHŌBEI: That's easy enough for you to say, but we are the ones who will suffer. We've decided to go away and lie low for a while, but we need some travel money.

IEMON: I would like to give you something, but I'm scraping by myself.

CHŌBEI: In that case, do you want us to turn you in?

IEMON: Don't do that!

CHŌBEI: Then give me some money.

IEMON: I want to, but . . .

CHŌBEI: If not, I'm going to turn you in. What are you going to do about that?

IEMON: Well . . .

CHŌBEI: Well . . .

BOTH: Well, well, well. (*The exchange between the two becomes a* kuri-age *in which one character presses another for an answer. As the rhythm of the lines*

Iemon flips over the wooden door to hide Oiwa's body, only to find Kohei's body on the other side. The cross-eyed look expresses his astonishment. Kohei, bound to the door, extends his right arm, asking for the medicine.

intensifies, it culminates in a series of "wells" spoken first alternately and then together.)

CHŌBEI: What are you going to do about it? (Iemon reconsiders and brings out the document that Okuma earlier gave to him.)

IEMON: This document that my mother got me guarantees my future with Lord Moronao. For the time being, I will give it to you and, as soon as I get the money, I'll exchange it for this document. Listen (Whispers).

CHŌBEI: Got it. For the time being, I will keep this instead of cash.

IEMON: I'll pay you well when I can.

CHŌBEI: You'd better. See you later, Tamiya.

IEMON: Akiyama.

CHŌBEI: Take good care of yourself. (Music. Temple bell. Carrying the document, Chōbei exits running along the runway. Iemon gazes after him.)

IEMON: Because Chōbei showed up, I had to hand over the valuable document just to keep his mouth shut. What terrible luck. (Looks up at the sky) It will be dark soon. I should put away my fishing pole. (Eerie music. Temple bell. He picks up his fishing pole. A wooden door with a body on it covered with a straw mat comes floating down the river from stage left. When it reaches the center of the stage, it sinks in the water, then bobs up again and stands up

Iemon strikes Kohei's body with his sword, turning it into a skeleton that slides into the river.

against the dike. Without thinking, Iemon approaches and takes the mat off the door. Doro-doro drums from the geza, *the music room. The dead body of Oiwa appears. She is holding the amulet taken by the rat earlier in this scene. Then the corpse opens its eyes and glares at Iemon.*) Oiwa, forgive me. I was wrong.

OIWA: My hatred will not rest until the whole bloodline of the Tamiya family is dead and every branch and leaf of Itō Kihei's clan has withered. (*She holds out the amulet. Iemon cannot endure her gaze and covers the body with the straw mat again.*)

IEMON: Hail Amida Buddha, Hail Amida Buddha. The passion of a woman never dies. Haven't you found salvation yet, Oiwa? Maybe if the crows consume her body, her sins will disappear and she will find rest. (*Without thinking about it, he turns over the door. This side of the door is covered with a thick layer of water weeds.*) Oh no, there is something on the other side too. (*With soft mysterious drums, the water weeds drop, revealing Kohei's body. Kohei opens his eyes.*)

KOHEI: Master, master, lend me the medicine. (*He stares entreatingly at Iemon.*)

IEMON: Another ghost!

Iemon draws his sword and strikes at the body. With doro-doro drums, the body immediately turns into a skeleton that falls apart and drops into the water.

This woodblock print by Utagawa Toyokuni III (1786–1864) depicts the discovery of the bodies of Oiwa and Kohei at the dike. The actors portrayed here starred in the 1861 performance at the Nakamura Theater in Edo. In this triptych, the central images, of Kohei and Oiwa, can be interchanged by flipping a piece of paper. Playing Satō Yomoshichi (*left*) is Bandō Hikosaburō V (1832–1877); Iemon, holding the long sword and pulling up the door, is acted by Kataoka Nizaemon VIII (1810–1863); both Kohei and Oiwa, clutching an amulet and strapped to the door, are played by Bandō Hikosaburō V; and Naosuke (Gonbei), carrying an eel rake from which a fishing basket is suspended, is acted by Seki Sanjūrō III (1805–1870). Phrases promoting the play, such as "big hit" and "great success," are written on the wooden stupas in the background. (Courtesy of the National Theatre of Japan)

Iemon releases his breath in relief but does not relax his defensive pose. With a loud clack from the tsuke clappers, several characters appear. From the shadow of the statue of Jizo, Naosuke appears holding his eel rake. The sluice gate below opens, and Yomoshichi (Osode's former lover, played by the same actor who plays Oiwa and Kohei) appears dressed in a colorful, handsome cotton kimono. He has a secret letter wrapped in oiled paper hanging from his neck and carries his swords wrapped in a straw mat. This is followed by a dammari, *or fight in the dark. To slow, dreamy music, all the characters grope through the dark. Their dance-like movements reveal their personalities as they confront one another, and the objects they carry move from person to person. The problems created by the loss or discovery of these objects will motivate the plot of later acts. Iemon grabs the letter around Yomoshichi's neck, and the three of them fight over it. Then, when Naosuke holds out his eel rake, Iemon cuts at it with his sword and ends up with the head of the rake; Yomoshichi ends up with the handle of the rake, which has Naosuke's name "Gonbei" burned into it; and Naosuke ends up with the letter. All three take hold of Iemon's fishing basket, and suddenly, with a sudden flaring up of a spirit flame and mysterious drums, the basket turns into the face of Oiwa. They throw away the basket and part as the curtain is pulled shut to the continuous clapping of the ki clappers.*

Curtain

[*Tōkaidō Yotsuya kaidan*, SNKS 45: 122–225, translated by Mark Oshima]

Chapter 22

LATE YOMIHON: HISTORY AND THE

SUPERNATURAL REVISITED

The early yomihon—those of the late eighteenth century—generally were historical narratives describing the supernatural, the fantastic, and the miraculous. Their elegant style contained many allusions to Chinese and Japanese classical texts. The yomihon of the early nineteenth century, however, were quite different. As the center of literary activity gradually moved to Edo in the Anei-Tenmei era (1772–1789), the yomihon, which had emerged in the Kyoto-Osaka area, increasingly shifted into the hands of professional Edo writers and publishers, reaching its highest level in the Bunka-Bunsei era (1804–1830) with the works of Santō Kyōden (1761–1816) and Kyokutei Bakin (1767–1848).

Like the earlier yomihon, the nineteenth-century versions focused on history and the supernatural, with many references to both Chinese and Japanese classics, but in contrast to the earlier Kyoto-Osaka yomihon, which usually were collections of short stories, these later works were extended narratives featuring complex plots. They also had a greater emphasis on didacticism, especially on the Confucian principle of "encouraging good and chastising evil" (*kanzen chōaku*), or on the Buddhist principle of karmic cause and effect, both of which helped sustain their extended narratives. These later yomihon, which often took the form of military conflicts, vendettas, or struggles for clan or house succession, tended to revolve around powerful male heroes, legendary warriors, and supernatural figures. They also borrowed from Buddhist folktales and the tales of the miraculous. Like the earlier yomihon, the later ones were written in an elegant, mixed Japanese and Chinese style and were intended as much for the ear as for the eye. While the nineteenth-century yomihon adapted Chinese fiction to Japanese settings, as the earlier yomihon had, the chief interest was now in extended Ming novels like *Water Margin* (*Suikoden,* Ch. *Shuihu zhuan*), which became a model for many Edo yomihon.

As a result of the Kansei Reforms in the 1790s, the sharebon were banned, and the authors of sharebon and kibyōshi were punished, so writers and readers had to develop new forms that would avoid censorship. This need was first answered by various Japanese adaptations of *Water Margin,* beginning with Takebe Ayatari's *Japanese Water Margin* (*Honchō suikoden,* 1773). Between 1799 and 1801, Santō Kyōden, who became a leading yomihon writer, wrote *Chūshingura Water Margin* (*Chūshingura suikoden*), which combined the world of the puppet drama *Chūshingura: The Storehouse of Loyal Retainers* (*Kanadehon Chūshingura*) with the events and characters of the Ming novel. *Chūshingura Water Margin,* in the "half-book" (*hanshibon*) size (roughly 8.5 inches high and 6 inches wide) with relatively small illustrations, became extremely popular and marked the beginning, at least in format, of the late yomihon. In fact, the term *yomihon* (literally, books for reading) derives from this format, in which the text took precedent over the pictures. In 1813, Kyōden wrote his last yomihon, leaving the stage to be monopolized by his former protégé Bakin. In the following year, Bakin published the first part of *The Eight Dog Chronicles* (*Nansō Satomi hakkenden*), his greatest work.

KYOKUTEI BAKIN

Kyokutei Bakin (1767–1848), also known as Takizawa Bakin, was born in Edo, the third son of a samurai in the service of Matsudaira Nobunari, a retainer of the shōgun. Bakin's father died when Bakin was nine years old, and both his older brothers died, so Bakin inherited the family title. He then served the grandson of the Matsudaira lord but was treated so cruelly that he ran away from the lord's mansion when he was only fourteen.

From an early age, Bakin had had a deep interest in picture books, haikai, Chinese studies, and Japanese classics and loved jōruri texts and contemporary vernacular fiction. In 1790 he gave up his plans to become an herbal doctor and any hope of reentering the warrior class and began to visit and live with the writer-artist Santō Kyōden (1761–1816), who recognized Bakin's talent and opened the way for his career as a writer of popular fiction. Under Kyōden, Bakin began writing kibyōshi and then became a clerk for a publishing house that produced Yoshiwara guides, sharebon, kibyōshi, and illustrated kyōka books. When he was twenty-seven, Bakin married a commoner who owned a general goods store.

Bakin quickly became a prolific professional writer and produced a number of popular works. His *Strange Tales of the Crescent Moon* (*Chinsetsu yumiharizuki*), published serially between 1807 and 1811, achieved unprecedented popularity as a yomihon. In this long work of historical fiction about the early medieval Minamoto warrior Tametomo and his mythical involvement in the Ryūkyū Islands royal line, Bakin clearly displayed his Confucian intention to praise virtue and punish evil as well as his lifelong sympathy for marginal or exploited figures.

THE EIGHT DOG CHRONICLES
(NANSŌ SATOMI HAKKENDEN, 1814–1842)

In 1814 Bakin began writing The Eight Dog Chronicles, a historical novel of the strange and supernatural set in a time of medieval war. By the time he had completed it, in 1842, the work spanned 106 volumes, making it one of the world's longest novels. Because Bakin's eyesight began to fail in 1839, he temporarily stopped writing Eight Dogs but finally was able to complete the work with the help of a scribe. The popularity of Bakin's yomihon reached unprecedented heights in the late Tokugawa and early Meiji periods. Even though it was severely criticized by the influential Meiji critic Tsubouchi Shōyō for its lack of realism and for its didactic framework of "encouraging good and chastising evil," the popularity of Eight Dogs continued unabated through the late Meiji period.

One of the outstanding characteristics of The Eight Dog Chronicles, considered the epitome of the yomihon, is its elegant style, which uses classical diction and Chinese compounds as well as classical rhetorical flourishes such as engo (word associations) and kakekotoba (homonyms), often in a melodious 5–7 syllabic rhythm. At the same time, Bakin sought to create a work on the kind of vast scale found in Water Margin, a narrative that would be the Japanese equal of that great Ming novel. Besides sharing the hallmarks of earlier yomihon—the interest in the supernatural and the use of the principles of rewarding good and punishing evil and karmic causality—The Eight Dog Chronicles stresses the need to overcome attachment and seek enlightenment.

Bakin's primary interest, however, was in human psychology and behavior. His favorite Japanese text was the Taiheiki (Record of Great Peace), the mid-fourteenth-century medieval chronicle that describes the war-torn period of the Northern and Southern Courts. He admired the samurai ideals found in such historical and legendary narratives, but he also sympathized with the oppressed and those who had met with misfortune in the past. In The Eight Dog Chronicles, he gives them new life in an imaginary world. The full title of the book is The Chronicles of the Eight Dog Heroes of the Satomi Clan of Nansō (Nansō Satomi hakkenden), which refers to eight little-known fifteenth-century heroes (each with "dog" in his name) who helped the Satomi clan reestablish itself in Awa Province (Chiba) and later expand north to the area known as Nansō, thus establishing its rule over most of the peninsula east across the bay from what later became Edo. Despite its praise for warrior values, the book may be obliquely criticizing Tokugawa corruption, especially under the shōgun Tokugawa Ienari (r. 1787–1837). The Tokugawa shōgunate regarded the Satomi as enemies and confiscated the clan's lands in 1614.

The Eight Dog Chronicles revolves around conflicting issues of morality, spirituality, fate, duty, sincerity, filial piety, and chastity, enforced in different ways by Confucian, samurai, and Buddhist values (of detachment, enlightenment, and karmic retribution) and complicated by the simultaneous associations of animality (carnal desire) and virtue (fidelity, self-sacrifice) implicit in the various dog figures. While praising warrior-class and Buddhist values, *The Eight Dog Chronicles* reveals Bakin's obvious fascination with carnality and commoner culture, which gives a compelling quality to a wide variety of characters, even those who are morally weak or evil. The book also raises fascinating issues of gender and human-nonhuman relations. The book presents a number of strong female characters, such as the brave young woman Fusehime, who is the spiritual creator and inspiration of all eight heroes. *The Eight Dog Chronicles* also contains many suggestions of androgyny, a common late-Edo theme. In the scenes translated here, Fusehime is described as being manlike, and by spreading her seedlike soul beads, she becomes the virtual mother-father of the eight heroes. Yatsufusa, who marries Fusehime, is a male dog possessed by a female soul. Shino, the first dog-hero to appear in the story, grows up disguised as a girl and imitates a female god. Fusehime is faced with the tragic dilemma of attempting both to achieve spiritual purity and preserve her chastity and to accept her destiny of bearing the children of a dog.

A different kind of tragedy faces Hamaji, the woman engaged to Shino. *Eight Dogs* generally describes male–female love relationships outside marriage negatively, as spoiling the moral purity of the warrior. In this regard, *Eight Dogs* was faithful to the Confucian ethics of the ruling samurai class. In the famous Hamaji-Shino separation scene translated here, Shino's aunt and uncle have declared that Shino, the son of a warrior, and Hamaji, their daughter, are engaged, even though they secretly have no intention of allowing such a marriage. Hamaji naively believes her parents' promise and thinks that she is as good as married. (The parental word was absolute in an age in which marriage was determined by the parents.) The ideal wife, particularly in a Confucian, warrior-class context, was to show her devotion to her husband, which Hamaji does. But Shino has discovered that the engagement has been made only to keep up appearances while his stepuncle tries to steal his sword, and he knows that accepting Hamaji's love would force him to break his promise to his father and to return his sword, which his father had been keeping for the Ashikaga ruling clan. Equally important, as a son filial to the spirit of his dead father, Shino is determined to restore the fortunes of his own real family and, to achieve this goal, must leave behind the family into which he has been adopted. This scene brings together two ideals, the traditional warrior-class way of the wife and the traditional way of the warrior, in a moving and revealing conflict.

CHARACTERS

(SATOMI) YOSHIZANE, a warrior, governor of Awa, and Fusehime's father

FUSEHIME, daughter of Yoshizane, gives birth to the spirits of the eight dog-heroes

YATSUFUSA (Eight Spots), the dog who "marries" Fusehime

KANAMARI, Yoshizane's retainer and Fusehime's fiancé

(INUZUKA) SHINO, the first of Fusehime's eight soul-sons to appear in the book. Like the other seven, he has "dog" in his name (Inuzuka means Dog Burial Mound). The son of an infirm warrior, he rides his beloved dog Yoshirō, is adopted by his aunt and uncle, and is engaged to Hamaji. He receives from his father a priceless sword that his father has been protecting for the Ashikaga rulers since they were defeated in battle.

HAMAJI, adopted daughter of Shino's aunt and uncle, who tell people she is engaged to Shino

In the opening chapters, Satomi Yoshizane, the son of a warrior leader who died aiding the sons of the defeated rebel deputy shōgun Ashikaga Mochiuji, escapes with two retainers just before the fall of Yūki Castle (in Ibaraki) in 1441. Yoshizane reaches Awa Province and leads a revolt of commoners against their immoral, exploitative ruler by appealing to their sense of justice. The victorious Yoshizane gives back the ruler's great wealth to the people and becomes the ruler of the area. He promises to save the life of Tamazusa, the sensual wife of the previous ruler, but at the insistence of his adviser, he goes against his word and executes her. Before she is executed, the fearless Tamazusa uses her powers to curse the Satomi clan, declaring that its members will become "dogs of worldly desire." Tamazusa's soul soon appears and causes the adviser who argued for her execution to commit ritual suicide. Several years pass, and Yoshizane finds a large male puppy at the foot of Mount Toyama in Awa and names him Yatsufusa (Eight Spots). His mother having been killed, the puppy was nursed by a mother raccoon, later revealed to be the soul of the dead Tamazusa, whose soul passed into the dog. Years later, in 1457, during a siege of his castle, Yoshizane jokingly offers his daughter Fusehime in marriage to the dog Yatsufusa if he kills the besieging general. The dog returns shortly with the general's head, and Yoshizane becomes ruler of all Awa. The dog then reveals his intention to marry Fusehime. Although Yoshizane wants to kill the dog, Fusehime reprimands him, reminding him that a ruler must always keep his word. Fusehime, unaware that the dog is possessed by Tamazusa's soul, agrees to go with him to his mountain home.

Fusehime at Toyama Cave

CHAPTER 12

In our present late age, immersed in delusion and attachment, what human can achieve liberation from the material desire of the five senses and step safely from the burning house of attachment? The bell of Jetavana Park, where the Buddha taught, still rings out daily to remind us that all things are impermanent, yet sensual people are not enlightened by it, hearing only the hated sound of the dawn bell telling them they must separate from their lovers after a night of passion.[1] And the teak trees that broke into white blossoms when the Buddha died under their branches and entered nirvana, did they not display the truth that all things that flourish must pass away? Yet now people vainly seek only to enjoy the beauty of blossoms and wish that spring, and their own youth, would last forever. How deeply they resent the wind and rain that scatter the blossoms from the branches!

For the enlightened, the world is a changing, insubstantial dream. Even without enlightenment, can anything be found that is not dreamlike? All the many people in the world subject to delusion may finally find enlightenment when Maitreya Buddha appears many eons in the future and preaches to them from beneath a dragon-flower tree, but in our own age there is no simple way for an ordinary human to cast off attachments and leave the world behind. Those who do manage to achieve enlightenment, however, know the great joy of buddhahood even in a tiger's lair or a water serpent's pool. Fusehime was one of these. While she lived through the end of one year and then through spring and fall in a second year in a cave on Toyama Mountain, she completely gave up all worldly thoughts.

Fusehime was the daughter of Satomi Yoshizane, governor of Awa Province and bearer of a court title. For the sake of her father and for Awa Province, she gave up everything and set off on her father's large dog Yatsufusa for Toyama, Mountain of Fertility, in the depths of the Awa Mountains, in order to show the people of Awa that they could believe in the truth of every one of their ruler's words—even when he jokingly promised his daughter to his dog.[2] Fusehime went into complete seclusion in the depths of the mountain, and not a single person discovered where she was.

Above the red clay banks of a rushing river, Fusehime spread stalks of sedge inside a cave and made a place to sleep, and there she spent the winter. Then spring came. Early one morning, as birds called to one another, Fusehime gazed at the flowers growing on the slopes of the high, mist-enfolded mountain and began to think about many things. It must be the Third Month already, she was sure, and girls in villages and towns were celebrating the Girl's Festival with special dolls. With attractive haircuts, they were also going out in pairs to pick asters, mother-daughter flowers, for the festivities. She remembered how she used to pick flowers with her own mother—dear, dear Mother! The lozenge-shaped rock in the cave that Fusehime liked to sit on reminded her of the large

---

1. The opening lines are directly inspired by the opening to *The Tale of the Heike*, which sets out similar Buddhist themes.

2. Yoshizane had broken his word with regard to saving Tamazusa's life. Now Fusehime sacrifices herself out of a sense of righteousness, since a ruler must always uphold his word. In a manifestation of karmic causality, Yoshizane pays for his earlier broken promise by losing his daughter to a dog.

Fusehime, in a fan-and-cherry-blossom brocade robe, with her sleeves held up with a white cord (*tasuki*), rides off on the dog Yatsufusa to his mountain home. "The most beloved dog of Satomi Yoshizane" (according to the cartouche) still carries the head of Yoshizane's enemy in his mouth. The illustration is by Yanagawa Shigenobu I (d. 1832), the favorite disciple of the noted ukiyo-e master Katsushika Hokusai (1760?–1849) and the artist for Tamenaga Shunsui's *Spring-Color Plum Calendar*. From the 1816 edition.

rice cakes she and her mother had made, with mother-daughter grass mixed inside. How delicious they had tasted on the third of the Third Month!

Day after day, the temperature of the moss-covered stone changed, and when it felt warm to her skin, she knew the Fourth Month had come. People in the world were all putting on their early summer clothes, but she had no other robes to change into. In summer, winds blowing through the mountain pines cooled her as they turned back her long sleeves. Her only comb was the wind, and she washed her hair in the sudden showers that fell in the evening, letting it dry after the rain had passed. Her hair had become as tangled as the mountain bushes and vines.

Then, from under the thick wild grasses, came the cries of autumn insects. In the valley around the cave the leaves of the trees shimmered bright colors in the sun and were woven by the light into a great brocade. Deer lay down in the many-colored mountain beds. Did they realize they could stay in them only briefly? Fusehime was filled with sadness. The loving cries of the deer for their absent mates made her even sadder. And then came the never-ending sounds of cold rains striking the marsh water. Finally, the wild mountain expanses were covered with snow for as far as Fusehime could see. The great boulders lost their sharp edges, and the limbs of the cedars and other evergreens blossomed with white snow.

Each season brought with it new and moving beauty. But Fusehime sat in her desolate cave and never left it, devoting herself to prayers for a better rebirth in her next life and chanting and copying out the Lotus Sutra. As day followed day, she grew used to the hardships that had earlier caused her so much suffering. She cared nothing about what was happening in the outside world, and she came to feel that even the songs of the birds and the cries of the animals around her were urging her on, as if they were her friends, in her fervent quest for enlightenment. Fusehime had a superbly tough mind.

Earlier, when her father's large dog Yatsufusa brought Fusehime on his back to Mount Toyama, deep in the mountains, he came to a cave on the lower slopes above a wide river that wound between Mount Toyama and the mountains around it. The boulders at the cave entrance looked as if they had been cleanly cut with a chisel, and pines and oaks soared upward to the northwest,[3] forming a natural fence protecting the cave mouth. The cave opened toward the south and was quite bright inside. Yatsufusa had stopped in front of the cave and gotten down on his forelegs. Fusehime understood immediately and slid gently off the dog's back. When she looked inside, she saw a torn straw mat and traces of ashes. Someone seemed to have lived here before.

"Then I'm not the only one!" she exclaimed out loud. "Not the only one who came to this mountain to forget the world . . . and be forgotten by it." Then she went inside and sat down. Yatsufusa followed her and sat quietly nearby.

When Fusehime left her father's castle in Takita, she took nothing with her but the eight volumes of the Lotus Sutra, some good-quality paper for copying it out, and a brush and inkstone set. Feeling lonely and depressed, Fusehime spent her first night at the front of the cave reading the Lotus Sutra by the light of the moon. Around her neck she wore the string of crystal prayer beads she had received as a girl from the mountain god En no Gyōja.[4] Shortly after the dog had killed her father's enemy, the eight largest of the beads—each of which had earlier displayed a written character with one of the eight Confucian virtues[5]—had suddenly shown eight characters forming the words "Animals can achieve enlightenment." All Fusehime had to protect her now were gods and buddhas.

Yatsufusa probably understands human language perfectly, Fusehime thought to herself. Surely he understood me when I told him I wouldn't go with him unless he promised not to come near me. Still, he's just an animal. He may have brought me all the way here into these mountains as a trick. And even if he has no bad intentions, he may be unable to control his desire for me. He may forget the vow of spiritual respect he made to me before we left

---

3. *Inui* (northwest), governed in yin-yang geomancy by the Dog and the Boar. This is the "divine gate," worshiped as the direction of ancestral spirits, human fertility, and good fortune.

4. A half-shamanic, half-Buddhist deity believed to be the soul of the eighth-century ascetic mountain monk En no Gyōja.

5. The eight are humanness, rightness, courtesy, wisdom, loyalty, sincerity, filial piety, and respect for elders. Bakin mixes them syncretically with Buddhism. In Buddhism, the 108 beads represent the 108 worldly desires.

my father's castle. If he gives in to lust and comes anywhere near me, he'll be guilty of deceiving his master. I'll have to stab him.

Fusehime's heart was pounding, but she managed to calm herself. As inconspicuously as she could, she untied the string around the opening of the pouch in her robe that held her dagger, and she took the weapon out. She placed it beside her right hand and went on chanting the Lotus Sutra.

Yatsufusa had been watching Fusehime, and he must have understood what she was thinking, because he did not try to approach her. He lay still, gazing at her face with an expression of deep longing. From time to time he got up, but he never stopped staring. His tongue hung out of his wide-open mouth, he drooled, he licked his fur, and he licked his nose, all the while watching Fusehime and breathing hard. Yatsufusa stared at Fusehime desirously through the night.

Early the next morning, Yatsufusa left the cave and went down into the valley. There he picked berries, fern roots, and other edible things and brought them back to Fusehime between his teeth and placed them before her. He did the same thing the next day, and the next. After he had been doing this for more than a hundred days, he gradually began to listen to the words of the Lotus Sutra that Fusehime was chanting. Eventually his desire seemed to clear from his mind, and he never again stared at Fusehime in that way. . . .[6]

Early each morning Fusehime rubbed her prayer beads between her palms and prayed southward in the direction of the faraway Susaki Shrine and its sacred cave devoted to the mountain god En no Gyōja, in whom she and her mother believed so deeply.[7] Sometimes Fusehime would also copy four-verse Buddhist poems and float them out on the river below the cave, praying that their power would protect her parents. During the spring she picked flowers and presented them to the buddhas, and when fall came, she recited various poems while the moon went down in the west, longing with all her heart for Amida Buddha's Pure Land paradise far away in the western sky. The wild fruits and nuts that fell down into her lap when the autumn winds shook the trees were all the food she needed, and her thin robes and the brushwood ends burning in her fire were enough to keep her warm on cold nights. The slopes of the mountain were so steep she had to lean forward as she climbed, but she did not mind the slopes or resent eating mountain ferns—hadn't righteous

---

6. The journey to a mountain cave with a dog implied both the animal carnality associated with the dog and the spiritual awakening associated with the holy mountain. As a result of the efficacy of the Lotus Sutra, Yatsufusa, to whom the spirit of the desire-filled Tamazusa had been transferred, goes from being a dog with animal lust to one who awakens spiritually, eventually revealing that "animals can achieve enlightenment."

7. As a small girl, Fusehime was sickly and unable to talk, so when she was three, her mother sent her to pray at Susaki. After seven days, the mountain god En no Gyōja appeared and put the beads around Fusehime's neck, protecting her and giving her the power of speech.

exiles in ancient China eaten them? The plum blossoms announced spring outside her rough cave window much later here than they had while she was growing up, but that did not bother her. At least, she thought, she did not have to study a whole new language the way the sad court lady Wang Zhaojun did after she was sent off by a Han emperor to marry a nomad chieftain.

Fusehime was not yet twenty years old, and she had a natural, jewel-like beauty. She was as voluptuous as the shaman woman of Mount Wu, who would turn into dawn clouds after a dreamlike night of love with a human lover, and she had the radiance of the poet Ono no Komachi, who compared herself in one of her poems to cherry blossoms. Fusehime still had the refined charm she had acquired growing up in her parent's castle, and even now, after living so long in the mountains and wearing torn, dirty clothes, her skin was whiter than the patches of snow remaining on the slopes. She had no comb for her lustrous black hair, but it was more fragrant than the spring flowers. Her narrow waist had grown as slim as a bending willow, and her long, slender fingers were becoming as thin as young bamboo.

A worthy daughter of the governor of Awa, Fusehime was as dedicated to Buddhist meditation as Chūjōhime, a young woman of centuries before who likewise lived alone, far from her noble father and dead mother, and wove lotus fibers into a great mandala of the Pure Land paradise. Fusehime also knew how to write even the most sinuous calligraphy and read difficult books. She had received an extensive education in the classics from her father, and she had a natural intelligence and ability to see the truth. From her mother she had learned not only sewing but music, and she played pieces of exceeding beauty. Yet for some reason, the god of marriage must have disliked this talented young woman, since she was forced to marry a dog and live a wretched life. My brush refuses to describe it further, and my heart aches. You must imagine her exact circumstances for yourself.

The year ended, and then grass appeared again along the river, and the trees in the valley were once more covered with green leaves. Fusehime would leave her cave to get fresh water for her inkstone, and one day, as she scooped pure river water with her hands, she noticed her reflection in a moving pool beside her. The body she saw on the water was human, but her head was definitely a dog's. Screaming, she ran back from the river. Then she returned and looked at her reflection once more. This time she saw her own image. She concluded that what she'd seen was only an illusion clouding her mind. She'd been shocked about nothing at all! Then she began to chant the name of Amida and other buddhas and spent the rest of the day copying out the Lotus Sutra. But she felt a strange pain in her lower chest. The next day she still didn't feel normal, and after that she found that she was no longer menstruating.

As days and then months went by, Fusehime's belly began to swell until she was quite uncomfortable. She guessed this might be the sickness that people called "dropsy," and she hoped she would die quickly. But she didn't, and spring

The ailing Fusehime and Yatsufusa in their mountain abode. In contrast to her days at the castle, Fusehime wears a simple white robe tied in front with a sash, her long hair dangling wildly. On her writing table are implements for copying the Lotus Sutra: her writing box, an inkstone, a brush, and a handscroll. In the right frame, a hint of future events, Kanamari shoots Yatsufusa and, by mistake, Fusehime. From the 1819 edition.

turned into summer, followed by an even more bitter autumn. When she counted, she realized it was the same month in which she had left her parents behind in Takita Castle and come all the way here. A year ago already! Her pain made her imagine the pain her mother must have felt when she lost her daughter to a dog. How Mother wept when she saw me off, Fusehime remembered, and how I wept, too, as I said good-bye to her. All I could see then was her dear face, and even now I see it before me always. I can't forget it, no matter how hard I try. And Mother must always see my face before her, too. . . .

Fusehime hears a flute and then encounters a boy on an ox who claims that he is collecting medicinal herbs but who later turns out to be a manifestation of the mountain god En no Gyōja. Mysteriously, the boy tells Fusehime about her mother's deep concern for her. When Fusehime asks the boy about her own ailment, the boy reveals that she has become pregnant by Yatsufusa through "mutual interfeeling between similars" because she sympathized so deeply with the dog and regarded him as her partner in their joint search for enlightenment. The spirit of Tamazusa, who had been executed with such terrible resentment against Fusehime's father Yoshizane, has become the dog Yatsufusa and has punished both the father and the daughter. But Yatsufusa did not try to rape Fusehime, and through the efficacy of the Lotus Sutra, which Fusehime has de-

voutly recited, they both have freed themselves from Tamazusa's resentful spirit and achieved spiritual awakening. As a reward, Fusehime will bear eight children, although they all will be "empty" or virtual souls rather than physical bodies. Formless, the souls will then have to be born again to physical mothers in order to acquire bodies. The number eight is linked to Yatsufusa's eight spots and to the eight volumes of the Lotus Sutra. The eight children, born to various mothers, will have good karma and, as a result of Fusehime's meditations, grow up to be the eight heroes who will come together and reestablish the Satomi as a great clan. Before leaving, the boy tells Fusehime that she will go into labor in her sixth month, that is, within less than a month.

Fusehime's Decision

CHAPTER 13

After hearing many surprising things from the mysterious boy, Fusehime realized for the first time how little she had known about herself. It was as if she were opening her eyes after a long sleep. But the boy was now nowhere in sight. Perhaps the boy and the conversation were just a dream. The explanations she had heard were very strange, and she wasn't completely convinced they were true. She sobbed long and hard, beset by fears that the worst would happen.

But Fusehime's mind was exceedingly strong, and recently she had become quite manly, so she managed to calm her violent feelings. She brushed her hair away from her face, wiped her eyes, and tried to analyze the situation. "What a horrible thought," she said, thinking out loud as if someone could hear her. "Some terrible deed in one of my former lives must have caught up with me. And I can't even know what it was! How tenacious that woman Tamazusa is, holding such a deep grudge against Father that she's willing to do even this to me. So be it. The boy said it was a curse that should have fallen on Mother. Well then, I'll gladly take it on myself instead. For Mother, I'd gladly sink to the bottom of hell in my next life, and in my life after that, too! But there's one thing that makes me feel very ashamed and sad. I haven't had a single lustful thought, and yet I have no way to explain to my parents and other people why I have a baby animal inside me—how I somehow got pregnant from the spirit of an animal!

"Since the first day I came here, I've done nothing but think of the various buddhas with all my heart and mind and read the Lotus Sutra. When I walk through these wild trees, for me they are the Crane Grove, where the Buddha entered nirvana. And the mountain I see above me is Eagle Peak, where the Buddha preached. I've done nothing else at all. And yet no buddha is willing to save me, and no god will help me. What if I really am pregnant? I've never slept with Yatsufusa, but still, I have no way to prove it. I'll be humiliated, and my parents will, too. Their names will never be redeemed, and I'll be known forever as an animal's wife. I'll have to live with this shame for the rest of my life, and after that, my soul will turn into pure resentment and never gain enlightenment. Could there be anything more terrible than this?

"I didn't have the slightest idea anything like this was going to happen. Why couldn't I just have let my father kill that dog when he wanted to? I could have died together with Yatsufusa in the castle. But it's too late now. Perhaps it was karma from a past life that kept me from dying. Or it could have been a karmic sign that was supposed to teach me something. But there's nothing this awful in all the parables and allegories in the Buddhist books. It's simply too terrible to be karma. Even supposing I had the babies and they made my parents and brother happy and helped the Satomi clan prosper, it would still be an unspeakable shame. How could anything this bad possibly happen?" Fusehime was very intelligent, and the more she tried to analyze what she'd heard from the boy, the more distressed she became. Finally, unable to endure it any more, she collapsed on the ground, weeping amid the long, thin stems of tufted wild grass that swayed in the wind.

Although the mysterious boy reveals to Fusehime the principle of karmic causality and the cause for her pregnancy, Fusehime decides not to have the babies and to kill herself, hoping that her soul will go to the Pure Land. She also invites Yatsufusa to join in committing religious suicide in hopes that his soul will also be purified. In this way, she hopes that Yatsufusa, who has been possessed by Tamazusa's resentful spirit, will be freed from Tamazusa's influence. Finally, Yatsufusa is freed from that attachment.

Kanamari, a retainer of Fusehime's father (whom her father hopes will marry Fusehime), has a vision and discovers Fusehime's cave just as she and Yatsufusa are preparing to enter the river. Kanamari shoots Yatsufusa, but one bullet also strikes Fusehime and kills her as well. Horrified, Kanamari tries to commit suicide but is stopped by Fusehime's father, who also arrives, having been sent by Fusehime's mother, who also had a vision. Kanamari sees that Fusehime has died of only a light wound, and he takes the prayer beads, places them on her forehead, and hangs them around her neck. Mysteriously, the words in the beads once more show the eight Confucian virtues. As Kanamari prays to the mountain god En no Gyōja, Fusehime comes back to life. When she sees what has happened, however, she weeps and admonishes her father.

Fusehime repeatedly wiped away the tears in her eyes. "Father," she said, "if my body were the way it used to be, how could I possibly oppose what you have come all the way here to ask? But some terrible karma is following me from a previous life, and I was shot down by a hunter like a wild animal. For most people, that would have been enough atonement. But apparently not for me. My karma is so bad I've been forced to come back to life again. How could I possibly abandon all shame and appear in this horrible shape in front of my parents and those in the place where I was born? The proverb says parents love a disabled child many times more than their other children, just as parents of a bird care for a chick with only one wing that can't fly from its nest. I wonder, though, if it's really true.

"Actually, Father, I'm sure that if I went home, you and Mother would care for me like parent cranes covering their young with their wings, or pheasants searching for their young in a burning field and leading them to safety. Yes, I suppose I am like a young pheasant, crying alone without a husband and separated from its parents. The world has brought me nothing but pain and constant tears, and today I decided to leave it completely behind. I even wrote out a will. You've seen it. What do you think of what I've written? Yatsufusa wasn't just a lustful animal. He escaped burning desires and attachments, and we set out together on a journey toward enlightenment. He protected me, and my body is still pure. He never touched me, much less forced himself on me. Still, my body does seem to be pregnant, although nothing at all happened to make it that way. I can't tell whether or not I'm really going to have children.

"Father, you may have hopes for me to marry that young man over there. That would be a mistake. And it would make things worse to start talking about your private wishes at the moment when I am about to die. So please, don't mention the subject. Neither Kanamari nor I am married, but if you had such a match in mind, then it would have been the height of infidelity for me to have abandoned my fiancé and gone off with the dog.

"There was no way for me to know some man had been chosen to be my husband. If I knew nothing about it and Kanamari also knew nothing about it and it's only in your mind, Father, then it all has no meaning, like the sword that was delivered too late to a man and had to be placed in front of his grave. And not only that. If Yatsufusa were my husband, then Kanamari would be my worst enemy, because he killed Yatsufusa. But the fact is, Yatsufusa isn't my husband, and neither is Kanamari. I was alone when I came into this world, and now I set out for the other world alone. Please don't try to stop me. If love goes too far, it turns into cruelty.

"I owe you a debt of gratitude too great ever to repay, Father. So when I refuse your offer to take me back into your house, I realize it is the height of disobedience and shows a lack of filial respect. I also realize that we will never meet again. But remember, there is a reason I can't return with you. I'm entangled in some terrible, uncontrollable karma, and it's blocking my way to buddhahood. So please give up your hopes for me and reconcile yourself to what I am going to do. And please explain things to Mother. Convey to her how deep my apologies are, and tell her that I am praying that she may live for many more years.

"There's no use hiding my body after I die. You've already seen me in this terrible condition. They say that when the souls of pregnant women reach the other world, they sink into a lake in hell that's filled with blood. It wouldn't be something I could escape or even dislike. It would simply be due to my karma. But these children that are supposed to be growing inside me without any father, they're too strange for me to believe. If I don't cut myself open and see what they are, I'll always suspect myself. And other people will always suspect me, too. Watch closely!"

Several episodes are pictured here. Kanamari Daisuke, who earlier shot Yatsufusa and Fusehime, kneels, chanting the name of En no Gyōja in hopes of reviving Fusehime. Unsheathing his long sword, Satomi Yoshizane, Fusehime's father, and his retainer Horiuchi Sadayuki (*far right*) look up at the eight dog-spirit shapes in the air. Fusehime, next to Yatsufusa's body, takes the short sword out of her belly with blood-smeared hands. The elderly lady-in-waiting with her eyes closed and hands clasped together and the young lady-in-waiting at Fusehime's side are her guardians. Text: "Cutting herself open, Fusehime releases the eight dog children."

Fusehime reached for her short sword, unsheathed it, and thrust it into her belly. She moved the blade sideways, cutting herself open in a straight line. A strange white mist rushed out of the wound. Undulating, the mist enveloped the string of 108 crystal prayer beads around her neck and lifted them up into the air. Suddenly the string broke and fell to the ground, carrying with it a hundred clattering beads. The eight larger beads remained in the air, giving off light and circling. Their paths crossed as if they were bright comets passing through the sky.

Fusehime's father, Yoshizane, and the others could do nothing to stop her. Dazed, they looked up at the still blue sky and tried to follow the dazzling globes of light. As they watched entranced, a harsh wind roared down from the mountains and carried off the eight soul-lights in different directions until they disappeared from sight. Finally, only the early evening moon remained above the mountains in the east. This was the beginning of the eight dog-heroes who would appear separately in the world and years later gather together in the Satomi clan.

Gravely wounded, Fusehime gazed steadily at the strange lights until they finally disappeared. "So!" she said. "At last I can feel happy. There actually weren't any babies inside me at all. The gods obviously didn't want me pregnant. Now I don't need to doubt myself any longer. And no one else can doubt me, either. My mind is clear—as clear as that moon. I'll be leaving with it, heading for the Pure Land beyond the western sky. Amida Buddha, please show me the way!"

As Fusehime chanted that final prayer, she pulled out the blood-spattered sword with her bloody hands and collapsed onto the ground. Her mind was so strong and her words so courageous that she hardly seemed to be a woman. Her death deeply moved everyone who saw it.

Fusehime counters Tamazusa's resentful spirit with her even stronger spiritual power, and both she and the dog achieve enlightenment. The eight soul beads from Fusehime's womb are reborn in the following two years as eight baby boys born to women in various locations around the Kantō Plain, later the site of Edo. Each of the boys has inu (dog) in his name, has a peony-shaped birthmark on his body, and comes into possession of one of the eight beads marked with the virtue he exemplifies. The grieving Kanamari becomes a monk named Chūdai (a name made up of two characters that, put together, mean "dog") and wanders around the Kantō area, praying for Fusehime's soul and searching for the eight soul beads. Eventually he finds them and explains to the possessors their relationship to one another and their future as virtuous fighters for justice and for the Satomi clan.

In the passage translated here, the first dog-hero to appear becomes partly aware of his identity. Inuzuka (literally, Dog Burial Mound)[8] Shino is the son of a noted but now infirm warrior who lives in poverty near his elder half sister in the farming village of Ōtsuka (on the outskirts of what later became Edo). Shino's grandfather, a trusted retainer of rebel Ashikaga deputy shōgun Mochiuji, has passed on to Shino's father a precious sword—called Rain Shower (Murasame)—that possesses mysterious powers. It was entrusted to him by Mochiuji's eldest son before he was killed and must be returned to the Ashikaga. Shino's parents raise him as a girl in an effort to protect him. Dressed as a girl, Shino resembles Fusehime by constantly riding on his beloved dog, Yoshirō. Just before Shino was conceived, a female deity (Fusehime's soul) riding on a flying dog threw one of the eight soul beads at Shino's mother, suggesting that Shino is Fusehime's virtual child.

Meanwhile, Shino's mother dies, and Shino's aunt Kamezasa and her husband, Hikiroku, covet the precious sword kept by Shino's father. When Shino's dog runs into his aunt's house after killing her cat, his uncle severely wounds the dog with a bamboo spear, claiming that he destroyed an entitling document from the deputy shōgun. As

---

8. Especially in the area just east of Edo, female dogs were revered for their power to ensure a safe, easy childbirth. If a female dog died during labor, her body was buried near a crossroad and her soul prayed to. Such a grave was called a Dog Mound.

punishment for this alleged crime, he demands the powerful sword, but Shino's father refuses and commits suicide instead. Before he dies, Shino's father tells the boy, now eleven, that from now on he must dress and act like a man, and he gives his son an additional warrior name, Moritaka, or Protector of Filial Devotion. It will now be Shino's filial duty as a man to return the sword to the present Ashikaga deputy shōgun in Koga Castle. In the following scene, Shino's dog Yoshirō has been seriously wounded by Hikiroku, and Shino's father has just committed ritual suicide to take responsibility for the incident, leaving Shino in shock.

Shino in Ōtsuka Village

CHAPTER 19

. . . The dog lay on the straw mat that Shino had spread for him on the ground under the eaves. His deep wounds seemed to be too painful for him to bear, and he gave off a long howl. Anxiously, Shino looked over at him.

"Yoshirō's still alive," he said out loud to himself. "Right after Mother took him in, she got pregnant with me. But then, also because of him, Father had to kill himself. When I think about Yoshirō and then about Father, I love and hate the dog at the same time. But I can't just let him lie there in pain. He's been speared too many times and will never recover. If I leave him like this, he'll suffer terribly tonight. It would be kinder to put him out of his misery. I could use the sword that Father left me. But I shouldn't get it stained just to help an animal. Still, the blade's supposed to have the power to repel blood. Why shouldn't I use it on my dog?

"Yoshirō, let me put you out of your misery. Did you understand what I was saying?"

Shino took the sword and jumped down onto the ground. When he unsheathed the sword and raised it, the dog did not show the slightest fear. He calmly extended his forelegs and turned his neck toward the blade. Moved by the dog's courage, Shino's fingers loosened their grip around the handle. You're a year older than I am, he thought. My parents raised you and took care of you all these years, and I'm used to seeing you every single day. I'm very fond of you. How could I possibly kill you? Shino hesitated, unsure of himself. Still, he thought, even if Yoshirō stays alive a little longer, my uncle's going to kill him. I'm losing my nerve. Even animals can achieve buddhahood,[9] he chanted silently, repeating the phrase as if it were a prayer, as the glinting blade cut through the dog's neck. He heard the sound of the head hitting the ground.

---

9. The same Buddhist phrase appeared in Fusehime's beads when she left with Yatsufusa.

Then, with a loud roar, the dog's red blood shot five feet up into the air. Shino could see something gleaming inside the blood, and when he reached out and grabbed it with his left hand, the spurting blood quickly subsided and stopped.

Mysteriously, just as his father had said, there was no blood on the sword blade. Only evening dew dripped from its tip. The sword had lived up to its name Rain Shower. Shino quickly wiped off the blade with his sleeve and put it back in its sheath at his waist. Then he rubbed the clotting blood off the object that had come out of the dog's cut throat and examined it. It was about twice the size of a large pea, round and clear like crystal, with a hole through it. Perhaps it was a decoration for a pouch string, or more probably, a prayer bead. Curious, Shino held it up to the bright moonlight. He was sure he could see a character inside it. Yes, there it was, the character for filial devotion. It wasn't carved by a knife or made of lacquer. It had appeared on its own.

"What a strange object!" Shino said out loud, slapping his knee. "And what mysterious writing! I don't know much about what happened, but this might be related to something Mother told me. One day she was going to make her daily prayer at the Benzaiten Shrine by the Takino River.[10] On her way home, she saw a very cute puppy. As she was hurrying home with the puppy, a female god appeared in front of her and gave her a small bead. But Mother said she dropped it, and it fell near the puppy. Mother looked very hard for the bead but could never find it. She also said that around this time she discovered she was pregnant. Then in the Seventh Month of the next year,[11] she gave birth to me. Later, Mother was sick for a long time, and our prayers to the gods and buddhas got no response at all, and she seemed to be dying. I wondered whether it was all because she'd lost that bead. For a while I thought she might recover if I could only find it, but I'd never seen it myself. I wouldn't recognize it even if I saw it. The next winter Mother died. Then, almost three years later, Father committed suicide. And just when I'm about to set out with him to the other world, a mysterious bead comes out of my dog's throat, a bead with the character for 'filial devotion,' the second character of the name Father gave me. I discover this after I've already lost my parents and I've made up my mind to die! But it's too late to be thinking about caring for my parents. What good is this thing now?" Angry, Shino threw the bead away. It struck the ground with a sharp sound and then rebounded back and fell through the front of his robe. Shino was amazed. He reached into his robe, found the bead, and threw it away again. But it rebounded back into the front of his robe. After this happened a third time, Shino folded his arms, trying to figure out what was happening. Finally he nodded his head as if he had understood.

"This bead surely has a soul in it," he mumbled to himself. "When Mother

---

10. In what was later Edo. Benzaiten is a female deity from India worshiped by Buddhists.
11. In 1460, almost two years after Fusehime's death.

Inside a dilapidated farmhouse, Bansaku, Shino's father, has committed suicide and is lying on the floor, with bloody handprints surrounding him. After cutting off his dog's head with a mysterious sword, Shino watches a soul bead fly up in the dog's blood. The covetous Kamezasa and Hikiroku secretly witness the scene from behind the fence (*upper left*). Text: "Deciding to commit suicide, Shino beheads Yoshirō."

dropped it, Yoshirō must have swallowed it. Even twelve years later, that dog still had good teeth and shiny hair, and he jumped around like a puppy. It must have been because of the bead inside him. This bead could be the most valuable treasure in the world, the priceless jewel of the marquis of Sui or the jewel of Bian He in ancient China. Still, I won't let a jewel make me cling to life. They say aristocrats are sometimes buried with jewels in their mouths—but those jewels were just wasted. After I'm dead, if someone wants this sword and the bead, they're welcome to take them. It's time to catch up with Father. I'm too far behind him already!"

Shino went back inside the room. Sitting down beside his father's body, he prepared himself mentally to die. He took the sword his father had given him and held it up. Three times he lifted it above his head to show his respect. Then he slipped off the top of his robe and bared himself to the waist. He noticed a large peony-shaped mark on his left arm. Surprised, he bent his arm and carefully tried to wipe it off. It was black, but it wasn't ink or anything else that would rub off. Suddenly he struck his arm.

"This mark wasn't here yesterday," he said. "Or even earlier today. When that bead came flying back into my robe, it hit my left arm. It stung for a moment, but it couldn't have caused a mark this big. Father told me mysterious things happen when a country is in decline or when a person is about to die.

I've read the same thing in Chinese books. I must be seeing something like that. But it's just my own mind. I'm worrying too much. After I die, my body will turn back to dirt. Why should I care about spots or moles on my skin?"

Shino was a gifted, godlike child. His bravery was supported by an unshakable will, and his intelligence and ability with words equaled those of the best of the ancients. He was already as wise as Gan Luo, a royal adviser and diplomat at twelve, or the boy genius Kong Rong, both of whom gained such fame in ancient China. What a pity it was that he had decided to kill himself.

Before he can commit suicide, Shino is stopped by a friendly local farmer and by his aunt and uncle, who take him into their family and dress him as a boy. The aunt and uncle adopt Shino, hoping to steal the precious sword, and to keep up the appearance of intimacy with Shino, they announce that Shino will marry their stepdaughter Hamaji when the two become old enough. When Kyūroku, a rich representative of the Kamakura regime, asks to marry Hamaji, the couple secretly agrees and persuades Shino to go to Koga Castle to return the sword to the Ashikaga shōgunal deputy. Early on the night before Shino's departure, they have the sword stolen and replaced with an ordinary one and plan to force Hamaji to marry Kyūroku after Shino leaves. Shino is attended by a servant, Gakuzō, who also turns out to have a peony-shaped birthmark and a bead with the word "justice" in it. An orphan, Gakuzō reveals to Shino that his family name is Inukawa (Dog River), and they become sworn brothers. Later he is revealed to be one of the dog-heroes.

Hamaji and Shino

CHAPTER 25

. . . Shino lay down, but he longed for dawn to come and couldn't fall asleep. All alone in the world, he lay thinking about his journey and his future. No one would stop him now, yet his parents' graves were here, and Ōtsuka was where he was born. It made him very sad to leave this place. His fiancée, Hamaji, was filled with a sadness just as fierce. She had endless things she wanted to tell Shino to stop his going, but she had no way to say them. Quietly she got up and left her bedroom. In the storeroom nearby, where her parents slept, she could hear snoring. Her parents kept her strictly away from her fiancé, and she was filled with fear that they would wake up. The path between her room and Shino's was always closely guarded during the day, and tonight, as she walked freely toward the room of the man she loved, she moved quickly, terrified that someone might be watching. Very softly Hamaji opened the door to Shino's room. Her knees shook violently as she stepped inside. She knew life was uncertain and constantly changing, but were she and Shino really never going to see each other again? Life seemed sad, full of pain, bitterness, and cruelty.

As Hamaji came closer to Shino, he sensed someone approaching and pulled his sword to his side. Suddenly he jumped up, shouting, "Who is it?" But there was only silence. Shino suspected someone might be listening for the sound of his breathing and trying to find out where he was sleeping in order to put a sword through him in the dark. Sure that he was in danger, Shino turned the lamp in the direction of the intruder. It was Hamaji. She had stopped, modestly, at the back edge of the mosquito netting covering his bed. She lay face down on the floor, sobbing silently, doing her best to muffle her sobs, but Shino could see tears coming from her eyes. She was obviously very upset and in great pain.

Shino was a brave man and had never feared anyone, but now his heart was pounding. He tried to calm himself as he stepped outside the netting, unhooked it, and put his bedding away.

"Hamaji," he said, "why have you come here in the middle of the night when you should be sleeping? Don't you know the saying, 'Don't bend down to adjust your shoes while you're in a watermelon patch, or reach up to straighten your headpiece while you're under a plum tree'? People will suspect us."

Hamaji, indignant, wiped away her tears and raised her head. "You ask as though you didn't know why I've come. Has our relationship come to nothing more than this? Yes, I know, we're only engaged, and our marriage is still nothing but a promise. We haven't gone through with the final ceremonies, so you have a certain right to speak like that. But haven't my parents declared to everyone that we're going to be married? And on tonight of all nights, when you're about to leave this house forever, there would be nothing shameful in saying a few words of good-bye to me. But no, you act as if nothing were happening, even up to the moment you leave. And you don't make the slightest attempt to say even a single word to me. Do you have any feelings at all?"

Shino sighed deeply. "I'm a human being. I'm not made of wood or stone. I'm very aware of what you feel for me. But my aunt and her husband hate me every minute I'm here, so there was no way I could meet you and tell you what I was planning. I know how real your love for me is. Even though I have to hide my feelings, I'm sure you know how deeply I love you. Koga's just forty miles from here. They say a round trip takes only three or four days, so please be patient until I come back."

"Now," Hamaji said, wiping away her tears, "you're lying to me. Once you leave, there's no reason for you ever to come back again. Here you'd be a caged bird longing to be in the sky with your friends. When a man leaves the village he was born in, it means he wants to find a lord who'll take him in and give him a stipend for life. As you know, my stepparents are unreliable, and now they've decided to get rid of you. They're sending you on this trip, and they don't expect you to come back. And you, you can hardly wait to leave. So once you leave, that's the end. Tonight is the last time we'll ever see each other.

"I have four parents." Hamaji continued. "You've probably already heard about all of them, but my stepparents won't tell me anything about my real parents. From what I've been able to put together from rumors, my real father is Nerima Heizaemon's retainer, and I have brothers. I don't know our family name, though. My stepparents have shown me much kindness by bringing me up, but I also owe a great debt of gratitude to my real parents, who brought me into the world. So I'd like very much to know more about my real parents. But I'm a woman, and I haven't been able to talk to anyone about this. I keep it inside myself and worry, and many nights I don't sleep at all. I've prayed with all my heart to every god there is to let me see my real parents for a moment in a dawn dream. But no.

"This has been going on for many years. It's almost more than I can bear. And then, in the Fourth Month of last year, everyone was saying that the To-shima and Nerima clans, with all their retainers and servants, had been cut down by their enemies. People said no one at all was left alive. When I try to imagine how my parents and brothers were killed, it grieves me until I can't think about anything else. Often I can't control my feelings, and I have to be very careful not to let my stepparents see me crying. I thought that if I confessed to you, you could help me learn the names of my real parents and brothers. You're the only one I can ask. Please, find out where they died and pray for their souls. I can't hide anything from you. Why should I? You'll be my husband for as long as I live.

"I've tried hard to find a moment when we could be alone, but they're always watching. Last year in the Seventh Month, I was about to tell you all this, but just when I was going to approach you, I realized Mother was following me. So I panicked and walked the other way. After that they've kept us completely apart, and we haven't seen each other even once. But they haven't been able to keep me from secretly sending you my love. It never stops or changes. It's an underground stream running from my heart to yours. Every single day I pray from morning to night that you'll be safe and find success and wealth.

"But you can't expect me to endure your coldness forever. Is it really your duty to your aunt to abandon your own wife? If you felt for me even a hundredth of what I feel for you, you would have explained to me clearly that you didn't know whether you would ever come back here, and you would have asked me to go away with you secretly. We're already engaged, after all, and no one would have accused us of being immoral. You're very cold. But the more I pity you, the more I don't want to be apart from you. It's my woman's true heart. So I want you to kill me with your sword. It's much better to die right now than to stay on in this village, abandoned, slowly dying of a love you ignore completely. I'll be waiting for you in the other world until we can meet again, no matter how many years it takes."

Hamaji explained her many objections and appealed to Shino with the utmost feeling. She refused to cry, fearing someone would hear them, but tears found their way down her cheeks and covered her sleeves.

"Don't speak so loudly," Shino wanted to say, "or someone will hear us. It would look pretty bad, wouldn't it, our being together like this?" Overwhelmed by the strength of Hamaji's feelings, however, he said nothing. There was no way for him to try to explain that their engagement had been only a temporary convenience for her stepparents. Overcome with sadness, he unfolded his arms and rested his hands on his knees.

"Hamaji," he said finally, "everything you say is reasonable and justified. But I didn't choose to go. I'm making this trip because my aunt and her husband ordered me to make it. The real reason is that they want me out of the way so they can ask another man to come to live here as your husband. From the very beginning, I've been your husband in name only. They were just using me until they could find the right man. Your stepparents can't tell you this directly, but surely you can guess their motives. Not only that. If I gave in to my feelings and invited you to go with me, everyone would think we did it only out of lust. If you could only control your desire to go with me and stay here instead, you would actually be acting for my sake. By forcing myself to leave, I'll be acting for your sake, won't I? Even if we're separated for a while, as long as we stay true to each other, we'll surely be together again someday. Quick, go back to your bedroom before your stepparents wake up. I won't forget about your real parents, either. Somehow or other I'm sure I'll be able to find out whether they're still alive. Please, you'd better go now."

Hamaji remained where she was and shook her head. "I've come this far," she said, "and I'm not going back now. If my parents wake up and criticize me for coming here, so be it. I have some things I'd like to say to say to them, too. Unless I hear you tell me you're going to take me with you, I'm not going to leave this room alive. Please, kill me!" Women are usually weak, but Hamaji's will was unshakable, and she refused to move.

Shino was stunned. "Now you're being unreasonable," he said in a low yet emotional voice. "As long as we're alive, we'll surely meet again sometime. How can anyone possibly show she's true to someone else by dying? And now, if you keep me from going out and making a career for myself as a warrior just when my aunt and her husband have finally given me permission to leave, if you block me now, then you're not my wife! What are you, anyway? A karmic enemy from a previous life?"

Hamaji broke down and cried. Finally she spoke. "When I try to persuade you from the bottom of my heart, you call me an avenging enemy! All right. There's no way to get through to you. This is due to my own pettiness. All right. I give up. I'll stay here in this house. Well then, please have a safe trip. The days have been getting very hot recently, so don't stay out in the sun too long or you'll get sick. Go on to Koga, make a name for yourself, and establish a clan with a line of descendants. Stay inside in winter, and when the storms come down from the northern mountains, send me messages on the wind. I'll be content just to know the man I love is living safely on this side of Mount Tsukuba. I don't think I'll live very long after we separate, so this will be the last time we ever see each other in this world. Yet I'm sure we'll meet again in the other world. They say husbands and wives are linked for two lives. Always remember we're going to be married in our next lives, too, and never be untrue to me." Hamaji's sorrowful words and her prayer to meet Shino in the next life reflected the fervent, pathetic wishes of a bright young woman who still did not know enough about the world.

Shino, strong as he was, sat dejected, feeling helpless to comfort Hamaji. He nodded his head at whatever she said and was unable to reply.

Outside, roosters began to crow, and Shino grew anxious. "Your parents in the back room," he said, "they'll be waking up any moment. Hurry! Hurry!"

At last Hamaji stood up. As she did, she recited a poem:

> "When dawn comes
> I'll feed them to a fox,
> the damn roosters—
> though it's still dark,
> they've made my lover leave.[12]

"This was once a love poem sent by a country woman to a traveler who stayed only half the night. Now it's from a wife to a husband who's about to leave on a long trip. If the roosters hadn't crowed, dawn wouldn't have come. And if dawn hadn't come, people wouldn't be waking up. I hate the sound of their crowing! No night will ever hide us and allow us to meet again. For us, the open gate at Meeting Barrier[13] is closed forever. How pitiful—the moon is at dawn."

As Hamaji turned to leave, someone coughed in the hallway outside and rapped on the sliding door. "The roosters are crowing already," a man's voice said. "Aren't you up yet?" It was Gakuzō, Shino's sworn blood brother who was leaving with him. Shino replied in a hurried voice, and Gakuzō went back to the kitchen.

"Quick, before he comes again!" Shino said, pushing Hamaji out the door. With swollen eyes she looked back at Shino from the dark hall a final time. Through her tears she couldn't see anything clearly. Leaning against the mountain-patterned wallpaper for support, she made her way back to her room, weeping. Truly, nothing is sadder than separating forever from someone who is still alive. It is even harder than parting from someone who has died.

---

12. A poem from *The Tales of Ise*, sec. 14.

13. Ausaka (Osaka, as it was pronounced in Bakin's time) no seki (Meeting Barrier), associated with the meeting of lovers in classical poetry. Hamaji is alluding to a poem by Sei Shōnagon in sec. 139 of the *Pillow Book*, later included in *Hundred Poets, One Poem Each* (*Hyakunin isshu*, no. 62).

Hamaji, lying on the floor beside the floor lamp, delivers her complaint. Shino (*left*) has left the mosquito netting and has his hand on his sword. His traveling gear lies ready under the lattice window, and the light of the full moon shines through bamboo leaves. The servant and future dog-hero Gakuzō (*right*), wearing a robe with the character "gaku" on it, stands in the next room, urging Shino to leave. Text: "Sugawara Michizane: 'Such painful partings because roosters have crowed! Ah, for a dawn in a village where roosters are not heard.'"

What a rare young woman Hamaji was. She and Shino had never shared the same covers, and they had yet to join their bodies as one, but their love was greater than that of a couple married for many years. Shino's love was equally strong, but he never let it sway his mind. Although he acted from love, he knew that men and women should keep a proper distance. In our world the wise and the foolish alike lose themselves in sensual pleasure. How many young people are drawn to these pleasures—and, once they come to the edge, how few do not fall in and drown! But here was a husband who was virtuous and a wife whose heart was completely true. Hamaji's passion did not come simply from a desire to enjoy lovemaking, and Shino's great sadness did not cause him to give in. Hamaji's love is a model for all, and Shino's equal is rarely found.

[*Nansō Satomi hakkenden*, Iwanami shoten, 1985, 1: 207–210, 219–220, 237–239, 337–342; 2: 81–87, translated by Chris Drake]

Chapter 23

NATIVIZING POETRY AND PROSE IN CHINESE

From the mid-eighteenth century, *kanshi* (poetry written only in Chinese characters) became the most respected literary form of poetry among intellectuals, and the number of kanshi poets and the quantity of kanshi vastly increased. These new kanshi poets attacked the style of Ogyū Sorai's Edo-based school, or the Ancient Rhetoric (*kobunji*) school, which had dominated the kanshi world and had attempted to imitate the poetry of the high Tang. In the view of these new poets, Sorai's school, which had insisted on an "elegant and grand" (*kōka yūkon*) style, using only diction from high-Tang poetry, tended to depart from reality and fall into hyperbolic rhetoric and did not answer their need to express the emotions and thoughts of contemporary, everyday life. This criticism gradually grew, coming from various kanshi groups outside Edo, particularly the Kyoto-Osaka region, and finally from within the Edo kanshi groups, most dramatically from Yamamoto Hokuzan, who wrote a blistering critique of the Sorai school's style in *Thoughts on Composing Poetry* (*Sakushi shikō*) in 1783.

YAMAMOTO HOKUZAN

The poetics espoused by Yamamoto Hokuzan (1752–1812) initiated a major shift in the nature and style of kanshi poetry, resulting in the demise of the neoclassical style and the birth of what has been called the "Fresh Spirit" (*seishin*) school. Poets such as Ichikawa Kansai (1749–1820) led the trend, turning not to the high Tang but to Song poetry, particularly the Southern Song poets concerned with everyday, commoner life. With the emergence of the Fresh Spirit school and the incorporation of everyday, easy-to-understand subject matter and vocabulary, kanshi became a more integral part of the native literature and was widely composed and appreciated. In the late Tokugawa period as the vernacular poetic forms—haikai, senryū, and kyōka—became more and more vulgarized, kanshi and waka were the only two genres in which serious men and women of letters could engage without any sense of embarrassment. Of these two forms, kanshi was the more recently liberated form, thus seeming both fresher and newer. With the disappearance of the neoclassicism represented by Sorai's Ancient Rhetoric school, which tried to write Chinese as a Chinese poet would have, the kanshi poets actively embraced "Japanese" kanshi (Chinese poetry that would have seemed strange to Chinese), expressing themselves as they pleased without concern for Chinese grammar and rules of pitch and rhyming—a major shift that popularized kanshi, especially from the beginning of the nineteenth century onward. By the Bunka-Bunsei era (1804–1830), kanshi poetry groups had sprung up across the country, among all the four classes (warriors, farmers, artisans, and merchants), and kanshi was being composed in the kind of relaxed setting and manner that had hitherto been associated with haikai.

THOUGHTS ON COMPOSING POETRY (SAKUSHI SHIKŌ, 1783)

In *Thoughts on Composing Poetry*, Yamamoto Hokuzan argues that the value or objective of kanshi lies not in the imitation of classical models, which marks the Sorai school poets (such as Hattori Nankaku), but in the direct expression of one's own "spirit" (*seirei*) through new and "fresh" (*seishin*) words: "When one imitates others in composing poetry [*shi*], it is someone else's poetry, not one's own poetry" (NKBT 94: 285). That is, when composing kanshi, one must not be concerned with only the poetic form and rhythm (*kakuchō*), as the Sorai school was; instead, one must value and reveal one's own true feelings (*jiko no shinjō*), the unrestricted expression of which would result in fresh and true poetry. In the following passage, Hokuzan distinguishes between Li Panlong, the Ming poet who advocated imitating high-Tang poetry and who was revered by the Sorai school, and Yuan Hongdao, a late Ming poet who valued "freshness" and the individual "spirit" and whom Hokuzan holds up as a model for the new kanshi poetry.

On Spirit and Freshness

The poetry of the Ming can generally be divided between that of Li Panlong and of Yuan Hongdao. When people of today hear of Ming poetry, they generally think only of the style of Li Panlong. Li Panlong and Yuan Hongdao are as different as water and fire or ice and hot coals. Hongdao stresses sentiment [*omomuki*], while Panlong stresses form and rhythm [*kakuchō*]. Yuan Hongdao is refreshing [*seishin*] and fluent; Li Panlong is stale and repetitious. Yuan Hongdao uses all the historical periods freely and does not single out one period from among the high Tang, late Tang, Song, and Yuan, whereas Li Panlong draws a strict division between the high Tang and the middle Tang.[1] He devotes himself to plagiarism and claims that "by basing ourselves on models, we bring about variations."[2] Yuan Hongdao's poetry is based on spirit [*seirei*], while Li Panlong seeks poetry in words [*ji*]. Yuan Hongdao's poetry is endlessly changing; Li Panlong's poetry is always the same.

Yuan Hongdao writes in his critique of Li Panlong, ". . . if people of today try to continue writing Tang poetry unchanged, then they will produce not the poetry of today but, rather, create counterfeit Tang poetry. Why should great men discard the true poetry they possess within themselves and plagiarize and imitate the poetry of others?"[3] Su Shi makes an excellent point when he writes, "To judge a painting based on its resemblance to the object it depicts is a view no different from that of a child. When composing poetry on a set topic, one who insists on a certain kind of poem is truly not one who knows poetry."[4] So those who compose poetry by imitating others produce only the poetry of others and not their own. When Yuan Hongdao writes, "In the Tang there is no poetry; poetry is found in the illustrious writers of the Song,"[5] he does not mean to say that Tang poetry is deficient but, instead, that the way in which Su Shi and Ouyang Xiu in the Song period did not imitate the Tang represents true poetry.

Today those of shallow learning and no discernment, who are ignorant of the Way of poetry and who have been duped by Ogyū Sorai and Hattori Nankaku, are steeped in the bad poetry produced by plagiarism. They declare that it is not poetry if it includes even a single word they are not used to hearing or a single character they are not used to seeing. This is what Yuan Hongdao deplored, and it persists to this day.

---

1. Hokuzan makes the high Tang the poetic ideal while automatically rejecting everything from the middle Tang. He is contrasting Li Panlong's dogmatism with Yuan Hongdao's willingness to draw on what is best from each particular period.

2. A quotation from the *Commentary on Appended Judgments* (*Xici zhuan*), a commentary on the *Book of Changes* (*Yi jing*) traditionally attributed to Confucius. The quotation originally refers to how the hexagrams, together with the judgments appended to them, offer us a way to bring our actions in line with the workings of the universe. Li Panlong borrows this passage to describe his own poetic ideals.

3. In this section, Hokuzan is paraphrasing ideas that appear in such texts such as Yuan Hongdao's "Letter to Qiu Zhangru" and his "Preface to the Poetry Collection of Yuan Zhongdao" (*Xiao xiu shi*).

4. From the first of "Two poems composed on the brushwood painted by Assistant Magistrate Wang of Yanling" by Su Shi (1037–1101).

5. From Yuan Hongdao's "Letter to Zhang Youyu."

The Conclusion

The two words "freshness" [*shinsei*] and "spirit" [*seirei*] are the lifeblood of poetry. When one does not imitate and plagiarize, one will always have freshness and spirit. When one lacks freshness and spirit, one will have imitation and plagiarism. Therefore, the Way of poetry can generally be divided between Yuan Hongdao and Li Panlong. . . . Today the poets of this country have long swallowed the poison of Li Panlong and Hattori Nankaku, so when they open their mouths, their poetry is rotted and fetid. If they are to rid themselves of this habit, they should do as Yuan Hongdao does. When I say that they should do as Yuan Hongdao does, I do not mean that they should imitate and plagiarize the poetry of Yuan Hongdao. Rather, they should follow Yuan Hongdao in not imitating or plagiarizing.

[*Kinsei bungaku ronshū*, NKBT 94: 284–285, 328, translated by Peter Flueckiger]

KAN CHAZAN

Kan Chazan (1748–1828), also called Kan Sazan, was a Confucian scholar and a kanshi poet. He was born in Kannabe in Bingo Province (Hiroshima), went to Kyoto in 1766, but in 1770 returned to Kannabe. In 1781 he opened what became a noted private school called the Yellow Leaf Sunset Lodge (Kōyō sekiyō sonsha). Chazan adopted the style of Song poetry, excelled in the seven-word quatrain, and is remembered for his collection of kanshi, *Yellow Leaf Sunset Lodge Poetry Collection* (*Kōyō sekiyō sonsha shishū*), and also his collection of essays in Japanese *Pleasures of the Brush* (*Fude no susabi*).

KANSHI

READING A BOOK ON A WINTER NIGHT

The snow envelops the mountain house; the tree shadows darken.
The wind chime remains still; the night grows deeper and deeper.
Quietly, I gather the scattered books and ponder the difficult words.
An ear of blue lamplight: the heart of the ancients.[6]

[Translated by Haruo Shirane]

---

6. In this seven-word quatrain, which he wrote at his home in Kannabe in the winter of 1811 when he was sixty-three, Chazan composes on the pleasures of reading alone and the joy of encountering the hearts of the ancient sage-kings of China. The flame of the lamp, which resembles the ear of rice, casts light on the heart of the ancients.

RAI SANYŌ

Rai Sanyō (1780–1832), one of the best-known kanshi poets and a noted histo-rian, was born in Osaka, the first son of Rai Shunsui, a Confucian scholar in the employ of the Aki (Hiroshima) Domain. At a young age Sanyō showed a talent for writing Chinese poetry, and when he was eighteen, he was taken to Edo to study at the Shōheikō, the bakufu school, and returned home the next year. In 1800, apparently wanting to study in the big city, he suddenly fled from his domain. He was caught in Kyoto and brought back to his home, where he was placed under house arrest for three years and then disinherited. During his confinement he began writing *The Unofficial History of Japan* (*Nihon gaishi*), a twenty-two-volume outsider's history of Japan's military clans, which he worked on for twenty years. Like most other scholars of his time, he wrote the history in kanbun, or Chinese prose. Sanyō was befriended by Kan Chazan, his father's friend and a noted kanshi poet in Bingo Province (Hiroshima), and later moved to Kyoto where he opened his own school, becoming one of the leading kanshi poets and teachers in the Kyoto-Osaka region.

When Sanyō was thirty-six, he met Ema Saikō, a woman who became both a kanshi disciple and a lifelong companion. Three years later he traveled to the west, to various parts of Kyūshū, during which time he composed the famous poem "Stopping at Amakusa Sea." In 1826 Sanyō completed his *Unofficial History*, which he dedicated to the retired *rōjū* (elder councillor) Matsudaira Sadanobu. In addition, he wrote *Record of Japan's Government* (*Nihon seiki*), a chronological history from Emperor Jinmu to Emperor GoYōzei (r. 1586–1611), which he almost completed before his death in 1832. Many of his kanshi can be found in *Selections from Sanyō's Poetry* (*Sanyō shishō*, 1833), a collection that he edited. *The Unofficial History of Japan* was not published until after his death, but in the late Tokugawa period, it was widely read by young samurai, who admired its pro-emperor stance, and brought its author posthumous fame.

THE UNOFFICIAL HISTORY OF JAPAN (*NIHON GAISHI*, 1826)

The Unofficial History of Japan is notable not only as a major work of history but also as a highly literary text, inspired by the format of Sima Qian's *Record of History* (*Shiki*) and written in a concise kanbun style that made it popular reading in the late Toku-gawa period. It is a history of the leading military clans, beginning with the Heike (Taira) and the Genji (Minamoto) and continuing through the Hōjō, Kusunoki, Nitta, Ashikaga, Takeda, Uesugi, Mōri, Oda, and others, until the Tokugawa clan. Through-out, Rai Sanyō stresses the importance of loyalty and service to the emperor and of the continuity of the imperial line. Sanyō saw the workings of heaven (*ten*) in both the position of the emperor, which he associated with an unchanging moral law or ethical principle, and the unavoidable "momentum" (*ikio*) that caused military rule to be constantly changed. Although this "momentum" transcended the power of any single individual, it made heroes of those who manifested it, thus creating a perspective in which the individual could—as happened in the waning years of the Tokugawa period—participate in history and contribute to change. Drawing on his talents as a poet, Sanyō wrote in a vivid, dramatic style that made historical figures come alive. After his death, when the "revere the emperor" (sonnō), anti-bakufu movement came to the fore, Sanyō's Unofficial History became a best-seller and a source of inspiration for many would-be reformers and activists.

Kusunoki

One of the most frequently noted passages in The Unofficial History of Japan is the concluding commentary on the significance of Kusunoki Masashige's role in the Kenmu Restoration (1333–1336), a three-year period when Emperor GoDaigo (r. 1318–1339) tried to resurrect direct imperial rule after the overthrow of the Hōjō clan, the shōgunate at Kamakura. In 1331, in response to a request from Emperor GoDaigo, Kusunoki Masashige (1294–1336), a low-ranking samurai, raised an army and helped the renegade shōgunate generals Ashikaga Takauji (1305–1358) and Nitta Yoshisada defeat the Hōjō clan. This was followed by a conflict between Ashikaga Takauji, who opposed GoDaigo and supported the Northern Court side of the imperial family, and Nitta Yoshisada and Kusunoki, who supported GoDaigo and his Southern Court lineage. Ashikaga Takauji prevailed and eventually established the Muromachi shōgunate, of which he served as the first shōgun. In the following passage, from volume 5, Rai Sanyō visits the post station at Sakurai (near present-day Osaka), where Kusunoki Masashige, aware of his impending death, met with his eleven-year-old son Masatsura (1326–1348), who wanted to follow his father in death on the battlefield, and asked Masatsura to remain loyal to the emperor. Masashige returned Masatsura to Kōchi Province because he wanted his descendants to protect the imperial throne after his death.

The unofficial historian said: I frequently traveled back and forth to Settsu and Harima Provinces[7] and on one of those occasions sought out the so-called post station at Sakurai and found it on the Yamazaki Road. It is only a small village. Some people pass through without realizing that these are the remains of the post station. As the Ashikaga, the Oda, the Toyotomi, and other clans came and went, the ways of the world changed, as did the post station, leaving the place unrecognizable. Filled with thoughts of the past, I was unable to leave. When I saw Kongō Hill[8] rising up to the edge of the clouds, I could see before my

---

7. Settsu and Harima are in present-day Osaka and Hyōgo Prefectures. Yamazaki is a mountain road between Kyoto and Osaka.
8. Kongō is a hill in southeast Osaka, where Masashige built Chihaya Castle.

eyes the autumn when Kusunoki led his troops for a just cause and when his descendants made this mountain their base as they protected the imperial family.

According to the records, when Kusunoki visited Emperor GoDaigo's temporary residence,[9] he said, "As long as I am alive and your subject, you do not have to worry about destroying the traitors." This was an imperial guard of the third rank who remained steadfast and took on his shoulders the heavy weight of the land. Deeply moved by his fortunate encounter with the emperor, Kusunoki sacrificed himself for the sake of the country. He accomplished great feats, stopping a great river with an empty hand and making the sun that had set rise again.[10] How magisterial!

Kusunoki enticed the elite troops of the Hōjō clan to the base of Chihaya Castle on Kongō Mountain and had the forces of Nitta Yoshisada and Ashikaga Takauji attack the positions vacated by the Hōjō and destroy the Hōjō leaders.[11] When the emperor returned to the throne and rewarded Kusunoki with a title and an official post, he should have offered him the highest position. Instead, Kusunoki's position was just barely comparable to that of his colleagues Yūki and Nawa. From the failure of this action, one can understand the failure of the Kenmu Imperial Restoration.

With the betrayal by the Ashikaga clan, the imperial court had to rely heavily on the Nitta clan. Kusunoki was simply turned into the Nitta's vice general and made to assist them. The only reason for this was that he did not have the pedigree of the Nitta clan. But wasn't the victory in Kyoto and the fact that they almost destroyed the traitors a result of Kusunoki's strategy? If the responsibility that was left to the Nitta had been given to Kusunoki, would he have caused the traitors—the dogs, sheep, foxes, and mice—to step on our imperial court?[12]

But when Kusunoki faced death, he cautioned his son with these words: "When I die, everything under heaven will revert to the Ashikaga." Even though he knew that the matters of the world could not be controlled, he left behind descendants to protect the emperor. His concern was equal to that of the great ministers of ancient times. His descendants faithfully obeyed his last words, looked after the rightful emperor in the confined place of Yoshino, and protected His Majesty from traitors for three reigns and more than fifty years. Kusunoki's descendants sacrificed the life of their entire clan for a country in

---

9. This temporary residence refers to Kasagi Mountain near Kyoto, where Emperor GoDaigo stayed in 1331.

10. The sinking sun was GoDaigo's exile to Oki. Kusunoki enabled GoDaigo to return to the capital, thus bringing the sun back up.

11. Takauji and Yoshisada attacked Kamakura and Rokuhara (in Kyoto) while the Hōjō were on the move and destroyed Hōjō Takatoki (d. 1333) and others.

12. Sanyō regrets the mistake made by the emperor in leaving the power to the Nitta clan rather than to Kusunoki after Ashikaga Takauji's betrayal.

crisis. It was only after Kusunoki's clan was destroyed that the Ashikaga clan was able, for the first time, to exercise out its will fully across the country.

Indeed, the imperial court was not able to give much responsibility to the Kusunoki clan. No more needs to be added—beyond the fact of their loyalty to the emperor—about why the Kusunoki clan took the responsibility on themselves. Today, when we evaluate the various generals involved in that imperial restoration, we evaluate them according to family lineage and social prestige and do not grasp the deeper reality of the situation—a view that is no better than that held at that time. If the Kusunoki clan had not existed, even if the Southern Court had the three imperial treasures, to whom could they have turned to keep alive the hopes of the country? The significance of the dream that the emperor had at Kasagi Mountain looms large here.[13] But the Southern wind[14] could not compete, and both the Southern Court and the Kusunoki clan were wounded and vanquished. How sad it is that since the distant past, no one has sympathized with the labors of the Kusunoki clan!

Even though the legitimate emperor and the unauthorized emperor differed, in the end they returned to being one, and the honored name of the emperor has been transmitted eternally.[15] If we could inform Kusunoki Masashige about this, he would no doubt be able to sleep peacefully. Then his great loyalty to the emperor would rise high and exist together with the mountains and rivers and be sufficient to maintain forever, for ten thousand years, the human spirit of those who follow the proper way of the world.[16] When we compare this to the evil heroes of China, who constantly fought one another and stayed in power for a mere few hundred years, this kind of gain and loss is nothing.

Uesugi Kenshin and Takeda Shingen

Uesugi Kenshin, a leader from Echigo Province (Niigata), and Takeda Shingen, from Kai Province (Yamanashi), were bitter rivals during the Warring States period (1477–1573), before the unification of the country by Oda Nobunaga. For twelve years, from 1553 to 1564, the two leaders fought five deadly battles at Kawanakajima, where the

---

13. According to the *Taiheiki*, Emperor GoDaigo had a dream while at Kasagi Mountain that the seat of the throne was placed under a "southern tree" (two radicals of the character for Kusunoki) of the main building in the imperial palace, and he consequently summoned Kusunoki Masashige.

14. The Southern Court.

15. In 1392, the Northern and Southern Courts were reconciled, and Emperor GoKameyama of the Southern Court ceded the throne to Emperor GoKomatsu (r. 1382–1412) of the Northern Court, thereby reunifying the imperial line.

16. Sanyō is implying that Kusunoki's greatest accomplishment was establishing respect and loyalty for the emperor. By sacrificing himself to the Southern Court and showing unswerving loyalty to GoDaigo, he helped maintain the imperial line for eternity.

Chikuma and Saikawa Rivers merge, in Shinano Province (Nagano) — battles that were dramatized in jōruri and kabuki by Chikamatsu Monzaemon, Chikamatsu Hanji, and Kawatake Mokuami. The following passage, which reveals the compact, dramatic style of *The Unofficial History of Japan*, describes one of the most famous of these encounters, which Rai Sanyō believes to have occurred in 1554.

In the Eighth Month, Kenshin again entered Shinano Province with eight thousand mounted soldiers and mused to himself, "In this battle, I must fight Shingen personally to determine victory or defeat." He advanced across the Saikawa River and set up camp on the opposite shore. On the sixteenth, Shingen set out, taking with him twenty thousand troops, and came face to face with Kenshin's forces. Shingen strengthened his defenses and did not go out to battle. After a day had passed, Kenshin had Murakami Yoshikiyo and others hide their troops during the night, and when the dawn arrived, Kenshin had woodcutters go out and approach the Kai defenses. The Kai troops came out and pursued the woodcutters, falling into the trap set by the hidden troops, and all died. The various units followed and clashed in a fierce battle. During the day there were seventeen engagements, with victories and defeats on both sides. Shingen secretly issued an order, had a large rope stretched across the Saikawa River, crossed the water, hid the flags and banners, passed through the reeds, and immediately attacked Kenshin's closest retainers, who collapsed and fled.

Riding on his success, Shingen advanced. At that point, Usami Sadayuki and others took their own soldiers and launched a surprise attack on Shingen from the side, broke through, and pushed Shingen's troops into the river. Shingen fled with twenty to thirty mounted soldiers. At that point, a warrior mounted on a chestnut horse and wearing a yellow battle cloak, emerged. Covering his face with a white cloth, the mounted warrior drew out a large sword and came forward, shouting, "Where's Shingen?" Shingen spurred on his horse, entered the river, and tried to escape. The mounted warrior followed, yelling, "Hey you there, punk!"[17] Raising his sword, the mounted warrior attacked. Shingen did not have time to draw his sword. Instead, he took what was in his hand, the command fan, and used it to fend off the blow. The fan broke. The mounted warrior swung again, cutting into Shingen's shoulder. The Kai retainers tried to save their commander, but the water was flowing quickly, preventing them from getting close.

At this point Hara Oosumi, a Kai unit commander, took his spear and stabbed at the mounted warrior in the yellow cloak but missed. Raising his spear, Oosumi thrust forward again, hitting the horse's neck. The horse jumped in fright and plunged into the rapids. Shingen barely managed to escape. Ta-

---

17. The mounted warrior uses a derogatory term for inexperienced youth, "punk" (*jushi*), intended to insult and draw out Shingen.

keda Nobushige,[18] hearing that Shingen was in danger, turned and came back, called out to the mounted warrior, demanding a duel, and died in the ensuing fight. The number of soldiers who died on both sides on this day was staggering. Having been wounded, Shingen gathered his troops at night and retreated. Later Shingen took a prisoner from Echigo,[19] who told him: "The mounted warrior who faced you was Kenshin."

[Vol. 11, *Later Records of the Ashikaga Clan*, translated by Haruo Shirane]

KANSHI

Although Rai Sanyō made a career of writing histories, he was equally noted as a poet of kanshi, especially for his history poems (*eishi*; Ch. *yongshi*). Some of them are quite long and unique in the Japanese kanshi tradition. In these poems, Sanyō recreates an event in the distant past or assumes the persona of a historical figure, as in the following, his most famous history poem. This quatrain describes the famous battle at Kawanakajima, in the Ninth Month of 1561, when Kenshin and Shingen accidentally came into direct contact with each other, as described in the preceding passage from *The Unofficial History of Japan*.

ON A PAINTING OF KENSHIN ATTACKING SHINGEN

Sound of the horse whips, softly, softly, crossing the river at night.
At dawn the sight of a thousand soldiers protecting the great tusk.
A lasting regret! For ten years, polishing one sword
Beneath the light of a falling star, the long snake escapes.[20]

[*Gozan bungaku shū, Edo kanshi shū*, NKBT 89: 294, translated by Haruo Shirane]

STOPPING AT AMAKUSA SEA

Is it clouds? Or mountains? Is it Wu? Or Yue?
The water and the heavens separated by a single hair
After countless miles, anchoring the boat in the Sea of Amakusa
The mist moving past my window, the sun gradually sinks.

---

18. By calling out to the mounted rider, Takeda Nobushige (1525–1561), the younger brother of Takeda Shingen, deflected attention to himself and ended up sacrificing his life for his brother.

19. Echigo was Kenshin's home province.

20. The poem is written from Kenshin's perspective. The opening line describes Kenshin's army, which is quietly crossing the river in preparation for an attack. The "great tusk" is a banner topped with a large tusk, marking the main camp of the general (Kenshin). The first four characters in the fourth line have been interpreted as either the momentary light of a shooting star or the momentary light beneath a drawn sword. In either case, the phrase refers to the moment of opportunity that Kenshin let slip. The "long snake" represents Takeda Shingen. The poem, which is still recited today, is noted for its rhythm and sound, which match the dramatic content.

I glimpse a giant fish jumping between the waves.
The light of Venus, bright as the moon, strikes the boat.[21]

[Translated by Haruo Shirane]

ESCORTING MY MOTHER HOME: A SHORT SONG FOR THE ROAD

East winds to greet my mother when she came;
North winds to see her on the way back home.
She arrived when roads were fragrant with blossoms,
Now suddenly this cold of frost and snow!
At cockcrow already I'm trying my footgear,
Waiting by her palanquin, legs a bit unsteady.
Never mind if the son's legs are tired,
Just worry whether her palanquin's fit for riding.
I pour her a cup of wine, a drink for myself too,
First sunlight flooding the inn, frost already dried.
Fifty-year-old son, seventy-year-old mother—
Not often you find a pair as lucky as us!
Off to the south, in from the north, streams of people—
Who among them happy as this mother and son?[22]

[*Gozan bungaku shū, Edo kanshi shū*, NKBT 89: 297, translated by Burton Watson]

RYŌKAN

Ryōkan (1758–1831) was a Zen monk renowned for his distinctive calligraphy and poetry in Chinese and Japanese. He was born in the village of Izumozaki in Echigo Province (Niigata), on the Japan Sea coast. His father, a practicing haiku poet, was the village headman and the custodian of the local Shintō

---

21. Sanyō composed this seven-word old-style (*koshi*) kanshi in 1818, during a journey in Kyūshū. In the first line, the speaker wonders whether what he is seeing is Wu (Go), a kingdom in the Spring and Autumn Warring States Period (eighth century–third century B.C.E.), or Yue (Etsu). Yue, a small kingdom in the south of China, defeated the kingdom of Wu in a war around 473 B.C.E. Amakusanada (literally, Sea of Heavenly Grass), the waters between present-day Kumamoto and Nagasaki Prefectures, faces China, although it would be impossible to see China from Amakusa. The poem is notable for its vast physical and temporal scale, reaching back into the past and up to the stars. Lines 1, 2, 4, and 6—*Etsu, hatsu* (hair), *botsu* (sink), and *tsuki* (moon)—rhyme. The "old-style" or "ancient-style" poem became popular in the Han and Wei (403–225 B.C.E.) periods.

22. Sanyō has also been admired as a poet of everyday life. A good example is this five-word old-style kanshi, considered to be one of his masterpieces. In the spring of 1829, Sanyō's sixty-eight-year-old mother came to visit him in Kyoto. In the winter of the same year, he escorted her part of the way back home to Hiroshima. The simple expressions combine in parallel couplets to create a buoyant rhythm, suggesting the poet's joy in being able to accompany his elderly mother.

shrine. As the eldest son, Ryōkan was in position to succeed his father as village headman, but at the age of seventeen, he abruptly entered a local Zen temple and began religious training, adopting the religious name of Ryōkan. His younger brother Yoshiyuki replaced him as the family heir. In 1779, he became a disciple of the Soto Zen master Kokusen, head of the Entsū-ji temple in Bitchū Province (Okayama Prefecture), and spent the next ten years or so under Kokusen's guidance, eventually becoming a Zen master himself. After Kokusen's death in 1791, Ryōkan left Entsū-ji and, after five years of wandering, returned to his native region of Echigo, where he remained for the rest of his life. In 1804, he settled down in the Gogō-an, or Five Measures of Rice Retreat, a small one-room hut on the slopes of Mount Kugami, near the Japan Sea. He died in the vicinity when he was seventy-three.

Unlike most prominent Buddhist priests, who became heads of temples, Ryōkan lived alone, devoted himself to meditation and poetry, and supported himself through the practice of *takuhatsu*, begging expeditions to nearby villages. Some of his best poems are on the begging bowl (*hachi*), a symbol of his life as a mendicant priest. He is also known for his poems about playing with children, his wanderings, his meditations, and his life in a small hut. Ryōkan's poems are marked by their interest in a natural, simple, and unpretentious life and by his strong persona, particularly as a compassionate, warm, and crazy monk—reminiscent of such other madcap Zen monks as Ikkyū or, in China, Hanshan (Cold Mountain). This aspect of Ryōkan's personality is reflected in the second religious name that he adopted: Taigu, or Great Fool. In 1826, he became close friends with a Zen Buddhist nun, Teishin (1798–1872), forty years his junior, with whom he exchanged numerous poems. After his death, she collected these poems in *Dew on the Lotus* (*Hachisu no tsuyu*, 1835).

KANSHI

Ryōkan was particularly inspired by the poetry of Hanshan, a Chinese lay follower of Zen Buddhism and a poet noted for his simplicity of language and directness in depicting a spartan life of ease and detachment. Ryōkan composed two types of kanshi: those that are Buddhist poems, which lay out doctrinal principles, and those that confess to worldly concerns or praise everyday life in the farm village. The latter depict many of the same activities that his poems in Japanese do—winters in the small hut, begging expeditions, playing with children, wanderings, visits with friends.

> Who says my poems are poems?
> My poems are not poems at all.
> Only when you understand that my poems are not poems,
> Can we begin to talk about poems.[23]

> [RZ 1: 222, translated by Burton Watson]

---

23. Many poems by Ryōkan, like this one, have no title. The word "poetry" (*shi*) in the first

How admirable—the fine gentleman,
In spare moments so often trying his hand at poetry!
His old-style verse is modeled on Han and Wei works;
For modern style, he makes the Tang his teacher;
With what elegance he shapes his compositions,
Adding touches that are striking and new.
But since he never writes of things in the heart,
However many he may turn out, what's the point?[24]

> [RZ 1: 232–233, translated by Burton Watson]

All my life I've had no interest in worldly success
I take it easy, leaving things to nature.
In my pocket, three cups of rice
By the stove, a bundle of brushwood
Why should I ask about ignorance or enlightenment?
Why should I know about the dust of profit and fame?
During the evening rain, inside the hut
I stretch out my two legs as I please.[25]

> [RZ 1: 216, translated by Haruo Shirane]

In my sleeve the colored ball worth a thousand in gold:
I dare say no one's as good at handball as me!
And if you ask what it's all about—
One—two—three—four—five—six—seven.[26]

> [RZ 1: 62, translated by Burton Watson]

---

two lines refers to traditional notions of kanshi, or poetry, which follow complex rules and form (such as rhyme schemes and the number of lines) and which describe nature in beautiful language. Ryōkan is warning the reader—and, more important, himself—that it is only when one gets beyond such conceptions that one truly begins to compose poetry.

24. Under the influence of Ogyū Sorai's (1666–1728) Ancient Rhetoric school, kanshi was dominated by a neoclassical style in which the poet aimed for the "elegant" style admired in the high Tang. Ryōkan supported those, such as Yamamoto Hokuzan, who rejected this approach as imitative.

25. "Leaving things to nature" means following what "heaven" or "nature" gives us. Ryōkan clings to neither ignorance (lack of spiritual awareness) nor enlightenment (satori). Instead, he goes with the flow, being satisfied with a simple, spartan lifestyle and a life of ease.

26. A temari (handball) is a cloth ball wound with colored thread and used for various children's games, to which songs are sung. The temari frequently appears in Ryōkan's letters, calligraphy, and poetry—in both his kanshi and his waka—as the primary means by which Ryōkan plays with children.

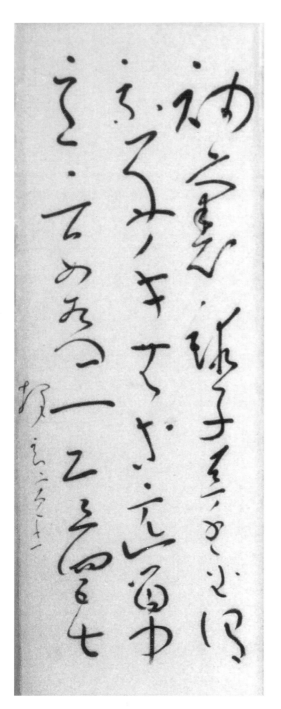

Calligraphy by Ryōkan. One of his favorite poems, the four-line kanshi "In my sleeve the colored ball worth a thousand in gold," is written in cursive script (*sōsho*), abbreviating and connecting the strokes of the characters. The soft, round contours and the uniform width of the flickering brushstrokes are characteristic of Ryōkan's style. The Japanese reading of the three calligraphic lines is *shūri no kyūshi atai senkin omohu / ware kōshu tōhitsu nashi to kachū no / ishi moshi ai towaba hi fu mi yo i mu na.* (Courtesy of Northern Culture Museum, Niigata)

I lie alone in my grass hut,
all day not seeing a soul.
Alms bag—how long now it's hung on the wall,
walking stick left wholly in the dust.
Dreams wing away to mountain meadows;
waking, my spirit roams the city—
along the roadside, the little boys—
as always, they'll be waiting for me to come.[27]

[RZ 1: 309–310, translated by Burton Watson]

27. This poem describes a period when Ryōkan was ill and lying in a mountain dwelling. Unable to move physically, his spirit travels to the city and thinks of the children with whom he has always played.

Chapter 24

THE MISCELLANY

The *zuihitsu* (literally, following the brush), or miscellany, is usually traced back to Sei Shōnagon's *Pillowbook* (*Makura no sōshi*, ca. 1000) and is regarded as reaching a peak with Yoshida Kenkō's *Essays in Idleness* (*Tsurezuregusa*, ca. 1310–1331). The zuihitsu varied in form but usually consisted of a collection of short sections, often randomly ordered, written in relatively short sentences, although it could also be an extended and unified essay. The contents of the individual sections ranged from diarylike entries to meditative or philosophical reflections, instructions on living, observations of society, lists of interesting things, transmissions of folk stories (*setsuwa*), and repositories of useful knowledge. In the early modern period, the zuihitsu became a defined and important genre when a number of intellectuals and writers—ranging from Confucian scholars, bunjin (literati), and nativist scholars to poets and writers of various types—took up the form. Perhaps the most famous of these collections is Matsudaira Sadanobu's *Blossoms and the Moon* (*Kagetsu sōshi*).

MATSUDAIRA SADANOBU

Matsudaira Sadanobu (1758–1828), the son of Tayasu Munetake (1715–1771), a noted kokugaku scholar and poet and the grandson of the shōgun Tokugawa Yoshimune (r. 1716–1745), became the lord of Shirakawa Domain in northern

Japan. In 1787 he became senior councillor (rōjū) to the eleventh shōgun, Tokugawa Ienari (r. 1787–1837), and engineered the Kansei Reforms (1789–1801), which reined in what Sadanobu considered to be the excesses of the former period. After only seven years of service, however, he retired to Shirakawa where he turned to writing and other leisurely activities.

BLOSSOMS AND THE MOON (KAGETSU SŌSHI, 1818)

Blossoms and the Moon, which Sadanobu wrote around 1812 after his retirement to Shirakawa and published privately after 1817, consists of six volumes and 156 sections on a wide range of topics, including literature, learning, gods, medicine, ethics, and military affairs. *Blossoms and the Moon* reveals the author's position as a social and political leader and became standard reading in textbooks from the Meiji period onward. It has been particularly admired for its elegant neoclassical style (*gabun*) and its observations on nature.

On Blossoms

To speak against what you are told, wanting to say yes when someone says no, or to call good what someone calls bad—that is perverse indeed. Still, even knowing that the cherry blossom supposedly was unique to our country, I thought it must surely exist in China as well and did a good deal of searching, only to find no Chinese paintings of cherry blossoms and not a poem that seemed to refer to that plant. Thus I must conclude that cherry blossoms do not exist in China.

Now then, even if one said only "blossoms" and not "cherry blossoms," no one would mistake the cherry for any other tree. It would be frivolous to mention only the sight of blossoms so grand on a mountain ridge lit by faint dawn light that one would think they might be clouds or snow, or so bright on a hazy evening that a faint view of them would seem to reveal one place where the day had not yet ended. And all the more haughty would it seem, then, to say that the long calyx of the blossoms makes them less excellent when viewed up close. Whether tossed on wind or drenched by rain, viewed on far-off mountains or close-up near the eaves of one's house, at dawn or in evening light; still one never takes one's eyes off them, not even for the moment it takes for the dew to fade away. Moreover, the plant seems especially suited to the ways of our country, with branches so gentle, flowers so delicate in shape, and hues so simple that the total effect is perfect beyond belief. And yet it is true that they are found everywhere, and to add words insisting they are more alluring at dawn or at dusk means only that one has not yet considered the matter deeply. Only those of shallow feeling would think abundant words could account for such things.

Leaving It to Heaven

The saying goes, "I will leave it up to the distant skies and not depend on my own insignificant talents," but one must think deeply before leaving things up to Heaven. For even when one can see starlight, a rough wind may be in the offing; to get on a boat knowing beforehand that the winds will blow here around noon tomorrow—that is leaving things up to Heaven. To not even ask about whether the wind is blowing offshore and just row out because the waves are calm where one is at the moment—that should not be called leaving things up to Heaven. The same is true even of eating: One should leave one's life or death up to Heaven only after taking the greatest care and doing all one can to nurture one's body—although I suppose there are also those who say they are leaving everything up to Heaven by giving no attention to nourishment and just following their desires.

Study

Someone says, "That man has spent years by his window, gathering snow and fireflies for light, using all his energy in looking at books, and so he is quite removed from things of the world," and then proceeds to praise such a person, saying he is one who truly pursues the Way of Learning. But to pursue the Way of Learning—what can this mean but to begin with the Five Ways,[1] learning to govern others and govern oneself? We should praise as a Pursuer of the Way of Learning only that person who knows not just about his own world at the present but is also enlightened about everything else—things of a thousand years ago, unseen things in China now or long ago, the signs of prosperity and decline, the thoughts of people's hearts, indeed, everything down to the details of how to serve one's lord. "How can one call a man who is ignorant of the world around him one who truly pursues the Way of Learning?" someone once asked.

On Skies Clearing and Rain Falling

One day in a time of drought, the east wind blows your way, clouds form, and you think, "Ah, today it will rain"—until the wind suddenly dies, the clouds break up, and the sunlight begins to beam down once more. Or again, when the rains have continued for some time, you hear the wind sounding strong in the pines, and it looks as if it will begin clearing up as you watch clumps of clouds turn green here and deep red over where the sun is going down, making

---

1. Probably a reference to the Confucian virtues: benevolence, righteousness, propriety, knowledge, and trustworthiness.

you think, "Ah, the moon will shine brightly tonight!"—but then clouds form when the moon does come out, and you hear the sound of raindrops. I hear it said that this is the way also with times of unrest and times of order and with the state of our hearts.

Rain

"On a moonlit night, no worries trouble one's thoughts and one's heart is clear down to its very bottom," I say, "yet I feel that a dark night, when the sky is free of clouds and the stars are shining bright, with the wind coursing high above, is still superior."

To this another replies, "Ah, but a rainy night is even better."

"How so?" I counter.

"Well, take rain in a time of drought—that goes without saying. Then, too, the flowers that bloom on grasses and trees are a result of the rain's blessing, are they not? And if one speaks of the most profound feelings, think of the first day of the year when the rain comes softly down, creating a mist all around that makes one feel that indeed spring has come. Or think how intrigued one is by the gentle rain on the last day of the old year that seems to be waiting for spring to begin.

"In spring the rains are always mild. Out from the eaves spreads a mist so fine that one's robes become damp, even though no rain seems to be falling at all. Everything about the scene is peaceful—the way an abandoned spider's web is strung with water beads, out beneath the eaves where the sound of falling drops seems more far away; the way green growth begins to show low on the withered grasses of the garden; the way droplets increase on willow branches still unmoved by wind. When one lights a lamp, its light seems moist, and the faint tolling of the evening bell clears the heart. Furthermore, the moist scent of plum blossoms spreading abroad in the depths of night, and even one's complaints against the rain on behalf of the blossoms—these, too, are most touching. Then as spring grows old, how amusing are the frogs croaking, as if to claim the time their own.

"One is wondering when the first cuckoo will call, when one hears the pitter-patter of raindrops coming down. Or one may be spending all one's hours leafing through books as the rains of the Fifth Month go on and on, making one feel more and more distant from the ways of the world as time goes on. Or just when the heat seems most unbearable, the clouds above may roil with rain, the winds descend in a rush, and the leaves and the willows and lotus leaves appear to turn white—a most cooling sight. When the big raindrops that had seemed far away finally come, falling so hard now that one can hear nothing else, one catches the scent of wet earth and feels renewed. A curtain of raindrops hangs from the eaves and the constant downpour makes the garden into a lake, here a waterfall, there a running stream, with people—most amusingly—just watching it all in silence. Then the clouds thin out as a few raindrops still splash here and there on the pond, and the birds prance out into the garden searching for food. Off where the clouds first arose, the sky shows blue, and a rainbow appears; and how cool one feels looking at the reflections of trees in the puddles in the garden! Startled by the thunder, an old woman crawls out and says, 'How nicely the sky has cleared, just like when I was young; these days it rarely clears up so well,' and babbles on while the people around laugh at her for making such a fuss. 'There won't be many mosquitoes today, with the thunder sounding so faintly; you can almost forget how hot it's been,' one says, going out onto the veranda to enjoy the captivating sight of light from the evening moon shining everywhere, making water drops on the bushes shine like jewels while fat frogs, gazing up into the sky as if waiting for something, call out in clumsy voices.

"The rain of autumn seems changed from what it was just days before and somehow forlorn. The wind blowing over the reeds, the voice of a deer crying in the foothills—these seem to strike more deeply into the heart than even the moon. The sound of the bamboo water-pipe that one is so used to hearing even seems sadder.

"Also captivating are rain showers passing before the moon. And more moving still is the sound of crickets in the chill of night, their voices hoarse from wear, calling out feebly near one's pillow during a short break in the rain. 'Surely this rain will be dyeing the leaves,' one thinks, only to hear a different reaction from one's children, who, crowded round the lamp, chatter forlornly: 'The bamboo shoots will be coming up, and the chestnuts will be falling.'

"Always damp is the sound of a bell ringing out late at night, but in autumn the sound takes on a chill, calling to mind nights spent waiting or times of parting, so much so that one's feelings grow even deeper, reaching out in sympathy even to the one who strikes the bell. The deep color of the autumn leaves, the final flourishing of faded chrysanthemums in the moment before they fall, the resentful look of gentian in bloom while the eulalia declines under heavy dew—all seem somehow appropriate to the season. And how moving it is that the morning glories, blooming in bright purple amid the general withering, should stave off their decline until after noon.

"Monsoon winds are a fearsome thing, and the rain they bring is no less fierce than the rain of a summer thunderstorm, so the lonely feeling they inspire can be attributed only to autumn's melancholy. Suddenly one hears the sound of showers falling whitely in the evening sunlight—a different sound and very alluring.

"'So—don't you agree?' the man says. 'Isn't a rainy night more moving than a moonlit night, or a night of darkness?'

"'When one runs through all those examples, one is quite ready to agree,' I think to myself, quite amused as I listened, 'but listening to you go through them makes me feel like I've been through a whole year of rain. This rain we're having now started just the day before yesterday, and already I'm sick of it—and that hasn't changed!'"

Comments Made by Bystanders

Comments made by bystanders often turn out to be true. Someone says, "My, how that fellow has aged," even though the man himself doesn't see it when he looks in the mirror. Or someone says, "Now he acts this way, but later he will regret it," whereas the one referred to is totally oblivious. If not for our self-centeredness, we might see just what those next to us see.

On the Ainu

I gave some rice to an Ainu, and he took it happily but then spilled a lot of it in the process of eating. "Hey you," I said, "don't you know rice is what sustains the string of life? How can you waste it so?" "But we don't depend on rice for life," he said. "Instead, we rely on a fish called salmon." So I said, "If that's so—if you sustain life by eating salmon—then you should respect salmon, right? But aren't those things on your feet made of salmon skin?" At this the man cocked his head a moment and then said, "But those sandals you are wearing—aren't they made of grass from the rice plant?"

We shouldn't ridicule the Ainu, someone said. Since people of our country know little about outsiders, many of us think that just because they don't look like us, all the Ainu are stupid and ignorant. This is why some people laugh out loud when they see someone who looks unusual or laugh when they hear words that they cannot understand, be it someone from China or an Ainu. This is because such people are narrow-minded and have not seen the outside world.

Fox Stupidity

Once there was a man who would always give food to a fox that came every night. Since the fox was one of the most intelligent of beasts, he thought, he will someday repay me for my generosity. So every day without fail, he left food, until the fox became accustomed to it. Then one day the man's horse foaled, and he was so busy that for two days he forgot to put food out, at which the fox—out of resentment, perhaps—ate the foal.

Bugs in a Hawk

There was a kind of bug that lived in the feathers of a hawk. When the hawk flew high into the sky, looking down on the houses of men far below, he thought to himself, "I am truly without peer, for without moving my wings I can sail more than a thousand *li*, rising even beyond the clouds; and I send other birds fleeing in fright, for there is none that can best me." Yet in this same hawk's feathers lived bugs that pierced his flesh and sucked his blood until—because they became so numerous—the hawk collapsed. At this, the bugs first tried to fly away themselves but could not succeed in getting off the ground, and then they tried to run but could not get up any speed. With the hawk's blood all gone and his flesh dried up, the bugs had no way to sustain life, and so they left. Just as they succeeded in making their way out from among the hawk's feathers, a baby sparrow showed up. "Certainly he will fear us," the bugs thought, but the baby sparrow paid no attention, and when they crawled over toward the bird thinking that he could not fail to notice them, the bird suddenly became happy, stuck out his beak, and began to peck at them. So amazed were the bugs that they became frightened and hid themselves—so said the friend who told me this story.

[*Kagetsu sōshi*, Iwanami shoten, 1964, pp. 21–22, 24–25, 27, 36–37, 43–46, 88, 139–140, translated by Steven Carter]

Chapter 25

EARLY-NINETEENTH-CENTURY HAIKU

With the spread of education in the eighteenth century, the haikai "population" gradually expanded to the point that even maids and grooms were said to be composing haiku for entertainment. Not surprisingly, the quality of the poetry suffered, and so in the mid-eighteenth century, Buson and his circle attempted in various ways to reelevate it, such as staging a Bashō revival. By the early nineteenth century, Buson and his successors had died, but haiku continued to be popular. The most talented haiku poet of this time was Kobayashi Issa, whose main interest was in everyday, contemporary life. This disregard for established poetic topics and the satirical quality of Issa's haiku—which often shaded into senryū—were typical of haikai of this time.

KOBAYASHI ISSA

Issa, born Kobayashi Yatarō (1763–1827), was the first son of a middle-class farmer in Kashiwabara, at the northern tip of Shinano Province (Nagano Prefecture), facing the Japan Sea side, a region referred to as snow country (*yukiguni*). Issa's mother died when he was three, and his father remarried three years later. Because of his stepmother's coldness, Issa left home in 1777 when he was fourteen and went to Edo, where he struggled as an apprentice-servant. Around 1787, he began studying haikai with Chikua (1710–1790) and other poets of the haikai Katsushika group, which was part of the larger Bashō revival taking place at this time, and he adopted the haikai pen name Issa (Cup of Tea). In 1792, he began a six-year journey through the Kyoto-Osaka region, Shikoku, and Kyūshū, after which he went back to Edo and took over Chikua's school. Issa had difficulty making a living as a teacher, however, and depended on friends to survive.

In 1801, when he was thirty-eight, Issa returned to Kashiwabara because his father was dying, an experience described in *Journal of My Father's Last Days* (*Chichi no shūen nikki*). In his will, Issa's father split the inheritance between Issa and his stepbrother, which his stepmother contested, leading to a long dispute. In 1813, Issa finally won his share of the property and returned to his home village. Shortly thereafter, he married a twenty-eight-year-old woman named Kiku, who bore him four children, none of whom survived for long. The birth and death of his second child and first daughter, Sato, prompted Issa to write *My Spring* (*Ora ga haru*) in 1819. In 1823, his wife of ten years also died, and then in 1827, he lost his house to a massive fire. Issa died soon afterward, at the age of sixty-four. The poems he wrote after returning to Kashiwabara were gathered in various collections such as *Seventh Diary* (*Shichiban nikki*, 1810–1818).

Issa is considered a highly unorthodox poet, although he was exposed to the different currents of haikai prevailing at that time: first, the Bashō-revival style of the Katsushika school, which is apparent in Issa's travel literature; then the comic style of the Danrin school in Osaka, with which Issa came into contact during his journey to Kyūshū; and finally the "provincial (*inaka*) style," which is characterized by colloquial language and dialect and is deliberately focused on provincial topics and which came into prominence in Edo in the first two decades of the nineteenth century. In contrast to the Edo haikai poets, for whom the provincial style was a kind of fashion and form of play, Issa wrote from experience and with striking individuality, reflecting both his roots in a provincial farming village and his uncertain existence in the city. The "Issa style" is noted for its dynamic and liberal use of colloquial language and dialect and for its fresh perspective, of someone looking at city life as an outsider. His poetry tends to straddle the border between the seventeen-syllable senryū (comic haiku), with its satiric and social concerns, and orthodox haikai, with its emphasis on nature and the seasons. In this sense, Issa reacted strongly against the tendency of earlier haikai poets to write on fixed seasonal topics. He is known for his sympathy for animals, insects, and small creatures; his use of personification; his humor; and the autobiographical character of his writing and poetry, particularly with regard to his position as an oppressed stepson and as a person consumed by poverty and misfortune. He created what one might call the "poetry of one's life." Recently, the autobiographical authenticity of his writings has been questioned, as some critics believe that they may contain significant fictional elements, but there is no doubt that he created a gripping poetic persona.

JOURNAL OF MY FATHER'S LAST DAYS
(CHICHI NO SHŪEN NIKKI, 1807)

In *Journal of My Father's Last Days*, Issa describes the last month of his father's life in the summer of 1801 and the bitter struggle with his stepmother and stepbrother, Senroku. In contrast to earlier death diaries (*shūenki*), which honor and idealize the dead, Issa's journal, which he probably wrote between 1801 and 1806 or 1807, is noteworthy for its realistic and frank description. It drew attention in the modern period as a pioneering work in the Naturalist mode. Recent scholars also see this diary as an attempt by Issa to justify his position vis-à-vis his stepmother and stepbrother.

Fourth Month, Twenty-third Day

A clear, calm, cloudless day, filled with the first songs of the mountain cuckoos. . . . As Father stood there, sprinkling water on the eggplant shoots, something came over him. He suddenly hunched down, turning his back to the early summer sun.

"Why are you lying in such a place?" I asked as I helped him up.

Later I realized that this was a portent of the flower about to fade. It must have been an inauspicious day for my father. He had just said, "I'm feeling a little poorly," when he was suddenly struck by a high fever. His body was as if on fire. I offered him some cooked rice, but he could not swallow a single grain. I was alarmed and wondered what could be the matter. I was at my wit's end, and for lack of anything else to do, I just massaged him. . . .

Fourth Month, Twenty-ninth Day

As my father's illness worsened, he must have begun to worry about my future as an orphan, for he began dividing his meager holdings between his two offspring. With painful breaths, he gave his instructions. He said he would give the rice field at Nakajima and the one at Kawara to my younger brother, but Senroku did not seem to take kindly to this and grew hostile toward Father and his wishes. Father and Senroku quarreled all day, and that's where the matter ended. It all started because greed, perversity, and guile had blinded Senroku and driven him out of his senses. How sad it was to see him turning his back on his father and revealing this world of men as it is in these evil days of the Five Defilements.[1]

This evening Father's pulse was exceptionally weak, and I felt anxious about his being left alone. Although Senroku might not be a son who measured up

---

1. The Five Defilements (*gojoku*) mark the Latter Age of the Buddhist Law or Dharma (*mappō*).

to his father's expectations, I felt that since he was a blood relation, he would regret it if he was not at his father's deathbed. Concerned for my brother's feelings, I had him sleep next to Father. Turning toward Father's sleeping face in the lamplight, I lay there watching over his resting body. Throughout the night Father gasped painful breaths, and it was hard to watch. I felt relieved when at last it became evident that the tide had turned and he seemed better.

Father had said that he wanted to try the bear-gall medicine that the doctor at Nojiri was said to have at his place.[2] Although it was barely two and a half miles down the road, I felt that were I to go and get the medicine, Father would not be properly taken care of in my absence, since he and my stepmother had had a quarrel the day before. So, without telling my father, I gave Senroku instructions and sent him off. The early summer rains had lifted overnight, but water was washing over the grass, arousing people's concern about flooding in the rice paddies. And then Father asked where Senroku had gone. I could hardly hide the truth any longer, so I told him what had happened. Father's rage was uncontrollable, and he would not listen to me.

He fumed, "Why do you send him out to pick up the bear gall without consulting me? Even *you* slight me!"

From the bedroom, my stepmother, raising her voice, seized the opportunity to revile me as though there was no one else around, saying things like "It was that lazybones Issa who sent out Senroku without breakfast. Doesn't he care at all if his brother's stomach is empty?"

There was no way to remedy the situation, so I suffered in silence. Pressing my head to the floor and rubbing my palms in supplication, I repented tearfully, promising, "I'll be more careful in the future." Father's rage abated somewhat.

Because all of Father's admonitions, whether given gently or in anger, were for my own benefit, how could I resent them? But how pitiful was his weakened voice raised in anger. After I had spent the previous night brooding about our pending eternal separation, my joy at suffering Father's scolding this morning could hardly be surpassed even by the joy of a blind tortoise finding a piece of driftwood.[3] Thus did the sun slowly rise higher in the sky, and Senroku came home dragging his feet. . . .

Fifth Month, Second Day

Father took a turn for the worse. Although he was in great pain, my stepmother took no notice and was as contentious as usual. Ever since the business of the

---

2. Bear-gall bladder (*kumanoi*) was considered a rare and efficacious medicine.

3. A Buddhist metaphor expressing the difficulty of being born as a human and thus having the chance to hear the Buddhist dharma. Here Issa extends the meaning of this metaphor to describe an extremely rare situation.

land distribution, relations between my brother and Father had not been good. And although Senroku and I had different mothers, I couldn't help but think that the real reason for his unpleasant hostility was that we had been enemies in some previous life.

Father felt bad about my not getting any sleep at night and kindly suggested, "Why don't you take a nap and catch up on some sleep, or go outside and clear your head a bit?"

Hearing this, my stepmother became as nasty as ever toward Father, criticizing his every fault and forgetting all about the Three Obligations.[4] I realized with regret that my stepmother made Father suffer like this because I, whom she despised, was in close attendance at his bedside. But where else could I go if I were to get up and leave? . . .

Fifth Month, Sixth Day

Since the sky was clear and I thought that Father might be bored just lying around, I folded up his bedclothes and helped him prop himself up on them. Then he began to talk about old times.

"Well now, you've been without your real mother from the time you were three years old. And ever since you began to grow up, you haven't been on good terms with your stepmother. Day after day there was fighting, night after night the fires of hatred burned. There wasn't a moment when my heart knew any peace. It struck me that as long as we were together in one place, it would always be like that. So I sent you to far-off Edo in the spring of your fourteenth year, thinking that once you were away from home, we all might be closer. Ah, if only I had been your father in different circumstances. I would have passed on this house to you after three or four years, making you settle down and leaving me free to enjoy my retirement. You must have thought me a cruel parent indeed to have hired you out as an apprentice while you were still just a young skinny-bones. I hope you'll accept all this as fate resulting from our previous lives. This year I had intended to make a pilgrimage to the sites of the Twenty-four Disciples[5] and hoped that once in Edo I might meet up with you, so that even if I were to die from the rigors of the trip, you would be there keeping vigil. But now, for you to have come all the way here and to have nursed me like this—surely the connections between us in our past lives could not have been weak ones. So even though I might die right now, what regrets would I have?"

---

4. The Three Obligations (*sanjū*) for a woman are those of a daughter to her father, a wife to her husband, and a widow to her son.

5. These were the twenty-four disciples of Shinran who went out to preach throughout the land.

Tears were streaming down his face. I just sat there, looking down and unable to say anything. Because of his kindness, my debt to Father is deeper than the matchless snows of Mount Fuji, unmelted by the summer sun, and deeper than a twice-dyed crimson. Yet I hadn't stayed at home and taken care of him. Instead, I had drifted around like a floating cloud. Before I could wonder whether I had gone east, off I was to the west. The days and nights rolled on like a wheel going downhill, and twenty-five years had passed. To have stayed away from my father's side until my hair was white as frost—I wondered whether even the Five Violations could be worse than this.[6] In my heart, I prostrated myself and prayed for forgiveness.

But if I were to shed tears openly, it would surely make him feel even worse. So I wiped my eyes and said with a smile, "Now put things like that out of your mind. Just hurry up and get well." I gave him some medicine and added, "If you get better soon, I'll become the perfect farmer's son, the Yatarō you used to know. I'll cut hay, plow the land, and really set your mind at rest. Please forgive me for what I've been until now." When Father heard this, his joy was boundless. . . .

Fifth Month, Thirteenth Day

"I feel so good this morning that I want some saké," Father said. But since saké was strictly forbidden by the doctor, I decided I couldn't give him even a drop until he recovered. But someone who'd come to visit him said, "If you go this far in stopping him from doing what he likes, you may regret it later if he should die. Your regrets then will be to no avail. It would only be kind to give him a little of whatever he wants, just one or two mouthfuls."

And those people who were just waiting for any chance to do their mischief pricked up their ears and sat there listening.[7] They said, "This morning why don't you trust the patient's wishes? Give him some saké! Give him some saké!"

So I did. Like a boat that had reached its mooring, Father drank as if a long-desired dream had been realized. Like a whale gulping seawater, he downed about a quart during the morning. For a man who had not eaten solid food in twenty days to do such a thing—why, even a three-year-old would frown if he heard about it. I alone wrung my hands, but it was difficult to stand up to the two of them, and in the end I did not speak out. How it galled me the way they pretended to be outwardly caring for Father, when in fact they were rejoicing in their hearts at his impending death. . . .

---

6. The Five Violations (*gogyakuzai*)—patricide, matricide, killing an arhat, upsetting the harmony of a Buddhist monastery, and causing a buddha to bleed—cause a person to be denied entry into the Pure Land.

7. A reference to Satsu, the stepmother, and Senroku.

Fifth Month, Twentieth Day

Father's fever was gradually rising. In the morning he hardly ate anything; from around noon, his face was ghastly pale, his eyes swollen and half-shut, and he moved his lips as though he wanted to say something. With each inhalation and exhalation, his life was being sucked away in the rattling of the mucus. His breathing was getting progressively weaker. Through the window entered the light of the sun as it moved toward its end like a lamb to the slaughter. Father could no longer distinguish people's faces. There seemed to be no hope left.

Oh the pain of it! Would that I could have exchanged my life for his and just once more have seen him healthy again. When he had said he wanted something to eat, I had prohibited it, telling him it would be bad for him. Now I felt that all the resources of Jivaka or Bian Que would not be enough,[8] that the power of all the gods would not suffice, and that there was nothing else to do but recite the *nenbutsu*.

nesugata no	His sleeping form—
hae ou mo kyō	I shoo away the flies today.
ga kagiri kana	There's nothing more to do.

As the day drew to a close, I vainly tried to wet his lips with water from a vessel by his bedside. The twentieth-night moon shone in through the window, and all the neighborhood was sleeping quietly. As a cock's crow could be heard in the distance announcing the dawn, Father's breathing became increasingly shallow, and the mucus that I'd been concerned about from the very beginning was now time and again blocking his throat. If the thread of his life was to be cut, I wanted at least to remove the mucus. But I was not Hua Tuo[9] and so did not know any of his skillful techniques. Dejected, I threw up my hands in despair. The suffering, the grief in my heart as I could do nothing but wait for his final moments. . . . Even the gods showed no mercy. The night moved brightly into dawn, and about six o'clock, as though he had fallen into a deep sleep, Father breathed his last.

I took hold of his empty, pitiful body. Would that this were all a dream from which I could awake! But dream or reality, I felt I was wandering in darkness without a lamp, on a cold dawn in this fleeting world.

The impermanent spring flowers are seduced and scattered by the wind; this ignorant world's autumn moon is surrounded and hidden by clouds. The world knows—need I repeat it?—"That which lives must perish; that which is joined

---

8. Giba (Skt: Jivaka), one of the Buddha's disciples, was renowned for his medical skill. Bian Que was a famous Chinese doctor during the Warring States period who became the subject of a Chinese saying: "Even Bian Que cannot raise the dead."

9. Hua Tuo was a famous physician in the Latter Han period.

together will certainly fall apart."[10] And although this is the road that all must travel, yesterday I was foolish enough not to believe that my own father could go as soon as today.[11]

Those people who just two days before had defied my father and quarreled with him were now clinging to his body, tears streaming down their faces. Amid the clouds of their repetitions of Amida's name, I realized that the eternal vows of husband and wife—to grow old together, to be buried together—were in fact ever binding.[12]

[Buson shū, Issa shū, NKBT 58: 404–425, translated by Robert Huey]

HOKKU

kore ga maa	This, I guess, is
tsui no sumika ka	my last resting place—
yuki goshaku	five feet of snow![13]

Shichiban nikki, Eleventh Month of 1812

furusato ya	My old home—
yoru mo sawaru mo	wherever I turn, whatever I touch
ibara no hana	thorned roses[14]

Shichiban nikki

10. A well-known quotation from the Nirvana Sutra.

11. A reference to a well-known poem by Ariwara no Narihira: "Although I had already heard that everyone must travel down this road, I never thought that it would be today" (Kokinshū, no. 861).

12. This vow is found in the Book of Songs, 3:6, 4; 6:9, 3.

13. This poem encapsulates Issa's emotions when in 1813, at the age of fifty, after a long dispute with his stepmother and stepbrother, he was able to claim his portion of his father's inheritance and return to his hometown of Kashiwabara. Having decided to stay there for the rest of his life, he looks at the deep snow and imagines it covering his grave. An earlier version had shinu tokoro ka yo (the place where I will die!) for the middle line, which apparently was too blunt. Kaneko Toota observes that the first line is colloquial, the second is classical, and the last is harsh reality. The five feet of snow is not the beautiful snow found in classical poetry but the snow that implicitly oppresses, that is harsh and powerful.

14. The wild rose (ibara), a seasonal word for early summer, is associated with nostalgia, much like the "old home" (furusato), but instead of enjoying the fond memories of the past, Issa is wounded everywhere he turns by the thorns on the rose. According to the Seventh Diary, which includes this poem, in the Fifth Month of 1810, Issa traveled from Edo to his home town of Kashiwabara, where he unsuccessfully attempted to obtain from the mayor the will left by his deceased father. The cold reception given him by the mayor, his stepmother and stepbrother, and others in his hometown provides the backdrop for this poem.

umasō na	Delicious looking!
yuki ga fūwari	the snow
fūwari kana	falling softly, softly—[15]

Shichiban nikki, Eleventh Month of 1813

yuki tokete	Melting snow
mura ippai no	and the village overflowing
kodomo kana	with children![16]

Shichiban nikki, First Month of 1814

suzukaze no	Cool breeze—
magarikunete	twisting and turning
kitarikeri	it comes along[17]

Shichiban nikki, Sixth Month of 1815

yasegaeru	Skinny frog,
makeru na Issa	don't give up the fight!
kore ni ari	Issa is here![18]

Shichiban nikki, Fourth Month of 1816

---

15. Issa, who grew up in Japan's "snow country," wrote frequently about snow. In this poem he focuses on big flakes of snow, falling down slowly, almost as if they could be eaten like candy. *Fūwari, fūwari* suggests the snowflakes' light, floating movement. The hokku is typical of Issa in taking the perspective of a child. But Kuriyama Riichi points out that the poem is unusual for Issa, since he usually treats snow as an enemy.

16. *Yukidoke* (snow thawing) is a seasonal word for midspring. In the snow country, the heavy accumulations of the snow begin to melt with the arrival of strong sunshine in midspring. Instead of the expected floodwaters, the village is suddenly filled with children, eager to play outside in the sunshine. Because of spring's late arrival, the transition to warmth is sudden and festive, a mood captured in the phrase *mura ippai* (village overflowing).

17. This poem is about Issa's life as a transient in Edo. Here the *suzukaze*, a cool breeze bringing relief on a hot summer day, has to bend and twist; that is, it has to travel through the crooked backstreets of Edo, where the poor people live, to get to the poet's house, which is at the farthest remove. The poem suggests that Issa, now with a house in Kashiwabara, is looking back on his Edo days with considerable detachment and amusement.

18. This poem notes that Issa has seen a frog battle. In the spring, during the mating season, male frogs gathered to fight over a single female frog. In this context, the poet is calling out encouragement to a frog that appears to be losing the battle. The poem has been interpreted as showing Issa's sympathy for the small, weak, and vulnerable creatures (like himself). In this larger context, it also may mean that Issa, single and without a family for most of his life, is talking to himself about his marital prospects. "Don't give up!" (*makeru na Issa kore ni ari*) is a military phrase used by a commander to urge on his troops.

ari no michi	The line of ants
kumo ni mine yori	seems to start
tsuzukiken	from the towering clouds[19]

Ora ga haru, Sixth Month of 1819

suzume no ko	Little sparrows,
sokonoke sokonoke	step aside, step aside,
ouma ga tōru	Master Horse is coming through[20]

Ora ga haru, Shichiban nikki, Second Month of 1819

yare utsu na	Hey, don't swat the fly!
hae ga te o suri	he wrings his hands,
ashi o suru	wrings his feet[21]

Hachiban nikki, Sixth Month of 1821

[*Buson shū, Issa shū*, NKBT 58: 322–362, translated by Haruo Shirane]

MY SPRING (*ORA GA HARU*, 1819)

Each year Issa collected in a single volume the poetry and prose that he had composed. The best example is *My Spring* (*Ora ga haru*), a collection of haibun in his mature style that he wrote in 1819, the year in which he finally settled down in Kashiwabara. The three recurring themes in *My Spring* are his life as an oppressed stepson; his love for his daughter Sato, born to him late in his life; and his belief in the power of the Buddha (Issa was a follower of the True Pure Land sect). The climax of the book is the section referred to as "A World of Dew" (Tsuyu no yo), which describes the death of his daughter.

---

19. *Ari* (ants), a word that does not appear in waka, and *kumo no mine* (towering clouds, with flat bottoms rising straight up into the sky) are seasonal words for summer. The poem sets up a striking contrast between the black ants and the white clouds, the small and the large, the close and the distant.

20. This poem suggests a bystander warning the little sparrows to step aside as a horse approaches. A more interesting interpretation is that a child is on a bamboo play-horse, telling the baby sparrows to get out of the way. The phrase "step aside, step aside" (*sokonoke, sokonoke*) was the command used to clear the road when a samurai procession was passing through. The honorific word *ouma* (honorable horse) implies that the horse belongs to a samurai, a member of the social elite, whereas baby sparrows (*suzume no ko*), a seasonal word for spring, suggest someone of low status.

21. This poem is frequently cited as an example of Issa's compassion for helpless creatures. In typical Issa fashion, the fly (*hae*)—a summer seasonal word that does not appear in waka—is personified. Issa liked to write about those creatures—flies, mosquitoes, lice—that were hated by humans and on which he projected his own sense of victimization and alienation.

Orphan

Despondent when the other children chant, "You can always tell an orphan: standing in a doorway, gnawing at his nails!"—never joining in with the others, spending the livelong day in the field out back, crouched in the shadow of a pile of thatching—what a forlorn figure I cut, even to myself!

ware to kite	Come and
asobe ya oya no	play with me,
nai suzume	orphan sparrow!

Yatarō, at age six[22]

Giving the Breast

Last summer, around bamboo-planting time, my daughter was born into this world of sorrow. In order that, though ignorant, she might come to comprehend the way of things, we named her Sato.[23] Since celebrating her birthday this year, she has delighted in such little games as "Clappety, clappety, ah-wa-wa! Pat-a-pate, pat-a-pate, this-a-way, that-a-way!"[24] Yet once when she saw another child her age with a windmill toy, she wanted it so badly that she put up a huge fuss. We immediately got her one, but in no time she had put it in her mouth, drooled all over it, and cast it aside, and with nary a dewdrop of attachment, straightaway shifted her attention to something else. Just when it seemed she was absorbed in smashing a rice bowl to bits, she quickly wearied of that and began tearing the thin paper off the sliding *shōji* door. When I praised her, saying, "Good job, good job!" she took me at my word and, squealing with laughter, began ripping away at it for all she was worth.

She has not one speck of dust in her heart, which shines bright and pure as the harvest moon; she smoothes the furrows of my heart, just as if I were watching a performance by a peerless actor. When someone comes over and says to her, "Where's the bow-wow?" she will point to a dog. When asked, "Where's the caw-caw?" she will point to a crow. From her mouth down to the tips of her nails, she is sweet and overflowing with lovableness, and it seems to me she is gentler than a butterfly flitting among the first tender shoots of spring.

---

22. Yatarō was Kobayashi Issa's given name. The poetic persona here is that of a child who feels deep sympathy for the orphaned sparrow; Issa himself had lost his mother at an early age. An 1814 entry in *Seventh Diary* suggests, as here, that Issa was six or eight years old when he wrote this, but he was in fact about fifty-one.

23. A name suggesting *satoru*, or to achieve spiritual awakening.

24. This refers to a sequence of nursery games in which an adult and/or a child claps his hands together, pats his open mouth to make an "ah-wa-wa-wa!" sound, pats his head with both hands, and then shakes his head from side to side. The names Issa uses to describe these amusements (*te-uchi te-uchi a-wa-wa, otsumu ten-ten, kaburi kaburi*) are onomatopoeic baby talk.

This child must be under Buddha's protection, for on the night before memorial services,[25] as soon as we light the altar candles and sound the bell, no matter where she is, she quickly crawls over and folds her tiny fern-bud hands in prayer. Her voice as she chants "*Nanmu, nanmu!*"[26] is so appealing, so beguiling, so irresistible, so angelic! Whereas I, who am at an age when numerous white hairs now frost my head and rippling waves furrow my brow, do not know how to entrust myself to Amida, and shilly-shally my days away, put to shame by a two-year-old.[27] Yet the moment I leave the altar, I am sowing the seeds of hell: detesting the flies that swarm around my knee, cursing the mosquitoes that circle my table, and even drinking the saké forbidden by the Buddha.

Just about the time when the moon slips through our gate and the air grows quite cool, from outside comes the sound of dancing children's voices. She promptly throws down her little bowl and scoots out, half-crawling on one knee, calling out and gesticulating in her joy. Watching her like this, it occurs to me that one day soon I will see her grown to the age when she'll wear her hair parted[28] and I will see *her* dance — a performance surely far more beguiling than the music of the Twenty-five Bodhisattvas[29] — and I forget my waxing years, and all my cares evaporate.

She never stops moving her arms and legs for a split second all day long; she plays herself into exhaustion and sleeps until the morning sun is high. Her mother takes that time as her only holiday: she boils the rice and sweeps and tidies up the place, and fans herself to cool the sweat. Then, taking the sound of crying from the bedroom as her signal that the baby has awakened, she deftly takes her up in her arms and brings her to the field out back to pee. After that she nurses her; and as the child avidly suckles, patting her mother's chest and beaming, her mother, forgetting utterly the pain she suffered during the long months the baby was in the womb and the daily round of dirty diapers, strokes her as tenderly as if she had found a precious jewel in the lining of her robe.[30] How extraordinarily happy she looks!

---

25. For deceased relatives.

26. A childish attempt to say *Namu Amida Butsu*, a ritual invocation meaning "Hail Amida Buddha!" The chanting of this formulaic salutation, known as the *nenbutsu*, or meditating on the Buddha, was the core practice of members of the Pure Land sects of Japanese Buddhism. It was seen as a means of attaining salvation by rebirth in the Western Pure Land of Amida Buddha.

27. Sato (who was born on June 6, 1818) is one year old. Issa, following the contemporary Japanese system of counting a child as one year old at birth, calls her a two-year-old.

28. That is, in the style worn by children five to eight years old: shoulder length and parted in the middle.

29. The twenty-five bodhisattvas who, together with Amida Buddha himself, are said to come to Pure Land believers at the moment of death, mounted on purple clouds and playing exquisite music, to escort them to their rebirth in the Pure Land.

30. This refers to a parable related in chapter 8 of the Lotus Sutra, the "Prophecy of Enlightenment for Five Hundred Disciples," about a man who dines at the home of a prosperous friend, gets drunk, and falls asleep. While he is sleeping, the friend sews a priceless jewel into the lining

nomi no ato   Counting
kazoenagara ni   fleabites as she
soeji ka na   gives the breast[31]

Issa

A World of Dew

At the height of our enjoyment comes anguish.[32] This is indeed the way of this world of sorrow, but for this seedling thousand-year-old pine that had known not even half life's joys—for this sprig of but two leaflets, at the peak of her young laughter, to be possessed, unexpectedly as water in a sleeper's ear, by the savage god of pox! At the height of the eruption, she was like a budding first blossom that had no sooner bloomed than it was beaten down by muddy rains; just watching by her side was agony. Then two or three days passed and the pustules began to dry, and like mud sliding down a hillside when the snow thaws, the scabs came off; so we held a joyous celebration, wove a disk of rice straw, sprinkled it with saké and hot water, and sent the god on his way.[33] Yet she grew weaker and weaker, and our hopes each day ebbed lower than the day before, and finally, on the twenty-first day of the Sixth Month, together with the morning glories, she faded from this world.[34] Her mother clung to her dead face, sobbing and sobbing, and who could blame her? When things have reached this pass, one may put on a face of mature resignation, telling oneself that it does no good to wail, for "flowing water returns not to its source, nor the fallen blossom to the branch"[35]—but hard indeed to sever are the bonds of love.

---

of his robe and then leaves. The man awakens and sets out on a long journey full of hardships. Years later he encounters his friend again, and the friend, who symbolizes the Buddha, rebukes him and shows him the jewel, a metaphor for the innate buddha wisdom, which he had in his possession all the while.

31. That is, the mother tenderly touches each tiny wound on the infant's skin as she nurses her. The word *soeji*, rendered here as "gives the breast," actually indicates lying side by side with one's baby while nursing.

32. A paraphrase of a famous line from the *yuefu* "Song of the Autumn Wind" (*Qiufeng ci*), by China's Han emperor Wu (156–87 B.C.E.): "At the height of our enjoyment, sorrow burgeons."

33. A traditional ceremony to purify the afflicted person of the disease. The deity having been enticed aboard, the straw disk was floated off downstream.

34. Sato died on August 10, 1819, at the age of fourteen months.

35. Paraphrased from similar passages found in numerous Japanese and Chinese classical works. For example, a waka by Fujiwara no Tadafusa reads: "That I did not go before you—regrets for this come eight thousand times; sad it is that flowing water comes not back again" (*Kokinshū*, no. 837). And from fascicle 17 of the Chinese Chan (Zen) Buddhist classic *The Jingde-Era Record of the Transmission of the Lamp* (Ch. *Jingde chuan deng lu*, J. *Keitoku dentōroku*), compiled by Daoyuan in 1004: "A broken mirror reflects no more; a fallen blossom cannot waft up to the branch."

tsuyu no yo wa	This world of dew's
tsuyu no yo nagara	a world of dew, and yet—
sarinagara	and yet . . .

Issa

Come What May

Those believers who proclaim their "faith in other-power, faith in other-power!" and pray with all their effort concentrated solely on other-power, end up bound by the rope of other-power and fall into the flames of the hell of self-power.[36] Again, those who put in an order to Amida Buddha to "make this dirty world-ling's skin a gorgeous gold!"[37] and then, just leaving their order on file, turn smug and act as though already steeped from head to toe in buddhahood— they, too, turn out to be self-power schemers.[38]

But you may ask, "Then what approach must one adopt to conform to the teachings of your sect?" And I will answer: So far as I am aware, it involves no especially difficult complexities. You simply take all that garbage about "other-power" and "self-power" and let it drift out to sea. And as for the crucial issue of your next rebirth, just prostrate yourself before the Buddha, requesting only, "Whether I be bound for heaven or for hell, dispose of me as you see fit."

With this kind of doubtless resolution, never again will you find that no sooner have the words "Hail Amida Buddha!" left your lips than already you are stretching your web of greed across spring meadows like a grasping spider and hoodwinking others, nor will you ever again entertain, for even the merest moment, the thievish mentality of drawing off your neighbor's water into your

---

36. The term *tariki* (other power) refers to the Pure Land Buddhist approach of seeking salvation by depending on the power and beneficence of Amida Buddha, in contrast to seeking salvation through one's own efforts, as advocated by other schools of Buddhism. Pure Land Buddhists refer, often derisively, to this latter approach as based on *jiriki*, or "self-power."

37. Beings reborn in Amida Buddha's Pure Land are said to be born with skin of gold, like that of Amida Buddha himself.

38. As a member of the True Pure Land sect, Issa follows the teachings of its founder, Shinran (1173–1263), who asserted that if performed with complete faith, even a single repetition of the *nenbutsu* was sufficient to ensure rebirth in the Pure Land. Here Issa is describing two extreme interpretations of Shinran's doctrine that Pure Land believers are liable to accept. The first extreme is trying too hard, concentrating so intensely on one's faith in Amida's salvational power that one's own concentration itself becomes the true object of concentration, leading to the bondage of excessive self-consciousness. This, he suggests, is in fact a self-power approach to an other-power discipline. The other extreme is being too lazy: taking Shinran's assertion too simplistically and arrogantly regarding oneself as already saved, as though Pure Land rebirth were something one could simply order up like a new kimono. This again, Issa argues, is a misconception based on an essentially self-power attitude. From this point, he goes on to expound his view of the true meaning of faith in other-power, in effect charting a middle way between these two extremes.

own field. Then you need not trouble yourself to solemnly intone the name of the Buddha—for even without your praying, the Buddha will protect you. This is what we call the resting-in-contentment of our sect. Oh, wondrous grace![39]

to mo kaku mo	Come what may,
anata makase no	I leave it up to Him
toshi no kure	this year's end[40]

Issa, age fifty-seven

Second year of Bunsei, Twelfth Month, twenty-ninth day[41]

[*Buson shū, Issa shū*, NKBT 58: 432–476, translated by Herschel Miller]

---

39. *Ana kashiko*: an auspicious interjection of awe and gratitude (a bit like "Hosanna!" or "Glory! Hallelujah!"). It was traditionally spoken at the end of every section when reciting a certain type of True Pure Land text.

40. That is, I simply leave everything in the hands of Amida Buddha.

41. February 13, 1820. By premodern Japanese reckoning, this was the last day of the year and the eve of a new spring. The book's opening verses are dated New Year's Day, the first day of the First Month of the second year of Bunsei. Complementing that date, this final passage rounds out both the volume and the year.

Chapter 26

WAKA IN THE LATE EDO PERIOD

Although the quality of prose fiction generally deteriorated toward the end of the Edo period, it was a rich and interesting period for waka, owing to the work of such talented provincial poets as Kagawa Kageki (1768–1843) from Tottori, Ryōkan (1758–1831) from Echigo, Tachibana Akemi (1828–1868) from Fukui, and Ōkuma Kotomichi (1798–1869) from Chikuzen. Both Ryōkan and Akemi were deeply influenced by the *Man'yōshū*, the eighth-century anthology of poetry, but wrote about everyday, commoner life. Kotomichi also wrote about everyday life and is noted for his poetic treatises, which stress individuality and freedom in vocabulary.

OZAWA ROAN

Ozawa Roan (1723–1801) was born in Osaka. Although his father had been a samurai in Matsuyama, a castle town in present-day Nara, he had left his position and moved to Osaka. Roan grew up in Osaka but moved to Kyoto, where he was adopted by Honjō Katsuna, a samurai there. When he was around thirty, Roan became the student of Reizei Tamemura (1712–1774), a noted court poet who had received the secret transmission of the *Kokinshū*, the early-tenth-century imperial anthology of waka, and was the leading member of the aristocratic Reizei school. Roan took his Ozawa family name again when he was about thirty-five and entered the service of another samurai. In 1765, his position as a samurai was terminated, and for the remainder of his life he concentrated on waka, while working as a teacher, poet, and scholar of the classics and Chinese studies.

Roan greatly admired the *Kokinshū* and loved the *Kokinwaka rokujō*, another Heian anthology of waka. He is best known for his advocacy of "direct-word poetry" (*tadakoto uta*), in which the poet expresses his or her thoughts as they are naturally, without restriction in language or rhetoric. Roan became known during the Kansei era (1789–1801) as one of Kyoto's "four kings" of commoner (*jige*) waka—as opposed to the court (*dōjō*) waka of his teacher Tamemura, who eventually expelled him from the Reizei school. Roan had close relationships with such men of letters as Ban Kōkei, Ueda Akinari, Motoori Norinaga, and Rai Sanyō and produced a number of outstanding disciples, the most notable being Kagawa Kageki (1768–1843), who became the leader of Kyoto-Osaka commoner waka in the late Edo period.

WAKA

Ōigawa	By the Ōi River
tsuki to hana to no	the moon and the cherry blossoms
oboroyo ni	enveloped by the evening mist—
hitori kasumanu	all that remains unclouded:
nami no oto kana	the sound of the waves![1]
Uzumasa no	The fierce roar
fukaki hayashi o	of the wind
hibikikuru	echoing through the deep forest
kaze no to sugoki	of Uzumasa—
aki no yūgure	autumn dusk[2]

[*Kinsei wakashū*, NKBT 93: 262, 282, translated by Peter Flueckiger]

---

1. Roan composed this spring poem by the banks of the Ōi River, at the foot of Arashiyama, in Kyoto, where he was relaxing with his friends after a day spent viewing the cherry blossoms. The poem presents an implicit contrast between the unobstructed afternoon view and the misty evening. The verb *kasumu* (to be obscured by spring haze), which is usually associated with visual phenomena, brings into sharp focus the sound of waves, which break the implicit quiet of the misty evening scene.

2. Roan composed this poem while living in Uzumasa, on the western edge of Kyoto, where he moved temporarily after his house was destroyed in the Great Tenmei Fire of 1788 and where he remained until 1792. Roan presents here a dynamic, powerful perspective on "autumn dusk" (*aki no yūgure*) that differs dramatically from the quiet, meditative, static view of autumn dusk in the famous "three evening" (*sanseki*) poems in the *Shinkokinshū*.

THE ANCIENT MIDDLE ROAD THROUGH FURU
(*FURU NO NAKAMICHI*, 1790)

Roan's pronouncements in *The Ancient Middle Road Through Furu*,[3] which he wrote late in life and portions of which are translated here, represent a major break with earlier views of waka. Roan attacked Kamo no Mabuchi for what he regarded as a serious contradiction: Mabuchi attempted to express human emotions directly, but he composed in the *Man'yōshū* style and with *Man'yōshū* vocabulary, which were foreign to contemporary readers. Roan, by contrast, argued that poetry should be without rhetorical artifice and should express thoughts and emotions using the language of the present, a poetic ideal he referred to as *tadakoto uta* (direct-word poetry). This term appears in Ki no Tsurayuki's kana preface to the *Kokinshū*, where it is listed as one of the "six poetic styles" (*rikugi*). Roan, however, offers his own interpretation of it, that it refers to poetry produced from a correct (*tadashi*) heart using direct or ordinary (*tada*) words (*koto*). In the first passage from the section called "Dust and Dirt"[4] and in the last passage from "Responses to Questions," Roan presents another theory, that of the notions of "universal emotion" (*dōjō*) and "fresh emotion" (*shinjō*), which have been compared with Bashō's haikai notion of the "unchanging and ever-changing" (*fueki ryūkō*). Here Roan contends that human emotions (*ninjō*) as expressed in poetry remain unchanged over time and thus are the "same emotions" (*dōjō*) in both past and present. At the same time, however, poetry directly expresses an individual's heart and in this sense has no poetic predecessors. That is, the constant changing of individual emotions is what gives poetry its freshness and vitality.

Dust and Dirt

There is nothing that comes before one's own heart. One does not compose poetry by following others, nor does one compose based on precedent. This shows that poetry is without rules and without teachers.

Although this principle is apparent, when I see what has been composed by the ancients, my own ignorance and incapacity drive me to want to imitate them. This is the second principle of poetry. But when we view this from the perspective of what I described earlier, we find that all our own feelings are in accord with what has been composed by the ancients.

As far as heaven and earth extend, in both past and present, human emotions

---

3. Furu is a poetic place-name (*utamakura*) located in Isonokami in Nara. The title of Roan's treatise alludes to a poem by Ki no Tsurayuki: "Had we never met, I would not long for you with a longing as long as the ancient middle road through Furu in Isonokami" (*Kokinshū*, no. 679).

4. This phrase appears in the kana preface to the *Kokinshū*: "Just as a long journey begins with the first step and continues for months and years, and a tall mountain grows from the dust and dirt [*chirihiji*] at its base until it reaches up to where the heavenly clouds trail, so too must poetry have developed."

are the same. Therefore when I concentrate my heart fully, it is completely in agreement with the spirit [*kokoro*] of the poetry of the ancients. This should not be confused with the "freshness" that I spoke of earlier. The universal character of human emotions is unchanged from past to present. "Freshness" refers to the way in which these emotions constantly change. Whether we come to know emotions through the poetry of the ancients or whether we come to know them through what we originally feel, we come to know the same thing. . . .

Ki no Tsurayuki spoke of direct-word poetry [*tadakoto uta*]. His personal poetry collection[5] is based on this notion. Its poetry flows easily, and its meaning is clearly expressed. In this style, it is easy to speak one's heart. In judgments of poetry matches, when the comment is made that a poem is "too direct," it refers to this style. The fact that directness is despised is surely a sign of the decline of poetry. I consider it good for the heart to be correct and the words to flow freely, and bad for the heart to be labored and the words to be crafted.

Reed Sprouts

Poetry is the natural Way [*onozukaranaru michi*] of this country, so when composing, we should not try to be clever, nor should we try to be exalted. We should not try to be entertaining, or graceful, or unusual. It is a natural Way, so if we seek a certain manner, we will lose naturalness. Poetry simply involves expressing the things we feel in the present moment, using words that are intelligible and that we use in our own speech.

For example, in a moment when I feel joyful, upon seeing blossoms I will compose the words "The flowers too bloom with the color of joy!" In a moment when I feel sad, upon hearing a bird, I will compose something like "Does the bird cry out because it too is sad?" The preface to the *Kokinshū* says that poetry "expresses what is felt upon seeing and hearing things."

There is nothing, then, that comes before our own heart. Day and night, it is constantly in motion and never stands still, and the thoughts that we have at each moment are always in flux. There is nothing fresher in the heart than this, and we express these feelings directly.

For example, "hot!" is a poem, and "cold!" is also a poem. The preface to the *Kokinshū* says, "Upon hearing the warblers crying among the blossoms and the voices of the frogs in the water, can we say that there is any living thing that does not produce poetry?" Living things do not cry out if they do not feel anything in their hearts. To express this in two or three lines is also a poem. To express it in a *konponka*, in a thirty-one-syllable waka, in a sedōka, or in a chōka is all poetry.[6] When there are many lines, they can express the heart at greater length.

---

5. A reference to the *Tsurayuki Collection* (*Tsurayuki shū*).

6. The *konponka*, ambiguously defined in the Chinese preface to the *Kokinshū*, may be a

Responses to Questions

The distinction between universal emotions [dōjō] and fresh emotions [shinjō] can be explained using a metaphor. From the beginning of the universe until the present day, it has remained the case that even though many rivers flow into the sea, the sea is able to receive them all without overflowing. This represents what is the same in both past and present. But day and night, the water never ceases to gush forth from the sources of these rivers. It is constantly in motion, together with the creative force of the universe, and is not the same water as in the past. The water that we can see gushing forth in each successive moment is like the human emotions that are spontaneously produced anew upon contact with external things.

[Kinsei kabunshū ge, SNKBT 68: 39, 44–47, 67, translated by Peter Flueckiger]

RYŌKAN

Besides being a noted kanshi poet, the Zen monk Ryōkan (1758–1831) also wrote various kinds of poetry in Japanese: the thirty-one-syllable waka, the thirty-eight-syllable sedōka, and the chōka (long poem). The latter two forms are found in the Man'yōshū but afterward were used only infrequently. Ryōkan deeply admired the Man'yōshū for its seeming simplicity and openness, and he often borrowed its archaic diction and "pillow words" (makurakotoba), or epithets, to depict the everyday life around him. He also stressed rhythm and melody in his poems.

WAKA

Yamakage no	Faint trickle of
iwama wo tsutau	mossy water from
koke mizu no	a crevice in the mountain rock:
kasuka ni ware wa	the clear still way
sumitaru kamo	I pass through the world.[7]

[RZ 1: 89, translated by Burton Watson]

---

twenty-four-syllable poem in a 5–7–5–7 format. Roan is listing poetic forms in order of increasing length. The sedōka is a thirty-eight-syllable poem in a 5–7–7–5–7–7 format. The chōka is a long poem of indeterminate length, consisting of alternating five- and seven-syllable lines and ending with two, seven-syllable lines.

7. The first three lines are a "preface" (jo) to the word "faintly" (kasuka ni), which describes both the moss stream and the poet's life. The verb sumu in the last line is a pun meaning both "to live" in the world and "to be clear" spiritually, like the water of the mountain stream. Note the repeated "a" vowel.

Hachi no ko wo   I've forgotten
waga wasururedomo   my begging bowl
toru hito wa nashi   but no one would take it
toru hito wa nashi   no one would take it—
hachi no ko aware   how sad for my begging bowl.[8]

[*Kinsei wakashū*, NKBT 93: 217, translated by Burton Watson]

Kasumi tatsu   On a long misty
nagaki haru hi ni   spring day—
kodomora to   hitting the handball
temari tsukitsutsu   with the children,
kono hi kurashitsu   I pass the whole day.[9]

[*Kinsei wakashū*, NKBT 93: 180, translated by Haruo Shirane]

Tsukiyumi no   Wait for the moonlight
hikari wo machite   before you try
kaherimase   to go home—
yamaji wa kuri no   the mountain trail's
iga no shigeki ni   so thick with chestnut burs![10]

[*Kinsei wakashū*, NKBT 93: 232, translated by Burton Watson]

Composed on the evening of the fifteenth day of the Seventh Month:

Kaze wa kiyoshi   The breeze is fresh,
tsuki wa sayakeshi   the moonlight bright—
iza tomo ni   let's dance together

---

8. Ryōkan composed many poems about the begging bowl, which priests carried for receiving money and rice but was normally considered to be of no value or interest. This is the second envoy (*hanka*) to a long poem (*chōka*).

9. This waka is an envoy (*hanka*), following a long poem (*chōka*) on the same subject. "Misty" (*kasumi tatsu*) is an epithet for "spring" (*haru*), the kind of phrase found in the *Man'yōshū*, no. 846). But the rest of the poem, which describes his everyday life, avoids such archaic rhetoric. This stylistic mixture is typical of Ryōkan's waka. The long spring days, which Ryōkan spends playing handball with the children, implicitly feel all too short after the long severe winters in Echigo. Ryōkan generates a rhythm through the repeated use of the vowel *tsu* at the end of lines 1, 4, and 5.

10. This poem was written when Abe Sadayoshi, Ryōkan's friend at the bottom of Mount Kugami, visited his hut, the Gogō-an (Five Measures of Rice Retreat), on the slope of Mount Kugami, and they drank saké together. A variant text has for the first word *tsukiyomi*, a *Man'yōshū* word that originally referred to the god of the moon and, later, the moon. This term has rich mythic and poetic associations, including a sense of warm hospitality for neighbors, as in "Come under the light of the moon—we're at the mountain edge, not far away" (*Man'yōshū*, no. 670). The poem mixes the suggestion that Ryōkan wants to detain his guest as long as possible with the suggestion that he is concerned about his friend's safety at night.

odori akasamu	the whole night through,
oi no nagori ni	a lasting memory for my old age.[11]

[*Kinsei wakashū*, NKBT 93: 198, translated by Burton Watson]

KAGAWA KAGEKI

Kagawa Kageki (1768–1843) was the second son of a samurai in Inaba Province (Tottori Prefecture). When Kagawa Kageki was seven, his father died, and he was adopted by his uncle. At the age of twenty-six, he moved to Kyoto to study waka and work as a masseur, using the name Arai Genzō. Three years later Kageki was adopted as the son of a Nijō school waka master, Kagawa Kagemoto, and assumed the name by which we know him. But after he became acquainted with Ozawa Roan and was influenced by his notion of "direct-word poetry" (*tadakoto uta*), he turned against the Nijō school, which had maintained its authority through the Kokin denju (secret transmissions of the *Kokinshū*), had an amicable separation from his adopted father, and set up his own school, the Keien school. Although Kageki composed in the *Kokinshū* style, he also used colloquial language and emphasized actual feelings and direct observation, giving his poetry a highly modern tone. The Keien school, which gained a national following and came to include as many as a thousand adherents, remained a major force in waka through the early Meiji period. Kageki's most famous collection of poetry is *Katsura Garden, a Branch* (*Keien isshi*), in which the following poems appear.

WAKA

Fuji no ne o	Looking back upon
konoma konoma ni	the peak of Fuji
kaherimite	through the trees, through the branches,
matsu no kage fumu	walking in the shade of pines
ukishimagahara	at Ukishimagahara[12]

---

11. The headnote, "Composed on the evening of the fifteenth day of the Seventh Month," suggests that this is a poem about Bon odori, Festival of the Dead dances. Apparently, Ryōkan loved dancing. The poem breaks after the first two parallel lines, both of which end with the syllable *shi*, giving it a dance rhythm. The last three lines, marked by two opening o's and two closing ni's, continue the strong pulse. Faced with his own impending death and a profound sense of impermanence, Ryōkan takes a buoyant, active approach to life, creating a sense of both joy and sadness, youth and old age.

12. Ukishimagahara is a swampy area at the southern foot of Mount Fuji. According to his travel diary, Kageki wrote this winter poem on the ninth day of the Eleventh Month in 1818 while traveling from Edo to Nagoya on the Tōkaidō, or Eastern Seaboard Highway. The poem establishes an implicit contrast between the green of the pines and the white of the snow-bound peak of Mount Fuji as well as between the near trees and the far mountain.

TOPIC UNKNOWN

Tomoshibi no	While reading
kage nite miru to	under the light of a lamp,
omohu ma ni	before I know it,
fumi no uhe shiroku	the day has arrived white
yo ha akenikeri	on top of the page.[13]

PLACE WHERE THEY SELL BLACK LOGS

Mese ya mese	Buy it! Buy it!
yuhuke no tsumaki	firewood for your dinner
hayaku mese	Buy it quick!
kaherusa tooshi	It's a long way home
Ōhara no sato	to Ōhara![14]

[*Kinsei wakashū*, NKBT 93: 357, 364, 378, translated by Haruo Shirane]

OBJECTIONS TO NEW LEARNING
(*NIIMANABI IKEN*, 1811, PUBLISHED 1815)

In *Objections to New Learning*, a selection from which is translated here, Kageki criticized the archaic revival in waka, attacking Kamo no Mabuchi's earlier poetic treatise *New Learning* (*Niimanabi*) for its attempt to return to the eighth-century *Man'yōshū*. Despite his respect for the *Kokinshū*, Kageki, under the heavy influence of Ozawa Roan, argued for modernity in poetry and offered his famous "theory of rhythm" (*shirabe no setsu*), which meant composing poetry that expressed natural feelings in a mellifluous rhythm (*shirabe*). Roan had contended that "the poetry of the current age should use the language of the current age and the rhythm of the current age," a position that had a profound influence on the future direction of waka.

Mabuchi wrote in *New Learning*, "In ancient poetry it is rhythm [*shirabe*] that is primary, and this is because it is sung."

In my opinion, the only reason both the rhythm and the content in ancient poetry are well ordered is that this poetry was produced by the true

---

13. A "Miscellaneous" topic poem.
14. This "haikai" waka takes the voice of an "Ōhara woman" (*Ōharame*), a term used to refer to the women who came to Kyoto from the village of Ōhara (north of the city) to sell blackened firewood, which they balanced on their heads. The repetition of the *se* and *sa* syllables recreates the rhythmic voice of the seller.

heart [*magokoro*]. Poetry that comes from the true heart is filled with the rhythm of heaven and earth. Just as the wind gusting in the skies makes sounds when it blows against something, everything the true heart encounters has a rhythm.

This process can be compared to clouds and water. When clouds form, they rise up like waves or hang down in the shape of flowers or flow out like women's sleeves or gather in the form of a peak. When water flows, it forms chaotic patterns or gathers in deep pools and acquires a bluish tinge or freezes and becomes like a mirror or forms a jewel-like spray. Although clouds and water go through hundreds and thousands of such transformations, they do not do so out of any conscious intention. Rather, the clouds simply float along with the breeze, and the water just flows along the ground.

The language of poetry is like this as well. When a poem is short, it takes the form of a *tanka* [short poem], and when it is long, it becomes a *chōka* [long poem], and everything is manifested just as it is seen and heard. Poetry is the form taken by the emotions upon encountering things. This form naturally has rhythm, and the fact that its patterning [*aya*] is unparalleled and appears to be constructed and embellished is because there is nothing in heaven and earth more graceful and beautiful than the sincerity [*makoto*] out of which this poetry emerges. We should say, then, that the rhythm of ancient poetry is produced naturally [*onozukara*]. It is greatly mistaken to think that it was consciously given rhythm. . . .

Mabuchi wrote, "Always look to the *Man'yōshū* to learn the spirit of poetry. If over time, one composes with the aim of making one's own poetry like that of the *Man'yōshū*, its rhythm and spirit will surely enter one's heart."

I consider this to be greatly in error. Poetry naturally acquires rhythm in accordance with the movement of the heart. It is not something to which one gives conscious thought, so how could there be time to imitate the past? If one were to imitate the past, it would just be an embellished falsehood. And even if one tried to imitate the past, could one really do so successfully? It is quite ridiculous to think that one has been successful in imitating the past. The emergence and transformations of the rhythm of poetry originated in heaven and earth, and unconsciously this rhythm takes on the form of each age. In addition, each person is born with a particular rhythm. It is different for each person, just as each person's face is different. But although each person's rhythm is different, it adheres to the style of the age. . . . Poetry of the current age should use the language of the current age and the rhythm of the current age. Still, among the various rhythms with which each person is individually endowed, some naturally resemble the style of the *Man'yōshū* or the *Kokinshū* or various other styles. The rhythm cannot go outside the style of the current age, though, so in reality it is not the style of the *Man'yōshū* or the *Kokinshū* but, rather, the style of the current age.

[*Karonshū*, NKBZ 50: 585–586, 597–599, translated by Peter Flueckiger]

TACHIBANA AKEMI

Tachibana Akemi (1812–1868) was born the eldest son of a paper merchant in Echizen (Fukui Prefecture), on the Japan Sea coast. Akemi's parents died when he was young. He became a priest for a short time but then returned to secular life and studied *kokugaku* (nativist studies) with Tanaka Ōhide, a disciple of Motoori Norinaga. Akemi's poetry, however, differed significantly from Norinaga's in being fresh in both expression and subject matter. Akemi was a "life" poet, drawing his material from everyday life. After returning to Echizen, he handed over the family business to his half brother and became a recluse, occasionally becoming impoverished.

During his lifetime, Akemi's waka were known only to those from Echizen, but in 1899, Masaoka Shiki, the pioneer of the modern tanka (thirty-one-syllable modern waka) movement, wrote in the newspaper *Japan* (*Nihon*) that Akemi "learned from the *Man'yōshū* and went beyond the *Man'yōshū*. With regard to sight, sound, and touch, there is nothing that he does not include in his thirty-one syllables. . . . As a poet, there has been no one like him since Sanetomo." The article made Akemi nationally famous, and his poetry about his personal experiences came to have considerable influence on modern tanka.

WAKA

Although it was the *kokugaku* poet Kamo no Mabuchi who had called for serial composition (*rensaku*), a series of waka on the same topic, it was Akemi who was probably its most successful practitioner. The following selections are from serial compositions in the *Poetry Collection of Shinobunoya* (*Shinobunoya kashū*), a title taken from one of Akemi's pen names. The first two poems are from a sequence of eight poems on mining, which begins with the entrance into the mines and ends with the excavation of the ore. Akemi's friend Tomita Iyahiko had received an order from the bakufu in 1859 to open a silver mine in Echizen. Akemi visited the mine the next year. This is probably the first waka to be composed on hard labor and is notable for its focus on the human body and the suffering of the miners.

WALKING AROUND WATCHING THE MINERS DIGGING

Hi no hikari   Deep in mountain caves
itaranu yama no   where no sun rays reach
hora no uchi ni   they enter,
hi tomoshi irite   torches flaming
kane horiidasu   digging out metal

Mahadaka no   Stark naked,
wonoko murewite   the men crowd forward,

aragane no
marogarikudaku
tsuchiuchifurite

flailing hammers
to smash
lumps of ore

[*Kinsei wakashū*, NKBT 93: 406, translated by Burton Watson]

GATHERED ANTS

Ari to ari
unazukiahite
nani ka koto
arige ni hashiru
nishi he higashi he

One ant and another
nodding to each other,
something seems to have
happened—they rush
to the west, to the east[15]

[*Kinsei wakashū*, NKBT 93: 441, translated by Haruo Shirane]

The next two poems are from *Compositions on Solitary Pleasures* (*Dokurakugin*), a series of fifty-two waka that begin with the phrase "Pleasure is" (*tanoshimi wa*). This series is reminiscent of the lists created by Sei Shōnagon in *The Pillow Book*, but unlike her elegant lists, Akemi focuses on everyday, commoner life. Married with three sons, Akemi took delight in the simple pleasures in life, especially with regard to family life. In the second poem, it is clear that he is poor (only rarely eating fish) but finds happiness in his children's enjoying this rare treat.

Tanoshimi ha
mare ni uwo nite
kora mina ga
umashi umashi to
ihite kuhu toki

Pleasure is
when you rarely cook
fish, and the children
all say "Yum, yum"
as they eat.

Tanoshimi ha
yo ni tokigataku
suru fumi no
kokoro wo hitori
satorieshi toki

Pleasure is
when you understand
all by yourself
a book that people
find impenetrable.

[*Kinsei wakashū*, NKBT 93: 429, translated by Haruo Shirane]

---

15. This poem, which embeds the word *ari* (ant) in the phrase *arige* (seems to have) and creates syntactic symmetry in the first and last lines, belongs to a series of nine poems on the topic of "Gathered Ants." Insects that traditionally appear in waka include fireflies, crickets, and butterflies, but there are almost no earlier examples of ants. Akemi also wrote a series of three poems on lice, another unusual insect topic. Here the personification of the ants, which are presented as a microcosm of human society, gives the poem a humorous haikai flavor.

ŌKUMA KOTOMICHI

Ōkuma Kotomichi (1798–1868) was born into a merchant family in Chikuzen (Fukuoka Prefecture), in Kyūshū. When he was thirty-nine, he turned over his family business to his younger brother and concentrated on composing waka. Later he became a student of kanshi poetry, and in his waka he was influenced by Kagawa Kageki's notion of expressing one's true emotions (but not by his notion of rhythm, or *shirabe*). When he was sixty, Kotomichi moved to Osaka, and five years later, in 1863, he published *The Grass Path Collection (Sōkei shū)*, a compendium of his own poetry. Kotomichi returned to Fukuoka in 1867 and died the following year.

WAKA

Kotomichi wrote a number of poems about children that capture their innocence and charm. In the second poem here, the poet does not notice the sound of the evening temple bell until he hears the last ring, which seems to linger. This kind of attention to the small surprises in everyday life is typical of Kotomichi, who avoids traditional poetic associations and instead looks directly at everyday life, in a way anticipating modern tanka.

Warahabe no	The kite
makura no moto no	at the child's
ikanobori	bedside
yume no sora ni ya	must be soaring high
maiagaruramu	in the sky of his dreams.

[*Ōkuma Kotomichi to sono uta*, p. 107, translated by Haruo Shirane]

VESPERS

Itsu yori ka	Since when
iriahi no kane ha	has the temple bell
naritsuramu	been ringing?
kokorozukitaru	noticing
hate no hito koe	the last sound

[*Kinsei wakashū*, NKBT 93: 463, translated by Haruo Shirane]

A PINWHEEL

Imo ga se ni	Sleeping on
neburu waraha no	the mother's back—

utsutsu naki
te ni sahe meguru
kazaguruma kana

the pinwheel spins
even in the baby's
unconscious hand.

[*Kinsei wakashū*, NKBT 93: 468, translated by Peter Flueckiger]

WORDS TO MYSELF (*HITORIGOCHI*, 1844)

In a poetic treatise entitled *Words to Myself*, some of which is translated here, Koto-michi condemns those who study the ancients (specifically the nativist scholar Motoori Norinaga) and try to imitate ancient poetry but end up creating only "wood-puppet poetry" (*deku uta*). He argues that those who do not imitate the ancients—which Kotomichi certainly did not—and instead compose with fresh eyes and emotions actually come closer in spirit to the ancients.

There is something I will, for now, refer to as "wood-puppet poetry" [*deku uta*]. It lacks a spirit [*tamashii*], and both its form and its content are from the past. No matter how many such poems one composes, it is like trying to scoop up water with a net. There is little in the poetry of people today that does not resemble such a leaky net. How long will it be before these puppets acquire a spirit? When I examine the poems of rural people, I find many who spend their entire lives as puppets.

The ancients are my teachers, but they are not me. I am a person of the Tenpō era [1830–1844]; I am not one of the ancients. When people pointlessly follow the ancients, they forget who they are. On the surface, they assume the appearance of high ministers, and the poetry they compose indeed seems exalted, but this is like a merchant dressing up as a nobleman. It is entirely an imitation, like what one sees when watching kabuki.

As I advised a certain poet, imitation is easy—even a kabuki actor can make himself into Sugawara no Michizane.[16] But can those who truly wish to become like Sugawara no Michizane do so by acting? And can those who wish to compose poetry resembling that of the ancients do so through artistry? If one wants to be a good person, one must begin with one's heart, and if one wants to compose good poetry, one must also begin with one's heart. When one composes poetry by taking one's heart as the seed, at first it will naturally contain lowly and vulgar [*zoku*] sentiments and will not resemble the appropriate form. With the passage of time, though, it will gradually come closer to the ancients. I consider those who do not resemble the ancients at all to be close to them, and those who greatly resemble the ancients to be distant from them. . . .

Poetry expresses human emotions [*ninjō*] and does not contain anything else.

---

16. Sugawara no Michizane (845–903), a scholar and high-ranking minister, famous for his poetry in Chinese. After his death he was deified as the god of learning.

As I said earlier, poetry cannot be created by reflecting on things, so the Way of poetry does not insist that things be a particular way but, rather, is entirely based on human emotion. Therefore, if the Chinese heart is my true heart [*magokoro*], there is nothing I can do about it. If the Buddhist heart is my true heart, I cannot help it. If we compose poetry by avoiding the Chinese heart and the Buddhist heart, we may believe that we are producing poetry in the style of our country. But our country has used Confucianism and Buddhism since ancient times, and people today have absorbed them since they were born. Therefore it is difficult to get rid of them, and moreover, Confucianism and Buddhism are not things that we should try to get rid of.

[NKT 8: 473, 479, translated by Peter Flueckiger]

Chapter 27

RAKUGO

Rakugo is the modern word for the art of oral storytelling, a performance genre that can be traced back to the late medieval period when *otogishū*, or storytellers, were retained by samurai generals for entertainment and sometimes advice. The term *rakugo* (literally, words with a twist) was first used around 1887, in the Meiji period (1868–1912), and the art continues to be popular today. In the seventeenth century, the humorous stories of the more aristocratic storytellers in Kyoto were collected in *Today's Tales of Yesterday* (*Kinō wa kyō no monogatari*, ca. 1615), which now is classified as a kana-zōshi. By the late seventeenth century, such performance conventions as the gestures of the storyteller and the assumption that the story was fictional had been established. Typically, the rakugo performer sits on a cushion, simultaneously employs mime and speech, uses a different voice for each character, and presents one or more humorous or frightening stories, each of which has an unexpected twist (*ochi*) at the end. The rakugo performer usually uses a fan or towel as a prop, abbreviates the kind of lyrical description found in *naniwa-bushi*, a late-Edo form of storytelling to musical accompaniment, and moves the story forward through quick dialogue and action. By the late eighteenth century, this art of storytelling had spread from the Kyoto-Osaka region, where it was established, to Edo, where it was called *otoshibanashi* (stories with a twist) and flourished alongside sharebon, kibyōshi, kyōka, senryū, and other humorous genres. Male geisha or jesters (*hōkan*) in the licensed quarters also used this art form. By the beginning of the nineteenth century, there were more than 120 storytelling halls (*yose*) in Edo alone.

SANYŪTEI ENCHŌ

Sanyūtei Enchō (1839–1900), considered the founder of modern rakugo, was born in Yushima in Edo and started to perform at the age of seven. He became a master of Edo rakugo, specializing in love stories (*ninjōbanashi*) and ghost stories (*kaidanbanashi*), the short-hand transcriptions of which became critical to the establishment of the movement in Japan to unify the written and spoken languages (*genbun itchi*). When he was seventeen, he took the performance name of Enchō, began performing his own compositions, and became noted for the composition and performance of long ghost-love stories such as *Peony Lantern Ghost Story*.

PEONY LANTERN GHOST STORY
(*KAIDAN BOTAN DŌRŌ*, 1861, PUBLISHED 1884)

Peony Lantern Ghost Story, part of which is translated here, greatly expands Asai Ryōi's short story "The Peony Lantern" (Botan tōrō), part of Ryōi's *Hand Puppets* (*Otogi bōko*, 1666) collection, and combines it with other ghost stories and real events. (In addition, the name of Ogihara, the male protagonist in Ryōi's version, has been changed to Hagiwara in Enchō's rendition.) In 1861 Enchō first performed *Peony Lantern Ghost Story* over a period of twenty-two nights. Then in 1884 Enchō's performance was transcribed by the scribe Wakabayashi Kanzō and published as a twelve-volume book, the first printing of a rakugo performance. Enchō's spellbinding performances of the tale became immensely popular, and in 1892 it became a hit kabuki play, starring Onoe Kikugorō V, who simultaneously played Kōsuke and Tomozō, the good and bad servants, and even the ghost of the maid Oyone.

The story takes place in Edo in 1743. A *hatamoto* (direct vassal of the shogun) named Iijima Heizaemon, better known as Heitarō, kills an insolent and drunken samurai and then, by chance, hires the samurai's son Kōsuke as a servant. Heitarō's wife, Oyuki, gives birth to a daughter, Otsuyu, and dies, and Oyuki's maid Okuni becomes Heitarō's mistress. Okuni, however, is having a secret affair with the neighbor Miyagino Genjirō, and the two decide to kill Heitarō. Kōsuke discovers the plot and tries to stab Genjirō but mistakenly strikes Heitarō. Knowing that Kōsuke has been faithful to him and that he earlier killed his father, Heitarō allows himself to be slain. Okuni and Genjirō at this point flee while Kōsuke prepares to avenge his master's death. Meanwhile, the daughter Otsuyu has fallen in love with Hagiwara Shinzaburō, a masterless samurai, whom Heitarō rejects. Otsuyu thereby dies of longing and becomes a ghost. Each night, she, led by her maid Oyone carrying a peony-design lantern, visits Hagiwara's house. Learning from his servant Tomozō that he has been making love every night to a ghost, Hagiwara requests the protective prayers of a Buddhist priest and obtains a miniature Buddha statue, which he places around his neck, and also a paper talisman, which he places on his window. The thwarted ghosts thus turn to Tomozō and his wife, Omine, whom they bribe with a hundred *ryō* of gold to remove the talisman and statue. Possessed by the vengeful spirit of Oyuki, Hagiwara dies. Fearing that they will be discovered, Tomozō and Omine flee to Kurihashi (present-day Saitama Prefecture) where, using the hundred pieces of gold, they set up a hardware store. Tomozō, however, has an affair with Okuni and kills his wife, Omine, when she goes crazy with jealousy. Whereas Tomozō finally is arrested in Edo, Kōsuke remains faithful to his master and eventually avenges his death and restores his own family's fortunes. The following translation is of the famous scene leading up to the entrance of the ghosts of Otsuyu and Oyone into Hagiwara's house, in which Enchō used the sound of the wooden clogs (*karan koron*) to signal their approach.

Volume 5, part 12

While Tomozō talked with the ghosts, his wife hid in the closet with old clothes over her head, perspiring profusely and trying to breathe as quietly as she could. Finally the ghost maid Oyone left, followed by the young woman ghost. After their shapes had grown dim and disappeared, Tomozō knocked on the closet door.

"Omine," he said, "you can come out now."

"Are you sure they're not doing something horrible out there?" she answered.

"They're gone now. Come out! Come out!"

"How did it go?" she said, leaving the closet.

"Well, it went this way and that way, and I negotiated as hard as I could, so all the saké wore off. When I have saké in me, I'm not afraid of anything, even a samurai. But when those ghosts came right up near me, you know, it was like someone poured a bucket of cold water on my head. I was completely sober again, and I couldn't say things the way I wanted to."

"In the closet sometimes I listened, and I could hear your voice talking with them. I was terrified."

"I told the ghosts to bring a hundred gold coins. Both of us, I said, depend on what we get from Hagiwara. If something should happen to him, I said, you and I would have no way to get along. I said that if they brought us a hundred gold coins, I'd pull off the paper charm pasted on the back wall of his house by the window. The ghosts promised to come with the money tomorrow night and asked me again to pull off the paper charm. They also told me they couldn't go inside Hagiwara's house as long as he has a little statue of Kaion Buddha around his neck to protect him. So they also asked me to find a way to steal it and take it outside the house. They said the statue was pure gold and a little more than four inches high. I saw it myself when the temple was showing it a while back. The priest said something or other about it. Yes, let's see, well, he definitely did. It's supposed to be some sort of priceless masterpiece. The ghosts want me to steal it. What do you think?"

"This has possibilities," Omine said. "Luck's beginning to come our way now. We could sell the statue somewhere, couldn't we?"

"We could never sell it in Edo. But we could take it somewhere in the country and sell it. Even melted down, it would still be worth a lot. We'd get a hundred gold coins for it minimum. Maybe two hundred."

"Two hundred? Really? We'd be set for the rest of our lives. So be careful, won't you? Do this right."

"I will, I will. But it's around his neck. Getting him to take it off won't be easy. Have any ideas?"

"Hagiwara hasn't been bathing at all these days," said Omine. "He just sits there inside his mosquito net chanting his sutra. Tell him he smells and get him to wash. Then while I'm bathing him, you go where he can't see and steal the statue."

"Yes. Yes, that's good. But how can we get him outside?"

"If he won't go outside, take out three sections of the mat floor in the living room and have him wash there."

Omine and Tomozō talked their plan over carefully. The next day they warmed a large basin of water, and Tomozō carried it over to his employer's house.

"Mr. Hagiwara, sir," he said, "we've heated some water today, so please use it to bathe yourself. I brought this right over so you could wash first."

"No," Hagiwara said, "no, really, I can't. Something's come up, and I'm not supposed to bathe right now."

"If you don't bathe when it gets this hot," Tomozō said, "your body will suffer. Your sleeping robe's dripping with sweat, and the weather's good today. You can't go out and wash if it rains. They say it's very bad for your body if you don't bathe."

"I go out and wash only after sundown. It's a bit complicated to explain, but I just can't do it right now."

"Well then," Tomozō said, "take out three sections of the mat floor over there."

"That won't work, either. I'd have to take off my clothes. I'm not supposed to."

"Don't you know what Dr. Hakuōdō, the diviner next door, says? He says that when people let themselves get dirty, then pretty soon they get sick or ghosts and other bad spirits get inside. As long as you keep yourself clean, he says, ghosts and things like that have no way to get inside you. You let yourself get all grubby and grimy, and well, the sickness appears from inside your own mind. And not only that. If you stay dirty for a long time, ghosts will get in."

"You mean ghosts will come inside if I stay dirty too long?"

"Come inside?" Tomozō said. "They'll come in pairs holding hands!"

"I can't let that happen," Hagiwara said. "Pull up three sections of the mat floor. I'll wash inside."

Tomozō and his wife knew they had Hagiwara now, and they got ready as quickly as they could.

"Bring the basin, will you?"

"Get a bucket and fill it with hot water."

Hagiwara took off his robe, and then he took off the buddha statue hanging around his neck in a long pouch and handed it to Tomozō. "This is a very precious protective image. Go put it on the altar while I'm bathing."

"Yes, sir, right away. Omine, wash him, will you? Well, but gently, understand?"

"Mr. Hagiwara," said Omine, "please don't move around. Stand still while I wash the back of your neck. Please hold your head down so I can get to it. Lean over, please. Farther than that, farther."

Pretending that the back of Hagiwara's neck needed a lot of washing, Omine made sure he wasn't able to see what was happening. As she washed, Tomozō squeezed the long, belt-like pouch and pushed out the black lacquer box inside. He opened the small double doors in front and found layers of black silk inside cushioning the statue. Unwrapping the silk, he took out the four-inch pure gold Kaion Buddha statue and put it inside the front of his robe. In its place he put a tile statue of the fierce buddha Fudō he'd brought with him that was almost the same weight. Then he put everything back just as it had been before and placed the pouch belt on the altar to Hagiwara's patron god.

"Hey Omine," Tomozō said, "you're sure taking a long time. If you wash him too long, the blood will go to his head. How about finishing up?"

"That's enough," Hagiwara said. He dried himself off and put on a clean bathrobe, feeling refreshed and satisfied. Being only human, he had no way of knowing that his bathrobe would also be his shroud and that his bath had also been his corpse's final washing. He was in a wonderful mood as he had Tomozō lock the doors and windows, and when it got dark, he strung up his mosquito net, went inside, and began fervently reciting the Uhō Dharani Sutra.

Meanwhile, Tomozō and Omine were in their house congratulating themselves for obtaining something they could never have expected to possess.

"It's impressive," Omine said. "It must be extremely valuable."

"We have no way of knowing why, but this buddha's so powerful the ghosts can't get in as long as it's in the house."

"Luck really is coming our way, isn't it?"

"Yeah, but what about tonight?" Tomozō said. "The ghosts are coming with a hundred gold coins tonight. And if we have this thing, they won't be able to get in. We've got a problem."

"Well, go outside and meet them before they get here."

"Are you crazy? How could I possibly do that?"

"Then ask someone to keep it for you tonight."

"Ask someone? Everyone knows I don't have anything worth anything. If they asked me what it was, they'd know I stole it and turn me in. I can't pawn it, either. And if I keep the statue here, well, if I pull off the paper charm the ghosts will get in through Hagiwara's window, and then they'll bite him to death or possess him and kill him somehow or other. When people examine the body, they'll find his protective buddha's missing and guess it was stolen. Naturally they'll suspect the diviner and me. But the diviner's an old man, and everybody knows he's honest, so they'll suspect me right off. They'll search the whole house for this thing. If they ever found it, I'd be in big, big trouble. So I know what I'll do. I'll put it inside an old jelly cake box and bury it in the garden. I can stand a bamboo pole above it so I won't forget where it is. Even if they search the house, they'll never find it there. If we go somewhere else for a while, in six months or a year nobody will even remember it, and we can go dig it up again. We won't need to worry about anything."

"Sounds promising. Go on out, then. Dig a deep hole and bury it. That'll be that."

Tomozō quickly found an old jelly cake box and put the statue in it. Then he carried it out to the garden, buried it deep in the ground between some vegetables, stuck in a bamboo pole above it, and came back again. Now all he had to do was wait for the ghosts to bring the coins. Celebrating early, Tomozō and Omine toasted each other and exchanged many cups of saké.

At last, Omine said she thought it must be almost two, and she went and hid in the closet. Tomozō sat alone, drinking and waiting for the ghosts. Soon he heard the two o'clock bell booming nearby in Ueno. Then there was only silence. The sounds of trickling water stopped, and even the grasses and trees seemed to be sleeping. All Tomozō could hear were the faint, melancholy cries of crickets by the wall of the house. There was something eerie about the dark, and he shuddered. Then from the direction of Shimizudani, he heard the familiar sound of women's wooden clogs coming steadily closer. Clack-clock, clack-clock, clack-clock. Tomozō knew the ghosts had come. He was so frightened that the hairs curled up on his skin. He hunched over and made himself as small as he could and watched. He thought he saw them at the hedge, but before he knew it they were on the low veranda.

"Tomozō! Tomozō!"

Tomozō was unable to speak. Finally he replied, "Yes, I'm here."

"We're very sorry to bother you every night with our request," came back the voice of the servant ghost. "But the paper charm is still pasted beside Mr. Hagiwara's back window. Won't you please pull it off? The young woman is anxious to meet Mr. Hagiwara, and she's beginning to criticize me and act very cross. I just don't know what to do any more. Please, pity us both and pull off the paper."

"I'll pull it off for you. Yes, I will. I certainly will. I'm definitely going to pull it off. Did you bring the hundred gold coins?"

Tomozō lies on his back beneath the ladder while the women ghosts enter the house through the window. From the 1884 edition.

"We've brought the full amount with us. Did you dispose of the Kaion Buddha statue around his neck?"

"Yes. I took it outside and hid it."

"Well, then, here are the hundred gold coins."

The ghost thrust the money toward Tomozō, and he took it, imagining it was a trick of some sort. But as he lifted the coins, he realized they had the full weight of gold, and when he looked at them closely, he saw they were real. He'd never seen this much money in one place before. He quickly forgot his fear, and trembling all over, he went outside.

"Won't you both come with me?" he asked the ghosts. He got out a twelve-foot ladder and walked across the garden, leaning it up against the window grating on the back side of Hagiwara's house. Controlling the shaking in his legs, he climbed carefully up the rungs and finally reached the top. Then he reached out his hand and tried to pull off the paper charm. But by then he was shaking so hard that he couldn't get it to come off. Finally he decided just to rip it off all at once, and he pulled so hard that the ladder began to shake and sway. Surprised, Tomozō lost his footing and fell backward onto the ground. He was unable to get up again and lay there with the paper in one fist. All he could manage to do was chant Amida Buddha's name again and again in a quavering voice.

The ghosts looked at each other happily. "Tonight you'll be able to meet

Mr. Hagiwara again," the servant ghost said. "You'll have all the time you need to explain to him how you feel about his not letting you in like this."

The servant ghost took the hand of the young woman ghost. When they looked at Tomozō, he was still lying on his back clutching the paper charm. Hiding their faces with their sleeves, the two ghosts went right through the back window and into the house.

[*Sanyūtei Enchō shū, Meiji bungaku zenshū,* 1965, 10: 38–40,
translated by Chris Drake]

ENGLISH-LANGUAGE BIBLIOGRAPHY

GENERAL READINGS FOR THE EARLY MODERN PERIOD

Gerstle, Andrew C., ed. *Eighteenth-Century Japan: Culture and Society*. Sydney: Allen & Unwin, 1989.

Guth, Christine. *Art of Edo Japan: The Artist and the City, 1615–1868*. New York: Abrams, 1996.

Hall, John Whitney, ed. *The Cambridge History of Japan*. Vol. 4, *Early Modern Japan*. Cambridge: Cambridge University Press, 1988.

Keene, Donald. *World Within Walls: Japanese Literature of the Pre-Modern Era, 1600–1868*. New York: Holt, Rinehart and Winston, 1976.

Nakane, Chie, and Shinzaburō Ōishi, eds. *Tokugawa Japan: The Social and Economic Antecedents of Modern Japan*. Tokyo: University of Tokyo Press, 1991.

Nishiyama, Matsunosuke. *Edo Culture: Daily Life and Diversions in Urban Japan, 1600–1868*. Honolulu: University of Hawai'i Press, 1997.

Totman, Conrad. *Early Modern Japan*. Berkeley and Los Angeles: University of California Press, 1993.

EARLY MODERN POETRY AND POETIC PROSE

Early Haikai

Hibbett, Howard S. "The Japanese Comic Linked-Verse Tradition." *Harvard Journal of Asiatic Studies* 23 (1961): 76–92.

Imoto, Noichi. "Independence of Hokku in Haikai and Its Significance." *Acta Asiatica* 9 (1964): 20–35.

Matsuo Bashō and Hokku

Fujikawa, Fumiko. "The Influence of Tu Fu on Bashō." *Monumenta Nipponica* 20 (1965): 374–388.

Kawamoto, Kōji. *The Poetics of Japanese Verse: Imagery, Structure, Meter.* Tokyo: University of Tokyo Press, 2000.

Ogata, Tsutomu. "Five Methods for Appreciating Bashō's Haiku." *Acta Asiatica* 28 (1975): 42–61.

Shirane, Haruo. *Traces of Dreams: Landscape, Cultural Memory, and the Poetry of Bashō.* Stanford, Calif.: Stanford University Press, 1997.

Ueda, Makoto, trans. *Bashō and His Interpreters: Selected Hokku with Commentary.* Stanford, Calif.: Stanford University Press, 1992.

Ueda, Makoto. *Matsuo Bashō: The Master Haiku Poet.* Tokyo: Kōdansha International, 1982.

Bashō's Linked Verse

Mayhew, Lenore, trans. *Monkey's Raincoat (Sarumino): Linked Poetry of the Bashō School with Haiku Selections.* Rutland, Vt.: Tuttle, 1985.

Miner, Earl, trans. *Japanese Linked Poetry.* Princeton, N.J.: Princeton University Press, 1979.

Miner, Earl, and Hiroko Odagiri, trans. *The Monkey's Straw Raincoat and Other Poetry of the Bashō School.* Princeton, N.J.: Princeton University Press, 1981.

Shirane, Haruo. "Matsuo Bashō and the Poetics of Scent." *Harvard Journal of Asiatic Studies* 52 (1991): 77–110.

Terasaki, Etsuko. "*Hatsushigure:* A Linked Verse Sequence by Bashō and His Disciples." *Harvard Journal of Asiatic Studies* 36 (1976): 204–239.

Oku no hosomichi and Other Poetic Diaries by Bashō

Britton, Dorothy, trans. *A Haiku Journey: Bashō's "Narrow Road to a Far Province."* Tokyo: Kōdansha International, 1980.

Corman, Cid, and Susumu Kamaike, trans. *Back Roads to Far Towns.* New York: Mushinsha/Grossman, 1968.

Keene, Donald. "Bashō's Diaries." *Japan Quarterly* 32 (1985): 374–383.

Keene, Donald. "Bashō's Journey of 1684." *Asia Major*, n.s., 7 (1959): 131–144.

Keene, Donald, trans. *The Narrow Road to Oku.* New York: Kodansha International, 1996.

McCullough, Helen, trans. "The Narrow Road of the Interior." In *Classical Japanese Prose: An Anthology,* edited by Helen McCullough, pp. 522–551. Stanford, Calif.: Stanford University Press, 1990.

Sato, Hiroaki, trans. *Bashō's Narrow Road: Spring and Autumn Passages: Two Works.* Berkeley, Calif.: Stone Bridge Press, 1996.

Shirane, Haruo. "Aisatsu: The Poet as Guest." In *New Leaves: Studies and Translations in Honor of Edward Seidensticker*, edited by Aileen Gatten and Anthony H. Chambers, pp. 89–113. Ann Arbor: University of Michigan, Center for Japanese Studies, 1993.

Shirane, Haruo. "Matsuo Bashō's *Oku no hosomichi* and the Anxiety of Influence." In *Currents in Japanese Culture: Translations and Transformations*, edited by Amy Vladeck Heinrich, pp. 171–183. New York: Columbia University Press, 1997.

Shirane, Haruo. *Traces of Dreams: Landscape, Cultural Memory, and the Poetry of Bashō.* Stanford, Calif.: Stanford University Press, 1997.

Yuasa, Nobuyuki, trans. *Bashō: The Narrow Road to the Deep North and Other Travel Sketches.* London: Penguin Books, 1968.

Yosa Buson

Morris, Mark. "Buson and Shiki." *Harvard Journal of Asiatic Studies* 44 (1984): 381–425.

Morris, Mark. "Buson and Shiki." *Harvard Journal of Asiatic Studies* 45 (1985): 256–319.

Nippon gakujutsu shinkōkai, ed. *Haikai and Haiku*, pp. 41–51. Tokyo: Nippon gakujutsu shinkōkai, 1958.

Sawa, Yuki, and Edith M. Shiffert. *Haiku Master Buson.* San Francisco: Heian International, 1978.

Ueda, Makoto. *The Path of Flowering Thorn: The Life and Poetry of Yosa Buson.* Stanford, Calif.: Stanford University Press, 1998.

Zolbrod, Leon M. "Buson's Poetic Ideals: The Theory and Practice of Haikai in the Age of Revival, 1771–1784." *Journal of the Association of Teachers of Japanese* 9 (1974): 1–20.

Zolbrod, Leon M. "The Busy Year: Buson's Life and Work, 1777." *Transactions of the Asiatic Society of Japan* 3 (1988): 53–81.

Zolbrod, Leon M. "Death of a Poet-Painter: Yosa Buson's Last Year, 1783–84." In *Studies on Japanese Culture*, vol. 1, edited by Saburo Ota and Rikutaro Fukuda, pp. 146–154. Tokyo: Japan P.E.N. Club, 1973.

Zolbrod, Leon M. "Talking Poetry: Buson's View of the Art of Haiku." *Literature East and West* 15–16 (1971–1972): 719–734.

Kobayashi Issa

Hamill, Sam, trans. *The Spring of My Life and Selected Haiku.* Boston: Shambhala, 1997.

Huey, Robert N. "Journal of My Father's Last Days: Issa's *Chichi no shūen no ki.*" *Monumenta Nipponica* 39 (1984): 25–54.

Mackenzie, Lewis, trans. *The Autumn Wind.* London: Murray, 1957.

Nippon gakujutsu shinkōkai, ed. *Haikai and Haiku*, pp. 69–78. Tokyo: Nippon gakujutsu shinkōkai, 1958.

Yuasa, Nobuyuki, trans. *The Year of My Life: A Translation of Issa's "Oraga haru."* Berkeley and Los Angeles: University of California Press, 1960.

Other Haiku Poets and Haibun

Blyth, Reginald H. *Haiku.* 4 vols. Tokyo: Hokuseidō Press, 1949–1952.

Blyth, Reginald H. *A History of Haiku.* Vol. 1, *From the Beginnings up to Issa.* Tokyo: Hokuseidō Press, 1963.

Blyth, Reginald H. *A History of Haiku.* Vol. 2, *From Issa up to the Present.* Tokyo: Hokuseidō Press, 1964.

Carter, Steven, trans. *Traditional Japanese Poetry: An Anthology.* Stanford, Calif.: Stanford University Press, 1991.

Donegan, Patricia, and Yoshie Ishibashi, eds. and trans. *Chiyo-ni: Woman Haiku Master.* Tokyo: Tuttle, 1996.

Hass, Robert. *The Essential Haiku: Versions of Basho, Buson, and Issa.* Hopewell, N.J.: Ecco Press, 1994.

Henderson, Harold G., ed. and trans. *An Introduction to Haiku: An Anthology of Poems and Poets from Bashō to Shiki.* Garden City, N.Y.: Doubleday Anchor Books, 1958.

Nippon gakujutsu shinkōkai, ed. *Haikai and Haiku.* Tokyo: Nippon gakujutsu shinkōkai, 1958.

Rogers, Laurence. "Rags and Tatters: The *Uzuragoromo* of Yokoi Yayu." *Monumenta Nipponica* 34 (1979): 279–310.

Yasuda, Kenneth. *The Japanese Haiku: Its Essential Nature, History, and Possibilities in English, with Selected Examples.* Rutland, Vt.: Tuttle, 1957.

Senryū: Comic Haiku

Blyth, Reginald H. *Japanese Life and Characters in Senryū.* Tokyo: Hokuseidō Press, 1961.

Blyth, Reginald H., ed. *Edo Satirical Verse Anthologies.* Tokyo: Hokuseidō Press, 1961.

Ueda, Makoto, ed. and trans. *Light Verse from the Floating World: An Anthology of Premodern Japanese Senryu.* New York: Columbia University Press, 1999.

Poetry in Chinese: Kanshi and Kyōshi

Bradstock, Timothy, and Judith Rabinovitch, eds. *An Anthology of Kanshi (Chinese Verse) by Japanese Poets of the Edo Period (1603–1868).* Lewiston, Maine: Mellen, 1997.

Markus, Andrew. "Dōmyaku Sensei and 'The Housemaid's Ballad' (1769)." *Harvard Journal of Asiatic Studies* 58 (1998): 5–58.

Pollack, David. "Kyōshi: Japanese 'Wild Poetry.'" *Journal of Asian Studies* 38 (1979): 499–517.

Watson, Burton, trans. *Grass Hill: Poems and Prose by the Japanese Monk Gensei.* New York: Columbia University Press, 1983.

Watson, Burton, trans. *Kanshi: The Poetry of Ishikawa Jōzan and Other Edo Period Poets.* San Francisco: North Point Press, 1990.

Ryōkan

Abe, Ryūichi, and Peter Haskel, trans. *Great Fool: Zen Master Ryōkan — Poems, Letters, and Other Writings.* Honolulu: University of Hawai'i Press, 1996.

Watson, Burton, trans. *Ryōkan: Zen Monk-Poet of Japan.* New York: Columbia University Press, 1977.

Yuasa, Nobuyuki, trans. *The Zen Poems of Ryōkan.* Princeton, N.J.: Princeton University Press, 1981.

PROSE FICTION

Kana-zōshi

Lane, Richard. "The Beginnings of the Modern Japanese Novel: *Kana-zōshi,* 1600–1682." *Harvard Journal of Asiatic Studies* 20 (1957): 644–701.

Mori, Maryellen Toman, trans. *The Peony Lantern,* by Asai Ryōi. Hollywood, Calif.: Highmoonoon, 2000.

Putzar, Edward. "'Inu makura': The Dog Pillow." *Harvard Journal of Asiatic Studies* 28 (1968): 98–113.

Putzar, Edward, trans. *"Chikusai monogatari:* A Partial Translation." *Monumenta Nipponica* 16 (1960–1961): 161–195.

Rucinski, Jack. "A Japanese Burlesque: *Nise monogatari.*" *Monumenta Nipponica* 30 (1975): 39–62.

Ihara Saikaku

Befu, Ben, trans. *Worldly Mental Calculations: An Annotated Translation of Ihara Saikaku's "Seken munezan'yo."* Berkeley and Los Angeles: University of California Press, 1976.

Callahan, Caryl Ann. *Tales of Samurai Honor.* Tokyo: Monumenta Nipponica, 1981.

de Bary, William Theodore, trans. *Five Women Who Loved Love.* Rutland, Vt.: Tuttle, 1956.

Hamada, Kengi, trans. *The Life of an Amorous Man.* Rutland, Vt.: Tuttle, 1964.

Hibbett, Howard S. *The Floating World in Japanese Fiction.* New York: Oxford University Press, 1959.

Hibbett, Howard S. "Saikaku and Burlesque Fiction." *Harvard Journal of Asiatic Studies* 20 (1957): 53–73.

Lane, Richard. "Saikaku and the Japanese Novel of Realism." *Japan Quarterly* 4 (1957): 178–188.

Lane, Richard, trans. "Three Stories from Saikaku." *Japan Quarterly* 5 (1958): 71–82.

Lane, Richard, trans. "Two Samurai Tales: Romance and Realism in Old Japan." *Atlantic Monthly* 195 (1955): 126–127.

Leutner, Robert. "Saikaku's Parting Gift—Translations from Saikaku's *Okimiyage.*" *Monumenta Nipponica* 30 (1975): 357–391.

Marcus, Virginia. "A Miscellany of Old Letters: Saikaku's *Yorozu no fumihogu.*" *Monumenta Nipponica* 40 (1985): 257–282.

Morris, Ivan, trans. *The Life of an Amorous Woman.* New York: New Directions, 1963.

Nōma, Kōshin. "Saikaku's Adoption of *Shukō* from *Kabuki* and *Joruri.*" *Acta Asiatica* 28 (1975): 62–83.

Nosco, Peter, trans. *Some Final Words of Advice.* Rutland, Vt.: Tuttle, 1980.

Sargent, G. W., trans. *The Japanese Family Storehouse or the Millionaire's Gospel Modernized.* Cambridge: Cambridge University Press, 1959.

Schalow, Paul Gordon, trans. *The Great Mirror of Male Love.* Stanford, Calif.: Stanford University Press, 1990.

Ejima Kiseki and Later Ukiyo-zōshi

Fox, Charles E. "Old Stories, New Modes: Ejima Kiseki's *Ukiyo oyaji katagi.*" *Monumenta Nipponica* 43 (1988): 63–93.

Hibbett, Howard S. *The Floating World in Japanese Fiction.* New York: Oxford University Press, 1959.

Lane, Richard. "Saikaku's Contemporaries and Followers: The Ukiyo-zōshi, 1680–1780." *Monumenta Nipponica* 14 (1958–1959): 125–137.

Hiraga Gennai

Jones, Stanleigh H., Jr. "Scholar, Scientist, Popular Author, Hiraga Gennai, 1728–1780." Ph.D. diss., Columbia University, 1971.

Ueda Akinari

Araki, James T. "A Critical Approach to the 'Ugetsu monogatari.'" *Monumenta Nipponica* 22 (1967): 49–64.

Chambers, Anthony H., trans. "Hankai: A Translation from *Harusame mongatari* by Ueda Akinari." *Monumenta Nipponica* 25 (1970): 371–406.

Hamada, Kengi, trans. *Tales of Moonlight and Rain: Japanese Gothic Tales.* Tokyo: University of Tokyo Press, 1971.

Jackman, Barry, trans. *Tales of the Spring Rain: "Harusame monogatari" by Ueda Akinari.* Tokyo: Japan Foundation, 1975.

Saunders, Dale, trans. "*Ugetsu monogatari* or *Tales of Moonlight and Rain.*" *Monumenta Nipponica* 21 (1966): 171–202.

Washburn, Dennis. "Ghostwriters and Literary Haunts: Subordinating Ethics to Art in *Ugetsu monogatari.*" *Monumenta Nipponica* 45 (1990): 39–74.

Young, Blake Morgan. *Ueda Akinari.* Vancouver: University of British Columbia Press, 1982.

Zolbrod, Leon M., trans. *Ugetsu monogatari: Tales of Moonlight and Rain*. Vancouver: University of British Columbia Press, 1974.

Takebe Ayatari

Marceau, Lawrence E. "Portraying the Sense: Takebe Ayatari's Literary and Painting Theories." *Transactions of the International Conference of Orientalists in Japan* 37 (1992): 85–103.
Young, Blake Morgan, trans. "A Tale of the Western Hills: Takebe Ayatari's *Nishiyama monogatari*." *Monumenta Nipponica* 37 (1982): 77–121.

Sharebon

Araki, James T. "Sharebon: Books for Men of Mode." *Monumenta Nipponica* 24 (1969): 31–45.
Kornicki, Peter F. "*Nishiki no ura:* An Instance of Censorship and the Structure of a Sharebon." *Monumenta Nipponica* 32 (1977): 153–188.
Miller, J. Scott. "The Hybrid Narrative of Kyoden's Sharebon." *Monumenta Nipponica* 43 (1988): 133–152.

Kibyōshi

Araki, James T. "The Dream Pillow in Edo Fiction, 1772–81." *Monumenta Nipponica* 25 (1970): 43–105.
Jones, Sumie. "William Hogarth and Kitao Masanobu: Reading Eighteenth-Century Pictorial Narratives." *Yearbook of Comparative and General Literature* 34 (1985): 37–73.
Iwasaki, Haruko. "The Literature of Wit and Humor in Late-Eighteenth-Century Edo." In *The Floating World Revisited,* edited by Donald Jenkins, pp. 47–61. Portland, Ore.: Portland Art Museum, 1993.

Kokkeibon: Shikitei Sanba and Jippensha Ikku

Leutner, Robert. *Shikitei Sanba and the Comic Tradition in Edo Fiction*. Cambridge, Mass.: Harvard University, Council on East Asian Studies, 1985.
Satchell, Thomas, trans. *Shanks' Mare: Being a Translation of the Tokaido Volumes of Hizakurige, Japan's Great Comic Novel of Travel and Ribaldry.* 1929. Reprint, Rutland, Vt.: Tuttle, 1988.

Yomihon

Zolbrod, Leon M. "The Allegory of Evil in Satomi and the Eight 'Dogs.'" In *Essays on Japanese Literature,* edited by Katushiko Takeda, pp. 76–94. Tokyo: Waseda University Press, 1977.

Zolbrod, Leon M. "The Autumn of the Epic Romance in Japan: Theme and Motif in Takizawa Bakin's Historical Novels." *Literature East and West* 14 (1970): 172–184.

Zolbrod, Leon M. *Takizawa Bakin.* New York: Twayne, 1967.

Zolbrod, Leon M. "Tigers, Boars, and Severed Heads: Parallel Series of Episodes in Eight 'Dogs' and 'Men of the Marshes.'" *Chung Chi Journal* 7 (1967): 30–39.

Zolbrod, Leon M. "Yomihon: The Appearance of the Historical Novel in Late Eighteenth Century and Early Nineteenth Century Japan." *Journal of Asian Studies* 25 (1966): 485–498.

Ryūtei Tanehiko

Markus, Andrew Lawrence. *The Willow in Autumn: Ryūtei Tanehiko, 1783–1842.* Cambridge, Mass.: Harvard University, Council on East Asian Studies, 1993.

Early Modern Books and Publishing

Chibbett, David. *The History of Japanese Printing and Book Illustration.* Tokyo: Kodansha International, 1977.

Hillier, Jack. *The Art of the Japanese Book.* 2 vols. London: Philip Wilson for Sotheby's, 1987.

Kornicki, Peter. *The Book in Japan: A Cultural History from the Beginnings to the Nineteenth Century.* Leiden: Brill, 1998.

Japanese Theater in General

Arnott, Peter D. *The Theatres of Japan.* New York: St. Martin's Press, 1969.

Bowers, Faubion. *Japanese Theatre.* Parts 2 and 3. New York: Hill & Wang, 1959.

Brandon, James. *The Cambridge Guide to Asian Theatre.* Cambridge: Cambridge University Press, 1993.

Brazell, Karen, ed. *Traditional Japanese Theater: An Anthology of Plays.* New York: Columbia University Press, 1998.

Inoura, Yoshinobu, and Toshio Kawatake. *The Traditional Theater of Japan.* New York: Weatherhill, in collaboration with the Japan Foundation, 1981.

Kawatake, Toshio. *A History of Japanese Theatre.* Vol. 2, *Bunraku and Kabuki.* Tokyo: Kokusai bunka shinkōkai, 1971.

Ortolani, Benito. *The Japanese Theatre: From Shamanistic Ritual to Contemporary Pluralism.* Rev. ed. Princeton, N.J.: Princeton University Press, 1995.

Bunraku in General

Adachi, Barbara Curtis. *Backstage at Bunraku: A Behind the Scenes Look at Japan's Traditional Puppet Theater.* New York: Weatherhill, 1985.

Adachi, Barbara Curtis. *The Voices and Hands of Bunraku.* Tokyo: Kōdansha International, 1978.

Dunn, C. U. *The Early Japanese Puppet Drama.* London: Luzac, 1966.

Keene, Donald. *Bunraku: The Art of the Japanese Puppet Theatre.* Tokyo: Kōdansha International, 1965.

Scott, Adolphe Clarence. *The Puppet Theater of Japan.* Rutland, Vt.: Tuttle, 1963.

Yūda, Yoshio. "The Formation of Early Modern *Jōruri.*" *Acta Asiatica* 28 (1975): 20–41.

Chikamatsu Monzaemon

Gerstle, C. Andrew, trans. *Chikamatsu: Five Late Plays.* New York: Columbia University Press, 2001.

Gerstle, C. Andrew. *Circles of Fantasy: Convention in the Plays of Chikamatsu.* Cambridge, Mass.: Harvard University, Council on East Asian Studies, 1986.

Gerstle, C. Andrew. "Hero as Murderer in Chikamatsu." *Monumenta Nipponica* 51 (1996): 317–356.

Gerstle, C. Andrew. "Heroic Honor: Chikamatsu and the Samurai Ideal." *Harvard Journal of Asiatic Studies* 57 (1997): 307–382.

Keene, Donald, trans. *Four Major Plays of Chikamatsu.* New York: Columbia University Press, 1969.

Keene, Donald, trans. *Major Plays of Chikamatsu.* New York: Columbia University Press, 1961.

Mueller, Jacqueline. "A Chronicle of Great Peace Played Out on a Chessboard: Chikamatsu Mon'zaemon's *Goban taiheiki.*" *Harvard Journal of Asiatic Studies* 46 (1986): 221–267.

Shively, Donald H. "Chikamatsu's Satire on the Dog Shogun." *Harvard Journal of Asiatic Studies* 18 (1955): 159–180.

Shively, Donald H., trans. *The Love Suicide at Amijima.* Cambridge, Mass.: Harvard University Press, 1953.

Golden Age of Puppet Theater

Gerstle, C. Andrew, Kiyoshi Inobe, and William P. Malm. *Theater as Music: The Bunraku Play "Mt. Imo and Mt. Se: An Exemplary Tale of Womanly Virtue."* Ann Arbor: University of Michigan, Center for Japanese Studies, 1990.

Jones, Stanleigh H., Jr., trans. *Sugawara and the Secrets of Calligraphy.* New York: Columbia University Press, 1985.

Jones, Stanleigh H., Jr., trans. *Yoshitsune and the Thousand Cherry Trees: A Masterpiece of the Eighteenth-Century Japanese Puppet Theater.* New York: Columbia University Press, 1993.

Keene, Donald, trans. *Chūshingura: The Treasury of Loyal Retainers.* New York: Columbia University Press, 1971.

Kabuki in General

Brandon, James. ed. *Chūshingura: Studies in Kabuki and the Puppet Theater.* Honolulu: University of Hawai'i Press, 1982.

Brandon, James R., ed. and trans. *Kabuki: Five Classic Plays*. 1975. Reprint, Honolulu: University of Hawai'i Press, 1992.

Brandon, James R., William P. Malm, and Donald H. Shively. *Studies in Kabuki: Its Acting, Music, and Historical Context*. Honolulu: University of Hawai'i Press, 1978.

Brazell, Karen, ed. *Traditional Japanese Theater: An Anthology of Plays*. New York: Columbia University Press, 1998.

Dunn, Charles, and Bunzo Torigoe. *The Actors' Analects*. New York: Columbia University Press, 1969 [translation of *Yakusha rongo*].

Ernst, Earle. *The Kabuki Theatre*. New York: Grove Press, 1956.

Gerstle, C. Andrew. "Flowers of Edo: Eighteenth-Century *Kabuki* and Its Patrons." *Asian Theatre Journal* 4 (1987): 52–75.

Kominz, Laurence R. *Avatars of Vengeance: Japanese Drama and the Soga Literary Tradition*. Ann Arbor: University of Michigan, Center for Japanese Studies, 1995.

Kominz, Laurence. *The Stars Who Created Kabuki*. Tokyo: Kōdansha International, 1997.

Kominz, Laurence. "*Ya no Ne*: The Genesis of a Kabuki Aragoto Classic." *Monumenta Nipponica* 38 (1983): 387–407.

Leiter, Samuel L., trans. *The Art of Kabuki: Famous Plays in Performance*. Berkeley and Los Angeles: University of California Press, 1979.

Leiter, Samuel L. "The Frozen Moment: A Kabuki Technique." *Drama Survey* 6 (1967): 74–80.

Leiter, Samuel L. "'Kumagai's Battle Camp': Form and Tradition in Kabuki Acting." *Asian Theatre Journal* 8 (1991): 1–34.

Leiter, Samuel L. *New Kabuki Encyclopedia*. Rev. ed. Westport, Conn.: Greenwood Press, 1997.

Motofuji, Frank T., trans. *The Love of Izayoi and Seishin: A Kabuki Play by Kawatake Mokuami*. Rutland, Vt.: Tuttle, 1966.

Scott, Adolphe Clarence, trans. *Gendayana: A Japanese Kabuki Play and Kanjincho: A Japanese Kabuki Play*. Tokyo: Hokuseidō, 1953.

Scott, Adolphe Clarence. *The Kabuki Theater of Japan*. London: Allen & Unwin, 1956.

Thornbury, Barbara E. *Sukeroku's Double Identity: The Dramatic Structure of Edo Kabuki*. Ann Arbor: University of Michigan, Center for Japanese Studies, 1982.

Matsudaira Sadanobu

Iwasaki, Haruko. "Portrait of a Daimyō: Comical Fiction by Matsudaira Sadanobu." *Monumenta Nipponica* 38 (1983): 1–19.

Ooms, Herman. *Charismatic Bureaucrat: A Political Biography of Matsudaira Sadanobu, 1758–1829*. Chicago: University of Chicago Press, 1975.

Women and the Pleasure Quarters

Seigle, Cecilia Segawa. *Yoshiwara: The Glittering World of the Japanese Courtesan*. Honolulu: University of Hawai'i Press, 1993.

Swinton, Elizabeth, ed. *The Women of the Pleasure Quarter: Japanese Paintings and Prints of the Floating World*. New York: Hudson Hills Press, 1995.

Diaries and Essays in the Middle to Late Edo Period

Markus, Andrew, trans. *An Account of the Prosperity of Edo*, by Terakado Seiken. Hollywood, Calif.: Highmoonoon, 2000 [translations of "Asakusa Kannon" and "Ryōgoku Bridge," from *Edo hanjōki* (1832–1836)].

Markus, Andrew, trans. *Tips for Travelers: Advice for Wayfarers from Late Edo Travel Literature*, by Tachibana Nankei, Kyokutei Bakin, and Yasumi Kageyama (Roan). Hollywood, Calif.: Highmoonoon, 2000.

Confucian Studies and Ancient Learning

Backus, Robert. "The Motivation of Confucian Orthodoxy in Tokugawa Japan." *Harvard Journal of Asiatic Studies* 39 (1979): 275–338.

Kassel, Marleen. *Tokugawa Confucian Education: The Kangien Academy of Hirose Tansō (1782–1856)*. Albany: State University of New York Press, 1996.

Kurozumi Makoto. "The Nature of Early Tokugawa Confucianism." Translated by Herman Ooms. *Journal of Japanese Studies* 20 (1994): 331–376.

Lidin, Olof G. *The Life of Ogyū Sorai, a Tokugawa Confucian Philosopher*. Lund: Studentlitt., 1973.

Marceau, Lawrence E. "*Ninjō* and the Affective Value of Literature at the Kogidō Academy." *Sino-Japanese Studies* 9 (1996): 47–55.

Maruyama, Masao. *Studies in the Intellectual History of Tokugawa Japan*. Translated by Mikiso Hane. Princeton, N.J.: Princeton University Press, 1974.

McMullen, James. *"Genji gaiden": The Origins of Kumazawa Banzan's Commentary on "The Tale of Genji."* Reading: Ithaca Press, for the Board of the Faculty of Oriental Studies, Oxford University, 1991.

McMullen, James. *Idealism, Protest, and "The Tale of Genji."* Oxford: Oxford University Press, 1999.

Najita, Tetsuo, ed. *Readings in Tokugawa Thought*. 2d ed. Chicago: University of Chicago Press, 1994.

Nakai, Kate Wildman. "The Nationalization of Confucianism in Tokugawa Japan: The Problem of Sinocentrism." *Harvard Journal of Asiatic Studies* 40 (1980): 157–199.

Nosco, Peter, ed. *Confucianism and Tokugawa Culture*. Princeton, N.J.: Princeton University Press, 1984.

Ooms, Herman. "'Primeval Chaos' and 'Mental Void' in Early Tokugawa Ideology: Fujiwara Seika, Suzuki Shōsan and Yamazaki Ansai." *Japanese Journal of Religious Studies* 13 (1986): 245–260.

Ooms, Herman. *Tokugawa Ideology: Early Constructs, 1570–1680*. Princeton, N.J.: Princeton University Press, 1985.

Pollack, David. *The Fracture of Meaning: Japan's Synthesis of China from the Eighth Through the Eighteenth Centuries*. Princeton, N.J.: Princeton University Press, 1986.

Sakai, Naoki. *Voices of the Past: The Status of Language in Eighteenth-Century Japanese Discourse*. Ithaca, N.Y.: Cornell University Press, 1991.

Smits, Gregory J. "The Sages' Scale in Japan: Nakae Toju (1608–1648) and Situational Weighing." *Transactions of the Asiatic Society of Japan* 6 (1991): 1–25.

Spae, Joseph John. *Itō Jinsai: A Philosopher, Educator and Sinologist of the Tokugawa Period*. New York: Paragon, 1967.

Tucker, John Allen. *Itō Jinsai's Gomō Jigi and the Philosophical Definition of Early Modern Japan*. Leiden: Brill, 1998.

Tucker, Mary Evelyn. *Moral and Spiritual Cultivation in Japanese Neo-Confucianism: The Life and Thought of Kaibara Ekken (1630–1714)*. Albany: State University of New York Press, 1989.

Tucker, Mary Evelyn. "Religious Aspects of Japanese Neo-Confucianism: The Thought of Nakae Tōju and Kaibara Ekken." *Japanese Journal of Religious Studies* 15 (1988): 55–69.

Yamashita, Samuel Hideo. "The Early Life and Thought of Itō Jinsai." *Harvard Journal of Asiatic Studies* 43 (1983): 453–480.

Yamashita, Samuel Hideo, trans. *Master Sorai's Responsals: An Annotated Translation of "Sorai sensei tōmonsho."* Honolulu: University of Hawai'i Press, 1994.

Yoshikawa, Kōjirō. *Jinsai, Sorai, Norinaga: Three Classical Philologists in Mid-Tokugawa Japan*. Translated by Kikuchi Yūji. Tokyo: Tōhō gakkai, 1983.

Arai Hakuseki

Ackroyd, Joyce, trans. *Lessons from History: Arai Hakuseki's Tokushi Yoron*. Brisbane: University of Queensland Press, 1982.

Ackroyd, Joyce, trans. *Told Round a Brushwood Fire: The Autobiography of Arai Hakuseki*. Tokyo: University of Tokyo Press, 1979.

Nakai, Kate Wildman. *Shogunal Politics: Arai Hakuseki and the Premises of Tokugawa Rule*. Cambridge, Mass.: Harvard University, Council on East Asian Studies, 1988.

Waka and Nativist Studies

Harootunian, H. D. *Things Seen and Unseen: Discourse and Ideology in Tokugawa Nativism*. Chicago: University of Chicago Press, 1988.

Marceau, Lawrence E. "The Emperor's Old Clothes: Classical Narratives in Early Modern Japan." *Proceedings of the Midwest Association for Japanese Literary Studies* 3 (1997): 182–203.

Nosco, Peter. "Keichū (1640–1701): Forerunner of National Learning." *Asian Thought and Society: An International Review* 5 (1980): 237–252.

Nosco, Peter. "Nature, Invention, and National Learning: The *Kokka hachiron* Controversy: 1742–46." *Harvard Journal of Asiatic Studies* 41 (1981): 75–91.

Nosco, Peter. *Remembering Paradise: Nativism and Nostalgia in Eighteenth-Century Japan*. Harvard Yenching Monograph Series, no. 31. Cambridge, Mass.: Harvard University, Council on East Asian Studies, 1990.

Ōkubo, Tadashi. "The Thought of Mabuchi and Norinaga." *Acta Asiatica* 25 (1973): 68–90.

Tahara, Tsuguo. "The Kokugaku Thought." *Acta Asiatica* 25 (1973): 54–67.

Thomas, Roger K. "Macroscopic vs. Microscopic: Spatial Sensibilities in Waka of the Bakumatsu Period." *Harvard Journal of Asiatic Studies* 58 (1998): 513–542.

Thomas, Roger K. "Ōkuma Kotomichi and the Re-Visioning of *Kokinshū* Elegance." *Proceedings of the Midwest Association for Japanese Literary Studies* 3 (1997): 160–181.

Motoori Norinaga

Brownlee, John S. "The Jeweled Comb-Box: Motoori Norinaga's *Tamakushige*." *Monumenta Nipponica* 43 (1988): 35–61.

Harper, Thomas James. "Motoori Norinaga's Criticism of the *Genji monogatari*: A Study of the Background and Critical Content of His *Genji monogatari Tama no ogushi*." Ph.D. diss., University of Michigan, 1971.

Matsumoto, Shigeru. *Motoori Norinaga*. Cambridge, Mass.: Harvard University Press, 1970.

Nishimura, Sey. "First Steps into the Mountains: Motoori Norinaga's *Uiyamabumi*." *Monumenta Nipponica* 42 (1987): 449–493.

Nishimura, Sey. "The Way of the Gods: Motoori Norinaga's *Naobi no Mitama*." *Monumenta Nipponica* 46 (1991): 21–41.

Wehmeyer, Ann, trans. *Kojiki-den, Book 1, Motoori Norinaga*. Ithaca, N.Y.: Cornell University, East Asia Program, 1997.

MISCELLANEOUS

Hare, Thomas Blenman. "'The Raven at First Light': A Shinnai Ballad." In *New Leaves: Studies and Translations of Japanese Literature in Honor of Edward Seidensticker*, edited by Aileen Gatten and Anthony H. Chambers, pp. 115–125. Ann Arbor: University of Michigan Press, 1993.

Jones, Sumie Amikura. "Comic Fiction During the Later Edo Period." Ph.D. diss., University of Washington, 1979.

Nakamura, Yukihiko. "Modes of Expression in a Historical Context." *Acta Asiatica* 28 (1975): 1–19.

Rogers, Lawrence. "She Loves Me, She Loves Me Not: *Shinjū* and *Shikidō Ōkagami*." *Monumenta Nipponica* 49 (1994): 31–60.

Sawada, Janine Anderson. *Confucian Values and Popular Zen: Sekimon Shingaku in Eighteenth-Century Japan*. Honolulu: University of Hawai'i Press, 1993.

Schalow, Paul Gordon. "Literature and Legitimacy: Uses of Irony and Humor in Seventeenth-Century Japanese Depictions of Male Love." In *Literary History, Narrative, and Culture*, edited by Wimal Dissanayake and Steven Bradbury, pp. 53–60. Honolulu: University of Hawai'i Press, 1989.

Schalow, Paul Gordon. "Male Lovers in Early Modern Japan: A Literary Depiction of the Youth." In *Hidden from History: Reclaiming the Gay and Lesbian Past*, edited by Martin Bauml Duberman, Martha Vicinus, and George Chauncey Jr., pp. 118–128. New York: New American Library, 1989.

INDEX

Account of My Hut, An (*Hōjōki*; Kamo
no Chōmei), 473n.55
*Account of Rewards and Retribution for
Good and Evil in Japan, An* (*Nihon
ryōiki*), 33
Actor's Vocal Shamisen (*Yakusha kuchijamisen*; Ejima Kiseki), 163
*Additional Gatherings for the Willow
Barrel* (*Yanagidaru shūi*), 522
adultery, 14, 259–260; punishment of, 15,
60, 61, 74, 81–82
Agatai *waka* school, 606
ageya (performance house), 10, 236
ageya-iri (entering the performance
house), 10
ai (love), 355, 357
Aigonowaka (seventeenth-century
miracle play), 435
Ainu tribe, 221n.67, 373
Akahito (ancient poet), 473n.57
akahon (red books), 673
akebono (faint light of early dawn),
183n.2

Akera Kankō, 528, 529, 530
aki fukaki (late autumn), 186n.15
aki no kure (autumn's end; autumn
evening), 186n.16
akikaze (autumn wind), 217nn.63, 64
akuba (evil older woman), 843
akudama (bad souls), 711, 712
akusho (bad places), 16, 21, 46, 121,
236
Amaterasu Ōmikami, 59n.31, 625–629
Amenomori Hōshū, 373
Analects (*Lunyu*; J. *Rongo*; Confucius),
354, 479n.63, 489, 509, 526n.13; as
Chinese classic, 352, 366; and good
behavior, 489; imitations of, 632;
quoted, 300n.57, 379, 568n.5, 689;
and study of ancient meanings,
362–363; and the Way, 509
*Ancient Middle Road Through Furu,
The* (*Furu no nakamichi*; Ozawa
Roan), 949–951
Ancient Rhetoric (*guwenci*; J.
kobunji) school, 367, 384, 910–913;

PERMISSIONS

OTHER WORKS IN THE

COLUMBIA ASIAN STUDIES SERIES

TRANSLATIONS FROM THE ASIAN CLASSICS

Major Plays of Chikamatsu, tr. Donald Keene 1961

Four Major Plays of Chikamatsu, tr. Donald Keene. Paperback ed. only. 1961; rev. ed. 1997

Records of the Grand Historian of China, translated from the Shih chi of Ssu-ma Ch'ien, tr. Burton Watson, 2 vols. 1961

Instructions for Practical Living and Other Neo-Confucian Writings by Wang Yang-ming, tr. Wing-tsit Chan 1963

Hsün Tzu: Basic Writings, tr. Burton Watson, paperback ed. only. 1963; rev. ed. 1996

Chuang Tzu: Basic Writings, tr. Burton Watson, paperback ed. only. 1964; rev. ed. 1996

The Mahābhārata, tr. Chakravarthi V. Narasimhan. Also in paperback ed. 1965; rev. ed. 1997

The Manyōshū, Nippon Gakujutsu Shinkōkai edition 1965

Su Tung-p'o: Selections from a Sung Dynasty Poet, tr. Burton Watson. Also in paperback ed. 1965

Bhartrihari: Poems, tr. Barbara Stoler Miller. Also in paperback ed. 1967

Basic Writings of Mo Tzu, Hsün Tzu, and Han Fei Tzu, tr. Burton Watson. Also in separate paperback eds. 1967

The Awakening of Faith, Attributed to Aśvaghosha, tr. Yoshito S. Hakeda. Also in paperback ed. 1967

Reflections on Things at Hand: The Neo-Confucian Anthology, comp. Chu Hsi and Lü Tsu-ch'ien, tr. Wing-tsit Chan 1967

The Platform Sutra of the Sixth Patriarch, tr. Philip B. Yampolsky. Also in paperback ed. 1967

Essays in Idleness: The Tsurezuregusa of Kenkō, tr. Donald Keene. Also in paperback ed. 1967

The Pillow Book of Sei Shōnagon, tr. Ivan Morris, 2 vols. 1967

Two Plays of Ancient India: The Little Clay Cart and the Minister's Seal, tr. J. A. B. van Buitenen 1968

The Complete Works of Chuang Tzu, tr. Burton Watson 1968

The Romance of the Western Chamber (Hsi Hsiang chi), tr. S. I. Hsiung. Also in paperback ed. 1968

The Manyōshū, Nippon Gakujutsu Shinkōkai edition. Paperback ed. only. 1969

Records of the Historian: Chapters from the Shih chi of Ssu-ma Ch'ien, tr. Burton Watson. Paperback ed. only. 1969

Cold Mountain: 100 Poems by the T'ang Poet Han-shan, tr. Burton Watson. Also in paperback ed. 1970

Twenty Plays of the Nō Theatre, ed. Donald Keene. Also in paperback ed. 1970

Chūshingura: The Treasury of Loyal Retainers, tr. Donald Keene. Also in paperback ed. 1971; rev. ed. 1997

The Zen Master Hakuin: Selected Writings, tr. Philip B. Yampolsky 1971

Chinese Rhyme-Prose: Poems in the Fu Form from the Han and Six Dynasties Periods, tr. Burton Watson. Also in paperback ed. 1971

Kūkai: Major Works, tr. Yoshito S. Hakeda. Also in paperback ed. 1972

The Old Man Who Does as He Pleases: Selections from the Poetry and Prose of Lu Yu, tr. Burton Watson 1973

The Lion's Roar of Queen Śrīmālā, tr. Alex and Hideko Wayman 1974

Courtier and Commoner in Ancient China: Selections from the History of the Former Han by Pan Ku, tr. Burton Watson. Also in paperback ed. 1974

Japanese Literature in Chinese, vol. 1: Poetry and Prose in Chinese by Japanese Writers of the Early Period, tr. Burton Watson 1975

Japanese Literature in Chinese, vol. 2: Poetry and Prose in Chinese by Japanese Writers of the Later Period, tr. Burton Watson 1976

Scripture of the Lotus Blossom of the Fine Dharma, tr. Leon Hurvitz. Also in paperback ed. 1976

Love Song of the Dark Lord: Jayadeva's Gītagovinda, tr. Barbara Stoler Miller. Also in paperback ed. Cloth ed. includes critical text of the Sanskrit. 1977; rev. ed. 1997

Ryōkan: Zen Monk-Poet of Japan, tr. Burton Watson 1977

Calming the Mind and Discerning the Real: From the Lam rim chen mo of Tsoṇ-kha-pa, tr. Alex Wayman 1978

The Hermit and the Love-Thief: Sanskrit Poems of Bhartrihari and Bilhaṇa, tr. Barbara Stoler Miller 1978

The Lute: Kao Ming's P'i-p'a chi, tr. Jean Mulligan. Also in paperback ed. 1980

A Chronicle of Gods and Sovereigns: Jinnō Shōtōki of Kitabatake Chikafusa, tr. H. Paul Varley 1980

Among the Flowers: The Hua-chien chi, tr. Lois Fusek 1982

Grass Hill: Poems and Prose by the Japanese Monk Gensei, tr. Burton Watson 1983

Doctors, Diviners, and Magicians of Ancient China: Biographies of Fang-shih, tr. Kenneth J. DeWoskin. Also in paperback ed. 1983

Theater of Memory: The Plays of Kālidāsa, ed. Barbara Stoler Miller. Also in paperback ed. 1984

The Columbia Book of Chinese Poetry: From Early Times to the Thirteenth Century, ed. and tr. Burton Watson. Also in paperback ed. 1984

Poems of Love and War: From the Eight Anthologies and the Ten Long Poems of Classical Tamil, tr. A. K. Ramanujan. Also in paperback ed. 1985

The Bhagavad Gita: Krishna's Counsel in Time of War, tr. Barbara Stoler Miller 1986

The Columbia Book of Later Chinese Poetry, ed. and tr. Jonathan Chaves. Also in paperback ed. 1986

The Tso Chuan: Selections from China's Oldest Narrative History, tr. Burton Watson 1989

Waiting for the Wind: Thirty-six Poets of Japan's Late Medieval Age, tr. Steven Carter 1989

Selected Writings of Nichiren, ed. Philip B. Yampolsky 1990

Saigyō, Poems of a Mountain Home, tr. Burton Watson 1990

The Book of Lieh Tzu: A Classic of the Tao, tr. A. C. Graham. Morningside ed. 1990

The Tale of an Anklet: An Epic of South India—The Cilappatikāram of Iḷaṅkō Aṭikaḷ, tr. R. Parthasarathy 1993

Waiting for the Dawn: A Plan for the Prince, tr. and introduction by Wm. Theodore de Bary 1993

Yoshitsune and the Thousand Cherry Trees: A Masterpiece of the Eighteenth-Century Japanese Puppet Theater, tr., annotated, and with introduction by Stanleigh H. Jones, Jr. 1993

The Lotus Sutra, tr. Burton Watson. Also in paperback ed. 1993

The Classic of Changes: A New Translation of the I Ching as Interpreted by Wang Bi, tr. Richard John Lynn 1994

Beyond Spring: Tz'u Poems of the Sung Dynasty, tr. Julie Landau 1994

The Columbia Anthology of Traditional Chinese Literature, ed. Victor H. Mair 1994

Scenes for Mandarins: The Elite Theater of the Ming, tr. Cyril Birch 1995

Letters of Nichiren, ed. Philip B. Yampolsky; tr. Burton Watson et al. 1996

Unforgotten Dreams: Poems by the Zen Monk Shōtetsu, tr. Steven D. Carter 1997

The Vimalakirti Sutra, tr. Burton Watson 1997

Japanese and Chinese Poems to Sing: The Wakan rōei shū, tr. J. Thomas Rimer and Jonathan Chaves 1997

A Tower for the Summer Heat, Li Yu, tr. Patrick Hanan 1998

Traditional Japanese Theater: An Anthology of Plays, Karen Brazell 1998

The Original Analects: Sayings of Confucius and His Successors (0479–0249), E. Bruce Brooks and A. Taeko Brooks 1998

The Classic of the Way and Virtue: A New Translation of the Tao-te ching of Laozi as Interpreted by Wang Bi, tr. Richard John Lynn 1999

The Four Hundred Songs of War and Wisdom: An Anthology of Poems from Classical Tamil, The Puranānūṟu, eds. and trans. George L. Hart and Hank Heifetz 1999

Original Tao: Inward Training (Nei-yeh) and the Foundations of Taoist Mysticism, by Harold D. Roth 1999

Lao Tzu's Tao Te Ching: *A Translation of the Startling New Documents Found at Guodian*, Robert G. Henricks 2000

The Shorter Columbia Anthology of Traditional Chinese Literature, ed. Victor H. Mair 2000

Mistress and Maid (Jiaohongji) by Meng Chengshun, tr. Cyril Birch 2001

Chikamatsu: Five Late Plays, tr. and ed. C. Andrew Gerstle

The Essential Lotus: Selections from the Lotus Sutra, tr. Burton Watson 2002

MODERN ASIAN LITERATURE

Modern Japanese Drama: An Anthology, ed. and tr. Ted. Takaya. Also in paperback ed. 1979

Mask and Sword: Two Plays for the Contemporary Japanese Theater, by Yamazaki Masakazu, tr. J. Thomas Rimer 1980

Yokomitsu Riichi, Modernist, Dennis Keene 1980

Nepali Visions, Nepali Dreams: The Poetry of Laxmiprasad Devkota, tr. David Rubin 1980

Literature of the Hundred Flowers, vol. 1: *Criticism and Polemics*, ed. Hualing Nieh 1981

Literature of the Hundred Flowers, vol. 2: *Poetry and Fiction*, ed. Hualing Nieh 1981

Modern Chinese Stories and Novellas, 1919 1949, ed. Joseph S. M. Lau, C. T. Hsia, and Leo Ou-fan Lee. Also in paperback ed. 1984

A View by the Sea, by Yasuoka Shōtarō, tr. Kären Wigen Lewis 1984

Other Worlds: Arishima Takeo and the Bounds of Modern Japanese Fiction, by Paul Anderer 1984

Selected Poems of Sō Chōngju, tr. with introduction by David R. McCann 1989

The Sting of Life: Four Contemporary Japanese Novelists, by Van C. Gessel 1989

Stories of Osaka Life, by Oda Sakunosuke, tr. Burton Watson 1990

The Bodhisattva, or Samantabhadra, by Ishikawa Jun, tr. with introduction by William Jefferson Tyler 1990

The Travels of Lao Ts'an, by Liu T'ieh-yün, tr. Harold Shadick. Morningside ed. 1990

Three Plays by Kōbō Abe, tr. with introduction by Donald Keene 1993

The Columbia Anthology of Modern Chinese Literature, ed. Joseph S. M. Lau and Howard Goldblatt 1995

Modern Japanese Tanka, ed. and tr. by Makoto Ueda 1996

Masaoka Shiki: Selected Poems, ed. and tr. by Burton Watson 1997

Writing Women in Modern China: An Anthology of Women's Literature from the Early Twentieth Century, ed. and tr. by Amy D. Dooling and Kristina M. Torgeson 1998

American Stories, by Nagai Kafū, tr. Mitsuko Iriye 2000

The Paper Door and Other Stories, by Shiga Naoya, tr. Lane Dunlop 2001

STUDIES IN ASIAN CULTURE

The Ōnin War: History of Its Origins and Background, with a Selective Translation of the Chronicle of Ōnin, by H. Paul Varley 1967

Chinese Government in Ming Times: Seven Studies, ed. Charles O. Hucker 1969

The Actors' Analects (Yakusha Rongo), ed. and tr. by Charles J. Dunn and Bungō
 Torigoe 1969
Self and Society in Ming Thought, by Wm. Theodore de Bary and the Conference on
 Ming Thought. Also in paperback ed. 1970
A History of Islamic Philosophy, by Majid Fakhry, 2d ed. 1983
Phantasies of a Love Thief: The Caurapañatcāśikā Attributed to Bilhaṇa, by Barbara
 Stoler Miller 1971
Iqbal: Poet-Philosopher of Pakistan, ed. Hafeez Malik 1971
The Golden Tradition: An Anthology of Urdu Poetry, ed. and tr. Ahmed Ali. Also in
 paperback ed. 1973
Conquerors and Confucians: Aspects of Political Change in Late Yüan China, by John
 W. Dardess 1973
The Unfolding of Neo-Confucianism, by Wm. Theodore de Bary and the Conference
 on Seventeenth-Century Chinese Thought. Also in paperback ed. 1975
To Acquire Wisdom: The Way of Wang Yang-ming, by Julia Ching 1976
Gods, Priests, and Warriors: The Bhrgus of the Mahābhārata, by Robert P. Goldman
 1977
Mei Yao-ch'en and the Development of Early Sung Poetry, by Jonathan Chaves 1976
The Legend of Semimaru, Blind Musician of Japan, by Susan Matisoff 1977
Sir Sayyid Ahmad Khan and Muslim Modernization in India and Pakistan, by Hafeez
 Malik 1980
The Khilafat Movement: Religious Symbolism and Political Mobilization in India, by
 Gail Minault 1982
The World of K'ung Shang-jen: A Man of Letters in Early Ch'ing China, by Richard
 Strassberg 1983
The Lotus Boat: The Origins of Chinese Tz'u Poetry in T'ang Popular Culture, by
 Marsha L. Wagner 1984
Expressions of Self in Chinese Literature, ed. Robert E. Hegel and Richard C. Hessney
 1985
Songs for the Bride: Women's Voices and Wedding Rites of Rural India, by W. G. Archer;
 eds. Barbara Stoler Miller and Mildred Archer 1986
The Confucian Kingship in Korea: Yŏngjo and the Politics of Sagacity, by JaHyun Kim
 Haboush 1988

COMPANIONS TO ASIAN STUDIES

Approaches to the Oriental Classics, ed. Wm. Theodore de Bary 1959
Early Chinese Literature, by Burton Watson. Also in paperback ed. 1962
Approaches to Asian Civilizations, eds. Wm. Theodore de Bary and Ainslie T. Embree
 1964
The Classic Chinese Novel: A Critical Introduction, by C. T. Hsia. Also in paperback
 ed. 1968
Chinese Lyricism: Shih Poetry from the Second to the Twelfth Century, tr. Burton Wat-
 son. Also in paperback ed. 1971
A Syllabus of Indian Civilization, by Leonard A. Gordon and Barbara Stoler Miller
 1971

Twentieth-Century Chinese Stories, ed. C. T. Hsia and Joseph S. M. Lau. Also in paperback ed. 1971

A Syllabus of Chinese Civilization, by J. Mason Gentzler, 2d ed. 1972

A Syllabus of Japanese Civilization, by H. Paul Varley, 2d ed. 1972

An Introduction to Chinese Civilization, ed. John Meskill, with the assistance of J. Mason Gentzler 1973

An Introduction to Japanese Civilization, ed. Arthur E. Tiedemann 1974

Ukifune: Love in the Tale of Genji, ed. Andrew Pekarik 1982

The Pleasures of Japanese Literature, by Donald Keene 1988

A Guide to Oriental Classics, eds. Wm. Theodore de Bary and Ainslie T. Embree; 3d edition ed. Amy Vladeck Heinrich, 2 vols. 1989

INTRODUCTION TO ASIAN CIVILIZATIONS

Wm. Theodore de Bary, General Editor

Sources of Japanese Tradition, 1958; paperback ed., 2 vols., 1964. 2d ed., vol. 1, 2001, compiled by Wm. Theodore de Bary, Donald Keene, George Tanabe, and Paul Varley

Sources of Indian Tradition, 1958; paperback ed., 2 vols., 1964. 2d ed., 2 vols., 1988

Sources of Chinese Tradition, 1960, paperback ed., 2 vols., 1964. 2d ed., vol. 1, 1999, compiled by Wm. Theodore de Bary and Irene Bloom; vol. 2, 2000, compiled by Wm. Theodore de Bary and Richard Lufrano

Sources of Korean Tradition, 1997; 2 vols., vol. 1, 1997, compiled by Peter H. Lee and Wm. Theodore de Bary; vol. 2, 2001, compiled by Yŏngho Ch'oe, Peter H. Lee, and Wm. Theodore de Bary

NEO-CONFUCIAN STUDIES

Instructions for Practical Living and Other Neo-Confucian Writings by Wang Yang-ming, tr. Wing-tsit Chan 1963

Reflections on Things at Hand: The Neo-Confucian Anthology, comp. Chu Hsi and Lü Tsu-ch'ien, tr. Wing-tsit Chan 1967

Self and Society in Ming Thought, by Wm. Theodore de Bary and the Conference on Ming Thought. Also in paperback ed. 1970

The Unfolding of Neo-Confucianism, by Wm. Theodore de Bary and the Conference on Seventeenth-Century Chinese Thought. Also in paperback ed. 1975

Principle and Practicality: Essays in Neo-Confucianism and Practical Learning, eds. Wm. Theodore de Bary and Irene Bloom. Also in paperback ed. 1979

The Syncretic Religion of Lin Chao-en, by Judith A. Berling 1980

The Renewal of Buddhism in China: Chu-hung and the Late Ming Synthesis, by Chün-fang Yü 1981

Neo-Confucian Orthodoxy and the Learning of the Mind-and-Heart, by Wm. Theodore de Bary 1981

Yüan Thought: Chinese Thought and Religion Under the Mongols, eds. Hok-lam Chan and Wm. Theodore de Bary 1982

The Liberal Tradition in China, by Wm. Theodore de Bary 1983

The Development and Decline of Chinese Cosmology, by John B. Henderson 1984

The Rise of Neo-Confucianism in Korea, by Wm. Theodore de Bary and JaHyun Kim Haboush 1985

Chiao Hung and the Restructuring of Neo-Confucianism in Late Ming, by Edward T. Ch'ien 1985

Neo-Confucian Terms Explained: Pei-hsi tzu-i, by Ch'en Ch'un, ed. and trans. Wing-tsit Chan 1986

Knowledge Painfully Acquired: K'un-chih chi, by Lo Ch'in-shun, ed. and trans. Irene Bloom 1987

To Become a Sage: The Ten Diagrams on Sage Learning, by Yi T'oegye, ed. and trans. Michael C. Kalton 1988

The Message of the Mind in Neo-Confucian Thought, by Wm. Theodore de Bary 1989